PROFESSIONAL AND PERSONAL RESPONSIBILITIES OF THE LAWYER

by

JOHN T. NOONAN, JR.
Judge, United States Court of Appeals for the Ninth Circuit
Robbins Professor of Law Emeritus
University of California at Berkeley

RICHARD W. PAINTER
Associate Professor of Law
University of Oregon

WESTBURY, NEW YORK
THE FOUNDATION PRESS, INC.
1997

COPYRIGHT © 1997 By THE FOUNDATION PRESS, INC.
615 Merrick Ave.
Westbury, N.Y. 11590–6607
(516) 832–6950

Library of Congress Cataloging-in-Publication Data

Noonan, John Thomas, 1926–
    Professional and personal responsibilities of the lawyer / by John T.
Noonan, Jr., Richard W. Painter.
       p.   cm. — (University casebook series)
    Includes index.
    ISBN 1–56662–477–0 (hardcover)
    1. Legal ethics—United States—Cases.   I. Painter, Richard W.,
1961–   .   II. Title.   III. Series.
KF306.A4N66   1997
174'.3'0973—dc21   97–7143

to
Mary Lee Noonan
and
William and Marion Painter

*

ACKNOWLEDGEMENTS

The Donald Walker—Norman Wiener Research Fund at the University of Oregon provided financial support for work on this casebook during the summers of 1995 and 1996. Karyn Smith and Pat Bray at the University of Oregon School of Law, and Dee Falls at the University of Illinois College of Law, provided valuable secretarial support. Boston University School of Law also provided secretarial and research support during the 1997 spring semester.

Portions of the Relevant Background sections in this casebook are based on research by students at the University of Oregon, including Sara Burke, Delphine Cherewick, Jodie Chusid, Tama Ewers, Joseph Fette, Richard George, Jed Goldfried, Rick Giolitti, Eric Hsu, Matthew Kemmy, Lori Kliewer, Shannon Kmetic, Jeannette Lavander, Cary McReynolds, Anne Nichol, Dainard Paulson, Kurt Wanless and Cory Zion. I am particularly indebted to Jennifer Duggan and Shane Goudey for supervision of these student research projects and for editorial assistance. I am also grateful for the research assistance of Beth Herrington, Jennifer Hua and Chuck Thompson at the University of Illinois.

Karen Painter gave important and much appreciated moral support for my work.

RICHARD W. PAINTER

Eugene, Oregon
May, 1997

*

FOREWORD

It is obvious from the table of contents that this casebook is different from most others, and perhaps an explanation is in order. Instead of relying primarily on cases which apply rules derived from the Model Rules or Model Code of the American Bar Association, this book includes cases from throughout the history of our legal system in which lawyers, and sometimes judges, make ethical decisions. Our emphasis is on the lawyers and judges themselves, not exclusively on legal rules. Some of these lawyers and judges make honest attempts to behave ethically. Others ignore ethical problems. Still others behave in a blatantly unethical fashion. Our selections are designed to explore the impact of human values of professional ethics and to expose students to the complexities of circumstances in which people act.

A lawyer, like any other person, is ultimately responsible not only to legal and professional standards, but also to his own conscience. Conduct which is in complete accordance with rules of professional conduct and other law may still violate a lawyer's own sense of right and wrong. If so, she should consider an alternative course of action. The materials in this casebook ask students to identify situations in which a course of professional conduct conflicts with their personal ethics, and hopefully prepare students to confront similar situations in their own practice.

This casebook emphasizes ethical problems in human and professional relationships. It is therefore more economical than most casebooks in its interpretation and criticism of formal rules. Its discussion of ABA rules and "black letter" law, while extensive, is designed to fit into a larger framework exploring relationships that create ethical problems and ways in which those problems can be resolved.

Our objective is to teach students to think about ethics proactively rather than reactively. After reading the cases, students should ask "what would I have done in this situation?" or "how could this problem have been avoided?" not merely "should the lawyer in this case be sanctioned?" and "what is the rule here?" This approach reflects our belief that professional responsibility should be taught as an approach to practicing law rather than as a distinct body of law, and that legal educators should be at least as concerned with promoting ethical conduct as with drafting rules and analyzing caselaw concerning unethical conduct. A professional responsibility course should focus more than other courses in the curriculum on developing standards of behavior and training students to anticipate ethical problems and less on interpreting judicial opinions, statutes and rules. Our pedagogical objective in the classroom is discerning not what the lawyer in each situation can get away with but what he or she should do.

The casebook emphasizes real situations instead of hypotheticals. Law professors know that life is never as simple as a hypothetical. Yet hypotheticals are widely popular as a pedagogical device, precisely because of their simplicity. The one or two dimensional examination of a problem allowed by a hypothetical makes it easy to explain a legal rule while keeping "extraneous" concerns from entering into the discussion. Real cases, or rather brief excerpts from real cases, can then conveniently be plugged into the hypothetical. While hypotheticals are often useful pedagogically—particularly for instructors who want to cover many legal concepts in little time—hypotheticals, standing alone, can be a shallow teaching device in a course concerned with the role of lawyers as ethical actors. Ethical decision making, problem solving and problem avoidance are each best learned by examining actual situations and the conduct of actors who are real people.

This book does include, however, as an additional instructional tool, a substantial number of problems after many of the selections. Unlike the selections themselves, these problems do not reflect the complexities of real life. Many of the problems do explore variations on problems actually confronted by lawyers and judges in the selections. Others are derived from case law or bar opinions and explore issues of professional ethics which we address in the text but, due to space limitations, cannot address in the larger selections. Finally, the selections and text often are followed by questions which probe deeper into the actors' motivations or explore the rationale behind certain ethical principles. Both the problems and questions provide ample material for extensive classroom discussion.

From 1908 to 1969 the ABA Canons of Professional Ethics embodied the ABA's formal position on matters of professional responsibility. In 1969, the Canons were replaced by the Code of Professional Responsibility. Since 1983, about 40 states have adopted the newer Model Rules of Professional Conduct in whole or in part, and other states appear ready to do so as well. While the rules adopted in many states are similar in many respects to the Model Code or the Model Rules, the ABA rules are not themselves law. Far too often, the proposed ABA rules are cited, in legal briefs and even by courts themselves, as if they were law. They are not, and in some areas, such as disclosure of client crimes or frauds, discussed in chapter 2 below, many states have chosen to depart from ABA-proposed rules. Despite the emphasis placed on the ABA rules in most professional responsibility courses and on the Multistate Professional Responsibility Exam (MPRE), students should be reminded that ABA rules are the legal profession's own view of the rules by which lawyers should be governed. The rules which actually govern lawyers are made by state legislatures and the courts.

Several of our selections are not contemporary. The prosecution of Sir Walter Raleigh dates from the seventeenth century and several of our cases date from the eighteenth and nineteenth centuries. These materials illustrate an important point: long before the ABA Model Rules or other formal codes of professional conduct came into existence, lawyers and judges thought about and debated legal ethics. Furthermore, freeing our discussion from exclusive reliance on contemporary case law underscores the permanence of certain principles in the legal profession: preservation of client confidences, zealous representation, candor to a tribunal and avoiding undue influence on a tribunal, to name a few. Some of our materials underscore the inevitability of tensions between these principles. For example in *Annesley v. Anglesea* (1743), the court explored the tension between the duty of a lawyer to preserve client confidences and the duty of a lawyer, when asked by a client to assist with an unlawful act, to protect the public. These materials demonstrate that professional ethics are defined not by the latest articulation of rules, but by general ethical principles, by consensus within the profession, and by human experience.

Part I of this casebook is organized around the relationship between clients and their lawyers. Part II explores multiple relationships such as the client and society, client and political superior, successive clients, partners, and concurrent relationships. Students reading Parts I and II will discover how the relationships discussed therein can create ethical problems and how lawyer conduct can help solve those problems or make them worse. Part III is organized around the tribunal as paradigm and the problems arising when lawyers and clients interact with adjudicative bodies. Part IV focuses on lawyers' cooperation with the system and ethical implications of lawyers' and judges' work within a larger political framework. In reading and discussing the materials in part IV, students will begin to understand the role of lawyers in implementing a society's political objectives, whether those objectives encompass the pluralistic democracy Tocqueville envisioned in America or the genocidal dictatorship that flourished in Nazi Germany. Analytically distinct, each part of this book overlaps with every other part.

Each selection in the casebook is preceded or followed by discussion of current law relevant to that particular selection under the heading "relevant background." This discussion includes comprehensive coverage of both the Model Rules and the Model Code, which, although not themselves substantive law, are models for many state codes of professional conduct. We also cover procedural rules governing lawyer conduct, such as F.R.C.P., Rule 11. We emphasize areas of substantive law under which attorneys can be sanctioned by administrative agencies or assessed civil damages and penalties in connection with their conduct. Although lawyers should consider this background material when making decisions, ethical decisions are essentially personal rather than legalistic in nature. The reading selections themselves, which are the core of this casebook, allow students to explore the relationship between legal decision making and their own sense of right and wrong.

A final word about the editorial approach here taken: we avoid a recent trend toward filling casebooks with shorter and shorter passages from more and more cases. Such abbreviated cases may restate legal rules, but do not explore interesting fact patterns. Instead, we rely primarily on text to describe legal rules; large number of cases are not required because each important rule need not appear in a case. The cases we do select, while edited to remove extraneous material, are complete in their description of a situation and of the actors involved.

The Division of Labor. Judge Noonan began teaching this subject at Notre Dame in 1961 and has taught it for over 25 years at Berkeley, with visiting appointments to teach it at Boston College, Harvard, and Southern Methodist. This book follows the structure of his course, and he has selected the bulk of the cases focused on. Editing, supplementary cases, questions, problems, and commentary are the work of Professor Painter, although some of the questions are based on teaching notes prepared by Judge Noonan.

SUMMARY OF CONTENTS

I. LAWYER AND CLIENT

II. MULTIPLE RELATIONSHIPS

*

TABLE OF CONTENTS

I. LAWYER AND CLIENT

II. MULTIPLE RELATIONSHIPS

*

TABLE OF CASES

Principal cases are in bold type. Non-principal cases are in roman type. References are to Pages.

*

TABLE OF ABA DISCIPLINARY RULES AND MODEL RULES

PROFESSIONAL AND PERSONAL RESPONSIBILITIES OF THE LAWYER

*

I. Lawyer and Client

CHAPTER 1

Lawyer and Client

A. The Client Perjury Dilemma

Gary A. Robinson, b. Torrance, California; B.A., Drake College, Iowa 1968; J.D., Western States Law School 1977; admitted to the Iowa bar in 1977 (had only recently been practicing law when assigned to represent defendant Whiteside in this case).

Crispus Nix, Warden, Petitioner v. Emanuel Charles Whiteside

475 U.S. 157 (1986).

■ CHIEF JUSTICE BURGER delivered the opinion of the Court.

We granted certiorari to decide whether the Sixth Amendment right of a criminal defendant to assistance of counsel is violated when an attorney refuses to cooperate with the defendant in presenting perjured testimony at his trial.

I

A

Whiteside was convicted of second-degree murder by a jury verdict which was affirmed by the Iowa courts. The killing took place on February 8, 1977, in Cedar Rapids, Iowa. Whiteside and two others went to one Calvin Love's apartment late that night, seeking marihuana. Love was in bed when Whiteside and his companions arrived; an argument between Whiteside and Love over the marihuana ensued. At one point, Love directed his girlfriend to get his "piece," and at another point got up, then returned to his bed. According to Whiteside's testimony, Love then started

1

to reach under his pillow and moved toward Whiteside. Whiteside stabbed Love in the chest, inflicting a fatal wound.

Whiteside was charged with murder, and when counsel was appointed he objected to the lawyer initially appointed, claiming that he felt uncomfortable with a lawyer who had formerly been a prosecutor. Gary L. Robinson was then appointed and immediately began an investigation. Whiteside gave him a statement that he had stabbed Love as the latter "was pulling a pistol from underneath the pillow on the bed." Upon questioning by Robinson, however, Whiteside indicated that he had not actually seen a gun, but that he was convinced that Love had a gun. No pistol was found on the premises; shortly after the police search following the stabbing, which had revealed no weapon, the victim's family had removed all of the victim's possessions from the apartment. Robinson interviewed Whiteside's companions who were present during the stabbing, and none had seen a gun during the incident. Robinson advised Whiteside that the existence of a gun was not necessary to establish the claim of self-defense, and that only a reasonable belief that the victim had a gun nearby was necessary even though no gun was actually present.

Until shortly before trial, Whiteside consistently stated to Robinson that he had not actually seen a gun, but that he was convinced that Love had a gun in his hand. About a week before trial, during preparation for direct examination, Whiteside for the first time told Robinson and his associate Donna Paulsen that he had seen something "metallic" in Love's hand. When asked about this, Whiteside responded: "[I]n Howard Cook's case there was a gun. If I don't say I saw a gun, I'm dead." Robinson told Whiteside that such testimony would be perjury and repeated that it was not necessary to prove that a gun was available but only that Whiteside reasonably believed that he was in danger. On Whiteside's insisting that he would testify that he saw "something metallic" Robinson told him, according to Robinson's testimony: "[W]e could not allow him to [testify falsely] because that would be perjury, and as officers of the court we would be suborning perjury if we allowed him to do it; . . . I advised him that if he did do that it would be my duty to advise the Court of what he was doing and that I felt he was committing perjury; also, that I probably would be allowed to attempt to impeach that particular testimony." App. to Pet. for Cert. A–85. Robinson also indicated he would seek to withdraw from the representation if Whiteside insisted on committing perjury.[2]

Whiteside testified in his own defense at trial and stated that he "knew" that Love had a gun and that he believed Love was reaching for a gun and he had acted swiftly in self-defense. On cross-examination, he admitted that he had not actually seen a gun in Love's hand. Robinson

---

2. Whiteside's version of the events at this pretrial meeting is considerably more cryptic: "Q. And as you went over the questions, did the two of you come into conflict with regard to whether or not there was a weapon?" A. "I couldn't—I couldn't say a conflict. But I got the impression at one time that maybe if I didn't go along with—with what was happening, that it was no gun being involved, maybe that he will pull out of my trial."

presented evidence that Love had been seen with a sawed-off shotgun on other occasions, that the police search of the apartment may have been careless, and that the victim's family had removed everything from the apartment shortly after the crime. Robinson presented this evidence to show a basis for Whiteside's asserted fear that Love had a gun.

The jury returned a verdict of second-degree murder, and Whiteside moved for a new trial, claiming that he had been deprived of a fair trial by Robinson's admonitions not to state that he saw a gun or "something metallic." The trial court held a hearing, heard testimony by Whiteside and Robinson, and denied the motion. The trial court made specific findings that the facts were as related by Robinson.

The Supreme Court of Iowa affirmed respondent's conviction. State v. Whiteside, 272 N.W.2d 468 (1978). That court held that the right to have counsel present all appropriate defenses does not extend to using perjury, and that an attorney's duty to a client does not extend to assisting a client in committing perjury. Relying on DR 7–102(A)(4) of the Iowa Code of Professional Responsibility for Lawyers, which expressly prohibits an attorney from using perjured testimony, and Iowa Code § 721.2 (now Iowa Code § 720.3 (1985)), which criminalizes subornation of perjury, the Iowa court concluded that not only were Robinson's actions permissible, but were required. The court commended "both Mr. Robinson and Ms. Paulsen for the high ethical manner in which this matter was handled."

B

Whiteside then petitioned for a writ of habeas corpus in the United States District Court for the Southern District of Iowa. In that petition Whiteside alleged that he had been denied effective assistance of counsel and of his right to present a defense by Robinson's refusal to allow him to testify as he had proposed. The District Court denied the writ. Accepting the state trial court's factual finding that Whiteside's intended testimony would have been perjurious, it concluded that there could be no grounds for habeas relief since there is no constitutional right to present a perjured defense.

The United States Court of Appeals for the Eighth Circuit reversed and directed that the writ of habeas corpus be granted. Whiteside v. Scurr, 744 F.2d 1323 (1984). The Court of Appeals accepted the findings of the trial judge, affirmed by the Iowa Supreme Court, that trial counsel believed with good cause that Whiteside would testify falsely and acknowledged that under Harris v. New York, 401 U.S. 222, 91 S.Ct. 643, 28 L.Ed.2d 1 (1971), a criminal defendant's privilege to testify in his own behalf does not include a right to commit perjury. Nevertheless, the court reasoned that an intent to commit perjury, communicated to counsel, does not alter a defendant's right to effective assistance of counsel and that Robinson's admonition to Whiteside that he would inform the court of Whiteside's perjury constituted a threat to violate the attorney's duty to preserve client confidences. According to the Court of Appeals, this threatened violation of client confidences breached the standards of effective representation set down in

Strickland v. Washington, 466 U.S. 668, 104 S.Ct. 2052, 80 L.Ed.2d 674 (1984). The court also concluded that Strickland 's prejudice requirement was satisfied by an implication of prejudice from the conflict between Robinson's duty of loyalty to his client and his ethical duties. A petition for rehearing en banc was denied, with Judges Gibson, Ross, Fagg, and Bowman dissenting. Whiteside v. Scurr, 750 F.2d 713 (1984). We granted certiorari, 471 U.S. 1014, 105 S.Ct. 2016, 85 L.Ed.2d 298 (1985), and we reverse.

II

A

The right of an accused to testify in his defense is of relatively recent origin. Until the latter part of the preceding century, criminal defendants in this country, as at common law, were considered to be disqualified from giving sworn testimony at their own trial by reason of their interest as a party to the case [citations omitted].

By the end of the 19th century, however, the disqualification was finally abolished by statute in most states and in the federal courts. Act of Mar. 16, 1878, ch. 37, 20 Stat. 30–31; see Thayer, A Chapter of Legal History in Massachusetts, 9 Harv.L.Rev. 1, 12 (1895). Although this Court has never explicitly held that a criminal defendant has a due process right to testify in his own behalf, cases in several Circuits have so held, and the right has long been assumed. [citations omitted] We have also suggested that such a right exists as a corollary to the Fifth Amendment privilege against compelled testimony, see Harris v. New York, supra [citations omitted].

B

In Strickland v. Washington, we held that to obtain relief by way of federal habeas corpus on a claim of a deprivation of effective assistance of counsel under the Sixth Amendment, the movant must establish both serious attorney error and prejudice. To show such error, it must be established that the assistance rendered by counsel was constitutionally deficient in that "counsel made errors so serious that counsel was not functioning as 'counsel' guaranteed the defendant by the Sixth Amendment." Strickland, 466 U.S., at 687, 104 S.Ct., at 2064. To show prejudice, it must be established that the claimed lapses in counsel's performance rendered the trial unfair so as to "undermine confidence in the outcome" of the trial. Id., at 694, 104 S.Ct., at 2068.

In Strickland, we acknowledged that the Sixth Amendment does not require any particular response by counsel to a problem that may arise. Rather, the Sixth Amendment inquiry is into whether the attorney's conduct was "reasonably effective." To counteract the natural tendency to fault an unsuccessful defense, a court reviewing a claim of ineffective assistance must "indulge a strong presumption that counsel's conduct falls within the wide range of reasonable professional assistance." Id., at 689, 104 S.Ct., at 2066. In giving shape to the perimeters of this range of reasonable professional assistance, Strickland mandates that "[p]revailing norms of practice as reflected in American Bar Association Standards and the like, ... are guides to determining what is reasonable, but they are only guides." Id., at 688, 104 S.Ct., at 2065.

Under the Strickland standard, breach of an ethical standard does not necessarily make out a denial of the Sixth Amendment guarantee of assistance of counsel. When examining attorney conduct, a court must be careful not to narrow the wide range of conduct acceptable under the Sixth Amendment so restrictively as to constitutionalize particular standards of professional conduct and thereby intrude into the state's proper authority to define and apply the standards of professional conduct applicable to those it admits to practice in its courts. In some future case challenging attorney conduct in the course of a state-court trial, we may need to define with greater precision the weight to be given to recognized canons of ethics, the standards established by the state in statutes or professional codes, and the Sixth Amendment, in defining the proper scope and limits on that conduct. Here we need not face that question, since virtually all of the sources speak with one voice.

C

We turn next to the question presented: the definition of the range of "reasonable professional" responses to a criminal defendant client who informs counsel that he will perjure himself on the stand. We must determine whether, in this setting, Robinson's conduct fell within the wide range of professional responses to threatened client perjury acceptable under the Sixth Amendment.

In Strickland, we recognized counsel's duty of loyalty and his "overarching duty to advocate the defendant's cause." Id. Plainly, that duty is limited to legitimate, lawful conduct compatible with the very nature of a trial as a search for truth. Although counsel must take all reasonable lawful means to attain the objectives of the client, counsel is precluded from taking steps or in any way assisting the client in presenting false evidence or otherwise violating the law. This principle has consistently been recognized in most unequivocal terms by expositors of the norms of professional conduct since the first Canons of Professional Ethics were adopted by the American Bar Association in 1908. The 1908 Canon 32 provided: "No client, corporate or individual, however powerful, nor any cause, civil or political, however important, is entitled to receive nor should any lawyer render any service or advice involving disloyalty to the law whose ministers we are, or disrespect of the judicial office, which we are bound to uphold, or corruption of any person or persons exercising a public office or private trust, or deception or betrayal of the public.... He must ... observe and advise his client to observe the statute law...." Of course, this Canon did no more than articulate centuries of accepted standards of conduct. Similarly, Canon 37, adopted in 1928, explicitly acknowledges as an exception to the attorney's duty of confidentiality a client's announced intention to commit a crime: "The announced intention of a client to commit a crime is not included within the confidences which [the attorney] is bound to respect.''

These principles have been carried through to contemporary codifications of an attorney's professional responsibility. Disciplinary Rule 7–102 of the Model Code of Professional Responsibility (1980), entitled ''Representing a Client Within the Bounds of the Law,'' provides:

''(A) In his representation of a client, a lawyer shall not:

* * *

''(4) Knowingly use perjured testimony or false evidence.

* * *

''(7) Counsel or assist his client in conduct that the lawyer knows to be illegal or fraudulent.'' This provision has been adopted by Iowa, and is binding on all lawyers who appear in its courts. See Iowa Code of Professional Responsibility for Lawyers (1985). The more recent Model Rules of Professional Conduct (1983) similarly admonish attorneys to obey all laws in the course of representing a client:

''RULE 1.2 Scope of Representation

* * *

''(d) A lawyer shall not counsel a client to engage, or assist a client, in conduct that the lawyer knows is criminal or fraudulent....'' Both the Model Code of Professional Responsibility and the Model Rules of Professional Conduct also adopt the specific exception from the attorney-client privilege for disclosure of perjury that his client intends to commit or has committed. DR 4–101(C)(3) (intention of client to commit a crime); Rule 3.3 (lawyer has duty to disclose falsity of evidence even if disclosure compromises client confidences). Indeed, both the Model Code and the Model Rules do not merely *authorize* disclosure by counsel of client perjury; they *require* such disclosure. See Rule 3.3(a)(4); DR 7–102(B)(1); Committee on Professional Ethics and Conduct of Iowa State Bar Assn. v. Crary, 245 N.W.2d 298 (Iowa 1976).

These standards confirm that the legal profession has accepted that an attorney's ethical duty to advance the interests of his client is limited by an equally solemn duty to comply with the law and standards of professional conduct; it specifically ensures that the client may not use false evidence. This special duty of an attorney to prevent and disclose frauds upon the court derives from the recognition that perjury is as much a crime as tampering with witnesses or jurors by way of promises and threats, and undermines the administration of justice. See 1 W. Burdick, Law of Crime §§ 293, 300, 318–336 (1946).

The offense of perjury was a crime recognized at common law, id., at p. 475, and has been made a felony in most states by statute, including Iowa. Iowa Code § 720.2 (1985). See generally 4 C. Torcia, Wharton's Criminal Law § 631 (14th ed. 1981). An attorney who aids false testimony by questioning a witness when perjurious responses can be anticipated risks prosecution for subornation of perjury under Iowa Code § 720.3 (1985).

It is universally agreed that at a minimum the attorney's first duty when confronted with a proposal for perjurious testimony is to attempt to dissuade the client from the unlawful course of conduct. Model Rules of Professional Conduct, Rule 3.3, Comment; Wolfram, Client Perjury, 50 S.Cal.L.Rev. 809, 846 (1977). A statement directly in point is found in the commentary to the Model Rules of Professional Conduct under the heading "False Evidence": "When false evidence is offered by the client, however, a conflict may arise between the lawyer's duty to keep the client's revelations confidential and the duty of candor to the court. Upon ascertaining that material evidence is false, the lawyer *should seek to persuade the client that the evidence should not be offered* or, if it has been offered, that its false character should immediately be disclosed." Model Rules of Professional Conduct, Rule 3.3, Comment (1983) (emphasis added). The commentary thus also suggests that an attorney's revelation of his client's perjury to the court is a professionally responsible and acceptable response to the conduct of a client who has actually given perjured testimony. Similarly, the Model Rules and the commentary, as well as the Code of Professional Responsibility adopted in Iowa, expressly permit withdrawal from representation as an appropriate response of an attorney when the client threatens to commit perjury. Model Rules of Professional Conduct, Rule 1.16(a)(1), Rule 1.6, Comment (1983); Code of Professional Responsibility, DR 2–110(B), (C) (1980). Withdrawal of counsel when this situation arises at trial gives rise to many difficult questions including possible mistrial and claims of double jeopardy.

The essence of the brief amicus of the American Bar Association reviewing practices long accepted by ethical lawyers is that under no circumstance may a lawyer either advocate or passively tolerate a client's giving false testimony. This, of course, is consistent with the governance of trial conduct in what we have long called "a search for truth." The suggestion sometimes made that "a lawyer must believe his client, not judge him" in no sense means a lawyer can honorably be a party to or in any way give aid to presenting known perjury.

D

Considering Robinson's representation of respondent in light of these accepted norms of professional conduct, we discern no failure to adhere to reasonable professional standards that would in any sense make out a deprivation of the Sixth Amendment right to counsel. Whether Robinson's conduct is seen as a successful attempt to dissuade his client from committing the crime of perjury, or whether seen as a "threat" to withdraw from representation and disclose the illegal scheme, Robinson's representation of Whiteside falls well within accepted standards of professional conduct and the range of reasonable professional conduct acceptable under Strickland.

The Court of Appeals assumed for the purpose of the decision that Whiteside would have given false testimony had counsel not intervened; its opinion denying a rehearing en banc states: "[W]e presume that appellant would have testified falsely.

* * *

"... Counsel's actions prevented [Whiteside] from testifying falsely. We hold that counsel's action deprived appellant of due process and effective assistance of counsel.

* * *

"Counsel's actions also impermissibly compromised appellant's right to testify in his own defense by conditioning continued representation by counsel and confidentiality upon appellant's restricted testimony." 750 F.2d, at 714–715. While purporting to follow Iowa's highest court "on all questions of state law," 744 F.2d., at 1330, the Court of Appeals reached its conclusions on the basis of federal constitutional due process and right to counsel.

The Court of Appeals' holding that Robinson's "action deprived [Whiteside] of due process and effective assistance of counsel" is not supported by the record since Robinson's action, at most, deprived Whiteside of his contemplated perjury. Nothing counsel did in any way undermined Whiteside's claim that he believed the victim was reaching for a gun. Similarly, the record gives no support for holding that Robinson's action "also impermissibly compromised [Whiteside's] right to testify in his own defense by conditioning continued representation ... and confidentiality upon [Whiteside's] *restricted* testimony." The record in fact shows the contrary: (a) that Whiteside did testify, and (b) he was "restricted" or restrained only from testifying falsely and was aided by Robinson in developing the basis for the fear that Love was reaching for a gun. Robinson divulged no client communications until he was compelled to do so in response to Whiteside's post-trial challenge to the quality of his performance. We see this as a case in which the attorney successfully dissuaded the client from committing the crime of perjury.

Paradoxically, even while accepting the conclusion of the Iowa trial court that Whiteside's proposed testimony would have been a criminal act, the Court of Appeals held that Robinson's efforts to persuade Whiteside not to commit that crime were improper, *first*, as forcing an impermissible choice between the right to counsel and the right to testify; and, *second*, as compromising client confidences because of Robinson's threat to disclose the contemplated perjury.[7]

---

7. The Court of Appeals also determined that Robinson's efforts to persuade Whiteside to testify truthfully constituted an impermissible threat to testify against his own client. We find no support for a threat to testify against Whiteside while he was acting as counsel. The record reflects testimony by Robinson that he had admonished Whiteside that if he withdrew he "probably would be allowed to attempt to impeach that particular testimony," if Whiteside testified falsely. The trial court accepted this version of the conversation as true.

Whatever the scope of a constitutional right to testify, it is elementary that such a right does not extend to testifying *falsely*. In Harris v. New York, we assumed the right of an accused to testify "in his own defense, or to refuse to do so" and went on to hold: "[T]hat privilege cannot be construed to include the right to commit perjury. See United States v. Knox, 396 U.S. 77 [90 S.Ct. 363, 24 L.Ed.2d 275] (1969); cf. Dennis v. United States, 384 U.S. 855 [86 S.Ct. 1840, 16 L.Ed.2d 973] (1966). Having voluntarily taken the stand, petitioner was under an obligation to speak truthfully...." 401 U.S., at 225, 91 S.Ct., at 645. In Harris we held the defendant could be impeached by prior contrary statements which had been ruled inadmissible under Miranda v. Arizona, 384 U.S. 436, 86 S.Ct. 1602, 16 L.Ed.2d 694 (1966). Harris and other cases make it crystal clear that there is no right whatever—constitutional or otherwise—for a defendant to use false evidence. See also United States v. Havens, 446 U.S. 620, 626–627, 100 S.Ct. 1912, 1916–1917, 64 L.Ed.2d 559 (1980).

The paucity of authority on the subject of any such "right" may be explained by the fact that such a notion has never been responsibly advanced; the right to counsel includes no right to have a lawyer who will cooperate with planned perjury. A lawyer who would so cooperate would be at risk of prosecution for suborning perjury, and disciplinary proceedings, including suspension or disbarment.

Robinson's admonitions to his client can in no sense be said to have forced respondent into an *impermissible* choice between his right to counsel and his right to testify as he proposed for there was no *permissible* choice to testify falsely. For defense counsel to take steps to persuade a criminal defendant to testify truthfully, or to withdraw, deprives the defendant of neither his right to counsel nor the right to testify truthfully. In United States v. Havens, supra, we made clear that "when defendants testify, they must testify truthfully or suffer the consequences." Id., at 626, 100 S.Ct., at 1916. When an accused proposes to resort to perjury or to produce false evidence, one consequence is the risk of withdrawal of counsel.

On this record, the accused enjoyed continued representation within the bounds of reasonable professional conduct and did in fact exercise his right to testify; at most he was denied the right to have the assistance of counsel in the presentation of false testimony. Similarly, we can discern no breach of professional duty in Robinson's admonition to respondent that he would disclose respondent's perjury to the court. The crime of perjury in this setting is indistinguishable in substance from the crime of threatening or tampering with a witness or a juror. A defendant who informed his counsel that he was arranging to bribe or threaten witnesses or members of the jury would have no "right" to insist on counsel's assistance or silence. Counsel would not be limited to advising against that conduct. An attorney's duty of confidentiality, which totally covers the client's admission of guilt, does not extend to a client's announced plans to engage in future criminal conduct. See Clark v. United States, 289 U.S. 1, 15, 53 S.Ct. 465, 469, 77 L.Ed. 993 (1933). In short, the responsibility of an ethical lawyer, as an officer of the court and a key component of a system of justice, dedicated to a search for truth, is essentially the same whether the client announces an intention to bribe or threaten witnesses or jurors or to commit or procure perjury. No system of justice worthy of the name can tolerate a lesser standard.

The rule adopted by the Court of Appeals, which seemingly would require an attorney to remain silent while his client committed perjury, is wholly incompatible with the established standards of ethical conduct and the laws of Iowa and contrary to professional standards promulgated by that State. The position advocated by petitioner, on the contrary, is wholly consistent with the Iowa standards of professional conduct and law, with the overwhelming majority of courts, and with codes of professional ethics. Since there has been no breach of any recognized professional duty, it follows that there can be no deprivation of the right to assistance of counsel under the Strickland standard.

E

We hold that, as a matter of law, counsel's conduct complained of here cannot establish the prejudice required for relief under the second strand of the Strickland inquiry. Although a defendant need not establish that the attorney's deficient performance more likely than not altered the outcome in order to establish prejudice under Strickland, a defendant must show that "there is a reasonable probability that, but for counsel's unprofessional errors, the result of the proceeding would have been different." 466 U.S., at 694, 104 S.Ct., at 2068. According to Strickland, "[a] reasonable probability is a probability sufficient to undermine confidence in the outcome." Ibid. The Strickland Court noted that the "benchmark" of an ineffective-assistance claim is the fairness of the adversary proceeding, and that in judging prejudice and the likelihood of a different outcome, "[a] defendant has no entitlement to the luck of a lawless decisionmaker." Id., at 695, 104 S.Ct., at 2068.

Whether he was persuaded or compelled to desist from perjury, Whiteside has no valid claim that confidence in the result of his trial has been diminished by his desisting from the contemplated perjury. Even if we were to assume that the jury might have believed his perjury, it does not follow that Whiteside was prejudiced.

In his attempt to evade the prejudice requirement of Strickland, Whiteside relies on cases involving conflicting loyalties of counsel. In Cuyler v. Sullivan, 446 U.S. 335, 100 S.Ct. 1708, 64 L.Ed.2d 333 (1980),* we held that a defendant could obtain relief without pointing to a specific prejudicial default on the part of his counsel, provided it is established that the attorney was "actively represent[ing] conflicting interests." Id., at 350, 100 S.Ct., at 1719.

Here, there was indeed a "conflict," but of a quite different kind; it was one imposed on the attorney by the client's proposal to commit the

---

* Conflicts created by concurrent representation of two or more criminal defendants are discussed more extensively in Chapter 6 infra.—Ed.

crime of fabricating testimony without which, as he put it, "I'm dead." This is not remotely the kind of conflict of interests dealt with in Cuyler v. Sullivan. Even in that case we did not suggest that all multiple representations necessarily resulted in an active conflict rendering the representation constitutionally infirm. If a "conflict" between a client's proposal and counsel's ethical obligation gives rise to a presumption that counsel's assistance was prejudicially ineffective, every guilty criminal's conviction would be suspect if the defendant had sought to obtain an acquittal by illegal means. Can anyone doubt what practices and problems would be spawned by such a rule and what volumes of litigation it would generate?

Whiteside's attorney treated Whiteside's proposed perjury in accord with professional standards, and since Whiteside's truthful testimony could not have prejudiced the result of his trial, the Court of Appeals was in error to direct the issuance of a writ of habeas corpus and must be reversed. Reversed.

■ JUSTICE BRENNAN, concurring in the judgment.

This Court has no constitutional authority to establish rules of ethical conduct for lawyers practicing in the state courts. Nor does the Court enjoy any statutory grant of jurisdiction over legal ethics.

Accordingly, it is not surprising that the Court emphasizes that it "must be careful not to narrow the wide range of conduct acceptable under the Sixth Amendment so restrictively as to constitutionalize particular standards of professional conduct and thereby intrude into the state's proper authority to define and apply the standards of professional conduct applicable to those it admits to practice in its courts." Ante, at 165. I read this as saying in another way that the Court *cannot* tell the States or the lawyers in the States how to behave in their courts, unless and until federal rights are violated.

Unfortunately, the Court seems unable to resist the temptation of sharing with the legal community its vision of ethical conduct. But let there be no mistake: the Court's essay regarding what constitutes the correct response to a criminal client's suggestion that he will perjure himself is pure discourse without force of law. As Justice Blackmun observes, *that* issue is a thorny one, post, at 177–78, but it is not an issue presented by this case. Lawyers, judges, bar associations, students, and others should understand that the problem has not now been "decided."

I join Justice Blackmun's concurrence because I agree that respondent has failed to prove the kind of prejudice necessary to make out a claim under Strickland v. Washington, 466 U.S. 668, 104 S.Ct. 2052, 80 L.Ed.2d 674 (1984).

■ JUSTICE BLACKMUN filed an opinion concurring in the judgment in which JUSTICES BRENNAN, MARSHALL, and STEVENS, joined.

■ JUSTICE STEVENS filed an opinion concurring in the judgment.

QUESTIONS

1. What was the rationale for the common law rule that criminal defendants were disqualified from giving sworn testimony at their own trials?

2. As the Court points out, by the late nineteenth century the disqualification was abolished in favor of a right to testify on one's own behalf. Would this change have come about if courts had thought that lawyers would knowingly allow their clients to testify falsely?

3. The Court observes that Canon 32 "did no more than articulate centuries of accepted standards of conduct." What are these standards? If a trial is a search for truth, should a lawyer's duty to her client be limited to conduct that is compatible with seeking truth?

4. The Court quotes from the 1908 Canons of Professional Ethics, the 1980 Model Code of Professional Responsibility and the 1983 Model Rules. Are these texts "authority" on the client perjury issue? Which of these texts is legally binding on Robinson? Does the opinion mention a criminal statute that is binding on Robinson?

5. The Eighth Circuit, in reversing the Federal District Court applied the *Strickland* standards, and held that (i) Robinson was not properly functioning as counsel when he threatened to disclose Whiteside's intention to testify falsely and when he threatened to testify against Whiteside, and (ii) that Whiteside had been prejudiced by this conduct. The Circuit Court held that Robinson had undermined the trust that must exist between a client and lawyer and noted in passing that counsel should act not as "triers of fact, but advocates." Whiteside v. Scurr, 744 F.2d 1323, 1328 (8th Cir. 1984). However, when the case was argued before the Supreme Court, the American Bar Association supported the state in seeking reversal, and the Supreme Court unanimously reversed. Was the Eighth Circuit wrong in its conception of what it means to be "functioning as counsel?" Is there a difference between a lawyer acting as a "trier of fact" and making an ethical decision when faced with facts?

6. A lawyer is prohibited from assisting a client with bribing or coercing witnesses. Is there any reason to allow lawyers to assist perjury?

7. Some criminal defense lawyers might have asked Whiteside for his version of the facts only after informing him that a lawyer is required to disclose client perjury and advising him not to say something to his lawyer that will conflict with his testimony on the stand. Is it ethical for a lawyer to begin a discussion with a client in this manner?

8. Some criminal defense lawyers would have asked Whiteside for his version of the facts only after explaining to him the law on self defense. Is this approach ethical?

9. Assume that Whiteside had testified that he saw a gun in Love's hand. What should Robinson have done?

10. Justice Brennan's concurrence argues that "the Court's essay regarding what constitutes the correct response to a criminal client's suggestion that he will perjure himself is pure discourse without force of law."

Nonetheless, the "pure discourse" in *Whiteside* has carried weight in state courts. See State v. Waggoner, 124 Idaho 716, 864 P.2d 162 (App.1993) (criminal defendant's attorney properly disclosed to the court that defendant was testifying against advice of counsel when defendant insisted on testifying falsely); Stephenson v. State, 206 Ga.App. 273, 424 S.E.2d 816 (Ga.App.1992) (also citing *Whiteside* in holding that counsel's refusal to call defendant to testify perjuriously was not ineffective assistance).

Do you agree with Justice Brennan's concurring opinion in *Whiteside*? Can the Supreme Court speak with authority as to what is ethical conduct for an attorney?

Relevant Background

At various places, this casebook will discuss, under this heading **Relevant Background**, some of the case law, statutes and model codes of professional conduct that are relevant to a particular topic. The model codes mentioned most frequently are the ABA Model Code of Professional Responsibility (as originally adopted in 1969 and subsequently amended) (hereinafter referred to as the "Model Code") and the ABA Model Rules of Professional Conduct (as originally adopted in 1982 and subsequently amended) (hereinafter referred to as the "Model Rules" or a "Model Rule" for a single rule.). You should read provisions of the Model Code and Model Rules separately from a statutory supplement. See Thomas D. Morgan and Ronald D. Rotunda, Selected Standards on Professional Responsibility (1996). Other bar association materials referred to herein include ABA Committee on Ethics and Professional Responsibility Formal Opinions (each hereinafter referred to as an "ABA Formal Opinion") and the American Legal Institute (ALI) draft Restatement Third of the Law Governing Lawyers (hereinafter referred to as the "Restatement, The Law Governing Lawyers"). It is important, however, to realize that these model codes and bar opinions are not law and that each lawyer must be familiar with the rules in her own particular jurisdiction. A lawyer also is accountable for her actions under tort, contract, criminal or other applicable law.

Furthermore, a lawyer is responsible not only to professional standards, but also to her own conscience, and black letter ethics codes may reduce rather than enhance a lawyer's chances of being a good ethical decision maker. See Heidi Li Feldman, Codes and Virtues: Can Good Lawyers Be Good Ethical Deliberators, 69 S. Cal. L. Rev. 885, 948 (1996). A course of action which is completely in accordance with rules of professional conduct and other applicable law, may violate a lawyer's own sense of right and wrong. If so, she should look for an alternative course of action. The rules discussed under this heading may or may not provide guidance as to what that alternative should be.

Client Perjury

Commentary on the client perjury issue generally falls into one of two general categories: one prioritizing the lawyer as advocate, the other prioritizing the lawyer as officer of the court. Two articles represent the opposing sides in the debate. Monroe Freedman thirty years ago argued that a criminal defense lawyer unable to dissuade her client from committing perjury should allow the client to testify, question him like any other, and argue his perjured testimony to a jury. Monroe Freedman, Professional Responsibility of the Criminal Defense Lawyer: The Three Hardest Questions, 64 Mich. L. Rev. 1469, 1477–8 (1966). In other words, a client's decision to commit perjury should not affect the lawyer's obligation to fully assist her client at trial or to maintain her client's confidences. One of the authors of this casebook, writing in response to Professor Freedman, argued that "partisanship involved in keeping a communication confidential must be restricted when it leads to conduct which destroys the truth or presents perjury to the fact finder." John T. Noonan, Jr., The Purposes of Advocacy and the Limits of Confidentiality, 64 Mich. L. Rev. 1485, 1489 (1966). Furthermore, the lawyer's duty to obey his own conscience is greater than the duty owed to a particular client who chooses to lie. Id. at 1491.

Both the Model Code and the Model Rules clearly prohibit a lawyer from knowingly presenting false testimony or other false evidence. However, under Model Code DR 7–102(B)(1), a lawyer's duty to reveal perjury after it has occurred is qualified by the lawyer's duty not to reveal a client's "privileged communication." ABA Formal Opinion 341 (1975) interprets the words "privileged communication" in DR 7–102(B)(1) to include both "confidences" (information communicated to the lawyer by the client) *and* "secrets" (any other information learned in the course of the professional relationship). It is hard to imagine how a lawyer could learn about client perjury except through a "confidence" or a "secret." The exception to DR 7–102(B)(1) thus swallows the rule.

Model Rule 3.3 reverses this position. According to ABA Formal Opinion 87–353 (1987), "[i]t is now mandatory under these Model Rule provisions, for a lawyer, who knows the client has committed perjury, to disclose this knowledge to the tribunal if the lawyer cannot persuade the client to rectify the perjury . . . [this] represents a reversal of prior opinions of this Committee given under earlier rules of professional conduct." If the lawyer believes the client is going to commit perjury, the Opinion advises disclosure of such knowledge to the court, unless the lawyer can change her client's mind, avoid the perjury, or withdraw from the case. Id. More recently, ABA Formal Opinion 93–376 (1993) addresses situations where a client lies in response to discovery requests. The ABA recommends the same course of action it would at trial: attempt persuasion and withdrawal, and if these approaches fail, disclose to opposing counsel or to the court. Also, Model Rule 3.9 provides that a lawyer shall conform to Model Rule 3.3 when representing a client in a legislative or administrative proceeding.

The Comment to Model Rule 3.3 discusses perjury involving a criminal defendant. The lawyer's duty to disclose in a criminal case "has been intensely debated," and the Comment mentions two solutions to the dilemma: allow the client to give narrative testimony without guidance by the lawyer's questions, or excuse the lawyer of a criminal client from any duty to disclose. The Comment expresses dissatisfaction with both solutions, as both compromise the lawyer's duty of candor to the court. A third solution is to require a lawyer to reveal her client's perjury to the court. In support of this approach, the Comment points out that a lawyer has a duty to avoid falsification of evidence, and that a client does not have a right to assistance of counsel in committing perjury. Although the comment observes that "the lawyer's ethical duty in such a situation may be qualified by constitutional provisions for due process and the right to counsel in criminal cases," the Supreme Court subsequently addressed these concerns in *Nix v. Whiteside*. The Justices were unanimous in refusing to create a new constitutional right to legal representation that includes a lawyer's tolerance of perjury. See also United States v. Henkel, 799 F.2d 369, 370 (7th Cir.1986) (defendant "had no right to lie" and, therefore, was not deprived of right to counsel because his lawyer refused to present testimony which the lawyer knew would be false).

Although jurisdictions differ in their approach to the client perjury problem, there is significant unanimity on one point: it is simply not an option for a lawyer to put her client on the stand and ask him questions if the lawyer knows the client is going to lie and the lawyer will not disclose the perjury to the court. See Model Rule 1.2(d) (prohibiting a lawyer from counseling or assisting a client in criminal conduct). As the Supreme Court points out in *Nix*, "[a] lawyer who would so cooperate would be at risk of prosecution for suborning perjury, and disciplinary proceedings, including suspension or disbarment." 475 U.S. at 173.

Disciplinary penalties for using perjured testimony can be severe. ABA Standards for Imposing Lawyer Discipline, Section 6.12 provides that "Suspension is generally appropriate when a lawyer knows that false statements ... are being submitted to the court ... and takes no remedial action, and causes injury or potential injury to a party to the legal proceeding, or causes an adverse or potentially adverse effect on the legal proceeding." The ABA Model Rules for Lawyer Disciplinary Enforcement provide for immediate suspension of a lawyer convicted of a "serious crime," defined as a crime that "reflects adversely on the lawyer's honesty, trustworthiness or fitness as a lawyer in other respects, or any crime a necessary element of which ... involves interference with the administration of justice...." Rule 19—Lawyers Convicted of a Crime, paragraphs B and D. Furthermore, "[i]t is difficult to understand ... why a lawyer convicted of conspiracy to suborn perjury can continue to try cases and present witnesses. Immediate suspension of a lawyer so convicted, regardless of the pendency of any appeal, is essential to preserve public confidence." Commentary to Rule 19, paragraph 3.

Disciplinary proceedings have been brought against lawyers who help clients to perjure themselves, or who simply allow perjury to occur. In In re Mack, 519 N.W.2d 900 (Minn.1994), John Mack's client, an insured seeking to collect from her insurance company after an accident, falsely claimed in a deposition that she had mailed her premium payment on time. In fact, she had left the envelope containing payment in the post office a few days after the accident, and several days after the due date, hoping to blame the delay on the post office. Mack later learned that the client had lied, but assured her that she could simply remain silent. However, the client reiterated her false testimony under direct examination by another lawyer who took Mack's place at trial. The truth came out when the client was cross-examined, and the court ordered that Mack be suspended from practice. The court found that "[n]ot only did Mack's silence in the face of his client's perjury violate Rule 3.3, but it was deceitful and prejudicial to the administration of justice.... Mack's silence was tantamount to acquiescence to the deception." Id. at 902. See In re Salmen, 484 N.W.2d 253, 254 (Minn.1992) ("[F]alse testimony strikes at the very heart of the administration of justice.").

More often, decisions concerning client perjury arise not in the disciplinary context, but in criminal appeals where a client claims ineffective assistance of counsel, or in cases where an attorney seeks to withdraw from a representation. Almost all case law supports the conclusion reached by the Supreme Court in *Nix v. Whiteside* that a lawyer must fulfill his duty of honesty to the court, even if doing so harms his client or results in a conviction. Even before *Whiteside*, it was recognized that a lawyer's duty to represent her client "must be met in conjunction with, rather than in opposition to, other professional obligations." Thornton v. United States, 357 A.2d 429, 437 (D.C.App.), cert. denied, 429 U.S. 1024 (1976).

Some courts require that, particularly in the context of a criminal representation, a lawyer have a firm factual basis before refusing to present testimony or revealing perjury to the court. "Because of the gravity of a decision to notify a court of potential client perjury, a reasonable lawyer would only act on a firm factual basis." United States v. Long, 857 F.2d 436, 445, n. 5 (8th Cir.1988). "The most weighty decision in a case of possible client perjury is made by the lawyer who decides to inform the court and perhaps incidentally his adversary and the jury ... of his client's possible perjury. This occurs when the lawyer makes a motion for withdrawal, usually for unstated reasons ... or allows his client to testify in narrative form.... Once this has been done, the die is cast. The prejudice will have occurred." Id. at 447. But see United States v. Curtis, 742 F.2d 1070, 1076 (7th Cir.1984) (defendant has no right to testify against his lawyer's advice where it is "apparent" that defendant would lie).

QUESTIONS

1. Model Rule 3.3 *permits* a lawyer to refuse to present evidence that she "reasonably believes" is false, and *prohibits* her from "knowingly" offering false evidence. Also, Model Rule 3.3, like the Model Code, provides that only when a lawyer knows that evidence she already has offered is false, shall she take reasonable remedial measures which might require breach of client confidentiality. What does it take for a lawyer to know that evidence is false? Does a lawyer have an obligation to investigate further if she suspects that her client is lying?

2. Much of the scholarship on client perjury written after the Freedman and Noonan articles discusses how a lawyer knows that a client is lying. For example, Professor Hazard observes that "as the matter unfolds, it may appear to the lawyer that the portents of abuse are strong or weak, clear or ambiguous, firm or wavering," and inquires, "[w]hen are these portents sufficiently certain so that the lawyer 'knows' that the client intends an illegal objective and is bent on its accomplishment?" Geoffrey C. Hazard, Jr., How Far May a Lawyer Go in Assisting a Client in Legally Wrongful Conduct? 35 U. Miami L. Rev. 669, 672 (1981). Norman Lefstein observes that, despite guidelines available for handling a client perjury situation, determining whether a client is lying is often difficult. Lefstein, Client Perjury in Criminal Cases: Still in Search of an Answer, 1 Geo. J. Legal Ethics 521, 527–533 (1988).

(a) How did Robinson know that Whiteside was lying? Could he prove it? Should proof have been required for Robinson to refuse to allow Whiteside to testify that he saw a gun?

(b) Can the "dimension of uncertainty" described by Professor Hazard become an excuse for not confronting obvious facts, particularly if those facts require a lawyer to make a difficult decision?

(c) Professor Subin has suggested that a defense lawyer can determine the truth after the lawyer examines all available evidence in support of her client's defense and weighs it with a strong presumption in favor of the client. See Harry Subin, The Criminal Lawyer's "Different Mission": Reflections on the "Right" to Present a False Case, 1 Geo. J. Legal Ethics 125, 141–143 (1987). "The attorney should be able to present a defense unless he or she 'knew' beyond a reasonable doubt that the defense was false." Id. at 142. "The standard proposed here does not require actual or subjective knowledge of the falsity of the defense. It holds the attorney to the standard of a reasonably competent attorney who has made an adequate investigation of a particular defense." Id., n. 82. Do you agree with Professor Subin's standard for determining when a lawyer is forbidden to present a defense? Is a different standard appropriate for determining whether a lawyer *may* refuse to present a defense?

3. May a lawyer allow a client to testify falsely in narrative form rather than answer questions from the lawyer? This "narrative approach" was endorsed in ABA Defense Function Standard 7.7 (1971), but then rejected as "no longer applicable" because "under Model Rule 3.3(a)(2) and the recent Supreme Court decision in *Nix v. Whiteside* the lawyer can no longer rely on the narrative approach to insulate the lawyer from a charge of assisting the client's perjury." ABA Formal Opinion 353 (1987). Nonetheless, narrative testimony remains popular among some criminal defense lawyers. The Connecticut Bar Association has supported the narrative approach in criminal trials: "A lawyer may not assist a client to commit perjury, but must allow a criminal defendant to take the stand and testify in narrative form." 67 Conn. B. J. 153 (April, 1993). Commonwealth v. Jermyn, 533 Pa. 194, 620 A.2d 1128 (Pa.1993), ruled that the trial counsel of a man convicted of murder acted reasonably when he asked his client if he would like to make a general statement to the jury, but refrained from asking the defendant questions that would be answered untruthfully. However, most courts reject this approach. See United States v. Curtis, 742 F.2d 1070 (7th Cir.1984) (defendant's constitutional rights not violated where attorney refused to put defendant on the witness stand because it was apparent that defendant would offer perjured testimony); McKissick v. United States, 379 F.2d 754 (5th Cir.1967), aff'd after remand, 398 F.2d 342 (5th Cir.1968) (where attorney is made aware that client has committed perjury or will attempt to do so, it is the attorney's professional, ethical and public duty to make the court aware of such conduct). Do you think the narrative approach is ethical?

4.   The Florida Bar v. Rubin, 549 So.2d 1000 (Fla.1989) is one of the most controversial cases in which a court endorsed the narrative approach. Ellis Rubin attempted to withdraw from representing a client about to commit perjury on the grounds that Rubin was ethically opposed to the narrative testimony approach then used by Florida courts. The court repeatedly denied his motion to withdraw, and when Rubin would not go to trial, he was cited with contempt and sentenced to thirty days in jail. The Florida Supreme Court had to decide "whether a lawyer may disobey a court order because he or she believes that order to be erroneous." Id. at 1001. The court decided that Rubin was "not permitted to ignore and refuse to follow a court order based upon his personal belief in the invalidity of that order," regardless of whether the ABA or anybody else would agree with his views. Id. at 1003. The dissenting opinion is more sympathetic to Rubin's dilemma, and points out that "[b]y refusing to participate in the crime of perjury, he chose the course of conduct that he believed constituted the least grievous violation, and his choice has been vindicated by [a number of authorities], all of which have condemned the narrative approach." Id. at 1004–5.

(a) Rubin was willing to go to jail rather than obey a judge's order that he offer perjured testimony in a criminal trial. In Chapter 11, you will read about how Thomas More faced execution for his refusal to take an oath that violated his religious principles. Under what circumstances should a lawyer disobey a court order rather than do something he believes to be wrong?

(b) Although a lawyer's conscience is important, the legal system would not function if each lawyer could make up her own rules of professional responsibility. How far should a judge go in seeking to require a lawyer to do something that the lawyer sincerely believes is wrong? What discipline should be imposed on a lawyer who violates a court order or an ethical rule because her conscience forbids obedience? See Maura Strassberg, Taking Ethics Seriously: Beyond Positivist Jurisprudence in Legal Ethics, 80 Iowa L. Rev. 901, 952 (1995) ("At a minimum, express acknowledgment of moral motivation as a mitigating factor would reduce, although certainly not eliminate, the threat of career-threatening discipline as a consequence of reasonable attempts to act ethically, while what is ethical behavior is recognized as fundamentally controversial.")

5. Iowa State Bar Ass'n v. Crary, 245 N.W.2d 298 (Iowa 1976), revoked a lawyer's license because of his participation in the perjury of his client. The court found that "[i]f [an attorney] knowingly suffers a witness to lie, he undermines the integrity of the fact-finding system of which he himself is an integral part." Id. at 305. Quoting the Canons of Professional Ethics, Canon 15 (1957), the court reiterated that the "office of attorney does not permit, much less does it demand of him for any client, violation of law or any manner of fraud or chicane. He must obey his own conscience and not that of his client." Id. at 306. The *Crary* court even stated that "no duty exists to the client when the client perjures himself to the knowledge of the attorney." Id. at 306.

(a) Why must a lawyer obey his own conscience rather than that of his client?

(b) Do you agree that no duty exists to a client who perjures himself? What duty might a lawyer have to such a client?

6. A lawyer may want to resign from a case before perjured testimony is offered. In People v. Schultheis, 638 P.2d 8 (Colo.1981), the court held that an attorney was allowed to withdraw rather than call witnesses who would testify falsely. However, the attorney did not have to disclose the nature of the intended false testimony to the trial judge. But see People v. Albaracon Salquerro, 107 Misc.2d 155, 433 N.Y.S.2d 711 (Sup. Ct. N.Y. Co.1980) (holding that an attorney *should* disclose and *should not* withdraw because the client would probably ask another lawyer to assist with the perjured testimony). Should Robinson have resigned instead of threaten to disclose Whiteside's perjury?

Attorney Competence

The Sixth Amendment guarantees all defendants in criminal cases the right to assistance of counsel and the Supreme Court has ruled that the assistance must be effective. McMann v. Richardson, 397 U.S. 759, 771 (1970). As the Court pointed out in *Whiteside, Strickland v. Washington* developed a two part test to determine if assistance of counsel was constitutionally defective. 466 U.S. 668, 694 (1984). A defendant challenging a conviction "bears the burden of showing: (1) that counsel's performance was deficient; and (2) that the deficient performance prejudiced the defense." Kubat v. Thieret, 867 F.2d 351, 359 (7th Cir.)(citing *Strickland*), cert. denied, 493 U.S. 874 (1989). It is important to remember, however, that work done by an attorney for a criminal defendant need not be constitutionally defective to fall below the standards of professional competence required in the lawyer's jurisdiction and thus subject the lawyer to discipline or suit for malpractice.

Generally, attorneys should not handle matters which they are not competent to handle, handle matters without adequate preparation or neglect matters entrusted to them. Model Code of Professional Responsibility DR 6–101(A)(1) (1980). The Code does not, however, define "competence." The Model Rules seek to clarify these standards. "A lawyer shall provide competent representation to a client. Competent representation requires the legal knowledge, skill, thoroughness and preparation reasonably necessary for the representation." Model Rule 1.1. The comment to Model Rule 1.1 goes on to state that factors relevant to determining knowledge and skill are:

> the relative complexity and specialized nature of the matter, the lawyer's general experience, the lawyer's training and experience in the field in question, the preparation and study the lawyer is able to give the matter and whether it is feasible to refer the matter to, or associate or consult with, a lawyer of established competence in the field is question. In many instances, the required proficiency is that of a general practitioner. Expertise in a particular field of law may be required in some circumstances.

Id., cmt. The ALI's draft Restatement also points out that a lawyer must "act with reasonable competence and diligence." Restatement, The Law Governing Lawyers, Section 28 (1996), citing Restatement, Second, Agency, Section 379. A lawyer should "perform the services called for by the client's objectives, including appropriate factual research, legal analysis, and exercise of professional judgment." Id., cmt. d. See also, A Model Peer Review System: Excerpts From Discussion Draft (ALI–ABA, 1980).

The Paradigm of Zealous Representation

ABA Canon 7 states that "[a] lawyer should represent a client zealously within the bounds of the law." However, putting a lying witness on the stand, and thereby defrauding the court, is one of the most extreme deeds a lawyer can commit out of supposed loyalty to his client. Such "loyalty" of course presumes that no harm will come to the client from lying under oath, a doubtful assumption at best. This loyalty paradigm has such a powerful grip on the principles of the profession that it arises in many other contexts where a client asks a lawyer to do something that the lawyer knows is wrong. As you read through this casebook, you will encounter lawyers who consider doing just about anything on behalf of their clients, whether it be bribing a judge (see *Report on the Conduct of Albert W. Johnson*, Chapter 2 infra), misleading Congress to cover up for a political superior (see *United States v. Kleindienst*, Chapter 3 infra), or invoking anti-immigrant prejudice to obtain a conviction in a capital case (*Commonwealth v. Sacco*, Chapter 8 infra). In each of these cases, you should ask yourself if the lawyers are truly loyal to their clients. Are they acting in the client's best interests? Is such "loyalty" justified?

QUESTIONS

1. Did Robinson "zealously" represent Whiteside?

2. The American Heritage Dictionary (2d. Ed. 1985) defines "zealous" to mean "filled with or motivated by zeal; fervent," and "zeal" to mean "enthusiastic and diligent devotion in pursuit of a cause, ideal, or goal; fervor." Does ABA Canon 7 use appropriate language to describe the duty of a lawyer to her client? Does this language lack the sense of balance required for a lawyer to honor her other obligations (such as to the court and to her own conscience)?

3. Is it possible to "zealously" represent a client whom you know is lying? What about a cause that you know is wrong? You will come back to this question when you read about Abraham Lincoln's argument of a pro-slavery case in Chapter 7 infra.

PROBLEMS

1. You represent Towntrust, a commercial bank that has been sued by the Justice Department for violating the antitrust laws by fixing rates on consumer loans. In preparation for trial, you interview three executives in charge of the loan department. Two of them insist that there is no price fixing with other banks. However, the third tells you that the three officers meet once a month with senior loan officers at two other local banks to discuss "current economic conditions," including interest rates. When you confront the other two, they tell you that no such meeting ever took place and that their colleague is "living in a fantasy world." The third loan officer does not have any grievances against Towntrust and you have no reason to believe that he would make things up. However, the third officer dies before trial and before being deposed in pretrial discovery. Do you put the other two loan officers on the stand?

2. Towntrust is also being sued by its shareholders for making loans without sufficient collateral to a real estate company owned by the directors of Towntrust. Because a critical issue in the case is the value of the real estate used as collateral for the loans, you hire an appraiser to determine its value and to testify at trial. The appraiser reviews records of rental income from the real estate before preparing her appraisal. After the appraiser's testimony at trial, and right before closing arguments, an employee of the real estate company tells you that the appraiser was given falsified records showing inflated rents. What do you do?

3. In the above scenario, you tell the appraiser what the actual rents were and she tells you that her valuation of the real estate would not change. Nonetheless, records showing the inflated rents were attached to the appraisal submitted to the court as an exhibit at trial. What do you do?

B. USE AND ABUSE OF CIVIL PROCESS

Relevant Background

Lawyers in the Labor Arena

Civil process can be used in many different settings, and the *Bill Johnson's Restaurants* case, infra, illustrates how lawsuits are sometimes used in labor disputes. It is not surprising that labor disputes, historically associated with more than occasional violence on both sides, are prone to abusive tactics at the bar as well as on the picket line.

Lawyer participation in labor disputes dates back to the Nineteenth Century. For example, Philander C. Knox, who later was appointed Secretary of State by President McKinley, was the attorney for steel magnate Henry Clay Frick in connection with a strike outside Pittsburgh in 1892. Their preferred tactics against striking workers were perhaps best described by an accountant in Knox's office who recalled overhearing,

> Henry C. Frick in the Firm's office excitedly, loudly and acrimoniously blame Mr. Knox for originating what had turned out to be the ill-advised and ill-fated plan of sending 150 armed Pinkerton detectives up the Monongahela River in two covered barges pushed by a steamboat named "Little Bill" in an unsuccessful attempt to take over the beleaguered Homestead Steel Works on the south bank of the river.

R. Demmler, Reed Smith Shaw & McClay 20 (1977) (quoting recollection of Robert Russell). Whether or not Knox conceived the plan of sending in the Pinkerton detectives, he was responsible for requesting that the Allegheny County sheriff deputize them after they arrived. Id. at 20–21.

After the unionization of much of the workforce in the first half of this century and passage of the National Labor Relations Act in 1935, confrontation in labor-management relations became more legal than physical, and what used to be the work of armed Pinkerton detectives became the work of lawyers armed with their ability to interpret, and sometimes manipulate, the law. Labor and management now use the bargaining process to exert pressure on each other and sometimes engage in "strategic behavior," such as boycotts and lockouts. See Kenneth G. Dau–Schmidt, A Bargaining Analysis of American Labor Law and the Search for Bargaining Equity and Industrial Peace, 91 Mich. L. Rev. 419, 475–478 (1992) (discussing various types of strategic behavior in the collective bargaining process and the role of labor law in regulating and deterring the same).

Lawyers have assisted clients with labor negotiations by becoming experts in federal regulation of strikes, lockouts and the collective bargaining process. Indeed, during the frequent strikes of the late 1940's and 1950's, lawyers often spent the duration of a strike on site monitoring "strategic behavior" of both management and labor. One second-year associate at Reed, Smith, Shaw & McClay, the successor to Knox's firm, recalled spending much of 1955 at Westinghouse's Small Motors Division plants in Lima, Ohio and Union City, Indiana. His,

> . . . activities involved legal advice concerning the "back to work" movement at Union City, Indiana, securing an injunction against violence on the picket line, processing criminal charges, representing the Company in a Grand Jury investigation, preparing a daily report of picket line activities, advising [the] Company concerning the discipline of striking employees and the preparation of strike discipline cases for arbitration.

Demmler, supra at 172.

Parties to a labor dispute thus often ask lawyers to assist with instigating or opposing strategic behavior. See Richard W. Painter, The

Moral Interdependence of Corporate Lawyers and Their Clients, 67 S. Cal. L. Rev. 507, 535–38 (1994) (discussing the above-mentioned examples of strategic behavior). Such strategic behavior may include filing a lawsuit in order to accomplish objectives outside the parameters of the suit itself. As you read the following case, ask yourself if the lawsuit filed against the waitresses at Bill Johnson's Restaurants is an acceptable form of strategic behavior. Is this a use for which the judicial system was designed?

Lawrence A. Katz, b. 1942, New York, New York; B.A., Harvard 1964; J.D., Boston College 1967 (Editor-in-chief of the Law Review); practiced law in New York City 1967–75; admitted to the Arizona bar 1975; partner of Streich, Lang, Weeks and Cardon (Phoenix); represented the restaurant in the proceedings referred to below.

Bill Johnson's Restaurants, Inc., Petitioner v. National Labor Relations Board

461 U.S. 731 (1983).

■ JUSTICE WHITE delivered the opinion of the Court.

We must decide whether the Board may issue a cease-and-desist order to halt the prosecution of a state court civil suit brought by an employer to retaliate against employees for exercising federally-protected labor rights, without also finding that the suit lacks a reasonable basis in fact or law.

I

The present controversy arises out of a labor dispute at "Bill Johnson's Big Apple East," one of four restaurants owned and operated by the petitioner in Phoenix, Arizona. It began on August 8, 1978, when petitioner fired Myrland Helton, one of the most senior waitresses at the restaurant. Believing that her termination was the result of her efforts to organize a union, she filed unfair labor practice charges against the restaurant with the Board.

On September 20, after an investigation, the Board's General Counsel issued a complaint. On the same day, Helton, joined by three co-waitresses and a few others, picketed the restaurant. The picketers carried signs asking customers to boycott the restaurant because its management was unfair to the waitresses. Petitioner's manager confronted the picketers and threatened to "get even" with them "if it's the last thing I do." Petitioner's president telephoned the husband of one of the picketing waitresses and impliedly threatened that the couple would "get hurt" and lose their new home if the wife continued to participate in the protest. The picketing continued on September 21 and 22. In addition, the picketers distributed a leaflet that accused management of making "[u]nwarranted sexual advances" and maintaining a "filthy restroom for women employees." The leaflet also stated that a complaint against the restaurant had been filed by the Board and that Helton had been fired after suggesting that a union be organized.

On the morning of September 25, petitioner and three of its co-owners filed a verified complaint against Helton and the other demonstrators in an Arizona state court. Plaintiffs alleged that the defendants had engaged in mass picketing, harassed customers, blocked public ingress to and egress from the restaurant, and created a threat to public safety. The complaint also contained a libel count, alleging that the leaflet contained false and outrageous statements published by the defendants with the malicious intent to injure the plaintiffs. The complaint sought a temporary restraining order and preliminary and permanent injunctive relief, as well as compensatory damages, $500,000 in punitive damages, and appropriate further legal and equitable relief. App. 3–9. After a hearing, the state court declined to enjoin the distribution of leaflets but otherwise issued the requested restraining order. Id. 19–23. Expedited depositions were also permitted. The defendants retained counsel and, after a hearing on the plaintiffs' motion for a preliminary injunction on November 16, the court dissolved the temporary restraining order and denied preliminary injunctive relief. Id. 52.

Meanwhile, on the day after the state-court suit was filed, Helton filed a second charge with the Board alleging that petitioner had committed a number of new unfair labor practices in connection with the dispute between the waitresses and the restaurant. Among these was a charge that petitioner had filed the civil suit in retaliation for the defendants' protected, concerted activities, and because they had filed charges under the Act. The General Counsel issued a complaint based on these new charges on October 23. As relevant here, the complaint alleged that petitioner, by filing and prosecuting the state suit, was attempting to retaliate against Helton and the others, in violation of §§ 8(a)(1) and (4) of the National Labor Relations Act (NLRA or Act), 29 U.S.C.A. §§ 158(a)(1) and (4).[1]

In December 1978, an Administrative Law Judge (ALJ) held a four-day consolidated hearing on the two unfair-labor-practice complaints. On September 27, 1979, the ALJ rendered a decision concluding that petitioner had committed a total of seven unfair labor practices during the course of the labor dispute. 249 N.L.R.B. 155, 168–169 (1980). With regard to the matter presently before us, the ALJ agreed with the General Counsel that the prosecution of the civil suit violated §§ 8(a)(1) and (4). The ALJ applied the rationale of Power Systems, Inc., 239 N.L.R.B. 445, 449–450 (1978), enforcement denied, 601 F.2d 936 (C.A.7 1979), in which the Board held that it is an unfair labor practice for an employer to institute a civil lawsuit for the purpose of penalizing or discouraging its employees from filing charges with the Board or seeking access to the Board's processes.

---

1. These provisions state: "It shall be an unfair labor practice for an employer—(1) to interfere with, restrain, or coerce employees in the exercise of rights guaranteed in [§ 7 of the Act]; . . . (4) to discharge or otherwise discriminate against an employee because he has filed charges or given testimony under this subchapter." 29 U.S.C.A. §§ 158(a)(1) and (4). Section 7 guarantees employees "the right to self-organization, to form, join, or assist labor organizations, . . . and to engage in other concerted activities for the purpose of collective bargaining or other mutual aid or protection." 29 U.S.C.A. § 157.

In Power Systems, the Board inferred that the employer had acted with retaliatory animus from the fact that the employer lacked "a reasonable basis upon which to assert" that its suit had merit. Similarly, in the present case, the ALJ found that petitioner's suit lacked a reasonable basis and then concluded from this fact that the suit violated the Act because it was "an attempt to penalize Helton for having filed charges with the Board, and to penalize the other defendants for assisting Helton in her protest of the unfair labor practice committed against her." 249 N.L.R.B. at 165. He bolstered his conclusion by noting the direct evidence that the suit had been filed for a retaliatory purpose, i.e., the threats to "get even with" and "hurt" the defendants. Id.

The ALJ reached his conclusion that petitioner's state suit lacked a reasonable basis "on the basis of the record and from [his] observation of the witnesses, including their demeanor, and upon the extensive briefs of the parties." Id. at 164. In the view of the ALJ, the "evidence failed to support" the complaint's allegations that the picketers clogged the sidewalks, harassed customers, or blocked entrances and exits to the restaurant. Id. at 165. The libel count was deemed baseless because "the evidence establishe[d] the truthfulness" of everything stated in the leaflet.

On petitioner's appeal, the Board adopted, with minor exceptions, the ALJ's findings, conclusions of law and recommended order. Id. at 155. Accordingly, petitioner was ordered to undertake a number of remedial measures. Among other things, petitioner was required to withdraw its state-court complaint and to reimburse the defendants for all their legal expenses in connection with the suit. Id. at 169–170.

The Court of Appeals enforced the Board's order in its entirety, 660 F.2d 1335 (C.A.9 1981), holding that substantial evidence supported both the Board's findings that the employer's "lawsuit lacked a reasonable basis in fact, and that it was filed to penalize Helton [and] the picketers for engaging in protected activity." Id. at 1342. Petitioner sought certiorari, urging that it could not properly be enjoined from maintaining its state-court action. We granted the writ, 459 U.S. 942, 103 S.Ct. 253, 74 L.Ed.2d 198 (1982), and we now vacate and remand for further proceedings.

II

The question whether the Board may issue a cease-and-desist order to halt an allegedly retaliatory lawsuit filed by an employer in a state court has had a checkered history before the Board.[5] [The Court describes the Board's wavering position on this issue from 1950 through 1978]....

... Since 1978, the Board has consistently adhered to the Power Systems rule that an employer or union who sues an employee for a retaliatory motive is guilty of a violation of the Act. Under this line of

---

5. It should be kept in mind that what is involved here is an employer's lawsuit that the federal law would not bar except for its allegedly retaliatory motivation. We are not dealing with a suit that is claimed to be beyond the jurisdiction of the state courts because of federal-law preemption, or a suit that has an objective that is illegal under federal law....

cases, as the Board's brief and its counsel's remarks at oral argument in the present case confirm, the Board does not regard lack of merit in the employer's suit as an independent element of the § 8(a)(1) and § 8(a)(4) unfair labor practice. Rather, it asserts that the *only* essential element of a violation is retaliatory motive.

III

A

At first blush, the Board's position seems to have substance. Sections 8(a)(1) and (4) of the Act are broad, remedial provisions that guarantee that employees will be able to enjoy their rights secured by § 7 of the Act—including the right to unionize, the right to engage in concerted activity for mutual aid and protection, and the right to utilize the Board's processes—without fear of restraint, coercion, discrimination, or interference from their employer. The Court has liberally construed these laws as prohibiting a wide variety of employer conduct that is intended to restrain, or that has the likely effect of restraining, employees in the exercise of protected activities. A lawsuit no doubt may be used by an employer as a powerful instrument of coercion or retaliation. As the Board has observed, by suing an employee who files charges with the Board or engages in other protected activities, an employer can place its employees on notice that anyone who engages in such conduct is subjecting himself to the possibility of a burdensome lawsuit. Regardless of how unmeritorious the employer's suit is, the employee will most likely have to retain counsel and incur substantial legal expenses to defend against it. Power Systems, supra, at 449. Furthermore, as the Court of Appeals in the present case noted, the chilling effect of a state lawsuit upon an employee's willingness to engage in protected activity is multiplied where the complaint seeks damages in addition to injunctive relief. 660 F.2d at 1343, n.3. Where, as here, such a suit is filed against hourly-wage waitresses or other individuals who lack the backing of a union, the need to allow the Board to intervene and provide a remedy is at its greatest.

There are weighty countervailing considerations, however, that militate against allowing the Board to condemn the filing of a suit as an unfair labor practice and to enjoin its prosecution. In California Motor Transport Co. v. Trucking Unlimited, 404 U.S. 508, 510, 92 S.Ct. 609, 611, 30 L.Ed.2d 642 (1972), we recognized that the right of access to the courts is an aspect of the First Amendment right to petition the Government for redress of grievances. Accordingly, we construed the antitrust laws as not prohibiting the filing of a lawsuit, regardless of the plaintiff's anticompetitive intent or purpose in doing so, unless the suit was a "mere sham" filed for harassment purposes. Id. at 511, 92 S.Ct. at 612. We should be sensitive to these First Amendment values in construing the NLRA in the present context. As the Board itself has recognized, "going to a judicial body for redress of alleged wrongs ... stands apart from other forms of action directed at the alleged wrongdoer. The right of access to a court is too important to be called an unfair labor practice solely on the ground that what is sought in court is to enjoin employees from exercising a protected right." Peddie

Buildings, 203 N.L.R.B. 265, 272 (1973), enforcement denied on other grounds, NLRB v. Visceglia, 498 F.2d 43 (C.A.3 1974). See also Clyde Taylor Co., 127 N.L.R.B. 103, 109 (1960).

Moreover, in recognition of the States' compelling interest in the maintenance of domestic peace, the Court has construed the Act as not preempting the States from providing a civil remedy for conduct touching interests "deeply rooted in local feeling and responsibility." San Diego Building Trades Council v. Garmon, 359 U.S. 236, 244, 79 S.Ct. 773, 779, 3 L.Ed.2d 775 (1959). It has therefore repeatedly been held that an employer has the right to seek local judicial protection from tortious conduct during a labor dispute. See, e.g., Sears, Roebuck & Co. v. Carpenters, 436 U.S. 180, 98 S.Ct. 1745, 56 L.Ed.2d 209 (1978)....

In Linn v. Plant Guard Workers, ... [383 U.S. at 65, 86 S.Ct. at 664 (1966)], we held that an employer can properly recover damages in a tort action arising out of a labor dispute if it can prove malice and actual injury. See also Farmer v. Carpenters, ... [430 U.S., at 306, 97 S.Ct., at 1066 (1977)]. If the Board is allowed to enjoin the prosecution of a well-grounded state lawsuit, it necessarily follows that any state plaintiff subject to such an injunction will be totally deprived of a remedy for an actual injury, since the "Board can award no damages, impose no penalty, or give any other relief" to the plaintiff. Linn, supra, 383 U.S. at 63, 86 S.Ct. at 663. Thus, to the extent the Board asserts the right to declare the filing of a meritorious suit to be a violation of the Act, it runs headlong into the basic rationale of Linn, Farmer, and other cases in which we declined to infer a congressional intent to ignore the substantial State interest "in protecting the health and well-being of its citizens." Farmer, supra, 430 U.S. at 302–303, 97 S.Ct. at 1064–65....

Of course, in light of the Board's special competence in applying the general provisions of the Act to the complexities of industrial life, its interpretations of the Act are entitled to deference, even where, as here, its position has not been entirely consistent.... And here, were only the literal language of §§ 8(a)(1) and 8(a)(4) to be considered, we would be inclined to uphold the Board, because its present construction of the statute is not irrational. Considering the First Amendment right of access to the courts and the State interests identified in cases such as Linn and Farmer, however, we conclude that the Board's interpretation of the Act is untenable. The filing and prosecution of a well-founded lawsuit may not be enjoined as an unfair labor practice, even if it would not have been commenced but for the plaintiff's desire to retaliate against the defendant for exercising rights protected by the Act.

B

Although it is not unlawful under the Act to prosecute a meritorious action, the same is not true of suits based on insubstantial claims—suits that lack, to use the term coined by the Board, a "reasonable basis." Such suits are not within the scope of First Amendment protection: "The first amendment interests involved in private litigation—compensation for violated rights and interests, the psychological benefits of vindication, public airing of disputed facts—are not advanced when the litigation is based on intentional falsehoods or on knowingly frivolous claims. Furthermore, since sham litigation by definition does not involve a bona fide grievance, it does not come within the first amendment right to petition."[10]

Just as false statements are not immunized by the First Amendment right to freedom of speech, see Herbert v. Lando, 441 U.S. 153, 171, 99 S.Ct. 1635, 1646, 60 L.Ed.2d 115 (1979); Gertz v. Robert Welch, Inc., 418 U.S. 323, 340, 94 S.Ct. 2997, 3007, 41 L.Ed.2d 789 (1974), baseless litigation is not immunized by the First Amendment right to petition.

Similarly, the State interests recognized in the Farmer line of cases do not enter into play when the state-court suit has no basis. Since, by definition, the plaintiff in a baseless suit has not suffered a legally-protected injury, the State's interest "in protecting the health and well-being of its citizens," Farmer, supra, 430 U.S. at 303, 97 S.Ct. at 1065, is not implicated. States have only a negligible interest, if any, in having insubstantial claims adjudicated by their courts, particularly in the face of the strong federal interest in vindicating the rights protected by the national labor laws.

Considerations analogous to these led us in the antitrust context to adopt the "mere sham" exception in California Motor Transport, supra. We should follow a similar course under the NLRA. The right to litigate is an important one, and the Board should consider the evidence with utmost care before ordering the cessation of a state-court lawsuit. In a proper case, however, we believe that Congress intended to allow the Board to provide this remedy. Therefore, we hold that it is an enjoinable unfair labor practice to prosecute a baseless lawsuit with the intent of retaliating against an employee for the exercise of rights protected by § 7 of the NLRA.

IV

Having concluded that the prosecution of an improperly motivated suit lacking a reasonable basis constitutes a violation of the Act that may be enjoined by the Board, we now inquire into what steps the Board may take in evaluating whether a state-court suit lacks the requisite basis. Petitioner insists that the Board's pre-judgment inquiry must not go beyond the four corners of the complaint. Its position is that as long as the complaint seeks lawful relief that the state court has jurisdiction to grant, the Board must allow the state litigation to proceed. The Board, on the other hand, apparently perceives no limitations on the scope of its pre-judgment determination as to whether a lawsuit has a reasonable basis. In the present case, for example, the ALJ conducted a virtual trial on the merits of petitioner's state-court claims. Based on this de facto trial, the ALJ concluded, in his independent judgment, based in part on "his observation of

---

10. Balmer, Sham Litigation and the   (1980)....
Antitrust Laws, 29 Buffalo L.Rev. 39, 60

the witnesses, including their demeanor,'' that petitioner's suit lacked a reasonable basis.

We cannot agree with either party. Although the Board's reasonable basis inquiry need not be limited to the bare pleadings, if there is a genuine issue of material fact that turns on the credibility of witnesses or on the proper inferences to be drawn from undisputed facts, it cannot, in our view, be concluded that the suit should be enjoined. When a suit presents genuine factual issues, the state plaintiff's First Amendment interest in petitioning the state court for redress of his grievance, his interest in having the factual dispute resolved by a jury, and the State's interest in protecting the health and welfare of its citizens, lead us to construe the Act as not permitting the Board to usurp the traditional fact-finding function of the state-court jury or judge. Hence, we conclude that if a state plaintiff is able to present the Board with evidence that shows his lawsuit raises genuine issues of material fact, the Board should proceed no further with the § 8(a)(1)-§ 8(a)(4) unfair labor practice proceedings but should stay those proceedings until the state-court suit has been concluded.

In the present case, the only disputed issues in the state lawsuit appear to be factual in nature. There will be cases, however, in which the state plaintiff's case turns on issues of state law or upon a mixed question of fact and law. Just as the Board must refrain from deciding genuinely disputed material factual issues with respect to a state suit, it likewise must not deprive a litigant of his right to have genuine state-law legal questions decided by the state judiciary. While the Board need not stay its hand if the plaintiff's position is plainly foreclosed as a matter of law or is otherwise frivolous, the Board should allow such issues to be decided by the state tribunals if there is any realistic chance that the plaintiff's legal theory might be adopted.

In instances where the Board must allow the lawsuit to proceed, if the employer's case in the state court ultimately proves meritorious and he has judgment against the employees, the employer should also prevail before the Board, for the filing of a meritorious law suit, even for a retaliatory motive, is not an unfair labor practice. If judgment goes against the employer in the state court, however, or if his suit is withdrawn or is otherwise shown to be without merit, the employer has had its day in court, the interest of the state in providing a forum for its citizens has been vindicated, and the Board may then proceed to adjudicate the § 8(a)(1) and 8(a)(4) unfair labor practice case. The employer's suit having proved unmeritorious, the Board would be warranted in taking that fact into account in determining whether the suit had been filed in retaliation for the exercise of the employees' § 7 rights. If a violation is found, the Board may order the employer to reimburse the employees whom he had wrongfully sued for their attorneys' fees and other expenses. It may also order any other proper relief that would effectuate the policies of the Act. 29 U.S.C.A. § 160(c).

V

The Board argues that, since petitioner has not sought review of the factual findings below that the state suit in the present case lacked a reasonable basis and was filed for a retaliatory motive, the judgment should be affirmed once it is concluded that the Board may enjoin a suit under these circumstances. Petitioner does, however, challenge the right of the Board to issue a cease-and-desist order in the circumstances present here, and the Board did not reach its reasonable basis determination in accordance with this opinion. As noted above, the ALJ had no reservations about weighing the evidence and making credibility judgments. Based on his own evaluation of the evidence, he concluded that the libel count in petitioner's suit lacked merit, because the statements in the leaflet were true, and that the business interference counts were groundless, because the evidence failed to support petitioner's factual allegations. 249 N.L.R.B. at 164–165. See supra, at 2166–2167. It was not the ALJ's province to make such factual determinations. What he should have determined is not whether the statements in the leaflet were true, but rather whether there was a genuine issue as to whether they were knowingly false. Similarly, he should not have decided the facts regarding the business interference counts; rather, he should have limited his inquiry to the question whether petitioner's evidence raised factual issues that were genuine and material. Furthermore, because, in enforcing the Board's order, the Court of Appeals ultimately relied on the fact that "substantial evidence" supported the Board's finding that the prosecution of the lawsuit violated the Act, 660 F.2d at 1343, the Board's error has not been cured. Accordingly, without expressing a view as to whether petitioner's suit is in fact enjoinable, we shall return this case to the Board for further consideration in light of the proper standards.

VI

To summarize, we hold that the Board may not halt the prosecution of a state-court lawsuit, regardless of the plaintiff's motive, unless the suit lacks a reasonable basis in fact or law. Retaliatory motive and lack of reasonable basis are both essential prerequisites to the issuance of a cease-and-desist order against a state suit. The Board's reasonable basis inquiry must be structured in a manner that will preserve the state plaintiff's right to have a state court jury or judge resolve genuine material factual or state-law legal disputes pertaining to the lawsuit. Therefore, if the Board is called upon to determine whether a suit is unlawful prior to the time that the state court renders final judgment, and if the state plaintiff can show that such genuine material factual or legal issues exist, the Board must await the results of the state-court adjudication with respect to the merits of the state suit. If the state proceedings result in a judgment adverse to the plaintiff, the Board may then consider the matter further and, if it is found that the lawsuit was filed with retaliatory intent, the Board may find a violation and order appropriate relief. In short, then, although it is an unfair labor practice to prosecute an unmeritorious lawsuit for a retaliatory purpose, the offense is not enjoinable unless the suit lacks a reasonable basis.

In view of the foregoing, the judgment of the Court of Appeals is vacated, and the case is remanded to that court with instructions to remand the case to the Board for further proceedings consistent with this opinion.

So ordered.

■ JUSTICE BRENNAN filed a concurring opinion.

QUESTIONS

1. The Court acknowledged that "regardless of how unmeritorious the employer's suit is, the employee will most likely have to retain counsel and incur substantial legal expenses to defend it." The Court also recognized that the waitresses were hourly-wage employees without the backing of a union. Nonetheless, the Court emphasized the employer's "right to litigate." Is this a case where a right to litigate interferes with a right to justice?

2. Does this holding encourage employers to use collateral actions in state court to undermine the NLRB's authority over labor disputes? How are ethical standards among labor lawyers likely to be affected by the holding?

3. This holding creates an opportunity for either side to change the parameters and forum of a labor dispute by use of civil process in state court. Should a lawyer take advantage of this opportunity if it would further her client's objectives? If so, when?

4. The Court holds that "[r]etaliatory motive *and* lack of reasonable basis are both essential prerequisites to the issuance of a cease and desist order against a state suit" by the NLRB. Is retaliation an acceptable motive for a lawsuit? Should a lawyer filing a lawsuit concern herself with her client's motive?

5. A lawsuit with only a 30% chance of winning is still reasonable in most circumstances. What about a 10% chance of winning? At what point does a lawsuit lack a reasonable basis?

Relevant Background

Model Code DR 7–102(A)(1) provides that a lawyer may not "[f]ile a suit, assert a position, conduct a defense, delay a trial, or take other action on behalf of his client when he knows or when it is obvious that such action would serve merely to harass or maliciously injure another." Also, DR 2–110 explicitly states that withdrawal is required where the lawyer knows that her client is bringing an action or asserting a defense merely for the purpose of harassing or maliciously injuring any person.

Under Model Rule 3.1, a lawyer may not bring an action, assert a defense or controvert an issue "unless there is a basis for doing so that is not frivolous." The Comment to Model Rule 3.1 states that the lawyer must balance her duty to the client's cause with her duty "not to abuse the legal procedure." The Comment explains that an action is not frivolous "merely because the facts have not first been fully substantiated" or because the lawyer expects to obtain evidence later:

> Such action is not frivolous even though the lawyer believes that the client's position ultimately will not prevail. *The action is frivolous, however, if the client desires to have the action taken primarily for the purpose of harassing or maliciously injuring a person*, or, if the lawyer is unable either to make a good faith argument on the merits of the action taken or to support the action taken by a good faith argument for an extension, modification or reversal of existing law.

Model Rule 3.1, cmt. (emphasis added)

Although Model Rule 3.1 explicitly allows criminal defense lawyers to require prosecutors to establish every element of crimes charged, neither this Rule nor DR 7–102 allows frivolous defenses in criminal cases. Furthermore, a criminal appellate lawyer can be even more selective, as a defendant does not have a constitutional right to have counsel raise every nonfrivolous issue on appeal. Jones v. Barnes, 463 U.S. 745, 752 (1983) ("There can hardly be any question about the importance of having the appellate advocate examine the record with a view to selecting the most promising issues for review.")

Disciplinary penalties for frivolous litigation can be severe. In In re Varakin, 1994 WL 606153 (Cal.Bar Ct.1994), attorney Varakin waged a four-year campaign of harassment against his ex-wife by filing suits and then appeals on behalf of himself and his mother. The Bar recommended Varakin's disbarment because he had "engaged in conduct intended to harass others, delay court proceedings, obstruct justice and abuse the legal process," without showing any remorse and was "no longer worthy of membership in the bar." Id. at 10–11. The California Supreme Court later ordered Varakin disbarred.

Furthermore, persons who believe themselves to be frequent defendants in frivolous lawsuits, such as doctors and hospitals, have sought to slow the onslaught of litigation by filing their own claims against plaintiffs and their attorneys. Malicious civil prosecution and abuse of process are the two main causes of action at tort that arise after a plaintiff's lawsuit is dismissed as unmeritorious.

In Crowley v. Katleman, 8 Cal.4th 666, 34 Cal.Rptr.2d 386, 881 P.2d 1083 (1994), the Supreme Court of California, ruling *en banc*, held that three elements must be shown to establish a claim for malicious civil prosecution: the suit was commenced by the defendant and ended in the plaintiff's favor; the suit was brought without probable cause; and the suit was brought with malice. The court also held that malicious prosecution may be shown as to only some of the counts in a suit; all of the counts need not be without reasonable basis and with the requisite degree of malice. Id. The second element, lack of probable cause, can be shown if, on the basis of facts known by the attorney, a reasonable attorney would not have thought that the prior action was legally tenable. Sheldon Appel Co. v. Albert & Oliker, 47 Cal.3d 863, 254 Cal.Rptr. 336, 349, 765 P.2d 498, 511 (1989). The Supreme Court of Nevada ruled in Dutt v. Kremp, 108 Nev. 1076, 844 P.2d 786 (1992), that this standard is purely objective and, if an attorney's belief is not reasonable, "does not permit the court to consider whether the attorney subjectively believed that the prior action was legally tenable." Id. at 789, citing *Sheldon Appel*. But see Smith v. Lucia, 173 Ariz. 290, 842 P.2d 1303 (App.1992) (inquiring into both the subjective and objective reasonableness of the lawyer's belief that the complaint was legally tenable). In Meiksin v. Howard Hanna Company, Inc., 404 Pa.Super. 417, 590 A.2d 1303, 1307 (1991), the court held that lawyers are entitled to rely upon facts given to them by their clients if they do so in good faith. The third element of malicious civil prosecution is malice, which clearly concerns the subjective intent or purpose of the attorney in prosecuting the action. The attorney's motivation is a question of fact to be determined by a jury. Dutt v. Kremp, 844 P.2d at 790.

A second, related tort is abuse of process, which is sometimes easier to show than malicious civil prosecution. A claim for abuse of process has two elements: (1) use of legal process; and (2) use of the legal process in an improper or unauthorized manner. See Restatement (Second) of Torts, Section 682, Abuse of Process. An improper purpose is "ordinarily an attempt to secure from another some collateral advantage not properly includable in the process itself." Wilson v. Hayes, 464 N.W.2d 250, 266 (Iowa 1990). Most important, abuse of process can occur even though there is probable cause to bring the action and the original action terminates in favor of the plaintiff. Id. "The usual case of abuse of process is one of some form of extortion, using the process to put pressure upon the other to compel him to pay a different debt or to take some other action or refrain from it." Restatement (Second) of Torts, Abuse of Process, Section 682, cmt. b.

Courts are cognizant not only of the need to control frivolous litigation but also that lawyers should be allowed to pursue legitimate, although difficult, claims. "The law tries to avoid both too much discouragement and too much encouragement of litigation. Some sort of balance has to be struck between the social interests in preventing unconscionable suits and in permitting honest assertion of supposed rights." Soffos v. Eaton, 152 F.2d 682, 683 (D.C.Cir.1945). Because the elements of either malicious civil prosecution or abuse of process can be difficult to prove, civil procedure rules give judges an alternative approach, the power to sanction lawyers and parties for wrongful suits and unmeritorious pleading. See John W. Wade, On Frivolous Litigation: A Study of Tort Liability and Procedural Sanctions, 14 Hofstra L. Rev. 433 (1986); Federal Rule of Civil Procedure 11. You will read more extensively about Rule 11 in Chapter 9 infra. For a lawyer seeking to avoid either tort claims or sanctions under these procedural rules, the best approach is to carefully ascertain facts and research legal issues *before* filing a lawsuit or any other pleading.

QUESTIONS

1. In Wilson v. Hayes, 464 N.W.2d 250 (Iowa 1990), Michael and Kathleen Wilson, a surgeon and an internist who were married to each other, treated a patient who had been in an accident. The patient was treated and released, but then suffered an aneurysm and died. Hayes, the attorney for the deceased patient's husband, met with the patient's family, did some legal research, and filed a malpractice claim against the Wilsons. After it became clear that the lawsuit had little factual basis, Hayes attempted to settle and then to withdraw, at which point the deceased's husband "made some vague threats as to what would happen if Hayes withdrew." Id. at 257. Hayes, however, eventually did withdraw, and the suit was dismissed. The Wilsons then sued Hayes for malicious prosecution and abuse of process, claiming that Hayes should have sought dismissal of the case instead of merely withdrawing. The Court, however, concluded that Hayes had probable cause for initiating the suit and that, when it later began to appear that probable cause was lacking, he requested a release from the representation. Although Hayes was not held liable for malicious prosecution, this case illustrates the impact that groundless claims can have on human lives. The Wilsons were so disturbed by the suit that they both decided to enter the military "believing that in the military they could practice medicine without fear of personal suits for malpractice." Id. at 254.

(a) What should a lawyer do when he discovers that a claim that he has already filed is without merit? Is withdrawal from the representation a sufficient remedial action?

(b) What should a lawyer do if a client tries to coerce him into pursuing a groundless claim?

(c) Do lawyers' economic incentives encourage them to take into account harm suffered by people like the Wilsons? Should lawyers' ethical decisions take into account harm that lawsuits might cause to persons other than their clients?

2. In Mirka v. Fairfield of America, Inc., 627 N.E.2d 449 (Ind.App. 3 Dist.1994), the Indiana appellate court dismissed an action for negligent filing of a lawsuit. The court found that no such action was available or recognized under Indiana law. "To create liability only for negligence, for the bringing of a weak case, would be to destroy an attorney's efficacy as advocate of his client and his value to the court, since only the rare attorney would have the courage to take other than the easy case." Id. at 452.

A lawyer ordinarily is liable to his client for negligence. Would extending such liability to third parties destroy an attorney's efficacy as an advocate for his client?

PROBLEMS

1. You represent a savings and loan being investigated for unsound lending practices by federal regulators. The regulators have been demanding access to documents which they have a right to see under federal banking laws. Nonetheless, based on the facts you are aware of, you believe that the regulators' requests are more frequent and burdensome than usual and that a lawsuit filed by your client seeking an injunction cutting back on the document requests is likely at least to survive summary judgment. However, you also know something that the regulators do not: your client is operating in an unsound manner and otherwise violating federal banking regulations. If the regulators find out, they will close the institution down. Suing the regulators, or even threatening to sue, could substantially delay the investigation. What should you do? See Susan Beck, Keating's Bouncer, Am. Law., Jan.–Feb., 1990, at 40 (describing how lawyers for Lincoln Savings and Loan allegedly threatened lawsuits against federal regulators in order to deflect a regulatory crackdown) and further discussion of the Lincoln matter at Chapter 2 infra.

2. Your client, a commercial landlord, leases space in a shopping center to a convenience store owner who has been complaining that the landlord has not made repairs required to be made by law. The tenant's lease is about to expire. The landlord tells you that he will not renew the lease and wants you to sue to evict the tenant if she won't leave, "to teach her a lesson and set an example for other tenants who also are complaining about repairs." Under state law applicable to commercial leases, a landlord may evict a tenant for any reason. The tenant refuses to leave. Do you file the lawsuit?

3. You represent an environmental group concerned about cutting of old growth forest in the Pacific Northwest. The group wants to sue Timber Co. for violation of a federal statute that restricts logging to protect the environment. As the statute exists today, it is clear that Timber Co. is in compliance with the law and there are no grounds for the lawsuit. Nonetheless, your client believes that the lawsuit, even if it is dismissed, will focus public attention on certain loopholes in the statute that allow Timber Co. to cut more timber than it should. The ensuing public debate, your client believes, will force Congress to amend the statute to close these loopholes. Should you file the lawsuit?

4. In the above example, assume that Timber Co. has violated the law by building a wood processing plant on land zoned for agriculture only. Your client, the environmental group, owns land adjacent to the plant and has standing to sue for violation of the local zoning ordinance and thus force Timber Co. to take down the processing plant at great expense. Your client has threatened to sue under the zoning ordinance unless Timber Co. agrees to voluntarily reduce its timber cut by 50%, even though its cut is currently in complete compliance with existing law. Should you file the lawsuit?

5. You represent a man who wants to sue his wife for divorce. He tells you that he does not want custody of their two children, but wants to keep his alimony and child support payments as low as possible. He also says that, although he intends to sue, he wants if at all possible to settle the case without going to trial. A friend of yours, a prominent member of the divorce bar, tells you that your client should demand custody in his complaint in order to have a "bargaining chip" in negotiations over alimony and child support. What is wrong with this approach?

Will Making Losers Pay Legal Fees Discourage Frivolous Lawsuits?

Frivolous litigation has become a heated political issue. Some reform proponents seek to address what is essentially a problem of shoddy professional ethics by realigning the economic incentives of our civil litigation system. As you read through the following discussion, ask yourself if penalizing unsuccessful litigants is the best way to discourage lawyers from filing frivolous lawsuits.

Although England allows judges some discretion in determining both the amount of costs and who shall pay those costs, the usual English rule is that the loser pays both parties' legal fees. There is considerable controversy over whether the English rule should be implemented in the United States. See H.R. 10, A Bill to Reform the Federal Justice System, Section 101 (104th Cong., 1st Session, 1995) (proposing adoption of a loser-pays rule). For a sampling of the intense debate on this issue, see John F. Vargo, The American Rule on Attorney Fee Allocation: The Injured Person's Access to Justice, 42 Am. U. L. Rev. 1567 (1993); Gregory E. Maggs and Michael D. Weiss, Progress on Attorney's Fees: Expanding the "Loser Pays" Rule in Texas, 30 Hous. L. Rev. 1915 (Spring 1994); and various articles in Symposium on Fee Shifting, 71 Chi. Kent L. Rev. 415 (1995).

American courts premise their refusal to include attorneys' fees in judgments for costs on the view that penalties for losing decrease access to courts. See Alyeska Pipeline Serv. Co. v. Wilderness Soc'y., 421 U.S. 240 (1975). However, it is not clear exactly how the American Rule evolved. "No adequate historical explanation for the [American] departure has ever been advanced, and in any event, the reasons commonly given—the spirit of individualism in frontier societies, the conception in earlier times of lawsuits as sporting contests, and the widespread hostility toward lawyers—are not persuasive now." John P. Dawson, Lawyers and Involuntary Clients: Attorney Fees From Funds, 87 Harv. L. Rev. 1597, 1598 (1974).

It has been suggested that the American rule of denying attorneys' fees to prevailing parties creates incentives to prosecute improperly motivated suits and suits without reasonable basis. See Stanley Shavell, Suit, Settlement and Trial: A Theoretical Analysis Under Alternative Methods for the Allocation of Legal Costs, 11 J. Legal Stud. 55 (1982). Indeed, the American rule may encourage *both* frivolous lawsuits and frivolous defenses because it fails to impose on losing parties the full cost of litigation. By contrast, the English rule, by increasing rewards for winning and penalties for losing, may deter litigation and induce settlement. See Richard Posner, An Economic Approach to Legal Procedure and Judicial Administration, 2 J. Legal Studies 399, 439 (1973). But see Thomas D. Rowe, Jr., The Legal Theory of Attorney Fee Shifting: A Critical Overview, 1982 Duke L.J. 651, 661 (fee shifting in some circumstances may encourage litigation and "may not be the correct approach even when punishment of a litigant's conduct seems called for").

Thus, an advantage of the English rule is that costs of litigation may more often be borne by persons in the best position avoid those costs: plaintiffs who bring lawsuits with poor chances of winning and defendants who should settle without litigating. The primary disadvantage of the English rule is that it cuts off impecunious and risk-adverse litigants from access to the courts. These litigants, if they lose, not only must pay their own lawyers, but must pay their opponents' lawyers as well. The course of settlement discussions thus could be determined by litigants' financial resources and tolerance for risk as much as the merits of their respective claims. Large corporate defendants, for example, might have an advantage over middle or lower income plaintiffs.

Moreover, there already are some instances in which successful defendants are allowed attorneys' fees in American courts. One such instance is where opposing counsel signs a frivolous or unsubstantiated pleading and is sanctioned under Rule 11 of the Federal Rules of Civil Procedure or a state-law equivalent. See Sussman v. Salem, Saxon, and Nielsen, 152 F.R.D. 648 (M.D.Fla.1994) (sanction for violation of Rule 11 may include reasonable attorneys' fees and expenses); Silva v. Witschen, 19 F.3d 725 (1st Cir.1994) (Rule 11 sanction against attorney for filing groundless complaint); In re Kunstler, Nakell, Pitts, and Robeson Defense Committee v. Britt, 914 F.2d 505, 516 (4th Cir.1990) ("a complaint containing allegations unsupported by any information obtained prior to filing, or allegations based on information which minimal factual inquiry would disprove, will subject the author to sanctions."). Rule 11 (as amended, effective December 1, 1993) is discussed more fully in Chapter 9 infra.

In addition, some statutes allow successful litigants to recover attorneys' fees. State security for expenses statutes, for example, require shareholder derivative suit plaintiffs to post bond at the outset of litigation to reimburse the legal expenses of corporations that successfully defend. See New York Bus. Corp. Law § 627; Cohen v. Beneficial Industrial Loan Corp., 337 U.S. 541 (1949) (state security for expenses statutes applicable under *Erie* doctrine to diversity cases in federal courts). The Model Business Corporation Act § 7.46 provides that on termination of a derivative proceeding, the court may order the plaintiff to pay any defendant's reasonable expenses if the proceeding was commenced without reasonable cause or for improper purpose. Statutes under which a successful *plaintiff* may recover legal fees are discussed at page 61 infra.

QUESTIONS

1. Which rule (English or American) assumes a higher standard of professional ethics on the part of plaintiffs' lawyers?

2. Do lawyers have as powerful an incentive not to file frivolous lawsuits in jurisdictions that rely on judicially imposed sanctions as they do in jurisdictions that include attorneys' fees in costs?

3. Will the American rule remain viable if judges are not willing to impose sanctions on lawyers who file frivolous lawsuits?

C. THE LAWYER AS AGENT AND FIDUCIARY

Armand P. D'Amato, b. Newark, N.J. 1944; B.B.A. St. John's University 1966; J.D. Suffolk University 1969; admitted to the New York bar in 1970; started a law partnership with Jeffrey Forchelli in 1976 that later became D'Amato, Forchelli, Libert, Schwartz, Mineo & Carlino in Mineola, New York; brother of United States Senator Alfonse D'Amato.

The case was argued for Mr. D'Amato by **John Warden**, a partner of Sullivan & Cromwell, but came into the firm through an associate, **Robert Giuffra, Jr.** who assisted with defending the case at trial and with writing the appellate brief. A complete biographical sketch for Mr. Giuffra, later Chief Counsel of the United States Senate Banking Committee, appears in Chapter 3 infra before the materials on *In re Whitewater*.

United States of America v. Armand P. D'Amato

39 F.3d 1249 (2d Cir.1994).

■ Before: WINTER and JACOBS, CIRCUIT JUDGES, and POLLACK, DISTRICT JUDGE (sitting by designation).

■ WINTER, CIRCUIT JUDGE:

Armand P. D'Amato appeals from his conviction by a jury before Judge Mishler. D'Amato was convicted of seven counts of mail fraud in violation of 18 U.S.C.A. § 1341 and sentenced principally to a term of five months imprisonment, two years of supervised release including five months of home detention, and payment of $7,500 restitution. D'Amato's conviction arises from services he provided to the Unisys Corporation ("Unisys"). The government claimed at trial that D'Amato was hired by a "rogue" Unisys employee, Charles Gardner, and that D'Amato, with Gardner's aid, defrauded Unisys in two ways. First, the government maintained that D'Amato committed mail fraud by structuring his billings to conceal from those in control of corporate funds the nature of his relationship with Unisys and the fact that his actual services involved lobbying his brother, a United States Senator and member of the Senate Appropriations Committee. We will style this theory the "right to control theory." The government maintained, second, that D'Amato committed mail fraud by contracting with Unisys to provide written reports on Senate proceedings while never intending to provide those reports. We will style this theory the "false pretenses theory."

Because the evidence of criminal intent was insufficient on either theory, we reverse the judgment of conviction and order the indictment dismissed.

. . .

D'Amato, an attorney, started a law partnership with Jeffrey Forchelli in 1976. By 1988, the two were practicing as partners of D'Amato, Forchelli, Libert, Schwartz, Mineo & Carlino ("D'Amato Forchelli"), a firm of roughly twenty lawyers based in Mineola, New York. D'Amato's brother, Alfonse D'Amato, was a United States Senator from the State of New York throughout the period of relevant events. Senator D'Amato was a member of the Senate Appropriations Committee, the Senate committee charged with oversight of defense procurement programs.

Unisys, a Fortune 100 company, maintained a Surveillance and Fire Control Systems Division ("S & FCS") in Great Neck, New York. This division manufactured radar missile control systems that were sold to the United States government. Charles Gardner served as a Unisys vice president in charge of marketing for S & FCS from the early 1980's until March 1988. Throughout the pertinent period, Gardner bribed Navy officials, made illegal campaign contributions to Congressmen, and personally profited through kickbacks. The government has stipulated, however, that none of these illegal activities involved D'Amato or Senator D'Amato, and there was no evidence that D'Amato was aware of any of Gardner's illegal activities.

Gardner first met D'Amato in spring 1984. At the time, Gardner was seeking to obtain support for the purchase of Unisys products in the Senate Appropriations Committee. Over the course of two meetings, Gardner expressed his interest in gaining Senator D'Amato's support and told Armand D'Amato that he was being hired to further that purpose. Gardner told D'Amato that he would be paid by means of a purchase order, and that these purchase orders would generally call for the production of some form of reports on Congressional proceedings. D'Amato apparently agreed to represent Unisys, although the work was to be done by Peter Iovino, who was joining D'Amato Forchelli to open a Washington, D.C. office.

In 1985, Gardner, dissatisfied with Iovino, sent Herbert Chodosh, a Unisys marketing manager, to ask D'Amato to work for Unisys personally. D'Amato agreed, and the parties discussed another purchase order arrangement, this time through Coastal Energy Enterprises ("Coastal"), a Unisys subsidiary. In a subsequent meeting with D'Amato, Gardner made clear that Unisys was hiring D'Amato to "support our programs in the Senate Appropriations Committee through Senator D'Amato's office." Gardner told D'Amato that he would receive $5,000 per month for his services and would be paid through Coastal's issuance of a purchase order calling for the production of reports on Congressional proceedings. Gardner further indicated to D'Amato that Unisys "would offer to help to do the report."

Pursuant to this agreement, in April 1986 Coastal sent D'Amato a purchase order to cover the period from June 1, 1986 to May 31, 1987. The purchase order called for D'Amato Forchelli to "[p]rovide technical services to advise Coastal on matters as specified in the attached Statement of Work." The statement of work contained directives such as "[a]nalyze matters within the purview of Coastal Energy Enterprises in such areas as Federal budgeting, legislative action, likelihood of program funding" and "[p]rovide reports to Coastal relative to performance of competitive companies' offerings of products."

Pursuant to the purchase order, D'Amato Forchelli sent monthly bills on its letterhead to Coastal seeking payment "For Professional Services Rendered: Re: Coastal Energy Enterprises, Inc. Monthly Retainer." By December 1986, Coastal had raised D'Amato Forchelli's retainer to $6,500 a month, and in May 1987 the agreement was extended for another year. In or around July 1986 and December 1987, Unisys employees asked D'Amato to transmit to Senator D'Amato's office draft letters to the Secretary of the Navy composed by Unisys employees. D'Amato apparently complied on both occasions, and letters bearing Senator D'Amato's signature were in fact sent to the Secretary of the Navy.

In fall 1987, Unisys began an internal investigation of alleged unethical behavior by Unisys employees. The investigation was headed by Lawrence Cresce, the Unisys ombudsman, who in turn reported to Henry Ruth, counsel to Unisys's corporate ethics committee. Cresce received information that Gardner was involved in unethical lobbying activities and began an investigation. Cresce's investigation discovered that Gardner had entered into numerous technical service agreements on behalf of Unisys that called for the production of reports. Upon examining the reports, Cresce became suspicious that many of the reports had been plagiarized from public sources.

In November 1987, Cresce questioned Gardner about his activities. Gardner acknowledged that the reports mentioned in the purchase orders "just weren't worth the money," and that the "reports were window dressing, and simply paper so that the consultants can get paid." Gardner further maintained that the consultants he hired were performing valuable work for Unisys. Gardner, however, did not tell Cresce that he had bribed Navy officials. Gardner also falsely denied receiving kickbacks.

In early 1988, Gardner met with senior management and explained the benefits to Unisys of the technical service agreements. Cresce also informed senior Unisys officials, including the Chairman of the Board and the General Counsel, of Gardner's procedure for paying political consultants. Subsequent to his November 1987 meeting with Gardner, Cresce received information that Gardner had used D'Amato Forchelli as a "contact point" with Senator D'Amato's office. Cresce eventually prepared a report dated May 1988 that concluded that Gardner had, among other activities, used D'Amato Forchelli to gain access to Senator D'Amato.

Meanwhile, Gardner had closed Coastal in 1987. Coastal's last payment to D'Amato Forchelli came in November 1987, bringing the total of payments to D'Amato Forchelli by Coastal to $88,000. Gardner decided, however, to continue to retain D'Amato's services through Unisys. Unisys internal procedures dictated that purchase orders to law firms had to be released and controlled by Unisys's law department. Gardner and Dennis Mitchell, a Unisys marketing manager, conceived the idea of circumventing this requirement by issuing the purchase order in the name of Jeffrey Forchelli, the second name on the firm's letterhead. At a subsequent meeting attended by Norm Steiger, head of the Unisys legal department at its Great Neck facility, it was mutually agreed that purchase orders would be issued in the name of Forchelli. Gardner further testified that the decision to use Forchelli's name rather than D'Amato's was "made because it was considered to be in the interest of Unisys company[ ] not to have the D'Amato name out there, because it . . . could be politically embarrassing." At Gardner's direction, Mitchell called the D'Amato Forchelli firm and confirmed that the law firm would accept a check made out to Forchelli alone.

Gardner also spoke to D'Amato about the payment of D'Amato Forchelli's outstanding bills. Gardner told D'Amato that he would be issuing a purchase order directly from Unisys, and that the purchase order, like the ones before, would "use the reports as a means to the end. And we would be supplying reports or helping him do the reports."

Thereafter, in February 1988, Mitchell issued a purchase order from Unisys in the name "J. Forchelli" at D'Amato Forchelli's address. The purchase order, dated February 2, 1988, covered the period of November and December 1987, in order to compensate D'Amato for two months he was not paid due to the closing of Coastal. The purchase order provided for payment of $13,000, per the prior agreement of $6,500 per month. The purchase order required the seller to "[p]rovide technical services to produce two survey reports evaluating the proceedings of the U.S. Senate" in accordance with an attached statement of work. The statement of work read as follows:

> Provide technical services to produce two reports on senatorial proceedings. Each report is to provide a quantitative and qualitative statement of senatorial action during the period for each program of concern to Unisys. Also provide an assessment of ultimate senatorial direction and any outside or competitive actions that may adversely influence the outcome of these programs.

The purchase order also provided, "Reports and invoices to be approved by C.F. Gardner Prior to payment." Mitchell testified that he did not understand the purchase order to require that D'Amato produce the reports.

The purchase order was mailed to Forchelli in February 1988. Forchelli and the firm's bookkeeper, Marlene Schwartz, met briefly with D'Amato in Schwartz's office. Forchelli asked D'Amato if he had "done the work." After looking at the purchase order, D'Amato responded affirmatively and mentioned traveling to Washington, D.C. for "work." Forchelli then signed the order. The government presented no evidence that the counter-signed order was returned to Unisys.

On March 7, 1988, D'Amato Forchelli sent another bill to Unisys on the firm's letterhead. The bill, which again requested payment "For Professional Services Rendered: Re: Monthly Retainer," showed a previous balance of $26,000 and a March 1988 balance of $6,500, for a total due of $32,500.

On March 15, 1988, Unisys issued a "Purchase Order Change" form to Forchelli. The form changed the dates of the most-recently issued purchase order to run from November 1, 1987 to March 31, 1988, and provided for payment of $32,500. The description of work stated, "Provide technical services to produce five survey reports as per orig. P.O." As with the prior purchase order, there was no evidence that Forchelli ever returned the purchase order to Unisys.

In April 1988, Unisys sent D'Amato Forchelli a discrepant invoice form indicating that Unisys could not make payment on the invoice received from D'Amato Forchelli because the name of the firm on the invoice diverged from the name on the purchase order Unisys had issued (i.e., Forchelli's name alone). Mitchell, after discussing the problem with Gardner, called Forchelli's secretary and asked that the invoice be resubmitted on letterhead with Forchelli's name alone. D'Amato also asked Forchelli to submit a bill in Forchelli's name, because "that's what the client wanted." Forchelli thereafter met with Schwartz and instructed her to generate letterhead with Forchelli's name alone and to prepare three new bills on this letterhead. The three new bills all called for payment "For Professional Services Rendered: Re: Monthly Retainer." The bills cumulatively covered six months of services (January 1988 to June 1988) and called for payment of $39,000. Unisys subsequently sent checks of $13,000 and $19,500 in April and June 1988 respectively in partial payment of the bills submitted.

Throughout D'Amato's relationship with Unisys, he never supplied Unisys with any written reports. Gardner testified, however, that he told D'Amato that D'Amato would not be responsible for the preparation of the reports. In fact, Unisys employees prepared five brief (less than half-a-page) reports and attached them to Forchelli's bills.

In connection with the sentencing, the district court found that D'Amato spent approximately 100 hours performing lobbying services for Unisys. The court further found that D'Amato traveled three times to Washington, D.C., at least in part on behalf of Unisys. In addition, D'Amato met with Unisys employee Lynch around ten times in his office, where Lynch briefed D'Amato on Unisys's programs and needs. D'Amato also helped cause two letters by Senator D'Amato and one by Congressman Norman Lent to be sent to Navy and Commerce Department officials concerning defense contracts.

. . .

A grand jury returned an indictment charging D'Amato with twenty-four counts of mail fraud. In particular, the indictment charged that twenty-four separate mailings constituted mail fraud under two separate legal theories. First, the indictment charged that the mailings were used as part of a scheme and artifice to "defraud Sperry/Unisys and its uninvolved officers, directors and shareholders, of the right to control the expenditure of corporate funds and to decide the manner and purpose of those expenditures" (the "right to control theory"). Second, the indictment charged that the mailings were part of a scheme to "obtain money and property from

Sperry/Unisys, by means of false and fraudulent pretenses, representations and promises" (the "false pretenses theory"). . . .

. . . D'Amato was acquitted of the charges stemming from his work on behalf of Coastal (Counts 1–17), but convicted of the charges relating to his representation of Unisys (Counts 18–24). . . . This appeal followed.

DISCUSSION

. . .

The mail fraud statute criminalizes use of the mails in furtherance of a "scheme or artifice to defraud, or for obtaining money or property by means of false or fraudulent pretenses. . . ." 18 U.S.C.A. § 1341. Therefore, an essential element of any mail fraud prosecution is proof of a "scheme or artifice to defraud." Id.; see also United States v. Starr, 816 F.2d 94, 98 (2d Cir.1987). . . .

Because the defendant must intend to harm the fraud's victims, "[m]isrepresentations amounting only to a deceit are insufficient to maintain a mail or wire fraud prosecution." Starr, 816 F.2d at 98. "Instead, the deceit must be coupled with a contemplated harm to the victim." Id. In many cases, this requirement poses no additional obstacle for the government. When the "necessary result" of the actor's scheme is to injure others, fraudulent intent may be inferred from the scheme itself. [Citation omitted]. Where the scheme does not cause injury to the alleged victim as its necessary result, the government must produce evidence independent of the alleged scheme to show the defendant's fraudulent intent. See, e.g., Starr, 816 F.2d at 98–99.

1. The Right to Control Theory

(a) The Elements.

We first address the right to control theory. That "theory is predicated on a showing that some person or entity has been deprived of potentially valuable economic information." [United States v. Wallach, 935 F.2d 445] at 462–63 (2d Cir. 1991). Thus, "the withholding or inaccurate reporting of information that could impact on economic decisions can provide the basis for a mail fraud prosecution." Id. A person charged with mail fraud under the right to control theory must intend to injure the person or entity misled—here Unisys, its management, and/or its shareholders—and the person or entity must thus be a specific target of the inaccurate or concealed information. Mail fraud cannot be charged against a corporate agent who in good faith believes that his or her (otherwise legal) misleading or inaccurate conduct is in the corporation's best interests.

Where no rule otherwise provides, persons acting on behalf of a corporation may well find it necessary to disguise or conceal certain matters in the interests of that corporation. For example, failure to disclose the nature of a service provided or the identity of the entity performing such a service may minimize the risk of disclosure of information that would enable competitors to learn of a corporation's future activities or plans. Mining companies may thus conceal the hiring of geologists and the site of their work. Such measures may be necessary also to protect company assets. A company may thus disguise the hiring of forensic accountants in order to avoid giving warning to an undetected embezzler. The preservation of a positive public relations image is a proper corporate goal and may be pursued by a policy of concealment. Such a policy may be necessary also to prevent insider trading. Firms planning a takeover may thus wish to conceal relationships with law firms, accountants, or banks until required to disclose under the Williams Act. 15 U.S.C.A. §§ 78m(d), (e) & 78n(d)–(f) (1988).

. . .

In the instant matter, of course, the defendant is not someone in corporate management but a person hired to perform services for the corporation. Such a person cannot be found to intend to harm a corporation or its shareholders through otherwise lawful misleading conduct if he or she follows the instructions of an appropriate corporate agent who appears to be unconflicted and acting in good faith. So far as the duty of a party contracting to provide ordinary business or professional services to the corporation is concerned, therefore, that party may rely upon instructions from a corporate agent with apparent authority and no ostensible conflict of interest to determine the contracting party's obligations and appropriate billing practices.

Additional considerations apply to a claim that shareholders have been deprived of their right to control. Unlike management, shareholders have no right to manage the business. Wallach, 935 F.2d at 462. Nevertheless, they do have property rights of which they may not be fraudulently deprived by "the withholding or inaccurate reporting of information that could impact on economic decisions." Id. at 463.

These property rights are defined by (i) state law concerning access to the company's books and records and the fiduciary obligations of management and (ii) the law of fraud concerning corporate information that is public. An inaccurate statement in documents that are not lawfully available for inspection by shareholders, and do not materially affect information that is available, can hardly be said, without more, to defraud, or to be intended to defraud, such shareholders. . . .

The otherwise lawful "withholding or inaccurate reporting of information" must thus relate to: (i) information available to shareholders as provided by the state of incorporation's laws providing access to corporate books and records, see Wallach, 935 F.2d at 463 (maintenance of accurate books and records is of "central importance" to preservation of shareholders' property interest); (ii) information that, if withheld or inaccurate, would result in rendering information that is public materially misleading, see id. (right to public information, required to be disclosed by law, is important component of shareholders' property rights), and (iii) information that would materially aid shareholders in enforcing management's fiduciary obligations under state law, see id. ("complete information" enables a stockholder to take "steps" to prevent corporate actions of which he or she disapproves). Where a third party acting upon instructions from a corporate agent is charged with depriving shareholders of their right to control, the government must prove that the third party knew that the concealment would involve (i), (ii), or (iii).

(b) Sufficiency of the Evidence.

The government's claim that D'Amato intended to injure Unisys by depriving its management or its shareholders of their right to control was not based on legally sufficient evidence. The jury could have found that D'Amato knew that his services on behalf of Unisys were disguised. However, the government concedes that the payments to D'Amato for the purpose of gaining "access" to his brother were not illegal. From D'Amato's point of view, if such access resulted in political support from the Senator that helped Unisys's sales, Unisys and its shareholders would benefit. Also from D'Amato's point of view, it was evident that Unisys might desire to keep its source of access to the Senator confidential because the means of access could easily become controversial and self-defeating if disclosed. D'Amato thus could have intended to deprive Unisys management (or shareholders) of "valuable" information that "could impact" on economic decisions only if (i) Gardner had no authority to instruct D'Amato to disguise his services in billing Unisys and D'Amato knew it, (ii) the payments to D'Amato were otherwise unlawful and D'Amato knew it, or (iii) Gardner was personally profiting from the concealed arrangement with D'Amato and D'Amato knew it. None of these conditions has been met in the instant matter.

The government does not claim that the payments were otherwise unlawful. Nor does it claim that Gardner received kickbacks from D'Amato or otherwise profited from the concealed arrangement. Conditions (ii) and (iii) are thus not at issue. With regard to (i), there is no evidence that D'Amato complied with Unisys's request to disguise his services through Forchelli in order to further a scheme to injure Unisys rather than because he thought it was a reasonable request by his client. Gardner testified that he met with Unisys in-house lawyers and that they agreed that D'Amato should bill through Forchelli because it was "in the interest of Unisys" and otherwise could be "politically embarrassing." Likewise, D'Amato testified that he and Forchelli determined that Unisys must have decided to suppress D'Amato's name to avoid negative publicity. They thought this especially likely because Unisys was a Long Island company and Senator D'Amato was at the time receiving critical attention from the Long Island-based newspaper, Newsday. The government thus offered no reason why anyone in D'Amato's position would think that he or she was injuring Unisys by complying with the request to use the Forchelli invoice. See Mulheren, 938 F.2d at 372 (fraudulent intent cannot be inferred from evidence "at least as consistent with innocence as with guilt").

.   .   .

2. The False Pretenses Theory

The false pretenses theory, simply stated, is a claim that D'Amato represented to Unisys that he would prepare reports in exchange for the fees he received, and took the money but prepared no reports. The government's false pretenses theory thus rests on the allegation that D'Amato did not perform the services that he contracted to perform for Unisys and for which he was paid.

D'Amato admits that he never intended to produce any reports in exchange for the fees he received. Criminal intent was not proven, however. As noted, there was no evidence that D'Amato ever believed, or even had reason to believe, that Gardner and others lacked authority to represent and bind Unisys in their dealings with D'Amato, and the record unambiguously demonstrates that Gardner told D'Amato that he did not have to prepare reports. Gardner testified that his understanding had been that Unisys employees would supply the reports. Indeed, the government in its argument stresses that Gardner, Chodosh, and other Unisys employees repeatedly told D'Amato that the reports would be written by Unisys staffers. Moreover, Dennis Mitchell, the Unisys official who issued the relevant purchase order, testified that he did not understand the purchase order to require D'Amato to produce the reports.

D'Amato could hardly have believed that he was supposed to provide written reports. From the beginning of the relationship, all the purchase orders contained roughly the same description of work. D'Amato had consistently been paid without comment by Unisys concerning his failure to submit reports. Given this consistent course of dealing, D'Amato had no reason whatsoever to believe that the most recent purchase order required him to submit a written report. ... There is thus no dispute that D'Amato performed all the services for Unisys that were requested of him. The government's theory was and is that D'Amato was paid for lobbying his Senator brother, concededly lawful conduct. There is no evidence that he did not perform such services. It is inconceivable on this record that Unisys could survive a motion for summary judgment in a civil suit to recover fees from D'Amato based on a false pretenses theory, even under the lower burden of proof applicable to civil cases.

Finally, the government argues that D'Amato's services were not worth what Unisys paid for them. This argument is seriously misguided. The mail fraud statute does not criminalize the charging of an allegedly excessive fee, where, as here, a corporate agent with at least apparent authority to do so agreed to the fee, received no personal benefit from the fee, and was not deceived by the payee. Retainer agreements that keep providers of services available are commonplace, and sometimes those services are not needed. We decline the government's invitation to infer fraudulent intent on the part of an attorney who accepts a retainer arrangement and is subsequently not called upon to perform services that the government or trier of fact deems worth the fee paid. Moreover, the government offered no evidence that access to the Senator was not worth the fees paid.

We vacate the conviction, and order dismissal of the indictment.

QUESTIONS

1. Because almost every commercial or professional relationship to some extent uses the mails, the mail fraud statute has a potentially very broad reach. The New York Civil Liberties Union pointed out in its brief supporting D'Amato's appeal that the prosecution had succeeded in applying the mail fraud statute "well beyond the concealment of economically material information." What are the dangers of allowing federal prosecutors to file mail fraud charges whenever a misrepresentation is allegedly made by use of the mails? What specific dangers arise when the statute is used against lawyers?

2. If this had been a disciplinary proceeding under New York's version of the Model Code of Professional Responsibility instead of a criminal prosecution for mail fraud, would the same line of reasoning used by Judge Winter here support a finding that D'Amato had not violated DR 1–102(A)(4) by engaging in conduct involving "dishonesty, deceit, and misrepresentation?"

3. Judge Winter points out that "the mail fraud statute does not criminalize the charging of an allegedly excessive fee." Is there any evidence here that D'Amato's fee was excessive under applicable standards (see DR 2–106)?

4. Judge Winter points out that D'Amato's lobbying activities were legal. If such lobbying activities had been illegal, how might the result in this case have been different?

5. Did D'Amato's billing practices "avoid even the appearance of professional impropriety" (Model Code, Canon 9)? When can following the directions of an officer of a corporate client be improper or create the appearance of impropriety?

6. "D'Amato's bills did not expressly state that he was engaged in lobbying, but neither did these bills expressly describe any of his activities. As the trial Judge, Jacob Mishler, observed, 'maybe one out of 100 [lawyers] would say no' to the billing arrangement at issue in this case." Richard W. Painter, If This is Mail Fraud, Then Most Lawyers are Guilty, Wall Street Journal, May 4, 1994, at A15 (op-ed). What would you say to a corporate officer who requested this type of billing arrangement for lobbying services?

7. The indictment against D'Amato did not allege that his lobbying services themselves were illegal or improper. Is there any evidence that D'Amato did anything to "state or imply that he [was] able to influence improperly or upon irrelevant grounds" a legislative body or public official (see DR 9–101(C))?

8. Judge Winter concludes his opinion by observing that "[m]oreover, the government offered no evidence that access to the Senator was not worth the fees paid." Besides Gardner's fiduciary duty to Unisys, are other fiduciary duties at issue here (see Chapter 3 infra).

9. Judge Winter observes that "[Armand] D'Amato testified that he and Forchelli determined that Unisys must have decided to suppress D'Amato's name to avoid negative publicity." Later, when Hillary Rodham Clinton became embroiled in some controversial decisions in the Whitehouse, negative publicity led to an investigation by the United States Senate. Senator D'Amato chaired the investigation. See In re Whitewater, Chapter 3 infra. Should siblings and spouses of public officials refrain from involvement in public policy merely to avoid an appearance of impropriety? What can a public official do in such a situation to avoid an appearance of impropriety?

10. Were any of Judge Winter's former law clerks involved in this case?

Relevant Background

Agency and Fiduciary Relationships

A lawyer is an agent of her client. The Supreme Court describes lawyers as " 'trusted agents of their clients, and as assistants to the court in search of a just solution....' " Ohralik v. Ohio State Bar Association, 436 U.S. 447, 460 (1978), quoting Cohen v. Hurley, 366 U.S. 117, 124 (1961). The Court has also emphasized the importance of a lawyer's "honored and traditional role as an authorized *but independent* agent acting to vindicate the legal rights of a client." In re Griffiths, 413 U.S. 717, 724 n. 14 (1973) (emphasis added).

What exactly is this relationship called "agency?" According to the Restatement (Second) of Agency § 1, "Agency is the fiduciary relation which results from the manifestation of consent by one person to another that the other shall act on his behalf and subject to his control, and consent by the other so to act." Restatement § 387 states that "[u]nless otherwise agreed, an agent is subject to a duty to his principal to act solely for the benefit of the principal in all matters connected with his agency." An agent also has a duty to act with care and skill in matters concerning the agency (Restatement § 379), to act only as authorized by her principal (Restatement § 383), and to give her principal information relevant to affairs entrusted to her (Restatement § 381). Professional conduct rules parallel these agency-based duties by imposing on a lawyer a duty, among other things, to provide competent representation (Model Rule 1.1), to act with reasonable diligence and promptness in a representation (Model Rule 1.3), to abide by a client's decisions concerning overall objectives, settlement of litigation and other matters (Model Rule 1.2), and to keep a client reasonably informed about the status of a matter and promptly comply with a client's request for information (Model Rule 1.4). Looking back at the D'Amato case, how well do you think D'Amato performed each of these functions?

As an agent, a lawyer also is a fiduciary for her client. A fiduciary relationship is such that one party to the relation (often referred to as "the entrustor") is dependent on the other (the fiduciary) for a particular service. Tamar Frankel, Fiduciary Law, 71 Cal. L. Rev. 795, 800 (1983). Fiduciary law is for the most part a one way street—it aims to protect the entrustor, not the fiduciary (whose rights are derived instead from contractual terms, such as a fee agreement). Id. at 801. Courts will require the fiduciary to act with loyalty and skill in the entrustor's best interests, and the entrustor cannot waive a court's supervision over the fiduciary's performance. Furthermore, courts prohibit, supervise or limit self dealing by the fiduciary, and any consents obtained by the fiduciary from the entrustor, whether to self dealing, conflicts of interest or otherwise, will be scrutinized to determine whether such consents were informed and independent. Id. at 821–25. As you read this casebook, you will see fiduciary concepts appear frequently in rules of professional responsibility and in judicial scrutiny of attorney-client relationships.

Keeping the Client Informed

One of the critical issues in the *D'Amato* case is who D'Amato should have informed at Unisys about the nature of his work for the company and his billing arrangements. As Judge Winter's opinion points out, the Company's shareholders were not entitled to be informed about D'Amato's lobbying activities. Also, for purposes of the mail fraud statute, D'Amato's following of Gardner's instructions was sufficient to establish that he did not intend to deceive his client, Unisys. Nonetheless, should he have informed a broader range of persons at Unisys about the arrangement? The comment to Model Rule 1.4 points out that, "[w]hen the client is an organization or group, it is often impossible or inappropriate to inform every one of its members about its legal affairs; ordinarily, the lawyer should address communications to the appropriate officials of the organization." See also Model Rule 1.13. If D'Amato knew or suspected that Gardner was violating company policy, Gardner clearly would not have been the only "appropriate person" for D'Amato to keep informed. Because, however, there was no evidence showing that D'Amato knew of Gardner's derelictions, the next step would have been for D'Amato to consider Gardner's role within Unisys and any policies Unisys might have concerning communications with lawyers. Although D'Amato was probably within the bounds of propriety to deal exclusively with Gardner, he could have saved himself substantial aggravation if he had informed a broader range of people within Unisys about what he was doing.

In other circumstances also, failure to communicate about a matter with a client can lead to serious difficulties for both the lawyer and client. See Nichols v. Keller, 15 Cal.App.4th 1672, 19 Cal.Rptr.2d 601 (1993) (malpractice action allowed against lawyer who failed to communicate with a client about availability of other legal remedies for workplace injury in addition to workman's compensation claim against his employer); Moores v. Greenberg, 834 F.2d 1105 (1st Cir.1987) (lawyer could be sued for malpractice because he failed to communicate a settlement offer to his client, even though lawyer at the time believed the settlement offer to be very inadequate). Indeed, such mundane offenses as failure to return telephone calls or to answer letters from clients are frequently grounds for imposition of discipline on lawyers. See also Model Code, EC 7–8 ("A lawyer should exert his best efforts to insure that decisions of his client are made only after the client has been informed of relevant considerations.'').

QUESTIONS

1. A general agent with actual or apparent authority can subject his principal to liability for acts done on his account within the scope of the agency. Restatement (Second) of Agency, § 161. Thus, a lawyer with actual or apparent authority to take action on behalf of a client may bind the client. "[A] client may clothe his attorney with the apparent authority to settle through the client's representations to the opposing party." Edwards v. Born, Inc., 792 F.2d 387, 390 (3d Cir. 1986); see also Glazer v. J.C. Bradford & Co., 616 F.2d 167, 168 (5th Cir.1980) (where client asked his attorney to see what could be done to effect settlement without spelling out precise terms that would be acceptable, settlement made by attorney was binding).

(a) What consequences are likely to ensue from a lawyer's failure to consult her client both before and during settlement discussions with opposing counsel?

(b) Is it ethical for a lawyer to represent that she has more authority to settle litigation or to negotiate a transaction than she does? How does such a strategy affect the lawyer's credibility with third parties?

2. Even criminal courts have held defendants responsible for the acts of their attorneys. In Taylor v. Illinois, 484 U.S. 400 (1988), defendant Taylor's lawyer willfully violated a procedural rule requiring that a list of anticipated witnesses be provided in response to a prosecutorial demand. The trial judge sanctioned Taylor by refusing to allow him to call a witness, and Taylor was convicted of attempted murder. The Supreme Court held that this sanction did not violate due process, observing that "the lawyer has—and must have—full authority to manage the conduct of the trial. The adversary process could not function effectively if every tactical decision required client approval." Id. at 418.

(a) Do you agree with the decision of the Court in *Taylor* that criminal defendants may be penalized for the negligence or unethical conduct of their attorneys?

(b) What bearing does the holding in *Taylor* have on a lawyer's obligation to practice law ethically and competently?

3. As a fiduciary of his client, a lawyer is presumptively barred from self dealing at the expense of his client. See Maksym v. Loesch, 937 F.2d 1237, 1241 (7th Cir.1991). See also Nolan v. Foreman, 665 F.2d 738, 739 n. 3 (5th Cir.1982) ("the fiduciary relationship between an attorney and his client extends even to preliminary consultations between the client and the attorney regarding the attorney's possible retention"); Archer v. Griffith, 390 S.W.2d 735, 739 (Tex.1964) ("The relation between an attorney and his client is highly fiduciary in nature, and their dealings with each other are subject to the same scrutiny, intendments and imputations as a transaction between an ordinary trustee and his cestui que trust'').

(a) What aspects of negotiating a lawyer-client relationship pose the greatest threat of overreaching on the part of the lawyer?

(b) Should courts enforce all agreements between lawyers and their clients? For discussion of some of the more controversial subjects of such agreements, see pages 63–67 (contingent fees); 62 (nonrefundable retainers); 363–364 (agreements in contravention of the client's right to fire her lawyer); 71–72 (lawyer-client business transactions); and 423–24 (waiver of conflicts of interest).

PROBLEM

1. You are the attorney for the husband in a divorce proceeding. He requests that you prevent unsupervised visits between his former wife and their child. You take no action to secure the appropriate court order. The former wife kidnaps the child. Are you liable for malpractice?

D.   FEE ARRANGEMENTS

What does a lawyer do when faced with an opportunity to give up all or part of his fee in exchange for a better settlement for his clients? In the following case, a class action defendant proposed a settlement that put a plaintiff's lawyer in just such a quandary. The Supreme Court decided that the Civil Rights Fees Act of 1976 permitted the fee waiver. The plaintiff's lawyer did the right thing in this case, but the Supreme Court opened the door to settlement proposals that allow one lawyer to exploit another lawyer's duty of loyalty to his clients.

Luvern Charles Johnson III, b. 1954; B.S. University of Utah 1976; J.D. University of Idaho 1979; employee of the Idaho Legal Aid Society at the time the underlying class action in *Evans v. Jeff* was filed in 1980; now a member of Johnson, Olson, Chartered, in Pocatello, Idaho.

William T. Coleman, b. 1920; A.B. University of Pennsylvania 1941; LL.B. Harvard University 1946; law clerk to Justice Felix Frankfurter 1975–77; Secretary of Transportation 1975–77; partner in the Washington, D.C. office of O'Melveny and Myers; argued the *Evans v. Jeff* case for the respondents.

James T. Jones, b. 1942; B.A. University of Oregon 1967; J.D. Northwestern 1970; Attorney General of Idaho.

John V. Evans, et al., Petitioners v. Jeff D. et al.

475 U.S. 717 (1986).

■ STEVENS, J., delivered the opinion of the Court, in which BURGER, C.J., and WHITE, POWELL, REHNQUIST, and O'CONNOR, JJ., joined. BRENNAN, J., filed a dissenting opinion, in which MARSHALL and BLACKMUN, JJ., joined.

The Civil Rights Attorney's Fees Awards Act of 1976 (Fees Act) provides that "the court, in its discretion, may allow the prevailing party ... a reasonable attorney's fee" in enumerated civil rights actions. 90 Stat. 2641, 42 U.S.C.A. § 1988. In Maher v. Gagne, 448 U.S. 122, 100 S.Ct. 2570, 65 L.Ed.2d 653 (1980), we held that fees may be assessed against state officials after a case has been settled by the entry of a consent decree. In this case, we consider the question whether attorney's fees must be assessed when the case has been settled by a consent decree granting prospective relief to the plaintiff class but providing that the defendants shall not pay any part of the prevailing party's fees or costs. We hold that the District Court has the power, in its sound discretion, to refuse to award fees.

I

The petitioners are the Governor and other public officials of the State of Idaho responsible for the education and treatment of children who suffer from emotional and mental handicaps. Respondents are a class of such children who have been or will be placed in petitioners' care.[1]

On August 4, 1980, respondents commenced this action by filing a complaint against petitioners in the United States District Court for the District of Idaho. The factual allegations in the complaint described deficiencies in both the educational programs and the health care services provided respondents. These deficiencies allegedly violated the United States Constitution, the Idaho Constitution, four federal statutes, and certain provisions of the Idaho Code. The complaint prayed for injunctive relief and for an award of costs and attorney's fees, but it did not seek damages.

On the day the complaint was filed, the District Court entered two orders, one granting the respondents leave to proceed *in forma pauperis*, and a second appointing Charles Johnson as their next friend for the sole purpose of instituting and prosecuting the action. At that time Johnson was employed by the Idaho Legal Aid Society, Inc., a private, nonprofit corporation that provides free legal services to qualified low-income persons.[2] Because the Idaho Legal Aid Society is prohibited from representing clients who are capable of paying their own fees, it made no agreement requiring any of the respondents to pay for the costs of litigation or the legal services it provided through Johnson. Moreover, the special character of both the class and its attorney-client relationship with Johnson explains why it did not enter into any agreement covering the various contingencies that might arise during the course of settlement negotiations of a class action of this kind.

---

1. The number of children in petitioners' custody, as well as the duration of that custody, fluctuates to a certain degree. Although it appears that only 40 or 50 children are in custody at any one moment, the membership in respondents' class is apparently well over 2,000.

2. Although Johnson subsequently entered private practice and apparently bore some of the financial burden of the litigation himself, any award of costs or fees would inure to the benefit of Idaho Legal Aid.

Shortly after petitioners filed their answer, and before substantial work had been done on the case, the parties entered into settlement negotiations. They were able to reach agreement concerning that part of the complaint relating to educational services with relative ease and, on October 14, 1981, entered into a stipulation disposing of that part of the case. The stipulation provided that each party would bear its "own attorney's fees and costs thus far incurred." App. 54. The District Court promptly entered an order approving the partial settlement.

Negotiations concerning the treatment claims broke down, however, and the parties filed cross-motions for summary judgment. Although the District Court dismissed several of respondents' claims, it held that the federal constitutional claims raised genuine issues of fact to be resolved at trial. Thereafter, the parties stipulated to the entry of a class certification order, engaged in discovery, and otherwise prepared to try the case in the spring of 1983.

In March 1983, one week before trial, petitioners presented respondents with a new settlement proposal. As respondents themselves characterize it, the proposal "offered virtually all of the injunctive relief [they] had sought in their complaint." Brief for Respondents 5. See App. 89. The Court of Appeals agreed with this characterization, and further noted that the proposed relief was "more than the district court in earlier hearings had indicated it was willing to grant." 743 F.2d 648, 650 (C.A.9 1984). As was true of the earlier partial settlement, however, petitioners' offer included a provision for a waiver by respondents of any claim to fees or costs.[4] Originally, this waiver was unacceptable to the Idaho Legal Aid Society, which had instructed Johnson to reject any settlement offer conditioned upon a waiver of fees, but Johnson ultimately determined that his ethical obligation to his clients mandated acceptance of the proposal. The parties conditioned the waiver on approval by the District Court.[5]

After the stipulation was signed, Johnson filed a written motion requesting the District Court to approve the settlement "except for the provision on costs and attorney's fees," and to allow respondents to present a bill of costs and fees for consideration by the court. App. 87. At the oral argument on that motion, Johnson contended that petitioners' offer had exploited his ethical duty to his clients—that he was "forced," by an offer giving his clients "the best result [they] could have gotten in this court or any other court," to waive his attorney's fees.[6] The District Court, however,

---

[4]. Petitioners append to their brief on the merits the parties' correspondence setting forth their respective positions on settlement. Without embarking on a letter-by-letter discussion of the status of the fee waiver in the bargaining, it is clear that petitioners' proposals uniformly included fee waivers while respondents' almost always did not.

[5]. Paragraph 25 of the settlement agreement provides: "Plaintiffs and defendants shall each bear their own costs and

attorney's fees thus far incurred, if so approved by the Court." App. 104. In addition, the entire settlement agreement was conditioned on the District Court's approval of the waiver provision under Federal Rule of Civil Procedure 23(e).

[6]. Johnson's oral presentation to the District Court reads in full as follows: "In other words, an attorney like myself can be put in the position of either negotiating for

evaluated the waiver in the context of the entire settlement and rejected the ethical underpinnings of Johnson's argument. Explaining that although petitioners were "not willing to concede that they were obligated to [make the changes in their practices required by the stipulation], ... they were willing to do them as long as their costs were outlined and they didn't face additional costs," it concluded that "it doesn't violate any ethical considerations for an attorney to give up his attorney fees in the interest of getting a better bargain for his client[s]." Id. at 93. Accordingly, the District Court approved the settlement and denied the motion to submit a costs bill.

When respondents appealed from the order denying attorney's fees and costs, petitioners filed a motion requesting the District Court to suspend or stay their obligation to comply with the substantive terms of the settlement. Because the District Court regarded the fee waiver as a material term of the complete settlement, it granted the motion. The Court of Appeals, however, granted two emergency motions for stays requiring enforcement of the substantive terms of the consent decree pending the appeal. More dramatically, after ordering preliminary relief, it invalidated the fee waiver and left standing the remainder of the settlement; it then instructed the District Court to "make its own determination of the fees that are reasonable" and remanded for that limited purpose. 743 F.2d at 652.

In explaining its holding, the Court of Appeals emphasized that Rule 23(e) of the Federal Rules of Civil Procedure gives the court the power to approve the terms of all settlements of class actions, and that the strong federal policy embodied in the Fees Act normally requires an award of fees to prevailing plaintiffs in civil rights actions, including those who have prevailed through settlement. The court added that "[w]hen attorney's fees are negotiated as part of a class action settlement, a conflict frequently exists between the class lawyers' interest in compensation and the class members' interest in relief." 743 F.2d, at 651–652. "To avoid this conflict," the Court of Appeals relied on Circuit precedent which had "disapproved simultaneous negotiation of settlements and attorney's fees" absent a showing of "unusual circumstances." Id., at 652. In this case, the Court of Appeals found no such "unusual circumstances" and therefore held that an agreement on fees "should not have been a part of the settlement of the claims of the class." Id. It concluded:

> The historical background of both Rule 23 and section 1988, as well as our experience since their enactment, compel the conclusion that a

his client or negotiating for his attorney's fees, and I think that that is pretty much the situation that occurred in this instance. I was forced, because of what I perceived to be a result favorable to the plaintiff class, a result that I didn't want to see jeopardized by a trial or by any other possible problems that might have occurred. And the result is the best result I could have gotten in this court or any other court and it is really a fair and just result in any instance and what should have occurred years earlier and which in fact should have been the case all along. That result I didn't want to see disturbed on the basis that my attorney's fees would cause a problem and cause that result to be jeopardized." App. 90–91.

stipulated waiver of all attorney's fees obtained solely as a condition for obtaining relief for the class should not be accepted by the court. Id.

The importance of the question decided by the Court of Appeals, together with the conflict between its decision and the decisions of other Courts of Appeals, led us to grant certiorari. 471 U.S. 1098, 105 S.Ct. 2319, 85 L.Ed.2d 838 (1985). We now reverse.

II

The disagreement between the parties and *amici* as to what exactly is at issue in this case makes it appropriate to put certain aspects of the case to one side in order to state precisely the question that the case does present.

To begin with, the Court of Appeals' decision rested on an erroneous view of the District Court's power to approve settlements in class actions. Rule 23(e) wisely requires court approval of the terms of any settlement of a class action, but the power to approve or reject a settlement negotiated by the parties before trial does not authorize the court to require the parties to accept a settlement to which they have not agreed. Although changed circumstances may justify a court-ordered modification of a consent decree over the objections of a party after the decree has been entered, and the District Court might have advised petitioners and respondents that it would not approve their proposal unless one or more of its provisions was deleted or modified, Rule 23(e) does not give the court the power, in advance of trial, to modify a proposed consent decree and order its acceptance over either party's objection. The options available to the District Court were essentially the same as those available to respondents: it could have accepted the proposed settlement; it could have rejected the proposal and postponed the trial to see if a different settlement could be achieved; or it could have decided to try the case. The District Court could not enforce the settlement on the merits and award attorney's fees anymore than it could, in a situation in which the attorney had negotiated a large fee at the expense of the plaintiff class, preserve the fee award and order greater relief on the merits. The question we must decide, therefore, is whether the District Court had a duty to reject the proposed settlement because it included a waiver of statutorily authorized attorney's fees.

That duty, whether it takes the form of a general prophylactic rule or arises out of the special circumstances of this case, derives ultimately from the Fees Act rather than from the strictures of professional ethics. Although respondents contend that Johnson, as counsel for the class, was faced with an "ethical dilemma" when petitioners offered him relief greater than that which he could reasonably have expected to obtain for his clients at trial (if only he would stipulate to a waiver of the statutory fee award), and although we recognize Johnson's conflicting interests between pursuing relief for the class and a fee for the Idaho Legal Aid Society, we do not believe that the "dilemma" was an "ethical" one in the sense that Johnson had to choose between conflicting duties under the prevailing norms of professional conduct. Plainly, Johnson had no *ethical* obligation to seek a statutory fee award. His ethical duty was to serve his clients loyally and competently.[14] Since the proposal to settle the merits was more favorable than the probable outcome of the trial, Johnson's decision to recommend acceptance was consistent with the highest standards of our profession. The District Court, therefore, correctly concluded that approval of the settlement involved no breach of ethics in this case.

The defect, if any, in the negotiated fee waiver must be traced not to the rules of ethics but to the Fees Act.[15] Following this tack, respondents argue that the statute must be construed to forbid a fee waiver that is the product of "coercion." They submit that a "coercive waiver" results when the defendant in a civil rights action (1) offers a settlement on the merits of equal or greater value than that which plaintiffs could reasonably expect to achieve at trial but (2) conditions the offer on a waiver of plaintiffs' statutory eligibility for attorney's fees. Such an offer, they claim, exploits the ethical obligation of plaintiffs' counsel to recommend settlement in order to avoid defendant's statutory liability for its opponents' fees and costs.[16]

The question this case presents, then, is whether the Fees Act requires a district court to disapprove a stipulation seeking to settle a civil rights class action under Rule 23 when the offered relief equals or exceeds the probable outcome at trial but is expressly conditioned on waiver of statutory eligibility for attorney's fees. For reasons set out below, we are not persuaded that Congress has commanded that all such settlements must be rejected by the District Court. Moreover, on the facts of record in this case, we are satisfied that the District Court did not abuse its discretion by approving the fee waiver.

III

The text of the Fees Act provides no support for the proposition that Congress intended to ban all fee waivers offered in connection with substantial relief on the merits. On the contrary, the language of the Act, as

---

14. Generally speaking, a lawyer is under an ethical obligation to exercise independent professional judgment on behalf of his client; he must not allow his own interests, financial or otherwise, to influence his professional advice. ABA, Model Code of Professional Responsibility EC 5–1, 5–2 (as amended 1980); ABA, Model Rules of Professional Conduct 1.7(b), 2.1 (as amended 1984). Accordingly, it is argued that an attorney is required to evaluate a settlement offer on the basis of his client's interest, without considering his own interest in obtaining a fee; upon recommending settlement, he must abide by the client's decision whether or not to accept the offer, see Model Code of Professional Responsibility EC 7–7 to EC 7–9; Model Rules of Professional Conduct 1.2(a).

15. Even state bar opinions holding it unethical for defendants to request fee waivers in exchange for relief on the merits of plaintiffs' claims are bottomed ultimately on § 1988. [citations omitted]

16. See Committee on Professional and Judicial Ethics of the New York City Bar Association, Op. No. 80–94, reprinted in 36 Record of N.Y.C.B.A., at 508 ("Defense counsel thus are in a uniquely favorable position when they condition settlement on the waiver of the statutory fee: they make a demand for a benefit which the plaintiff's lawyer cannot resist as a matter of ethics and which the plaintiff will not resist due to lack of interest"). Accord, District of Columbia Bar Legal Ethics Committee, Op. No. 147, reprinted in 113 Daily Wash.L.Rep., at 394.

well as its legislative history, indicates that Congress bestowed on the *"prevailing party"* (generally plaintiffs) a statutory eligibility for a discretionary award of attorney's fees in specified civil rights actions. It did not prevent the party from waiving this eligibility anymore than it legislated against assignment of this right to an attorney, such as effectively occurred here. Instead, Congress enacted the fee-shifting provision as "an integral part of the remedies necessary to obtain" compliance with civil rights laws, S.Rep. No. 94–1011, p. 5 (1976), U.S.Code Cong. & Admin.News 1976, p. 5912, to further the same general purpose—promotion of respect for civil rights—that led it to provide damages and injunctive relief. The statute and its legislative history nowhere suggest that Congress intended to forbid *all* waivers of attorney's fees—even those insisted upon by a civil rights plaintiff in exchange for some other relief to which he is indisputably not entitled—anymore than it intended to bar a concession on damages to secure broader injunctive relief. Thus, while it is undoubtedly true that Congress expected fee shifting to attract competent counsel to represent citizens deprived of their civil rights, it neither bestowed fee awards upon attorneys nor rendered them nonwaivable or nonnegotiable; instead, it added them to the arsenal of remedies available to combat violations of civil rights, a goal not invariably inconsistent with conditioning settlement on the merits on a waiver of statutory attorney's fees.

In fact, we believe that a general proscription against negotiated waiver of attorney's fees in exchange for a settlement on the merits would itself impede vindication of civil rights, at least in some cases, by reducing the attractiveness of settlement. Of particular relevance in this regard is our recent decision in Marek v. Chesny, 473 U.S. 1, 105 S.Ct. 3012, 87 L.Ed.2d 1 (1985). . . .

In approving the package offer in Marek v. Chesny we recognized that a rule prohibiting the comprehensive negotiation of all outstanding issues in a pending case might well preclude the settlement of a substantial number of cases: "If defendants are not allowed to make lump-sum offers that would, if accepted, represent their total liability, they would understandably be reluctant to make settlement offers. . . ."

Most defendants are unlikely to settle unless the cost of the predicted judgment, discounted by its probability, plus the transaction costs of further litigation, are greater than the cost of the settlement package. If fee waivers cannot be negotiated, the settlement package must either contain an attorney's fee component of potentially large and typically uncertain magnitude, or else the parties must agree to have the fee fixed by the court. Although either of these alternatives may well be acceptable in many cases, there surely is a significant number in which neither alternative will be as satisfactory as a decision to try the entire case.

The adverse impact of removing attorney's fees and costs from bargaining might be tolerable if the uncertainty introduced into settlement negotiations were small. But it is not. The defendants' potential liability for fees in this kind of litigation can be as significant as, and sometimes even more significant than, their potential liability on the merits. . . . Indeed, in this very case "[c]ounsel for defendants viewed the risk of an attorney's fees award as the most significant liability in the case." Brief for Defendants in Support of Approval of Compromise in Jeff D. v. Evans, No. 80–4091 (D.Idaho), p. 5. Undoubtedly there are many other civil rights actions in which potential liability for attorney's fees may overshadow the potential cost of relief on the merits and darken prospects for settlement if fees cannot be negotiated.

The unpredictability of attorney's fees may be just as important as their magnitude when a defendant is striving to fix its liability. Unlike a determination of costs, which ordinarily involve smaller outlays and are more susceptible of calculation, see Marek v. Chesny, 473 U.S. at 7, 105 S.Ct. at 3015, "[t]here is no precise rule or formula" for determining attorney's fees, Hensley v. Eckerhart, 461 U.S. 424, 436, 103 S.Ct. 1933, 1941, 76 L.Ed.2d 40 (1983). Among other considerations, the district court must determine what hours were reasonably expended on what claims, whether that expenditure was reasonable in light of the success obtained, see id. at 436, 440, 103 S.Ct. at 1941, 1943, and what is an appropriate hourly rate for the services rendered. Some District Courts have also considered whether a "multiplier" or other adjustment is appropriate. The consequence of this succession of necessarily judgmental decisions for the ultimate fee award is inescapable: a defendant's liability for his opponent's attorney's fees in a civil rights action cannot be fixed with a sufficient degree of confidence to make defendants indifferent to their exclusion from negotiation. It is therefore not implausible to anticipate that parties to a significant number of civil rights cases will refuse to settle if liability for attorney's fees remains open, thereby forcing more cases to trial, unnecessarily burdening the judicial system, and disserving civil rights litigants. Respondents' own waiver of attorney's fees and costs to obtain settlement of their educational claims is eloquent testimony to the utility of fee waivers in vindicating civil rights claims. We conclude, therefore, that it is not necessary to construe the Fees Act as embodying a general rule prohibiting settlements conditioned on the waiver of fees in order to be faithful to the purposes of that Act.

IV

The question remains whether the District Court abused its discretion in this case by approving a settlement which included a complete fee waiver. As noted earlier, Rule 23(e) wisely requires court approval of the terms of any settlement of a class action. The potential conflict among members of the class—in this case, for example, the possible conflict between children primarily interested in better educational programs and those primarily interested in improved health care—fully justifies the requirement of court approval.

The Court of Appeals, respondents, and various amici supporting their position, however, suggest that the court's authority to pass on settlements, typically invoked to ensure fair treatment of class members, must be exercised in accordance with the Fees Act to promote the availability of attorneys in civil rights cases. Specifically, respondents assert that the State of Idaho could not pass a valid statute precluding the payment of attorney's fees in settlements of civil rights cases to which the Fees Act applies. From this they reason that the Fees Act must equally preclude the adoption of a uniform state-wide policy that serves the same end.....

We find it unnecessary to evaluate this argument, however, because the record in this case does not indicate that Idaho has adopted such a statute, policy, or practice. Nor does the record support the narrower proposition that petitioners' request to waive fees was a vindictive effort to deter attorneys from representing plaintiffs in civil rights suits against Idaho. It is true that a fee waiver was requested and obtained as a part of the early settlement of the education claims, but we do not understand respondents to be challenging that waiver, see Tr. of Oral Arg. 31–32, and they have not offered to prove that petitioners' tactics in this case merely implemented a routine state policy designed to frustrate the objectives of the Fees Act. Our own examination of the record reveals no such policy.

In light of the record, respondents must—to sustain the judgment in their favor—confront the District Court's finding that the extensive structural relief they obtained constituted an adequate quid pro quo for their waiver of attorney's fees. The Court of Appeals did not overturn this finding. Indeed, even that court did not suggest that the option of rejecting the entire settlement and requiring the parties either to try the case or to attempt to negotiate a different settlement would have served the interests of justice. Only by making the unsupported assumption that the respondent class was entitled to retain the favorable portions of the settlement while rejecting the fee waiver could the Court of Appeals conclude that the District Court had acted unwisely.

What the outcome of this settlement illustrates is that the Fees Act has given the victims of civil rights violations a powerful weapon that improves their ability to employ counsel, to obtain access to the courts, and thereafter to vindicate their rights by means of settlement or trial. For aught that appears, it was the "coercive" effect of respondents' statutory right to seek a fee award that motivated petitioners' exceptionally generous offer. Whether this weapon might be even more powerful if fee waivers were prohibited in cases like this is another question,[34] but it is in any event a question that Congress is best equipped to answer. Thus far, the Legislature has not commanded that fees be paid whenever a case is settled. Unless it issues such a command, we shall rely primarily on the sound

---

34. We are cognizant of the possibility that decisions by individual clients to bargain away fee awards may, in the aggregate and in the long run, diminish lawyers' expectations of statutory fees in civil rights cases. If this occurred, the pool of lawyers willing to represent plaintiffs in such cases might shrink, constricting the "effective access to the judicial process" for persons with civil rights grievances which the Fees Act was intended to provide. H.R.Rep. No. 94–1558, p. 1 (1976). That the "tyranny of small decisions" may operate in this fashion is not to say that there is any reason or documentation to support such a concern at the present time. Comment on this issue is therefore premature at this juncture. We believe, however, that as a practical matter the likelihood of this circumstance arising is remote....

discretion of the district courts to appraise the reasonableness of particular class-action settlements on a case-by-case basis, in the light of all the relevant circumstances. In this case, the District Court did not abuse its discretion in upholding a fee waiver which secured broad injunctive relief, relief greater than that which plaintiffs could reasonably have expected to achieve at trial.

The judgment of the Court of Appeals is reversed.

It is so ordered.

■ JUSTICE BRENNAN, with whom JUSTICE MARSHALL and JUSTICE BLACKMUN join, dissenting. . . .

QUESTIONS

1. The Court observes that "the special character of both the class and its attorney-client relationship with Johnson explains why it did not enter into any agreement covering the various contingencies that might arise during the course of settlement negotiations of a class action of this kind." Why, in these circumstances, is negotiation of an agreement between attorney and client concerning settlement and legal fees difficult, if not impossible?

2. Why did the Legal Aid Society instruct Johnson not to take a settlement offer that included a fee waiver? What are the long term implications for the Legal Aid Society of the type of settlement approved by the Court in this case?

3. The Court points out that a lawyer "must not allow his own interests, financial or otherwise, to influence his professional advice." (citing Model Code, EC 5–1, 5–2, Model Rule 1.7(b)). Johnson therefore properly recommended acceptance of the proposed settlement. The Court did not believe that its decision would discourage lawyers from taking civil rights cases. Do you agree?

4. Do you agree with Justice Stevens's statement that the Supreme Court's decision in this case promotes settlement of civil rights suits?

5. The Court found no evidence that Idaho had a statute, policy, or practice of requiring fee waivers, or that it made the request to waive "in a vindictive effort to deter attorneys from representing plaintiffs in civil rights suits in Idaho." Do you think it was ethical for Idaho's lawyers to propose a settlement that forced Johnson to choose between getting paid and serving the best interests of his clients? See Note: Fee Waivers and Civil Rights Settlement Offers: State Ethics Prohibitions After Evans v. Jeff D., 87 Colum. L. Rev. 1214 (1987).

6. Consider Johnson's role as a lawyer within a social framework extending beyond the particular clients in this case. Did this litigation benefit persons beyond this class of plaintiffs? If so, did Johnson have an ethical obligation to take into account the public interest in this suit?

Relevant Background

One–Way Fee Shifting Statutes

As shown in the *Evans* case, the fiduciary relationship between attorney and client can be tested when attorneys' fees are part of an award or settlement of a class action. Attorneys may be asked by defendants to bargain away their fees in return for major concessions to their clients. Alternatively, attorneys may be tempted to go to the other extreme and urge clients to accept settlement offers that maximize attorneys' fees in return for less injunctive relief or lower money damages. For these reasons, settlements of class actions usually must be reviewed and approved by the court.

Although the usual "American Rule" is that each party to a lawsuit bears its own attorneys' fees, some statutes, including the Civil Rights Attorney's Fees Act of 1976, award attorneys' fees to successful plaintiffs. The Supreme Court has held that, while the amount of damages a plaintiff recovers is certainly relevant to the amount awarded under the Fees Act, the fees need not be proportional to the amount of damages a plaintiff actually recovers. City of Riverside v. Rivera, 477 U.S. 561 (1986) (award of $245,456.25 in attorneys' fees upheld where respondents were awarded $33,350 in compensatory and punitive damages). Other federal statutes in which attorneys' fees are allowed for successful plaintiffs include actions brought under the Truth in Lending Act, 15 U.S.C.A. § 1640(a)(3), federal minimum wage laws, 29 U.S.C.A. § 216(b), and antitrust laws, 15 U.S.C.A. § 15(a). Under some circumstances, a public interest organization rather than an individual plaintiff can be the beneficiary of a fee shifting statute. See Jordan v. United States Department of Justice, 691 F.2d 514, 517 (D.C.Cir.1982) (fee awarded to a law school clinic).

The Supreme Court has sharply restricted district courts' discretion under fee shifting statutes to make upward adjustment of court-awarded fees based on risk counsel assumed that the case would be lost. See Pennsylvania v. Delaware Valley Citizens' Council, 483 U.S. 711 (1987) (concurring opinion of Justice O'Connor) (fee shifting provisions of the Clean Air Act do not allow for risk enhancement unless, without an adjustment for risk, the applicant would have had substantial difficulties in finding counsel). Justice Blackmun, writing for the dissent, argued that such a risk adjustment is needed to assure access to counsel. Id. at 735. See also Samuel Berger, Court Awarded Attorneys' Fees: What Is "Reasonable"?, 126 U. Pa. L.Rev. 281 (1977), and John Leubsdorf, The Contingency Factor in Attorney Fee Awards, 90 Yale L.J. 473 (1981).

Some state statutes also award attorneys' fees to successful plaintiffs, but not to defendants, unless a plaintiff's claim is frivolous. See Oregon Unlawful Trade Practices Act, O.R.S. Section 646.638(3) (1993). Furthermore, winning parties' attorneys' fees also may be allowed against unsuccessful defendants as punitive damages. See Lenz v. CNA Assurance Company, 42 Conn.Sup. 514, 630 A.2d 1082 (1993) (plaintiff employee awarded punitive damages on complaint alleging unjustified reduction of state worker's compensation benefits by insurer).

Reasonableness of Fees

In negotiating a fee arrangement, a lawyer acts as a principal representing her own interests at the same time as she is beginning an agency and fiduciary relationship with her client. Furthermore, the lawyer often knows a lot more about the legal services involved and what fees are reasonable than does the client. Thus, a fiduciary standard should apply when lawyers negotiate fees with their clients. As Professor Hazard has observed, "[a] contract for a fee is, under general principles of law, a contract between a fiduciary and his protected dependent. As such, it is unenforceable unless its terms are fair to the client." G. Hazard, Ethics in the Practice of Law 99 (1978). A fee arrangement should be fair both *ex-ante* (when it is entered into) and *ex-post* (when payment is sought). As the Court observed in McKenzie Construction, Inc. v. Maynard, 823 F.2d 43, 45 (3d Cir. 1987), "[a]lthough reasonableness at the time of contracting is relevant, consideration should also be given to whether events occurred after the fee arrangement was made which rendered a contract fair at the time unfair in its enforcement."

Although substantial retainers can be requested by lawyers representing large corporations or well-to-do individuals, lawyers are required by Model Rule 1.16(d) to refund "any advance payment of fee that has not been earned" upon termination of a representation. While the Model Rules do not explicitly prohibit an agreement whereby a client agrees to pay for a specified minimum amount of legal services, courts may invalidate such arrangements. The New York Court of Appeals has held that it is unethical for a lawyer to charge "a nonrefundable fee for specific services, in advance and irrespective of whether any professional services are actually rendered." Matter of Cooperman, 83 N.Y.2d 465, 611 N.Y.S.2d 465, 466, 633 N.E.2d 1069, 1070 (1994). See Lester Brickman & Lawrence Cunningham, Nonrefundable Retainers Revisited, 72 N.C. L.Rev. 1, 4 (1993) (nonrefundable retainers "deprive a client of the right, granted in early case law and recognized by the majority of states, to discharge a lawyer with or without cause, at any time, without penalty"). See Model Rule 1.16(d), DR 2–110(A)(3) (a lawyer who withdraws from employment shall refund promptly any part of a fee paid in advance that has not been earned). Even in jurisdictions where nonrefundable retainers are allowed, they are not appropriate for matters requiring little lawyer time, particularly if charged to clients of limited means. See Bushman v. State Bar of California, 11 Cal.3d 558, 113 Cal.Rptr. 904, 522 P.2d 312 (1974) (lawyer suspended from practice for one year because $5,000 retainer charged for representing 16 year old daughter of a family on welfare in divorce action was unconscionable where only simple and routine documents were filed by the attorney on the client's behalf).

Model Rule 1.5 states that a lawyer's fee shall be reasonable, and DR 2–106(A) states that a lawyer "shall not enter into an agreement for, charge or collect an illegal or clearly excessive fee." Model Rule 1.5 and DR 2–106 also list similar criteria for determining whether a fee is reasonable or excessive. These include, the amount of work done, its difficulty, the skill required, the likelihood that the work will preclude the lawyer from other employment, the fee customarily charged in the same locality for similar services, the amount of money involved in the matter and the results obtained, any time limitations or deadlines imposed by the client, the nature and length of the lawyer's relationship with the client, the experience, reputation and ability of the lawyer and whether the fee is fixed or contingent. Also, as pointed out in ABA Canon 12, "[a] client's ability to pay cannot justify a charge in excess of the value of the service, though poverty may require a lower charge, or none at all." Furthermore, when a lawyer has not regularly represented a client, the basis for the lawyer's fee should be communicated to the client, preferably in writing, within a reasonable period of time after commencing the representation. Model Rule 1.5

Prior to 1975, some state bar associations imposed minimum fee schedules to prevent lawyers from discounting their services. This practice ended with Goldfarb v. Virginia State Bar, 421 U.S. 773 (1975), in which the petitioner unsuccessfully tried to find a lawyer who would perform a title examination for less than the fee prescribed in a minimum fee schedule published by the county bar. The petitioner brought a class action against the state and county bar associations for injunctive relief and damages, alleging that fee schedules for residential real estate transactions constituted price-fixing in violation of the Sherman Antitrust Act. The Supreme Court agreed and held that the rigid price floor established in the fee schedule violated the Sherman Act. See also Arizona v. Maricopa County Medical Society, 457 U.S. 332 (1982) (fact that doctors, rather than nonprofessionals, were parties to agreements setting maximum prices did not save the agreements from the Sherman Act).

Contingent Fees[10]

The respondents in the *Evans* case raise an important issue: persons with just claims but little or no money may not get legal representation if their lawyers have no assurance of getting paid. Fee shifting under the Fees Act alleviates this problem and is an integral part of suits for injunctive relief under the civil rights laws. In suits for money damages, the American legal system facilitates access to legal services through a different mechanism: the contingent fee.

The contingent fee, for the most part unique to this country, is one of the most controversial topics in legal ethics. Charging on a contingency, a practice which began, and is still most prevalent, in the personal injury arena, has spread to many areas of law practice, including antitrust litigation, patent litigation and mergers and acquisitions work. See Milton Handler, The Shift from Substantive to Procedural Innovations in Antitrust Suits—The Twenty–Third Annual Antitrust Review, 71 Colum. L. Rev. 1, 9–10 (1971); Andrea Gerlin, Patent Lawyers Forgo Sure Fees on a

---

10. This discussion of contingent fees is derived in part from Richard W. Painter, Litigating on a Contingency: A Monopoly of Champions or a Market for Champerty, 71 Chi. Kent L. Rev. 625, 644–653 (1995).

Bet, Wall St. J, June 24, 1994 at B1; and Daniel Hertzberg & James B. Stewart, Contingency Legal Fee for Merger Breaks Ground, Stirs Controversy, Wall St. J., Oct. 24, 1986, at 31 (discussing "performance fees" charged by Wall Street law firms).

Contingent fees are commonplace in class actions under the securities laws, although some courts require lawyers to bid against each other to represent shareholders. See In re Oracle Securities Litigation, 131 F.R.D. 688, 697 (N.D.Cal.1990), 132 F.R.D. 538, 539, 542 (N.D.Cal.1990), 136 F.R.D. 639, 641 (N.D.Cal.1991) (outlining bidding procedures imposed on lawyers seeking to become lead counsel in securities class action against accountants). In derivative suits, as in securities class actions, attorneys' fees are paid under the "common fund" doctrine that allows a named plaintiff who creates a fund benefiting others to recover attorneys' fees therefrom. Attorneys' fees for successful derivative suits can be quite substantial, leading Judge Ralph Winter to observe that, "[t]he real incentive to bring derivative actions is usually not the hope of return to the corporation but the hope of handsome fees to be recovered by plaintiffs' counsel." Joy v. North, 692 F.2d 880, 887 (2d Cir.1982), cert. denied, 460 U.S. 1051 (1983). See also Roberta Romano, The Shareholder Suit: Litigation Without Foundation?, 7 J. Law. Econ. & Org. 55, 63–65, 84 (1991) (study of settlement results has shown that the principal beneficiaries of derivative litigation are not shareholders, but attorneys). Nonetheless, the fact remains that, without contingent fees, litigation on behalf of widely dispersed shareholders might very well be impossible.

A substantial body of academic literature discusses the effect contingent fees have on both settlement discussions and litigation. Skeptics insist that contingent fees overcompensate lawyers and encourage unethical conduct by plaintiffs' lawyers. Others point out that contingent fees provide access to the courts by plaintiffs who cannot afford lawyers. Many commentators argue that, while contingent fees should be permitted, they easily can become excessive.

Professor Brickman argues that "many contingency fees are invalid as a matter of ethics, policy, and law since they are often used in situations where there is either no contingency or, although a contingency exists, the contingent fee far exceeds any legitimate risk premium for the anticipated effort. On the other hand, contingent fees in excess of fifty percent, which are typically precluded by court rule, statute, or custom, should be upheld in cases where the risks of nonrecovery and greater effort than anticipated are high." Lester Brickman, Contingent Fees Without Contingencies: Hamlet Without the Prince of Denmark, 37 UCLA L.Rev. 29, 32 (1989). Other scholars contest Brickman's findings and contend that contingent fees are for the most part reasonable. See Herbert M. Kritzer, Rhetoric and Reality ... Uses and Abuses ... Contingencies and Certainties: The Political Economy of the American Contingent Fee (Wisconsin Institute for Legal Studies 1995).

Unfortunately, there is no bright line test for determining when contingent fees are excessive. In In re Swartz, 141 Ariz. 266, 686 P.2d 1236,

1243 (1984), the Supreme Court of Arizona considered, in addition to the factors listed in DR 2–106, "a number of factors including: . . . the degree of uncertainty or contingency with respect to liability, amount of damages which may be recovered, or the funds available from which to collect any judgment. . . ." In that particular case a contingent fee of one-third of the client's recovery was determined to be excessive, although the Court recognized that a lawyer working on a contingency may receive a much larger fee than if working on an hourly basis. See also McKenzie Constr., Inc. v. Maynard, 823 F.2d 43, 45, 49 (3d Cir. 1987) (contingent fee not unreasonable where attorney earned $790 per hour rather than his normal hourly rate of $60). "On the other hand, when a case is virtually certain to result in a large verdict, when both liability and great damages are easy to prove, the small chances of nonrecovery or of a small award can justify a correspondingly smaller increase in the attorney's fee." Rosquist v. Soo Line Railroad, 692 F.2d 1107, 1114 (7th Cir.1982). See also Anderson v. Kenelly, 37 Colo.App. 217, 547 P.2d 260, 260–61 (Colo.Ct.App.1975) (one-third contingent fee unreasonable where lawyer's only action to assist widow in collection of claim from life insurance company was to inform insurer of the correct date her deceased husband enlisted in the Air Force); Horton v. Butler, 387 So.2d 1315, 1317 (La.Ct.App.1980) (one-quarter contingent fee unreasonable where lawyer's only actions to collect insurance were contacting insurer and accepting a check).

In addition to determining reasonableness on a case by case basis, some jurisdictions impose outer limits on contingent fee percentages by rules of court. See N.J.R. 1:21–7(c) (West 1995)(New Jersey's schedule of contingent fees allows "(1) 33 ⅓% on the first $250,000 recovered; (2) 25% on the next $250,000 recovered; (3) 20% on the next $500,000 recovered;" and on all additional amounts a reasonable fee by application to the court). American Trial Lawyers Ass'n v. New Jersey Supreme Court, 66 N.J. 258, 330 A.2d 350 (1974) (New Jersey's Supreme Court had authority under its rule-making power to establish this fee schedule).

Some recent proposals have sought to address allegedly excessive contingent fees by linking fees to early settlement offers rather than to fixed fee schedules. The Manhattan Institute has proposed that when a defendant makes an early settlement offer which is then rejected by a plaintiff, the plaintiff's lawyer should be permitted to charge only an hourly rate on work done before the settlement offer plus a percentage of any recovery in excess of the offer. This proposal is designed for personal injury litigation, although with some modification it could apply to other litigation as well. Its five principal features are:

(1) Contingency fees may not be charged against settlement offers made prior to plaintiff's retention of counsel.

(2) All defendants are given an opportunity to make settlement offers covered by the proposal, but no later than 60 days from the receipt of a demand for settlement from plaintiff's counsel. If the offer is accepted by the plaintiff, counsel fees are limited to hourly rate charges and are

capped at 10% of the first $100,000 of the offer and 5% of any greater amounts.

(3) Demands for settlement submitted by plaintiffs' counsel are required to include basic, routinely discoverable information designed to assist defendants in evaluating plaintiff's claims. In turn, to assist plaintiffs in evaluating defendants' offers, discoverable material "in the . . . [defendant's] possession concerning the alleged injury upon which [the defendant] relied in making his offer of settlement must be made available to plaintiffs for a settlement offer to be effective."

(4) When plaintiffs reject defendants' early offers, contingency fees may only be charged against net recoveries in excess of such offers.

(5) If no offer is made within the 60 day period, contingency fee contracts are unaffected by the proposal.

Lester Brickman, Michael Horowitz and Jeffrey O'Connell, Rethinking Contingency Fees 27–28 (Manhattan Institute, 1994; Foreword by Judge John T. Noonan, Jr. and Preface by Derek C. Bok).

The Model Rules and Model Code for the most part address procedural fairness—whether clients are informed of their options before agreeing to contingent fees—rather than substantive fairness—whether a fee is excessive. Model Code, EC 2–20 provides that "[c]ontingent fee arrangements in civil cases have long been commonly accepted in the United States . . ." but that ". . . a lawyer generally should decline to accept employment on a contingent fee basis by one who is able to pay a reasonable fixed fee." Model Rule 1.5(c) requires that a contingent fee agreement be in writing, and Model Code, EC 2–19 states that it is "usually beneficial to reduce to writing the understanding of the parties regarding the fee, particularly where it is contingent."

If there is doubt as to whether a contingent fee is in a client's best interest, the lawyer should "offer the client alternative bases for the fee and explain their implications." Model Rule 1.5, cmt. Furthermore, use of a contingent fee should be appropriate under the circumstances. "[B]ecause [the lawyer] is in a better position to evaluate a cause of action, [the lawyer] should enter into a contingent fee arrangement only in those instances where the arrangement will be beneficial to the client." Model Code, EC 5–7.

Although contingent fees are allowed in a wide variety of circumstances, they are prohibited in some forms of litigation, most notably criminal and divorce cases. See DR 2–106(C); EC 2–20; Model Rule 1.5(d)(1) and (2). Most states adhere to these prohibitions on contingent fees in criminal and divorce cases. See Meister v. Moore, 96 U.S. 76 (1877); Roberds v. Sweitzer, 733 S.W.2d 444, 445 (Mo.1987). But see Krieger v. Bulpitt, 40 Cal.2d 97, 251 P.2d 673, 674 (Cal. 1953) (contingent fee allowed in divorce action).

Under Model Rule 1.8(e)(1), a lawyer not only may devote time to a case, but may advance court costs and expenses of litigation, repayment of which is contingent on the outcome. By contrast, Model Code DR 5–103(B) requires that the client ultimately be responsible for costs and expenses: " ... a lawyer may advance or guarantee the expenses of litigation, including court costs, expenses of investigation, expenses of medical examination, and costs of obtaining and presenting evidence, provided the client remains ultimately liable for such expenses." See Janet E. Findlater, The Proposed Revision of DR 5–103(B): Champerty and Class Actions, 36 Bus. Law. 1667 (1981).

Finally, if a lawyer is discharged by her client, "[t]he rule, which is now recognized in almost every state ... is that a client's discharge of a lawyer ends the lawyer's right to recover on the contract of employment." Charles W. Wolfram, Modern Legal Ethics 546 (1986). Most jurisdictions award a discharged attorney *quantum meruit* recovery for the fair value of her services although an exception might exist where an attorney working for a contingent fee is discharged at the conclusion of the litigation. Fracasse v. Brent, 6 Cal.3d 784, 100 Cal.Rptr. 385, 390, 494 P.2d 9, 14 (Cal. 1972) (when the "discharge occurs 'on the courthouse steps,' where the client executes a settlement obtained after much work by the attorney, the factors involved in a determination of reasonableness would certainly justify a finding that the entire fee was the reasonable value of the attorney's services.") In most cases, however, the discharged lawyer is likely to be paid less than she would have been if she had completed the representation. Furthermore, if the case is lost, a lawyer discharged from a contingent fee contract may not even be entitled to *quantum meruit* recovery. See Lester Brickman, Setting the Fee When the Client Discharges a Contingent Fee Attorney, 41 Emory Law Journal 367 (1992) (clients who employ an attorney under a contingent fee arrangement, and thereafter discharge the attorney, should not be forced to pay a *quantum meruit* fee unless the underlying suit is successful).

In summary, before taking a case for a contingent fee, a lawyer should consider (i) whether a contingent fee is permitted for the type of case, (ii) whether a contingent fee is in the best interests of the client, (iii) whether the client wants to pay a contingent fee after being informed of the other options available, and (iv) what percentage fee is reasonable in view of all relevant factors, including the size of the case and the likelihood of success. The lawyer also should know that, if she is discharged, she will most likely receive *quantum meruit* recovery rather than the contingent fee she bargained for.

QUESTIONS

1. Does the Manhattan Institute proposal solve the problem that Professor Brickman identifies in his law review article?

2. Does the Manhattan Institute proposal make it less likely that plaintiffs will be able to find lawyers to take their cases?

3. Does the Manhattan Institute proposal suggest limits on contingent fees that lawyers should observe voluntarily, even if the proposal is not imposed by statute or rule of court?

4. In what types of litigation are plaintiffs likely to have significant bargaining power in negotiating contingent fees with lawyers? In what types of litigation are they not?

5. Other than through a contingent fee, a lawyer may not acquire a proprietary interest in a cause of action. "A lawyer may accept property in payment for services, such as an ownership interest in an enterprise, providing this does not involve acquisition of a proprietary interest in the cause of action or subject matter of the litigation contrary to Rule 1.8(j)." Model Rule 1.5, cmt. See Model Rule 1.8(j) (prohibiting a lawyer from acquiring a proprietary interest in the cause of action or subject matter of litigation); EC 5–7 (1981). ("The possibility of an adverse effect upon the exercise of free judgment by a lawyer on behalf of his client during litigation generally makes it undesirable for the lawyer to acquire a proprietary interest in the cause of his client or otherwise to become financially interested in the outcome of the litigation."). How is a contingent fee different from some other proprietary interest in a cause of action?

PROBLEMS

1. You are asked to represent the 17 year old son of a millionaire on a drunk driving charge. You ask for a $4,000 nonrefundable retainer to take the case, expecting to spend substantial time defending against the charges. Instead, after you work three hours on the matter, the prosecutor agrees to dismiss the charges if your client enters a treatment program. Is it ethical for you to keep the retainer as agreed?

2. Your client in the above example is the 17 year old son of a family on welfare. You take $1,000 cash and a $3,000 note for the retainer and get the same results after spending the same amount of time on the case. Is it ethical for you to keep the retainer and demand payment on the note as agreed?

3. You are retained by a man who suffered a broken leg in an automobile accident. It is clear from the police reports that the other driver was at fault. From your practice experience, you know that the other driver's insurance company routinely settles such cases for between $10,000 and $15,000 upon receiving a demand letter from an injured party's attorney with police reports and medical records attached. You have a form of demand letter on your word processor, and expect to spend approximately one hour reviewing the facts and preparing the letter. Nonetheless, your client has been convinced by friends and family that insurance companies never settle such cases without going to court. Your client asks you to take the case on a contingent fee of 33% of the amount recovered in a judgment or settlement. What do you say to your client before entering into the fee agreement?

4. You are asked to take two plaintiffs' personal injury cases on a contingency. You estimate that one case has an expected value of $50,000 (meaning that amount is your best estimate of what the client will recover at trial, and you would advise the client to settle for that amount or more).

You estimate that the other case has an expected value of $750,000. You also estimate that you will have to spend the same amount of time, approximately 200 hours, on each case before it is settled or you obtain a judgment. Should you charge the same percentage contingent fee for the two cases?

E. DIVISION OF FEES

"A division of a fee is a single billing to a client covering the fee of two or more lawyers who are not in the same firm." Model Rule 1.5, cmt. Such an arrangement allows unaffiliated lawyers to join together to provide representation to a client who benefits from the lawyers' different areas of expertise. While lawyers within the same firm are free to divide fees as they see fit (usually in accordance with a partnership agreement), the Model Code prohibits unaffiliated lawyers from dividing fees except in proportion to the work that they actually perform for a client. Furthermore, the client must be told of, and consent to, the arrangement. See DR 2–107(A). The practical effect of the Model Code restrictions is to prohibit fees for "referral." Lawyers refer work to each other out of professional courtesy, often hoping to receive a referral in return, but they may not share in fees for work that they do not do.

However, many jurisdictions have chosen the more liberal approach in Model Rule 1.5(e), which allows a fee division so long as either the division is in proportion to the services performed by each lawyer or each lawyer in writing assumes joint responsibility for the representation. This Rule "permits the lawyers to divide a fee on either the basis of the proportion of services they render or by agreement between the participating lawyers if all assume responsibility for the representation as a whole and the client is advised and does not object." Rule 1.5, cmt. Such arrangements are often used by lawyers who initiate contingent fee representations and then pass cases on to other lawyers more experienced in trial work, keeping for themselves "finder's" fees consisting of a percentage of the judgments obtained.

For discussion of fee splitting with nonlawyer third parties, see Concurrent Conflicts with Lay Intermediaries, Chapter 6 infra.

QUESTION

1. The liberalized fee splitting rule in Model Rule 1.5 broadens the range of allowed contractual arrangements between lawyers and their clients. Allowing a portion of a fee to go to the lawyer who originates a representation may encourage lawyers to refer cases to lawyers who can handle them more competently. However, fee splitting can be subject to some abuses, particularly if lawyers are compensated for drumming up cases which they have no intention of prosecuting themselves. In what contexts might such "finders' fees" be particularly prone to abuse?

F. Payment of Legal Fees

Payment in Cash

Some clients are happy to pay their lawyers up front—in cash. Internal Revenue Code Section 6050I, 26 U.S.C.A. Section 6050I, requires recipients of over $10,000 in cash to file an informational return with the IRS. Although some state bar associations have objected, lawyers are subject to this rule. United States v. Goldberger & Dubin, 935 F.2d 501 (2d Cir. 1991) (a client's name and amount of cash payment are not protected by the attorney-client privilege even though such information might incriminate the client). See Daniel Capra, Disclosure of Client Identity, Payment of Fees and Communication by Fiduciaries, 4 Geo. J. Legal Ethics 235 (1990) (urging protection of clients' names and consultations from disclosure in most circumstances).

Fee Forfeitures in Criminal Cases

The Organized Crime Control Act of 1970, see 18 U.S.C.A. Section 1963, and Comprehensive Forfeiture Act of 1984, see 21 U.S.C.A. Section 853, empower the government to seize proceeds from certain criminal offenses as well as real and personal property used to commit those offenses. The seized property can sometimes include the money an accused defendant needs to pay a lawyer.

In Caplin & Drysdale v. United States, 491 U.S. 617 (1989), a defendant was charged with running a massive drug distribution scheme. The petitioner, a law firm representing the defendant, argued that the defendant needed his assets to pay his lawyers and that forfeiture of the defendant's assets under the Forfeiture Act violated the Due Process Clause of the Fifth Amendment as well as the Sixth Amendment right of the defendant to hire counsel of his choice. The Court held that nothing in the statute prevents a defendant from hiring counsel of his choice, that the government has a legitimate pecuniary interest in the forfeiture, and that the statute did not violate the Fifth Amendment in part because it permits "rightful owners of forfeited assets to make claims for forfeited assets before they are retained by the Government." Id. at 629. In United States v. Monsanto, 491 U.S. 600 (1989), decided the same day as *Caplin & Drysdale*, respondent was indicted for directing a large scale heroin distribution network. The indictment alleged that assets, including a home, an apartment and $35,000 in cash, had been accumulated as a direct result of the narcotics trafficking, making them subject to forfeiture under the Comprehensive Forfeiture Act of 1984. The government froze the respondent's assets pending trial, and the respondent argued that the government's refusal to allow him to use his assets to pay a lawyer violated his Sixth Amendment right to counsel of his choice. Relying on its decision in *Caplin & Drysdale*, the Court held that the Sixth Amendment did not require Congress to permit a defendant to use forfeited assets to pay legal fees.

G. TRANSACTIONS INVOLVING CLIENTS

As a fiduciary of his client, a lawyer is presumptively barred from self dealing at the expense of his client. Maksym v. Loesch, 937 F.2d 1237, 1241 (7th Cir.1991). Model Rule 1.8 carves out a very limited exception to a blanket prohibition against lawyer-client transactions and DR 5–104 a somewhat more flexible exception. However, whatever rule applies in a particular jurisdiction, a court reviewing a lawyer-client transaction is likely to evaluate its overall fairness. Any fiduciary, whether a director dealing with her corporation or a lawyer dealing with his client, "has the burden of justifying self dealing transactions." Tamar Frankel, Fiduciary Law, 71 Cal. L. Rev. 795, 824–25 (1983). Furthermore, "attorneys at law, in dealing with their clients, are required to exercise the highest order of good faith and to disclose to clients all information in their possession" arising out of the attorney-client relationship that might influence clients' decisions about such dealings. Huston v. Schohr, 63 Cal.App.2d 267, 146 P.2d 730, 734 (1944) (promissory note from client to attorney held enforceable after jury found attorney had met the required standard of good faith and fair dealing).

In addition to unfairness and nondisclosure, another area of potential abuse is use of client information. Model Rule 1.8(b) provides that a lawyer shall not "use information relating to representation of a client to the disadvantage of the client unless the client consents after consultation." For example, a lawyer who learns that a client intends to invest in certain real estate, may not, without the client's consent, acquire nearby property where doing so will adversely affect the client's development plans. Model Rule 1.8, cmt.

Furthermore, a lawyer must be careful not to carry out a representation in a manner that benefits, or appears to benefit, herself rather than her client. Model Rule 1.8(c) provides that a lawyer shall not prepare an instrument giving the lawyer or certain relations of the lawyer any substantial gift or legacy from the client except where the client is related to the donee. Otherwise, a lawyer may accept a gift from a client, if the transaction meets standards of fairness. Id., cmt. Model Rule 1.8(d) prohibits a lawyer from negotiating with a client for literary or media rights prior to the conclusion of a representation. Model Rule 1.8(e) prohibits a lawyer from providing financial assistance to a client in connection with pending or contemplated litigation except to advance court costs and expenses (see discussion of this rule in the discussion of contingent fees supra). Finally, Rule 1.8(h) prohibits a lawyer from making an agreement prospectively limiting the lawyer's liability for malpractice unless the client is independently represented, and also prohibits a lawyer from settling a malpractice claim without first advising the client in writing to consult another lawyer.

The remaining provisions of Rule 1.8, Rule 1.8(f) concerning concurrent conflicts which arise with lay intermediaries and Rules 1.8(g) and (i) concerning concurrent conflicts between two or more clients, are discussed in Chapter 6 infra.

H. CLIENT AND THIRD-PARTY FUNDS

One of the most important fiduciary obligations of a lawyer is to properly handle money entrusted to her by clients and third parties. Unfortunately, many lawyers fail to handle other people's money properly, and such failure, even if unintentional, is a common cause for disbarment and other severe discipline. Although the Model Code and Model Rules are a useful guide, it is critical that a lawyer know and meticulously follow the rules in her own jurisdiction.

Model Rule 1.15(a) provides that if a lawyer comes into possession of property of clients or third persons, the lawyer must hold the property separate from the lawyer's own property. Money is to be kept in a separate bank account (usually called an "attorney trust account"), and other property (stock certificates, deeds, etc.) is to be identified as such and appropriately safeguarded. Complete records of bank accounts and other property must be kept by the lawyer and preserved for a specified period of time (in many jurisdictions for a period of five years). DR 9–102(A) imposes a similar requirement that "funds of clients" be kept in an identifiable bank account. Although the Disciplinary Rule does not specifically mention the property of third parties, as does Model Rule 1.15, segregation of *any* funds held by a lawyer that do not belong to the lawyer is not only a good business practice, but the only way to avoid an appearance of impropriety. Commingling of other people's funds in the same bank account with a lawyer's own funds is one of the surest ways for a lawyer to find herself being accused of improper use of the funds, or even of embezzlement.

Also, upon receiving any funds belonging to a client or third person, a lawyer shall promptly notify the client or third person and, except as specifically permitted by law or by agreement, shall promptly deliver to the client or third person any funds that that person is entitled to receive. Upon request, a lawyer must render a full accounting regarding property held by the lawyer. Model Rule 1.15(b). See also DR 9–102(B).

Finally, a lawyer must keep in a separate fund any property the ownership of which is in dispute (either between the lawyer and the client or between the client and another person) until after the dispute is resolved. See Model Rule 1.15(c); DR 9–102(A)(2).

I. TERMINATION OF REPRESENTATION

Rules on withdrawal from a representation vary among jurisdictions, and a lawyer should know the local rules of court as well as state ethics rules. Generally, a lawyer shall not represent a client, and shall withdraw from a representation that has begun, if the representation will violate rules of professional conduct. Model Rule 1.16(a)(1). Perhaps the best example is where the representation would conflict with a previous or concurrent representation of another person by the same lawyer, a problem discussed in more detail in Chapters 4 and 6 infra. A lawyer also shall not represent a client, and shall withdraw from representing a client, if the lawyer's physical or mental condition materially impairs the lawyer's ability to represent the client, or if the lawyer is discharged by the client. See Martin v. Camp, 219 N.Y. 170, 114 N.E. 46 (N.Y. 1916) (a client can discharge his attorney at any time without cause and without penalty). DR 2–110(B) also explicitly states that withdrawal is required where the lawyer knows that her client is bringing an action or asserting a defense merely for the purpose of harassing or maliciously injuring any person. See discussion of abuse of process supra.

A lawyer furthermore *may* withdraw from a representation if withdrawal can be accomplished without material adverse effect on the client, and in certain other circumstances, including if the client persists in a course of action involving the lawyer's services that the lawyer reasonably believes is criminal or fraudulent, the client has used the lawyer's services to perpetrate a crime or fraud, or the client insists upon pursuing an objective that the lawyer considers repugnant or imprudent. Model Rule 1.16(b). If a lawyer has a moral objection to her client's conduct, this option of withdrawing is an important one to remember, although it is of course better not to undertake such a representation in the first place.

Model Rule 1.16(b)(4) allows a lawyer to resign from a representation, even where an adverse effect on the client results, if the client fails to fulfill an obligation to the lawyer regarding the lawyer's services (for example, paying the lawyer's fee), the representation will impose an unreasonable financial burden on the lawyer, the representation has been made unreasonably difficult by the client, or other good cause for withdrawal exists. Notwithstanding good cause for withdrawal, Model Rule 1.16(c) requires a lawyer to continue a representation when ordered to do so by a tribunal.

In terminating a representation, a lawyer must take steps to protect the client's interests, including giving reasonable notice of termination, allowing time for employment of other counsel, surrendering papers and property, and refunding any advance payment of unearned fees. Model Rule 1.16(d). See DR 2–110(A)(2); Disciplinary Proceedings Against Lesperance, 165 Wis.2d 723, 478 N.W.2d 587 (Wis. 1992) (lawyer's license revoked for numerous violations of professional conduct rules, including withdrawing from representation without protecting clients' interests).

Finally, the duty to preserve client confidences continues after termination of a lawyer's employment, and a lawyer cannot accept employment against a former client that may require the lawyer to use confidential information obtained by the lawyer in the course of his professional relations with the client. Slater v. Rimar, Inc. et al., 462 Pa. 138, 338 A.2d 584, 587–88 (Pa. 1975) (lawyer disqualified from representing plaintiff in derivative action where he served as an officer and director of, and was counsel to defendant corporations prior to commencement of derivative action). See also Goldstein v. Lees, 46 Cal.App.3d 614, 120 Cal.Rptr. 253 (1975), Chapter 4 infra.

J.   REPRESENTATION PRO BONO PUBLICO

Rethinking "Professionalism"

41 Emory L.J. 403 (1992).
Timothy P. Terrell.
James H. Wildman.

A Responsibility for Adequate Distribution of Legal Services

The final value we would include within the essence of professionalism is a lawyer's special responsibility to assist in the effort to distribute legal services widely in our society. This moral duty, like the others we have discussed, follows from the importance of law to our culture. Because law pervades all significant social arrangements and institutions, legal services must be widely available to the citizenry, and the legal system should be functioning adequately on their behalf. The remarkable significance of law in this country means that the government, representing all of the population, has a responsibility, at a minimum, to fund courts, prosecutors, and other agencies adequately, and perhaps a broader duty to subsidize indigent legal services agencies of various kinds as well. But regardless of the government's proper role in this regard, lawyers have a special professional responsibility here as well.

* * *

We believe that professionalism creates an "enabling," as opposed to a "personal," responsibility for the distribution of legal services. Our responsibility as lawyers is to see that the Bar as an entity assists and enables those in the profession who desire to do so to distribute legal services widely in society. Professionalism does not necessarily demand, then, that each of us personally pledge to devote time and effort to legal help for the poor. Instead, appropriate professional behavior would entail other individual and institutional actions. Personally, lawyers at the very least should not interfere with the efforts of other lawyers who seek to provide this wide distribution. For example, law firms should not have internal policies, practices, or incentives that actively discourage partners and associates from becoming involved in pro bono projects. Beyond this, however, a firm, legal department, or agency should actively encourage such commitment to outside legal activities. But the decision to make that commitment should remain an individual moral choice not forced by the concept of professionalism.

In addition, because the responsibility here is "enabling" rather than personal, one way for the Bar as an entity to fulfill the profession's duty to foster wider distribution of legal services would be for it to impose a special tax or fee on its members that would be used to subsidize the efforts of those Bar members interested in providing legal services to indigents. We recognize how controversial such a tax would be, but we believe that opposition to the idea is based in part on an inadequate understanding of the justification such a tax has from the perspective of the Bar's professional heritage.

This "distributional" responsibility within professionalism would not entail much more, however. And it cannot. Any purported personal moral requirement on lawyers to give legal assistance to the poor would mean that lawyers would lack the traditional individual freedom to choose not to work on behalf of others they would not otherwise willingly assist. The reason for this refusal should not matter to professionalism—it could be based simply in economics in that the client cannot pay full market value for the lawyer's services, or in philosophy in that the lawyer is not convinced of the legitimacy of the claim espoused by the client, or in any other explanation. To impose a personal obligation nevertheless would create a most unfortunate and sadly perverted form of professionalism: professionalism as indentured servanthood. A coerced, false, and politically biased morality of this kind has no place in this debate.

Rethinking "The Practice of Law"

41 Emory L.J. 451 (1992).
Jennifer Gerarda Brown.

* * *

Even as the members of the legal profession take time away from pro bono matters to spend more time serving paying clients, the vast demand for legal services among people of low and moderate income goes unmet. It has been said that eighty-five percent of Americans cannot afford the services of an attorney. Writing for a majority of the Supreme Court in Mallard v. United States District Court of the Southern District of Iowa, Justice Brennan stated, "[I]n a time when the need for legal services among the poor is growing and public funding for such services has not kept pace, lawyers' ethical obligation to volunteer their time and skills pro bono publico is manifest." [490 U.S. 296, 310 (1989)] In the early and mid–1970s, the United States Supreme Court and the American Bar Association acknowledged that "the middle seventy percent of our population is not being reached or served adequately by the legal profession." More recent ABA studies show that eighty percent of the legal problems experienced by low-income households are not handled or resolved with the assistance of counsel.

Such statistics suggest at the very least that a small percentage of potential clients absorb a very large portion of legal services, and that some segment of society (it may be the poor; it may be members of the middle class dealing with domestic relations, real estate, and bankruptcy problems) is proportionately under-served by the legal profession. When lawyers work toward an equitable distribution of legal services throughout society, then, they should bear in mind the broad spectrum of potential clients who may not be able to afford their ordinary rates. Contrary to Terrell and Wildman's assumptions, legal assistance, particularly in civil and administrative matters, remains a "luxury available only to a small segment of society." Because lawyers are uniquely qualified to provide this assistance, it is appropriate for the profession to continue to impose pro bono obligations on individual lawyers as a part of their professional duties.

Furthermore, we should not distinguish the responsibility to serve the public from other professional responsibilities imposed upon the practicing lawyer; we should accept it as an integral part of being a lawyer. A rule requiring public service might reduce the time and effort a lawyer can devote to any individual client, but other rules of professional conduct do the same thing. Lawyers engage in this kind of balancing all the time, allocating their time and attention between clients as events and the needs of their clients require. Though taking additional fee-paying clients necessarily means that a lawyer may have less time to give to any individual fee-paying client, we assume that the lawyer will nonetheless take as many additional clients as the lawyer can competently serve. Each additional paying client is not considered an imposition on the other paying clients; Terrell and Wildman do not explain why non-paying clients would present a greater imposition.

A public service requirement might also reduce lawyers' revenues, but other rules of professional responsibility have the same effect. Rules requiring competence and diligence limit the number of clients a lawyer can serve, and this restricts revenues. Rules restricting the fee a lawyer may ethically charge reduce revenues. Rules regarding conflicts of interest may restrict the number of clients a lawyer can represent competently and diligently and therefore have the effect of reducing revenues. Regulations on solicitation and advertising may also reduce some lawyers' revenues. As a profession, however, we accept—even expect—that ethical duties may from time to time compromise profits.

When Terrell and Wildman argue that "[a]ny purported personal moral requirement on lawyers to give legal assistance to the poor would mean that lawyers would lack the traditional individual freedom to choose not to work on behalf of others they would not otherwise willingly assist," they underestimate the importance of the choices people make when deciding to become lawyers. When public service is again firmly rooted as an integral part of being a lawyer, people will make moral choices, but they will make those choices early in the game, as they try to discern whether they are in fact called to the profession, the vocation, of the law. A group of people can decide collectively to set some standard of behavior for members of the group. Some, even many, may decide that compliance with that standard is too costly; they would rather suffer exclusion from the group than comply. People are always able to decide what they value more.

* * *

III. Conclusion

Mark Twain said: "To do right is noble; to advise others to do right is also noble and much less trouble for yourself." In Rethinking "Professionalism," Terrell and Wildman put a different spin on the Twain adage and argue that paying others to do right is also noble and much less trouble for yourself. The point of pro bono service, however, is not just that the profession should contribute something to others—though such contributions are sorely needed. If this giving were the whole of pro bono service, then perhaps we could fulfill our obligation by collectively supporting lawyers who were interested in public service, as Terrell and Wildman suggest. Pro bono service is also important to professionalism because service to a different group of clients, on different terms than lawyers ordinarily establish, enriches professional life and improves the lawyer's delivery of services to paying clients. This aspect of pro bono service comes through only as individual lawyers are actively involved in serving the public good. Paying others to serve misses the point entirely.

Relevant Background

Pro bono publico means "for the public good."

Mandatory pro bono is not a new concept. In fifteenth century England, Parliament enacted a law requiring court appointed attorneys to provide no cost legal representation for poor litigants. See 11 Hen. 7, ch.12 (1495) (providing that for every poor person having a cause of action against any person in the realm "the justices shall appoint attorney and attornies for the same poor person and persons, and all of the officers requisite and necessary to be had for the speed of the said suits to be had and made, which shall do their duties without any reward for their counsels help, and business in the same."); 2 W. Holdsworth, A History of English Law 491 (1936); David L Shapiro, The Enigma of the Lawyer's Duty to Serve, 55 N.Y.U. L. Rev. 735, 740–50 (1980); Michael Millemann, Mandatory Pro Bono in Civil Cases: A Partial Answer to the Right Question, 49 Md. L. Rev. 18, 42–43 (1990).

Model Rule 6.1, approved by the ABA House of Delegates in August 1983, stated that "A lawyer *should* render public interest legal service." Model Rule 6.1 (1983) (emphasis added). In 1993 Model Rule 6.1 was amended to provide that a lawyer should "aspire to render at least (50) hours of pro bono publico legal services per year." The Rule also includes guidelines for how that time should be spent, and states that a substantial majority of the 50 hours should be spent representing persons of limited means or organizations in matters that address the needs of persons of limited means. Model Rule 6.1(a) (1993). See B. George Ballman Jr., Amended Rule 6.1: Another Move Towards Mandatory Pro Bono? Is That What We Want? 7 Geo. J. Legal Ethics 1139 (Spring 1994).

In 1990 the Florida Supreme Court found "that lawyers had an obligation, upon admission to the Florida Bar, to render legal services to the poor when appointed by the court." In re Amendments to Rules Regulating the Florida Bar–1–3.1(a) and Rules of Judicial Administration–

2.065 (Legal Aid), 598 So.2d 41 (Fla.1992), *cited in* Omar J. Arcia, Comment, Objections, Administrative Difficulties and Alternatives to Mandatory Pro Bono Legal Services in Florida, 22 Fla. St. U. L. Rev. 771, 774 (Winter 1995). However, the court was not willing to change existing bar rules and instead requested recommendations from a Florida Bar Commission on how to increase legal services for the poor. The Commission proposed Rule 4–6.1, calling for twenty hours of legal service each year or an annual donation of $350 to a legal aid organization. Although aspirational rather than mandatory, the rule does require attorneys to report whether or not they have met the pro bono requirement. Failure to report can result in disciplinary action. Arcia, supra, at 775.

In November 1994 the State Bar of Nevada Board of Governors (Nevada Board) attempted to go a step further than Florida and institute the first mandatory pro bono requirement. Had it been adopted, the plan would have required Nevada attorneys to perform twenty hours of pro bono work per year. However, opposition was strong, and the Nevada Board decided to withdraw the proposal and instead increase promotion of voluntary pro bono. Kendra Emi Nitta, Note and Comment, An Ethical Evaluation of Mandatory Pro Bono, 29 Loy. L.A. L. Rev. 909, 910 (1996), citing Margo Piscevich, A View From the Top, Nev. Law., Nov. 1994 at 2, 4, and Ed Vogel, Nevada Bar Abandons Pro Bono Requirement, Las Vegas Rev. J., Jan. 14, 1995, at 3B.

Mandatory pro bono will likely remain a controversial topic as bar associations confront increasing numbers of individuals unable to afford legal services. Many attorneys support pro bono and gain personal and professional satisfaction from representing the poor. However, most attorneys want to frame their response to this ethical obligation on their own terms. For this reason, attempts to mandate pro bono may continue to meet with strong resistance.

QUESTIONS

1. How persuasive is each of the following arguments for mandatory pro bono?

(a) The historical tradition of pro bono mandates "that attorneys, as officers of the court, must assist in the administration of justice...." Debra Burke, Reagan McLaurin, and James W. Pearce, Pro Bono Publico: Issues and Implications, 26 Loy. U. Chi. L.J. 61, 63 (Fall, 1994).

(b) The advocacy paradigm, see Chapter 8 infra, does not work if only one side can afford legal representation.

(c) Doctors are in at least some circumstances required to help persons in need regardless of ability to pay. Lawyers should do the same.

2. How persuasive is each of the following arguments against mandatory pro bono?

(a) Attorneys should not be singled out as the only state licensed profession to have to donate services. Burke, McLaurin and Pearce, supra at 72.

(b) Poverty law is a specialized field and average attorneys may not possess adequate expertise to render effective legal service. Id. at 74.

(c) It would be more efficient to tax legal services generally and use the tax revenues to provide legal services to the poor.

3. Are poor persons more in need of legal services today than in 1495 when Parliament passed a statute requiring that court appointed attorneys for poor persons "do their duties without any reward for their counsels help"?

II. Multiple Relationships

CHAPTER 2

The Client and Society

A. Disclosure of Client Confidences

John Giffard was coroner in Devon for 12 to 14 years and a lawyer for 20 odd years since about 1722. From 1722 to 1741, Giffard worked for Anglesea in nine or more cases concerning a great variety of matters, including *Rex v. Richard Annesley* (at Lord Anglesea's direction) and *Risden v. Richard Annesley* in 1722, *Earl v. His Wife*, *Lord Haversham v. Earl*, and *In Re Anglesea Will* in 1737, and *Earl v. Mrs. Simpson*, *Earl v. Henderson, a Quaker*, *Banks v. Henderson* (at Lord Angelsea's direction), and *Earl v. Rachael Cooper* in 1741.

The Court of Exchequer, established by William the Conqueror, originally had jurisdiction over revenue cases arising out of nonpayment of debts to the Crown. This jurisdiction was extended over time to include all personal actions, until the Judicature Act of 1873 transferred the business of the Court of Exchequer to the High Court of Justice which was in turn merged into the Queen's Bench Division.

Annesley v. Anglesea

17 How. St. Tr. 1140 (Exchequer 1743).

The plaintiff James Annesley, brought an action against Richard, Earl of Anglesea for certain property in Ireland. The plaintiff's contention was that he was the rightful heir of the property, as the only son and sole heir of the previous owner, Lord Altham. The defendant, the brother of Lord Altham, denied that the plaintiff was the legitimate son of Lord Altham.

The plaintiff's story was that he had been born in 1715 to Lord and Lady Altham; that in 1716 his parents had separated; that he had been still brought up affectionately by his father until 1722 when his father took as a mistress Miss Gregory; that in 1724 due to the influence of Miss Gregory and his father's desire to raise money by the selling of reversions, which were encumbered by fee tails, it was arranged by his father to have it appear that he was dead and he was brought up in a butcher's house; that in 1727 his father died and his uncle, the defendant, wishing to have the property himself, had kidnaped him and sold him into slavery in America; that he was in Delaware as a slave for 13 years; that he had returned to Great Britain to vindicate his rights; that he had accidentally shot a gamekeeper on his return; that his uncle had tried to have him convicted of murder; that he had been tried at Old Bailey and acquitted; and he now was able at last to assert his rights.

Technically, the action was one of ejectment brought by a lessee of Annesley for certain lands in Meath. Indirectly involved was the title to the earldom and one of the largest estates in Ireland. The value was said to be the largest ever litigated to that date in an English court. Sergeant Marshall appeared for the plaintiff, assisted by 13 other lawyers; Sergeant Malone for the defendant, assisted by 16 lawyers. Three Exchequer judges presided over a jury of 12 composed of "gentlemen of the greatest property in Ireland, and most all members of Parliament." According to a report of the "General Evening Post" of London, December 6, 1743, several of the jurors had financial or blood ties to the defendant. Fifty-nine witnesses were called for the plaintiff; thirty-one for the defendant. There was a great deal of contradiction on the question of whether Lady Altham had given birth to a son. The woman alleged by the defense to be the true mother was not called; presumably the defense believed their claim and thought she would lie for her son; the plaintiff feared she had been bought by the incumbent Earl. As to the kidnaping and prosecution for murder, the defendant merely sought to impeach the plaintiff's witnesses or explain away the circumstances, arguing that a fatherless boy of twelve might well have indentured himself for service in America. With the factual issues much in doubt, the plaintiff called the defendant's former solicitor, John Giffard.

GEORGE II, Trial in Ejectment between J. Annesley, esq. and Richard Earl of Anglesea

Wednesday, November 16

The counsel for the plaintiff proposed to examine Mr. John Giffard to what he had heard the defendant say concerning the lessor of the plaintiff, and his title; and being called upon to open the nature of that evidence;

Mr. Harward, of counsel for the plaintiff, spoke as follows: My lord, the conversation Mr. Giffard had with lord Anglesea was to this purpose: Mr. Giffard is an attorney of reputation in England, and as such has been twenty years or thereabouts employed by this noble earl in his business, as he had occasion for him. When my unfortunate client was to be tried at the

Old Bailey, that was the time lord Anglesea had greatest occasion for this Mr. Giffard; and it will appear to your lordship that lord Anglesea disclosed his intentions to him in this manner: "I am advised that it is not prudent for me to appear publicly in the prosecution, but I would give 10,000£ to have him hanged. Mr. Jans my agent shall always attend you. I am in great distress; I am worried by my wife in Ireland; Mr. Charles Annesley is at law with me for part of my estate, and," says he, "If I cannot hang James Annesley, it is better for me to quit this kingdom and go to France, and let Jemmy have his right, if he will remit me into France 3,000£ a year; I will learn French before I go."

Mr. Daley, of counsel for the defendant, objects to Mr. Giffard's being examined, since as an attorney he was to keep the secrets of his client, and if he is a gentleman of character, he will not, and as an attorney he ought not to disclose them. . . .

Serj. Marshall, for the plaintiff. But if an attorney will voluntarily come and disclose any secret, he ought to be heard.

Mr. Blake, of counsel for the defendant. An attorney or solicitor might not, nor is he compellable to disclose the secrets of his client; this is a privilege inherent in the office of an attorney or solicitor: but as this privilege has its source in a public consideration, I shall, with submission to better judgment, insist that this exemptive privilege is not merely and solely the privilege of the solicitor or attorney, but is, in law and reason, the right and privilege of the client. . . .

Mr. Recorder, for the defendant. My lord, formerly persons appeared in court themselves; but as business multiplied and became more intricate, and titles more perplexed, both the distance of places, and the multiplicity of businesses, made it absolutely necessary that there should be a set of people who should stand in the place of the suitors, and these persons are called attornies. Since this has been thought necessary, all people and all courts have looked upon that confidence between the party and attorney to be so great, that it would be destructive to all business, if attornies were to disclose the business of their clients. In many cases men hold their estates without titles; in others, but such titles, that if their deeds could be got out of their hands, they must lose their fortunes. When persons become purchasers for valuable considerations, and get a deed that makes against them, they are not obliged to disclose whether they have that deed. Now, if an attorney was to be examined in every case, what man would trust an attorney with the secret of his estate, if he should be permitted to offer himself as a witness? If an attorney had it in his option to be examined, there would be an entire stop to business; nobody would trust an attorney with the state of his affairs.

The reason why attornies are not to be examined to any thing relating to their clients or their affairs, is, because they would destroy the confidence that is necessary to be preserved between them. This confidence between the employer and the person employed, is so sacred a thing, that if they were at liberty, when the present cause was over that they were employed in, to give testimony in favour of any other person, it would not answer the end for which it was instituted. The end is, that persons with safety may substitute others in their room; and therefore if you cannot ask me, you cannot ask that man; for everything said to him, is as if I had said it to myself, and he is not to answer it. Now, the question will be, for whose sake it was instituted? Be sure, for the sake of the person employing him. Who then has the option that he should be examined? Why, the employer; because otherwise it would be in vain to fix a confidence in persons, if that person was at liberty on any account to shake him off, and say, While I was employed by you, it was not in my option to disclose it, but now that I am not, I will unravel all. As it was for the sake of the employer that attorneys were instituted, they cannot in civil suits become witnesses without the consent of the employer; therefore, I submit it, whether the option is in the attorney or in the person who is the employer; and if in the employer, as I think it be both for his safety and advantage, the attorney neither can nor ought to reveal what is entrusted to him. In pleading, it is "ponit in loco suo attornatum," the attorney is as himself. And it is contrary to the rules of natural justice and equity, that any man should betray himself. I apprehend it is not material whether this be a "turpis causa" or not; as this man was employed by my lord Anglesea, he can be asked no other questions than my lord Anglesea himself.

My lord, I must submit it, whether an attorney's testimony should be received, although he offers to give it? And in the next place, I submit it, whether this kind of testimony is this criminal case ought to be received? It would be very little satisfaction to a client to be put to apply to the Court for an attachment against this person who offers to lay his evidence before the jury, if his testimony could be received. I apprehend that person is in the place of the client, and as he entrusts him with secrets, he is not to disclose them without his leave; and if he should disclose them out of court, an action of deceit lies against him. And though an attorney should not insist upon his privilege, yet it is in the power of the employer to insist upon that privilege, and to say he is the person entrusted with his secrets. Now, in this case it is much stronger, for here it is said, that he is employed by my lord Anglesea. Now, if that party cannot disclose those secrets in a civil case, he ought not, for a strong reason, in a criminal case; because that is subjecting his client perhaps to a criminal prosecution.

Mr. Lee, of counsel for the defendant. My lord, if the attorney confess judgment upon record, it shall bind the [party], though done without warrant; and the reason is, that the attorney appearing for the party is, since the statute of Merton, considered as the party himself.* If then the attorney and party are considered as one person, why shall the one be offered to be examined in this cause, when the other cannot?

Serj. Marshall. I do admit in some cases the attorney ought not to be permitted to disclose the secrets of his clients; but that must be where the confidence was necessary and lawful: but here the trust was unlawful, and the attorney could not conceal it without breach of his oath, as an attorney,

---

* See discussion of lawyers as agents for their clients in Chapter 1 *supra.*—ed.

which was to do right to all men. This was a criminal secret, that was not only to affect the plaintiff's property and life, but also to acquire a title in which the public were interested; so that it became the duty of the attorney to disclose it.

Upon which the Lord Chief Baron desired to ask Mr. Giffard a few questions, and he was called up accordingly.

Mr. John Giffard sworn.

Q. Are you an attorney of any, and what court?—A. I am an attorney of the Common Pleas in England, and a solicitor of the High Court of Chancery, and sworn and admitted as such by virtue of the act of Parliament.

Q. Did you know the defendant the earl of Anglesea?—A. Yes.

Q. Were you ever agent or solicitor for him in any, and what cause? A. In the year 1722, Lord Anglesea employed me to assist him on a particular occasion to make his defense.

Q. Name the parties.—A. He was persecuted, the king against him, as Richard Annesley, esq.

Q. Were you employed in any other cause?—A. In the year 1722, the same year when an action was brought against him at the suite on one George Risden. But from the year 1722, until he became earl of Anglesea, I never heard of him. In the year 1737 I met him in London, and he desired me to solicit an affair between him and his countess that lived at Biddiford.

Q. Name the next cause.—A. Between the right honourable Maurice Thompson lord Haversham, and the earl of Anglesea.

Q. The next.—A. I was concerned in another, the same year, and attended it, (it is very well known through the Houses of Lords and Commons in England) in order to throw a Bill out of the House of Commons, for the exemplifying the late earl of Anglesea's will.

Q. Go on.—A. I was likewise concerned in a particular cause, between my lord Anglesea, in the year 1741, and one Mrs. Simpson of this place; and have also sued out several writs out of the Court of Common Pleas, at the suit of my lord Anglesea, against one Henderson a Quaker.

Q. Go on.—A. I likewise was employed by lord Anglesea in a cause, wherein his lordship was plaintiff, and one Rachael Cooper was defendant.

Q. Go on.—A. I issued out writs against Henderson, at the suit of one Banks, by lord Anglesea's directions.

Q. Go on.—A. I was sent for, and commanded by him to solicit and carry on a prosecution against the plaintiff Mr. Annesley.

Q. Have you been retained as agent or solicitor for the earl of Anglesea, in any other causes within these three years?—A. I do not know; some frivolous thing might have slipped my memory, but I was not concerned in any other cause, since the prosecution of Mr. Annesley.

Q. Name the time when you were retained by the earl to prosecute that murder.—A. The second day of May, 1742.

Q. The conversation that passed between you and my lord, to which you are now produced as an evidence, was it before, or after, that time?—A. There were several declarations, some before, and some after. The conversations were from the 7th of December 1741, to the time of Mr. Annesley's being discharged at the Old Bailey.

Q. When was the bill of indictment found against Mr. Annesley?—A. The bill was found in June, and he was admitted to bail in July sessions, 1742.

Q. On what day is the murder laid in the indictment?—A. On the first of May, 1742, the 15th year of the present king.

Q. Were you agent or solicitor for lord Anglesea at the time that the conversation passed, before the 2d of May?—A. Not for the cause of Mr. Annesley.

Q. Were not the other causes subsisting?—A. The causes were writs which were never executed.

Q. I desire you may answer directly, whether the conversation before the 2d of May was not on some affair in which my lord Anglesea, consulted and advised with you as his agent or solicitor, designing to employ you in that affair?—A. No, my lord, it was not; for I did not expect to be employed by him again, he having employed Mr. George Garden and Mr. Adam Gordon.

Q. Name the people.—A. Mr. Garden and Mr. Gordon. They are attornies, they are partners, and I received my instructions, in a great part, from them; my lord ordered me to take directions from them, and I have instructions under Gordon's own handwriting.

Q. Had my lord Anglesea those conversations with you relative to the plaintiff, between the 7th of December and 2d of May, as intending to employ you, or not?—A. I never was employed, not intended to be employed, in any suit for or against him, during that time.

Q. When did you first receive instructions from Garden and Gordon?—A. In a week after the first of May.

Q. Had you any instruction from them, except what were relative to the prosecution, in relation to the plaintiff?—A. No; no instructions but what were relative to the prosecution.

Q. Did you charge lord Anglesea with any term fees in the year 1741, relative to particular suits?—A. I believed I charged 10s. 4d. for lord Haversham's suit.

Q. In what term did you charge it?—A. I find that cause was in the vacation between Hilary and Easter term, and was concluded before Easter term came. It was depending in Hilary term 1741, and was concluded before the next term.

Q. Was it depending for any time before Hilary term?—A. The beginning of it was the 20th of January, the essoin day before Hilary term.

Q. Were you concerned for lord Anglesea from the latter end of November to the beginning of January 1741?—A. I was concerned in issuing out some writs.

Q. And do not you think, if any suit had depended upon them, you would have been concerned?—A. I do not know but I might.

The witness goes off the table.

Mr. Prim Serjeant, (Anthony Malone, esq.) for the defendant. An attorney shall not disclose any thing whatsoever in a collateral question, that shall affect the property of the client.

Serj. Tisdall, for the plaintiff. My lord, we propose to examine to no fact which came to his knowledge as an attorney, in any suit in which he was employed for lord Anglesea: but he declares he never was employed in any suit relating to the lessor of the plaintiff, nor was even intended to be employed in any suit relating to this trial. We hope, therefore, we are proper to give in evidence several declarations and conversations lord Anglesea had with the witness concerning the lessor, his title to this estate, and the necessity he apprehended himself under of putting him out of the way at that time. We do not propose to examine him as to any facts relating to the prosecution of that suit in which he was then employed; we desire only to examine him as to the conversations with lord Anglesea concerning this cause; and I apprehend we have undoubtedly a right to examine him as to these points.

I cannot say, but the gentlemen on the other side have good reason to oppose this evidence, which, if it appears in the manner we are instructed it will, must be an evidence of great weight. I shall first beg leave to consider, whether an attorney may be examined to any matter which came to his knowledge as an attorney. If he is employed as an attorney in any unlawful or wicked act, his duty to the public obliges him to disclose it; no private obligations can dispense with that universal one, which lies on every member of the society, to discover every design which may be formed, contrary to the laws of the society, to destroy the public welfare. For this reason I apprehend, that if a secret, which is contrary to the public good, such as a design to commit treason, murder, or perjury, comes to the knowledge of an attorney, even in a cause wherein he is concerned, the obligation to the public must dispense with the private obligation to the client: but in this case the witness proposed to be examined was not attorney to the defendant in any case relative to this testimony. And the secrecy of the attorney is necessary to the client in that cause only, for the carrying on of which he is under a necessity to entrust him. For this reason I agree, that whatever is communicated to him from that necessity ought not to be disclosed, even in a future cause, wherein he is not concerned; but as the client is not obliged to entrust his attorney with any of his secrets, but such only as are relative to, or may be useful for carrying on the cause in which he is employed; if he trusts him with any matter foreign to that, even during the time that he is employed, with any matter which was not necessary or any way material or immaterial, to the cause depending, he is not obliged to conceal it.

I beg leave to say, as there was no necessity upon the client to entrust him with it, so mutually there can be no obligation upon the attorney to conceal it; for as the only obligation which lies on the attorney to secrecy, arises from the necessity of confidence between him and his employer, from the necessity the client must be under to entrust him, it cannot extend to any case where that confidence was not necessary, where the client was not under such a necessity. If this be admitted, the matters we propose to examine to are quite foreign to those suits in which the witness was employed for the defendant. My lord Anglesea was indeed under a necessity of entrusting him with all the evidence that he thought necessary for the prosecution carried on against the plaintiff in England, and the attorney is under an obligation of concealing that evidence: but was he under a necessity of telling the attorney he wanted to put this man out of the way, or that he was entitled to his honours and estate? This was a secret he ought in prudence to have kept within his own breast, and not to have discovered. This was a secret not necessary to be communicated, and therefore not to be concealed.

Upon these principles, therefore, I should submit it to your lordship, that we must be at liberty to examine Mr. Giffard as to those conversations which were no way relative to the matter in which he was then employed by the defendant, and which, if true, as they are represented to us, import a design contrary to all laws of nature and society.

Mr. Walsh, for the plaintiff. I do admit that an attorney shall not be examined to any fact disclosed to him by his client as an attorney, relative to a cause wherein he was employed; because a client must of necessity entrust the secrets of his title to his attorney, to enable him to conduct his suit; and therefore the attorney stands in the place of his client, who cannot be examined as a witness against himself. But this rule can never be extended either to a case where the matter was not communicated to him as a secret, in the cause wherein he was employed, or before he was employed as attorney in that cause; because there the client was not under any necessity of disclosing the fact to him; and if it were otherwise, this inconvenience must happen, that no attorney could ever be a witness against a person, if he ever happened, upon any occasion whatsoever, to be his attorney. The question then is, whether the fact to which we want to examine Mr. Giffard was communicated to him by lord Anglesea, as his lordship's attorney, or not? Or whether he was actually employed by him in the prosecution of Mr. Annesley, at the time the discourse we would examine him to happened? It is true, Mr. Giffard had been attorney to lord Anglesea in several suits before this conversation happened; but he could not be at the time employed in the prosecution of Mr. Annesley; because it appears, that his discourse happened before the coroner's inquest sat, or any prosecution began on that account; so that I apprehend this case does not come within the rule I mentioned, and that Mr. Giffard ought to be examined. But besides, what we would examine him to is, not as to any secret in the prosecution itself, but only as to lord Anglesea's intention and design in engaging himself in the prosecution. But I must mention another reason, which puts this matter out of doubt, and that is, that this prosecution was at the suit of the crown; if any secrets were in that suit, they were the king's secrets, the revealing of which could be no inconvenience to lord Anglesea, or affect his property; if an attorney is a subscribing witness to the execution of a deed by his client, he does not attest it as attorney, and therefore he may reveal his client's having executed such deed.

If a conversation happened between an attorney and his client, even relating to a cause he is concerned in, but before he was concerned, he may disclose it; and therefore, my lord, I apprehend, for these reasons, that Mr. Giffard ought to be examined as to the point we have opened.

Mr. Harward* ... I take the distinction to be, that where an attorney comes to the knowledge of a thing that is "malum in se," against the common rules of morality and honesty, though from his client, and necessary to procure success in the cause, yet it is no breach of trust in him to disclose it, as it can't be presumed an honest man would engage in a trust that by law prevented him from discharging that moral duty all are bound to, nor can private obligation cancel the justice owing by us to the public. But the trust reposed in this attorney was, to carry on a prosecution of murder. The matter disclosed by this lord to him was foreign concerning the title to an estate; then, how can the revealing of that be a breach of trust, when not within the trust he was employed in? . . . .

And lastly, as it is a discovery to the agent to contrive the death of an innocent man, that there is no protection whatsoever can be given to dispense with that moral engagement he was under to the discovery of it; if this unfortunate gentleman had come to the discovery, that the lord Anglesea and his attorney had entered into a conspiracy to bribe witnesses, could the Court stand by and say, That this witness should not be examined? How can he now then, in a civil case, wherein he never was concerned, have that protection? ...

* * *

Solicitor General, (Warden Flood, esq.) for the defendant. I humbly hope your lordship will not admit this person to be examined in this cause. If the

---

* In the "Trial at Bar," &c. this speech of Mr. Harward begins thus:

"If even an act of parliament was made, that no attorney should disclose the secrets of his client, yet that act, in numberless cases, would have no weight, because no act whatsoever can be consistent with reason which would subvert the laws of God. And to conceal a crime, is in some measure to become a party to it. Surely there never was a stranger instance of iniquity than the present; a de-sign of the blackest dye against the life of an innocent person. And shall a man; because he has once been concerned as attorney for the assassin, have his mouth shut for ever? Such a doctrine would be to protect villainy against all virtue and innocence. Shall an attorney stand by and see a man kept out of his estate and honour, and all that is dear to him, and not speak, because the criminal has once been his client? No sure, unless he has a mind to become a party to the crime by the concealment of it."

question were only to his credit, surely he can deserve none; for he appears under the circumstances of a person who was employed from the year 1722, by this noble person as his attorney: a man willingly betraying those secrets, which, in point of duty and common honesty, he ought to keep. Besides, the secrets he pretends to disclose are such as it is not necessary for my lord to communicate to him, and such as no man in his wits could disclose to any person, under what obligation soever of secrecy, without an unavoidable necessity, which does in no sort appear to be the case here; and this makes what he says less credible, and him the less bit to be believed as to his competency....

* * *

Mr. Smith, for the defendant.... Before I speak to these points, I shall beg leave to observe in general, that breach of trust and confidence is a thing in no ways to be favoured in any man whatsoever, whether he is or is not an attorney; for mutual trust and confidence is one of the strongest cements of human society, and without which it could not subsist; and therefore I apprehend, that the Court will always go as far in every case, as by law they can, to prevent a person from being guilty of so base an action as violation of trust and confidence, although he should be ever so willing to do it.

As to the first point, whether Mr. Giffard ought to be at liberty to wave his privilege; I think the case of my lord Say and Seal, in the book called Macclesfield's Cases, fol. 41, mentioned by Mr. Prim Serjeant, seems to be an express authority that he ought not. In that case, the Court in giving their opinion, lay it down as a general rule, "That an attorney's privilege is the privilege of his client; and that an attorney, though he would, yet shall not be allowed to discover the secrets of his client."

.... Mr. Giffard says, That my lord, at several times before, and particularly in the year 1741, had employed him in several suits; that he, after those disclosures, employed him again, and in the month of May 1742 discharged him. So that the general confidence my lord reposed in him as his attorney, must be presumed actually to subsist from the time he first retained Mr. Giffard, till the time he discharged him; and whatever my lord said to him during that space of time, touching his affairs, was plainly said to him under confidence as his attorney; my lord had employed him as an attorney before, and plainly intended to employ him as his attorney afterwards; and because there was an interval, during that space of time, in which my lord was at peace, and happened to have no suits on his hands, to say that his attorney shall therefore be at liberty to disclose what was in that interval revealed to him, would be equally productive of all the ill consequences that would attend his being permitted to disclose what he was entrusted with relative to a suit actually depending; the confidence reposed in the attorney, is the same in the one case as in the other, and his violation of that confidence equally prejudicial both to the client and the public....

* * *

L.C. Baron. The objections to Mr. Giffard's being admitted to give the evidence proposed by the plaintiff's counsel, have been argued with great strength and undoubtedly the public is interested in the event of this question, so far as it may affect the necessary confidence between the client and his attorney or agent, which will make me cautious of fixing boundaries to that trust. The proper way will be to determine this and every like case upon their own circumstances. What has been urged to take the present case out of the general rule, was, that the conversation to which they would examine Mr. Giffard, was neither in any cause wherein he was concerned for the defendant; or relative to any in which he was consulted, or intended to be employed by the defendant. If so, the question will be whether an attorney shall be permitted to disclose the general conversation he had with his client, without relation to him as his attorney? Now, admitting the policy of the law in protecting secrets disclosed by the client to his attorney, to be, as has been said, in favor of the client, and principally for his service, and that the attorney is in loco of the client, and therefore his trustee, does it follow from thence, that every thing said by a client to his attorney, falls under the same reason? I own, I think not; because there is not the same necessity upon the client to trust him in one case as in the other; and of this the Court may judge, from the particulars of the conversation. Nor do I see any impropriety in supposing the same person to be trusted in one case as an attorney or agent, and in another as a common acquaintance. In the first instance, the court will not permit him, though willing, to discover what came to his knowledge as an attorney, because it would be in breach of that trust which the law supposes to be necessary between him and his employer; but where the client talks to him at large as a friend, and not in the way of his profession, I think the Court is not under the same obligations to guard such secrets, though in the breast of an attorney. If I employ an attorney, and entrust to him secrets relative to the suit, that trust is not to be violated; but when I depart from that subject wherein I employed him, he is no more than another man, especially when the cause I did employ him in is over; because he is not to be supposed, as an attorney to be a general confident. When the cause is ended, he is then only to be considered with respect to his former employer, as one man to another; and then the breach of trust does not fall within the jurisdiction of this court; for the Court can't determine what is honour but what is law, and all the cases fall under this distinction. . . .

What I found myself upon is, the nature of the testimony proposed, which appears to me to have been casual conversation between the witness and the earl of Anglesea, which was not necessary to have been communicated to Giffard by his lordship. As to the private trusts between man and man, we cannot interpose. Besides, as this was in part a wicked secret, it ought not to have been concealed; though, if earlier disclosed, it might have been more for the credit of the witness. I therefore think Mr. Giffard may be examined to the defendant's declarations concerning the plaintiff's person and title.

* * *

Mr. Baron Mounteney

. . . . the question now before us will receive a very easy, clear, and short determination, and that in favour of the evidence proposed. I the rather say so, because I think, that upon the very principles laid down, and upon the authority of the very cases cited by the defendant's counsel, it is to demonstration clear that the evidence now offered ought to be admitted.

Mr. Recorder hath very properly mentioned the foundation upon which it hath been held, and is certainly undoubted law, that attornies ought to keep inviolably the secrets of their clients, viz. That an increase of legal business, and the inability of parties to transact that business themselves, made it necessary for them to employ (and as the law properly expresses it, *poncre in loco suo*) other persons who might transact that business for them. That this necessity introduced with it the necessity of what the law hath very justly established, an inviolable secrecy to be observed by attornies, in order to render it safe for clients to communicate to their attornies all proper instruction for the carrying on those causes which they found themselves under a necessity of intrusting to their care. And if this original principle be kept constantly in view, I think it cannot be difficult to determine either the present question, or any other which may arise upon this head; for upon this principle, whatever either is, or by the party concerned can naturally be supposed, necessary to be communicated to the attorney, in order to the carrying on any suit or prosecution, in which he is retained, that the attorney shall inviolably keep secret.

On the other hand, whatever is not, nor can possibly by any man living be supposed to be, necessary for that purpose, that the attorney is at liberty, and in many cases, as particularly, I think, in the present case, the attorney ought to disclose.

The declarations of the defendant to his attorney, which are now offered to be proved, I shall not mention at large, but shall only take notice of one, which was, that (speaking of Mr. Annesley, the now lessor of the plaintiff) he declared, he did not care if it cost him 10,000£. if he could get him hanged. Does any man living, who hears these words pronounced, hesitate one moment as to the meaning and import of them? They would speak too plainly to be misunderstood, or doubted of. For God's sake then let us consider, what will be the consequence of the doctrine, now laid down, and so earnestly contended for, that such a declaration made by any person to his attorney, ought not by that attorney to be proved? A man (without any natural call to it) promotes a prosecution against another for a capital offence—he is desirous and determined, at all events, to get him hanged—he retains an attorney to carry on the prosecution, and makes such a declaration to him as I have before mentioned, (the meaning and intention of which, if the attorney hath common understanding about him, it is impossible he should mistake)—he happens to be too honest a man to engage in such an affair—he declines the prosecution—but he must never discover this declaration, because he was retained as attorney. This prosecutor applies in the same manner to a second, a third, and so on, who still refuse, but are still to keep this inviolably secret; at last, he finds an attorney wicked enough to carry his iniquitous scheme into execution—and after all, none of these persons are to be admitted to prove this, in order either to bring the guilty party to condign punishment, or to prevent the evil consequences of his crime with regard to civil property. Is this law? Is this reason? I think it is absolutely contrary to both.

.... The declaration now offered to be proved, is of that nature, and so highly criminal, that, in my opinion, mankind is interested in the discovery; and whoever it was made to, attorney or not attorney, lies under an obligation to society in general, prior and superior to any obligation he can lie under to a particular individual, to make it known.

* * *

Mr. Baron Dawson. If there had been no objection made on the part of the defendant that the attorney had been employed by him, the plaintiff would have had a right prima facie for his being admitted a witness; therefore to deprive the plaintiff of this right, it must be shewn, that the particulars offered here to be given in evidence came to the knowledge of Giffard merely as attorney for the defendant. Nothing that came properly to the knowledge of the attorney in defense of his client's cause ought to be revealed. I will suppose an unknowing man to have twenty deeds by him, and he delivers them all to his attorney to see which were relative to the suit; he looks them over, and finds not half of them to be relative thereto; I apprehend the attorney is not compellable to disclose the contents of any one of those deeds; neither do I think it necessary that there should be a suit actually depending. If I have an apprehension that a man intends a suit against me and I employ an attorney to draw a state of the case from my papers, though there is no cause depending, there I apprehend it would be a breach of trust to disclose the contents of those papers, and that the attorney ought not to be admitted to disclose what has been so intrusted to him: and I think, the Court must, in this case, be satisfied, first, that what came to this man's knowledge was not necessary to his client's affairs; and in the next place, that the client could not think it necessary. The cause to be carried on, was a prosecution for the killing of a man; what was necessary for the carrying on that prosecution, I think the attorney ought not to disclose. I think further, that any thing that the client thought necessary, ought likewise not to be disclosed. The motive for carrying on the prosecution against the plaintiff is said to be, because he has a right to the estate the defendant was in possession of. Can any man think that this was necessary to tell the attorney, or that the defendant could have thought it so? What was necessary, or what a man might have thought necessary, ought not to be disclosed. But if the defendant in this case, has gone any thing further, he has trusted him, not as an attorney, but as an acquaintance. The attorney is to keep secret what comes to him as an attorney; but this conversation I don't think was necessary for carrying on the cause. Besides, the prosecution was at the suit of the king, so that he could not be looked upon as attorney for Lord Anglesea. I agree therefore with my lord chief baron and my brother Mounteney, that the evidence is proper to be given.

* * *

Mr. John Giffard sworn.

Q. Do You Know the Present Earl of Anglesea? Giffard. Yes, Sir. Pray Sir, Do You Know the Present Plaintiff, Mr. Annesley—yes—sir

Pray had you at any time any conversation, and when, with the present Lord Anglesea concerning the plaintiff, or his title to the lands in this ejectment, or any other lands?—It was some time between the 7th of December 1741, and May 1742, my Lord Anglesea had an appeal from this kingdom to the House of Lords in England between Charles Annesley, esq. and him, which appeal was heard on the 10th of March 1741.

Court. Answer the question directly—A. I am only giving you the reasons of this discourse.—My Lord Anglesea having that suit, and a good many others, with my Lord Haversham, Francis Annesley, and Mrs. Simpson, he was very uneasy at it. He said, he would be very glad to send to the present plaintiff, and if he would give him 2 or 3,000£ a year, he would surrender up to him the titles of Anglesea and Altham, and the estate, and go over to France and live there; and then he should be much easier and happier than to be tormented with those people that were suing of him, for that he would rather his brother's son should have it than any other person.

Go on.—For if Jemmy had the estate on those terms, he should live much happier and easier in France than he was here, as he was tormented by law; for it was his right, and he would surrender it to him, (for he did not value the title) rather than Frank and Charles Annesley, and those that were striving to take it from him should have it; and that he would send for a gentleman to teach him the French tongue, to qualify him to live in that kingdom; and accordingly he sent for one Mr. Stephen Hayes.

What is he?—He was an officer in the French service, as Hayes himself and my lord told me; and my lord had him in the house a considerable time, on purpose to converse with him in French.

Did you ever see him there?—I did, my lord, forty times.

Can you recollect any particular time when this conversation happened?—I told you, my lord, it was about March 1741, when he had the appeal in England.

Was it before or after the determination of that appeal?—I believe it was both before and after; the appeal was determined the 10th of March, and he continued in that resolution till May 1742.

And, pray, what altered his resolution then?—Why, on the 1st of May, Mr. Annesley had shot a man at Staines; it was on Saturday, as appears by the indictment and coroner's inquest; upon which, the 2d of May, my lord sent for me, and ordered me to go to Staines, and to enquire into the affair, and to collect the evidence, and carry on the prosecution, and to follow the directions of Mr. Garden and Mr. Gordon, with the assistance of one Mr. Jans, who was a surgeon; which I accordingly did. My lord told me further, that I should follow their directions, and in some small time after (perhaps 3 or 4 days) told me, that they had consulted together, and advised him not to be seen to converse with me, for that it was not proper for him to appear in the prosecution, for fear of its hurting him in the cause that was coming on between him and the plaintiff; and, that he did not care if it cost him 10,000£ if he could get the plaintiff hanged; for then he should be easy in his title and estate.

After he told you that he did not care if it cost him 10,000£ if he could get the plaintiff hanged, for then he should be easy in his titles and estate, who laid out the money in carrying on this prosecution of this unfortunate man?—Money came privately from Mr. Jans; my lord told me. He was determined, as he was advised, not to appear in it himself, but that I should apply, from time to time, to Mr. Jans, and Mr. Jans should, from time to time, supply me, for that he had ordered him to provide money; and accordingly I had money from him.

What was Jans to my Lord Anglesea?—His companion, and manager, and agent, and managed everything for him.

Cross Examination

* * *

Sir, I see you have refreshed your memory with papers and memorandums as to periods of time, are they of your own handwriting?—They are.

I should be glad to know when it was that you put down those periods of time in writing.

—Sir, I put down the days as they came on. I could shew you every day where I was for seven years last past.

Were they wrote about the time the transactions happened?—I always did, since I was a practitioner of the law, keep a day book of everything I did; and the first thing I do in a morning is, to set down the preceding day's work.

You say, my lord used some words to this purpose; that he did not care if it cost him 10,000£ if he could get the plaintiff hanged; and you were the agent under Garden and Gordon, to carry on that prosecution?—I was.

How came you to be employed?—The reason I was sent for was, that I had been a coroner myself in the county of Devon for some years (a dozen or fourteen), and was thought a proper person because of that.

Did you go with that prosecution till there was a verdict?—I did, Sir.

Pray now, did you inform yourself of the nature of that fact at any time before the trial came on?—I attended the coroner's inquest, Sir, and did inform myself of it. I collected evidences, and drew the brief. I have the brief here.

Did you see, or had you a copy of, the examinations upon which the indictment was found?—I was present at the examination of the witnesses before the coroner, and took some notes of my own at that time, which I have with me.

How was the indictment found?—The indictment was upon the coroner's inquest.

* * *

... Pray, now, did the case appear, for the most part, to be the same upon the trial, as upon the examinations before the coroner?—No, Sir, it differed vastly.

What was the finding on the coroner's inquest?—Willful murder.

Recollect some one material circumstance wherein the evidence varied?—I tell you, Sir,—

Was the evidence stronger on the coroner's inquest than it was in court on the trial?—Yes, it was stronger against Mr. Annesley, because the main evidence was taken off upon the trial, for reasons—-

Had my Lord Anglesea any hand in taking off the main evidence?—No.

Who took it off?—It was the prisoner who took it off. His evidence was rendered invalid; his evidence was given in court, but his evidence was discredited in court by reason of his character; and there was a strong reason given for it in court by a witness.

What was that witness's name?—It was Paul Keating.

Were there any persons produced upon that trial to the character of Paul Keating?—Yes.

Was Paul Keating for or against the prisoner?—He was for the prisoner.

Who was the main witness that swore against the plaintiff on his trial?—It was John Egglestone.

Had you any conversation with that John Egglestone before the trial, touching his evidence?—I had. He was brought to me by one Williams, that keeps the White–Horse in Piccadilly, and he varied from his evidence that he gave before sir Thomas Reynell.

Were you present when he gave that evidence?—I was not.

How do you know it?—It was declared so in court, and you asked me what passed in court.

Tell us, whether this fact, for which Mr. Annesley was prosecuted, was committed by day or night?—By day. The fact was committed at Staines.

What time of day was it?—As it appeared upon the examination, one or two o'clock in the afternoon.

Did it appear to have been done in a public place?—In a meadow.

Did it appear on the trial that there were any number of persons present?—There were present, John Egglestone, John Fisher, and John Bettesworth, and one more, I think.

Were there any other of the witnesses that appeared on that prosecution that were discredited on account of their character, besides Egglestone?—There was a variation in their testimony, but that they were discredited for their character, I cannot say.

What time was the trial?—The trial, I believe, was the 14th of July 1742.

What time was the coroner's inquest held?—The 4th of May, 1742.

Pray, now, when my Lord Anglesea said to you, that he did not care if it cost him 10,000£ to get the plaintiff hanged, did you understand that it was his resolution to destroy him if he could?—I did, Sir.

Did you advise my Lord Anglesea not to carry on that prosecution?—I did not advise him not to carry it on; I did not presume to undertake to advise him.

Did you say anything in answer to my lord, and what, when he told you, he did not care if it cost him 10,000£ if he could get the plaintiff hanged?—I do not know any particular answer that I made him.

Did you approve or disapprove of his expressions and design together?—I cannot say that I did either.

Did not you go on as effectually after, with the prosecution, as you could?—I did, to be sure, Sir. Indeed, I advised my Lord Anglesea not to appear upon the trial.

Since my lord had told you, that he would agree with the plaintiff, and go to France, and disappoint Charles Annesley, how came you not to tell him, that if he hanged this pretender, it would frustrate his designs, and the expectations he had?—In answer to what you say (that if the pretender, as you call him, were hanged, there would be a greater fund left than 2 or 3,000£ a year to go abroad with), it certainly would destroy that project of disappointing Mess. Annesleys; but then it would put a greater estate in his own pocket.

Was not the intention of the prosecution to disappoint the Annesleys?—No, the intention was to put this man out of the way, that he might enjoy the estate easy and quiet.

When my Lord Anglesea said, that he would not care if it cost him 10,000£ so he could get the plaintiff hanged, did you apprehend from thence, that he would be willing to go to that expense in the prosecution?—I did.

Did you suppose from thence that he would dispose of that 10,000£ in any shape to bring about the death of the plaintiff?—I did.

Did you not apprehend that to be a most wicked crime?—I did.

If so, how could you, who set yourself out as a man of business, engage in that project, without making any objection to it?—I may as well ask you, how you came to be engaged for the defendant in this suit.

Was it before, or after the coroner's inquest, that my Lord Anglesea told you, he did not care if it cost him ten thousand pounds to get the plaintiff hang'd?—I can't charge my memory; it was there, or thereabouts.

Look in your diary, and see—I'll look in my diary. I cannot exactly tell you, Sir. The second of May was the day I was sent for to my lord, at the White Horse in Piccadilly; and I believe one Thompson Gregory was sent for me, and with a great deal of joy they said that Mr. Annesley had killed a man, and would be hanged. The 3rd of May I went to Colebrook, within three miles of Staines. The 4th of May I went to Staines, and the inquest was held there.

Was it after the 4th of May it was held?—I came home the 5th, and I believe it was that day; for my lord met me at Hounslow, in his coach-and-six, to know how things went on.

Was it at the meeting he said this to you?—I cannot tell. It was within a day or two, up or down. I did not take particular notice.

Did you ever enter down in writing any conversation between you?—I have made memorandums about my business, but private conversation in company I never entered in writing.

Was it not upon the day he sent for you to go down to Staines that he said these words?—I can't say more than I know. I believe it was not. And I believe it was after, or just upon, holding the coroner's inquest.

Did not you understand from thence, that he would lay out that money, in any shape, to compass the death of this man?—I cannot tell. But my lord is very apt to be flashy in his discourse.

Did not you apprehend it to be a bad purpose to lay out money to compass the death of another man?—I do not know but I did. I do believe it, Sir: But I was not to undertake that bad purpose. If there was any dirty work, I was not concerned in it.

If you believe this, I ask you, how came you to engage in this prosecution without objection?—I make a distinction between carrying on a prosecution, and compassing the death of a man.

How came you to make that distinction?—I may as well ask, how the counsel came to plead the cause?

Did you ever mention to any of your counsel, that my lord made that declaration?—I did not.

If you had told any of them that my lord made that declaration, would they have appeared for you?—I can't tell whether they would or not.

Do you believe any honest man would? * * *—Yes, I believe they would, or else I would not have carried it on, Sir. And I do assure you, it is the only cause I was concerned in at the Old Bailey in my life, and shall be the last.

Don't you believe, that my lord's engaging in that prosecution was, because the man set up a title to his estate, and not on account of his killing the man at Staines?—I believe it was; and believed it then, and do now.

Do you not believe it was an unlawful purpose?—I cannot help that. I was employed by the church-warden of Staines to prosecute. I should not have been concerned upon any account whatsoever, had not I the sanction of the coroner's inquest for willful murder, which I thought a justification of the prosecution.

When was it that the church-warden employed you?—The 8th of May, 1742. He wrote a letter to me, "Pray, prosecute James Annesley," &c. Signed Stephen Bolton.

Was not this after my lord declared he would spend 10,000£ to get him hanged?—It was.

Sir, I ask you, was there any money given to any witness to appear and give evidence?—I don't know of any.

What sum was given for their attendance?—About half a crown a day for their attendance. If there was any dirty work, I knew nothing of it.

Are you paid your bill of costs?—Not all of it.

How much does it come to?—The prosecution cost 800£: but the total remaining due me is 330£.

Was there any body present, when you had this conversation with my lord?—No, I believe not; for we used to converse together alone frequently.

Was Mr. Jans ever present?—No, never.

Was Thompson Gregory present when he went and brought you to my lord?—He came with me.

Did he remain in the room?—I believe he did, all that night.

Was this the 2nd of May?—Yes.

Had you that day any discourse about the sum of money that my lord would spend?—No, not that day.

Was it by your advice and directions that that letter was sent to you by the church-warden of Staines?—No, it was by Garden's and Gordon's advice.

Were you privy to it?—Yes, I was. And this letter was advised in order that the defendant might not appear in the prosecution.

Did not you know this was to give a colour?—I did.

Did you think this was for a good purpose?—Mr. Garden, Gordon, Jans, and Lord Anglesea had a consultation, and it was thought proper that I should have another person to my assistance, because they would not appear, and my instructions were, to send this order to the church-warden and get it signed; that my lord should not appear in it; and the reason was, that if my lord should appear in it, they thought it would be attended with ill consequences.

Did you know at the time of the trial that Mr. Annesley intended to sue for the title and estate of Lord Anglesea?—It was reported he would, that he intended it; and this was in order to prevent it.

Did you know one Mr. Thomas Smith?—Yes, Sir.

I desire to know, if Mr. Annesley gets this suit, whether you will be paid your bill of costs?—No, Sir, if he gets it, I shall lose every shilling of it.

Where do you lodge?—At one Parson's in King Street.

Are you acquainted with Thomas Smith the cabinet-maker?—I am very well acquainted with him.

Had you any discourse with him about this evidence that you have given today?—I have had some discourse with him about it.

Did you not tell him that you had been ill used, and that that provoked you to give in this evidence?—No, I never did; for he knew that I had been ill used. I will tell you what I have said to him: that it was a wrong step in my lord; that this bill of costs of mine would never have come to light, had not I been obliged to sue for my right. That my lord filed a bill in the Exchequer against me in England, to disclose what business I had done for him, and that I was obliged in my justification to annex in a schedule this my bill of costs.

Did not you look upon my Lord Anglesea as your real client in the prosecution of the plaintiff?—He promised to pay me, but I did not look upon him as my immediate employer; for my lord told me he had directed Mr. Jans to employ me.

Did you look upon Mr. Jans at this time as your client?—I did look upon him as my client.

Do not you believe that my lord had these discourses with you as his attorney?—No, Sir, for I knew I was never to be concerned in the cause.

In what light then did you look upon the discourse?—I looked upon it to be a discourse to me as a friend.

Was not the discourse with you on the 4th and 5th of May, as his attorney or solicitor?—I looked upon him to be my client.

And therefore did not he look upon you as his solicitor?—I cannot tell what he did.

Did he meet you as his friend, or solicitor?—Sir, there was another man with me.

Were not you employed by him to see the inquest held?—I was. I wish you would produce any person to attempt to prove that I am a dishonest man.

How long have you been a practitioner?—I have had a great many clients in the course of twenty and odd years.

Do not you look upon it as a rule of prudence and honour, for attornies to keep religiously the secrets of their clients?—I do, indeed.

Do not you think, that if a solicitor or an attorney discloses these secrets, he is a very bad man?—I think he is.

And how came you to disclose this secret?—I would not have disclosed this, if I had not been obliged to do it; and the reason which obliged me to do it, was, my lord's filing a bill in the Exchequer to disclose what business I had done for him; when I was obliged to answer the interrogatories I am now asked.

* * *

In charging the jury, Lord Baron Bowes, Baron Mounteney and Baron Dawson left all of the evidence as to the prosecution of Annesley for their consideration on the grounds that the evidence of the attorney John Giffard showed that the defendant was conscious of the goodness of the plaintiff's title and distrusted his own. The jury gave its verdict for the plaintiff James Annesley.

QUESTIONS

1.   The following justifications for the attorney-client privilege appear in the arguments and opinions in *Annesley v. Anglesea*:

(a) *The normative argument*: A "gentleman of character" does not disclose his client's secrets.

(b) *The natural equity argument*: An attorney is in the place of the client and therefore identifies himself with his client. It would be "contrary to the rules of natural justice and equity" for an individual to betray himself.

(c) *The business necessity argument*: Attorneys are necessary for the conduct of business, and business would be harmed if attorneys were to disclose communications with their clients.

How persuasive is each of these justifications? How do you respond to the following observations:

(a) is too general (apart from referring only to the male gender);

(b) depends on a metaphor which could include all agents, not just attorneys, and does not address how far protection against self incrimination should go, particularly in a *civil* suit; and

(c) arguably includes all business agents, including officers, directors and accountants as well as lawyers, and therefore could, if taken to its logical conclusion, make the business world immune from answering in a lawsuit.

2.   Are there additional, perhaps better, justifications for the attorney-client privilege? How convincing is each of the following:

(a) *the necessity of lawyers in criminal trials:* A criminal defendant needs a lawyer who will keep client confidences, in part to equalize the power of the state.

(b) *the civilizing influence of lawyers:* It is desirable that lawyers know about unlawful behavior so they can counsel lawful behavior.

If you accept these latter two justifications, what conclusions can you draw about the relative importance of the privilege in criminal and civil trials?

3. At what times and for what purposes was Anglesea Giffard's client? Is Mr. Smith right in arguing that the privilege extends to communications made by Anglesea to Giffard during intervals between suits?

4. Was the communication to be elicited from Giffard told to him in connection with a pending action? Should the attorney-client privilege be limited to information imparted in connection with a pending action? What were Baron Dawson's observations on this point?

5. Was the communication essential to the matter for which Anglesea consulted Giffard?

6. Even if there had been sufficient evidence to prosecute Annesley, Anglesea was doing so in order to obtain a collateral advantage in another matter. This itself is troubling. See Model Code, DR 7–105 ("A lawyer shall not present, participate in presenting, or threaten to present criminal charges solely to obtain an advantage in a civil matter."). Did the communication at issue here concern a purpose to which Giffard could lawfully lend his assistance?

7. Should the attorney-client privilege extend to "a secret, which is contrary to the public good, such as a design to commit treason, murder, or perjury?" What were Baron Mounteney's observations on this point?

8. The Court allowed the testimony to be received. What standard did each of Lord Baron Bowes, Baron Mounteney and Baron Dawson use to determine when the attorney-client privilege should apply?

9. Serj. Tisdall argues that if an attorney is employed "in any unlawful or wicked act, his duty to the public obliges him to disclose it; no private obligations can dispense with that universal one." The client perjury issue discussed in Chapter 1 is another situation where "private obligations" of an attorney arguably conflict with obligations to the public. Does it make sense to argue that an attorney, as an officer of the court, can incur a private obligation to conceal a client's intent to commit an unlawful act?

10. The principal issue in this case is framed very early on as whether a lawyer who is a "gentleman of character" would reveal client confidences. However, whether Giffard is a "gentleman of character" in the first place becomes doubtful once he takes the stand. Giffard replies on cross-examination that "If there was any dirty work, I was not concerned in it," and that "I make a distinction between carrying on a prosecution, and compassing the death of a man." Is this a valid distinction? Does Giffard's willingness to carry on the prosecution of Annesley undermine his credibility?

11. Lord Baron Bowes points out that if Giffard had revealed Anglesea's plan to prosecute Annesley earlier, "it might be more for the credit of the witness." Anglesea's "secret" came out, not because Giffard had a moral or other objection to the scheme to prosecute Annesley, but in a dispute over

Giffard's fee. Is a dispute over a lawyer's fee a justification for revealing a client confidence? *See* Model Rule 1.6 (permitting disclosure to establish a claim on behalf of the lawyer but not to avoid financial injury to the public). Do Giffard's conduct and Model Rule 1.6 reflect the same ordering of priorities? Is this the right ordering of priorities?

12. The Annesley case involved many different instances of impropriety and corruption (a lawyer's participation in a wrongful prosecution for murder, jurors related to the defendant, bought witnesses, conflicts of interest, and more). This case, like many of the others in this casebook, involves more than one incident of improper conduct, and illustrates how ethical problems tend to arise in "clusters." There is indeed often a correlation between the moral character of the parties involved in a case and the likelihood that lawyers in the case will face ethical dilemmas. What are the practical as well as moral justifications for a lawyer refusing to represent a client whom she finds to be unethical?

13. In Catherine Drinker Bowen's account of the trial of Sir Walter Raleigh (Chapter 8) you will read about how trial "by accusation" in early Seventeenth Century England differed from trial "by inquisition" on the Continent. Presumably fairer to the defendant, the accusatory model still has its drawbacks, as accusations can have as much to do with the accusers' or other persons' ulterior motives as with the truth. It is not surprising that many of the witnesses who presumably accused Annesley of murder at the coroner's inquest were discredited at trial. Nonetheless, until the nineteenth century, England allowed private criminal prosecutions in addition to those brought by the Crown. What are the dangers of allowing private citizens to bring criminal actions against each other? What is the primary responsibility of lawyers retained to prosecute such cases—to represent the prosecuting persons or to see that justice is done?

14. This case suggests that ethical responsibilities of lawyers conducting criminal prosecutions may differ from responsibilities of lawyers acting in other capacities, a topic that will be explored more extensively in Chapters 7 and 8 infra. Did Giffard act responsibly in prosecuting the case against Annesley? Why or why not?

Relevant Background

The Limits of Confidentiality

One of the most controversial debates in legal ethics is over whether lawyers should disclose client fraud or other illegal acts. Disclosure is favored by those who believe lawyers' obligations to the legal system and to society are at least as important as obligations to clients. See Deborah Rhode, Ethical Perspectives on Legal Practice, 37 Stan. L. Rev. 589, 616 (1985); Sissela Bok, Secrets: On the Ethics of Concealment and Revelation 116–35 (1982); David Luban, Lawyers and Justice, An Ethical Study 233 (1988). Disclosure is disfavored by those who emphasize lawyers' obligations to clients. See Monroe Freedman, Professional Responsibility of the Criminal Defense Lawyer: The Three Hardest Questions, 64 Mich. L. Rev. 1469 (1966).

As pointed out in Chapter 1, there is similar controversy over whether a lawyer must disclose a client's intent to commit perjury, although there is near unanimity on the point that a lawyer may not assist with this crime by examining the perjurer under oath. With respect to crimes and frauds other than perjury, bar associations, state legislatures, regulators and the courts have each sought to articulate their own rules on when lawyers must or may disclose client confidences. Unfortunately, the multitude of different rules and conflicting interpretations of the same rules can create confusion.

As in the client perjury situation, however, it is clear what a lawyer should *not* do: provide legal services to a client in furtherance of a crime or fraud. Thus, at a minimum, a lawyer who cannot persuade her client to desist from a crime or fraud, should resign. See Model Rule 1.16(a) (a lawyer shall not represent a client, and shall withdraw from a representation that has commenced, if the representation will violate rules of professional conduct); Model Rule 1.2(d) (a lawyer may not assist a client in criminal or fraudulent conduct); Model Code, DR 7–102(A)(7) (same). What elements of crime, fraud or other improper conduct do you see in Lord Anglesea's attempt to prosecute Annesley? Should Giffard have refused to take the case?

Whether a lawyer should disclose a client's crime or fraud is a more difficult question. The ABA's Model Rule 1.6 is very protective of client confidences, but has been adopted in relatively few states in its existing form. The Rule permits disclosure of confidential client information only to prevent commission of a crime likely to result in death or substantial bodily harm. If the client only intends to commit fraud or crimes causing financial injury, disclosure is not permitted. Furthermore, even if death or substantial bodily injury is likely, disclosure under the Model Rule is optional; it is not required (although other substantive law may require it). Ironically, Rule 1.6, as restrictive as it is, still allows disclosure necessary for a lawyer to establish his own claim or defense in a dispute with a client (including over unpaid fees) or to defend himself in an action based on conduct in connection with a representation. Indeed, this is exactly what happened in the *Annesley* case; Giffard disclosed Anglesea's secret in a suit for his fee.

Rule 1.6 does not prohibit a lawyer from withdrawing on account of the client's conduct, and the comment to the Rule specifically gives the lawyer a way to suggest, but not to fully disclose, to third parties the reasons for the withdrawal. "Neither this rule nor Rule 1.8(b) nor Rule 1.16(d) prevents the lawyer from giving notice of the fact of withdrawal, and the lawyer may also withdraw or disaffirm any opinion, document, affirmation, or the like." Comment to Rule 1.6, paragraph 16. See ABA Formal Ethics Opinion 92–366 (1992) (interpreting this "noisy withdrawal" provision); and Ronald D. Rotunda, The Notice of Withdrawal and the New Model Rules of Professional Conduct: Blowing the Whistle and Waving the Red Flag, 63 Or. L. Rev. 455, 484 (1984) (although the final version of Rule 1.6 differs from an earlier draft of the Rule by the ABA's Kutak Commission that allowed disclosure to prevent a crime or fraud, a lawyer still can disaffirm her own prior representations and thereby put everyone on notice).

The predecessor to the Model Rules, the ABA Model Code, is somewhat more flexible than Rule 1.6 and allows disclosure when a client intends to commit a crime. "A lawyer *may* reveal: . . . (3) the intention of his client to commit a crime and the information necessary to prevent the crime." D–R 4–101(C). The Code does not, however, allow disclosure when the intended conduct is an intentional tort, a civil fraud or any other act which does not amount to a crime. The Code also, like the Model Rules, is permissive; in no circumstances is a lawyer required to disclose (although, once again, other areas of substantive law may require it). Furthermore, the Code, like the Model Rules, does not allow disclosure in order to rectify results of past crimes. *See* New York State Opinion 479 (1978) (discussing 1973 murder case in which an accused murderer's lawyers saw and took photographs of victims' bodies, and opining that the lawyers were dutybound not to disclose the location of the bodies to the authorities or the victims' families); People v. Belge, 83 Misc.2d 186, 372 N.Y.S.2d 798 (Co.Ct.), aff'd, 50 A.D.2d 1088, 376 N.Y.S.2d 771 (4th Dep't.1975), aff'd, 41 N.Y.2d 60, 390 N.Y.S.2d 867, 359 N.E.2d 377 (1976) (attorney in same case acquitted on charge of violating health law by not providing a decent burial). See also Monroe H. Freedman, Lawyers Ethics in an Adversary System 1–2 (1975) (approving of the same). However, even the court in *Belge* rejected the defendant's argument for an absolute attorney-client privilege, noting that "[w]e believe that an attorney must protect his client's interests, but also must observe basic human standards of decency." 376 N.Y.S.2d at 771.

The American Law Institute (ALI) addresses disclosure of client confidences in its drafts of the Restatement of the Law Governing Lawyers. Section 117A of the draft Restatement permits disclosure to prevent death or serious bodily injury. However, the extent of disagreement within the ALI, as within other bar associations, on lawyer "whistleblowing" is best revealed by the two versions of § 117A(1)(b) that permit disclosure if a client has committed or intends to commit a crime or fraud that threatens to cause substantial financial loss. The Reporters' proposed version permits disclosure necessary to prevent the loss following a good faith attempt to dissuade the client from committing the crime or fraud. The alternative version, preferred by the ALI Director upon consultation with a four-person ad hoc subcommittee of the ALI Council, only permits disclosure of a crime or fraud "in the commission of which the lawyer's services were or are being employed." ALI Proposed Final Draft, § 117A. As the Reporters point out, the Section "does not apply to a past act of a client, no matter how clearly illegal and serious, if all of the harmful consequences of the act have already occurred," id., comment a, and nowhere does § 117 *require* disclosure by the lawyer to prevent death, serious bodily injury or financial loss (although other applicable law may require it). Apart from the circumstances described in § 117, the ALI Preliminary Draft allows a lawyer to disclose confidential client information when a client consents (§ 114), when other law so requires (§ 115), when reasonably necessary in the lawyer's self defense of a malpractice or other action (§ 116) or in a dispute over the lawyer's compensation (§ 117).

These ABA and ALI rules set forth what the ABA and ALI believe the law should be, but are not themselves law. Indeed, state codes of professional conduct have taken very different approaches to disclosure of client confidences. Many state supreme courts have rewritten Model Rule 1.6 to allow or even require disclosure in a broader range of circumstances, and the disarray in the rules on this subject can be confusing. For example, "[i]f you are in Wilmington, Delaware, confronted by a client's intended fraudulent conduct that will likely cause substantial financial harm, and you practice law also in Pennsylvania and New Jersey, you are subject to three different rules. New Jersey requires disclosure to the proper authorities. Delaware forbids disclosure. Pennsylvania permits but does not require disclosure." Harris Weinstein, Attorney Liability in the Savings and Loan Crisis 1993 U. Ill. L. Rev. 53, 64 (1993). See N.J. Rules of Professional Conduct Rule 1.6(b)(1) (1992) (requiring a lawyer to disclose information necessary to prevent a client "from committing a criminal, illegal or fraudulent act that the lawyer believes is likely to result in death or substantial bodily harm or substantial injury to the financial interest or property of another."); Del. Rules of Professional Responsibility Rule 1.6 (1983) (following Model Rule 1.6); and Penn. Rules of Professional Conduct Rule 1.6(c)(1) (1992)(lawyer may disclose a client's illegal acts). Although many states follow Pennsylvania in making disclosure optional, Florida follows New Jersey in requiring disclosure. See Florida Rules of Professional Conduct Rule 1.6(B)(1).

QUESTIONS

1. How is the "noisy withdrawal" permitted under the comment to Model Rule 1.6 different from outright disclosure? Is there any reason why the ABA might want to allow one, but not the other?

2. Could the wording of Model Rule 1.6 and the comment thereto be the result of political compromise more than policy considerations?

3. Why have many state courts and other rule making bodies rejected Model Rule 1.6 as drafted by the ABA?

4. Is the ALI draft Restatement a significant improvement over Model Rule 1.6?

PROBLEM

1. Defense lawyers in a tort case discover through a medical exam that the plaintiff has a life threatening aneurysm. The plaintiff and his doctors are unaware of the condition and the defense lawyers' clients insist that the information not be disclosed. Should the lawyers inform the plaintiff of his condition so he can seek medical attention? See Spaulding v. Zimmerman, 263 Minn. 346, 116 N.W.2d 704 (Minn. 1962).

The Attorney–Client Privilege and the Work Product Doctrine

A lawyer's duty to protect client confidences arises from many of the same policy considerations as two important evidentiary privileges: the attorney-client privilege and the work product doctrine. The duty, however, should be distinguished from these two privileges. The former focuses on a lawyer's ethical obligations. The latter concern the power of a court to require production of documents and to compel testimony. As the ABA points out, "[t]he attorney-client privilege is more limited than the ethical obligation of a lawyer to guard the confidences and secrets of his client." Model Code, EC4–4.

These privileges compromise the truth finding function of a tribunal as do other exclusionary rules (for example, rules excluding from criminal trials evidence that is acquired in an illegal search and seizure). Because these privileges exclude certain communications from pretrial discovery and admission into evidence, judges and juries will sometimes make decisions that are based on inaccurate or incomplete information. The justice system reluctantly tolerates this result to accomplish important policy objectives: here, to allow a lawyer and client to discuss the client's legal problems without worry that client communications or attorney work product will later be used against the client.

The attorney-client privilege thus creates a zone of privacy where a client may refuse to disclose, and prevent others from disclosing, confidential communications made for the purpose of facilitating legal services to the client. See Richard O. Lempert & Stephen A. Saltzburg, A Modern Approach to Evidence 652 (2d ed. 1982). The lawyer or client invoking the privilege carries the burden of showing that the information withheld actually qualifies as a privileged communication. For background on the development of the privilege, see Geoffrey C. Hazard Jr., A Historical Perspective on the Attorney–Client Privilege, 66 Cal. L. Rev. 1061 (1978).

The privilege is limited, and only certain communications fall within its reach. An initial requirement for a communication to be privileged is that it must be relevant to a legal problem about which the client seeks a lawyer's advice. Furthermore, although protected communications may include advice given by the lawyer to the client, or disclosures made by the client to the lawyer, facts that are objectively discoverable are not protected. For example, documents that pre-exist an attorney-client relationship are no more protected after they are handed over to the lawyer then they were before the transfer of possession. The identity or whereabouts of a client also are usually not protected; if demanded by a court or in a lawful subpoena this information must be disclosed by the lawyer. Finally, if the client has in mind anything but a "legitimate" purpose in consulting a lawyer—perhaps a scheme to defraud someone or commit a crime—it is doubtful that the communication is a "professional" confidence in the course of an attorney-client relationship. Hazard, supra at 1064, citing The Queen v. Cox and Railton, 14 Q.B.D. 153, 168 (1885) ("In order that the rule may apply there must be both professional confidence and professional employment, but if the client has a criminal object in view in his communications with his solicitor one of these elements must necessarily be absent. The client must either conspire with the solicitor or deceive him.") Using similar reasoning, the Court in *Annesley v. Anglesea* allowed Giffard to be examined on Anglesea's plot to have Annesley hung for murder.

The client need not specifically request that his lawyer keep information confidential, but the privilege may be waived explicitly, as when the client allows his lawyer to testify about the communication. The privilege also may be waived implicitly by actions inconsistent with confidentiality such as communicating the privileged information to third parties. The privilege generally continues past the end of litigation and often continues even after the death of the client.

Perhaps the most common way the privilege is lost inadvertently is by showing a privileged document to a third person or allowing a third person to sit in on a private conversation between an attorney and her client. Once this happens, the privilege is lost and *anybody* with a proper purpose can subpoena the document or demand testimony on the content of the document or conversation. See Westinghouse Electric Corporation v. Republic of the Philippines, 951 F.2d 1414, 1424 (3d Cir. 1991) (when client voluntarily discloses privileged communications to third party, privilege is waived); International Honeycomb Corporation v. Transtech Service Network, Inc., 1992 WL 314897 (E.D.N.Y.) (disclosure of confidential information to outsiders for commercial purposes waives attorney-client privilege). Part of an attorney's professional responsibility to her client is to take care that the privilege is not lost inadvertently.

A requirement for the privilege to apply is thus that the client's communication only be made to a lawyer or to a third-party agent of a lawyer (such as a paralegal). Third parties from outside the lawyer's firm may be necessary to the attorney-client communication being made in the first place, and, if so, their presence usually will not destroy the privilege. For example, although a friend or relative is not "necessary" for a client to communicate with her attorney, and in most circumstances should not be present, the presence of a foreign language translator, if needed, will not destroy the privilege. In United States v. Kovel, 296 F.2d 918 (2d Cir.1961), Louis Kovel, a former IRS agent, was employed by a law firm and did some work with clients' accounting problems. The privilege had been extended to lawyer support staff such as paralegals, but it was unclear whether the privilege could extend to other specialists, such as accountants. When Kovel was subpoenaed to appear before a grand jury in connection with an investigation of one of the firm's clients, he refused to answer certain questions. Cited with contempt, he was told that the attorney-client privilege applied only to attorneys. On appeal, Judge Friendly wrote for the Second Circuit in vacating the contempt finding: "[I]n contrast to the Tudor times when the privilege was first recognized, ... the complexities of modern existence prevent attorneys from effectively handling clients' affairs without the help of others...." Id. at 921 (citations omitted). "[The] analogy of the client speaking a foreign language is by no means irrelevant to the appeal at hand. Accounting concepts are a foreign language to some lawyers in almost all cases, and to almost all lawyers in some cases." Id. at 922. See also State v. Rickabaugh, 361 N.W.2d 623 (S.D.1985) (protecting confidentiality of statements made to polygraph test administrator under attorney-client privilege where administrator was the attorney's representative); Rodriguez v. Superior Court, 14 Cal.App.4th 1260, 18 Cal.Rptr.2d 120 (Ct. App.1993) (protecting statements made by defendant to psychologist at request of counsel under attorney-client privilege). But see Linde Thomson Langworthy Kohn & Van Dyke v. Resolution Trust Corp., 5 F.3d 1508 (D.C.Cir.1993) (refusing, under federal law, to extend attorney-client privilege to statements made by insured to insurer when not made strictly for the purpose of obtaining legal advice).

The work product doctrine is related to the attorney-client privilege, but, instead of protecting communications, protects material that is prepared by a lawyer in anticipation of litigation. Like the attorney-client privilege, this doctrine is intended to improve a lawyer's ability to represent her client by allowing the lawyer to prepare for litigation without fear that her work product will be revealed to the other side. Such work product might, but need not, include communications that are also covered by the attorney-client privilege. For example, notes on an interview with a witness and notes on an interview with a client both can qualify as work product, although only the latter are covered by the attorney-client privilege. To be covered by the work product doctrine, material need not originate from the client, nor must the information be kept secret from third parties.

In Hickman v. Taylor, 329 U.S. 495 (1947), the Supreme Court developed the modern work product doctrine that was later incorporated into the Federal Rules of Civil Procedure as well as into most state law. *Hickman* created two categories of protected material: (1) factual material (such as notes on an interview with a witness), which is protected from discovery unless the demanding party shows that production of these facts is essential to preparation of its case; and (2) the attorney's mental impressions (such as often found in private notes or in a legal memorandum), which are covered by an absolute privilege that continues regardless of the other party's need for the information. 329 U.S. at 511–512. Under F.R.C.P. 26(b)(3), material prepared in anticipation of litigation is discoverable only upon a showing that the party seeking discovery has a substantial need for the materials in the preparation of the party's case and that the party is unable without undue hardship to obtain the substantial equivalent of the materials by other means. In ordering discovery, the court shall protect against disclosure of the mental impressions, conclusions, opinions, or legal theories of an attorney or other representative of a party.

The Attorney–Client Privilege and Work Product Doctrine in Organizations

Upjohn v. United States, 449 U.S. 383 (1981), defines the scope of the attorney-client privilege and the work product doctrine as they apply to communications within a corporation or other organization. In *Upjohn*, the general counsel of Upjohn, a pharmaceutical company, in the course of an internal investigation of possible illegal payments to foreign governments, sent questionnaires to employees to get details of the transactions. The IRS, in its own investigation, sought production of the questionnaires and notes on interviews with the employees. Upjohn refused, asserting the attorney-client privilege and the work product doctrine. The Sixth Circuit found that the privilege did not apply because the communications were made to Upjohn's attorney by persons outside of a "control group," mostly high level executives responsible for directing Upjohn's actions in response to legal advice. The Circuit Court found that applying the privilege to communications from employees outside of this "control group" would create too large a "zone of silence" that would obstruct litigation. Id. at 395.

The Supreme Court reversed, holding that the privilege applies to responses given by an organization's employees to its counsel. The Court disapproved of the control group test used by the Sixth Circuit, because it undermines the purpose of the privilege, to encourage free exchange of information and sound legal advice. Chief Justice Burger's concurring opinion proposed an alternative standard hinging on whether an employee is communicating with a lawyer at the direction of management for certain enumerated purposes, in which case the privilege would apply. However, the majority opinion did not articulate an alternative to the control group test and instead endorsed a case-by-case determination.

The Court also held that the work product doctrine probably justified Upjohn's refusal to submit notes which revealed its attorney's mental processes. The Court pointed out that the Sixth Circuit, in refusing to apply the work product doctrine, had misapplied the "necessity" standard in *Hickman*. Under FRCP 26 and *Hickman,* therefore, disclosure of the attorney's mental processes was not mandated just because the IRS had substantial need for the information. Id. at 401.

QUESTION

1. Are communications by cellular phones and electronic mail privileged? What can an attorney do to protect confidentiality when using these means of communication?

PROBLEMS

1. You are the attorney for Emerald City Distributing, a distributor of beverages. An employee of Emerald, Diane Johnson, was involved in an accident while driving a company vehicle in connection with her duties. Emerald requests that you interview Johnson for them. Before the interview, you tell Johnson that in addition to representing Emerald, you will represent her at no cost. During the interview, Johnson makes statements to you indicating that she may have been at fault in the accident. Must you maintain the confidentiality of her statements? May you disclose her statements to Emerald?

2. As the attorney for Emerald you are asked to investigate another accident. Dave Jones, accompanied by a trainee, was making a delivery when he collided with another vehicle. Afterwards, you interview Dave and Tina, the trainee who witnessed the accident but was not driving. Which, if any, of these communications are within the attorney-client privilege?

Marshall was a "bright"—i.e. light skinned—African American man living in or around Mobile, Alabama.

B.B. Breeden was a white man and an attorney, also living in or around Mobile. Besides his relationship with Marshall that is mentioned in this case, he presumably had no past contacts with Marshall.

The State v. Marshall, A Slave

8 Ala. 302 (1845).

Novel and difficult questions from Mobile.

The prisoner was indicted in the Circuit Court of Mobile, for burglary. The indictment contained two counts, in one of which the prisoner is charged to be the property of Joseph Bryan, and in the other, the property of some one unknown. The jury found a general verdict of guilty, upon which the Court passed sentence....

Upon the trial, the prisoner proved that he was a bright mulatto, and that for a number of years he had acted as a free person—that he owned property, or claimed it, and had made contracts as a free person. To prove that he was a slave, the State offered as a witness Joseph Bryan, charged in the first count of the indictment, to be the owner of the prisoner, who stated that he did not consider himself to be the owner of the prisoner. That some six or seven years before, a bill of sale of the prisoner had been transferred to him, by Isaac H. Erwin; that in his opinion he had acquired no right of ownership under the bill of sale, that it was brought to him by the prisoner—that he had not given Erwin any consideration for it, nor had he ever conversed with Erwin in relation to it. The prisoner objected to the testimony, because of the interest of the witness, and because he could not speak of an instrument of writing not in Court. The Court overruled the objection, and permitted the witness to testify.

The State then offered B.B. Breeden, Esq. who testified that several years before, the prisoner had applied to him to draw up a petition to the Legislature for his freedom. Witness said, that he prepared the petition, but that the prisoner never called for it, nor had he paid witness for it. The witness was an attorney at law, and the application was made to him at his office. The prisoner objected to this testimony going to the jury, because the facts were confidentially disclosed to the witness as an attorney at law, and because the prisoner could not admit that he was a slave. The Court overruled the objection.

The prisoner being convicted, moved in arrest of judgment because the verdict of the jury was general, and did not state upon which count of the indictment they found the prisoner guilty, and did not ascertain whether he was the slave of Joseph Bryan, or of some person unknown. The court refused to arrest the judgment, and certified the several matters above as novel and difficult. . . .

Confidential communications between attorney and client are privileged, and cannot be divulged. The rule is not confined to communications in reference to suits in existence, or expected to be brought; it is sufficient if the attorney is consulted professionally. *Walker v. Wildman*, 6 Madd. 47. As if he be employed to draw a deed, (*Parker v. Carter*, 4 Munf. 285 [6 Am. Dec. 458]) or to procure a sale under a mortgage, where there is a statutory foreclosure. *Wilson v. Troup*, 2 Cow. 197 [14 Am.Dec. 458]. No inference can arise from the statement upon the bill of exceptions, that the communication was confidential, but the inference must be that it was not, as the only fact disclosed was one which it was proper to make public. If the disclosure had been of the facts upon which the prisoner rested his application to the Legislature, it might be different. It is not sufficient to exclude the testimony, that the witness was an attorney at law. The privilege of withholding the facts disclosed does not depend upon the circumstance, but that the disclosure was made to him professionally. That does not appear from the facts disclosed, or from the nature of the employment, which was such as did not require legal skill in its execution. We think, therefore, that this case is not brought within the rule.

The propriety of the admissions of the witness Bryan, depend upon the question of interest. An interest to disqualify a witness must be a pecuniary interest in the event of the suit, inclining him to one side of the party calling him. He was called to prove that the prisoner was a slave, being charged in one count of the indictment to be the owner of the prisoner.

Upon the assumption that he was the owner of the prisoner, he was clearly competent to testify for the State, as it was his interest to prevent a conviction, the consequence of which would be the certain loss of one half his value, and the possible loss of his entire value.

It is however urged, that he has an interest in the record which disqualifies him from being a witness. This argument is founded on the statute making compensation to owners of slaves executed for crimes, and is as follows: "Whenever, on the trial of any slave for a capital offence, the jury shall return a verdict of guilty, the presiding judge shall have the same jury sworn to assess the value of said slave, and the verdict of said jury, shall be entered on the record of the Court, and the master or owner of such slave, producing to the Comptroller of Public Accounts, a transcript from the record of the Court, regularly certified by the clerk, and the certificate of the sheriff, that any slave has been executed in pursuance of the sentence of the Court, shall be entitled to receive a warrant on the Treasurer for one half of the amount assessed by the jury, to be paid out of the funds hereinafter provided for that purpose." Clay's Dig. 474 Sec. 19.

The succeeding section authorizes the jury to refuse compensation to the master, when he has been to blame for the offence committed by the slave.

From this it appears that the verdict, and judgment against the slave, does not entitle the owner, or master, to the compensation provided by the statute; that right is to be ascertained by a subsequent proceeding and may be refused upon that proceeding. The previous verdict and judgment establishes nothing but the condemnation of the slave; the right of the master to compensation, and its amount, depends upon the evidence to be adduced upon the subsequent proceeding.

Objection was also made to the testimony itself; what the objection was does not very distinctly appear; but giving to the bill of exceptions a liberal interpretation, it may be considered as a motion to exclude that portion of the testimony of the witness, which related to the bill of sale from Erwin, upon the ground that it was secondary evidence. It is very clear that the bill of sale was not evidence before the jury, it not being produced, and its execution proved or its absence accounted for, so as to let in secondary evidence of its contents; and if the object of the testimony was to prove that the prisoner had once been the slave of Erwin, it should have been excluded.

It does not, however, distinctly appear, that this was the purpose for which the testimony was offered, as there is an aspect of the case in which it was certainly competent.

It appears that the prisoner brought to the witness a bill of sale of himself, which had been transferred by Erwin to the witness, who had never conversed with Erwin in relation to it, or had ever paid any consideration for it. This transaction occurred some six or seven years before the trial, since which time it appears, the prisoner has been acting as a free man, as the witness stated, that he did not consider himself as the owner of the prisoner.

Upon the assumption that the prisoner knew that the paper he gave to the witness was a bill of sale of himself, transferred to the witness, which we think from the circumstances may be fairly presumed, it was an act distinctly admitting his status and can be understood in no other light than that of a request to the witness to stand as his nominal owner. Considered in this aspect, the mention by the witness of the fact that the prisoner brought him a bill of sale, was wholly unimportant, as it proved nothing but the admission of the prisoner that he was a slave, which would have been quite as potent without the bill of sale, as with it.

It is probable, however, that the jury considered the bill of sale in evidence before them, and establishing the fact that the prisoner either was then, or had been the slave of Erwin, and in favorem vitae, as the jury may have been and probably were misled by the permission to the witness to speak of the bill of sale, without limiting the evidence to the fact of the admission of the prisoner, to be inferred from the act, we think there should be a new trial. This renders it unnecessary to consider the matters urged in arrest of judgment.

Let the judgment be reversed and the cause remanded for another trial; or until the prisoner is discharged by due course of law.

COLLIER, C.J.—I am inclined to think that the fact of the prisoner's carrying a bill of sale from Erwin to the witness cannot be construed as an admission by the former that he was a slave. There is no proof that the prisoner was aware of the contents of the bill of sale, or that previous or subsequent to that time he had spoken to the witness on the subject, requested the witness to purchase him, or admitted that he was in servitude to Erwin or any one else. In other respects I concur in the opinion pronounced by my brother Ormond.

GOLDTHWAITE, J.—My judgment, uninfluenced by the opinions of my colleagues, would lead to an affirmance of the judgment of the Circuit Court, on all the questions reserved; but in a capital conviction, I cannot consent that it shall stand when any member of the Court entertains a serious doubt of its correctness.

QUESTIONS

1. Is there any evidence that Breeden is being compelled to testify, or is it likely that he is volunteering? Why is Breeden betraying his client in a matter affecting his client's very existence?

2. It is hard to imagine a person with less power than an African American in Alabama in the 1840's. By contrast, lawyers were perceived at the time to have extensive power. See Alexis de Tocqueville, "Mitigation of the Tyranny of the Majority" from Democracy in America, Chapter 11 infra. Lawyers representing some clients, such as children or aliens, also have far more power than do their clients. This power imbalance is vulnerable to abuse by the lawyer, and one possible abuse is collaboration with the client's adversary. Did such collaboration occur here?

3. The Court finds that it may be "fairly presumed" that "the prisoner knew that the paper he gave to the witness was a bill of sale of himself," and that this "was an act distinctly admitting his status." The Court thus acknowledges that Marshall can understand a legal document, yet refuses to find that he could impart confidential communications to an attorney. Why?

4. The Court holds that the nature of Breeden's employment, drawing up a petition to the Legislature for Marshall's freedom, "was such as did not require legal skill in its execution." Is the Court right in concluding that legal skill is not required for this task? Could a butcher or a farmer have drawn up the petition just as well?

5. What skills are required of a lawyer seeking to influence a legislature? How are those skills different from the skills of a courtroom advocate on the one hand or a nonlawyer lobbyist on the other?

6. This case rules on admissibility of a communication between a client and his attorney about facts that are very relevant to a capital case. Should the admissibility of lawyer-client communications be determined differently in a capital case?

7. Did the legal system's denial of Marshall's basic rights require the complicity of lawyers as well as that of judges and legislators?

8. The critical issue in this case is whether Marshall was a slave. Alabama's legal system in 1845 made legal status more important than personal conduct in defining the penalty for a crime. Is race still an important factor in determining who will get the death penalty? In cases where it is, are lawyers in part responsible for this result?

Relevant Background

Lawyers as Witnesses

As demonstrated in the *Annesley* case, calling a lawyer as a witness can raise complex issues surrounding the attorney-client privilege. In *State v. Marshall*, these issues were even more paramount, but were given short shrift by a legal system hardly concerned with any of Marshall's legal rights, much less his right to consult an attorney in confidence.

Lawyers called as witnesses are generally precluded from representing a client in the matter in which they have testified. Giffard, for example, was not representing Anglesea in Annesley's ejectment action, and his testimony would probably have made it inappropriate for him to later represent any party in the case.

Indeed, evidentiary rules at the time generally prohibited any person who might be interested in a case from testifying. 3 Jack B. Weinstein & Margaret A. Berger, Weinstein's Evidence 601, 604 (1991). Gradually courts began to allow interested witnesses, including lawyers, to testify. In French v. Hall, 119 U.S. 152, 154–55 (1886), the Supreme Court stated that

"[t]here is nothing in the policy of the law, and there is no positive enactment, which hinders the attorney of a party prosecuting or defending in a civil action from testifying at the call of his client. In some cases it may be unseemly, especially if counsel is in a position to comment on his own testimony, and the practice, therefore, may very properly be discouraged; but there are cases, also, in which it may be quite important, if not necessary, that the testimony should be admitted to prevent injustice or to redress wrong."

Subsequently, the American Bar Association, in Canon 19 of its 1908 Canons of Professional Ethics, stated its own view that an advocate should not testify except when the testimony concerned "purely formal matters," or if it was "essential to the ends of justice."

If a lawyer's testimony is required and concerns matters important to the case, a court ordinarily will disqualify the lawyer from further participation in the case. This restriction "avoid[s] putting a lawyer in the obviously embarrassing predicament of testifying and then having to argue the credibility and effect of his own testimony. It was not designed to permit a lawyer to call opposing counsel as a witness and thereby disqualify him as counsel." Galarowicz v. Ward, 119 Utah 611, 230 P.2d 576, 580 (Utah 1951). For this reason, courts will be circumspect in deciding whether to require existing counsel to testify. Generally, the adversary who calls opposing counsel to testify will be required to show that the testimony cannot be elicited from any other source. See Richard C. Wydick, Trial-Counsel as Witness: The Code and The Model Rules, 15 U. Cal. Davis L. Rev. 651, 677 (1982).

A good rationale for separating the role of an advocate from that of a witness is that the two roles are premised on different ethical obligations. As discussed in Chapter 1, both a witness and an advocate must be truthful. However, an advocate must also be partial, and her testimony as a witness may be affected by her partiality. Even if the advocate's testimony is unaffected, her partiality may be used to attack her credibility, meaning that her testimony will carry less weight than it would have carried, and therefore be less useful to the party seeking to offer it. Furthermore, if the lawyer is impeached as a witness, the judge or jury may later distrust the lawyer as an advocate as well. See Wolfram, Modern Legal Ethics 377 (1986).

Another rationale for disqualification, pointed out in both French v. Hall, supra, and in Galarowicz v. Ward, supra, is that, if an advocate is also a witness, she may comment in summation upon her own testimony. What she was required to testify to objectively, she later restates in the form of an argument. A jury, and even a judge, could easily confuse the lawyer's two roles and have a difficult time differentiating between testimony and argument. See Roxanne Malaspina, Disqualifying House Counsel under the Advocate–Witness Rule, 67 N.Y.U. L. Rev. 1073, 1088 (1992).

A third rationale for the advocate-witness rule is avoiding the appearance of impropriety (see Canon 9). A judge or jury may wonder if a lawyer is testifying truthfully or slanting her testimony while zealously representing her client. The appearance of impropriety could not only affect the outcome of the case, but the public's view of the legal profession as well.

However, a client's right to counsel of his choosing is a compelling reason for courts to be cautious in either disqualifying an attorney or deciding that the lawyer's testimony is required to begin with. Because disqualification interferes with the client's choice of counsel, courts will usually evaluate both the necessity and the nature of the testimony before forcing the client to retain another lawyer. See Malaspina, supra, at 1097. Furthermore, the judge in a particular dispute has discretion to balance the interests of both parties in determining whether one of the parties has made a compelling case for requiring counsel for the other to testify. Finally, disqualification of a lawyer-witness from representing a client at trial does not extend to representation of the client in other matters. See, e.g., Nakasian v. Incontrade, Inc., 78 F.R.D. 229, 232 n. 3 (S.D.N.Y.1978) (testifying lawyer only disqualified from the role of trial counsel, not from other facets of representation).

QUESTION

1. Look at Model Code, DR 5–101(B) (stating that a lawyer shall not accept employment in pending or contemplated litigation if the lawyer knows or it is obvious that she or a lawyer in her firm ought to be called as a witness); DR 5–102(A) (stating that, if a lawyer or lawyer in her firm is already employed by a client, the lawyer or firm must withdraw if it becomes obvious later that the lawyer or a lawyer in the firm ought to be called as a witness *on behalf of the client*); and Model Rule 3.7(a) ("a lawyer shall not act as advocate at a trial in which the lawyer is likely to be a necessary witness.") What are the differences between the approach of the Model Code and the Model Rules. Which approach do you prefer?

Edward Fretwell Prichard, Jr. graduated from Harvard Law School in 1939 and was a clerk to Justice Felix Frankfurter. He was also a former clerk to the Attorney General and to the Secretary of the Treasury as well as a former general counsel to the Democratic National Committee. He was influential in Kentucky politics and planned to be governor. Admired and envied, he was the country boy back in the country. Judge Ardery had known Prichard all his life. Prichard was a schoolmate and law partner of Ardery's son.

Prichard v. United States

181 F.2d 326 (6th Cir.1950).

■ Before SIMONS, ALLEN and McALLISTER, CIRCUIT JUDGES.

■ SIMONS, CIRCUIT JUDGE.

The appellant and his law partner, A. E. Funk, Jr., were indicted under Sec. 241, Title 18 U.S.C.A. for conspiracy to stuff ballot boxes in certain precincts of Bourbon County, Kentucky, at the general election in November, 1948, which was, of course, a national election. Funk was acquitted but Prichard was convicted and sentenced. He contends that the district court erred in admitting the testimony of Judge Ardery in respect to a confession, over his claim of privilege; that there was no corroborative evidence of Judge Ardery's testimony to warrant submitting the case to a jury; that Funk, having been acquitted and the charge being conspiracy, the judgment against him should have been set aside, and finally, that the proofs failed to establish a federal offense.

The principal ground for the appeal as argued and briefed, relates to the testimony of Judge Ardery as to an interview solicited from him by Prichard, and this necessitates a recital of the circumstances which led to the conversation and the status of the parties at the time. Prichard is a lawyer with a career of marked distinction. Graduated from college and with a law degree from Harvard Law School, admitted to the bar in 1939, he had been research secretary to one and probably two of the present Justices of the Supreme Court, to the Attorney General of the United States and the Secretary of the Treasury, and was, at one time, general counsel of the Democratic National Committee. Returning from Washington to Kentucky a number of years before the incidents here involved, he practiced law in the Circuit Court of his county and in the Court of Appeals of the Commonwealth of Kentucky. He became a man of great influence in the politics of his state and county. Judge Ardery is a judge of the 14th Judicial Circuit of the State of Kentucky, had known Prichard all his life, especially since Prichard had been a school mate and later a law partner of his son, Philip. At the election 254 forged ballots had been placed in the ballot boxes of a number of the precincts in Bourbon County prior to the opening of the polls. On the night that the appellant, accompanied by Philip Ardery, sought the interview with the judge, the latter had already called a grand jury to investigate election frauds in the county. The grand jury was to meet the following morning at which time Judge Ardery was expected to instruct the grand jurors as to their duties and the scope of the investigation, as required by Kentucky law.

Prichard had gone to Philip Ardery, his former law partner, on Sunday evening, November 7, 1948, for legal advice. Whatever conversation there was between them at that time was held by the district judge to be within the attorney-client relationship, so privileged, and is not here involved. Prichard and Philip Ardery, however, decided to consult Judge Ardery and drove to the judge's house, arriving there about 11 o'clock. Being advised that the interview which then transpired would be met by the claim of privilege on behalf of Prichard, the district judge heard evidence and argument in camera as to the nature of the evidence expected to be solicited from the judge, and limited interrogation with scrupulous concern for Prichard's rights. In view of Judge Ardery's official position, the duties he was then engaged upon in reference to the grand jury, the command of Kentucky statutes and the public interest, he concluded that one who seeks the advice of the judge of the court in which his case is to be tried is not entitled to the privilege accorded by law to confidential communications between an attorney and client. To allow the privilege under such circumstances would invite frustration of the administration of the courts by their duly elected and qualified judges. Such application would seem inimical to the public interest and a perversion of the purpose and spirit of the rule. He decided that Judge Ardery's testimony was admissible and would be received by the jury with caution as to its lack of bearing upon the guilt of the co-defendant.

At the preliminary hearing the judge had told the court that when Mr. Prichard appeared at his door that night he said, "Judge, I am in deep trouble and I want your advice." He then invited him into his home. To the jury the judge testified, "Mr. Prichard told me that he and two other young men prepared the ballots here in issue and put them in the ballot boxes before the election began." He said that he felt he could give Prichard legal advice and that if anything transpired later he would not sit in the case. Prichard gave him two details in regard to it. He said one of the young men wrote the names of the election officers on the ballots and that he stamped the ballot which scratched Senator Chapman. Prichard appeared greatly disturbed, both mentally and emotionally. His mind was not on the past. It was on the future, at what it might hold for him. "He asked me if I had a suggestion which would help him. I had none at that time." Asked whether Prichard had requested suggestions at any other time, the judge testified that he had on the following Wednesday. At this point the court excused the jury for the purpose of considering the competency of this additional evidence. Judge Ardery then explained, "I suggested to him that he go to his pastor and talk over the matter he had told me of. He didn't seem inclined to receive that suggestion favorably, and then I told him that in my opinion the sooner he got this question over and disposed of, the better it would be. My grand jury was then in session. * * * We understood each other as to what my words meant." While this second conversation was not permitted to go to the jury it has bearing upon the problem here involved.

The privilege that attaches to the communications of a man to his lawyer is of ancient origin. "It is a salutary rule designed to secure the client's freedom of mind in committing his affairs to the attorney's knowledge." 5 Wigmore on Evidence, (2d) Ed. § 2306. "It is designed to influence him when he may be hesitating between the positive action of disclosure and the inaction of secrecy." It is the privilege, however, of the client which the attorney is bound to respect. As Wigmore elucidates it, Sec. 2291, "It is worth preserving for the sake of a general policy; but it is none the less an obstacle to the investigation of the truth. It ought to be strictly confined within the narrowest possible limits consistent with the logic of its principle." As one court has put it, "The privilege is an anomaly, and ought not to be extended." Foster v. Hall, 12 Pick.,Mass., 89, 97, 22 Am.Dec. 400. In the endeavor to phrase the general principle so as to represent all of its essential, Wigmore undertakes to fashion a formula by which this may be accomplished. Its elements are (1) where legal advice of any kind is sought (2) from a professional legal adviser in his capacity as such, (3) the communications relating to that purpose, (4) made in confidence (5) by the client, (6) are at his instance permanently protected (7) from disclosure by himself or by the legal adviser, (8) except the protection be waived.

We concern ourselves here primarily with the second element of the formula, and this leads us first to a consideration of Kentucky law. Section 30.120, par. 1 of the Kentucky Revised Statutes, provides: "The Governor, the Lieutenant Governor when serving as Governor, a judge of the Court of Appeals or circuit judge shall not practice law in any court of the state except in cases in which he was employed previous to his election, or in which he is personally interested." Prichard contends that this does not impose general prohibition against the practice of law by circuit judges. It merely provides that circuit judges shall not practice law in any court of the state and the giving of legal advice carried on outside the courtroom does not constitute practicing law "in any court" within the meaning of the prohibition. There are no Kentucky cases construing the statute. There are state cases which would seem to indicate that a statute of such limited purport does not disqualify a judge from giving legal advice. People ex rel. Colorado Bar Ass'n v. Class, 70 Colo. 381, 201 P. 883; Appeal of Clark, 119 Me. 150, 109 A. 752. There are also cases which hold that even though a judge acts as a legal adviser in violation of statute, this does not affect his status as a lawyer so as to impair the rights of his client. They are noted in 48 C.J.S., Judges, § 9.

The present case, however, is sui generis. Judge Ardery was not merely a judge giving, as a lawyer, legal advice to a client—he was the presiding circuit judge of Bourbon County and as such had impaneled a grand jury which he was about to instruct concerning reported infractions of law upon which his advice was sought. By all standards of ethical conduct which govern the conduct of a judge it was morally, if not legally, impossible for Judge Ardery to enter into an attorney-client relationship with one whose conduct was to be investigated by a grand jury already called and about to be instructed, and this Prichard knew or must have known. It is true that no indictment against Prichard was returned by the local grand jury, but this was because the Federal Bureau of Investigation had taken over the inquiry and the state grand jury investigation was never completed. Prichard testified in camera that he knew Judge Ardery would be disqualified in sitting upon his case if an indictment against him were returned. By all the modern concepts of judicial ethics, the judge was not only disqualified from sitting on Prichard's case, but doubtless was also disqualified from organizing and instructing the grand jury once he was advised that the investigation would likely bring within the ambit of the inquest matters bearing upon the conduct of one who, upon the eve of inquiry, had already discussed with him participation in the very alleged unlawful conduct about to be investigated. We are not confined to the narrow limits of the Kentucky prohibition. The Kentucky Statute commendably reaches out toward a standard of judicial and professional propriety. It approaches but may not yet have reached materialization of prevailing modern thought upon the subject.

Canon 31 of Judicial Ethics promulgated by the American Bar Association on July 9, 1924, Reports of American Bar Association, Vol. 62, 1937, recites: "In many states the practice of law by one holding judicial position is forbidden. In superior courts of general jurisdiction, it should never be permitted." Canon 24 provides: "A judge should not accept inconsistent duties; nor incur obligations, pecuniary or otherwise, which will in any way interfere or appear to interfere with his devotion to the expeditious and proper administration of his official functions." Rule 209(B) of the American Law Institute's Model Code of Evidence, defines "lawyer" for the purpose of the sections dealing with privilege as "a person authorized, or reasonably believed by the client to be authorized, to practice law in any state or nation the law of which recognizes a privilege against disclosure of confidential communications between client and lawyer." These concepts of propriety must have been known to a lawyer of the attainments and experience of Prichard. In our view they prohibit the possibility of existence between Prichard and the judge of any attorney-client relationship. To this may perhaps be added the general understanding of an informed laity that judges, at least those of appellate and the higher trial courts, should not and do not practice law.

While Prichard asserts he went to the judge for legal advice, and while the judge thought he might give such advice and then withdraw from any case that might result from the grand jury investigation, there is no suggestion in the record as to any advice sought or given that would constitute legal advice. Rather there is strong inference that Prichard sought the interview to ease a troubled conscience and sought it of Judge Ardery not in his professional capacity as a lawyer capable of giving legal counsel but as a wise and valued friend who had known him all his life. "I am in deep trouble and I want your advice," and so the judge seemingly interpreted it. "I suggested to him that he go to his pastor and talk over the matter he had told me of. * * * We understood each other as to what my words meant." So the second element of the Wigmore formula disappears.

Finally, Prichard's request for advice was robbed of the element of good faith once he knew, as know he did, that the judge was about to charge a grand jury in respect to election frauds. Whether we conceive the function of the judge in organizing and instructing a grand jury to be judicial or administrative is immaterial. In either capacity, knowledge of law violation may not be reposed in him under the cloak of privilege. As Wigmore puts it, Sec. 2300, "A consultation with a judge, in his capacity as such, falls unquestionably outside the present privilege." Judge Ardery was currently engaged in ferreting out election frauds under the authority and command of the laws of his state. Knowledge that came to him while exercising this function could not be received by him in confidence. Whether judges of superior courts may ever enter into an attorney-client relationship, we need not presently decide, even though voicing our doubts. It is sufficient to say for purpose of present decision, that a judge circumstanced as was Judge Ardery, may not enter into such relationship with a lawyer who may not deny knowledge of accepted notions of judicial propriety. There was no error in receiving Judge Ardery's evidence.

A subordinate contention of the appellant is that even if the testimony of Judge Ardery was properly admitted there was insufficient corroborative evidence to justify the submission of the case to the jury or support the verdict in reliance upon the well-established rule that an extra-judicial confession is not in itself sufficient to support a conviction. Isaacs v. United States, 159 U.S. 487, 490, 16 S.Ct. 51, 40 L.Ed. 229; Anderson v. United States, 6 Cir., 124 F.2d 58; Wigmore, Evidence, 3d Ed. Sec. 2071. But there is corroborative evidence. After the fraudulent ballots were discovered Prichard visited the State Police Commissioner to inquire whether the ballot paper would retain fingerprints, and in at least one precinct Prichard asked the election board to go ahead with the voting even after the discovery of illegal ballots in the box. In Anderson v. United States, supra, we held that corroborative proof need not be such as independently of the confession will establish the corpus delicti or the defendant's guilt beyond a reasonable doubt.

Again it is contended that the acquittal of Funk required the setting aside of Prichard's conviction on the ground that one person may not be guilty of a conspiracy. The indictment, however, charged Prichard with conspiring not only with Funk but with other persons unknown. It is the rule that all parties to a conspiracy need not be named in the indictment. Didenti v. United States, 9 Cir., 44 F.2d 537. If the indictment charges a conspiracy among named defendants and other persons unknown to the grand jury, and it appears at the trial that there was such conspiracy but that only one of the named defendants was a member of it, it is sufficient to support a conviction if it is shown by substantial evidence that the parties unknown at the time the indictment was returned committed overt acts therein alleged. Such evidence there was. The alleged conspiracy could not have been carried out by one person because it required access to the clerk's office, a careful removal of the stolen ballots so that their theft could not be detected, and the forgery of approximately 44 different signatures on 254 ballots, deposited in the ballot boxes of 11 precincts. The signatures on the ballots were not the signature of Prichard but were, according to the evidence, made in a number of different handwritings. It is the rule that the existence of a conspiracy may be established by inferences from circumstantial evidence. Johnson v. United States, 6 Cir., 82 F.2d 500, 504.

It is also urged that the charges in the indictment and the proofs of the government failed to establish an offense in violation of Sec. 241. The indictment charges a conspiracy to injure and oppress specifically described citizens, namely, the voters of the particularly named precincts who voted for the Republican candidates. Section 241 penalizes conspiracies "to injure, oppress, threaten, or intimidate any citizen in the free exercise or enjoyment of any right or privilege secured to him by the Constitution or laws of the United States." It is argued by the appellant that so phrased the section is limited to the protection of the individual rights of citizens and was not intended to vindicate a general interest in the purity of elections; that 254 forged ballots constituted but an infinitesimal fraction of the votes cast in the election and did not affect the outcome of a single contest in any precinct; that this, together with the fact that Bourbon County is traditionally Democratic, shows complete absence of any intent to affect the outcome of the election. The argument has no merit. It was rejected by the Supreme Court in United States v. Saylor, 322 U.S. 385, 64 S.Ct. 1101, 88 L.Ed. 1341. The deposit of forged ballots in the ballot boxes, no matter how small or great their number, dilutes the influence of honest votes in an election, and whether in greater or less degree is immaterial. The right to an honest count is a right possessed by each voting elector, and to the extent that the importance of his vote is nullified, wholly or in part, he has been injured in the free exercise of a right or privilege secured to him by the laws and Constitution of the United States.

Finally, it is contended that the court's instructions to the jury that it might find one of the defendants guilty and the other not guilty is ambiguous and misleading. However, when read in context, and considered in the light of the entire charge to the jury, the ambiguity, if one exists, disappears, since the court was careful to charge the jury fully as to all of the essential elements of the offense and the requirements of proof.

The judgment below is affirmed.

NOTES AND QUESTIONS

This scenario is perhaps difficult to believe: a target of grand jury proceedings shows up on the judge's doorstep at eleven o'clock on a Sunday evening with the judge's son, an attorney, to talk about the case. Even more shocking is Prichard's claim that his communications to Judge Ardery were within the attorney-client privilege.

It could be said that this fact pattern is "too easy" to study in a professional responsibility course—how could a lawyer stuff ballot boxes and then claim that an ex-parte communication with the judge assigned to his case was an attorney-client communication? It is obvious that Prichard was wrong; however, his complete lack of respect for, or understanding of, professional ethics is more difficult to explain. So is the fact that other lawyers in Bourbon County, including Judge Ardery's son, showed similar insensitivity to ethical concerns. In this respect, the most outrageous cases are sometimes the most puzzling.

1.   Prichard is accused of stuffing ballot boxes with 254 forged ballots. What was his motive—to win the election or to show his strength as party boss in Bourbon County, a Democratic stronghold in a divided state?

2.   Was Prichard's crime less or more serious than Anglesea's assault on life and on the judicial process?

3.   The amount of respect for the democratic process in Bourbon County says something about the amount of respect likely to be shown for judicial process. Do ethical standards at the bar depend in part on ethical standards in society as a whole?

4.   Prichard's substantive defense—that there were too few Republicans in Bourbon County for Democratic election fraud to change an outcome—implies that society should tolerate corruption where a specific harm cannot be shown. Does your answer to Question 3 above suggest that corruption has its own cost to society, apart from the specific harm caused?

5.   How did the government learn of Prichard's conversations with Judge Ardery? Presumably, Ardery turned Prichard in. Should he have done so? In this case, the ethics of friendship clearly conflict with the ethics of citizenship. Which should get priority?

6.   The court holds that an attorney-client relationship must exist for communications to be privileged and that it was "morally if not legally impossible" for Judge Ardery to enter into an attorney client relationship with Prichard. First, Ardery had a preexisting duty as a judge which conflicted with any possible attorney-client relationship with Prichard. Second, Prichard appeared to have come to Ardery as a friend, not as a lawyer, and Ardery's advice was personal: "Go to your pastor." Why, however, are such communications between friends not privileged? Are lawyers more important in such situations than friends?

PROBLEMS

1.   You represent a man accused of robbing a bank. He comes into your office with his brother, who was not present at the crime scene and has not been charged in the crime. He says that he wants to tell you everything that happened on the day of the robbery and asks if his brother can come into your office to be with him while he talks with you. How do you respond?

2. You are advising the general counsel of a large corporation on its compliance with the antitrust laws and send her a memorandum discussing certain practices of the corporation that could be illegal. The memo is marked "Privileged and Confidential." Five months later, the corporation is planning to sell some assets to another corporation and the same general counsel asks you to send a copy of the memo to the general counsel for the prospective buyer. The prospective buyer, she tells you, has promised not to disclose the contents of the memo to anybody. How do you respond?

3. You are the general counsel for a bank. A loan officer from the bank comes into your office and tells you "in confidence" that he embezzled $50,000 from the bank. You consult with the President of the bank and an agreement is reached whereby the loan officer will return the money and resign from his position; the crime will not be reported to the authorities. However, another employee tells the district attorney about the incident and the district attorney wants to question you. Is your conversation with the loan officer privileged?

4. A suspected drug dealer comes into your office and asks you to represent him in his upcoming trial on charges of selling heroin. After hearing the facts of his case, you tell him that you do not want to represent him. The district attorney wants to question you about the conversation. Is it privileged?

5. You represent a large manufacturing concern. Last year, your client paid an environmental audit firm to perform ground tests at several of its manufacturing sites to detect the presence of hazardous wastes and to prepare a report. One month ago, your client was sued by the EPA in a complaint alleging improper disposal of hazardous wastes. The EPA has subpoenaed the environmental audit report. Is the report privileged?

6. In the above situation, you ask the environmental audit firm to perform more tests and prepare another report to help you prepare for litigation against the EPA. Is this report privileged?

B. DISCLOSURES TO REGULATORS AND INVESTORS

Arthur R.G. Solmssen, b. 1928 in New York City; B.A. Harvard College 1950; J.D. University of Pennsylvania 1953; admitted in Pennsylvania in 1954; associate, partner, and then of counsel in Saul, Ewing, Remick & Saul (specializing in corporate and municipal securities law) 1953 to present; author of several novels.

The Comfort Letter

As this chapter of Solmssen's novel The Comfort Letter begins, Charlie Conroy, President and CEO of Conroy Concepts Corporation ("CCC"), a conglomerate, is planning to acquire Bromberg Instruments, which manufactures calculators. The merger has already been approved by Bromberg shareholders, whose stock has already appreciated considerably with news of the merger. At the same time, Conroy is planning for CCC to close a $100 million offering of debentures, the proceeds of which will be used to pay off short term debt. As with any new issue, CCC has to register the debentures with the SEC. The underwriting syndicate, managed by First Hudson, will not go through with closing the debenture offering without a "comfort letter" from Pennypacker Poole & Co. ("PP"), an accounting firm. The comfort letter is to essentially state that no material changes to CCC's financial condition have occurred since the time CCC's financial statements were prepared and published in the prospectus.

Darby Turbine is a recently-acquired subsidiary of CCC primarily engaged in the construction of power plants. Just prior to the beginning of this chapter, a design defect is discovered at a nearly-completed plant that Darby has been building. With the closing of the CCC debenture offering just days away, investors are already lined up to purchase the debentures and the merger with Bromberg is about to be consummated. The problem with Darby's construction contract comes to a head.

The narrator is Ordway Smith; the year is 1969.

Charlie Conroy is President and CEO of CCC.

Ordway Smith is a partner of Conyers & Dean in Philadelphia and represents CCC.

Tommy Sharp is a young associate at Conyers & Dean and is assisting Ordway Smith on the deal.

Harry Hatch is a partner at Iselin Brothers & Devereaux in New York City and is counsel for the underwriters.

Bernard Bromberg is President and CEO of Bromberg Instruments.

Justin Silverstone is lead counsel for Bromberg Instruments.

Sandy Simon is also counsel for Bromberg Instruments.

Hewitt Robinson is President of Darby Turbine.

Alex Morrisson is Chief Engineer at Darby Turbine.

John Lundquist, CPA is the partner in charge of Pennypacker Poole & Co.

Jack Renfrew is Executive Vice President of CCC.

Frank Fonseca (the Frenchman) is corporate secretary of CCC.

The Comfort Letter

The Limestone Scrubber

Mr. Alex Morrisson, chief engineer of Darby Turbine, had apparently been to church. He wore a blue suit and a white shirt and a gold watch chain over his vest and a Masonic emblem in his lapel, and there was one thing that he wanted made entirely crystal clear right from the outset, and that was that his people were not going to take the blame for this, because this is exactly the kind of thing he'd been warning about, exactly the kind of thing that will happen if you bring in fancy hotshot atomic energy people from General Electric and Westinghouse who don't know a goddamned thing about coal-burning furnaces and give them fancy titles and fancy salaries and put them over top of people who have been building coal furnaces all over the world for forty years, and let them make decisions about how to bid and what to guarantee and not to guarantee, and anybody who isn't wet behind the ears will tell you that at this stage of development you don't promise that a limestone scrubber is going to work no matter how bad you want to get any particular contract, and his people had explained this until they were blue in the face, but no, nobody will listen to what engineering people with forty years in the coal business have to say, they let a kid just out of engineering school call the shots about bidding a coal-burning power plant—

"Simmer down, Alex," said Hewitt Robinson, president of Darby Turbine, formerly a divisional vice president at Westinghouse. "That kind of talk isn't going to get us anywhere, and we didn't guarantee the scrubbers anyway."

"Tell that to the power company lawyers," said Alex Morrisson.

"Could we start at the beginning?" I asked. "Would somebody tell me what a limestone scrubber is?"

Sunshine was streaming through the windows of Conference Room A, and the place smelled of the coffee Tommy Sharp had concocted in the adjoining kitchenette. John Lundquist and his accountants hadn't said a word yet, but they looked unhappy, even more unhappy than Hewitt Robinson and Jack Renfrew, who wore tweed sport jackets and seemed angry at being summoned to town on Sunday morning to deal with yet another crisis the lawyers had dreamed up. Everybody leaned forward to watch as one of Morrisson's engineers flipped open a fat book of specifications to show me a schematic diagram.

His boss explained:

The electric generating plant on the Turkey River was designed to burn local West Virginia coal, 2 ½ percent sulphur content; furnace gases consist of sulphur dioxide and fly ash; a full-scale stack gas cleaning system was required by the state environmental control agency and specified by the electric company; Darby agreed to include the newest type system, utilizing limestone injection into the furnace and wet scrubbers for particulate and sulphur dioxide removal....

The other engineers joined in, and I tried to follow as best I could. First the coal is ground as fine as talcum powder, then it is burned in a mixture of air and powdered limestone. Hot gases from the furnace are forced into enormous tanks, in which they are "scrubbed" by a spray of water and limestone, a "slurry." This mixture of water and gas and limestone is forced up through a bed of crushed marble. The sulphur dioxide and fly ash are turned into other chemicals and washed out the bottom. The scrubbed gases rise through a "demister"—which heats out the water that would create white clouds—and finally up the tall smoke-stack.

"And now it isn't working?" I asked.

Well, they were having a lot of trouble. The fly ash and the limestone slurry tended to form hard cement-like deposits that clogged the marble beds, clogged the demisters, clogged the water jets, and clogged the inlets to the scrubbers. They were having so much trouble that the electric company had just refused to pay the last installment of the construction contract.

"Can't they operate the plant without the scrubbers?" asked Tommy Sharp.

Alex Morrisson shook his head. "Ever seen that valley? River's a hundred yards wide, then there's a railroad track, a highway, a half mile of bottom land, then mountains straight up on both sides. Unless you get a wind blowing down the river the smoke will lie in there, there's three little factory towns strung along that valley, they had to close a chemical plant because they couldn't get rid of the fumes—"

"Could bring in low-sulphur coal," said one of his men.

"Yeah. From Wyoming or someplace. Know what that would do to their electric rates? They're sitting right on top of the cheapest coal in the country, they'd be nuts to haul in expensive coal—"

"That's not really the point, is it?" John Lundquist looks like an intelligent college student, but he is one of the youngest and most brilliant partners in the worldwide accounting firm of Pennypacker Poole & Co. He has published a book on accounting and flies about the country explaining the latest pronouncements of the Accounting Principles Board to less sophisticated colleagues.

"The point is that the electric company is disputing payment of the contract price, on the ground that they can't operate their plant. If they hook up the limestone scrubbers they clog and choke the furnaces, and if they bypass the scrubbers and put the smoke right up the stack, then the State of West Virginia will close them down—so we've got a dispute over a very substantial amount of money here—we don't even know how much, but the full contract price is about a hundred and seventy million dol-lars—"

"A hundred and—*what?*" I couldn't believe my ears.

"That's right, and thirty-five million of that represents the sulphur dioxide removal system—which doesn't work—and the unpaid part of the contract is . . . how much?"

"Ten percent," said Larry Lenz, CCC's comptroller. "Roughly seventeen million, of which maybe a million-five is profit—"

"And that's profit Darby's already taken into income," said John Lundquist.

I still didn't understand. "How could they have taken it into income if they didn't get it yet?"

Lundquist folded a copy of CCC's Prospectus back to page sixty-five, and pointed his gold pencil: "Take a look at Note D again. Percentage-of-completion method. Typical in long-term construction contracts." He leaned back, took off his glasses, and settled into what was obviously a familiar lecture. "The trouble with contracts that run over several years is that they cause a conflict between two principles of accounting. One principle says that income is recognized only when the right to payment has become unconditional. That would mean no income on a long-term contract until the work is accepted—none. On the other hand, we also have a principle that says you must give an accurate picture of the results in each accounting period—each year—and that means you should take the profit in the same year you expend the costs, the same year you're doing the work. For example, if it takes you five years to build a plant, you're spending money those five years but if you only take the profit when they accept the plant and finish paying you, in year five, then you've distorted your results in years one through four. Does that make sense?"

I said I guessed it did.

"Of course you can also use what we call the completed-contract method: defer *both* cost and revenues into the year the contract is finished—say year five—but what does that do to your results in years one, two, three and four? You're really working those years, you're really earning money but it doesn't show in your results, so you're distorting again. So the Accounting Principles Board recommends the percentage-of-completion method for long-term construction contracts when you can make reasonable estimates of costs to complete and reasonable estimates of how long it's going to take—which you can, in Darby's case. Usually. So that's the method Darby uses. Perfectly correct, generally accepted accounting principles. Clear so far?"

"Yes." I began to see where he was going. Tommy Sharp, way ahead of me as usual, had turned the pages of the Prospectus to CCC's earnings statement and was making computations with his slide rule.

John Lundquist continued. "Okay, percentage-of-completion method, we tell them that there in Note D, we tell them in effect we're estimating some profit factor in each year's earnings, we're taking in some earnings in each year even though we haven't finished the job. But what happens now? Now instead of a profit on this Turkey River contract, it looks like we might have a loss, Because of this fight about the limestone scrubbers—"

"*No Way* are we going to have a loss on Turkey River!" Hewitt Robinson interrupted angrily. "Despite Alex, we never guaranteed those scrubbers, and anyway we're going to get them to work, and we'll get paid for them too!"

"Okay, fine," said Lundquist. "If Conyers & Dean will give us a bulletproof opinion that the electric company has to pay you the full contract price, then maybe we're all right. But if not, then we've got to set up reserves for losses, and what does that do to the earnings we've reported in the Prospectus? They'll have to be adjusted."

Numbers filled the air. How big would the reserves have to be? What would the effect on CCC's per share earnings be?

My mind was reeling. "Are you trying to tell me this Prospectus is *wrong*? After six months of work? After two hundred thousand dollars of accounting fees and legal fees and printing costs?"

"No," said Lundquist, looking up from his computations. "The financials weren't wrong as of the time we reported on them, as a matter of fact I don't think the Prospectus was wrong as of last Wednesday, when it became effective—"

"—and you delivered your first comfort letter."

"That's right, but then something happened, you see, a subsequent event that changed the facts. So in the light of these new facts we obviously can't deliver the same letter on Tuesday—at least not in the form required by the underwriters. I can't very well say that nothing has come to my attention that would indicate a material adverse change in consolidated results of operations—unless, as I say, your firm is willing to go on the hook with the opinion that the electric company will have to pay for the scrubbers whether they work or not."

"This is ridiculous," I said. "They've been building this plant for what . . . four or five years? And up to last Wednesday nobody knew there might be trouble about these scrubbers? After four or five years of work something like this is discovered between Thursday and Saturday? Is anybody going to believe that?"

"My God, we climbed all over that plant," said Tommy Sharp. "The underwriters were there, the people from Iselin Brothers were there, nobody said a *word* about this!"

I didn't like the way he sounded. He sounded frightened, and Tommy isn't easily frightened.

"Of course *they* didn't say a word about it." Alex Morrisson was not frightened at all. On the contrary, he sounded pleased. "This was *their* baby, *their* brilliant idea, Mike Barkus practically invented the scrubbers, you know—"

"Who's Mike Barkus?" I asked.

"Mike Barkus is a kid six years out of Carnegie Tech, a kid who's going to show the whole profession how to build coal-fired power plants, a kid who sold this whole ball of wax to people who know all about atomic energy—"

Jack Renfrew cut in. "Ordway, could Hewitt and I see you alone?" He sounded very tired.

The three of us stepped out into the musty corridor.

"Jesus Christ!" said Hewitt Robinson.

"Shoulda gotten rid of him *years* ago," said Jack Renfrew. "Didn't I tell you? Look, Ordway, what we got here, as you can see, is company politics, Darby politics. Alex is a holdover from the old gang, from before

Charlie got control, he's got a chip on his shoulder because other people have been put on top of him, and underneath him too."

"That's right," said Hewitt Robinson. "Now this kid Barkus is a good example, a brilliant kid, a real nut on coal, comes from Pittsburgh, claims that coal is going to solve all our problems, he's done a hell of a lot of work on these stack gas cleaning systems, he's a real pioneer in this field and that's how we got the Turkey River contract, because he convinced those people that we could make the thing work, they could burn their own coal in that valley—"

"So you did guarantee the scrubbers?"

"No, we did *not* guarantee them, we said we'd build the plant to specifications—"

"Did our firm prepare the contracts?"

"No, we still had the Openshaw firm, they worked it out with the electric company lawyers in Wheeling."

"But we must have reviewed it in connection with this underwriting."

"Ordway, we've got these agreements all over the world, I don't think you had to read every one of them."

"Well, in any case we'd better look at it right away, and you'll have to bring young Mr. Barkus over from West Virginia—in fact you'd better send the Learjet out for him this afternoon.... How much does Charlie know about this?"

They looked at each other.

"Not a damn thing," said Jack Renfrew.

"This hasn't ever come up in discussion?"

They shook their heads. "Ordway, this is just an engineering problem, we assumed the thing would be built according to the specs, that it would work the way they said it would—"

"Even though Morrisson warned you that it wouldn't?"

"Ordway, you don't know Alex Morrisson! He's been crying the blues ever since CCC acquired Darby! Everything's been done wrong, everything's screwed up, nothing's going to work—we just don't pay attention to him, we let him talk. Jack's right, I should have got him out a long time ago, but he knows the utility engineering departments, they like him, he does have his uses, and he has to retire this year anyhow—"

I opened the door and led them back into the conference room.

"—personally no skin off *my* ass," Alex Morrisson was telling the accountants. "Pension's vested, condominium in Lauderdale is paid for, sold my Darby stock to Conroy and bought triple A utilities—"

I had to interrupt him. "Tommy, will you find a copy of the Turkey River contract? We'd better take a look at that right away.... Gentlemen, I think we might as well disband for the moment. John, if your people could sit down with Larry and come up with some numbers, some estimate of what kind of reserves you're talking about and what effect they would have on the earnings. . . . I think we've got to set up a meeting with the underwriters tomorrow morning, first thing. They are going to be very unhappy underwriters."

* * *

Bernard Bromberg was taking a walk with Justin Silverstone. They stood outside the big ironwork gates of the Hyde Place and saw us coming, galloping all the way down the long easy slope from the ridge and around the orchards.

"That's quite a sight," said Justin Silverstone as we reined in.

"I thought Karin would be with you," said Bernard Bromberg.

"She went driving with Mr. Anders," shouted Ailsa before I could say anything.

I dismounted and handed my reins to Ailsa. "I guess she's just doing some sightseeing, Bernard." His expression revealed nothing. "Is Charlie around?" I asked. "I'm afraid we've got a problem."

They looked at each other. "Apparently Charlie isn't granting audiences today," said Bernard Bromberg. "Frank Ferguson and two directors of Manayunk Steel just drove away, madder than hornets. Seems that last night Charlie asked them to come over and talk about the merger, maybe watch the Redskins, drink some beer ... But then he wouldn't come downstairs. Justin and I tried to entertain them as best we could, but they didn't seem very happy about it. Ferguson left word that Charlie knew where to find him if he wanted him."

"Is Charlie sick?" I asked. "He was pretty high last night. . . ."

"We wouldn't know, Ordway. As I say, we haven't seen him." Bernard was angry too. Justin Silverstone said nothing.

The hell with this, I thought, and marched upstairs. The door to the master apartment was shut. I knocked. No answer. I knocked again. When I opened the heavy oak door, I heard the television, Redskins and Dallas Cowboys, but it was dark as I turned through the dressing room into the master bedroom, and the smell was stale beer and cigarette smoke. The curtains were closed and the only light came from the television set.

Charlie slouched in a leather armchair, enormous, dressed in striped pajamas, black silk kimono, slippers. Around him, empty beer cans and overflowing ashtrays.

"Are you all right?" I asked, still standing by the door.

No answer.

I walked in, walked past him, turned off the sound of the television. Still no comment.

I pulled one of the curtains just a little bit, so that a beam of sunlight pierced the smoky darkness.

"Cut that out," Charlie snarled. "The light hurts my eyes."

He rubbed his hands across his face, then looked up angrily. He hadn't shaved or combed his hair, but he sounded sober.

"Have you got a hangover?" I asked. "What you need is some coffee and some fresh air."

"What I need is peace and quiet. I slept two hours last night. Can't I have some privacy and quiet in my own home?"

"Charlie, we've got a problem with the accountants, they've turned up a serious mess at Darby Turbine—"

I sat down on the unmade bed and told him about the limestone scrubbers.

I suppose I expected an explosion: shouts of rage, galvanic action, telephone calls, threats, decapitations . . . .

There was no reaction at all. He seemed to be listening, but his eyes strayed back to the television screen.

"Charlie, you understand what this means? If P–P doesn't give comfort, Harry Hatch won't let the underwriters close, won't let them pay for the Debentures, and that in turn means we can't merge with Bromberg—"

"—and I can't pay off the banks," said Charlie, his voice like lead, still staring at the silent football game. He understood, all right. I waited.

After a long time he said: "It also means I'm a shitty manager, a guy who doesn't know what's going on in his own companies." He looked at me with an expression I'd never seen before. "It confirms what you and a lot of other people have known for years—Conroy's a big fraud, CCC's a house of cards."

"Now wait a second, Charlie—"

"A fucking house of cards! You know it better than anybody! Bank debt, convertible debentures, stock trading at crazy price-earnings ratios, earnings based on creative accounting . . . What's going to happen if I can't pay off the banks? You know what those loan agreements say!" With that he sank back into the chair and lit a cigarette, his hands shaking.

I'd never seen him like this. I knew he had his ups and downs, but I couldn't believe this was the same man who soared to the skies last night, who was going to buy Manayunk Steel, who was going to build his tower sixty stories over Thirtieth Street Station—

"And you know it better than anybody," he said again, through a cloud of cigarette smoke. "Charlie Conroy, the gardener's son who had to wear patched knickers, who had to walk down to the road to meet the school bus, whose father stank of cheap rye, whose mother cried. And now he's a big shot! I can hear all of you laughing!"

I suddenly thought about the Frenchman who had always gotten him out, diverted him somehow, protected him when such a mood hit. Where was the Frenchman?

I did the best I could.

"Nobody's laughing at you, Charlie. You've built an empire with your own energy, your own courage and brains, you've built yourself an empire out of nothing, but every empire has troubles out along the borders, and it's a long way from the emperor's palace to the places where troubles develop, so you've got communications problems. But when you see the trouble you've got to jump in and deal with it. Now we have this mess down in West Virginia, it's no use crying over it, we've got to decide what to do. We've got a meeting with the underwriters in New York tomorrow. We've sent for the engineers to explain the problem to everybody, but you're going to have to be there, Charlie! They'll want to hear what *you* plan to do about it."

He sat there and stared at the football game.

"I've done what I can, Charlie. I've told Renfrew to send the Learjet out for the engineers. I've got our best people reviewing the construction contract, to see if they can tell whose responsibility those scrubbers are. I've arranged for the helicopter to take us to New York first thing in the morning. But when we meet with the underwriters they'll be looking at you! You're going to have to convince them that you're on top of the situation."

"Never should have bought Darby. That's what changed everything. If I was so damned smart, why did I go into hock to buy Darby?"

"Charlie, you're stuck with Darby! You've got to deal with this particular crisis tomorrow morning, and I've got to tell Bromberg and Silverstone about it, right now before they find out from somebody else. We've got to have them on our side in this, or the whole house of cards really will collapse." I stood up. "Will you be ready at dawn? I want to see the engineers for an hour or so before the underwriters have a go at them."

No answer.

"Charlie? Would you rather I go over first thing with Tommy Sharp and send the chopper back for you and Bernard? I've got to be there when Harry Hatch examines the engineers."

He stared at the football game, smoking a cigarette.

"Charlie?"

"What difference does it make? Do what you want, just leave me alone."

I got up and left him alone and went downstairs to tell Bernard Bromberg and Justin Silverstone about the limestone scrubbers.

What Would It Do to the Bottom Line?

First Hudson's conference room was packed. Outside the big windows a breathtaking view of New York harbor, blazing sunshine, a stiff ocean breeze raising sparkling whitecaps on the water; inside, fifty worried men ignoring the view, glumly listening to a tall young engineer preaching his particular gospel.

It was the same working team that assembled in Philadelphia so long ago, plus First Hudson's chairman, First Hudson's syndicate manager, their assistants, two professors of engineering called in to advise First Hudson about this crisis, Hewitt Robinson with a battery of Darby Turbine engineers, and Sandy Simon, flown in from San Francisco on Sunday night to represent the Bromberg interests.

Mike Barkus wore a Zapata moustache, a striped shirt with fat necktie, and a knitted suit with bell-bottom trousers. "Some funny-looking engineer," muttered First Hudson's slicked-down pinstriped chairman, but they listened attentively to his message about how the world was running out of oil, about the cost and danger of atomic fission, about a five-hundred-year supply of coal right here in the United States, about how we would *have* to use our coal to generate power, would *have* to burn it without polluting the air . . . .

This was in 1969. Nobody gave a damn about energy shortages. The underwriters became impatient. They wanted to hear whether Darby would get paid for the Turkey River plant, and the questions came.

What was the matter with the limestone scrubbers? Could they be fixed? Why hadn't anybody anticipated that this would happen?

Harry Hatch's spectacles glistened as he warmed to his cross-examination: Why hadn't anything been mentioned when the underwriters visited the plant? How many other limestone scrubbers were in operation? Had they been inspected by Darby's engineers? Did they clog too? What was being done about them?

Mike Barkus stood in front of his photographs and his blueprints and held his ground like any true believer. Nothing was mentioned when the underwriters came because nothing was wrong: the scrubbers hadn't even been assembled then. A few other plants were installing scrubbers, and they were having trouble too, all different kinds of trouble depending on the type of plant, the type of coal . . . you always have trouble with new processes. Did we know how much trouble they were having with the nuclear installations?

He was young and he was smart and he believed in his cause, and even the professors of engineering couldn't shake him. The limestone scrubbers were going to work.

"But who is going to pay for making them work?" demanded Harry Hatch. "And how much is it going to cost?"

Mike Barkus had some thoughts about what it might cost, but he guessed the lawyers would decide who had to pay for it. All eyes swiveled to me, and I turned to Tommy Sharp, who had been up all night too. While I talked he distributed the memorandum of law our people had prepared.

I cleared my throat. "Now in the first place, I want to explain that the contract for construction of the Turkey River plant provides that it be interpreted under the law of West Virginia, and of course we can't give a formal opinion on the law of another state—"

"Oh now, wait a minute," said John Lundquist.

"—but we've reviewed all the decisions we could find, in West Virginia and elsewhere, we've prepared this memorandum Tommy is distributing, and we hope to get it backed up by a formal opinion from West Virginia counsel."

"By tomorrow morning?" asked Harry Hatch.

"We're working on it."

Everybody read the memorandum—ten pages of discussion and citations, put together by young lawyers working all Sunday afternoon, revised by Ames Mahoney Sunday evening, retyped Sunday night.... The silence was deafening.

Harry Hatch to John Lundquist: "Is this the bulletproof opinion you wanted?"

John Lundquist: "No."

Ordway Smith: "Well, we don't claim it's bulletproof, but it's all we can say in the circumstances."

I knew it sounded lame, but if you can't predict a result you can't predict it.

Another silence. The underwriters looked at each other.

Sandy Simon piped up: "Could somebody give us hard numbers? If reserves have to be set up, what would it do to the bottom line?"

That's what they really wanted to know. Larry Lenz and John Lundquist began to talk. The gold pencils came out and the slide rules. Of course there was no way of knowing exactly what it might cost to put the scrubbers into operating condition, or what would happened to the contract if that couldn't be done, but Mike Barkus's boys had supplied a safe high number and a minimum low number and so we've worked out the adjustments on two levels....

"All right, call it five cents a share for the quarter," Harry Hatch was saying, bent over his pad.

Grunts of agreement around the room.

"Why don't we sticker the Prospectus?" somebody asked. "Postpone the closing one day, print a sticker explaining the problem, show what the adjustment might do to the earnings, paste the explanation on the cover of each Prospectus, let each bondholder make his own decision?"

Harry Hatch turned to look at his underwriters. "Want to sticker?"

Dubious faces. "Doesn't that mean the customers could back out? Wouldn't have to take the bonds they ordered?"

"That's what it means," said Harry Hatch. "Of course in theory they never have to take securities until they get the final Prospectus with their confirmation—"

"In practice people don't back out," said First Hudson's syndicate manager, "not if they want to keep doing business with us." "But if we wave a sticker under their noses and say, 'Look at this terrible thing that happened, are you sure you don't want to change your mind?'"

"That's different."

"You're goddamned right it's different."

"Maybe we'd better go out and call our people."

Harry Hatch followed them out. I had the feeling he had some solution up his sleeve-everything that can happen must have happened at Iselin Bros. & Devereaux at least once before—and Harry wanted to produce the rabbit that would save the deal, but only at the moment providing the maximum glory for the magician, the moment just before the apocalypse. Intermission. The meeting fragmented into separate discussions. Secretaries brought sandwiches, and coffee in Styrofoam cups. The engineers bent over their rolled blue prints. I looked out across the harbor, then forced myself to focus on a new debate between Tommy Sharp and Sandy Simon.

"What good would a sticker do you?" asked Tommy, munching. "Even if the underwriters let us sticker their Prospectuses, what about your Bromberg stockholders? They got the same financials in their Proxy Statement. Are you going to send them another Proxy Statement, hold another meeting, have them vote on the merger all over again?"

Sandy lighted his pipe, looking profound. "Mm. We've considered that."

Tommy plowed ahead. "And if you postpone the merger, call another stockholders' meeting, then our Prospectus is wrong again because it contains the Bromberg earnings and it says the Bromberg holders *have* approved the merger!"

Sandy nodded. "Fortunately, you'll recall the merger agreement says that Bromberg's officers can waive certain conditions of closing, if it appears to be in the best interests of Bromberg's stockholders."

That was the first time the word "waive" was heard in the room.

Now Tommy Sharp looked skeptical. "You're going to waive the comfort letter?"

"Not the whole letter, of course, but perhaps we could work out some change in the wording...." At the other end of the table, the accountants stopped talking among themselves. Sandy Simon rose and went over to confer with John Lundquist.

Tommy Sharp leaned toward my left ear: "I don't know if Bromberg realizes it, but he's really in something of a box."

"Why?"

"Well look, when the merger was first announced, before it was announced, Bromberg stock was worth what? Sixteen—seventeen dollars a share, something like that? But now it's traded as if the merger's accomplished, and CCC is up, so right now Bromberg stock is worth about forty. Right?"

"Right."

"So let's say the merger aborts, the merger doesn't take place because the Bromberg control people—that's Bernard and Bob—insist that every technical closing requirement be met, that the comfort letter says word for word what the merger agreement requires . . . so the merger doesn't come off, what happens? Each and every Bromberg stockholder has a loss of twenty-three or twenty-four dollars a share. Who are they going to go after for that loss?"

"Charlie?"

"No, not if Charlie was willing to go ahead with the merger. They're going to go after Bernard and Bob, that's what they're going to do!"

A girl came in. Telephone call for Mr. Sharp. He was back a moment later. Two young lawyers from Conyers & Dean had arrived at Iselin Bros. & Devereaux with the Trust Indentures, our final legal opinions and the other closing papers, and people from First Hudson were already at the bank, counting and packaging the executed Debentures for delivery tomorrow.

"They want to know should they go ahead with the preclosing," said Tommy. "The Trust Indentures are signed but it'll take all afternoon to go over the other things with Harry Hatch's people . . . ."

"But nothing is delivered until tomorrow, when the underwriters bring their checks?"

"That's correct."

"Well sure, they'd better get everything ready on the assumption that we'll close on schedule."

Tommy went off to transmit the order

* * *

I returned just as the second act began. Charlie Conroy, Bernard Bromberg and Justin Silverstone were at the table now, and the underwriters were crowding back into the room.

"All right, is the fire out?" demanded Charlie. He seemed completely recovered.

I turned to Harry Hatch. "Are you going to sticker the Prospectus?"

"No sticker. Market's off six points this afternoon. If we offer people an excuse to get out from under their orders, there may be some doubt if the syndicate will hold together—"

"Not *our* customers," interjected First Hudson's chairman. "No problem with our customers. But we had to form one hell of a big group, and some of the smaller houses can't promise they won't have cancellations in a down market, and of course nobody wants this deal to turn sticky—"

"I think we'd like to hear from the engineers," said Bernard Bromberg.

So Mike Barkus had the floor again, the same story but in more detail, the blueprints, the photographs, the conviction that he knew what he was talking about, that he was right, that the scrubbers would work. It was just a matter of trial and error, adjusting the pH control, changing the acid content in the slurry, speeding up the movement of the slurry through the pipes. This time the engineering professors were nodding in agreement.

Bernard Bromberg leaned forward, listening, completely absorbed.

Charlie Conroy's scowl reflected anger and impatience. "So what's the big problem?" he finally interrupted. "It's a new concept, it's going to take some time to make it work, why are we making such a big deal about it?"

Patiently John Lundquist explained again: percentage-of-completion method, earnings already taken in might have to be backed out, adjustments might be required. . . .

"So what? So we'll make the adjustments! It can't amount to more than a couple of cents a share. . . ."

"But you see, the comfort letter requires us to say. . . ."

Back and forth, a Ping–Pong match. The sun moved behind the city and rain clouds blew in from the sea. A tanker came out of the East River. An army transport approached Fort Hamilton. A white seaplane flitted behind the towers, landed in the water, and taxied toward the foot of Wall Street. Surreptitiously, some of the younger brokers began to peek at their wristwatches.

Suddenly Charlie exploded: "All right, let's cut out all this bullshit! What are we going to do? I've got sixty-five million in bank notes coming due next week. Are you people trying to tell me you're walking away from this deal on account of some trouble at one power plant in West Virginia? One project out of two dozen we've got going all over the world? On account of a possible adjustment of five cents a share? Is that what you're trying to tell me? We're going to write off six months of work and two hundred thousand in expenses and tell the banks, 'Sorry, fellas, our limestone scrubbers got clogged, you'll have to wait a while!'? And what about Bernard's stockholders? They think their stock's worth forty bucks a share because they're merging with CCC tomorrow. What are we going to tell them? Now come on, wake up! We're paying you guys the kind of fees we're paying you because you're supposed to be the best lawyers, and the best accountants and the best investment bankers in the country, and I'm telling you you'd better come up with the answer!"

In the silence, Harry Hatch took off his glasses and began to polish them with his handkerchief. His moment had come. "Gentlemen," he said quietly, "let's consider our options."

* * *

Cold Comfort

I mainly remember the faces. In the huge conference room of Iselin Bros. & Devereaux, young lawyers frowning over closing documents; the Frenchman, for once without sunglasses, squinting his ugly little eyes, signing things; Tommy Sharp looking at me across the room, looking at me and not at the closing papers; a squadron of brokers filing in, talking, shaking hands, smiling; Charlie Conroy also shaking hands, also smiling, a white carnation in his lapel—where had they found him a carnation in Wall Street? Bernard Bromberg, Justin Silverstone, Sandy Simon, all carrying their suitcases for the flight home—where was Karin? Harry Hatch, all subdued triumph behind vest and gold rimmed spectacles . . .

"Harry, could I borrow an office somewhere? I've got to talk with Charlie."

"Sure thing. Come on back and use my room."

Charlie's smile vanished. "Now what?" but he followed me down the hall.

Harry Hatch is a clean-desk man: no papers, no junk, leather swivel chair, leather sofa, telephone, diplomas, chaste photograph of smiling wife and solemn children, the partners in dinner jackets around tables at the Union Club. . . . His secretary withdrew and closed the door.

At first Charlie didn't understand. "What do you mean you can't give an opinion? We all agreed it was okay, we'll make the scrubbers work and if it costs us money we'll adjust the earnings. . . . They've all agreed it's okay!"

"They're kidding themselves, Charlie. It's not okay. We've either got to put on a sticker to tell people about the problem, or we can't take their money."

"They *won't* put on a sticker, you heard them explain that yesterday!"

"Then we can't close."

The color left his face. "You gotta be kidding."

"You really think I'd be kidding about something like this? This is the hardest thing I've ever done in my life, Charlie, but I've got to do it. There's going to be holy hell to pay about this Turkey River thing. You know there is! A hundred-and-seventy-million-dollar project *and they can't use it?* What's going to happen when that gets into the papers? Where are they going to get their power? Are they going to close down those factories? Is Darby going to get the blame for that? We could all wind up in front of some committee, on television—"

"Ordway, what the hell has gotten into you? You heard the engineers, they spent all day explaining, they're going to use the plant, it's just a question of working out some bugs in a new process—"

"Charlie, I hope to God the scrubbers will work, but that isn't the point. The point is we've got to tell people we've got a problem. This is the kind of thing an investor would want to be told, isn't it? Wouldn't you want to be told? We've somehow talked ourselves into the position that it's not a big problem, it's not what they call material—well, that's bullshit, it is material, and both of us know it!''

He stared at me for a long moment. His face changed.

"You're chicken!"

"Aw Charlie!"

"We run into a few problems and the Messrs. Conyers & Dean develop cold feet. Oh, they don't mind collecting two or three hundred grand in fees every year, even from the gardener's son—it's all money, after all—but when we get down to the nitty-gritty, when the client really has his balls in the wringer, then the Messrs. Conyers & Dean suddenly develop very high ethics—"

"That's unfair, Charlie! You know we've overcome one hurdle after another, we've moved heaven and earth for you—"

"For Christ's sake, Harry Hatch thinks it's okay. Are you smarter than he is? One of the biggest law firms in the world?"

"I think he's wrong. This thing is going to come back to haunt us all—"

"Sandy Simon thinks it's okay, one of the biggest firms on the Coast. Are you so much smarter than they are, Ordway? Would you really call yourself a top-notch lawyer? Or would you call yourself a guy who's had every goddamned thing in life handed to him on a silver platter." He was shouting now, his face red. I was thankful the door was shut, but even so— "Now wait a minute—"

"Every goddamned *thing*! While I had to work my ass to the bone morning noon and night since I was sixteen years old and I built a four-hundred-million-dollar company out of nothing. Out of nothing! A sick old sheet and tube company eighteen months away from bankruptcy, and I built it all up by myself, and you're supposed to be my lawyer! Aren't you supposed to be my lawyer?"

"Yes, I am your lawyer."

"You're my lawyer? A lawyer is supposed to help when his client gets in trouble, isn't he? Here we run into a little flak and it isn't the other guys' lawyers that shoot me down, *it's my own lawyer!*"

There was no use arguing with him. He was frantic. I knew it would be bad but I didn't think it would be this bad. I looked down at the carpet while he struggled to control himself, breathing heavily.

"House of cards," he said, more quietly, his voice shaking. "Banks going to move in—"

"We'll work out something with the banks—"

"We'll work out *shit*!" It came quietly now, through clenched teeth. "You and I are through, Ordway!"

"I'm sorry."

"Are you? Really? Now that everything is going to hit the fan? Or are you just as glad to get those fine gentlemen at Conyers & Dean out of the line of fire?"

"No, I'm as sorry as I've ever been about anything in my life, Charlie. We could really help you, but you've got to play it our way."

"Yeah. Play it your way. You know where I'd be today if I always played it your way? You wouldn't even *know* me, Ordway!" He was speaking more quietly now, but his eyes were still wild and he couldn't catch his breath. "I'm going out there now . . . and I'm going to tell them . . . I'm going to tell them what the great firm of Conyers & Dean has done to me . . . what my own lawyer . . . has done to me—"

"Wait a minute, Charlie." I stood up and blocked his way.

We stared into each other's eyes. He was sweating. I thought he was going to hit me. "If you go out there in this state, you'll really blow everything. Just look at yourself. What are they going to think when they see you? The only way to handle this—after you've calmed down—is to tell them it's *your* decision: you've decided to withdraw the issue—on advice of counsel, of course—because of the Turkey River contract, because you may have to restate your earnings and you want the investment community to know that before you put out the Debentures. Honest to God, Charlie, it's the only way!"

A curtain fell over his eyes. "I need legal advice," he muttered, turning away from me, opening the door. . . .

As long as I live I won't forget the horrified looks on the faces of the youngest men from Conyers & Dean—the ones who had prepared the closing papers—nor the gleam of surprise in the eyes of Thomas Sharp, Esq., as Charlie Conroy calmly read the announcement Harry Hatch had written out for him. Every eye in the room focused on me. The Frenchman had his sunglasses on again, but it seemed to me that I could see his eyes right through them.

One of the brokers, sotto voce: "That's the ballgame. We're in the red for sixty-nine. Bye-bye bonus."

"Bye-bye Conroy," whispered his neighbor.

Harry Hatch's first reaction had been an icy stare: "I take it you know something we don't?"

"No, you have all the facts we have, Harry. I'm just drawing a different conclusion."

For a moment he continued to stare at me, genuinely puzzled. If he knew how, he would have shrugged. Then he swung into action. Young lawyers from Iselin Bros. & Devereaux were suddenly all over the place, very competently moving in, taking charge, calling the branch chief at the SEC, calling the New York Stock Exchange, calling Dow Jones, calling a financial writer on the New York *Times*. Listening to their smooth self-assured explanations of Charlie's statesmanlike decision ("Right ... Right ... Under the circumstances we all felt that it was the only proper course...."), you would think it was based on their advice.

I stood in one corner, very much alone, watching Tommy and the others collect the useless closing papers into their briefcases. Bernard Bromberg shouldered his way through the crowd and stood in front of me. He looked better than he had yesterday. There was a small enigmatic smile on his face.

"Had second thoughts, didn't you?"

I nodded.

"Want to hear something strange?" He glanced over his shoulder and moved closer. "I'm relieved. Can you imagine that? Four months of work, four months of negotiations, four months wasted time, fifty-sixty-seventy thousand dollars of expenses down the tube, a paper loss of twenty-four dollars a share, stockholders who will be climbing the walls ... and I'm *relieved*? What do you make of that?"

"That's not hard to figure out," I said.

"It's not, huh?"

"You didn't really want to sell."

He put his hands into his pockets and stood beside me, facing the room. He said nothing. "You really want to be your own boss," I said feeling light headed, feeling numb, feeling that I was saying something I wouldn't say under normal circumstances. "And maybe you really want to give your son a chance to show what he can do."

It caught him off guard. He stared at me. Was he angry? I couldn't tell.

"My fine-feathered friend," he said very slowly. "You certainly turned out to be full of surprises." He put out his hand. "I'll say goodbye now, Justin and I are going to round up our people and catch our plane. We'll leave Sandy behind to clean up. It's been quite an experience, Ordway. Maybe our paths will cross again."

The room was emptying. Justin Silverstone shook hands, Sandy Simon shook hands. The First Hudson people shook hands, but they were embarrassed, shaking hands with a dead man. Tommy Sharp said: "All the papers are packed, we can leave any time."

"No time like the present," I said. "Where's Harry?"

Harry was closeted with Charlie Conroy and the Frenchman, it turned out. His young lawyers were embarrassed too. Piles of CCC Prospectuses overflowed the wastebaskets. We said goodbye, and I led my team of briefcase-laden lawyers out of the room.

We were alone in the elevator. The two youngest men looked straight ahead, stunned.

"I'm sorry, fellows," I said. "You've all done a splendid job on this deal, and I appreciate it. I'm sorry it turned into such a mess."

"Ordway," said Tommy Sharp, "I'd like to say ... I'd like you to know ... that I've never been so impressed in my life. I want you to know that."

The other two exchanged glances.

"Object lesson," I said. "How to lose your biggest client."

Tommy Sharp shook his head. "Had to be done. But I wonder who else would have done it. I'm never going to forget this."

"Thanks. That's very nice of you. I guess I'm not going to forget it either."

Tommy smiled. "The subway's in the basement here. May I assume we're not heading for the helicopter pad?"

"Basement, please." The numbness was wearing off now, the bad pain was just beginning, but for a moment I felt a little better.

Copyright © by Arthur R.G. Solmssen, 1975

QUESTIONS

1. What is Charlie Conroy's view of the role of a lawyer in a lawyer-client relationship? Do some of the lawyers in this story appear to share his view?

2. Charlie Conroy, the entrepreneur, and Ordway Smith, the Philadelphia lawyer who lives on the Main Line, clearly come from different social backgrounds. In Charlie's argument with Ordway, is Charlie implying that his self-made status entitles him to play by different rules? Does he imply that the rules were made to prevent people like him from getting ahead? Does Ordway effectively deal with this argument?

3. What is the purpose of the comfort letter in this transaction? Why do the accountants not want to provide an unqualified comfort letter?

4. What is the purpose of "stickering" a prospectus?

5. Why does Harry Hatch want to go ahead and close the deal? What is his "solution" to the problem?

6. What would happen if they closed the deal without the comfort letter and without stickering the prospectus?

7. Is there an obligation to resolicit the shareholders who voted to approve the merger? Why?

8. Why is it important for Ordway that it be Charlie's decision to withdraw the issue? Why is this important for Charlie?

Relevant Background

The Comfort Letter is based on a true story about New York and Chicago lawyers who were sued by the SEC as aiders and abettors of a client's violations of the 1934 Securities Exchange Act's antifraud provisions in SEC v. National Student Marketing Corp., 457 F.Supp. 682

(D.D.C.1978). National Student Marketing's attorneys discovered that National's earnings had been overstated in financial statements, yet allowed a merger of National into another company to go forward without resoliciting approval from both companies' shareholders. Federal District Judge Parker held that the attorneys aided and abetted their client's violation of Section 10–b of the 1934 Act because the attorneys neglected their duty to protest National's decision to go ahead with the merger. "Their silence was not only a breach of this duty to speak, but in addition lent the appearance of legitimacy to the closing." Id. at 713. Unfortunately, Judge Parker was less clear on exactly what the lawyers should have done. "[I]t is unnecessary to determine the precise extent of their obligations here, since . . . they took no steps whatsoever to delay the closing." Id.

As evident from the *National Student Marketing* case, some lawyers have a critical role in the process by which their clients make disclosure to regulators and investors. Two federal agencies in particular, the SEC and the Office of Thrift Supervision (OTS), have assumed an increasingly aggressive posture toward lawyers who fail to act, or who act in a deceptive or evasive manner, while their clients misrepresent material facts to regulators or investors.

The Organization as Client

Although some of the tension between regulators and the bar turns on regulators' perception that lawyers are themselves engaging in misrepresentations and malfeasance, there is another issue: do lawyers have an affirmative duty to disclose to regulators information that organizational clients are required to disclose but do not? Some commentators argue that mandating such disclosure by lawyers would interfere with the legitimate objectives of legal representation. See Joseph C. Daly and Roberta S. Karmel, Attorneys' Responsibilities: Adversaries at the Bar of the SEC, 24 Emory L.J. 747 (1975). Professor Kraakman argues that "whistleblowing leaves all regulatory targets at the mercy of their private monitors" and creates for clients "a powerful incentive to withhold information from potential whistleblowers." Reinier H. Kraakman, Gatekeepers: The Anatomy of a Third–Party Enforcement Strategy, 2 J. of L. Econ & Org. 53, 60 (1986). However, other commentators argue that "[u]sing lawyers as gatekeepers and whistleblowers is a relatively inexpensive mechanism to achieve widespread compliance with the law." George H. Brown, Financial Institution Lawyers as Quasi–Public Enforcers, 7 Geo. J. L. Ethics 637, 718 (1994).

Model Rule 1.13 and § 155 of the draft ALI Restatement of the Law Governing Lawyers, both distinguish between individual and organizational clients. Although an organizational client is itself the lawyer's client—not its officers or directors—it is far too easy for a lawyer to lose sight of this fact and view the officers and directors as if *they* were the client. Armand D'Amato, even though he was not aware of Gardner's wrongful acts, probably should have consulted more people within Unisys about his billing arrangement instead of relying on a single officer to speak on behalf of the entire corporation. See *United States v. D'Amato*, Chapter 1 supra. Furthermore, when a lawyer does learn that an officer or director is acting in a way that could harm an organizational client, the lawyer must act in the best interest of the organization, not the individual officer or director concerned.

Model Rule 1.13 states that if a lawyer representing an organization knows that a constituent of the organization is acting in violation of the law in a manner that could be harmful to the organization, "the lawyer shall proceed as is reasonably necessary in the best interest of the organization," and his options include "referring the matter to higher authority in the organization." Although the Rule does not require the lawyer to make such a report, the comment to the Rule states that if asking the constituent to reconsider the matter fails, "it may be *reasonably necessary* for the lawyer to take steps to have the matter reviewed by a higher authority in the organization." Id. at comment 4.

Under the ALI Restatement, if a lawyer representing an organization as an entity,

> "knows that a constituent of the organization has engaged in action or intends to act in a way that violates a legal obligation to the organization and that will cause substantial injury to it or that reasonably can be foreseen to be imputable to and thus likely [to] result in substantial injury to it, the lawyer must proceed in what the lawyer reasonably believes to be the best interests of the organization."

Id., Section 155(3). Section 155(4) specifically states that, in such circumstances, the lawyer may ask the constituent to reconsider the matter, recommend that a legal opinion be sought, and seek review by an appropriate supervisory authority within the organization (including referral to the highest authority that can act on behalf of the organization).

Up to this point, the language in the ALI Restatement is remarkably similar to Model Rule 1.13, under which a lawyer may "resign in accordance with Rule 1.16" if she cannot deter the highest authority within an organization from action or refusal to act that is clearly a violation of law and likely to substantially injure the organization. However, the ALI provision is broader than Rule 1.13 and allows the lawyer to (i) withdraw from the representation or

> "(ii) disclose the breach of legal duty to persons outside the organization when the lawyer reasonably believes that:

> (a) the harm to the organization of the threatened breach is likely to exceed substantially the costs and other disadvantages of such disclosure;

> (b) no other measure could reasonably be taken by the lawyer within the organization to protect its interests adequately;

> (c) disclosure is reasonably likely to prevent or limit the harm to the organization in a substantial way; and

(d) following reasonable inquiry by the lawyer, no constituent of the organization who is authorized to act with respect to the question and is not complicit in the breach is available to make a decision about such disclosure.

In making disclosure, the lawyer must take reasonable measures to restrict disclosure outside the organization to the extent consistent with protecting the interest of the organization."

Id. § 155(4).

Disclosure to Securities and Banking Regulators

For a securities lawyer, the SEC's view of lawyer responsibility can be as important as any code of conduct based on the Model Rules, Model Code or ALI Restatement. Under Rule 2(e) of the SEC Rules of Practice, 17 C.F.R. 201.2(e), the Commission may disqualify from appearing or practicing before it, temporarily or permanently, any attorney found to have violated or aided and abetted a violation of the securities laws or the rules and regulations thereunder. See In re Emmanuel Fields, 45 S.E.C. 262 (1973) (administrative proceeding under Rule 2(e)), aff'd without opinion, 495 F.2d 1075 (D.C.Cir.1974). See also, James R. Doty, Regulatory Expectations Regarding the Conduct of Attorneys in the Enforcement of the Federal Securities Laws: Recent Developments and Lessons for the Future, 48 Bus. Law. 1543, 1544–1548 (1993); Harvey L. Pitt & Karen L. Shapiro, Securities Regulation by Enforcement: A Look at the Next Decade, 7 Yale J. on Reg., 149, 176–77 (1990); Daniel L. Goelzer & Susan Ferris Wyderko, Rule 2(e): Securities and Exchange Commission Discipline of Professionals, 85 N.W. U. Law Rev. 652 (1991).

In In the Matter of William B. Carter and Charles J. Johnson, Jr., Release No. 34–17597, CCH Sec. L. Rep. 82,847 at 84,172 (1981), Carter and Johnson, two partners of New York City's Brown and Wood, represented National Telephone, a company that installed and leased telephone equipment. For over a year and a half, National ignored Carter and Johnson's legal advice and repeatedly failed to make required disclosures in a 1933 Act registration statement, 1934 Act periodic filing and letters to shareholders. The SEC found that Carter and Johnson each had an affirmative obligation to correct National's disclosure violations, including either to approach the rest of National's board of directors or to resign.

After an initial decision by an SEC administrative law judge that Carter and Johnson should be sanctioned under Rule 2(e) for aiding and abetting National's violations of Section 10(b) of the Securities Exchange Act, the full Commission dismissed the charges against Carter and Johnson. The Commission explicitly stated that the two attorneys "could not be sanctioned under Rule 2(e)(1)(iii) for willfully aiding and abetting [a client's securities law] violations unless they 'were aware or knew that their role was part of an activity that was improper or illegal.' " Id. at 84,167. Furthermore, the Commission held that Carter and Johnson should not be sanctioned because standards for professional conduct in securities practice had not yet been satisfactorily developed. Instead, the Commission articulated standards that lawyers presumably must adhere to in the future:

> [W]hen a lawyer ... becomes aware that his client is engaged in a substantial and continuing failure to satisfy [SEC] disclosure requirements, his continued participation violates professional standards unless he takes prompt steps to end the client's noncompliance [with the securities laws].

Id. See Richard W. Painter and Jennifer E. Duggan, Lawyer Disclosure of Corporate Fraud: Establishing a Firm Foundation, 50 SMU L. Rev. 225 (1996) (discussing Carter and Johnson and other SEC administrative proceedings against lawyers).

After *Carter and Johnson*, the SEC pursued several actions against attorneys whom it believed were substantially responsible for their clients' violations of the securities laws. In *In re Kern*, the SEC held that George Kern, a mergers and acquisitions partner at Sullivan & Cromwell, "caused" his client Allied Signal to violate § 14(2)(4) of the 1934 Act (the Williams Act) by advising Allied not to disclose negotiations for the sale of a substantial amount of assets to a potential "white knight" when Allied was the subject of a tender offer. *In re Kern* [1988–1989 Transfer Binder] Fed. Sec. L. Rep. (CCH) ¶ 84,342. Kern, the administrative law judge found, had

> "assumed sole responsibility for determining when an amendment to Allied's Schedule 14D–9 would be filed.... In the usual relationship of lawyer and client Kern would have had only the responsibility of giving legal advice to [officers] of Allied who in turn would have made decisions whether amendments to Allied's Schedule 14D–9 were required. When Kern accepted discretionary authority to make those decisions he also accepted the responsibility the Allied officers had for compliance with Rule 14D–9...."

Id. at 89,592. This holding was never reviewed by the Commission on the merits because the proceeding was later dismissed on jurisdictional grounds.

The SEC has found in other proceedings that lawyers have "caused" clients not to make proper disclosures. See In the Matter of Jeffrey Feldman, Securities Act Release No. 7014, 55 SEC Docket (CCH) 9, 12 (September 20, 1993) (lawyer for three Pakistani banks "aided and abetted and caused" violations of Sections 5(a) and (c) of the 1933 Act by incorrectly advising his client that offering of rupee-denominated foreign exchange bearer certificates did not involve securities required to be registered prior to sale in the U.S.). Furthermore, the SEC recently stated that inside counsel for a broker-dealer, if confronted with client misconduct, must take steps to assure that it is reported. See In Re John H. Gutfreund, Thomas W. Strauss & John W. Meriwether, Exchange Act Release No. 31,554, [1992 Transfer Binder] Fed. Sec. L. Rep. (CCH) ¶ 85,067 (Dec. 3, 1992). Although Salomon Brothers' chief legal officer Donald M. Feuerstein repeatedly advised C.E.O. Gutfreund to report unauthorized U.S. Treasury auction bids by trader Paul Mozer to the Federal Reserve, Gutfreund did not do so. The Commission concluded that Feuerstein was Mozer's "supervisor" for purposes of Sections 15(b)(4)(E) and 15(b)(6) of the 1934 Act, 15 U.S.C.A. §§ 78o(b)(4), 78(b)(6) (1988), and as such was obligated to take appropriate steps to deal with Mozer's misconduct. Appropriate steps, the SEC suggested, included approaching senior management, but if that failed, (i) approaching the board of directors, (ii) resigning, or (iii) disclosing the misconduct to regulators. Id. at 83,609.

Perhaps even more ominous for industry lawyers than these SEC enforcement actions, are the aggressive enforcement actions brought by the OTS and the Resolution Trust Corporation (RTC) in the wake of the savings and loan debacle of the late 1980's and early 1990's. Unlike SEC proceedings, which for the most part accuse lawyers of "causing," or not doing enough to prevent, misleading statements to the SEC or to investors, OTS proceedings often allege that lawyers breached duties to their clients as well as to federal regulators. After taking over federally insured institutions and paying off insured depositors, regulators prosecute claims that they believe the institutions have against third parties, including malpractice claims against lawyers and accountants. Public harm and harm to the insured institutions are often perceived to be one and the same. For example, the Ninth Circuit observed in a savings and loan case that under California law, "a lawyer has to act competently to avoid public harm when he learns that his is a dishonest client." FDIC v. O'Melveny & Meyers, 969 F.2d 744, 748 (9th Cir.1992), rev'd on other grounds, 512 U.S. 79 (1994) (malpractice action brought by a thrift's receiver against its former counsel is governed by state, not federal, law).

In March of 1992, the OTS charged that lawyers at Kaye, Scholer, Fierman, Hays & Handler caused actual losses to the federal insurance fund of at least $275 million in connection with their representation of Charles Keating's notorious Lincoln Savings & Loan. See Notice of Charges, Office of Thrift Supervision v. Fishbein, OTS AP–92–19 (Mar. 1, 1992). Many of the allegations in the Notice of Charges state that Kaye, Scholer actively participated in Lincoln's efforts to mislead regulators. These allegations, if proven, would certainly have been grounds for liability. However, in the Third Claim in the Notice of Charges, the OTS also alleges that Kaye, Scholer made itself Lincoln's agent for purposes of making the required disclosures. Kaye, Scholer, according to the OTS, indicated its willingness to assume responsibility for Lincoln's disclosures by "demand[ing] that all FHLBB [Federal Home Loan Bank Board] requests for information made in connection with the 1986 Examination be directed to ... Kaye, Scholer" instead of to Lincoln. Notice of Charges, *Fishbein*, at parag. 20. Kaye, Scholer furthermore chose to disclose facts to regulators in place of Lincoln. Id.

The OTS Acting Chief Counsel later elaborated: "If a lawyer chooses to make statements of fact to an examiner in place of a client, as Peter Fishbein and Kaye, Scholer did in representing Lincoln Savings, then the lawyer is subject to the same disclosure requirements as the client." Carolyn B. Lieberman, OTS's Position on Lawyer Ethics, Wall St. J., Jan 12, 1994, at A–11. Harris Weinstein, former Chief Counsel of the OTS, has pointed out that "[the Kaye, Scholer matter] was a case where the lawyers were alleged to have assumed an unusual responsibility for factual representations made to the regulators...." Harris Weinstein and Michael P. Socarras, Lincoln Savings and Loan: An Engine of Professional Liability 25 (Practicing Law Institute, 1993). Kaye, Scholer allegedly assumed the responsibility for making the same disclosures about Lincoln's operations which were required to be made by Lincoln. Notice of Charges, parag. 46–48. This Kaye, Scholer allegedly did not do.

The OTS sued Kaye, Scholer for $275 million and imposed a very controversial freeze on Kaye, Scholer's assets. See Attachment of Law Firm Assets by Federal Regulatory Agencies, The Record of the Association of the Bar of the City of New York 116 (March 1992) (criticizing attachment of Kaye, Scholer's assets by the OTS but not addressing the substantive allegations in the Notice of Charges). Kaye, Scholer, rather than contest the charges and the asset freeze, settled the case weeks later for $41 million.

Almost all of the actions by the OTS and other federal banking regulators against law firms have also been settled prior to trial. These include settlements against Jones, Day, Reavis & Pogue ($50 million), Paul, Weiss, Rifkind, Wharton & Garrison ($45 million), and Troutman, Sanders, Lockerman & Ashmore ($20 million). John H. Cushman, Jr., Paul, Weiss Law Firm to Pay U.S. $45 Million, New York Times, Sept. 29, 1993 at C1. Most of these actions alleged that attorneys who represented failed institutions facilitated their clients' efforts to mislead federal regulators. The Financial Institutions Reform, Recovery, and Enforcement Act of 1989 (FIRREA), enacted after much of the conduct in these actions was alleged to have occurred, now expressly includes attorneys within its definition of "institution affiliated parties" subject to OTS enforcement remedies. FIRREA § 204(f)(6), 12 U.S.C.A. 1813(u)(4) (Supp. II 1990).

QUESTIONS

1. Should federal regulators promulgate their own professional conduct rules for lawyers practicing before them? What should lawyers do when regulators' rules arguably conflict with professional conduct rules in the state in which they practice?

2. The Private Securities Litigation Reform Act of 1995, Title III, Section 301, requires accountants to follow specified procedures when confronted with client fraud. The Act amends the Securities Exchange Act of 1934 by inserting a Section 10A providing that each audit performed pursuant to the securities laws must include procedures designed to discover illegal acts having a material effect on financial statements. In addition, the new act requires accountants who discover information indicating that an illegal act may have occurred to report the illegal act to the appropriate level of management. If the accountant does make a report to management, and the accountant is unsatisfied that management has remedied the problem, then the accountant must go to the full board of directors. The statute then requires the board within one day of the accountant's report to disclose the problem to the SEC; if the board does not, the statute requires disclosure by the accountant to the SEC.

Should the same rules apply to lawyers? If not, what rules should apply? See Richard W. Painter and Jennifer E. Duggan, Lawyer Disclosure of Corporate Fraud: Establishing a Firm Foundation, 50 SMU L. Rev. 225 (1996) (suggesting that, although different standards should apply to lawyers than to accountants, clear standards on lawyer disclosure of corporate fraud should be adopted by statute or SEC rules).

3. The ABA stated as early as 1975:

"Efforts by the government to impose responsibility upon lawyers to assure the quality of their clients' compliance with the law or to compel lawyers to give advice resolving all doubts in favor of regulatory restrictions would evoke serious and far-reaching disruption in the role of the lawyer as counselor, which would be detrimental to the public, clients and the legal profession."

ABA Report to the House of Delegates, Section on Corporation, Banking and Business Law (1975). See also Stephen J. Friedman, Reflections on Carter–Johnson, Thirteenth Annual Institute on Securities Regulation 297 (A. Fleischer, M. Lipton, R. Mundheim, & R. Santoni eds. 1982); Werner Kronstein, SEC Practice: The Carter & Johnson Case: A Higher Threshold for SEC Actions Against Lawyers, 9 Sec. Reg. L.J. 293 (1981); Michael Klein, SEC Reopens Old Wounds with its Proceeding Against George C. Kern, Jr., Insights, September 1987 at 32.

(a) Should lawyers as counselors, "assure the quality of their clients' compliance with the law?" If so, should lawyers be held responsible for doing this job right?

(b) Should a lawyer resign if her client refuses to comply with the law?

4. The SEC, in *In Re John H. Gutfreund, et al.*, observed that Salomon Brothers' chief legal officer Donald Feuerstein should have taken action to cause Paul Mozer's illicit trades to be reported to the Treasury Department. Nonetheless, the SEC did not bring formal charges against Feuerstein as it did against the other senior executives at Salomon who failed to report the trades. Client misconduct can be even more troubling for inside counsel than for outside counsel, particularly when reporting misconduct or resigning from a representation means losing one's job rather than only a single client. Do these different circumstances justify different standards of professional conduct for inside corporate counsel or merely more sympathy when conduct does not measure up to our expectations?

5. The bar was very critical of the 1992 OTS action against Kaye, Scholer. Bernard W. Nussbaum, a prominent New York lawyer, was retained to defend Kaye, Scholer against the OTS allegations. Nussbaum insisted even after the case was settled that the OTS had gone too far:

"[W]hat's going on in this country [is] a desire to break lawyers, first in the S & L area or in the regulated areas, and then it'll extend elsewhere.... People are entitled to go to lawyers, people are entitled to impose confidences in lawyers, to consult with lawyers, to get the lawyer's best judgment and best advice, and that should be encouraged not discouraged."

Special Report, Kaye, Scholer and the New Ethics Imperative, Am. Law., Sept., 1992, at 64, 74 (comments of Bernard W. Nussbaum).

(a) Do you think the OTS action against Kaye, Scholer was motivated by a desire to "break lawyers," or does Nussbaum's observation strike you as self defensive? For an alternative theory of why the OTS went after lawyers so aggressively, see Jonathan R. Macey & Geoffrey P. Miller, Kaye, Scholer, FIRREA, and the Desirability of Early Closure: A View of the Kaye, Scholer Case from the Perspective of Bank Regulatory Policy, 66 S. Cal. L. Rev. 1115, 1132–39 (1993) (arguing that the OTS charged Kaye, Scholer in part to cover up its own ineptitude).

(b) Do you agree with Nussbaum's view that people like Charles Keating are entitled to a lawyer's services, and indeed should be encouraged to go to lawyers and impose confidences in lawyers? Does your answer to this question depend on what lawyers will do for such a client?

For discussion of developments in Mr. Nussbaum's legal career after he left New York practice to became White House Counsel, see Chapter 3 infra.

6. What practical steps can a lawyer take to assure that regulators do not believe she has "assumed an unusual responsibility for factual representations made to the regulators?"

7. In response to the *Kaye, Scholer* matter, the ABA not only repudiated a requirement that lawyers disclose client fraud, but also rejected the OTS's position that attorneys, when confronted with client fraud, should take at least one of several actions usually seen as alternatives to whistleblowing. See American Bar Association, Working Group on Lawyers' Representation of Regulated Clients Report to the House of Delegates (1993) reprinted in Invitational Conference Materials on Lawyer and Accountant Liability and Responsibility (ALI–ABA 1993) 575–76. The Working Group complains that, among the OTS's "novel theories of professional responsibility" is the notion that lawyers have an obligation to report misconduct to superiors, going "all the way to the client's board of directors." Id. at 583. Regulators, according to the Working Group, are also wrong to "seek to impose a duty of due diligence on lawyers with respect to the accuracy of any statements made to federal banking agencies by *the lawyers*." Id. at 583 (emphasis added). Finally, "[T]he regulators have sometimes taken the view that the lawyer must resign if his or her efforts to prevent the wrongdoing prove unsuccessful. The Working Group again believes this to be an incorrect reading of Rule 1.13 and Rule 1.16." Id. at 583. The Working Group takes this position despite the fact that the ABA's own ethics opinions require a lawyer to withdraw when her services will further a client's fraud. See ABA Formal Opinion No. 92–366, Withdrawal When a Lawyer's Services Will Otherwise be Used to Perpetrate a Fraud (August 8, 1992).

(a) Do you agree with the ABA Working Group that it is a "novel theor[y] of professional responsibility" that lawyers have an obligation to report misconduct to superiors, going all the way to the client's board of directors?

(b) Do you agree with the ABA Working Group that it is wrong for regulators to seek to impose a duty of due diligence on lawyers with respect to the accuracy of statements made to federal banking agencies by the lawyers?

(c) Should a lawyer continue representing a client if her efforts to dissuade the client from wrongdoing are unsuccessful?

(d) Is it sufficient to withdraw from representing a client who intends to commit a fraud? Is disclosure or some other action to prevent the fraud appropriate?

PROBLEM

1. You advise a large chemicals manufacturer about its compliance with state and federal environmental regulations. In the course of your review of company records, you learn that your client has been dumping hazardous waste in a landfill even though state law prohibits dumping anything in the landfill other than household garbage. You also learn that the dumping occurs at night and regular payments are made to the night watchman. You advise the chief executive officer of your client that the dumping should stop immediately. She refuses, saying that there is no other "economically feasible" place to dump the waste. How do each of (i) the ABA Model Rules, (ii) the Model Code and (iii) the ALI Restatement suggest that you deal with this situation? What do *you* think is an appropriate response?

C.   FACILITATION OF CLIENT FRAUD

Robert Swaine, The Cravath Firm and Its Predecessors (1946)

Biographical sketch of Hoyt Augustus Moore

Hoyt Augustus Moore, the son of Augustus Edwin and Susan Tucker Moore, was born at Ellsworth, Maine, September 15, 1870.

From his grandfather, Edward Moore (1816–1896), he traces his ancestry back to his eleventh great-grandfather, Edward Moore, of Scotland, who was custodian in 1447 of Loudoun Castle.... [there follows a one-and-a-half page description of Moore's English and Scottish ancestry]

Hoyt Moore was educated in the Ellsworth schools and at Bowdoin College. At Bowdoin he was a member of Delta Kappa Epsilon; he took an interest in forensic work, winning the sophomore prize for declamation. He was graduated with a B.A. in 1895, a Phi Beta Kappa, and received an LL.D. in 1939. He has continued an active interest in Bowdoin, having been elected an overseer in 1929 and a trustee in 1933, and has given the college Augustus E. Moore Hall, a dormitory for 64 boys. He was one of the original 200 Phi Beta Kappa Associates, organized in 1940 to give financial support to the United Chapters.

For six years after graduating from Bowdoin, Moore taught school: as assistant principal of Wilton Academy, Wilton, Maine; Superintendent of Schools at Ellsworth; principal of the Ellsworth High School; and principal of the high school of Putnam, Conn.

In 1901 Moore decided to study law and went to Harvard Law School, receiving his LL.B. in 1904. He entered the Cravath office September 1, 1904.

He is a member of the Maine Society of New York (president for two years), Bowdoin Alumni Association of New York City (a former president), Academy of Political Science of New York, New York Genealogical and Biographical Society, New England Historical Society, American Academy of Political and Social Science and Society of Colonial Wars, of New York.

He married, at Ellsworth, October 10, 1906, Lora Parsons, daughter of James E. Parsons, an Ellsworth banker. They have a son and a daughter.

Hoyt Moore's hard, driving work far into the night, through Sundays and holidays, has become as much a tradition of the Cravath office as Governor Seward's night work at Auburn a century ago. As the Governor wore out his young men and kept working when they had to go home for sleep, so Hoyt Moore has outstayed the succession of his young associates. He has a constitution of iron; save for a serious operation in 1910, which kept him home for several months, he has never admitted illness; and no one has ever seen him exhausted. The story, doubtless apocryphal, has long been told that when some of his partners urged that the office was under such pressure as to make additions to the staff imperative, Moore replied: "That's silly. No one is under pressure. There wasn't a light on when I left at two o'clock this morning."

Even more meticulous than Henderson in the drafting of corporate papers, he is even harder to satisfy. In the early years of Moore's partnership when he was under great pressure in a matter for Bethlehem, Cravath assigned one of his own assistants to help Moore. Never having worked for Moore, but knowing his reputation, the associate carefully examined all the recent products of Moore's draftsmanship within the scope of the current project and, with them as a basis and making the modifications required by the statutes of the governing state, prepared papers which he thought conformed to Moore's best models. They met a scathing denunciation as a shoddy job. When the assistant explained that the drafts had their origin in some of Moore's own recent documents, Moore gave a reply which typifies his approach to every job: "Haven't you been here long enough to know that what was good yesterday isn't good enough today?"

Arthur LeVine of Ad Press tells many stories of long, sleepless nights spent at the printers' by Moore's assistants "in their shirt sleeves, bleary-eyed and exhausted, comparing the last bit of copy." A young associate, who had not worked long with Moore, according to LeVine, "felt impelled to correct the grammar and phraseology [of a document], but I cautioned him that if I were he, I wouldn't change the dot of an *i*, knowing that this was written by 'H.A.' himself. But the young man insisted, and about midnight called Mr. Moore. For one hour he held the receiver, listening to a lecture on the correct usage of past participles."

The expanding work for Bethlehem Steel Corporation and its many subsidiaries has been Moore's principal concern. No lawyer ever unreservedly gave more of himself to a client than Hoyt Moore has given to Bethlehem.

Judge Albert Johnson, a Republican state legislator and a county judge in Scranton, Pennsylvania, was appointed in 1925 by President Calvin Coolidge on the recommendation of Senator George Warton Pepper. There were a number of protests at the time. His minor crimes in office included making federal employees rent from him and perform work in his home, and setting up the Spring Lodge, a hunting lodge which Judge Johnson coerced lawyers into joining for $500 each. Johnson's major crimes included demanding and receiving payoffs in receiverships and bankruptcies and payoffs from criminal defendants. Judge Johnson had three sons and two sons-in-law, all of whom were lawyers.

Judge Johnson's bagmen: **Jacob Greens** was a beer salesman. **John Memolo**, local counsel for the receivers, was a small-town lawyer and part-time farmer. **H. W. Mumford** was Bethlehem Steel's local lawyer.

Committee on Judiciary, Report on the Official Conduct of Albert W. Johnson and Albert L. Watson

House of Representatives 1639, Feb. 25, 1946, 79th Cong. 2nd Session.

OFFICIAL CONDUCT OF ALBERT W. JOHNSON AND ALBERT L. WATSON, DISTRICT JUDGES OF THE UNITED STATES DISTRICT COURT FOR THE MIDDLE DISTRICT OF PENNSYLVANIA

Mr. KEFAUVER, from the Committee on the Judiciary, submitted the following

REPORT

[Pursuant to H. Res. 138]

* * *

WILLIAMSPORT WIRE ROPE CO.

The Williamsport Wire Rope Co. was a Pennsylvania corporation engaged from 1887 in the manufacture of wire rope and strand. Its principal place of business was located at Williamsport, Pa. A great portion of its stock, both common and preferred, was owned by the people of that community, especially by those employed in the company plant.

In 1926 the Bethlehem Steel Co. purchased 2,000 of the 9,380 shares of common stock and arranged a loan of $133,000 to Robert Gilmore, the new president of the Williamsport company. With this purchase the Bethlehem Steel Co. obtained from the Williamsport company an exclusive purchasing agreement for 90 percent of the Williamsport company's steel requirements for a 10–year period. Bethlehem Steel was interested in expanding the Williamsport company's business, and in 1927 Bethlehem Steel Co.'s officials prevailed upon the National City Co. of New York to float a mortgage bond issue for the Williamsport company in the amount of $1,221,000. The money was to refinance the Williamsport company and provide for the expansion of its plant.

During the depression the Williamsport Co. became involved financially, and in the spring of 1932 was in difficult need of working capital. In September of 1932 Bethlehem Steel officials arranged for the filing of a creditor's bill in equity against the Williamsport Co. in the Federal Court for the middle district of Pennsylvania. The bill was filed September 16, 1932, in the name of Guaranty Trust Co. of New York, a creditor on an unsecured note in the sum of $211,789. This, the Williamsport Co. was led to believe, was a friendly suit and was filed with its consent. The bill alleged that the Williamsport Co. was solvent, that its properties had a fair valuation considerably in excess of the amount of its liabilities, but that it was unable to secure funds necessary to meet its obligations that were due or about to become due. It prayed for the appointment of receivers and for the administration of the property in the usual form of a creditor's bill. The receivership was an involved proceeding covering the period from September 1932 to December 1938. Two plans of reorganization were filed, and a foreclosure was instituted with numerous motions and hearings.

Hoyt A. Moore, senior member of the New York law firm of Cravath, deGersdorff, Swaine & Wood (now Cravath, Swaine & Moore), general counsel for Bethlehem Steel Co., was in charge of the proceedings for Bethlehem Steel. He arranged to have a Williamsport attorney, Oliver J. Decker, file the bill for the Guaranty Trust Co. Decker reported to Moore that Judge Johnson wanted the judge's son-in-law, Carl A. Schug, appointed one of the receivers and had suggested that the bill be presented to Judge J. Warren Davis of the Third Circuit. Moore testified that Bethlehem wanted Charles M. Ballard, vice president and sales manager of the Williamsport Co., as receiver, and assumed that the court would also appoint Robert Gilmore, president, as coreceiver. To his knowledge, no creditor or any other party in interest in the cause requested or desired the appointment of Schug. Judge Davis appointed Gilmore, Ballard, and Schug as receivers. Three days later Judge Johnson appointed Decker as attorney for the receivers. On October 24, 1932, Judge Johnson fixed the compensation of the three receivers, including his son-in-law, and their attorney, Decker, at $1,000 each a month.

A reputable New York accounting firm, Arthur Anderson & Co., was appointed by Judge Johnson to audit the Williamsport Co.'s books as of September 19, 1932. This audit reflects assets of $7,534,375, and the following liabilities:

First-mortgage 6–percent bonds	$1,221,000.00
Notes payable (Guaranty Trust Co., New York; Baltimore Trust Co., Baltimore; Philadelphia National Bank, Philadelphia)	628,676.01
Accounts payable (due principally to Bethlehem Steel Co.)	749,302.63
Accrued liabilities	66,903.79
Total	2,665,882.43

Cash on hand amounted to only $11,113.28.

On March 3, 1933, Judge Johnson vacated his order fixing compensation for the receivers and their attorney, on his own motion, without giving any reason therefor. The receivers and the attorney then applied to the circuit court for the fixing of fees. At a hearing held on the fees Judge Joseph Buffington, of the circuit court, sitting with Judge Davis, expressed surprise at the request for an allowance of $1,000 a month to Carl Schug, considering that he was an attorney without knowledge of the wire-rope business. He pointed out that at $1,000 a month, Schug would be earning more than a circuit-court judge. He asked whether an attempt was being made to have the circuit court approve the appointment of Judge Johnson's son-in-law by getting it to fix his fee. On the following day Schug resigned. This was all made known to Hoyt A. Moore at the time.

On June 16, 1933, Judges Buffington and Davis referred, in an order, to the profitable operation of the plant and observed that

> shortly the management of the corporation may with advantage be restored to the stockholders and officers thereof, it further appearing that in recognition of this situation the third receiver, Carl A. Schug, has tendered his resignation.

Compensation for the two continuing receivers was fixed at $1,000 a month, and that of their attorney at $500 a month. On June 29, 1933, Judge Buffington signed an order assigning the conduct of the receivership to Judge Johnson. By September 30, 1933, the receivers had accumulated cash on hand in the sum of $173,636.35.

On April 3, 1934, Judge Johnson, on his own motion, while an investigation of his official conduct was in process, issued an order for a hearing for a progress report on the receivership. Decker told Moore that it was rumored that the judge intended to appoint a receiver to replace Schug. By letter dated April 7, 1934, Moore wrote to Decker as follows:

> I, too, am surprised by Judge Johnson's order. It is almost unthinkable that he, having gotten the favorable decision from the Attorney Gener-

al which you mention in your letter, and having had power handed back to him by the judges of the circuit court of appeals, as covered by the letter which is set forth in the copy of the order which you enclosed with your letter, Judge Johnson would propose now to go back to the practices of which he was accused as improper. Such, however, may be the case. If it is, then the only thing that I can think of is that he might appoint another receiver.

(The favorable decision referred to was an exoneration after a previous investigation of his official conduct.)

On April 26, 1934, Judge Johnson, notwithstanding the order of Judges Buffington and Davis of June 16, appointed Delmar K. Townsend additional receiver at the same compensation of $1,000 a month.

Under date of May 2, 1934, Moore wrote to Decker:

Absence from my office since Saturday has delayed me in acknowledging receipt of your letter of the 27th ultimo, wherein you advised me of the appointment by Judge Johnson of a third receiver for the Wire Rope Co.

I am not surprised by Judge Johnson's action, although it seems to me that it is quite unnecessary. As I see it, the opportunity had presented itself. Apparently the judge could not refrain from embracing it.

Miller A. Johnson, another son of Judge Johnson, called Townsend to the courthouse at Lewisburg, Pa., for a conference. He told Townsend that Donald M. Johnson and Albert W. Johnson, Jr., two other sons of Judge Johnson, were in some financial difficulty, and he asked Townsend to agree to give half of his compensation as receiver to them. (These three sons of Judge Johnson all were lawyers.) Miller Johnson said it should be paid "in cash" to Albert, Jr. Townsend paid in cash, to Albert W. Johnson, Jr., one-half of his fees as receiver from April 1934 to August 1937. Townsend's fees for that period amounted to approximately $42,443.55. Although from time to time he withheld payments sufficient to cover income taxes, he estimated that he paid Albert W. Johnson, Jr., approximately $17,000.

At about the time the receivership started, a Bondholders Protective Committee was organized through the efforts of Bethlehem Steel Co. Joseph P. Ripley, a former official of the National City Co., was chairman, and John M. Fisher, a former employee of National City Co., was secretary. On July 21, 1933, Fisher submitted a memorandum to Ripley containing the following:

The [National] City Co. was brought into this picture by Bethlehem Steel. It was a piece of financing we could not ordinarily have undertaken but, because of its sponsorship, we undertook it and naturally we assumed that Bethlehem would keep "parental eye" on the situation. In the light of subsequent events, it is evident that Bethlehem let the management of the company run wild, maybe intentionally. The mortgage bondholders are the sufferers, and the moral obligation which Bethlehem had, thus has been thrown into the discard and, in fact, it has never even been acknowledged. They are now trying to obtain the company for as small a price as possible, and it is felt by us, and rightly so, that maybe they should not get away with it.

Through the Bondholders Protective Committee, Bethlehem Steel submitted a plan of reorganization which provided for an exchange of securities as follows: $700 of Bethlehem securities for each $1,000 Williamsport bonds, and $433 of Bethlehem securities for each $1,000 of unsecured claims. It made no provision for preferred or common stockholders. Subsequently, for the purpose of blocking a plan of reorganization sponsored by the stockholders, the Bethlehem Steel Co. bought the bonds on deposit with the Bondholders Protective Committee for $700 cash, thus obtaining over 90 percent of Williamsport's outstanding bonds.

While Judge Johnson took jurisdiction and accepted the supervision of the proposed plan of reorganization, it never was moved for adoption, and he subsequently stated that it was not acceptable. Johnson stated that

> The Bethlehem plan ... does not fairly and equitably provide for the interests of the bondholders, creditors, or stockholders, and would not be approved by the court in its present form.

On April 12, 1935, in an opinion, Judge Johnson stated that the assets of the company, exclusive of good will, were in excess of $4,000,000 with secured and unsecured debts amounting to about $2,600,000:

> It therefore appears there is an equity in favor of the stockholders. In view of this equity, any plan of reorganization that does not adequately provide for the stockholders should not be acceptable.

This indicated an equity in favor of stockholders of at least $1,400,000 after all claims are paid in full.

On May 29, 1935, Judge Johnson appointed a Scranton attorney, John Memolo, as associate counsel for the receivers, at $500 a month. The order of appointment recited that the receivers and their counsel had been consulted and had approved the appointment. The evidence is overwhelming that there was no such consultation or approval, and that no petition was filed requesting additional counsel. Townsend testified that there was no need for this appointment. Memolo testified before the committee that he had obtained his appointment through Jacob Greenes, as he had in an earlier case, upon an agreement to split half of his fee with Greenes. In fact, on June 3, 1935, a few days after this appointment, Memolo paid Greenes $2,500 on account of the fee split, and subsequently gave him an additional $1,600 for the same purpose. Both payments are evidenced by cashier's drafts, bearing both of their endorsements. Memolo also paid Greenes other sums out of his Williamsport fees, or in anticipation of fees, for a total payment of approximately $34,000. Greenes corroborated the agreement, the receipt of the split fees, and payment of the "split" to Donald Johnson. Greenes further testified that Memolo's appointment was suggested and arranged by Donald Johnson, son of Judge Johnson, upon condition that Memolo split his fees 50-50.

On August 28, 1935, Memolo and Decker, attorneys for the receivers, petitioned Judge Johnson for an increase of compensation to $1,000 a month. Judge Johnson granted that, making it retroactive to July 1, 1935. Memolo testified before the committee that the increase was at Greenes' suggestion, and that he, Memolo, specifically urged against its being made retroactive.

When the receivers, Ballard and Gilmore, learned of the increase granted the attorneys they were provoked, because the attorneys were devoting only part time to the receivership, while the receivers themselves actually were operating the business for the same fee of $1,000 a month. They were ready to quit, but Townsend urged them not to do so. They then asked him to speak to Judge Johnson about increasing their monthly allowance. Townsend conferred with the judge about the attitude of Gilmore and Ballard, but told him that he considered himself well compensated and was not seeking an increase for himself. Judge Johnson then directed that all three salaries be increased to $1,500 a month. Albert W. Johnson, Jr., who had been receiving half of Townsend's monthly $1,000 compensation, now collected half of his $1,500 monthly fee.

Meanwhile the receivership was being operated successfully. As of July 1, 1936, the receivers had accumulated cash on hand in the sum of $734,148.34. Neither litigation nor appeal were pending at that time, and the future of the Williamsport Wire Rope Co. looked promising. On July 8, 1936, in open court, Judge Johnson told stockholders that he had supervised personally the operation of the receivership and expressed great pride in its accomplishments. He pointed out that there was over $700,000 in the treasury, although the receivers had started with practically nothing in cash; that an additional factory had been bought by the receivers for $87,000, which had been paid for in cash; that the plant was running at full blast; that it had been kept modern by the receivers; that new and improved machinery had been installed; that all back taxes had been paid; that bills had been kept current; and that orders and production were increasing. * * *

It is quite obvious from the remarks of the judge made on July 8, 1936, as to the cash position of the company, and the figures submitted by Dershem, that a feasible plan of reorganization was possible. Furthermore, Dershem pointed out that on September 21, 1936, $600,000 out of the $777,763 cash on hand was immediately available to apply on the complete debt. Obviously, any substantial reduction of the debt would have entitled the company to borrow, or to refund its obligations, even if at the time it could not pay off in full out of earnings. Yet Judge Johnson never took any action on the information furnished by Dershem. Neither creditors nor bondholders were consulted on these proposed plans of reorganization. In fact, there was no discussion or consideration of any reorganization from that time on.

The record shows that shortly thereafter Bethlehem caused the foreclosure of the mortgage, securing the bonds it had purchased at 70 cents on the dollar, and that Judge Johnson ordered the sale of the property. He confirmed the sale price of $3,300,000 to Bethlehem, thereby wiping out the preferred and common stockholders. Bethlehem came to the sale prepared to bid four and a half million dollars, which in the opinion of the judge, dated April 12, 1935, created approximately the equity which he had indicated the stockholders had, exclusive of good will. A rather ridiculous feature of the sale was that the assets sold included over $1,000,000 in cash and that the bond issue under which the foreclosure was prosecuted amounted to $1,221,000. As part of the purchase price, Bethlehem turned in for full credit $1,174,000 par value in Williamsport bonds which it had acquired at 70 cents on the dollar, and $541,742, the principal amount of notes which it had acquired from other creditors during the receivership at 49 cents on the dollar. These items, plus its own open account and accrued interest on all items, required Bethlehem to make an outlay of only $89,000 on the $3,300,000 bid.

The reason for this sudden liquidation at the expense of the Williamsport stockholders, when the company was about to work itself out, was clearly established to have been due to the corrupt connivance of John Memolo, attorney for the receivers; Hoyt A. Moore, attorney for Bethlehem Steel Co.; Judge Johnson; and his son, Donald Johnson; while Robert E. McMath, for Bethlehem Steel Co., bought off certain opposition.

John Memolo offered his service to Bethlehem Steel Co. through Hoyt A. Moore to influence Judge Johnson to terminate the proceedings in Bethlehem's favor in consideration of the payment of approximately $250,000 to cover "administration" expenses to be paid out under Memolo's direction, of which $210,000 was to be divided among Memolo, Greenes, Donald Johnson, and the Judge.

The sale was scheduled for May 12, 1937, but was postponed until May 20 because of objections raised by stockholders to the form of the decree of sale. On May 17, 1937, Donald Johnson telephoned Judge Johnson's law clerk, Houck, to ascertain whether the opinion on this motion was filed, and instructed Houck not to file it until "the boss" (Judge Johnson) said so. Later the same day Donald Johnson instructed Houck to mail the opinion by special delivery to Judge Johnson in New York. As the opinion dismissed the objections of the stockholders, the sale could have proceeded on May 20, 1937. However, Judge Johnson postponed the sale until May 27. He did not file his opinion until May 26, thus providing an opportunity for Memolo to confer with Moore on May 18, 19, and 25.

During this interval Greenes suggested to Memolo that Bethlehem Steel should put a substantial part of the "administration expenses" in a safe deposit box with keys to be held by Memolo and Moore. Memolo insisted that this was not necessary, but he passed it on to Moore. Moore refused to adopt this procedure, saying, "Well, I'll be damned if I'll listen to a thing like that. No one can put a gun to my temple." Memolo offered to have him meet Judge Johnson, who was then in New York. Moore again declined, with the comment that he didn't want to meet anyone, and that "these country judges were always trying to hold someone up." During the course of the negotiations Moore told H. W. Mumford, one of Bethlehem's officials, that Memolo wanted to be paid in cash, but that it couldn't be done that way. The nature of the relationship between Bethlehem Steel Co.

and Memolo may well be gaged by the testimony of H. W. Mumford to the effect that on July 27, 1936, he discussed with McMath whether John Memolo was a "bagman for Judge Johnson."

Memolo made a bargain with Moore, and accomplished the desired result. He told Moore that he was prepared to assist Bethlehem. They discussed "administration" expenses, which Memolo said "ought to run in the neighborhood of $250,000." Moore replied that he "had estimated himself between $150,000 and $200,000, but that $250,000 was not excessive and it was not objectionable to him." Memolo, further referring to Moore, said: "I told him that whatever they would require to put the property ultimately under sale would be taken care of favorably." "Well, I told Moore that there was a certain little Jew boy—pretty smart, that was able to do things and get things done in that court." He was referring to Jacob Greenes, Donald Johnson's friend. Memolo fixed the date of the conversation as "it wasn't so very much before the foreclosure, nor was it so very long after my first meeting with him." He added, "Oh, we had a number of conversations before the bill was filed because I believe that I did see Mr. Moore during the course of the preparation of the pleadings, the bill and incidental matters, at least 1 or 2 days in each week for a period of over a year and a half or two." He admitted helping prepare the petition to make the receivers party defendant, and the bill to foreclose. He also prepared the receivers' answer opposing both the petition and the bill. Before ordering the sale, Judge Johnson asked Memolo if he would take care of "the boys" out of the fund which Bethlehem had agreed to pay. Memolo agreed, and the decree was signed.

The receivers and stockholders of the Williamsport Wire Rope Co. filed answers in opposition to the foreclosure, setting up that Bethlehem was not a bona fide holder of Williamsport bonds and that by its recent purchase of preferred stock at $40 a share, it thereby admitted the stockholders' equity. It was alleged that Bethlehem had also purchased Williamsport common stock at $10 a share, and that to foreclose would make it possible for Bethlehem to make a huge profit at the expense of stockholders and creditors. The court's attention was called to the fact that the receivership was operating at such a profit that within a reasonable length of time it would be able to pay off all bonds and other indebtedness of the company.

On March 27, 1937, J. M. Fisher, secretary of the Bondholders Protective Committee, expressed to Joseph P. Ripley and to Moore's firm his "alarm" at the amount of cash accumulated by the receivers ($923,000), and noted a profit for the last 2 months of 1936 in excess of $102,000. He wrote:

> In the light of the outlook for the company, [it] looks to me as if the time is not far distant when the cash item alone will be sufficient to pay the old bank loans, the old current liabilities, and maybe the present liabilities.

It should be noted that Mr. Fisher's concern was not for the bondholders. The Bondholders Protective Committee having sold all of its bonds to the Bethlehem Steel Co., it no longer represented any creditors of the

Williamsport Co. He realized that the success of the receivership would reflect unfavorably on the Bondholder's Committee sale of the bonds to Bethlehem at $700.

In the face of the ability of the receivership soon to pay off all its obligations and return the plant to its stockholders, Judge Johnson struck out the answers filed by the receivers and stockholders, and ordered the foreclosure sale in a written opinion in which he recited that although all current expenses had been met, almost a million dollars in cash accumulated, additional property acquired, plant and equipment maintained in excellent condition, and enhanced in value, he was not warranted in operating the receivership indefinitely, especially in view of the fact that "a receivership is only temporary and the creditors and bondholders are entitled to their money."

After the sale Memolo, Donald Johnson, and Greenes conferred to decide on a means of distributing the funds to be paid by Bethlehem as a check to Memolo for the entire amount would have been indefensible. It was decided that three persons whom they could control should be appointed as officers of the court in the case as conduits through whom Bethlehem Steel would pay the sum agreed upon. These persons were John W. Crolly, special master; E. J. Maloney, accountant; and Martin Memolo, brother of John Memolo, as agent of the court to oversee the operations of the Williamsport plant while in Bethlehem's control pending the appeal of the stockholders. Judge Johnson in pursuance of the conference made the appointments agreed upon.

It is of interest to note that although the decree of foreclosure named John Taylor as special master to conduct the sale, receive and allow claims against the estate, prepare a schedule for distribution, and make such distribution as the court would thereafter direct, Judge Johnson, after conferring with Memolo and Donald Johnson, named Crolly, an office associate of Memolo, as special master to make distribution. Taylor was required and did turn over the cash deposited for the sale and the list of allowed claims to Crolly for distribution. Bethlehem Steel subsequently paid Crolly for his services in the sum of $30,850.01, most of which he in turn delivered to Memolo. He did get about $1,000 for his services. Greenes and Donald Johnson had promised Crolly that for his cooperation Judge Johnson would appoint him referee in bankruptcy. This was subsequently done. Martin Memolo's duties as agent of the court have been described as that of a "watchman." Ostensibly he was to protect the assets of the Wire Rope Co. while in Bethlehem's control pending the appeal. There appears to be no reason why the receivers or any one of them could not have been retained at $1,000 a month for that purpose.

J. V. Ferguson, superintendent of the wire-rope plant for Bethlehem Steel Co., testified that he did not know what services Martin Memolo had performed and had never been questioned by Bethlehem Steel Co. officials in that regard. Notwithstanding these facts, Bethlehem Steel Co. paid Martin Memolo the sum of $66,990 for less than 9 months' work, which is understandable only in connection with the agreement between Moore and

Memolo on the cost of administration. John Memolo admits that this sum was turned over to him by his brother for "safekeeping."

E. J. Maloney was appointed to audit the accounts of the receivers from September 1932 to August 1937, although the books had already been audited by order of the court up to July 1, 1936. Correspondence between Decker and Moore discloses that Moore was at one point considering closing out the case without an audit, or upon a brief audit, and that Judge Johnson had been so informed by Decker. Upon the approval of John Memolo, Bethlehem paid Maloney for his services the sum of $31,750 by check, which Bethlehem mailed to Memolo. After Maloney endorsed the check Memolo gave him $1,200, plus the money to pay the income tax on the $31,750 for the work done on the audit. Memolo retained the balance. Apparently neither Bethlehem nor the Cravath firm were interested in how the money was distributed, because they raised none of the obvious objections to these three appointments.

On July 9, 1938, a conference was held by Judge Johnson with the receivers, their attorneys, and H. W. Mumford, representing Bethlehem Steel Co., for consideration of additional final compensation to the court officers for their services in the receivership. The judge stated that he considered $5,000 as adequate additional final compensation for each of them and suggested that Bethlehem Steel further might cancel the indebtedness of Ballard and Gilmore to the Wire Rope Co. Moore's letter to Decker shows he knew that this conference was to be held, and Mumford reported the results of the conference to Moore. Since Judge Johnson knew that Bethlehem had agreed upon a stipulated amount out of which all administration fees were to be paid, it is quite obvious that the purpose of this conference was to fix at a low figure the fees of the court officers not in the deal in order to leave a large balance for division with the Johnsons. To carry out the scheme the judge fixed Memolo's fee also at $5,000 with the others. Bethlehem Steel paid him the $5,000 by separate check and later voluntarily paid him the balance, totaling $81,084.99. This was in addition to approximately $18,000 paid out of the estate by order of the judge in interim allowances to Memolo during the receivership.

These off-the-record fees were made possible by the form of the decree of sale, which provided that the successful bidder would have to pay the costs of administration in addition to the price bid, to be fixed by the judge only in the event the parties could not agree privately. Stockholders objected to these provisions of the decree on the ground that it would stifle bidding, since a prospective bidder would have no idea of how much the administration expenses might total. Judge Johnson dismissed this objection on the ground that the fees would be an "inconsequential" amount. The decree in that form was drafted by Moore's firm apparently with the intention that they could thereby cover up the payment by Bethlehem Steel of approximately $210,000 to John Memolo.

As to these payments some interesting comparisons may be made as follows:

The Cravath firm, which prepared practically all pleadings, briefs, appeal briefs, and papers for the bondholders protective committee, Bethlehem Steel Co., and the trustee (National City Bank) in foreclosure, from September 1932 to December 1938, billed Bethlehem Steel Co. for its services $125,209.

John Memolo, as co-counsel for the receivers, from May 1, 1935, to December 1938, was paid directly $98,000. Oliver J. Decker, attorney for the receivers, from September 1932 to December 1938, was paid a total of $40,596.

Arthur Anderson & Co., for audit of the Williamsport Co.'s books at the beginning of the receivership, received $3,500 by order of the judge. Price, Waterhouse & Co., for audit of Bethlehem's acquisition of Williamsport assets, charged $2,500, and was paid by order of the judge. Frank Dershem for audit from September 1932 to June 30, 1936, was paid $8,805 by order of the judge. E. J. Maloney was paid $31,075 by Bethlehem for audit. Martin Memolo, "agent of the court," was paid $66,990 by Bethlehem Steel for less than 8 months' service as "watchman."

Robert E. McMath's annual salary, as secretary of Bethlehem Steel Co., in charge of its financial and law departments, was $60,000. John T. Taylor, special master, who conducted the foreclosure sale, received and passed on all claims against the estate and prepared the statement for distribution, was paid $10,000 by order of Judge Johnson. John W. Crolly, special master, who made the distribution, received $30,850.01 from Bethlehem Steel.

This contrast in the amount of fees paid to syphon the proceeds out of the agreed cost of administration with those paid for work actually performed is extreme indeed.

Moore and McMath say there is nothing unusual about the payment or the amount of these fees. McMath insists the fees were paid on Moore's recommendation. Moore in turn denies that fees or administration expenses were discussed with Memolo prior to the sale, although admitting that he may have set $250,000 as the top figure to cover administration expenses. Moore's files were found to be strangely bare of evidence of negotiations of these fees, although considerable correspondence and memoranda relating to the settlement of the fee for the attorney for the foreclosing trustee were found. For approximately 6 years Moore kept memoranda concerning those fees in his personal desk, apart from the regular office files. These notations made by Moore at the time, show that $250,000 was fixed as the figure to cover the fees of the court appointees, and that Memolo's direct share was the residue of that fund. The fees of Crolly, Maloney, and Martin Memolo were negotiated by John Memolo with Moore, and Moore's personal file contains small slips of paper which had been attached to those bills marked "O. K. J. M." Moore admits that this indicated that Memolo had approved the amount of the bills. He said that the determination of their propriety had not been delegated by him and could not be, although he offered no explanation of any independent research or consideration. Memolo testified flatly that the "O. K." slips were attached to the bills at Moore's request to bind Memolo to the deduction of these sums from the $250,000. The notations of Moore, the testimony of Greenes and Memolo, establish that the fund of $250,000 was divided as follows:

John T. Taylor	$10,000
Oliver J. Decker	5,000
Delmar K. Townsend	5,000
Charles M. Ballard	5,000
Robert Gilmore	5,000
Reserve for settlement with Robert Gilmore and applied on his debt to Williamsport	10,000
Total	40,000

These persons were not participants in the arrangement between Moore and Memolo.

A total of $203,000 was paid by the issuance of checks to John Memolo and persons controlled by Memolo, and the checks themselves were delivered directly to John Memolo by Hoyt A. Moore. That total is made up as follows:

E. J. Maloney	$ 31,075.00
John W. Crolly	30,850.01
Martin Memolo	59,990.00
John Memolo	81,084.99
Total	203,000.00

These two items plus the $7,000 paid by order of Judge Johnson to Martin Memolo make the grand total of $250,000.

On one occasion Memolo prepared an opinion for Judge Johnson. Houck, Judge Johnson's law clerk, characterized such procedure as "quite unusual." Memolo identified his draft of the opinion, found among Judge Johnson's papers submitted as a grand jury exhibit. Memolo also identified a note which he had attached to the draft, which reads in part as follows: "This is a draft for order to dismiss the petition to require Bethlehem to submit a plan of reorganization; this must be done in order to carry out the distribution of the proceeds of sale. Unless the petition is dismissed the distribution cannot be made nor the case wound up." It is obvious that the concern is for "distribution", and not for the merits of the petition. The four-page draft of the opinion as submitted by Memolo and the signed opinion filed by the judge are identical.

The testimony shows that Memolo suppressed the facts even from Greenes and the Johnsons by indicating that the stipulated sum was for only $150,000. He also failed to split as he originally had agreed to do. For a long time he told Greenes and Judge Johnson that he had not received the final payments from Bethlehem. Memolo testified that in January or February, 1939, Judge Johnson had asked him how much he had paid Greenes, and that he later had furnished the judge with a tabulating-machine tape showing payments totaling $34,000. Although the judge had indicated some surprise at the total, he had made no comment. At that time Judge Johnson requested Memolo to pay the balance to him directly, and suggested that Memolo was entitled to retain only one-third instead of 50 percent.

Judge Johnson categorically denies any improper conduct or action on his part in this case and denies knowledge of any deal or the receipt of any money. An examination of his books and records shows that for the years 1935, 1936, 1937, 1938, and 1939, he had at least $24,830 in cash in excess of his salary or other explained income. He has given no satisfactory explanation of this cash. During the year 1934 he had no funds in excess of known income. To offset the obvious implication of this evidence, Judge Johnson testified that he had "a tin box" containing $20,000 which he had saved prior to his appointment as a Federal judge in 1925, and suggested that the unexplained cash may also have come from honorariums paid him for making speeches to high schools, patriotic organizations, and clubs, which he estimated totaled $2,000 a year. An examination of his books and records shows that for an 11–year period, 1934–44, his total receipts for making speeches did not exceed $211. Of 200 such speeches that he claimed to have made, he was able to furnish the committee with the name of only a single organization that paid him.

There was convincing testimony that in July 1938, Memolo paid $6,000 to Greenes out of a $25,000 payment from Bethlehem Steel to Martin Memolo. Memolo stated that Greenes told him this money was to be used by Judge Johnson to buy a summer home. Donald Johnson got the $6,000 share of Martin Memolo's fee. A deed for Judge Johnson's summer home at Cherry Run, Pa., is dated the same day on which Martin Memolo's check was cashed, July 22, 1938. Judge Johnson testified that all he paid on that contract was $250 and that the deed was received by him through the mail. He thought that the balance of the purchase price of $5,750 was paid or canceled because of his aid to the seller and another man in acquiring an adjacent piece of property. In the 7 years after the receipt of the deed he had never ascertained who his benefactor was. The seller, however, has testified that he received the full $6,000 from Judge Johnson's attorney, who is now deceased. It would be difficult to come to any other conclusion than that the $6,000 share of Martin Memolo's fee was the purchase price of the Cherry Run property.

Reference has been made to the fact that during the proceedings Bethlehem Steel Co. bought off certain opposition. The evidence is that Bethlehem Steel Co. entered into a contract in December 1935 to pay Lee Warren James $45,600 to withdraw his opposition to Bethlehem and to influence George W. Hartke, comptroller, and Robert Gilmore, receiver, to obtain discontinuance of certain litigation that obstructed Bethlehem's plans. Bethlehem later settled with James for $15,000, since he had not been entirely successful.

In November 1936, Robert E. McMath, secretary of Bethlehem Steel Co., promised to pay Charles M. Ballard, then one of the receivers of the Williamsport Co., compensation in addition to that which he would receive from the court, to cancel Ballard's debt of $14,000 to the Williamsport Co. (this was before the bill of foreclosure was filed) and to arrange a loan for him through a Philadelphia bank with which he could pay off another debt. This additional compensation which Bethlehem paid to Ballard totaled approximately $49,000. After the receivership Ballard was retained in a lucrative position by Bethlehem Steel. Bethlehem Steel paid George W. Hartke $34,255 for his services, canceled his indebtedness of $15,144 to the Williamsport Co., and purchased his home (which Bethlehem had valued at $12,000) for $20,000. Hartke was paid $6,000 while employed by the receivers.

The highest price paid publicly by Bethlehem Steel for Williamsport Wire Rope preferred stock was $40. Moore and McMath, however, purchased the stock of Mrs. Edward S. Lyon for $45 a share. Moore's records identify Mrs. Lyon as the mother-in-law of Albert W. Johnson, Jr. This stock was purchased after the foreclosure sale and at a time when McMath told other holders of preferred stock that it was worthless.

Because he withdrew himself as a witness and signed a waiver of all his rights and privileges of retirement, Judge Johnson was not examined by the committee as to his conduct in the Williamsport Wire Rope receivership.

Your committee is of the opinion that the evidence presented in the foregoing cases establishes conclusively that Judge Albert W. Johnson is guilty of such high crimes and misdemeanors as in the contemplation of the Constitution ordinarily require the interposition of the constitutional powers of impeachment of the House; that in the actual administration of justice between private individuals, corporate entities, and the Government and its citizens, he was guilty over a long number of years of such misconduct as to constitute a continuing impeachable offense; that such judicial misconduct was manifested during the exercise of his judicial authority, in the discharge of his judicial duties in his official judicial capacity. . . .

Here, indeed, are presented derelictions from standards of judicial rectitude and canons of judicial ethics to shock the conscience of all honest citizens—lay as well as members of the bench and the bar. Albert W. Johnson was appointed to the federal bench in 1925. Almost from the beginning of his tenure, as disclosed in the Mount Jessup Coal Co. case, he entered into a conspiracy against justice that was to continue in increasing degree until the investigation undertaken by this committee forced him to resign and waive all the privileges and rights to which his exalted position and his long tenure as a judicial officer otherwise entitled him.

These derelictions and this conspiracy are all the more flagrant and culpable in that they were participated in, or perhaps initiated by, the judge's own son, Donald, and later shared in by two other sons all members of the bar and all admitted to practice before their father in a Federal court. Bankruptcy, a system adopted by the Government of the United States to aid unfortunate individuals and corporations to liquidate their debts and begin anew their existence, especially those aspects intended by reorganization and receivership to keep potentially solvent concerns alive and in operation until they can work out of temporary financial difficulties, were among the major causes that fell afoul of the cupidity of this Federal judge. In those cases an evil, wicked, and malicious intent appears to have accompanied all his judgments, opinions, decrees, and orders. Certainly that appears to be true of those presented herein. He appears to have been motivated by a wicked endeavor to subvert the statutes enacted by Congress for the benefit of potentially solvent debtors, or at least he found such cases to offer opportunity to satisfy his own cupidity as well as that of his son, Donald, and his coconspirators. He did so at times under the color of judicial authority and propriety. . . .

There is evidence before your committee to show that petitioners in bankruptcy desirous of continuing their operations under owner management in order to avoid burdensome administration costs often found themselves saddled with all the expenses and fees of trustees, appraisers, and other court officers arbitrarily, suddenly, and unexpectedly appointed by Judge Johnson. Indeed, the evidence shows that even creditors complained against such appointments in cases in which their confidence in the debtor was such as to request that the operations be continued by the debtor in order to prevent the excessive costs of administration. Yet such appointments were made and the appointees were among the inner circle who in previous cases had demonstrated their willingness to participate in the conspiracy and share the loot. And the evidence shows further that when these sharks had received their looted fees and compensation there frequently was so little operating capital left that survival of the estate thereafter was but short-lived. . . .

Many of the bankruptcy cases that came before Judge Johnson naturally were those involving corporations. Corporate enterprise has become increasingly general. Although it appears from the evidence that individual citizens involved in bankruptcy usually were at the mercy of this court, it is even more apparent that corporations so involved were regarded as fit prey. Perhaps the Johnsons and their coconspirators looked upon corporations as soulless and, therefore, meriting destruction at their hands. The evidence shows certainly that they had but little regard for those provisions of the bankruptcy laws enacted by Congress for the conservation and preservation and the revival of temporarily bankrupt concerns. Their obsession for pillage and plunder appears to have overshadowed all else. The evidence shows further and conclusively that they were not loathe to enter into conspiracy with the agents, officers, and attorneys of competitor corporations in order to bring about any liquidation or absorption that might prove of profit to themselves. And when the judge's sons were unavailable or otherwise inappropriate to aid in such conspiracies, the judge nevertheless kept the benefits within the family circle by arranging for the appointment of a son-in-law, at a compensation at times of $1,000 a month.

Regardless of any conclusions concerning the soullessness of corporations, it will not be contended seriously that Judge Johnson was divinely appointed to crush them. Certainly it will not be contended that he was appointed divinely or otherwise to crush thousands of innocent and often otherwise impecunious stockholders and bondholders who because of their faith in the free enterprise and independent industry of America often had invested their life savings in these institutions. Yet that was notoriously the effect of some of his decrees and orders. The evidence before your committee shows it conclusively. Protective committees, either of little bondholders or little stockholders, had but slight chance against the unscrupulous conspirators who operated in and out of this court. Despite occasional judicial pretense there apparently never was any real or honest intent to provide either fairly or equitably for the interests of bondholders, stockholders, or creditors. The sole intent, the sole motive, appears at all times to have been only that of booty, or graft, or plunder. . . .

Subsequent Developments

In 1945, Judge Johnson resigned his judicial office and pension after a single day of hearings before a subcommittee of the House Judiciary Committee charged with investigating his corrupt handling of ten cases—all bankruptcies, receiverships, or reorganizations. Johnson and his bagmen, Memolo and Greenes, were tried in 1947 for conspiracy to defraud the United States. Greenes and Memolo refused to testify against Judge Johnson and were convicted. Johnson was acquitted, returned to law practice and was elected president of his local bar association. John T. Noonan, Jr., BRIBES 573 (1984).

Hoyt Moore also would have been tried in 1947, but the charges were dismissed under a three-year statute of limitations. None of the New York City bar associations brought disciplinary charges against him. The Cravath Firm, which had become Cravath, Swaine, and Moore in 1944, retains his name to this day. See id. at 574.

NOTES AND QUESTIONS

As Learned Hand discovered shortly after his appointment as a federal district judge in 1909, the legions of lawyers seeking favors can be deeply troubling for a judge. Hand, faced with many of the same temptations as Judge Johnson, responded very differently, but could not conceal his disdain for those who constantly sought to chip away at his integrity:

Early in June, [Hand] was assigned to handle bankruptcy cases for the first time—cases that produced more than half of his written opinions during his first year on the bench. After a day of it, he reported to his mother, "I seem to be all tired out, but I have recovered now, and I think that after a little I shall get along well." Promptly, his mother asked who was responsible for heaping such difficult work upon him. "It is not that the bankruptcy cases are more difficult to decide than others," he replied patiently, "only there are so many of them, and I get mixed up; and besides that, I am constantly interrupted by people who come in asking usually for what they ought not to have." All he had tried to say, he explained, was that "the strain of four hours' attention to one thing after another and being talked at continually was very wearing, but I think that was only because it was the first, and I am enjoying it a great deal." In his passing remark about interruptions by those "asking usually for what they ought not to have," Hand tried to make light of a problem that in fact he took very seriously. When creditors of insolvent businesses asked a court to appoint a receiver to manage and wind up the insolvent's estate, federal judges traditionally appointed private lawyers. Appointment as a receiver was considered a plum by attorneys eager to supplement their incomes, and political pressures on judges to appoint loyal clubhouse workers were a routine aspect of the patronage system.

Hand was the rare judge who had not been appointed because of his political connections, but he was not exempt from these pressures. As he wrote to C.C. Burlingham, more frankly than he had to his mother: "I wish some benevolent person would abolish the power to appoint receivers and substitute standing receivers [permanent functionaries], like the referees. I find that I have about half my time taken up by obsequious gentlemen who come in with letters either from [Congressman] Herbert Parsons, who did the best be could to keep me out, or the politicians to whom my appointment must be equally grateful." For years, Hand struggled with these annoying requests for political favors. He tried his best to appoint receivers only on the basis of merit, and he repeatedly pressed for reform of the system, without success.

Gerald Gunther, Learned Hand: The Man and the Judge 137–38 (1994).

1. The Committee Report on the conduct of Judge Johnson mentions Bethlehem's purchase of 2,000 of the 9,380 shares of Williamsport, putting Bethlehem well on its way to being Williamsport's dominant shareholder. Bethlehem also received a contract to be the exclusive purchasing agent for Williamsport and arranged a $133,000 loan to the President of Williamsport.

(a) Even though the stock sale, the exclusive purchasing agreement, and the loan were not illegal, should the conflict of interest created by these transactions have alerted Bethlehem's lawyers that Bethlehem was putting itself in a position to abuse its relationship with Williamsport?

(b) Was Hoyt Moore good at anticipating when ethical problems were likely to arise? If so, did he care?

(c) Do these early developments suggest that conflicts of interest and abuses of power, if tolerated by lawyers and businesspeople, tend to foster new conflicts and abuses of power?

2. What was the ratio of Williamsport's assets to liabilities at the beginning and at the end of the receivership? What was Williamsport's cash position? Was a liquidation of Williamsport's assets at the expense of the preferred and common stockholders necessary? Was Bethlehem taking advantage of the situation? How?

3. Judge Johnson's sons were all three lawyers. What was their role in the Williamsport Wire and Rope case? In what other case in this chapter did a lawyer misuse his father's role as a judge?

4. Judge Johnson clearly looked after the material well being of his sons. Was he a better father than he was a judge?

5. Do the events in this case suggest a need for rules against fee splitting? See Model Rule 1.5 (e); Model Code, DR 2–107 (A), Chapter 1 supra.

6. The Report concludes that the liquidation was "due to the corrupt connivance of John Memolo, attorney for the receivers; Hoyt A. Moore, attorney for Bethlehem Steel Co.; Judge Johnson; and his son, Donald Johnson; while Robert E. McMath, for Bethlehem Steel Co., bought off certain opposition." What specifically was the role of each of these persons in what happened and how did each benefit from his conduct?

7. What specific conduct on Judge Johnson's part was Moore willing to tolerate to secure the objectives of his client, Bethlehem?

8. Hoyt Moore participated in the scheme to bribe Judge Johnson by approving John Memolo's proposal that administration expenses "not exceed $250,000" (an exorbitant amount at the time) and sending Memolo checks totaling $203,000 for the payoffs (Moore kept in his personal files bills for these payments with the notation "O.K. J.M."). Although Moore's files were "strangely bare of evidence," he gave himself away by keeping memoranda documenting these "fees" away from the office files in his own desk. Moore was 67 at the time of this incident. Bethlehem Steel was a longstanding client of his and its legal fees probably were a substantial part of his income. Nonetheless, was money Moore's real motivation? Was he more likely motivated by obsession with serving his client and solving its problems? Is there anything in Swaine's biography of Moore suggesting that he might suffer from tunnel vision and compulsiveness?

9. Swaine observes in the last line of the biographical sketch that "[n]o lawyer ever unreservedly gave more of himself to a client than Hoyt Moore has given to Bethlehem." What did Hoyt Moore give of himself to Bethlehem? Can a lawyer give too much for a client?

10. The first half of Swaine's biography discusses Moore's English and Scottish ancestry, which were typical of Cravath and many other Wall Street firms at the time (see *Lucido v. Cravath*, alleging discrimination against Italians, Catholics and others, Chapter 5 infra). In the Committee Report, Memolo, the alleged "bagman for Judge Johnson," refers to Jacob Greenes not by name but as a "Jew boy, pretty smart, that was able to do things and get things done in that court." Who actually was able to get things done in Judge Johnson's court? What do these selections reveal about how ethnic stereotypes can be used to obfuscate dishonesty and corruption?

11. Why does John Memolo double cross Judge Johnson and tell him that he is only receiving $150,000? Is he indeed a lawyer entirely without ethics?

Relevant Background

Harsh penalties may be imposed on an attorney who knowingly assists a client in conduct that is illegal or fraudulent. In Office of Disciplinary Counsel v. Peter M. Stern, 515 Pa. 68, 526 A.2d 1180 (Pa. 1987), the Supreme Court of Pennsylvania held that facilitation of illegal payment to a union official warranted disbarment. Peter Stern was approached by one of his clients who was having difficulty dealing with a local union. The client asked Stern to deliver $5,000 to the union president to see if he would "back off" from his position opposing any concessions in labor negotiations. After initially declining, Stern agreed when the client threatened to seek different legal counsel. The court held that Stern "knew he was being requested to violate the law and made a deliberate decision to do so rather than suffer what he perceived as a setback to his career." Id. at 79, 526 A.2d at 1185.

In another case involving bribery, the Supreme Court of Illinois found that a lawyer, John Leonard, participated in preparation of fraudulent corporate income tax returns and in a scheme to funnel substantial amounts of money as bribes to the late Paul Powell, Secretary of State of Illinois, in connection with a license plate contract. In re John M. Leonard, Jr., 64 Ill.2d 398, 1 Ill.Dec. 62, 356 N.E.2d 62 (1976). Additionally, Leonard maintained a corporate checkbook in which he falsely recorded compensation to employees of the corporation and which he furnished to the accountant who prepared the corporation's income tax forms. The court found that Leonard had a clear duty to dissuade his client from the bribery and tax fraud and at the very least was required to withdraw his services. Id. at 405, 356 N.E.2d at 65, 66. Leonard's conduct, the court found, warranted a suspension for three years.

QUESTION

1. In a particularly bizarre case, Attorney Grievance Commission of Maryland v. Stanley E. Protokowicz, Jr., 329 Md. 252, 619 A.2d 100 (1993), the Court of Appeals of Maryland upheld an order suspending for one year Stanley Protokowicz, an attorney who assisted his client in illegal activities arising out of a divorce proceeding. Protokowicz participated in numerous illegal activities, including breaking into and entering a house belonging to the father of his client's former wife with intent to take materials of evidentiary value in pending divorce litigation, taking items of personal property, and killing the family cat in a microwave oven. The Court found such behavior to be "a world apart from what this Court, the profession, and the public is entitled to expect from members of the bar." Id. at 261, 262, 619 A.2d at 104. Although Protokowicz and Hoyt Moore practiced in very different areas of the law and for very different clients, they may have shared some psychological characteristics. What might these be?

Attorney Liability for Facilitation of Securities Fraud

Lawyers who assist client wrongdoing in securities transactions can be subject not only to disciplinary action, but to suit by investors under federal and state securities laws. For example, under exceptional circumstances a lawyer representing a client selling securities can become a "seller" of the securities, and therefore liable in a suit for misrepresentation under Section 12(2) of the 1933 Securities Act. See Wilson v. Saintine Exploration and Drilling Corp., 872 F.2d 1124, 1126 (2d Cir. 1989) (lawyers for issuer of securities are not "sellers" under Section 12(2) if they perform only their usual professional functions in preparing documents for an offering, "but may be 'sellers' if they actively engage in solicitation of prospective buyers for the securities). Furthermore, state securities laws may deem a lawyer to be the equivalent of a "seller" of securities even if she only performs her normal professional functions in an offering. See Prince v. Brydon, 307 Or. 146, 764 P.2d 1370 (1988) (lawyer for issuer of unregistered securities liable under state law because lawyer substantially assisted in the sale by preparing a tax opinion and other documentation for the transaction).

Courts have held that an attorney must not knowingly assist in a sale of securities that violates the securities laws. See SEC v. Frank, 388 F.2d 486, 489 (2d Cir.1968) (reversing for procedural defects an injunction against an attorney committing future violations of Section 10(b) of the 1934 Act after misrepresentations were discovered in an offering circular drafted in part by the attorney). See SEC v. National Student Marketing Corp., 457 F.Supp. 682 (D.D.C.1978), supra; In re American Continental Corp./Lincoln Savings & Loan Securities Litigation, 794 F.Supp. 1424 (D.Ariz.1992). "An attorney may not continue to provide services to corporate clients when the attorney knows the client is engaged in a course of conduct designed to deceive others, and where it is obvious that the attorney's compliant legal service may be a substantial factor in permitting the deceit to continue." Id. at 1452.

The Supreme Court decided in Central Bank of Denver v. First Interstate Bank, 511 U.S. 164 (1994) that private plaintiffs cannot sue alleged aiders and abetters of violations of the antifraud provisions of the 1934 Securities Exchange Act. However, Section 104 of the 1995 Private Securities Litigation Reform Act specifically gives the SEC authority to prosecute aiders and abetters, including accountants and lawyers. Furthermore, lawyers can still be sued by private plaintiffs for primary violations of the securities laws.

PROBLEMS

1. You represent a United States bank in connection with loans to a multinational corporation that you learn is bribing foreign officials in violation of the Foreign Corrupt Practices Act. You inform loan officers at your client, and they tell you that what the borrower does in other countries is not their concern so long as the bank gets a good interest rate on its loans. Should you continue representing the bank in connection with the loans to this corporation?

2. You represent the owner of a hotel in negotiating a contract for its sale. The purchase and sale agreement specifically states that all fixtures, furniture, machinery, art work and other property located inside the hotel as of noon on the day the agreement is signed shall become the property of the purchaser. You have reason to believe that your client, the seller, will shortly before noon on the day the agreement is signed remove some of the art work from the hotel. At noon, the art work will not be in the hotel and consequently title to the artwork will not pass to the buyer. The agreement is being negotiated in an office several blocks away from the hotel, with signing scheduled for shortly before noon. Your client tells you that you are not to make any representations whatsoever to the buyer about the art work other than what is in the plain language of the agreement. Should you participate in negotiations for sale of the hotel as directed by your client?

D.   LEGAL OPINIONS

Lawyers frequently interpose their own reputations to certify clients' reliability. Indeed, it may be considerably less costly for lawyers to investigate clients' affairs than for third parties to do so. Model Rule 2.3 specifically addresses lawyers' role in selling information *about* their clients as well as services *to* clients by allowing a lawyer, with a client's permission, to "undertake an evaluation of a matter affecting a client for the use of someone other than the client." The Comment to Rule 2.3 points out that the evaluation, while performed at the client's direction, may be for the "primary purpose of establishing information for the benefit of third parties." In such circumstances, "a legal duty to that [third] person may or may not arise." Id.

Formal opinion letters from lawyers and accountants are usually required to close corporate and commercial real-estate financing transactions. The routine lawyer's letter to auditors is another example of lawyers certifying facts about their clients.

Legal opinions can create ethical dilemmas for lawyers, even where they do not create liability. A legally correct opinion from a reputable lawyer may lend legitimacy to an unscrupulous client, even if the opinion concerns an issue as trivial as whether the client is duly incorporated. A more complex opinion may be passed off by an unscrupulous client as opining on more than it actually does. A lawyer who opines for a client thus lends her reputation to that client, and the lawyer should trust the client generally, not just in those matters addressed in the opinion. If she cannot, the opinion should not be given.

The ABA has sought to standardize both opinion language and procedures. See ABA Committee on Legal Opinions, Third–Party Legal Opinion Report, Including the Legal Opinion Accord, of the Section of Business Law, American Bar Association, 47 Bus. Law. 167 (1991). This ABA Opinion Accord is sometimes referred to as the "Silverado Accord." While a legal opinion does not have to conform to the guidelines set forth in the Accord, the Accord defines preferred opinion writing practice, and an opinion letter may incorporate provisions of the Accord by reference. ABA Opinion Accord at 219, Section 22.

When lawyers certify clients' representations, and third parties rely on such representations, courts may hold the lawyers liable if the representations turn out to be misleading. For example, a borrower's lawyer who certified incorrectly to a lender that the borrower's farm machinery was free of encumbrances was held liable to the lender for negligent misrepresentation. As Judge Posner pointed out in affirming for the Seventh Circuit, where "the defendant makes the negligent misrepresentation directly to the plaintiff in the course of the defendant's business or profession, the courts have little difficulty in finding a duty of care." Greycas v. Proud, 826 F.2d 1560, 1563 (7th Cir.1987), cert. denied, 484 U.S. 1043 (1988). See also Capital Bank & Trust v. Core, 343 So.2d 284 (La.App.1977) (lawyer for corporate borrower could be liable to lender for fraud when opinion letter addressed to lender stated that lawyer had examined certain records of his client when in fact he had not); Prudential Insurance Co. v. Dewey, Ballantine, Bushby, Palmer & Wood, 80 N.Y.2d 377, 590 N.Y.S.2d 831, 605 N.E.2d 318 (N.Y. 1992) (borrower's lawyer owes lender a duty of care with respect to opinion addressed to the lender). See also Morgan Shipman, The Liabilities of Lawyers in Corporate and Securities Work, 62 Cin. L. Rev. 513, 523–25 (1993) (discussing lawyer's duties to opinion letter addressees who are not clients); Jonathan R. Macey, Third Party Legal Opinions (1993).

Legal opinions and letters to auditors for the most part make representations about a client's affairs at a particular moment in time (such as the closing of a loan or the end of a fiscal year). Generally, the lawyer has no legal obligation to advise the opinion recipient (or any third party) of changes of law or fact that occur after the date of the opinion letter. ABA Opinion Accord at 196–97. However, a lawyer who writes an opinion letter, if he later doubts factual or legal representations contained therein, should not allow her client to continue to use the opinion to induce reliance on the part of third parties. See Ackerman v. Schwartz, 947 F.2d 841, 848–49 (7th Cir.1991) (lawyer may be liable for securities fraud for allowing a client to circulate an inaccurate opinion letter). Furthermore, although most opinion letters recite factual assumptions before opining on legal issues, the opinion giver should not assume facts which she doubts are true. An "Opinion Giver may not rely on information (including certificates or other documentation) or assumptions, otherwise appropriate in the circumstances, if the Opinion Giver has Actual Knowledge that the information or assumptions are false or the Opinion Giver has Actual Knowledge of facts that under the circumstances would make the reliance unreasonable." Opinion Accord at 190, Section 5. The Opinion Accord defines "Actual Knowledge" as "conscious awareness of facts or other information" by the lawyer signing the opinion or another lawyer in the same firm who is active in preparing the opinion, in negotiating the underlying transaction or in providing a response concerning the particular opinion issue or confirmation. Id. at 190–91, Section 6–A and 6–B.

Finally, it is unethical to provide even a factually and legally correct opinion letter to a client engaged in a fraudulent transaction. "A lawyer should not give an opinion (including one based on hypothetical facts or one that is legally correct as to the limited matters to which it is addressed), if he knows or suspects that the opinion is being sought to further an illegal securities transaction" Association of the Bar of the City of New York, Report by the Special Committee on Lawyers' Role in Securities Transactions, 32 Bus. Law. 1879, 1887 (1977).

PROBLEMS

1. Your client is selling a shopping center, and you furnish an opinion concerning compliance with state and federal health and safety regulations. The opinion begins with a recitation of assumed facts about the property, including the statement that "this opinion assumes that there is no asbestos on the premises." Based on these facts, you reach a legal conclusion that the property is in complete compliance with state and federal health and safety regulations. Two months after the closing of the sale, you learn that there is asbestos on the premises. What do you do?

2. In the above example, you learn about the asbestos before delivering the opinion at closing. The opinion merely contains legal conclusions that would follow if facts assumed in the opinion were correct and does not make any factual representations as to whether there actually is asbestos on the premises. Should you deliver the opinion?

3. You are a tax law expert and are asked by your client, a real-estate limited partnership, to prepare an opinion letter concerning tax deductions that will accrue to persons buying limited partnership interests from your client. You prepare the opinion and it is inserted, along with financial statements and other information, in the offering circular that will be distributed to prospective investors. You have nothing to do with drafting the promotion materials or preparing your client's financial statements, but, shortly before the offering circular is distributed, your client's accountant tells you that the financial statements intentionally overstate the net income of the limited partnership. Although your opinion makes no reference to the financial statements and is legally correct, the false financial statements are to be distributed with your opinion to prospective investors. Do you allow your client to send out the offering circular with your tax opinion included therein?

CLIENT AND POLITICAL SUPERIOR

Do We Have Enough Ethics in Government Yet?: An Answer From Fiduciary Theory

by Kathleen Clark.
1996 U. Ill. L. Rev. 57, 63–68.

* * *

I. The Continuing Expansion of Federal Ethics Regulation

Government ethics were a matter of concern even at the founding of this nation. The Constitution contains at least three provisions aimed at government officials' conflicts of interest: one forbids federal officials from accepting gifts, employment, or titles from foreign governments [art. I, sect. 9, cl.8]; another prohibits members of Congress from being appointed to a federal office that was created or whose salary was increased during that member's term in Congress [art. 1, sect. 6, cl.2]; and a third prevents members of Congress from receiving an increase in salary until after they stand for reelection [amend XXVII, ratified in 1992].

The first wave of ethics reform legislation occurred in the mid-nineteenth century, in the wake of wide-scale influence peddling and procurement fraud during the Civil War. Among other reforms, Congress made it a crime for government employees to act as agents or attorneys on behalf of parties who had monetary claims against the United States. These statutes remained on the books, with few prosecutions, for nearly a century. During the 1950s, however, they significantly complicated the government's ability to hire consultants on a temporary or intermittent basis. In 1962, Congress enacted legislation that recodified and reorganized the nineteenth century conflict of interest statutes [Pub. L. No. 87–849, 76 Stat. 1119 (current version at 18 U.S.C.A. sections 201–218) (1994)]. This legislation also created a new category of government employment for persons employed by the federal government on a temporary or intermittent basis, and provided that the conflict of interest laws would operate differently on this type of employee.

The next major change in the federal conflict of interest laws came after Watergate with passage of the Ethics in Government Act of 1978. The Act required certain employees of the government to disclose their finances, placed restrictions on post-government employment for executive branch employees, and established the Office of Government Ethics. In response to continued perceptions of abuse in both the executive and legislative branches, Congress passed the Ethics Reform Act of 1989, which imposed tougher post-government employment restrictions on certain high-level executive branch officials, created post-employment restrictions for members of Congress and highly paid congressional staff, established a rule restricting the ability of employees in all three branches of government to accept gifts, and banned honoraria for almost all government employees. On his first day in office, President Clinton imposed significant new restrictions on high-level political appointees, including a five-year ban on their ability to lobby their former departments and a life-time ban on their ability to lobby on behalf of foreign companies. And in 1995, both Houses of Congress adopted more restrictions on the ability of members and staff to accept gifts. As this short recitation suggests, Congress's periodic tightening of ethics regulation are responses to specific, perceived abuses; moreover, Congress often has undertaken such action without considering the underlying purposes of ethics regulation.

The current federal ethics regulatory structure, including statutes, regulations, and executive orders, is highly detailed and complicated. As the director of the office charged with writing executive branch ethics regulations explains, "even an employee who sincerely wants to follow the rules doesn't have the remotest chance of understanding them."[1] For example, the government has issued detailed regulations distinguishing donuts from sandwiches, compensation for giving a series of speeches from compensation for teaching, compensation for writing a chapter in a book from compensation for writing an article, and lobbying on behalf of a private university from lobbying on behalf of a private high school. The Office of Government Ethics presently employs eighty-seven people. Twelve hundred employees in other agencies spend more than half of their time on ethics issues, and more than 13,000 other employees have some responsibility for government ethics. In fact, an entire cottage industry has arisen to interpret the statutes, promulgate regulations, and provide guidance to employees.

There continues to be pressure to place additional restrictions on the activities of government employees. Under the current system, no obvious benchmark exists for determining when the government has reached an adequate or optimal level of ethics regulation. Thus, other factors tend to drive the adoption of ethics laws. For example, when members of Congress and the President tighten ethics regulation, they can claim that they are promoting more ethical government. Only rarely has there been political pressure to loosen these regulations. Given this political reality, one reasonably could expect the tide of government ethics regulation to increase with no apparent end.

* * *

[Professor Clark proposes that fiduciary theory be a "unifying principle" for "determining the appropriateness of a particular set of ethics regulations" for public officials. The fiduciary obligation, she explains, can be

---

1. Jacob Weisberg, Springtime for Lobbyists, New Republic, Feb. 1, 1993, at 33, 38 (quoting Stephen J. Potts, director of the Office of Government Ethics).

broken down into four component parts: (i) a *conflict* component that "prohibits a fiduciary from placing herself in a position where her own interest conflicts with her duty toward the beneficiary," (ii) an *influence* component that "subjects transactions between certain fiduciaries and their beneficiaries to heightened scrutiny to ensure that the fiduciary has not unduly influenced the beneficiary's decision to enter the transaction," (iii) a *partiality* component that "requires fiduciaries who have responsibility for allocating benefits among beneficiaries to treat beneficiaries of the same class equally and beneficiaries of different classes fairly," and (iv) an *avoidance* component that "prohibits certain fiduciaries from delegating their duties to others or putting themselves in a position where, because of conflict or other concerns, they could not act on behalf of the beneficiary." Id. at 71, citing Robert Flannigan, The Fiduciary Obligation, 9 Oxford J. Legal Stud. 285, 311–13 (1989). A "key characteristic of fiduciaries is that the law limits their freedom of action by the imposition of prophylactic rules—rules that prohibit more than just those activities that actually harm the beneficiary," and "a wide range of remedies are available for breach" of these rules. Clark, supra, at 71–72.

"[C]ourts have recognized the fiduciary obligation of government employees, even in the absence of specific legislative or regulatory endorsements of such duties." Id. at 74. For example, the conflict component is applied in situations involving bribes, kickbacks, conflicts created by the employee's business holdings and use of government property, and the influence component is applied to government contracts and to state legislators who, as lawyers, represent private parties before government agencies. Id.

Professor Clark develops a methodology for identifying which components of the fiduciary obligation are implicated by a particular activity and for determining "how these components can be expressed through specific restrictions" with due consideration of any other values that are implicated by the restrictions. Id. at 78. For example, the conflicts component of a government employee's fiduciary obligation is implicated when she accepts a gift of a certain size by or on behalf of someone likely to be affected by the government employee's discretionary decisions. Other values, however, could be implicated by prohibiting such gifts; for example, a legislator with the power to lower everybody's taxes, including those of his own family, should still be allowed to receive gifts from family members. Comparing the rules suggested by the fiduciary theory analysis to existing rules restricting gifts, Professor Clark finds that the existing rules are over broad in that they apply to government employees at all levels, whether or not they have discretionary power that could be influenced by the gift. The existing rules also apply to a larger than necessary category of gift givers, for example all persons who "conduct activities regulated by [the employee's] employing entity," rather than merely those persons likely to be affected by the gift recipient's discretionary decisions. Finally, until recently, the restrictions on gifts were not broad enough in that they did not cover a class of recipients whose receipt of a gift is very likely to implicate the conflicts component: members of Congress. Id. at 81–83.]

Will regulation of government employees based on fiduciary principles effectively promote ethical behavior? Why or why not? As you read through the selections in this chapter, think about what types of regulation, if any, would encourage government employees to be more faithful to their task.

The ITT Case

The following materials describe how Deputy Attorney General Richard Kleindienst was ordered by President Nixon to drop the appeal of a politically sensitive antitrust suit against ITT. Attorney General John Mitchell recused himself from the case because his law firm, of which Nixon had also been a partner, had represented ITT (Mitchell, however, continued to intervene behind the scenes). Kleindienst first had to decide how to respond to the President's order and later had to decide whether to reveal the President's order to the Senate Judiciary Committee in his own confirmation hearings to replace Mitchell as Attorney General.

The materials that follow on the ITT case raise a number of questions concerning the conduct of high ranking officials in the Nixon Administration. Questions to consider are: (i) did the President act properly in ordering that the jurisdictional statement for an appeal not be filed; (ii) did Deputy Attorney General Kleindienst act properly in ignoring the President's order; (iii) did Attorney General Mitchell act properly when he involved himself with the case after his former law firm had represented ITT; (iv) did ITT's contribution to the cost of the 1972 Republican National Convention influence the way the Administration handled the case; and (v) did Kleindienst tell the truth when he was asked about the case under oath by the Senate Judiciary Committee?

Richard M. Nixon, b. 1913, d. 1994; A.B. Whittier College 1934; LL.B. with honors from Duke University 1937; admitted to California bar in 1937 and New York bar in 1963; practiced law in Whittier, California 1937–42; attorney, Office of Price Administration, Washington, D.C. January–August 1942; United States House of Representatives 1946–50 (spearheaded the investigation of Alger Hiss for alleged spying and perjury); United States Senator from California 1951–53; Vice President of the United States 1953–60; Republican nominee for President 1960; of counsel, Adams Duque & Hazeltine, Los Angeles 1961–63; Nixon Mudge Rose Guthrie & Alexander, New York City 1964–68 (firm clients included ITT); President of the United States 1969–74; disbarred.

Spiro T. Agnew, b. 1918, d. 1996; LL.D. Drexel University, University of Maryland; LL.B. University of Baltimore 1947; bar-certified in Maryland; Chairman, Baltimore County Board of Appeals 1958–61; Chairman, Transportation Committee of National Association of Counties 1963; Executive of Baltimore County 1962–66; Governor of Maryland 1967–69; Vice President of the United States 1969–73 (forced to resign after pleading guilty to a mail fraud charge); disbarred.

John D. Ehrlichman, b. 1925; B.A. U.C.L.A. 1948; J.D. Stanford University 1951; Huyllin, Ehrlichman, Roberts & Hodge, Seattle, Washington 1952–68; Director of Convention Activities, Tour Director for Nixon Presidential campaign 1968; counsel to President Nixon 1969; assistant to President Nixon for domestic affairs, also Executive Director of Staff, Domestic Council 1969–73; sentenced in 1974 to 20 months in prison for his role in the break-in to the office of Daniel Ellsberg's psychiatrist; disbarred.

Charles W. Colson, b. 1931; B.A. Brown University 1954; J.D. George Washington University 1961; assistant to the Assistant Secretary of the Navy 1955–56; administrative assistant to Senator Leverett Saltonstall 1956–61; private practice in Washington, D.C. 1961–69; special counsel to President Nixon 1969–72; partner, Colson & Shapiro, Washington, D.C. 1973–74; sentenced to 1 to 3 years in prison in 1974 for obstructing justice in the Daniel Ellsberg case (served seven months); after a religious conversion in prison, organized the Association Prison Fellowship in 1976; disbarred.

John N. Mitchell, b. 1913, d. 1988; B.A. Fordham University 1935; J.D. Fordham University 1938; admitted to the New York bar in 1938; private practice in New York; partner, Nixon Mudge Rose Guthrie & Alexander, New York 1967–68; 1968 campaign manager for Richard Nixon; chaired Committee to Re-elect the President 1972; Attorney General 1969–72; served 19 months in prison for conspiracy, obstruction of justice and perjury in connection with the Watergate scandal; disbarred.

Richard G. Kleindienst, b. 1923; A.B. Harvard University 1947; LL.B Harvard University 1950; admitted to Arizona bar in 1950; associate and later partner, Jennings, Strous, Salmon & Trask in Phoenix, Arizona 1950–57; Arizona state representative 1953–54; senior partner, Shimmel, Hill, Kleindienst & Bishop in Phoenix, Arizona 1958–69; national director of field operations, Goldwater for President Committee 1964; national director of field of operations, Nixon for President Committee 1968; general counsel to Republican National Committee 1968; Deputy Attorney General 1969–72; Attorney General 1972–73; member, Johnson, Dowdall & Kleindienst in Tucson, Arizona.

Richard W. McLaren, b. 1918, d. 1976; B.A. Yale University 1939; LL.B Yale University 1942; admitted to the New York bar in 1944 and Illinois bar in 1950; associated with Hodges, Reavis, Pantaleoni & Downey, New York City 1946–49; partner, Chadwell, Keck, Kayser, Ruggles, & McLaren in Chicago, Illinois 1950–69; Assistant Attorney General, anti-trust division, Justice Department 1969–72; U.S. District Judge, Northern District of Illinois, 1972–76.

Erwin N. Griswold, b. 1904, d. 1994; A.B., A.M. Oberlin College 1925; LL.B. Harvard University 1928; S.J.D. Harvard University 1929; bar admission in Ohio 1929, Massachusetts 1935 and Washington, D.C. 1973; Griswold, Green, Palmer & Hadden, Cleveland, Ohio 1929; attorney for the Office of the Solicitor General, Special Assistant to the Attorney General, Washington, D.C. 1929–34; assistant professor of law, Harvard University 1934–35; professor of law, Harvard University 1935–46; dean, Charles Stebbins Fairchild professor of law 1946–50; dean, Langdell professor of law 1950–67; Solicitor General of the United States 1967–73; partner, Jones, Day, Reavis & Pogue, Washington, D.C. 1973–94.

Lawrence E. Walsh, b. 1912; A.B. Columbia University 1932; LL.B. Columbia University 1935; special assistant to attorney general Drukman Investigation 1936–38; deputy assistant district attorney, New York County 1938–41; counsel to the Governor of New York 1950–51; counsel for Public Service Commission 1951–53; U.S. District Judge, Southern District of New York 1954–57; U.S. Deputy Attorney General 1957–60; partner, Davis Polk & Wardwell 1961–81 (counsel for ITT); Special Prosecutor for investigation of Iran–Contra affair 1986–92.

Henry P. Sailer, a partner of Covington & Burling in Washington, D.C., was trial counsel for ITT in the *Grinnell* and *Hartford* cases; **Hammond E. Chaffetz**, a partner of Kirkland & Ellis in Chicago, was counsel for ITT in the *Canteen* case and **Felix Rohatyn**, a partner of Lazard Freres & Co., a New York investment banking firm, was advisor to ITT in formulating its overall mergers and acquisitions policy.

Abstract

From the New York Times
August 3, 1973, Friday.

On August 2, the New York Times obtained copies of ITT documents referred to in a March 30, 1972 memo from former Presidential special assistant C. W. Colson to former White House chief of staff H. R. Haldeman. These documents revealed a "well-orchestrated" effort by ITT to enlist the aid of top Administration officials in blocking an antitrust suit against ITT's merger with Hartford Fire Insurance Company . . .

A Memo by ITT lobbyist Mrs. D. D. Beard, dated June 25, 1971, to ITT chief of Washington relations W. R. Merriam, said that ITT's "noble commitment" of $400,000 for the Republican National Convention had greatly aided ITT's negotiations on a merger with Hartford Insurance and that negotiations would "eventually" come out as ITT president Harold S. Geneen "wants them." The second ITT document cited by the New York Times [see page 182 infra] is an August 7, 1970 letter with an enclosed memo written by ITT vice president E. J. Gerrity following a meeting of John Mitchell, then Attorney General, with Geneen and Gerrity. The letter expresses appreciation for Agnew's "assistance concerning the attached memo," and states that the "problem" faced by Geneen and Gerrity is to alert Mitchell to the "attitude" of Richard W. McLaren, then Assistant Attorney General for the antitrust division, because McLaren "is more responsive" to Congress than to Nixon Administration policy. . . .

The fourth ITT document is a April 22, 1971 letter from Merriam to then Treasury Secretary Connally expressing thanks for the Justice Department's agreement to postpone for 30 days the filing of jurisdictional papers in a case concerning ITT's divestiture of subsidiary Grinnell Corp. The Justice Department, which had brought three antitrust suits against ITT concerning Grinnell, Hartford Insurance and Canteen Corp, was in the process of appealing the Grinnell and Canteen cases to the U.S. Supreme Court after U.S. District Courts ruled against the Justice Department, when Solicitor General Erwin N. Griswold asked for and was granted the delay; the delay was very much desired by ITT and gave ITT a chance to seek settlement of both cases. . . .

Chronology

4/28/69 Suit filed in *U.S. v. ITT re Canteen* (Kleindienst and Ehrlichman approve)

8/1/69 Suit filed in *U.S. v. ITT re Hartford & Grinnell* (Kleindienst and Ehrlichman approve)

8/7/70 Ned Gerrity approached Vice President Agnew

12/31/70 Judgment for ITT in *Grinnell*

3/1/71 U.S. motion to file appeal

3/20/71 U.S. motion to extend time to perfect appeal for one month

Friday 4/16/71 Walsh letter to Kleindienst requesting an extension of jurisdictional statement

Monday 4/19/71 Nixon telephone call to Kleindienst; Kleindienst to Griswold

5/12/71 Sheraton pledge to San Diego Tourist Bureau discussed by ITT executives

6/17/71 McLaren presents plan to Kleindienst; approved in one hour

7/21/71 $200,000 Sheraton pledge to San Diego

7/31/71 Settlement Agreement with ITT

1/26/72 McLaren nominated for District Court

2/15/72 Kleindienst nominated for Attorney General

ITT VICE PRESIDENT "NED" GERRITY LETTER
AUGUST 7, 1970, WITH ATTACHMENT
PERSONAL & CONFIDENTIAL

August 7, 1970

The Honorable Spiro T. Agnew

Ted:

I deeply appreciate your assistance concerning the attached memo. Our problem is to get to John [Mitchell] the facts concerning McLaren's attitude because, as my memo indicates, McLaren seems to be running all by himself.

I think it is rather strange that he is more responsive to Phil Hart[1] and Manny Celler[2] than to the policy of the Administration.

After you read this, I would appreciate your reaction on how we should proceed.

NED

PERSONAL & CONFIDENTIAL

MEMORANDUM

August 7, 1970

You will recall at our meeting on Tuesday I told you of our efforts to try and settle the three antitrust suits that Mr. McLaren has brought. Before we met, Hal [ITT C.E.O. Harold Geneen] had a very friendly session with John [Mitchell], whom, as you know, he admires greatly and in whom he has the greatest confidence. John made plain to him that the President was not opposed to mergers per se, that he believed some mergers were good and that in no case had we been sued because "bigness is bad." Hal discussed this in detail because McLaren has said and in his complaints indicated strongly that bigness is bad. John made plain that was not the case. Hal said on that basis he was certain we could work out something. John said he would talk with McLaren and get back to Hal.

While you and I were at lunch, Hal and Bill Merriam, who runs our local office, met with Chuck Colson and John Ehrlichman, and Hal told them of his meeting with John. Ehrlichman said flatly that the President was not enforcing a bigness-is-bad policy and that the President had instructed the Justice Department along these lines. He supported strongly what John had told Hal. Again, Hal was encouraged. I learned the details of this meeting after our lunch.

Yesterday our outside counsel from Chicago, Ham Chaffetz, who represents us in the Canteen Case vs. The Justice Department, had a pretrial meeting with McLaren and his trial people. They reviewed the case, and Chaffetz said he was ready to settle since Justice really had no case, i.e., they could not show reciprocity, etc., and that all that was alleged was [that] ITT was getting too big. McLaren, ignoring the evidence, said that ITT must be stopped, that the merger movement must be stopped, etc., in effect saying he was running a campaign based on his own beliefs and he intended to prosecute diligently. It is quite plain that Mr. McLaren's approach to the entire merger movement in the United States is keyed into the present cases involving ITT. Therefore, it is equally plain that he feels that if a judgment is obtained against ITT in any of these cases then the merger movement in the United States will be stopped. His approach obviously becomes an emotional one regardless of fact.

It was plain that McLaren's views were not and are not consistent with those of the Attorney General and the White House. We are being pursued,

---

1. U.S. Congressman (D–Michigan)—   **2.** U.S. Congressman (D–New York)—
ed.   ed.

contrary to what John told Hal, not on law but on theory bordering on the fanatic.

In his conversation with Hal, John agreed that the steam had gone out of the merger movement because of tax reform legislation, the new accounting principles and general developments in the economy. John agreed with Hal that there was no need for a "crusade" to halt the merger movement because of the reasons I have indicated above. It is plain, therefore, that McLaren is operating on a completely different basis from John and the White House. I believe it has reached the point where he is more concerned about his personal views than those of his superior or the President.

My question to you is, should we get this development back to John, so he is aware, and how do we do it? What is the best way? I would appreciate your help and advice.

JOHN EHRLICHMAN MEMORANDUM, SEPTEMBER 17, 1970
PERSONAL & CONFIDENTIAL

September 17, 1970

MEMORANDUM FOR THE ATTORNEY GENERAL

Re: The United States v. ITT

I was disappointed to learn that the ITT case had gone to trial with apparently no further effort on the part of Mr. McLaren to settle this case with ITT on the basis of our understanding that "largeness" was not really an issue in the case.

ITT has passed word to us that the gravamen of the case remains "largeness" which is contrary to the understanding that I believe you and I had during the time that we each talked to Mr. Geneen.

I think we are in a rather awkward position with ITT in view of the assurances that both you and I must have given Geneen on this subject.

I'll be out of touch for about two weeks, but I would appreciate your reexamining our position in the case in view of these conversations. Geneen is, of course, entitled to assume the Administration meant what it said to him.

John D. Ehrlichman

JDE:JDE:korn

bcc: Colson

Cole

CONFIDENTIAL

EYES ONLY

CHARLES COLSON MEMORANDUM, OCTOBER 1, 1970
THE WHITE HOUSE
Washington

October 1, 1970

EYES ONLY

MEMORANDUM FOR JOHN EHRLICHMAN

I am enclosing a copy of the speech which Mr. McLaren gave on September 17th. He does not, as you will see, defend the proposition that under the existing anti-trust laws a case can be brought on the grounds of bigness per se. What he does argue is that bigness is not good, and that the thrust of the anti-trust laws should be directed to economic concentration and bigness. He points out that while *legislation might be needed*, Justice can and is doing things, short of obtaining new legislation (note the last paragraph in particular).

In sum, I think that we still have a problem here, which is a serious one and which is manifesting itself in Mr. McLaren's conduct of the ITT case.

Charles W. Colson

EYES ONLY

————————

LAWRENCE WALSH LETTER, APRIL 16, 1971, WITH
ATTACHED MEMORANDUM OF LAW

Davis, Polk & Wardwell,
New York, N.Y., April 16, 1971.

Hon. Richard G. Kleindienst,
Deputy Attorney General,
U.S. Department of Justice,
Washington, D.C.

Dear Dick: As I told you over the telephone, our firm has represented ITT, as outside counsel, ever since its incorporation over fifty years ago. A few weeks ago, Mr. Harold S. Geneen, Chairman and President of ITT, asked me to prepare a presentation to you as Acting Attorney General and, through you, to the National Administration on the question of whether diversification mergers should be barred and, more specifically, urging that the Department of Justice not advocate any position before the Supreme Court which would be tantamount to barring such mergers without a full study of the economic consequences of such a step.

To us this is not a question of the conduct of litigation in the narrow sense. Looking back at the results of government antitrust cases in the

Supreme Court, one must realize that if the government urges an expanded interpretation of the vague language of the Clayton Act, there is a high probability that it will succeed. Indeed, the court has at times adopted a position more extreme than that urged by the Department. We therefore believe that the Department should not take such a step without all of the usual precautions that precede a recommendation for new legislation. If the antitrust laws were to be expanded by legislation, rather than by litigation, the Department's views would, in the first instance, be collected by the Deputy Attorney General and then cleared with the Bureau of the Budget which would give all of the other interested federal departments an opportunity to comment. We believe that any major expansion of the antitrust laws should be accompanied by these steps whether the expansion is by litigation or by legislation. It is our understanding that the Secretary of the Treasury, the Secretary of Commerce, and the Chairman of the President's Council of Economic Advisors all have some views with respect to the question under consideration.

Ordinarily I would have first seen Dick McLaren, but I understand that you, as Acting Attorney General, have already been consulted with respect to the ITT problem and that the Solicitor General also has under consideration the perfection of an appeal from the District Court decision in the *ITT-Grinnell* case.

It is our hope that after reading the enclosed memorandum, which is merely a preliminary presentation, you and Dick McLaren and the Solicitor General would be willing to delay the submission of the jurisdictional statement in the Grinnell case long enough to permit us to make a more adequate presentation on this question. ITT of course will join in any application for an extension of time. It is obvious that this case cannot be heard at this term of court and it would therefore seem that a delay of a relatively short period would not be harmful to the public interest.

> With kindest regards,
> Sincerely yours,
>
> Ed
> Lawrence E. Walsh.

MEMORANDUM FOR THE DEPARTMENT OF JUSTICE IN SUPPORT OF A COMPREHENSIVE REVIEW OF ADMINISTRATION POLICY TOWARD DIVERSIFICATION BY MERGER

This memorandum is submitted to demonstrate that the Department of Justice should initiate a comprehensive, Government-wide review of the national interest implications of diversification by merger before making any argument to the United States Supreme Court which, if accepted by the Court, would have the effect of banning all significant mergers and diversification. We submit that such a sweeping ban should not be adopted as the policy of the Administration and the Nation without the most careful review....

I

A BAN ON SIGNIFICANT MERGERS AND DIVERSIFICATION WOULD INJURE VITAL NATIONAL INTERESTS

* * *

CONCLUSION

For the reasons given above, a comprehensive, Government-wide review of Administration policy toward mergers and diversification should be undertaken.

Respectfully submitted.

LAWRENCE E. WALSH,

FREDERICK A. O. SCHWARZ,

GUY M. STRUVZ,
(*Of counsel*),
*Attorneys for International
Telephone & Telegraph Corp.*

TRANSCRIPT PREPARED BY THE IMPEACHMENT INQUIRY STAFF FOR THE HOUSE JUDICIARY COMMITTEE OF A RECORDING OF A MEETING AMONG THE PRESIDENT, JOHN EHRLICHMAN AND GEORGE SHULTZ ON APRIL 19, 1971 FROM 3:03 TO 3:34 P.M.

PRESIDENT: Yeah. Let's see (unintelligible)

EHRLICHMAN: Yeah. (Unintelligible) antitrust thing.

PRESIDENT: No (unintelligible)

UNIDENTIFIED: Um Hm.

EHRLICHMAN: We are going to see the Attorney General tomorrow, and by then it may be too late, in a sense.

PRESIDENT: No. Honestly?

EHRLICHMAN: ITT case, where God knows we have made your position as clear as we could to Mr. What's-his-name over there.

PRESIDENT: McLaren.

EHRLICHMAN: And, uh, John [Mitchell] has said because ITT is involved, he's not involved because he's got a conflict of interest going back to the old law firm.

PRESIDENT: Huh, (unintelligible)

EHRLICHMAN: Richard Kleindienst, uh, uh, has been supervising McLaren's work. It's the Grinnell case. It involves an attack on, uh, conglomerates, on a theory which specifically had been contemplated by the Johnson administration and laid aside as too anti-business.

PRESIDENT: Kleindienst is in this? (Picks up telephone.)

EHRLICHMAN: Yes.

PRESIDENT: (To telephone operator) Dick Kleindienst. (Hangs up.)

EHRLICHMAN: And—

PRESIDENT: How long before that (unintelligible) do you expect a moratorium?

EHRLICHMAN: Well, they filed a notice of appeal. If

PRESIDENT: Who did?

EHRLICHMAN: we do not file a statement of jurisdiction by tomorrow the case is dead, and, uh,

PRESIDENT: Who?

EHRLICHMAN: Uh—the Justice Department.

PRESIDENT: They're not going to file.

EHRLICHMAN: Well, I thought that was your position.

PRESIDENT: Oh, hell.

EHRLICHMAN: I've been trying to give, I've been trying to give them signals on this, and, uh, they've been horsing us pretty steadily. Uh, uh, Geneen—

PRESIDENT: Statement of jurisdiction.

EHRLICHMAN: Right.

PRESIDENT: I don't want to know anything about the case. Don't tell me a

EHRLICHMAN: Yeah, I won't.

PRESIDENT: thing about it. I don't want to know about Geneen. I've met him and I don't know—I don't know whether ITT is bad, good, or indifferent. But there is not going to be any more antitrust actions as long as I am in this chair.

EHRLICHMAN: Well, there's one—

PRESIDENT: God damn it, we're going to stop it.

EHRLICHMAN: All right. There's this other one that you are going to talk to John about tomorrow on the networks.

PRESIDENT: Well, I don't want him to do that, for other reasons.

EHRLICHMAN: Well, that's right. This, that's

PRESIDENT: This is the wrong time.

EHRLICHMAN: These are all coming together.

PRESIDENT: We wanted to do that at another time.

EHRLICHMAN: Okay, but that's all coming together you see at this point in time, so uh, uh, it's (unintelligible)

PRESIDENT: Where's Kleindienst? Isn't he in town?

EHRLICHMAN: Yeah. He's in his office. I just talked to him about an hour ago, and, uh—

PRESIDENT: Well, we'll take care of it.

EHRLICHMAN: Okay. Beyond that, uh—

PRESIDENT: (Unintelligible) cut out this damn thing, Bob,—John.

SHULTZ: In this, uh, talk that I am making speeches—

PRESIDENT: Yeah, you talking economic,

SHULTZ: Yeah,

PRESIDENT: (unintelligible) great.

SHULTZ: which I quote you with, uh—I'd like to get you to riffle through it when I'm done to

PRESIDENT: Sure, I will.

SHULTZ: see what kind of shape, but there is a section on the question of is there something new about the economy today. Has business become more monopolistic, and so on. And I go through the various studies of (Telephone buzzes) concentration and the vertical integration and—

PRESIDENT: (Picks up telephone.) Yeah.

      * * *

TRANSCRIPT PREPARED BY THE IMPEACHMENT INQUIRY STAFF FOR THE HOUSE JUDICIARY COMMITTEE OF A RECORDING OF A TELEPHONE CONVERSATION BETWEEN THE PRESIDENT AND RICHARD KLEINDIENST ON APRIL 19, 1971, FROM 3:04 TO 3:09 P.M.

PRESIDENT: Yeah.

SECRETARY: Mr. Kleindienst, Mr. President.

KLEINDIENST: Hi, Mr. President.

PRESIDENT: Hi, Dick, how are you?

KLEINDIENST: Good, how are you, sir?

PRESIDENT: Fine, fine. I'm going to talk to John tomorrow about my general attitude on antitrust,

KLEINDIENST: Yes sir.

PRESIDENT: and in the meantime, I know that he has left with you, uh, the IT & T thing because apparently he says he had something to do with them once.

KLEINDIENST: (Laughs) Yeah. Yeah.

PRESIDENT: Well, I have, I have nothing to do with them, and I want something clearly understood, and, if it is not understood, McLaren's ass is to be out within one hour. The IT & T thing—stay the hell out of it. Is that clear? That's an order.

KLEINDIENST: Well, you mean the order is to—.

PRESIDENT: The order is to leave the God damned thing alone. Now, I've said this, Dick, a number of times, and you fellows apparently don't get the me—, the message over there. I do not want McLaren to run around prosecuting people, raising hell about conglomerates, stirring things up at this point. Now you keep him the hell out of that. Is that clear?

KLEINDIENST: Well, Mr. President—

PRESIDENT: Or either he resigns. I'd rather have him out anyway. I don't like the son-of-a-bitch.

KLEINDIENST: The, the question then is—

PRESIDENT: The question is, I know, that the jurisdiction—I know all the legal things, Dick, you don't have to spell out the legal—

KLEINDIENST: (Unintelligible) the appeal filed.

PRESIDENT: That's right.

KLEINDIENST: That brief has to be filed tomorrow.

PRESIDENT: That's right. Don't file the brief.

KLEINDIENST: Your order is not to file a brief?

PRESIDENT: Your—my order is to drop the God damn thing. Is that clear?

KLEINDIENST: (Laughs) Yeah, I understand that.

PRESIDENT: Okay.

KLEINDIENST: (Unintelligible)

(President hangs up.)

* * *

RESUMPTION OF TRANSCRIPT PREPARED BY THE IMPEACH-MENT INQUIRY STAFF FOR THE HOUSE JUDICIARY COMMIT-TEE OF A RECORDING OF A MEETING AMONG THE PRESI-DENT, JOHN EHRLICHMAN AND GEORGE SHULTZ ON APRIL 19, 1971 FROM 3:03 TO 3:34 P.M.

SHULTZ: Anyway, looking—

PRESIDENT: I hope he resigns. He may.

SHULTZ: If you look at concentration ratios over a period of time, on horizontal integration, if you look at ratios of sales to value added on vertical integration, what you find is no evidence of any increase in, in monopoly in American business. In fact, over a thirty-year period, and I checked this over with my friend

Stigler who has made a lot of these studies. If anything, you see a decline. And in the conglomerate area that is what I think we are witnessing, is, uh, a sort of a reaction to the buildup of conglomerates, which is perhaps affected somewhat by the antitrust. . . .

EHRLICHMAN: You're not the only one.

SHULTZ: From the standpoint of the economics of it, uh, I would be the last to say we should not continue, uh, to, uh, pursue the antitrust laws in the proper way, but, the, uh—I think the conglomerates have taken a bum rap.

PRESIDENT: This is, this is the problem. The problem is McLaren's a nice little fellow who's a good little antitrust lawyer out in Chicago. Now he comes in and all these bright little bastards that worked for the Antitrust Department for years and years and years and who hate business with a passion—any business—have taken him over. They haven't taken him over. Then of course McLaren is the man. They go into— Kleindienst is busy appointing judges; Mitchell is busy doing other things, so they're afraid to overrule him. By God they're not going to do it. I mean the point is that on this antitrust they had deliberately gone into a number of areas which have no relationship with each other, to—whether it's a question of operating more, more efficiently than the rest. There's simply a question of tactically, they've gone off on a kick, that'll make them big God damn trust busters. That was all right fifty years ago. Fifty years ago maybe it was a good thing for the country. It's not a good thing for the country today. That's my views about it, and I am not— We've been, been through this crap. They've done several of them already about—They have raised holy hell with the people that we, uh, uh,—Well, Geneen, hell, he's no contributor. He's nothing to us. I don't care about him. So you can—I've only met him once, twice—uh, we've, I'm just, uh—I can't understand what the trouble is.

EHRLICHMAN: Well,

PRESIDENT: It's McLaren, isn't it?

EHRLICHMAN: McLaren has a very strong sense of mission here.

PRESIDENT: Good—Jesus, he's—Get him out. In one hour.

EHRLICHMAN: He's got a

PRESIDENT: One hour.

EHRLICHMAN: Very strong—

PRESIDENT: And he's not going to be a judge, either. He is out of the God damn government. You know, just like that regional office man in, in, in San Francisco. I put an order into Haldeman today that he be fired today.

EHRLICHMAN: Yeah.

PRESIDENT: Today. Anybody that didn't follow what we've done per the latest'd have his ass out. Unless he is a—What is he, is he a Republican hack or something!

EHRLICHMAN: No, I don't even know what he is.

PRESIDENT: Now could he—I mean, that's ridiculous that he went through there with one

EHRLICHMAN: Five—

PRESIDENT: applications out of four thousand he'd been processing. He didn't follow what we said. To hell with him. We've got to be a little bit more effective here. You're not going to (unintelligible). Oh, I know what McLaren is, he believes this.

EHRLICHMAN: Yeah.

PRESIDENT: I know. Who the hell—he wasn't elected (unintelligible)

EHRLICHMAN: That's the point—

PRESIDENT: He is here by sufferance.

EHRLICHMAN: That's the point.

PRESIDENT: And he is not going to stay one, uh, another minute. Not a minute. Because he's going after everybody, you know, just—Why the hell doesn't he go after somebody that, uh—

EHRLICHMAN: (Laughs) That's been suggested.

PRESIDENT: Oh.

* * *

After the President's telephone call Kleindienst met with McLaren and Solicitor General Erwin Griswold and directed that the Solicitor General apply to the Supreme Court for another extension of time. At 4:30 p.m. Kleindienst telephoned Walsh and informed him that the Solicitor General was arranging for an extension of time for the government to perfect its appeal.

CONFIRMATION HEARINGS FOR THE NOMINATION OF RICHARD KLEINDIENST TO BE ATTORNEY GENERAL

RICHARD McLAREN TESTIMONY, (the attached memorandum appears as an exhibit)

March 2, 1972

U.S. SENATE

COMMITTEE ON THE JUDICIARY

Washington, D.C.

Department of Justice,

Washington, D.C., June 17, 1971.

MEMORANDUM FOR THE DEPUTY ATTORNEY GENERAL

Re: Proposed Procedure in ITT Merger Cases

Background—We have three anti-merger cases pending, against ITT: the *Grinnell* case (sprinkler systems), which was tried and lost in the District Court and is now on appeal to the Supreme Court; the *Canteen* case (vending and food service), which was tried and is now *sub judice*; and the *Hartford Fire Insurance Co.* case, which is set for trial in September.

About six weeks ago, representatives of ITT made a confidential presentation to the Department, the gist of which was that if we are successful in obtaining a divestiture order in the ITT–Hartford Fire Insurance Company case, this will cripple ITT financially and seriously injure its 250,000 stockholders. . . .

Under the circumstances, I think we are compelled to weigh the need for divestiture in this case—including its deterrent effect as well as the elimination of anti-competitive effects to be expected from divestiture—against the damage which divestiture would occasion. Or, to refine the issue a little more: Is a decree against ITT containing injunctive relief and a divestiture order worth enough more than a decree containing only injunctive relief to justify the projected adverse effects on ITT and its stockholders, and the risk of adverse effects on the stock market and the economy?

I come to the reluctant conclusion that the answer is "no." I say reluctant because ITT's management consummated the Hartford acquisition knowing it violated our antitrust policy; knowing we intended to sue; and in effect, representing to the court that he need not issue a preliminary injunction because ITT would hold Hartford separate and thus minimize any divestiture problem if violation were found. . . .

Proposed Procedures—In order that we do not lose the deterrent we have developed in this field, I propose the following terms of settlement of the ITT cases:

1. *Grinnell*—divestiture. This would require a joint motion in the Supreme Court to refer the case back to the District Court for entry of consent order. . . .

2. *Canteen*—divestiture by consent order.

3. *Hartford*—injunction along lines of *LTV*, including [prohibitions against certain future acquisitions and requirement of certain divestitures].

Finally, in all three cases, I think we should have the right to approve ITT's press releases. We want no great protestations of innocence, government abuse, etc., etc.

I recommend that you approve a program along the lines of the foregoing—allowing, of course, for some leeway in negotiating.

Richard W. McLaren,
Assistant Attorney General,
Antitrust Division.

Approved, 6/17/71.

R. G. K. [Richard Kleindienst]

[Testimony of Richard McLaren]

Mr. McLaren. This plan contemplated divestiture of Grinnell and Canteen; divestiture of Avis and Levitt; prohibition for 10 years of acquisitions of any corporation with assets of $100 million or more, or acquisitions of any corporation with assets of more than $10 million except on a showing that it would not tend to lessen competition. . . .

At the conclusion of my meeting with Mr. Kleindienst, I telephoned Mr. Felix Rohatyn from Mr. Kleindienst's office—while he was present—and outlined my proposal to him. This was at approximately 10 o'clock in the morning on June 17. Mr. Rohatyn asked certain questions about points in the proposal and repeated his understanding of the proposal as—it appeared to me—he took notes on it. I told Mr. Rohatyn that if the proposal was acceptable to ITT as a basis for a settlement, he should have ITT's trial counsel get in touch with me. I made clear that if ITT was unwilling to accept the basic outline of the proposal, with negotiation only as to details, I did not care to discuss the matter further. . . .

Thereafter Mr. Henry Sailer, of the Covington & Burling law firm, who was trial counsel for ITT in the *Grinnell* and *Hartford* cases, as I said before, telephoned me for an appointment. Judging from the telephone record maintained by my secretary, this apparently was on June 18; we made an appointment for a preliminary discussion on June 24. At the meeting on June 24, Mr. Sailer showed by his comments that he received a rather full and accurate account of the proposal which we had made to Mr. Rohatyn, and he inquired as to various specifics of our proposal. . . . He protested that there was no good antitrust reason why ITT should be forced to divest Avis. Then he asked about the negotiatibility of our provision on no acquisitions over $10 million, and so forth. I told him we would negotiate on details, but that the basic provisions of the proposal were firm.

Within the next few days we agreed internally that [Justice Department Lawyers] Carlson and Widmar should handle the negotiations, and by June 30 Carlson and Widmar had so advised Sailer, and had had a discussion with him concerning procedure.

On July 1, I met with Sailer, Carlson and Widmar and after a very short session, principally covering the points I had discussed with Sailer on June 24, I left Carlson and Widmar with Sailer to continue the negotiations.

Negotiations between Carlson and Widmar on the one hand and Sailer on the other hand continued through the month of July—a part of which time I think from about July 10 to July 20, I was in London at the ABA meeting—and in the last few days of the month, Carlson and Widmar advised me that the matter was about wound up and that it would be helpful if I would sit in on one or two sessions to cover some final points. . . .

In conclusion, I want to emphasize that the decision to enter into settlement negotiations with ITT was my own personal decision; I was not pressured to reach this decision. Furthermore, the plan of the settlement was devised, and the final terms were negotiated, by me with the advice of other members of the Antitrust Division, and by no one else.

* * *

[Testimony of ITT Chairman Harold Geneen]

Senator KENNEDY. Where do you think everyone, like Congressman Wilson, who is very much involved in the negotiations, as I understand, got the idea of $400,000?

Mr. GENEEN. Well, I think I covered that, Senator, in the statement yesterday. I said this thing was brought up to my first knowledge—we were out during our annual meeting at a party we gave, a dinner party, for about 70 people, and we were enthusiastic about it, but I didn't figure any kind of a figure was a commitment. He was talking in terms of the use of hotel rooms, which may not be otherwise used; and we talked in general terms. I don't remember a figure of $400,000 by any means. But in any event, before the site selection made its bid for the convention, we sent a telegram to the San Diego Tourist and Convention Bureau, care of Congressman Wilson, which spelled out clearly what our total commitment was, and it was in writing and that is the only commitment that we have.

Now, I appreciate there has been some mixup on it, misstatement, but that is the only commitment we have and it was given in writing before the site selection was made.

Senator KENNEDY. Why was Congressman Wilson—why was the telegram sent to him?

Mr. GENEEN. He asked to have such a telegram sent to the bureau in care of him—it was not sent to him—in order to have it at the meeting, I presume, and I am assuming now because I don't know what he was going to do with it, where they were going to select the site.

Senator KENNEDY. Was he involved in the negotiations, then, between ITT and the selection committee?

Mr. GENEEN. We had no—

Senator KENNEDY. Was he the go-between?

Mr. GENEEN. We had no negotiations with the selection committee at all. We undertook to make a contribution to the convention bureau, and that is whom the check has been made out and that is to whom the telegram is addressed, and he asked to have a copy of the telegram sent to him before they went out there and it was sent to the convention bureau, care of Congressman Wilson; that is his district and he is naturally interested in it.

Senator KENNEDY. Do we have a copy of the telegram?

Mr. GENEEN. I think we said we would make it available yesterday, and if it hasn't been we can.

Mr. GILBERT. There are several here, Senator.

Mr. GENEEN. And the check is made out in the same manner.

(The telegram referred to follows:)

July 21, 1971.

To: San Diego County Convention and Tourist Bureau.

C/o: Congressman Bob Wilson, 2235 Rayburn House Office Building, Washington, D.C.

As you know Sheraton Corporation of America will have, with the completion of the Sheraton Harbor Island Hotel, a 700 room hotel being located on land owned and created by San Diego Port Authority, three hotels in San Diego. In consideration of the naming of the Sheraton Harbor Island Hotel as Presidential headquarters hotel in conjunction with its opening at the time of the convention, and as part of the general community effort to establish San Diego as a convention center by bringing the 1972 Republican National Convention to the City, Sheraton is prepared to commit a total of $200,000 to the Bureau for its promotional activities, if San Diego is designated as the convention site, on the following basis: $100,000 in cash to be available to the bureau on August 1, 1971 and a balance to be paid as a matching contribution when the bureau has raised an additional $200,000 in cash from other non-public sources.

HOWARD JAMES,

President, Sheraton Corporation of America

Senator KENNEDY. Now, Mr. Geneen, was this a personal pledge on your behalf, in behalf of the corporation; was it?

Mr. GENEEN. That is a question, Senator?

Senator KENNEDY. Pardon?

Mr. GENEEN. That is a question?

Senator KENNEDY. Yes.

Mr. GENEEN. Let me say I can make no personal pledge on behalf of the corporation. The corporation can only carry out ordinary and necessary business, and as I said a moment ago, the decision on what we would do and what was reasonable to do and what was a good business investment to do was made by Mr. James, the president of the Sheraton chain. He made the decision and that is what is in our telegram and that is the only commitment we have.

* * *

*CONFIRMATION HEARINGS FOR THE NOMINATION OF RICHARD
KLEINDIENST TO BE ATTORNEY GENERAL*

March 2, 1972

U.S. SENATE,

COMMITTEE ON THE JUDICIARY,

Washington, D.C.

THE CHAIRMAN (Senator James O. Eastland). The committee will be in order.

Mr. Kleindienst, hold up your hand.

Do you solemnly swear to tell the truth, the whole truth, and nothing but the truth, so help you God?

Mr. KLEINDIENST. I do.

Mr. McLAREN. I do.

Mr. ROHATYN. I do.

[questioning ensued]

* * *

March 3, 1972

U.S. SENATE

COMMITTEE OF THE JUDICIARY,

Washington, D.C.

The committee met, pursuant to recess, at 10:50 a.m., in room 2228, New Senate Office Building, Senator James O. Eastland, chairman, presiding. . . .

* * *

Senator BAYH. Could I ask just one question? I am not certain that this was asked yesterday of both Mr. Kleindienst and Judge McLaren.

Did either of you gentlemen talk to Mr. Geneen or any other officials in the hierarchy of ITT?

Mr. KLEINDIENST. I have never met Mr. Geneen, I have never talked to Mr. Geneen. I would not recognize him if I saw him. . . .

Senator BAYH. Now, I ask one other question. I wonder if you have had a chance to reflect, overnight, on whether you had ever talked to anybody down at the White House about the ITT case, and it would be—

Mr. KLEINDIENST. No, sir. No, sir. To the best of my recollection, but as I qualified that yesterday, I am talking to somebody at the White House almost constantly about a variety of problems, and it is not inconceivable that somebody up there could have made reference to the status of the ITT cases, you know, or something like that.

So far as consulting about, reporting to, getting directions from, going into depth on these matters or any other antitrust case, I have never had that experience.

Senator BAYH. How about Members of Congress?

Mr. KLEINDIENST. On I.T. & T.?

Senator BAYH. Yes.

Mr. KLEINDIENST. Not to my recollection. Not to my recollection.

Senator BAYH. Or members of the Republican National Committee?

Mr. KLEINDIENST. No. No; not to my recollection.

* * *

[Questioning of Mr. ROHATYN, Mr. MCLAREN and Mr. KLEINDIENST]

Senator KENNEDY. And then on April 18, you telephoned Mr. Kleindienst, is that right, on or about April 18?

Mr. ROHATYN. On or about April 18, before April 20.

Senator KENNEDY. Now, as I understand, on April 19, the Justice Department requested a last-minute delay for its filing of an appeal in *Grinnell*. This is the *ITT* case in the Supreme Court, is that right, Mr. Kleindienst?

Mr. KLEINDIENST. I beg your pardon, Senator Kennedy?

Senator KENNEDY. That on April 19, this is the day after Mr. Rohatyn's phone call to you, the Justice Department requests a last minute delay for its filing of appeal in *Grinnell*, is that correct? I believe that—

Mr. KLEINDIENST. We requested a delay, but I do not remember the date, Senator Kennedy.

Senator KENNEDY. Mr. McLaren, do you remember? I believe that is the date.

Mr. MCLAREN. I could not place the date, Senator.

. . .

Senator KENNEDY. OK. As I understand, if we can get back now, we have the phone call of the 18th, the 19th is the request by the Department in the *Grinnell* case. Would you tell us, Mr. Kleindienst, why this request was filed since there had already been a 30–day extension in the *Grinnell* case?

Mr. KLEINDIENST. Well, there was just a problem as to whether this thing was to be filed in the request for the delay. Excuse me just a minute.

Senator KENNEDY. Yes.

(Short pause.)

Senator KENNEDY. If I could—

Mr. KLEINDIENST. Senator Kennedy, I do not recollect why that extension was asked.

Senator KENNEDY. Well, does Mr. McLaren have the petition there?

Mr. McLAREN. I was just looking at the memorandum we filed, or the Solicitor General filed, rather, as to the precise details as to why we filed it at the time. I think that we said "additional time is needed for further study of the case and to permit consultation among various interested Government agencies with regard to whether the Government should perfect its appeal."

Senator KENNEDY. What was the doubt, Mr. Kleindienst, as to whether the Government should perfect its appeal?

Mr. KLEINDIENST. I do not know.

. . .

Senator FONG. Mr. Kleindienst, there seems to be some talk that your testimony is in conflict with that of Mr. Flanigan [a White House staff member] and I would like you to speak to that. Would you mind clarifying this alleged conflict to us?

Mr. KLEINDIENST. Yes, I would, because I would like to refer to the committee to the testimony that I gave and I am referring now to page 157. Senator Bayh, in a question to me, said:

> Could you be a bit more definitive? It leaves an uneasy feeling in the pit of my stomach when you talk about casual references when you realize the significance of this case, politically, economically, financially.

And I replied:

> You asked me did I discuss the ITT matter with the White House. I do not recollect doing so. But I am on the telephone almost constantly, throughout a day or a week, with somebody on the White House staff or another with respect to some aspect of the operations of the Department of Justice.

> For me to say that no one in the White House with whom I might have talked would not have raised the ITT question, I would not be prepared to say that.

> So far as discussing with anybody on the staff of the White House what I was doing, what do you think I ought to do, what do you feel about it, what are your recommendations—no.

And then, likewise, on page 353 in response to a question from Senator Kennedy, I said:

> Well, I also know this, Senator Kennedy, as I have testified fully: In the discharge of my responsibilities as the Acting Attorney General in these cases, I was not interfered with by anybody at the White House. I was not importuned; I was not pressured; I was not directed. I did not have conferences with respect to what I should or should not do. So I know that. And, then, I was dealing directly with Judge McLaren, as I have indicated. So, there has been nothing, to my knowledge, based upon my experience and participation or anything that I have heard

here that even just by innuendo or conjecture or by implication would suggest that in this case there was any improper conduct by anybody or interference, or anything like that.

Because I tried to make it clear, Senator Fong, that in view of the posture I put myself in, in this case, I could have had several conversations but I would have had a vivid recollection if someone at the White House had called me up and said, "Look, Kleindienst, this is the way we are going to handle that case." People who know me, I don't think would talk to me that way, but if anybody did it would be a very sharp impact on my mind because I believe I know how I would have responded.

No such conversation occurred.

THE NEW YORK TIMES
NOVEMBER 1, 1973
PAGE 33; COL. 1
TEXT OF KLEINDIENST STATEMENT ON I.T.T.

WASHINGTON; Oct. 31—Following is the text of a statement issued by former Attorney General Richard G. Kleindienst in defense of his role in an antitrust case against the International Telephone and Telegraph Corporation.

Three weeks ago I had a conversation at the Special Prosecutor's office with Mr. Cox and two of his assistants concerning the handling of the I.T.T. antitrust case during my tenure as Deputy Attorney General. A story in The New York Times yesterday, which was repeated on the networks and in newspapers around the country, contained a very specific report of one part of that conversation.

As a result of the leak to The Times, I have been accused on national television of having given false information to the Senate Judiciary Committee at the time of my nomination as Attorney General. That accusation is false.

My conversation with Professor Cox was held under strict assurances of confidentiality, and as Professor Cox has stated, was a serious breach of faith on the part of the Special Prosecutor. I continue to regard my conversation with Professor Cox as confidential, but because of the distorted and misleading accounts of my conduct that have appeared in the press, I feel compelled at this time to relate an important aspect of the event which was not leaked.

On Monday afternoon, April 19th, 1971, Mr. Ehrlichman abruptly called and stated that the President directed me not to file that appeal in the Grinnell case. That was the last day in which that appeal could be taken. I informed him that we had determined to take that appeal, and that he should so inform the President. Minutes later the President called me and, without any discussion ordered me to drop the appeal immediately.

Thereafter, I sent word to the President that if he persisted in this direction I would be compelled to submit my resignation. Because that was the last day in which the appeal could be perfected, I obtained an extension of time from the Supreme Court to enable the President to consider my position.

The President changed his mind and the appeal was filed 30 days later in the exact form it would have been filed one month earlier. Thus, but for my for my threat to resign, the Grinnell case would never have been appealed and we would never have been able to obtain what even Professor Cox has characterized as a settlement highly advantageous to the United States.

At the time of my testimony before the Senate Judiciary Committee, I was not asked whether I had had any contacts with the White House at the time of this decision, and I did not deny any such contacts.

Focus of the Hearings

The focus of the hearings dealing with the I.T.T. affair was the negotiations in May, June and July of 1971 leading to settlement of the pending cases on July 31. I was questioned at length concerning these negotiations and particularly with reference to any conversations or meetings I might have had with Mr. Peter Flanigan of the White House staff. It was in the context of those questions that I made the statement quoted on C.B.S. news last evening as follows:

"In the discharge of my responsibilities as the Acting Attorney General in these cases, I was not interfered with by anybody at the White House, I was not importuned; I was not pressured; I was not directed."

It was also in response to a question by Senator Fong concerning Mr. Flanigan that I made the other statement quoted by C.B.S. as follows:

"... I would have had a vivid recollection if someone at the White House had called me up and said, 'Look, Kleindienst, this is the way we are going to handle that case.' People who know me, I don't think would talk to me that way, but if anybody did it would be a very sharp impact on my mind because I believe I know how I would have responded. No such conversation occurred."

Both of these statements, taken in the context in which they were made, were completely accurate.

In short, I did not perjure myself or give false information to the Senate Judiciary Committee. A fair and objective reading of the transcript of my testimony will so indicate.

I deeply regret the circumstances which have compelled me to make this statement. However, in view of the serious breach of faith by the Special Prosecutor and the distorted treatment of my testimony in the press, I have no other choice. I have done no wrong.

UNITED STATES v. KLEINDIENST INFORMATION,
MAY 16, 1974, WITH ATTACHMENT
UNITED STATES DISTRICT COURT

FOR THE DISTRICT OF COLUMBIA

UNITED STATES OF AMERICA)	
)	
v.)	Defendant
)	
RICHARD G. KLEINDIENST)	

INFORMATION

The Special Prosecutor charges:

1. From on or about the 2nd day of March, 1972 up to on or about the 27th day of April, 1972, in accordance with Article II, Section 2 of the Constitution of the United States, Rule 38 of the rules of the United States Senate and the customs and practices of the United States Senate, an inquiry was being had by the Committee on the Judiciary of the United States Senate, pursuant to the referral to said committee of the nomination of RICHARD G. KLEINDIENST to be Attorney General of the United States into the qualifications of RICHARD G. KLEINDIENST to hold said office. As a material part of said inquiry said Committee was inquiring into the manner in which the United States Department of Justice had processed certain antitrust matters involving mergers made and contemplated by the International Telephone and Telegraph Corporation (hereinafter ITT), matters for which RICHARD G. KLEINDIENST had been Acting Attorney General.

2. During the course of the inquiry described in paragraph one, on or about the 2nd, 3rd, 7th and 8th days of March, 1972 and the 27th day of April, 1972, in the District of Columbia, RICHARD G. KLEINDIENST, the defendant, having appeared as a witness before the Committee on the Judiciary of the Senate of the United States to give testimony upon the inquiry as described in paragraph one, did refuse and fail to answer accurately and fully questions pertinent to said inquiry, thereby withholding from said Committee the fact that he had received an order from Richard M. Nixon, President of the United States, relating to the filing of the jurisdictional statement by the United States before the Supreme court of the United States in the case of *United States of America v. International Telephone and Telegraph Corporation* and, in testifying in said manner did thereby refuse to answer questions relating to the following:

1. Communications in relation to antitrust cases involving ITT between the President of the United States, Richard M. Nixon and members of the staff of said President, and the said RICHARD G. KLEINDIENST and Attorney General John N. Mitchell;

2. Communications in relation to antitrust cases involving ITT between Attorney General John N. Mitchell, who was disqualified from said cases, and himself;

3. The circumstances surrounding an application made on April 19, 1971, before the Supreme Court of the United States by and on behalf of the United States, which application requested that the time in which the United States could file its jurisdictional statement in the above described case be extended for thirty days.

(Title 2, United States Code, Section 192)

/s/_____

Leon Jaworski
Special Prosecutor

_____

ATTACHMENT TO RICHARD KLEINDIENST INFORMATION

Watergate Special Prosecution Force

1425 K Street, N.W.
Washington, D.C. 20005

May 16, 1974

FOR IMMEDIATE RELEASE

The following information was filed in U.S. District Court, Washington, D.C., today:

NAME: RICHARD G. KLEINDIENST

ADDRESS: WASHINGTON, D.C.

AGE: 50

CHARGE: One count. Violation of Title 2, USC, Section 192. copy attached.

PENALTY: Violation of Title 2, USC, Section 192, is punishable by a fine of not more than $1,000 nor less than $100 and imprisonment not less than one month nor more than twelve months.

_____

LEON JAWORSKI LETTER, MAY 10, 1974

Herbert J. Miller, Jr., Esq.
Miller, Cassidy, Larroca & Lewin
1320 19th Street, N.W.
Washington, D.C. 20036

Dear Mr. Miller:

This letter will record the understandings between you, your client, Richard G. Kleindienst, and my office relating to his agreement to plead guilty to a one-count information charging him with violating Title 2, United States Code, Section 192.

The understandings are that Mr. Kleindienst will enter this plea in the district court for the District of Columbia, that he will waive any possible objection to the bringing of this charge by virtue of the failure of the Senate to certify this matter to the Department of Justice and that he will waive defenses he might have to this charge. Based on the legal brief you have submitted, both you and your client agree that his conduct violates Section 192. If Mr. Kleindienst enters this plea, this will dispose of all charges of which this office is presently aware arising out of his testimony at his confirmation hearings, arising out of his handling of documents during his hearings and arising out of his appearance before the August, 1973 Grand Jury on December 21, 1973, unless substantial new evidence develops demonstrating that Mr. Kleindienst has failed to disclose material matters relating to the ITT matter.

One significant factor in my determination is that our investigation has failed to disclose any criminal conduct by Mr. Kleindienst in the manner in which he handled the ITT antitrust cases. In one of the cases he successfully opposed a direct Presidential order to abandon an appeal and leave the Government without any relief.

Another important factor in my agreeing to this plea relates to Mr. Kleindienst having come forward voluntarily and disclosed information material to the investigation conducted by this office on his understanding that he would be given some consideration for doing so. It is my belief that he is entitled to consideration in arriving at an appropriate disposition of this matter. After a full review of the facts, my conception of a fair disposition is for Mr. Kleindienst to plead to a violation of Title 2, United States Code, Section 192.

This disposition will not bar prosecution of Mr. Kleindienst for any other serious offenses about which evidence may develop. It is thus specifically understood that if evidence is developed that Mr. Kleindienst was involved in any criminal obstruction of the ITT antitrust cases or any other matter within the Department of Justice, this disposition will not bar his prosecution for that offense.

Sincerely,

/s/_____

Leon Jaworski
Special Prosecutor

STATE BAR OF ARIZONA v. RICHARD G. KLEINDIENST (1975)

Concurring opinion of Stanley Feldman, Governor, State Bar of Arizona

I concur with the recommendations of the Board of Governors, but differ on some matters of importance. I have therefore decided to set forth my views separately. Admittedly, such a procedure is unusual, but so is the case. To me, this case involves issues which go to the heart of the legal profession. I feel, therefore, that the Board's report should not be transmitted to the Supreme Court without expressing reasons for the decision in more detail than that which the Board majority adopted.

In writing this, I do not speak for the Board, or even its majority. I state my own opinions, with which some members of the Board might agree, and others would not.

By a vote of eight to six, one member not voting, the Board of Governors recommended that Respondent be found guilty of a violation of Disciplinary Rule 1–102(A)(6). The majority voted to censure Respondent for that violation. Of the six who voted against those findings and recommendations, three specifically indicated that they did so because they thought the punishment recommended was insufficient to fit the offense. I tended to agree with them, but voted for the motion to censure because otherwise it would have been impossible to reach a decision, a "majority of the entire Board" being required on disciplinary matters.

The facts of this matter are found in the volumes of the transcript of the testimony given by Respondent before the Senate Judiciary Committee. Those facts are amplified and explained by the statement Respondent made before the Special Local Administrative Committee of the State Bar, by the summary letter authored by the office of the Watergate Prosecutor, by a letter written by Respondent and filed in this case, and by Respondent's answers to questions put to him at the hearing before the Board of Governors. The entire problem must also be placed within the context of the political situation which existed at the time of the offense, for no one could fairly consider the matter without reference to the political partisanship which colored the questioning put to Respondent before the Senate Judiciary Committee and the reactions of anyone placed in Respondent's position.

Despite all this, the *operative facts* are clear and mostly uncontroverted. During the period 1969 to 1970, Respondent was Deputy Attorney General of the United States. Before that he had actively practiced law in Arizona. He has a reputation as a competent, honest practitioner. He had been involved in politics and had run for the office of Governor of Arizona. He had worked hard for the election of Richard Nixon as President of the United States. His stature in the Bar, and his efforts on behalf of the Republican Party, had resulted in his being offered the position of Deputy

Attorney General; his acceptance of that position cast him as a participant in a Byzantine political drama.

While Respondent was Deputy Attorney General of the United States, Richard McLaren was Assistant Attorney General with direct responsibility for handling three proposed anti-trust cases where in the United States proposed to challenge the acquisition by International Telephone and Telegraph of Canteen Corporation, Hartford Insurance and Grinnell Corporation. Regulations of the Justice Department required the Attorney General's approval for filing of anti-trust cases. The Attorney General, John Mitchell, had recused himself[1] and Mr. Kleindienst was therefore responsible for granting or denying approval of the filing of the ITT cases. Mr. McLaren requested and was given approval to file.

As of April, 1971, the United States had filed all three cases. The trial courts had ruled against the United States in *Grinnell*, and had refused to issue a preliminary injunction in *Hartford*. The Government was awaiting the decision of the Court in *Canteen*. The appeal process had been commenced in *Grinnell* and the Government's jurisdictional statement in that case was due in the Supreme Court on April 20, 1971.

On April 16, 1971, an attorney for ITT filed a written request with Mr. Kleindienst asking that the Government seek an extension of time for filing the jurisdictional statement. Mr. McLaren opposed this request. Mr. Kleindienst told ITT's attorney on April 19, 1971, that it was not likely that the Government would seek an extension. That same day, Mr. Kleindienst received a call from Mr. Ehrlichman, who said he was calling on behalf of President Nixon and was instructing Mr. Kleindienst not to file the *Grinnell* appeal.[2] Mr. Kleindienst replied that filing could not be withheld. A few minutes later, Mr. Kleindienst received a call from the President, who ordered him to drop the case and not to file the appeal.[3]

Mr. Kleindienst then called Mr. Mitchell and protested the President's orders, threatened resignation and asked Mr. Mitchell to intercede with the President and persuade him to change the orders. Before Mr. Mitchell called back, Respondent talked to Mr. McLaren and the Solicitor General, informed them of the situation and they all agreed not to file the jurisdictional statement but instead to seek an extension. They did so on April 19, 1971. Mr. Mitchell later told Respondent the President ("your friend at the White House") would let Mr. Kleindienst handle it his own way. In effect,

1. His former law firm, and the President's, had represented ITT in the past.

2. The appeal had been filed; it was the jurisdictional statement which was to be filed. Mr. Ehrlichman evidently had not gotten his facts straight, no doubt because of factual distortions produced by getting information through various intermediaries.

3. See Footnote 2. Also, the call (which was taped) is indicative of some sense of urgency on the part of the President. The ancestors of both Kleindienst and McLaren were described in uncomplimentary terms; the President refused to listen to Kleindienst's attempts to explain why the appeal should not be dismissed, and ended up giving Kleindienst a direct order to dismiss. Mr. Nixon then hung up.

the President rescinded his orders to drop the case. Mr. Kleindienst had thus refused the direct orders of the President, withstood the pressure and preserved the Government's position. The cases were thereafter settled by Mr. McLaren's office and on terms favorable to the Government.

During his confirmation hearing in March, 1972, Respondent testified under oath to the Senate Judiciary Committee that he had never "discussed" any aspect of the ITT case with Mr. Mitchell or with anyone on the White House staff; that he had received no suggestions from the White House regarding the cases, and had not been pressured or directed by anyone at the White House; he testified that he had changed his mind and instructed Mr. McLaren and the Solicitor General to obtain the extension of time within which to file the jurisdictional statement because of the request from ITT's attorney and the lack of prejudice to the Government in granting that request. Respondent failed to mention his conversations with John Ehrlichman, John Mitchell and Richard M. Nixon. Respondent did not disclose that the true reason for filing the request for the extension was to allow for time to get the President to change his mind or, if he did not, to resign.

On May 16, 1974, Richard G. Kleindienst entered a plea of guilty to an information accusing him of the misdemeanor of violating Title 2, Section 192, United States Code, by refusing or failing to give accurate and complete answers to questions propounded to him while he was testifying under oath before the Senate Judiciary committee in regard to the matters hereinabove set forth.

The transcripts of the proceedings before the Senate Judiciary Committee, before the Special Local Administrative Committee and before the Board of Governors, together with analysis of the documents forming part of the file (including the comments of Judge Hart at the time of sentencing of Respondent on the misdemeanor conviction, the comments of Mr. Jaworski and of Justice Udall in the dissenting opinion before the Special Local Administrative Committee) all lead to the compelling conclusion that we are dealing with a situation which, while simple from a factual standpoint, is more complex from a moral standpoint.

Factually, Mr. Kleindienst found himself in an untenable situation at the hearings on his confirmation. He felt that the *settlement* of the ITT anti-trust case had been accomplished free from pressure and in a manner advantageous to the Government.[4] He felt he had withstood an intense amount of political pressure and had performed in an exemplary manner by refusing the President's order to dismiss the cases and by proceeding to work out the best settlement obtainable from the United States' viewpoint. He felt, probably correctly, that he deserved commendation for refusing an improper order from the President. On the other hand, he was loyal to his political party and was especially loyal to Richard Nixon, a man for whom

---

4. This feeling was no doubt justified. The pressure came before settlement and was resisted by Kleindienst. The settlement was worked out later and appears advantageous to the Government's position. Kleindienst did not participate in the settlement negotiations and appears not to have pressured McLaren to be indulgent to ITT.

he had worked, in whom he believed, and who was then a popular President. He knew the President's attempt to pressure him was wrong; he felt that it had produced no harm and that, for reasons unknown to him, the President had backed off. He also knew that if he revealed the attempt of the President and his counsel to bring pressure on the Attorney General's office on behalf of ITT he would have precipitated a political storm, damaging to the President, though it would certainly have helped insure Mr. Kleindienst's confirmation as Attorney General.

In the final analysis, Respondent tried to protect the President and the Administration by adopting a policy of non-disclosure, unless direct questions were asked. In other words, he did not intend to commit perjury, only to come as close to the line as necessary in order to protect the Administration, but to stop short of perjury. The problem is that it is difficult in the heat of interrogation to tell just where the line between non-disclosure and lying by non-disclosure exists. Whether Respondent's non-disclosure constituted perjury or not is a nice question which, in my mind, is not answered in the record, and perhaps is unanswerable.[5] Certainly, it is fair to say that Respondent probably did not *consciously* intend to commit perjury.

So, we have a man who has been nominated for the office of Attorney General of the United States, whose qualifications are unquestioned, who has resisted serious political pressure in order to protect the Government's interests but who, it must be said, misled a Senate inquiry in order to protect those in whom he had political faith and to whom he owed political loyalty.

Respondent's answers to questions from the Senate Judiciary Committee, while arguably not perjury, were certainly short of a full and frank description of the events which had occurred. If we take the oath which was administered literally, i.e., "tell the truth, the whole truth and nothing but the truth," we must find that Respondent failed to tell "the whole truth." He himself admits he answered incompletely, although, he claims, not inaccurately. I would say that his answers were so incomplete as to be inaccurate.

The best method for a witness to keep out of trouble is to tell the whole truth as he knows it. Of course, if Respondent had done that, he would have brought political troubles on the Administration. However, he would not have found himself in his present position. In the long run, he, like Archibald Cox and Elliott Richardson, would have preserved both personal honor and the honor of his profession. If his loyalty motivated him to resist disclosure, his alternative course could well have been to claim executive privilege. If the claim of executive privilege was one which he was unwilling or unable to take, he could simply ask that his name be withdrawn from consideration and pass up the opportunity to become Attorney

---

5. Most of the questions were propounded in the context of what influenced and produced the *settlement*. This in fact was the subject of the hearing before the Senate Committee. In that context it could be argued that Kleindienst was not pressured, had not "discussed" the matter with Mitchell, etc.; all that had occurred before the settlement negotiations commenced.

General. Instead, he chose to take his chances on a policy on non-disclosure and made answers which were incomplete, despite the fact he took the oath to tell " ... the whole truth ..." and despite the fact he was a lawyer, being examined under oath with regard to his qualifications to become Attorney General of the United States.

I think it not overly idealistic to feel that Respondent's acts under those circumstances involved moral turpitude and, regardless of moral turpitude, also involved a violation of several portions of Disciplinary Rule 1–102(A).[6] One must consider the situation *and the duty thereby created*:

> EC 8–5 "Fraudulent, deceptive, or otherwise illegal conduct by a participant in a proceeding before a tribunal or legislative body is inconsistent with fair administration of justice, and it should never be participated in or condoned by lawyers. Unless constrained by his obligation to preserve the confidences and secrets of his client, a lawyer should reveal to appropriate authorities any knowledge he may have of such improper conduct."

Under Rule 29(c), conviction of the offense is proof of commission of the act, and, with respect to a misdemeanor, the only inquiry is whether that misdemeanor was one involving moral turpitude. The Special Local Administrative Committee found that it was. A majority of the Board of Governors disagreed and is of the opinion that no moral turpitude can be found because the legal definition of that term requires motives which are absent from this case:

> "Moral turpitude is an elusive concept incapable of precise definition. One dramatic exposition of the term ... has since been consistently followed: An act of baseness, vileness or depravity in the private and social duties which a man owes to his fellow men or to society in general, ..." *In Re Higbie*, 99 Cal. Rptr. § 65, 493 P.2d 97.

I do not concur with the majority on their finding of an absence of moral turpitude. It is true that we deal with understandable human frailty rather than evil or base motives. However, the definition of moral turpitude must vary somewhat with the circumstances. Non-disclosure may be acceptable between two businessmen dealing at arm's length and with equal means of knowledge. If not acceptable in such circumstances, it would ordinarily not involve moral turpitude. On the other hand, non-disclosure between attorney and client may well involve moral turpitude, and non-disclosure between a man who has been nominated for the highest legal office in the country and the elected representatives of the people of that country is, to my mind, sufficient moral turpitude to warrant imposition of discipline.

---

6. Disciplinary Rule 1–102: "*Misconduct.* (A) a lawyer shall not: * * * (3) Engage in illegal conduct involving moral turpitude. (4) Engage in conduct involving dishonesty, fraud, deceit, or misrepresentation. (5) Engage in conduct that is prejudicial to the administration of justice. (6) Engage in any other conduct that adversely reflects on his fitness to practice law."

Of course, even if the misdemeanor of which Respondent was convicted did not involve moral turpitude, he may be disciplined for breach of some of the disciplinary rules which members of our profession must observe. Here we have an even more interesting concept. Respondent was not an ordinary lawyer involved in an ordinary situation. He was the acting Attorney General at the time of the hearings before the Senate Judiciary Committee, and he was the nominee for the position of Attorney General of the United States. His acts must be judged by the office to which he aspired. Some members of the Board were of the opinion that to be fair to Respondent we must take cognizance of the fact that he was involved in "politics" (and certainly one must admit that any Cabinet position is in a greater or lesser sense "political"), and some members of the Board thought that some additional allowance must be made to Respondent because of the fact. Pragmatically, that may be right. However, my view is diametrically opposed. I feel that simply because he was a lawyer, and was the nominee for the highest legal office of the country the duty he owed was higher and not lower; I am unwilling, as a matter of principle, to make any allowance.

Thus, like the majority of the Special Administrative Committee and at least ten members of the Board of Governors, I feel that discipline should be imposed.

The question of what that discipline should be is to my mind considerably less clear. I am cognizant that there is considerable public clamor for disbarment and that many of those who have little knowledge of the facts are most vocal in their recommendation. Interestingly enough, no member of the Board of Governors was in favor of disbarment and I think that even a minimal degree of human understanding of Respondent's predicament would make it impossible to impose such punishment. After all, in the final analysis, Respondent is not convicted of failing to show the degree of candor and honesty of the normal person; but rather of failing to display that greater amount which is to be expected of a person in a much higher position than normal. Punishment for that failure will come from the history books and from Respondent's own feelings of remorse. The basic purpose of the Bar's disciplinary proceedings is not to punish but to protect the public from those lawyers who may fail to properly represent their clients or who may practice in a dishonest manner. No such danger exists with respect to the Respondent.

The problem, however, is that while one can understand, one cannot justify Respondent's failure to disclose and lack of candor; because he was a lawyer in a high place he, of all people, should have been completely candid. To impose no discipline would be to condone, and this the profession cannot do. To disbar the Respondent would be to mete punishment unsuited to the situation. To some extent the same could be said about suspension of Respondent. Somewhere between public censure and a brief suspension the principle is established, the importance of the matter is confirmed and, to my mind, justice is done. I would, therefore, have suspended Respondent for a short period, not for the purpose of "punishing" him, since history has already done that, but for the purpose of establishing a precedent and making it clear that the profession demands more of itself than of other people and that it demands most of those members who seek high office. I think that censure is not enough to establish that precedent; I voted for it since otherwise there would have been insufficient votes to find for imposition of any discipline. However, I felt unable to agree to censure in the absence of some explanation of what was done and why.

QUESTIONS

1. McLaren was paid by the United States Treasury from the Justice Department budget; he was hired by the Attorney General after approval from the White House; he reported to the Attorney General. Who was McLaren's "client" in the ITT case?

2. If McLaren's duty was to represent the public interest, who was to determine what was in the public interest? The President? The Attorney General? McLaren?

3. Should McLaren have resigned if his orders from the President and Attorney General were contrary to his conscience?

4. As pointed out in Lawrence Walsh's letter to Kleindienst, the antitrust laws could be interpreted in a number of ways, some of which would have been favorable to ITT. Walsh also pointed out that this was a case where the antitrust laws could be expanded through litigation "without all of the usual precautions that precede a recommendation for new legislation." Do the President and the White House staff have a role in determining the Justice Department's position on how the antitrust laws should be interpreted and how to proceed in a particular case? Is Stanley Feldman correct in implying that the President's attempt to pressure Kleindienst was wrong?

5. Why was McLaren appointed to a judgeship? Should he have declined the appointment?

6. The "Dear Ted" letter to Vice President Spiro Agnew from ITT Vice President Edward Gerrity, dated August 7, 1970, discussed meetings 3 days earlier of Harold Geneen with John Mitchell, John D. Ehrlichman and Charles W. Colson, and of Gerrity with Agnew. Why did Attorney General Mitchell recuse himself from the ITT case? Why did he still meet with Geneen and subsequently talk with McLaren and Nixon about the case?

7. Government lawyers sometimes have authority that in private litigation ordinarily reposes in the client, such as authority to appeal or settle a case without consulting political superiors. Did Kleindienst and McLaren properly use their discretionary authority in handling the ITT case or should they have been more responsive to President Nixon's wishes?

8. ITT's financial support for the Republican convention appeared to have been a promotional effort for a new hotel, but there were gratuitous elements in the transaction as well. Looking back at Professor Clark's fiduciary analysis of government ethics, can a political party be identified as a fiduciary? Is so, for whom? What types of restrictions on financial support for political parties and for political conventions would have reinforced fiduciary principles in this case?

9. When Kleindienst was asked by the Senate Judiciary Committee about contacts with the White House concerning ITT, should he have claimed attorney-client or executive privilege, thereby forcing the Committee to seek to compel his testimony if it chose? Would he have risked losing his confirmation vote if he had claimed privilege?

10. Although government lawyers are not excepted from the client confidentiality provisions of Model Rule 1.6, most (but not all) public business should be conducted under the public eye. Should attorney-client confidences be protected even in circumstances where public officials should act publicly and secrecy can be a badge of evil?

11. Kleindienst, in his statement of October 31, 1973, said, "In short, I did not perjure myself or give false information to the Senate Judiciary Committee. A fair and objective reading of the transcript of my testimony will so indicate." Do you agree? If not, did his effort to excuse his conduct compound the wrongdoing?

12. Do you agree with Stanley Feldman's finding that Kleindienst's conduct involved moral turpitude?

The Vincent Foster Papers

On July 20, 1993, Deputy White House Counsel Vincent Foster, Jr. died of gunshot wounds to the head in an apparent suicide. The following materials describe how White House Counsel Bernard W. Nussbaum handled the subsequent inquiry by the Park Police and the Justice Department into the circumstances surrounding Mr. Foster's death.

Vincent Foster, Jr., b. 1945, d. 1993; A.B. Davidson College 1967; J.D. University of Arkansas 1971 (Managing Editor, Arkansas Law Review); admitted to the Arkansas bar in 1971; member, Arkansas House of Delegates 1973–76 and 1990–93; president, Pulaski County Bar Association 1981–82; chairman, Arkansas Executive Council 1987–88; partner, Rose Law Firm, Little Rock, Arkansas, through January 1993 (partner of Hillary Rodham Clinton); fellow, American College of Trial Lawyers; Deputy Counsel to the President of the United States, January to July 1993.

Bernard W. Nussbaum, b. 1937; A.B. Columbia University 1958; LL.B. Harvard University 1961; admitted to the New York bar in 1962; Assistant U.S. Attorney, Southern Dist. of New York 1962–66; Senior Associate Special Counsel, House Judiciary Committee Impeachment Inquiry 1974 (supervised a staff of attorneys, including Hillary Rodham, a recent graduate of Yale Law School!); member, Wachtell, Lipton, Rosen & Katz, New York City 1966–93, 1994 to present (represented Kaye, Scholer in 1992 proceeding by the Office of Thrift Supervision for that firm's role in the Lincoln Savings and Loan failure); White House counsel from 1993 to 1994.

Philip B. Heymann, b. 1932; B.A. Yale University 1954; LL.B. Harvard University 1960; admitted to the District of Columbia bar in 1960 and Massachusetts bar in 1970; law clerk, Justice John Harlan, United States Supreme Court 1960–61; Assistant to the Solicitor General, United States Department of Justice 1961–65; Acting Administrator, Bureau of Security and Consular Affairs, United States Department of State 1966–67; Deputy Assistant Secretary of State, Bureau of International Organizations 1967; Executive Assistant to the Undersecretary of State, United States Department of State 1967–69; Assistant Attorney General, Criminal Division, United States Department of Justice 1978–81 (played a significant role in investigations into charges against Bert Lance, Hamilton Jordon and others); professor, Harvard Law School since 1981; Deputy Attorney General, United States Department of Justice 1993–94.

David Gergen was an advisor to President Clinton, **Susan Thomases** was a high level advisor to First Lady Hillary Rodham Clinton and **Thomas F. "Mack" McLarty** was White House Chief of Staff.

RESIGNATION LETTER OF BERNARD W. NUSSBAUM TO PRESIDENT CLINTON
March 5, 1994
New York Times, March 6, 1994 at A–12

The following is the text of the letter of resignation sent to President Clinton today by Bernard W. Nussbaum, the White House counsel, and excerpts from the President's letter in response:

Dear Mr. President:

It has been a great honor and privilege to serve you as Counsel to the accomplishments of this Administration and those that I know will be achieved in the months and years to come. I am also proud of the many contributions my office has made to the wide array of policy initiatives of your administration.

It was also an honor to have assisted in your choice of Janet Reno to be Attorney General of the United States, Louis J. Freeh to be the Director of the Federal Bureau of Investigation, and Ruth Bader Ginsburg to sit on the Supreme Court of the United States. I am particularly proud of assisting in your selection of more than 60 men and women of the most distinguished and diverse backgrounds ever to serve on the Federal bench.

As I know you know, from the day I became Counsel, my sole objective was to serve you as well and as effectively as I could, consistent with the rules of law, standards of ethics, and the highest traditions of the Bar. At all times I have conducted the Office of the White House Counsel and performed the duties of Counsel to the President in an absolutely legal and ethical manner. Unfortunately, as a result of controversy generated by those who do not understand, nor wish to understand the role and obligations of a lawyer, even one acting as White House Counsel, I now believe I can best serve you by returning to private life. With this letter I am therefore tendering my resignation. It will be effective April 5, 1994, to assist you in arranging for an orderly transition in the Counsel's office.

I will always value your friendship and that of the First Lady, and will always be grateful for the opportunity you gave me to serve. I wish you both the very best.

Bernard W. Nussbaum

Dear Bernie:

With deep regret, I accept your decision to resign as Counsel to the President. Your friendship and advice have meant a great deal to me over the years.

During your tenure, this Administration named the highest percentage of women and minorities to the Federal Judiciary in history, while meeting, in a vast number of cases, the highest standards set by the American Bar Association.

. . . .

It has been said that the best a man can give is his living spirit to a service that is not easy. And we have worked together in Washington at a time when serving is hard. But you gave this Administration one of its liveliest spirits and keenest minds, along with your special reverence for duty and friendship. For these contributions, I will be forever grateful; for your accomplishments, I hope you will be forever proud.

Bill Clinton

HEARINGS BEFORE SENATE SPECIAL WHITEWATER DEVELOPMENT CORPORATION AND RELATED MATTERS COMMITTEE

AUGUST 2, 1995, WEDNESDAY

WITNESS: PHILIP B. HEYMANN, FORMER DEPUTY ATTORNEY GENERAL

CHAIRED BY:
SENATOR ALFONSE D'AMATO
(R–NY)
216 HART SENATE OFFICE
BUILDING

* * *

MR. HEYMANN: Thank you very much, Senator D'Amato. Mr. Chairman and members of the committee, I greatly appreciate the opportunity to make a short opening statement. I think it'll help the committee to understand my thought processes at the time of Vince Foster's death and will put my answers in a useful context. I managed the efforts of the Department of Justice to assist the investigative agency responsible in this case, the Park Police, assisted by the FBI. I believed then and continue to believe that there was one central question that had to be addressed with regard to the handling of files in Vince Foster's office. That question was, who should determine, who should determine what documents would be made available to the investigators. I thought White House counsels should not decide, largely alone, whether particular documents were relevant to the Foster investigation, whether executive privilege attached to any particular document, and whether the need of the Park Police and the Federal Bureau of Investigation for a particular document as part of their investigation justified overriding any such privilege.

Who should decide is not a question of personal trust but a matter of assuring that there's a trustworthy process. It isn't a technical legal question but an issue as to the necessary conditions for maintaining the credibility of federal law enforcement and of the presidency. I thought that for the White House counsel's office to make these decisions largely by itself, as it did, was simply not an acceptable way of addressing them. A player with significant stakes in the matter cannot also be referee.

. . .

A few lessons were very much in my mind when I learned of Vince Foster's death. An investigation that requires access to White House papers is always difficult because there are legitimate investigative claims by law enforcement that must somehow be reconciled with recognized and legitimate claims of confidentiality by the White House and the president. Reconciliation is not an abstract process. It requires balancing interests document by document. Not every document is equally entitled to protection in terms of confidentiality. Not every document is essential or even relevant to an investigation. The obvious stakes in reconciling these competing demands are getting the truth in the investigation and not defeating any of the purposes of executive privilege, particularly allowing frankness in White House discussions and protecting national security secrets.

. . .

The Department of Justice was not entitled to subpoena all the documents in Vince Foster's office. The general presumption of confidentiality access in *U.S. v. Nixon*, the Watergate case, forcing President Nixon to turn over papers and tapes, was overcome in that case only by the special prosecutor being able to identify specific documents as relevant and essential to the criminal investigation. We knew of no specific documents in Foster's office that would be relevant or essential to determining whether he had killed himself. But the fact that a court would not have intervened does not leave the question of a fair and credible process just a matter of choice for an administration. The federal law enforcement authorities have a responsibility to assure a process that credibly promises objectivity when high officials are part of the investigation. To keep this promise of objectivity even in a case that showed all the early signs of being a suicide, the White House counsel could not be the one to decide what documents would be shown to the investigators and which would be retained or distributed as irrelevant to the investigation or as privileged, despite potential usefulness to the investigation.

. . .

[Senator Shelby is asking Mr. Heymann about Roger Adams and David Margolis, two career Justice Department lawyers]

MR. HEYMANN: That's Roger Adams and David Margolis.

SEN. SHELBY: And what were their positions in the Justice Department?

MR. HEYMANN: Both of them were then temporarily on detail to my office as Deputy Attorney General. They were long time career prosecutors in the Criminal Division of the Justice Department.

SEN. SHELBY: With a lot of experience?

MR. HEYMANN: Many, many, many years of experience.

. . .

SEN. SHELBY: At some point on the 21st it was determined that Roger Adams and David Margolis would be sent over to the White House, as I've said, to review documents regarding the relevance and privilege dealing with the Foster investigation. You said that was right.

MR. HEYMANN: That's correct, Senator Shelby.

SEN. SHELBY: And the scope of this review according to your notes would be looking for anything to do with this violent death. Do you want to refer to your notes?

MR. HEYMANN: Yes. I have my notes here and that's correct.

SEN. SHELBY: Okay, is that correct?

MR. HEYMANN: That's correct.

SEN. SHELBY: And it was your—was it your understanding by the end of the 21st that an agreement or understanding had been reached between the Department of Justice, the Park Police and the White House over how the search would be conducted, the search of the Deputy Counsel's office?

MR. HEYMANN: Yes, Senator Shelby, in the sense that we all had agreed on how it would be done, and in what I still think was a very sensible way.

SEN. SHELBY: Would you relate what you recall of how—what you agreed to or thought you had agreed to.

MR. HEYMANN: I would be happy to. I just wanted to make clear, Senator Shelby, I didn't feel that I had a binding commitment by Mr. Nussbaum or anyone else. We simply all had talked about it by then and we all were on the same track, we all were on the same page, we all thought it would be done in the way I'm about to describe.

SEN. SHELBY: Did you think when you sent Mr. Adams and Mr. Margolis over there that it would turn into an adversarial relationship or something close to that?

MR. HEYMANN: No, I did not.

SEN. SHELBY: You did not.

MR. HEYMANN: You had asked me to describe what the understanding was, Senator Shelby.

SEN. SHELBY: Yes, sir. Absolutely, right. You go ahead.

MR. HEYMANN: The understanding was that they would see these two senior prosecutors, not the investigators, but the prosecutors would see enough of every document to be able to determine whether it was relevant to the investigation or not. Now, I've been handed some pages from my transcript, but let's assume this is a document and it's about 30 pages long.

SEN. SHELBY: Yes, sir.

MR. HEYMANN: They would look at this and it says, deposition of Philip Heymann re: Whitewater, and they would know that that didn't seem to have any likely baring on the cause of Vince Foster's death. If need be, they might have to look a page or two into it. But the object was to maintain the confidentiality of White House papers to the largest extent possible with satisfying ourselves that we were learning of every [potentially relevant] document. If there was a relevant document, it would be set aside in a separate pile. If the White House counsel's office believed that it was entitled to executive privilege, and therefore should not be turned over to us, we would then have to resolve that. There would be a separate pile of documents, some relevant that would go directly to the investigators, some relevant but executive privilege claims, in which case we would have to resolve it, perhaps with the assistance of the legal counsel's office at the Justice Department.

SEN. SHELBY: Mr. Heymann, did you contemplate that this would be done jointly or just done by the White House counsel?

MR. HEYMANN: I thought it was essential, Senator Shelby, that it be done jointly with these two prosecutors being able to satisfy themselves and through them, satisfy the investigative agencies that whatever might be relevant was being made available to us.

. . .

SEN. SHELBY: Okay. Your notes mention, I believe, Mr. Heymann, that Steve Neuwirth objected to this agreement, but that Mr. Nussbaum agreed with Margolis that it was a done deal, is that correct? Do you want to refer—

MR. HEYMANN: That is what they reported to me when Mr. Margolis and Mr. Adams returned that evening, the evening of Wednesday the 21st—

SEN. SHELBY: What do you know it to reflect? I was paraphrasing.

MR. HEYMANN: It said they discussed the system that had been agreed upon, I've just described it to you.

SEN. SHELBY: Yes, sir.

MR. HEYMANN: BN, that stands for Mr. Nussbaum, agreed. SN, that stands for Steve Neuwirth, said no, we shouldn't do it that way; the Justice Department attorneys should not have direct access to the files. David Margolis, the Justice Department attorney said it's a done deal, and Mr. Nussbaum at that point said, yes, we've agreed to that.

SEN. SHELBY: Was it important to you and to the Department of Justice that you represented that the documents be reviewed independently? Is that why it was important that the Department of Justice look for relevance and privilege jointly in this undertaking?

MR. HEYMANN: Yes, Senator Shelby. Again, I did not think it was necessary and do not think it was necessary to review documents which we could quickly determine had no relevance to Vince Foster's death. So our attorneys would not have looked at those. That was a clear part of the understanding—or pages.

SEN. SHELBY: Yes, sir. I understand that you received a call from David Margolis the next morning from the White House about the search. Is that correct? You want to refer to your notes?

MR. HEYMANN: That's correct, Senator Shelby.

SEN. SHELBY: What was his call about?

MR. HEYMANN: He and Roger and Adams had gone over with the Park Police and the FBI to do the review we planned.

SEN. SHELBY: This was pursuant to the understanding you had with Mr. Nussbaum.

MR. HEYMANN: Pursuant to the understanding of the 21st.

SEN. SHELBY: Okay.

MR. HEYMANN: Mr. Margolis told me that Mr. Nussbaum had said to me that they had changed the plan; that only the White House counsel's office would see the actual documents. Mr. Margolis had asked Mr. Nussbaum whether that had been discussed with me, and Mr. Nussbaum had said no. I told Mr. Margolis at that point to put Mr. Nussbaum on the phone, and I was—

SEN. SHELBY: Did he get on the phone with you?

MR. HEYMANN: He got on the phone.

SEN. SHELBY: Okay, what did you say to him?

MR. HEYMANN: I told him that this was a terrible mistake; that—

SEN. SHELBY: A terrible mistake. Go ahead.

MR. HEYMANN: Well, please don't—

SEN. SHELBY: That was your words, is that right?

MR. HEYMANN: Yeah, no, no please don't assume that what I now paraphrase would be the words I actually used. This is 740 days ago, and it would be quite unreliable to think that those were the exact words. I remember, very clearly, sitting in the deputy attorney general's conference room, picking up the phone in that very big room. I remember being very angry and very adamant and saying, this is a bad mistake. This is not the right way to do it. And I don't think I'm going to let Margolis and Adams stay there if you're going to do it that way, because they would have no useful function, and it would simply look like they were performing a useful function, and I don't want this to happen.

. . .

SEN. SHELBY: You later found out, sir, that the search was conducted with Mr. Nussbaum calling the shots that night, is that right?

MR. HEYMANN: That's correct.

SEN. SHELBY: Did you talk to Mr. Nussbaum after that?

MR. HEYMANN: I found that out at about—when Mr. Margolis and Mr. Adams returned the evening of the 22nd—

SEN. SHELBY: Returned to your office.

MR. HEYMANN: To my office.

SEN. SHELBY: Yes, sir.

MR. HEYMANN: I went home to an apartment we were renting then, and I picked up the phone and I called Mr. Nussbaum, and I told him that I couldn't imagine why he would have treated me that way. How could he have told me that he was going to call back before he made any decision on how the search would be done, and then not call back?

SEN. SHELBY: What did [he] say to that?

MR. HEYMANN: I don't honestly remember, Senator Shelby. He was, again, polite. He didn't—there was no explanation given that I would remember. And I remember saying to him, "Bernie, are you hiding something?" And he said, "No, Phil, I promise you we're not hiding something."

. . .

[Steven Neuwirth had found a suicide note in Vincent Foster's briefcase on the following Monday, July 26]

SEN. SHELBY: When you and the attorney general—Janet Reno—were summoned to the White House and given the note—

MR. HEYMANN: Yes.

SEN. SHELBY:—at that meeting, were any discussions of concerns raised to you or the attorney general about what to do with the note? Would you just relate to us, when you went to the White House, what transpired?

MR. HEYMANN: I rode over with the attorney general on the evening of Tuesday the 27th. We had a 7:00 meeting. We had not been told what it was about—though, I thought it was probably about the Foster matter. We were shown into Mr. McLarty's office. The only—I think, at first, only Mr. Gergen—David Gergen was there. Then Mr. Nussbaum came in. Then Mr. Burton, I believe, and certainly Mr. McLarty. We—there had been some small talk before that. Mr. Nussbaum sat down on the couch. There are two couches that face each other across a coffee table. He pulled out an envelope, and he said, "Yesterday, we found these—we found a torn up note." I do not believe he assembled it for us. I think he may have taken out the yellow pages and shown it to us. I can't remember exactly. He had written down what the note said, and he read us the note. They wanted to know what we thought should be done with it. They attorney general said, "Turn it over to the Park Police immediately." She then asked, "Why did we just—why are we just getting it now, if we—if it was found—" I guess it's 30 hours—it was 30 hours before then? The White House people—I don't know whether it was Mr. Nussbaum or who said that there was—they wanted first to show it to Mrs. Foster, and they wanted to show it to the President, who might—if he had wanted to—have exerted executive privilege, they said. They said they were not able to get to the President until late on the 27th. And as soon as they got the President and made the President aware of the note, they had called us.

          * * *

SEN. SHELBY: Mr. Heymann, the next day, I believe your notes reveal—the 28th—the Department of Justice called the FBI. Is that you, or someone asked, is that right, sir?

MR. HEYMANN: I directed Mr. Margolis, who was the person who was in contact with the investigative agencies—particularly the FBI most—to call the FBI and ask them to do a thorough investigation of the finding of the note.

SEN. SHELBY: And was your words in the note, "do an aggressive investigation?"

MR. HEYMANN: Yes, I told them to be very aggressive.

SEN. SHELBY: Okay. And then the next day—the 29th, according to your notes—you received a call from Mr. Collier, the chief of staff to the Secretary of the Interior. What was the substance of that call?

MR. HEYMANN: I had never met him. He asked me—he sounded quite worried about something. He identified who he was and asked if he could come over and see me. I said, "Sure, come right away." He came over and he went into my office and he expressed—he said, "The Park Police are very, very upset about the investigation." This was the first time something like that had been told to me. In fact, of course it was the day after the note had been found, and they probably felt that they were looking bad with a note having been found four or five days later. He said that he wondered whether the Park Police were capable of doing an investigation in the White House. He said that they felt that they really couldn't get the cooperation that they wanted. And he said that he wanted to pull the Park Police out, and he'd like me to substitute the FBI for the Park Police.

SEN. SHELBY: What did you say?

MR. HEYMANN: I told him that the FBI was already in there at my request investigating the finding of the note, and that I would see to it that he had no more trouble with the White House in his investigation. I think I called Mr. Gergen, and I said to him that—

SEN. SHELBY: These notes flashed up now—does that reflect that you called Mr. Gergen? And also you had in that call [to] Mr. Gergen? Is that correct?

MR. HEYMANN: I called Mr. Gergen, and I said we have a very serious problem on our hands, and I described it to him, and Mr. Gergen said, "Look, I'd like you to call back, or I'll call you back." What he obviously wanted to do, and then did, was assemble a large number of people from the White House—I don't know whether it was five or eight or more—in an office, and put me—and then had me call back, and put me on a speaker phone. And I told them all that they had a major disaster brewing, that I wasn't going to put up with it any more, that the FBI was in there, that the FBI was going to interview anybody it wanted to, and the Park Police were going to interview anybody they wanted to, that I wanted full cooperation, that White House counsel could not attend the interviews—that seemed to be an issue of some contention. And that if they did everything as I described it they might manage to avoid prolonged Senate hearings in the summer of 1995. Now, that last was not true, Senator Shelby. (Laughter.) They did everything as I told them.

* * *

DAY 12 OF HEARINGS INTO WHITEWATER DEVELOPMENT CORPORATION AND HANDLING OF DOCUMENTS FROM OFFICE OF WHITE HOUSE COUNSEL VINCE FOSTER.

Senate Whitewater Special Committee

August 9, 1995

Chair: Senator Alfonse D'Amato, (R–NY)

Witness: Bernard Nussbaum, Former White House Counsel

SEN. D'AMATO: . . . Do you swear or affirm that the testimony you are about to give is the truth, the whole truth, and nothing but the truth so help you God.

MR. NUSSBAUM: I do affirm.

SEN. D'AMATO: Thank you. Mr. Nussbaum, I understand that you have a prepared statement that you'd like to give to the Committee for the record, and we'd be prepared to receive your testimony on it at this point.

* * *

MR. NUSSBAUM: Thank you. Mr. Chairman. . . .

As you know, I was counsel to the President of the United States from January 20, 1993 until April 5, 1994. Vincent Foster was my deputy. He was a superb lawyer, an individual of great integrity, and a magnificent human being. Vince was the co-senior partner of the little law firm we created in the White House, the White House Counsel's office. It is hard to imagine having a finer colleague. I miss him. I miss him a great deal. So do so many others who knew him well.

This Committee is looking into the following question. Did improper conduct occur regarding the way in which White House officials handled documents in Mr. Foster's office following his death. I have an answer to that question, Mr. Chairman. It is a categorical no. There was nothing improper in the way White House officials handled documents in Vince Foster's office following his death.

As this Committee has heard, there were differences of opinion with the Justice Department as to how a search of Vince's office for a suicide note or similar such document should be conducted. That office contained numerous confidential files, as well as sensitive documents, such as briefing reports on Supreme Court nominees and other high administration officials.

Before any review by me of the documents in that office, Justice Department officials wanted to read a part of each document. They also [were] concerned with maintaining the credibility of federal law enforcement. But I was bound to act in accordance with my obligation as a lawyer and I did not believe that doing so, that acting in accordance with my obligations as a lawyer would undermine the credibility of federal law enforcement. It was my ethical duty, as a lawyer and as White House counsel, to protect a client's information and confidences, and not to disclose them without a prior review by me.

It was my duty to preserve the right of the White House, of this President, and future presidents to exert executive privilege, attorney-client privilege, and work product privilege. It was my duty to do nothing that could result in an inadvertent waiver of these privileges. It was my duty to protect the confidentiality of other matters as well, including sensitive government documents in that office. These were solemn professional obligations that I was sworn as a lawyer to uphold.

. . .

Mr. Heymann apparently believes that all lawyers, even Justice Department lawyers, are "co-players" with a "significant stake in the matter." He believes they cannot, and indeed they must not, be trusted to act as a "referee"—his words—when it comes to reviewing and producing documents. That notion is foreign to our system of civil and criminal justice. It is contrary to how our system functions.

All lawyers, whether they are White House lawyers, private lawyers or Justice Department lawyers are bound by the same ethical obligations. No one of us stands on a higher pedestal than the other. No one of us is more or less of a player with a stake than the other. No one of us is more or less deserving of trust than the other. In our system of justice, tens of thousands of lawyers each day act as referees under strict ethical rules, when it comes to reviewing and producing documents. This is how our system functions. These lawyers are subject, of course, to that ultimate referee, our judges.

Still, Heymann's view that when it comes to the President's documents, the public will only trust and accept the word of a Justice Department lawyer, and not a White House Counsel, or a private lawyer, is not only disappointing, it is destructive. For it feeds the very cynicism it creates; the very distrust that he claims to be combating. I've known Phil Heymann a long time. Phil is a good, and decent, and honest person. Here in my judgement, he just happens to be profoundly wrong. And so, as I will describe later, while I sought to accommodate the legitimate needs of law enforcement, I fulfilled my professional obligations. And as you will hear, I was also concerned, as Mr. Heymann appears to be, about appearances.

· · ·

Let me now describe, in some detail, those fateful days in July 1993.

· · ·

Patsy Thomasson and Maggie Williams, two White House staff members, were in Vince's office. Maggie was sitting on Vince's sofa crying. Patsy, who was sitting behind Vince's desk said they had just arrived. She told me, Patsy told me, she was looking for a suicide note. Patsy and I checked the surfaces in Vince's office. We opened a drawer or two, looking for a note. No one, no one looked through Vince's files. Patsy did not examine any individual file. She did not rummage through or examine any individual file, nor did I. We did not find a note. We spoke about Vince and what a tragedy this was. Each of us, all of us, were quite emotional that night. The three of us then left. The [off]ice itself did not have a lock on the door, but the counsel's suite did. Initially I did not think about securing the office in any special manner. It was not a crime scene. Vince did not die there. One does not typically seal the workplace of a person who commits suicide. No one, the night before, suggested to me that Vince's office should be sealed. But, on the morning of July 21, after talking about the issue with two of my staff members, we called the Secret Service. We asked to have an agent stand outside of, and control access to, Vince's office. The Secret Service promptly complied with that request. That evening a lock was installed on the office door.

That morning of July 21, I also attended a meeting in the White House with the Park Police. They told us about the discovery of Vince Foster's body and the scene of his death. They said they believed that Vince had committed suicide. The President came to the counsel suite on July 21. He came to console the people who worked there. While the President was with us, I briefly entered Vince's office. I removed and showed to the President an early 1950's photograph of Miss Mary's Kindergarten class in Hope, Arkansas.

That photograph, which Vince cherished, showed a five-year-old Vince Foster and a five-year-old Bill Clinton. Nothing else was removed from Vince's office that day.

Later that afternoon, the President, Mack McLarty, and I addressed the entire White House staff to try to comfort them. It was not easy.

Midday, members of the Park Police contacted me. They asked me to review—they asked to review the contents of Mr. Foster's office to see if there was a suicide note, an extortion note or some other similar document. They also asked to interview me and members of my staff. I thought there might be multiple requests for information, so I called Mr. Heymann, Philip Heymann, the deputy attorney general, and asked if the Justice Department would agree to coordinate the investigations of Foster's death. He said the department would do so.

In the late afternoon, I met with representatives of the Park Police, the Department of Justice, and others. We agreed that interviews of my staff members, many of whom were still shaken, would be held the next morning. We also agreed after some discussion that a search of Vince's office would take place the next day to search more thoroughly for a suicide note or similar such document. I will return shortly to this meeting with the Justice Department on July 21.

Thursday, July 22. The next day, on July 22, the Park Police interviews of staff members took place, as scheduled. The search of Vince's office began in the early afternoon.

How the search of Vince Foster's office was conducted. Prior to the search of Mr. Foster's office, I gave a good deal of thought about how it should be done.

Vince's office was the office of a senior executive branch lawyer. It contained numerous, numerous confidential and privileged files. It had extremely sensitive documents, such as briefing books on Supreme Court nominees and sensitive reports, background reports, on other high administration officials. I believed there also might be national security information in the office.

As a lawyer, as a former Justice Department prosecutor—I was an assistant United States attorney in New York in the 1960s under Robert Kennedy, the attorney general, and Bob Morgenthau, the U.S. attorney. As a former federal prosecutor myself, I understood and respected the desire of law enforcement officials to examine the office promptly. I understood their need to see if there was a suicide note or some other such document that might help explain Vince Foster's death.

It is important to understand what we were being asked to do on July 22, to understand what the search was for and what it was not for. The search was for a suicide note, an extortion note or some similar document which reflected depression or acute mental anguish. That is the request law enforcement officials made of me.

They did not ask to read every piece of paper in Foster's office, every official White House record there, every personal file there, to see if there was any indication of concern about any matter Vince had been working on. I was not faced with a request for some general excursion through documents to determine Vince's state of mind about matters he was working on.

But even as to the limited request made of me on July 22, it was my duty, as a lawyer and as a White House counsel, to protect client confidences, including highly sensitive government documents in that office. It was my duty to preserve the ability of the White House to exert the executive, attorney/client and work product privileges and to be concerned about institutional precedent.

This was a duty that I could not ignore. This was my professional obligation under the code of professional responsibility and the model rules of professional conduct, which in one form or another, govern the conduct of all lawyers and protect the confidences and secrets of all clients.

Before deciding on how to balance the competing interests I was facing, I spoke with other attorneys in the White House on the morning of July 22. I talked to a number of people about this issue, as to how a search for a suicide note should be conducted, but I did not speak to the President or the first lady about this matter, nor did Susan Thomases, or anyone else convey a message to me from either of them. Susan Thomases did not discuss the first lady's views with me. But, I should say, I assumed from the outset of this tragedy, that the first lady, who's a very good lawyer, like every other good lawyer in or out of the White House would believe that permitting unfettered access to a lawyer's office is not proper. That was my assumption. It was not the result of any conversation with her.

. . .

I decided I was not going to keep law enforcement officials out of Vince's office. I chose a middle ground. I chose a procedure that balanced and accommodated the interests of confidentiality and law enforcement interests. I chose a procedure that provided the agents with immediate access to Vince's office, avoiding, I hoped by doing so, unnecessary conflict with the agents and unfortunate appearances.

This is the procedure I followed. This is what we did on July 22. I entered Mr. Foster's office together with the law enforcement officials.

No one sat in the hallway, the agents were with me at all times during the search in Vince's office. As the agents watched, I personally pulled out each of the files in that office. I briefly reviewed the files. As I was doing so, I gave the agents a general description of the documents, and I checked to see if there was a suicide note or an extortion note or other similar document in those files. Which is what this search, after all, was all about.

But the agents did not sit, as cigar store dummies, as I conducted the search.

I also accepted a request from the agents to read for themselves any document I was describing. As I went through the files in Vince Foster's office, the agents did [raise the] possibility of allowing Justice Department lawyers to look at a portion of each document, to see if it was privileged. I said, I did say, I would consider that option. I did not say I would agree to it. I did consider it very carefully. By the next day I had determined that this would create an unacceptable risk of disclosure of confidences and equally unacceptable risks of waiver of the privileges I was obligated to protect.

As for privileged matters, the law regarding waiver is both strict and uncertain. A party cannot selectively disclose portions of attorney/client privileged documents without running a serious risk of forfeiting the right to keep other documents and communications on that subject matter privileged. I could not take such a risk of waiver consistent with my obligations to preserve the right to assert privilege.

If the Justice Department officials believe that we reached an agreement after our July 21 meeting, then a misunderstanding and a miscommunication occurred. And I may be responsible for that. But I do not believe, nor as you have heard, do my colleagues in the White House counsel's office believe, who were also present at those meetings, that we reached any agreement on July 21.

. . .

The vast majority of the files reviewed during the office search on July 22 were Mr. Foster's working files, matters that he was working on in his role as Deputy White House Counsel. When the agents left, the search was over. I wanted to get on with the work of the office, to reassign Foster's matters to other attorney's.

As this committee has heard, the Justice Department attorneys were aware that Foster's working files would be immediately distributed to other attorneys in the office. I began this process immediately. Now, let me turn to the Clinton personal files. During the office search on July 22, I saw a number of files that concerned personal matters of the Clintons. I identified them to the agent present, to the agents present. I said, "These were Clinton personal files." I said, "These involve investments, taxes, other financial matters and the like." Included was a file on the Clintons' Whitewater real estate investment.

I knew that Vince had been assisting the first family in completing financial disclosure statements, filing tax returns, and creating a blind trust. A President and his family are officially required to perform such acts. As such is proper, it is proper and indeed traditional, for the White House Counsel's office to assist in that official function.

Mr. Foster needed access to the Clinton personal files for these official purposes. They were, therefore, properly in the White House Counsel's office. But that did not make them any less personal files even though the first family has to file financial disclosure forms and other similar documents, blind trust and the like.

And even though it must use its personal financial files as the basis for that disclosure, it does not follow that every such file becomes a Presidential record. That would be a ludicrous result. Those files had nothing to do with the transaction of government business. Although they were needed to file official forms. They remained personal files. They remained the Clinton's personal files. I knew that the work on the project for which the personal files were needed had recently been completed. But, Vince's death, and the work done, the reason for our office possessing these personal files was at an end. Just as I believed, the Foster personal files should go to the Foster family lawyers, I believed the Clinton personal files belonged in the hands of the first family or their personal lawyers.

Shortly after the search of Vince's office was completed, I asked Maggie Williams, the first lady's Chief of Staff, to help me transfer these files to the Clintons, and to their personal lawyers. I told Maggie that I thought the Clintons would probably want to send the files to Williams and Connolly, a Washington law firm that had been working with Vince, and was representing them personally. I said she should confirm that with the first family. The Clinton personal files were sent to the White House residence on the evening of July 22. They were sent to the residence because it was late in the day, and we were leaving for the funeral in Arkansas early the next morning. . . .

* * *

On Friday, July 23rd, we flew to Arkansas with the President to attend Vince's funeral. I returned to the White House on July 26th. During that period of time Mr. Foster's office was locked. Before we left for the funeral, I had asked Steve Neuwirth to pack up the remaining personal items in Vince's office, such as photographs and wall hangings, and send them to the Foster family.

On Monday, July 26th, Steve turned to his task. . . .

* * *

Steven R. Neuwirth, b. 1962; B.A. Yale University 1984; J.D. Yale University 1987; associated with Wachtell, Lipton, Rosen & Katz, New York City 1987–93; Associate Counsel to the President of the United States since 1993.

Robert J. Giuffra, b. 1960; A.B. Princeton University 1983; J.D. Yale University 1987; staff assistant, White House Office of Public Liaison, 1981–82; law clerk, Judge Ralph K. Winter, Jr. (2nd. Cir.) 1987–88; law clerk, Chief Justice William Rehnquist 1988–89; associated with Sullivan & Cromwell, New York City 1989–94, 1996–___ (cases included *United States v. Armand D'Amato,* Chapter 1 supra); Chief Counsel, United States Senate

Committee on Banking, Housing and Urban Affairs, Jan. 1995 to Nov. 1996.

Robert Giuffra deposed his law school classmate Steven Neuwirth in July of 1995 concerning the circumstances surrounding Neuwirth's discovery of a handwritten "suicide note" in the bottom of Vince Foster's briefcase.

DEPOSITION OF STEPHEN R. NEUWIRTH (IN RE: WHITEWATER) JULY 10, 1995 (9:35 A.M.)

Whereupon,

STEPHEN R. NEUWIRTH

was called as a witness herein, and having been first duly sworn, was examined and testified as follows:

EXAMINATION

BY MR. GIUFFRA:

Q *Good morning, Mr. Neuwirth, my name is Robert Giuffra. I'm Chief Counsel of the Senate Banking Committee. . . .*

Would you please state your name for the record?

A Stephen Neuwirth.

* * *

Q *If you could just state, going backwards, your employment history from law school to the present.*

A After I graduated from law school, I clerked for a year for Peter Leisure, who's a Federal District Court Judge in the Southern District of New York.

From December of 1988 through January of 1993, I was employed by Wachtell, Lipton, Rosen & Katz, a law firm in New York. Since January 26, 1993, I've been Associate Counsel for the President.

Q *While you were at Wachtell, Lipton, what was your area of specialization?*

A I was a litigator.

Q *Did you work with Mr. Nussbaum while you were a litigator at Wachtell, Lipton?*

A Yes.

Q *How closely did you work with Mr. Nussbaum while you were a litigator at Wachtell, Lipton?*

A It depended on the matter we were working on.

Q *Did you work with Mr. Nussbaum on a number of matters at Wachtell, Lipton?*

A Yes.

Q *Do you recall roughly what portion of your time you spent working on matters on which Mr. Nussbaum was the supervising partner?*

A I don't know. It's difficult for me to calculate an exact percentage.

Q *How about a rough percentage?*

A At this point, it's hard for me to go back and reconstruct what it was, but Mr. Nussbaum was one of the heads of the litigation department at the firm.

Q *Did Mr. Nussbaum hire you as an associate counsel to the President?*

A He was the White House counsel at the time I was hired.

Q *Was he the person responsible, though, for the fact that you were hired as a White House counsel, associate White House counsel?*

A I think so.

* * *

Q *What was your understanding as to Mr. Foster's areas of responsibility during this period of January through July 1993?*

A He was the Deputy White House Counsel and he worked with Mr. Nussbaum on running the White House Counsel's Office and helping to supervise all of the matters handled by the office.

Q *Did Mr. Foster have any specific areas of responsibility?*

A My understanding of his responsibilities were what I just described.

Q *Did you have any understanding as to how management of the office was delineated between Mr. Nussbaum and Mr. Foster?*

A Well, I think Mr. Nussbaum liked to say that the White House Counsel's Office was like a small law firm, and that he and Vince were like the senior partners in the law firm.

* * *

Q *What did Mr. Nussbaum say to you about his conversation with Ms. Thomases?*

A I don't remember what exact words Mr. Nussbaum used in his conversation with me.

Q *Would this conversation have been before the review actually occurred on the 22nd?*

A I'm not sure. I think it may have been but I'm not positive.

. . .

Q *What did Mr. Nussbaum tell you about the conversation that he had with Ms. Thomases?*

A Again, while I don't remember his exact words, in a very brief discussion, my understanding was that Mr. Nussbaum felt that Ms. Thomases and the First Lady may have been concerned about anyone having unfettered access to Mr. Foster's office.

Q *Did Mr. Nussbaum indicate to you that Ms. Thomases had spoken to the First Lady?*

A No.

* * *

Q *Do you recall how may [sic] briefcases Mr. Foster had?*

A I don't know how many briefcases Mr. Foster had.

Q *Do you recall how many briefcases were in his office on July 22nd, when you conducted the review?*

A I was only aware of one.

Q *Could you describe that briefcase for the record?*

A It was a leather briefbag, is the term I would use, that expanded slightly. I don't know whether it had a zipper on top but it had handles on top that allowed you to carry it.

Q *Was this a soft leather?*

A It was not hard like a briefcase, it was more like, as I said, a leather briefbag, and it was not much larger than the length of a legal pad, maybe a little bit longer.

Q *At the outset of the review process, where was this briefcase located?*

A I believe it was behind Mr. Foster's desk under the window, leaning against the wall under the window.

Q *What was the color of this briefcase?*

A I think it was a brownish color.

Q *Did there come a time during the course of the review when Mr. Nussbaum reviewed the contents of this briefcase?*

A I know that at the start of the review, he advised the people in the room that there was a briefbag behind Mr. Foster's desk, because I don't know that the agents could see it from where they were standing or sitting.

And so Mr. Nussbaum advised them that it was there. I'm not certain whether I was in the room at the time he reviewed the contents of the briefbag, but it was certainly my understanding that he reviewed the contents of the briefbag, and I may have been there, I'm just not certain.

Q *Do you recall seeing him review the contents of the briefbag?*

A As I said, I'm not sure. The briefbag did not stand out in a way that made it more significant than any other items that he looked at during the review, so it's hard for me to be sure whether anything he did related to the briefbag or some other location in the office.

Q *Do you remember Mr. Nussbaum ever indicating that the briefbag was empty during the course of the review?*

A I don't have a recollection of him saying that it was empty. But, again, I was not necessarily present at every moment when he would have talked about the bag.

Q *Did you ever look in the briefcase on July 22nd, 1993?*

A No.

* * *

Q *Mr. Neuwirth, directing your attention to July 26th, did there come a time when you entered Mr. Foster's office and reviewed certain documents contained therein?*

A Yes.

Q *Could you please describe for the record the circumstances under which you reviewed these documents?*

A Mr. Nussbaum, I believe the previous Thursday, had asked me to make an inventory of the files in Mr. Foster's office.

* * *

Q *Did there come a time in the course of preparing this inventory that you found scraps of paper in Mr. Foster's briefcase?*

A After I had completed the inventory, and when I was packing personal items that I found, like photographs, into a box, I saw the briefcase against the wall under the window behind Mr. Foster's desk. I knew it belonged to Mr. Foster and I understood that it was empty, and I picked it up and carried it over to put it into the box. And because I didn't want to destroy the pictures that were lying across the top of the box, I turned the briefbag to try to fit it into the box without causing such damage. While I was doing that, scraps of yellow paper fell out.

Q *Why did you understand the briefcase was empty?*

A Because it both looked empty, it felt empty, and my understanding was that whatever contents were in the briefbag had been handled by Mr. Nussbaum during the review that occurred the previous Thursday.

Q *Approximately how many scraps of paper fell out of the briefcase as you were trying to place it in the box?*

A I don't remember what the exact number was, but it was fewer than the total number of scraps of paper that were in the briefbag.

Q *When you saw these scraps of paper, what did you do?*

A I picked them up and noticed that they had handwriting on them that was like Mr. Foster's. And when I saw that there were a number of pieces of these paper scraps, I brought the scraps of paper into Mr. Nussbaum's office, which no one was in at time, but which had a conference table, and on my way in, I asked—I think either on my way in or after I noticed that I had the scraps of paper that looked like a piece of paper once they were put together, or going to, I asked one of the assistants in the outer office to call Mr. Nussbaum, either by paging him or phoning him, and I went back into Mr. Nussbaum's office to try to put the scraps of paper together.

And Mr. Nussbaum arrived very shortly thereafter.

* * *

Q *Did Mr. Nussbaum try to contact anyone upon the discovery of the note?*

A Yes.

Q *Who did he contact?*

A He asked me to wait in his office while he went to get Mack McLarty, the Chief of Staff. He came back with Bill Burden from Mr. McLarty's office and told me that Mr. McLarty was traveling with the President in Chicago.

Q *Did Mr. Nussbaum attempt to locate the First Lady?*

A He did later.

Q *Do you recall when that was?*

A I don't know the exact time, but the sequence of events was that after Mr. Burden saw the note, an effort was made to contact Mr. McLarty, who was in Chicago, and there was a brief discussion with Mr. McLarty, who said he would call back.

And after that discussion, Mr. Nussbaum went to the First Lady's office and came back with her.

Q *And she was in her office in the West Wing of the White House?*

A I actually don't know whether she was in her office at the time Mr. Nussbaum located her.

Q *The First Lady came to Mr. Nussbaum's office in the West Wing, correct?*

A That's correct.

    Q *What did the First Lady do or say?*

A Mr. Nussbaum told the First Lady that this note in Mr. Foster's handwriting had been found and he showed it to her, laid out on the conference table in his office.

I don't think the First Lady actually read it, as opposed to having had it described to her.

Very soon after the First Lady came into the office, the call came back from Mr. McLarty in Chicago, and once that discussion began, the First Lady left.

* * *

    Q *After the First Lady left the office, you testified that Mr. McLarty had called?*

A He called back.

    Q *What happened in that conversation?*

A Mr. McLarty called back, and David Gergen, who was with Mr. McLarty in Chicago, was also on the call, and it was a conversation that, at the White House, included Mr. Nussbaum and Mr. Burden, and I was also present in Bernie's office during the conversation.

* * *

    Q *What do you recall about this conversation with McLarty and Burden?*

A I recall that Mr. Nussbaum used his speaker phone because more people than himself were in the office. I think that the focus of the call was the appropriate steps to take, now that the note had been discovered, and I think by the conclusion of the call, it was agreed that, one, it was appropriate to show the note to Mrs. Foster before anything was done with it, and that she would be in Washington the next day. That the President was tied up on his trip, and that it would be appropriate at least to tell the President about the note when he got back, before taking any further steps.

I don't think there was ever a question about whether the note would be turned over to law enforcement officials but it was felt that there should be research done on some questions in case issues came up the next day and that people were going to have a response to.

    Q *What sort of issues might come up the next day that people would want a response to?*

A Whether a note like this, that talked about matters that Mr. Foster was working on in his capacity as White House Counsel was privileged in any way. Whether something like this, which was not dated and did not talk about suicide, could be considered a suicide note as opposed to some other type of writing. Whether there was some sort of legal obligation that was unambiguous with respect to turning it over to law enforcement officials. And, as I said, I didn't understand this research to be for the purpose of constructing arguments against turning over the note. I think that it was because people anticipated that questions of this type could come up in discussions about the note, and that it was appropriate to have answers to those questions.

Q *Were law enforcement officials notified of the note's existence on July 26th?*

A July 26th is Monday. I'm not aware of any such notification.

Q *Do you know why they were not notified of the note's existence, as opposed to having the note turned over?*

A My understanding was that, as I said earlier, in terms of the question of timing, it was felt that it would be appropriate to let Mrs. Foster know that such a note had been discovered, and since she was coming to Washington, to do so in person, before turning it over. And I think the feeling was—my understanding was that the feeling was that Mrs. Foster deserved to learn about this before she read about it in the newspaper and I think there was also a feeling that it would be appropriate to be able to tell the President about at least the existence of the note before turning it over.

Q *What about just notifying law enforcement officials of the note's existence?*

A I think I already told you that that, to my knowledge, did not occur on the 26th.

* * *

Q *Let me show you a document that bears Park Police 68.*

(Handing document to witness.)

[The document reads:

I made mistakes from ignorance, inexperience and overwork

I did not knowingly violate any law or standard of conduct

No one in the White House, to my knowledge, violated any law or standard of conduct, including any action in the travel office. There was no intent to benefit any individual or specific group

The FBI lied in their report to the AG (Attorney General)

The press is covering up the illegal benefits they received from the travel staff

The GOP has lied and misrepresented its knowledge and role and covered up a prior investigation

The Ushers Office plotted to have excessive costs incurred, taking advantage of Khaki (Katherine Hockersmith, a Little Rock interior designer brought in to redecorate the White House) and HRC (Hillary Rodham Clinton)

The public will never believe the innocence of the Clintons and their loyal staff

The WSJ (Wall Street Journal) editors lie without consequence

I was not meant for the job or the spotlight of public life in Washington. Here ruining people is considered sport.]

BY MR. GIUFFRA:

Q *What is this document?*

A It appears to be a photocopy of what looks to be the note that I found in Mr. Foster's office.

* * *

Q ... *Do you know when the note was disclosed to law enforcement authorities?*

A I don't know the exact time. I know that it was on Tuesday the 27th.

Q *Do you remember if it was early in the day or late in the day?*

A I believe it was in the latter part of the afternoon.

QUESTIONS

1. Nussbaum was paid by the United States Treasury from the White House budget; he was hired by the President to be White House Counsel and reported to the President. When Park Service Police, and later Justice Department lawyers, showed up to inspect the files in Vincent Foster's office, who was Nussbaum's "client" in the matter?

2. Who do you think was right, Bernard Nussbaum or Philip Heymann?

3. At the outset, Nussbaum observes that "Vince was the co-senior partner of the little law firm we created in the White House, the White House Counsel's office." Steven Neuwirth also refers to Nussbaum making this same analogy. Is this a good analogy? Does this analogy erect an unnecessary barrier between the White House Counsel's office and other parts of the government?

4. Nussbaum observes that "[a]ll lawyers, whether they are White House lawyers, private lawyers or Justice Department lawyers are bound by the same ethical obligations." Is this true? Does the context in which a lawyer practices make a difference? See David B. Wilkins, Legal Realism for Lawyers, 104 Harv. L. Rev. 468 (1990) (context must replace traditional model's commitment to general, universally applicable ethical rules); David B. Wilkins, Making Context Count: Regulating Lawyers After Kaye, Scholer, 66 S. Cal. L. Rev. 1145, 1151–60 (1993) (the traditional model of legal ethics incorrectly assumes uniformity among different practice areas). Had Nussbaum, even before entering government service, generalized about lawyers' roles? See Question 5 following discussion of the *Kaye, Scholer* matter in Chapter 2, supra.

5. How is the adversarial lawyering for private interests that is predominant in New York similar to or different from the way government lawyers interact with each other in Washington? Was Nussbaum hurt by presuppositions about law practice that he brought with him to his new job?

6. Were documents in Vincent Foster's office that concerned official government business, such as the selection of judges, covered by the attorney-client privilege? If so, should Nussbaum have prevented lawyers from the Justice Department from looking at these documents?

7. Were documents in Vincent Foster's office that concerned the private business of President and Mrs. Clinton covered by the attorney-client privilege? Had this privilege been waived?

8. Both Heymann and Neuwirth refer to White House lawyers having at least contemplated assertion of attorney-client or executive privilege with respect to the suicide note. Is there anything in the note that is arguably privileged?

9. Events occurring after the Justice Department review of papers in Foster's office compounded whatever negative appearances were created by Nussbaum's handling of the review. These events included Neuwirth's finding of the note and Neuwirth's statement that "Mr. Nussbaum felt that Ms. Thomases and the First Lady may have been concerned about anyone having unfettered access to Mr. Foster's office." The later political furor over the Whitewater land transactions and the controversy over the White House travel office made the situation worse. Does a government lawyer need to "plan for the worst" when deciding how to handle a situation that might look very different two years later? Even if Nussbaum should have handled the situation differently, were his actions still ethical?

10. It is clear from both Nussbaum's and Neuwirth's testimony that the White House lawyers were making difficult ethical decisions at a time when they were emotionally upset. Were they too close to the situation to make the best decision? Would it have been better if someone in the White House who was not as close to Foster, perhaps David Gergen, had decided how to handle the Justice Department investigation?

11. The "revolving door" between private law firms and government, discussed more extensively in Chapter 4 infra, is illustrated by the biographical sketches of the lawyers involved in both this matter and the ITT matter. Here, Vincent Foster had a professional relationship with Hillary Clinton while in private practice, and Mrs. Clinton had worked for Bernard Nussbaum in the Watergate investigation almost twenty years earlier. What relationships did Robert Giuffra and Steven Neuwirth have in the private sector with persons they would later work under in the public sector? Are these relationships relevant to the issues raised here?

CHAPTER 3 CLIENT AND POLITICAL SUPERIOR   **237**

12. Nussbaum's testimony and Neuwirth's deposition gave varying, if not inconsistent, accounts of Nussbaum's conversations with Susan Thomases. Neuwirth's deposition also raised the possibility that Nussbaum looked in the briefcase prior to Neuwirth's discovery of the note, although Neuwirth did not say that Nussbaum did look in the briefcase, and Nussbaum denied having done so. Why was the Senate Committee interested in these apparent inconsistencies?

13. What does Foster's note say about ethical standards in the political arena? Is he right?

Relevant Background

Government lawyers hold many different positions—Attorney General, Solicitor General, Department of Justice attorneys, federal agency attorneys, and White House Counsel, to name a few. Many other attorneys perform similar functions in state and local governments.

A lawyer representing the federal government is required by Congress to be "duly licensed and authorized to practice as an attorney under the laws of a State, territory, or the District of Columbia." Department of Justice Appropriation Authorization Act, Pub.L.No. 96–132, § 3(a), 93 Stat. 1040, 1044 (1980). Lawyers representing state and local governments must also be licensed in their own jurisdictions. Government attorneys thus are generally bound by the same rules of professional responsibility as other attorneys, although some problems are unique to their practice.

Who is the Client?*

Often, several different entities or individuals make competing demands on the government lawyer, all claiming the right to make decisions, insist on confidentiality and exercise other rights ordinarily associated with the lawyer's "client." Arguably, the government attorney should not seek to identify the client at all, but should stick to a more limited inquiry asking whose directions should be followed, whose confidences must be kept, and what role her own judgment has in deciding what to do. Robert P. Lawry, *Who is the Client of the Federal Government Lawyer? An Analysis of the Wrong Question.* 37:4 Fed. Bar J. 61, 62 (1978). Nonetheless, it is helpful to understand the different interests that from time to time claim to be the government attorney's "client."

The Public Interest

The government attorney ultimately represents the public. However, it is not easy to determine what exactly the public interest is when there are many competing interests in our society. Indeed, the District of Columbia Bar Association has gone so far as to proclaim that the notion of "public interest" is too amorphous to give useful guidance to government attorneys. Report by the District of Columbia Bar Special Committee on Govern-

---

* This discussion is based in part on Beth Nolan, Removing Conflicts from the Administration of Justice: Conflicts of Interest and Independent Counsels Under the Ethics in Government Act, 79 Geo. L. J. 1, 36–43 (1990).

ment Lawyers and the Model Rules of Professional Conduct, reprinted in Wash. Law, Sept.-Oct. 1988, at 53; see also Keith W. Donahoe, The Model Rules and the Government Lawyer, A Sword or Shield? A Response to the D.C. Bar Special Committee on Government Lawyers and The Model Rules of Professional Conduct, 2 Geo. J. Legal Ethics 987, 1000–05 (1989) (criticizing the D.C. Bar for emphasizing government interests rather than reflecting "the true consensus of the profession's conscience.").

Also, government attorneys do not always know when to use their own judgment in determining the public interest and when instead to adopt the vision of their political superiors. Some commentators emphasize the attorney's reliance on her own moral character and personal sense of the public good, justice and fairness. See Robert P. Lawry, Confidences and the Government Lawyer, 57 N.C. L. Rev. 625, 627 (1979)(government attorneys have a "duty to justice" or at least to "fairness" above and beyond that of other lawyers); Charles Fahy, Special Ethical Problems of Counsel for the Government, 33 Fed. Bar J. 331, 339–40 (1974) (Judge Fahy observes that "the surest means perhaps to the ethical performance of government counsel is the development of his own character and determination to maintain it intact."). Other commentators point out that governmental institutions mirror the public will as much as possible, and that a government attorney "acts unethically when she substitutes her individual moral judgment for that of a political process which is generally accepted as legitimate." Geoffrey P. Miller, Government Lawyers' Ethics in a System of Checks and Balances, 54 U. Chi. L. Rev. 1293, 1294 (1987). The responsible government attorney, according to this view, recognizes that, in order to function effectively as a counselor or advisor, he must have the confidence of his superiors that he will not be influenced by a personal vision of the public good.

Which of these two views should prevail depends on the particular circumstances involved. Government certainly would not function well if each government attorney could decide for herself what is in the public interest and act accordingly with no deference to political authority. On the other hand, an attorney can act unethically if he goes to the opposite extreme and allows the political process to completely consume his own moral judgment. Attorney General Kleindienst may have been right to do what he could to delay implementation of President Nixon's order to drop the appeal of the ITT case, at least until Attorney General Mitchell had a chance to urge Nixon to reconsider. In Chapter 12, you will read about a far more extreme example: prosecutors and judges in Nazi Germany who clearly should have resisted orders that they participate in judicially sanctioned murder.

The Executive Branch and the President

As a practical matter the government attorney works within a system of checks and balances between the various branches of government, and there are sometimes even conflicts between different constituencies within a single branch. See Miller, supra, at 1296. For example, the Justice

Department and the White House Counsel, both part of the executive branch, were sharply divided on how to review the papers left in Vincent Foster's office after his suicide.

Some commentators argue that, because executive department employees report ultimately to the President, the executive-branch attorney is responsible to "[that] branch as a whole and to the President as its head." Id. at 1298. However, as a practical matter, the attorney usually does not report to the President, but instead to a department head. As President Nixon discovered in confronting McLaren's refusal to drop the ITT antitrust suit, a department head like Kleindienst may exercise considerable independence in shaping policy. As President Nixon later learned in firing Attorney General Elliott Richardson (for his own refusal to fire Watergate Special Prosecutor Archibald Cox), firing a department head can be a costly political decision. Complete domination of the executive branch by the President thus is averted by the limited independence that executive agencies can preserve for themselves in the political process.

The Agency or Department

The government attorney's client is perhaps best described as the agency or department to which the attorney is assigned. The attorney is usually employed by the agency, and carries out his day to day activities under its administration. Generally, the attorney follows the instructions, and keeps the confidences, of superior officers who make policy decisions. Although this hierarchy usually relieves the attorney from having to determine policy objectives on her own, the attorney still must remember the obligations of the agency to the public. See Note, Developments in the Law—Conflicts of Interest in the Legal Profession, 94 Harv. L. Rev. 1244, 1415 (1981); see also, Lawry, Who is the Client, supra.

How are the Duties of Government Attorneys Unique?

Government attorneys, like other attorneys, owe their clients duties of competence, loyalty, and confidentiality. Although the duty of competence is relatively straightforward, client loyalty and confidentiality can be muddled if the client is difficult to identify in the first place.

The description in Canon 7 of the duty of loyalty as one of "zealous representation," suggests, perhaps incorrectly, that an attorney must devote herself without reservation to her client's interests. In the context of government service, it is easy for this duty of loyalty not only to be exaggerated, but also to be misplaced. For example, does the Attorney General "zealously represent" the Justice Department, the President, the United States government or the public, and who is to determine what are in the interests of each? Indeed, zealous representation can all too easily translate into advocacy of a political agenda or protection of the careers of political superiors. The "zealous representation" paradigm thus can be particularly troubling if embraced by government attorneys who, perhaps even more than other lawyers, should "temper their advocacy in the interests of 'justice'." Catherine J. Lanctot, The Duty of Zealous Advocacy and the Ethics of the Federal Government Lawyer: The Three Hardest Questions, 64 S. Cal. L. Rev. 951, 955 (1991).

Confidentiality also depends on the identity of the client. When should a government lawyer disclose a government official's fraud, waste or abuse of power, even at the expense of disclosing confidential "client" information? See Roger C. Cramton, The Lawyer as Whistleblower: Confidentiality and the Government Lawyer, 5 Geo J. Legal Ethics 291 (1991). When a government lawyer is called to testify in an investigation, there may not be much difference between refusal to blow the whistle on a superior and outright perjury or obstruction of justice. Attorney General Kleindienst clearly went too far when he misled Congress in order to conceal Nixon's order that the ITT appeal be dropped, even though Nixon's order itself was not on its face illegal. On the other hand, if Kleindienst had not been asked about the ITT matter under oath, one could hardly expect him to have volunteered information about President Nixon's involvement in the case.

White House counsel Bernard Nussbaum may have gone too far when he prevented lawyers from the Justice Department, itself part of the executive branch, from viewing confidential papers in the files of Deputy White House Counsel Vincent Foster. His insistence on protecting confidences from other executive branch lawyers did little to protect the reputation of the President (assuming the papers did not incriminate the President) and did create the "appearance of impropriety" (see Model Code, Canon 9). Indeed, the majority of the Senate Committee, voting along party lines, concluded that "White House officials engaged in highly improper conduct in handling documents in Vincent Foster's office following his death." Final Report of the Special Committee to Investigate Whitewater Development Corporation and Related Matters, Together with Minority Views, Report 104–280, 104th Cong., 2nd Sess. 14 (1996). On the other hand, the minority of the Senators on the Committee concluded that Nussbaum's handling of the documents did not hinder the investigation into Foster's suicide, Id. at 650, and that the majority's Report was politically motivated. Id. at 395. Nonetheless, the highly charged political atmosphere of the Senate hearings demonstrated one point that Nussbaum may have overlooked: for government lawyers and their clients, appearances can make a big difference. See Jennifer Wang, Raising the Stakes at the White House: Legal and Ethical Duties of the White House Counsel, 8 Geo. J. Legal Ethics 115, 120 (1994).

Conflicting Loyalties

Besides the "client" focused duties of competence, loyalty and confidentiality, a government attorney also has a duty to the judicial system as an "officer of the court." Although attorneys in the private sector have a similar duty, government attorneys' obligations take on a special dimension. For example, the government attorney who files a lawsuit has an obligation to consider the judicial resources that will be spent as well as the resources of her particular agency. Furthermore, the attorney should be sensitive to legitimate arguments made on the other side of a lawsuit or administrative proceeding. Even though the attorney will advocate a position, usually one determined by her political superiors, her opponent may advocate a position that reflects interests and values of a significant portion of the public. If circumstances warrant, the attorney may want to advise her political superiors that the government's position should be modified. See Rex E. Lee, Lawyering for the Government: Politics, Polemics & Principle, 47 Ohio St. L.J. 595, 596 (1986).

The government attorney also can face situations in which two or more persons or entities he represents have conflicting interests. First, the attorney may have a client relationship with both sides in a conflict between officers, agencies or subdivisions of agencies. For example, when an individual executive officer is accused of acting improperly, the officer may have an existing relationship with the attorney for the agency as a whole.

Second, a government attorney might be asked to represent both an officer of an agency and the agency itself in the same matter. For example, in Suffolk County, New York a civil rights action was brought against a police officer and against the police department and County. The County lawyer represented all of the defendants, and a conflict of interest arose when the lawyer attempted to clear the department and County by showing that the police officer acted outside of the scope of his employment. On appeal, the court vacated the judgment against the officer after finding that his lawyer acted contrary to his interests. Dunton v. County of Suffolk, 729 F.2d 903, 907 (2d Cir.), modified, 748 F.2d 69, 71 (2d Cir.1984).

Third, an attorney might have a client relationship with both an agency and a party appearing before it. In Civil Serv. Comm'n v. Superior Court, 163 Cal.App.3d 70, 209 Cal.Rptr. 159 (1984), for example, two San Diego County Department of Social Services employees were demoted during budget cut-backs and filed complaints with the County Personnel Commission. The Commission ordered reinstatement of the employees, but the County disagreed with the Commission's rulings and filed suit. The court found a conflict of interest because the municipal attorney bringing the County's suit had also advised the Commission in the same matter, and the attorney was disqualified. See also ABA Comm. on Ethics and Professional Responsibility Informal Op. 1433 (1978) (discussing a municipal law department's representation of two parties with opposing views in the same litigation) ("We see no way that, consistent with the Model Code, these opposing positions can be properly advocated in the same litigation by members of the same law department, who work from the same office and who are responsible to and presumably subject to the supervision and direction of the same department head.")

In each of these situations, the attorney should not continue to blindly profess loyalty to both interests, but instead should encourage the persons or entities involved to recognize conflicts where they exist and, if appropriate, to obtain separate counsel. See generally Beth Nolan, Removing Conflicts from the Administration of Justice: Conflicts of Interest and

Independent Counsels Under the Ethics in Government Act, supra; and further discussion of concurrent conflicts in Chapter 6, infra.

Personal Conflicts of Interest

In addition to her unique responsibilities as a lawyer, the government lawyer has the same ethical obligations that other government employees have with respect to personal conflicts of interest. She must avoid conflicts of interest between her official duties and both her own financial interests and her prior or subsequent employment in the private sector or in another branch of government. Occasionally, the government lawyer will also have to concern herself with real or perceived conflicts between her work and her personal moral beliefs.

Financial conflicts of interest can take many forms, including bribes, exploitation of public office for financial gain and any financial interest (such as stock holdings) that compromises the performance of an attorney's official duties. The federal government and most states have statutes addressing financial conflicts of interest, violation of which can result in criminal sanctions. For example, 18 U.S.C.A. § 208 requires a government employee to recuse herself from a matter in which she or her family has a financial interest. See also 28 C.F.R. §§ 45.735–4, 735–5 (1989) (requiring recusal of Justice Department employees); Nolan, supra, at 11. Financial conflicts of interest affecting judicial and administrative tribunals are discussed more extensively in Chapter 10, infra.

Conflicts of interest between official duties and concurrent private employment are relatively rare because most government attorneys are severely limited in their outside employment options. On the other hand, conflicts of interest between official duties and past and future employment often arise when government attorneys move through the "revolving door" from public service to private practice. See 18 U.S.C.A. § 207(b) (imposing one year post-employment ineligibility as to matters in which the attorney was previously responsible). These and similar successive conflicts are discussed in Chapter 4, infra.

Finally, it is important to point out that the government attorney may express her personal beliefs, even when those beliefs and the position of her government "client" conflict. For example, in Johnston v. Koppes, 850 F.2d 594 (9th Cir.1988), Joyce Johnston, an attorney for the California Department of Health Services, requested vacation leave to attend a hearing on state funding for abortion, but was instructed not to attend because her views in favor of state funded abortion differed from the policies of her office. Johnston nonetheless attended the hearing, but did not speak her views. She was subsequently transferred to another department in part because she had attended the hearing. Both the district court and the Ninth Circuit found that Johnston's attendance did not put her in a conflict of interest with her employer because she acted in her capacity as a public citizen. "[L]oyalty to a client does not require extinguishment of a lawyer's deepest convictions; and there are occasions where exercise of these convictions—even an exercise debatable in professional terms—is protected by the Constitution." Id. at 596 (Noonan, J.).

QUESTION

1. Both the ITT case and the controversy over Vincent Foster's papers raised important issues concerning the powers and privileges of the President. Another controversial issue is when, if ever, the President can be sued.

"Vice President John Adams did not attend the Philadelphia convention, but in a 1789 conversation with Connecticut delegate Oliver Ellsworth, Adams asserted the immunity of the President from any process whatsoever. The conversation occurred in the Senate chamber and was overhead by another Senator, William Maclay of Pennsylvania. Adams was a staunch advocate of a strong central government and of greater ceremony and prestige for the members of the new government; Maclay dismissed their views because Adams and Ellsworth were 'amazingly fond of the old leaven.' For Adams to be correct on this point, the President must enjoy greater privileges than Members of Congress. Yet, whereas Congress's privileges are specifically enumerated in Article I, the President's are nowhere mentioned." Bradford E. Biegon, Note: Presidential Immunity in Civil Actions: An Analysis Based upon Text, History and Blackstone's Commentaries, 82 Va. L. Rev. 677 (1996), citing, Journal of William Maclay 167–68 (Edgar S. Maclay ed., 1890).

Presidential immunity continues to be a controversial issue to this day. See Nixon v. Fitzgerald, 457 U.S. 731, 749 (1982) (President has absolute immunity from damages arising from official acts); Jones v. Clinton, 72 F.3d 1354 (8th Cir.) ("[T]he Constitution does not confer upon an incumbent President any immunity from civil actions that arise from his unofficial acts," and trial may proceed on complaint by former state employee alleging that President Clinton sexually harassed her while Governor of Arkansas), cert. granted, 116 S.Ct. 2545 (1996).

Who do you think was right, Adams or Maclay? If the President should be immune from suit while in office, should immunity extend only to suits concerning official acts, as in *Nixon*, or also to acts alleged to have occurred before the beginning of the President's term, as claimed by President Clinton?

CHAPTER 4

SUCCESSIVE CLIENTS

A. THE REVOLVING DOOR: LAWYERS IN GOVERNMENT SERVICE AND PRIVATE PRACTICE

Arthur H. Dean, b. Ithaca, N.Y. 1898, d. 1987; A.B. Cornell University 1921; LL.B. Cornell University 1923; joined Sullivan & Cromwell (S & C) in 1923; became a partner in 1930 and head of the firm in 1949 (helped draft the Securities Act of 1933, the Bankruptcy Act of 1938, the Trust Indenture Act of 1939, and the Investment Company Act of 1940); represented the United States on numerous occasions negotiating for the release of prisoners following the Korean Conflict in 1953 and at the nuclear test-ban negotiations in Geneva in 1961 and 1962.

Garfield H. Horn, b. Aberdeen, S.D. 1919; B.A. Harvard University 1940; LL.B. Harvard University 1946 (President of the Harvard Law Review); Naval service 1942–46; joined S & C in 1946; left S & C in May 1949 to become General Counsel to the United States Special Representative in Europe of the Economic Cooperation Administration; returned to S & C in 1951 and became a partner in 1953; resident partner at the firm's Paris office 1962–65.

The Firm:

Algernon Sydney Sullivan (1826–87), a native Virginian, moved to New York to practice law and distinguished himself in defending the crew of the Confederate raider *Savannah* who had been captured and brought to New York to be tried for piracy. Although the crew members were eventually exchanged as prisoners of war, Sullivan was himself imprisoned off New York Harbor for several weeks for his role in defending their cause. William Nelson Cromwell (1854–1948) grew up in Brooklyn under extreme financial difficulties after his father was killed in the Civil War. He was employed by Sullivan as an accountant beginning in 1874, and, with Sullivan's financial support, completed what was then a two year course at Columbia Law School. S & C was founded in 1879 when Sullivan signed articles of partnership with Cromwell, then aged 25; after Sullivan's death, eight years later, Cromwell was head of the firm for nearly forty years. In the 1890's Cromwell was counsel to the French Panama Canal Company, and is perhaps best known for his role in orchestrating the acquisition of the canal by the United States. John Foster Dulles (1888–1959), was also a managing partner of S & C before he became Secretary of State under President Eisenhower. Other S & C partners, including Arthur Dean and Garfield Horn, have also played prominent roles in government. See Arthur

H. Dean, William Nelson Cromwell 1854–1948 An American Pioneer 4–7, 23–24, 129–153 (1957).

United States of America v. Standard Oil Company (New Jersey) and Esso Export Corporation

136 F. Supp. 345 (S.D.N.Y.1955).

■ IRVING R. KAUFMAN, District Judge.

In a civil suit by the United States Government to recover refunds from Standard Oil Company (New Jersey) and its subsidiary, Esso Export Corporation, for alleged overcharges in ECA financed transactions, defendant Esso Export moved for an order decreeing that the law firm of Sullivan & Cromwell, its counsel, may properly represent Esso Export in this action, and the government cross-moved for an order disqualifying Sullivan & Cromwell from acting as attorneys for defendant in this suit. The basis for the motion and cross-motion was a request made by the Department of Justice on June 2, 1955 that Sullivan & Cromwell withdraw as attorneys because one of their partners, Mr. Garfield Horn, who is actively working on the case, was a government counsel for a Paris office of the Economic Co-operation Administration (ECA) during the period in question. The government contends that Mr. Horn and his firm are barred from participation in this suit by Canons 6, 36 and 37 of the Canons of Legal Ethics adopted as Rules of this Court. Succinctly stated, these Canons forbid an attorney to accept employment in matters adversely affecting any interest of a former client with respect to which confidence has been reposed. They forbid his revealing or using such confidences to the disadvantage of the former client even though there are other available sources of this information. Further, they forbid a former government attorney to accept employment "in connection with any matter which he has investigated or passed upon while in such office or employ." Canon 36. In order to intelligently decide whether Mr. Horn and his firm have in fact violated these Canons, a thorough understanding of the factual and legal questions posed by the main controversy is necessary.

The Main Action

In the main action, the United States seeks recovery of $35,862,288.08 claiming that Esso Export charged excessive prices in sales of Arabian crude oil to private importers in European countries participating in the Marshall Plan. Under this plan, authorized by the Economic Cooperation Act of 1948, 22 U.S.C.A. 1501, et seq., the ECA allocated funds in United States currency to various European nations participating in the program through the issuance of "procurement authorizations" setting forth the conditions for procurement of commodities. Firms in participating countries which desired crude oil, for example, after obtaining the approval of their respective governments, contracted to purchase such crude oil from various suppliers (including Esso Export). Such purchasers made payment to their local governments in local currencies and the money so paid was placed in "counterpart fund" accounts for use locally in connection with foreign aid programs. The suppliers were paid in the United States currency allocated by ECA, payment being made either through the participating countries or through designated banks in accordance with the type of procurement authorization which had been issued. Thus although the money was not paid directly by ECA to the suppliers, suppliers were paid in money provided by the United States; the local moneys paid out by the importers were retained in their respective countries for ECA approved projects aimed at the economic rehabilitation of Europe.

With regard to the specific transactions which are the subject matter of this suit, the United States claims that the prices charged by Esso Export for Arabian crude oil were higher than the maximum prices permitted by the Act and by the ECA Regulations which were promulgated (purportedly) pursuant to the Act. The government claims that these price maximums were the allegedly lower prices charged by Esso Export and other companies in comparable sales not financed by ECA and in shipments of Arabian crude oil to Western Hemisphere destinations. The period in question dates from April 3, 1948, effective date of the Economic Cooperation Act of 1948, until August 1952, the month of the commencement of this law suit and of the last shipment of Arabian oil in any ECA transactions.

Defendant, Esso Export, in its answer, denied any violation either of the price provisions of the Act or of the ECA regulations promulgated under them, assuming these to be valid. Defendant further contended that these Regulations are invalid. For an affirmative defense, the defendant alleged that the United States continued to reimburse participating countries with respect to these purchases of Arabian crude oil although it had full knowledge of all data material to applying the price maximums of the Act and Regulations to the prices Esso Export charged for such crude oil. It alleged further that by the government's failure to notify defendant that the prices charged were considered excessive, it represented to the defendant that the prices charged were not in excess of maximum prices, and that the government knew or should have known that the defendant would rely on this representation by continuing to sell crude oil at those prices. In good faith, defendant alleged, it did rely on such representation, and it pleaded estoppel against the government. Another defense averred that under the Marshall Plan, for each dollar of assistance provided by the United States to a participating country, that country deposited an amount of its local currency commensurate to the United States dollar cost in counterpart funds. Defendant asserted that since these funds were expended for various economic rehabilitation projects consistent with the purposes of the Act, and therefore with the purposes of the United States, the government has had full benefit of the moneys it expended and has sustained no damages.

It is against this background of the case that we must examine the government service and private employment record of Mr. Garfield Horn, the partner in Sullivan & Cromwell whose former employment by ECA is the cause of these motions.[4]

Mr. Horn's Employment Record

Mr. Horn joined the staff of Sullivan & Cromwell as a salaried associate upon his graduation from Harvard Law School in 1946. A major part of his work for the firm was in the area of foreign legal and economic problems, an area of work for which he had specially prepared during his undergraduate training. In April 1949, Mr. Horn completely terminated his relationship with Sullivan & Cromwell, and on May 31, 1949, he entered the employ of ECA. At the time he left the employ of Sullivan & Cromwell there was no understanding with respect to his being re-employed by the firm; rather he was clearly told that any application for re-employment would have to be considered anew on the basis of the situation at the time such application was made. Mr. Horn served with the ECA until October 11, 1951, and in November 1951, he again entered the employ of Sullivan & Cromwell, pursuant to arrangements made during the summer of 1951, and he became a partner of the firm on January 1, 1953. Since his return to the firm, he has continued to concentrate on problems with foreign aspects. In the spring of 1952, Sullivan & Cromwell was retained to represent Esso Export in this case; the retainer came personally to Arthur H. Dean, senior partner of the firm, who is also quite familiar with aspects of the Marshall Plan and related problems. Since Mr. Horn had often worked under Mr. Dean in such matters before, Mr. Dean chose Mr. Horn to act as his assistant in this case. Mr. Horn assured Mr. Dean at that time that while in ECA he had never worked on the subject of the present controversy, that he had never investigated or passed upon it, and that in all respects the matter was completely new to him, and he had never heard of it while he was with ECA.

The government has been aware of Mr. Horn's active participation in the case since the fall of 1952, but not until June 2, 1955 did it make a request for Mr. Horn's and his firm's withdrawal. The government contends that it was not until Mr. Horn displayed "peculiar knowledge" of the inner workings of ECA during a conference in March of 1955 that it considered whether there might be any impropriety in his serving as attorney for defendant and that an investigation then of Mr. Horn's government service record convinced it that a request for withdrawal was necessary.[6]

---

4. It is conceded by Sullivan & Cromwell that if Mr. Horn is disqualified, the entire firm is disqualified ... [subsequent to Judge Kaufman's ruling in this case, the ABA and many jurisdictions adopted rules relieving a law firm of such imputed disqualification if the former government attorney is screened from participation in the matter. See Model Rule 1.11–ed.]

6. Attorney for the defense has raised the question of laches here because of this two and a half year interval during which the government maintained silence though it knew of Mr. Horn's former employment and present connection with this case. Since a court may disqualify an attorney on its own motion for violation of the Canons of Ethics, see Porter v. Huber, D.C.W.D.Wash.1946, 68 F.Supp. 132, the government's laches, if any,

During the entire two and a half years Mr. Horn served with the ECA he was in the General Counsel's Office of the Office of the Special Representative in Paris (OSR/Paris). The only periods during which he was in Washington were ten days of personnel processing and indoctrination at the time of his initial assignment to Paris, approximately two days personnel processing at the termination of his duties, and two trips to Washington on OSR/Paris business. He was initially hired as an Attorney and served in that capacity until February, 1950 when he was promoted to Assistant General Counsel, a position he held for eight months. On October 15, 1950 he was appointed Deputy General Counsel, having served during one or two periods in the interim as Acting General Counsel of OSR. He continued to be Acting General Counsel of OSR from October 15, 1950 until January 21, 1951, when he was appointed General Counsel of OSR/Paris, a position he retained until his resignation in October 1951. I reiterate; all these positions were held in Paris. The General Counsel of OSR/Paris was chief legal representative and adviser of the United States Special Representative in Europe. The Special Representative, holding the rank of Ambassador, was the representative in Europe of the Administrator of the Economic Cooperation Act.

Respective Interpretations of Mr. Horn's Government Service Record

Mr. Horn's period of service with ECA from May 1949 to October 1951 falls entirely within the period of time during which the contested transactions occurred, i.e., April 1948 to August 1952. His position in the OSR/Paris hierarchy was an important one. Nevertheless, defendant contends that due to a division in functions between ECA/Washington and OSR/Paris, Mr. Horn's office in OSR/Paris knew nothing of the subject matter of these transactions, and none of his work for OSR/Paris was related to the subject of this case.

Defendant contends that OSR/Paris was concerned with implementing the operating phases of the ECA program, that its function in chief was to work closely with the various European countries and the ECA Missions in them on problems such as eliminating trade restrictions between the participating countries, clearing European payments and working out foreign currency problems, the allocation of scarce materials, and problems of manpower supply. It claims that the General Counsel's Office furnished legal advice on such problems, its chief job being the determination of whether various activities could be undertaken under the terms of the Act or financed with counterpart funds. Defendant further asserts that the only petroleum problems considered by OSR/Paris were those that dealt with the compiling of data estimating the oil requirements of the various countries, and recommending where and how much additional refinery capacity should be built in Europe. It is defendant's contention that ECA/Washington had exclusive responsibility for the drafting, promul-

cannot prevent an adjudication of this question once a possible violation of the Canons has been called to the court's attention....

gation and enforcement of the ECA policies relating to procurement and prices set forth in ECA Regulation 1, the Regulation which implemented the Marshall Plan procurement program. Defendant further says that this sharp division in functions between ECA/Washington and OSR/Paris also applied to the two separate General Counsel's Offices; that while the General Counsel's Office in Washington played an active part in the drafting, promulgation and enforcement of the procurement and price provisions of Regulation 1, the General Counsel's Office in Paris played no role in these matters, and that as to the very controversy on which the lawsuit is based, the General Counsel in Washington was continuously involved in the controversy while the Paris office played no part in it. The defendant urges, therefore, that Mr. Horn never received any confidences of the government with regard to the subject matter of this case; that he cannot be considered as having represented the government in matters relating to this case; that he never investigated or passed upon the matters involved in this controversy; and that he is, therefore, free to act as attorney for defendant, Esso Export.

The government's reply to defendant's contentions is largely based on the key legal position Mr. Horn held during the time of the transactions in question. It urges that his duties in Paris included proposing legislation necessary to implement the operating phases of the program, solving legal problems arising under the Act, interpreting legislative provisions under the Act and drafting new legislative provisions. The government contends, therefore, that while Mr. Horn was employed by the government, he should have pointed out any invalidity in Regulation 1 which defendant now asserts. It is the government's position that whether or not Mr. Horn ever actually considered the validity of Regulation 1, he is disqualified because he should have done so. Further, it claims that he actually did pass on Regulation 1 and pricing problems under it, more specifically, petroleum pricing problems.

It is urged further by the government that Mr. Horn had access to confidential data relating to the present controversy, and that in connection with the broad estoppel defense urged by defendant, many of the matters which must necessarily have come to Mr. Horn's attention while he was counsel and General Counsel in Paris, and because of his official position, are closely related to and interwoven with the question of the government's knowledge of the purported overcharges. It points out that many of his duties related to the counterpart funds mentioned in defendant's answer as having been expended for the benefit of the United States thus nullifying the government's claim of damages, and asserts that this fact also disqualifies him. The government summarizes its position by asserting that Mr. Horn is disqualified from acting in this case by Canons 6 and 37 because he had access to and obtained confidential information from the plaintiff and because he owed a duty of fidelity to plaintiff; and that he is further disqualified by Canon 36 because he passed upon or should have passed upon matters relating to the present controversy.

It is obvious, therefore, that the extent, if any, of Mr. Horn's involvement in matters related to the present case is in sharp conflict. The legal consequences of any relationship found will depend, of course, on the pertinent Canons of Ethics as interpreted by the courts and various bar association committees on professional ethics which have dealt with these Canons.

The Canons of Ethics Involved

The pertinent provisions of these Canons follow:

Canon 6. Adverse Influences and Conflicting Interests

"* * *

The obligation to represent the client with undivided fidelity and not to divulge his secrets or confidences forbids also the subsequent acceptance of retainers or employment from others in matters adversely affecting any interest of the client with respect to which confidence has been reposed."

Canon 37. Confidences of a Client

"It is the duty of a lawyer to preserve his client's confidences. This duty outlasts the lawyer's employment, and extends as well to his employees; and neither of them should accept employment which involves or may involve the disclosure or use of these confidences, either for the private advantage of the lawyer or his employees or to the disadvantage of the client, without his knowledge and consent, and even though there are other available sources of such information. A lawyer should not continue employment when he discovers that this obligation prevents the performance of his full duty to his former or to his new client.

* * *"

Canon 36. Retirement from Judicial Position or Public Employment

"* * *

A lawyer, having once held public office or having been in the public employ, should not after his retirement accept employment in connection with any matter which he has investigated or passed upon while in such office or employ."

Inferences Arising Under the Canons

Decisions interpreting these Canons have created three inferences operating against the attorney in question which the government contends are operative here. These must be examined to determine if they are applicable in the present case.

I.   Inference of Access to Confidential Information

Insofar as these canons relate to the question of preservation of a former client's confidences, they disqualify an attorney who has received confidences which might possibly be relevant to the controversy at hand as they seek to avoid unconscious as well as conscious betrayal.

As to who must carry the burden of showing that relevant confidences were reposed, an inference favorable to complainant has been reaffirmed recently in this Circuit. In T. C. Theatre Corp. v. Warner Bros. Pictures, Inc., D.C.S.D.N.Y.1953, 113 F.Supp. 265, 268, Judge Weinfeld said:

> "A lawyer's duty of absolute loyalty to his client's interests does not end with his retainer. He is enjoined for all time, except as he may be released by law, from disclosing matters revealed to him by reason of the confidential relationship. Related to this principle is the rule that where any substantial relationship can be shown between the subject matter of a former representation and that of a subsequent adverse representation, the latter will be prohibited."

The court disagreed with the contention of the attorney whose conduct was questioned in the T. C. Theatre case. The attorney urged that the former client was required to show that it had disclosed to the attorney confidential matters related to the instant case. The court stated:

> "The former client need show no more than that the matters embraced within the pending suit wherein his former attorney appears on behalf of his adversary are substantially related to the matters or cause of action wherein the attorney previously represented him, the former client. *The Court will assume that during the course of the former representation confidences were disclosed to the attorney bearing on the subject matter of the representation.*" (Italics supplied.) at page 268

In Consolidated Theatres, Inc., v. Warner Bros. Circuit Management Corporation, 2 Cir., 1954, 216 F.2d 920, the Court of Appeals for the Second Circuit adopted Judge Weinfeld's reasoning as related to the issue of burden of proof of disqualification under the Canons of Ethics. In that case there were no findings—and perhaps no evidence—of specific information given by the former client to the attorney, the use of which would adversely affect the former client in the instant suit. The Court said:

> "There is no suggestion in the Canons that to invoke an obligation defined therein the proof thereof must be by direct evidence. We think that the professional obligation therein defined, like any legal relationship, may be *established by reasonable inference.*" (Second emphasis supplied.) at page 924.

The rule is clear, therefore, that complainant's burden extends only to showing the existence of a substantial relationship between the subject matter of the lawsuit and the matters in which the attorney represented his former client. This substantial relationship creates an inference that confidential information was reposed. Further, complainant need only show access to such substantially related material and the inference that defendant received these confidences will follow.

The rationale behind this rule is as sound as it is elementary. The confidences communicated by a client to his attorney must remain inviolate for all time if the public is to have reverence for the law and confidence in its guardians. It is traditional in the legal profession that the fidelity of a lawyer to his client can be depended upon. The client must be secure in his belief that the lawyer will be forever barred from disclosing confidences reposed in him. It follows that if, in order to protect his secret utterances to counsel, the client or former client is required to reveal these utterances, the very purpose of the rule of secrecy will be destroyed, and the free flow of information from client to attorney, so vital to our system of justice, will be irreparably damaged. Therefore, to guarantee that these confidences remain inviolate, the courts will assume that when a client entrusts an attorney with the handling of a particular matter, the client will reveal to that counsel all the information at his disposal, including confidential matter. It is upon this assumption that the courts will bar an attorney from taking a position adverse to a former client in regard to any matters substantially related to those in which the attorney represented that client. This assumption, however, is reasonable only so long as there is a substantial relationship between those former matters and the lawsuit in which the confidence question is raised.

A. Substantial Relationship of Subject Matter

Unfortunately, the cases furnish no applicable guide as to what creates a "substantial" relationship. In both of the cited cases, the attorney in question had served as defense counsel for motion picture producers in anti-trust actions brought by the United States government charging defendants with a nationwide conspiracy in violation of Sections 1 and 2 of the Sherman Act, 15 U.S.C.A. 1, 2. They were later retained by independent exhibitors as counsel for plaintiffs in treble damage actions against these producers alleging the same type of conspiracy in violation of the Sherman Act. The evidence disclosed that the attorneys in question had had access to the files of their former clients which showed in detail their clients' modus operandi, and that they had made extensive use of these files in preparing a defense against the government. The relationship between the first anti-trust litigation and the second case was in each instance patently clear; indeed, the finding of a nation-wide conspiracy in the government's case was prima facie proof of a conspiracy in the later private actions. No such glaringly obvious relationship exists in this case.

Guidance on this point cannot be found either in those other decisions by courts or Ethics Committees which have dealt with the problem of representing adverse interests and the question of confidence betrayal raised thereby. In the majority of the cases decided by both bench and bar committees on the question of representing interests adverse to a former client, the offending attorney had either accepted a retainer from the other side in a retrial of the same case in which he had formerly represented complainant, or he had taken a position adverse to the former client in a matter in which he had specifically represented him. In most of these cases, the link between the subject matter of the first litigation or first representation by offending counsel, and the second, adverse litigation was comparatively simple to detect—the same accident, the same documents, the same litigation, etc.

There appears to be no case where the question of whether a substantial relationship existed between the former representation and the second suit presented serious factual problems. But, clearly, the word "substantial" must be given some restrictive content.

B.   Defendant's Contention: No Substantial Relationship

In the present case, Mr. Horn was formerly employed in a Paris office of the very agency which is making a claim against his client. His job was concerned with legal questions arising during the implementation in Europe of the operating phases of the ECA program, the program under which the contested transactions occurred. However, ECA was a vast agency with a network of offices throughout Europe and in Washington, D.C. It administered a billion dollar foreign aid program which dealt with almost every sort of problem that could arise in financing a project aimed at helping Europe recover from the devastations of World War II. It is easy to visualize a situation where an official in one office of that agency would be unaware of some of the functions of other branches of the agency. Indeed, this is the very contention that defendant makes here. It claims that the job of implementing the operating phases of the program in no way involved consideration of any pricing, procurement or refund problems of the type involved in the present controversy. Defendant supports its assertion that Mr. Horn's former duties had nothing to do with any matters relating to the present controversy by the affidavits of 13 men who held key positions in ECA in Paris and in Washington during the period in question. Typical of their recollections is the affidavit of Isaac N. P. Stokes, who served as Acting General Counsel, General Counsel and Acting Special Representative in OSR/Paris from February 1949 through September 1952, at which time he became General Counsel in Washington, a position in which he served until March 1953. In his affidavit of September 26, 1955, he states:

> "In connection with the preparation of this affidavit, I have carefully searched my recollection as to all aspects of this case of which I had any knowledge and as to the functions, responsibilities, and activities of GC/Paris. I am unable to recall any instance in which there was referred to or considered by GC/Paris any question relating to the promulgation, interpretation, operation, or validity of any of the pricing or refund provisions of ECA Regulation 1, either in connection with Arabian crude oil or any other commodity; any question involving the consideration of whether prices charged in ECA-financed sales of Arabian crude oil complied or failed to comply with the provisions of ECA Regulation 1; any question concerning prices charged for Arabian crude oil, whether in ECA-financed sales or non-ECA-financed sales; any question involving comparisons between prices of Arabian crude oil shipped

to European destinations and prices of Arabian crude oil shipped to Western Hemisphere or other destinations; or any question concerning refunds to be obtained in respect of ECA-financed shipments of Arabian crude oil. Nor can I recall any other instance in which GC/Paris would have had any occasion to acquire any information regarding any of the above mentioned questions, or any instance when or any reason why any member of the staff of GC/Paris would have had any occasion, on his own initiative, to inquire into the subject matter of this case.

"Any reference of any such questions to GC/Paris or to any other part of OSR/Paris would have been inconsistent with the recognized division of responsibilities and functions as between Washington and Paris."

I find that these affidavits establish that there was no such substantial relationship between Mr. Horn's former work and his present position as would disqualify him in this suit. Any other ruling would delete all meaning from the word "substantial." These affidavits deprive of any significance the fact that Horn had access to the file rooms of OSR/Paris by their assertion that the functions of that office were such that it would not maintain relevant files.[21]

C. Rebutting Defendant's Affidavits Re: No Substantial Relationship

The government had two alternative methods of rebutting the import of these affidavits:

(1) It could show that no such functional division actually existed, and that substantially related affairs were handled by Paris, thereby raising the inference of access to substantially related material.

(2) If it could not disprove the existence of the functional split, it could show that despite this division, Mr. Horn did actually work on matters substantially related to the present controversy.

The government has attempted to pursue both courses by submitting a series of documents with which Mr. Horn had some contact while working for OSR and which, it claims, show that he actually did work on or have access to documents on matters substantially related to the present controversy, and that he received confidences relevant to the present case. By choosing to rest its case on specific documents, however, the government has withdrawn itself in part from the sphere of the access-substantial relationship-confidence inference. If any of these documents tends to show that Mr. Horn's job did actually bring him into contact with relevant confidences or substantially related affairs generally, the government will have carried its point—not by inference but by direct proof. If none of the documents is itself indicative of such a connection between his former job

---

21. In his affidavit of September 26, 1955, Mr. Horn avers (pp. 188 and 225) that he never consulted or had access to any files other than the files of the General Counsel's Office of OSR/Paris during his tenure in the department, and he further avers that he never consulted the oil folders of the files in the General Counsel's Office. . . .

and the present lawsuit, the government will not have sustained its burden of showing substantial relationship in light of the affidavit evidence of a division in functions, and the inference flowing from such a relationship will not be applicable. Only if these documents fail to show action by Mr. Horn, but do disprove the asserted division in functions will the question of an inference arising from access be presented.

II. Inferences Arising From the Appearance of Evil

Interpretations of the Canons of Ethics have held that it is the duty of an attorney to avoid not only the actuality but the appearance of evil. In discussing Canon 36, H. S. Drinker in his Legal Ethics, p. 130, points out that one of the reasons for the rule forbidding the former public attorney to act in relation to any matter he passed upon while in government service is to prevent the appearance of evil—i.e. to prevent even the appearance that the government servant may take a certain stand in the hope of later being privately employed to uphold or upset what he had done. This rule finds application here in the government's contention that Mr. Horn should be disqualified if he passed upon or should have passed upon the validity of the pricing regulations in question in this controversy. Of course, if Mr. Horn did actually pass on the validity of these regulations, he is barred from participating in this case by the language of Canon 36. However, if he did not actually consider the question of whether these regulations were valid, I find that there is no appearance of evil arising from his now questioning their validity unless it is proven that he was specifically ordered to consider that question while in government employ. If he was so ordered, he cannot now be heard to urge that he shirked his duty in the past and is, therefore, free to raise the question presently. This exception to the necessity of proving actual investigation of the matter in question will be applied, however, only when the attorney's duty to pass upon that particular matter, was very clear.

The factual questions raised by this rule as applied to this case will be discussed after consideration of one more inference arising under these Canons.

III. Inference of Imputed Knowledge Within a Partnership

It has been repeatedly held by courts and ethics committees which have considered these canons, that the knowledge of one member of a law firm will be imputed by inference to all members of that firm. In Laskey Bros. of West Virginia v. Warner Bros. Pictures, Inc., 2 Cir., 1955, 224 F.2d 824, 826–827, the Court said:

> "[A]ll authorities agree that all members of a partnership are barred from participating in a case from which one partner is disqualified.
>
> "* * *
>
> "Within the framework of the original partnership the fact of access to confidential information through the person of the partner with such specialized knowledge is sufficient to bar the other

partners, whether or not they actually profit from such access. Such a result, although an extension of the literal wording of Canons 6 and 37 of the Canons of Professional Ethics of the American Bar Association, is necessary to facilitate maximum disclosure of relevant facts on the part of clients.''

This chain of imputed knowledge has been held to extend, not only to the partners in a law firm, but to salaried law clerks in a firm. Applied to the instant case, treating the entire OSR/Paris office as a partnership, the government argues that if anyone in the OSR/Paris office would have been barred from taking part in this controversy, then Horn is barred. It then urges that there was such a close association between the Counsel's Office in Washington and the Counsel's Office in Paris, that the chain of disqualification must necessarily extend from one office to another, and the Washington Counsel's Office was clearly involved in the present controversy from its inception.

The major premise on which the partnership disqualification theory is based, however, is that there was in the partnership office confidential information pertinent to the pending law suit to which all the partners had access. In this case, that basic premise is challenged by affidavits denying this alleged closeness between Washington and Paris, and the government has attempted to meet that challenge by producing documents from its files. If none of the documents the government has introduced rebut the import of those affidavits, the basic premise of knowledge within the office fails, the inference fails also, and the government is again left with the burden of proving actual knowledge.

Applying Doctrine of Imputed Knowledge to Government Attorney

Applying this doctrine of imputed knowledge within a partnership to the present case, however, presents a difficulty not found when dealing with private law firms. As stated, the doctrine's basic premise is that there is a free flow of information within a partnership office so that the knowledge of one member is the knowledge of all. When dealing with a government attorney, the question remains, within what office is that free flow of information assumed to exist. In this case, for example, is the office the overall ECA agency itself, OSR/Paris, or the General Counsel's Office of OSR/Paris.

This question arises in analogous form with relation to the inference set forth in the T.C. Theatre case that if an attorney had access to materials of the former client which are substantially related to the present controversy, it will be presumed that he came into contact with confidential information relating to the controversy, and he will be disqualified. Who is the client which the former government attorney represented and to whose files will access be presumed? Through what divisions and sub-divisions of a large government office will an attorney, who actually can go to any file, be presumed to have gone to such files regardless of his personal job assignments? At this point, when dealing with the government attorney, the client he represented and the partnership of which he was a member become merged. This is so because the basic problem is not merely to identify the former client here, which is in a larger sense the United States Government in toto, but rather to identify the interests with respect to which the attorney represented the client, for it is only as to these interests that he is disqualified. In identifying these interests one is confronted by the question of whether this attorney is to be considered as having represented the government in matters pending within his immediate office, or within a broader agency to which that office is attached, or solely in matters which he himself handled. In other words, the full circle has been swung and a decision must be made as to whether the theory of imputed knowledge as applied to members of a law partnership applies to attorneys working for the government; if it does, what office marks the boundary of imputation?

Guidance on this point can be taken from the language of Canon 36 which was enacted in 1928, twenty years after the American Bar Association originally adopted the first 32 Canons, and which deals specifically with lawyers retiring from public positions. This Canon forbids a former government attorney to accept employment "in connection with any matter which he has *investigated or passed upon* while in such office or employ." (Italics supplied.) The main purpose of this Canon was to clarify the duties in Canon 6 as related to government attorneys—chiefly, it avoids the "client" language of Canon 6 which presents serious difficulties in this sphere. Although it cannot be considered as completely superseding Canon 6 in dealing with a lawyer's duty to a former client, Canon 36 undoubtedly serves as a guide to the chief purpose of the ethical principle involved and the words "investigated" or "passed upon" imply a test of actual personal knowledge or action. However, it is also undoubtedly the purpose of the Canons generally to avoid the appearance that an attorney has taken a position contradictory to his former client's interests although, in fact, he may not have done so. This second purpose makes it impossible to hold that Canon 36 permits of none of the previously discussed inferences where a former government attorney is involved. The language of that Canon, however, must be held to require that a practical test be employed in determining when an appearance of evil exists: i.e. in each instance the fact finder must determine whether it was likely that the particular government attorney would have attained knowledge of or taken a stand on the subject matter of the particular controversy. If there is no practical likelihood, there is no appearance of evil.

Vertical and Horizontal Imputation of Knowledge to Government Attorneys

Where an attorney is head of his office or a subdivision of it, as was Mr. Horn during part of his tenure, there is, of course, imputed to him knowledge of the proceedings taken by his juniors. This is a vertical theory of imputed knowledge well founded in rules of ultimate responsibility. However, for such an official there is still the problem of horizontal imputation of the knowledge of another division head of coordinate rank within the same larger agency. Again, there may sometimes be a rebuttable presumption of imputed knowledge, but this is the kind of question which must be decided on an ad hoc basis depending on the particular factual relationship between the two divisions or the two personalities involved and the likelihood that knowledge passed freely between them. In the instant case, the decision as to imputed knowledge, if any, must await closer examination of these facts.

In view of the importance of the determination being made in the instant case in a virgin area of the law, further discussion is in order of those unique problems which arise when these Canons are applied to government attorneys.

Unique Problems Presented in Cases of Public Employment

Support for applying this practical, factual test in cases involving the disqualification of former government attorneys can be found in recognition of the serious problems which would otherwise arise—problems particularly acute where the employment was with the United States Government as opposed to some smaller public body. The government itself does not expect to bar a former government servant from participating in any case against the government involving in any way the agency in which he was employed. The size and diversity of function of many government agencies prohibit any such broad conclusion. The fact that the government is a client difficult to identify, and that the "firm" of which the government attorney is a part is difficult to limit in scope, were factors in the establishment of the more specific "investigated" or "passed upon" language of Canon 36. Although the confidence and adverse interests rules of Canons 6 and 37 still bind the former government attorney with a duty of fidelity, that duty must be given a practical scope. This is important for the benefit of the government which must constantly recruit attorneys from private practice. If service with the government will tend to sterilize an attorney in too large an area of law for too long a time, or will prevent him from engaging in practice of the very specialty for which the government sought his service—and if that sterilization will spread to the firm with which he becomes associated—the sacrifices of entering government service will be too great for most men to make. As for those men willing to make these sacrifices, not only will they and their firms suffer a restricted practice thereafter, but clients will find it difficult to obtain counsel, particularly in those specialties and suits dealing with the government.[34]

---

34. A converse problem arises when an attorney who has represented several corporate clients enters government service as the head of a department or as a lower ranking official, and that department wishes to undertake an investigation of or lawsuit against his former clients. If he is head of the department, knowledge of his subordinates' activities is imputed to him as is responsibility for their actions. A former department chief is barred from undertaking to represent in private practice any interests adverse to the government in any matters which were pending in his department during his tenure; why should not the present chief be barred while in government service from undertaking any activities adverse to interests of his former client. And if he is barred, why not his subordinates since he is held responsible for their actions. The answer which has been reached is that the hands of the government cannot be tied because of the former associations of one of its officials; therefore, that top person disqualifies himself from handling that particular matter, and the conflict of interest

Ethical Problems Cannot Be Viewed in a Vacuum

These practical problems undoubtedly were factors leading to the formulation of Canon 36; they have been given recent consideration by the Court of Appeals for the Second Circuit, and have been recently discussed by both the Yale Law Journal and the Harvard Law Review.[35]

In Laskey Bros. of West Virginia v. Warner Bros. Pictures, Inc., 2 Cir., 1955, 224 F.2d 824, in a disqualification proceeding, the Second Circuit was confronted with a former partner in a private law firm, who would have been barred from taking the case in question if he had remained a member of that firm because of the theory of imputed knowledge. The Court held that although the presumption of imputed knowledge is irrebuttable while a partnership exists, after its dissolution or after an attorney leaves the firm, a former partner barred only by imputed knowledge may rebut the inference that he received confidential information from the attorney with actual knowledge. It held further that the testimony of the former partner was itself sufficient rebuttal. Discussing the practical problems which would be raised by any stricter application of the partnership-imputed knowledge rule, the Court said:

> "Since the degree of association to effect disqualification need not necessarily be that of a partner, young lawyers might seriously jeopardize their careers by temporary affiliation with large law firms. But even more important is the effect on litigants who may seriously feel they have claims worthy of judicial testing, but are prejudiced in securing proper representation. For the net effect of an over harsh rule of disqualification must be to hinder adequate protection of clients' interests in view of the difficulty in discovering technically trained attorneys in specialized areas who were not disqualified, due to their peripheral or temporally remote connections with attorneys for the other side. See Note, 64 Yale L.J. 917, 928. The necessity of judicial recognition of the contingent fee is an appropriate analogy."

Aside from these practical problems, it is doubtful if the Canons of Ethics are intended to disqualify an attorney who did not actually come into contact with materials substantially related to the controversy at hand when he was acting as attorney for a former client now adverse to his position. I agree, that where there is a close question as to whether particular confidences of the former client will be pertinent to the instant case, an attorney should be disqualified to avoid the appearance if not the

question is considered resolved. Similarly, the particular lower ranking attorney disqualifies himself and another attorney handles the matter. No such opportunity is given to one partner in a law firm to disqualify himself and qualify the firm. The only explanation for the difference in result is that the practical exigencies are more compelling in the former situation than the latter. This is another illustration of the fact that ethical problems cannot be viewed in a vacuum; practical, everyday facts of life must be considered.

35. See Note, Disqualification of Attorneys for Representing Interests Adverse to Former Clients, 64 Yale L.J. 917, 927–928 (1955); Casenote, 68 Harvard L.Rev. 1084 (1955).

actuality of evil. But, where an attorney has worked for a vast agency of the United States government, as in the instant case, it is hardly reasonable to hold that an appearance of evil can be found in his undertaking a case against the government where there is not some closer factual relationship between his former job and the case at hand other than that the same vast agency is involved.

Application of Principles to Instant Case

Recapitulating the positions, defendant rests its case on the alleged fact that there was a clearcut division in functions between the Washington and Paris offices, and that the former office had sole responsibility for and actually solely handled all problems relating to pricing, procurement and refunds, including the drafting, promulgation and enforcement of the various regulations which are the subject matter of this controversy. It supports this contention chiefly with two lengthy affidavits by Mr. Horn: the first sets forth in detail the specific nature of all the duties of the personnel of the OSR/Paris General Counsel's Office while he was a member of its staff; the second is a document-by-document explanation of the papers on which the government rests its case. Mr. Horn's affidavits are supported by the affidavits of 13 key officials of OSR/Paris and/or ECA/Washington who attest to that same functional division, and by the affidavits of Arthur H. Dean as to the background of the present controversy. These affidavits establish that the work of the Paris office was unrelated to the instant controversy and refute any actuality or appearance of evil.

The government, complainant herein, had the burden of coming forward with evidence to dispel the effect of these affidavits. Specifically, to show grounds for disqualifying Mr. Horn in the present controversy, the government had the burden of either showing that he actually received relevant confidences or passed on the subject of the controversy, or that, although such personal active participation cannot be proved, his former duties were so substantially related to the present controversy that an appearance of evil arises from his taking part in this suit.

To support its contention that Mr. Horn's duties did bring him into contact with the subject matter of the present controversy in such a way as to disqualify him from proceeding as attorney for defendant in this action, the government has submitted some 25 assorted documents from its files, and two explanatory affidavits by Judge Stanley N. Barnes, Assistant Attorney General in charge of the Anti-trust Division, United States Department of Justice. Unlike the affidavits submitted by defendant, Judge Barnes' affidavits are based, not upon personal knowledge of ECA and OSR operations during the time in question, but upon interpretations which he has given the submitted documents without such personal knowledge.

Conclusion

After careful study of these documents, the government's interpretation of their significance as set forth in the Barnes affidavits and government oral argument, Mr. Horn's explanation of their significance in his affidavits of August 3 and September 26, 1955, and the supporting affidavits submitted by Sullivan & Cromwell—it is my considered opinion that the government has failed to present grounds for ordering the disqualification of Mr. Horn and his firm as defense attorneys in this case, and that the division in functions between OSR/Paris and ECA/Washington has been clearly established.

Specifically, the government has failed to prove:

(1) that Mr. Horn had access to documents substantially related to the subject matter of the instant case;

(2) that he ever had access to and/or actually saw or worked on any relevant confidential materials;

(3) that he ever investigated or passed upon the subject matter of the instant case;

(4) that he ever rendered any legal advice or opinion in relation to the regulations which are the subject matter of the instant case; and

(5) that despite these conclusions, Mr. Horn's present position creates an appearance of evil requiring disqualification.

These conclusions have been reached after a thorough document-by-document analysis of the papers upon which the government bases its motion. Many of these documents fail on their face to show any conceivable disqualifying relationship between their content and the subject matter of the present controversy. Others bear a surface relationship, but can be and are satisfactorily explained as unrelated owing to the functional division between ECA/Washington and OSR/Paris, a division which the government does not either disprove or place in substantial doubt. For example, the government placed great reliance on Civil Service Job Description Sheets which imposed upon the General Counsel and his staff the duty of drafting and interpreting legislation on the operating phases of the program, but it made no attempt to show why the word "operating" should not be read as limiting that office's duties to the problems encountered in European operations—operations in no way concerned with pricing and procurement policies. The latter interpretation is supported by thirteen knowledgeable affiants and contradicted only by the speculations of Judge Barnes and Mr. Olson, the Special Assistant who presented the government's argument on the instant application. Neither of these proponents has any personal knowledge as to the operations of either ECA or OSR during the period in question.

Similarly, another series of documents upon which the government placed considerable stress consisted of three missives dealing with a publicized change in price policy—a change which ultimately took effect as Amendment 5 to Regulation 1. In presenting these documents, the government did not consider it relevant that the Amendment in question dealt with petroleum products and not crude oil; that the missives did not in any way discuss whether defendant had been charging over ECA maximum prices for such products; that two of the three missives in question were copies of letters sent directly to defendant and other oil companies; that Paris was clearly being told what Washington had done, not being asked its opinion on whether the new policy was sound; and that the last missive was a request for information sent from Paris to Washington which clearly reflected complete ignorance of that price policy on the part of the Paris office.

Most of the other government exhibits go even further afield. Examination of them leads me to the conclusion that, in preparing its case, the mere mention of the word "petroleum" in a document caused the government to assume its relevancy to the instant case and its pertinence to the instant motion. But, it must be borne in mind that a word appearing in empty space, with no history, expresses nothing. To be expressive of any meaning, the word must be considered in its context and background.

When dealing with ethical principles, it is apparent that we cannot paint with broad strokes. The lines are fine and must be so marked. Guideposts can be established when virgin ground is being explored, and the conclusion in a particular case can be reached only after painstaking analysis of the facts and precise application of precedent. After full consideration of all applicable principles, I hold that the motion of the government to disqualify Mr. Horn and his firm as defense attorneys is denied, and the motion of Sullivan & Cromwell for an order decreeing them to be qualified as attorneys herein is granted. So ordered.

QUESTIONS

1. Who was Horn's client when he was working at the ECA—the entire U.S. Government, its executive branch, the ECA or the ECA in Paris? See discussion of this issue in Chapter 3 supra.

2. Does it make sense to say that Horn had different clients for different purposes? If so, who was his client for purposes of deciding whether there was a conflict?

3. What reasons does Judge Kaufman articulate for not imposing excessively strict conflict rules on ex-government lawyers?

4. What would be the result if the rule imputing a lawyer's knowledge of confidential information to all lawyers in her firm (horizontal imputation) were applied to government lawyers, with the entire U.S. Government being viewed as a "firm?" Is this an application of the "firm" analogy that may not work for government lawyers?

5. What complications would arise if vertical imputation were used to disqualify government lawyers when a private sector lawyer goes to work for the government as their superior? What is the best solution to this problem? (See *In Re Kleindienst,* supra Chapter 3, where Deputy Attorney General Kleindienst took over supervision of the ITT case because Attorney General Mitchell's old law firm previously represented ITT).

6. Judge Kaufman discusses three types of inferences that arise under the Canons: the inference of access to confidential information, inferences arising from the appearance of evil, and the inference of imputed knowledge within a partnership. Does Judge Kaufman give less attention to one of these inferences than to the others?

7. After this holding, the ABA endorsed, and many jurisdictions adopted, rules allowing firms to escape imputed disqualification from a former government lawyer if that lawyer is screened from participation in the matter. See Model Rule 1.11; New York Code of Professional Responsibility DR 9–101. Would it have been better to disqualify Horn, but allow Sullivan & Cromwell to remain on the case? Would such a "middle ground" have removed the appearance of impropriety that the government alluded to in its motion?

8. Would this case have been a lot easier to decide if the only issue in the underlying litigation had been whether Esso overcharged for the crude oil?

9. Judge Kaufman observes that ethical problems cannot be viewed in a vacuum. How is his holding in this case influenced by that observation? Is that same observation relevant to any of the other cases you have read in this casebook so far?

George D. Reycraft, b. 1924; B.A. Wesleyan University 1947; LL.B. Harvard University 1950; admitted to the District of Columbia bar in 1951 and to the New York bar in 1964; trial attorney for the U.S. Department of Justice (DOJ) 1952–57; assistant chief of the general litigation section of the DOJ 1957–58; chief of the special trial section of the DOJ 1958–60; chief of section operations for the antitrust division of the DOJ 1960–63; became a partner at Cadwalader, Wickersham & Taft in New York City in 1963.

General Motors Corporation, Defendant–Appellant, v. City of New York, for itself and all other persons similarly situated, Plaintiff–Appellee.

501 F.2d 639 (2d Cir. 1974).

■ Before KAUFMAN, Chief Judge, MANSFIELD and MULLIGAN, Circuit Judges.

■ IRVING R. KAUFMAN, Chief Judge:

Suits involving large damage claims inevitably spark intensive pretrial skirmishing, as the litigants bombard each other and the district court with a variety of motions. In this case, brought by the City of New York (City), which alone has a $12,000,000 claim, as a class action alleging that General Motors Corporation (GM) has violated the antitrust laws principally by monopolizing or attempting to monopolize the nationwide market for city buses, we face appeals by GM from interlocutory orders deciding two bitterly contested pretrial, although unrelated, motions. The first is the City's successful motion to permit the suit to proceed as a class action; the second, GM's unsuccessful motion to have the City's privately-retained counsel, George D. Reycraft, disqualified for breach of the ethical precepts embodied in Canon 9 of the Code of Professional Responsibility.[1] After carefully applying the *Cohen*[2] collateral order doctrine to separate the appealable from the non-appealable order, we dismiss the appeal from the court's order determining that this action may proceed as a class action because in the context of this case that order is not appealable. With respect to the motion to disqualify counsel, however, we conclude, without intending to suggest any actual impropriety on the part of Reycraft, that his disqualification is required to "avoid even the appearance of professional impropriety."[3] Accordingly, the court's order denying disqualification of Reycraft is reversed.

I.　Factual Background

The facts necessary to an understanding of our disposition of these appeals have been gleaned, in the main, from the complaint and from the affidavits filed by the parties in support of and in opposition to the respective motions at issue. They are, thankfully, rather straightforward and, in all material respects, undisputed.

On October 4, 1972, the City filed a complaint alleging that GM had violated Section 2 of the Sherman Act by attempting to monopolize and monopolizing "trade and commerce in the manufacture and sale of city buses." The complaint contained, as a second cause of action, the allegation that GM had breached Section 7 of the Clayton Act by acquiring, in 1925, a controlling interest in Yellow Truck & Coach Manufacturing Co. (Yellow Coach)—an acquisition which purportedly "threatens substantially to lessen competition and to tend to create a monopoly in the manufacture and sale of buses within the United States...." The action, furthermore, was commenced on behalf of a class consisting of "all non-federal governmental units and instrumentalities in the United States which have purchased or have contributed to the purchase of city buses or city bus parts...." The relief sought was, *inter alia*, for appropriate divestiture, treble damages, costs and attorneys' fees.

According to Reycraft's affidavit, filed in opposition to the disqualification motion, he was asked by the Office of the Corporation Counsel, sometime in July 1972, to assist in the preparation of the complaint. When approached by the Corporation Counsel, then J. Lee Rankin, Reycraft responded by informing Rankin of his prior and substantial involvement in an action brought by the United States against GM, under Section 2 of the Sherman Act, based on GM's alleged monopolization of a nation-wide market for the manufacture and sale of city and intercity buses. United States v. General Motors (No. 15816, E.D.Mich.1956) (1956 *Bus* case).

---

1. Canon 9 of the Code of Professional Responsibility provides that "A lawyer should avoid even the appearance of professional impropriety." More particularly, Disciplinary Rule (DR) 9–101(B), prohibits "A lawyer ... (from accepting) private employment in a matter in which he had substantial responsibility while he was a public employee."

2. Cohen v. Beneficial Industrial Loan Corp., 337 U.S. 541, 69 S.Ct. 1221, 93 L.Ed. 1528 (1949).

3. Canon 9, supra note 1.

In his affidavit, Reycraft described his participation in the 1956 *Bus* case, and his work for the Antitrust Division of the Department of Justice, in these words:

> I was employed as an attorney for the Antitrust Division of the Department of Justice from the end of December, 1952 through the end of December, 1962. From sometime during the middle of 1954 through the end of 1962 I was employed in the Washington Office of the Antitrust Division. My initial assignment in the Washington Office of the Antitrust Division in 1954 was as a trial attorney in the General Litigation Section.
>
> One of my first assignments as a member of the General Litigation Section was to work on an investigation of alleged monopolization by General Motors of the city and intercity bus business. The chief counsel in that matter from at least 1954 until the case was settled by Consent Decree in 1965 was Walter D. Murphy. At no time was I in active charge of the case. *That investigation culminated in the Complaint filed on July 6, 1956 which I signed and in the preparation of which I participated substantially.*
>
> In 1958, I became Chief of the Special Trial Section of the Antitrust Division and no longer had any direct or indirect involvement with the 1956 *Bus* case. Subsequently in 1961 I became Chief of Section Operations of the Antitrust Division and had technical responsibility for all matters within the Washington Office of the Antitrust Division, including the 1956 *Bus* case. I have no recollection of any active participation on my part in the 1956 *Bus* case from 1958 through the time I departed from the Antitrust Division in December of 1962. The case was in the charge of Walter D. Murphy from its inception and he continued in charge until the Consent Decree was entered on December 31, 1965 *(emphasis added)*.[6]

In light of his substantial involvement as an employee of the Department of Justice in a matter which, at the very least, was similar to the dispute for which his retention was sought, Reycraft initially consulted his partners in the firm of Cadwalader, Wickersham & Taft and, subsequently, requested the advice of the Antitrust Division on the applicability of the Federal conflict of interest statute [18 U.S.C.A. § 207]. That statute, we note, is penal in nature and its prohibitory rules, only two in number, must therefore be specifically defined and strictly construed. With that in mind, the Justice Department had little difficulty in concluding that the statute

---

6. In addition to his contact with GM during the course of investigating and preparing the 1956 Bus case, Reycraft also was in charge of a Grand Jury inquiry from 1959 to 1961, which delved into the workings of GM's Electromotive Division. Although GM argued below that Reycraft gained information about the bus industry, and GM's participation in it, through this Grand Jury investigation, Judge Carter after lengthy consideration rejected that contention. We need not review that finding here, for we conclude that disqualification is necessary without regard to Reycraft's Grand Jury assignment.

placed no bar on Reycraft's employment by the City. Its response to Reycraft states, in pertinent part:

> It is clear that section 207(b) (which applies for only one year after separation from government employ) has no bearing on your case. As for section 207(a) (which applies only where the United States is a party or has a direct and substantial interest in the matter), although it appears that you participated personally and substantially in the case brought by the United States against General Motors, the Antitrust Division advises us that the United States will not be a party to or have a direct and substantial interest in the private antitrust suit by the City of New York against General Motors. Therefore, section 207(a) has no application.

Accordingly, with Cadwalader's approval and the absence of any barrier posed by federal law, Reycraft agreed to represent the City on a contingent fee basis, a not infrequent arrangement in actions where recovery is at the same time uncertain but potentially great.

On February 22, 1973, the City moved before Judge Carter for a determination that its suit could proceed as a class action pursuant to Fed.R.Civ.P. 23(a) and 23(b)(3). GM responded by opposing the class determination and, in turn, moved for the disqualification of Reycraft. Argument on both motions was subsequently heard by the court.

. . .

In August 1973, Judge Carter entered his order, and filed an accompanying memorandum opinion, granting the City's motion for class action status and denying GM's motion to disqualify Reycraft....

* * *

III. Disqualification of Counsel

We turn now to GM's unsuccessful motion to disqualify the City's privately-retained counsel, George Reycraft. It is necessary that we begin our discussion by focusing again on the language of Canon 9 of the Code of Professional Responsibility:

> A lawyer should avoid even the appearance of professional impropriety.

Providing a measure of specificity to this general caveat, DR9–101(B) commands:

> A lawyer shall not accept private employment in a matter in which he had substantial responsibility while he was a public employee.

The purpose behind this plain interdiction is not difficult to discern. Indeed, the City recognizes its salutary goal, as stated by the ABA Comm. on Professional Ethics, Opinions, No. 37 (1931) to be:

> (to avoid) the manifest possibility that ... (a former Government lawyer's) action as a public legal official might be influenced (or open to the charge that it had been influenced) by the hope of later being employed privately to *uphold or upset* what he had done.

Id. at 124. (emphasis added) Viewed in this light, the question before us is whether Reycraft's decision to represent the City on a contingent fee basis in an antitrust suit strikingly similar, though perhaps not identical in every respect, to an antitrust action brought over his signature by the Department of Justice would raise an "appearance of impropriety," as private employment "to uphold ... what he had done" as a Government lawyer. Unlike the court below, we are constrained to answer in the affirmative.

Before we commence our analysis, we would do well to recall the following description of our task:

> We approach our task as a reviewing court in this case conscious of our responsibility to preserve a balance, delicate though it may be, between an individual's right to his own freely chosen counsel (we do not presume the City to have a lesser right) and the need to maintain the highest ethical standards of professional responsibility. This balance is essential if the public's trust in the integrity of the Bar is to be preserved.

Emle Industries, Inc. v. Patentex, Inc., 478 F.2d 562, 564–565 (2d Cir. 1973).

Indeed, the "public's trust" is the raison d'etre for Canon 9's "appearance-of-evil" doctrine. Now explicitly incorporated in the profession's ethical Code,[19] this doctrine is directed at maintaining, in the public mind, a high regard for the legal profession. The standard it sets—i.e. what creates an appearance of evil—is largely a question of current ethical-legal mores. See Kaufman, The Former Government Attorney and the Canons of Professional Ethics, 70 Harv.L.Rev. 657, 660 (1957).

Nor can we overlook that the Code of Professional Responsibility is not designed for Holmes' proverbial "bad man" who wants to know just how many corners he may cut, how close to the line he may play, without running into trouble with the law. Holmes, The Path of the Law, in Collected Legal Papers 170 (1920). Rather, it is drawn for the "good man," as a beacon to assist him in navigating an ethical course through the sometimes murky waters of professional conduct. Accordingly, without in the least even intimating that Reycraft himself was improperly influenced while in Government service, or that he is guilty of any actual impropriety in agreeing to represent the City here, we must act with scrupulous care to avoid any appearance of impropriety lest it taint both the public and private segments of the legal profession.

It is undisputed that Reycraft had "substantial responsibility" in initiating the Government's Sherman 2 claim against GM for monopolizing or attempting to monopolize the nationwide market for city and intercity

---

19. Although Canon 36 of the old Canons of Professional Ethics was uniformly interpreted to espouse the "appearance-of-evil" doctrine, see e.g. United States v. Standard Oil Co. (N.J.), 136 F.Supp. 345, 359 (D.C.N.Y. 1955); H. Drinker, Legal Ethics 130, it was not until the adoption of Canon 9 of the Code of Professional Responsibility that the canons of ethics expressly enunciated that doctrine.

buses. Thus, we are left to determine whether the City's antitrust suit is the same "matter" as the Government's action and whether Reycraft's contingent fee arrangement with the City constitutes "private employment."

Directing our attention to the simpler question first, we are convinced beyond doubt that Reycraft's and, indeed, his firm's opportunity to earn a substantial fee for Reycraft's services is plainly "private employment" under DR9–101(B). The district judge apparently grounded his contrary decision on the rationale that Reycraft "has not changed sides"—i.e. "there is nothing antithetical in the postures of the two governments in the actions in question. . . ." But, as we have already noted, Opinion No. 37 of the ABA Commission on Professional Ethics unequivocally applies the ethical precepts of Canon 9 and DR9–101(B) irrespective of the side chosen in private practice. And see Allied Realty of St. Paul v. Exchange Nat. Bank of Chicago, 283 F. Supp. 464, 466 (D.Minn.1968). We believe, moreover, that this is as it should be for there lurks great potential for lucrative returns in following into private practice the course already charted with the aid of governmental resources. And, with such a large contingent fee at stake, we could hardly accept "pro bono publico" as a proper characterization of Reycraft's work, simply because the keeper of the purse is the City of New York or other governmental entities in the class.

It is manifest also, from an examination of the respective complaints (see the appendix to this opinion), that the City's antitrust action is sufficiently similar to the 1956 *Bus* case to be the same "matter" under DR9–101(B). Indeed, virtually every overt act of attempted monopolization alleged in the City's complaint is lifted *in haec verba* from the Justice Department complaint. We cite, merely by way of illustration, paragraphs appearing in both complaints alleging the withdrawal of more than 20 companies from bus manufacturing, the coincidence of directors on the boards of GM and another bus manufacturer, the Flxible Company, and GM's acquisition of a controlling stock interest in Yellow Coach in 1925.

To be sure, as the City urges, the four-year statute of limitations, embodied in 15 U.S.C.A. 15b, requires the City to focus on market conditions since 1968, some ten years after Reycraft ceased his involvement in the *Bus* case. But, an equally essential element in proving a violation of Section 2 of the Sherman Act is either an intent to monopolize or an abuse of monopoly power. [citations omitted.] Moreover, to decide the question whether GM is a passive recipient of monopoly power, a history of its operations will be imperative. See e.g. United States v. Aluminum Co. of America, supra (included an exhaustive study of Alcoa's operations from 1902 to the date of the lawsuit). Accordingly, at the very forefront of the City's case will be proof of alleged predatory practices amassed by the United States, with the substantial participation of Reycraft, when the Justice Department built its case against GM in 1956.

The addition of the Clayton Act claim, based solely on the same 1925 Yellow Coach acquisition which was part of the Sherman Act violation alleged by both the United States and the City, hardly alters the nuclear identity of these two suits.[22] Both, after all, allege monopolization or attempted monopolization of the same product line—city buses—and, in the same geographic market—the United States. The subtleties of differential proof will not obviate the "appearance of impropriety" to an unsophisticated public. We opined in Emle:

> Nowhere is Shakespeare's observation that "there is nothing either good or bad but thinking makes it so," more apt than in the realm of ethical considerations. Emle Industries, Inc. v. Patentex, Inc., supra, 478 F.2d at 571.

The City maintains, in the end, that if we reverse the court below and disqualify Reycraft, we will chill the ardor for Government service by rendering worthless the experience gained in Government employ. Indeed, the author of this opinion is hardly unaware of this claim, for he has cautioned:

> If the government service will tend to sterilize an attorney in too large an area of law for too long a time, or will prevent him from engaging in the practice of a technical specialty which he has devoted years in acquiring, and if that sterilization will spread to the firm with which he becomes associated, the sacrifice of entering government service will be too great for most men to make.

Kaufman, supra, 70 Harv.L.Rev. at 668. But, in that commentary, and the case upon which it was based (United States v. Standard Oil Co. (N.J.), 136 F.Supp. 345 (S.D.N.Y.1955)—Esso Export Case), the accommodation between maintaining high ethical standards for former Government employees, on the one hand, and encouraging entry into Government service, on the other, was struck under far different circumstances. Unlike the instant case, in which Reycraft's "substantial responsibility" in the *Bus* case is undisputed, the writer of this opinion concluded in Esso Export that the lawyer:

> never investigated or passed upon the subject matter of the pending case ... never rendered or had any specific duty to render any legal advice in relation to the regulations involved in the litigation.

Kaufman, supra, 70 Harv.L.Rev. at 664. More to the point, therefore, is another admonition voiced in that article:

> If there was a likelihood that information pertaining to the pending matter reached the attorney, although he did not "investigate" or "pass upon" it, ... there would undoubtedly be an appearance of evil if he were not disqualified.

Id. at 665.

---

22. As to this, the district court set forth the proper test (60 F.R.D. at 402):

In determining whether this case involves the same matter as the 1956 *Bus* case, the most important consideration is not whether the two actions rely for their foundation upon the same section of the law, but whether the facts necessary to support the two claims are sufficiently similar.

Esso Export unquestionably presented a case for the cautious application of the "appearance-of-evil doctrine," because the former Government lawyer's connection with the matter at issue was the tenuous one of mere employment in the same Government agency. If, for example, Reycraft had not worked on the 1956 *Bus* case, but was simply a member of the Antitrust Division at that time, a case not unlike Esso Export would be before us. To the contrary, however, Reycraft not only participated in the *Bus* case, but he signed the complaint in that action and admittedly had "substantial responsibility" in its investigatory and preparatory stages. Where the overlap of issues is so plain, and the involvement while in Government employ so direct, the resulting appearance of impropriety must be avoided through disqualification.

Accordingly, we dismiss the appeal from the order granting class action status, and reverse the court's order denying disqualification of Reycraft.

APPENDIX

The following comparison of portions of the complaints filed by the United States in the 1956 *Bus* case and by the City in the instant ease was included in the record below:

United States v. General Motors Corporation (1956 *Bus* case)	City of New York v. General Motors Corporation
15. Between 1925 and 1955 more than 20 manufacturers of buses withdrew from the bus manufacturing business. Among these companies are the following:	16. Between 1925 and 1971, more than 20 bus manufacturers or bus assemblers withdrew from business. Among these companies were the following:
Ford Motor Company	Ford Motor Company
ACF–Brill Motors Company	ACF–Brill Motors Company
The White Motor Company	The White Motor Company
Twin Coach Company	Twin Coach Company
General American Aerocoach Company	General American Aerocoach Company
Studebaker Corporation	Studebaker Corporation
Dodge Brothers Corporation	Dodge Brothers Corporation
International Harvester Co.	International Harvester Co.
Reo Motors, Inc.	Reo Motors, Inc.
Fifth Avenue Coach Company	Fifth Avenue Coach Company
The Pickwick Nitecoach Corporation	The Pickwick Nitecoach Corporation
C. H. Will Motors Corporation	C. H. Will Motors Corporation
Pacific Car & Foundry Company	Pacific Car & Foundry Company
Diamond T. Motor Car Company	Diamond T. Motor Car Company
Kenworth Motor Truck Corporation	Kenworth Motor Truck Corporation
Beaver Metropolitan Coaches, Inc.	Beaver Metropolitan Coaches, Inc.
Kalamazoo Coaches, Inc.	Kalamazoo Coaches, Inc.
Superior Coach Corporation	Superior Coach Corporation
Transicoach, Inc.	Transicoach, Inc.
Cub Industries, Inc.	Cub Industries, Inc.
	Mack Trucks, Inc.

United States v. General Motors Corporation (1956 *Bus* case)

City of New York v. General Motors Corporation

Southern Coach Manufacturing Co., Inc.

16. After 1946, no concern not theretofore engaged in the manufacture of buses has commenced the manufacture of this product.

17. Defendant manufactured approximately 85 percent of the new buses delivered in the United States during 1955. In that year it delivered 2,724 buses, having a value of approximately $55,000,000. Defendant has manufactured at least 65 percent of the new buses delivered in the United States during each year from 1952 to 1955 inclusive.

20. The Flxible Company (hereinafter referred to as "Flxible"), has been engaged in the manufacture of buses for more than twenty-five years.... For many years Charles F. Kettering has been the Chairman of the Board of Directors of Flxible and holder of more Flxible stock than any other stockholder of Flxible. During much of the same period of time he also was an officer and director of General Motors.

22. For many years continuously up to the date of the filing of this complaint, the defendant has been monopolizing the above-described trade and commerce in the manufacture and sale of buses in violation of Section 2 of the Sherman Act (15 U.S.C.A. § 2). The defendant threatens to continue said offense and will continue it unless the relief hereinafter prayed for is granted.

23. Pursuant to and in effectuation of the aforesaid monopolization, the defendant directly and through its subsidiaries, among other things, has done the following:

(a) Acquired a controlling interest in one bus manufacturer ...;

17. After 1946, no concern not theretofore engaged in the manufacture of buses has commenced the manufacture of buses.

11. Since 1956, General Motors has manufactured over 80 percent of all buses manufactured in the United States. Since 1965, it has manufactured and sold between 85 percent to 100 percent of all city and intercity buses manufactured in the United States.

19. The Flxible Company ("Flxible") has been in business for over 40 years. For many years, Charles F. Kettering was Chairman of the Board of Directors of Flxible and the largest individual stockholder of Flxible; during much of the same period, Mr. Kettering was also an officer and director of General Motors.

21. For many years continuously up to the date of the filing of this complaint, defendant has violated Section 2 of the Sherman Act (15 U.S.C.A. § 2) by attempting to monopolize and by monopolizing the above-described trade and commerce in the manufacture and sale of city buses. The defendant threatens to continue said offenses and violations and will continue them unless the relief hereinafter prayed for is granted.

22. Pursuant to and in effectuation of the aforesaid attempt to monopolize and monopolization, the defendant directly and through its subsidiaries has done, among other things, the following:

(a) Acquired controlling stock interest in one bus manufacturer.

United States v. General Motors Corporation (1956 *Bus* case)

(b) Acquired the power to influence the policies of its principal existing competitor in the manufacture of intercity buses by having an officer and director of General Motors as Chairman of the Board of Directors and principal stockholder of that company;

(c) Acquired the power to control some bus operating companies, and influenced the policies of others by:

(1) purchasing their capital stock;

(2) having officers and employees of General Motors own their capital stock;

(3) having officers or directors of General Motors on their boards of directors;

(4) promoting their formation and assisting in their organization and expansion.

(d) Entered into contracts with bus-operating companies which required them to purchase stated percentage of their requirements of buses from defendant;

(e) Induced some bus operating companies to purchase buses from defendant exclusively or on a preferential basis by:

(1) agreeing to refuse and refusing to sell buses to competitors of some of said companies;

(2) offering to sell and selling some of said companies buses and parts for buses at prices lower or on terms more favorable, or both, than the prices or terms offered by defendant to other bus operating companies; and

(3) making substantial loans of money to some of said companies.

(f) Offered to finance and financed the sale of buses through GMAC on terms which General Motors' competitors with more limited resources have been unable to meet;

(g) Induced officials of municipally-owned transit systems to adopt

City of New York v. General Motors Corporation

(d) Acquired the power to influence the policies of its principal existing competitor in the manufacture of intercity buses by having an officer and director of General Motors as Chairman of the Board of Directors and principal stockholder of that company;

(e) Acquired the power to control some bus operating companies, and influenced the policies of others by:

(1) purchasing their capital stock;

(2) having officers and employees of General Motors own their capital stock;

(3) having officers or directors of General Motors on their boards of directors;

(4) promoting their formation and assisting in their organization and expansion.

(f) Entered into contracts with bus operating companies which required them to purchase stated percentages of their requirements of buses from defendant.

(g) Induced some bus operating companies to purchase buses from defendant exclusively or on a preferential basis by:

(1) agreeing to refuse and refusing to sell buses to competitors of some of said companies;

(2) offering to sell and selling some of said companies buses and parts for buses at prices lower or on terms more favorable, or both, than the prices or terms offered by defendant to other bus operating companies; and

(3) making substantial loans of money to some of said companies.

(h) Offered to finance and financed the sale of buses on terms which General Motors' competitors with more limited resources have been unable to meet.

(i) Persuaded officials of municipally-owned transit systems to

United States v. General Motors Corporation (1956 *Bus* case)	City of New York v. General Motors Corporation

bus specifications for use in obtaining so-called competitive bids which prevented other bus manufacturers from competing;

(h) Refused to sell to other bus manufacturing companies and to their suppliers, various parts, including automatic transmissions and diesel engines, for use in the manufacture of buses;

(i) Entered into contracts under the terms of which defendant was granted the exclusive right to use various improvements (patented and unpatented), including "air suspension" and automatic transmissions, in the design and manufacture of buses;

(j) Made surveys of bus operating companies for the purpose and with the effect of inducing said companies to agree to purchase or to purchase buses from defendant on an exclusionary basis;

26. The effects of the aforesaid offenses, among others, have been and are:

(a) To drive most of General Motors' competitors out of the bus manufacturing business;

(b) To curtail the supply of new buses readily available for purchase;

(c) To deprive bus operating companies and the bus-riding public of the benefits of competition in the manufacture of buses;

(d) To increase prices paid by bus operating companies for some types of buses;

(e) To prevent other concerns from entering the bus manufacturing business;

---

adopt bus specifications for use in obtaining so-called competitive bids which prevented other bus manufacturers from competing.

(j) Refused to sell to other bus manufacturing companies, and to their suppliers, various parts, including automatic transmissions and diesel engines, for use in the manufacture of buses.

(k) Entered into contracts under the terms of which defendant was granted the exclusive right to use various improvements (patented and unpatented), including "air suspension" and automatic transmissions, in the design and manufacture of buses.

(*l*) Made surveys of bus operating companies for the purpose and with the effect of inducing said companies to agree to purchase or to purchase buses from defendant on an exclusionary basis.

26. The effects of the aforesaid offenses and violations by defendant, among others, have been and are:

(a) To drive all of General Motors' competitors in the United States out of the new bus manufacturing business;

(c) To curtail the supply of new city buses readily available for purchase;

(e) To deprive bus operators, the bus-riding public, the plaintiff, and the other members of the class of the benefits of competition in the manufacture and sale of new City buses . . . ;

(d) To cause and maintain excessive and noncompetitive prices to be paid by bus operators . . . for new city buses and bus parts;

(f) To prevent or discourage other concerns from entering into the bus manufacturing business in the United States;

QUESTIONS

1.   Is there any inconsistency between Judge Kaufman's approach in this case and his approach in *United States v. Standard Oil*? Does he convincingly distinguish the two cases?

2.   Should whether a former government attorney "switches sides" or stays on the same side have any bearing on disqualification?

3.   Assume that you had drafted the complaints in *United States v. General Motors* and in *City of New York v. General Motors*. Would you hand them in for credit as drafting exercises in two separate classes? What would happen if you did?

4.   By contrast to an academic setting where work is assumed to be original unless credited to a specific source, lawyers sometimes use and reuse forms and boilerplate sections of pleadings and briefs. In what circumstances may a lawyer use work prepared for one client in her work for another client? Should the second client be billed as if the work were original?

5.   Should General Motors have standing to object to Reycraft's use of work product from his government service, or should the United States Department of Justice be the only party with standing to object?

6.   Should Reycraft have been allowed to stay in the case if the United States Department of Justice, perhaps to encourage private plaintiffs under the antitrust laws, had consented to Reycraft's use of its work product to litigate on behalf of the City of New York?

Relevant Background

What is the Revolving Door?

The metaphor of a "revolving door" is sometimes used to describe movement of attorneys between government service and private practice. Because government service provides valuable experience and contacts, many attorneys begin their career with a government agency and then move after a few years to the private sector. However, the revolving door can also move in the opposite direction or full circle; some attorneys move from private practice to government while others begin in government, enter private practice and then return to a different government job. Still other attorneys move from one branch of government to another, as does a law clerk for a judge who takes a job with Congress or the executive branch at the end of her clerkship.

After moving from government to private practice, an attorney is disqualified from representing a party to a matter substantially similar to a matter that the attorney handled while working for the government. The attorney's law firm will sometimes be disqualified as well. At a minimum, a law firm must take steps to screen a former government attorney from cases that pose conflicts of interest. These restrictions are needed to prevent government attorneys from unfairly exploiting, either during or after their government employment, the information and influence gained therefrom.

Similar restrictions apply when an attorney leaves private practice for government or leaves one branch of government for another. A prosecutor, for example, should not participate in the investigation or prosecution of a former client. See Havens v. Indiana, 793 F.2d 143, 145 (7th Cir.), cert. denied, 479 U.S. 935 (1986) (although no constitutional violation existed because prosecutor had represented defendant on unrelated charges four and five years earlier, "ethical concerns dictate that it may have been the better course of action for [the prosecutor] to recuse himself from the entire case.") However, disqualification is not as sweeping in government agencies as in private law firms; as pointed out in the *Standard Oil* case, supra, the rule imputing knowledge of confidential information to all the members of a law firm (horizontal imputation) is not ordinarily applied so as to impute knowledge of one government lawyer to all lawyers in her agency. For example, a criminal defense lawyer can become a United States Attorney without disqualifying the entire office from prosecuting one of his former clients.

Advantages of the Revolving Door

There are policy reasons for a flexible approach to private-sector representations by former government lawyers. Ethics rules, statutes and case law thus strive to balance the detriments of successive conflicts with the benefits of lawyer mobility in and out of government.

First, restrictions that impair job mobility also may impair recruitment of government lawyers who do not want to limit their future opportunities for private practice employment. Able attorneys will accept lower government salaries because they can use the experience they gain elsewhere. See Charles W. Wolfram, Modern Legal Ethics 456–62 (1986). This concern is raised in United States v. Standard Oil Co., supra, at 363, and again by the Second Circuit in Armstrong v. McAlpin, 625 F.2d 433, 443 (2d Cir.1980) (en banc), vacated on other grounds, 449 U.S. 1106 (1981).

Second, movement from government to private practice often furthers government policy objectives. Because the former government attorney is familiar with statutes, regulations and administrative procedures, he is well equipped to facilitate client compliance. Of course, there is also a downside; the same lawyer might use his government experience to find loopholes in laws and regulations and then use these loopholes to undermine the government's interests. Wolfram, supra, at 461.

Third, because attorneys often receive excellent training in government service, the revolving door helps private parties obtain experienced counsel. This is especially true in many areas of regulatory law and criminal litigation, where government employment can significantly enhance the value of a lawyer's services.

Finally, easy access to employment in the private sector helps government attorneys maintain some degree of independence from political superiors. Many of the ethical problems discussed in Chapter 3 are easier to confront without caving in to political pressures if government attorneys know that opportunities are available to them if they are discharged or choose to leave. See generally Note, Developments in the Law—Conflicts of Interest in the Legal Profession, 94 Harv. L. Rev. 1244, 1428–30 (1981).

Conflicts of Interest

Two types of successive conflicts of interest arise from movement of attorneys in and out of government: adverse-interest conflicts and congruent-interest conflicts. Wolfram, supra, at 457. As discussed in *Standard Oil*, supra, an adverse-interest conflict arises where a new matter is substantially related to a matter from the attorney's government practice, and the interests of the two clients are opposed to one another. Because the attorney may not breach his duty of loyalty to his former government employer or his duty not to disclose confidential information, he must refer the new matter to another attorney.

Congruent-interest representation, on the other hand, involves matters where the interests of the new client parallel those of the former government client. In *General Motors Corp. v. City of New York*, supra, for example, the allegations in the City's complaint were substantially similar to those made by the Justice Department in the 1956 *Bus* case. Although the potential for abuse is not as strong as in an adverse-interest representation, such a congruent-interest representation can allow a lawyer to use his position in government to curry favor with potential future clients in the private sector. Thus, as pointed out in *General Motors*, regardless of whether an attorney's former and current interests are consistent, all that is required for disqualification of a former government attorney is that the attorney, while in government service, assumed substantial responsibility for the "same matter," often interpreted to mean a "strikingly similar" or "substantially related" matter. See Comment, Disqualification of Counsel: Adverse Interests and Revolving Doors, 81 Colum. L. Rev. 199, 203 (1981); W.J. Michael Cody, Special Ethical Duties for Attorneys who Hold Public Positions, 23 Mem. St. U. L. Rev. 453, 466 (1993); Note, Developments in the Law, supra, at 1430.

Perhaps the most compelling reason that an attorney should not be allowed to represent a new client on a matter that is substantially related to a matter in which he represented a government entity, is the risk that confidential information will be disclosed or misused. The government attorney, like any other attorney, owes a duty to his client not to disclose *or to use* confidential information for his own benefit or for the benefit of another client (as discussed in Chapter 3 supra, in most circumstances the government attorney's "client" for purposes of confidentiality is the agency by which he is employed). Even if use of the information does not harm the government agency, its use may still allow a person employing the attorney to obtain an unfair advantage over private sector competitors dealing with the same agency. Also, a government agency will hesitate to give an attorney all of the information necessary to do his job if it is not assured that the attorney will keep its confidences. See Irving R. Kaufman, Comment, The Former Government Attorney and the Canons of Professional Ethics, 70 Harv. L. Rev. 657, 659 (1957). Perhaps the best way of providing such assurance is to prohibit the attorney from representing a subsequent client on a substantially related matter, regardless of whether that client's interests are adverse or congruent with the interests of the government agency.

Furthermore, successive representation on substantially related matters gives an appearance of impropriety that erodes public confidence in the integrity of government. See DR 9–101 and Canon 9 of the Model Code; Report of the President's Comm. on Fed. Ethics Law Reform, To Serve With Honor 1 (1989) (The duty of a public official "is to conduct one's office not only with honor but with perceived honor"). Prohibition of lawyer conduct that creates an appearance of impropriety thus is particularly important when a lawyer represents a government agency that ultimately needs public confidence. Indeed, "appearance of impropriety" is in some circumstances a good reason for vicarious disqualification of a former government lawyer's firm as well as the lawyer.

Restrictions on the Revolving Door

Federal and state statutes as well as state bar ethics rules regulate the work of former government attorneys in private practice. The Ethics in Government Act of 1978 § 207, 18 U.S.C.A. § 207 (1994), amended after the *General Motors* case, is the principal federal statute governing this issue. The statute (i) prohibits a former government lawyer from representing any client before a federal agency or court in a matter in which the lawyer "participated personally and substantially" while in government employment, (ii) prevents certain government employees from having any contact with their employing agency for one year after their government service, and (iii) prohibits for two years a former government employee from acting before an agency or court on any matter that was actually pending under his official responsibility. 18 U.S.C.A. § 207 (a)–(c) (1994). Violations of § 207 can result in criminal sanctions. Id. For a comparable state statute, see Fla. Stat. Ann. § 112.313(9) (West 1992), as amended, 1995 Fla. Sess. Law Serv. 95–147 (West) (no state officer or employee shall personally represent another person or entity for compensation before a government body or agency of which he or she was an officer or employee for a period of two years after vacating the office or position; violators are subject to removal from office, civil fines or criminal punishment).

Model Code, DR 9–101(B) disqualifies a private practice attorney from working on a matter with respect to which he had substantial responsibility while a government employee. Although merely working in the same government office that handled a matter is not "substantial responsibility," being an important actor in the matter is. This determination becomes much more difficult when an attorney only had a slight involvement in the matter, or worked in a supervisory role. For example, should a senior attorney in the Justice Department, such as the Attorney General, later be disqualified from an antitrust suit brought by her subordinates in the Department with her knowledge but without her personal involvement? *General Motors Corp. v. City of New York*, supra, discusses the equally difficult question of what comprises the same "matter" and suggests that the test is not whether two cases rely on the same rule of law, but whether the underlying facts are "sufficiently similar." Id. at 651, n.22. For an example of a very close case, see United States v. Smith, 653 F.2d 126 (4th Cir.1981), in which the defendant Smith hired a former prosecutor who previously had prosecuted him for gambling to defend him on an unrelated gambling charge. The Fourth Circuit narrowly defined the "matter" in the second trial as distinct from that of the first and concluded that the former prosecutor was not disqualified. See ABA Formal Opinion 342 (Nov. 24, 1975) (discussing what is a "matter" and what constitutes "substantial responsibility"); Note, Developments in the Law, supra at 1440.

DR 5–105(D) vicariously disqualifies an attorney's entire firm whenever the attorney is individually disqualified. However, this rule could easily disqualify too many law firms from too many cases, particularly antitrust and other cases to which government agencies regularly assign large numbers of attorneys. Thus ABA opinions and courts have allowed for exceptions to firm disqualification when firms screen former government attorneys from participation in, and discussion with other attorneys about, the cases involved. See Samuel R. Miller & Irwin H. Warren, Conflicts of Interest and Ethical Issues for the Inside and Outside Counsel, 40 Bus. Law. 631, 651 (1985).

In Kesselhaut v. United States, 555 F.2d 791 (Ct.Cl.1977), an attorney who was formerly employed as General Counsel to the Federal Housing Administration (FHA) joined the firm of Krooth & Altman which represented the plaintiff in a fee claim against the FHA for services it had rendered. The court, instead of disqualifying Krooth & Altman from the case, allowed Krooth & Altman to construct a "Chinese Wall" separating the attorney who had worked for the FHA from involvement with the case. See Comment, The Chinese Wall Defense to Law–Firm Disqualification, 128 U. Pa. L. Rev. 677 (1980); Sheldon Raab, New Frontiers in Conflicts of Interest: The Mobile Attorney—When to Build a Chinese Wall, in Legal Ethics 1990: What Every Lawyer Needs to Know at 173, 328 (PLI Litig. & Admin. Practice Course Handbook Series No. H4–5099, 1990).

In *Armstrong v. McAlpin*, 625 F.2d 433 (2d Cir.1980) (en banc), vacated on other grounds, 449 U.S. 1106 (1981), the Second Circuit elaborated on what constitutes adequate screening. Attorney Altman, while at the Securities Exchange Commission (SEC) had supervisory responsibility over litigation against appellant McAlpin and others for looting millions of dollars from a group of investment companies collectively called the Capital Growth companies. Altman resigned from the SEC and joined the firm that was carrying out litigation against McAlpin to recover the misappropriated funds. Altman was excluded from participation in the ensuing litigation, did not receive a share of the fees from the new representation and did not have access to the files. The Court further found that Altman had not discussed the case with his colleagues in any way. Although the court did not specifically evaluate the screening, appellants' motion to disqualify the firm was denied. Id. at 445.

What constitutes adequate screening is thus not always easy to determine when a law firm seeks to avoid disqualification of the entire firm by putting a former government attorney behind a "Chinese Wall." See Note, Ethical Problems for the Law Firm of a Former Government Attorney: Firm or Individual Disqualification?, 1977 Duke L.J. 512, 528. Furthermore, it is important to remember that, although screening devices can avoid disqualification of a firm that hires a former government attorney, such devices generally are not sufficient to resolve conflicts in successive matters handled for two private clients. See discussion in Section B infra.

Having the benefit of much of the case law discussed above, the drafters of the Model Rules sought to clarify some of the ambiguities in the Model Code. Model Rule 1.11 provides that "a lawyer shall not represent a private client in connection with a matter in which the lawyer participated personally and substantially as a public officer or employee." Additionally, the firm of the former government attorney will be disqualified unless the attorney is screened from participation in the matter, is not apportioned any part of the fee from the matter, and written notice is given to the government to enable it to ascertain compliance with the rule. Model Rule 1.11(a) and (b). Finally, under Model Rule 1.11(a), if the appropriate government agency consents to the attorney's involvement after consultation, then disqualification is not necessary. Many states which otherwise still adhere to variations of the Model Code have adopted this approach as well. See New York Code of Professional Responsibility DR 9–101(B).

The Revolving Door to the Underworld

Law enforcement officials estimate that the Columbia Cali Cocaine Cartel has been responsible for importing over 200,000 kilograms of cocaine into the United States since the mid 1980's. The Cali Cartel is exceptionally well organized and has been described as a large multi-national corporation which uses murder as a management tool. See David Lyons, Fourth Guilty Plea in Cali Case/Ex–Federal Prosecutor Expected to Turn State's Evidence, Hous. Chron., July 4, 1995, at 8; In Service of the Cali Cartel, Wash. Post, June 7, 1995, Editorial at A20; David Adams, Cartel's Lawyers, Legal Profession Also on Trial in Miami Series: The Cali Connection, St. Petersburg Times, Aug. 1, 1995, at 1A, 1B.

On June 2, 1995, 60 people connected with the Cali Cartel were indicted, including six American lawyers, three of whom were former federal prosecutors. The accusations against the lawyers included money laundering, drug conspiracy, racketeering, obstruction of justice, passing death threats to potential witnesses and, in one case, revealing the identity of an informant who was later murdered. Prosecutors working on the case also suspect that these lawyers used experience gained as federal officials to educate Cartel members on how to evade American law. In Service of the Cali Cartel, supra, at A20. Three of the accused lawyers, Miami defense attorneys Robert Moore and Francisco Laguna, and former federal prosecutor Joel Rosenthal, pleaded guilty to reduced charges even before the indictment was unsealed. Deal May Aid U.S. in Cartel Case, Chic. Trib., July 4, 1995 at 4.

48 year-old Boca Raton lawyer Donald Ferguson, an Assistant United States Attorney in Miami between 1973 and 1976, also admitted to charges of conspiracy to obstruct justice, and money laundering. The obstruction charges stemmed from Ferguson's efforts to secure false statements from drug defendants to help cartel leaders. Ferguson agreed to cooperate in the government case against the remaining two lawyers who were indicted: Cartel defense lawyer Michael Abbell and Miami attorney William Moran. See Ex–Prosecutor Pleads Guilty in Cali Cartel Probe, Wash. Post, July 4, 1995 at A10; Deal May Aid U.S. in Cartel Case, supra, at 4.

Abbell was a former federal Department of Justice official who had specialized in extraditing drug kingpins. In 1985, he started to represent Columbian cartel leaders on legal matters and he recruited Ferguson to help him in 1990. Id. Moran, a former Dade County assistant state attorney, for years represented some of Colombia's biggest accused drug lords including Jorge Ochoa from the Medellin Cartel and Rodriguez, one of the Cali leaders. Moran retained Albert Krieger, a nationally prominent criminal defense attorney best known for defending New York Mafia boss John Gotti, for his own defense. Lawyers for both Moran and Abbell asserted that what their clients did was completely within the law, and that this was a case of government retaliation against lawyers who represented drug defendants well. See Adams, supra, at A1.

QUESTION

1. Apart from obviously illegal activity such as money laundering and threatening witnesses, what should a former prosecutor refrain from doing on behalf of clients who are criminal defendants? Consider each of the following:

(a) providing a client with the names of government informants;

(b) describing to clients the details of government "sting" operations;

(c) using knowledge about government "sting" operations to argue that a particular operation involving the lawyer's client was entrapment;

(d) providing a client with the names of persons under investigation when the prosecutor left government service; and

(e) providing a client with details about government plea bargaining strategy.

PROBLEMS

1. You represent a prominent politician in connection with personal matters, including several real-estate transactions. After your client is elected President of the United States, he offers you a job as Deputy White

House Counsel and you accept. The Deputy White House Counsel, like other White House lawyers, represents the President in his official capacity. In moving files from your law firm office to your new office in the White House, you come across files concerning one of the President's personal real estate transactions. Should you move these files into your new office in the White House? Would doing so affect the status of the attorney-client privilege?

2. You have worked for two years as a staff attorney for a congressional committee that is drafting revisions to the securities laws. Morgan Goldman & Co., a New York investment bank and one of the largest underwriters of securities in the country, offers you a high paying job on its legal staff, which you accept. However, your current boss, Senator Smith, asks you to delay your departure for New York and remain on the committee staff for another two months to assist with drafting the new legislation. Morgan Goldman tells you that you may stay on the committee staff for as long as it takes to finish the job. What should you do?

B.   SUCCESSIVE CLIENTS IN THE PRIVATE SECTOR

Charles H. Goldstein, b. 1939; B.A. Case Western Reserve University 1961; J.D. George Washington University 1964; admitted to the bar in Virginia in 1964 and California in 1972; currently a managing partner of Goldstein, Kennedy & Petito in Los Angeles (labor and public employment relations law).

Norman H. Kirshman, b. 1930; B.S. Columbia University 1955; J.D. Cornell University 1958; U.S. Army JAGC 1959–63; admitted to the bar in New York in 1958 and California in 1965; outside counsel to Diodes, Inc. beginning in 1965; Executive Vice President, Secretary and general counsel of Diodes 1967–69; partner of Goldstein, Gentile and Kirshman beginning in 1969; currently a partner of Kirshman & Harris in Los Angeles (general civil and trial practice; employment relations law and corporate securities law).

Charles H. Goldstein et al., Plaintiffs and Respondents, v. Alan B. Lees and Florenza Lees, Defendants and Appellants.

46 Cal.App.3d 614, 120 Cal.Rptr. 253 (2 Dist.1975).

■ STEPHENS, Acting Presiding Justice.

On January 31, 1972, the law firm of Charles H. Goldstein, Joseph F. Gentile, and Norman H. Kirshman filed its amended complaint claiming money due for the reasonable value of legal services rendered by Norman H. Kirshman. Defendants Alan B. Lees and Florenza Lees contended at trial that the monies prayed for in the complaint exceeded the amount specified in an oral agreement between Alan Lees and Norman Kirshman.

Plaintiffs contended that there was no such agreement, and the trial judge agreed. The defendants have appealed.

The basic question presented in this case is whether or not a former counsel to a corporation can properly render legal services on behalf of a minority shareholder and director in a proxy fight designed to gain control of the same corporation under circumstances where the former counsel holds corporate confidences and secrets which are relevant to the proxy fight. We hold that such representation is improper and that a contract to provide such services is void for reasons of public policy.

Facts

Norman Kirshman served as Executive Vice President, Secretary, and general counsel to Diodes, Inc. from April 1967 to October 1969. Before assuming the position of general counsel, he had been retained by Diodes as outside counsel, beginning February 1965. In his position as an officer and as general counsel to Diodes, Kirshman became privy to its innermost secrets. In fact, Kirshman testified that he "knew the operations of the corporation intimately ... all of the subsidiaries had been acquired either as a result of my negotiations or as a result of my participation that I had as a member of the board of directors.... I think I knew the company more intimately than anybody other than Mr. Lloyd ... the chief executive officer."

Early in 1971, Kirshman and Alan Lees (a director of Diodes, who owned more than 107,000 shares of its stock) discussed the possibility of a proxy solicitation to gain control of the corporation. After a series of preliminary discussions, the decision to initiate the proxy battle was made, and Lees agreed to assume the cost of soliciting proxies. Initially, Lees, at Kirshman's suggestion, retained the legal services of Goldstein and Moffitt. After two months, Lees discharged Goldstein and Moffitt and hired Kirshman as counsel for the proxy effort. Kirshman testified that he felt he could perform the work "very effectively because of my insight to the facts, whereas some other attorney who was a total stranger to the Diodes scene would not have, and I agreed to accept full responsibility for the Diodes contest." Thus there is no question that Kirshman's "insight to the facts" of Diodes was a critical component in the retention of his services as counsel. Indeed, as Kirshman explained, the decision to initiate the proxy struggle was preceded by "many questions by Dr. Lees to me about the intricacies and inside information that I had because I had been very close to Mr. Lloyd as his No. 2 man...."

Discussion

It is settled in California that an attorney may not recover for services rendered if those services are rendered in contradiction to the requirements of professional responsibility. As the California Supreme Court explained in Clark v. Millsap, 197 Cal. 765, 785, 242 P. 918, 926 (quoting 6 C.J. 722, 723), "Fraud or unfairness on the part of the attorney will prevent him from recovering for services rendered; *as will ... acts of impropriety inconsistent with the character of the profession, and incompatible with the faithful discharge of its duties."* (Emphasis added.) (See also Priester v. Citizens Nat'l Trust & Sav. Bank of Los Angeles, 131 Cal.App.2d 314, 322, 280 P.2d 835; Denton v. Smith, 101 Cal.App.2d 841, 845, 226 P.2d 723.) Contracts to render such services even if not tainted with actual fraud have been held to be "clearly against public policy and void." (Anderson v. Eaton, 211 Cal. 113, 116, 293 P. 788, 789.) Thus the facts and law applicable to this case require us to decide a question of first impression in California—whether a former counsel to a corporation can properly represent a minority shareholder and director of the same corporation in a proxy contest in circumstances where counsel holds corporate secrets that are material to the proxy fight.

At the time of the performance of the services for which compensation is demanded here, Rule 5 of the Rules of Professional Conduct provided that: "A member of the State Bar shall not accept employment adverse to a client or former client, relating to a matter in reference to which he has obtained confidential information by reason of or in the course of his employment by such client or former client." (See Bus. & Prof.Code, § 6076.) The primary purpose of this rule is to protect the confidential relationship which exists between attorney and client. (Jacuzzi v. Jacuzzi Bros., Inc., 218 Cal.App.2d 24, 28, 32 Cal.Rptr. 188.) Thus, nothing in the rule prohibits an attorney from accepting employment adverse to a former client if the matter has no relationship to confidential information acquired by reason of or in the course of his employment by the former client. Similarly, nothing in the rule prohibits an attorney from accepting employment relating to a matter in which he has obtained confidential information provided that the new employment is not adverse to the interests of the former client. Plaintiffs contend that Kirshman's representation was not adverse to the interests of the corporation.

In one sense, plaintiffs are correct. There is no basis in the record which would permit an appellate court to conclude that the proxy fight itself was adverse to the interests of the corporation. This conclusion follows even though Kirshman and Lees failed in their attempt to gain control of the corporation. We cannot say that this exercise in corporate democracy was inimical to the interests of the corporation. Certainly if the proxy fight itself were in fact adverse to the interests of the corporation, a violation of Rule 5 would be apparent. Although the conclusion that the proxy fight may have been consistent with the interests of the corporation is necessary to preserve the plaintiffs' judgment, it is not sufficient. The question is whether or not the employment of Kirshman was adverse to the interests of the former client. Clearly, it was.

Business and Professions Code section 6068 subdivision (e) states: "It is the duty of an attorney: . . . (t)o maintain inviolate the confidence, and at every peril to himself to preserve the secrets, of his client." In this instance, Kirshman accepted employment which surely at best must have tempted him to reveal or to improperly monopolize the confidences and secrets of his former client. As the Supreme Court recognized in Anderson

v. Eaton, supra (211 Cal. at p. 117, 293 P. at p. 790), "Conscience and good morals dictate that an attorney should not so conduct himself as to be open to the temptation of violating his obligation of fidelity and confidence." Clearly, the acceptance of employment which threatens the revelation or improper monopolization of a former client's confidences is adverse to the interests of the former client. To be sure, Rule 5 implies that an attorney may accept employment on a matter in reference to which he has before obtained confidential information, but nothing in Rule 5 sanctions the acceptance of such employment when the representation of the interests of the new client inherently tempts the attorney to reveal or improperly monopolize the confidences of the old. Such a reading of Rule 5 would conflict with the policies underlying section 6068, subdivision (e) of the Business and Professions Code; it would needlessly permit attorneys to create the appearance of impropriety. Nor would such an interpretation offer assistance to the new client. Clients are entitled to vigorous and determined representation by counsel. It is difficult to believe that a counsel who scrupulously attempts to avoid the revelation of former client confidences—i.e., who makes every effort to steer clear of the danger zone—can offer the kind of undivided loyalty that a client has every right to expect and that our legal system demands. Rule 5 operates to preclude any impediment to the fulfillment of an attorney's professional obligation to his client by proscribing any conflict of interest in his representation of past and present clients. "It is better to remain on safe and secure professional ground, to the end that the ancient and honored profession of the law and its representatives may not be brought into disrepute. Courts have consistently held the members of the profession to the strictest account in matters affecting the relation of attorney and client." (Tomblin v. Hill, 206 Cal. 689, 694, 275 P. 941, 943, quoting Addison v. Cope, 210 Mo.App. 569, 243 S.W. 212, 215.)

It could be argued that as a shareholder and as a director, Lees was entitled to be apprised of corporate confidences and secrets. Since Lees' status as a shareholder and his status as a director give rise to different issues, we treat the questions separately.

Clearly, the duty stated in section 6068, subdivision (e) applies in the corporate context. As the California Supreme Court stated in discussing the narrower[5] but related question of the attorney-client privilege, "Certainly the public policy behind the attorney-client privilege requires that an artificial person be given equal opportunity with a natural person to communicate with its attorney, within the professional relationship, without fear that its communication will be made public. As one writer has said, 'The more deeply one is convinced of the social necessity of permitting corporations to consult frankly and privately with their legal advisers, the more willing one should be to accord them a flexible and generous protection.'" (D. I. Chadbourne, Inc. v. Superior Court, 60 Cal.2d 723, 736, 36

---

5. The attorney-client privilege is more limited than the ethical obligation of a lawyer to guard the confidences and secrets of his client. (American Bar Assn., Code of Professional Responsibility EC4—4.)

Cal.Rptr. 468, 477, 388 P.2d 700, 709, quoting Simon, The Attorney–Client Privilege as Applied to Corporations (1956) 65 Yale L.J. 953, 990.)

Moreover, it is apparent that although shareholders have some rights to corporate information not available to the general public, shareholder status does not in and of itself entitle an individual to unfettered access to corporate confidences and secrets. For example, Corporations Code section 3003 confines the shareholder's right to inspect corporate records to three categories of documents: (1) the share register or duplicate share register; (2) the books of account; and (3) the minutes of proceedings of the shareholders and the board of directors, and of executive committees of the directors. Thus, by statute, shareholders have less right to acquire corporate information than do directors. This proposition is also supported by the interpretations governing the scope of the attorney-client privilege. It is generally conceded that a communication coming from a mere stockholder would not be privileged. (See D. I. Chadbourne, Inc. v. Superior Court, supra; Ann. 98 A.L.R.2d 241, 245—247.) The logical counterpart of this concession would appear to be that the privilege may be invoked "against all whose communications are not covered by the scope of the privilege— among others, the stockholders of the corporation." (Com., The Attorney–Client Privilege in Shareholders' Suits, 69 Colum.L.Rev. 309, 318, n. 39.) This, of course, does not mean that such a privilege is absolute. It may, for example, give way in shareholders' derivative suits on a proper showing (Garner v. Wolfinbarger (5th Cir.1970) 430 F.2d 1093), but the fact that the availability of the privilege may be denied by a judicial officer on a proper showing does not mean that a former attorney may divulge corporate secrets to a shareholder in the absence of a corporate waiver, or in the absence of judicial compulsion.

On the other hand, Lees' position as a director of the corporation would ordinarily entitle him to the receipt of confidential information. Thus it can be argued that Kirshman's employment did not threaten the revelation of corporate confidences to anyone who would not otherwise be entitled to receive them. This superficially acceptable argument cannot withstand analysis.

Clearly, if Kirshman were counsel to the corporation, he could not, consistently with his position as general counsel, act as proxy for one contending group of shareholders. As the Committee on Professional Ethics and Grievances of the American Bar Association stated in Opinion 86: "In acting as the corporation's legal advisor he must refrain from taking part in any controversies or factional differences which may exist among shareholders as to its control. When his opinion is sought by those entitled to it, or when it becomes his duty to voice it, he must be in a position to give it without bias or prejudice and to have it recognized as being so given. Unless he is in that position his usefulness to his client is impaired." This duty to act without bias or prejudice does not dissolve merely because the attorney has been discharged. Any contrary ruling would conflict with California's commitment to the principle that "the client's power to discharge an attorney, with or without cause, is absolute." (Code Civ.Proc.,

§ 284; Fracasse v. Brent, 6 Cal.3d 784, 790, 100 Cal.Rptr. 385, 389, 494 P.2d 9, 13.)

The board of directors, not corporate counsel, has the right to control the affairs of the corporation. (Corp.Code, § 800.) The board of directors thus has the power to retain and discharge corporate counsel. It would serve no useful purpose to burden the exercise of that power with the fear that discharged[8] counsel could make his services available to the highest bidding minority shareholder. Thus, even though a director has a right to receive confidential information, he has no exclusive right to receive such information from former counsel. To the extent that Lees had a claim on Kirshman's knowledge by virtue of his status as director, so did all of the other directors of the corporation.

Thus the argument that Less had a right to the confidences of the corporation proves too much. It proves that Kirshman had a duty to serve both Lees and the adversaries in the proxy contest. Conflicts of interest such as these cannot be tolerated.

Finally, we note that there is no force to the objection that the result announced here will work a windfall for defendants. This decision is not rendered for the sake of defendants. Indeed, it is enough to say that "(c)ourts do not sit to give effect to ... illegal contracts. The law is not to be subsidized to overthrow itself...." (Valentine v. Stewart, 15 Cal. 387, 405.)

The judgment is reversed.

ASHBY and HASTINGS, JJ., concur.

Hearing denied; MOSK, J., dissenting.

QUESTIONS

1. The Court begins its opinion by stating that the question it confronts is whether or not a former counsel to a corporation may render legal services in a proxy fight for a minority shareholder and director "under circumstances where the former counsel holds corporate confidences and secrets which are relevant to the proxy fight." How important are "corporate confidences and secrets" to the Court's final analysis of the problem? What is the likelihood that Lees had access to the same confidences and secrets that Kirshman did?

2. Why is it important that a former lawyer for a corporation not take sides when a shareholder seeks to gain control of the corporation in a proxy fight?

3. If Kirshman had remained counsel to Diodes, could he have represented the incumbent directors in opposing Lees in the proxy fight? Why or why not?

8. We do not intend to suggest that the operation of this rule would vary if the attor-ney resigns before discharge or resigns because of a disagreement over company policy.

Relevant Background

Successive conflicts generally occur where a law firm represents a client whose interests conflict with those of a former client or where an attorney moves from one firm to another and works against the interests of a former client. The two clients need not actually be involved in the same legal dispute; if work that the lawyer is asked to do for one client is detrimental to the other, then the lawyer should seriously consider whether or not there is an impermissible successive conflict. See John S. Dzienkowski, Positional Conflicts of Interest, 71 Tex. L. Rev. 457, 460 (1993); Samuel R. Miller, Richard E. Rochman & Ray Cannon, Conflicts of Interest in Corporate Litigation, 48 Bus. Law. 141, 145 (1992).

It is also important to distinguish conflicts in successive representations from conflicts in concurrent representations, which are discussed in Chapter 6, infra. Concurrent representation of adverse clients nearly always warrants automatic disqualification, whereas only some successive conflicts are impermissible. Occasionally, an attorney will fire a client in order to avoid a concurrent conflict and take advantage of the more flexible rules governing successive conflicts by accepting a new case that is more lucrative. Such jumping from one client to another before a matter is completed violates the attorney's duty of loyalty to the first client and is widely condemned as unethical. See Picker Int'l, Inc. v. Varian Assocs., Inc., 670 F.Supp. 1363, 1365 (N.D.Ohio 1987) ("A firm may not drop a client like a hot potato, especially if it is in order to keep happy a far more lucrative client.").

Duties of Confidentiality and Loyalty

The two duties that underlie restrictions on successive representations are the duty to preserve client confidences and the duty of loyalty to clients. In addition, even if client confidences and loyalty are not compromised, some successive representations create the appearance of impropriety, which itself can damage an attorney-client relationship, an attorney's reputation, and the reputation of the legal profession as a whole. See Steven H. Goldberg, The Former Client's Disqualification Gambit: A Bad Move in Pursuit of an Ethical Anomaly, 72 Minn. L. Rev. 227, 233–34 (1987).

Although ethics rules prohibit both non-adverse and adverse disclosure or use of confidential client information (see Model Rule 1.6, DR 4–101), the further step of disqualifying an attorney from representing a new client is taken in adverse situations, where breach of confidence is most likely. Indeed, a lawyer's breach of her duty of confidentiality may be difficult to prevent, particularly in situations where she could unconsciously disclose or use confidential information. Equally important, restrictions on successive conflicts alleviate former clients' concerns that their confidences will be disclosed or used to further an adverse cause.

Finally, it is often difficult as an evidentiary matter to determine when confidential information is misused by an attorney, and a hearing designed to uncover whether information was misused will itself reveal that which was sought to be kept secret. See Wolfram, supra, at 360. Just such a dilemma arose in Government of India v. Cook Indus., Inc., 569 F.2d 737 (2d Cir.1978), where attorney Frederick W. Meeker previously represented Cook Industries (Cook) in breach of contract actions against Cook for failing to ship the proper tonnage of soybeans to Taiwanese plaintiffs. Meeker then joined a new firm which represented Indian plaintiffs suing Cook for a similar failure to ship the proper amounts of soybeans described in bills of lading. The Second Circuit determined that the two actions were substantially related, and that Meeker's involvement in the prior case made it likely that he had come across privileged information. The Court deemed it unnecessary to find that Meeker actually learned confidential information, and observed that such a requirement "would put the former client to the Hobson's choice of either having to disclose his privileged information in order to disqualify his former attorney or having to refrain from the disqualification motion altogether." Id. at 740.

The second duty, the duty of loyalty, is often described as zealous representation of a current client. Loyalty, however, is also owed to a former client. Although disclosure or use of client confidences is one way in which an attorney can be disloyal, there are other types of disloyalty. A lawyer might: 1) misuse a former client's trust to convince her to do something, for example to undertake a risky transaction that benefits a current client; 2) conduct a representation in such a way as to facilitate a future representation of another client; or 3) attack legal arguments or documents that the lawyer has made or prepared for a former client. Restrictions on successive conflicts help prevent such abuses and recognize that, while loyalty is obviously owed to a current client, loyalty to past clients should not be ignored. See Wolfram, supra, at 362; Mark I. Steinberg & Timonthy U. Sharpe, Attorney Conflicts of Interest: The Need for a Coherent Framework, 66 Notre Dame L. Rev. 1, 6 (1990); Donald R. McMinn, Note, ABA Formal Opinion 88–356: New Justification for Increased Use of Screening Devices to Avert Attorney Disqualification, 65 N.Y.U. L. Rev. 1231, 1241 (1990).

Finally, even if an attorney does not misuse client confidences or act in a disloyal manner toward a former client, appearances created by successive conflicts cause clients to distrust their lawyers and the public to distrust the legal profession generally. Disqualifying attorneys from successive conflicts thus keeps the "appearance of impropriety" at a minimum and helps restore trust where it is urgently needed.

Disqualification as a Mechanism of Enforcement

Although the motion to disqualify is the most common means of restricting successive conflicts, this enforcement mechanism can create as many problems as it solves. First, disqualification may impinge on a client's right to choose a lawyer, particularly in specialized areas where a lawyer may have unique expertise not generally available in the community. Second, disqualification, and even a motion for disqualification, can tarnish the reputation of a lawyer, and unjustifiably so in close cases where the lawyer's responsibilities are less than clear. Third, a motion to disqualify can be misused to delay a trial and as a tactical device. See Max Gitter, Conflicts with Former Clients, in Legal Ethics: Everything a Lawyer Needs to Know and Should Not be Afraid to Ask, at 7 (PLI Litig. & Admin. Practice Course Handbook Series No. H4–5043, 1988). An irony of the motion to disqualify is that while conflict rules are designed to protect former clients, it is often third persons who file motions to disqualify (for example, General Motors filed the motion in *General Motors v. City of New York*, supra). In these circumstances, disqualification can become a court-room strategy, rather than a mechanism for enforcing ethical standards in the profession.

The Substantial Relationship Doctrine

Disqualification from successive representation of private-sector clients generally requires that there be a "substantial relationship" as well as adversity between the prior and current representations. This rule is credited to T.C. Theatre Corp. v. Warner Bros. Pictures, Inc., 113 F.Supp. 265 (S.D.N.Y.1953), which held that "[w]here any substantial relationship can be shown between the subject matter of a former representation and that of a subsequent adverse representation, the latter will be prohibited." Id. at 268. As pointed out in *General Motors Corp. v. City of New York*, supra, the disqualification net is cast far more broadly in the case of a former government attorney: regardless of whether the two interests are adverse or congruent, all that is required for disqualification is that the attorney, while in government service, assumed substantial responsibility for the "same matter." See generally Note, Developments in the Law—Conflicts of Interest in the Legal Profession, 94 Harv. L. Rev. 1244 (1981).

The former representation need not be a formal attorney-client relationship for the rule to apply; anyone who imparts confidential communications to an attorney—whether clients, prospective clients, or other people with whom the attorney has had a professional relationship—will usually be considered a "client" for purposes of the substantial relationship test. The former client may also be a one-time client, a client on retainer, or someone who is serially-represented. Charles W. Wolfram, The Uncertain Realm of Former–Client Conflicts, in Legal Ethics 1990: What Every Lawyer Needs to Know, at 165 (PLI Litig. & Admin. Practice Course Handbook Series No. H4–5099, 1990). In close cases, it may be difficult to determine what actually is a substantial relationship between former and current interests. There are three general approaches: 1) the Second Circuit looks to similarity of legal issues, 2) the Seventh Circuit looks to relevance of information disclosed in the prior representation, and 3) the Ninth Circuit (and probably most other courts) look to factual similarity. See Silver Chrysler Plymouth, Inc. v. Chrysler Motors Corp., 518 F.2d 751, 754 (2d Cir.1975), overruled on other grounds; Armstrong v. McAlpin, 625 F.2d 433 (2d Cir. 1980) (en banc); Westinghouse Elec. Corp. v. Gulf Oil Corp., 588 F.2d 221, 225 (7th Cir.1978); and Trone v. Smith, 621 F.2d 994,

998 (9th Cir.1980); see also Miller, Rochman & Cannon supra, at 148; Note, Developments in the Law, supra at 1325.

Successive conflicts can be difficult for attorneys to resolve, particularly when a prospective client asks a lawyer to accept or turn down a representation within a short time frame. Nonetheless, an attorney should be careful to obtain complete and accurate information about both representations before making a decision, as a court later will decide whether or not to disqualify based on the information at its disposal, not what the attorney knew at the time. If a substantial relationship is found, a presumption arises that the attorney received confidential information from his client, and this presumption warrants disqualification of the attorney.

Rebutting the Presumption

Occasionally, a lawyer who can demonstrate that she was not privy to client confidences in the first place will be allowed to rebut the presumption of the substantial relationship doctrine. See Wolfram, supra, at 372. For example, some courts allow for a so called "scrivener exception" to the substantial-relationship standard in situations where the former representation was of a type that no confidential information would pass, and the former client could not reasonably expect loyalty to continue after the representation was completed. This exception usually is allowed only where the lawyer is retained by the former client for a brief period of time for a limited purpose or to draft public documents (such as a permit application or a mortgage). Appellate lawyers occasionally have also been excused from the substantial relationship standard when accepting subsequent adverse representations, on the theory that the prior representation worked only with information that was a matter of public record. See Phillips v. Phillips, 242 Ga. 577, 250 S.E.2d 418 (Ga. 1978) (lawyer drafted deeds which he later sought to set aside); People v. Jones, 105 Ill.App.3d 1143, 62 Ill.Dec. 25, 435 N.E.2d 823 (Ill. App.1982) (less rigorous criteria for determining conflict of interest applied to appellate representation).

However, in the vast majority of representations, a lawyer is not a mere "scrivener." This label is convenient for the lawyer when a substantially related, and lucrative, subsequent adverse representation is proposed, just as it can be convenient when a lawyer is accused of facilitating client fraud or other misconduct. See discussion in Chapter 2, supra. It is important to recognize that in most litigation matters and transactional work a lawyer is not a mere "scrivener" for her client, but an advocate and advisor who helps her client make decisions, often after being exposed to confidential information. In evaluating subsequent adverse representations, lawyers should be aware that the "scrivener" exception, if applied at all, will most likely be narrowly construed.

The Model Code and Model Rules

Under Model Code, DR 5–105(A), a lawyer should not accept employment if the interests of another client may impair the independent professional judgment of the lawyer. Additionally, under EC 4–5, a lawyer should take care to avoid disclosure of confidences from one client to another. Finally, Canon 6 (competence), Canon 7 (zealous representation), and Canon 9 (avoiding appearance of professional impropriety) are relevant to a lawyer's responsibility in a successive client situation.

Model Rule 1.9(a) prohibits representation of a new client in a matter substantially related to a matter that a lawyer worked on for a former client, if the new client's interest in the matter is materially adverse to an interest of the former client. This rule is essentially the same as the *T.C.* substantial relationship standard, supra, but also specifically includes a consent provision. Thus, under Model Rule 1.9(a), an attorney may accept a substantially related adverse representation if the former client consents after consultation. Rule 1.9(c) prohibits any use of a former client's information that is to the disadvantage of the former client, except where the information has become generally known or is permitted to be disclosed under the narrow exceptions set forth in Model Rule 1.6. From their wording, Rule 1.9(a) and Rule 1.9(c) appear to have similar objectives and to overlap in scope. Professor Wolfram has suggested that Rule 1.9(c) (designated as Rule 1.9(b) prior to 1989) may have been designed as a backstop to prevent leaks of information where the substantial relationship test fails. See Wolfram, supra, at 365.

Model Rule 1.9(b) provides that "a lawyer shall not knowingly represent a person in the same or a substantially related matter in which a firm with which the lawyer formerly was associated had previously represented a client, (1) whose interests are materially adverse to that person; and (2) about whom the lawyer had acquired information protected by Rules 1.6 [confidentiality of information] and 1.9(c) that is material to the matter." However, the former firm's client may consent to such a representation after consultation.

Imputed Disqualification in Successive Representations

Imputed disqualification applies to lawyers in private practice as well as to government lawyers. See Model Rule 1.10 and Model Rule 1.11. Thus, if a lawyer should not represent a new client because of a conflict with a former client, the lawyer's firm generally is disqualified as well. For example, if an attorney is representing client A in a matter and then moves to a new firm where another attorney is representing client B in a matter substantially related and adverse to client A's interest in the first matter, the second attorney might be disqualified from representing client B once the first attorney joins his firm.

The rationale for such imputed disqualification is sometimes phrased as a rebuttable presumption that a lawyer will share information with members of her firm, even if doing so would violate the confidences of a previous client. A problem with this rationale is that it presumes that an attorney will do something unethical, which is not a very good starting place for defining rules of professional ethics. An alternative rationale for imputed disqualification is that it removes the temptation to misuse client confidences within law firms and gives former clients greater peace of mind.

Occasionally, courts allow law firms to use screening devices to shelter a conflicted attorney from the rest of the firm so as to continue a representation. On the other hand, the Model Rules and most state ethics codes do not specifically allow for screening of attorneys moving between law firms. See Note, New Justification for Increased Use of Screening Devices, supra, at 1233. But see ABA Formal Opinion 88–356 (1988) (sanctioning use of screening devices in law firms for temporary attorneys facing conflicts of interest from successive representations)

Successive Conflicts in the Corporate Context

An important issue in successive representations is whether an organization's lawyer may be disqualified in a suit by the organization against a former employee when the employee previously consulted with the lawyer. In E.F. Hutton & Co. v. Brown, 305 F.Supp. 371 (S.D.Tex.1969), a lawyer represented both E.F. Hutton and Brown, a former Houston regional vice-president of E.F. Hutton, in a formal SEC investigation. The court held that, even though no secrets had been kept between Brown and E.F. Hutton, and Brown had not communicated any confidential information to the lawyer that was not also communicated to E.F. Hutton, the lawyer still could not later represent E.F. Hutton in a lawsuit against Brown for alleged negligence and breach of fiduciary duty in connection with the same matter. Id. at 395. On the other hand, some courts have found that employees are not represented personally by an employer's lawyer, and thus are not joint clients with their employer. If so, no successive representation problem results. See Meehan v. Hopps, 144 Cal.App.2d 284, 301 P.2d 10 (Cal.Dist.Ct.App.1956).

As vividly illustrated in *Goldstein v. Lees*, supra, successive conflicts can also arise in changes of corporate control and other intra-corporate disputes in which attorneys are asked to take sides. See Miller, Rochman and Cannon, *Conflicts of Interest*, supra, at 150. For example, in Allegaert v. Perot, 565 F.2d 246 (2d Cir.1977), two law firms, Weil, Gotschal & Manges and Leva, Hawes, Symington, represented duPont Glore Forgan, Inc. (DGF), a brokerage firm controlled by business interests aligned with H. Ross Perot. Pursuant to the terms of a realignment or joint venture agreement between DGF and another brokerage firm, Walston Incorporated (Walston), the two law firms also represented Walston. Later, a trustee in bankruptcy for Walston sought to disqualify the law firms from representing DGF as a defendant in a lawsuit brought by the trustee alleging fraudulent conduct by DGF in connection with the realignment agreement. The Second Circuit, however, found that Walston knew that information it had disclosed to both law firms during the previous representation would certainly have been conveyed to the firms' primary client, DGF, and therefore held that the substantial-relationship test was inapplicable. Id. at 250.

PROBLEMS

1. You represented X Corp. for ten years lobbying on environmental issues arising out of its offshore oil exploration and drilling. In the course of the representation, you learn how X Corp. makes its exploration and drilling decisions. You are now asked to represent Y Corp., a purchaser of crude oil, in an antitrust suit alleging that X Corp. and other oil companies artificially restricted their production to keep prices up. Y Corp.'s claims against X Corp. will probably include allegations concerning the exploration and drilling decisions you learned about earlier. Are the two matters substantially related? May you take the case?

2. You were the General Counsel to A Corp. for ten years. You did a good job on work that included all aspects of A Corp.'s business, but were dismissed after a new group of investors gained control of A Corp. B Corp. asks you to represent it in suing A Corp. for antitrust violations that occurred after you left A Corp. The violations were allegedly part of a pattern of anticompetitive conduct going back to your time as General Counsel of A Corp. May you take the case?

3. For three years, you represented Smith, a real estate developer, in closing sales of lots in the Mountaincrest subdivision outside a major city. Your work for these closings mostly concerned marketability of title. A month ago, Smith stopped retaining you and retained his nephew, a recent law school graduate, instead. Jones now asks you to represent him in bringing suit against Smith concerning the marketability of title to a lot that Smith sold Jones in the Hilltop subdivision, located two miles south of the Mountaincrest subdivision. May you take the case?

See Restatement, The Law Governing Lawyers, Proposed Final Draft No. 1, section 213, Illustrations 2–4 (March 29, 1996).

CHAPTER 5

PROFESSIONAL RELATIONSHIPS: PEERS, ASSOCIATES AND PARTNERS

A. PEERS

A professional career does not begin with admission to the bar, but more than three years earlier with enrollment in law school. It is in law school that a lawyer begins to form professional relationships—many of which will last a lifetime—and it is in law school that she must begin to act like a professional. Conduct that may be tolerated in an undergraduate college usually has far more drastic consequences in law school. Misconduct by a law student, particularly if it involves dishonesty, can also delay or prevent admission to the bar.

Academic Dishonesty

Ultimately the moral character of the legal profession is only as good as the moral character of the persons who enter it. As you read the next selection, ask yourself how you would handle the problem that Chip Benedict confronts. Are Chip's motives in acting as he does entirely honorable? What is the meaning of honor?

Louis Stanton Auchincloss, b. 1917 in Lawrence, New York; Groton School 1933; attended Yale College (editor, Yale Literary Magazine); LL.B. University of Virginia 1941 (editor, Virginia Law Review); U.S. Navy 1941–45; associate, Sullivan & Cromwell 1941, 1946–51; creative writer 1951–54; partner of Hawkins, Delafield & Wood 1954–86 (specializing in trusts and estates); member, Executive Committee of the Association of the Bar of the City of New York; author of fifty books, including novels and collections of short stories, many of which focus on the life and work of lawyers.

Many of Louis Auchincloss's novels take place in a setting unfamiliar to today's young lawyers, the "uppercrust" world of prep-school and Ivy League educated lawyers and investment bankers who dominated the legal and financial community in the East and in pockets of the Midwest and West until well into the 1960's. His women characters, although sometimes caricatures from the era before women's liberation, often show more understanding than their male counterparts of moral complexities in a professional world then dominated almost exclusively by men. Although today's lawyers happily confront a more diverse environment than do Auchincloss's protagonists, his novels depict the ethical dilemmas of professional life in a way that transcends what might at first appear to be his limited selection of places and personalities.

Excerpt From Louis Auchincloss, Honorable Men (1985)

Chip Benedict, a graduate of Yale College, is in his third year of law school at the University of Virginia in the early 1940's. Chip has done well in law school and is the Editor-in-Chief of the Virginia Law Review. **Chessy Bogart**, also a graduate of Yale, is in the same class as Chip in law school and is an editor of the Law Review. Chip and Chessy also attended boarding school together at St. Luke's in Massachusetts. Chip graduated from St. Luke's, but Chessy was expelled for misconduct in which he unsuccessfully tried to implicate Chip. Chip and Chessy have had a cordial but strained relationship ever since.

The story is told by Chip's wife **Alida Benedict**:

. . . A greater crisis for Chip and me came shortly after this, just before Christmas in his last year at law school.

I have not spoken of Chessy Bogart, though he continued to play a considerable role in our lives. He had come to Virginia Law School with Chip, and he was very much a part of the weekend group that met every Saturday night for dinner and bridge or poker, sometimes at our house, sometimes at the house of one of the other law school couples who lived in the Farmington area. . . .

Chessy, anyway, seemed assured of a good future. He was too much of a party-goer, even by Virginia standards, and he did the minimum homework, but he listened to the lectures, and his remarkable memory taped, as it were, every spoken word of his professors.

"They're all peacocks," he explained to me, "in love with their own tails. Spell it *t-a-l-e-s*. So long as you have the wit to toss back their own garbage on an exam, you have it made. Actually, you don't have to crack a book, except just enough to be able to answer occasionally in class."

His brilliance won him an editorship in the contest for the Law Review, but it proved a poor substitute for industry in the writing of articles, and his failure to pull his oar soon became a bone of bitter contention between him and Chip. When the final rift between them came, however, it was over something much graver than Chessy's omissions. It was not nonfeasance but actual malfeasance that now confronted us. You see, I had picked up some legal terms from Chip.

When I saw one morning from the living room window Chessy's blue Chevrolet pull up by our door, I thought at first it was [Chessy's wife] Suzy. Chip had gone to school, as I assumed his friend had. But then I recognized Chessy at the front door alone, looking graver than I had ever seen him.

"I've got to talk to you, Alida."

"You look as if you could do with a cup of coffee."

"I'd rather have a whiskey, thank you."

"At ten o'clock in the morning? Well, you know where it is."

When we were settled by the fire, which I had lit, for it was a cold day, he began.

"Do you remember Bob Reardon?"

I did. He had been a classmate of Chip and Chessy's, a Virginian, from Norfolk, an agreeable but silent young man, an editor of the Review, who had shot himself in the cellar of his fraternity house the spring before for no reason that anyone had ever been able to determine. But Virginia men could be like that, I had learned—inscrutable, mysterious.

"Of course. Chip asked him out here a couple of times. He didn't say much, but his silences were better than our yacking. Have they ever found out . . . ?"

"Why he did it? No. But that's not why I bring him up. His mother recently sent Chip a folder of his Law Review notes. She thought they might be of some use."

"How considerate. And were they?"

"Wait. You will be the judge of that. Do you recall how hotly Chip has been after me to write a note for the February issue?"

"Oh, yes. I really don't see why, Chessy, you make it so hard for him."

"Well, I wrote the damn note. It was on what constitutes a failure to bargain collectively under the Labor Relations Act. It was a subject that I had assigned last year to Bob Reardon and on which he had submitted an outline. I decided not to use the poor fellow's outline, and I wrote the note. Chip accepted it and scheduled it for the February issue."

I looked at him blankly. "Is there some question of plagiarism? Surely an outline's nothing."

"A mere outline is nothing, I agree. But there's more to come. In Reardon's portfolio there was an almost completed note that bore a curious resemblance to mine. Enough so for Chip to accuse me of plagiarism."

My little world, bounded by the Blue Ridge and Mr. Jefferson's rotunda, tottered. "But if you didn't have Bob's draft . . . ?"

"Ah, but Chip says I must have. He has removed my note from the galleys of the February issue. He has replaced it with an old one of his own that he brought up to date."

"So that's why he worked till dawn the last two nights! I wondered what had happened."

"Yes. He said he had to fill the space somehow."

"But how do you explain it, Chessy? A fantastic coincidence?"

"A coincidence. They happen, you know. Possibly Reardon and I had discussed his note in more detail than I remember. But I promise you, Alida, I did not have a copy of that draft."

"Why couldn't Chip have published the note with both yours and Reardon's initials on it?"

"I suggested that. He turned it down flat. He said it would be compounding a crime. That he could not do such a thing under the university's honor system. Or, he added, under his own."

I looked hard at Chessy's oddly constricted countenance. Was he, who laughed at everything, restraining a laugh at this? I groped for a spar amid the swish of sinking vessels.

"Anyway, it's over."

"But it's not. Chip says if I don't resign from law school, he'll report the matter to the Honor Court."

"You're not serious!"

"Would even I be guilty of that joke? You must talk to Chip, Alida. You must make him see some kind of sense. I verily believe the man's gone mad!"

"Then what can I do?" I moaned.

Chessy and I discussed the matter passionately for another forty minutes, but we added nothing to what I have already described. It was an hour after he left before Chip came home for lunch, and I had had two stiff drinks out of the bottle Chessy had opened. Chip picked up the glass by my chair, sniffed it and said tersely, "Chessy, of course, has been here."

"Darling, let me get *you* a drink before we discuss it."

"I have no need of one. You know how I feel about drinking before six."

"But this is a crisis."

"I don't know that it's a crisis. It's a tragedy. For Chessy, anyway. And, to a lesser extent, for me. Because our friendship will hardly survive it. It's certainly not a crisis in the sense that there's anything to do about it. It's done."

"You mean the note's withdrawn."

"Well, that of course. I was referring to my ultimatum to Chessy."

"Surely you won't stick to it!"

"What are you talking about, Alida? Of course I'll stick to it."

"You mean you'll deliberately ruin Chessy's law career? Maybe his whole life as well?"

Oh, how tightly Chip set his lips! He was silent for a few minutes while he controlled his impatience. When he spoke, his tone was clipped, almost condescending. "You are being dramatic. Chessy's career will not be ruined unless he chooses to go before the Honor Court. If he does that and is convicted—as I have little doubt he would be—he will be expelled from the university without credit. If on the other hand he resigns, on any grounds he chooses—health, lack of funds, ailing parents—he will be able to transfer to another law school. The Wall Street firm that has already offered him a job will probably not be too concerned. Actually, I am doing him a great favor. For I'm not at all sure that my failing to report him isn't in itself a violation of the honor code."

"But, darling, how can you be so sure that he copied that note? Couldn't the resemblance be a coincidence? Chessy swears it was!"

"You can judge for yourself. I've got both notes in my briefcase."

"But what do I know about collective bargaining?"

"You don't have to know anything about it. The similarities are obvious. A child could see that Chessy was a plagiarist. And I don't think any more of him for coming weeping to you and lying in his teeth."

In his now handsome indignation, so much more appealing than his cold contempt, he might have been Sir Galahad. I shook my head to dispel a reluctant admiration.

"But this is you and Chessy, Chip!" I cried, as the full grotesqueness of the situation suddenly struck me. "You and Chessy and a cribbed note, if you like. It's been taken out of the Review. There's nothing left of it! Chessy isn't going to do anything like that again. He only did it, anyway, because you put so much heat on him. Can't you forgive him?"

"It's not a question of forgiveness. We took the pledge to observe the honor code when we came down here. One of the principal duties is to report a violation. And there is no question in my mind that Chessy violated the code when he submitted a paper that was not his."

"But you caught it in time, darling!"

"Fortunately for Chessy, yes. If it had already been published, I should have had no alternative but to report him."

"Isn't that what we used to call snitching?"

Chip did not flinch. "That's what we should have called it at Saint Luke's or Yale. But in Virginia they think differently about these matters. The university is full of stories of men turning in their closest friends. I didn't have to come down here, but having come, I certainly intend to abide by their rules."

I stamped my foot. "I can't see it! Here we are, you and I and Chessy. In a few more months we'll be out of this place. How can you let some crazy code designed by ancient slaveholders control what *we* three do in a matter known only to us?"

"That is your way of looking at it. I've told you mine."

"But doesn't it kill you, Chip?"

"Kill me?"

"To hurt Chessy this way? Your dearest friend? Who introduced us?"

Chip could quote Shakespeare at the damndest times! He actually smiled now. " 'What? Michael Cassio, that came awooing with you?' "

I saw then that it was hopeless. "You'll be smothering me next," I muttered. "Like Desdemona."

. . .

I did not see Chessy before he left school. He explained to people that he had to move back to Brooklyn to be closer to his mother, who had had a stroke. He transferred without difficulty to New York University Law

School. I believe that Mr. Benedict [Chip's father], who was a trustee of that university, provided some assistance at Chip's request. I doubt that Chessy told the true story to anyone, including his wife, though I suppose he must have squared his mother in some fashion to make her feign a temporary ailment. But from what little I knew of Mrs. Bogart, she was putty in her clever son's hands. Certainly Chip never told anyone, so the secret is revealed for the first time on this page.

No, that is not true. I have just remembered that I *did* tell somebody; my mother-in-law. When Chip graduated, she and Mr. Benedict came down to Charlottesville for several days, and she and I took a couple of long walks in the spring countryside. On one of these I told her the story of Chessy and confessed my doubts as to the rectitude of what Chip had done. Mrs. Benedict stopped short and looked at me in surprise.

"But Alida, what else could he possibly have done? I think he behaved admirably! And with the greatest kindness and consideration, too. I suppose you will not want me to speak to him about it, but otherwise, I should offer him my heartiest congratulations!"

"Well, please don't" was all I could murmur. These Benedicts!

QUESTIONS

1. Chessy is almost certainly lying to Alida about the extent of his use of Reardon's law review note to write his own. Does she believe him? If not, why does she still urge Chip to be lenient?

2. Chessy plagiarized his note from a law student who killed himself without telling anybody why. Chip displays little emotion in forcing Chessy out of law school and makes fun of Alida's plea for compassion by quoting Shakespeare. Both the silence surrounding Reardon's suicide and Chip's reliance on rules in a situation where a friend does something dishonest, reveal a moral code that is purposely detached from the human actors behind moral problems. What are the good and the bad aspects of this approach? Will the sense of honor instilled in these law students be a sound basis for an ethical law practice?

3. Carol Gilligan has argued that women often evaluate moral choices differently than men. Rather than rely on abstract principles of "right" and "wrong," women are more likely to ask who will be harmed in a situation and to choose the course of action that causes the least harm. See Carol Gilligan, In a Different Voice (1982). Might women law students have approached these problems (both the suicide and the plagiarized law review note) differently than the male students who attended Virginia at the time? How?

4. Is Alida's proposal merely to forget about the plagiarized note ethically acceptable? Why or why not?

5. Alida refers to Virginia's honor code as a "crazy code designed by ancient slaveholders." Is she right to question the moral authority of law that comes from an immoral legal system? What are the dangers inherent in her argument?

6. The title of the novel, Honorable Men, is itself revealing, and both Chip and Alida display stereotypical attitudes about male and female roles and the relative importance of men's and women's opinions. What are these attitudes? How are these men, who graduated from law school in the 1940's, likely to react to the entrance of women into the profession in large numbers after the 1960's? See *Hishon v. King and Spalding*, and subsequent discussion, infra page 336.

7. An honor code that relies principally on student accusations reinforces a sense of communal responsibility for ethical standards, but can also be abused. For example, at the time of this story, the University of Virginia was almost exclusively white. Today, Virginia retains its 150–year-old honor code, although the code was reviewed in 1991 "after a task force on African–American affairs found a disproportionate number of blacks were accused of infractions." Year in Review Virginia Education, United Press International, December 21, 1991. What abuses are possible under an honor code that requires students to report infractions by their peers? Are these abuses likely to carry over into the legal profession?

The Zbiegien Case

In re John A. Zbiegien, 433 N.W.2d 871 (Minn.1988), relates a plagiarism scenario that takes place in a vastly different setting than Chessy Bogart's cribbed note for the Virginia Law Review. On November 11, 1986, fourth-year law student John A. Zbiegien submitted a first draft of a research paper to Professor Michael Steenson at William Mitchell College of Law. On December 5, 1986, Professor Steenson informed Zbiegien that 12 pages out of the 30 page paper were plagiarized. "Nearly all of the first 12 pages were taken verbatim or nearly verbatim from a number of law review articles without proper citation in the endnotes." Id. at 872. Other portions of the paper were paraphrased with phrases both substituted and omitted without proper citation. Professor Steenson recommended that Zbiegien be expelled from school.

Associate Dean Matthew Downs decided to give Zbiegien an "F" grade in the products liability seminar taught by Professor Steenson. Zbiegien also lost credit and tuition for the course, but he was allowed to continue law school. "When [Zbiegien was] asked for an explanation of his circumstances, he replied that he had been under the stress of time pressures, that he had just begun a new job, and that his wife had been injured in an automobile accident, causing additional stress at home." Id.

Zbiegien applied for admission to the Minnesota Bar in April 1987. "In response to the question, 'Where [sic] you ever placed on probation, disciplined, dropped, suspended, or expelled from school, college, university or law school?,'" Zbiegien explained that he had submitted a paper that was unacceptable due to incomplete endnotes and direct quotes without citation, and further stated that Dean Downs had "found that the paper defects were ones of omission rather than intent." Id. at 876.

Zbiegien passed the Minnesota Bar Examination in July 1987.

Four months later he had a formal hearing with the Committee on Character and Fitness of the Board of Law Examiners. Zbiegien testified that he "completed his GED while in the army. He had then gone on to night classes at two community colleges in Iowa where he received his bachelor's degree. Both his military record and his previous academic record were unblemished." Id. at 873. Zbiegien admitted to plagiarizing but said that computer problems had contributed to the flaws. Furthermore, both he and his wife testified about his wife's condition

> which caused her to be confined to the house, under heavy medication, unable to work, and unable to do household chores. She had done the typing of the paper on a computer using unfamiliar software. Neither had actually proofread the paper, although both had apparently glanced through the text. No copy was saved.

Id. Furthermore, Zbiegien's teenage son ran away from home on the Thursday before his paper was due. Although his son returned Saturday, he was suspended from school for three days because of truancy.

The Board decided that Zbiegien had plagiarized published sources without proper citation and that he had also "attempted to deceive the Board in his untruthful explanations on his application and in testimony at the hearing." Id. at 874. The Board found that Zbiegien's computer problems did not explain away the plagiarism, nor did he demonstrate that he understood the seriousness of the matter.

Zbiegien appealed the Board's decision to the Supreme Court of Minnesota. The Court concluded that a "single incident of plagiarism while in law school is [not] necessarily sufficient evidence to prove lack of good character and fitness to practice law." Id. at 875. The Court also concluded that Zbiegien's conduct did not demonstrate "such a lack of character that he must be barred from the practice of law." Id. at 877. In dicta, the Court stated that he had been punished enough because he was ashamed of his actions and his admission to the bar had been delayed for over a year. The court wanted to give Zbiegien a second chance as William Mitchell College of Law had done a year earlier. Zbiegien was admitted to the bar.

In subsequent cases, the Supreme Court of Minnesota has denied admission to the bar for intentionally evading the truth on the bar application. See In re Brown, 467 N.W.2d 622 (Minn.1991) (per curiam) (misleading the Board as to guilt in prior arson case); In re Cunningham, 502 N.W.2d 53 (Minn.1993) (per curiam) (failing to note default on paternity payments on bar application).

QUESTIONS

1. Chessy Bogart appears to have plagiarized his law review note because he was lazy, whereas John Zbiegien was apparently taking a short cut when working under pressure. To what extent should circumstances such as those in Zbiegien's case be grounds for mitigation of the discipline imposed?

2. Is taking a short cut when working under pressure sometimes an explanation for other forms of misconduct in law school? What will happen to a lawyer who looks for an easy "out" from a high pressure situation?

Other forms of dishonesty

In re John Wali Mustafa II

An Applicant for Admission to the Bar of the District of Columbia.
631 A.2d 45 (D.C.App.1993).

■ Before King and Sullivan, Associate Judges, and Belson, Senior Judge.

■ Sullivan, Associate Judge:

John W. Mustafa II, passed the July 1991 Bar examination and is an applicant for admission to the Bar of the District of Columbia. The Committee on Admissions ("the Committee") recommended that he be admitted to the Bar, despite its finding that Mustafa "converted to his personal use funds entrusted to him for expenditure in a law school program." We conclude, however, that on the record here, particularly the short period of time that has elapsed since his misconduct, Mustafa has failed to establish that he has the good moral character required for admission to the Bar. Accordingly, we deny his application for admission.

I.

In his third year of law school at the University of California at Los Angeles, Mustafa and Larry Brennan served as co-chief justices of the law school's moot court program, and shared access to and control over the program's checking account. Over a five-month period, between October 1990 and February 1991, Mustafa wrote thirteen checks totaling $4,331, approximately $3,510 of which he converted to his personal use.[2] On at least seven occasions, he wrote checks to reimburse himself for expenditures which had been, or would be, reimbursed by the university's accounting department. At other times, he failed to make any notation about the use of the money or falsified the purpose of the checks.[3]

---

2. Mustafa explained that he used the funds principally to pay his rent and other bills, to pay a $1,000 bail for his sister, to lend another sister $750 so she could leave an abusive husband, and to pay expenses for a law student to compete in a Chicago moot court competition. Mustafa also assumed responsibility for approximately $811 which he claimed were legitimate moot court program expenses for which he could provide no documentation.

3. In particular, on November 28, 1990, he wrote a check to himself for $1,500, stating falsely on the check stub that it was for air fare to a competition in New York. Mustafa returned this amount to the fund via a personal check on January 2, 1991. Again, on February 28, 1991, he wrote a check for $1,500, indicating on the stub that the check was for $75.00 for Girl Scout cookies.

Mustafa admitted to Brennan on June 14, 1991, that he had taken $1,000 from the fund to pay his sister's bail and that he would repay the money from a loan he had arranged from his then-prospective employer. Several days later, Brennan discovered that less than $800 remained in the account, rather than the $1,300 he had expected; Brennan closed the account. On June 25th, Mustafa presented Brennan with a cashier's check for $2,200. On June 28th, Brennan disclosed Mustafa's misconduct to the law school dean; on the same day, Mustafa disclosed his misconduct to a law school professor and to the Committee. After an investigation, the university was satisfied that Mustafa had made full restitution and disposed of the matter by issuing a letter of censure to be placed in his confidential student discipline file for four years. As required by the university, Mustafa disclosed his misconduct to the law firm at which he is presently employed as a law clerk.

Following a hearing, the Committee found that Mustafa always intended to repay the sums taken from the fund, principally because he repaid $1,500 on January 2, 1991, kept an accurate mental record of how much he had taken from the fund, and made full restitution before there was any threatened action by the law school. The Committee was also impressed by Mustafa's honesty and forthrightness before the Committee and during the law school investigation. Moreover, Mustafa's references from two law school professors, three former members of the moot court program board, a former employer, and three partners and two associates from the law firm where Mustafa is employed, were, to the Committee, powerful testimony of his current good character. The Committee unanimously recommended that Mustafa be admitted to the Bar.

II.

In order to gain admission to the Bar, an applicant must demonstrate "by clear and convincing evidence, that the applicant possessed good moral character and general fitness to practice law in the District of Columbia" at the time of the applicant's admission. D.C.App.R. 46(e); see In re Manville, 538 A.2d 1128, 1132 (D.C.1988) (en banc) ("Manville II"). This court will "accept findings of fact made by the Committee unless they are unsupported by substantial evidence of record," will "make due allowance for the Committee's opportunity to observe and evaluate the demeanor of the applicant where relevant," and will "afford the Committee's recommendations some deference...." In re Manville, 494 A.2d 1289, 1293 (D.C.1985) (citations omitted) ("Manville I").

Mustafa candidly acknowledges that he, like few others in his position, was placed in a position of trust in handling others' money and that he "failed that test." As the Committee recognized, Mustafa's conduct, while it did not result in a criminal conviction, "was sufficiently serious to require analysis under the principles laid down in [Manville I]." Of particular significance is the Committee's finding that Mustafa's conduct "could be considered criminal in nature and would almost invariably have resulted in the disbarment of an attorney admitted to practice." There is no doubt that an attorney who mismanages the funds of a client will ordinarily face disbarment. In re Addams, 579 A.2d 190, 191 (D.C.1990) (en banc). Similarly, an attorney convicted of a crime involving moral turpitude faces automatic disbarment. D.C.Code § 11–2503(a) (1989); In re Hopmayer, 625 A.2d 290, 292 (D.C.1993) In re McBride, 602 A.2d 626, 629 (D.C.1992) (en banc). A disbarred attorney would be ineligible to apply for reinstatement for five years. D.C.Bar R. XI, § 16(e); Hopmayer, supra, 625 A.2d at 292. While we do not hold as a matter of law that an applicant for admission to the Bar, like a disbarred attorney, must necessarily wait a minimum of five years from the date of proven misconduct before applying for admission to the Bar, we conclude that on the record here, particularly the relatively short period of time that has elapsed since the date of his misconduct, Mustafa has failed to establish that he has the good moral character required for admission to the Bar. Cf. In re Polin, 630 A.2d 1140, 1142 (D.C.1993) ("Polin II") (applicant admitted to the Bar six and one-half years after his conviction of conspiracy to distribute cocaine and two years after being denied admission to the Bar).

In reaching this conclusion, we are mindful of Mustafa's outstanding law school record[5] and his appropriate conduct since the embezzlement: he cooperated with the university and the Committee; he has married; and he has volunteered in several community projects since coming to the District of Columbia. As we said in In re Polin, 596 A.2d 50, 55 (D.C.1991) ("Polin I"), "[i]t is by no means our purpose to discourage the applicant" from continuing his positive personal and professional development. Id. Indeed, on the record here, it appears likely that Mustafa will be able to establish the requisite good moral character at some future time. At present, however, "[o]ur consideration of the entire record leaves us unpersuaded that [Mustafa] now possesses 'those qualities of truth-speaking, of a high sense of honor, of granite discretion, of the strictest observation of fiduciary responsibility, that have ... been compendiously described as [the] "moral character" necessary for the practice of law.' " id. at 55 (quoting Schware v. Board of Bar Examiners, 353 U.S. 232, 247, 77 S.Ct. 752, 761, 1 L.Ed.2d 796 (1957) (Frankfurter, J., concurring)). In sum, Mustafa has not demonstrated his present fitness for the privilege of membership in the District of Columbia Bar.

Accordingly we deny Mustafa's application for admission to the Bar of the District of Columbia.

So Ordered.

QUESTIONS

1. Mustafa receives a far harsher penalty than did John Zbiegien. Is theft of money that much worse than theft of ideas? Are the circumstances of these two cases different?

5. Mustafa was a staff member and editor of the law review; he was one of two co-chief justices of the moot court program; was named one of twelve outstanding advocates during his second year of law school; and was one of three graduating law students selected by the law school Dean, Susan Westerberg Prager, to attend an annual donors' dinner. He also participated in several other law school activities.

2. Is it relevant that Mustafa made other contributions to the life of UCLA Law School? Does his position on the law review, the moot court and as a representative of the School at fundraising events, see note 5, weigh for him or against him in assessing the culpability of his conduct?

3. Why is misappropriation of money such a serious offense for a law student to commit? See page 72, on lawyer use of client funds.

Relevant Background

Applying for Admission to the Bar

Every jurisdiction in the United States requires a showing of good moral character for admission to the bar. The Bar Examiners Handbook 122 (Stuart Duhl, ed., 2d ed. 1980); see also Rules for Admission to the Bar in the United States and Territories (West 1982). Some critics have pointed out that the criteria used to evaluate applicants are artificial and do little to screen out persons likely to be dishonest or ineffective lawyers. See Deborah L. Rhode, Moral Character as a Professional Credential, 94 Yale L.J. 491, 509 (1985). Nonetheless, applicants should be aware that factors such as prior crimes, academic dishonesty, untreated drug and alcohol abuse and dishonesty in the application process itself, can result in denial of admission. The United States Supreme Court has held that the good moral character requirement is constitutionally permissible if the conduct which is the basis for denying bar admission has a "rational connection with the applicant's fitness or capacity to practice law." Schware v. Board of Bar Examiners, 353 U.S. 232, 239 (1957).

It is imperative that applicants answer all questions completely and truthfully. See Model Code, DR 1–101(A), Model Rules, Rule 8.1. Indeed, an applicant's failure to truthfully disclose material information in the bar admission process is one of the most frequently cited reasons for denial of admission on moral character grounds. See Michael K. McChrystal, A Structural Analysis of the Good Moral Character Requirement for Bar Admission, 60 Notre Dame L. Rev. 67, 78 (1984). Most misleading answers to application questions concern prior arrests, illegal conduct and academic dishonesty. See, e.g., In re Mitan, 75 Ill.2d 118, 25 Ill.Dec. 622, 387 N.E.2d 278 (applicant failed to disclose name change trying to hide felony conviction), cert. denied, 444 U.S. 916 (1979); In re Bowen, 84 Nev. 681, 447 P.2d 658 (1968) (applicant gave false statements about prior convictions). Such lack of candor on the bar application is often far more harmful to the applicant than the incident that she failed to disclose and raises the presumption of bad moral character because dishonesty is occurring at the moment the applicant seeks admission to the bar. See Florida Bd. of Bar Examiners re F.O.L., 646 So.2d 185 (Fla.1994); In re Legg, 325 N.C. 658, 386 S.E.2d 174 (N.C. 1989).

The Supreme Court has held that an applicant may be denied bar admission on moral character grounds for refusing to answer questions that are substantially relevant to his qualifications. Konigsberg v. State Bar of Cal., 366 U.S. 36 (1961). However, an applicant may not be denied admission solely because she is a member of a political organization or holds certain beliefs. Baird v. State Bar of Ariz., 401 U.S. 1, 6 (1971). Furthermore, some courts have held that, when an applicant refuses to answer questions concerning conduct of a political nature, the most equitable approach is to make a balanced assessment considering the full record rather than to deny admission on account of the refusal. In re Jolles, 235 Or. 262, 383 P.2d 388 (1963). See McChrystal, supra at 81.

B. The Associate

Howard L. Wieder, B.A. Yeshiva University 1975; J.D. New York University 1978; associate, Feder, Kaszovitz, Isaacson, Weber & Skala, June 1986 to March 1988; unemployed for nine months; subsequently associated with Harvis, Trien & Beck in New York; presently a court attorney in Brooklyn State Supreme Court.

Howard L. Wieder, Appellant, v. Murray L. Skala et al., Respondents, et al., Defendant

80 N.Y.2d 628, 593 N.Y.S.2d 752, 609 N.E.2d 105 (1992).

■ Hancock, Judge.

Plaintiff, a member of the Bar, has sued his former employer, a law firm. He claims he was wrongfully discharged as an associate because of his insistence that the firm comply with the governing disciplinary rules by reporting professional misconduct allegedly committed by another associate. The question presented is whether plaintiff has stated a claim for relief either for breach of contract or for the tort of wrongful discharge in violation of this State's public policy. The lower courts have dismissed both causes of action on motion as legally insufficient under CPLR 3211(a)(7) on the strength of New York's employment-at-will doctrine. For reasons which follow, we modify the order and reinstate plaintiff's cause of action for breach of contract.

I.

In the complaint, which must be accepted as true on a dismissal motion under CPLR 3211(a)(7), plaintiff alleges that he was a commercial litigation attorney associated with defendant law firm from June 16, 1986 until March 18, 1988. In early 1987, plaintiff requested that the law firm represent him in the purchase of a condominium apartment. The firm agreed and assigned a fellow associate (L.L.) "to do 'everything that needs to be done.'" For several months, L.L. neglected plaintiff's real estate transaction and, to conceal his neglect, made several "false and fraudulent material misrepresentations." In September 1987, when plaintiff learned of L.L.'s neglect and false statements, he advised two of the firm's senior partners. They conceded that the firm was aware "that [L.L.] was a pathological liar and that [L.L.] had previously lied to [members of the firm] regarding the status of other pending legal matters." When plaintiff confronted L.L., he acknowledged that he had lied about the real estate transaction and later admitted in writing that he had committed "several acts of legal malpractice and fraud and deceit upon plaintiff and several other clients of the firm."

The complaint further alleges that, after plaintiff asked the firm partners to report L.L.'s misconduct to the Appellate Division Disciplinary Committee as required under DR 1–103(A) of the Code of Professional Responsibility,[1] they declined to act. Later, in an effort to dissuade plaintiff from making the report himself, the partners told him that they would reimburse his losses. Plaintiff nonetheless met with the Committee "to discuss the entire matter." He withdrew his complaint, however, "because the [f]irm had indicated that it would fire plaintiff if he reported [L.L.'s] misconduct." Ultimately, in December 1987—as a result of plaintiff's insistence—the firm made a report concerning L.L.'s "numerous misrepresentations and [acts of] malpractice against clients of the [f]irm and acts of forgery of checks drawn on the [f]irm's account." Thereafter, two partners "continuously berated plaintiff for having caused them to report [the] misconduct." The firm nevertheless continued to employ plaintiff "because he was in charge of handling the most important litigation in the [f]irm." Plaintiff was fired in March 1988, a few days after he filed motion papers in that important case.

Plaintiff asserts that defendants wrongfully discharged him as a result of his insistence that L.L.'s misconduct be reported as required by DR 1–103(A). In his fourth cause of action, he alleges that the firm's termination constituted a breach of the employment relationship. In the fifth cause of action, he claims that his discharge was in violation of public policy and constituted a tort for which he seeks compensatory and punitive damages.

Defendants moved to dismiss the fourth and fifth causes of action as legally insufficient pursuant to CPLR 3211(a)(7). Supreme Court granted defendants' motion because his employment relationship was at will, holding: "since [the] 'Whistleblowers Law' [Labor Law § 740] is not applicable to the facts of this case, and plaintiff has not pleaded facts to come within the exception set forth in Weiner v. McGraw–Hill, Inc., 57 N.Y.2d 458, 457 N.Y.S.2d 193, 443 N.E.2d 441 (1982); the rules governing the causes of action for wrongful discharge are those set forth in Murphy [v. American Home Prods. Corp., 58 N.Y.2d 293, 461 N.Y.S.2d 232, (448 N.E.2d 86)]. Accordingly, since under the facts pleaded herein, the law firm had the right to terminate plaintiff, the fourth and fifth causes of action are dismissed." The Appellate Division affirmed, 167 A.D.2d 265, 562 N.Y.S.2d 930. It also concluded that plaintiff failed to state a cause of action because, as an at-will employee, the firm could terminate him without cause. This Court granted leave to appeal.

---

1. DR 1–103(A) provides: "A lawyer possessing knowledge, not protected as a confidence or secret, of a violation of DR 1–103 that raises a substantial question as to another lawyer's honesty, trustworthiness or fit- ness in other respects as a lawyer shall report such knowledge to a tribunal or other authority empowered to investigate or act upon such violation."

II.

We discuss first whether, notwithstanding our firmly established employment-at-will doctrine, plaintiff has stated a legal claim for breach of contract in the fourth cause of action. The answer requires a review of the three cases in which that doctrine is fully explained.

The employment-at-will doctrine is a judicially created common-law rule "that where an employment is for an indefinite term it is presumed to be a hiring at will which may be freely terminated by either party at any time for any reason or even for no reason" (Murphy v. American Home Prods. Corp., 58 N.Y.2d 293, 300, 461 N.Y.S.2d 232, 448 N.E.2d 86, supra [citing Martin v. New York Life Ins. Co., 148 N.Y. 117, 42 N.E. 416]). In Murphy, this Court dismissed the claim of an employee who alleged he had been discharged in bad faith in retaliation for his disclosure of accounting improprieties. In so doing, we expressly declined to follow other jurisdictions in adopting the tort-based abusive discharge cause of action for imposing "liability on employers where employees have been discharged for disclosing illegal activities on the part of their employers," being of the view "that such a significant change in our law is best left to the Legislature" (id., 58 N.Y.2d at 301, 461 N.Y.S.2d 232, 448 N.E.2d 86).

With respect to the contract cause of action asserted in Murphy, the Court held that plaintiff had not shown evidence of any express agreement limiting the employer's unfettered right to fire the employee. For this reason, the Court distinguished Weiner v. McGraw-Hill, Inc., 57 N.Y.2d 458, 457 N.Y.S.2d 193, 443 N.E.2d 441, supra, where such an express limitation had been found in language in the employer's personnel handbook. Finally, in Murphy, the Court rejected the argument that plaintiff's discharge for disclosing improprieties violated a legally implied obligation in the employment contract requiring the employer to deal fairly and in good faith with the employee, explaining: "No New York case upholding any such broad proposition is cited to us by plaintiff (or identified by our dissenting colleague), and we know of none. . . ."

Four years after Murphy, the Court decided Sabetay v. Sterling Drug, 69 N.Y.2d 329, 514 N.Y.S.2d 209, 506 N.E.2d 919. There, the Court dismissed the complaint of an employee who claimed he was fired for "blowing the whistle" and refusing to engage in improper and unethical activities. As in Murphy, the Court found no basis for an express limitation on the employer's right to discharge an at-will employee and, adhering to Murphy as a precedent, declined to base any such limitation on an implied-in-law obligation of dealing fairly and in good faith with its employee.

Not surprisingly, defendants' position here with respect to plaintiff's breach of contract cause of action is simple and direct, i.e., that: (1) as in Murphy and Sabetay, plaintiff has shown no factual basis for an express limitation on the right to terminate of the type upheld in Weiner; and (2) Murphy and Sabetay rule out any basis for contractual relief under an obligation implied-in-law. We agree that plaintiff's complaint does not contain allegations that could come within the Weiner exception for express contractual limitations (see, Weiner v. McGraw–Hill, Inc., supra, 57 N.Y.2d at 465, 457 N.Y.S.2d 193, 443 N.E.2d 441). As to an implied-in-law duty, however, a different analysis and other considerations pertain.

In arguing that the law imposes no implied duty which would curtail their unlimited right to terminate the employment contract, defendants rely on the holding in Murphy that "[n]o obligation can be implied, however, which would be inconsistent with other terms of the contractual relationship * * * [and] it would be incongruous to say that an inference may be drawn that the employer impliedly agreed to a provision which would be destructive of his right of termination" (58 N.Y.2d 293, 304–305, 461 N.Y.S.2d 232, 448 N.E.2d 86, supra; accord, Sabetay v. Sterling Drug, supra, 69 N.Y.2d at 335–336, 514 N.Y.S.2d 209, 506 N.E.2d 919). The decisions in Murphy and Sabetay, however, are not controlling here.

As plaintiff points out, his employment as a lawyer to render professional services as an associate with a law firm differs in several respects from the employments in Murphy and Sabetay. The plaintiffs in those cases were in the financial departments of their employers, both large companies. Although they performed accounting services, they did so in furtherance of their primary line responsibilities as part of corporate management. In contrast, plaintiff's performance of professional services for the firm's clients as a duly admitted member of the Bar was at the very core and, indeed, the only purpose of his association with defendants. Associates are, to be sure, employees of the firm but they remain independent officers of the court responsible in a broader public sense for their professional obligations. Practically speaking, plaintiff's duties and responsibilities as a lawyer and as an associate of the firm were so closely linked as to be incapable of separation. It is in this distinctive relationship between a law firm and a lawyer hired as an associate that plaintiff finds the implied-in-law obligation on which he founds his claim.

We agree with plaintiff that in any hiring of an attorney as an associate to practice law with a firm there is implied an understanding so fundamental to the relationship and essential to its purpose as to require no expression: that both the associate and the firm in conducting the practice will do so in accordance with the ethical standards of the profession. Erecting or countenancing disincentives to compliance with the applicable rules of professional conduct, plaintiff contends, would subvert the central professional purpose of his relationship with the firm—the lawful and ethical practice of law.

The particular rule of professional conduct implicated here (DR 1–103[A]), it must be noted, is critical to the unique function of self-regulation belonging to the legal profession. Although the Bar admission requirements provide some safeguards against the enrollment of unethical applicants, the Legislature has delegated the responsibility for maintaining the standards of ethics and competence to the Departments of the Appellate Division (see, Judiciary Law § 90[2]; and see, e.g., Rules of App.Div., 1st Dept. [22 NYCRR] § 603.2). To assure that the legal profession fulfills its responsibility of self-regulation, DR 1–103(A) places upon each lawyer and Judge the duty to report to the Disciplinary Committee of the Appellate Division any potential violations of the Disciplinary Rules that raise a "substantial question as to another lawyer's honesty, trustworthiness or fitness in other respects." Indeed, one commentator has noted that, "[t]he reporting requirement is nothing less than essential to the survival of the profession" (Gentile, Professional Responsibility—Reporting Misconduct By Other Lawyers, N.Y.L.J., Oct. 23, 1984, at 1, col. 1; at 2, col. 2; see also, Olsson, Reporting Peer Misconduct: Lip Service to Ethical Standards is Not Enough, 31 Ariz.L.Rev. 657, 658–659).

Moreover, as plaintiff points out, failure to comply with the reporting requirement may result in suspension or disbarment (see, e.g., Matter of Dowd, 160 A.D.2d 78, 559 N.Y.S.2d 365). Thus, by insisting that plaintiff disregard DR 1–103(A) defendants were not only making it impossible for plaintiff to fulfill his professional obligations but placing him in the position of having to choose between continued employment and his own potential suspension and disbarment. We agree with plaintiff that these unique characteristics of the legal profession in respect to this core Disciplinary Rule make the relationship of an associate to a law firm employer intrinsically different from that of the financial managers to the corporate employers in Murphy and Sabetay. The critical question is whether this distinction calls for a different rule regarding the implied obligation of good faith and fair dealing from that applied in Murphy and Sabetay. We believe that it does in this case, but we, by no means, suggest that each provision of the Code of Professional Responsibility should be deemed incorporated as an implied-in-law term in every contractual relationship between or among lawyers.

It is the law that in "every contract there is an implied undertaking on the part of each party that he will not intentionally and purposely do anything to prevent the other party from carrying out the agreement on his part" [citations omitted]. The idea is simply that when A and B agree that B will do something it is understood that A will not prevent B from doing it. The concept is rooted in notions of common sense and fairness (see, Farnsworth, The Law of the Contract § 7.16, at 524 [1982]). "What courts are doing [when an omitted term is implied]," Professor Corbin explains, "whether calling the process 'implication' of promises, or interpreting the requirements of 'good faith,' as the current fashion may be, is but a recognition that the parties occasionally have understandings or expectations that were so fundamental that they did not need to negotiate about those expectations" (3 Corbin, Contracts § 570, 1992 Supp., at 411).

Just such fundamental understanding, though unexpressed, was inherent in the relationship between plaintiff and defendant law firm (see also, Wakefield v. Northern Telecom, 769 F.2d 109, 112, supra ["Implied contractual obligations may coexist with express provisions which seemingly negate them where common expectations or the relationship of the parties as structured by the contract so dictate" (emphasis added)]). Defendants, a firm of lawyers, hired plaintiff to practice law and this objective was the only basis for the employment relationship. Intrinsic to this relationship, of course, was the unstated but essential compact that in conducting the firm's legal practice both plaintiff and the firm would do so in compliance with the prevailing rules of conduct and ethical standards of the profession. Insisting that as an associate in their employ plaintiff must act unethically and in violation of one of the primary professional rules amounted to nothing less than a frustration of the only legitimate purpose of the employment relationship.

From the foregoing, it is evident that both Murphy and Sabetay are markedly different. The defendants in those cases were large manufacturing concerns—not law firms engaged with their employee in a common professional enterprise, as here. In neither Murphy nor Sabetay was the plaintiff required to act in a way that subverted the core purpose of the employment. The company rules underlying the firing of Murphy and Sabetay were not, as in this case, general rules of conduct and ethical standards governing both plaintiff and defendants in carrying out the sole aim of their joint enterprise, the practice of their profession (see, Judiciary Law § 90[2]; and see, e.g., Rules of App.Div., 1st Dept. [22 NYCRR] § 603.2). Unlike Murphy and Sabetay, giving effect to an implied understanding—that in their common endeavor of providing legal services plaintiff and the firm would comply with the governing rules and standards and that the firm would not act in any way to impede or discourage plaintiff's compliance—would be "in aid and furtherance of [the central purpose] of the agreement of the parties" (Murphy v. American Home Prods. Corp., supra, 58 N.Y.2d at 304, 461 N.Y.S.2d 232, 448 N.E.2d 86). Thus, the case is distinguishable from Murphy and Sabetay where giving effect to the implied obligation would have been "inconsistent with" and "destructive of" an elemental term in the agreement (id., at 304–305, 461 N.Y.S.2d 232, 448 N.E.2d 86). We conclude, therefore, that plaintiff has stated a valid claim for breach of contract based on an implied-in-law obligation in his relationship with defendants.

III.

Plaintiff argues, moreover, citing our decision in Cohen v. Lord, Day & Lord[3], 75 N.Y.2d 95, 101, 551 N.Y.S.2d 157, (550 N.E.2d 410), that the dictates of public policy in DR 1–103(A) have such force as to warrant our recognition of the tort of abusive discharge pleaded in the fifth cause of action. While the arguments are persuasive and the circumstances here compelling, we have consistently held that "significant alteration of employment relationships, such as the plaintiff urges, is best left to the Legislature" [citations omitted]. We believe that the same rationale applies here. In 1984, the Legislature enacted a "Whistleblower" statute (Labor Law § 740, added by L.1984, ch. 660, § 2). We have noted that, although the present "statute has been criticized by commentators for not affording sufficient safeguards against retaliatory discharge (see, Minda and Raab,

---

3. In Cohen, the Court held that a term in a law firm partnership agreement which conditions payment of earned but uncollected partnership revenues upon a withdrawing partner's refraining from practicing law in competition with the firm restricts the practice of law in violation of DR 2–108(A) and is, therefore, unenforceable as against public policy. [Ed.—see discussion of covenants not to compete in this Chapter 5 infra]

Time for an Unjust Dismissal Statute in New York, 54 Brooklyn L.Rev. 1137, 1138, 1182–1187 [1989]; Dworkin and Near, Whistleblowing Statutes: Are They Working?, 25 Amer.Bus.L.J. 241, 253 [1987]), any additional protection must come from the Legislature" (Remba v. Federation Empl. & Guidance Serv., 76 N.Y.2d 801, 803, 559 N.Y.S.2d 961, 559 N.E.2d 655).

Accordingly, the judgment appealed from and the order of the Appellate Division brought up for review should be modified, with costs to plaintiff, by denying defendant's motion to dismiss the fourth cause of action and, as so modified, affirmed.

■ SIMONS, Acting C.J., and KAYE, TITONE and BELLACOSA, JJ., concur.

■ SMITH, J., taking no part.

Judgment appealed from and order of the Appellate Division brought up for review modified, etc.

QUESTIONS

1. What would you have done in Wieder's situation?

2. The Court describes DR 1–103(a) as a "core Disciplinary Rule" and states that "we, by no means, suggest that each provision of the Code of Professional Responsibility should be deemed incorporated as an implied-in-law term in every contractual relationship between or among lawyers." How should a court determine which provisions of the Code are implied-in-law terms to an employment relationship and which are not? Should a law firm in a Model Code jurisdiction have the right to fire an associate for following an Ethical Consideration that is not a Disciplinary Rule?

3. In Balla v. Gambro, Inc., 145 Ill.2d 492, 164 Ill.Dec. 892, 584 N.E.2d 104 (Ill. 1991), Roger J. Balla, the general counsel for a manufacturer of dialyzers, was fired for telling the President of the company that "he would do whatever necessary to stop the sale" of dialyzers that did not comply with FDA regulations. The Supreme Court of Illinois steadfastly refused to protect Balla from termination. First, under Illinois's version of Model Rule 1.6(b) "[a] lawyer shall reveal information about a client to the extent it appears necessary to prevent the client from committing an act that would result in death or serious bodily injury." Balla thus had no choice as to whether or not to report, and no public policy objective would be met by allowing him to sue for retaliatory discharge. Id. at 109. Furthermore, allowing such a lawsuit by an in-house lawyer could interfere with the client's right to discharge its attorney at any time. Id. Although *Balla* involved a duty to report client conduct rather than lawyer conduct, this case, like *Wieder*, involved a lawyer who was fired for following a mandatory reporting requirement. Do you think the Illinois court is naive in its assumption that a mandatory reporting requirement is itself sufficient inducement to report misconduct, even absent protection from retaliatory discharge?

4. Even in a jurisdiction that adheres to *Wieder*, do you think an associate in a law firm is likely to report the professional misconduct of another lawyer in the firm? Is it reasonable to expect her to do so?

5. In July, 1995, dozens of New York City police officers, while visiting Washington D.C. to attend a memorial service for slain colleagues, went on a drunken rampage, damaging property and discharging their weapons into the air. The ensuing investigation was frustrated because almost none of the officers who attended were willing to speak about the incident. "There's a white wall of silence in the medical profession, a black wall of silence for lawyers and a blue wall for police," Police Commissioner William Bratton observed at a news conference. Reuters North American Wire, July 11, 1995. Is a "wall of silence" appropriate in professions that are supposedly concerned with enforcing and upholding the law?

Relevant Background

Model Rule 8.3 requires that a lawyer "having knowledge that another lawyer has committed a violation of the Rules of Professional Conduct that raises a substantial question as to that lawyer's honesty, trustworthiness or fitness as a lawyer in other respects, shall inform the appropriate professional authority." Rule 8.3 expressly exempts client confidences from disclosure.

As pointed out in the *Wieder* case, the Model Code also requires a lawyer to disclose misconduct of another lawyer. See DR 1–103(a) (requiring lawyer possessing unprivileged knowledge of a violation of disciplinary rules to report such knowledge to a tribunal or authority empowered to investigate). See also The Attorney's Duties to Report the Misconduct of Other Attorneys and to Report Fraud on a Tribunal, Report of the Committee on Professional Responsibility, 47 The Record of the Association of the Bar of the City of New York 905 (1992) (discussing New York's version of DR 1–103(a) as well as DR 7–102(B)(2), requiring report of a fraud on a tribunal).

Delayed Reporting

A report of another lawyer's misconduct should be prompt and without delay. See ABA Comm. on Ethics and Professional Responsibility, Formal Opinion 94–383 (1994) ("A lawyer who becomes aware of professional misconduct that raises a substantial question as to a lawyer's honesty, trustworthiness or fitness as a lawyer in other respects should report that misconduct promptly, to the extent required by Rule 8.3(a), and not use it as a bargaining chip in [a] civil case."); ABA Annotated Model Rules of Professional Conduct, Rule 8.3 (1995) ("[O]nce a lawyer delays reporting misconduct, he or she might be subject to discipline for such delay"); Ethics Committee of North Dakota State Bar, Formal Op. 42 (1990) ("Once a lawyer has concluded that he or she has actual knowledge of a reportable violation, he or she may not postpone the reporting...." The language of Model Rule 8.3(a) suggests no basis for postponing the reporting of a violation.)

As the New York City Bar Association points out, this duty to report promptly can outweigh even a lawyer's duty to act in the best interests of a client:

> This Committee previously has addressed the question of whether it is permissible to delay reporting misconduct of another lawyer in order to protect the interests of a client. We determined that notwithstanding a lawyer's duty under Canon 7 to represent a client loyally and zealously and to avoid prejudicing the client's interest "a report of misconduct must be made promptly upon discovery in order to protect the public." NY City 82–79. . . . While it may be permissible in certain limited circumstances to postpone reporting for a brief period of time, we reiterate our caution in N.Y. City 81–40 that "once a lawyer decides that he or she must disclose under DR 1–103(A), any substantial delay in reporting would be improper."

N.Y.C. Assn. B. Comm. Prof. Jud. Eth. Op. 1990–3 (1990). See Also in re Himmel, 125 Ill.2d 531, 127 Ill.Dec. 708, 533 N.E.2d 790 (1988) (Himmel learned in April 1983 that his client's previous attorney had converted client funds, but did not disclose the conversion until he filed suit against the previous attorney over a year and a half later in February 1985; Himmel was suspended for one year for his failure to report).

Indeed, a delayed report not only reflects poorly on the judgment of the lawyer making the report, but may also raise questions about the integrity of the report itself. Such a delay is particularly ominous if the reporting attorney knows that he is making a report so late that evidence needed to establish the guilt or innocence of the accused attorney is no longer available (perhaps because relevant documents have been lost or destroyed).* Even if the charge is dismissed, the delay may make it difficult for the accused attorney to definitively disprove the allegation.

Bad Faith Reporting

Bad faith reporting of alleged attorney misconduct, like bad faith litigation (see Chapter 2 supra) is a problem in the profession:

> It bears emphasis that this right to report misconduct, though generally serving the salutary purpose of assisting courts, disciplinary agencies and other authorities in policing members of the bar, is unquestionably susceptible to abuse by attorneys seeking to gain advantages or concessions from other lawyers in the course of litigation, in private business transactions, or in interpersonal relationships, or by attorneys acting purely out of spite.

N. Y. B. Assn. Comm. Prof. Eth. Op. 635 (1992).** As pointed out by Professor Geoffrey Hazard:

---

* Furthermore, Model Rule 8.4(d) provides that it is professional misconduct for a lawyer to "engage in conduct that is prejudicial to the administration of justice." A delayed report can be very prejudicial to the administration of justice in a disciplinary proceeding, particularly if evidence has been lost or destroyed during the delay.

** Accusations motivated by anger and vengefulness are not unique to the legal pro-

Another development raising questions about the mandatory reporting rule emerging in several jurisdictions is the practice of filing a disciplinary charge whenever a dispute between lawyers gets heated. The result has been a surge of petty disciplinary matters. These grievances are ostensibly justified but often are motivated by anger or vengefulness. They add a burden to overloaded disciplinary systems and corrode already fragile relations within the bar.

Geoffrey C. Hazard, "Squeal Rule" Considered for Change, 12 The National Law Journal 13–14 (1990). Bad faith reporting trivializes the disciplinary process and engenders allegations which most likely will never be proved or disproved, but merely allowed to linger on to stain an attorney's reputation. Nonetheless, as the legal profession becomes increasingly competitive, abuse of reporting rules may become more common.

Libel and Slander

A report of lawyer misconduct is privileged under libel law if made only to a disciplinary authority. "Complainants should be absolutely immune from civil liability for all communications to the agency, but disclosure of the information to anyone else should not be protected." ABA Standards for Professional Discipline for Lawyers and Judges, Section 8.3. A lawyer thus exposes herself to liability for defamation if she discusses alleged misconduct with persons outside the parameters of the disciplinary system, although a qualified privilege applies if a communication is made to protect a genuine private interest of the person making it or of the person hearing it (for example in a reference check for employment). This qualified privilege usually requires that malice be shown in a suit for defamation. Casual conversation and gossip about alleged professional misconduct, however, are clearly outside the scope of any privilege. See Conley v. Southern Import Sales, Inc. 382 F.Supp. 121, 124 (M.D.Ala.1974) ("[a] statement imputing a want of integrity or capacity in an attorney is actionable per se.") (qualified privilege applied to accusatory letter sent to bar association); Sassower v. Himwich, 236 N.Y.S.2d 491, 494 (1962), aff'd, 19 A.D.2d 946, 245 N.Y.S.2d 971 (1963) ("[w]hile the right of the public to make proper complaints concerning the conduct of attorneys is to be guarded, the right of members of the Bar to protect themselves from baseless and malicious complaints, similarly must be protected"). See also 9 A.L.R. 4th 807, 822–24 (discussing circumstances where qualified privilege warranted).

Also, a lawyer can be disciplined for making an unjustified public accusation of improper conduct by other members of the bar. An attorney in Nebraska was disbarred for casting public disparagements in a political

fession, or even to modern society. Ancient Israel experienced similar problems. Although lying is generally prohibited under Old Testament law, false accusations alone are mentioned in the ten commandments to Moses. Exo. 20: 16 ("thou shalt not bear false witness against thy neighbor"). Any rule that requires people to make accusations thus works against a backdrop of human nature inclined not only to conceal evil where it exists, but also to invent evil where it does not exist.

campaign on other members of the bar that he knew, or with ordinary care should have known, were false. Nebraska v. Michaelis, 210 Neb. 545, 316 N.W.2d 46 (Neb. 1982).

PROBLEMS

1. You are an associate in a law firm with ten partners. Every Friday, one of the partners drinks three or four two-ounce glasses of scotch at the office after work and drives home. What should you do?

2. Another associate in your office tells you that he has been consistently padding his time sheets by as much as forty hours a month for the past year. What should you do?

3. A client asks you to sue her previous lawyer for malpractice and for mishandling money the lawyer held in escrow. You take the case on a 33% contingency. Before you bring suit, you discover that the other lawyer actually embezzled $5,000 from the escrow fund. When you confront him, the other lawyer agrees to return the money to your client and to settle the malpractice claim for $50,000 if you and the client will agree to keep the facts of the matter confidential. What should you do?

4. Wieder v. Skala—imagine a less conscientious Howard Wieder, and a perhaps less culpable L.L. The facts are not as in the case, but instead are as follows: Wieder honestly believes, but is not absolutely certain, that from January to March 1993, L.L. neglected Wieder's real estate transaction and, to conceal his neglect, made several misrepresentations. Wieder considers reporting L.L.'s alleged misconduct to the Attorney Disciplinary Committee, but Wieder knows that a decision to report will not be looked upon favorably by the partners of the Firm. He decides not to report L.L.'s alleged misconduct, at least before his own candidacy for partner in the Firm is voted on. However, Wieder tells two other associates at the Firm—Smith and Jones—that L.L. neglected the condominium transaction and subsequently lied about it. Smith and Jones do not have any independent verification of whether or not Wieder's allegations are accurate and decide not to report their second-hand information concerning L.L.'s alleged misconduct.

Wieder's condominium purchase is closed in March, 1993. The Firm has a policy of destroying all drafts and attorney work product on real-estate transactions 14 months from the date the transaction is closed. Wieder, Smith and Jones all know of this policy and also know that it will be very difficult, if not impossible, to establish whether or not L.L. violated any rules of professional responsibility once the drafts and attorney work product in the file are destroyed. The documents in question are destroyed in May of 1994 pursuant to the above mentioned policy.

In September of 1994, the Firm holds partnership elections. L.L. is elected a partner; Wieder, Smith and Jones are not. Four weeks later, Smith and Jones tell Wieder that under DR 1–103(A) Wieder should have reported L.L.'s alleged misconduct. They threaten to report the alleged misconduct if Wieder does not. Wieder decides to make a report. The Disciplinary Committee considers the report in October of 1994, but, not having the drafts and attorney work product for the condominium transaction, unanimously dismisses the allegations. What are the ethical and practical consequences of the actions of (i) Wieder, (ii) Smith and Jones, and (iii) the Firm (particularly with respect to its document retention policy).

C.   PROMOTION TO PARTNER

The Selection Process

Robert T. Swaine, b. 1886 in Iowa; A.B. University of Iowa 1905; taught history for two years in Iowa; LL.B. Harvard University 1910 (President of the Harvard Law Review); considered a career in law teaching, but instead entered the Cravath office as an associate in 1910 where his interests began in litigation but quickly shifted to corporate finance; promoted to partner in 1917; author of two-volume firm history.

This excerpt is from Swaine's account of the policies of the Cravath Firm as they existed in the 1940's:

Robert T. Swaine, description of "the Cravath System," from The Cravath Firm and its Predecessors (1946).

The Cravath Firm

Since 1906

The dominant personality of this volume is Paul D. Cravath. He was the authoritative head of the firm until his death in 1940, and his conceptions of the management of a law office still control its operations.

* * *

As to recruiting the legal staff:

Cravath believed that a staff trained within the office would be better adapted to its methods of work than a staff recruited from older men who, in practice elsewhere, might have acquired habits inconsistent with Cravath methods, and hence he insisted that the staff should be recruited, so far as possible, from men just out of the law schools. . . .

The best men, too, are most likely to be found in the law schools which have established reputations by reason of their distinguished faculties and rigorous curricula, and which, by that very fact, attract the more scholarly college graduates. . . .

The scholastic standards of the "Cravath system" thus made a Phi Beta Kappa man from a good college who had become a law review editor at Harvard, Columbia or Yale the first choice. Such standards are commonplace today among New York offices; when Cravath came to the Seward firm in 1899 they were regarded as somewhat eccentric—not to say stuffy....

Cravath did not, however, want colorless, narrow-minded bookworms. From applicants who met his standards of scholarship, he wanted those who also had warmth and force of personality and physical stamina adequate to the pressure to which they would often be subject because of the rugged character of the work. It is, of course, difficult to judge these qualities in the brief interviews which the partners are able to have with most of the many applicants. This was especially true during the conventional "rushing season" of December which prevailed prior to World War II, when applicants came to the office in scores in a concentrated period of a few weeks....

As to training associates:

. . .

At the outset of their practice Cravath men are not thrown into deep water and told to swim; rather, they are taken into shallow water and carefully taught strokes. The Cravath office does not follow the practice of many other offices of leaving small routine matters entirely to young men fresh from law school without much supervision, on the theory that a man best learns how to handle cases by actually handling them. Under the "Cravath system" a young man watches his senior break a large problem down into its component parts, is given one of the small parts and does thoroughly and exhaustively the part assigned to him—a process impracticable in the handling of small routine matters. Cravath believed that the man who learns to analyze the component parts of a large problem involving complicated facts, and to do each detailed part well, becomes a better lawyer faster than the man who is not taught in such detail.

. . .

As to choosing partners:

. . .

Obviously not all the men competent to be partners can be taken into the firm—for that would make the firm unwieldy. The choice is difficult; factors which control ultimate decisions are intangible; admittedly they are affected by the idiosyncrasies of the existing partners. Mental ability there must be, but in addition, personality, judgment, character. No pretense is made that the ultimate decisions are infallible. Only infrequently have mistakes been made in taking men into the firm; more often, mistakes not so easily remedied have been made in not admitting others....

The problem of the firm is to do the business which comes to it; by so doing that business, more comes in. Hence, business-getting ability is not a factor in advancement of a man within the office at any level, except in so far as that ability arises out of competence in doing law work, as contrasted with family or social connections.

Cravath early came to believe that in most cases the client is best advised by a lawyer who maintains an objective point of view and that such objectivity may be impeded by any financial interest in the client's business or any participation in its management. Accordingly, he made it the policy of the firm that neither its partners nor its associates should hold equity securities of any client, or serve as a director of a corporate client, or have a financial interest, direct or indirect, in any transaction in which the firm was acting as counsel. Occasionally, more frequently in recent years, clients have insisted upon exceptions permitting partners to occupy directorships and own qualifying equity securities, but the exceptions have been few.

QUESTIONS

1. It is no surprise that in 1946 Swaine referred to recruitment of "men" for Cravath's legal staff. What else does his description of the law schools recruited from at the time, and his reference to a December "rushing season," tell you about the process and the types of people that were likely to be chosen?

2. Swaine distinguished the Cravath method of training associates from that used by firms where associates were immersed in law practice by giving them substantial responsibility for entire matters. Were lawyers trained under the "Cravath System" likely to be prepared for work at smaller firms after they left Cravath? How much courtroom experience was a litigation associate likely to get? If you were an associate in a large firm, which method of training would you prefer?

3. As to choosing partners, Swaine admitted that "[t]he choice is difficult; factors which control ultimate decisions are intangible; admittedly they are affected by the idiosyncrasies of the existing partners." What types of "intangible" factors and "idiosyncrasies" were likely to determine who made partner?

4. Cravath and some other large firms did not consider business-getting ability in selecting partners, making it unlikely that associates would learn how to generate new business. Presumably, these firms had enough large clients that they did not need more business, particularly from the smaller clients that a young associate might attract. How important, however, are business-getting skills to a young lawyer's professional development, particularly if he leaves a large firm? In what other ways may large firms sometimes deny associates valuable training that they might need elsewhere?

5. Mark Galanter and Tom Palay describe the law firm promotion process as a partner-sponsored "tournament" in which associates are encouraged to compete with each other for billable hours and overall productivity in hopes of receiving the "prize" of admission to the partnership. Marc Galanter and Thomas Palay, Tournament of Lawyers: The Transformation of the Big Law Firm 77–120 (1991). Galanter and Palay argue that this tournament drives law firm growth. On the other hand, Professor Lambert has argued that "availability of legal business is a far more significant factor in law firm growth than are promotional structures." Frederick W. Lambert, An Academic Visit to the Modern Law Firm: Considering a Theory of Promotion–Driven Growth, 90 Mich. L. Rev. 1719 (1992). Although the Cravath firm reputedly has among the highest profits per partner in New York City (well over $1 million annually), the firm has grown less quickly than some of its rivals (Cravath has slightly more than 300 lawyers, whereas another, younger, New York City firm, Skadden, Arps, Slate, Meagher & Flom, has approximately 1000 lawyers). Why do some firms promote so few associates to partner? Why do associates agree to participate in partnership tournaments sponsored by firms that do not promote many associates to partner?

6. What are the advantages of Cravath's policy of prohibiting lawyers from serving as directors of clients? Was this policy effective at maintaining Hoyt Moore's objectivity in his work for Bethlehem Steel (Chapter 2 supra)? For further discussion of this topic, see Chapter 12 *infra*.

Discrimination on Account of Religion, Race and Ethnicity

John Anthony Lucido B.S. St. Louis University, *cum laude* 1959; M.A. Washington University, St. Louis 1961 (University Fellow 1960–61); Johns Hopkins University (Woodrow Wilson Foundation Fellow 1960–61); J.D. University of Notre Dame 1965; Notre Dame Law School Scholar 1962–65; Editor-in-Chief, Notre Dame Law Review 1964–65; Article, *Antitrust— Section 5 of the Clayton Act,* 38 Notre Dame L. Rev. 467 (1963); Note, *Religious Institutions and Values*, 39 Notre Dame L. Rev. 466 (1964); Farabaugh Prize for outstanding academic work.

Commendation: "We regret the fact that [Mr. Lucido's civil rights suit against Cravath, Swaine and Moore] was resolved without a full evidentiary hearing or subsequent appeals, and further regret any part which the decision to pursue his claim has played in his inability to secure employment." "John Lucido is a talented and conscientious lawyer with much to offer the legal profession and society. It is a tragedy that his current employment situation prevents the use of his considerable legal ability." Resolutions of the Law Faculty of the University of Notre Dame, South Bend, Indiana, on file in the office of the Dean of the Law School, October, 1984.

Alan M. Dershowitz, b. 1938; B.A. Brooklyn College 1959; LL.B. Yale University 1962; law clerk to Chief Judge David L. Bazelon, U.S. Court of Appeals 1962–63; law clerk to Justice Arthur J. Goldberg, U.S. Supreme Court 1963–64; admitted in the District of Columbia in 1963 and Massachusetts in 1968; member of the Harvard Law School faculty since 1964. More recently, Professor Dershowitz has taken part in the defense of high profile criminal trials, including that of Claus Von Bulow (acquitted of murdering his wife); Mike Tyson (convicted of rape); Leona Helmsley (convicted of tax evasion); and O.J. Simpson (acquitted of murdering his ex-wife and a male acquaintance).

Simon H. Rifkind, b. 1901, d. 1995; B.S. City College of New York 1922; LL.B. Columbia University 1925; legislative secretary to U.S. Senator

Robert F. Wagner 1927–33; partner, Wagner, Quillinan & Rifkind, New York City 1930–4; United States District Judge, Southern District of New York 1941–50; advisor to General Eisenhower on Jewish matters in the American occupation 1945; partner, Paul, Weiss, Rifkind, Wharton & Garrison 1950–95.

The following complaint was filed on December 19, 1975 in federal district court. Because the case was never heard on the merits, there has not been any finding of fact as to the truth of the matters alleged therein:

UNITED STATES DISTRICT COURT
SOUTHERN DISTRICT OF NEW YORK

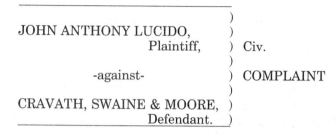

JOHN ANTHONY LUCIDO, Plaintiff,	Civ.
-against-	COMPLAINT
CRAVATH, SWAINE & MOORE, Defendant.	

Count I

1.   ... This action is authorized and instituted pursuant to Title VII of The Civil Rights Act of 1964, 42 U.S.C.A. §§ 2000e et seq., as amended by P.L. 92–261, known as the Equal Employment Opportunity Act of 1972. The jurisdiction of this court is invoked to secure protection of and to redress deprivation of rights secured by 42 U.S.C.A. §§ 2000e et seq., providing for injunctive and other relief against discrimination in employment on the basis of national origin and religion.

2.   Plaintiff, JOHN ANTHONY LUCIDO, is a citizen of the United States and State of New Jersey. He resides at 227 McMane Avenue, Berkeley Heights, New Jersey. There is diversity of citizenship between the parties and the amount in controversy, exclusive of interest and costs, exceeds $10,000.

3.   Plaintiff is of Italian ancestry and is a Catholic. He attended St. Louis University on a scholarship and in 1959 received a B.S. degree cum laude in the Honors Program. Thereafter, during the 1959–1960 academic year he pursued graduate studies at Johns Hopkins University on a Woodrow Wilson Fellowship. He continued his studies the next year on a fellowship at Washington University where he was awarded an M.A. degree in 1961. Following a year of Government service, plaintiff accepted a scholarship to attend the Notre Dame Law School in 1962. In 1963, plaintiff became a member of the staff of the school's law review, the *Notre Dame Lawyer*, and in 1964 was elected editor-in-chief. He received his LL.B. in 1965 after graduating second in his class and being awarded the school's Farabaugh Prize for outstanding academic work. While attending law school plaintiff also taught labor law at St. Mary's College and was a research assistant to the editor of the *Natural Law Forum*.

4. The defendant, CRAVATH, SWAINE & MOORE ("Cravath") is a law firm organized as a partnership and its principal place of business is located at One Chase Manhattan Plaza, New York, New York. Cravath also maintains European offices in London and Paris. The unlawful acts complained of hereinafter occurred within the Southern District of New York.

5. Cravath's operations as a law firm include operations in interstate commerce. [A]s of March 2, 1973, it had a total employment of 492 employees, including 178 lawyers, of whom 48 were classified by Cravath as employees in the job category of "partner" and 130 were classified by Cravath as employees in the job category of "professionals." The 130 employees classified as professionals were the associate attorneys at the firm. Cravath is an employer within the meaning of 42 U.S.C.A. § 2000e (b) in that it is engaged in an industry affecting commerce and employs more than fifteen persons.

. . .

8. Promotion to partnership at defendant means greatly increased earnings, status, prestige and privileges. It is the primary inducement and consideration that defendant holds out to its many young associates who are hired each year to compete for the partnership promotional opportunity.

9. Cravath is organized in departments or sections based on types of practice or areas of specialization. The departments include corporate, litigation, trusts and estates, tax and real estate. The corporate and litigation departments are the most desirable departments. The great majority of the lawyers are in those two departments. . . .

10. In the summer of 1964, while working in New York City as a summer clerk in the law department of a corporation, plaintiff wrote to defendant requesting an interview for the position of associate attorney upon graduation from law school. The request was granted and plaintiff was interviewed at defendant's offices on or about September 2, 1964. Although plaintiff had expressed an interest in litigation, he was interviewed by two corporate partners and one partner from the trusts and estates department. The interviewing partners described the so-called "Cravath system" of law firm organization. They explained the terms, conditions and privileges of Cravath's employment of associates and also discussed defendant's policies and practices, including:

(a) employing associates only immediately upon graduation from law school except for those few associates who are employed immediately after completion of a clerkship, fellowship, military service and the like;

(b) allowing new associates to select the department or area of specialty in which they intend to practice and thereafter not transferring them to a different department or area of specialty unless they request a transfer;

(c) rotating associates among partners and changing associates' work assignments periodically to ensure that associates have experience with as many partners and in as many different types of work in their department or area of specialty as possible without undue specialization in any one type and to enable as many partners in their departments or area of specialty as possible to evaluate their work;

(d) requiring associates and partners to work full time on defendant's law firm business, devoting their regular working hours primarily to defendant's law practice, without pursuing outside business or financial interests;

(e) filling partnership positions exclusively by promoting associates from within defendant law firm; and

(f) requiring associates who are not promoted to partnership to seek other employment (hereinafter referred to as Cravath's "up or out" policy).

11. .... Defendant's interviewers also assured plaintiff that, if an associate performed his professional duties satisfactorily and thereby demonstrated that he was qualified for the partnership position, he could expect to be promoted to partnership after a reasonable period of time as an associate attorney; that an associate's progress to partnership would depend on his own efforts and ability without regard to such factors as capacity to bring in business, social background, contacts or being from the "right schools"; that defendant had a system of evaluating associates that ensured fairness in the promotional process, including a procedure under which defendant annually prepared and maintained records evaluating each associate for use, not only in determining annual raises and giving progress reports to associates each year, but also for reference in considering each associate for promotion to partnership; that defendant did not, and would not, employ relatives of partners or clients on the legal staff; and that an associate would not be discriminated against in terms, conditions or privileges of employment including opportunities for promotion to partnership.

12.   At the conclusion of the interviews, plaintiff received an offer of employment as an associate attorney at an annual salary of $7,800.00. . . . In reliance upon defendant's representations and assurances, as stated above, plaintiff accepted defendant's offer.

13.   Plaintiff was employed by defendant from July 19, 1965, through March 16, 1973, when he was constructively discharged. During this time plaintiff was employed as an associate attorney in the litigation department of defendant.

14.   At all times during his employment by the defendant, plaintiff performed his duties as an associate satisfactorily, excelling in all of the tasks assigned to him and earning the praise of partners inside and outside the litigation department. Throughout his period of employment, plaintiff received what he was told were the maximum raise in annual salary and maximum bonus given to any associate in his law school graduating class.

The raises plaintiff received after April 1968 were based strictly on merit in keeping with a new policy defendant announced to its associates in late 1967 or early 1968.

15. On October 17, 1972, plaintiff was informed by defendant that its litigation partners had decided not to recommend him for promotion to partnership.

16. Thereafter, in two conferences with one of defendant's litigation partners on October 19 and 20, 1972, plaintiff strongly protested the decision of the litigation partners. As a result of his protests, the litigation partner to whom plaintiff spoke stated that he wished to consult further with his partners. Thereafter, plaintiff received a negative report from this litigation partner concerning the outcome of his consultations whereupon on November 2, 1972, plaintiff sent a memorandum to defendant's managing partner in charge of the litigation legal staff formally requesting reconsideration and setting forth reasons for his request. One of the reasons he provided was that the decision of the litigation partners was based on unlawful discriminatory grounds.

17. On November 3, 1972, defendant's managing partner of the litigation legal staff denied plaintiff's charges and insisted that the decision was final. At the same time, he disparaged plaintiff, suggested that his charge of discrimination was irrational and warned plaintiff that for the sake of his family he had better forget his charges and start thinking about his future career.

18. Defendant's response to plaintiff's memorandum was an act of retaliation against plaintiff for having charged defendant with discrimination and was intended to intimidate plaintiff in the hope that as a result he would not pursue his claim of discrimination.

19. On November 8, 1972, plaintiff appealed the denial of his request for reconsideration to defendant's presiding partner. Defendant's presiding partner summoned plaintiff to his office and, in retaliation for charging Cravath with discrimination, abruptly suspended plaintiff from his duties at the defendant firm as an associate attorney without affording plaintiff any opportunity to be heard and coldly told him to go see a psychiatrist. Plaintiff immediately left the presiding partner's office without having said a word. The presiding partner and three of defendant's litigation partners hurriedly followed plaintiff to plaintiff's office. On the way to his office, one of the defendant's litigation partners repeatedly ordered plaintiff to leave the office immediately and made disparaging comments about plaintiff. A number of associates and other employees witnessed the commotion and defendant's humiliating treatment of plaintiff. Once inside plaintiff's office, one of defendant's partners guarded the door to divert curious associates while the other three again tried to intimidate plaintiff. Plaintiff strongly protested his suspension but his protest was rejected and defendant's partners threatened plaintiff that, if he pressed his charges, his family and career would suffer.

. . .

21. On information and belief, on November 11, 1972, defendant held a meeting of all of its partners. At such meeting defendant confirmed and finalized the decision not to promote plaintiff to the position of partner.

22. On November 15, 1972, plaintiff formally protested his suspension and requested clarification of his status.

23. Defendant lifted plaintiff's suspension on December 5, 1972, and permitted him to return to Cravath as an associate attorney on the condition that he immediately seek other employment in accordance with a strict and unfair application of defendant's "up or out" policy. Plaintiff was also warned that, if he continued to press his discrimination claim, defendant would have to keep him under surveillance and begin building a case against him.

24. Defendant's conditional lifting of plaintiff's suspension and its threats to keep him under surveillance and to begin building a case against him were acts done in further retaliation against plaintiff for having charged defendant with discrimination.

25. On information and belief, during the period that plaintiff was suspended from his duties as an associate attorney and thereafter, defendant spoke disparagingly of plaintiff to associates, clients and other persons.

26. During the remaining period of plaintiff's employment until his constructive discharge on March 16, 1973, defendant harassed plaintiff by, among other things, continuing to disparage him, carrying out its aforesaid threats and taking other steps to ensure that plaintiff would soon terminate his employment relationship.

27. During the period that plaintiff was employed by defendant, Cravath engaged in unlawful employment practices against him because of his national origin or religion or both, in violation of Title VII of the Civil Rights Act of 1964 as amended. Such discrimination was part of a continuing pattern and practice of discrimination by Cravath against persons of Italian ancestry, including Italian-surnamed persons, and persons of the Catholic religion in terms, conditions and privileges of employment including recruiting, hiring, compensating, assigning, training, transferring and promoting associate attorneys to the partnership position. . . .

. . .

28. Cravath has a history of failing and refusing to hire Americans of Italian ancestry, including Italian-surnamed Americans, as summer interns and associate attorneys. During the period from May 1, 1906, through June 1, 1964, the Cravath firm hired 685 associates, of whom one percent or less were Italian-surnamed associates. During the period from November 15, 1959, through July 13, 1965, defendant did not have in its employ any Italian-surnamed associates. On information and belief, plaintiff was the first associate of Italian ancestry or the first Italian-surnamed associate ever to be hired into the litigation department. He was the only Italian-surnamed associate at the firm from July 19, 1965, until November 26,

1967, although throughout that period Cravath had approximately 100 associates and had hired 49 new associates to replace associates who had left the firm. The Italian-surnamed American hired by defendant on November 27, 1967, was assigned to the real estate department, a less desirable department at the defendant firm, and was not hired on a line of progression leading to partnership. Americans of Italian ancestry, including Italian-surnamed Americans, in the summer intern and associate attorney position remained underrepresented throughout plaintiff's period of employment.

29. One effect of Cravath's continuing pattern and practice of discrimination is that as of January 1, 1973, Cravath did not have, and had never had, a partner of Italian ancestry or an Italian-surnamed partner. As of January 1, 1973, the Cravath firm and its predecessor firms had had a total of 105 partners.

30. Cravath has a history of systematically limiting its employment of Catholics, including Italian-surnamed Catholics and Catholics of Italian ancestry, as summer interns and associate attorneys with the result that as of January 1, 1973, and for years prior thereto Catholics were not represented or were under represented at the firm in the associate attorney and partnership positions.

31. Defendant's selection criteria for recruiting and hiring summer interns and associate attorneys have an adverse and discriminatory impact on Catholics, including Catholics of Italian ancestry and Italian-surnamed Catholics. Although defendant has repeatedly stated that its partners and associates are "drawn from many different law schools," in fact defendant for years has recruited and hired the great majority of its associates from certain preferred law schools at which, on information and belief, Catholics, including Catholics of Italian ancestry and Italian-surnamed Catholics, have been under represented. . . .

32. On information and belief, for years the students who have attended Catholic law schools have included a disproportionately large number of Catholics, including Catholics of Italian ancestry and Italian-surnamed Catholics. Defendant discourages graduates of Catholic law schools from seeking employment at Cravath. One of defendant's litigation partners, in plaintiff's presence, declined to even interview a Catholic law school applicant who ranked third in his class and disparaged the law school in question. Another of defendant's partners, attempting to explain Cravath's refusal regularly to recruit at any Catholic law school, has suggested that Catholic law school students lack a "substantial interest" in Wall Street law firms. . . .

33. The single most important source of associates for defendant is Cravath's summer internship program for students between their second and third year of law school. . . . Students from Catholic law schools have been systematically excluded from Cravath's summer intern program regardless of their qualifications.

34.   Defendant's selection criteria for recruiting and hiring summer interns and associate attorneys are not job related and have never been validated. In 1969 plaintiff complained to defendant's then managing partner concerning Cravath's recruitment policies as they affected Catholics and was told that Catholic law schools were "inferior". When plaintiff inquired as to the basis for defendant's selection of the law schools at which Cravath concentrates its recruiting and hiring efforts, defendant's managing partner responded that Cravath goes by what it hears through the "grapevine" concerning the quality of various law schools. In December 1972 that same partner told plaintiff that he had a "ghetto mentality" because he had elected to attend the Notre Dame Law School.

35.   Defendant's selection criteria for promoting associate attorneys to partnership are not job related and have never been validated. Defendant told plaintiff that the reason the litigation partners had decided not to recommend him for promotion to partnership was because of "imponderables". At the same time, defendant told plaintiff that he was qualified to be a partner at Sullivan & Cromwell.

36.   The selection criteria which resulted in defendant recruiting and hiring its summer interns and associate attorneys in disproportionately large numbers from a few preferred law schools, also determines or influences defendant's promotional policies. Most of its partners are graduates of those same preferred law schools. Since 1963, the firm has promoted 18 associates to partnership, one of whom did not graduate from any law school.... During the period between May 1, 1906, and January 1, 1973, the Cravath firm had a total of 78 partners, two of whom did not graduate from any law school. Of the 76 who did graduate from law school, 67 or 88% graduated from Harvard, Yale, Columbia or Virginia law school. sixty–two or 82% graduated from just three law schools (*i.e.*, Harvard, Yale and Columbia)....

37.   Cravath's selection criteria for promotion of associate attorneys to partnership have had and continue to have an adverse differential impact on Catholics. Of 78 partners at the Cravath firm between May 1, 1906, and January 1, 1973, only one graduated from a Catholic law school. He was promoted to partnership in 1961, after serving more than three years longer as an associate than the average period of associateship served by all partners from Harvard, Yale and Columbia law schools who were promoted during the period from 1950 through 1973. On information and belief, he was the first Catholic to be promoted to partnership in decades.

38.   On information and belief, as of January 1, 1973, Cravath had 12 litigation partners, none of whom was Catholic. On information and belief, as of that date the Cravath firm and its predecessor firms had not had a Catholic partner in its litigation department since 1906 when William D. Guthrie, a Catholic senior litigation partner and another Catholic partner left the firm, then known as Guthrie, Cravath & Henderson, as the result of a bitter dispute with the founder of the modern Cravath firm, Paul D. Cravath, who then became and remained the authoritative head of the law firm until his death in 1940. Mr. Cravath conceived, and succeeding

presiding partners have continued, the so-called Cravath system including the policy of limiting associate attorney employment opportunities to graduates of a few preferred law schools....

43. On information and belief, plaintiff was not promoted to partnership because of the prejudice of one or more of defendant's litigation partners against Americans of the Catholic religion, Americans of Italian Ancestry or Italian-surnamed Americans.

44. The facts set forth in the preceding paragraphs establish that Cravath has engaged in a continuing pattern and practice of discrimination on the grounds of national origin and religion in violation of 42 U.S.C.A. § 2000e–2(a) against persons of the Catholic religion, including Catholics of Italian ancestry and Italian-surnamed Catholics. That pattern and practice of discrimination is part of a larger continuing pattern and practice of discrimination, in favor of white Protestant males generally of Northern European ancestry in recruiting, hiring, compensating, assigning, training, transferring and promoting associate attorneys to partnership in violation of 42 U.S.C § 2000e. [The result of this larger pattern and practice has been:]

(a) Cravath for years did not have any Jewish partner at the firm. On information and belief, the first Jewish partner was promoted to partnership in 1958. On information and belief, Cravath promoted its next Jewish partners to partnership effective January 1, 1965, when three were promoted—all in the corporate department.... As of January 1, 1973, only two of defendant's 12 litigation partners were Jewish.

(b) Cravath has had only one female partner. On January 1, 1971, she was promoted to partnership in the trusts and estates department, one of the less desirable departments at Cravath and one in which Cravath has traditionally had female jobs.

(c) Cravath has never had a black partner nor a Spanish-surnamed partner.

(d) Cravath for years has limited, classified and segregated its lawyers in such a manner that female and minority group members, including Catholics and Jews, in disproportionately large numbers have been hired into less desirable positions at the firm, including the position of permanent associate, assigned to less desirable departments and given less desirable work at the firm. The less desirable departments and the permanent associate positions at the firm for years have contained or been filled by a disproportionately large number of graduates of Catholic law schools.

45. On or about June 13, 1973, plaintiff timely filed, under oath, a written Charge of Discrimination with the Equal Employment Opportunity Commission ("EEOC") regional office in New York. At the same time plaintiff filed a substantially identical complaint with the New York City Commission on Human Rights.

46. Those agencies thereafter attempted to investigate plaintiff's charges, but defendant objected to, and refused to comply with, certain of the information requests of the EEOC and the City Commission.

47. On September 4, 1975, plaintiff requested a right-to-sue letter from the EEOC. On September 22, 1975, the EEOC sent a 90–day letter to plaintiff advising him that he had the right to sue defendant. A copy of that letter is attached hereto as Exhibit A.

48. The plaintiff has exhausted all of his available administrative remedies within applicable federal, state and local agencies.

WHEREFORE, plaintiff respectfully requests that this Court:

A. Enter a judgement in favor of plaintiff and against defendant declaring that the aforesaid acts and practices of defendant are in violation of the laws of the United States and in violation of rights guaranteed plaintiff by those laws;

B. Issue a permanent injunction: [seeking reinstatement, promotion, back pay, attorneys fees and an order that defendant "cease and desist its discriminatory conduct in recruiting, hiring, assigning, transferring, training, compensating and promoting summer interns and associate attorneys and to take appropriate affirmative action to remedy the present effects of past discrimination"].

COUNT II

1. Plaintiff repeats and realleges the statements contained in paragraphs 1 through 48 of Count I.

2. Plaintiff and defendant entered into an employment contract under the terms of which defendant promised and agreed, among other things, to promote plaintiff to partnership after a reasonable period of associateship if plaintiff performed his professional duties satisfactorily and thereby demonstrated that he was qualified for the partnership position.

3. In reliance on the aforesaid contract, including defendant's representations and assurances as confirmed by defendant's partners from time to time during plaintiff's employment by defendant, plaintiff fully performed the obligations of the employment contract on his part to be performed but defendant refused, and continues to refuse, to promote plaintiff to partnership.

4. By reason of the foregoing, defendant breached its employment contract with plaintiff to plaintiff's great damage.

WHEREFORE, plaintiff respectfully requests that this Court:

[order reinstatement and promotion, back pay and other compensatory damages]

Respectfully submitted,

Michael Pollet
Marpatkin, Pollet & LeMoult
1345 Avenue of the Americas
New York, New York 10019

Alan Dershowitz
Harvard Law School
Cambridge, Massachusetts 02138

Attorneys for Plaintiff
New York, New York
December 19, 1975

DEFENDANT'S BRIEF IN SUPPORT OF ITS MOTION TO DISMISS THE COMPLAINT

PAUL, WEISS, RIFKIND, WHARTON & GARRISON
Attorneys and Counselors at Law
345 Park Avenue, New York, NY 10022

Preliminary Statements

. . .

Because of the nature of the charges made in this case; because, on a motion to dismiss, well-pleaded averments must be assumed to be true for the technical purposes of the motion; and because that assumption here is so blatantly contrary to reality, we wish to emphasize at the outset that this motion should not be construed to imply even the slightest concurrence in fact with the basic assertions of the complaint. Were a sound legal and constitutional foundation for this complaint found to exist, and the motion denied, we would show that plaintiff was in fact treated fairly and honorably throughout his employments; that his charge of bias is not merely false but mendacious; and that this action is a disservice to the high purposes of the Act under which it is purportedly brought.

But it is also true that the suit is baseless in law; and we believe the time to show that is now, rather than proceeding further with the processes warranted in the litigation of colorable claims.

Argument

I.

AS A MATTER OF STATUTORY AND CONSTITUTIONAL LAW, THE STRICTURES OF TITLE VII OF THE CIVIL RIGHTS ACT OF 1964, AS AMENDED, DO NOT APPLY TO THE PROCESS BY WHICH THE MEMBERS OF A LAW PARTNERSHIP DECIDE TO INVITE AN ATTORNEY TO BECOME THEIR PARTNER.

A. *Title VII of the Civil Rights Act of 1964, as amended, applies to employer–employee relationships, but does not purport to regulate a partnership's choice of its members.*

Section 703 of Title VII of the Civil Rights Act of 1964, as amended by the Equal Employment Opportunity Act of 1972, 42 U.S.C.A. § 2000e–2 (1972), proscribes certain discriminatory employment practices, but does not purport to regulate the relationship among members of a partnership. The section reads in relevant part:

"(a) It shall be an unlawful employment practice for an employer—

(1) to fail or refuse to hire or to discharge any individual, or otherwise to discriminate against any individual with respect to his compensation, terms, conditions or privileges of employment, because of such individual's race, color, religion, sex or national origin; or

(2) to limit, segregate, or classify his employees or applicants for employment in any way which would deprive or tend to deprive any individual of employment opportunities or otherwise adversely affect his status as an employee, because of such individual's race, color, religion, sex or national origin."

. . .

A partnership is a unique legal relationship, governed by statute in New York. Our law defines a partnership as "an association of two or more persons to carry on as co-owners a business for profit," N.Y. Partnership L. § 10(1) (McKinney 1948).

By statute in New York, and in common law as well, no person can become a member of a partnership without the consent of all the partners, and the members of a partnership need not accept as an unwelcome member of their partnership anyone who is thrust upon them. . . .

Consent, unlike obedience, cannot be decreed. The supposition that Title VII is applicable to the membership of a partnership necessarily assumes that Congress rewrote the law of partnership in New York and 49 other states, altering its nature in this, its most fundamental respect. Whether or not Congress had the constitutional power to do so, there is nothing in the language of the Act or its legislative history to suggest that it intended to do so.

These principles are particularly appropriate to a partnership for the practice of law. The members of a law firm must necessarily have mutual trust and confidence in each other, for each is capable of involving the others in extraordinary responsibility or liability: Each partner has authority to contract on behalf of the firm and bind his copartners, N.Y. Partnership L. § 20 (1); each has equal rights in the management and conduct of the partnership business, N.Y. Partnership L. § 40 (5); yet all of the partners are jointly and severally liable to third persons for any partner's wrongful act or omission, or for a partner's malpractice or breach of trust, N.Y. Partnership L. §§ 24, 25, 26.

Moreover, in a partnership of lawyers, each member to an appreciable extent places his own professional reputation and standing at the Bar in the hands of his partners: an error or omission by one partner could adversely affect the standing and professional reputation of the others.

Because of these extraordinary responsibilities and liabilities of partners for each other's acts, the invitation to partnership must be a very personal one—much more intimate, for instance, than an invitation to membership of the board of directors of a commercial company. . . .

For these reasons, we submit, the decision to invite an attorney to membership in a law firm is not an employment decision governed by the requirements of Title VII. The scope of the Act does not extend to regulation of the association of self-employed lawyers.

B. *The First Amendment Prohibits Governmental Regulation of a Law Firm's Choice of Partners.*

If, contrary to the language of the statute, Title VII were interpreted to extend to regulation of the partners' decisions about who shall be invited to membership in a law firm, such an interpretation would render the statute constitutionally invalid.

* * *

In a concurring opinion in Bell v. Maryland, 378 U.S. 226, 313 (1964), Justice Goldberg was joined by Chief Justice Warren and Justice Douglas in writing:

> "It is the constitutional right of every person to close his home or club to any person or to choose his social intimates and business partners solely on the basis of personal prejudices including race."

. . .

Under our constitutional system, there are areas of private action upon which the state is not permitted to intrude. The individual is protected in his right to make certain decisions for himself—what he shall read or believe, whom he shall marry, what children he shall adopt, those friends with whom he shall have social intercourse. The state cannot compel such relationships or beliefs, no matter what the grounds on which the individuals involved may have eschewed them.

In like context, there are protected forms of association that pertain to the professional relationship of the members. If two or three attorneys choose to enter into a partnership for the practice of law, there is no statute, however noble in purpose, which can regulate their choice of partners. There presently are 45 partners in the Cravath firm, but the rights, responsibilities and liabilities of each toward the others and the public are the same as those of the members of a two-partner firm. We submit that government cannot, consistently with the freedoms established by our Constitution, compel a lawyer to practice his profession in partnership with another. That choice involves a right of association protected from governmental intrusion under the penumbra of the First Amendment. . . .

If the members of a law partnership were actually to predicate their choice of partners on religious or ethnic grounds, such conduct would be socially and morally reprehensible as well as a self-defeating course from which the partnership would ultimately suffer in terms of recruitment, public esteem, breadth of experience, and in scores of other intangible and unpredictable ways. Yet, from a constitutional standpoint, there are compelling reasons why a partnership decision to invite or not invite new members should not be made the subject of litigation by each aspirant disappointed in the result. Given the nature of a law partnership, the high level of mutual trust required, and the personal relationships involved, for the government to assert the power to control the members' choice of those with whom they wish to join in partnership in the practice of their profession would imperil more than it protects.

* * *

II

IF COUNT I IS DISMISSED, COUNT II MUST ALSO BE DISMISSED, BECAUSE THERE IS NEITHER DIVERSITY JURISDICTION NOR PENDENT JURISDICTION FOR THE STATE LAW CLAIM.

* * *

New York, New York
March 9, 1976

> Respectfully submitted,
> PAUL, WEISS, RIFKIND,
> WHARTON & GARRISON
> Attorneys for Defendant
> 345 Park Avenue
> New York, New York 10022

Subsequent Developments

In Lucido v. Cravath Swaine & Moore, 425 F.Supp. 123 (S.D.N.Y.1977) (Gagliardi, J.), the court held that the opportunity to be promoted to partner at Cravath was ". . . 'a term, condition, or privilege of employment' . . ." and an "employment opportunity" under Section 703 of Title VII. Because a clear employer-employee relationship between Cravath and Lucido existed, the Court determined that any ethnic or religious discrimination during that relationship was covered by Title VII, and, therefore, unabatedly prohibited. As a result, Lucido had stated a claim upon which relief could be granted. The court further stated that its decision did not infringe upon any First Amendment right of Cravath because the Court did not "recognize any First Amendment privacy or associational rights for a commercial, profit-making business organization of the nature of the Cravath partnership." Id. at 129. Title VII's application, in the court's view, would not prevent the partners from "associating for political, social and economic goals" or limit the use of discretionary subjective judgment in the partnership promotion process. It only prevented the partners from considering such factors as religion, national origin, race, color and sex. Id.

Following this denial of its motion to dismiss the complaint for failure to state a claim, Cravath served upon Lucido its first set of interrogatories in April, 1977. Lucido was asked to identify and set forth certain information regarding "each oral statement upon which [he] relies to prove" the principal substantive allegations of the complaint. Lucido v. Cravath, 25 F. R. Serv.2d (Callaghan) 1050 (May 25, 1978). There ensued a controversy over whether Lucido's answers should be a matter of public record:

> In November 1977, plaintiff served his answers upon Cravath but did not file them with the clerk of the court as part of the public record. Upon receipt and review of these answers, which specify 86 oral statements and run for 104 pages, Cravath moved for a protective order pursuant to Rule 26(c), Fed. R. Civ. P. . . . In December 1977, Cravath submitted a proposed order of confidentiality which would have placed *all* of the interrogatory answers under court seal and prevented the parties or counsel from disclosing their contents to any third party without prior notice to the opposing party and the opportunity to apply to the court for a hearing on the propriety of disclosure.

Id. at 1051. The Court found that "[m]any of the statements contained in the answers impugned the professional qualifications, personal values and character of particular present and past partners and associates of defendant, and charged them with ethnic bigotry, lack of intelligence, laziness and various unethical practices." Id. at 1050 Cravath's motion for a protective order therefore was granted. Id.

On July 20, 1981, after extensive and controversial discovery, Lucido's case was dismissed with prejudice for want of prosecution when Lucido failed to appear at a pretrial conference.

QUESTIONS

1. How do the allegations in the *Lucido* complaint compare with Swaine's account of how partners were chosen at Cravath?

2. Even if there is no intent to discriminate, is it still unethical to employ and evaluate associates based on criteria that facilitate *de facto* discrimination? For example, is a firm acting ethically if, even without facially discriminatory policies, it recruits only in regions of the country and from law schools where African Americans, Italian Americans or Jews are not well represented?

3. Defendant's brief acknowledges that "[i]f the members of a law partnership were actually to predicate their choice of partners on religious or ethnic grounds, such conduct would be socially and morally reprehensible . . . ," but still insists that discrimination within a partnership is outside the scope of Title VII, and that indeed the federal government could not constitutionally prohibit such discrimination even it wanted to. Why didn't Cravath proceed directly to litigate the claim on the merits to show that it did not discriminate against Lucido instead of moving for dismissal on these grounds? If you were Cravath's lawyer, would you encourage the firm to make the arguments that it does in its brief? Why or why not?

4. Compare Lucido's contract claim (Count II) to the implied contract claim upheld in *Wieder v. Skala*. How are the two similar? How are they different? Is an associate likely to prevail on a claim that his law firm breached oral understandings about evaluation and promotion?

5. The brief in support of Cravath's motion to dismiss is correct in pointing out that a partnership is a unique form of business organization in which partners share responsibility, and ultimately liability, for each other's actions. Do any of these considerations justify making partnership decisions based on the criteria that Lucido's complaint alleges were used by Cravath?

6. What reasons might Cravath have had for retaining Paul, Weiss, Rifkind, Wharton & Garrison to defend this case? Should Paul, Weiss have accepted the case to make the arguments it did in the motion to dismiss? Should Paul, Weiss have accepted the case, but only for a trial on the merits?

7. Lucido's case was dismissed for want of prosecution in 1981 after extensive and controversial discovery. Lucido apparently gave up at this point, almost nine years after he had been informed that he would not make partner at Cravath. Is it right that a litigant should have to wait so long for the legal system to resolve his claim?

Discrimination on Account of Sex

Elizabeth Anderson Hishon, b. 1944; B.A. Wellesley College; J.D. Columbia University 1972; admitted to the Georgia Bar in 1972; associated with King & Spalding 1972–79; partner Callaghan, Saunders & Sturm, Atlanta, Georgia beginning in 1980 (specialist in commercial real estate and commercial contracts).

Emmet J. Bondurant II, b. 1937; A.B. University of Georgia 1958; LL.B. University of Georgia 1960; LL.M. Harvard University 1962; law clerk to Clement F. Haynsworth, Jr., U.S. Court of Appeals, Fourth Circuit 1960–61; senior partner of Bondurant, Mixson & Elmore in Atlanta, Georgia and counsel for Elizabeth Hishon in her suit against King & Spalding.

Paul M. Bator, filed a brief for the United States as amicus curiae at the direction of the Reagan Administration. The Administration's brief urged the Supreme Court to rule that law firms may not discriminate on the basis of sex in deciding who becomes a partner. Griffin Bell, who served as Attorney General under President Carter, was a member of the defendant law firm.

Elizabeth Anderson Hishon, Petitioner v. King & Spalding

467 U.S. 69 (1984).

■ CHIEF JUSTICE BURGER delivered the opinion of the Court.

We granted certiorari to determine whether the District Court properly dismissed a Title VII complaint alleging that a law partnership discriminated against petitioner, a woman lawyer employed as an associate, when it failed to invite her to become a partner.

I

A

In 1972 petitioner Elizabeth Anderson Hishon accepted a position as an associate with respondent, a large Atlanta law firm established as a general partnership. When this suit was filed in 1980, the firm had more than 50 partners and employed approximately 50 attorneys as associates. Up to that time, no woman had ever served as a partner at the firm.

Petitioner alleges that the prospect of partnership was an important factor in her initial decision to accept employment with respondent. She alleges that respondent used the possibility of ultimate partnership as a recruiting device to induce petitioner and other young lawyers to become associates at the firm. According to the complaint, respondent represented that advancement to partnership after five or six years was "a matter of course" for associates "who receive[d] satisfactory evaluations" and that associates were promoted to partnership "on a fair and equal basis." Petitioner alleges that she relied on these representations when she accepted employment with respondent. The complaint further alleges that respondent's promise to consider her on a "fair and equal basis" created a binding employment contract.

In May 1978 the partnership considered and rejected Hishon for admission to the partnership; one year later, the partners again declined to invite her to become a partner. Once an associate is passed over for partnership at respondent's firm, the associate is notified to begin seeking employment elsewhere. Petitioner's employment as an associate terminated on December 31, 1979.

B

Hishon filed a charge with the Equal Employment Opportunity Commission on November 19, 1979, claiming that respondent had discriminated against her on the basis of her sex in violation of Title VII of the Civil Rights Act of 1964, 78 Stat. 241, as amended, 42 U.S.C.A. § 2000e et seq. Ten days later the Commission issued a notice of right to sue, and on February 27, 1980, Hishon brought this action in the United States District Court for the Northern District of Georgia. She sought declaratory and injunctive relief, backpay, and compensatory damages "in lieu of reinstatement and promotion to partnership." This, of course, negates any claim for specific performance of the contract alleged.

The District Court dismissed the complaint on the ground that Title VII was inapplicable to the selection of partners by a partnership. A divided panel of the United States Court of Appeals for the Eleventh Circuit affirmed. 678 F.2d 1022 (1982). We granted certiorari, 459 U.S. 1169, and we reverse.

II

At this stage of the litigation, we must accept petitioner's allegations as true.... The issue before us is whether petitioner's allegations state a claim under Title VII, the relevant portion of which provides as follows: " '(a) *It shall be an unlawful employment practice for an employer—*' (1) to fail or refuse to hire or to discharge any individual, or otherwise *to discriminate against any individual with respect to his* compensation, *terms, conditions, or privileges of employment, because of such individual's* race, color, religion, *sex,* or national origin." 42 U.S.C.A. § 2000e–2(a) (emphasis added).

A

Petitioner alleges that respondent is an "employer" to whom Title VII is addressed. She then asserts that consideration for partnership was one of the "terms, conditions, or privileges of employment" as an associate with respondent. See § 2000e–2(a)(1). If this is correct, respondent could not base an adverse partnership decision on "race, color, religion, sex, or national origin."

Once a contractual relationship of employment is established, the provisions of Title VII attach and govern certain aspects of that relationship. In the context of Title VII, the contract of employment may be written or oral, formal or informal; an informal contract of employment may arise by the simple act of handing a job applicant a shovel and providing a workplace. The contractual relationship of employment triggers the provision of Title VII governing "terms, conditions, or privileges of employment." Title VII in turn forbids discrimination on the basis of "race, color, religion, sex, or national origin."

Because the underlying employment relationship is contractual, it follows that the "terms, conditions, or privileges of employment" clearly include benefits that are part of an employment contract. Here, petitioner in essence alleges that respondent made a contract to consider her for partnership.[6] Indeed, this promise was allegedly a key contractual provision which induced her to accept employment. If the evidence at trial establishes that the parties contracted to have petitioner considered for partnership,

---

6. Petitioner alleges not only that respondent promised to consider her for partnership, but also that it promised to consider her on a "fair and equal basis." This latter promise is not necessary to petitioner's Title VII claim. Even if the employment contract did not afford a basis for an implied condition that the ultimate decision would be fairly made on the merits, Title VII itself would impose such a requirement. If the promised consideration for partnership is a term, condition, or privilege of employment, then the partnership decision must be without regard to "race, color, religion, sex, or national origin."

that promise clearly was a term, condition, or privilege of her employment. Title VII would then bind respondent to consider petitioner for partnership as the statute provides, i.e., without regard to petitioner's sex. The contract she alleges would lead to the same result.

Petitioner's claim that a contract was made, however, is not the only allegation that would qualify respondent's consideration of petitioner for partnership as a term, condition, or privilege of employment. An employer may provide its employees with many benefits that it is under no obligation to furnish by any express or implied contract. Such a benefit, though not a contractual right of employment, may qualify as a "privileg[e]" of employment under Title VII. A benefit that is part and parcel of the employment relationship may not be doled out in a discriminatory fashion, even if the employer would be free under the employment contract simply not to provide the benefit at all. Those benefits that comprise the "incidents of employment," S.Rep. No. 867, 88th Cong., 2d Sess., 11 (1964), or that form "an aspect of the relationship between the employer and employees," Chemical & Alkali Workers v. Pittsburgh Plate Glass Co., 404 U.S. 157, 178, 92 S.Ct. 383, 397, 30 L.Ed.2d 341 (1971), may not be afforded in a manner contrary to Title VII.

Several allegations in petitioner's complaint would support the conclusion that the opportunity to become a partner was part and parcel of an associate's status as an employee at respondent's firm, independent of any allegation that such an opportunity was included in associates' employment contracts. Petitioner alleges that respondent's associates could regularly expect to be considered for partnership at the end of their "apprenticeships," and it appears that lawyers outside the firm were not routinely so considered.[9] Thus, the benefit of partnership consideration was allegedly linked directly with an associate's status as an employee, and this linkage was far more than coincidental: petitioner alleges that respondent explicitly used the prospect of ultimate partnership to induce young lawyers to join the firm. Indeed, the importance of the partnership decision to a lawyer's status as an associate is underscored by the allegation that associates' employment is terminated if they are not elected to become partners. These allegations, if proved at trial, would suffice to show that partnership consideration was a term, condition, or privilege of an associate's employment at respondent's firm, and accordingly that partnership consideration must be without regard to sex.

B

Respondent contends that advancement to partnership may never qualify as a term, condition, or privilege of employment for purposes of Title VII. First, respondent asserts that elevation to partnership entails a change in status from an "employee" to an "employer." However, even if respondent is correct that a partnership invitation is not itself an offer of

---

9. Respondent's own submissions indicate that most of respondent's partners in fact were selected from the ranks of associates who had spent their entire prepartnership legal careers (excluding judicial clerkships) with the firm. See App. 45.

employment, Title VII would nonetheless apply and preclude discrimination on the basis of sex. The benefit a plaintiff is denied need not be employment to fall within Title VII's protection; it need only be a term, condition, or privilege of employment. It is also of no consequence that employment as an associate necessarily ends when an associate becomes a partner. A benefit need not accrue before a person's employment is completed to be a term, condition, or privilege of that employment relationship. Pension benefits, for example, qualify as terms, conditions, or privileges of employment even though they are received only after employment terminates. Arizona Governing Committee for Tax Deferred Annuity & Deferred Compensation Plans v. Norris, 463 U.S. 1073, 103 S.Ct. 3492, 77 L.Ed.2d 1236 (1983) (opinion of Marshall, J.). Accordingly, nothing in the change in status that advancement to partnership might entail means that partnership consideration falls outside the terms of the statute. See Lucido v. Cravath, Swaine & Moore, 425 F.Supp. 123, 128–129 (S.D.N.Y.1977).

Second, respondent argues that Title VII categorically exempts partnership decisions from scrutiny. However, respondent points to nothing in the statute or the legislative history that would support such a per se exemption. When Congress wanted to grant an employer complete immunity, it expressly did so.

Third, respondent argues that application of Title VII in this case would infringe constitutional rights of expression or association. Although we have recognized that the activities of lawyers may make a "distinctive contribution ... to the ideas and beliefs of our society," NAACP v. Button, 371 U.S. 415, 431, 83 S.Ct. 328, 337, 9 L.Ed.2d 405 (1963), respondent has not shown how its ability to fulfill such a function would be inhibited by a requirement that it consider petitioner for partnership on her merits. Moreover, as we have held in another context, "[i]nvidious private discrimination may be characterized as a form of exercising freedom of association protected by the First Amendment, but it has never been accorded affirmative constitutional protections." Norwood v. Harrison, 413 U.S. 455, 470, 93 S.Ct. 2804, 2813, 37 L.Ed.2d 723 (1973). There is no constitutional right, for example, to discriminate in the selection of who may attend a private school or join a labor union. [Citations omitted].

III

We conclude that petitioner's complaint states a claim cognizable under Title VII. Petitioner therefore is entitled to her day in court to prove her allegations. The judgment of the Court of Appeals is reversed, and the case is remanded for further proceedings consistent with this opinion.

It is so ordered.

■ JUSTICE POWELL, concurring.

I join the Court's opinion holding that petitioner's complaint alleges a violation of Title VII and that the motion to dismiss should not have been granted. Petitioner's complaint avers that the law firm violated its promise that she would be considered for partnership on a "fair and equal basis" within the time span that associates generally are so considered. Petitioner is entitled to the opportunity to prove these averments.

I write to make clear my understanding that the Court's opinion should not be read as extending Title VII to the management of a law firm by its partners. The reasoning of the Court's opinion does not require that the relationship among partners be characterized as an "employment" relationship to which Title VII would apply. The relationship among law partners differs markedly from that between employer and employee—including that between the partnership and its associates. The judgmental and sensitive decisions that must be made among the partners embrace a wide range of subjects. The essence of the law partnership is the common conduct of a shared enterprise. The relationship among law partners contemplates that decisions important to the partnership normally will be made by common agreement, see, e.g., Memorandum of Agreement, King & Spalding, App. 153–164 (respondent's partnership agreement), or consent among the partners.

Respondent contends that for these reasons application of Title VII to the decision whether to admit petitioner to the firm implicates the constitutional right to association. But here it is alleged that respondent as an employer is obligated by contract to consider petitioner for partnership on equal terms without regard to sex. I agree that enforcement of this obligation, voluntarily assumed, would impair no right of association.

In admission decisions made by law firms, it is now widely recognized—as it should be—that in fact neither race nor sex is relevant. The qualities of mind, capacity to reason logically, ability to work under pressure, leadership, and the like are unrelated to race or sex. This is demonstrated by the success of women and minorities in law schools, in the practice of law, on the bench, and in positions of community, state, and national leadership. Law firms—and, of course, society—are the better for these changes.

Relevant Background

Hiring of women attorneys by large law firms has increased slowly in the last decade. A 1993 Chicago survey showed that women made up 38.2% of associates at polled firms, up from 36.3% in 1992 and 35.6% in 1987. Ed Finkel, Women's Survey Results: Women's Gains Measured by the Inch in Largest Law Firms, Chicago Lawyer May 1993. Women attorneys also still face many obstacles which make it hard to advance in a firm once they are hired. In 1989, Judge Patricia Wald observed that women still only represented 8% of total partners in the nation's 250 largest law firms. Patricia M. Wald, Breaking the Glass Ceiling: Will We Ever Rid the Legal Profession of "The Ugly Residue of Gender Discrimination"?, 16 A.B.A. Sec. Individual Rts. & Resp. (1989). Even once they are admitted to partnership, women may be undercompensated, excluded from important firm committees and denied opportunities to work for important clients. Nonetheless, Justice Powell's concurring opinion in *Hishon* presumably puts such matters well beyond the reach of Title VII.

Also, despite the Supreme Court's holding in *Hishon*, as a practical matter courts are often unwilling to review partnership decisions. In Ezold v. Wolf et al., 983 F.2d 509 (3d Cir. 1992), the plaintiff, an associate with the Philadelphia firm of Wolf, Block, Schorr and Solis-Cohen, sued the firm under Title VII for failing to promote her to partner. She won her case in the district court, but the firm won reversal from an appellate panel that was skeptical about the ability of trial courts to determine whether an associate should have been promoted in a firm. Id. at 512–13.

Sexual harassment is one of the most common forms of gender bias. In a recent survey by Prentice–Hall, 56% of female litigators surveyed said that they had experienced sexual harassment by either opposing counsel or law firm colleagues, and surveys by the National Law Journal and the ABA Journal showed similar figures. Lisa Pfenninger, Sexual Harassment in the Legal Profession: Workplace Education and Reform, Civil Remedies and Professional Discipline. 22 Fla. St. U. L. Rev. 171, 175 (1994). Another recent survey showed that sexual harassment by clients is also a serious problem. See Toby Pilsner, Recurrent Gender Biases Continue to Block Progress of Women Lawyers, N.Y.L.J. May 3, 1993 at col. 1.

Sexual harassment in the workplace violates Section 703 of Title VII. 42 U.S.C.A. Section 2000e et seq. Sexual harassment is defined for purposes of Title VII as unwelcome sexual advances, requests for sexual favors, and other verbal or physical conduct of a sexual nature when (1) submission to such conduct is made either explicitly or implicitly a term or condition of employment, or rejection of such conduct is used as a basis for employment decisions, or (2) the conduct unreasonably interferes with an individual's work performance or otherwise creates a hostile work environment. 29 C.F.R. Section 1604.11(a). Many states have similar statutes and regulations prohibiting sexual harassment by employers. In 1994 California went one step further and enacted a statute providing a civil cause of action for sexual harassment that occurs within the context of a "professional relationship," such as that between a lawyer and another lawyer he retains as co-counsel or between a lawyer and a client. See California Civil Code, Section 51.9. Some states, including Oregon, impose an outright ban on sexual relations between lawyers and clients, although not between lawyers working in the same office.

The New York based firm of Milbank, Tweed, Hadley & McCloy has one of the most comprehensive policies to combat sex-discrimination. The firm sends a four-page policy statement to all employees twice a year and has a committee composed of 13 employees from all levels of the firm to hear sexual harassment complaints. Many law firms' sexual harassment policies, however, are not as thorough as Milbank's. See Edward A. Adams, Gender Bias at Law Firms: A Rising Tide of Litigation, Model Harassment Policy Devised by Milbank, N.Y.L.J. October 5, 1992 at col. 4.

Unfortunately, sexual harassment laws and litigation can also have a "chilling effect" on professional relationships. Male partners may choose to avoid mentoring relationships with female attorneys instead of treading what they perceive to be a thin line between friendship and sexual harassment. Pfenninger supra at 174. Although such a reaction usually demonstrates ignorance about what sexual harassment is, workplace policies that are not designed with education rather than merely litigation avoidance in mind, can deprive female attorneys of mentoring relationships that are essential to their careers.

In response to incidents of gender discrimination in the courtroom, the ABA incorporated provisions aimed at curbing gender discrimination in the Model Code of Judicial Conduct Canon 3 (1990). The official commentary to this canon is explicit: "A judge must refrain from speech, gestures or other conduct that could reasonably be perceived as sexual harassment and must require the same standard of conduct of others subject to the judge's direction and control." Unfortunately, abuses continue, provoking sharp criticism from advocates of women's equality in the courtroom. See *Matter of Holtzman*, infra, Chapter 12.

QUESTIONS

1. How would each of the following practices affect a firm's recruiting and promotion outcomes? Which of the following are inappropriate?

a. Holding a summer outing at a country club known to exclude African Americans and Jews from membership.

b. Requiring associates to work on Saturdays or Sundays despite religious objections, or taking into account willingness to work on religious holidays when evaluating associates.

c. Representing clients who complain when lawyers cannot be reached on Saturdays and religious holidays.

d. Taking clients to a lunch club that does not have women members but allows women to use the dining room as guests.

e. Representing clients who insist that their work not be assigned to women lawyers.

f. Establishing a rigid seven-year up-or-out partnership track and refusing to allow an associate to work part time on account of his or her family responsibilities.

2. What other recruiting and promotion practices might discriminate on the basis of sex, race, religion or national origin?

3. Some economic theorists have argued that unfettered market competition will drive out race and sex discrimination. See Gary Becker, The Economics of Discrimination 14 (2d ed. 1971) ("if an individual has a 'taste for discrimination,' he must act as if he were willing to pay something, either directly or in the form of a reduced income, to be associated with some persons instead of others."). Under this line of reasoning, market forces make discrimination laws unnecessary and inefficient. See Richard A. Epstein, Forbidden Grounds: The Case Against Employment Discrimination Laws 33–41 (1992). However, other scholars use economic theory to explain that discrimination results from people deriving esteem from group identity and making material sacrifices to promote group status at the expense of other groups. "[D]esire for inter-group status causes inter-group conflict," which in turn manifests itself in discriminatory practices. Richard H. McAdams, Cooperation and Conflict: The Economics of Group Status Production and Race Discrimination, 108 Harv. L. Rev. 1003, 1007 (1995). Which theory is more consistent with your own observations? What other explanations are there for prejudice and discrimination?

4. One survey of students enrolled at the University of Pennsylvania Law School between 1987 and 1992 concluded that "the law school experience of women in the aggregate differs markedly from that of their male peers." Lani Guinier, Michelle Fine, Jane Balin, Ann Bartow and Deborah Lee Stachel, Becoming Gentlemen: Women's Experiences at One Ivy League Law School, 143 U. Pa. L. Rev. 1 (1994). The authors concluded, among other things, that "by the end of their first year in law school, men are three times more likely than women to be in the top 10% of their law school class," first-year women are "far more critical than their first-year male peers of the social status quo, of legal education, and of themselves as students," and women "self-report much lower rates of class participation than do men for all three years of law school." Id. at 3–4. Assuming the authors' survey accurately portrays gender imbalances at the University of Pennsylvania, what explanations might there be for these differences? What practical suggestions would you make to improve the law school environment for women students?

Discrimination on Account of Sexual Orientation and Disability

Philadelphia, starring Tom Hanks (1993)

This movie is based on an actual lawsuit alleging that a large Philadelphia law firm fired an associate because he developed AIDS. After renting and viewing the movie, you should consider the following questions:

1. Scientific research has shown that AIDS cannot be transmitted through casual contact. Why are many people, like the plaintiff's lawyer in this movie, still apprehensive when around people with AIDS? Even absent overt discrimination, how does this apprehension affect an infected person's work environment?

2. The plaintiff's lawyer here appears willing to try just about any case for other clients. Why is he initially so unwilling to take the discrimination claim in this suit?

3. This case involves efforts by at least one lawyer to sabotage another lawyer's work within a firm, here by removing documents from his desk and sending them to central files. What other more subtle tactics might a lawyer use to "sandbag" another lawyer in a law firm? Can you identify provisions of the Model Rules or Model Code that would prohibit such conduct?

4. Is it more likely that women lawyers, minority lawyers, gay and lesbian lawyers and lawyers with disabilities will be unfairly blamed when something goes wrong in a law firm? What should law firms do to assure that personnel policies are fairly applied?

Relevant Background

Doe v. Kohn Nast & Graf, P.C., 862 F.Supp. 1310 (E.D.Pa.1994) relates facts essentially similar to the movie *Philadelphia*. In this case, the plaintiff (identified only as "Doe" in the case), was employed in July, 1991 on a contract basis by the defendant, a Philadelphia law firm. Six months later, he was praised for exceptionally good work and given a substantial raise. However, in the fall of 1992, the plaintiff learned that he had AIDS, and on November 25, 1992 received a letter concerning his infection from a physician. The letter, addressed to the plaintiff at Kohn Nast & Graf, was presumably kept in his office where it could have been seen by a co-worker. The plaintiff contended that several days after receiving the letter, his mentor in the firm "stopped assigning him work, stopped speaking with him, and avoided physical contact with him." Id. at 1315. The Plaintiff sued, claiming violation of several federal and state statutes, including the Americans with Disabilities Act (ADA), 42 U.S.C.A. section 12101, et seq, and the Employee Retirement Income Security Act of 1974 (ERISA), 29 U.S.C.A. section 1140. In denying the firm's motion for summary judgment, the court held that the plaintiff's HIV infection imposed "substantial limits on major life activities," and brought him within the protection of the ADA, and that a question of fact existed as to whether the plaintiff's discharge had been discriminatory. The court also noted that the plaintiff's mentor at the firm kept in a personal file a document entitled "Disability income proposal for [Mr. Doe]." This and other circumstantial evidence created a question of fact as to whether the plaintiff had been discharged in order to "interfere with the vesting of [his] disability plan" with the firm, a clear violation of ERISA. Id. at 1324. The case later settled out of court after a four week trial.

Another well known case brought against a law firm by a gay associate was the 1993 case of Bowers v. Baker & McKenzie, 1993 WL 766865 (N.Y.Div. of Human Rights). Also disturbingly similar to the movie *Philadelphia*, this case involved Geoffrey Bowers's termination from the firm in 1986, which he alleged was motivated by the discovery of his homosexuality and his affliction with AIDS. Although the firm maintained that the firing was based on performance factors, the New York State Division of Human Rights, in its 1993 decision, awarded Bowers's estate damages amounting to $500,000 (Bowers died before he had a chance to see his case to trial). In 1994 New York University Law School's recruitment committee promised to ban the firm from recruiting on campus for a year if New York's Appellate Division upheld the case. When the parties settled before the case was appealed, the recruitment committee imposed the ban anyway. Edward W. Adams, NYU Bans Baker & McKenzie's New York Office From Recruiting, N.Y.L.J., March 14, 1995.

Unfortunately, a lawyer's concealment of sexual orientation out of fear of discrimination can have even more devastating emotional and other consequences than the discrimination itself. The death of New York lawyer David Schwartz is a chilling illustration of how a lawyer's "secret" life on the side can go wrong. Schwartz was a partner at Cravath, Swaine & Moore, earning about $2.5 million a year. In November of 1992, he was murdered in a Bronx motel room by an eighteen-year-old man whom he had picked up and who claimed he killed Schwartz in self defense after Schwartz made a sexual overture to him. Only after his death did his partners, colleagues and friends realize that Schwartz was gay. See Rita Henley Jensen, The Private Life and Public Death of David Schwartz, Nat'l L. J., Jan. 25, 1993.

In the past decade, the federal and many state governments have taken an active stand against discrimination on account of sexual orientation. Many states have passed legislation prohibiting such discrimination in employment, housing and other basic economic relationships. In 1996, an Oregon trial court ruled that denial of spousal benefits to lesbian couples violated state law. Brown v. Starbucks Corp., Civil No. 96–269–MA (July 1, 1996).

D.   PARTNERS

"Power in Trust", from Louis Auchincloss, Powers of Attorney (1955).

When Clitus Tilney heard Tower, Tilney & Webb criticized as a "law factory" and its opinions described as "assembly line products," it did not bother him in the least. He knew the fashion among lawyers to affect an aversion to administrative detail, to boast that their own firms were totally disorganized, that they practiced law in a bookish, informal atmosphere, suggestive of Victorian lithographs of county solicitors seated at rolltop desks and listening with wise smiles to the problems of youth and beauty. But he also knew, from his own early days, the price paid for that kind of atmosphere: clerks unpromoted and underpaid, or kept dangling in the hope of partnership until they were too old to get other jobs, aged partners grabbing too much of the profits, an office staff bullied by those spoiled old tartars whom the hoodwinked regarded sentimentally as "treasures." And he knew what disorganization did to overhead. It might be feasible in a firm of twenty lawyers, but when Tilney had joined Tower & Strong it already numbered thirty-four, and now, under his leadership, it had risen to seventy. These, with a staff of a hundred, occupied two great gleaming floors in a new glass cube at 65 Wall Street, with modern paintings and a marble spiral staircase and a reception hall paneled in white and gold. It had not been enough for Tilney to make himself the finest securities lawyer in New York. For every sixty minutes dedicated to the law he had to devote twenty to administration. He had to be a housekeeper, a headmaster, a führer.

His only concession to the other school was that he looked like one of them. He had a large, shaggy grey head and a strong, furrowed, pensive face, and his bulging shoulders and thick frame, usually covered in unpressed tweed, were supported on long thin legs and matchstick ankles. But whether he was being charming as an after-dinner speaker, or stern with troublemakers at a stockholders' meeting, or whimsically philosophical with the chosen group of his favorite clerks, his "disciples," as they were known in the office, he liked to think that his associates recognized that, however speculative and adventurous they found his mind, it was still an instrument capable of recalling the difference in price between roller towels and evaporating units for the washrooms.

Every leader must be prepared to tolerate expressions of individuality where they are harmless or even useful, and Tilney had had the wisdom to interfere as little as possible with such prima donnas as the litigators. But there was one member of the firm in whose continued independence of action he saw something more dangerous than the theatrical gesticulations dear to the hearts of trial lawyers. Francis Hyde, a thin, bald, bony, long-jawed old bachelor, as morose as he was dusty, represented that almost extinct species, the nonspecialist lawyer. He would take on anything, without consulting his partners, from a corporate reorganization to a scandalous murder trial, and he blandly regarded Tilney's reorganized firm, in which he found himself a rare survivor from the old Tower days, as a mere depot to supply him with stationery and law clerks. Worse still, he made no secret of his contempt for the senior partner's high concept of the role of the bar in modern society. Lawyers to Francis Hyde were simple opportunists, and he considered as hypocrites those who argued otherwise. A client's case was no more than the hand that he had been dealt. Whether or not he could win it was an elementary question of skill, as in the bridge rubbers that he played night after night over too many whiskeys in the Hone Club where he had lived for thirty-five years.

"When he came to Tower & Strong we were a law firm," Hyde used sneeringly to say of Clitus Tilney. "Now we're a boys' church school."

Matters between the two were brought to a crisis on the spring outing at the Glenville Beach Club. As Tilney was passing through the bar, after playing his eighteen holes of golf, he noticed a little group of associates, still in their city clothes, who must have been passing the beautiful morning drinking in their dark cool corner, and his lips tightened with the disgust of one whose faith was in hard play when it was not in hard work. It did not surprise him to spot Francis Hyde's gleaming pate at the end of the table, the only partner in the nonathletic little group. As Tilney paused now, perspiring freely, his sweater and flannels a reproach to their urban darkness, all the eyes at the table turned on him. But if there was in Tilney's gaze, unconcealed by his perfunctory grin, some of the sternness of Abraham contemplating Sodom, there was no corresponding guilt in those answering eyes. To his surprise and indignation he found himself surveyed as if he were something quaint and ridiculous, a sort of vaudeville charac-ter, vaguely suggestive of Edwardian sports and fatuity, of blazers and straw hats and boating on rivers. They might have expected him to tip his hat forward over one eyebrow, tuck a cane under his arm, wink and burst into a song about playing the game. It came over him that they must have been actually talking about him, for the sudden silence of their concerted stare conveyed an awkward sense of interruption.

"I don't know what I'm going to do about these fellows, Clitus," Hyde called over in his harsh nasal tone. "All they want to do is booze. How are they ever going to make the varsity team in Tower, Tilney?"

The laugh that followed had the boldness of a rebel group that has found at last a leader. Tilney turned aside without a word and pursued his way to the locker room. But in that brief moment he had made, and made finally, his grim decision. He could no longer afford to wait for Hyde's retirement.

There was considerable discussion in Wall Street at just this time over the contested will of Harry P. Granger, the president of a great drug firm, who had left an estate of forty million, half to his widow and half to the Granger Foundation. He had had no children, but a sister, Mrs. Crimmins, a whining, petulant creature whose six sons had been educated by the decedent and who had herself been provided for in his lifetime, had chosen to attack the will as the product of undue influence. Tilney had followed the proceedings with a lively interest because Mrs. Granger, the widow, had been a childhood friend of his in Ulrica, a small, upstate town.

"We have an interesting situation here," he announced at the weekly partners' lunch in a private dining room at the Down Town Association. "This Crimmins woman is making a tour of the big firms looking for someone shady enough to take her case. It really puts it up to them, because no matter how little she has to go on, she can always settle for something."

"What makes you so sure she has nothing to go on?" Waldron Webb, the senior litigator, demanded. "If you were a court lawyer, Clitus, you'd learn not to be so positive."

"But I knew Harry Granger well," Tilney explained. "A violent man, but an utterly sane one. And one who knew exactly what he wanted to do with every penny he'd earned."

"Well, if she has no case, why should the executors settle? Or do you just assume they can't be bothered to work for their commissions?"

"No, it's not that. I know the executors. They're all right. But nobody likes to take chances with forty million bucks. Haven't you always told me, Waldron, that juries are unpredictable? Besides, it may be cheaper to pay Mrs. Crimmins off than to win the case. While it's going on, the executors can't qualify. That means there has to be a temporary administration, and the Granger Drug Company, which Harry controlled, would be run in the Surrogate's Court. Any businessman knows that a few months of that would cost more than even a whacking settlement. It's simply another example of the way our law favors the grabbers and shysters."

At this point the nasal drawl of Francis Hyde came down the table to Tilney's astonished ears: "It may interest you to know, Clitus, that you have just described a client of this office as a grabber and one of your own partners as a shyster. I agreed only last night to represent Mrs. Crimmins in her honest efforts to rectify the injustice done her by her brother's will."

In the profound silence that followed, Tilney knew that every eye at the table was on him. But he stared back only at Hyde, fascinated by the bleak cynicism in the latter's long, arrogant leathery face. "Do you think you should have made that decision without consulting the firm?" he asked now in a mild tone. "Do you think you should have taken on a client so controversial without asking your partners?"

"She's only controversial to you, Clitus," Hyde retorted, "because you've made up your mind about her case without knowing the facts. I wonder if she appears so bad to the rest of us." He turned now to address the table. "Here's a man with one of the great fortunes of the city, who cuts out his closest blood relative to leave more to his widow than she could ever spend. Who are we to say that his only sister isn't entitled to her day in court?" He paused for effect and then actually dared to wink. "Particularly when I've taken her on a contingent fee basis under which we are to receive fifty percent of any recovery." There was a gasp around the table. "Some of you gentlemen who thought that Clitus was a bit grandiose in moving into our sumptuous new quarters may be less inclined to slam our expensive front door in the face of a poor supplicant like Mrs. Crimmins."

Tilney glanced around the table and saw at once that his partners were not prepared to condemn Hyde. It was not only that the new rent was high; they were not inclined to take moral issues seriously where women were the litigants. In his sudden violent anger he knew he would go too far. "Look," he said curtly, "it's a question of what you are, what you stand for. It depends on what your philosophy of being a lawyer is. Do you want to be the kind of person who helps society to make a better thing of itself, or do you want to make your money out of simple blackmail?"

This was followed by an outburst from the whole table.

"Really, Clitus," Morris Madison, the senior tax partner objected, "isn't that a bit rough on Frank? Is it so unreasonable for the closest blood relative to expect *some* remembrance in an estate of that size?"

"I think these foundations get entirely too much anyhow," Waldron Webb broke in. "It's become a racket."

"Wouldn't the sister have taken half the estate if there'd been no will?" somebody asked.

"But there *was* a will," Tilney exclaimed impatiently. "It's only a question of what Harry Granger wanted to do with his money. And it's clear as daylight that he didn't want to leave Mrs. Crimmins a red cent!"

"But you're begging the question," Madison pointed out reasonably. "How do you know that Granger was in the full possession of his faculties when he signed the will?"

"Because I knew Granger!" Tilney almost shouted. "Anyone who knew Granger knew that he was sane!"

The constrained silence that followed this second explosion was of a painful duration. It was almost a relief to everybody to have it broken, even by Francis Hyde's mocking tone. "However well our friend Clitus knew the late Mr. Granger, he obviously did not know him well enough to be his lawyer. And that would be the only thing that would keep me from accepting Mrs. Crimmins' retainer. Does anyone but Mr. Tilney disagree with me?"

Tilney, correctly reading his defeat in the renewal of silence around him, was unable to resist a last fling at his opponent. "If I know Margaret Granger, you may have bitten off more than you can chew. I doubt if *she*'ll settle, even if it costs her double to lick you!"

"With admirable foresight the late Mr. Granger did not make his widow an executor," Hyde retorted, smiling down the table. "I have two very realistic officers of the Granger Drug Company to deal with. You said yourself, Clitus, that they were all right. But I tell you what. If I settle this case for a penny under four hundred grand—which is a mere one percent of the gross estate—I'll be glad to tender you my resignation from the firm."

"You'd better be careful," Tilney muttered grimly. "I just may accept it."

For several minutes thereafter there was no sound at the table but the chink of silver and the lapping of soup, and the dirty joke with which Waldron Webb at length broke the silence was greeted with a burst of relieved laughter.

The next months were terrible ones for Clitus Tilney. Hyde initiated in the Surrogate's Court a lengthy series of pre-trial examinations, or what was known in the legal world as a "fishing expedition." He examined and re-examined, with exhaustive and exhausting care, the three witnesses to Mr. Granger's will, but he uncovered nothing but the fact that the decedent had drunk two cocktails—*after* the execution of the document. He interrogated the servants in the house, the nurses and doctors who had attended Granger's last illness, and the employees of the drug company whom the president had known personally. He showed particular interest in any evidence of the frequent manifestations of the decedent's lively temper. But above all he procrastinated. He complained to the court about his difficulties in rounding up witnesses; he pleaded illnesses and accidents; he insisted mysteriously that he was on the trail of new leads. He made motion after motion and appealed from decisions denying them. As Tilney put it disgustedly to his wife, the whole procedure, written up, would have made a perfect textbook for incipient shysters in the art of delaying tactics. The surrogate was impatient, the press caustic and the executors and their counsel livid, but time passed, and time, of course, was Hyde's trump card.

Reaching deeper and deeper into waters that he himself had muddied, Hyde at last plucked out one small, faintly wriggling eel, in the form of a modest trust fund that Granger had set up years before for a retired actress who had presumably been at one point his mistress. By showing that his client, Mrs. Crimmins, had been a friend of the actress, Hyde sought to establish a basis for Mrs. Granger's "psychopathic hatred" of her sister-in-law and her reason for "hounding the decedent until he had removed his sister from the will." At this point Mrs. Granger, driven to exasperation by her own long interrogations, snapped in answer to one of Hyde's sneering questions that Mrs. Crimmins was "a cheat and a liar." The words hit the headlines of the evening papers, and people began to shrug and say that the case was simply a mud-slinging competition between two angry women. When Hyde announced confidentially at a firm lunch that he had received a settlement offer of half a million, Tilney, sick at heart, assumed that all was over.

That evening he and his wife went to a private harpsichord concert in an old brownstone on lower Park Avenue. He had hoped that the music would settle his nerves, but he found that the twanging exasperated him, and he slipped out to the dining room where the butler, an old friend, gave him a whiskey and soda. He had settled down to drink it when he saw approaching him across the empty chamber the small, neat, grey, compact figure of Margaret Granger. So might Queen Victoria have crossed a room, with dignity, with intent, with relentlessness. As he rose to greet her, he noticed how everything about her, her pale round unpowdered cheeks, her thin pale, set lips, her straight grey hair held in a knot in back, her simple satin grey dress and slippers, her single strand of tiny pearls, proclaimed, and proclaimed sincerely, that her money was but a burden and a duty.

"Sit down, Clitus," she said severely, "I want to have a word with you." They sat facing each other, on two high-backed Italian chairs, while she eyed him for a cool moment. "I'd like to know what you think you're up to."

"I'm up to very little. My partner, Mr. Hyde, seems to be up to more."

"He's a disgrace to the bar!"

Tilney glanced stealthily to his left and right and then leaned forward to whisper hoarsely: "I agree with you!"

"No, Clitus, I won't let you joke your way out of this. I really won't. He's your partner, and you should have stopped him. You owed me that much, as an old friend."

"I tried, Margaret, believe me. My partners wouldn't go along."

"I thought you were the senior."

"There's a limit to what we seniors can do."

"Well, I don't understand it," she said, shaking her head. "But I should think there was some way a man in your position could have stopped it. And now I suppose you'll get a large fee?"

"Hyde gets no fee at all if he loses the case, and he can't possibly win if you fight. What's all this settlement talk? Have your lawyers lost their guts?"

Mrs. Granger was taken aback by his sudden offensive.

"They tell me it costs less to settle. No matter how sure we are of winning."

"And is costing less the only criterion?" Tilney protested. "Is there no moral issue involved?"

"You talk to me of moral issues, Clitus!" she exclaimed indignantly. "You, the partner of a man who's dragged my poor Harry's name through the mire!"

"Yes, *I* talk to you of moral issues, Margaret!" he retorted. "I have the unmitigated gall, if you will, to remind you of your moral obligation, as Harry's widow, not to give away a penny of his hard-earned money to his swindling sister."

Mrs. Granger really gaped at this. "Your *client*," she murmured in astonishment. "Is that the way you talk about your clients?"

"When I tell you that it could get me into the hottest kind of water with the Bar Association, will you believe I'm sincere?"

Mrs. Granger leaned over now to rest her small hand for just a moment on top of his large one. "Oh, Clitus, my good old friend, forgive me. Tell me what I should do." Her voice trembled. "Everyone keeps telling me it's best to settle the wretched thing. They talk about the publicity and the cost, and they tell me that Harry's foundation will pay Mrs. Crimmins out of its half of the estate, so it won't make any difference to me anyway. But I don't *care* about the publicity and the cost. And I don't care about who pays what. All I care is that Harry's horrible sister and her horrible lawyer should not be rewarded for what they've done to his memory. And I know that Harry would gladly have paid out his last dollar to lick them!"

"You believe that?"

"Passionately!" she exclaimed and clasped her hands together. "Oh, Clitus, tell me what to do."

He hesitated a moment. "Do you still walk your poodles in the park in the early morning?"

She stared. "Yes. Every morning at seven."

"I'll meet you tomorrow at seven. At the Ninetieth Street gate."

They both rose in startled guilt at the sudden burst of applause from the next room. It was the intermission.

Tilney, of course, had made a careful study of the Granger will. It was a simple document, perfectly designed by competent counsel to effectuate the testator's twofold design: to provide sumptuously for his widow and to deprive the United States of its last penny of tax. The primary function of the Granger Foundation, at least in the mind of its benefactor, was less the study of incurable diseases than keeping the money away from the federal bureaucrats. And so the forty millions had been divided neatly in half, without a single outside bequest: twenty outright to the Granger Foundation, and twenty in trust to the widow for her life and then to the

Foundation. But to qualify the widow's trust for the widow's tax exemption it had been necessary for Granger's lawyers to give her a power to dispose of her trust by will. Of course, it was understood between her and her husband that she would not exercise this power and that on her death the foundation would come into possession of the reunited halves of the estate, still virgin to the tax collector. Nonetheless, she had it. She had it, and on this Tilney had based his little plan.

The morning of his meeting with Mrs. Granger was a bright mild day of early spring, and seated on a park bench watching the pigeons and squirrels, Tilney felt as exhilarated as a young man at a romantic assignation. He jumped up when he saw her approaching, with her three absurd miniature poodles, and, taking the dogs' leashes, led her to a bench.

"Give me the little darlings, Margaret, and take this pencil and paper. I want to dictate a letter of just three lines. To the Director of the Granger Foundation. Of course, you will wish to add your own embellishments. But so long as the final version contains the gist of my message, we'll be all right, and Frank Hyde will be all wrong."

"Dear Clitus," she murmured affectionately as she sat down, "what a true friend you are. I wonder if having my faith restored in you isn't worth as much to me as frustrating Mrs. Crimmins."

"You can have both," he assured her as she took the pad and pencil and waited. "Now then. 'Dear Bill or Jim, or whatever you call him: This is to inform you of my irrevocable decision.'" He paused and smiled while she hastily scribbled. "'If a single penny of my husband's estate, or any money previously contributed by him to the Granger Foundation, is, under any circumstances whatever, given to Mrs. Crimmins ...'" He paused again, this time even longer than was needed.

"Go on, Clitus!"

"'I will immediately execute a new will, by the terms of which the entire principle of my trust will be given to charities *other* than the Granger Foundation.'"

Mrs. Granger scribbled busily until she had finished, but when she looked up, she was frowning. "I couldn't do it. I gave Harry my word."

"And, of course, I wouldn't ask you to break it. But you never promised Harry you wouldn't do a little bluffing, did you? You never gave him your word that you wouldn't try to trick his foundation into showing a little backbone?"

"No," she said doubtfully. "I didn't. The matter never came up. Do you think he'd have approved of that kind of stratagem?"

"I think he'd have been tickled pink. I think he'd have clapped his hands and shouted!"

"And you really think this ..." She glanced down at the pad on which she had scribbled his message. "You really think it will work?"

"It will work like a charm. Can you imagine a foundation tossing away twenty sure millions to save a possible few hundred grand? They're not madmen, you know. Even if they suspected you were bluffing, how would they dare take the chance that you weren't?"

As the beauty of the scheme sank into her mind, she smiled at last at this vision of the perfect weapon. "But then it will cost your firm a great fee," she protested. "Is there any way I can make it up to you? Can *I* give you a fee?"

Tilney threw back his head with a roar of laughter. "My dear Margaret, what sort of crook do you take me for? Haven't I been unethical enough for one day?" He rose and reached out a hand. "Come now. Go home and write that letter. Make me proud of you. That's all the fee I could ever ask."

The next days were delectable ones for Tilney. He never missed the chance, passing Hyde in a corridor, to boom a hearty question at him as to how the great case was going, and he would chuckle loudly at the other's evasive and discomfited answers. After a fortnight had passed, he felt that it was time, at a firm lunch, to call down the table to Hyde for a report on the Granger case.

"When you last spoke of it," he added, "you told us it was as good as settled. Has the agreement been signed?"

Hyde stared back at him with unconcealed malevolence. "I suppose the word's out by now that the settlement has fallen through." He snorted in disgust as he directed a less baleful stare around the table at the other partners. "I was going to tell you all today, anyway. Frankly, gentlemen, it's the dangdest thing that's ever happened to me. The agreement was all hashed out, typed and ready to sign. We'd even told the surrogate about it in chambers. And then, whambo, somebody gets cold feet, the widow or the foundation, and refuses to go through with it. Oh, I can tell you, their counsel's face was *really* red. Old John Gales, of Gales & Martin, admitted to me he was thunderstruck. He actually apologized!"

"What are they trying to do ?" Waldron Webb demanded hotly. "Shake you down a hundred grand at the last moment? It's the most unscrupulous thing I ever heard!"

"That may be it, I don't know. But Gales says they won't settle for a penny. Somebody seems to have got religion on the Granger Foundation."

"In that case, what do we do now?" Tilney demanded, frowning. "Fold our tents and steal away?"

"No such luck, Clitus," Hyde retorted angrily. "If it's a fight they want, they'll get a fight. And if it's dirt they want, they'll get their fill!"

"That's a pleasant prospect," said Tilney with an acid smile. "But first of all, there's one little matter that I feel obliged to bring to the attention of the firm. I note on the monthly statement that more than thirteen thousand dollars of cash disbursements have been charged to Mrs. Crimmins' account. Of course, I understand that the fee basis is contingent, and that we get nothing if we lose, but you must surely know, Frank, that lawyers can't pay clients' disbursements. Isn't that champerty?"

"What am I expected to do? Mrs. Crimmins hasn't got that kind of money."

"Well, Mrs. Crimmins had better find it, I'm afraid," Tilney continued in a sharper tone. "She'd better beg, borrow or steal it. The firm has suffered enough from the bad publicity of this case without having the Grievance Committee of the City Bar breathing down our neck. In the meanwhile I have given the cashier instructions that no further sums are to be charged to that account."

"Does that mean," Hyde demanded irately, "that I can no longer sign a chit for a taxi to go to court?"

"It means precisely that. If you go to court on the Granger case."

Hyde pushed his chair roughly back and strode from the room while the partners exchanged uneasy glances.

"Does anyone think I'm wrong?" Tilney demanded in his highest, most challenging tone. "Does anyone want to see us continue in champertous practices?"

"I'm sure nobody thinks you're wrong, Clitus," Morris Madison put in his reasonable tone. "But I do think it was a bit rough on Frank, springing it that way. He'll have to make up those disbursements out of his own pocket."

"Well, I don't want to know about it if he does," Tilney exclaimed. "It's just as bad for him to do it as the firm."

"You won't know it," Madison said quietly. "He'll simply deposit the money in Mrs. Crimmins' checking account, and she'd pay us. Frank may love his booze, and me may be crusty, but he'll give a client the shirt off his back. And he's not a rich man, either."

"You're breaking my heart," Tilney sneered, and he was defiantly glad to note, taking in the table with a rapid glance as he lowered his head over his soup bowl, that he had shocked them all.

Hyde was good to his word about giving the Granger estate a fight full of dirt, and the trial attracted even more publicity than the pre-trial hearings. Tilney was sure that his partner had privately hired a press agent and fervently prayed that the latter's bill would be a large one. But for all the dirt and the headlines, for all the weeks of idle testimony, for all the tricks and chicaneries, the defense remained adamant. The legal world found such intransigence hard to understand. It was widely rumored that Hyde had offered to settle for less than half the sum originally rendered him, and the executors made no secret of their dissatisfaction at having their hands tied by legatees. The other stockholders of the Granger Drug Company, worried by the effect of the delayed probate on the affairs of the corporation, had appealed in vain to the widow, and an editorial appeared in a morning paper questioning the right of a charitable foundation to spend more of its money in litigation than a settlement would cost. It was no use. The board of trustees of the Granger Foundation, with a disregard of public opinion unique in the gentle field of charities, issued a statement to the press that because of "the aspersions cast on the name of their distinguished founder," not even a nominal settlement would be considered.

After that Hyde's case, if case it could be really called, collapsed. When he had called the last of his witnesses, the estate moved for a directed verdict which the surrogate granted. Six weeks later the Appellate Division unanimously rejected Hyde's appeal and denied him leave to appeal higher. Two months after that the Court of Appeals in Albany refused to hear his appeal, and Harry P. Granger's fortune was safe at last from the attacks of his sister and her embittered counsel. Clitus Tilney felt a greater exultation in his heart than he had known at the most splendid of his firm's past triumphs.

Only a week after the end of the Granger case Tilney was dressing at home to attend a dinner at the Bar association in honor of the visiting Lord Chancellor of England. Ada Tilney, whose high pale brow under her faded straight brown hair, parted in the middle in mid-Victorian fashion, was like a rock washed clean by the years of his absences, absences at conventions, testimonial dinners, committee meetings, or simply at the office, sat beside his dresser, fitting the pearl studs in his shirt.

"I left something on the bureau for you," she said in her placid tone. "Have you seen it yet?"

Tilney noticed a magazine, folded open under his silver-handled hairbrush, and picked it up. It was the *Gotham Gazette*, a periodical sent out free to addresses east of Central Park for the sake of the fashionable advertising. Tilney saw the title of an article, "Early-morning Dog-walking" and beneath it a small photograph of Mrs. Granger and her poodles. Behind her, of course, loomed himself, although he was not identified in the caption which read: "Mrs. Harry P. Granger, widow of the drug magnate, is up and out with her 'toy' poodles as early as seven o'clock."

"Most women seem to have trouble with their husbands going out at night," Ada continued. "It's so like you to make time for infidelity only in the early morning."

"Ada, you're wonderful!" he exclaimed with a chuckle as he tossed the magazine in the scrap basket. "Let me tell you something funny about that picture. There *is* someone who might make trouble about it. But that someone doesn't happen to be you."

"Still another woman, no doubt."

"No, a man."

The sudden hint of grimness in his tone aroused her apprehension. "Oh, Clitus, does it have something to do with that horrible case? Is it Frank Hyde?"

"It's Frank, all right." He took his shirt from her. "But do you know something, Ada? I'm a man who's missed two wars. Too young for the first and too old for the second. I've always wondered how I would have behaved under fire. Well, tonight perhaps, I shall find out."

"But surely Frank would never see a silly magazine like that?"

"There are those in the office who would be only too glad to send it to him. Besides, it's elementary in military intelligence to assume that the enemy knows anything he *could* have known."

As Tilney entered the long somber portrait-lined reception hall of the Bar Association, filled with black ties and grey heads, Chambers Todd, straight nosed, square jawed, black haired, the "business getting" partner of the office, came up to complain about Hyde.

"He's over there, talking to Judge Caulkins," he said with a brief nod of his head towards a corner. "He's half plastered already. Something's got to be done about him, Clitus. He's giving the firm a terrible black eye. Suppose he passes out at an affair like this?"

But nothing could dull the curious sense of elation that his little talk with Ada had given Tilney. "It wouldn't be what Madison Avenue calls a good 'image,' would it?" he asked with a rumbling laugh. "Think of it. Whenever the words 'Tower, Tilney & Webb' are uttered, the picture flashed on the mental screen is one of an elderly man, inebriated, sinking slowly to his knees."

"I'm glad you find it so funny," Todd retorted.

"Leave him to me, Chambers. I'll go and speak to him now."

As Tilney approached, Judge Caulkins greeted him with the fulsomeness of one anxious to escape an embarrassing colloquy. Hyde, swaying slightly, stared after the retreating jurist with narrowed eyes. He did not look at Tilney.

"What do *you* want?" he muttered.

"I'd like to persuade you to shift to soda water. Just until dinner, old man."

"Don't 'old man' me. You had the gall to talk to me about champerty. What about betraying one's own client? Which is worse?" Hyde turned suddenly on Tilney and almost shouted as he repeated the question. "Which?"

"Do you imply that I betrayed a client?" Tilney asked calmly. "Whom?"

"You tricked Mrs. Crimmins out of a half a million bucks! By some kind of rinky-dink with Mrs. Granger. What do you think the Grievance Committee will think of *that*?"

"Ask them."

Hyde steadied himself against the back of the sofa. "Do you know how many copies of that picture I found on my desk this morning? *Three!*"

"My wife had one for me," Tilney announced with a laugh. "She had a couple of questions herself." His spirits rose to a peak as he felt the dizzy joy of danger, and he regretted the wars he had missed. "But if you think you can make something out of my old friendship with Margaret Granger, by all means go ahead. Drag the poor woman to the Grievance Committee. Drag me. And don't blame anyone but Francis Hyde when you've made the biggest fool of yourself in all New York!"

Hyde's watery eyes began to twitch. He glanced around at the bar. "I think I'll get myself one more little drink before we go in."

Tilney laughed again, an elated laugh, as he saw that he had won. And won, too, not in the sneaky way of his conference in the park, but with all his cards on the table. There was bluffing indeed! But the foe had not only to be routed; he had to be destroyed. "Tarry, Frank," he called softly after him, and the other turned back in surprise. "You and I can't go on this way. You have threatened me, and we can no longer be partners. You promised to resign from the firm if you lost the Granger case. I should like to invoke that promise now."

Hyde's eyes peered at Tilney as if he had not fully grasped his meaning. "Have you discussed this with the firm?"

"They can choose between you and me."

"I see." Hyde nodded vaguely. "Between you and me."

"I would assume that an adequate pension would be arranged for which ever has to go."

"An adequate pension," Hyde mumbled with a thickening tone. "Yes, no doubt."

Tilney watched him as he ambled off to the bar, and for the first time it occurred to him that Hyde might be an object of pity. He seemed old now and frail, and the prospect of lonely days as well as nights at the Hone Club seemed dismal enough. Still, there might be work that the firm could send him, or legal aid, or committee work for the Bar Association, or even writing law review articles. And the pension would be adequate; he would see to that.

He saw that Hyde was arguing with the bartender, who was reluctant to give him another drink. The dining room doors were open, and the guests were beginning to move forward.

"Look at him, Clitus! Shall I take him home?"

It was Todd again at his elbow, and Tilney in a single grim second saw all the fatuity of his own reasoning. Frank Hyde was doomed to a lonely, miserable, alcoholic old age, and nothing on earth was going to alter that doom. But was it any sadder than the withering of a leaf or the eating of flesh by carnivores? The senior partner of Tower, Tilney & Webb had not created the universe.

"Oh, God, there he goes!" moaned Todd as Hyde fell suddenly forward on the bar table. The noise was slight and attracted only the notice of those in the immediate vicinity, but when Hyde tried to get up his right arm suddenly swept a whole tray of glasses to the floor, and the hideous crash brought silence to the entire vast chamber.

"There's your image, Todd!" Tilney called after the younger man who was hurrying to help their fallen partner. He resisted the impulse to go himself. He would spare Hyde the final mortification of having the victor help him to his feet. It was probably the last mortification that it would be in his power to spare him.

QUESTIONS

1. Hyde took a very weak case on a fifty percent contingency with the hopes that Mrs. Granger and the Foundation would settle for a relatively small amount rather than bear the costs of litigation. Was Hyde's conduct ethical? (See discussion of frivolous litigation in Chapter 1, supra). Is Tilney right in describing this case as "simple blackmail?"

2. For Tilney to avoid complicity with Hyde's conduct, he would have risked an open rupture with the other partners of the firm. How far should a lawyer, and particularly a managing partner, go to confront wrongdoing at the outset? Did Tilney fulfill his obligations to the firm when he allowed Hyde to proceed with the case? Should Tilney have reported Hyde's conduct to the Bar? See *Wieder v. Skala*, supra.

3. Tilney denounces a client of his firm, gives advice to his client's adversary, and destroys Hyde by tricking him into resignation from Tower, Tilney & Webb. However, Tilney has prevented Hyde from extracting a settlement from a meritless lawsuit. Does this end justify the means that Tilney uses?

4. Tilney's motives in betraying his firm's client, Mrs. Crimmins, have nothing to do with money; indeed, the firm would have realized a substantial fee if the case had settled as Hyde anticipated it would. What factors besides money influence how law firm partners act?

5. Intrafirm power struggles may influence the quality of service given to a client, and, in cases such as this one, even the firm's loyalty to a client. In what other cases in this casebook did office politics cause lawyers to act unethically?

6. Did Hyde make "reasonable efforts to expedite litigation consistent with the interests of the client?" See Model Rule 3.2 and cmt. ("[r]ealizing financial or other benefit from otherwise improper delay in litigation is not a legitimate interest of the client.") Are there any circumstances in which delay can be an ethical strategy in litigation?

7. Was it ethical for Hyde to give the Grangers a "fight full of dirt" in the press? See Model Rule 3.6(a) ("A lawyer shall not make an extrajudicial statement that a reasonable person would expect to be disseminated by means of public communication if the lawyer knows or reasonably should know that it will have a substantial likelihood of materially prejudicing an adjudicative proceeding.")

8. Was it appropriate for Hyde or the firm to advance expenses to Mrs. Crimmins? (Compare DR 5–103(b) with Model Rule 1.8(e)(1), and see discussion of fee arrangements in Chapter 1, supra).

Substance Abuse in the Legal Profession

Hyde's conduct in the Granger matter is clearly affected by his abuse of alcohol. His partners do little to confront Hyde with his problem, even though they are embarrassed when he drinks too heavily at the Bar Association. Indeed, Tilney appears to gloat in Hyde's sickness, knowing that alcohol abuse will impair Hyde's professional judgment and hurry his departure from the firm.

Nonetheless, lawyers who ignore substance abuse by other lawyers in their firm do so at substantial risk. If alcoholism or other forms of substance abuse result in malpractice and other types of unethical conduct, all of the lawyers with whom an abuser practices are at risk. Productivity declines, clients are lost, the firm's reputation suffers, and, in egregious circumstances, the partners can each be personally liable for damages caused by the professional misconduct of a colleague whom they should have confronted long before. Substance abuse may be involved in as many as 50 to 75 percent of major disciplinary cases. See Report of the AALS Special Committee on Problems of Substance Abuse in the Law Schools, 44 J. Legal Educ. 35 (1994). Oregon's Professional Liability Fund has estimated that more than half of attorneys admitted to its alcohol treatment program have already been sued for malpractice. Charles J. Santangelo & Donald W. Morrison, Alcohol Abuse on the Rise Among Lawyers: Stress at Work Takes Its Toll, 209 N.Y.L.J. 5 (1993).

Furthermore, substance abuse is a common way of dealing with the stress that comes from practicing law. Professionals, including lawyers, have difficulties with alcohol as much as 30 times as often as the general population, and it has been estimated that one-quarter of all practicing lawyers have a drug or alcohol problem. Id. A study in Washington State concluded that as many as 18 percent of lawyers there may be dependent on alcohol. AALS Special Committee on Problems of Substance Abuse, supra at 35. Alcohol is often readily available not only at bar associations but inside the offices of many law firms (the Association of the Bar of the City of New York regularly arranges for a full bar to be available at evening committee meetings; this perquisite of membership on any committee of the Association does not go unused).

In order to encourage lawyers to avail themselves of assistance programs, many of which focus on drug and alcohol abuse, the ABA House of Delegates in 1991 amended Model Rule 8.3, Reporting Professional Misconduct, to protect from disclosure information gained by a lawyer while working with a lawyer assistance program. It has also been suggested that there is an affirmative duty to report lawyers who are impaired by substance abuse:

> At first glance, it may appear to be time for a new Model Rule that specifically deals with impaired lawyers. It could include, for example,

providing ethical penalties for failure to report an impaired colleague to [a lawyer assistance program (LAP)]. The fact is, however, that most of the provisions necessary to achieve these goals already are in place. What is lacking is a major commitment on the part of the entire bar to effectively self-regulate. . . .

In writing about *In re Kersey*[10] for the ABA publication Litigation, associate editor Howard Gutman commented:

> The court also ignored the major villain: a local bar committed more to a skewered notion of friendship than to its oath and profession. How could lawyers and judges pretend for seven years not to notice the bloodshot eyes, peppermint breath, lost paperwork, blackouts, and missed court dates?

[Gutman, Drunk at the Bar, 13 Litigation 61 (1987).] Once Kersey could not control himself, others should have stopped him. The Board of Professional Responsibility should have sanctioned Kersey's so-called friends at the bar for choosing not to do so.

Why did not Kersey's so-called friends help? It is easy to place the blame on them. It is too easy, perhaps, because experience demonstrates that people generally are willing to help a friend with a problem. That is how friends and colleagues become trapped in the dilemma of "enabling" to begin with. Gutman's "skewered notion of friendship" demonstrates the insidious nature of alcoholism. It is highly unlikely that Kersey's friends and colleagues did not notice the changes in Kersey's behavior, personality, and professionalism. It is equally likely that they were without the knowledge and resources to successfully address the problem.

The current informal system of underfunded state and local bar organization programs is inadequate to confront a disease that affects more than ten percent of the bar (and perhaps as high as one in every five lawyers or more). The cost of identifying and offering help to lawyers afflicted with alcoholism cannot be viewed as a luxury. At the very least, lawyers are paying for their lack of concern with increased malpractice insurance premiums. An additional cost is the continual erosion of public confidence in the integrity of the bar. Even more important is the human cost, the damage to clients, the needless destruction of lawyers, their careers, and their families.

The conspiracy of silence surrounding lawyers and alcoholism must be broken. The time has come for a national policy which goes beyond acknowledging that alcoholism is a disease. The policy must advocate that the duty to report impaired lawyers is a critical element in self-regulation of the profession. Furthermore, it must advocate the use of

---

10. 520 A.2d 321 (D.C.App.1987) (alcoholic attorney's professional misconduct warranted disbarment, with execution of disbarment stayed and five years probation conditioned on total abstinence from use of alcohol and supervision of professional conduct and finances).

sanctions against lawyers who knowingly fail to meet this obligation of self-regulation. . . .

In purely human terms, we owe it to ourselves, as individuals and as a profession, to take care of our own."

Michael A. Bloom and Carol Lynn Wallinger, Lawyers and Alcoholism: Is it Time for a New Approach?, 61 Temp. L. Rev. 1409, 1428–29 (1988).

QUESTIONS

1. Do you have one or more law school classmates who appear to have trouble with alcohol or drugs? If so, what can you do to help?

2. Does a lawyer have an ethical obligation to help another lawyer who is having difficulty with alcohol or drugs?

Relevant Background

Supervising Other Attorneys

Law firm partners often claim that law school does not adequately prepare law students for practice. See Robert MacCrate, A Fresh Look at Lawyers' Education, 27 U. Rich. L. Rev. 21 (1992). Whether or not law schools could do a better job than they are now doing, it would be virtually impossible for law schools to fully prepare graduates for the complexities of legal practice. Much of a young lawyer's training will instead come from other attorneys in supervisory roles. Irwin D. Miller, Preventing Misconduct by Promoting the Ethics of Attorneys' Supervisory Duties, 70 Notre Dame L. Rev. 259, 266, 269 (1994).

Model Rule of Professional Conduct 5.1(a) states: "A partner in a law firm shall make reasonable efforts to ensure that the firm has in effect measures giving reasonable assurance that *all lawyers* in the firm conform to the Rules of Professional Conduct." (emphasis added). The meaning of "reasonable efforts" may depend on the type of firm; in small firms informal supervision may be enough, whereas large firms may have detailed supervisory procedures. See Model Rules of Professional Conduct 5.1 cmt. (1995).

Model Rule 5.1(b) states: "A lawyer having direct supervisory authority over another lawyer shall make reasonable efforts to ensure that the other lawyer conforms to the Rules of Professional Conduct." Although Rule 5.1(a) appears to cover only law firm partners, Rule 5.1(b) covers supervisory attorneys working for a variety of entities, including firms, government agencies, public interest groups and corporate law departments. Unlike Rule 5.1(a), Rule 5.1(b) does not impose on supervisory attorneys an entity-wide duty to ensure compliance. See Miller, supra at 278–283. A lawyer, however, is responsible for another lawyer's violations if the lawyer orders or ratifies the conduct involved. See Model Rule 5.1(c).

Supervising attorneys, however, are not always themselves in the right, and a subordinate lawyer must be willing to disobey orders from a superior if necessary. The subordinate lawyer thus is bound by rules of professional conduct notwithstanding directions from another person to the contrary. See Model Rule 5.2(a). However, "[a] subordinate lawyer does not violate rules of professional conduct if that lawyer acts in accordance with a supervisory lawyer's reasonable resolution of an arguable question of professional duty." Model Rule 5.2(b).

Discipline is sometimes, but not often, imposed on supervisory attorneys. In one case, a lawyer with two years of practice experience was left to fend for himself in a firm's new satellite office. He was subsequently suspended for neglecting a client's case and then falsifying documents to cover up his neglect. In re Yacavino, 100 N.J. 50, 57, 494 A.2d 801, 804 (N.J. 1985). Although the court did not discipline the supervising attorneys, it found that "[h]ad this young attorney received the collegial support and guidance expected of supervising attorneys, this incident might never have occurred." Id. In another case, an attorney was disbarred for neglecting his duties as administrator of an estate and commingling his own funds with funds of the estate. Although the disbarred attorney claimed that he had delegated the estate's affairs to an incompetent subordinate attorney, the Supreme Court of Illinois rejected this excuse. "An attorney cannot avoid his professional obligations to a client by the simple device of delegating work to others." In Re Weston, 92 Ill.2d 431, 437, 65 Ill.Dec. 925, 927, 442 N.E.2d 236, 238 (Ill. 1982)(citations omitted).

In 1993, the Association of the Bar of the City of New York suggested that supervision of lawyers would be facilitated if disciplinary sanctions were available against law firms as well as against individual lawyers. See Discipline of Law Firms, Report of the Committee on Professional Responsibility, 48 The Record of the Association of the Bar of the City of New York 628 (1993), reproduced in part in Chapter 12 infra. In 1996, New York adopted a disciplinary rule modeled on language proposed in this report. See Chapter 12 infra.

PROBLEM

1. You are a sole practitioner and give responsibility for most of your probate work to your legal secretary. He takes in money and writes checks on your client trust account. He gets behind and begins commingling funds from the trust account with your general account. Are you subject to discipline?

Sharing Profits

Although lawyers might enjoy their office environment more if they were more amenable to sharing profits with their partners, and perhaps with their associates as well, lawyers, like other people, sometimes resist sharing. Disputes over division of profits can make partners' meetings unpleasant and, if serious enough, can lead to dissolution of a firm. Occasionally, lawyers will abandon their partners in order to take a client or a large case for themselves. Clients sometimes are all too willing to facilitate such "grabbing and leaving."

Contingent-fee arrangements in particular can invite disputes.[11] First, a client may discover in the midst of litigation that his case is a lot stronger than at first believed and that another lawyer is willing to take the case for a lower percentage of judgment or settlement. Although the first lawyer may be winning her bet on the contingency, the client dismisses her and moves on. As Professor Wolfram correctly observes, "[t]he rule, which is now recognized in almost every state . . . is that a client's discharge of a lawyer ends the lawyer's right to recover on the contract of employment." Charles W. Wolfram, Modern Legal Ethics, 546 (1986). See Model Rule 1.16(a)(3) (providing that a lawyer shall not represent a client, and shall withdraw from a representation that has commenced, if the lawyer is discharged by the client); Model Code, DR 2–110(B)(4). Most jurisdictions award the discharged attorney *quantum meruit* recovery for the value of her services rendered. At most, the lawyer is entitled to a contingent percentage fee determined by a court either at the time of withdrawal or at the conclusion of the litigation. See Lai Ling Cheng v. Modansky Leasing Co., 73 N.Y.2d 454, 541 N.Y.S.2d 742, 539 N.E.2d 570 (N.Y.1989). In any event, the lawyer is likely to be paid less than she would have been if she had completed the representation.

The client's opportunity to take advantage of his lawyer in turn creates an opportunity for law partners to take advantage of each other by leaving their firms and encouraging one or more clients to follow. The temptation for a lawyer to do so is particularly high when the lawyer knows that a case is likely to result in a substantial judgment or settlement and that the client can fire and hire counsel at will. As Professor Hillman observes, ethical rules can act as "aids to grabbing and leaving." See Robert W. Hillman, Hillman On Lawyer Mobility, § 2.3 (1994).

One California case illustrates just the type of opportunistic conduct most feared by lawyers when their partners are working on a contingency. See Rosenfeld, Meyer & Susman v. Cohen, 146 Cal.App.3d 200, 194 Cal.Rptr. 180 (Ct.App.1983). Attorneys Cohen and Riorden spent five years working on an antitrust suit for Rectifier Corporation which was to pay their firm a contingent fee of one-third of recovery. Cohen and Riorden earned very little by way of fees for the firm during those five years, yet were paid their shares of the firm's profits under the partnership agreement. Then, as the antitrust case neared settlement, Cohen and Riorden demanded that the firm pay them double their share of profits from the antitrust suit. When the other partners refused, Cohen and Riorden resigned and formed a new firm. They asked Rectifier to fire their old firm and instead hire the new firm for a reduced 8 ¾% contingent fee. One year later, the litigation settled for $33 million. Client and lawyer opportunism thus came together to deprive Cohen and Riorden's partners of their share of the contingent fee.

---

11. The discussion of contingent-fee arrangements that follows is taken in part from Richard W. Painter, Symposium on Fee Shifting: Litigating on a Contingency: A Monopoly of Champions or a Market For Champerty?, 71 Chi. Kent. L. Rev. 625, 674–678 (1995).

The court held that Cohen and Riorden had breached their fiduciary duty to their partners both in wrongfully dissolving the old firm and in failing to complete Rectifier's case for the dissolved firm. This case is important not for its result, which in the end curtailed Cohen and Riorden's opportunistic conduct, but as an illustration of the difficulties that confront a firm in trying to control grabbing and leaving. Ethical rules prohibit the most obvious method of controlling such conduct, requiring the client to agree not to change lawyers. Furthermore, breach of fiduciary duty under a partnership agreement turns on facts specific to each case, making it difficult for either party to obtain summary judgment.

Most courts seek to discourage such "grabbing and leaving" by interpreting the Uniform Partnership Act to require that "attorneys' fees received on cases in progress upon dissolution of a law partnership are to be shared by the former partners according to their right to fees in the former partnership, regardless of which former partner provides legal services in the case after the dissolution. The fact that the client substitutes one of the former partners as attorney of record in place of the former partnership does not affect this result." Jewel v. Boxer, 156 Cal.App.3d 171, 203 Cal.Rptr. 13 (Ct.App.1984); accord Resnick v. Kaplan, 49 Md.App. 499, 434 A.2d 582, 588 (Md.Ct.Spec.App.1981).

Incentives to act opportunistically grow with the size of the case involved. It is the rare personal injury case that will make it worthwhile for a lawyer to leave his partners. However, larger cases present greater temptation. Furthermore, incentives to grab and leave intensify at larger firms where successful contingent-fee lawyers must share the fruits of their victories with a greater number of partners. Finally, even absent client or lawyer opportunism, a client's decision to change lawyers in a contingent-fee case is likely to create disputes between incoming and outgoing attorneys over the proper fee to be awarded to each.

Finally, law firm partners have an incentive to act opportunistically toward each other apart from the contingent fee context, often in circumstances surrounding the division of partnership profits. If a firm's partnership agreement divides profits according to a lock-step schedule of partnership shares, usually based on seniority at the firm or at the bar, older partners may slack off while taking the lion's share of the profits. Because younger partners usually resent such a scheme, many firms have switched to compensating partners based on billable hours, business generation and other contributions to overall firm profitability. See Marc Galanter & Thomas Palay, Tournament of Lawyers 53–54 (1991) (by around 1960, profits at most firms were divided "according to individualized shares, rather than a norm of equal participation"). Such schemes, however, are not without their own cost to a firm's collegiality, as intrafirm politics and struggles over clients can become instruments for increasing one's share of the profits.

Noncompetition Agreements

As far back as the eighteenth century, courts enforced restrictions on competition if they were found to be reasonable under a "rule of reason" test. E. Allan Farnsworth, Contracts § 5.3, 356 (2d ed. 1990). The Restatement of Contracts provides that covenants not to compete are valid if they are "ancillary to the selling of a business, to an employment contract, or to a partnership agreement." Restatement (Second) of Contracts § 188.

Nonetheless, Courts have historically rejected agreements which "restrict the right of an attorney to practice and the right of a client to choose representation." Kevin T. Caiaccio, Howard v. Babcock, The Business of Law Versus the Ethics of Lawyers: Are Noncompetition Covenants Among Law Partners Against Public Policy?, 28 Ga. L. Rev. 807 (1994). This approach was confirmed by the ABA Committee on Professional Ethics in Formal Opinion 300 (1961), which stated that restrictive noncompetition covenants among lawyers were per se violations of professional conduct rules. The ABA's growing animosity towards such covenants was further manifested in 1969 when it adopted DR 2–108, providing that:

> (A) A lawyer shall not be a party to or participate in a partnership or employment agreement with another lawyer that restricts the right of a lawyer to practice law after the termination of a relationship created by the agreement, except as a condition of retirement benefits.

> (B) In connection with the settlement of a controversy or suit, a lawyer shall not enter into an agreement that restricts his right to practice law.

Model Code, DR 2–108; see also Model Rule 5.6.

In Dwyer v. Jung, 133 N.J.Super. 343, 336 A.2d 498 (N.J.Super.Ct.Ch.Div.), aff'd per curiam, 137 N.J.Super. 135, 348 A.2d 208 (N.J.Super.Ct.App.Div.1975), the court applied DR 2–108(A) to nullify a partnership agreement that allocated a firm's clients among its partners upon dissolution. The court mentioned a client's right to choose her lawyer and the fiduciary nature of the attorney-client relationship. Several years later, in Gray v. Martin, 63 Or.App. 173, 663 P.2d 1285 (Or.Ct.App.1983), an Oregon appellate court invalidated a partnership agreement that required a departing attorney to surrender his remaining partnership interest if he competed with the firm (a forfeiture-for-competition clause). The court held that this forfeiture clause was prohibited under DR 2–108(A) because it restricted a lawyer's right to practice. Caiaccio, supra at 815.

In yet another major forfeiture-for-competition clause case, Cohen v. Lord, Day & Lord, 75 N.Y.2d 95, 551 N.Y.S.2d 157, 550 N.E.2d 410 (N.Y. 1989), the New York Court of Appeals refused to enforce a clause in a partnership agreement that conditioned collection of partnership profits upon a departing partner's promise not to practice in any state or jurisdiction where the firm had an office. The court believed that this economic threat would foreclose a departing partner from representing clients who might want to continue their business with the partner. As the New York Court of Appeals later observed in *Wieder*, "[i]n *Cohen*, the Court held that a term in a law firm partnership agreement which conditions payment of earned but uncollected partnership revenues upon a withdrawing partner's refraining from practicing law in competition with the firm restricts the practice of law in violation of DR 2–108(a) and is, therefore, unenforceable as against public policy." 609 N.E.2d at 110, n.3. See also Whiteside v. Griffis & Griffis, 902 S.W.2d 739 (Tex.App.1995); Weiss v. Carpenter, Bennett & Morrissey, 275 N.J.Super. 393, 646 A.2d 473 (N.J.1994); ABA Formal Opinion 94–381, Restrictions on Right to Practice (1994) (restrictive employment agreements infringe upon a lawyer's right to practice and interfere with the public's access to lawyers).

In 1991, the first significant departure from the per se prohibition on restrictive covenants came from the Second Appellate District in California in Haight, Brown & Bonesteel v. Superior Court, 234 Cal.App.3d 963, 285 Cal.Rptr. 845 (Cal.Ct.App.1991). The covenant at issue provided that a departing partner surrendered all his remaining partnership interest if he practiced law in the same geographic area as the firm and represented a client of the firm within 12 months. The court held that California's codification of DR 2–108 (Cal. Rule 1–500) disallowed only covenants that completely banned competition and did not apply to agreements providing that the departing partner must compensate the firm. See Kirstan Penasack, Abandoning the Per Se Rule Against Law Firm Agreements Anticipating Competition: Comment on Haight, Brown & Bonesteel v. Superior Court of Los Angeles County, 5 Geo. J. Legal Ethics 889, 892 (1992).

The leading California case eradicating the per se rule is Howard v. Babcock, 6 Cal.4th 409, 25 Cal.Rptr.2d 80, 863 P.2d 150 (Cal. 1993), in which the California Supreme Court upheld a covenant forfeiting departure benefits of withdrawing partners electing to practice in the same geographic area as the firm. The Court reasoned that the forfeiture-for-competition clause did not restrain a partner's ability to practice, rather it only required the partner to pay the firm for its lost clients. The Court held that noncompetition agreements among attorneys in a partnership are subject to a reasonableness standard and are not per se invalid. Id. at 152.

With these few exceptions, most courts still apply the per se rule to prohibit noncompetition agreements among attorneys. However, as the practice of law becomes increasingly competitive and business concerns of law firms come to the forefront, some jurisdictions may be tempted to follow the California courts in relaxing the per se ban on agreements not to compete.

QUESTIONS

1. Under what circumstances is an agreement not to compete allowed under Model Rule 5.6?

2. Why was Model Rule 1.17 adopted by the ABA in 1990?

CHAPTER 6

CONCURRENT RELATIONSHIPS

A. CONCURRENT ROLES

Report of the Joint Conference on Professional Responsibility of the Association of American Law Schools and American Bar Association[1]

Lon L. Fuller, Harvard University, Co–Chairman (AALS).
John D. Randall, Cedar Rapids, Iowa, Co–Chairman (ABA).
Reprinted with Permission of West Publishing Corporation.

INTRODUCTION

The Joint Conference on Professional Responsibility was established in 1952 by the American Bar Association and the Association of American Law Schools. At the first meeting of the Conference the general problem discussed was that of bringing home to the law student, the lawyer and the public an understanding of the nature of the lawyer's professional responsibilities. All present considered that the chief obstacle to the success of this undertaking lay in "the adversary system." Those who had attempted to arrange conferences on professional ethics between lawyers, on the one side, and philosophers and theologians, on the other, observed that communication broke down at this point. Similarly, those who had attempted to teach ethical principles to law students found that the students were uneasy about the adversary system, some thinking of it as an unwholesome compromise with the combativeness of human nature, others vaguely approving of it but disturbed by their inability to articulate its proper limits. Finally, it was observed that the legal profession is itself generally not very philosophic about this issue. Confronted by the layman's charge that he is nothing but a hired brain and voice, the lawyer often finds it difficult to convey an insight into the value of the adversary system or an understanding of the tacit restraints with which it is infused.

Accordingly, it was decided that the first need was for a reasoned statement of the lawyer's responsibilities, set in the context of the adversary system. The statement printed below is intended to meet that need. It

---

1. The Report of the Joint Conference on Professional Responsibility is published in the Program and Reports of Committees of the Association of American Law Schools, 1958 Annual Meeting, p. 111, and in the December 1958 issue of the American Bar Journal, Vol. 44, p. 1159. The Report was approved by the Association of American Law Schools at its Annual Meeting, December 28–30, 1958; it received the approval of the House of Delegates of the American Bar Association at the 1959 Midyear Meeting, February 23–24.

is not expected that all lawyers will agree with every detail of the statement, particularly in matters of emphasis. It was considered, however, that the statement would largely fail of its purpose if it were confined to generalities too broad to elicit dissent, but, by the same token, too broad to sharpen insight or to stimulate useful discussion.

PROFESSIONAL RESPONSIBILITY: A STATEMENT

I.

A profession to be worthy of the name must inculcate in its members a strong sense of the special obligations that attach to their calling. One who undertakes the practice of a profession cannot rest content with the faithful discharge of duties assigned to him by others. His work must find its direction within a larger frame. All that he does must evidence a dedication, not merely to a specific assignment, but to the enduring ideals of his vocation. Only such a dedication will enable him to reconcile fidelity to those he serves with an equal fidelity to an office that must at all times rise above the involvements of immediate interest.

The legal profession has its traditional standards of conduct, its codified canons of ethics. The lawyer must know and respect these rules established for the conduct of his professional life. At the same time he must realize that a letter-bound observance of the canons is not equivalent to the practice of professional responsibility.

A true sense of professional responsibility must derive from an understanding of the reasons that lie back of specific restraints, such as those embodied in the canons. The grounds for the lawyer's peculiar obligations are to be found in the nature of his calling. The lawyer who seeks a clear understanding of his duties will be led to reflect on the special services his profession renders to society and the services it might render if its full capacities were realized. When the lawyer fully understands the nature of his office, he will then discern what restraints are necessary to keep that office wholesome and effective.

Under the conditions of modern practice it is peculiarly necessary that the lawyer should understand, not merely the established standards of professional conduct, but the reasons underlying these standards. Today the lawyer plays a changing and increasingly varied role. In many developing fields the precise contribution of the legal profession is as yet undefined. In these areas the lawyer who determines what his own contribution shall be is at the same time helping to shape the future role of the profession itself. In the duties that the lawyer must now undertake, the inherited traditions of the bar often yield but an indirect guidance. Principles of conduct applicable to appearance in open court do not, for example, resolve the issues confronting the lawyer who must assume the delicate task of mediating among opposing interests. Where the lawyer's work is of sufficient public concern to become newsworthy, his audience is today often vastly expanded, while at the same time the issues in controversy are less readily understood than formerly. While performance under public scrutiny may at times reinforce the sense of professional obligation, it may also create grave temptations to unprofessional conduct.

For all these reasons the lawyer stands today in special need of a clear understanding of his obligations and of the vital connection between those obligations and the role his profession plays in society.

II.

In modern society the legal profession may be said to perform three major services. The most obvious of these relates to the lawyer's role as advocate and counselor. The second has to do with the lawyer as one who designs a framework that will give form and direction to collaborative effort. His third service runs not to particular clients, but to the public as a whole.

1.

The Lawyer's Service in the Administration and Development of the Law.
The Lawyer's Role as Advocate in Open Court.

The lawyer appearing as an advocate before a tribunal presents, as persuasively as he can, the facts and the law of the case as seen from the standpoint of his client's interest. It is essential that both the lawyer and the public understand clearly the nature of the role thus discharged. Such an understanding is required not only to appreciate the need for an adversary presentation of issues, but also in order to perceive truly the limits partisan advocacy must impose on itself if it is to remain wholesome and useful.

In a very real sense it may be said that the integrity of the adjudicative process itself depends upon the participation of the advocate. This becomes apparent when we contemplate the nature of the task assumed by any arbiter who attempts to decide a dispute without the aid of partisan advocacy.

Such an arbiter must undertake, not only the role of judge, but that of representative for both of the litigants. Each of these roles must be played to the full without being muted by qualifications derived from the others. When he is developing for each side the most effective statement of its case, the arbiter must put aside his neutrality and permit himself to be moved by a sympathetic identification sufficiently intense to draw from his mind all that it is capable of giving,—in analysis, patience and creative power. When he resumes his neutral position, he must be able to view with distrust the fruits of this identification and be ready to reject the products of his own best mental efforts. The difficulties of this undertaking are obvious. If it is true that a man in his time must play many parts, it is scarcely given to him to play them all at once.

It is small wonder, then, that failure generally attends the attempt to dispense with the distinct roles traditionally implied in adjudication. What generally occurs in practice is that at some early point a familiar pattern will seem to emerge from the evidence; an accustomed label is waiting for the case and, without awaiting further proofs, this label is promptly assigned to it. It is a mistake to suppose that this premature cataloguing must necessarily result from impatience, prejudice or mental sloth. Often it proceeds from a very understandable desire to bring the hearing into some order and coherence, for without some tentative theory of the case there is no standard of relevance by which testimony may be measured. But what starts as a preliminary diagnosis designed to direct the inquiry tends, quickly and imperceptibly, to become a fixed conclusion, as all that confirms the diagnosis makes a strong imprint on the mind, while all that runs counter to it is received with diverted attention.

An adversary presentation seems the only effective means for combating this natural human tendency to judge too swiftly in terms of the familiar that which is not yet fully known. The arguments of counsel hold the case, as it were, in suspension between two opposing interpretations of it. While the proper classification of the case is thus kept unresolved, there is time to explore all of its peculiarities and nuances.

These are the contributions made by partisan advocacy during the public hearing of the cause. When we take into account the preparations that must precede the hearing, the essential quality of the advocate's contribution becomes even more apparent. Preceding the hearing inquiries must be instituted to determine what facts can be proved or seem sufficiently established to warrant a formal test of their truth during the hearing. There must also be a preliminary analysis of the issues, so that the hearing may have form and direction. These preparatory measures are indispensable whether or not the parties involved in the controversy are represented by advocates.

Where that representation is present there is an obvious advantage in the fact that the area of dispute may be greatly reduced by an exchange of written pleadings or by stipulations of counsel. Without the participation of someone who can act responsibly for each of the parties, this essential narrowing of the issues becomes impossible. But here again the true significance of partisan advocacy lies deeper, touching once more the integrity of the adjudicative process itself. It is only through the advocate's participation that the hearing may remain in fact what it purports to be in theory: a public trial of the facts and issues. Each advocate comes to the hearing prepared to present his proofs and arguments, knowing at the same time that his arguments may fail to persuade and that his proofs may be rejected as inadequate. It is a part of his role to absorb these possible disappointments. The deciding tribunal, on the other hand, comes to the hearing uncommitted. It has not represented to the public that any fact can be proved, that any argument is sound, or that any particular way of stating a litigant's case is the most effective expression of its merits.

The matter assumes a very different aspect when the deciding tribunal is compelled to take into its own hands the preparations that must precede the public hearing. In such a case the tribunal cannot truly be said to come to the hearing uncommitted, for it has itself appointed the channels along which the public inquiry is to run. If an unexpected turn in the testimony reveals a miscalculation in the design of these channels, there is no advocate to absorb the blame. The deciding tribunal is under a strong temptation to keep the hearing moving within the boundaries originally set for it. The result may be that the hearing loses its character as an open trial of the facts and issues, and becomes instead a ritual designed to provide public confirmation for what the tribunal considers it has already established in private. When this occurs adjudication acquires the taint affecting all institutions that become subject to manipulation, presenting one aspect to the public, another to knowing participants.

These, then, are the reasons for believing that partisan advocacy plays a vital and essential role in one of the most fundamental procedures of a democratic society. But if we were to put all of these detailed considerations to one side, we should still be confronted by the fact that, in whatever form adjudication may appear, the experienced judge or arbitrator desires and actively seeks to obtain an adversary presentation of the issues. Only when he has had the benefit of intelligent and vigorous advocacy on both sides can he feel fully confident of his decision.

Viewed in this light, the role of the lawyer as a partisan advocate appears, not as a regrettable necessity, but as an indispensable part of a larger ordering of affairs. The institution of advocacy is not a concession to the frailties of human nature, but an expression of human insight in the design of a social framework without which man's capacity for impartial judgment can attain its fullest realization.

When advocacy is thus viewed, it becomes clear by what principle limits must be set to partisanship. The advocate plays his role well when zeal for his client's cause promotes a wise and informed decision of the case. He plays his role badly, and trespasses against the obligations of professional responsibility, when his desire to win leads him to muddy the headwaters of decision, when, instead of lending a needed perspective to the controversy, he distorts and obscures its true nature.

The Lawyer's Role as Counselor.

Vital as is the lawyer's role in adjudication, it should not be thought that it is only as an advocate pleading in open court that he contributes to the administration of the law. The most effective realization of the law's aims often takes place in the attorney's office, where litigation is forestalled by anticipating its outcome, where the lawyer's quiet counsel takes the place of public force. Contrary to popular belief, the compliance with the law thus brought about is not generally lipserving and narrow, for by reminding him of its long-run costs the lawyer often deters his client from a course of conduct technically permissible under existing law, though inconsistent with its underlying spirit and purpose.

Although the lawyer serves the administration of justice indispensably both as advocate and as office counselor, the demands imposed on him by these two roles must be sharply distinguished. The man who has been called into court to answer for his own actions is entitled to a fair hearing. Partisan advocacy plays its essential part in such a hearing, and the lawyer pleading his client's case may properly present it in the most favorable light. A similar resolution of doubts in one direction becomes inappropriate when the lawyer acts as counselor. The reasons that justify and even require partisan advocacy in the trial of a cause do not grant any license to the lawyer to participate as legal adviser in a line of conduct that is immoral, unfair, or of doubtful legality. In saving himself from this unworthy involvement, the lawyer cannot be guided solely by an unreflective inner sense of good faith; he must be at pains to preserve a sufficient detachment from his client's interests so that he remains capable of a sound and objective appraisal of the propriety of what his client proposes to do.

2.

The Lawyer as One Who Designs the Framework of Collaborative Effort.

In our society the great bulk of human relations are set, not by governmental decree, but by the voluntary action of the affected parties. Men come together to collaborate and to arrange their relations in many ways: by forming corporations, partnerships, labor unions, clubs and churches; by concluding contracts and leases; by entering a hundred other large and small transactions by which their rights and duties toward one another are defined.

Successful voluntary collaboration usually requires for its guidance something equivalent to a formal charter, defining the terms of the collaboration, anticipating and forfending against possible disputes, and generally providing a framework for the parties' future dealings. In our society the natural architect of this framework is the lawyer.

This is obvious where the transactions or relationship proposed must be fitted into existing law, either to insure legal enforcement or in order not to trespass against legal prohibitions. But the lawyer is also apt to be called upon to draft the by-laws of a social club or the terms of an agreement known to be unenforceable because cancelable by either party at any time. In these cases the lawyer functions, not as an expert in the rules of an existing government, but as one who brings into existence a government for the regulation of the parties' own relations. The skill thus exercised is essentially the same as that involved in drafting constitutions and international treaties. The fruits of this skill enter in large measure into the drafting of ordinary legal documents, though this fact is obscured by the mistaken notion that the lawyer's only concern in such cases is with possible future litigation, it being forgotten that an important part of his task is to design a framework of collaboration that will function in such a way that litigation will not arise.

As the examples just given have suggested, in devising charters of collaborative effort the lawyer often acts where all of the affected parties are present as participants. But the lawyer also performs a similar function in situations where this is not so, as, for example, in planning estates and drafting wills. Here the instrument defining the terms of collaboration may affect persons not present and often not born. Yet here, too, the good lawyer does not serve merely as a legal conduit for his client's desires, but as a wise counselor, experienced in the art of devising arrangements that will put in workable order the entangled affairs and interests of human beings.

The Lawyer's Opportunities and Obligations of Public Service.
Private Practice as a Form of Public Service.

There is a sense in which the lawyer must keep his obligations of public service distinct from the involvements of his private practice. This line of separation is aptly illustrated by an incident in the life of Thomas Talfourd. As a barrister Talfourd had successfully represented a father in a suit over the custody of a child. Judgment for Talfourd's client was based on his superior legal right, though the court recognized in the case at bar that the mother had a stronger moral claim to custody than the father. Having thus encountered in the course of his practice an injustice in the law as then applied by the courts, Talfourd later as a member of Parliament secured the enactment of a statute that would make impossible a repetition of the result his own advocacy had helped to bring about. Here the line is clearly drawn between the obligation of the advocate and the obligation of the public servant.

Yet in another sense, Talfourd's devotion to public service grew out of his own enlightened view of his role as an advocate. It is impossible to imagine a lawyer who was narrow, crafty, quibbling or ungenerous in his private practice having the conception of public responsibility displayed by Talfourd. A sure sense of the broader obligations of the legal profession must have its roots in the lawyer's own practice. His public service must begin at home.

Private practice is a form of public service when it is conducted with an appreciation of, and a respect for, the larger framework of government of which it forms a part, including under the term government those voluntary forms of self-regulation already discussed in this statement. It is within this larger framework that the lawyer must seek the answer to what he must do, the limits of what he may do.

Thus, partisan advocacy is a form of public service so long as it aids the process of adjudication; it ceases to be when it hinders that process, when it misleads, distorts and obfuscates, when it renders the task of the deciding tribunal not easier, but more difficult. Judges are inevitably the mirrors of the bar practicing before them; they can with difficulty rise above the sources on which they must depend in reaching their decision. The primary responsibility for preserving adjudication as a meaningful and useful social institution rests ultimately with the practicing legal profession.

Where the lawyer serves as negotiator and draftsman, he advances the public interest when he facilitates the processes of voluntary self-government; he works against the public interest when he obstructs the channels of collaborative effort, when he seeks petty advantages to the detriment of the larger processes in which he participates.

Private legal practice, properly pursued, is, then, itself a public service. This reflection should not induce a sense of complacency in the lawyer, nor lead him to disparage those forms of public service that fall outside the normal practice of law. On the contrary, a proper sense of the significance of his role as the representative of private clients will almost inevitably lead the lawyer into broader fields of public service.

The Lawyer as a Guardian of Due Process.

The lawyer's highest loyalty is at the same time the most intangible. It is a loyalty that runs, not to persons, but to procedures and institutions. The lawyer's role imposes on him a trusteeship for the integrity of those fundamental processes of government and self-government upon which the successful functioning of our society depends.

All institutions, however sound in purpose, present temptations to interested exploitation, to abusive short cuts, to corroding misinterpretations. The forms of democracy may be observed while means are found to circumvent inconvenient consequences resulting from a compliance with those forms. A lawyer recreant to his responsibilities can so disrupt the hearing of a cause as to undermine those rational foundations without which an adversary proceeding loses its meaning and its justification. Everywhere democratic and constitutional government is tragically dependent on voluntary and understanding cooperation in the maintenance of its fundamental processes and forms.

It is the lawyer's duty to preserve and advance this indispensable cooperation by keeping alive the willingness to engage in it and by imparting the understanding necessary to give it direction and effectiveness. This is a duty that attaches not only to his private practice, but to his relations with the public. In this matter he is not entitled to take public opinion as a datum by which to orient and justify his actions. He has an affirmative duty to help shape the growth and development of public attitudes toward fair procedures and due process.

Without this essential leadership, there is an inevitable tendency for practice to drift downward to the level of those who have the least understanding of the issues at stake, whose experience of life has not taught them the vital importance of preserving just and proper forms of procedure. It is chiefly for the lawyer that the term "due process" takes on tangible meaning, for whom it indicates what is allowable and what is not, who realizes what a ruinous cost is incurred when its demands are disregarded. For the lawyer the insidious dangers contained in the notion that "the end justifies the means" is not a matter of abstract philosophic conviction, but of direct professional experience. If the lawyer fails to do his part in educating the public to these dangers, he fails in one of his highest duties.

Making Legal Services Available to All Who Need Them.

If there is any fundamental proposition of government on which all would agree, it is that one of the highest goals of society must be to achieve and maintain equality before the law. Yet this ideal remains an empty form of words unless the legal profession is ready to provide adequate legal representation for those unable to pay the usual fees.

At present this representation is being supplied in some measure through the spontaneous generosity of individual lawyers, through legal aid societies, and—increasingly—through the organized efforts of the bar. If those who stand in need of this service know of its availability, and their need is in fact adequately met, the precise mechanism by which this service is provided becomes of secondary importance. It is of great importance, however, that both the impulse to render this service, and the plan for making that impulse effective, should arise within the legal profession itself.

The moral position of the advocate is here at stake. Partisan advocacy finds its justification in the contribution it makes to a sound and informed disposition of controversies. Where this contribution is lacking, the partisan position permitted to the advocate loses its reason for being. The legal profession has, therefore, a clear moral obligation to see to it that those already handicapped do not suffer the cumulative disadvantage of being without proper legal representation, for it is obvious that adjudication can neither be effective nor fair where only one side is represented by counsel.

In discharging this obligation, the legal profession can help to bring about a better understanding of the role of the advocate in our system of government. Popular misconceptions of the advocate's function disappear when the lawyer pleads without a fee, and the true value of his service to society is immediately perceived. The insight thus obtained by the public promotes a deeper understanding of the work of the legal profession as a whole.

The obligation to provide legal services for those actually caught up in litigation carries with it the obligation to make preventive legal advice accessible to all. It is among those unaccustomed to business affairs and fearful of the ways of the law that such advice is often most needed. If it is not received in time, the most valiant and skillful representation in court may come too late.

The Representation of Unpopular Causes.

One of the highest services the lawyer can render to society is to appear in court on behalf of clients whose causes are in disfavor with the general public.

Under our system of government the process of adjudication is surrounded by safeguards evolved from centuries of experience. These safeguards are not designed merely to lend formality and decorum to the trial of causes. They are predicated on the assumption that to secure for any controversy a truly informed and dispassionate decision is a difficult thing, requiring for its achievement a special summoning and organization of human effort and the adoption of measures to exclude the biases and prejudgments that have free play outside the courtroom. All of this goes for naught if the man with an unpopular cause is unable to find a competent lawyer courageous enough to represent him. His chance to have his day in court loses much of its meaning if his case is handicapped from the outset by the very kind of prejudgment our rules of evidence and procedure are intended to prevent.

Where a cause is in disfavor because of a misunderstanding by the public, the service of the lawyer representing it is obvious, since he helps to remove an obloquy unjustly attaching to his client's position. But the lawyer renders an equally important, though less readily understood service where the unfavorable public opinion of the client's cause is in fact justified. It is essential for a sound and wholesome development of public opinion that the disfavored cause have its full day in court, which includes, of necessity, representation by competent counsel. Where this does not occur, a fear arises that perhaps more might have been said for the losing side and suspicion is cast on the decision reached. Thus, confidence in the fundamental processes of government is diminished.

The extent to which the individual lawyer should feel himself bound to undertake the representation of unpopular causes must remain a matter for individual conscience. The legal profession as a whole, however, has a clear moral obligation with respect to this problem. By appointing one of its members to represent the client whose cause is in popular disfavor, the organized bar can not only discharge an obligation incumbent on it, but at the same time relieve the individual lawyer of the stigma that might otherwise unjustly attach to his appearance on behalf of such a cause. If the courage and the initiative of the individual lawyer make this step unnecessary, the legal profession should in any event strive to promote and maintain a moral atmosphere in which he may render this service without ruinous cost to himself. No member of the bar should indulge in public criticism of another lawyer because he has undertaken the representation of causes in general disfavor. Every member of the profession should, on the contrary, do what he can to promote a public understanding of the service rendered by the advocate in such situations.

The Lawyer and Legal Reform.

There are few great figures in the history of the bar who have not concerned themselves with the reform and improvement of the law. The special obligation of the profession with respect to legal reform rests on considerations too obvious to require enumeration. Certainly it is the lawyer who has both the best chance to know when the law is working badly and the special competence to put it in order.

Where the lawyer fails to interest himself in the improvement of the law, the reason does not ordinarily lie in a lack of perception. It lies rather in a desire to retain the comfortable fit of accustomed ways, in a distaste for stirring up controversy within the profession, or perhaps in a hope that if enough time is allowed to pass, the need for change will become so obvious that no special effort will be required to accomplish it.

The lawyer tempted by repose should recall the heavy costs paid by his profession when needed legal reform has to be accomplished through the initiative of public-spirited laymen. Where change must be thrust from without upon an unwilling bar, the public's least flattering picture of the lawyer seems confirmed. The lawyer concerned for the standing of his profession will, therefore, interest himself actively in the improvement of the law. In doing so he will not only help to maintain confidence in the bar, but will have the satisfaction of meeting a responsibility inhering in the nature of his calling.

The Lawyer as Citizen.

Law should be so practiced that the lawyer remains free to make up his own mind how he will vote, what causes he will support, what economic and political philosophy he will espouse. It is one of the glories of the profession that it admits of this freedom. Distinguished examples can be cited of lawyers whose views were at variance from those of their clients, lawyers whose skill and wisdom made them valued advisers to those who had little sympathy with their views as citizens.

Broad issues of social policy can and should, therefore, be approached by the lawyer without the encumbrance of any special obligation derived from his profession. To this proposition there is, perhaps, one important qualification. Every calling owes to the public a duty of leadership in those matters where its training and experience give it a special competence and insight. The practice of his profession brings the lawyer in daily touch with a problem that is at best imperfectly understood by the general public. This is, broadly speaking, the problem of implementation as it arises in human affairs. Where an objective has been selected as desirable, it is generally the lawyer who is called upon to design the framework that will put human relations in such an order that the objective will be achieved. For that reason it is likely to be the lawyer who best understands the difficulties encountered in this task.

A dangerously unreal atmosphere surrounds much public discussion of economic and political issues. The electorate is addressed in terms implying that it has only to decide which among proffered objectives it considers most attractive. Little attention is paid to the question of the procedures and institutional arrangements which these objectives will require for their realization. Yet the lawyer knows that the most difficult problems are usually first encountered in giving workable legal form to an objective which all may consider desirable in itself. Not uncommonly at this stage the original objective must be modified, redefined, or even abandoned as not being attainable without undue cost.

Out of his professional experience the lawyer can draw the insight needed to improve public discussion of political and economic issues. Whether he considers himself a conservative or a liberal, the lawyer should do what he can to rescue that discussion from a world of unreality in which it is assumed that ends can be selected without any consideration of means. Obviously if he is to be effective in this respect, the lawyer cannot permit himself to become indifferent and uninformed concerning public issues.

Special Obligations Attaching to Particular Positions Held by the Lawyer.

No general statement of the responsibilities of the legal profession can encompass all the situations in which the lawyer may be placed. Each position held by him makes its own peculiar demands. These demands the lawyer must clarify for himself in the light of the particular role in which he serves.

Two positions of public trust require special mention. The first of these is the office of public prosecutor. The manner in which the duties of this office are discharged is of prime importance, not only because the powers it confers are so readily subject to abuse, but also because in the public mind the whole administration of justice tends to be symbolized by its most dramatic branch, the criminal law.

The public prosecutor cannot take as a guide for the conduct of his office the standards of an attorney appearing on behalf of an individual client. The freedom elsewhere wisely granted to partisan advocacy must be severely curtailed if the prosecutor's duties are to be properly discharged. The public prosecutor must recall that he occupies a dual role, being obligated, on the one hand, to furnish that adversary element essential to the informed decision of any controversy, but being possessed, on the other, of important governmental powers that are pledged to the accomplishment of one objective only, that of impartial justice. Where the prosecutor is recreant to the trust implicit in his office, he undermines confidence, not only in his profession, but in government and the very ideal of justice itself.

Special fiduciary obligations are also incumbent on the lawyer who becomes a representative in the legislative branch of government, especially where he continues his private practice after assuming public office. Such a lawyer must be able to envisage the moral disaster that may result from a confusion of his role as legislator and his role as the representative of private clients. The fact that one in this position is sometimes faced with delicate issues difficult of resolution should not cause the lawyer to forget that a failure to face honestly and courageously the moral issues presented by his position may forfeit his integrity both as lawyer and as legislator and pervert the very meaning of representative government.

Mention of special positions of public trust should not be taken to imply that delicate moral issues are not confronted even in the course of the most humble private practice. The lawyer deciding whether to undertake a case must be able to judge objectively whether he is capable of handling it and whether he can assume its burdens without prejudice to previous commitments. In apportioning his time among cases already undertaken the lawyer must guard against the temptation to neglect clients whose needs are real but whose cases promise little financial reward. Even in meeting such everyday problems, good conscience must be fortified by reflection and a capacity to foresee the less immediate consequences of any contemplated course of action.

III.

To meet the highest demands of professional responsibility the lawyer must not only have a clear understanding of his duties, but must also possess the resolution necessary to carry into effect what his intellect tells him ought to be done.

For understanding is not of itself enough. Understanding may enable the lawyer to see the goal toward which he should strive, but it will not furnish the motive power that will impel him toward it. For this the lawyer requires a sense of attachment to something larger than himself.

For some this will be attainable only through religious faith. For others it may come from a feeling of identification with the legal profession and its great leaders of the past. Still others, looking to the future, may find it in the thought that they are applying their professional skills to help bring about a better life for all men.

These are problems each lawyer must solve in his own way. But in solving them he will remember, with Whitehead, that moral education cannot be complete without the habitual vision of greatness. And he will recall the concluding words of a famous essay by Holmes:

> Happiness, I am sure from having known many successful men, cannot be won simply by being counsel for great corporations and having an income of fifty thousand dollars. An intellect great enough to win the prize needs other food besides success. The remoter and more general aspects of the law are those which give it universal interest. It is through them that you not only become a great master in your calling, but connect your subject with the universe and catch an echo of the infinite, a glimpse of its unfathomable process, a hint of the universal law.

QUESTIONS

1. What is a calling? Why is the legal profession a calling rather than simply a business? What are the "special obligations" that attach to this calling?

2. What specific roles of a lawyer are identified in the Joint Conference Report? Can these roles sometimes conflict?

3. Why is private practice a form of public service?

4. Review the cases you have read so far in this casebook. What does this Report say about the issues raised in each one of them?

B.   CONCURRENT CONFLICTS IN FAMILY AND BUSINESS REPRESENTATIONS

The Warren Family Trust

Historical Note: The Brandeis Confirmation Hearings

The confirmation hearings for President Wilson's nomination of Louis D. Brandeis to the Supreme Court of the United States were fraught with debate over ethical issues that arose in the context of Brandeis's Boston law practice. Unfortunately, much of this debate also was clouded by the blatant anti-Semitism of many of Brandeis's opponents in the Boston bar and elsewhere. Even before the Brandeis nomination, President Wilson got a hint of what lay ahead when Brandeis was proposed for membership in Washington's exclusive Cosmos Club. Justice Hitz of the United States Court of Appeals for the District of Columbia wrote to President Wilson on January 30, 1915 that:

> Several members of the Club have started an opposition to Mr. Brandeis which bids fair to be successful unless his friends come strongly to his support. The grounds of opposition to Mr. Brandeis are stated to be that he is a reformer for revenue only; that he is a Jew; and that he would be a disturbing element in any club of gentlemen.

On February 1, 1915 President Wilson wrote to the Cosmos Club's admissions committee, saying that he held Brandeis in "highest esteem" and that "his admission to the Club would not only be an act of justice to him, but would add a member of very fine quality to its list." Brandeis eventually was elected to the Club. See Alpheus Thomas Mason, Brandeis: A Free Man's Life 466–67 (1956). For discussion of anti-semitism as it affected Brandeis's life and professional career, see A. Gal, Brandeis of Boston (1980); T. Karfunkel & T. Ryley, The Jewish Seat: Anti–Semitism and the Appointment of Jews to the Supreme Court (1978).

As discussed in the following selection, the Brandeis confirmation was also at the center of a political tempest over the makeup of the Supreme Court:

Appointment of Justices: Some Historical Perspectives

Paul A. Freund.
101 Harv. L. Rev. 1146 (1988).

* * *

From 1894 to 1930 there were no further rejections [of Supreme Court nominees], but the focus of concern in the Senate underwent a marked shift, coincident with the Court's increased activity in judging the merits of social and economic legislation under the due process clauses of the fifth, and especially the fourteenth, amendments. The turning point was President Wilson's nomination, in late January, 1916, of Louis D. Brandeis of Boston. He was one of the very few nominees to the Court who had held no public office, but he was a nationally-known public figure because of his challenges to such established practices and institutions as bankers' control of big business, interlocking corporate directorships, the New Haven railroad management, abuses in industrial life insurance, and inefficient corporate consolidations. In courts, in print, and in legislative hearings, he had championed savings bank life insurance, cooperatives, minimum-wage and maximum-hour laws, collective bargaining, and the responsibility of labor unions. He regarded himself as a conservative, in the sense of Macaulay's dictum that to reform is to preserve, but he was perceived in the upper reaches of Boston's financial and business community as a dangerous radical.

The opposition couched its attack in terms of questionable character and lack of judicial temperament, and occasionally anti-Semitism became overt, but essentially the campaign against the nominee rested on the repugnance of his social and economic views. Writing in The New Republic, Walter Lippmann put it concisely: Brandeis was deemed untrustworthy only by "the powerful but limited community which dominated the business and social life of Boston. He was untrustworthy because he was troublesome." Lippmann was responding to a petition opposing the nomination circulated by President A. Lawrence Lowell of Harvard, signed by fifty-five prominent Bostonians. Notably missing among the signatures was that of President Emeritus Charles W. Eliot, Boston's (and perhaps the nation's) first citizen, who wrote a deeply-felt, appreciative letter highly praising the nomination. On a lower level, of the eleven Harvard Law School professors, nine signed an endorsement, with one dissenting and one not voting. Labor unions signified their support. Opposed was the president of the American Bar Association, Elihu Root, joined by six of the sixteen living ex-presidents of the association, including William Howard Taft.

Four agitated months elapsed between the nomination and ultimate confirmation. Both sides mounted organized campaigns. During this period Brandeis himself made no public statement, but he was energetic in fortifying his lieutenants with suggestions and detailed documentation for their use. His law partner, Edward F. McClennen, took up residence in Washington, where he kept in touch with Attorney General Thomas Gregory, and was assisted at a distance, and through occasional conferences, by George W. Anderson, United States Attorney in Boston, Professor Felix Frankfurter, Norman Hapgood, editor of Harper's Weekly, and others. Briefs and counter-briefs, petitions, memoranda, and letters poured forth from both sides to the Judiciary Committee, the President, and the weekly and daily press. The hearings before a subcommittee, which were open to the public at the behest of Attorney General Gregory, produced two thousand printed pages.

The outcome was anticlimactic. The full committee voted favorably on strict party lines, ten to eight, and the Senate confirmed on June 1, 1916, by a vote of forty-seven to twenty-two, with only one Democrat breaking ranks. The successful outcome owed much to President Wilson, whose resolute support rested on close personal association with Brandeis, an unofficial adviser in the early years of the administration. "I can never live up to my Brandeis appointment," the President later remarked to Hapgood. Anticlimactic though the final result may have been, the whole episode was indeed a watershed; in the nature of the nominee, in the underlying conflict of forces, in the organized campaigning, and in the breadth of participation at the confirmation stage, it foreshadowed the shape of future appointment battles.

The Accusers and the Accused

Many of the scenarios discussed in this casebook involve dishonest lawyers and judges. Nonetheless, as Judge Irving Kaufman observes, "compliance or noncompliance with Canons of Ethics frequently do not involve morality or venality, but differences of opinions among honest men over the ethical propriety of conduct." Funds of Funds, Ltd. v. Arthur Andersen & Co., 567 F.2d 225, 227 (2d Cir.1977). Concurrent and successive conflicts are sometimes situations that involve differences of opinions among honest persons. As you read through the following testimony, you should evaluate the ethical propriety of Louis Brandeis's actions in the Warren representation. Did he conduct his law practice in a manner that created an appearance of impropriety (see Canon 9)? If so, were his misjudgments in this matter serious enough to disqualify him for a seat on the Supreme Court?

Louis Dembitz Brandeis, b. 1856 in Louisville, Kentucky to parents who emigrated from Prague, d. 1941; completed high school studies while visiting Dresden Germany with his family 1874–75; no college education; entered Harvard Law School in 1875 at age 18; financed law school through family support, loans and income from tutoring other students; graduated first in his class at age 20 in 1877 with one of the highest grade averages ever earned at Harvard Law School; practiced law in St. Louis, Missouri 1876–79; part time law clerk to Chief Justice Horace Gray, Supreme Judicial Court of Massachusetts 1879–81; partner, Warren and Brandeis (with law school classmate Samuel Dennis Warren, Jr.) 1879–97; partner, Brandeis, Dunbar & Nutter, Boston 1897–1916; involved in progressive politics 1911–15; active in Zionist movement 1912; author of numerous books, including Other People's Money and How the Bankers Use It (1914), and three articles in the Harvard Law Review (all with Samuel D. Warren, Jr.); Associate Justice of the United States Supreme Court 1916–39.

Samuel Dennis Warren, Jr. b. 1852, d. 1910; son of a wealthy paper manufacturer; B.A. Harvard University 1874, LL.B. Harvard University 1877 (graduated second in his class); partner, Warren and Brandeis 1879–97; left the law partnership to go into the family paper business in 1897; killed himself in 1910.

Hollis Russell Bailey, b. 1852 in North Andover, Massachusetts, d. 1934; prepared at Phillips Academy, Andover; B.A Harvard University 1877; LL.B. and A.M. Harvard University 1878, 1879 (worked his way through law school by tutoring; appointed a proctor at Harvard in 1877) (when Louis Brandeis's eyes gave out from excessive study, Bailey and other students were employed to read to him for hourly pay); law clerk to Chief Justice Horace Grey 1880; private practice in Boston beginning in 1880; wrote numerous articles in the Harvard Law Review on bankruptcy and other topics in the 1890's; edited *Bailey Genealogy, James, John, and Thomas and their Descendants* (1899); Chairman of the Board of Bar Examiners of Massachusetts 1901–16; member of the general council of the American Bar Association and the William E. Russell Democratic Club in Cambridge; Senior Deacon of the First Church in Cambridge (Unitarian); Board of Trustees, Cambridge Savings Bank; assisted in the formation of the Massachusetts Bar Association and served on its executive committee 1911–14; counsel to Edward Warren (a.k.a. "Ned") in the Warren Trust matter beginning in 1909; signer of the 1916 anti-Brandeis petition with fifty-five Boston lawyers.

William S. Youngman, b. 1872 in Williamsport, Pennsylvania, d. 1934; attended Williamsport High School; B.A. Harvard University 1895; LL.B. Harvard University 1898; private practice in Boston with Hollis Bailey; Ned Warren's principal lawyer in the Warren Trust matter beginning in 1903; testified in support of Bailey's accusations at the Brandeis confirmation hearings; State Senator from Norfolk and Suffolk, Massachusetts (elected in 1922); State Treasurer (elected in 1924); Lieutenant Governor (elected in 1930); Republican candidate for governor (1932); member of the Brookline Country Club and Boston City Club.

Sherman Whipple, LL.B. Harvard University, was in private practice in Boston where he was counsel to Ned Warren with Hollis Bailey and William Youngman in the Warren Trust matter. Whipple, who cross-examined Samuel Warren for 27 days immediately prior to Sam's suicide, was a supporter of the Brandeis nomination. **Moorfield Storey**, LL.B. Harvard University, was a member of the Board of Overseers of Harvard College and in private practice in Boston, where he was counsel to Fiske Warren in the Warren Trust matter. Storey was a severe critic of Brandeis who had opposed him in a number of cases, but did not sign the Boston fifty-five petition. **Edward F. McClennen**, LL.B. Harvard University, was an associate and later a partner of Brandeis. McClennen was counsel to Samuel Warren in the litigation over the Warren Trust matter.

Austen G. Fox, a lawyer in private practice in New York City, appeared before the Senate Judiciary Committee as counsel for the fifty-five Boston lawyers who had signed the protest to the confirmation of Brandeis. **George W. Anderson**, United States Attorney for the Massachusetts District, was retained to act for the Senate Judiciary Committee to present evidence in favor of Brandeis.

On December 19, 1909, Hollis Bailey and William Youngman brought a bill in equity on behalf of Edward Warren against his brother Samuel Warren as trustee, and against his brother Fiske Warren and sister Cornelia Warren as trust beneficiaries, and against the estate of a Mr. Mason, also a trustee, alleging that Samuel had from 1889 to 1909 disposed of family property in breach of Samuel's fiduciary duties as trustee. Louis Brandeis had represented the Warren Trust as well as his law partner Samuel Warren in Samuel's dealings with the Trust, but was not named as a defendant and was not present in the hearing room. In 1910 Samuel Warren was examined at length before a master by Sherman Whipple, but Samuel killed himself before the examination was completed. The case was settled shortly after Samuel's death when the other family members bought out Edward's interest in the trust.

On January 28, 1916, President Wilson nominated Brandeis to succeed Joseph R. Lamar as an Associate Justice of the United States Supreme Court. On February 15, 1916, Hollis Bailey appeared before the United

States Senate Committee on the Judiciary to accuse Brandeis of unethical conduct in connection with the Warren Trust.

As you read the following testimony, you should evaluate not only Brandeis's handling of the concurrent conflict, but also the accusers' actions and motives. Were Bailey and Youngman acting ethically in accusing Brandeis years later concerning facts that they had never testified to before? If they had believed that Brandeis's conduct was unethical, why had they not brought charges against him with the Massachusetts bar? Why did Bailey and Youngman not name Brandeis as a defendant in the complaint against Samuel Warren? What is the significance of the fact that Samuel Warren, perhaps the most crucial witness, had died six years before these accusations were first brought against Brandeis at his confirmation hearings?

NOMINATION OF LOUIS D. BRANDEIS.

Mr. Chilton, from the subcommittee of the Committee on the Judiciary, submitted the following

VIEWS.

[To accompany the nomination of Louis D. Brandeis.]

To the COMMITTEE ON THE JUDICIARY,

United States Senate:

As heretofore announced to the Committee on the Judiciary, your subcommittee decided to have open hearings, which were begun on February 9, 1916, and continued from time to time until March 15, 1916.

Very soon after your subcommittee was organized a protest against the confirmation was filed, signed by the following-named gentlemen:

Charles S. Rackemann.
Harrison M. Davis.
Joseph Sargent.
A. Lawrence Lowell.
John Noble.
Charles F. Adams.
I. Tucker Burr.
C. Minot Weld.
Nathaniel H. Stone.
Felix Rackemann.
Arthur Lyman.
Henry S. Grew.
George P. Gardner.
Roger Walcott.
Pierpont L. Stackpole.
Francis Peabody.
Edmund K. Arnold.
Willard B. Luther.
Charles A. Williams.
Moses Williams.

Reginald H. Johnson.
Henry Ware.
J. L. Thorndike.
Julian Codman.
Richard C. Storey.
Fred C. Bowditch.
W. L. Putnam.
Edward H. Warren (Prof.)
Roger S. Warner.
James M. Newell.
William S. Ball.
Clifton L. Bremer.
Lawrence Minot.
Henry E. Edes.
Hollis R. Bailey.
Edward S. Dodge.
F. Walker Johnson.
George B. Dabney.
Francis R. Boyd.

J. A. Lowell Blake.
Louis Bacon.
Lawrence P. Dodge.
George B. Harris.
Eugene J. Fabens.
Charles H. Fiske, Jr.
Harold Jefferson Coolidge.
P.T. Jackson, Jr.
Augustus P. Loring.
William W. Vaughn.
Samuel D. Parker.
Thomas N. Perkins.
R.W. Boyden.
Henry L. Shattuck.
A.R. Graustein.
James D. Colt.
Edmund A. Whitman.
William C. Indicott.

Albert E. Pillsbury.
William V. Kellen.
Frederic M. Stone.

Mr. Austen G. Fox, assisted by Mr. Kenneth M. Spence, appeared on behalf of those signing the petition, and the committee requested Mr. George W. Anderson to represent the committee in bringing out the facts. Quite a number of other protests and many letters of commendation of the nominee were filed before the committee in the shape of letters and telegrams, some to the committee and some to different members, all of which are made a part of the report.

Nomination of Louis D. Brandeis

"The Warren Trust", from, 64th Congress, 1st Sess. *Hearings Before the Subcommittee of the Senate Committee on the Judiciary on the Nomination of Louis D. Brandeis To Be An Associate Justice of the Supreme Court of the United States* (1916).

Testimony of Hollis Russell Bailey, Esq., of Boston.

(The witness was duly sworn by Senator Fletcher)

SENATOR FLETCHER. What is your name?

MR. BAILEY. Hollis Russell Bailey.

SENATOR FLETCHER. You reside where?

MR. BAILEY. In Cambridge, with my office in Boston.

SENATOR FLETCHER. How long have you resided there?

MR. BAILEY. In Cambridge since 1885, and my office in Boston since 1880.

SENATOR FLETCHER. Do you know Mr. Louis D. Brandeis?

MR. BAILEY. I do.

SENATOR FLETCHER. How long have you known him?

MR. BAILEY. Since 1878, when we were together in the Harvard Law School.

SENATOR FLETCHER. Some statement has been made here to the effect that you have knowledge of some facts or circumstances bearing upon the professional conduct of Mr. Brandeis, and the committee has asked you to come here to state what you know in that connection.

MR. BAILEY. I assume, your honor—I call the chairman "your honor," because we get used to that term—it is the Warren case which the chairman has in mind. I was counsel in that case, and prepared the bill in equity, which was filed in that case, and afterwards participated in the hearings that were had at which testimony was taken. There was that matter, and, perhaps, also the point of general reputation, if that is a point which is open. Those will be the only two points upon which I would have information.

SENATOR FLETCHER. Have you had any differences with Mr. Brandeis?

MR. BAILEY. No personal differences whatever, only that we have been on opposite sides in quite a number of cases in court since 1880.

SENATOR FLETCHER. What are your relations now?

MR. BAILEY. Our relations I consider friendly. I have never had an unpleasant word with Mr. Brandeis.

SENATOR WALSH. Just before proceeding, if you please. MR. BAILEY, has the matter of which you can speak been the subject of judicial investigation anywhere?

MR. BAILEY. The case came to an end by the death of the principal defendant, and following that, a settlement out of court, so there was no judicial adjudication.

SENATOR WALSH. What I desire to inquire is whether Mr. Brandeis's connection with the matter and his conduct in reference to it have ever been the subject of judicial investigation?

MR. BAILEY. Not at all. The matter ended in settlement, and that was the end of it.

SENATOR WALSH. So far as you know, the facts concerning which you would testify have never been testified to before?

MR. BAILEY. I think that is correct, so far as I know. I have never testified with reference to them, and, so far as I know, that is true.

Speaking first as to the Warren case, the gist of that is that Mr. Brandeis assisted his partner, Mr. Warren, in entering into a plan and framing a plan and carrying out a plan which placed his partner in a position individually antagonistic to the position of trustee, which he had assumed—as I will explain a moment later—which, as I shall undertake to state, resulted in a breach of trust, and that Mr. Brandeis acted for Mr. Warren as trustee; also acted for him in a position which was conflicting with his position as trustee, as I will explain a little more fully; and finally, defended Mr. Warren in what he had done, and that Mr. Brandeis and his firm acted for some 15 or 20 years as counsel for Mr. Warren and his associates, as trustees, under an annual retainer of $2000; and also acted for Mr. Warren and two associates individually under a like retainer of $2000 a year, those interests being, in some important points, conflicting, and the result being that beneficiaries of the trust—one of them was my client—suffered financially to a very considerable extent—some hundreds of thousands of dollars. Now, explaining a little more in detail, Mr. Brandeis's partner was in the law school with him.

SENATOR CLARK. What is the name of the partner?

MR. BAILEY. Samuel Dennis Warren was his partner, and they were in the law school together when I was there; they got through a year earlier than I did, and he began to practice law in 1879, and I began in 1880. Immediately on leaving the law school, Mr. Warren and Mr. Brandeis formed a law partnership, which continued for some 10 years, under the name of Warren & Brandeis, having their offices in Boston. Mr. Warren's father was also known as Samuel D. Warren, Sr. ..., and was engaged in the paper manufacturing and selling business, with paper mills in the State of Maine, and the selling end of the business and the offices in Boston. Mr. Samuel Warren died in 1888, or about that time, and the property amounted to some $2,000,000. He left a widow and five children, and left a will, in which he gave the property to the widow and the five children: I think, giving the widow a little larger proportion than the children: my memory is that the widow had five-fifteenths, and each of the children two-fifteenths. Then a year or about a year after the death of Samuel D. Warren, Sr. ..., the question arose of how to carry on the paper business for the best interests of all concerned. Mr. Edward Warren, who became my client a good many years later—about 1910 or 1912—was then residing in Europe most of the time, and engaged in antiquarian research and the purchase of antiquities, and work of that nature.

SENATOR FLETCHER. He was a brother of Mr. Brandeis's partner?

MR. BAILEY. A brother of Mr. Brandeis's partner. Mr. Edward Warren had never had any connection with the paper business or with the running of it; he had been educated in England, and had lived a large part of the time abroad, and was abroad at the time these transactions were going on. Another brother, Henry Warren, was a graduate of Harvard, and engaged in study and research, living in Cambridge, and had no connection with the paper business. There was a sister, Miss Cornelia Warren, who was not a woman of business experience. There was a brother Fiske Warren, who had, in a small way, helped his father in the paper business. Samuel D. Warren, while still a partner with Mr. Brandeis, had, during the last few years of his father's life, been consulted by his father and knew something, in a general way, about his father's business. The mother, the widow of Samuel D. Warren, Sr. ..., was a lady 61 years old, and had no acquaintance in a practical way with the affairs of her husband. The following arrangement was devised and carried out: First, that the widow and all the children should convey all their interest in the paper mills and the real estate used in carrying them on—something to the value of approaching $2,000,000 through a conduit—that is a dummy, a third party—to three trustees, consisting of Samuel D. Warren, Mr. Brandeis's partner, and a Mr. Mason, and Mrs. Warren, Sr.... Mr. Mason had been for some seven or eight years before the death of Mr. Warren, Sr...., a partner in the paper business, having no title, however, in the real estate, and having not exceeding $15,000 a year as his recompense for his services, or thereabouts; and the arrangement with Mr. Mason being such that the representatives of Samuel D. Warren, Sr...., had the right to terminate the partnership and terminate the arrangement which had existed with Mr. Mason, which was done.

Substantially all the property was then conveyed to three trustees, as I have stated—Mrs. Warren, Sr...., Mr. Samuel Warren, and Mr. Mason—upon a written deed of trust, a copy of which I have here; Mr. Youngman, I believe, is asked to come tomorrow, and he will bring a certified exemplified copy of the deed of trust from the court records of Massachusetts. The deed of trust provided that the trustees might, in their discretion, carry on the paper business. It provided clearly that they should act as trustees for the benefit of the children of Samuel D. Warren, including Mr. Edward Warren. It provided further that they might transfer the property to a firm, on suitable terms, by way of a lease, for a suitable compensation, for the firm to carry on the business. What was done was that the three trustees—Samuel D. Warren, Mr. Mason, and Mrs. Warren, Sr.—made a lease of the property to Mr. Brandeis, as a conduit, and through him or from him, to Mr. Warren individually, to Mr. Mason individually, and to Mr. Fiske Warren a small fractional interest. It was provided in the lease, first, that the rental should consist of 6 percent interest on the real estate leased to the firm, and half of the net profits of the firm, and it also provided that the lessees should make repairs and replacements, and the lessors, the trustees, should make additions.

That arrangement was entered into—I have given the outline of it—and it resulted in Mr. Samuel D. Warren—Mr. Brandeis's partner—receiving as compensation—as we say, for his services for the running of the business for the first two or three years, which were very profitable years—something approaching $75,000 or $100,000 instead of the income of about $10,000 which he had received as a practicing member of the law firm. It also resulted in Mr. Fiske Warren receiving as much as $30,000 or $10,000 for one or two years for doing very little as a partner, and in the end it resulted that Mr. Samuel D. Warren and Mr. Mason (Mr. Fiske Warren in a very small degree) had received something over $2,000,000 for carrying on the business.

SENATOR CUMMINS. For what length of time?

MR. BAILEY. For 19 or 20 years. The allegations in the bill of equity were that this was twice as much as they could fairly charge for the work of carrying on the business. That was the allegation. It also appeared in the hearings that, as I have already stated, Mr. Brandeis acted as counsel—he and his firm—for the lessees and also as counsel for the lessors, and for many years Mr. Brandeis and Mr. Samuel D. Warren had the trust and the confidence of all the beneficiaries. Mrs. Warren, Sr. ..., was receiving a very large income, of which she had occasion to spend only a part, so when she died, in 1898, 1899, or 1900 she had accumulated a very considerable amount of property out of her income.

My client, Mr. Edward Warren, was not shown a copy of the lease, or the lease itself. He did sign a deed conveying the property to the trustees, but he did see a copy of the deed of trust which provided that the trustees should either carry on the paper business or make a lease on suitable terms to someone else. He learned of the lease and what had taken place some time after 1903, when he employed independent counsel, Mr. Youngman, who has been asked to come before you.

I came into the matter with Mr. Youngman some time about 1910 or 1911 or 1912—I do not carry this date exactly—and had to do with the bringing of the suit and the carrying of it on.

In the hearings, which were had before a master, the time was spent with the testimony of Mr. Samuel D. Warren, and, in connection with his testimony, the documents, books, and papers; and Mr. Warren was represented by my friend, Mr. McClennen, who is here, a partner of Mr. Brandeis. Mr. Brandeis acted a little in the beginning of that litigation, but not afterwards, directly. The litigation was defended principally by Mr. McClennen, acting for Mr. Samuel D. Warren. It did appear that as a result of that provision in the lease, by which Mr. Samuel D. Warren personally, with his associates, was bound to make repairs and replacements, that Mr. Samuel D. Warren, as trustee, was bound to make additions; that considerable sums had been charged to the addition account and the improvements which, as we claim, should have gone and been properly charged to the repair account.

Our claim was that Mr. Brandeis was largely instrumental in making the plan. He wrote an opinion, which was sent to the different beneficiaries, saying that the plan was one that was legally correct and proper, that by means of the trust the beneficiaries would be protected from individual liability as partners, and that it was a proper arrangement.

None of the beneficiaries had independent counsel, nor were there any suggestions that they should have independent counsel to advise them about the arrangement until as late as 1903, when Mr. Edward Warren employed independent counsel. Mr. Brandeis had to do with drawing—I think he drew the will for Mrs. Warren, Sr. . . . He drew one will for Mr. Edward Warren and was counsel for all parties to, I think it is fair to say, 1903 and 1904. The claim of my client was that the lease that Mr. Samuel D. Warren, with the assistance of Mr. Brandeis, made personally was not fair to the beneficiaries, and was one in which regard was had to the personal interests of Mr. Samuel D. Warren rather than to his duty as trustee.

Now, I have given you that outline. I can leave with you a copy of the deed of trust and a copy of the lease made by the trustees to Mr. Brandeis, but Mr. Youngman will bring certified copies of all those. This [exhibiting] is a copy of the original bill. It was afterwards amended formally by making Mr. Mason's representatives parties defendant. Mr. Mason also had died. . . .

SENATOR FLETCHER. Let us see about this first. You have stated what was practically claimed in your bill of equity?

MR. BAILEY. Now, also, I would say that the testimony which was introduced during the three weeks of the hearing—very considerable being documentary—that as to all these documents there was no dispute; no dispute in the lease made to Mr. Brandeis from the trustees and from him to Mr. Samuel D. Warren and Mr. Mason, personally. There was no dispute about the fact that Mr. Brandies wrote an opinion, copies of which were sent to beneficiaries, that the trust arrangement was legally proper or was legal. There was no dispute about the fact that Mr. Brandeis and his firm acted for some 19 years under a retainer of $2,000 a year for Mr. Samuel D.

Warren, and his associates, as trustees, under a like retainer of $2,000 a year, for Mr. Samuel D. Warren and associates personally.

SENATOR WALSH. That is, as lessees?

MR. BAILEY. Yes, sir.

SENATOR FLETCHER. What you stated you say is practically what you claim in your bill of equity?

MR. BAILEY. Which we substantiate in documentary evidence.

SENATOR FLETCHER. Has that evidence ever been printed?

MR. BAILEY. The testimony was taken, and I think Mr. Youngman is going to bring typewritten copies of the testimony, which consists of the testimony by Mr. Samuel D. Warren and his admissions as to documents and as to quite a good many tabulations from the books of accounts. We finally, on behalf of Mr. Edward Warren, employed expert accountants, who examined the books and took off tabulated statements to how the divisions were, from year to year, from the beginning.

SENATOR FLETCHER. What became finally of the case?

MR. BAILEY. The case was settled within a year after the death of Mr. Samuel D. Warren. The hearings continued, commencing about the 1st of January to the 1st of February. Then a recess was taken, and during the recess Mr. Samuel D. Warren died, and then negotiations for settlement began and came to an end before the end of the year.

SENATOR FLETCHER. The final decree was by consent?

MR. BAILEY. Yes, sir: dismissing the bill.

SENATOR FLETCHER. That, of course, is a matter of record?

MR. BAILEY. Yes, sir.

SENATOR FLETCHER. Dismissed the bill?

MR. BAILEY. Yes, sir: by consent.

SENATOR FLETCHER. Now, who were the lessees under that arrangement?

MR. BAILEY. Samuel D. Warren and Mr. Mason, former copartner of Mr. Warren, Sr., and Mr. Fisk Warren, for a small fractional interest, which finally got down to one-fortieth, I believe.

SENATOR FLETCHER. Who were trustees?

MR. BAILEY. The trustees were Samuel D. Warren, Mr. Mason, and Mrs. Warren, Sr.

SENATOR FLETCHER. And Mr. Brandeis, you stated, was—

MR. BAILEY (interposing). Was the partner of Mr. Samuel D. Warren.

SENATOR FLETCHER. No; but, as you expressed it, a conduit.

MR. BAILEY. Yes, sir; being a transfer from Samuel D. Warren himself of an interest in real estate, under the law, as it was then [in] Massachusetts, he had to employ a dummy conduit, so the lease was made to Mr. Brandeis and then assigned by him to Mr. Samuel D. Warren personally, and with him, Mr. Mason, and Mr. Fiske Warren.

SENATOR FLETCHER. As lessees?

MR. BAILEY. Yes, sir.

SENATOR FLETCHER. And is it not a fact that Mr. Samuel D. Warren himself looked after the affairs of the Warren estate, while he was a partner of Mr. Brandeis, particularly?

MR. BAILEY. Well, the Warren estate continued—you mean after the death of Mr. Samuel D. Warren, Sr.?

SENATOR FLETCHER. Yes.

MR. BAILEY. That was less than a year that the business was carried on, and my memory was Mr. Samuel D. Warren was one of the executors in the will of the father, and Mr. Mason another, and I think Mrs. Warren another, and that during that period, of less than a year, that they did carry on the business, Mr. Mason being a practical manufacturer.

SENATOR FLETCHER. Throughout as long as Mr. Samuel D. Warren lived, it would seem not unusual that he would have personal charge of the affairs of the Warren estate.

MR. BAILEY. This is before or after the father's death?

SENATOR FLETCHER. Afterwards—during the time of his lifetime. Samuel D. Warren, Jr., is dead.

MR. BAILEY. After the death of the father first he became executor of the father's will and then became the trustee.

SENATOR FLETCHER. Yes.

MR. BAILEY. That is as I had stated it.

SENATOR FLETCHER. And then became lessee?

MR. BAILEY. Yes, sir.

SENATOR FLETCHER. And then during all that time was he not, while a member of the firm of Warren & Brandeis—was not Warren the partner who was giving attention to the affairs of the Warren estate?

MR. BAILEY. He left the law business about the time this began, and the firm of Warren & Brandeis was dissolved, and Mr. Warren gave up practicing law and no more practiced law.

SENATOR FLETCHER. About what time was that dissolution?

MR. BAILEY. That, I think, was 1898, 1899, or 1900, or just about the time that he became a member of the copartnership and managed the paper business, and he then gave up the law business. . . .

* * *

Testimony of Moorfield Storey, Esq., of Boston

* * *

MR. ANDERSON. I wanted to ask you one question about the Warren case. When that family controversy arose, or some time during it, you became counsel for Mr. Fiske Warren?

MR. STOREY. Yes, sir.

MR. ANDERSON. A brother of Samuel D. Warren?

MR. STOREY. Yes, sir.

MR. ANDERSON. And who was one of the defendants in the suit brought by Mr. Edward Warren, referred to by Mr. Bailey?

MR. STOREY. Yes, sir.

MR. ANDERSON. And advised Mr. Fiske Warren?

MR. STOREY. I advised him in that case, but not in the early part of the case.

MR. ANDERSON. You advised him in this case which MR. BAILEY referred to?

MR. STOREY. Yes, sir.

MR. ANDERSON. May I ask you to state whether you found anything, either in the attitude of Mr. Brandeis or Mr. Warren, dealing with the family, open to the charge of unethical conduct?

MR. STOREY. The position is this: When Mr. Samuel D. Warren, Sr. was alive, he owned the mills and was the controlling partner in the firm. The firm sold the goods, and there was some arrangement between the firm and Mr. Warren, personally, for a division of the expenses and profits. When he died that situation existed and something had to be done in order to carry on the business, and an arrangement was made whereby the property formerly held by Mr. Warren, personally, was vested in trustees, and Mr. Samuel Warren took his father's place in the firm, and Mr. Fiske Warren was also in the firm, but with a smaller interest. Mr. Edward Warren was in Europe engaged in the study of arts and curiosities, and was not in active business.

The arrangement which was made seemed to me, as I examined it, a perfectly fair arrangement. It probably, in view of what happened afterwards, would have been better if Mr. Edward Warren had independent advisers to counsel him. But the thing was submitted to him and agreed to by him, and I saw nothing in the arrangement as to which he could complain. I sat through the trial which had begun and Mr. Warren was on the stand, as I remember, about six weeks, and during that time was cross-examined by MR. WHIPPLE. There were about six weeks more, as I understand it. It looked as if the cross-examination might last longer, when Mr. Warren died. During the cross-examination nothing developed which reflected upon Mr. Samuel D. Warren in any way, or upon Mr. Brandeis.

SENATOR WALSH. You did not join for your client in the prosecution of the Edward Warren suit?

MR. STOREY. Mr. Fiske Warren was, so to speak, interested on both sides. He was a partner in the firm and sharing its profits, and he was as much interested in the estate as anybody else, and, therefore, more largely interested in its profits or losses.

Your question was—

MR. ANDERSON. I asked you if you joined with the others.

MR. STOREY. No, sir; he came to me, and my position was one of observation rather, but before the case went very far, just about the time of Mr. Warren's death, or afterwards, Mr. Fiske Warren recommended buying out Mr. Edward Warren's interest in the situation and that was done. It was erroneously represented to the newspapers that was a payment made in settlement of a claim for damages caused by somebody's mismanagement of the property. That is not true. The price paid to Mr. Edward Warren was an adequate price for the property received. It was purely a settlement for the property. As I say, I saw nothing in the case up to the time the case ended of which Mr. Warren could be in any way ashamed. It seemed to me he had treated his brother with great fairness. I should have done perhaps very much as Mr. Brandeis did if I had been in his place. It would have been a matter of caution, however, to have independent counsel, but apparently the family united—

MR. ANDERSON. Was there any more reason for suggesting independent counsel for Mr. Edward D. Warren than Mrs. Warren—I mean at the outset?

MR. STOREY. I do not know that there was.

MR. ANDERSON. Was there any more reason for suggesting separate counsel for Edward Warren than for Fiske Warren?

MR. STOREY. They were all of age, and Fiske Warren, up to that time, had not been very active as a business man, any more than Edward Warren, but he was on the ground and was in a position to employ counsel. Mr. Edward Warren was on the other side of the water. At the time, as I say, there was nothing in the relations between the different members of the family to suggest that there was any divergence of interests, or any reason why they should not act harmoniously, as they did.

As I understand the claim of the other side, it was not the original arrangement which was defective, or contracts between the estate and the firm, but certain terms of the contracts with relation to repairs which imposed upon the estate heavy expenses in keeping up the property. The money was, in effect, charged to the estate rather than the firm.

SENATOR WALSH. Mr. Bailey told us of that, but I do not understand that he connected up Mr. Brandeis in any way with what might seem to be an improper diversion of funds, but his charge related to the time of the making of the contract.

MR. STOREY. Of course, wherever the same person is interested on both sides to a contract, complications may arise, but where, as in that case, the parties were brothers and sister and mother, etc., there was no disposition, I am sure, on the part of anyone to take advantage of anybody else.

SENATOR WALSH. Let me ask you, Mr. Storey, whether it is or is not a common practice among lawyers in these family settlements, for a lawyer, who has the apparent confidence of all parties, to undertake to represent all of them, although eventually the interests may be disclosed to be, in a sense, conflicting?

MR. STOREY. I think it is a common practice, but, I think, a bad practice. I remember a case of my own, in which I was dealing with some people, and they and I concurred in the construction of a contract, and if our construction had been right, we would have received a large sum of money. I said, however, that we should have another counsel, and they engaged other counsel, and the other counsel put a different interpretation upon the contract, and we lost a large sum of money.

SENATOR WALSH. I am speaking principally of family situations.

MR. STOREY. As I have said to you already, if I had been in Mr. Brandeis's shoes when that situation came up, I think I would have taken the same course.

SENATOR FLETCHER. There is no criticism to make of the execution of the leases by these trustees, in which some of the trustees were lessees?

MR. STOREY. That seemed to be inevitable. The partner in the firm had been the owner of the property. On his death the property descended, under the will, to his heirs. They became the owners. It was important that the relation between the property and the selling agency should continue. It was inevitable that the arrangement should be made. From the very nature of the case, it was impossible for them [not] to be on both sides of the contract. The only question was whether the contract was fair, and was carried out. The contract was submitted to all parties and they agreed to it.

SENATOR FLETCHER. I understand the deed of trust contained a provision which authorized the trustees to lease and sell.

MR. STOREY. The purpose was to reestablish the same relations that existed between Mr. Warren, while he was alive, and his firm, as between his heirs and the new firm.

SENATOR FLETCHER. Exactly.

MR. STOREY. And of course Mr. Warren, in his life, was on both sides of that contract, and all that could be done was to make a fair contract. The contract was drawn and submitted to all parties. As I say, I saw nothing in it to criticize.

* * *

Testimony of Sherman Whipple, Esq., of Boston

MR. ANDERSON. Now, Mr. Whipple, you have known Mr. Brandeis a great many years?

MR. WHIPPLE. Yes, sir.

. . . .

MR. ANDERSON. Now, will you be good enough to give to the committee the statement you gave to the public when Mr. Brandeis's nomination was announced?

MR. WHIPPLE. I venture to say that immediately the nomination was announced in Boston, some of the newspapers called me by telephone. I think all of them called me within a few minutes, and I, therefore, dictated a statement which they were all at liberty to publish. It was as follows:

As a lawyer, Mr. Brandeis is able and learned. As a man, he is conscientious and high minded. The feature of his career which is the most striking and remarkable has been his unselfish and unswerving devotion to the social, moral, and industrial uplift of the lowly and less fortunate of our people. I believe that on the Supreme Bench of the United States he will exert a strong influence in establishing the ideals to which he has devoted his recent years.

MR. ANDERSON. You were counsel with Mr. Hollis Bailey and William S. Youngman in the Warren case?

MR. WHIPPLE. Yes, sir; after the bill in equity had been filed.

MR. ANDERSON. Were you brought in to try the case?

MR. WHIPPLE. I was the trial counsel. . . .

* * *

MR. ANDERSON. Coming now to the Warren case, in the preparation and control of that case, so far as it was tried, you became thoroughly conversant with all the aspects of the transaction, in which Messrs. Warren and Brandeis had been a large part?

MR. WHIPPLE. I thought I did.

MR. ANDERSON. And Mr. Warren was being examined by you at the time of his death?

MR. WHIPPLE. That is true.

MR. ANDERSON. Can you state any facts to the committee with relation to Mr. Brandeis's connection with the Warren case which you subject to its correction, think material?

MR. WHIPPLE. I have read the newspaper reports of Mr. Hollis Bailey's statement to the committee, and if what I have to say may be taken in that way, I agree with his statements of fact. I mean they accord with my own memory. I remember one fact, in addition, that he did not state, that impressed me at the time as important on the question of the lease. As I remember it, although I have not refreshed my mind from looking at the papers, the lease from the trustees, in effect to themselves, provided that the lessees might, upon giving a very short notice—comparatively short notice—terminate the lease, and thus the responsibility which they had assumed and the lease would be brought to an end, while, as I remember, the lessors were bound for quite a long term of years, which had the effect of permitting the lessees on short notice, if things were going against them, to terminate the lease and turn the property back so that its further operation or disposition would be upon the trust; that is, the trustees.

SENATOR CHILTON. Is that kind of lease legal in Massachusetts?

MR. WHIPPLE. I think so. I had not thought of the point, but I see no reason why any lease may not provide that it may be terminated by either party upon giving certain notice to the other party, but I presume it is a very material matter in the assumption of any risk on the part of the lessee, and it impressed my mind a good deal as I proceeded with the litigation, and I think, ultimately, impressed the minds of others who were connected with the litigation. We claimed—and I was convinced then and am now convinced—that the original transaction under the circumstances under which it was made involved a breach of trust, in that it gave to Mr. Samuel Warren, and perhaps one of the other trustees, this opportunity to make out of the trust a great deal more than he might probably have been allowed as trustee's fees, and it violated the general principle that a trustee may not make out of his trust personal or private profit. The question was then whether all parties who were involved—all the beneficiaries—knew it and assented to it, fully advised and with their eyes open, and it was contended in behalf of Mr. Edward Warren, who was at the time abroad and whose information all came by correspondence, that he entrusted the whole matter to Mr. Brandeis and was not fully informed, so that was the ground of the position which we took in the litigation and with reference to which my cross-examination of Mr. Samuel D. Warren proceeded; but Mr. Bailey, as I noticed by the public press, stated in response to a question by one member of the committee, that he believed that Mr. Brandeis intentionally framed this lease and other papers so as to give Mr. Warren this opportunity to make private profit. That belief I do not share with Mr. Bailey. I cross-examined Mr. Warren at length, and I was then impressed, and so expressed myself, that the idea of defrauding his brother or the other members of his family, or securing a personal advantage to which he was not entitled, did not enter his head; that the entire transaction was free from any taint of dishonest motives or intentional fraud.

I had the feeling with regard to Mr. Brandeis somewhat like Mr. Storey has just expressed, that he was possibly careless in not making very, very clear to Mr. Edward Warren just the whole transaction and its possible effect upon his rights, but I felt at the time, and I feel now, that Mr. Brandeis, who has been the family counselor and been trusted for many years, thought that there was a perfect understanding and accord among all the members of the family; that Mr. Samuel D. Warren, who, by the death of his father, became the head of the family, should be charged with the responsibility of handling and operating this large property and should have what he could make out of it. Of course, if that was so, and all parties assented, there was no violation of trust; and there was no moral wrong. Therefore, I reached the conclusion that there was a legal wrong; that there was a violation of that principle of law with regard to trusts which I have just pointed out, but that there was no reprehensible motive to secure a personal advantage secretly or in any way like that.

In that opinion I do not wish at all to minimize that of Mr. Bailey: he took a different view of it at the time, I think, from what I did. I was concerned merely with the prosecution of what I felt to be a perfectly just claim on the part of Edward Warren, who had not been informed or advised as to the significance of this transaction, his legal rights, and its effect upon his personal fortune.

MR. ANDERSON. Mr. Samuel D. Warren and his father both belonged to the class of men eminent in business and well-known for their personal integrity?

MR. WHIPPLE. That is true.

MR. ANDERSON. Men against whose character and reputation no breath had ever arisen?

MR. WHIPPLE. I can not say as to that, because I was not familiar enough with social or business life prior to this time to make a statement; but I have always understood that the elder Warren was an honorable merchant of very high standing, and certainly Mr. Samuel Warren stood very well in the community—stood very high in the community.

MR. ANDERSON. Mr. Brandeis has been counsel for three generations for that family, has he not; for the elder, and for Samuel D. Warren who died, and Samuel D. Warren the younger?

MR. WHIPPLE. I did not know that he was, personally, for the younger man, but I assume so.

MR. ANDERSON. After Samuel D. Warren's death the rest of the family united in buying out Mr. Edward Warren's interest in the estate, did they not?

MR. WHIPPLE. I am so informed.

MR. ANDERSON. You did not participate in that?

MR. WHIPPLE. I did, to the extent of advice that inasmuch as it was not, so to speak, my case—I was the trial lawyer; Mr. Bailey and Mr. Youngman carried through the settlement, which I must say, however, I understood to involve considerably more than what Mr. Storey stated. I cannot see, however, that it makes very much difference, because it was the adjustment of a very unfortunate and unhappy family dispute, in the shadow of the death of the head of the family.

MR. ANDERSON. Was not that settlement, to a considerable degree, finally negotiated between you and Mr. McClennen?

MR. WHIPPLE. If so, I have forgotten; but if Mr. McClennen's memory is clearer on that, I should trust him.

MR. ANDERSON. Mr. McClennen was the trial lawyer?

MR. WHIPPLE. Yes.

MR. ANDERSON. Mr. Brandeis had nothing to do with the transaction, except he might have advised Mr. Warren as to the original transaction?

MR. WHIPPLE. I always thought he advised Mr. McClennen in the trial of the case.

MR. ANDERSON. Was he not down here [in Washington, D. C.] trying the Ballinger case?

MR. WHIPPLE. If you say so, I assume he was; but that did not, necessarily, prevent that close communion between himself and Mr. McClennen. I never knew whether all that I was up against was Mr. McClennen's mental operations.

MR. ANDERSON. That was enough.

MR. WHIPPLE. I think that was enough, but I thought he got counsel from Mr. Brandeis.

* * *

Testimony of William S. Youngman, Esq., of Boston.

SENATOR WORKS. What was her age?

MR. YOUNGMAN. I think 64 years old when her husband died. She died in 1901. When she died they did not fill the vacancy. They proposed— and I think Mr. Brandeis participated in the proposal—to have another woman put on—the daughter. Mr. Edward Warren protested against that, and that was the beginning of the issue between Edward Warren and the others. It has been unjustly said of him that he wanted money. He wanted the protection of the interests of the whole trust, by the application to the situation, of the judgment of some independent mind, because by that time, say 1903, I think it was, when he first took that up, it was quite clear that something had gone wrong in the management of this trust. One thing that made it clear to Edward Warren was that he had either less or about the same income from this trust as he had when his father died, although there had been considerably more than a million dollars supposed to have been added to it, by way of capital. Most of his contributions from that came out of the shares of the earnings, but there were a great many thousand dollars of that given to new capital that came out of his property outside of the trust, and he very naturally questioned whether the trust was being managed on sound business principles. . . .

* * *

SENATOR FLETCHER. These trustees subsequently made a lease, did they not?

MR. YOUNGMAN. Yes, sir; I shall come to the lease. Before the lease we have to deal with a bill of sale which these heirs were asked to sign of all personal property of the estate that was in any way connected with the mills of S. D. Warren & Co. to Louis Brandeis, who, I believe, assigned his interest to the new trustee partners. It was in connection with that bill of sale that such things as the patents were left unconsidered, and they yielded a great many thousands of dollars a year, and the good will of the business, as I say, was passed over to the new firm without any consideration whatsoever.

That brings me now to the lease. The lease was made by these trustees to Louis D. Brandeis, and I should think that ought to go into the record.

* * *

SENATOR WORKS. I do not think it is material how he put him to sleep, whether by chloroform or not.

MR. ANDERSON. I thought it was probably some immoral chloroforming, and I wanted to get the transaction to which the anesthetic was applied.

That was a question, then, of drawing out profits that ought to be left in for capital?

MR. YOUNGMAN. No, sir; it was a question of whether Sam Warren should assent to this scheme and put it up to his brother Ned to sign all these papers to put it into effect.

MR. ANDERSON. Then this chloroforming had to do with the original transaction before your client had assented to it?

MR. YOUNGMAN. Yes, sir; getting the heirs into it.

MR. ANDERSON. Then I understand you mean by that you directly charge that when the plan was laid out, . . . Mr. Warren had doubts of its ethical quality, and Mr. Brandeis chloroformed him out of those doubts; is that a fair statement?

MR. YOUNGMAN. No: I object to the emphasis on the "chloroformed." I only used that word to indicate my high regard for Sam Warren's sense of honor and to indicate that Sam Warren had to be persuaded, and he was persuaded by Louis D. Brandeis, who wrote this letter, which will be in evidence here, and addressed "Dear Sam," that made Sam Warren think that he had an arrangement that took the risk of the business off the beneficiaries and made all the risk to be assumed by him and Mason, although he and Mason at that time had nothing. Sam Warren owed the estate $62,500, which Ned Warren forgave his share of. There was no bitterness between those men, as far as Ned was concerned.

MR. ANDERSON. Then, it was this: Sam Warren was a man of a high sense of honor, and this plan laid out for the family and consented to by the family, was one which his natural sense of honor rejected, but he was persuaded into it by the dishonorable Brandeis?

MR. YOUNGMAN. That is such an argumentative question I do not think I should be required to answer it. I am here to testify to facts.

MR. ANDERSON. Do you think you have done that this morning?

MR. YOUNGMAN. I beg you to realize I am a lawyer, and a lawyer always makes a poor witness, but I have endeavored to present these facts and allow the Senators and the United States to draw what conclusions they will.

MR. ANDERSON. I think on this long record that my question is perfectly fair and I should like an answer to it, because, as I understand it, you now intend to leave it that the original plan was rejected by the moral perception of Samuel D. Warren, and that he was finally persuaded into it by Louis D. Brandeis, whose firm was getting $4,000 a year in two parts out of the entire estate.

MR. YOUNGMAN. Well, they were getting additional favors from Mason and from Sam Warren.

MR. ANDERSON. Then your notion is that the fact that they were getting $4,000 and looked for additional favors was what induced Mr. Brandeis to persuade Mr. Warren into a fraudulent transaction, which Mr. Warren's better nature rejects?

MR. YOUNGMAN. No; that is not my notion. My notion is—

SENATOR WORKS. I do not think it is very important what your notions are about. The findings of the committee will be based on the facts you state.

MR. YOUNGMAN. I am glad I was not led to express it. I thank the committee.

* * *

MR. YOUNGMAN . . . . Furthermore, I feel that if Mr. Whipple had known of Mr. Brandeis's participation in the various things that happened and which Mr. Whipple, as you will find there in his own words all over that record, sought to have redress in this suit—if he had known of Mr. Brandeis's participation, he would not have expressed that opinion in that way. If he had known of it as I knew of it through those eight years previously, I believe he would not have expressed that opinion. You must bear in mind, in this connection, that Mr. Brandeis was not on trial in this Warren case and never was present in the hearing room.

SENATOR CHILTON. You think, then that this is a matter about which there should be no difference amongst honest men, so far as Mr. Brandeis is concerned?

MR. YOUNGMAN. I think this is a matter that is a question of fact, applying to it the principles of equity, which are indisputable. Nobody questions them. When a man accepts a fiduciary obligation he may be obligated at the same time to two people. That is perhaps an indiscreet position for him to get in—two people with adverse or antagonistic interests. But if he is so obligated and he accepts such a position, then he is morally bound to disclose to the man that is getting the worst of the bargain, who is receiving treatment that is different from what equity, if it steps in and just divided those profits as they should be according to the courts would decide.

SENATOR CHILTON. You do not attach any importance, as Mr. Whipple does, to the fact that Mr. Samuel D. Warren was the older brother of Edward Warren, and that they were very friendly, that they were very close to each other, and that it is entirely possible that Mr. Brandeis supposed that the elder brother would talk to the younger brother? You attach no importance to that at all?

MR. YOUNGMAN. I would attach some importance to that. But, beginning in 1902, certainly in 1903, it was known to Mr. Brandeis that the older brother had not talked to Mr. Edward Warren, and Mr. Brandeis continued thereafter, so long as Ned Warren had an interest in this trust, to draw his money to protect the interests of the beneficiaries.

SENATOR CHILTON. That is all.

SENATOR FLETCHER. Mr. Samuel D. Warren was a man of high integrity and excellent standing in every way, was he not?

MR. YOUNGMAN. He was: yes. And I think he was deceived into what he was doing. He did not realize or comprehend this thing until very shortly before his death. If anything was done that should not have been done, he had a less part in it in a way than Mr. Mason, because Mr. Mason owned no share in this property. He was not the elder brother. He was simply the hired man. The question is whether he hired himself at a reasonable compensation or whether he had a scheme that would give him an unreasonable compensation. What he knew about the business before this scheme was put into operation and afterwards tells the story.

SENATOR CHILTON. That seems to be all, Mr. Youngman. Thank you.

(The witness was excused.)

* * *

Testimony of Edward McClennen, Esq. of Boston

SENATOR CHILTON. Mr. Samuel D. Warren died before they concluded his cross-examination?

MR. McCLENNEN. Yes.

SENATOR CHILTON. I refer to the elder Warren.

MR. McCLENNEN. Yes.

SENATOR CHILTON. He was on the stand, and he was a witness for whom? By whom was he called?

MR. McCLENNEN. He was called as the first witness by his brother's counsel and cross-examined, and was never direct-examined.

SENATOR CHILTON. And that was as far as the case ever went?

MR. McCLENNEN. That is as far as the case ever went. It went through some 27 days of trial as I recall it; perhaps it was more than that.

SENATOR CHILTON. It is plain to me that what we are investigating, so far as the charge of Mr. Youngman is concerned, is that Mr. Brandeis had a trust relation which he violated; and Mr. Youngman devoted his time here to show us that the points in which he violated that trust in particular were that he charged to expenses what should have been charged to permanent improvements, or vice versa, under that agreement.

MR. McCLENNEN. That difference between repairs and improvements is a separate matter that I have not referred to as yet.

SENATOR CHILTON. I understand that is the point.

SENATOR CUMMINS. Those things relate to the merits of the case itself. I am more interested in knowing the relations Mr. Brandeis sustained toward the people who had conflicting interests in that matter. Up to the time, and including the time, of making the lease, Mr. Brandeis represented all of them, as I understand.

MR. McCLENNEN. I should say so; yes.

SENATOR CUMMINS. And your firm received pay from all of them for the work that you did in preparing the deed of trust and in preparing the lease.

MR. McCLENNEN. Not distinguishably from all of them. Mr. Warren and Mr. Brandeis had been counsel for S. D. Warren & Co., the old firm. When Mr. Warren died they were counsel for the executors, and they were paid as counsel for the executors. They then went right on for the following 20 years receiving a retainer, I think it was of $4,000 a year, which was paid half by S. D. Warren & Co. and half by the trustees, and they did any advising of any Warren, brother, sister, child, or grandchild, I should say, without any particular charge, as there was occasion, as they were asked.

SENATOR CUMMINS. Up to and including the making of the lease, Mr. Brandeis or his firm was paid by the executors under the will.

MR. McCLENNEN. You are now speaking of the period after the elder Warren's death?

SENATOR CUMMINS. Yes.

MR. McCLENNEN. Paid by the executors under the will a special charge for services, and the executors paid also as they had been, being paid before by the firm, I think.

SENATOR CUMMINS. That meant, of course, they were being paid by all who were interested in the property of the elder Warren.

MR. McCLENNEN. In the final suffering of the charge.

SENATOR CUMMINS. After the making of the lease, as I understand it, the new firm, together with the trustees paid whatever was paid.

MR. McCLENNEN. That is correct.

SENATOR CUMMINS. In the retainer or employment by the trustees, of course the firm represented all who were beneficiaries under the trust.

MR. McCLENNEN. In the same sense.

SENATOR CUMMINS. And in the payments that were made by the new firm they, I assume, represented as well those who constituted the new firm.

MR. McCLENNEN. Sam and Fiske and Mason were the members of the firm.

SENATOR WORKS. I think we would better adjourn at this point.

* * *

AFTER RECESS

Testimony of Edward F. McClennen, Esq.—Continued.

MR. McCLENNEN. Before the questions put to me had led me to speak of these matters of depreciation, I had wanted to call your attention to some more things indicating the full knowledge of the members of the Warren family as to this arrangement before it was executed at all.

MR. FOX. You mean other members than Edward?

MR. McCLENNEN. The members other than Edward.

MR. FOX. I suppose you meant so.

MR. McCLENNEN. In view of your inquiry I will say, that as far as I have been able to discover, up to the time that Edward signed these papers in the summer of 1889, the extent of his knowledge was contained in the papers that have been laid before the committee, except for this matter of the brief description of proposals or something like that—a document which is described in the letter of May 31, but which has not come to light in any way. What its contents are I never yet have discovered.

On May 4, 1889, four weeks before the papers were executed, there was a written letter which Sam Warren wrote to Henry, as follows:

Boston, May 4, 1889

My Dear Henry: I inclose you a copy of the original draft of the trust agreement and of an amended draft thereof. The latter is the result of my cogitations since I talked with you and, I believe, is an improvement on the old in one or two particulars.

First. It meets your point regarding a trustee not connected with the business.

Second. It provides for a reserve of income independent of improvements at the mills. Since you preferred not to have a general power of reinvestment for a specified fraction of the income, I think it necessary for the protection of the trust property, to have at least the power to reserve as a guaranty against future needs. The trustees, in other words, ought not to be called upon to pay out every cent of income at the end of each year, not expended for improvements, no matter what the needs or prospects of the coming or future years might be. This reserve would also make it possible to supply any deficiency of income below the normal expenditures of the beneficiaries in a bad year, making it up in a good.

Third. In order to meet a possible legal objection to an absolute period of 23 years for the duration of the trust, I have inserted the first limitation that it shall not endure beyond the life of the survivors of the residuary legatees. Please show to mother and Pussy.

Your affect.

Sam

Henry C. Warren, Esq.

MR. FOX. Was this put in evidence?

MR. McCLENNEN. "Pussy" meant Miss Cornelia Warren. This is a letter that was never put in evidence because we had not come to the time in the case when we were putting evidence.

On November 9, at page 293 of the Warren evidence, appears another letter to Edward, in which reference is made to the fact that the rate of rent is 6 per cent and the interest in the profits, without specifying, as has been specified in the May letter, just what that interest in the profits was. . . .

. . . As to the using of one-half for improvements, the report for 1890 recites the agreement. These reports have been put into the record as a part of Mr. Youngman's testimony.

SENATOR WORKS. Yes; I remember it.

MR. McCLENNEN. It is not necessary to reread them. Each report thereafter refers to that agreement or to the fact of the retention of one-half of the profits for use for making improvements.

The letters in the Warren record showed in Edward's comments on this subject never, as I recall it, prior to his mother's death, any objection, but quite to the contrary—such expressions as "the mills must be kept up at all cost," etc.

Along in the latter part of the nineties the correspondence showed that Edward was getting into the purchase of these antiquities and using a large amount of money in that way, and there began to be—perhaps I ought not to say a large amount of money, because it is also comparative—but he was using money in that way and feeling cramped to some extent in consequence of that, but no criticisms, as I recall it, of the way the money was being expended in improving the plant. Of course, the improvement of the plant was recognized by them all as being an investment of their funds in increasing their capital.

During these earlier years, up to the death of Henry, in 1899, I think it was—or possibly in 1897—each child had, outside of the business, this two-fifths interest, the mother having the five-fifteenths interest. When Henry died it increased by so much the interest of each child.

MR. ANDERSON. He died without a will and they inherited?

MR. McCLENNEN. I have forgotten whether he died without a will and they inherited, or whether he left a will under which they took. At all events, there is no question that his interest fell into the interests of the others.

The depreciation charged off I have already referred to, and Edward is mentioned in that connection in a letter of March 1, 1896, which is set out at page 920 of the Warren record.

One of the complaints made in the bill of complaint was that the mother's will had made this provision by which her money went to the trustees of the mill trust, as they were termed—that is, they then were herself and Mr. Warren and Mr. Mason. Her will provided that the trustees under her will should be the same persons who were at any time the trustees under the mill trust.

SENATOR WORKS. Do you know who prepared that will for her?

MR. McCLENNEN. I do not know whether Sam Warren drew that will or whether Mr. Brandeis drew it, but unquestionably it was one or the other, or both. It was a matter of correspondence between Edward and Sam.

On March 30, 1897, at page 998 of the Warren record, there is a letter from Sam to Ned referring to the fact that he is advising his mother to make the trustees her residuary, and on April 17, 1897, at page 1000, praises this, as far as he understands it, as the best change of all. There were certain other incidental changes relating to gifts to the museum. The whole family were more or less interested in the Boston Art Museum, in matters of art, and there run through the correspondence lots of references to that matter.

At page 1240, On October 2, 1900—that is, before the mother's death—Ned speaks in his letter of having read his mother's will some time before. At page 1289 Ned refers to having known the main facts of the will, and there never was any criticism of that.

The will that finally went into operation—this one of 1898, I think—was executed somewhere in Europe. Apart from the date that appeared on the will, showing its execution, there was some diary entry of Miss Cornelia, who was with her mother at the time, and neither Mr. Sam Warren nor Mr. Brandeis nor Ned Warren were at the place of execution. It was returned to Sam after the execution, and that will was as clearly the common property of all the Warren family as anything could possibly be, before the mother's death.

A reference has been made by Mr. Youngman in his testimony to the fact that the bill of complaint was sworn to by Ned with these various allegations relative to the improprieties running through the administration of the trust. In consequence this letter written at the time of the filing of the bill is of some significance. This is a letter which was received by Mr. Sam Warren on December 14, 1909, and reads as follows:

My Dear Sam: I have had to file the bill because otherwise it would have been difficult to obtain a satisfactory before Monday next, but—

First. I hope that you will make me contented to withdraw it; and

Second. The phrases are such as in a legal document I have felt obliged to sign, but are very far from representing my feelings toward you aside from the business of my desire for unanimous fraternal procedure.

Let us try to agree; it would be much pleasanter.

E[dward] P. Warren.

Bellevue Hotel, Boston
December 13, 1909

In the course of the hearings, a statement was made that there was not a claim of bad faith in the conduct of this affair. You will find such statement by Mr. Whipple on page 490 and pages 601 to 613, and pages 878 to 882 of the Warren record. Mr. Whipple's position, as briefly as you could state it there, was that the arrangement on the plan had resulted in an unfairness to these beneficiaries.

* * *

MR. McCLENNEN. . . . I had occasion in the course of the trial, to go into those items and find out the reasons which led to the distribution into the one account or the other. I went into them with the bookkeepers—I do not mean in the open course of the trial, but in connection with preparing the case and as the hearings were going on. These investigations I took up with the bookkeepers, with the mechanical men, with Mr. Warren himself. Of course, Mr. Mason was no longer living. I do not recall of ever hearing from any source, up to the time that Mr. Youngman testified before this committee, that Mr. Brandeis was in any way connected with that distribution. It was obviously a distribution which an accountant could not make as a matter of accounting. It involved the exercise of mechanical and business judgment. It was not a division that had been made according to any definite prescribed rule of division applying to all cases. It was not conceivable that you could get any rule that would fit every situation, because the question would arise in so many different ways. One could only form a judgment as to the correctness of the distribution of figures that had been made. I could not discover anything to indicate that the division had not been a correct one. It is certainly true, as true certainly as one can speak of the character and understanding of other men, that there was absolutely no bad faith or intention to rig the accounts in these transactions, and this suggestion of Mr. Youngman's that Sam Warren did not have to do with the matter does not conform to the facts, as I found them in going over the matter with Sam Warren. It was a matter, as I got it from dealing with all of these men—Fiske Warren, Sam Warren (Mr. Mason was no longer alive), and the other employees—that was worked out in the office by the ordinary means that business men would take in determining those questions.

MR. FOX. Would it be out of place to ask whether you yourself do not think you are testifying as to confidential communications made to you by your own client, who is now dead? I express no view. I am only asking what you think.

MR. McCLENNEN. I do not think that I am.

MR. FOX. That is for you to decide.

MR. McCLENNEN. I have endeavored not to, and certainly I believe that it is better for me to testify, even to confidential communications, than to leave an imputation upon his honesty, integrity, or fairness, projected into the case by the counsel for his adversary.

MR. FOX. Oh, very well.

MR. McCLENNEN. There never was a more unfounded assertion projected into any litigation than that there was the slightest bit of dishonesty or unfairness in the action of the people in this matter. . . .

* * *

SENATOR WORKS. The feature of that particular transaction that I want to know as much about as I can is Mr. Brandeis's relation to these various parties whose interest did, at a certain time, become conflicting relations, his being attorney originally for Mr. Warren and his being attorney for the estate, and was he the executor of that estate only, or of Mrs. Warren's estate?

MR. McCLENNEN. He was, I think, never an executor of any estate until Samuel D.'s death in 1910.

SENATOR WORKS. Then his being an attorney for the lessees under this lease and the partnership, after it was formed, and the fact that subsequently litigation came between the people that he had been representing altogether, and then he, through you, took one side of that litigation. Those are the things that seem to me to be important—not that transaction, not the result of the trial of the Warren case, or, in fact, any charges made in the Warren case, unless Mr. Brandeis has been connected with this case. I may say to you now that I do not think there is any evidence here that connects him with any wrongdoing in connection with the management of the property. I do not recall anything that would satisfy or even create any doubt in my mind as to whether he was connected with any wrongful transaction in the management of the property.

SENATOR WALSH. In connection with the matter to which your attention is now directed by Senator Works, my recollection is that the first gentleman who told us about this matter, Mr. Bailey, advanced that the only ground that he had to urge in the way of criticism of Mr. Brandeis in connection with the matter was that he did not, at the outset, advise Edward Warren that his interests were or might be adverse to the other, and that he should get independent counsel. I want to inquire of you whether there was any evidence of Mr. Edward Warren having taken counsel from any one other that Mr. Brandeis or Mr. Brandeis's firm until he employed Mr. Youngman?

MR. McCLENNEN. I do not think there was any indication whatever.

SENATOR WALSH. When did he first consult Mr. Youngman or other counsel outside of the Brandeis firm?

MR. McCLENNEN. In 1903 he consulted Mr. Youngman, and the first matter, I think, was in connection with an advance which S.D. Warren & Co. were to make him on the faith of his interest. I think that was money that was to be used in connection with these antiquities which he was collecting. Incidentally, while he was interested in art for art's sake this purchasing of antiquities was a business transaction.

SENATOR WALSH. It had a commercial aspect?

MR. McCLENNEN. It was a business transaction, and one of the things that produced some little friction which was just a brotherly friction. Sam Warren did not believe very much in the antiquity business, and Ned Warren maintained that there was money in it, and I think has since maintained that he proved his superior judgement to Sam's in the outcome.

SENATOR WALSH. He probably felt his brother knew more about paper making and he knew more about antiquities?

MR. McCLENNEN. I think that may be so.

SENATOR WORKS. As I understand it, Mr. Brandeis, or your firm, represented the estate and collected your fees from them?

MR. McCLENNEN. That, I think, is correct.

SENATOR WORKS. In that connection, I suppose you made these different contracts that resulted finally in the organization of this company. Who paid for that?

MR. McCLENNEN. I think that Mr. Sam Warren drew those contracts, undoubtedly with the advice and assistance of Mr. Brandeis; but I think the actual drafting was Sam Warren's. Of course, you realize that Mr. Sam Warren was likely just as good a lawyer as Mr. Brandeis at that time.

. . .

SENATOR WORKS. When this suit was brought that you have been talking about, was that included in that salary—your services there?

MR. McCLENNEN. This Edward Warren suit?

SENATOR WALSH. Yes.

MR. McCLENNEN. No; that was dealt with separately. That had a magnitude far beyond anything we had in contemplation.

SENATOR WORKS. Whom do you understand you were representing in that litigation?

MR. McCLENNEN. In that litigation Samuel D. Warren was a party as a trustee, and we represented him. Fiske Warren was in as a beneficiary, made a defendant, represented by Mr. Storey. Cornelia Warren was in as a beneficiary, made a defendant, represented by Mr. Gorham. Mr. Mason's executors were in as representatives of a deceased trustee, and they were represented by Stoughton Bell or their counsel. So that the only party in that suit for whom we appeared was Samuel D. Warren as trustee.

. . . .

SENATOR WORKS. Did it ever occur to your mind that there might be any reason why Mr. Brandeis should not represent one of these parties as against the other, considering the fact that it grew out of the trust transaction in which he was attorney, and the instrument that he drew?

MR. McCLENNEN. I had not thought and never had heard it suggested until to-day that that was one of the factors of possible criticism. It was a matter of absolute course as handled at the time that we should defend this trustee whose trust administration was being attacked.

SENATOR WORKS. Well, that would depend altogether upon whether Mr. Brandeis was in such a position that he really was a representative of all these parties. He had been up to that time, apparently, and of course had gained all of the information that one could have very well gained on account of his connection with the estate and with the trusteeship and the partnership in connection with the business, and all those things would be, at least, of immense advantage in dealing with the situation. I am only suggesting to you whether that relation was inconsistent with his duty to Ned Warren, as they call him, who may or may not have been fully informed of the condition, either through Mr. Brandeis or his brother.

MR. McCLENNEN. Well, I never had thought of that problem before. Of course, the only way in which in these matters Mr. Brandeis had ever represented Ned Warren at all was derivatively; that is, he had been counsel for these trustees and counsel for S. D. Warren & Co. As individual counsel, primarily for Ned Warren, he continued in these matters, and his only relation with Ned Warren was the relation counsel for a trustee bears to the beneficiaries of that trust; and I would have supposed that counsel for the trustee would ordinarily, as a matter of course, be expected to defend the administration of the trust upon which, in a measure, he had been advising.

SENATOR WORKS. That might be so if it is conceded that Mr. Brandeis, without any impropriety, could continue the attorneyship of the trustees, but it seems to have been assumed here all along, by you as well as by other witnesses, that the duty did rest on Mr. Brandeis to keep Mr. Ned Warren advised of what the situation was in dealing with the trust property. I do not know whether it was or not; but you have assumed that, because you have undertaken to show that he was advised, and that Mr. Brandeis and Mr. S. D. Warren did keep him informed of conditions. You must keep in mind all the time that in that matter Mr. Brandeis undoubtedly was representing all of these parties at least up to the time that this trust was formed and the property turned over to other parties, and there was no doubt about that, is there?

MR. McCLENNEN. In the sense that a man who represents an executor represents every beneficiary of the will. In no other sense did he ever represent S. D. Warren.

SENATOR WORKS. I suppose it was understood at the time this trust relation was created that this property was turned over to somebody else that Mr. Brandeis himself was representing, by these parties. Didn't you so regard it?

MR. McCLENNEN. Then, again, in the sense that any counsel of a trust intimately represents every member of that trust, but not in any primary sense.

SENATOR WORKS. As a test of the duty of an attorney under those circumstances, do you think Mr. Brandeis was under obligation to inform the members of the family of the conditions at the time they were proposing to execute this trust? Do you think any obligation rested upon him then?

MR. McCLENNEN. I should not have said that any such duty existed, under the circumstances that were there presented, if I may make that answer complete.

SENATOR WORKS. Oh, yes; I want it complete.

MR. McCLENNEN. What I have in mind is this: The subject matter of this proposed plan was the real estate of these heirs, and the plan was a negotiation between all those heirs. If Mr. Brandeis, under those circumstances, was under an obligation to disclose everything to Ned Warren, then he was under an obligation to Sam Warren to keep everything still, if that was the situation.

SENATOR WORKS. That would show, then, that there was absolute conflict of interest there, if your statement is true. I do not accept that as being so.

MR. McCLENNEN. Of course, every time there exists a partnership you may say there is a conflict of interest between the two partners, and I would not suppose it was affirmative duty of the counsel for that partnership to look out to see that one partner did not overreach the other in the transaction which those two partners were planning out and conducting between themselves.

SENATOR WORKS. Yes; but you are assuming that there is nothing involved here, MR. McCLENNEN, but a partnership. There was a trust established here under which this lease was executed, if I understand the situation. At that time the estate had not been closed. Your firm was representing the estate then?

MR. McCLENNEN. I think the estate was closed coincidentally.

* * *

SENATOR WALSH. I want to ask whether it ever occurred in the course of your practice that two gentlemen, desiring to enter into a contract, an elaborate contract, with many terms and conditions and mutual obligations, reposing entire confidence in your firm, came to you and asked you to draw the matter up to meet the views of both of them?

MR. McCLENNEN. That certainly has been, in my experience, not an uncommon situation.

SENATOR WALSH. Have you ever felt in those circumstances that you ought to advise each of them that he ought to be represented by counsel in the matter, or did you undertake to carry out what they desired to the best of your ability under the circumstances?

MR. McCLENNEN. I have done the latter. Under those circumstances, if I was wanted at all, as I understand it, it would involve getting three lawyers into the situation.

SENATOR WALSH. Just to give us your point of view about this matter, I wish you would tell us now if you had never been able to anticipate what followed, but the conditions arose as they existed in 1888 or 1889 when Mr. Brandeis was connected with this matter, and adjusting the family affair, would you have felt it necessary to advise each one of the interested parties that it would be prudent on their part, if not advisable, that each of them be represented in the negotiations by counsel?

MR. McCLENNEN. It would not have occurred to me personally to do anything of the kind; that is, this is one of the perhaps few occasions on which I can agree with Mr. Storey—that if this situation returned again, without the insight I now have, I should do just as was done by Mr. Brandeis under the situation that there presented itself.

SENATOR FLETCHER. Did you know Mr. S. D Warren, the partner of Mr. Brandeis?

MR. McCLENNEN. Oh, yes, indeed. I knew him slightly in 1895 and from that time down, and extremely well during the last short period of his life.

SENATOR FLETCHER. He was the senior member of the firm of Warren & Brandeis, was he not?

MR. McCLENNEN. He was the senior member of the firm of Warren & Brandeis up to 1889.

SENATOR FLETCHER. Was he the man who had his own views of things and asserted his opinions on questions, or did he rely solely and entirely on Mr. Brandeis's views?

MR. McCLENNEN. Mr. Warren was a man of unusual mental capacity and vigor and strength of purpose and mind. I do not know where a comparison of the respective mental capacities and legal attainments of Mr. Warren and Mr. Brandeis at that time would land. He was the senior member, and I always understood was the second man in his class in the law school, and a man who, about this time, I remember, collaborated with Mr. Brandeis on legal articles, or on one I have in my mind, anyway, that was published.

SENATOR FLETCHER. Mr. Youngman gives us this picture of Mr. Warren, if this impression on my mind is the one he desired to give—that Mr. Warren was a man of highest integrity and honor—

MR. McCLENNEN. There is not the slightest question but what that is so.

SENATOR FLETCHER. Let me finish, please (continuing). And that if Mr. Warren had been left free to act according to the dictates of his own conscience and according to his own judgment, and had not been—I think he used the word "hypnotized" on one occasion—

MR. McCLENNEN (interrupting). Chloroformed.

SENATOR FLETCHER (continuing). And chloroformed on another occasion by Mr. Brandeis, this sort of an arrangement would not have been entered into.

With your knowledge of Mr. Warren and his habits and his practice as a member of the firm, would you say he was a man who was subject to hypnotic influences and to being chloroformed in a large business undertaking?

MR. McCLENNEN. Of course I never saw Mr. Warren as a member of the law firm and I never saw his activities in the office. I can not answer that part of the question. So far as he was concerned, he was a dominant man in any situation in which he was placed, a leader in any course in which he was engaged; ready to some extent to take advice, but not at all over ready to take advice from anybody. Of course, a man who had a great respect for Mr. Brandeis's ability and judgment, and undoubtedly a man who would be influenced by that respect that he had, but not at all a man to be controlled except as his intelligence, which was of a very high order, was convinced.

* * *

SENATOR WORKS. Let me take Senator Walsh's illustration of two men being represented by the same attorney in a given matter. I do not see any reason why an attorney should not do that. But suppose litigation should occur over a contract involving a question of fact. Would you, in that case, have any delicacy about taking the litigation for one of the parties as against the other?

MR. McCLENNEN. If one was a detractor from the common agreement they had reached, I should think it was proper to act for the one who was pursuing the undertakings which I had been employed to put into concrete shape.

SENATOR WORKS. The very question might be the construction of a contract, as one or the other was violating its terms. Having drawn that contract, what would you think about taking sides on that question when litigation occurred? In other words, you might feel that one of the parties to the contract, as you construed it, was violating its terms, and that might be the very subject of litigation.

MR. McCLENNEN. The question of the propriety of acting then might, to my mind, well depend upon the debatable character of the contest that was being proposed.

SENATOR WORKS. It must be assumed that when two parties get into litigation there is a debatable question between them.

MR. McCLENNEN. I have found many times when that assumption was without foundation.

* * *

SENATOR CHILTON. As you said this morning, is it not a fact that the trust agreements and what should be done under the trust agreements was submitted to all the parties before it was signed and that the trust was made practically for the purpose of the lease, the terms of which had been agreed upon by the parties?

MR. McCLENNEN. That is true. Of course, I do not want to seem to assent too far. You understand that when this was fully agreed to by all the parties having the papers before them, Ned Warren was in Europe and had not seen the papers. They were then executed by all the parties, and went to him on the 31st of May, 1889, I should think, except the lease and that letter which explained the terms of the lease.

SENATOR CHILTON. In other words, when Mr. Edward Warren signed the trust agreement he understood it was for the purpose of making a lease, and the terms of the lease were set forth in the letter to him, and that was acted under for a number of years, and during that time Mr. Brandeis occupied the personal and professional relations which you have related?

MR. McCLENNEN. Yes.

SENATOR CHILTON. Therefore, when you spoke of a disagreement afterwards, the supposed case is not just on a par with that. There was not any controversy about the terms of agreements, was there? Mr. Edward Warren undertook, either through his counsel or personally, to impugn some actions of the elder Warren under him, and in doing that in that way it involved Mr. Brandeis, did it not?

MR. McCLENNEN. I never heard, until Mr. Youngman stated it here, that that involved Mr. Brandeis in any way.

SENATOR CHILTON. All right.

MR. McCLENNEN. Of course, it appeared in his bill of complaint that one of the things that he set up in painting the entire picture of the situation, according to his view, was the fact that Warren and Brandeis, or Mr. Brandeis, had been counsel for the trustees.

SENATOR CHILTON. I think we understand it now. Are there questions?

MR. FOX. May I ask one question?

SENATOR CHILTON. Certainly.

MR. FOX. It is not on that line.

SENATOR CHILTON. All right.

MR. FOX. You spoke of Warren being the senior member of the firm. How many years' difference in their graduation at college was there do you know. Of course, Mr. Brandeis was not a graduate of the college; he was a graduate of the law school, was he not?

MR. McCLENNEN. Mr. Brandeis was not a graduate of the college.

MR. FOX. No.

MR. McCLENNEN. Mr. Warren was a graduate of the college in the class of 1874. When I used the term "senior member," I referred really to the order of their names; but to make it more specific, I will say that at the time of putting this plan in operation, Mr. Warren was, I believe, 36 and Mr. Brandeis was 32. Ned Warren was 29.

MR. FOX. That is all.

* * *

QUESTIONS

1. The problem that the Warren family had to solve after the death of Samuel Warren, Sr. was finding a way to compensate Mason and family members interested in operating the business, while other family members received dividend payments. Such problems are common in representing family members after the death of the founder of a successful business. Why might family members in this situation not want to retain separate lawyers?

2. Should Brandeis and Samuel D. Warren, Jr. ("Sam") have discussed the potential conflicts of interest with the family members at the outset of the representation? Should the family members have been told to each consult a separate lawyer?

3. The conflict between Edward Warren ("Ned") and Sam had at least some of its roots in Ned's reaction to the puritanical self righteousness of nineteenth century Boston society. Ned knew that he was gay at a very early age, had bitter experiences as a boy "and because of it he hated Boston for the rest of his life. He suffered the derision of other boys, both for his failure in manly sports and tastes, and for his sexual 'abnormality.'" Martin Green, The Mount Vernon Street Warrens: A Boston Story, 1860–1910 41 (1989). This alienation not only instigated Ned's departure from Boston to collect art in the more tolerant city of Paris, but eventually led to ill will between Ned and the rest of his family, particularly Sam. Id. (note Senator Chilton's apparent ignorance of these matters in his exchange with Youngman on the relations between Sam and Ned). To the extent Brandeis was aware of these matters, should be have been more alert to the risks of representing both Ned and Sam? How much should a lawyer know about the personal lives of family members before beginning a family representation?

4. Sam was Brandeis's senior by four years, and this matter involved his family. Was he or Brandeis the lawyer on this matter? Was Sam too involved to be an effective lawyer? How did Brandeis's role change after Sam left the law partnership to go into the paper business in 1897?

5.   Was there a breach of trust from the start in that trustees were dealing with themselves? If so, who was responsible for this breach of trust?

6.   In what way could conflicts of interest have affected Sam's handling of the following discretionary features of the arrangement:

a.   the lessees' right to terminate on short notice;

b.   the rent due to the trust from the lessees (6 percent interest on the real estate plus half of the net profits of the firm);

c.   the financial return to the lessees (according to Bailey, Sam went from earning $10,000 in the law firm to earning "something approaching $75,000 or $100,000" during the first few years of the trust; Bailey alleged in the bill in equity that this was "twice as much as they could fairly charge for the work of carrying on the business");

d.   the lessees' right to determine what was a "repair" or "replacement" paid for by the lessees and what was an "addition" paid for by the lessor;

e.   the method of compensating the law firm ($4,000 per year; half from the trustees, half from lessees); and

f.   the calculation of depreciation on the property.

7.   Should an independent judgment have been sought on the repairs or the depreciation?

8.   What actual conflicts arose on account of each of the following:

a.   the death of Mrs. Samuel Warren, Sr. in 1901;

b.   Sam's preference for Cornelia to Ned in selecting a new trustee; and

c.   the fact that income did not increase although $1 million was added to capital;

9.   Brandeis had prepared Ned's will and had a duty of loyalty to Ned as well as to Sam. On the other hand, he had received no confidential communication from Ned and Ned knew all along that Brandeis had a strong loyalty to Sam. Should Brandeis have continued to represent Sam after the interests of Sam and Ned came into conflict?

10.   Should Brandeis have acted as counsel for the trustees and the lessees at the same time?

11.   Storey observes that it is "a common practice, but I think a bad practice" in family settlements for a lawyer to undertake to represent all of the parties, even though the interests may be conflicting. To what extent should a lawyer's conduct be judged by what other lawyers do? Is it likely that at least some of Brandeis's accusers in the Boston bar had involved themselves in similar concurrent conflicts?

12.   Bailey and Youngman had brought their bill in equity against Sam, not Brandeis. Nonetheless, Youngman testified at Brandeis's confirmation hearings that he had "high regard for Sam Warren's sense of honor," and that "Sam Warren had to be persuaded, and he was persuaded by Louis D. Brandeis" to proceed with the contemplated arrangement. Was Youngman unfairly shifting blame from Sam to Brandeis? Was this shifting of blame facilitated by the fact that these accusations against Brandeis were made after Sam was dead?

13. When Fox questions McClennen's testimony about confidential communications made to him by Sam, McClennen replies that it would be better for him to testify about Sam's confidential communications than to "leave an imputation upon his honesty, integrity, or fairness, projected into the case by the counsel for his adversary." Is this a good reason to reveal client confidences? See Chapter 2 supra.

14. Sherman Whipple cross-examined Sam for 27 days immediately prior to Sam's death, apparently of self inflicted gunshot wounds. See A. Gal, Brandeis of Boston 172 (1980) (based on interview with Sam's grandson); Martin Green, supra, at 197. Is wearing down a witness with lengthy questioning an acceptable trial tactic? Should a lawyer consider the emotional effect a trial can have on a witness?

15. "I do not recall having met Hollis R. Bailey in the Warren case," Brandeis wrote McClennen on February 17, 1916. "The last case I had against Bailey ... was the Henry E. Weston will case.... The question in that case was whether Weston was of sound mind. We contended that he was not and undertook to prove that he was affected by general paresis. I think there is little doubt but that the case was won on my closing argument.... As I think it over, it must be Bailey's wrong-headedness in this case that started him in opposition to me." Alpheus Thomas Mason, Brandeis: A Free Man's Life 484 (1956).

a. How common is it for petty jealousies to affect one lawyer's view of another lawyer? What do you think Bailey's motivations were in bringing these accusations forward at Brandeis's confirmation hearings?

b. If it is true that Bailey had never met Brandeis in the Warren case, did Bailey have an ethical obligation to at least hear Brandeis's side of the story before going public with his accusations?

16. An 1898 survey of William Youngman's class at Harvard College asked class members to identify their "religious views." Responses overwhelmingly indicated three denominations: Episcopalian, Unitarian and Congregationalist (no indication of what Youngman's affiliation was, and no mention of denomination in his own class notes). 5 out of 376 class members indicated that they were Jewish and 13 out of 376 that they were Catholic. *Harvard College Class of 1895, Secretary's Report No. 1* (1898).

After Hollis Bailey died in 1934, F.W. Smith, a classmate, wrote: "It was perfectly fitting that our classmate, Hollis Russell Bailey, a son of New England, of honorable New England ancestry, should pass from us on New England's most venerable and typical holiday, Thanksgiving Day—Thanksgiving Day, 1934." *Harvard College Class of 1877, Tenth Report* 20 (1937).

The Reverend A.A. Berle had written to Senator Chilton on February 18, 1916:

It would be fair to say that if any man bearing an old New England name and practicing at the Bar in Boston had everything which is alleged against Brandeis alleged against him, and were nominated for the Supreme Court, no one would dream of raising these questions.

Long and unchallenged control of everything in the Commonwealth has given many of these gentlemen the perfectly natural feeling that whoever is not approved by them is *ipso facto* a person who is either "dangerous" or lacking in "judicial temperament." They simply cannot realize, and do not, that a long New England ancestry is not *prima facie* a trusteeship for everything in New England. That is in my judgment the real spring of most of the opposition.

Mason, Brandeis: A Free Man's Life 481 (1956).

a. Was the sense of honor displayed by Bailey and others in Boston shaped by ethnic pride and self-righteousness or by genuine concern for ethical standards in the legal profession?

b. Are the Reverend Berle's observations correct, or were there multiple grounds for the opposition to Brandeis, of which he identifies one?

c. Do prejudices based on social class or ethnicity still influence our judgments of other people's ethics? How does lack of diversity in college and law school classes reinforce such prejudice?

d. Is the legal profession the best judge of the conduct of its own members, or is the profession still too insular, and perhaps even clubby, to do so evenhandedly?

17. In a brief autobiography appearing in *Harvard College Class of 1877 Seventh Report* (1917), Bailey discussed his extensive involvement in social clubs, civic organizations and bar association groups, but made no mention of his role in the Brandeis confirmation hearings. Youngman, however, remained adamant about the failed accusations years after his testimony. In 1920, Youngman wrote in his college reunion report:

I seem always to be engaged in some kind of battle, but I have tried at all times to be constructive and progressive. I have not sought to be safe or cozy, either in war or peace. I have regularly fought men who were snobs, liars and traitors to the public good. Some of these have been rich, and some have been powerful. I haven't gone out of my way to punish them, but when it came in the line of duty I must say that I enjoyed taking the conceit out of some men who had been very generous advertisers of themselves as extremely virtuous, when they were in reality hypocrites and secretly disloyal to the causes that they publicly espoused. I was summoned to appear before a committee of the United States Senate to do one job of this kind, and I do not regret the action, although persons concerned have endeavored to make me suffer severely for it.

Harvard Class of 1895, Report VI 558–559 (1920).

a.   Was Youngman's testimony given "in the line of duty?" What duty did he have in this situation? What type of "job" did he do before the United States Senate?

b.   After one lawyer has accused another lawyer of misconduct, and the matter has been investigated without an adverse finding against the second lawyer, is it proper for the first lawyer to continue to make the accusation publicly?

c.   Was it proper for Youngman to allege that "persons concerned," presumably Brandeis and his supporters, were on a vendetta against him without stating any evidence in support of such an accusation?

18.   In 1920, Youngman wrote: "I have had no ambition for power or wealth, nor to attain any so-called position in society." *Harvard Class of 1895, Report VI* 558–559 (1920). He was elected two years later as State Senator from Norfolk and Suffolk, four years later as State Treasurer, and ten years later as Lieutenant Governor. Could political ambition have had something to do with Youngman's enthusiasm to make an accusation against Brandeis?

The Brief in Opposition

A *Brief on Behalf of the Opposition to the Confirmation of Louis Brandeis as Associate Justice of the Supreme Court of the United States*, was filed by Austen Fox and Kenneth Spence, both of New York, with the United States Senate on March 28, 1916. The brief, ninety-nine pages in length, recited a litany of unfavorable character evidence and over a dozen specific charges against Brandeis.

HEARINGS BEFORE THE SUB–COMMITTEE OF THE COMMITTEE
ON THE JUDICIARY,
UNITED STATES SENATE, SIXTY–FOURTH CONGRESS,
FIRST SESSION, ON THE
NOMINATION
OF
LOUIS D. BRANDEIS
TO BE AN ASSOCIATE JUSTICE
OF THE
SUPREME COURT OF THE UNITED STATES.

**Brief on Behalf of the Opposition to the Confirmation
of Louis D. Brandeis as Associate Justice of the
Supreme Court of the United States**

AUSTEN G. FOX
KENNETH M. SPENCE
of New York
*Counsel in Opposition
to Confirmation*

Summary of Brief in Opposition.

———

PAGE

The President and seven former Presidents of the American Bar Association have opposed the confirmation of Mr. Brandeis   6–7

Character witnesses, called both in opposition and in support of confirmation testified that Mr. Brandeis's reputation among a considerable portion of the members of his home bar is that he is not straightforward and is unscrupulous   7–10

The proof shows that:

1.   THE NOMINEE HAS VIOLATED WELL ESTABLISHED CANONS OF PROFESSIONAL ETHICS IN THE FOLLOWING INSTANCES:

Mr. Brandeis "was retained and accepted the retainer * * * of James T. Lennox".

Mr. Brandeis advised Lennox to make an assignment for the benefit of creditors without informing him that the assignment constituted an act of bankruptcy and two and a half months thereafter at the instance of three creditors of Lennox, Mr. Brandeis filed a petition in bankruptcy against Lennox who thereafter was adjudged an involuntary bankrupt. Mr. Brandeis's law firm's fees from this bankruptcy proceeding arose in part from fees of his partner Mr. Nutter as assignee for the benefit of creditors, in part from Mr. Brandeis's fees as counsel for the assignee, in part from Mr. Nutter's fees as trustee in bankruptcy, and in part from Mr. Brandeis's fees as counsel for the trustee, and for the firm's services in bankruptcy proceeding. These fees amounted in all to $43,852.88. Mr. Lennox did not know that Mr. Brandeis was acting otherwise than his counsel until after the petition in bankruptcy had been filed 15–29

Mr. Brandeis, while acting as counsel to Edward P. Warren, failed for thirteen years to disclose to his client the essential features of a plan for operating the Warren paper mill, in which Edward P. Warren had an equal share with his brother, Samuel D. Warren, Jr., the partner of Mr. Brandeis. The plan was formulated and consummated by Mr. Brandeis. Under this plan Samuel D. Warren, Jr., one of the trustees, leased to himself, as one of the lessees, the trust property. The result of the plan was that Mr. Brandeis's partner, S.D. Warren, Jr., trustee, profited personally to an unconscionable amount. Mr. Brandeis subsequently appeared as attorney for S.D. Warren, Jr., as against his former client, Edward P. Warren, in respect to the very matter in which Edward P. Warren had reposed confidence in Mr. Brandeis   29–39

Mr. Brandeis participated in the organization of the United Shoe Machinery Company. As active director from 1899 to 1906, and as counsel from 1899 to 1907, he approved and defended, before the Massachusetts Legislature and elsewhere, the policy and leases of the Company. Soon after his employment as counsel had ceased, Mr. Brandeis became counsel for the Company's assailants, and promulgated opinions to the effect that the Company and its leases were monopolistic and unlawful. Before Committees of Congress and elsewhere, he made against the Company the very charges against which he had defended it prior to 1909

In 1905, Mr. Brandeis in a public address charged the directors of the Equitable Life Assurance Society with fraud and dishonesty in the handling of the funds of the Society, and shortly thereafter he became counsel for a Protective Committee of Equitable policyholders. At the same time his firm was acting as counsel for the Equitable Society in certain pending litigations. About a year after Mr. Brandeis had become counsel for this Protective Committee, his firm appeared as counsel for the Equitable Society in a suit brought against it by a policyholder alleging fraud and mismanagement upon the part of the directors, and for several years Mr. Brandeis's firm conducted this litigation on behalf of the Equitable Society, although the complaint was largely a reassertion of the very language which Mr. Brandeis himself had used in his attack against the Equitable

In suits brought by a stockholder against four directors of the Gillette Safety Razor Company, Mr. Brandeis appeared as attorney for all four directors. While acting as attorney for all four directors in these suits, Mr. Brandeis devised a plan whereby two of them might secure control of the Gillette Safety Razor company and oust the other two. Mr. Brandeis continued to appear as attorney for the other two until the plan to oust them was effected and they were ousted from control, meanwhile concealing the plan from them

2. IN THE COURSE OF THE PERFORMANCE OF HIS PROFESSIONAL DUTIES, THE NOMINEE HAS MADE FALSE AND MISLEADING STATEMENTS AND HAS BEEN GUILTY OF DUPLICITY:

In the Congressional investigation of the charges of Glavis against Secretary Ballinger,[2] Mr. Brandeis, though retained and paid by

---

2. Ed.—"Ballinger, [President] Taft's Secretary of the Interior, had fired a subordinate, Richard Glavis, for impugning his integrity before the President by reporting suspicions about Ballinger's dealings with the Guggenheim mining interests. Glavis had previously been in touch with the administration's chief forester, Gifford Pinchot, the leading progressive spokesman on conservation issues, and by this time an ardent opponent of Ballinger's policies. The two went to Collier's Weekly, which in turn published their story of frustration. Collier's Weekly, Nov. 13, 1909, at 15–17, 27. The administra-

tion called for a Congressional investigation to vindicate Ballinger, and also threatened to sue Collier's for libel. Brandeis, among other leading lawyers, was called in by Collier's, to represent Glavis. The Republicans on the committee sought to whitewash the matter and frustrated the lawyer at most turns. But Brandeis, smelling blood, sought the wounds. Soon, by his questioning and 'detective-work,' he discovered that Taft had exonerated Ballinger without being aware of all the facts and then, along with his attorney general, Wickersham, had antedated certain documents to conceal his neglect. It was a petty mistake by an elephant of a man, but Taft

PAGE

3. THE NOMINEE HAS PRESENTED INTERESTS OPPOSED TO THE PUBLIC WELFARE AND BEEN GUILTY OF SHARP PRACTICE:

continued to handle the press badly once found out." L. S. Zacharias, Legal Theory: Repaving the Brandeis Way: The Decline of Developmental Property, 82 Nw. U.L. Rev. 596, 610, n. 61 (1988).

NOTES AND QUESTIONS

None of the charges listed in the *Brief in Opposition* had been the subject of disciplinary proceedings or action against Brandeis by a court or bar committee, and apparently none of the charges was proved to the satisfaction of the majority of the Senate. Brandeis was confirmed by a vote of 47 to 22 as Progressive Republicans lined up with Democrats to approve the nomination (only one Democrat, Francis G. Newlands of Nevada, voted against confirmation). For a point-by-point rebuttal of most of these charges, see John P. Frank, The Legal Ethics of Louis D. Brandeis, 17 Stan. L. Rev. 683 (1965).

1. How accurate is the summary of the Warren Trust matter in the table of contents to Austen Fox's brief?

2. Does the brief's mention of the Ballinger affair (which preoccupied Brandeis during much of the Warren Trust litigation) suggest that the Republicans were trying to get back at Brandeis for his representation of Ballinger's opponents?

3. "The 1916 hearings were virtually one long inquiry into claims that, on various occasions, Brandeis had violated the ethical norms of law practice. And almost all of the charges played on a common theme—that Brandeis did not measure his duties as advocate according to the interest of an individual client, to whom he owed unqualified loyalty; in more modern terms, he had become embroiled in conflicts of interest and had failed to pursue his clients' interests with the zeal required by the canons of the bar. But the 'conflicts of interest' here were of an idiosyncratic kind: Brandeis was accused essentially of permitting his own vision to interfere with what should have been a deferential loyalty to his clients." Clyde Spillenger, Elusive Advocate: Reconsidering Brandeis as People's Lawyer, 105 Yale L. J. 1445, 1500 (1996). The problems with the Warren Trust matter "arose at least in part because Brandeis attempted to handle the needs and interests of everybody involved—that is, all the family members who were or might have been beneficiaries under Sam's will." Id., n. 192. Brandeis himself sometimes described his role in a case as being a "lawyer for the situation" rather than for a specific client. Is it possible that Brandeis allowed his own and Sam's vision for addressing the "situation" presented by the death of

Samuel Warren, Sr. to interfere with his duty to look after the interests of his clients?

4. Does the long litany of accusations recited in the *Brief in Opposition* shore up the case against Brandeis even though there was apparently no clear proof for any one of these accusations? Alternatively, is the opposition merely trying to smear Brandeis by replacing proof with multiple accusations of unethical conduct?

5. How much weight would you give to the number of accusations made against a lawyer's ethics absent proof for any one of the accusations? Do multiple accusations make it more or less likely that the other lawyer is unethical? Does the context in which you are assessing the other lawyer's ethics matter (for example, a decision whether to retain the lawyer as co-counsel on a case, compared to a decision whether to support that lawyer's nomination to the bench)?

6. What matters are "fair game" for testimony in Senate hearings for the confirmation of a Supreme Court justice? How, if at all, should the Senate confine its investigation? In 1916, it was not customary for the nominee to testify in his defense, and Brandeis did not do so. Is it better for the nominee to testify or to stay away from the hearings and allow others to come to his defense?

Relevant Background

What is a Concurrent Conflict?

A concurrent conflict arises when a lawyer simultaneously represents two or more clients with different interests. For example, clients may be opponents in litigation or co-parties who decide to file cross claims against each other. A concurrent conflict can also arise between clients that are parties to related but separate actions or even to entirely unrelated actions. Furthermore, concurrent conflicts can occur in non-litigation matters, as where clients have adverse business interests or the interests of family members represented by the same lawyer begin to diverge.

There are valid reasons for allowing many concurrent representations, despite the conflicts that may arise. Parties may be aligned in a lawsuit against a common opponent or seek to embark on a common enterprise, such as setting up a partnership or corporation. Hiring a single lawyer often saves legal fees, makes a representation more efficient, and facilitates sharing of information. Charles W. Wolfram, Modern Legal Ethics 349 (1986). Also, family members operating a business usually want to be represented by the same lawyer. However, Louis Brandeis discovered how problematic such a concurrent representation becomes once a specific conflict of interest emerges and the lawyer has to decide when to disqualify himself from representing some or all of his previous clients.

Generally, if clients have directly adverse interests, the concurrent representation is unacceptable unless it will not adversely affect the lawyer's relationship with either client and the lawyer obtains consent of *each client* after full disclosure of the risks of the representation. Full disclosure requires the lawyer to explain the nature of potential conflicts in sufficient detail that the client can see why it might be desirable to have independent counsel. L. Ray Patterson, An Analysis of Conflicts of Interest Problems, 37 Mercer L. Rev. 569, 580 (1986), citing In re Boivin, 271 Or. 419, 424, 533 P.2d 171, 174 (1975). This disclosure and consent process is primarily intended to protect the client, but also requires the lawyer to ponder existing problems with the representation and conflicts that could arise in the future.

The Model Code provides that a lawyer should not take part in a representation where her independent judgment is adversely affected by her representation of another client, or if she would be representing differing interests. See Model Code DR 5–105. Differing interests include "every interest that will adversely affect either the judgment or the loyalty of a lawyer to a client, whether it be a conflicting, inconsistent, diverse, or other interest." Id., definitions. Similarly, Mode Rule 1.7(a) prohibits a lawyer from representing a client when "representation of that client will be directly adverse to another client," although such representation is permitted if the lawyer reasonably believes that the lawyer's relationship with the other client will not be adversely affected and the client consents after consultation. Rule 1.7 and other conflicts rules in the Model Rules are discussed more extensively in Russell G. Pearce, *Family Values and Legal Ethics*, infra. See also Samuel R. Miller, et al., Conflicts of Interest in Corporate–Litigation, 48 Bus. Law. 141, 198 (1992).

Adversity and Potential Adversity

As illustrated by Brandeis's experience with the Warren Trust, concurrent representations are problematic not only where actual adversity exists, but also where potential adversity might later lead to full blown conflict. Another example would be co-plaintiffs or co-defendants who are represented by the same lawyer yet who also have possible cross claims against each other. Some courts have distinguished actual conflict from potential conflict and have required withdrawal or disqualification when the conflict is actual. See Clay v. Doherty, 608 F.Supp. 295, 302 (N.D.Ill.1985). Other courts recognize the need to prevent potential conflicts and distinguish between cases where conflicts are actual, likely, and unlikely. When conflict is actual the lawyer may be required to withdraw, regardless of whether consent is obtained, and when conflict is likely, the lawyer may be allowed to proceed, but only with the informed consent of both clients. See In re Conduct of Johnson, 300 Or. 52, 707 P.2d 573 (1985). However, economic competition between clients is generally not considered "conflict" until a legal dispute emerges between them (for example, one of a lawyer's clients begins to contemplate suing another client under the antitrust laws). In In re Ainsworth, 289 Or. 479, 487, 614 P.2d 1127, 1131 (1980), the Oregon Supreme Court found that there was no conflict of interest when a lawyer represented parties with adverse interests in two unrelated real-estate matters and when it was not likely that the "independent professional judgment" of the lawyer on behalf of either client would be adversely affected.

Even if the clients themselves are not adverse, their legal positions still can be. For example, if one client succeeds in court, the outcome could have a negative precedential effect on the other. Also, if in one case a lawyer attacks or undermines an argument that the lawyer is concurrently making on behalf of another client in another case, the second client's case may be weakened by the perceived inconsistency. This problem is accentuated if one of the clients may face the identical issue many times in the future. See John S. Dzienkowski, Positional Conflicts of Interest, 71 Tex. L. Rev. 457, 488–9 (1993). Courts proscribe such representations where a lawyer may consciously or unconsciously sacrifice one client's interest in favor of another. See Note, Developments in the Law: Conflicts of Interest in the Legal Profession, 94 Harv. L. Rev. 1244, 1296 (1981). For example, in Estates Theatres, Inc. v. Columbia Pictures Industries, Inc. 345 F.Supp. 93, 98–99 (S.D.N.Y.1972), the court held that a lawyer was disqualified from representing a plaintiff in a new antitrust matter because success in that case would conflict with a legal position that the lawyer had asserted for another client in a pending case. In Unified Sewerage Agency of Washington County, Oregon v. Jelco Inc. 646 F.2d 1339, 1345 (9th Cir.1981), the Ninth Circuit also observed that an adverse interest can occur when a lawyer takes a legal position that is adverse to a present client, even though the litigation does not involve that client.

Unrelated Matters and the Prima Facie Rule

Because concurrent representations are a greater threat to client loyalty and confidentiality than successive representations, lawyers are generally not permitted to represent at the same time two clients whose interests are adverse, whether or not the matters involved are related. This prima facie proscription of adverse concurrent conflicts was articulated in Cinema 5 Ltd. v. Cinerama, Inc., 528 F.2d 1384 (2d Cir.1976), where the Second Circuit held that the "substantial relationship" test, often used to evaluate successive conflicts with former clients (see Chapter 4 supra), was inadequate for concurrent conflicts. Instead, the court held that in concurrent representations, "where the relationship is a continuing one, adverse representation is prima facie improper." Id. at 1387. The court allowed a lawyer to rebut this prima facie showing with proof that there was no "actual or apparent conflict of loyalties or diminution in the vigor of representation." Id. In reality, however, the burden of overcoming the prima facie rule has been heavy and has rarely been met. Wolfram, supra, at 352 n. 22.

Arguably, the prima facie rule is too broad where the duty of loyalty to a current client might prevent other clients from obtaining adequate representation in a particular geographic location or in a specialized area of the law. Also, the prima facie rule may be too broad in large firm situations, where imputed conflicts are inevitable due to the large number of lawyers (see Model Rule 1.10; DR 5–105(D); and discussion of imputed disqualification in Chapter 4 supra). In such circumstances, it may be appropriate for courts to apply imputed disqualification rules less rigorously or to adopt the approach used for successive conflicts, under which a lawyer is only disqualified if matters are "substantially related." However, a lawyer contemplating a new representation which could conflict with the interests of a current client can save herself much aggravation by seeking the informed consent of both clients or asking a court for permission to proceed.

Remedies for a Concurrent Conflict

As in the case of successive conflicts, a motion to disqualify is the usual remedy for a concurrent conflict. In ruling on the motion and constructing a remedy, a court will have to weigh the loyalty and confidentiality interests of the client seeking disqualification against another client's right to retain counsel of its choice. Also, the court will have to guard against misuse of disqualification motions for strictly tactical purposes. Finally, most courts do not look favorably on a lawyer or law firm that accepts a potentially lucrative representation despite an obvious conflict with an existing client and then tells the existing client to consent or find a new lawyer. In such circumstances, a "law firm should not be allowed to abandon its absolute duty of loyalty to one of its clients so that it can benefit from a conflict of interest that it has created." Miller, supra, at 194, quoting Ex parte AmSouth Bank, N.A., 589 So.2d 715, 721 (Ala.1991).

PROBLEM

1. Grimy and Greenleaf ("Firm") is a twenty-lawyer firm in Los Angeles, California. Firm's largest client is Midpoint Realty, a commercial real-estate brokerage firm also in Los Angeles. 40% of Firm's total billable hours last year were for Midpoint and Firm anticipates similar billings to Midpoint this year. Firm usually represents Midpoint when Midpoint is agent for the seller of commercial property. Most of the properties that Midpoint sells are worth over $1 million, and Midpoint receives 10% of the selling price as a commission. Midpoint's counsel supervises a process known as "due diligence" whereby a prospective buyer's agents (including attorneys) inspect a seller's property prior to signing a purchase agreement. Concerns raised during due diligence, such as environmental concerns, are then addressed in the purchase agreement.

Firm is approached by a new client, Elf Acquisitions ("Elf"), a German manufacturing conglomerate, and asked if Firm will agree to represent Elf as the *buyer* of a paper manufacturing facility located at 111 Toxic Tort Road in Los Angeles (the "Toxic Tort Property"). The seller of the Toxic Tort Property, Jolly Not–So–Green Giant, Inc. ("Giant") has hired Midpoint to be the seller's broker. Midpoint has retained a different law firm to represent it for this transaction. After Firm consults with Midpoint and Elf, both clients consent that Firm may represent Elf in this transaction.

At the request of Elf, Firm sends an associate, Naive Novice, to inspect files kept at the Toxic Tort Property. Novice asks to see some inspection reports written by Giant's outside environmental auditing firm, but is told by Simon Salmon, an employee of Midpoint, that the inspection reports have been removed from the Toxic Tort Property to Giant's headquarters in Los Angeles where they will be very difficult to find, and that the reports therefore are unavailable. After several attempts to gain access to the inspection reports, Novice becomes frustrated and asks Salmon: "Is Giant trying to hide something?"

The next day, Salmon telephones Sidney Greenleaf, a partner of Firm to complain that Novice's insistence on seeing the inspection reports is obstructing the deal. "I know that I am not your client this time around," Salmon says, "but, if I were your client, I would get this associate off the deal—he asks too many unimportant questions and is a pain in the a—." Without consulting Elf, Greenleaf removes Novice from the deal.

Should firm have represented Elf in the first place? How should Greenleaf have handled Salmon's telephone call? What should Novice have done when he learned why he was removed from the deal?

2. You are an in-house attorney defending a company against a class action sex discrimination lawsuit. After several months of working on the case, you determine that you also have been discriminated against by your employer. You quit your job and contact the plaintiffs' attorneys who welcome you as a client. They assure the defendant, your former employer, that you have agreed not to reveal any information regarding the case which you acquired while employed as corporate counsel. Must the plaintiffs' law firm withdraw?

C.   Concurrent Conflicts in Spousal Representations

In the following selection, Professor Pearce discusses conflicts that arise in representing spouses with differing interests. His discussion focuses for the most part on the Model Rules as a "basic guide" to handling such conflicts. Although the Model Rules are not controlling authority in this or any other area of professional responsibility, it is useful to work through hypotheticals based on the Model Rules. Actual rules differ from jurisdiction to jurisdiction, but for the most part use a similar method of analysis. It is of course more difficult to resolve conflicts between clients who are real people, particularly if their pocketbook cannot afford the solution that first comes to mind: referring one of them to another lawyer. In all of these situations, the right course of action will be framed in part by the lawyer's own sense of what is right for the particular persons involved.

Family Values and Legal Ethics: Competing Approaches to Conflicts in Representing Spouses

by Russell G. Pearce
62 Fordham L. Rev. 1253 (1994).

I.   The Doctrinal Perspective

* * *

A.   Overview of Conflicts Rules

The lawyer's obligation to avoid representation of clients with conflicting interests is often derived from the lawyer's duty of loyalty to her client.

As Professors Hazard and Hodes observe in their treatise, however, conflicts issues broadly "implicate ... the basic duties a lawyer owes to a client—competence, confidentiality, communication, and loyalty."[3] The proposed [ALI] Restatement of the Law Governing Lawyers elaborates by noting that conflicts undermine a client's "trust" in her lawyer's "undivided loyalty," impair the lawyer's judgment and dedication necessary to competent representation, and increase the opportunity for "use of confidential information against interests of the client."[4] In addition, the prohibition of conflicts "protects interests of the legal system in obtaining adequate presentation of matters to tribunals." Professors Hazard and Hodes further note that duties of communication arise from the lawyer's obligation to consult with clients in obtaining waivers of conflicts.

The proposed Restatement acknowledges, however, that because "conflict avoidance can impose significant costs on lawyers and clients alike, any prohibition of conflicts of interest should reach no farther than necessary." These costs include the multiple clients obtaining separate representation, interference with client expectations of retaining a particular lawyer, disclosures or delays necessary to obtain consent to conflicts, and limits on "lawyers' own freedom to practice according to their own best judgment of appropriate professional behavior."

The established conflicts doctrine represents a "balancing of the interests involved." The doctrine does not bar all representation of clients with conflicting interests. It permits, however, such representation only with client consent and the lawyer's objective determination that the representation of, or relationship with, the clients will not be adversely affected.

Rule 1.7 of the Model Rules provides the basic guide for concurrent representation of clients with conflicting interests, whether the conflicts developed before or during the representations.* Rule 1.7 has two parts. Rule 1.7(a) applies where representation of one client will be "directly adverse to another client," while Rule 1.7(b) applies where the lawyer's responsibilities to one client may materially limit representation of another.

Under Rule 1.7(a), a lawyer may represent clients directly adverse to each other only where "each client consents after consultation" and "the lawyer reasonably believes the representation will not adversely affect the relationship with the other client." Professors Hazard and Hodes note that

---

3. Geoffrey C. Hazard, Jr. & William Hodes, The Law of Lawyering section 1.1:101 (2d ed. Supp. 1992 & 1993).

4. Restatement of the Law Governing Lawyers section 201 cmt. b (Tent. Draft No. 4 1991)

* The authors of this casebook would word this less strongly—the Model Rules are a guide for concurrent representations. However, the Model Rules are not law and each lawyer must consult the law in her own jurisdiction on this as well as other ethical considerations.—ed.

while client consent is "highly relevant in appraising the probable effect of the representation on the client-lawyer relationships," a lawyer's reasonable belief that the representation will not adversely affect the relationship will be "relatively rare." They suggest that "Rule 1.7(a) contemplates the practical equivalent of an absolute ban on concurrent representation of clients whose interests are in direct conflict." This "presumption against concurrent representation of clients with directly conflicting interests" is especially strong "where one of the clients is an individual, as opposed to a business or other entity, because the client's personal feelings will almost always be bound up in any legal transaction to which he or she is a party."

While Rule 1.7(a) applies to existing and direct adversity, Rule 1.7(b) applies even where the lawyer's responsibilities may only indirectly limit representation. Rule 1.7(b) governs situations where representation of a client "may be materially limited by the lawyer's responsibilities to another client." Rule 1.7(b) permits such representation only where "the client consents after consultation" and "the lawyer reasonably believes the representation will not be adversely affected." The Rule further specifies that the consultation for representing "multiple clients in a single matter ... shall include an explanation of the implications of the common representation and the advantages and risks involved." One of the risks is that "information received from one joint client about the subject matter of the joint representation is not privileged from disclosure against the other client, even though it may be a confidence that the lawyer has a duty not to disclose to the other client."

Professors Hazard and Hodes note that "Rule 1.7(b) is more flexible than Rule 1.7(a), for it speaks to material limitations on the representations and it forces a case-specific inquiry into the precise effect that a particular combination of conflicting responsibilities might engender." At the same time, Rule 1.7(b) is a "strong 'client-protecting' rule that will sometimes require a careful lawyer to decline representation of a client who very much wants to be represented by that lawyer" on account of "the long-term public interest in protecting clients against foolish waivers, or against waivers that will reflect poorly on the legal system." Indeed, the requirement of the lawyer's reasonable belief "may be somewhat more stringent" under Rule 1.7(b) than Rule 1.7(a) because the client can judge the "quality of the client-lawyer relationships ... at least as well as the lawyer," while "only the lawyer can fully judge ... the quality of the representation to be provided."

In addition to Rule 1.7, Rule 2.2 is relevant to conflicts issues arising in the representation of multiple clients in a single matter. Rule 2.2 applies to "intermediary" representation which occurs "when the lawyer represents two or more parties with potentially conflicting interests." In the intermediary role, the lawyer seeks "to establish or adjust a relationship between clients on an amicable and mutually advantageous basis.... The lawyer seeks to resolve potentially conflicting interests by developing the parties' mutual interests."

Rule 2.2 requires the same types of disclosures that Rule 1.7(b) requires for joint representation. Rule 2.2 specifies disclosure of "the effect on the attorney-client privileges" which presumably would fall within "advantages and risks" under Rule 1.7(b). Furthermore, Rule 2.2 substitutes two related provisions for Rule 1.7(b)'s requirement of the lawyer's reasonable belief that "the representation will not be adversely affected." Rule 2.2(a)(2) requires the lawyer's reasonable belief that the matter can be resolved on terms compatible with the clients' best interests, that each client will be able to make adequately informed decisions in the matter and that there is little risk of material prejudice to the interests of any of the clients if the contemplated resolution is unsuccessful. Rule 2.2(a)(3) requires the lawyer's reasonable belief "that the common representation can be undertaken impartially and without improper effect on other responsibilities the lawyer has to any of the clients."

Rule 2.2 was intended to provide an opportunity to "lawyer for the situation," as opposed to individual clients. The use of the term "common representation," in Rule 2.2 as opposed to the term "multiple clients" in Rule 1.7, could mean that Rule 2.2 envisions the lawyer representing the family entity rather than the individuals. Similarly, Rule 2.2 speaks of the "clients' best interests," rather than the interest of each client separately, and the Comment to the Rule discusses adjusting a "relationship." The language and intent of Rule 2.2 could therefore support a broader representation of individuals with conflicting interest than Rule 1.7.

Despite these considerations, most commentators have concluded that Rule 2.2 does not afford lawyers an opportunity to undertake or continue a representation that would be prohibited by Rule 1.7. Professor Thomas Shaffer observes that Rule 2.2's use of "a behavioral checklist to make exceptional, multiple-client employment possible" evidences that "the rule rests on the assumption that employment by individuals is the norm." Indeed, as noted above, the conditions that a lawyer must satisfy to represent clients under Rule 2.2 are only a more specific explication of Rule 1.7's requirements. Accordingly, Professors Hazard and Koniak observe that Rule 2.2 "may be considered a specific application of 1.7(b)."

In light of the similarities between Rules 1.7(b) and 2.2, it is unclear whether Rule 2.2 or Rule 1.7 governs a joint representation. The Comment to Rule 2.2 which applies the rule to all situations where "the lawyer represents two or more parties with potentially conflicting interests," suggests that it includes all joint representations. Such a construction, however, would be inconsistent with the express language of Rule 1.7(b) which contemplates "representation of multiple clients in a single matter." A more plausible interpretation is that the lawyer may choose to apply Rule 2.2 in appropriate cases where the lawyer makes the disclosures, obtains the consents, and reaches the objective conclusions required by Rule 2.2. Indeed, Professors Hazard and Hodes observe that the provisions of Rule 2.2 "are so confining that prudent lawyers often will not undertake this role, but will treat the representations as ... involving a 'consented conflict' under Rule 1.7(b)."

Another possibility for analyzing conflicts is to view the client as an organization. Under Rule 1.13, the lawyer represents the organization, not its constituents. If a conflict arises between a constituent and the organization, the lawyer's duty is to represent the organization. In such circumstances, the lawyer has an obligation to make sure that the constituent "understands that ... the lawyer for the organization cannot provide legal representation for that constituent individual and that discussions between the lawyer for the organization and the individual may not be privileged."

The last rule generally relevant to conflicts in family representation is Rule 1.9 which governs conflicts between current and former clients. Rule 1.9 bars representation of a client "in the same or a substantially related matter in which that person's interests are materially adverse to the interests of the former client unless the former client consents after consultation." If the concurrent representation is commenced under Rule 2.2, the restrictions on continuing to represent one multiple client after withdrawal from representing another are even stricter. Rule 2.2 requires the lawyer to withdraw from representing all multiple clients "if any of the clients so requests" or if any of the conditions of the representation are no longer satisfied.

B. Applying Conflicts Doctrine to Spousal Representation

As in any other matter, the lawyer should as a "first step ... identify whether a conflict exists." Professor Wolfram suggests that the lawyer "identify at the outset of the representation the legal and other interests that the several clients have and that they may wish to assert or seriously consider as the transaction proceeds."

If the lawyer discovers that the spouses' interests are directly adverse, Rule 1.7(a) virtually prevents her from representing both. One example of where some authorities permit representation of spouses whose interests are directly adverse is in the preparation of a dissolution agreement in an amicable situation where the spouses consent to joint representation and "reasonable prospects of an agreement exist."

Even where the lawyer does not find direct adversity, she may discover evidence that representation of one spouse "may be materially limited" by representation of the other under Rule 1.7(b). Although Rule 1.7(b) and its comment do not offer specific guidance for spousal representation, the authorities suggest that dual representation will often create a potential material limit because of the spouses' many potential differing interests. In estate planning, for example, spouses may have different interests regarding which assets should be provided to each other, their children together, other children they may have, relatives, friends, and charities; which assets are joint and separate; the implications of the rights each spouse might have to a statutory share and whether a waiver of such rights is appropriate; and whether to use trusts and asset transfers to minimize tax liabilities. In light of these difficult issues, Professor Jeffrey Pennell, a leading scholar in the area of trusts and estates, has observed that even when representation of spouses begins, "the risk of conflict is significant....

There always is the potential for conflicts of interest in a representation of both spouses." Similarly, the proposed Restatement of the Law Governing Lawyers finds that where the spouses ask a lawyer to draft "reciprocal wills" there exists "substantial risk that the lawyer's representation of one spouse would be materially and adversely affected by the lawyer's duties to the other."

Another common situation where differences potentially limit representation occurs where the lawyer "has had substantial prior dealings with one member of the couple but not the other." Professors Hazard and Hodes suggest two types of limits which may result. First, "it is likely that the lawyer will have confidences of the established client that he cannot reveal to the other client, but which the other client has a need to know." Second, the lawyer "may not trust his own ability to be fair to both by putting aside his prior relationship." In these cases, while "self-disqualification" is not "automatic," the lawyer "should be particularly careful to explain his concerns, and to make certain that the established client authorizes him to reveal all confidences to the other spouse." If the lawyer discovers "the slightest hesitation on the part of the established client, it is a warning that he or she considers himself or herself to be the 'main' client, and the lawyer must then refuse to represent the other."

In many instances of spousal representation, therefore, Rule 1.7(b) will require the lawyer to obtain the client's informed consent to the representation in light of the potential for material limits and to reach a reasonable belief that the representation of one will not adversely affect representation of the other. If the spouses are to be represented jointly, the consultation must include a discussion "of the implications of the common representation and the advantages and risks involved." In light of the potential differences, the lawyer could also represent the spouses under Rule 2.2. She would then have to satisfy the requirements of disclosure and consent, as well as the objective determinations required by that Rule.

If conflicts develop during representation, the lawyer will have to withdraw from representing one or both spouses. Under Rule 1.9, the lawyer could not continue to represent one spouse in the same or substantially related matter where the spouses' interests were materially adverse without the other spouse's consent. This would appear generally to bar a lawyer from continuing to represent one spouse where conflicts had developed in representing both. If the representation is under Rule 2.2, the lawyer must withdraw from representing both at the request of either or if the conditions for representation are no longer satisfied.

Rule 1.13 offers another possible perspective on conflicts in family representation. The text and comment to Rule 1.13 authorize a lawyer to represent an organization, as opposed to its constituents. The Rule applies to organizations of any size, whether incorporated or not. Rule 1.13 does not define the term "organization," but does describe Rule 1.13's purpose as providing representation for legal entities which "cannot act except through ... constituents." This would seem to include families which are often "legal entities" that can act only through constituent family members. Professors Hazard and Hodes further suggest that the crux of eligibility for representation under Rule 1.13 is whether "the group will be regarded as an entity that is distinct from its individual constituents." While formality of "the association, the longer its duration, and the more elaborate its purposes" evidence organizational status, "even a small group informally organized for a limited purpose can be considered an entity." Both traditional and non-traditional families have elements of formality, duration, and elaborate purposes sufficient to fall within this understanding of Rule 1.13.

Despite the existence of a reasonable fit between Rule 1.13 and family representation, no authority has yet applied Rule 1.13 to family representation. Perhaps this is due to the pervasiveness of the assumption in established doctrine that family members are separable individuals. Perhaps, too, authorities have understood Rule 1.13's use of corporate governance terminology, such as references to shareholders and boards of directors, to indicate an intent to limit the scope of Rule 1.13 to business or business-like organizations. In any event, the absence of authority for applying Rule 1.13 to families should make a practitioner leery of doing so.

* * *

Later in this article, Professor Pearce proposes "a new legal ethic for representing families. In addition to separate, joint, or intermediation representation under established doctrine, family members could choose Optional Family Representation. Optional Family Representation would permit representation of family members as a group even where actual or potential risks to individual interests would prohibit joint or intermediation representation under established doctrine." Id. at 1258. Each family member would have access to all information relevant to all family decisions including information imparted in communications to the attorney from other family members, and a family member would have the option to withdraw from the Optional Family Representation at any time.

QUESTIONS

Professor Pearce recognizes the following objections to Optional Family Representation:

1. The lawyer's function is to represent individuals, not families.

2. Families lack identifiable group characteristics needed for legal representation.

3. The lawyer could end up substituting her judgment for that of family members.

4. Power imbalances within the family may make representation of the entire family inappropriate.

In what circumstances would each of these objections most likely apply? If a lawyer practices in a jurisdiction that allows her to represent an entire family with consent of the family members, what "warning signs" should she look for before agreeing to do so?

PROBLEMS

1. John and Mary retain you for estate planning. They meet with you and ask you to prepare mirror wills for them. Can you represent them both? If so, what must you do first? See Pearce, supra, at 1257.

2. Two days after you agree to the representation, Mary calls you and asks you to prepare a different will for her and to keep confidential from John both the terms of her will and Mary's consultation with you. At this point, must you withdraw from the representation of both spouses? Can you disclose Mary's call to John? Id.

3. You are a legal services staff attorney and previously represented Ozzie and Harriet in a dispute with their landlord. They now tell you that Harriet has suffered a series of strokes and cannot take care of herself physically. While Harriet is periodically disoriented, she is competent at the time she consults you. Ozzie wants to put Harriet in a nursing home, but Harriet refuses. They love each other and want to resolve their differences amicably; they seek your advice on how to proceed. If they cannot work things out, Ozzie intends to take legal action and Harriet intends to defend herself. Can you represent both Ozzie and Harriet? Id.

D.   CONCURRENT CONFLICT WITH LAY INTERMEDIARIES

The **Brotherhood of Railroad Trainmen**, a powerful railway labor union, was merged with several other railway labor unions in 1969 to form the United Transportation Union.

Brotherhood of R.R. Trainmen v. Virginia ex rel. Virginia State Bar

377 U.S. 1 (1964).

■ MR. JUSTICE BLACK delivered the opinion of the Court.

The Virginia State Bar brought this suit in the Chancery Court of the City of Richmond, Virginia, against the Brotherhood of Railroad Trainmen, an investigator employed by the Brotherhood, and an attorney designated its "Regional Counsel," to enjoin them from carrying on activities which, the Bar charged, constituted the solicitation of legal business and the unauthorized practice of law in Virginia. It was conceded that in order to assist the prosecution of claims by injured railroad workers or by the families of workers killed on the job the Brotherhood maintains in Virginia and throughout the country a Department of Legal Counsel which recommends to Brotherhood members and their families the names of lawyers whom the Brotherhood believes to be honest and competent. Finding that the Brotherhood's plan resulted in "channeling all, or substantially all," the workers' claims to lawyers chosen by the Department of Legal Counsel, the court issued an injunction against the Brotherhood's carrying out its plan in Virginia. The Supreme Court of Appeals of Virginia affirmed summarily over objections that the injunction abridges the Brotherhood's rights under the First and Fourteenth Amendments, which guarantee freedom of speech, petition and assembly. We granted certiorari to consider this constitutional question in the light of our recent decision in NAACP v. Button, 371 U.S. 415.

The Brotherhood's plan is not a new one. Its roots go back to 1883, when the Brotherhood was founded as a fraternal and mutual benefit society to promote the welfare of the trainmen and "to protect their families by the exercise of benevolence, very needful in a calling so hazardous as ours...." Railroad work at that time was indeed dangerous. In 1888 the odds against a railroad brakeman's dying a natural death were almost four to one; the average life expectancy of a switchman in 1893 was seven years. It was quite natural, therefore, that railroad workers combined their strength and efforts in the Brotherhood in order to provide insurance and financial assistance to sick and injured members and to seek safer working conditions. The Trainmen and other railroad Brotherhoods were the moving forces that brought about the passage of the Safety Appliance Act in 1893 to make railroad work less dangerous; they also supported passage of the Federal Employers' Liability Act of 1908 to provide for recovery of damages for injured railroad workers and their families by doing away with harsh and technical common-law rules which sometimes made recovery difficult or even impossible. It soon became apparent to the railroad workers, however, that simply having these federal statutes on the books was not enough to assure that the workers would receive the full benefit of the compensatory damages Congress intended they should have. Injured workers or their families often fell prey on the one hand to persuasive claims adjusters eager to gain a quick and cheap settlement for their railroad employers, or on the other to lawyers either not competent to try these lawsuits against the able and experienced railroad counsel or too willing to settle a case for a quick dollar.

It was to protect against these obvious hazards to the injured man or his widow that the workers through their Brotherhood set up their Legal Aid Department, since renamed Department of Legal Counsel, the basic activities of which the court below has enjoined. Under their plan the United States was divided into sixteen regions and the Brotherhood selected, on the advice of local lawyers and federal and state judges, a lawyer or firm in each region with a reputation for honesty and skill in representing plaintiffs in railroad personal injury litigation. When a worker was injured or killed, the secretary of his local lodge would go to him or to his widow or children and recommend that the claim not be settled without first seeing a lawyer, and that in the Brotherhood's judgment the best lawyer to consult was the counsel selected by it for that area.[8]

---

8. The Brotherhood also provides a staff, now at its own expense, to investigate accidents to help gather evidence for use by the injured worker or his family should a trial be necessary to vindicate their rights.

There is a dispute between the parties as to the exact meaning of the decree rendered below, but the Brotherhood in this Court objects specifically to the provisions which enjoin it "... from holding out lawyers selected by it as the only approved lawyers to aid the members or their families; ... or in any other manner soliciting or encouraging such legal employment of the selected lawyers; ... and from doing any act or combination of acts, and from formulating and putting into practice any plan, pattern or design, the result of which is to channel legal employment to any particular lawyer or group of lawyers...."[9]

The Brotherhood admits that it advises injured members and their dependents to obtain legal advice before making settlement of their claims and that it recommends particular lawyers to handle such claims. The result of the plan, the Brotherhood admits, is to channel legal employment to the particular lawyers approved by the Brotherhood as legally and morally competent to handle injury claims for members and their families. It is the injunction against this particular practice which the Brotherhood, on behalf of its members, contends denies them rights guaranteed by the First and Fourteenth Amendments. We agree with this contention.

It cannot be seriously doubted that the First Amendment's guarantees of free speech, petition and assembly give railroad workers the right to gather together for the lawful purpose of helping and advising one another in asserting the rights Congress gave them in the Safety Appliance Act and the Federal Employers' Liability Act, statutory rights which would be vain and futile if the workers could not talk together freely as to the best course to follow. The right of members to consult with each other in a fraternal organization necessarily includes the right to select a spokesman from their number who could be expected to give the wisest counsel. That is the role played by the members who carry out the legal aid program. And the right of the workers personally or through a special department of their Brotherhood to advise concerning the need for legal assistance—and, most importantly, what lawyer a member could confidently rely on—is an inseparable part of this constitutionally guaranteed right to assist and advise each other.

Virginia undoubtedly has broad powers to regulate the practice of law

---

9. Certain other provisions of the decree enjoin the Brotherhood from sharing counsel fees with lawyers whom it recommended and from countenancing the sharing of fees by its regional investigators. The Brotherhood denies that it has engaged in such practices since 1959, in compliance with a decree of the Supreme Court of Illinois. See In re Brotherhood of Railroad Trainmen, 13 Ill. 2d 391, 150 N. E. 2d 163. Since the Brotherhood is not objecting to the other provisions of the decree except insofar as they might later be construed as barring the Brotherhood from helping injured workers or their families by recommending that they not settle without a lawyer and by recommending certain lawyers selected by the Brotherhood, it is only to that extent that we pass upon the validity of the other provisions. Because of our disposition of the case, we do not consider the Brotherhood's claim that the findings of the court were not supported by substantial evidence.

within its borders;[10] but we have had occasion in the past to recognize that in regulating the practice of law a State cannot ignore the rights of individuals secured by the Constitution. For as we said in NAACP v. Button, supra, 371 U.S., at 429, "a State cannot foreclose the exercise of constitutional rights by mere labels." Here what Virginia has sought to halt is not a commercialization of the legal profession which might threaten the moral and ethical fabric of the administration of justice. It is not "ambulance chasing." The railroad workers, by recommending competent lawyers to each other, obviously are not themselves engaging in the practice of law, nor are they or the lawyers whom they select parties to any soliciting of business. It is interesting to note that in Great Britain unions do not simply recommend lawyers to members in need of advice; they retain counsel, paid by the union, to represent members in personal lawsuits, a practice similar to that which we upheld in NAACP v. Button, supra.

A State could not, by invoking the power to regulate the professional conduct of attorneys, infringe in any way the right of individuals and the public to be fairly represented in lawsuits authorized by Congress to effectuate a basic public interest. Laymen cannot be expected to know how to protect their rights when dealing with practiced and carefully counseled adversaries, cf. Gideon v. Wainwright, 372 U.S. 335, and for them to associate together to help one another to preserve and enforce rights granted them under federal laws cannot be condemned as a threat to legal ethics. The State can no more keep these workers from using their cooperative plan to advise one another than it could use more direct means to bar them from resorting to the courts to vindicate their legal rights. The right to petition the courts cannot be so handicapped.

Only last Term we had occasion to consider an earlier attempt by Virginia to enjoin the National Association for the Advancement of Colored People from advising prospective litigants to seek the assistance of particular attorneys. In fact, in that case, unlike this one, the attorneys were actually employed by the association which recommended them, and recommendations were made even to nonmembers. NAACP v. Button, supra. We held that "although the petitioner has amply shown that its activities fall within the First Amendment's protections, the State has failed to advance any substantial regulatory interest, in the form of substantive evils flowing from petitioner's activities, which can justify the broad prohibitions which it has imposed." 371 U.S., at 444. In the present case the State again has failed to show any appreciable public interest in preventing the Brotherhood from carrying out its plan to recommend the lawyers it selects to represent injured workers. The Brotherhood's activities fall just as clearly

---

10. The Bar relies on the common law, the Canons of Ethics of the American Bar Association, adopted into the rules of the Supreme Court of Appeals of Virginia, 171 Va. xviii, and several Virginia statutes prohibiting the unauthorized practice of law. The Canons of Ethics to which the Bar refers prohibit respectively stirring up of litigation, control or exploitation by a lay agency of professional services of a lawyer, and aiding the unauthorized practice of law. Canons 28, 35, 47. The statutes respectively set the qualifications for the practice of law in the State and provide for injunctions against "running, capping, soliciting and maintenance." Virginia Code, 1950, §§ 54–42, 54–83.1.

within the protection of the First Amendment. And the Constitution protects the associational rights of the members of the union precisely as it does those of the NAACP.

We hold that the First and Fourteenth Amendments protect the right of the members through their Brotherhood to maintain and carry out their plan for advising workers who are injured to obtain legal advice and for recommending specific lawyers. Since the part of the decree to which the Brotherhood objects infringes those rights, it cannot stand; and to the extent any other part of the decree forbids these activities it too must fall. And, of course, lawyers accepting employment under this constitutionally protected plan have a like protection which the State cannot abridge.

The judgment and decree are vacated and the case is remanded for proceedings not inconsistent with this opinion.

It is so ordered.

Relevant Background

Lay Intermediaries and Legal Aid Services

The term lay intermediary generally applies to an organization that may "act as a neutral buffer between the lawyer and the potential client who is in need of legal services or a referral." Frederick C. Moss, The Ethics of Law Practice Marketing, 61 Notre Dame L. Rev. 601, 648 (1986). Such lay intermediaries include legal advocacy organizations such as labor unions, the NAACP, and the ACLU. When a member of a legal advocacy organization, or a person whose case the organization wishes to support, needs a lawyer, a lawyer is referred to her by the organization.

Ethical problems can arise from this intermediary role. First, the lawyer may compromise his independent judgment if it conflicts with the judgment of the lay intermediary. Second, the intermediary may engage in the unauthorized practice of law, as where the intermediary gives legal advice to the client prior to consultation with the lawyer.

A third problem arises when lay intermediaries split legal fees with lawyers, as do most public interest groups that sponsor litigation and require lawyers to pay over to them court-awarded fees. Under Model Rule 5.4(a), with very few exceptions, a lawyer or law firm may not share legal fees with a non-lawyer. Nonetheless, because legal fees are a significant source of funds, some organizations ignore these restrictions. Perhaps a better alternative is for an organization to avail itself of an exception which, in many jurisdictions, allows a lawyer to pay the "usual charges for a not-for-profit lawyer referral service or other legal service organization." See Model Rule 7.2(c). Because legal service organizations such as the ACLU and NAACP recommend lawyers, fee sharing may be possible in the form of such "usual charges." See Roy D. Simon, Jr., Fee Sharing Between Lawyers and Public Interest Groups, 98 Yale L.J. 1069 (1989).

A fourth problem raised by the interaction of a lay intermediary with a lawyer is the potential disclosure of confidential client information to the intermediary and the intermediary's subsequent misuse of such information (perhaps to further a political agenda or to raise funds). Finally, an organization might use underprivileged clients to gain access to court for the benefit of other clients or for some other reason only tangentially related to the clients' own welfare. Wolfram, Modern Legal Ethics 446 (1986).

Constitutional Issues

Four Supreme Court cases frame the constitutional right of legal service organizations to sponsor litigation and refer clients to lawyers. In the first, NAACP v. Button, 371 U.S. 415 (1963), the Court held that state bar rules could not interfere with the NAACP's First Amendment right to select and bring school desegregation cases and "to associate for the purpose of assisting persons who seek legal redress for infringements of their constitutionally guaranteed and other rights." Id. at 428. The second case, Brotherhood of Railroad Trainmen v. Virginia ex rel. Virginia State Bar, 377 U.S. 1 (1964), supra, applied similar reasoning and held that states could not prevent a union from advising injured members and their families to obtain legal assistance before settling their claims. The third case, United Mine Workers v. Illinois State Bar Association, 389 U.S. 217 (1967), held that a private practice lawyer could not be prevented from receiving a salary from a union to handle workers' compensation claims.

Finally, in United Transportation Union v. State Bar of Michigan, 401 U.S. 576 (1971), a Michigan trial court, under a state statute making it a misdemeanor to "solicit" damage suits against railroads, enjoined a union from: (1) giving legal advice to workers in filing damage suits under the Federal Employers' Liability Act; (2) furnishing lawyers with the names of injured members and information about their injuries; and (3) controlling the lawyer's fees, which the union had sought to limit to 25% of the amount recovered. After observing that "[t]he State Bar's complaint appears to be a plea for court protection of unlimited legal fees," 401 U.S. at 577–78, the Court held that the injunction violated the union's First Amendment right to give legal advice, employ counsel to represent its members, communicate with counsel and enable its members to obtain meaningful access to the courts by meeting the costs of legal representation.

QUESTIONS

1. What restrictions do the Model Code (DR 5–107) and the Model Rules (Rules 1.7(b), 1.8(f) and 5.4(c)) impose on third-party payment for legal services?

2. How do the Model Code (DR 2–103) and the Model Rules (Rules 5.4(a) and 6.3) differ in their restriction of payments by lawyers to lay intermediaries?

Insurers as Intermediaries

Concurrent conflicts arise whenever a lawyer is retained by an insurance company to represent an insured party. Liability insurance policies usually provide that the insurer will pay claims against the insured and also bear the costs of defending such claims. When a claim is made on the insured's policy, the insurer employs a lawyer to represent the insured under a separate, usually oral, retainer agreement. Some commentators observe that the liability insurance contract shapes the later retainer agreement and that "[b]ecause most of the duties a lawyer can owe a client are mutable—that is, are capable of being created and altered by agreement—the retainer agreement is of overwhelming importance in deciding what defense counsel's responsibilities are to be." Charles Silver and Kent Syverud, The Professional Responsibilities of Insurance Defense Lawyers 45 Duke L. J. 255, 270–271 (1995). There is, however, significant disagreement over the extent to which insurers should be permitted to bargain with their insureds ex-ante concerning the professional responsibilities of insurance defense lawyers. Id. at 361.

There is also disagreement over whether the insurance defense lawyer represents only the insured (the "one client" view) or both the insurer and the insured (the "two clients" view). Most jurisdictions have endorsed the "two clients" view, whereas tentative drafts of the ALI's Restatement of The Law Governing Lawyers endorsed the one client view. Silver and Syverud, supra, at 273–74. See also Atlanta International Insurance Co. v. Bell, 438 Mich. 512, 475 N.W.2d 294 (Mich.1991) (finding that there is no attorney client relationship between an insurer and a lawyer paid by the insurer to represent an insured). Professor Silver suggests that this issue is appropriately resolved by the lawyer's retainer agreement. "Defense counsel has one client if and when the retainer agreement provides that counsel shall represent only the insured; defense counsel has two clients if and when the retainer agreement requires counsel to represent the company as well." Id. at 274; see also Charles Silver, Does Insurance Defense Counsel Represent the Company or the Insured?, 72 Tex. L. Rev. 1583, 1604 (1994). Nonetheless, factors such as unequal bargaining power between insurers and insureds, the fact that many insurance policies are adhesion contracts, and most insureds' lack of familiarity with the types of concurrent conflicts that arise in insurance defense work, may caution against a strictly contractarian approach to lawyer professional responsibilities in this area.

Concurrent conflicts between the interests of the insurer and insured most often arise in contexts where an insurance defense lawyer is under pressure to accommodate the insurer in litigation strategy and in settlement negotiations. For example, if the plaintiff's claim exceeds the policy limits, the insured may want to settle at or near the policy limit rather than pursue litigation. The insurance company, however, might want to litigate. Also, the lawyer may face a conflict of interest when insured and uninsured claims are asserted in the same action, for example, where alternative claims of negligent and intentional tort are asserted, but the policy only covers liability for negligent acts. In such a case, the lawyer may minimize the insurer's liability on the covered allegations by providing a less than vigorous defense to the uncovered allegations. Finally, conflicts of interest may arise if the insured and the insurer have differing assessments of the facts, the insured doesn't want to provide information to the insurer, the insurer suspects that the insured is cooperating with the claimant, or there is a dispute between the insurer and the insured over the insurer's right under the policy to subrogation (the right to assert on its own behalf the insured's counterclaims and claims against third parties).

One approach is to require the lawyer to side with the insured whenever a conflict arises that cannot be waived. See Silver and Syverud, supra at 335, citing Montanez v. Irizarry–Rodriguez, 273 N.J.Super. 276, 641 A.2d 1079, 1084 (N.J.Super.Ct.App.Div.1994). Many jurisdictions, however, follow a "no subordination rule" forbidding the lawyer from favoring the interests of one client over another absent both clients' informed consent; if no course of action satisfies this criteria, the lawyer must withdraw. Yet another solution to these concurrent conflicts is to specify in the insurance policy and in the retainer agreement exactly what the lawyer's responsibilities are should such conflicts arise. Id. at 362.

Other Third–Party Intermediaries

Similar problems arise whenever a third party pays another person's legal expenses and the lawyer's loyalty could be influenced by the payor. For example, where one spouse pays a lawyer to represent the other, the resulting conflicts may be difficult to resolve. See People ex rel. Cortez v. Calvert, 200 Colo. 157, 617 P.2d 797 (Colo.1980) (where a "significant other" hired a lawyer to represent his girlfriend in a suit filed in her name to prevent a marriage to another man, the lawyer was disciplined for conflict of interest, charging an illegal or clearly excessive fee, and inadequate preparation).

Some of the most difficult situations arise when a parent hires a lawyer to represent a child. See People v. White, 127 Mich.App. 65, 338 N.W.2d 556 (1983) (child's lawyer rendered ineffective assistance of counsel due to his failure to plead insanity defense because the father of child refused to pay for independent psychiatric evaluation of child to support such a defense). Although allowing a parent such unfettered control over a child's representation is inappropriate, Professor Nancy Moore has observed that literal application of ethics codes can create the misimpression that parents do not have an important role in legal matters affecting their children:

> It is often (but not always) the case that parents expect not only to select and retain a lawyer for their child, but also to be actively involved in the representation. Nevertheless, the current ethics codes treat them as if they were third-party strangers with no more legitimate interest in their child's representation than if they were insurance companies or employers. While putting some distance between lawyer and parent will sometimes be appropriate (for example, in custody cases and when there are allegations of parental misconduct), in many situations it is simply absurd.

Nancy J. Moore, Conflicts of Interests in The Representation of Children, 64 Fordham L. Rev. 1819, 1856 (1996).

Different conflicts arise, and are indeed quite common, where a lawyer paid by an employer represents an employee. Although the employer and employee may be potentially liable for the same incident, their interests may conflict. The employee may seek contribution or indemnification from her employer under an employment agreement or under agency law by showing that she was acting within the scope of her employment. The employer, by contrast, may seek to escape vicarious liability to the injured party by showing that the employee was acting outside the scope of her employment.

Finally, as pointed out in *Evans v. Jeff D.*, supra chapter 1, a lawyer might face a conflict of interest created by the negotiation strategy of his adversary. While a lawyer ordinarily would not be influenced by an adversary, an adversary can wield considerable influence in situations where the adversary and the lawyer are negotiating over the "size of the lawyer's fee in relation to the share of the recovery by the lawyer's client from a settlement fund." Wolfram, supra, at 443. Luvern Johnson's decision in *Evans* to give up his fee in return for a favorable settlement for the disabled children he represented was clearly the right thing to do. His choice, however, was costly to him and to his employer, the Legal Aid Society. Unfortunately, some lawyers are tempted to do just the opposite and accept an inadequate settlement in return for a larger fee.

QUESTION

1. Professor Wallace Mlyniec asks the following question:

    When, if ever, is it appropriate in a juvenile delinquency proceeding for a lawyer to ignore a judgment or decision made by a child client and substitute her own judgment or that of the child's parent?

Wallace J. Mlyniec, Who Decides: Decision Making in Juvenile Delinquency Proceedings, in Ethical Problems Facing the Criminal Defense Lawyer 105 (Rodney J. Uphoff Ed.) (ABA 1995). How would you answer this question?

E. CONCURRENT CONFLICTS IN CLASS ACTIONS

Derrick A. Bell, Jr., b. 1930, A.B. Dusquesne University 1952; LL.B. University of Pittsburgh 1957 (Associate Editor-in-Chief, Pittsburgh Law Review); Staff Lawyer, U.S. Department of Justice 1957–59; Executive Secretary, NAACP Pittsburgh Branch 1959; First Assistant Counsel, NAACP Legal Defense Fund, New York City 1960–66; Office of Civil Rights, Department of Health Education and Welfare, Washington, D.C. 1966–68; Adjunct Professor, Harvard Law School 1968–69, Lecturer 1969–71, Professor 1971–80; Dean, University of Oregon School of Law 1981–85, Professor 1981–86; Professor, Harvard Law School 1986–92; Visiting Professor New York University since 1992.

Serving Two Masters: Integration Ideals and Client Interests in School Desegregation Litigation

by Derrick A. Bell, Jr.
85 Yale L. J. 470 (1976)

In the name of equity, we ... seek dramatic improvement in the quality of the education available to our children. Any steps to achieve desegregation must be reviewed in light of the black community's interest in improved pupil performance as the primary characteristic of educational equity. We define educational equity as the absence of discriminatory pupil placement and improved performance for all children who have been the objects of discrimination. We think it neither necessary, nor proper to endure the dislocations of desegregation without reasonable assurances that our children will instructionally profit.

Coalition of black community groups in Boston

* * *

At one time, expressions of disinterest and even disapproval of civil rights litigation by portions of the class may have been motivated by fear and by threats of physical and economic intimidation. But events in Atlanta, Detroit, and Boston provide the basis for judicial notice that many black parents oppose total reliance on racial balance remedies to cure the effects of school segregation. As one federal court of appeals judge has put it: "Almost predictably, changing circumstances during those years of litigation have dissolved the initial unity of the plaintiffs' position." Black parents who prefer alternative remedies are poorly served by the routine approval of plaintiffs' requests for class status in school desegregation litigation.

Basic principles of equity require courts to develop greater sensitivity to the growing disagreement in black communities over the nature of school relief. Existing class action rules provide ample authority for broadening representation in school cases to reflect the fact that views in the black community are no longer monolithic. One aspect of class action status requiring closer scrutiny is whether the representation provided by plaintiffs will "fairly and adequately protect the interests of the class." Because every person is entitled to be adequately represented when his rights and duties are being adjudicated, it is incumbent upon the courts to ensure the fairness of proceedings that will bind absent class members. The failure to exercise such care may violate due process rights guaranteed by the Fifth and Fourteenth Amendments.

These problems can be avoided if, instead of routinely assuming that school desegregation plaintiffs adequately represent the class, courts will apply carefully the standard tests for determining the validity of class action allegations and the standard procedures for protecting the interests of unnamed class members. Where objecting members of the class seek to intervene, their conflicting interests can be recognized under the provisions of Rule 23(d)(2). In this regard, the class action intervention provisions are in harmony with those contained in Rule 24.

Even with the exercise of great care, the adequacy of representation may be difficult to determine, particularly at the outset of the litigation. For this reason, Professor Owen Fiss has suggested that the standard for adequacy of representation for certifying a class action should differ from that used in allowing intervention. If the standards are the same, he reasons, the logical result will be that no member of the class will be allowed to intervene in a class action suit as a matter of right once it is determined that the representation is adequate as to the class. In some instances, although the representation by the named party is adequate as to a class, unnamed class members will have interests deserving of independent representation but not sufficiently important or conflicting to require that the class action be dismissed, the class representative replaced, or the class redefined to exclude the intervenors. The denial of intervention as of right whenever representation is adequate as to the class is particularly unacceptable to Fiss because the class representative is self-selected.

In Norwalk CORE v. Norwalk Board of Education, 298 F. Supp. 208 (D.Conn.1968), aff'd, 423 F.2d 121 (2d Cir.1970), groups seeking integration more extensive than that sought by the named plaintiffs became ensnared in the traditional reading of the class action rule. The district court denied a motion to intervene as of right under Rule 24(a)(2) by a group purportedly representing blacks and Puerto Ricans in the community. CORE, which represented a class similarly defined, had challenged the method of school desegregation (the closing of facilities in the black and Puerto Rican communities and the transporting of minority children to predominantly white outlying schools) rather than the objective of desegregation itself. It sought reopening of the school facilities in the minority communities. The proposed intervenors asserted that this would hamper the board's efforts to integrate the schools. In denying the motion to intervene, the court reasoned that since neither group opposed school integration and both sought integrated schools, the question was simply whether the original plaintiff had standing to bring the suit. However, the district court in effect satisfied the intervenors' request by refusing the two-way busing sought by the original plaintiffs.

Courts have been more sensitive to the differing interests of persons of varied racial, ethnic, and national backgrounds. While efforts of white parents to intervene as defendants in order to make arguments similar to those being made by school boards generally have not been successful, courts have allowed intervention in recognition of the distinct interests of Mexican- and Chinese–Americans. The disagreements among blacks as to whether racial balance remedies are the most appropriate relief for segregated schools, particularly in large urban districts, reflect interests as divergent as those which courts have recognized at the request of other ethnic minorities.

The failure to carefully monitor class status in accordance with the class action rules can frustrate the purposes of those rules and intensify the danger of attorney-client conflict inherent in class action litigation. To a measurable degree, the conflict can be traced to the civil rights lawyer's idealism and commitment to school integration. Such motivations do not become "unprofessional" because subjected to psychological scrutiny. They help explain the drive that enables the civil rights lawyer to survive discouragement and defeat and renew the challenge for change. But when challenges are made on behalf of large classes unable to speak effectively for themselves, courts should not refrain from making those inquiries under the Federal Rules that cannot fail, when properly undertaken, to strengthen the position of the class, the representative, and the counsel who serve them both.

V.   The Resolution of Lawyer–Client Conflicts

There is nothing revolutionary in any of the suggestions in this article. They are controversial only to the extent they suggest that some civil rights lawyers, like their more candid poverty law colleagues, are making decisions, setting priorities, and undertaking responsibilities that should be determined by their clients and shaped by the community. It is essential that lawyers "lawyer" and not attempt to lead clients and class. Commitment renders restraint more, not less, difficult, and the inability of black clients to pay handsome fees for legal services can cause their lawyers, unconsciously perhaps, to adopt an attitude of "we know what's best" in determining legal strategy. Unfortunately, clients are all too willing to turn everything over to the lawyers. In school cases, perhaps more than in any other civil rights field, the attorney must be more than a litigator. The willingness to innovate, organize, and negotiate—and the ability to perform each with skill and persistence—are of crucial importance. In this process of overall representation, the apparent—and sometimes real—conflicts of interest between lawyer and client can be resolved.

Finally, commitment to an integrated society should not be allowed to interfere with the ability to represent effectively parents who favor education-oriented remedies. Those civil rights lawyers, regardless of race, whose commitment to integration is buoyed by doubts about the effectiveness of predominantly black schools should reconsider seriously the propriety of representing blacks, at least in those school cases involving heavily minority districts.

This seemingly harsh suggestion is dictated by practical as well as professional considerations. Lacking more viable alternatives, the black community has turned to the courts. After several decades of frustration, the legal system, for a number of complex reasons, responded. Law and lawyers have received perhaps too much credit for that response.[136] The

---

136. Blacks lost in Plessy v. Ferguson, 163 U.S. 537 (1896), in part because the timing was not right. The Supreme Court and the nation had become reactionary on the issue of race. As LDF Director–Counsel Greenberg has acknowledged:

[Plaintiff's attorney in *Plessy*, Albion W.] Tourgée recognized that the tide of history was against him and spoke of an effort to overcome its effect by influencing public opinion. But this, too, was beyond his control. All the lawyer can realistically

quest for symbolic manifestations of new rights and the search for new legal theories have too often failed to prompt an assessment of the economic and political condition that so influence the progress and outcome of any social reform improvement.

In school desegregation blacks have a just cause, but that cause can be undermined as well as furthered by litigation. A test case can be an important means of calling attention to perceived injustice; more important, school litigation presents opportunities for improving the weak economic and political position which renders the black community vulnerable to the specific injustices the litigation is intended to correct. Litigation can and should serve lawyer and client as a community-organizing tool, an educational forum, a means of obtaining data, a method of exercising political leverage, and a rallying point for public support.

But even when directed by the most resourceful attorneys, civil rights litigation remains an unpredictable vehicle for gaining benefits, such as quality schooling, which a great many whites do not enjoy. The risks involved in such efforts increase dramatically when civil rights attorneys, for idealistic or other reasons, fail to consider continually the limits imposed by the social and political circumstances under which clients must function even if the case is won. In the closest of lawyer-client relationships this continual reexamination can be difficult; it becomes much harder where much of the representation takes place hundreds of miles from the site of the litigation.[138]

Professor Leroy Clark has written that the black community's belief in the efficacy of litigation inhibited the development of techniques involving popular participation and control that might have advanced school desegre-

do is marshall the evidence of what the claims of history may be and present them to the court. But no matter how skillful the presentation, *Plessy* and *Brown* had dynamics of their own. Tourgée would have won with *Plessy* in 1954. The lawyers who brought *Brown* would have lost in 1896.

Greenberg, Litigation for Social Change: Methods, Limits and Role in Democracy, 29 Record of N.Y.C.B.A. 320, 334 (1974).

138.   Marian Wright Edelman, a former LDF staff lawyer who lived and practiced in Mississippi before moving to Washington, has spoken of her concern about the distance between her and her clients. She stated:

"We are up here filing desegregation suits, but something else is going on in the black community. I sensed it before I left Mississippi. We hear more about non-desegregation, about 'our' schools, about money to build up black schools. I'm not sure we are doing the right thing

in the long run. We automatically assume that what we need to do is close lousy black schools. But desegregation is taking the best black teachers out of the black schools and putting lousy white teachers in black schools. It has become a very complex thing."

. . . .

The passage of time has left Ms. Edelman less uneasy. In 1975 she wrote, "School desegregation is a necessary, viable and important national goal." Acknowledging that the middle class can escape to the suburbs or private schools and that black children in desegregated schools are often classified as retarded or disciplined disproportionately, she nevertheless urged desegregation because "[t]he Constitution requires it. Minority children will never achieve equal educational opportunity without it. And our children will never learn to live together if they do not begin to learn together now." N.Y. Times, Sept. 22, 1975, at 33, col. 2.

gation in the South. He feels that civil rights lawyers were partly responsible for this unwise reliance on the law. They had studied "cases" in which the conflict involved easily identifiable adversaries, a limited number of variables, and issues which courts could resolve in a manageable way. A lawyer seeking social change, Clark advises, must "make clear that the major social and economic obstacles are not easily amenable to the legal process and that vigilance and continued activity by the disadvantaged are the crucial elements in social change." For reasons quite similar to those which enabled blacks to win in *Brown* in 1954 and caused them to lose in *Plessy* in 1896, even successful school litigation will bring little meaningful change unless there is continuing pressure for implementation from the black community. The problem of unjust laws, as Professor Gary Bellow has noted, is almost invariably a problem of distribution of political and economic power. The rules merely reflect a series of choices by the society made in response to these distributions. " '[R]ule' change, without a political base to support it, just doesn't produce any substantial result because rules are not self-executing: they require an enforcement mechanism."

In the last analysis, blacks must provide an enforcement mechanism that will give educational content to the constitutional right recognized in *Brown*. Simply placing black children in "white" schools will seldom suffice. Lawyers in school cases who fail to obtain judicial relief that reasonably promises to improve the education of black children serve poorly both their clients and their cause.

In 1935, W. E. B. DuBois, in the course of a national debate over the education of blacks which has not been significantly altered by *Brown*, expressed simply but eloquently the message of the coalition of black community groups in Boston with which this article began:

> [T]he Negro needs neither segregated schools nor mixed schools. What he needs is education. What he must remember is that there is no magic, either in mixed schools or in segregated schools. A mixed school with poor and unsympathetic teachers, with hostile public opinion, and no teaching of truth concerning black folk, is bad. A segregated school with ignorant placeholders, inadequate equipment, poor salaries, and wretched housing, is equally bad. Other things being equal, the mixed school is the broader, more natural basis for the education of all youth. It gives wider contacts; it inspires greater self-confidence; and suppresses the inferiority complex. But other things seldom are equal, and in that case, Sympathy, Knowledge, and the Truth, outweigh all that the mixed school can offer.[143]

DuBois spoke neither for the integrationist nor the separatist, but for poor black parents unable to choose, as can well-to-do of both races, which schools will educate their children. Effective representation of these par-

---

143. DuBois, *Does the Negro Need Separate Schools?*, 4 J. Negro Educ. 328, 335 (1935).

ents and their children presents a still unmet challenge for all lawyers committed to civil rights.

Conclusion

The tactics that worked for civil rights lawyers in the first decade of school desegregation—the careful selection and filing of class action suits seeking standardized relief in accordance with set, uncompromising national goals—are no longer unfailingly effective. In recent years, the relief sought and obtained in these suits has helped to precipitate a rise in militant white opposition and has seriously eroded carefully cultivated judicial support. Opposition to any civil rights program can be expected, but the hoped-for improvement in schooling for black children that might have justified the sacrifice and risk has proven minimal at best. It has been virtually nonexistent for the great mass of urban black children locked in all-black schools, many of which are today as separate and unequal as they were before 1954.

Political, economic, and social conditions have contributed to the loss of school desegregation momentum; but to the extent that civil rights lawyers have not recognized the shift of black parental priorities, they have sacrificed opportunities to negotiate with school boards and petition courts for the judicially enforceable educational improvements which all parents seek. The time has come for civil rights lawyers to end their single-minded commitment to racial balance, a goal which, standing alone, is increasingly inaccessible and all too often educationally impotent.

* * *

Professor Deborah Rhode has addressed some of Derrick Bell's concerns:

> "It does not follow, of course, that attorneys in these and comparable cases failed to represent class interests. Much depends on who one views as appropriate spokesmen for the class and how broadly one defines 'interest.' ... parents are often poorly situated to speak for all children who will be affected by judicial decree. But neither is an attorney with strong prudential or ideological preferences well positioned to decide which class members or guardians deserve a hearing and which do not."

Deborah L. Rhode, Class Conflicts in Class Actions, 34 Stan. L. Rev. 1183, 1212 (1982). Rhode suggests various strategies that could be deployed to encourage more responsiveness to the concerns of class members, including requiring class counsel to "submit statements detailing contacts with class members," and structuring attorney's fees awards to create more incentives for lawyer-client communication. Id. at 1250.

When the interests of class members are too disparate, the court will refuse to certify the class. Some courts also refuse to certify a class for settlement purposes only. In Georgine v. Amchem Products, Inc., 83 F.3d 610 (3d Cir. 1996), cert. granted. 117 S.Ct. 379 (1996) (No. 96–270) the district court approved a settlement between defendants and the "Georgine" class consisting of over 150,000 persons exposed to defendants' asbestos either on the job or from a spouse or housemate who was exposed on the job, plus family members of such persons. In reversing, the Third Circuit ordered that the district court decertify the "Georgine" settlement class for failure to meet typicality of claims and adequacy of representation requirements of F.R.C.P. Rule 23(a) and vacated the district court's injunction prohibiting absent class members from pursuing asbestos-related personal injury claims pending a final order in the suit. Law professors Charles Silver and Samuel Issacharoff filed an amicus brief with the Supreme Court expressing concern that application of Rule 23 to facilitate such settlements would "endanger absent class members by weakening the incentives plaintiffs' attorneys have to maximize the value of their claims, by encouraging collusive settlements judges will have difficulty policing, and by ignoring important respects in which some absent plaintiffs' interests conflict with others."

Note, The Attorney–Client Privilege in Class Actions: Fashioning an Exception to Promote Adequacy of Representation

97 Harv. L. Rev. 947 (1984).

* * *

II. The Class Action

A. The Definition and Importance of Adequate Representation

The class action enables groups of individuals lacking access to courts through traditional channels to seek judicial redress through a spokesperson who is bound to advocate their interests. By allowing courts to adjudicate the rights of individuals who have not pressed their claims individually, the class action necessarily strains the traditional principle that the parties affected by litigation control its course: judgments in class actions, unlike judgments in conventional suits, can bind individuals who have taken no part in the litigation.

Nonetheless, the legal system has established mechanisms designed to integrate the class suit into the conceptual framework of conventional litigation. The most important of these mechanisms is the requirement that class representatives and class counsel adequately represent the interests of absent class members, a requirement that serves as a surrogate for the traditional principle that only those who have participated in litigation can be legally bound by its outcome. The adequate-representation requirement can be seen either to provide absentees with a form of indirect participation or to extend to them enough of the benefits of involvement to justify dispensing with their actual participation. Under either rationale, the adequate-representation requirement is central to the idea of class action.

Federal Rule of Civil Procedure 23 and judicial interpretations of that provision attempt to set out a means of ensuring that representatives fulfill their duties to absentee class members. Rule 23(a)(4) provides that a court, before it may permit a suit to be conducted as a class action, must find that persons seeking class designation are adequate representatives of those for whom they desire to speak. The requirement of adequacy arises with the filing of the suit and remains in force until the suit's final disposition. Courts typically conceptualize the relationship between the representatives and the class in familiar legal terms by treating the representatives as fiduciaries for the absent members.

Despite these provisions, the task of ensuring that the interests of absentees are represented is formidable. Representatives are not elected by constituents; rather, they put themselves forward for approval by the court. Once the trial judge determines that the parties seeking representative status meet the criteria of rules 23(a) and 23(b), the class representatives' control over the conduct of litigation becomes sweeping: they need not keep absentees closely informed of their strategies or goals. Given the looseness of constraints on the representatives, it is not surprising that the case law contains numerous instances of class member dissatisfaction with representation. Dissent may arise over a wide variety of issues, including attorneys' fees, the structure and sufficiency of remedies sought by class representatives, and the desirability of any relief at all.

B.   Standards and Mechanisms for Evaluating Representation

Courts have enumerated broad criteria for evaluating the adequacy of representation. Many facets of named representatives' conduct of the litigation are relevant to the inquiry. Named representatives can be questioned on fee arrangements, on their knowledge of how other representatives joined the suit, and on their understanding of the goals of the litigation and their own responsibilities. In addition, the qualifications and experience of the named representatives' counsel are factors in evaluating the adequacy of representation. One court has held that a named plaintiff has an obligation to "question the class attorney to ensure that counsel is adequately performing his job," [Gill v. Monroe County Dep't of Social Servs., 92 F.R.D. 14, 16 (W.D.N.Y.1981)] and the Seventh Circuit has declared that the representatives' conduct of settlement negotiations is an important area for judicial scrutiny. [In re General Motors Corp. Engine Interchange Litig., 594 F.2d 1106, 1124–25 (7th Cir.), cert. denied, 444 U.S. 870 (1979)].

Scrutinizing adequacy of representation requires not only criteria of evaluation, but also mechanisms for raising and exploring the adequacy issue. The Federal Rules of Civil Procedure establish the trial court as the principal watchdog over representation, yet in practice, judicial oversight is limited. Although appellate courts admonish trial courts to play an active role, the adversarial nature of judicial proceedings places the onus of challenging adequacy of representation largely on the party opposing the class. Indeed, unless the opposing party makes such a challenge, courts typically treat the burden of demonstrating adequacy of representation—technically borne by the named representatives—as a formality. Thus, the protection of absentees' interests is left to opponents of the class, who naturally have strong incentives to resist certification of capable representatives and to acquiesce in the designation of less threatening ones.

Another potential guarantor of adequate representation is the class counsel, who is charged with an independent responsibility to protect the interests of class members. But the class counsel offers absentees only limited protection against inadequate representation. Because class representatives often relinquish to the class counsel all control over the litigation, the attorney does not police representation, but directs it. Moreover, the interests of the attorney may diverge significantly from the interests of class members. As a result, the conduct of the class attorney needs more scrutiny than that of the named representatives. Indeed, courts have maintained that named representatives owe absentees a duty to supervise class attorneys closely. In practice, class counsel and named representatives usually function as a unit rather than as independent actors capable of effectively overseeing each other.

By far the most reliable assurance of adequate representation is provided by the class itself. Although direct class member involvement may diminish the efficiency of class litigation, it avoids the conflicts of interest that may arise when other actors purport to police class representation. Additionally, direct challenges obviate the need—implicit in the courts' oversight of class representation—for judicial definition of class interests. The Federal Rules recognize the desirability of participation by absent members and are structured to facilitate such involvement. Rule 23 expressly requires the court to permit class members to enter an appearance through counsel, object to proposed settlements, and, in suits conducted under Rule 23(b)(3), opt out of the suit entirely. The stringent notice requirements for Rule 23(b)(3) actions and proposed settlements further facilitate class member participation. Moreover, courts have held that class members objecting to proposed settlements are entitled to develop their challenges through discovery aimed at both the opposition and their own representatives. Finally, class members can attempt to avoid the binding effects of a class action through collateral attack on the judgment.

Despite these opportunities, absent members participate in class litigation only infrequently. But the failure to participate cannot be taken as approval of the representatives' conduct of the suit, because the barriers to participation—including lack of effective notice, difficulty in securing legal representation, and lack of absentee interest because of the small size of individual claims—sharply curtail the level of actual involvement. In sum, the very factors that justify litigation by representative parties limit the potential participation of absentees.

C.   The Role of the Attorney–Client Privilege in Litigation Over Adequacy of Representation

The task of holding representatives accountable demands both curtailment of the courts' traditional deference to party control over litigation and close judicial scrutiny of representatives' conduct of litigation. Doctrines based on the conception that the attorney-client relationship requires insulation from judicial oversight may be inapplicable to class representation. In particular, the unqualified availability of the attorney-client privilege in the representational suit impedes the functioning of the mechanisms devised to hold representatives accountable. Although some lines of inquiry into adequacy of representation do not necessarily run afoul of the privilege, attorney-client communications may still be highly pertinent to resolution of the adequacy issue. Such communications are, naturally, some of the most probative sources of evidence about the nature of the lawyer-client relationship and thus about the adequacy of representation. By presenting a barrier to the scrutiny of representation, the privilege undercuts rather than underpins the participatory structure of the suit: it blocks the flow of information from representatives to absentees. Modifying the privilege might therefore facilitate class members' inquiry into adequacy of representation and improve their ability to scrutinize the performance of their spokesperson.

III.   Contours of the Proposed Exception

Any modification of the attorney-client privilege in class actions should reflect the fiduciary duties that class representatives and counsel owe to absent class members. Existing law on the scope and applicability of the privilege in other disputes between fiduciary and principal can guide consideration of how courts might modify the attorney-client privilege in class actions. In Garner v. Wolfinbarger, [430 F.2d 1093 (5th Cir.1970), cert. denied, 401 U.S. 974 (1971)] the Fifth Circuit recognized a limitation on the privilege in shareholder suits charging management with breach of fiduciary duty. In holding that a corporation's communications with its counsel were available to the plaintiff shareholders upon a showing of 'good cause,' the Garner court reasoned that management's obligations to stockholders barred it from concealing information by invoking the privilege. The objective of holding management accountable to shareholders took precedence over the goal of promoting communication between corporate management and counsel.

Because the reasoning of the Garner court "is not premised on concepts peculiar to corporate law," [see Donovan v. Fitzsimmons, 90 F.R.D. 583, 586 (N.D.Ill.1981) (applying the Garner exception by analogy to compel disclosure of communications between pension fund managers and counsel)] it can provide a doctrinal basis for shaping an exception to the attorney-client privilege in class actions. The parallels between the stockholder-management relationship and the absentee-representative relationship are clear. Corporate management and class representatives are both obliged to act in the interests of others. Their assertion of the attorney-client privilege against their principals is inconsistent with that obligation.

Garner is premised in part on the notion that client communications with an attorney representing a collective unit should be available to other members of the unit. This component of Garner can be discerned in the court's reliance on a long-recognized common law exception to the privilege in situations in which two or more individuals are represented by a single attorney in connection with a common interest and subsequently become adversaries. In the later litigation, the parties are barred from asserting the privilege with respect to communications relating to the earlier matter. Because class members, like shareholders, are by definition associated to protect common interests, the common law exception seems as applicable to class actions as to shareholder suits.

A class action exception to the privilege designed to facilitate policing of representation by absent class members would require courts to determine the precise scope of the class representatives' duties. In particular, courts would need to determine when the representatives' duties arise and, thus, when legal communications become subject to discovery. There are two points at which the representatives' duties might arise: the point at which the representatives seek class status (either the filing of the suit as a class action or the motion for certification), or the point at which the court certifies the class. Judicial decisions have tended to prefer the earlier point, the petition for certification. In Roper v. Consurve, Inc. [578 F.2d 1106, 1110 (5th Cir.1978)], the Fifth Circuit noted that "[b]y the very act of filing a class action, the class representatives assume responsibilities to members of the class." Moreover, courts generally scrutinize precertification settlements to ensure that the settlements do not adversely affect absent class members. This limitation on representatives' freedom to compromise their claims implies that representatives incur obligations to the class at an early stage. Furthermore, barring assertion of the privilege with respect to all communications occurring after the petition for certification is filed would serve to police adequacy of representation. Because key decisions are reached at the outset of litigation, precertification communications may be at least as important to the evaluation of representation issues as are those following the formal designation of the suit as a class action.

Limiting the attorney-client privilege would also require consideration of when the exception should terminate. In this regard, differences exist between the shareholder suit involved in Garner and the typical challenge to class representation. Shareholder suits generally concern events prior to and distinct from the litigation. Therefore, the attorney-client communications sought by shareholders relate not to trial strategies and plans, but rather to the management policies or acts that gave rise to the suit. In one shareholder suit in which the plaintiffs sought attorney-client communications, In re LTV Securities Litigation [89 F.R.D. 595 (N.D.Tex.1981)], the court distinguished Garner on the basis of this difference between communications during the sequence of events leading to the suit and communications exchanged in preparation for litigation over the contested acts. The court held that, once fiduciary and principal assume an adversarial relationship, the privilege exception terminates. LTV's reasoning, however, should not be adopted in the class action context, because class representatives' fiduciary duties to absentees continue after the absentees have initiated a challenge to the representatives. Although preserving the representatives' duties to dissenting class members can lead to seemingly unusual situations in which litigants are bound to protect the interests of their antagonists, it avoids the even more anomalous situations that would result from discharging representatives from their obligations. If the representatives' duties to absentees terminated when the absentees elected to participate directly, all attempts to hold representatives to fulfillment of their obligations would simply free them of those obligations.

The Garner court chose to retain the privilege in situations in which the plaintiff stockholders failed to show "good cause" for discovery, and rejected the trial court's broad ruling allowing the stockholders unimpeded access to the communications between management and counsel. [See Garner v. Wolfinbarger, 280 F. Supp. 1018, 1019 (N.D.Ala.1968), rev'd, 430 F.2d 1093 (5th Cir.1970)]. The appellate court's rationale was that "[d]ue regard must be paid to the interests of the nonparty stockholders, which may be affected by impinging on the privilege, sometimes injuriously." [Garner, 430 F.2d at 1101 n.17]. Similar considerations suggest that a "good cause" requirement would be sensible in class actions. Challenges to representation by factions within a class could injure non-objecting class members by impeding the representatives' ability to conduct the litigation. A "good cause" provision would enable the judge to safeguard class interests by allowing discovery only when the challengers have raised serious doubts regarding the adequacy of representation. Such a provision would also make it more difficult for opposing parties to exploit the exception by recruiting class members to uncover attorney-client communications. Similarly, orders for in camera review of communications could safeguard the class from harm caused by disclosure of attorney-client communications to the opposing party.

IV. Conclusion

Establishing a relatively narrow limitation on the attorney-client privilege in class actions would facilitate class members' challenges to representation and thus bolster the representational nature of class action procedure. The uncertainty of confidentiality would encourage class representatives to protect their absentees diligently. It might also discourage representatives from seeking certification of overinclusive classes likely to fracture during litigation. Narrowly defined, the exception would interfere minimally with achievement of the privilege's objectives. Moreover, the proposed exception would be burdensome only in the sense that it would further the enforcement of obligations that already exist. A class representative should be attentive to the absentees' interests in the planning and conduct of the litigation and aware of the public nature of the attorney-client relationship in class actions. An exception to the attorney-client privilege would most likely place additional burdens on representatives unconcerned with protecting the class. It would, however, impose few new constraints on those truly committed to effective representation.

Relevant Background

Securities Class Actions: A New Lead Plaintiff

Class actions brought under the securities laws (usually against an issuer for false or misleading statements to investors) are often initiated by a named plaintiff who owns a relatively small amount of stock. That plaintiff has traditionally been allowed to become the lead plaintiff, choosing the lawyer to represent the class and deciding on litigation and settlement strategy subject to oversight by the court. However, the fact that the lead plaintiff is such a small stakeholder can lead to allegations that the plaintiff's lawyers actually control the litigation and settlement negotiations, perhaps for their own benefit rather than that of the class. In 1995, Professor Eliott Weiss suggested that the issuer's largest shareholder should be presumed to be the class representative in securities class actions. Elliot J. Weiss, Let the Money Do the Monitoring: How Institutional Investors Can Reduce Agency Costs in Securities Class Actions, 104 Yale L. J. 2053 (1995). If the largest shareholder wants to perform this role, under Weiss's proposal, that shareholder would be substituted for the shareholder who originally brought the lawsuit, and could then choose whether to retain the lawyer who initiated the lawsuit or retain a new lawyer. Id. at 2105–07. Professor Weiss's proposal, having drawn the attention of the Senate Banking Committee, was enacted into law in substantially similar form in the Securities Litigation Reform Act of 1995, Section 101.

QUESTIONS

1. How is representing a class in a class action different from individually representing several persons with aligned interests in a lawsuit?

2. Compare the standards used for certification of a class with the standards used to evaluate concurrent conflicts in civil representations. How are the two problems different? Why are the applicable standards different?

3. In civil rights litigation, it may be possible for a lawyer to accomplish one important objective (for example, rapid school integration) at the expense of another objective (for example, quality of education at least in the short term). Who should decide which objectives are more important?

4. What practical strategies should a class action lawyer use to consult with individual class members and conform trial strategy to their interests?

5. When should a class action lawyer suggest that some members of the class form a separate class and get another lawyer?

6. Should a lawyer representing a class consider the interests of similarly situated persons outside the class (for example, school children in a different geographic location who may benefit from the precedential value of litigation)?

F. CONCURRENT CONFLICTS IN CRIMINAL REPRESENTATIONS

Eugene G. Iredale, b. Louisville, Kentucky 1951; B.A. Columbia University 1973; J.D. Harvard University 1976; admitted to the Massachusetts bar in 1977 and California bar in 1983; Member, National Association of Criminal Defense Lawyers; California Attorneys for Criminal Justice.

Wheat v. United States

486 U.S. 153 (1988).

■ Rehnquist, C. J., delivered the opinion of the Court, in which White, O'Connor, Scalia, and Kennedy, JJ., joined. Marshall, J., filed a dissenting opinion, in which Brennan, J., joined, Stevens, J., filed a dissenting opinion, in which Blackmun, J., joined.

■ Chief Justice Rehnquist delivered the opinion of the Court.

The issue in this case is whether the District Court erred in declining petitioner's waiver of his right to conflict-free counsel and by refusing to permit petitioner's proposed substitution of attorneys.

I

Petitioner Mark Wheat, along with numerous codefendants, was charged with participating in a far-flung drug distribution conspiracy. Over a period of several years, many thousands of pounds of marijuana were transported from Mexico and other locations to southern California. Petitioner acted primarily as an intermediary in the distribution ring; he received and stored large shipments of marijuana at his home, then distributed the marijuana to customers in the region.

Also charged in the conspiracy were Juvenal Gomez–Barajas and Javier Bravo, who were represented in their criminal proceedings by attorney Eugene Iredale. Gomez–Barajas was tried first and was acquitted on drug charges overlapping with those against petitioner. To avoid a second trial on other charges, however, Gomez–Barajas offered to plead guilty to tax evasion and illegal importation of merchandise. At the commencement of petitioner's trial, the District Court had not accepted the plea; Gomez–Barajas was thus free to withdraw his guilty plea and proceed to trial.

Bravo, evidently a lesser player in the conspiracy, decided to forgo trial and plead guilty to one count of transporting approximately 2,400 pounds of marijuana from Los Angeles to a residence controlled by Victor Vidal. At the conclusion of Bravo's guilty plea proceedings on August 22, 1985, Iredale notified the District Court that he had been contacted by petitioner and had been asked to try petitioner's case as well. In response, the Government registered substantial concern about the possibility of conflict in the representation. After entertaining some initial discussion of the substitution of counsel, the District Court instructed the parties to present more detailed arguments the following Monday, just one day before the scheduled start of petitioner's trial.

At the Monday hearing, the Government objected to petitioner's proposed substitution on the ground that Iredale's representation of Gomez–Barajas and Bravo created a serious conflict of interest. The Government's position was premised on two possible conflicts. First, the District Court had not yet accepted the plea and sentencing arrangement negotiated between Gomez–Barajas and the Government; in the event that arrangement were rejected by the court, Gomez–Barajas would be free to withdraw the plea and stand trial. He would then be faced with the prospect of representation by Iredale, who in the meantime would have acted as petitioner's attorney. Petitioner, through his participation in the drug distribution scheme, was familiar with the sources and size of Gomez–Barajas' income, and was thus likely to be called as a witness for the Government at any subsequent trial of Gomez–Barajas. This scenario would pose a conflict of interest for Iredale, who would be prevented from cross-examining petitioner and thereby from effectively representing Gomez–Barajas.

Second, and of more immediate concern, Iredale's representation of Bravo would directly affect his ability to act as counsel for petitioner. The Government believed that a portion of the marijuana delivered by Bravo to Vidal's residence eventually was transferred to petitioner. In this regard, the Government contacted Iredale and asked that Bravo be made available as a witness to testify against petitioner, and agreed in exchange to modify its position at the time of Bravo's sentencing. In the likely event that Bravo were called to testify, Iredale's position in representing both men would become untenable, for ethical proscriptions would forbid him to cross-examine Bravo in any meaningful way. By failing to do so, he would also fail to provide petitioner with effective assistance of counsel. Thus, because of Iredale's prior representation of Gomez–Barajas and Bravo and the potential for serious conflict of interest, the Government urged the District Court to reject the substitution of attorneys.

In response, petitioner emphasized his right to have counsel of his own choosing and the willingness of Gomez–Barajas, Bravo, and petitioner to waive the right to conflict-free counsel. Petitioner argued that the circumstances posited by the Government that would create a conflict for Iredale were highly speculative and bore no connection to the true relationship between the co-conspirators. If called to testify, Bravo would simply say that he did not know petitioner and had no dealings with him; no attempt by Iredale to impeach Bravo would be necessary. Further, in the unlikely event that Gomez–Barajas went to trial on the charges of tax evasion and illegal importation, petitioner's lack of involvement in those alleged crimes made his appearance as a witness highly improbable. Finally, and most importantly, all three defendants agreed to allow Iredale to represent petitioner and to waive any future claims of conflict of interest. In petitioner's view, the Government was manufacturing implausible conflicts in an attempt to disqualify Iredale, who had already proved extremely effective in representing Gomez–Barajas and Bravo.

After hearing argument from each side, the District Court noted that it was unfortunate that petitioner had not suggested the substitution sooner, rather than two court days before the commencement of trial. The court then ruled:

"[B]ased upon the representation of the Government in [its] memorandum that the Court really has no choice at this point other than to find that an irreconcilable conflict of interest exists. I don't think it can be waived, and accordingly, Mr. Wheat's request to substitute Mr. Iredale in as attorney of record is denied." App. 100–101.

Petitioner proceeded to trial with his original counsel and was convicted of conspiracy to possess more than 1,000 pounds of marijuana with intent to distribute, in violation of 21 U.S.C.A. § 846, and five counts of possessing marijuana with intent to distribute, in violation of § 841(a)(1).

The Court of Appeals for the Ninth Circuit affirmed petitioner's convictions, 813 F. 2d 1399 (1987), finding that, within the limits prescribed by the Sixth Amendment, the District Court has considerable discretion in allowing substitution of counsel. The Court of Appeals found that the District Court had correctly balanced two Sixth Amendment rights: (1) the qualified right to be represented by counsel of one's choice, and (2) the right to a defense conducted by an attorney who is free of conflicts of interest. Denial of either of these rights threatened the District Court with an appeal assigning the ruling as reversible error, and the Court of Appeals concluded that the District Court did not abuse its discretion in declining to allow the substitution or addition of Iredale as trial counsel for petitioner.

Because the Courts of Appeals have expressed substantial disagreement about when a district court may override a defendant's waiver of his attorney's conflict of interest, we granted certiorari, 484 U.S. 814 (1987).

II

The Sixth Amendment to the Constitution guarantees that "[i]n all criminal prosecutions, the accused shall enjoy the right ... to have the Assistance of Counsel for his defense." In United States v. Morrison, 449 U.S. 361, 364 (1981), we observed that this right was designed to assure fairness in the adversary criminal process. Realizing that an unaided layman may have little skill in arguing the law or in coping with an intricate procedural system, Powell v. Alabama, 287 U.S. 45, 69 (1932); United States v. Ash, 413 U.S. 300, 307 (1973), we have held that the Sixth Amendment secures the right to the assistance of counsel, by appointment if necessary, in a trial for any serious crime. Gideon v. Wainwright, 372 U.S. 335 (1963). We have further recognized that the purpose of providing assistance of counsel "is simply to ensure that criminal defendants receive a fair trial," Strickland v. Washington, 466 U.S. 668, 689 (1984), and that in evaluating Sixth Amendment claims, "the appropriate inquiry focuses on the adversarial process, not on the accused's relationship with his lawyer as such." United States v. Cronic, 466 U.S. 648, 657, n. 21 (1984). Thus, while the right to select and be represented by one's preferred attorney is comprehended by the Sixth Amendment, the essential aim of the Amendment is to guarantee an effective advocate for each criminal defendant rather than to ensure that a defendant will inexorably be represented by the lawyer whom he prefers. See Morris v. Slappy, 461 U.S. 1, 13–14 (1983); Jones v. Barnes, 463 U.S. 745 (1983).

The Sixth Amendment right to choose one's own counsel is circumscribed in several important respects. Regardless of his persuasive powers, an advocate who is not a member of the bar may not represent clients (other than himself) in court. Similarly, a defendant may not insist on representation by an attorney he cannot afford or who for other reasons declines to represent the defendant. Nor may a defendant insist on the counsel of an attorney who has a previous or ongoing relationship with an opposing party, even when the opposing party is the Government. The question raised in this case is the extent to which a criminal defendant's right under the Sixth Amendment to his chosen attorney is qualified by the fact that the attorney has represented other defendants charged in the same criminal conspiracy.

In previous cases, we have recognized that multiple representation of criminal defendants engenders special dangers of which a court must be aware. While "permitting a single lawyer to represent codefendants ... is not per se violative of constitutional guarantees of effective assistance of counsel," Holloway v. Arkansas, 435 U.S. 475, 482 (1978), a court confronted with and alerted to possible conflicts of interest must take adequate steps to ascertain whether the conflicts warrant separate counsel. See also Cuyler v. Sullivan, 446 U.S. 335 (1980). As we said in Holloway:

> "Joint representation of conflicting interests is suspect because of what it tends to prevent the lawyer from doing.... [A] conflict may ... prevent an attorney from challenging the admission of evidence prejudicial to one client but perhaps favorable to another, or from arguing at the sentencing hearing the relative involvement and culpability of his clients in order to minimize the culpability of one by emphasizing that of another." 435 U.S. at 489–490.

Petitioner insists that the provision of waivers by all affected defendants cures any problems created by the multiple representation. But no such flat rule can be deduced from the Sixth Amendment presumption in favor of counsel of choice. Federal courts have an independent interest in ensuring that criminal trials are conducted within the ethical standards of the profession and that legal proceedings appear fair to all who observe them. Both the American Bar Association's Model Code of Professional Responsibility and its Model Rules of Professional Conduct, as well as the rules of the California Bar Association (which governed the attorneys in this case), impose limitations on multiple representation of clients. See ABA Model Code of Professional Responsibility DR5–105(C) (1980); ABA Model Rules of Professional Conduct, Rule 1.7 (1984); Rules of Professional Conduct of the State Bar of California, Rules 5 and 7, Cal. Bus. & Prof. Code Ann. § 6076 (West 1974). Not only the interest of a criminal defendant but the institutional interest in the rendition of just verdicts in criminal cases may be jeopardized by unregulated multiple representation.

For this reason, the Federal Rules of Criminal Procedure direct trial judges to investigate specially cases involving joint representation. In pertinent part, Rule 44(c) provides:

"[T]he court shall promptly inquire with respect to such joint representation and shall personally advise each defendant of his right to the effective assistance of counsel, including separate representation. Unless it appears that there is good cause to believe no conflict of interest is likely to arise, the court shall take such measures as may be appropriate to protect each defendant's right to counsel."

Although Rule 44(c) does not specify what particular measures may be taken by a district court, one option suggested by the Notes of the Advisory Committee is an order by the court that the defendants be separately represented in subsequent proceedings in the case. 18 U. S. C. App., p. 650. This suggestion comports with our instructions in Holloway and in Glasser v. United States, 315 U.S. 60 (1942), that the trial courts, when alerted by objection from one of the parties, have an independent duty to ensure that criminal defendants receive a trial that is fair and does not contravene the Sixth Amendment.

To be sure, this need to investigate potential conflicts arises in part from the legitimate wish of district courts that their judgments remain intact on appeal. As the Court of Appeals accurately pointed out, trial courts confronted with multiple representations face the prospect of being "whipsawed" by assertions of error no matter which way they rule. If a district court agrees to the multiple representation, and the advocacy of counsel is thereafter impaired as a result, the defendant may well claim that he did not receive effective assistance. See, e. g., Burger v. Kemp, 483 U.S. 776 (1987). On the other hand, a district court's refusal to accede to the multiple representation may result in a challenge such as petitioner's in this case. Nor does a waiver by the defendant necessarily solve the problem, for we note, without passing judgment on, the apparent willingness of Courts of Appeals to entertain ineffective-assistance claims from defendants who have specifically waived the right to conflict-free counsel. See, e. g., United States ex rel. Tonaldi v. Elrod, 716 F. 2d 431, 436–437 (C.A.7 1983); United States v. Vowteras, 500 F. 2d 1210, 1211 (CA2), cert. denied, 419 U.S. 1069 (1974); see also Glasser, supra, at 70 ("To preserve the protection of the Bill of Rights for hard-pressed defendants, we indulge every reasonable presumption against the waiver of fundamental rights").

Thus, where a court justifiably finds an actual conflict of interest, there can be no doubt that it may decline a proffer of waiver, and insist that defendants be separately represented. As the Court of Appeals for the Third Circuit stated in United States v. Dolan, 570 F. 2d 1177, 1184 (1978):

"[W]hen a trial court finds an actual conflict of interest which impairs the ability of a criminal defendant's chosen counsel to conform with the ABA Code of Professional Responsibility, the court should not be required to tolerate an inadequate representation of a defendant. Such representation not only constitutes a breach of professional ethics and invites disrespect for the integrity of the court, but it is also detrimental to the independent interest of the trial judge to be free from future attacks over the adequacy of the waiver or the fairness of the proceedings in his own court and the subtle problems implicating the defendant's comprehension of the waiver.''

Unfortunately for all concerned, a district court must pass on the issue whether or not to allow a waiver of a conflict of interest by a criminal defendant not with the wisdom of hindsight after the trial has taken place, but in the murkier pretrial context when relationships between parties are seen through a glass, darkly. The likelihood and dimensions of nascent conflicts of interest are notoriously hard to predict, even for those thoroughly familiar with criminal trials. It is a rare attorney who will be fortunate enough to learn the entire truth from his own client, much less be fully apprised before trial of what each of the Government's witnesses will say on the stand. A few bits of unforeseen testimony or a single previously unknown or unnoticed document may significantly shift the relationship between multiple defendants. These imponderables are difficult enough for a lawyer to assess, and even more difficult to convey by way of explanation to a criminal defendant untutored in the niceties of legal ethics. Nor is it amiss to observe that the willingness of an attorney to obtain such waivers from his clients may bear an inverse relation to the care with which he conveys all the necessary information to them.

For these reasons we think the district court must be allowed substantial latitude in refusing waivers of conflicts of interest not only in those rare cases where an actual conflict may be demonstrated before trial, but in the more common cases where a potential for conflict exists which may or may not burgeon into an actual conflict as the trial progresses. In the circumstances of this case, with the motion for substitution of counsel made so close to the time of trial, the District Court relied on instinct and judgment based on experience in making its decision. We do not think it can be said that the court exceeded the broad latitude which must be accorded it in making this decision. Petitioner of course rightly points out that the Government may seek to ''manufacture'' a conflict in order to prevent a defendant from having a particularly able defense counsel at his side; but trial courts are undoubtedly aware of this possibility, and must take it into consideration along with all of the other factors which inform this sort of a decision.

Here the District Court was confronted not simply with an attorney who wished to represent two coequal defendants in a straightforward criminal prosecution; rather, Iredale proposed to defend three conspirators of varying stature in a complex drug distribution scheme. The Government intended to call Bravo as a witness for the prosecution at petitioner's trial.[4] The Government might readily have tied certain deliveries of marijuana by Bravo to petitioner, necessitating vigorous cross-examination of Bravo by

---

4. Bravo was in fact called as a witness at petitioner's trial. See Tr. 728 et seq. His testimony was elicited to demonstrate the transportation of drugs that the prosecution hoped to link to petitioner.

petitioner's counsel. Iredale, because of his prior representation of Bravo, would have been unable ethically to provide that cross-examination.

Iredale had also represented Gomez–Barajas, one of the alleged king-pins of the distribution ring, and had succeeded in obtaining a verdict of acquittal for him. Gomez–Barajas had agreed with the Government to plead guilty to other charges, but the District Court had not yet accepted the plea arrangement. If the agreement were rejected, petitioner's probable testimony at the resulting trial of Gomez–Barajas would create an ethical dilemma for Iredale from which one or the other of his clients would likely suffer.

Viewing the situation as it did before trial, we hold that the District Court's refusal to permit the substitution of counsel in this case was within its discretion and did not violate petitioner's Sixth Amendment rights. Other district courts might have reached differing or opposite conclusions with equal justification, but that does not mean that one conclusion was "right" and the other "wrong." The District Court must recognize a presumption in favor of petitioner's counsel of choice, but that presumption may be overcome not only by a demonstration of actual conflict but by a showing of a serious potential for conflict. The evaluation of the facts and circumstances of each case under this standard must be left primarily to the informed judgment of the trial court.

The judgment of the Court of Appeals is accordingly Affirmed.

Relevant Background

Joint representations in criminal cases are attractive to many co-defendants because using a single lawyer can save money, facilitate a unified defense strategy and prevent mutual recrimination. Gary T. Lowenthal, Joint Representation in Criminal Cases: A Critical Appraisal, 64 Va. L. Rev. 939, 940 (1978). Nonetheless, joint representations create numerous possibilities for concurrent conflicts. One of two co-defendants initially presenting a joint defense may turn against the other and portray himself to be less culpable than his co-defendant. Indeed, one defendant may seek to clear himself by implicating and testifying against one or more co-defendants, or by questioning the credibility of a co-defendant whose testimony implicates him. Id. at 944–946.

In each of these situations, the lawyer may find that it is suddenly impossible to be completely loyal to all of her clients. For example, she would breach her duty to provide effective counsel if she did not take advantage of opportunities to argue one defendant's innocence or lesser culpability, but such arguments might emphasize the higher culpability of another defendant. The problem is compounded, and the lawyer may have to withdraw from both representations, if she knows confidential information about both defendants. See Stewart Geer, Representation of Multiple Criminal Defendants: Conflicts of Interest and the Professional Responsibilities of the Defense Lawyer, 62 Minn. L. Rev. 119, 125–135 (1978) (describing different contexts in which conflicts can arise). Although joint representation of criminal defendants is not unconstitutional *per se*, a lawyer has an ethical obligation to inform the court if she believes that her client's defense could be impaired by a conflict of interest. Holloway v. Arkansas, 435 U.S. 475, 485–86 (1978).

Lawyers jointly representing co-defendants can also find themselves in a dilemma when plea bargain offers are made. The government may offer less culpable defendants lenient sentences in return for testimony against more culpable defendants. If a lawyer convinces one defendant to accept such a bargain, she may in turn sacrifice the interests of other defendants. On the other hand, if the lawyer does not advise less culpable defendants on the advantages of accepting the bargain, she fails to provide them effective counsel. Lowenthal, supra, at 948–49. Similar conflicts can arise at sentencing, where defendants, even if they have previously pursued a unified defense, may turn against each other, destroying counsel's ability to represent any defendant effectively. Id. at 949.

Perhaps the most extreme conflicts of interest arise where an illegal organization hires a lawyer to represent its members in criminal actions. The lawyer will usually place the organization's interests ahead of the defendant, whom the organization might be happy to see convicted so long as the lawyer can show that the defendant acted on his own initiative, rather than in the employ of the organization. See In re Abrams, 56 N.J. 271, 266 A.2d 275 (1970) (lawyer disciplined for conflict of interest while representing an employee of a gambling enterprise).

Limits on Concurrent Conflicts in Criminal Representations

As pointed out earlier in this chapter, under Model Rule 1.7(a) a lawyer may not represent a client when the interests of that client will be directly adverse to another client, unless the lawyer reasonably believes that the representation will not adversely affect the relationship with the other client and each client consents after consultation. Rule 1.7(b) prohibits a lawyer from representing a client when her ability to represent that client will be limited by the lawyer's responsibilities to another client or to a third party unless the lawyer reasonably believes that the representation will not be adversely affected and the clients consent after consultation. These rules apply to criminal as well as civil representations, and, as with civil representations, if a lawyer is disqualified from a representation, her entire law firm can be disqualified as well. See Model Rule 1.10.

Federal Rules of Criminal Procedure 44(c) provides courts with the means of enforcing such restrictions. Under Rule 44(c), when two or more defendants have been jointly charged pursuant to FRCP 8(b) or have been joined for trial pursuant to FRCP 13, and are represented by the same counsel, unless there is good cause to believe no conflict of interest is likely to arise, the court must take proper measures to protect and advise each defendant as to the right to effective counsel.

Constitutional Issues

One of the most fundamental rights of a criminal defendant is the Sixth Amendment right "to have the assistance of counsel for his defense." This right to counsel "includes two correlative rights, the right to adequate representation by an attorney of reasonable competence and the right to the attorney's undivided loyalty free of conflict of interest." United States v. Gambino, 864 F.2d 1064, 1069 (3d Cir.1988), citing Government of Virgin Islands v. Zepp, 748 F.2d 125, 131 (3d Cir.1984). A third right was derived from the right to effective counsel when the Supreme Court in Powell v. Alabama, 287 U.S. 45, 53 (1932), said that each defendant in a criminal trial "should be afforded a fair opportunity to secure counsel of his own choice." Today's jurisprudence on conflicts treads a narrow path between a defendant's right to counsel free of conflicting interests, and that same defendant's right to counsel of his own choice.

In *Glasser v. United States*, the Supreme Court held that the Sixth Amendment right to assistance of counsel "contemplates that such assistance be untrammeled and unimpaired by a court order requiring that one lawyer shall simultaneously represent conflicting interests." Glasser v. United States, 315 U.S. 60, 70 (1942) (defendant in a conspiracy case was deprived of assistance of counsel when, over his objection, the court on the day set for trial appointed his counsel also to represent a co-defendant). In situations where defendants voluntarily choose to be represented by the same lawyer, the test used in Cuyler v. Sullivan, 446 U.S. 335 (1980) controls: (1) a state trial court is not required under the Sixth Amendment to assume a lawyer's responsibility of recognizing and advising clients about potential conflicts; and (2) reversal of convictions (upon post-conviction review) will only be granted where a defendant can show both that there was an actual conflict of interest *and* that the conflict adversely affected the performance of the lawyer. Id. at 348. See also Margaret J. Ryan, The Sixth Amendment Right of Counsel: A Criminal Defendant's Right to Counsel of Choice v. Interest in Conflict–Free Representation, 14 S. Ill. U. L. J. 657 (1990).

Many defendants who want a joint representation choose to waive their right to conflict-free counsel in favor of their right to counsel of their choice. See United States v. Allen, 831 F.2d 1487 (9th Cir.1987) (trial court received waivers from defendants shortly after it became apparent that a number of defendants would be represented by a single group of lawyers); United States v. Beniach, 825 F.2d 1207 (7th Cir.1987) (defendant's waiver of his right to conflict-free representations precluded him from attacking his conviction by asserting ineffective assistance of counsel). A federal court under FRCP 44(c) must assure that a defendant is adequately informed of the significance of a conflict before waiving separate representation. See *United States v. Allen*, supra, at 1495, n. 12 and 1500. However, the defendant's subsequent waiver of the right to conflict-free counsel usually will be respected as long as the waiver was voluntary, knowing and intelligent. *Beniach*, supra, at 1210. Occasionally, courts will refuse to allow joint representation where the conflict is egregious. See *Wheat*, supra (upholding trial court's decision not to allow Wheat to replace his lawyer with attorney Iredale who had a potential conflict of interest).

Although courts will attempt to prevent conflicts at the outset of a trial, often the issue arises on postconviction review where a defendant argues that he wasn't provided with effective assistance of counsel. However, postconviction review can be difficult, in part because the reviewing court can only look to the trial record. While blatant and obvious conflicts of interest are usually apparent from the record, more subtle conflicts may escape review because the issue was not made clear in the record. Lowenthal, supra, at 978–79. Another problem, recognized by the court in Holloway v. Arkansas, 435 U.S. 475 (1978), is that joint representation is most dangerous in what it encourages lawyers *not* to do. For example, if a lawyer's ineffectiveness lies in omissions caused by conflicting interests (such as lost plea bargaining opportunities or unpursued lines of defense), the effects of the joint representation are not likely to be obvious from the trial record and therefore may not be recognized in the postconviction review.

QUESTIONS

1. Some commentators have suggested an absolute ban on joint criminal representations. See Geer, supra, at 157 (proposing that the ABA Model Code "should be interpreted to prohibit an attorney from representing multiple defendants in a criminal matter"). While such a ban may eliminate the conflicts of interest associated with joint representation, the ban would impede a defendant's freedom to choose his own counsel. Which objective do you think is more important?

2. Geoffrey Hazard and William Hodes observe that "[s]ome of the most difficult problems in the law of lawyering are problems of conflict of interest. These problems are not only pervasive, but intractable; many of them can at best be ameliorated—not 'solved.' " Geoffrey C. Hazard, Jr. and W. William Hodes, The Law of Lawyering: A Handbook on The Model Rules of Professional Conduct 217 (2d. ed. Supp. 1991). Joint criminal representations underscore limitations in "solving" the conflicts problem, and similar limits arise in the context of joint family representations (see discussion of Louis Brandeis's representation of the Warren family supra). In both situations, clients may ascertain certain advantages to joint representation, and some joint representations are indeed beneficial despite the inherent risks involved. Can you think of specific examples of how a lawyer's single-minded attempt to "solve" the conflict of interest problem, by avoiding even the most remote conflicts, may diminish the overall quality of legal representation?

III. THE TRIBUNAL AS PARADIGM

CHAPTER 7

REPRESENTATION

A. REPRESENTATION OF CRIMINAL DEFENDANTS

John Adams, b. 1735, d. 1826; B.A. Harvard University 1755; admitted to the Boston Bar in 1758; highly regarded lawyer and later a leader in the Revolutionary War; representative for Massachusetts in the Continental Congress 1774–78; Chief Justice of the Superior Court of Massachusetts 1775; signed the Declaration of Independence in 1776; Commissioner to France (negotiated the treaty ending the Revolutionary War); Vice President of the United States under President George Washington 1789–96; President of the United States 1796–1800. In 1770, John Adams was counsel for defendants Captain Preston and his men in the Boston Massacre trials.

Samuel Adams, b. 1722, d. 1803; B.A. Harvard University 1740; briefly studied law but dropped his studies to join his father in running the family brewery; joined various political groups, including the Caucus Club and the Sons of Liberty; member of the Massachusetts House of Representatives 1765–74; organized the Boston Tea Party in 1773; member of Congress 1775–81; signed the Declaration of Independence in 1776; member of the committee that drafted the Articles of Confederation. Samuel Adams led the political faction pressing for prompt prosecution of Captain Preston and his men.

Josiah Quincy, b. 1744, d. 1775; B.A. Harvard University 1763; studied law under Oxenbridge Thatcher, one of the most prominent lawyers in Boston, and took over Thatcher's practice after the latter's death in 1765; despite his youth and inexperience, was active in politics and published various articles supporting the patriot cause until his untimely death of tuberculosis. Josiah Quincy was co-counsel with John Adams for Captain Preston and his men.

Robert Treat Paine, b. 1731, d. 1814; B.A. Harvard University 1752; pursued a brief career in the ministry; admitted to the Massachusetts bar in 1757; active member of the Provincial Congress and Continental Congress; signed the Declaration of Independence; first Attorney General of Massachusetts 1777; Justice of the Massachusetts Supreme Judicial Court 1790–1804. Robert Paine was the special prosecutor assisting Josiah Quincy's older brother Samuel Quincy in prosecuting Captain Preston and his men.

The Boston Massacre Trials: 63. Rex v. Preston; 64. Rex v. Weems (Mass. Superior Ct. 1770) from 3 Legal Papers of John Adams

(L. Kinvin Wroth & Hiller B. Zobel Eds., 1965)
Reprinted by Permission of Harvard University Press. Copyright 1965 by the Massachusetts Historical Society.

Editorial Note

* * *

British troops had been garrisoned in Boston since 1768; thereafter friction between inhabitants and soldiers had increased steadily; this friction generated heat and even occasional sparks of violence; in the evening of 5 March 1770, the lone sentry before the Custom House on King Street became embroiled with a group of people as he stood his post; he called for help; in response, six soldiers, a corporal, and Captain Thomas Preston marched down to the Custom House from the Main Guard; the tumult continued; the soldiers fired, their bullets striking a number of persons, of whom three died instantly, one shortly thereafter, and a fifth in a few days.

* * *

The "Massacre" became interesting from a legal standpoint only after the dead, dying, and wounded had been removed, the eight soldiers had been handed over to the civil authorities, and Captain Preston had voluntarily surrendered to the sheriff. From the moment of the shooting, almost everyone, including Acting Governor Thomas Hutchinson and even General Thomas Gage, when the news reached him in New York, agreed that Preston, not having acted pursuant to orders received from a civilian authority, could justify his presence and his actions only by evidence of an actual attack; and the same applied to the soldiers. But, establishing proof of the danger Preston and his men faced meant nothing less than, in effect, prosecuting the entire town of Boston for assault with intent to kill. This would be a difficult burden of proof under ideal circumstances. The Massacre's timing, only eleven days after the so-called martyrdom of the little Seider boy (*Rex v. Richardson*, No. 59), rendered the defense impossible; the popular feeling was one not of self-criticism, but of blood-thirstiness and revenge.

It was clear that Preston and the men could not hope for a fair trial until the town's passions had been greatly reduced. Nonetheless, Sam Adams and his associates strove mightily to bring the hearings on at once. Although ostensibly trying not to disseminate in Boston the assorted depositions taken by the Town immediately after the shootings, lest such publication "may be supposed by the unhappy Persons now in custody for tryal as tending to give an undue Byass to the minds of the Jury who are to try the same," they were perfectly willing to march into court and press the judges physically as well as morally.

* * *

Meanwhile, the Grand Jury had indicted Preston and the eight soldiers in five separate indictments for the several murders of Crispus Attucks, Patrick Carr, Samuel Maverick, Samuel Gray, and James Caldwell, and had for good measure indicted four Customs employees, accused of firing out of a second-floor window of the Custom House. The Custom House seems to have been an object of the post-riot fury, if not of the mob itself.

* * *

We lack, unfortunately, any Adams diary entries between 26 February and 19 June 1770; our sole insight into the circumstances of his retainer comes from the account in the Autobiography written more than three decades later: "The next Morning [i.e. 6 March] I think it was, sitting in my Office, near the Steps of the Town house Stairs, Mr. Forrest came in, who was then called the Irish Infant. I had some Acquaintance with him. With tears streaming from his Eyes, he said I am come with a very solemn Message from a very unfortunate Man, Captain Preston in Prison. He wishes for Council, and can get none. I have waited on Mr. [*Josiah*] Quincy, who says he will engage if you will give him your Assistance: without it positively he will not. Even Mr. Auchmuty declines unless you will engage ... I had no hesitation in answering that Council ought to be the very last thing that an accused Person should want in a free Country. That the Bar ought in my opinion to be independent and impartial at all Times And in every Circumstance. And that Persons whose Lives were at Stake ought to have the Council they preferred: But he must be sensible this would be as important a Cause as ever was tryed in any Court or Country of the World: and that every Lawyer must hold himself responsible not only to his Country, but to the highest and most infallible of all Trybunals for the Part he should Act. He must therefore expect from me no Art of Address, No Sophistry or Prevarication in such a Cause; nor any thing more than Fact, Evidence and Law would justify. Captain Preston he said requested and desired no more: and that he had such an Opinion, from all he had heard from all Parties of me, that he could cheerfully trust his Life with me, upon those Principles. And said Forrest, as God almighty is my Judge I believe him an innocent Man. I replied, That must be ascertained by his Tryal, and if he thinks he cannot have a fair Tryal of that Issue without my Assistance, without hesitation he shall have it."

Of Josiah Quincy's engagement, we have a more contemporary if not more accurate account. On 22 March, Quincy's father wrote him from Braintree:

"My Dear Son, I am under great affliction at hearing the bitterest reproaches uttered against you, for having become an advocate for those criminals who are charged with the murder of their fellow-citizens. Good God! Is it possible? I will not believe it.

"Just before I returned home from Boston, I knew, indeed, that on the day those criminals were committed to prison, a sergeant had inquired for you at your brother's house; but I had no apprehension that it was possible an application would be made to you to undertake their defence. Since then I have been told that you have actually engaged for Captain Preston; and I have heard the severest reflections made upon the occasion, by men who had just before manifested the highest esteem for you, as one destined to be a savior of your country.

"I must own to you, it has filled the bosom of your aged and infirm parent with anxiety and distress, lest it should not only prove true, but destructive of your reputation and interest; and I repeat, I will not believe it, unless it be confirmed by your own mouth, or under your own hand.

"Your anxious and distressed parent, Josiah Quincy."

To this, on 26 March, Quincy replied in part:

"I have little leisure, and less inclination, either to know or to take notice of those ignorant slanderers who have dared to utter their 'bitter reproaches' in your hearing against me, for having become an advocate for criminals charged with murder.... Before pouring their reproaches into the ear of the aged and infirm, if they had been friends, they would have surely spared a little reflection on the nature of an attorney's oath and duty; some trifling scrutiny into the business and discharge of his office, and some small portion of patience in viewing my past and future conduct.

"Let such be told, Sir that these criminals, charged with murder, are *not yet legally proved guilty*, and therefore, however criminal, are entitled, by the laws of God and man, to all legal counsel and aid; that my duty as a man obliged me to undertake; that my duty as a lawyer strengthened the obligation; that from abundant caution, I at first declined being engaged; that after the best advice and most mature deliberation had determined my judgment, I waited on Captain Preston, and told him that I would afford him my assistance; but prior to this, in presence of two of his friends, I made the most explicit declaration to him of my real opinion on the contests (as I expressed it to him) of the times, and that my heart and hand were indissolubly attached to the cause of my country and finally that I refused all engagement, until advised and urged to undertake it, by an Adams, a Hancock, a Molineux, a Cushing, a Henshaw, a Pemberton, a Warren, a Cooper, and a Phillips. This and much more might be told with great truth; and I dare affirm that you and this whole people will one day REJOICE that I became an advocate for the aforesaid 'criminals' *charged* with the murder of our fellow-citizens."

But the military men were not the only parties to have difficulty obtaining counsel. Attorney General Jonathan Sewall, after drawing up the indictments, seems to have left Boston quasi-permanently. At first this assisted the effort to postpone the trial, because, with the Crown's chief law officer absent, the court could restrict itself to civil matters. But with the pressure for action which culminated in Richardson's arraignment, it became necessary to appoint a substitute for Sewall, and the court apparently chose Josiah Quincy's elder brother, Samuel. Meanwhile, on 13 March, the Town, probably afraid that the tory leanings of the prosecutors might soften the prosecution, resolved that "the Selectmen be desired to employ one or more Council to offer to the Kings Attorney as Assistance to him in the tryal of the Murtherers now committed; and in case the Kings Attorney should refuse such Assistance, and the Relatives of those Persons who were murthered should apply for it, that then the Town will bear the Expence that may accrue thereby." Accordingly, Robert Treat Paine entered the case as a kind of special prosecutor.

. . . .

* * *

The Town, too, had been active in collecting prospective evidence. At the meeting of 12 March, James Bowdoin, Joseph Warren, and Samuel Pemberton were voted a committee to obtain "a particular Account of all proceedings relative to the Massacre in King Street on Monday Night last, that a full and Just representation may be made thereof." The result was the famous *Short Narrative of the Horrid Massacre in Boston*, which, with its weighty appendix of 95 depositions, told the Town's side of the story. (But only about one-third of the deponents testified at any of the ensuing trials.)

With counsel retained and evidence prepared, only the trials themselves remained. During the month following Richardson's trial (21 April), the struggle continued between the radicals seeking to hurry on the hearings and the loyalists hoping to postpone them. "Party zeal has entirely got the better of reason, and I believe it may be added *justice*, procrastination is our only course, as things are now situated," wrote Dalrymple in May; and Hutchinson earlier had suggested that the judges' salaries were being delayed to prevent the continuance. According to Peter Oliver's later account, "The Judges ... refused to bring the Trial on; the Bar also advised to an Adjournment, as they theirselves, as well as the Court, had been fatigued with the business of the Term in this County, and the Country Terms were approaching in quick Succession. The Faction, upon hearing the Design of the Court, were very restive. The Leaders of the Faction met at the House of Mr. [John] *Temple*, a Commissioner of the Customs with £500 per year Salary; and from thence a party came into the Court, and insolently insisted on an immediate Trial of Captain *Preston* and his Soldiers. Two of the Heads of this Faction ... appeared in the Front, *John Hancock* and *Samuel Adams*."

* * *

During the summer two rumors circulated briskly through Boston, one alarming the prerogative side, the other the radicals. The first of these, fanned by newspaper publication of Preston's "Case," was simply that the mob planned to tear Preston (and probably the soldiers as well) from the jail and lynch them. . . .

The second of the rumors in a way fed the first. This was the report that, even if found guilty, Preston and the soldiers would be pardoned. The mob leaders reacted by recalling the fate of Captain John Porteous, who commanded the guard at the execution of the smuggler Andrew Wilson at Edinburgh in 1736. Because the guard fired into the crowd, killing eight or nine people, Porteous had been tried, convicted, and sentenced to death. He was reprieved, but a mob took him from prison and lynched him.

The second rumor was substantially true. Hutchinson's instructions were not to effect a pardon, but only to respite, or reprieve, the men if convicted, until a regular pardon could be obtained.

* * *

Hutchinson was also having trouble with the judges. On 28 August 1770 he wrote Bernard: "I have persuaded Judge Lynde who came twice to me with his resignation in his pocket to hold his place a little longer. Timid as he is I think Goffe is more so, the only difference is, little matters as well as great frighten Lynde, Goffe appears valiant until the danger or apprehensions of it, rise to considerable height, after that he is more terrified than the other. Judge Oliver appears to be very firm, tho threatened in yesterdays paper, and I hope Cushing will be so likewise. The prospect certainly is much better than with any new Judges I could have appointed who would be accepted."

* * *

Although Auchmuty, Adams, and Quincy had early been retained on behalf of Preston, the military men were troubled by the attorneys' lack of fire. Even the loyalist Auchmuty was something less than enthusiastic about his client's case. "I am afraid poor Preston has but little chance," Hutchinson wrote in March. "Mr. Auch[muty] who is his counsel tells me the evidence is very strong to prove that the firing upon the Inhabitants was by his order and he doubts whether the Assault could be an excuse for it." "It is to be hoped," Gage had written Dalrymple, "that Captain Preston and the Soldiers will have the best Advice to be procured. If there is any doubt either of the abilities or good Intentions of their Council; Lawyers should be procured from some of the other Provinces." Dalrymple had replied: "The best lawyers to be obtained here are engaged for Captain Preston, and I hope they will do their duty, but when I consider the spirit prevalent here, as well as the unfavourable ideas universally held to the prejudice of the kings servants, I cannot hope that their exertions will be proportionate to the goodness of the cause. Lawyers from other provinces would probably do better for their Client, not being residents here they might exert their abilities without apprehension of future enjuries; but where are any to be had; Mr. Auchmuty the Judge of the admiralty is engaged to appear, but I am much mistaken if he will not disappoint Captain Preston, when the Crown Lawyers fall off, the opinion of the others may be easily collected."

. . . .

A problem even more basic to the defense than the zeal of counsel was a conflict of interest which became more acute as the time for trial approached. The difficulty was this: If Preston should fail in his primary defense, that is, that the killings were justifiable, then he would probably have to argue that the men fired against or without his orders. The men, on the other hand, would argue that it was indeed Preston who gave the order to fire, and that they had merely obeyed his command.

Were the officer to be tried in the same proceedings with the men, the resultant mutual finger-pointing might well convince the jury to find all the defendants guilty. Perhaps in part to avoid this difficulty, the decision was taken at some time to sever the trials. That eased the immediate danger of a mass conviction, but it did not change the professional problem faced by Josiah Quincy and Adams (who was to argue in both trials). Engaged as they were for all the defendants, Quincy and Adams ran a substantial risk that their efforts in Preston's trial might seriously embarrass the defense of the men. No direct evidence that either lawyer considered the problem has been found, but it is inconceivable that they were not aware of it. On 24 October 1770, the day Preston's trial opened, three of the soldiers petitioned "the Honourable Judges of the Superior Court," raising the point squarely.

"May it please Your Honours we poor Distressed Prisoners Beg that ye Would be so good as to let us have our Trial at the same time with our Captain, for we did our Captains Orders and if we don't Obay his Command we should have been Confine'd and shott for not doing of it. We Humbly pray Your Honours that you would take it into your serious consideration and grant us that favour for we only desire to Open the truth before our Captains face, for it is very hard he being a Gentelman should have more chance for to save his life then we poor men that is Oblidged to Obay his command. We hope that Your Honours will grant this our petition, and we shall all be in duty Bound ever to pray for Your honours. Dated Boston Goal, October the 24th 1770. Hugh White, James Hartigan, Mathew (his X mark) Killroy." MB: Chamberlain Coll. By law, criminal defendants could not testify.

There is a suggestion that the decision to sever was not taken until the cases were actually called. "After repeated delays," William Palfrey wrote John Wilkes, "the Trial"—note the singular—"of Captain Preston and the Soldiers concern'd in the Massacre of the 5th of March was fix'd for the 23d inst. but the day has now elapsed and the Judges have not appear'd, what reason they may have for thus deferring the trial from time to time I know not."

At long last, at 8 A.M. on Wednesday, 24 October 1770, Preston's trial began. The first item was impaneling the jury. As *Rex v. Preston*, Documents II and III, indicate, there was a brief, preliminary skirmish on various technicalities, the most important being whether the prisoner should have received a list of the jury panel before the trial, and the number of challenges to which he was entitled. Palfrey's account to John Wilkes of the actual impaneling, while, like most of the contemporary accounts, perhaps not wholly objective, serves as a convenient introduction to this part of the proceedings. "By a Law of this Province, the Jurors are return'd by the Selectmen, after the choice has been made by the Town. The Method of Chusing them is the most fair and impartial that the wit of man could possibly devise. The freeholders names are roll'd in a Box in the same manner that Lotteries are usually drawn, and the first who are drawn out are return'd. In this manner the Jurors on Captain Preston's trial were chosen and return'd. but when any are challeng'd the Sheriff has a right to return Talesmen [alternate jurors]. Captain Preston on his trial challeng'd twenty-two of the Pannel, a number of his friends and most intimate acquaintances stood ready and were accordingly return'd by the Sheriff, among whom was a person that had been first drawn out by Lot by the Town and was excus'd because he alleged he was so much prejudic'd in Captain Preston's favour, that he could not return an impartial verdict, yet this very person intimately connected with Captain Preston was return'd as a Talesman by the Sheriff." Two of the talesmen, Palfrey continued, "were persons who from the time of Captain Preston's confinement had interested themselves in his behalf, and had been extremely busy in procuring evidence in his favour. One of these Mr. Phillip Dumaresq had repeatedly declared in presence of divers witnesses that he believed Captain Preston to be as innocent as the Child unborn, and that if he happened to be upon the Jury he would never convict him if he sat to all eternity.... The management to pack the Jury was evident to every impartial spectator.... Mr. Dumaresq, who I mentioned before, was drawn ... by the Town, and when he was notified of it by the Constable he went immediately to the Town meeting and desired to be excused as he was an intimate acquaintance of Captain Preston's and therefore consider'd himself as an improper person to serve upon the Jury, he was accordingly excused."

Palfrey's characterization of the jury as packed is not exaggerated. Of the twelve jurors, five, including Dumaresq, Gilbert Deblois, William Hill, Joseph Barrick, and William Wait Wallis, were later loyalist exiles. The available evidence indicates that these men were supporters of the King well before the trial. Hill, for example, was a baker who supplied the Fourteenth Regiment its bread; he stood surety for the soldiers accused during the Riley Riot of 1769. Barrick boasted of his open avowal of support. Deblois' case is even more interesting, as Preston pointed out in the 1780's in his testimony to the Board of Commissioners appointed to examine the losses sustained by the American loyalists:

"The testimony of Thomas Preston, late a Captain in His Majesty's 29th Regiment of Foot. Sheweth that he knew Gilbert Deblois Merchant in Boston, that he kept a large Store house filld with all sorts of European goods, and carried on as extensive a trade as most Merchants there, and that he was particularly connected with the Officers, to whom he was remarkably friendly and obliging.

"That when said Preston was thrown into Jail there, for what was call'd the bloody massacre, said Deblois got him several valuable evidences, and gave him the character of many of the persons return'd for Jurors, by which means he was enabled to set aside most of those return'd by the Town, who were men of violent principles, and pick out some of the moderate ones sent up from the Country. That on a deficiency of Jurors said Deblois attended, and got himself put on the Pannel, where during the tryal which lasted a week, he was confin'd in the Jail along with the other Jurors, to the great neglect of his business. That by his strict attention and close examination he detected some of the Evidences of perjury; And also that by his personal influence on the rest of the Jurors he was a great means of said Prestons being acquitted."

* * *

In the absence of a transcript, it is hard to say exactly how the lawyers divided the work. Existing documents suggest that Samuel Quincy opened for the Crown and handled the evidence, while Adams did the same for Preston; Auchmuty and Paine closed for the prisoner and Crown respectively. This division is supported by the usual practice, in which the junior counsel for the Crown opened the case and examined the witnesses, with the senior man closing the argument. Josiah Quincy, although apparently active in the pre-trial preparations, did not participate in the trial itself. The entries in Judge Lynde's diary indicate that of the five trial days which the case required, the lawyers' arguments and the judges' seriatim charges took up over two.

"The Counsel for the Crown or rather the town were but poor and manag'd poorly," Preston said later. "My Counsel on the contrary were men of parts, and exerted themselves with great spirit and cleverness, particularly Judge Auchmuty." Judge Oliver agreed. "I know you think," he wrote to Hutchinson on Saturday evening, 27 October, "you would have finished the Cause in half the Time and I know it would not have taken half a Day at the Old Bailey; but we must conform to the Times. We have not finished yet. Mr. Paine has now to close for the Crown, and he was so unfit, that to avoid as much as possible all popular Censure we indulged him till Monday morn; for Mr. Auchmuty did not finish till ½ past 4 o'clock.... Hard upon the Jury, you say, it is so, but we have allowed them the Liberty of the Court House tomorrow with their Keepers."

Finally, at 5 p.m. on Monday, 29 October, the case went to the jury. Court was immediately adjourned until the next day at 8 a.m. The jury, a later report had it, agreed within three hours after retiring, and the next morning brought in its verdict, not guilty.

The verdict was hardly unexpected. Even before the case went to the jury, Peter Oliver thought the evidence indicated acquittal. "I have," he wrote Hutchinson, "a Quarto Volume of Evidence which I have pretty minutely taken.... and it turns out to the Dishonour of the Inhabitants, and appears quite plain to me that he must be acquitted; that the Person who gave the Orders to *fire* was not the Captain, and indeed if it had been he, it at present appears justifiable."

* * *

The soldiers' trial was originally scheduled for 20 November 1770, the date to which the Suffolk Court had been adjourned following the conclusion of Preston's trial. But, despite Gage's hope that the Preston jury would try the soldiers, "from a defect of Jurors the Trial of the Soldiers has been postponed and is fixed for" 27 November.

The radicals apparently felt that lack of trial preparation had hurt the prosecution in the Preston trial. . . .

The defense, too, was taking extra precautions. "My great concern," Hutchinson told Gage, "is to obtain an unbiased Jury and for that purpose, principally, I advised Captain Preston to engage one of the Bar, over and above the Council to conduct the Cause in Court, in the character of an Attorney who should make a very diligent inquiry into the characters and principles of all who are returned which he has done and it may be to good purpose, but after all it will be extremely difficult to keep a Jury to the Rules of Law." That attorney was almost certainly Sampson Salter Blowers, who was associated in the defense, but who did not, so far as the *Weems Trial* shows, appear in court.

The jury problem was serious. A strong feeling prevailed that blood required blood, regardless of guilt. One of the prospective jurors at the soldiers' trail was reported to have said "he believed Captain Preston was innocent, but innocent blood had been shed and somebody ought to be hanged for it." There was also, apparently, a feeling "that the Verdict of the Jury in Favor of Captain Preston, arose from a Doubt whether he *gave Orders* to Fire: And that the soldiers who are to be tryed this Week expect to obtain a Verdict in their Favour, by bringing full Evidence that in firing they *obey'd the Orders of the Captain.*" Jurors with these considerations in mind could be dangerous. It may be significant that the jury as ultimately chosen contained not a single Bostonian.

* * *

And as for the slashing cross-examination, the confronting with prior inconsistent statements under oath, which one would have thought the very life of a case like this, these are almost wholly absent. There is little transcript evidence to support the familiar story, related by William Gordon, that Josiah Quincy pressed his cross-examination so far that Adams had to tell him to desist:

"While carrying on, Mr. Quincy pushes the examination and cross-examination of the witnesses to such an extent, that Mr. Adams, in order to check it, is obliged to tell him, that if he will not desist, he shall decline having anything further to do in the cause. The captain and his friends are alarmed, and consult about engaging another counsellor; but Mr. Adams has no intention of abandoning his client. He is sensible that there is sufficient evidence to obtain a favorable verdict from an impartial jury; and only feels for the honor of the town, which he apprehends will suffer yet more, if the witnesses are examined too closely and particularly, and by that mean[s] more truth be drawn from them than what has an immediate connection with the soldiers firing, by or without the orders of the captain." In Adams' personal copy of Gordon's book (now in the Boston Public Library), he wrote a rebutting marginal note: "Adams' Motive is not here perceived. His Clients lives were hazarded by Quincy's too youthful ardour."

While the trial was still going on there was "a Report in Town . . . that one of the Council is not so faithful as he ought to be." But Hutchinson, who passed the rumor to Gage, immediately noted his hope that "there is nothing more in it than a difference in opinion from some others of the necessity of entering into the examination of the Conduct of the Towns people previous to the Action itself, he being a Representative of the Town and a great Partisan wishes to blacken the people as little as may be consistent with his Duty to his Clients."

Like Gordon's, Hutchinson's version suggests that the problem arose at Preston's trial, as well as the men's. However, he too indicates that it was Josiah Quincy with whom Adams disagreed. Because Quincy does not seem to have participated in the actual trial of Preston's case, it is possible that the incident took place only at the trial of the men. Here is what Hutchinson says about Preston's trial:

"They [i.e. counsel] were faithful to their client unless the refusal of one to suffer evidence to be produced to shew that the expulsion of the Troops from the Town of Boston was a plan concerted among the inhabitants, can be urged to the contrary. Mr. Adams one of the counsel declined being further concerned if any further evidence of that sort was insisted upon probably having no doubt that the other evidence without it was sufficient for the acquittal of his client; while Mr. Quincy the other counsel was willing it should be produced."

And this is Hutchinson's comment on the soldiers' trial:

"The employing counsel who were warmly engaged in popular measures caused some of the evidence to be kept back which would otherwise have been produced for the prisoners. The counsel for the crown insisted upon producing evidence to prove the menaces of the soldiers preceding the action, and the counsel for the prisoners consented to it, provided they might have the like liberty with respect to the inhabitants. After the evidence had been given on the part of the crown, and divers witnesses had been examined to shew the premeditated plan of the inhabitants to drive out the soldiers, one of the counsel, Mr. John Adams, for the prisoners then declined proceeding any further, and declared that he would leave the cause, if such witnesses must be produced as served only to set the town in a bad light. A stop therefore was put to any further examination of such witnesses, by which means many facts were not brought to light which the friends to government thought would have been of service in the cause, though it must be presumed the counsel did not think them necessary, for it was allowed, that they acted with great fidelity to their clients, when it was evident, that a verdict in their favour, must be of general disservice to the popular cause, in which counsel had been, and afterwards continued to be, warmly engaged."

Hutchinson's account is probably more accurate than Adams'. The real significance of the incident is the potential conflict it reveals, a conflict which faces any lawyer defending an accused whose defense depends (or may depend) on pressuring, or even harming, the basic interests of his community or his country. . . .

In the Massacre trials, Adams resolved this conflict pragmatically: he won acquittals. At this distance, we cannot determine whether, as Hutchinson suggested, Adams allowed only the minimum of evidence necessary for acquittal, suppressing all the rest; or whether, as Adams himself put it, he acted merely to suppress evidence which would have actively harmed the defense's chances.

It is for questions like this one, and the somewhat more obvious lesson in control of vengeance, that the Massacre trials remain principally important today. But the points of interest to a lawyer likewise abound; we can here only suggest some of them. It is apparent from the transcript, for example, that the witnesses were not sequestrated, but remained in open court during the taking of other testimony; that witnesses were called out of order (Crown witnesses were called in the middle of the defense's case); that rebuttal witnesses were called immediately, to refute specific segments of testimony; that counsel stood approximately three feet from the witness, and the witness stood six feet from the bench; that when addressing the jury, counsel not only argued law but read directly from law books; and that to save time, counsel entered a kind of "cumulative testimony" agreement.

* * *

XII.   Adams' Minutes of Defense Evidence

* * *

30 November 1770

Dr. Richard Hyrons [a witness]. About 7 o Clock. Saw several soldiers at my own door a little after 8, passing and repassing, some with Clubbs, some with Bayonetts. The Noise and Confusion seemed to come from the Bottom of the Street towards the Markett. In 8 or 10 minutes I heard a Person run thro B[oylstones] Ally with great Violence from Cornhill. He ran towards the barrack Gate, and then ran back again crying Town born, turn out, *Town born* turn out, repeated 20 or 30 times. I heard a Voice I took it to be Lt. or Ensign Mall, say who is that fellow? lay hold of him. I heard nothing Said by the Centinel, to this Man, nor by him to them. This cry of Town born was continued for 6 or 7 minutes when I heard the foot steps of several more people. In a short Space there seemed to be a great many more passing backwards and forwards whether soldiers or Inhab[itants] cant tell. In about 20 minutes there seemed to be, a great Number of People in Boylstones Alley. I heard their Clubbs and sticks striking on the fence on both sides. I lockd my door, put out my Lights and went up stairs to the Chamber that fronts the barracks. Then I observed 4 or 5 officers of 29 Reg. standing upon their own Steps. About 20 or 30 of the Towns People facing of em. About that times comes a little Man, and asks why dont you keep your Soldiers in the Barracks. They answerd they had done and would do every Thing they could to keep em in their Barracks. On this the small Man said are the Inhabitants to be knocked down in the streets are they to be murdered in this manner? The officers still insisted they had done their Utmost and would do it. He said you know the Country has been used ill, the Town has been used ill. We did not send for you. We wont have you here. *We'll get rid of you, or drive you away*, I cant say which. The officers said they would do what they could to keep the Soldiers in and beggd that he would use his Influence to disperse the People that no Mischief might be done or Words to that [Effect]. Whether he did or no, I cant tell, as the Confusion was so great I could not distinguish. Immediately the Cry Home, Home was mentiond. And in 5 minutes after the Cry Home Home was repeated, and the greatest Part of em perhaps t[w]o thirds went up Boylstones Ally and huzzad for the main Guard. More Towns People came up from the Market Place. There was then a good deal of Squabble and Noise between the People and the Officers, no Blows—but could not distinguish. . . . .

At this Time, I saw Captn. Goldfinch of the 14th upon the Steps. Another little Man came up, much different from the other. He requested the officers that the soldiers might be kept in the Barracks. They Said they did all they could, and beggd that he would take the People away. This little Man said to the People, you hear what the officers say you had better go home. On which there was the Cry Home Home again, and many of em did say, again lets away to the main Guard, and went up Boylstones Alley. Goldfinch was still upon the Steps and while they were talking I heard the Report of a Musquet, not many Minutes after they cryd home home the last Time. In a few seconds I heard the 2d Musquet and the 3d & c. I heard Captn. Goldfinch say, I thought it would come to this it is time for me to go. A Soldier soon came and said as I thought, they had fired upon the main Guard. I then heard the drums at the main Guard beat to Arms. I went down Stairs and did not go out till I was sent for to some of the wounded People. I was call'd to Maverick and he told me he was running away from the soldiers and yet the Ball went into his Breast, thro a Portion of his Liver, wounded the stomack and one of the small Gutts and lodged between the 2 lower Ribbs on the left side. The Ball was bruisd as if it struck some object before him. Mr. Craft producd the Ball in Court.

* * *

XVI. Adams' Argument for the Defense

3–4 December 1770

> *May it please your Honours and you Gentlemen of the Jury,*

I am for the prisoners at the bar, and shall apologize for it only in the words of Marquis *Beccaria*: "If I can but be the instrument of preserving one life, his blessing and tears of transport, shall be a sufficient consolation to me, for the contempt of all mankind." As the prisoners stand before you for their lives, it may be proper, to recollect with what temper the law requires we should proceed to this trial. The form of proceeding at their arraignment, has discovered that the spirit of the law upon such occasions, is conformable to humanity, to common sense and feeling; that it is all benignity and candor. And the trial commences with the prayer of the Court, expressed by the Clerk, to the Supream JUDGE of Judges, empires and worlds: "God send you a good deliverance."

We find, in the rules laid down by the greatest English Judges, who have been the brightest of mankind; We are to look upon it as more beneficial, that many guilty persons should escape unpunished, than one innocent person should suffer. The reason is, because it's of more importance to community, that innocence should be protected, than it is, that guilt should be punished; for guilt and crimes are so frequent in the world, that all of them cannot be punished; and many times they happen in such a manner, that it is not of much consequence to the public, whether they are punished or not. But when innocence itself, is brought to the bar and condemned, especially to die, the subject will exclaim, it is immaterial to me, whether I behave well or ill; for virtue itself, is no security. And if such a sentiment as this, should take place in the mind of the subject, there would be an end to all security whatsoever. I will read the words of the law itself.

The rules I shall produce to you from Lord Chief Justice *Hale*, whose character as a lawyer, a man of learning and philosophy, and as a christian, will be disputed by nobody living; one of the greatest and best characters, the English nation ever produced: his words are these ... it is always safer to err in acquitting, than punishing, on the part of mercy, than the part of justice. The next is from the same authority ... it is always safer to err on the milder side, the side of mercy, H.H.P.C. 509, the best rule in doubtful cases, is, rather to incline to acquittal than conviction: and in page 300 . . . . Where you are doubtful never act; that is, if you doubt of the prisoner's guilt, never declare him guilty; this is always the rule, especially in cases of life. Another rule from the same Author, 289, where he says, In some cases, presumptive evidence go far to prove a person guilty, though there is no express proof of the fact, to be committed by him; but then it must be very warily pressed, for it is better, five guilty person should escape unpunished, than one innocent person should die.

* * *

I shall now consider the several divisions of law, under which the evidence will arrange itself.

Now suppose you should have a jealousy in your minds, that the people who made this attack on the Sentry, had nothing in their intention more than to take him off his post, and that was threatened by some; suppose they intended to go a little farther, and tar and feather him, or to ride him, (as the phrase is in *Hudibras*) he would have a good right to have stood upon his defence, the defence of his liberty, and if he could not preserve that without hazard to his own life, he would be warranted, in depriving those of life, who were endeavouring to deprive him of his; that is a point I would not give up for my right hand, nay, for my life.

Well, I say, if the people did this, or if this was only their intention, surely the officer and soldiers had a right to go to his relief, and therefore they set out upon a lawful errand, they were therefore a lawful assembly, if we only consider them as private subjects and fellow citizens, without regard to Mutiny Acts, Articles of War, or Soldiers Oaths; a private person, or any number of private persons, have a right to go to the assistance of their fellow subject in distress and danger of his life, when assaulted and in danger from a few or a multitude. *Keyl.* 136. "If a man perceives another by force to be injuriously treated, pressed and restrained of his liberty, tho' the person abused doth not complain, or call for aid or assistance; and others out of compassion shall come to his rescue, and kill any of those that shall so restrain him, that is manslaughter. . . ."

I am not insensible of Sir *Michael Foster's* observations on these cases, but apprehend they do not invalidate the authority of them as far as I now apply them to the purpose of my argument. If a stranger, a mere fellow subject may interpose to defend the liberty, he may to defend the life of another individual. But according to the evidence, some imprudent people before the Sentry, proposed to take him off his post, others threatened his life, and intelligence of this was carried to the *Main-guard*, before any of the prisoners turned out: They were then ordered out to relieve the Sentry, and any of our fellow citizens might lawfully have gone upon the same errand; they were therefore a lawful assembly.

I have but one point more of law to consider, and that is this: In the case before you, I do not pretend to prove that every one of the unhappy persons slain, were concerned in the riot; the authorities read to you just now, say, it would be endless to prove, whether every person that was present and in a riot, was concerned in planning the first enterprise or not: nay, I believe it but justice, to say, some were perfectly innocent of the occasion, I have reason to suppose, that one of them was, Mr. *Maverick*; he was a very worthy young man, as he has been represented to me, and had no concern in the riotous proceedings of that night; and I believe the same may be said, in favour of one more, at least, Mr. *Caldwell* who was slain; and therefore many people may think, that as he, and perhaps another was innocent, therefore innocent blood having been shed, that must be expiated by the death of somebody or other. I take notice of this, because one gentleman nominated by the sheriff, for a Juryman upon this trial, because he said, he believed Capt. *Preston* was innocent, but innocent blood had been shed, and therefore somebody ought to be hanged for it, which he thought was indirectly giving his opinion in this cause. I am afraid many other persons have formed such an opinion; I do not take it to be a rule, that where innocent blood is shed, the person must die. In the instance of the *Frenchmen* on the *Plains of Abraham*, they were innocent, fighting for their King and country, their blood is as innocent as any, there may be multitudes killed, when innocent blood is shed on all sides, so that it is not an invariable rule. I will put a case, in which, I dare say, all will agree with me: Here are two persons, the father and the son, go out a hunting, they take different roads, the father hears a rushing among the bushes, takes it to be game, fires and kills his son through a mistake; here is innocent blood shed, but yet nobody will say the father ought to die for it. So that the general rule of law, is, that whenever one person hath a right to do an act, and that act by any accident, takes away the life of another, it is excusable, it bears the same regard to the innocent as to the guilty. If two men are together, and attack me, and I have a right to kill them, I strike at them, and by mistake, strike a third and kill him, as I had a right to kill the first, my killing the other, will be excusable, as it happened by accident. If I in the heat of passion, aim a blow at the person who has assaulted me, aiming at him, I kill another person, it is but manslaughter. *Foster*, 261. § 3. "If an action unlawful in itself be done deliberately and with intention of mischief or great bodily harm to particulars, or of mischief indiscriminately, fall it where it may, and death ensues against or beside the original intention of the party, it will be murder. But if such mischievous intention doth not appear, which is matter of fact and to be collected from circumstances, and the act was done heedlessly and inconsiderately, it will be manslaughter: not accidental death, because the act upon which death ensued, was unlawful."

* * *

Supposing in this case, the Molatto man [Crispus Attucks] was the person made the assault, suppose he was concerned in the unlawful assembly, and this party of soldiers endeavouring to defend themselves against him, happened to kill another person who was innocent, though the soldiers had no reason that we know of, to think any person there, at least of that number who were crouding about them innocent, they might naturally enough presume all to be guilty of the riot and assault, and to come with the same design; I say, if on firing on these who were guilty, they accidentally killed an innocent person, it was not their faults, they were obliged to defend themselves against those who were pressing upon them, they are not answerable for it with their lives, for upon supposition it was justifiable or excusable to kill *Attucks* or any other person, it will be equally justifiable or excusable if in firing at him, they killed another who was innocent, or if the provocation was such as to mitigate the guilt to manslaughter, it will equally mitigate the guilt, if they killed an innocent man undesignedly, in aiming at him who gave the provocation, according to Judge *Foster*, and as this point is of such consequence, I must produce some more authorities for it. I. *Hawkins*, 84. "Also, if a third person accidentally happen to be killed, by one engaged in combat with another upon a sudden quarrel, it seems that he who kills him is guilty of manslaughter only." H.H.P.C. 442. To the same point, and I. H.H.P.C. 484 and 4 *Black*. 27.

* * *

Young Mr. *Davis* swears, that he saw *Gray* that evening, a little before the firing, that he had a stick under his arm, and said he would go to the riot, "I am glad of it, (that is that there was a rumpus) I will go and have a slap at them, if I lose my life." And when he was upon the spot, some witnesses swear, he did not act that peaceable inoffensive part, which *Langford* thinks he did. They swear, they thought him in liquor—that he run about clapping several people on the shoulders saying, "Dont run away"—"they dare not fire." *Langford* goes on "I saw twenty or five and twenty boys about the Sentinel—and I spoke to him, and bid him not be afraid."—How came the Watchman *Langford* to tell him not to be afraid. Does not this circumstance prove, that he thought there was danger, or at least that the Sentinel in fact, was terrified and did think himself in danger. *Langford* goes on "I saw about twenty or five and twenty boys that is young shavers."—We have been entertained with a great variety of phrases, to avoid calling this sort of people a mob.—Some call them shavers, some call them genius's.—The plain English is gentlemen, most probably a motley rabble of saucy boys, negroes and molattoes, Irish teagues and out landish jack tarrs.—And why we should scruple to call such a set a people a mob, I can't conceive, unless the name is too respectable for them:—The sun is not about to stand still or go out, nor the rivers to dry up because there was a mob in *Boston* on the 5th of *March* that attacked a party of soldiers.—Such things are not new in the world, nor in the British dominions, though they are comparatively, rareties and novelties in this town. *Carr* a native of *Ireland* had often been concerned in such attacks, and indeed, from the nature of things, soldiers quartered in a populous town, will always occasion two mobs, where they prevent one.— They are wretched conservators of the peace!

* * *

John Adams. Diary

1773. March 5th. Fryday.

Heard an Oration, at Mr. Hunts Meeting House, by Dr. Benja. Church, in Commemoration of the Massacre in Kings Street, 3 Years ago. That large Church was filled and crouded in every Pew, Seat, Alley, and Gallery, by an Audience of several Thousands of People of all Ages and Characters and of both Sexes.

I have Reason to remember that fatal Night. The Part I took in Defence of Captn. Preston and the Soldiers, procured me Anxiety, and Obloquy enough. It was, however, one of the most gallant, generous, manly and disinterested Actions of my whole Life, and one of the best Pieces of Service I ever rendered my Country. Judgment of Death against those

Soldiers would have been as foul a Stain upon this Country as the Executions of the Quakers or Witches, anciently. As the Evidence was, the Verdict of the Jury was exactly right.

This however is no Reason why the Town should not call the Action of that Night a Massacre, nor is it any Argument in favour of the Governor or Minister, who caused them to be sent here. But it is the strongest of Proofs of the Danger of standing Armies.

QUESTIONS

1. One reason John Adams gives for taking this case is sparing the defendants' lives. "If I can but be the instrument of preserving one life, his blessing—shall be sufficient consolation to me, for the contempt of all mankind." Does the possibility of a mistake taking the life of an innocent person make effective assistance of counsel more important in capital cases than in other cases? Does preservation of life justify helping even a guilty person escape conviction in a capital case?

2. Adams also gives a political reason for taking the case: "[c]ouncil ought to be the very last thing that an accused Person should want in a free Country." Why is the right to counsel important to preservation of other liberties?

3. Josiah Quincy writes to his father, "I dare affirm that you and this whole people will one day rejoice that I became an advocate for the aforesaid 'criminals' charged with the murder of our fellow-citizens." Why should the people have rejoiced in Quincy's representation of men whom the vast majority of Bostonians believed were guilty?

4. Josiah Quincy, in stating his reasons for taking the case, refers to the "nature of an attorney's oath and duty" and "the business and discharge of his office." Because legal training and experience are needed to assemble facts, recognize the bearing of the laws and argue their ambiguity, the advocacy paradigm will not work unless both sides of a case are adequately represented. See Lon Fuller's and John Randall's discussion of the advocacy paradigm in the Report of the Joint Conference on Professional Responsibility in Chapter 6 supra ("In a very real sense it may be said that the integrity of the adjudicative process itself depends upon the participation of the advocate"). Does the integrity of the adjudicative process require that attorneys be willing to represent unpopular clients? How about clients who cannot pay for legal services? See discussion of pro bono legal services in Chapter 1 supra.

5. The Report of the Joint Conference on Professional Responsibility observes that "[a]n adversary presentation seems the only effective means for combating th[e] natural human tendency to judge too swiftly in terms of the familiar that which is not yet fully known." How do the Boston Massacre trials illustrate this point?

6. Samuel Adams and his associates did not disseminate in Boston the depositions taken after the shootings. They apparently believed such publicity to be improper if it would prejudice the Jury (see also Model Rule

3.6). Nonetheless, these same persons were willing to press for immediate trial, knowing that heated passions in Boston made conviction of Preston and his men more likely. Is it ethical for prosecutors to take advantage of popular sentiment so long as the prosecutors themselves do not stir up the sentiment? Alternatively, should prosecutors do more to assure an impartial trial, for example by suggesting trial at a later date or at a different location?

7. Close relatives in both the Quincy and Adams families are on opposite sides of this case. Model Rule 1.8(i) requires that "a lawyer related to another lawyer as parent, child, sibling or spouse shall not represent a client in a representation directly adverse to a person who the lawyer knows is represented by the other lawyer except upon the consent by the client after consultation regarding the relationship." Why? How could family relationships have been problematic in the Boston Massacre case?

8. Look at John Adams's conduct more closely. Is he justified in (a) using challenges and other devices to pack the jury (one juror procured evidence for the defendants, while two were suppliers of the British); and (b) appealing to the jurors' emotions, for example in his speech on the "blessing" of saving life?

9. Adams appeals to juror prejudice when he describes the crowd as "a motley rabble of saucy boys, negroes and mulattoes, Irish [t]eagues and out landish jack tarrs." Referring to Crispus Attucks, one of the persons killed, he says, "[s]upposing in this case, the Mulatto man was the person made the assault, suppose he was concerned in the unlawful assembly, and this party of soldiers endeavoring to defend themselves against him, happened to kill another person who was innocent. . . ." Is Adams compensating for not "putting the town on trial" by blaming the incident on a portion of the town, including persons of Irish and African descent? If playing on ethnic prejudice is wrong for a prosecutor, is it also wrong for a defense attorney?

10. Adams represents both Captain Preston and his men, creating a concurrent conflict because the men claim to have followed Preston's orders to fire (see Kilroy's petition for a joint trial with Preston). Model Rule 1.7 states that a lawyer "shall not represent a client if the representation of that client will be directly adverse to another client" and "shall not represent a client if the representation of that client may be materially limited by the lawyer's responsibilities to another client or to a third person, or by the lawyer's own interests," unless the lawyer reasonably believes the representation will not be adversely affected and each client consents after consultation. Look back at the discussion of concurrent conflicts in criminal representations in Chapter 6, and particularly at question 2 on page 465 supra. What should Adams have done? What could he have done? Was this a concurrent conflict that could be "solved" without impairing the overall quality of representation?

Relevant Background

Dilatory Tactics in Criminal Trials

Although Adams wanted to delay the Boston Massacre trials because of unusual circumstances, delay can be a common defense strategy even in the most ordinary circumstances. Tactics used to delay trials range from requesting time to plea bargain to defense lawyers rearranging their schedules and asking judges to grant continuances. The objective of such delay is sometimes to foster forgetfulness and exhaustion on the part of the prosecution and its witnesses. See William H. Simon, The Ethics of Criminal Defense, 91 Mich. L. Rev. 1703, 1704 (1993). As one assistant district attorney has complained, "by and large defense lawyers here play a game. It's called delay. The more you delay your cases, the weaker they get for the prosecution." Steven Brill, Fighting Crime in a Crumbling System, American Lawyer, July–Aug. 1989, at 3.

Model Rule 3.2 states that "[a] lawyer shall make reasonable efforts to expedite litigation consistent with the interests of the client," and the comment to the Rule states that "[d]ilatory practices bring the administration of justice into disrepute." See also DR 7–102(A)(1). However, many defense lawyers see delay and other tactics as part of their duty to represent their clients zealously. Indeed, there are sometimes, although not often, sound reasons for a delay. What factors weighed in favor of seeking delay in the trial of the British soldiers? In what other types of situations might delay be justified?

Jury Selection

Jury selection was hotly contested in the Boston Massacre trial as it is in many high profile criminal trials. Eliminating bias in the jury pool may be the objective of voir dire, but as the Boston Massacre trial shows, this is sometimes difficult.

A lawyer may want to employ preemptory challenges based on race, sex, religion or other criteria to increase the chances of a favorable outcome. This practice is increasingly disfavored in all types of litigation, and the Supreme Court, in several cases where race or gender challenges were used in criminal trials, has held the practice to be unconstitutional. See Batson v. Kentucky, 476 U.S. 79, 86 (1986) ("The Equal Protection Clause guarantees the defendant that the state will not exclude members of his race from the jury venire on account of race …"); J.E.B. v. Alabama, 511 U.S. 127, 146 (1994)("[T]he Equal Protection Clause prohibits discrimination in jury selection on the basis of gender, or on the assumption that an individual will be biased in a particular case for no reason other than the fact that the person happens to be a woman or happens to be a man"). A similar rule could be justified for preemptory challenges based upon religion. See Julie D. Arp, Note, The Batson Analysis and Religious Discrimination, 74 Or. L. Rev. 721 (1995). Even apart from the constitutional mandate, prosecutors are ethically obligated to consider potential damage to the truth finding function of the adjudicative process caused by discriminatory jury selection tactics.

Disclosing Scandalous Evidence

Another tactic that a criminal defense lawyer might use is to disclose or threaten to disclose information injurious or embarrassing to the prosecution or its witnesses, but having little or no relevance to the merits of a case. Simon, supra at 1705. One of the most common examples of this strategy is introduction of evidence concerning the sexual history of a victim of rape or sexual assault at the criminal trial of his or her assailant. Rule 412 of the Federal Rules of Evidence precludes routine admissibility of a rape victim's prior sexual conduct or sexual predisposition in most circumstances. Many states have adopted similar evidentiary rules known as "rape shield statutes." An analogous situation arises in civil suits for sexual misconduct, including sexual harassment, where evidence is introduced concerning the sexual conduct and predisposition of the complainant. Federal Rules of Evidence, Rule 412(b)(2) provides that "[i]n a civil case, evidence offered to prove the sexual behavior or sexual predisposition of any alleged victim is admissible if it is otherwise admissible under these rules and its probative value substantially outweighs the danger of harm to any victim and of unfair prejudice to any party. Evidence of an alleged victim's reputation is admissible only if it has been placed in controversy by the alleged victim."

Whether or not specifically circumscribed by statute, introduction of irrelevant evidence or reference to unsupportable allegations violates ethical norms of the profession. A lawyer should not, for example, "state or allude to any matter that he has no reasonable basis to believe is relevant to the case or that will not be supported by admissible evidence." DR 7–106(C); see also Model Rule 3.4(e). However, "relevance" can be broadly or narrowly defined depending on one's objectives, and in a criminal trial full disclosure of facts touching on the prosecution's case and its witnesses is believed by many to be part of the aggressive defense to which a defendant is entitled.

John Adams insisted on drawing the line at the introduction of evidence "to shew that the expulsion of the Troops from the Town of Boston was a plan concerted among the inhabitants." Adams threatened to resign from the representation if such evidence was introduced, whereas his co-counsel, Quincy "was willing it should be produced." Was this evidence relevant? Who do you think was right?

Effective Assistance of Counsel

The representation of Captain Preston and his men ultimately was effective despite its flaws (for example, the conflicts of interest between the defendants and between Adams's own loyalty to his clients and to the citizens of Boston). However, without able lawyers like Adams and Quincy being willing to endure the hostility of an angry populace, the defendants would almost certainly have received ineffective assistance of counsel, or perhaps no counsel at all. Their conviction in such circumstances would have lacked moral force, and today might have been unconstitutional as well. The minimal levels of lawyer competence constitutionally required under Strickland v. Washington, 466 U.S. 668 (1984) and its progeny, and ethically required under Model Code DR 6–101(A) and Model Rule 1.1, are discussed in Chapter 1, supra (after the *Nix v. Whiteside* case). Although a lawyer should not represent a client whose case the lawyer is not competent to handle, John Adams's defense of the British soldiers is a good example of a situation where competence is best measured by availability of an alternative. Even if Adams was caught up in the emotional tumult following the Massacre and did not feel entirely comfortable with the representation, the fact that Captain Preston and his men might go without any counsel at all certainly weighed in favor of Adams accepting the case. As Dalrymple wrote to General Gage, " '[l]awyers from other provinces would probably do better for their Client, not being residents here they might exert their abilities without apprehension of future enjuries [sic]; but where are any to be had.' "

QUESTIONS

1. In Kimmelman v. Morrison, 477 U.S. 365 (1986), a bedsheet used as evidence in a rape trial was illegally seized by a police officer who entered the defendant's apartment without a search warrant. The defendant's attorney, however, failed to file a suppression motion, and the Supreme Court remanded the case for a hearing on the issue of prejudice resulting from the ineffective assistance of counsel. In Justice Powell's concurring opinion, he argued that *Strickland* "emphasized that ineffective-assistance claims were designed to protect defendants against fundamental unfairness," Id. at 394. "[T]he bedsheet may have provided critical evidence of respondent's guilt, evidence whose relevance and reliability cannot seriously be questioned." Id. at 397. Justice Powell further argues that all the evidence did was "[help] the factfinder make a well-informed determination of respondent's guilt or innocence." Id. He concludes that, although the evidence was wrongfully admitted, the defendant should not receive a windfall when the result of the error was not unfair. Do you agree? Regardless of the outcome for the defendant, should the defendant's lawyer be subject to discipline for failure to file a motion to exclude such damaging, yet illegally obtained, evidence?

2. In some jurisdictions, lawyers are not called for jury duty. In other jurisdictions, lawyers are called, but frequently excused by litigants exercising their preemptory challenges. Why are lawyers sometimes excused as jurors? What are the advantages and disadvantages of allowing lawyers to serve as jurors?

3. How would you answer the following question:

"Is defense counsel obligated to pursue a suppression motion requested by her client if she feels that the motion is strategically damaging to the defendant's case? If counsel wants to pursue a legal issue in a pretrial motion, but defendant does not, may counsel still go forward?"

George E. Bisharat, Pursuing a Questionable Suppression Motion, in Ethical Problems Facing the Criminal Defense Lawyer 63 (Rodney J. Uphoff ed., ABA 1995).

4. How would you answer the following question:

"Should an individual public defender be permitted to refuse to represent certain categories of clients for moral or ideological reasons? Does the public defender supervisor or agency have the right to limit a defender's ability to 'opt out' of certain cases?"

Abbe Smith, When Ideology and Duty Conflict, in Ethical Problems Facing the Criminal Defense Lawyer, supra, at 18.

B.   REPRESENTATION OF CIVIL LITIGANTS

Daniel Webster, b. 1782 in Salisbury, N.H., d. 1852; B.A. Dartmouth College 1801; studied law in the office of Thomas W. Thompson in Salisbury, N.H. and later in the office of Christopher Gore in Boston 1801–04; country and provincial seaport lawyer in Boscawen, N.H. 1805–07 and Portsmouth, N.H. 1807–16; elected to U.S. House of Representatives (from N.H.) in 1812; re-elected in 1814; moved his law practice to Boston in 1816; elected to Massachusetts General Court 1822; elected to U.S. House of Representatives (from Mass.) in 1822; elected to U.S. Senate (from Mass.) in 1827; re-elected in 1833 and 1839; resigned to serve as Secretary of State 1840–43; elected to U.S. Senate (from Mass.) in 1845; resigned to serve as Secretary of State 1850–52.

The Devil and Daniel Webster

Robert W. Gordon
94 Yale L. J. 445 (1984)
Book Review (Reviewing the Papers of Daniel Webster: Legal Papers. Vol. I: The New Hampshire Practice. Vol. II: The Boston Practice. Edited by Alfred S. Konefsky)

* * *

Webster's climb upward through the hierarchies of practice, for example, illuminates how law business came to be divided by the early nineteenth-century bar. When he started out in Boscawen, [New Hampshire in 1805], nearly all of his business came from routine debt-collection cases, mostly settled or sent to reference (arbitration) after filing, hardly ever (less than two percent) going to a jury trial. Even then, however, Webster was well off the bottom rung of the bar, since most of his clients were plaintiffs, and, most important, connections from his legal apprenticeship in Boston had given him a steady client in the Boston mercantile house of Gore, Miller & Parker. The lawyer for such a house served as its general business agent in dealing with its rural customers, reporting (in the days before Dun & Bradstreet) on their credit-worthiness and judging their motives if they were late in paying their bills. Indeed, Konefsky and King argue that the lawyer played a vital stabilizing role in the fragile web of credit connecting entrepot creditors and inland merchants. At the downturn of the business cycle, overeager debt collection could bring about a chain-reaction of defaults and unravel the entire web. The lawyer could keep everyone afloat by manipulating legal forms (delaying court proceedings or obtaining extra security through collusive agreements to waive statutes of limitations or usury bans), administering in effect an informal local bankruptcy. Contemporaries thought it neither uncommon nor (given this mediating function) unethical for Webster to appear in court for and against the same person, first to help him collect his own debts, and then to collect the proceeds for the benefit of Webster's primary creditor client.

Not surprisingly, Webster found his Boscawen practice–keeping "shop," as he called it, "for the manufacture of Justice writs"—fairly tedious:

> It is now eight months since I opened an office in this town, during which time I have led a life which I know not how to describe better than by calling it a life of writs and summonses.... My business has been just about so, so; its quantity less objectionable than its quality.[24]

He moved to Portsmouth as soon as he conveniently could–unfortunately, just in time to experience the beginning of its decline brought on by the Embargo Act of 1807. While dramatic improvement in his practice did not come immediately, Portsmouth provided a base from which Webster could diversify his practice. From 1807 to 1813, while he was still traveling on circuit through small New Hampshire towns, his cases consisted mostly (70 percent), though less than formerly, of collections on promissory notes. From 1813 to 1816, however, that figure was down to 34 percent. He was elected to his first term in Congress in 1812. In reflection of his growing reputation and ability to pick his own clients, his practice was increasingly concentrated in his home county of Rockingham. His other cases were chiefly contract cases, with a smattering of property, family law, and maritime law business. Yet even these offered him little scope to exercise his talents before a jury. As before, all but a few of his cases ended in defaults or dismissals. Nevertheless, he kept on the more prestigious side of these routines, maintaining his connections to Boston creditors and appearing mostly for merchant plaintiffs.

The character of his practice altered dramatically upon his move to Boston in 1816. The expansion of international trade after the Revolution created an entirely novel set of practice opportunities, founded upon longterm relationships with large mercantile concerns, particularly insurance companies. This new business involved litigation much more complex than the typical writ-issued/case-settled transaction of the provinces; it called for a good deal of office work (drafting, counseling, writing opinion letters), and brought in much higher fees. Though practice was still conducted solo or in two-man or temporary partnerships, it was in many other respects the recognizable ancestor of today's metropolitan corporate practice.

To appreciate the scope of these changes, consider that John Adams, while practicing in Braintree and Boston in the 1760's and 1770's, made do with a miscellany of bread-and-butter cases; these were predominantly debt-collection cases, but they also included land, defamation, enforcement of town regulations, and many criminal cases. He had to follow the

---

24. Letter from D. Webster to J.H. Bingham (Jan. 19, 1806).

Superior Court on its arduous circuits around New England. As the editors of his papers point out, his fees were modest: "Even at the peak of his career, Adams owed any financial success more to quantity of business than to high fees. His charges seem to have been standard for nearly all clients and in many cases were governed by statute."[31] His income was thus built up of a pile of twelve-shilling writs together with cases tried worth a couple of pounds apiece; in gross, this income never seems to have been very high. To move up as a lawyer in Adams' world meant to attract a greater volume of business, from richer and more socially prominent clients, but not to change one's way of life.

When Alexander Hamilton, by contrast, left the Secretaryship of the Treasury to return to private practice in New York City in 1795, he found the nature of that practice profoundly altered. One of his commercial contracts cases (an unusual one, to be sure) took eight lawsuits in three courts over a five-year period to resolve, and resulted in a judgment of almost $120,000. The great bulk of his counseling and litigation work came from marine insurance companies, especially the United Insurance Company, which held his services on annual retainer. In 1802 he recorded almost $13,000 in fees.

Webster's move from Portsmouth to Boston allowed him to trade, in effect, Adams' world for Hamilton's. By the mid–1830's his book of receipts records annual fees totaling as high as $21,793. A sizable part of this income consisted of retainers and fees from Webster's new urban clientele: mercantile and banking houses (including Baring Brothers of London, and the Bank of the United States, as well as Boston-based merchants), mill owners, canal and railroad companies, and, of course, insurance companies. By 1835 eight Boston insurance offices were each paying him annual retainers of $100. During much of this time (1821–24), he was also representing a consortium of Boston and Philadelphia merchants before a special Commission set up to adjudicate claims for losses to American ships at the hands of Spain: From this business, he eventually realized $70,000 in contingent fees. Such fees, though prohibited in Massachusetts, were becoming common elsewhere as rates for lawyers' services underwent general deregulation under the pressure of the bar's increasingly entrepreneurial attitudes towards practice.

Yet to achieve professional prestige, an early nineteenth-century lawyer required more than an office practice nourished by the retainers of large urban capitalists: He had to be a litigator as well. The leaders of the bar at that time were without exception the great courtroom performers, and success brought frequent opportunities to try jury cases and argue appeals–relatively rare events in a law industry, then as now, mainly occupied with "keeping shop for the manufacture of Justice writs." By the 1830's, having passed on the routine of his Boston practice to an associate, Webster occupied himself with appellate practice, much of it before the

---

31. The Adams Papers: The Legal Papers of John Adams (L. Wroth & H. Zobel eds. 1965) at lxix.

United States Supreme Court in Washington. Most of his appearances before that Court were on behalf of his regular commercial clients—the New England merchants and the Bank of the United States, and a number of inventors for whom he acted in patent disputes. Only a few (24 out of 168) of his Supreme Court arguments raised any Constitutional issues, much less the grand issues of his famous public causes.

Still, the famous and the ordinary cases were connected; success in one arena could lead to employment in another. This is one of the many complex relations, hostile as well as symbiotic, between a lawyer's private and public careers, upon which the Webster Legal Papers volumes throw considerable light.

* * *

Webster was not unmindful of the advantages of family connections. He calculatingly married into an influential mercantile family after his first wife's death, and his daughter married into the leading mercantile family of Boston, the Appletons. Nevertheless, for Webster, involvement in Federalist political circles was critical to his early success at the bar. In his first years of apprenticeship and practice he contributed articles to the Federalist literary organ, the Boston Anthology, and thus displayed before Boston's elite the Federalist virtues of classical cultivation, legal erudition, and savage invective against political radicals.

As a New Hampshireman in Congress (1812–14), Webster attracted national attention by opposing the War of 1812, accusing President Madison of keeping secret information that might have prevented the war, and commending the secession-minded Hartford Convention. When he moved his practice to Boston, the Federalist–Unitarian elite immediately adopted him as one of their chief political talents, accepted him in the highest ranks of society, and retained him as their lawyer. And it was his political prominence, as well as his rising fame as a trial lawyer, that encouraged the Federalist board of trustees of Dartmouth College to seek (in 1815) the help of their loyal alumnus in the litigation that established him as a national figure.[59]

This symbiosis of legal and political careers, convenient though it undoubtedly was for young men without capital as a way of getting ahead in life and for the polity as a way of attracting ambitious talent to office, often created severe tensions between lawyers' public and private roles. The source of most of these tensions was what we now tend to call "conflicts of interest," but what Webster's generation, employing "classical republican" terms of analysis, labeled "corruption." Corruption in individuals resulted from the surrender of the independent, public-regarding judgment that supported "virtue"; corruption leading to the decline of republics could follow from the loss of virtue among their chief citizens. Federalist–Whig lawyers like Webster subscribed to an ideal of representation supposedly controlling lawyers and politicians alike: that in neither role should one act simply as an extension of constituency or client, but in both preserve an independent judgment. To become overdependent upon or

---

59. Trustees of Dartmouth College v. Woodward, 17 U.S. (4 Wheat.) 518 (1819).

over-attached to a particular interest would subvert that independence. One would become prisoner of a faction, no longer able to perceive, much less pursue, the interests of the whole community. Among the forces creating the temptations to corruption were "ambition" and "commerce." Ambition could corrupt not only because it could raise the interests of the self over those of the public, but because the loyalties, debts, and compromises incurred to serve ambition could enslave one's judgment to one's factional patrons. Commerce could corrupt because the love of profit and luxury could distract one from the public business and deliver one's independence into the power of creditors. In the Federalist–Whig ideology, neither ambition nor commerce was despised as such; indeed, both were highly prized, but only if subordinated to virtue.

Webster was thoroughly saturated in this ideology, as his following observations indicate. He wrote the first while still at Dartmouth:

> Ambition is what? The grand nerve of human exertion; the producer of everything excellent in virtue and ... in vice.... Ambition in Caesar and in Washington is radically the same; in each it is the wish of excelling. But there is an essential difference in its direction. Caesar's ambition was not subordinate to his virtue.... In Washington ambition was a secondary principle. It was subordinate to his integrity....
>
> Thus various are the effects of ambition. It can enslave a nation, or it can burst the manacles of despotism, and make the oppressed rejoice....[62]

And this—somewhat less a rhetorical set-piece and more a bitter and deeply felt cri de coeur—while a struggling young lawyer in Boscawen:

> The evil is, that an accursed thirst for money violates everything. We cannot study, because we must pettifog. We learn the low recourses of attorneyism, when we should learn the conceptions, the reasonings, and the opinions of Cicero and Murray.... The liberal professions are resorted to, not to acquire reputation and consequence, but to get rich.... Our profession is good if practised in the spirit of it; it is damnable fraud and iniquity, when its true spirit is supplied by a spirit of mischief-making and money-catching.[63]

The fascination of Webster for his contemporaries was that he seemed to lead a life of allegory in which the forces of virtue and corruption battled for his mighty soul. We, who are insulated by Webster's death from the magnetic force of his personality, and by the culture of modernism from the power of his rhetoric, have difficulty appreciating that most antebellum Americans considered him the greatest man of his age, indeed one of the greatest men of all time, the very model of ambition subdued to virtue. His more enduring reputation is probably the one originated by the antislavery "Conscience Whigs" of Webster's party. They pictured him as a fallen Lucifer, who, in his support of the Fugitive Slave Law in the compromise

62. Unpublished manuscript, quoted in I. Bartlett, Daniel Webster 26 (1978).

63. Letter from D. Webster to J.H. Bingham, Jan. 19, 1806, quoted at The Papers of Daniel Webster: Legal Papers. Vol. I: The New Hampshire Practice at 69.

package of 1850, had sold out all his principles to his own ambitions for the Presidency and to his commercial clients.

The Webster Legal Papers make possible more concrete if less melodramatic insights into the temptations and tensions of a statesman who was simultaneously trying to practice law. Webster was under constant pressure (although much of it was self-generated) to use his office to pursue favors for clients. After winning big judgments for his mercantile clients before the Spanish Claims Commission, for example, Webster turned his attention to what he called "[m]y great business of the [House] Session,"[64] appropriation of the money to pay the claims, thus protecting both his constituents and his contingent fee.[65] As chairman of a Senate committee considering whether to set up a similar commission to pay losses suffered by American merchants through French attacks on their ships, Webster actually solicited Boston merchants to appoint him as their claims agent, assuring them that "[b]y proper pains, this Bill will assuredly pass the Senate."[66] He subsequently issued a statement denying he had ever been interested in or connected with the French–Spoliation claimants.[67] In 1831 Senator Webster sponsored legislation on behalf of one of his biggest clients, the Bank of the United States, enabling the Bank to obtain federal court jurisdiction when it brought suit in states that had no federal circuit courts. "Webster drafted the bill in general terms," the editors explain, for "if President Jackson knew it aided the Bank he would surely veto it."[68] The bill passed, and Webster charged $500 for his services.[69]

Such favors as these seem not to have troubled Webster or the mores of his time. What ultimately undermined Webster was not the money he earned, however tainted, but the money he borrowed. His financial base, a law-office clientele developed through advantageous political connections, solidified into a discrete constituency to which Webster was always in debt. Not just morally in debt, for having advanced his career and given him business, but literally: He was kept afloat by their extensive loans and other contributions. In one of many such transactions, forty Boston businessmen subscribed to a $100,000 fund in 1845 to enable Webster to return to the Senate. "This is at least the third time that the wind has been raised for him," a somewhat disillusioned patron wrote at the time, "and the most curious fact is that thousands are subscribed by many who hold his old notes for other thousands, and who have not been backward in their censures of his profusion."[70] He was constantly in debt to the Bank of the United States ($100,000 worth in 1841), which was a major political embarrassment while he was maneuvering to maintain his independence and play the mediator in Jackson's war with the Bank in the 1830's, and

64. Letter from D. Webster to J. Mason, April 19, 1824, quoted at The Papers of Daniel Webster: Legal Papers Vol. II: The Boston Practice at 251.

65. Id. at 251–52.

66. Letter from D. Webster to H.W. Kinsman, Jan. 11, 1834, reprinted in Legal Papers, Vol. II supra: 335.

67. II: 342–43.

68. II: 316–17.

69. II: 317.

70. Harrison Grey Otis, the doyen of Federalist–Whig Boston, quoted in R. Current, Daniel Webster and the Rise of National Conservatism 137 (1955). The very next year, probably calculating that with Webster a gift when he was appointed Secretary of State in the 1840's. These dealings made life easy for his political enemies, and eventually helped to cost him the Presidency.

They cost him some loss of vision as well. The "Conscience Whigs" were probably being unjust when they accused Webster of selling out in 1850 to his clients, the pro-slavery mercantile interests of State Street. His support of the Compromise was of course completely consistent with the overarching theme of all his political life, the cause of national Union. (His opponents were on much surer ground when they brought up his fight against the War of 1812 and his switch from opposing to favoring the tariff, both highly sectional positions.) But it is not far-fetched to suppose that by rooting his professional and social lives so solidly within a single class, Webster had become unable to conceive of a view of the national interest separate from his own interests and those of his crowd. He was unable to ally with the antislavery cause, or even to sympathize with it enough to understand what it was all about, and in consequence drastically underestimated its importance. This loss of perspective, rather than the cruder examples of bribe-taking, perhaps best illustrates the subtler meaning of "corruption."

QUESTIONS

1. In what specific areas of Webster's practice did he accept private practice representations that were substantially related to the subject matter of his government service? See Chapter 4, supra, for discussion of modern ethics rules concerning such conflicts.

2. Look back at the materials concerning Louis Brandeis's confirmation hearings, supra Chapter 6. Were the concurrent conflicts in Webster's law practice more or less serious than those alleged against Brandeis? Why did Webster have so much more support among prominent Bostonians in the 1830s and 1840's than Brandeis did seventy years later?

3. Unlike Brandeis, a vigorous opponent of concentrated banking and industrial interests, Webster appears to have been unable or unwilling to take stands in public life that went against the interests of his clients. Why?

4. Does this account of Webster's life underscore a relationship between personal finances and professional ethics? What is that relationship? Is keeping one's own finances in order part of being ethical?

5. Nicholas Biddle, the President of the Bank of the United States, kept a handwritten list of "congressmen, federal officials, and newspaper editors, liable to the Bank as borrowers or guarantors" including "James Monroe, down for $10,596; Henry Clay in the amount of $7,500; and Senator Daniel Webster of Massachusetts, liable for $17,782.86." John T. Noonan, Jr., Bribes 444 (1984).

was as good as a loan, a consortium of Boston subscribers established a $37,000 annuity for his benefit, "in evidence of their grateful sense to the valuable services you have rendered to your whole country." I. Bartlett, supra note [62], at 193.

A second way of acquiring influence—less open to political polemic if it became known—was to hire a member of Congress as one's lawyer.... The Bank of the United States found it useful to employ both Clay and Webster. In 1833, when the Bank was engaged in the mortal combat to keep its federal charter, Senator Webster coolly wrote Biddle, "Since I have arrived here, I have had an application to be concerned, professionally, against the Bank, which I have declined of course, although I believe my retainer has not been renewed, or *refreshed* as usual. If it be wished that my relation to the Bank should be continued, it may be well to send me the usual retainers." In these phrases there was the suggestion that only Webster's professional allegiance was at stake. Delivered at a time of peril for the Bank in Congress the letter scarcely failed to convey the importance of keeping the Senator satisfied. Id.

(a) Do politicians violate their fiduciary obligations to the public when they borrow from financial institutions under their regulatory authority? Should the practice be prohibited?

(b) Although members of the United States House and Senate no longer practice law on the side, many state legislators do. Is it possible to isolate a law practice from conflicts with a legislative role? How?

Abraham Lincoln, b. Larue County, Kentucky 1809, d. 1865; grew up near Springfield, Illinois; self educated; elected to the Illinois State Legislature in 1834; licensed to practice law in 1836; practiced in Springfield; elected to the U.S. House of Representatives in 1847; President of the United States 1860–65; assassinated while attending a theater performance in 1865.

Usher F. Linder, of Charleston, Illinois was a proslavery lawyer who with Abraham Lincoln represented Robert Matson of Bourbon County, Kentucky in seeking return of the Bryant family, allegedly five of Matson's slaves. Matson, had other difficulties with the law in Illinois, having been arrested for "criminal fornication" with his housekeeper, Mary Corbin.

Orlando B. Ficklin and **Charles Constable** were proslavery lawyers. In this case, however, they represented the abolitionists Gideon Ashmore and Dr. Hiram Rutherford in bringing a writ of habeas corpus on behalf of the Bryants.

Matson v. Rutherford
(Ill. Cir. Ct. 1847).

Abraham Lincoln Argues a Pro–slavery Case
Anton–Hermann Chroust
4 American Journal of Legal History (1960).

In 1843 a Kentucky slaveholder, "General" Robert Matson, purchased a tract of land called Black Grove in Coles County, Illinois. He worked his newly acquired property with the help of his two sons, his hired men and some slaves brought each spring from his plantation in Bourbon County, Kentucky. Each fall, after the harvest was in, he returned these slaves to Kentucky.

Since the slaves were returned each fall to Kentucky and, hence, were not permanently domiciled in Illinois, they did not, and could not, under the existing laws acquire the status of free men in the "free" State of Illinois. Thus Matson managed to maintain their status as slaves in Illinois. Being a meticulous and prudent man, he took extraordinary precautions to avoid any possible misunderstanding as to his avowed intentions to retain his slaves: every time he brought these slaves into Illinois, he made a formal declaration before a witness, Joe Drew (or, Joe Dean), one of his own hired hands, that "the slaves were here [in Coles County] temporarily and [were to be] returned shortly to his plantation in Bourbon." One slave, however, a certain Anthony Bryant, who acted as a sort of overseer of other slaves, regularly stayed behind in Black Grove, residing there the year round. Thus, Bryant, although at the time unaware of the fact and lacking a "certificate of freedom," became by virtue of his continuous residence technically a free man under the laws of Illinois.

In August 1847, it appears, some trouble developed on the Black Grove property involving Bryant and his wife Jane who had joined him that year with her four children. Fearing reprisals, Bryant fled to the town of Oakland in Coles County, where he sought protection with two abolitionists, Gideon M. Ashmore, an innkeeper, and Dr. Hiram Rutherford, a physician. Although at the time it was a criminal offense in Illinois to harbor or secrete a fugitive slave owing service to a citizen of another state, these two men advised Bryant to bring his wife and four children to Ashmore's inn without delay. They also notified some antislavery men in the neighborhood, requesting them to be in readiness in the event Matson should try to retrieve his escaped slaves by the use of force.

Matson made several attempts to persuade Bryant and his wife to return peaceably. Failing in this, he brought legal proceedings, retaining as his lawyer Usher F. Linder (and perhaps Thomas A. Marshall) of Charleston, the county seat of Coles County.[4] Acting under the provisions of the so-called "Black Laws" of Illinois or Fugitive Slave Laws—statutes enacted to discourage the settlement of fugitive Negroes in Illinois—Linder asked for and obtained from William Gilmore, the local Justice of the Peace in Charleston, a writ to produce the five Negroes (Jane and her four children) who then were promptly locked in the Charleston county jail as runaway slaves. Subsequently, a hearing was held before Justice Gilmore, a Captain Easton and a Mr. Shephard—the latter two acting as Gilmore's associates

---

4. Matson had been living, to use John J. Duff's whimsical expression, "in more or less respectable sin" with Mary Corbin, who apparently doubled as his housekeeper. Duff, A. Lincoln, Prairie Lawyer, 131 (1960). At about the time the Bryants fled to Oakland, he was arrested on the charge of "criminal fornication." The warrant of his arrest can be found in the William H. Herndon–Jesse W. Weik Collection, Illinois State Historical Library (microfilm). Presumably he was released on bail.

on the bench—in which the Negroes, at the request of Rutherford, were represented by Orlando B. Ficklin, a Charleston lawyer, who had also insisted that Gilmore, a pro-slavery man and a person known to be under Linder's influence, be "assisted" by Easton and Shephard. When, after a two day's hearing, Justice Gilmore denied that his court had jurisdiction in the matter, the Negroes, who, of course, lacked "certificates of freedom," were bound over to the sheriff to be advertised and sold for jail fees under the provisions of the Illinois "Black Laws." Immediately, Ashmore and Rutherford sued out a writ of *habeas corpus* in behalf of the Negroes. In the meantime Matson brought proceedings against Ashmore and Rutherford, demanding damages amounting to two thousand five hundred dollars for enticing his slaves. The *habeas corpus* proceedings, which apparently were joined with the suit for damages, were held at the October, 1847, term of the Coles County Circuit Court in Charleston, Chief Justice William Wilson (or Willson) of the Illinois Supreme Court and Judge Samuel H. Treat of the Eighth Illinois Circuit, presiding.

Abraham Lincoln, who since the year 1841 had appeared quite frequently before the Coles County Circuit Court, happened to be in Charleston during the same term. As a matter of fact, after he got to Charleston he was retained in two other cases that were to be argued there. Linder, it seems, took hold of Lincoln and succeeded in engaging his professional services as co-counsel for Matson. Undoubtedly, Lincoln was fully appraised of the facts in the Bryant case before he agreed to argue it. Somewhat later, it is believed, Rutherford, intending to defend himself against Matson's damage suit and also in order to have a prominent lawyer argue the case for the Negroes, likewise approached Lincoln, asking him to appear in his behalf as well as that of the Negroes. Lincoln, however, declined to do so on the ostensible grounds that he had previously been engaged by the other side. It has been alleged that Lincoln later let it be known that he would have liked to withdraw as Matson's counsel and be retained by Rutherford, but that Rutherford, incensed over Lincoln's original refusal, no longer wished to hire him. Rutherford subsequently engaged the professional services of Charles H. Constable, who thus became Ficklin's co-counsel. Thus it came about that Matson was represented by Linder and Lincoln, and the Negroes or, rather, Ashmore and Rutherford, by Ficklin and Constable. All but Lincoln were professed pro-slavery men, and of these the only actor in this court drama cast in his proper role was Linder.

The hearing on the writ of *habeas corpus*, as is the rule, was held before the court without a jury on October 16, 1847. Ficklin, arguing for Ashmore and Rutherford and, incidentally, for the Negroes, contended that the provisions of the Northwest Ordinance of 1787 and the Constitution of Illinois had conferred freedom on the Negroes—an argument, in fact, which Lincoln had already advanced successfully in 1841 in *Bailey v. Cromwell*.[12]

---

12. In Bailey v. Cromwell, 4 Ill. 71 (1841), Lincoln, representing the defendant-appellant, argued before the Illinois Supreme Court that in the State of Illinois a promisso- ry note made out by the vendee in payment for a slave was without proper consideration and, hence, void, inasmuch as it was given as the purchase price of a human being who in a

Inexcusably, and with an ineptitude bordering on professional incompetence, neither Ficklin nor his co-counsel, Constable, ever referred to this case which would have lent to their contentions the authority of established precedent. How embarrassing, not to say devastating, it would have been to confront Lincoln with the very argument he had presented so successfully some six years previously, namely, that a slave had been made free when his master had taken him into the State of Illinois where slavery was illegal. Constable limited himself to a long and somewhat irrelevant declamation on the English notion of liberty. ... Linder, in turn, argued that every American citizen, including Matson, must be protected in the enjoyment of his property rights—a commonplace argument in such cases. In addition, he alleged that Matson never intended the slaves to become permanently settled in Illinois. Beyond this he contributed little to the case.

Lincoln's argument, in the opinion of Ficklin, was one of "trenchant blows and cold logic and subtle knitting together and presenting of facts favorable to his side of the case." According to the same Ficklin, Lincoln reasoned as follows: "The fact that General Matson had at such a time when he placed a slave on his Illinois farm, publicly declared that he was not placed there for permanent settlement, and that no counter statement had ever been made publicly or privately by him, constituted the web and woof of the argument of Mr. Lincoln, and these facts were plausibly, ingeniously and forcibly presented to the court, so as to give them all the effect and significance to which they were entitled and more." From all this it appears that it was Lincoln's contention that Jane Bryant and her four children had come to Illinois together with a group of seasonal workers who happened to be slaves and who were to be returned to Kentucky every fall, in accordance with their master's annual custom and publicly declared intention. This being admittedly so, neither Jane nor her children ever, at any time, became or could become permanent residents of the State of Illinois and, hence, gain their freedom.

The judgment of the court, which went against Lincoln and Linder, declared that the Negroes "shall be and remain free and discharged from all servitude whatever to any person or persons from henceforward and forever." The court apparently followed the rule laid down in *Bailey v. Cromwell*, without, however, citing that case as authority. The order of Justice Gilmore and his two associates for the sale of the Negroes was set aside; the motion for the discharge of the Negroes from imprisonment was sustained, and their discharge from prison was ordered.

Because he lost the case for his client, the rather unfair charge has been made against Lincoln that since his heart allegedly was not in the case he "threw" it on purpose. It has also been claimed that his efforts in behalf

---

free state such as Illinois was not legally the subject of sale. Lincoln also contended that under the provisions of the Ordinance of 1787 and the Illinois State Constitution forbidding slavery, the Negro under consideration was a free person. It was this case which laid down the rule that in Illinois the presumption of law is that every person is free without regard to color, and that the sale of a free person is illegal. See also Pratt, "In Defense of Mr. Justice Browne," 56 Bulletin of the Abraham Lincoln Society (1939).

of Matson lacked enthusiasm and energy, and that his presentation "was pitiably weak" and "his arguments in behalf of a cause which his conscience detested were spiritless, half-hearted, and devoid of his usual wit, logic, and invective." Aside from the fact that these insinuations cast a most unfavorable light on Lincoln's professional ethics, honesty, and integrity by charging him with insensibility to his sworn duty as an attorney, they are definitely not in keeping with the events which transpired in the Charleston court house on October 16, 1847. Not only did Lincoln give by far the best forensic performance of all the lawyers connected with this case, but his arguments from a legal point of view were forceful, not to say convincing. His was the only persuasive presentation which under the circumstances could be made with any chance for success: the slaves never were, and never had been, intended to be permanent residents of the State of Illinois. This was the only rational conclusion which the defense could draw from the facts before the court. Lincoln, who displayed good courtroom tactics when handling the case, seized upon the only arguable point in favor of his client. Thus, in the light of Lincoln's forensic tactics it cannot possibly be maintained that he deliberately gave a lackluster and halfhearted performance. Any statement to the contrary, aside from being a serious attack on his professional ethics, is nothing more than an instance of that fantastic Lincoln adulation which refuses to permit even the slightest shadow of doubt regarding the "unimpeachable" character of its hero.

A final question might be raised here: what could possibly have induced Lincoln, the "Great Emancipator," to lend his professional skills to a slaveholder intent upon retrieving his runaway slave? The answer is not simple. Lincoln, as we know, had argued cases before in Coles County, and he did find some legal business there during the October, 1847, term. But, it will be noted, he picked up this legal business only *after* he got to Charleston. On the other hand, he had no "hold-overs" there from the spring term which would have necessitated his presence in Charleston. Also, some weight should be given to the fact that Lincoln, usually a most regular attender of his own circuit, passed up the fall term of 1847 in Vermillion County which started October 4, and in Edgar County which started October 11—two counties which belonged to the Eighth Illinois Judicial Circuit which was Lincoln's own circuit—solely to travel about eighty miles of poor roads to get to Charleston. From these facts it may be inferred that he went there primarily in the hope of being retained in the Matson case which must have attracted considerable attention throughout the state. In short, he was on the look-out for business, a not uncommon practice in those days. As it happened, Linder was the first to approach him and to engage his services as co-counsel.

Undoubtedly, Linder fully disclosed the facts of the case to Lincoln. Although he knew or must have known that by accepting the retainer he would unequivocally align himself with the pro-slavery people, he apparently had no qualms about undertaking the assignment or, perhaps, not the good sense to turn it down. This is the more astounding since on a previous occasion (*Bailey v. Cromwell*) he had so successfully argued the other side of the case. To be sure, Lincoln was one of Linder's closer acquaintances and, hence, might have accepted the retainer just as a "personal favor" to Linder. But Lincoln was also a friend of Rutherford. Indeed, the fact that he was a friend of Linder's should have made it more easy for him to decline. He accepted and, it could be said, he accepted hastily. Lincoln, it would appear, had made a grave mistake, but he was not prudent enough to get out of it. All this leaves but one conclusion: in 1847, to use the words of Benjamin P. Thomas, one of Lincoln's outstanding biographers, "the slave issue had not yet seared itself into his conscience to the point of inducing him to place the plight of a few hapless Negroes above the abstract legal aspects of the slavery question."

QUESTIONS

1.   Should Lincoln have taken this case? In arguing Matson's cause, was Lincoln acknowledging the legitimacy of legal rules that denied basic human rights to African Americans?

2.   Do you agree with the author that it would have been unethical for Lincoln, having taken the case, to argue it with less than full enthusiasm? What should a lawyer do when "his sworn duty as an attorney" comes into conflict with his duty to other human beings?

3.   Lincoln had argued the case of Bailey v. Cromwell, 4 Ill. 71 (1841), which created the presumption that a black person in Illinois was free and put the burden on the alleged slave owner to prove to the contrary. Lincoln now argued that the Bryants were brought into Illinois as seasonal workers and were legally in transit. Is this argument inconsistent with *Bailey v. Cromwell*? Is it unethical to make an argument on behalf of one client that is inconsistent with an argument made on behalf of another client? See discussion of successive conflicts in Chapter 4, supra, and of concurrent conflicts in Chapter 6, supra.

4.   Ficklin and Constable, "[i]nexcusably, and with ineptitude bordering on professional incompetence," did not argue *Bailey v. Cromwell* to the Court. The Court's opinion followed the rule in *Bailey* without citing that case as authority, indicating that none of the lawyers had directed the court's attention to *Bailey*. Should Lincoln have done so? See Model Rule 3.3(a)(3) ("A lawyer shall not knowingly: . . . fail to disclose to the tribunal legal authority in the controlling jurisdiction known to the lawyer to be directly adverse to the position of the client and not disclosed by opposing counsel").

5.   David Luban writes:

"We began with James Giffard, who, as a prisoner of his role, tried to hang the runaway slave James Annesley; perhaps it is not inappropriate to end with Abraham Lincoln, who in his Springfield law practice once heard out a client and said to him:

> Yes, we can doubtless gain your case for you; we can set a whole neighborhood at loggerheads; we can distress a widowed mother and

her six fatherless children and thereby get you six hundred dollars to which you seem to have a legal claim, but which rightfully belongs, it appears to me, as much to the woman and her children as it does to you. You must remember that some things legally right are not morally right. We shall not take your case, but will give you a little advice for which we will charge you nothing. You seem to be a sprightly, energetic man; we would advise you to try your hand at making six hundred dollars in some other way.

Lincoln freed the slaves; this may not be unconnected to the fact that in his practice of law he was himself no slave, not even to trade idioms that he surely thought were moral idioms as well." David Luban, Lawyers and Justice: An Ethical Study 173–74 (1988).

Do you agree with Luban's assessment of Lincoln?

6.   Abraham Lincoln and Daniel Webster in different ways and at different times took the wrong side in the slavery debate. Lincoln agreed to represent General Matson in this case, and as President only proclaimed an end to slavery in the middle of the Civil War. Webster, as a United States Senator from Massachusetts, hardly a pro-slavery state, supported a law designed to help persons like Matson retain their slaves—the Fugitive Slave Law in the Compromise of 1850. In the end, however, Lincoln had a positive and forceful impact on the slavery debate, whereas Webster did not. Why?

PROBLEM

1.   The Texas Commission on Human Rights (the "Human Rights Commission") seeks to compel the Texas Knights of the Ku Klux Klan ("KKK") to turn over its membership list to facilitate prosecution of Klan members for threats and intimidation directed at citizens seeking to integrate publicly funded housing. Anthony Griffin, a black lawyer working with the American Civil Liberties Union, is asked to represent the KKK in opposing the Human Rights Commission's demand on the ground that it violates the KKK's First Amendment rights under NAACP v. Alabama, 357 U.S. 449, 466 (1958) (holding that the NAACP may keep its membership list private from government authorities under the Fourteenth Amendment). Should Griffin accept the case? See David B. Wilkins, Race, Ethics and the First Amendment: Should a Black Lawyer Represent the Ku Klux Klan?, 63 Geo. Wash. L. Rev. 1030 (1995).

C.   REPRESENTATION OF BUSINESS

Relevant Background

The history of many of today's large law firms began at a time when "robber barons" built their business empires by buying up the stock of their competitors, suppliers or distributors.[13] For example, in the late 1860's David Dudley Field was counsel to Jim Fisk and Jay Gould in one of the most famous contests, the struggle of Fisk, Gould and Daniel Drew against Commodore Vanderbilt for control of the Erie Railroad. Drew and his cohorts, probably with Field's assistance, found and took advantage of a loophole in the General Railroad Act of 1850 which, while it prohibited railroads from issuing new stock, allowed bonds issued for construction or new equipment to be converted into stock. As Vanderbilt furiously bought up shares of the Erie, his opponents thus used their control of the Erie board of directors to dump a steady stream of new shares on the market. See Maury Klein, The Life and Legend of Jay Gould 81 (1986).

Judges and state legislators were bribed by both sides and, while Field himself probably did not directly participate in the bribery, "he was a general in the notorious war of injunctions in the lower courts." William Simon, Ethical Discretion in Lawyering, 101 Harv. L. Rev. 1083, 1136 (1988). Both sides accumulated judges as quickly as they retained lawyers, and many of the judges who granted injunctions had already been "persuaded" by Field's clients or their opponents before the lawyers ever walked into court. Drafting and copying these injunctions for judges to sign was the lawyers' job, and forty-odd lawyers were retained by Drew's Erie clique at a total cost of $334,416. Clarence Seward of Blatchford, Seward and Griswold, a predecessor firm to Cravath, Swaine & Moore, joined Field in this endeavor. Robert Swaine, The Cravath Firm at I: 241 (1946). John W. Sterling, a young associate in Field's office, wrote of the Erie episode,

> "Night and day, we have labored without extra compensation or reward or even thanks. Sundays, Mr. Field wished us to work; but I remonstrated, as it was contrary to my principales [sic] to work on the Lord's day. One Sunday however, he invited me to dinner, and afterward I found myself copying a half sheet of paper...."

Walter K. Earle, Mr. Shearman and Mr. Sterling and How They Grew 16 (Carl Purington Rollins Printing Office) (1963).

Field, however, defended his own integrity by asserting his independence from his clients. He cited Lord Erskine's famous defense of Thomas Paine on charges of seditious libel for publication of The Rights of Man as an articulation of the extent, and limitations, of a lawyer's responsibilities. Just as Lord Erskine was not responsible for publication of Paine's alleged libel, rather only for defending his client's right to publish it, likewise "legal opinions and arguing cases" were Field's own work, he argued, whereas the wrongdoing, if any, was the work of his clients. Samuel Bowles, editor of the Springfield Republican, however, did not agree:

> But the Republican had long ago maintained, and applied to cases in Massachusetts, the doctrine that a lawyer was responsible, in a decided

---

13. This discussion appears in lengthier form in Richard W. Painter, The Moral Inter- dependence of Corporate Lawyers and Their Clients, 67 S. Cal. L. Rev. 507 (1994).

degree, for the character of his clients and the character of the suits which he undertook in their behalf . . .

Do not deceive yourself, my dear sir; history may be relied upon to defend freedom of opinion, and to avenge its martyrs; but it will never put James Fisk, Jun., by the side of Thomas Paine, nor, for daring and losing for his cause, will it put David Dudley Field on a page parallel to that belonging to Erskine.

Correspondence of Messrs. David Dudley and Dudley Field, of the New York Bar, with Mr. Samuel Bowles of the Springfield Republican (1871), reprinted in A. Kaufman, Problems in Professional Responsibility 414–22 (3d ed. 1989). To some at least, the fallacy in asserting that lawyers have no responsibility for the conduct of their clients was quite apparent.

The Association of the Bar of the City of New York, shortly after its founding in 1869, conducted an investigation into charges filed with the Association against Field. The hearings, held in 1872 and 1873, were frequently interrupted by disturbances and cat-calls, but were finally adjourned without action. Field & Shearman then represented Jay Gould until Field retired and the newly formed Shearman & Sterling took over sixty-three lawsuits which concerned Mr. Gould. These suits were "based on fraud, breach of contract, conversion, trespass, and almost everything else which could support claims for money damages. . . . All of them were concerned with Gould's activities . . . in all of which many people suffered losses." Earle supra at 30.

Even in the early twentieth century, despite the changing nature of corporations and corporate representation, lawyers resisted the notion that they were in any way responsible for the conduct of their clients. As Robert T. Swaine stated in his history of the Cravath firm, during the period after the Spanish–American War, "[h]olding companies, with inflated capitalizations top-heavy with debt, popped up like puff balls, controlling production and distribution in many industries with little concern for the anti-trust laws." Swaine went on to observe, however, that,

> Those critics who ascribe to the corporate executives and bankers of the day and to the lawyers moral turpitude in these transactions are wrong, and unfairly so. Mistaken judgment there may have been—but not dishonesty or deliberate flouting of the law. As to lawyers, they did not regard the social and economic problems as theirs. Robert Swaine, The Cravath Firm, supra at I: 667.

These events concerned the founding partners of some of New York's premier law firms, including Cravath, Swaine & Moore and Shearman & Sterling. Space does not permit discussion here of the equally colorful exploits of their counterparts at other firms. A careful reading of these law firms' own histories, however, should dispel any illusion one might have that lawyers were more ethical in the "Gilded Age" than they are today. As the next selection illustrates, the views of Field and Swaine were reflected in the practice of many prominent lawyers. One of these lawyers was Elihu Root.

Elihu Root, b. 1845, d. 1937; LL.B. New York University School of Law 1867; U.S. Attorney in New York City 1883–85; Secretary of War under President McKinley 1899–1904; Secretary of State under President Theodore Roosevelt 1904–09; elected to the United States Senate in 1909; received the Nobel Peace Prize in 1912; co-founder of the American Legal Institute (ALI).

"The Clients of Elihu Root" from Philip C. Jessup, Elihu Root

(1937)

Chapter X

Years 1894–1899

Age 49–54

There was no lawyer practicing at the American Bar in the 1890's who was more sought-after than Elihu Root. It was the heyday of his practice. Although other lawyers excelled him in particular qualifications, none equaled him in his combination of wisdom, farsightedness, ingenuity and influence with the courts. His fees were large but he would rather send a receipt in full than quarrel over the amount. In his usual capacity as counsel, he constantly asked the attorneys to adjust his charges as they saw fit. His income from fees at this period ranged from about fifty to one hundred and ten thousand dollars a year. Even the great panic of 1893 with its ensuing depression seems to have had no appreciable effect upon the wide demand for his professional services....

A description of even the most important cases which Root handled in this period would require a somewhat extended history of business enterprise and a mass of legal detail which even a fellow lawyer would hardly peruse without a retainer and an occasional refresher. Look at a partial roster of his clients between 1890 and 1898: The Government of the United States; the Comptroller of the State of New York; the City of New York in the famous Aqueduct cases in which he saved the city millions of dollars; Theodore Roosevelt as Police Commissioner and as gubernatorial candidate; Dana as editor of the New York *Sun* when Root successfully resisted his extradition in a libel suit; The New York *Times* Publishing Company; The New York *Press* Company; his old friend Professor Peters in the famous "Star Catalogue" case; another old friend, Professor William H. Chandler of Lehigh University, in the matter of a publishing contract; Robert Ray Hamilton whose estate he protected in a sensational case from the machinations of the notorious Eva Mann; at least six railroads, several of the cases involving important reorganizations; the Metropolitan Street Railway Company of New York and the matter of the Chicago Elevated Syndicate Agreement; men like Frederick W. Vanderbilt, August Belmont, Thomas Fortune Ryan, Peter A. B. Widener and William C. Whitney; the National Cash Register Company; the Western Union Telegraph Company; the National Starch Manufacturing Company; the Consolidated Gas Company; the Union Tobacco Company and the United States Rubber Company; H. F. Havemeyer and the Sugar Trust; the Lead Trust, the Whiskey Trust, the Watch Trust and the Standard Oil Company.

The Sherman Anti–Trust Act of 1890 had made necessary some reorganizations in big business combinations, but neither the statute nor the early court decisions made large corporate organizations illegal. Nor did the *mores* of the time condemn them. The law had failed to keep pace with all the violent new methods of business. This was partly because the law rarely does; it waits until the evils have roused public opinion. Partly it was because legislatures were too much controlled by corporate wealth. There had been a few investigations, such as that of the Hepburn Committee of the New York Legislature which revealed in 1879 the secret agreements between the railroads and oil refiners. Yet little was done. Vanderbilt's partly innocent but widely heralded remark, "The public be damned," dates from this period and is not atypical of the business man's point of view. It remained for Theodore Roosevelt, not to discover the evils nor to eliminate monopolies from American business, but by the dramatic force of his character to awaken the public consciousness to some of the defects of the system.

Root, as it happened, never actually formed a "trust." He did advise on a number of important reorganizations which new laws made necessary. . . .

There are many forms of the remark, variously attributed to Thomas Fortune Ryan and to William C. Whitney: "I have had many lawyers who have told me what I cannot do; Mr. Root is the only lawyer who tells me how to do what I want to do." In one sense, the gist of the remark was true. A lawyer recalled in a letter to Mr. Root on his eightieth birthday a familiar scene in the suite at the Waldorf–Astoria which Whitney kept for conferences. Whitney would sit at the head of the table. When the talk was spent, he would say, "Well, gentlemen, this is the thing to do," and he would state it briefly. Meanwhile Root would be writing on small slips of paper and when Whitney had finished he would say, "This is the way to do it." But in the sense usually attributed to Whitney's (or Ryan's) remark, it is quite untrue. Samuel B. Clarke, who had been Root's Assistant in the District Attorney's office and his junior partner from 1886 to 1897, and who worked with him particularly on New York Street Railway matters, wrote on November 17th, 1908, to Joseph H. Choate in regard to an attack which the New York *World* had made on Root. "The gist of the *World*'s attack," Clarke wrote, "was that Root is a typical example of an able lawyer who cleverly and craftily and successfully devises legal forms to accomplish purposes of his clients which are essentially immoral and illegal. This charge, in form and substance, is false. There is no element of truth in it. The exact contrary is the truth. Root is the type of lawyer who, knowing the law and seeing the very right of the matter, advises his clients in accordance therewith, and insists upon his clients following his advice so long as the relation between them continues. Frequently have I heard him tell clients, including the two mentioned by the *World*, namely:—Mr. Whitney and Mr. Ryan, that this thing or that thing they wanted to do or were inclined to do they could not do." In 1924, Henry L. Stimson, also for many years Root's partner, sat next to Mr. Ryan at a dinner: "As usual he spoke very warmly of Mr. Root. He said: 'Root was always keeping me out of trouble and prevented me from doing many things that I wanted to do.' He said particularly of the matter of inflation of securities: 'In those days we generally issued bonds for the property but in the case of common stock and even preferred stock it was not considered necessary to have anything but water behind it—good will. Root always wanted to have value put in and to have the stock represent property.' "

To go back to one sentence in Mr. Clarke's letter, it is fair to point out that there are two irreconcilable points of view on these matters. As Abraham Lincoln once said, "There is a vague popular belief that lawyers are necessarily dishonest." There is a similar belief that the whole practice and spirit of American big business in the end of the nineteenth century was essentially non-moral. Persons who hold to both beliefs are particularly suspicious of the lawyer for big corporations. They think of big business men and their lawyers as being "unscrupulous," meaning, as Thurman Arnold says, "men who were not caught in the common ethics with regard to 'bigness' and who were therefore ready to use practical means to avoid the handicap which such ethics put upon the formation of organizations." "Everybody knows," Root once said, "that some rules for the conduct of life are matters of right and wrong, substantial, essential, and that other rules for the conduct of life are matters of convenience, of form, of method, desirable but not essential." Root kept the two categories perfectly distinct in his mind and neither advised nor countenanced what he considered wrong. He was never willing to be a "company lawyer" who becomes a mere employee devoting all his time to the corporation which employs him. He always kept himself free to drop any client if he chose to do so. He told Theodore Roosevelt that he had great difficulty in making up his mind whether he should act as attorney for the Whitney–Ryan traction interests in New York but finally reached the conclusion that there was no reason why he should not. Root came to realize later that the law had inadequately regulated business practices and he favored changes in the law, but he never doubted that as a lawyer he acted properly in advising clients regarding the rights which they had under the law as it was at the time.

One case may be described here because it illustrates the power of a newspaper story to fasten in the public mind a picture of an individual and of the system with which he is connected, and because it also demonstrates that the investigation of the facts behind such newspaper stories frequently gives the picture quite a different setting. In January, 1900, after Root had become Secretary of War, the New York *World* began the publication of a series of articles about the State Trust Company of which Root had been a director and counsel. The gist of the stories was that Root had advised the Company to make illegal loans, especially one of $2,000,000 to Daniel Shea, an office boy in Thomas Fortune Ryan's office, and one of $435,000 to Louis F. Payn while he was State Superintendent of Insurance. The latter loan was considered significant because the control of the State Trust Company was in the hands of the same men who controlled the American

Surety Company which was under Payn's official jurisdiction. This loan took on added significance because at the time Governor Roosevelt was faced with political difficulties in ousting Payn from his position.

In regard to the Payn loan, the facts were that Payn had what was then a perfectly usual margin loan with a broker who was carrying stocks for him; the actual extent of Payn's obligation was the amount of the margin required for carrying the loan. Payn's wife was dying; he wrote a pathetic letter to William C. Whitney asking him if he would not carry the loan for him. Whitney, who had just lost his own wife after a lingering illness, responded and asked the State Trust Company to take the loan with Payn's collateral and Whitney's personal written guarantee.

The $2,000,000 loan to Ryan's office boy, Daniel Shea, came about as follows: Ryan, P. A. B. Widener, Whitney and others, were members of a syndicate engaged in a merger or reorganization of the Electric Vehicle Company. According to the usual business practice of the times, pending the completion of the arrangement for the final transfer of stock, the stock was held in the name of a nominal holder, who in this case was Shea. Shea of course never had any vestige of interest in the stock. Shea signed a formal note to the Trust Company asking it to take up 20,000 shares of the preferred stock of the Electric Vehicle Company at par, and agreeing to reimburse them with interest at four per cent, the stock to be held by the bank until the loan was paid. The stock at the time had just paid an 8% dividend and was selling at 135, a total value of $2,700,000 for securing the loan of $2,000,000. In addition, Whitney and Widener signed a guarantee of the loan. As part of the same transaction, an additional loan of the same amount was extended and repaid in cash within a short time. The arrangement also provided that a substantial part of the loan was to remain on deposit with the Trust Company. When the cash balance fell just below one million dollars, additional collateral was deposited in the form of 20,000 shares of New York Gas, Light, Heat & Power Company, which shortly produced $2,000,000 Debenture Bonds of the Consolidated Gas Company. Moreover, other companies involved in the plans of the syndicate opened accounts at the Trust Company so that during the entire time the Trust Company had on deposit from these sources more than the face amount of the loan.

The transactions involved two technical violations of the banking law of the state: the law forbade any single secured loan in excess of fifty per cent of the paid-in capital and surplus of the banking institution. The law was so much of a dead letter that the President of the State Trust Company did not even know of its existence until this case was aired. He pointed out in a letter to Root that if they had known of the law, it would have been a simple matter to distribute the loan among the six members of the syndicate, any one of whom could have paid off the whole two million without embarrassment. The second legal provision, of which the President of the State Trust Company was also ignorant and which he considered entirely ridiculous, forbade loans to any director. The Shea loan was in part at least a loan to Ryan who was a director; Widener, his co-guarantor, was not even a stockholder. Since the business practice of the time considered such transactions perfectly proper, the transaction could have been made entirely in Widener's name had they considered such a course necessary. The legal technicalities are relatively unimportant; it is significant that this transaction was of such a usual type in those days that the admittedly able and diligent bank examiner, who had in routine course examined the State Trust Company a little while before, had made no comment on either the size of the loan or the fact that a director was involved. Superintendent of Banking Kilburn, in parts of his report which the *World* reproduced in fine print, indicated a belief in the general soundness and good management of the Trust Company. The newspaper scandal did not interrupt the steadily increasing prosperity of the Trust Company and despite the outraged protests of the *World*, the whole affair blew over quickly. It seems to have been inspired by a discharged employee of the State Trust Company and persons connected with a rival institution. Roosevelt's part in the matter is not wholly clear but it seems to have been satisfactorily explained to Ryan and Whitney and the brief scandal enabled Roosevelt to triumph in his row with Platt over the ouster of Payn and the appointment of his successor.

Despite the absorbing pressure of his law practice, however, Root continued to take an active interest in municipal affairs and to widen steadily his field of political influence in the state and the nation.

The Lexow Committee, appointed in January, 1894, had revealed almost every imaginable evil existing in New York City, with the Police Department protecting and promoting saloons, gambling dens and houses of prostitution. It was the kind of sensational revelation of scandal which New Yorkers need to stir them from their lethargic acquiescence in corrupt political misrule. Root was now a member of the Citizens' Committee of Seventy, reminiscent of the one which had organized to overthrow Tweed. His correspondence throws no light on the offer of the mayoralty nomination to Roosevelt who was tiring of the post of United States Civil Service Commissioner, although he had been glad to continue serving under Cleveland after Harrison's defeat in 1892. The Committee of Seventy put up William L. Strong, a respectable but not notable business man, and rallied to his support the Republicans, the State Democrats, the Independent County Democrats and the Anti–Tammany Democrats. The Committee's platform emphatically asserted that state and national party affiliations should play no part in city elections. The fusion candidate was elected over Tammany's Hugh J. Grant by a majority of 45,000.

March 28th, 1895, Root made an impressive and vigorous speech at a great mass meeting at Cooper Union in favor of the city's reform measures. Speaking of a bill designed to liberate legal real estate sales from the control of Richard Croker, the Tammany boss, Root went so far as to say that any Republican who voted against the bill in the Legislature would thereby prove conclusively that his vote had been bought. "That was a frank statement of Mr. Root's personal conviction," the *Tribune* remarked on April 5th, "and it necessarily carried much weight. . . ."

QUESTIONS

1. The charge was made against Root that he "devises legal forms to accomplish purposes of his clients which are essentially immoral and illegal." Jessup replies that Root "neither advised nor countenanced what he considered wrong." How likely is it that Root's sense of right and wrong was influenced by the perspective of his clients?

2. William Whitney observed that "I have had many lawyers who have told me what I cannot do. Mr. Root is the only lawyer to tell me how to do what I want to do." Does this comment suggest that Root was an exceptionally able lawyer, or that he was perhaps lacking in scruples? When does an able lawyer become an unethical lawyer?

3. Consider State Trust's loan to one of its directors and Jessup's observation that "[t]he legal technicalities are relatively unimportant" and that "it is significant that this transaction was of such a usual type in those days...." Is Jessup arguing that the loan was acceptable because "everybody did it?" How should Root have responded to the view of State Trust's President that the law prohibiting loans to directors was "ridiculous?" Is the bank examiner's failure to enforce the law relevant?

4. Consider the guarantee by William Whitney of the loan from State Trust to New York's Superintendent of Insurance Louis Payn. State Trust "was in the hands of the same men who controlled the American Surety Company which was under Payn's official jurisdiction." Was this loan a disguised bribe or an attempt to offer a bribe? How similar or dissimilar was Root's involvement in the loan to Hoyt Moore's participation in the corruption of Judge Johnson (see Chapter 2 supra)?

5. Was the State Trust loan to Payn in keeping with Root's aspirations to the ideals of public service? Did Root's work on behalf of business interests undermine his credibility in fighting government corruption at Tammany Hall?

D. GIVING ADVICE

Counseling at the Limits of the Law: An Exercise in the Jurisprudence and Ethics of Lawyering

Stephen L. Pepper
104 Yale L.J. 1545 (1995).

A. Summary of the Problem

The primary job of the lawyer is to give the client access to the law in its multitude of facets. The litigator provides access to the dispute resolution mechanisms that are our civil and criminal courts and to the substantive law that they apply; the "deal maker" provides access to the structuring aspects of the law, regimes of contract, corporate law, securities, property, and trust; the family law lawyer and the estate planner provide access to systems of law that include both court resolution and structuring by legal mechanisms; and so on with all sorts of law and lawyers. Each of these functions combines the lawyer's knowledge of the law with the client's need for or ability to profit from access to that law. This is true across the spectrum of law, whether procedural or substantive; whether concerning the mechanics and structures of various legal devices such as contracts, deeds, and trusts, or the legal entities that can be formed from combinations of such structures (a corporation or set of corporations, for example, or a condominium, the limited partnership that builds it, and the condominium association that will manage it).

The client often wants or needs to understand what the law is in order to evaluate options and make decisions about his or her life, and the most common function of lawyers (across specializations and areas of practice) is to provide that knowledge. Knowledge of the law, however, is an instrument that can be used to follow the law or to avoid it. Knowing that the speed limit is fifty-five miles per hour on an isolated, rarely patrolled stretch of rural highway will lead some to drive at or below fifty-five, but will lead others to drive at sixty-three miles per hour or faster. Similarly, knowing that the only penalty for engaging in unfair labor practices is back pay and reinstatement for individual harmed employees can lead the employer/client either to avoid such practices or to engage in them intentionally. Knowledge of the law thus is two-edged. When the lawyer is in a situation in which the client may well use the relevant knowledge of the law to violate the law or avoid its norms, what ought the lawyer to do? That question is the subject of this Article.

Two brief examples will set the stage. The client is negotiating a multiyear contract, anticipating that the first two or three years will be very profitable, and the subsequent two or three years significantly less so. This client's inquiries about the consequences of breach three years down the line and the docket delays in the relevant courts lead the lawyer to believe the client is considering breach of contract before he has entered into it. Or imagine the client whose elderly wife or parent is desperately ill and in immense pain, with no chance of recovery and no end in sight. The client wants legal advice about the possibility of consensual euthanasia, and the lawyer is wondering whether, in addition to informing the client that the substantive law would consider this to be murder, she also ought to include advice about the possibility of prosecutorial discretion or jury nullification. How ought these lawyers to proceed? Should they provide accurate information about the law that may well facilitate an intentional, planned breach of contract or a homicide? What guidance—what rules or principles—ought the profession or the law provide to lawyers in such situations?

Our legal system is premised on the assumption that law is intended to be known or knowable, that law is in its nature public information. The "rule of law" as we understand it requires promulgation. (Consider for a moment the alternative possibility of secret "law.") And one fundamental, well-understood aspect of the lawyer's role is to be the conduit for that promulgation. In a complex legal environment much law cannot be known and acted upon, cannot function as law, without lawyers to make it accessible to those for whom it is relevant. Thus, in our society lawyers are necessary for much of our law to be known, to be functional. The traditional understanding is that lawyers as professionals act for the client's benefit in providing that access to the law. Under this understanding, lawyers do not function as law enforcement officers or as judges of their clients in providing knowledge of the law; the choices to be made concern the client's life and affairs, and they are therefore primarily the client's choices to make.

The limits on the assistance lawyers may provide to their clients have commonly been articulated and thought of as the "bounds of the law." The lawyer may not become an active participant in the client's unlawful activity, and does not have immunity if she becomes an aider and abettor of unlawful conduct. The difficulty arises in deciding whether providing accurate, truthful information about the law—the core function of lawyering—can also be considered active assistance in violation of the law in situations in which the lawyer knows the information may well lead to or facilitate the client's unlawful conduct. The answers or guides to that inquiry are disturbingly unclear. There are no reported cases of civil or criminal liability on the part of the lawyer, or of professional discipline, clearly based only upon providing the client with accurate legal information. On the other hand, the legal limits are not stated in a way to make it clear that providing such advice is within the proper bounds of lawyering. Nor do these limits provide much assistance in knowing when giving the advice is proper and when it is not. And while the case law does not ground liability on such conduct, courts have rarely held or clearly stated that such conduct does not provide a basis for liability. The case law is for the most part silent. Does the client as citizen have an entitlement to knowledge of the law? Or does the lawyer have an ethical or legal obligation not to provide that knowledge when it may facilitate violation of the law or its norms?

* * *

H.   Distinctions, Guidance, and Complexity

. . . . The civil/criminal line is the one most accepted and articulated by lawyers. But that acceptance and articulation are not particularly deep or thought through, as the water pollution and tax audit examples show.*

---

* Earlier in this Article, *id.* at 1551, Professor Pepper raises two hypotheticals:

Assume an Environmental Protection Agency water pollution regulation, widely publicized to relevant industries, prohibiting discharge of ammonia at amounts greater than .050 grams per liter of effluent. The client owns a rural plant that discharges am- monia in its effluent, the removal of which would be very expensive. The lawyer knows from informal sources that: (1) violations of .075 grams per liter or less are ignored because of a limited enforcement budget; and (2) EPA inspection in rural areas is rare, and in such areas enforcement officials usually issue a warning prior to applying sanctions

Each of these presents a situation in which formally criminal conduct may well be facilitated, yet most lawyers would think it appropriate to provide the client with information about the law. For that reason, among others discussed above, the criminal/civil distinction is not nearly as helpful as it first appears. The malum in se/malum prohibitum distinction may well be the most helpful, but it has several quite different formulations. The combination of one or the other form of the malum in se/malum prohibitum distinction with the criminal/civil line probably comes closest to the operational limit applied by most lawyers. Although the conduct at issue in the water pollution and the tax audit examples is possibly criminal, because it is not malum in se, most lawyers would provide the information. And when both criminality and clear moral wrongfulness are combined, most lawyers will hesitate and may well not provide the facilitating information about the law. Unfortunately, the malum in se characterization is itself both unclear and intimately connected to personal morality, and thus subject to great dispute and difference of opinion. Any combination of the two factors includes the weaknesses of both. Thus the combination does not provide clear or rulelike guidance, although it is more determinative and helpful than either distinction alone.

We can try to join the factors together—perhaps in a grid, as on the chart on the following page—but this does not generate clarity either. Rather, it provides us with a graphic demonstration of complexity: seven possible distinctions, each of which, as discussed above, has significant problems and variations within it. (An attempt at including those variations would make for an even more bewildering chart.) The lawyer facing the kind of situation explored here could, having considered each of the factors, place a check in each appropriate box of the grid. The more checks on the left side of the grid, the more concerned the lawyer ought to be about providing the client with information about the law. Or the lawyer, as she goes through such a process, might give a weight to each check mark (a number from 1 to 4, perhaps) based upon the importance of each factor to the situation at issue. Attempting such an exercise with one or two of the examples is surprisingly interesting. The checks spread out in no clearly determinative pattern (usually a significant number on each side), but the process of deciding which side the check goes on, and how important that factor ought to be, is clearly helpful even though it provides no direct answer.

unless the violation is extreme (more than 1.5 grams per liter). Is it appropriate for the lawyer to educate the client concerning these enforcement-related facts even though it may motivate the client to violate the .050 gram limit?

A second, well-known example is the client who wants to file a tax return reporting a favorable outcome based upon an arguable interpretation of the law. The lawyer is confident the IRS would challenge the client's return if it became aware of this interpretation and would be highly likely to succeed in the event of litigation. If that were to occur, the penalties would likely be only the tax due plus interest. The lawyer knows that in the past the audit rate for this type of return has been less than two percent, and knows that this fact is likely to lead this client to take the dubious position on her return. Ought the lawyer to communicate this information to the client?

FIGURE 1. Distinctions Discussed in Part II

Criminal Violation (Law as prohibition)	Civil Violation (Law as cost)

Conduct *Malum in Se* (Conduct wrong in itself)	Conduct *Malum Prohibitum* (Conduct "merely" prohibited)

Enforced Law	Rarely Enforced Law	Unenforced Law

Enforcement of Law	Procedural Law	Substantive Legal Rules

Private Information	Public Information

Lawyer–Initiated Discussion	Client–Initiated Discussion

Likely information will be used to assist unlawful conduct	Unlikely information will be used to assist unlawful conduct

This suggests, in turn, that the value of the factors—or of the grid—is primarily in providing a process to help analyze problem situations. The distinctions draw the lawyer's attention to a number of different perspectives from which a particular situation can be seen, and allow for separate consideration of each. The process thus helps discipline a lawyer's consideration of the situation, providing a mechanism for initiating and refining the lawyer's intuition. Given the complexity and the lack of determinative guides, refined and reflective intuition may be the most one can seek. One aspect of the situation, one factor in the grid, will just seem more important. Often it will be the malum in se/malum prohibitum distinction: is there something fundamentally wrong with the conduct the lawyer may be assisting? Or it may seem that the advice is not really about "law," but is really about the enforcement of law and how to avoid it. And while the sense that one factor in the particular situation is more significant—that the conduct is really wrong (or not), or the advice is about avoiding detection rather than about more central aspects of "law"—leaves us relying essentially on the lawyer's intuition, it is at least an intuition that has been forced to consider the situation from the vantage of a number of possible distinguishing factors, a number of possibly significant perspectives. Thus, the explorations to this point are substantially useful, although far from providing lawyers with a rule or set of rules to use when confronted with the problem. . . .

[I]t should be noted that the questions we have been exploring could be consolidated and seen as aspects of three more inclusive questions. First, does the conduct of the client that may be facilitated involve real wrongfulness? The first two lines on the chart (the criminal/civil and malum in se/malum prohibitum distinctions) deal with that question. Second, is the advice or information to be conveyed about "law"? The middle three lines on the chart (dealing with the knot of issues connected to enforcement of law and with the distinction between private information and public information) are facets of that fundamental jurisprudential question, what is law? Third, will the advice or information incite the client to engage in the conduct? The bottom two lines on the chart (dealing with initiation of the subject and likelihood of the client acting unlawfully) relate to that final factor. My own sense is that such a consolidation masks more than it reveals, however. Each of the seven distinctions concerns a quite separate issue. . . .

* * *

V.   Conclusion

. . . . The first rule or principle is that the client has a presumptive right to know the law governing his or her situation, understanding "law" in the widely defined contemporary sense. The second rule or principle is that the lawyer has a presumptive moral obligation to engage in a counseling conversation if there is reason to foresee that the client may violate the law or a significant legal or moral norm. When applying these rules, and in determining when and why the presumptions have been overcome, the seven distinctions developed in this Article will be helpful. In addition to that analytic assistance, however, lawyers working their way through these problems ought to be aware that what is necessary to reach a solution is the exercise and development of their own practical wisdom. In such deliberations, reliance on character—on implicit perception and evaluation, on moral habit—is unavoidable. For this reason, in working on the professional ethics of lawyering in the larger sense we—practitioners, teachers, the profession—ought to (1) formulate a set of such tentative rules and principles and (2) work to create a culture that will cultivate a professional practical wisdom for applying them. The dualism here is an effort to suggest the compatibility of a "rights"-oriented perspective, which views the primary job of lawyers as providing clients with access to the law to which they have something resembling a right, with a "virtue"- and "character"-oriented approach to the professional life of the lawyer. We need the rules and principles to protect clients who are often vulnerable or dependent in relation to professionals, and to protect, in turn, third persons who often are vulnerable in relation to the conduct of clients. We need practical wisdom because the rules and principles simply will not be sufficient to deal with the moral questions of lawyering.

QUESTIONS

1. "Everybody knows," Phillip Jessup reports Elihu Root to have once said, "that some rules for the conduct of life are matters of right and wrong, substantial, essential, and that other rules for the conduct of life are matters of convenience, of form, of method, desirable but not essential." Does Root's distinction resemble Stephen Pepper's distinction between conduct *malum in se* and *malum prohibitum*? What are the dangers inherent in lawyers making these types of distinctions about the law?

2. Professor Pepper suggests including the following rule in the Model Rules: "When it appears more probable than not that the client will use legal information or advice to facilitate conduct which (1) is clearly prohibited by law and (2) involves what is by clear societal consensus a serious and substantial moral wrong, the lawyer shall not provide the client with the legal advice or information." Stephen L. Pepper, Counseling at the Limits of the Law, supra, at n.80. What difficulties could arise in applying this standard to the following situations:

(a) a lawyer in the 1850's advised an abolitionist operating an underground railroad as to which states in the North enforced fugitive slave laws;

(b) a lawyer in the 1950's advised a civil rights activist that refusing to leave a segregated lunch counter can at most result in a fine of $50 for unlawful trespass;

(c) a lawyer in the 1980's advised an antiabortion protestor that authorities were not enforcing laws prohibiting protestors from standing within a certain distance of an abortion clinic; and

(d) a lawyer in the 1980's advised the chief financial officer of a multinational corporation (i) that bribes of foreign officials are regularly described by other corporations on their financial statements as "fees" paid to foreign "consultants," (ii) that doing so is a clear violation of the Foreign Corrupt Practices Act, (iii) that such bribes are rarely detected by United States law enforcement authorities, and (iv) that his corporation was doing business in countries where there was a societal consensus that it was acceptable and at times even necessary to bribe government officials.

3. In The People of the State of Colorado v. Bernard D. Morley, 725 P.2d 510 (Colo.1986), Morley was disbarred for knowingly counseling undercover officers posing as clients in an illegal prostitution scheme. Morley was found to have received payment for advice concerning the Colorado Escort Service Code and ways to structure the prostitution scheme to avoid detection and prosecution. The court held that disbarment was appropriate because "[a]ny lesser sanction would unduly depreciate the seriousness of the respondent's misconduct in the eyes of both the public and the legal profession." Id. at 519. Was Morley's advice to his "clients" permissible under Professor Pepper's analysis distinguishing between conduct malum in se and malum prohibitum?

4. Although Professor Pepper organizes his approach to the client counseling problem schematically, he ultimately eschews a rigid categorical approach and falls back on stressing the connection between practical wisdom and the moral questions of lawyering. Anthony Kronman also connects professional ethics to practical wisdom:

> preeminent. . . . [is] the trait of prudence or practical wisdom, which even today we view as a quality of character. When we attribute good judgment to a person, we imply more than he has broad knowledge and a quick intelligence. We mean also to suggest that he shows a certain calmness in his deliberations, together with a balanced sympathy toward the various concerns of which his situation (or the situation of the client) requires that he take account.

Anthony Kronman, The Lost Lawyer 15–16 (1993).

(a) How would the practical wisdom described by Kronman help a lawyer resolve some of the problems described by Pepper?

(b) Practical wisdom is often the product of experience. However, more experienced lawyers are not always wise in their ethical decision making. Are there some very experienced lawyers mentioned in this casebook who did not display practical wisdom? How might experience, far from reinforcing practical wisdom, have undermined their sense of balance?

CHAPTER 8

THE ADVERSARY

A. THE ADVOCACY PARADIGM

Charles P. Curtis, "The Advocate" From *It's Your Law*
The Adversary Process

Justice is a chilly virtue. It is of high importance that we be introduced into the inhospitable halls of justice by a friend. I think we neglect the fact that the first function of the lawyer, and the first great purpose of the devotion which a lawyer owes to his client, is the overcoming of this feeling of unfriendliness. The first duty of the bar is to make sure that everyone who feels the need of a friend in court shall have one, and I am not talking only of the poor and indigent. They obviously need a friend, and a good judge will fill the need if the bar does not. Nor only of those whose cause we detest. A proper sense of advocacy will take care of them, and I will speak of that in its place. I mean everyone, including those who seem least to need a friend, those who have the most respect for the law and who are usually the least familiar with it and the most fearful.

But if the devotion a lawyer owes to his client were no more than friendliness, if it were simply to serve the purpose of taking the chill off justice, there would be no more to say. We make greater demands upon our lawyers than that. They must be not only our friends. They must be our champions. For the way we administer justice is by an adversary proceeding, which is as much as to say, we set the parties fighting. This has been so for some time; in fact, according to Max Radin, since about the fourth or the fifth century B.C. in Rome, when, Radin says, the judge's task changed from determining the truth to the umpiring of a competition. "At a certain special stage in the history of Western society," Radin said, "the way in which it was done was to call upon the judge to umpire a contest. His task was not to determine truth, but to decide who had the best of a competition—a competition that was not originally one of argument, though it soon became one. The place and time of this event can be set with fair probability at Rome somewhere in the fifth or fourth centuries B.C. For many modern lawyers it is difficult to conceive of a trial as anything else, although the words 'trial' and 'verdict' might have called attention to the fact that these things professed to be something quite different."

. . . .

I find it quite impossible to understand trial by ordeal, where justice apparently used to be put to the touch of a small miracle, but anyone who has been anywhere near a piece of determined litigation will readily understand trial by battle.

"One other method of proof was one introduced into England by the Normans, and this was trial by battle. In civil cases it was not fought between the parties themselves, but between their respective champions. . . . We very soon find from the rolls that there was a professional band of champions who undertook business all over the country; courts would arrange the dates of battle so that the champions could fit in their engagements conveniently. Some very great landowners, such as the large monasteries, were so constantly involved in litigation that they maintained their own full-time champions. But in criminal cases battle was a much more serious affair. It lay when a private person brought a criminal charge against another, and was fought by the accuser and accused in person. It was deadly; if the defeated defendant was not already slain in the battle he was immediately hanged on the gallows which stood ready." Theodore F. T. Plucknett, A Concise History of the Common Law 104–05 (1929).

There are some subjects of litigation in which the adversary proceeding is an admirable way of administering justice. One wise judge implied as much when Charles E. Wyzanski said, "A political libel suit is the modern substitute for ordeal by battle. It is the means which society has chosen to induce bitter partisans to wager money instead of exchanging bloody noses." But litigation by an adversary proceeding is the way we cut the knot of many disputes in which it is disastrously inappropriate. Divorces, the custody of children, will contests, almost any kind of dispute which springs from family or equally intimate dissension—there a broken bone is more easily mendable. And it is intolerably too often true that a criminal trial turns into an adversary proceeding. "Criminal justice is concerned with the pathology of the body politic. In administering the criminal law, judges wield the most awesome surgical instruments of society. A criminal trial, it has been well said, should have the atmosphere of the operating room. The presiding judge determines the atmosphere. He is not an umpire who enforces the rules of a game, or merely a moderator between contestants. If he is adequate to his functions, the moral authority which he radiates will impose the indispensable standards of dignity and austerity upon all those who participate in a criminal trial." Felix Frankfurter, dissenting in Sacher v. United States, 343 U.S. 1 at 37, 38 (1952).

What, then, is the justification for this approach to justice, other than the fact we are several centuries used to it and aside from the fact that spectators in small communities and newspaper readers in cities enjoy the spectacle? It seems to me that the justification of the adversary proceeding is the satisfaction of the parties, and not our satisfaction, except we too are prospective litigants. This is a rational justification of the adversary approach to justice. Along this line, what the law is trying to do is give the algebraic maximum of satisfaction to both parties. This is a crude, but indeed it is not a bad, definition of the justice which the adversary proceeding provides. The law is trying to do justice between the parties for the parties rather than for us, trying to give them their own justice so far as possible and so far as compatible with what may be distinguished as our justice.

. . . .

A Lawyer's Loyalties

. . . . Is not the lawyer an officer of the court? Why doesn't the court have first claim on his loyalty? No, in a paradoxical way. The lawyer's official duty, required of him indeed by the court, is to devote himself to the client. He has two masters, and it is sometimes hard to say which comes first. There are occasions when our system of justice seems to give the nod to the client.

Lord Brougham, in his defense of Queen Caroline in her divorce case, told the House of Lords, "I once before took occasion to remind your Lordships, which was unnecessary, but there are many whom it may be needful to remind, that an advocate, by the sacred duty which he owes his client, knows in the discharge of that office but one person in the world— that client and no other ... Nay, separating even the duties of a patriot from those of an advocate, and casting them if need be to the wind, he must go on reckless of the consequences, if his fate it should unhappily be to involve his country in confusion for his client's protection."

Lord Brougham was a great advocate, and when he made this statement he was arguing a great case, the divorce of Queen Caroline from George IV before the House of Lords. Plainly he was exerting more than his learning and more than his legal ability. Years later he explained this to William Forsyth, the author of a book on lawyers called *Hortensius*, who had asked him what he meant. Before you read Brougham's reply, let me remind you that the king, George IV, was the one who was pressing the divorce which Brougham was defending, and that George had contracted a secret marriage, while he was heir apparent, with Mrs. Fitzherbert, a Roman Catholic. Brougham knew this, and knew too that it was enough to deprive the king of his crown under the Act of Settlement. Brougham wrote:

"The real truth is, that the statement was anything rather than a deliberate and well-considered opinion. It was a menace, and it was addressed chiefly to George IV, but also to wiser men, such as Castlereagh and Wellington. I was prepared, *in case of necessity*, that is, in case the Bill passed the Lords, to do two things—first, to resist it in the Commons *with the country at my back*; but next, if need be, to dispute the King's title, to show he had forfeited the crown by marrying a Catholic, in the words of the Act, 'as if he were naturally dead.' What I said was fully understood by Geo. IV; perhaps by the Duke of Castlereagh, and I am confident it would have prevented them from pressing the Bill beyond a certain point."

Lord Brougham's menace has become the classic statement of the loyalty which a lawyer owes to his client, perhaps because, being a menace, it is so extreme. And yet the Canons of Ethics of the American Bar Association are scarcely more moderate. "The lawyer owes 'entire devotion to the interest of the client, warm zeal in the maintenance and defense of his rights and the exertion of his utmost learning and ability,' to the end that nothing be taken or withheld from him, save by the rules of law, legally applied." Canon 15

How entire is this devotion and how warm is this zeal? How much *alter* do they together put in the lawyer's *ego*? How far from himself do they draw a lawyer? How much less than himself, as a patriot and a citizen and an individual, do they require a lawyer to be? These are hard questions, as hard to ask as I think they are hard to answer.

. . . .

. . . . [A]cting for others is in a different category of behavior than acting for yourself and I think its ethics are different. Let me examine this proposition with some care and in some detail.

The person for whom you are acting very reasonably expects you to treat him better than you do other people, which is just another way of saying that you owe him a higher standard of conduct than you owe to others. This goes back a long way. It is the pre-platonic ethics which Socrates disposed of at the very outset of the *Republic*; that is, that justice consists of doing good to your friends and harm to your enemies. A lawyer, therefore, insensibly finds himself treating his client better than others; and therefore others worse than his client. A lawyer, or a trustee, or anyone acting for another, has lower standards of conduct toward outsiders than he has toward his clients or his beneficiaries against the outsiders. He is required to treat outsiders as if they were barbarians and enemies. The more devotion and zeal the lawyer owes to his client, the less he owes to others when he is acting for his client. It is as if a man had only so much virtue, and the more he gives to one, the less he has available for anyone else. The upshot is that a man whose business it is to act for others finds himself, in his dealings on his client's behalf with outsiders, acting on a lower standard than he would if he were acting for himself, lower than any standard his client himself would be willing to act on, lower in fact than anyone on his own.

. . . .

I will give you a personal case. I was a trustee under a will. My co-trustee was away, and had left me with the duty of trying to sell a piece of real estate. I got an offer of $50,000 which I agreed orally to accept. They left to draw up the agreement for me to sign, but before they had it ready I received a cash offer of $55,000. So I was on the spot, for under the Statute of Frauds, as any lawyer knows, I was not legally bound on an oral contract to sell real estate.

I didn't know quite what to do. I called up the purchaser and the broker and told them to bring their lawyer with them. And I said to them, "I have received an offer of $55,000, and either you are going to make me an offer of $55,000 cash or I am going to take up that offer and go back on my word, which I gave you. Unless you," then I turned to the lawyer, "can show me out of the correspondence that I am bound under the Statute of Frauds.'' By way of peroration I added, ''If you want to call me a son of a bitch, do, because I am going to do just that, and I heartily agree that I am a son of a bitch to do it.''

I didn't like it. They were very angry. Their lawyer was no help. He had the correspondence, but he didn't point to anything I had written which legally bound me.

I went back to my office, turned my file over to one of my partners, and said, ''Am I bound under the statute?'' My partner took the file, came back the next day, and to my great relief, he had spelled enough out of the correspondence to convince me that I was bound. I called up the lawyer and laughed at him somewhat, and everyone was happy; except that no one complimented me and no one expressed any disagreement with what I had called myself.

I did not enjoy the situation, but I was confident that I had done right. Years later Professor Austin W. Scott, who has written the one and only best book on trusts and trustees, told me there was an English case I ought to read. It was not so long ago—1950—in London. Mrs. Simpson—not the one you think—rented a house in London and decided she wanted to buy it. She offered the owners, who were three trustees, 6,000 pounds, and they agreed. All the terms of the sale were agreed to, except who should pay the expenses of the sale, which amounted to 142 pounds. At that point, one of the several beneficiaries of the trust, a Canon Buttle, also offered 6,000 pounds. Mrs. Simpson then agreed to pay the expenses. This made hers the better offer, and a contract of sale was drawn up, signed by Mrs. Simpson, and signed by one, only one, of the three trustees. Canon Buttle promptly offered 6,500 pounds, which made his the better offer. The trustees informed the canon that they felt that the sale to Mrs. Simpson could not properly be cancelled and Canon Buttle brought suit against them, to require them to sell the property to him for 6,500 pounds, substantially more than the 6,142 pounds which was Mrs. Simpson's offer.

Was the canon right? This is what Judge Wynn–Perry said. ''The trustees felt in a position of great embarrassment. They felt in honour bound to proceed with the proposed sale to Mrs. Simpson.... They felt that all considerations of commercial morality required that they should proceed with the contract.'' Let me interrupt to remind you that two of the three trustees had not signed it and that it had not yet been delivered to the lady. The judge went on, ''My view is that the trustees and their solicitors acted on an incorrect principle. The only consideration which was present to their minds was that they had gone so far in the negotiations with Mrs. Simpson that they could not properly, from the point of view of commercial morality, resile from those negotiations.''

Fortunately, these sad stories usually have a happier ending than you expect. Mrs. Simpson raised her offer to 6,600 pounds, and everyone, including Canon Buttle, felt better. It would have been interesting to have sat in on the conversations which we may suppose were held between the good canon and the solicitors for the trustees, while the churchman argued for the strict law and the lawyers argued for the principles of morality. But the law was against the lawyers and against the conscience of the trustees, as it was against mine.

The ethical problems of a lawyer are not so simple as the canon, either canon for that matter. . . .

.   .   .   .

The Guilty Client

.   .   .   .

No, there is nothing unethical in taking a bad case or defending the guilty or advocating what you don't believe in. It is ethically neutral. It's a free choice. . . .

I will give you as good an example as I know that a lawyer can make a case as noble as a cause. I want to tell you how Arthur D. Hill came into the Sacco–Vanzetti case.* It was through Felix Frankfurter, and it is his story. Frankfurter wrote some of it in the newspapers shortly after Arthur's death, and he told it to me in more detail just after the funeral.

When the conviction of Sacco and Vanzetti had been sustained by the Supreme Judicial Court of Massachusetts, there was left an all but hopeless appeal to the federal courts, that is, to the Supreme Court. "It was at this stage," Felix Frankfurter said, "that I was asked if I would try to enlist Arthur Hill's legal services to undertake a final effort on behalf of the men, hopeless as it seemed, by appeal to the Federal law."

Frankfurter called Arthur Hill up and said that he had a very serious matter to discuss with him. "In that case," said Arthur Hill, "we had better have a good lunch first. I will meet you at the Somerset Club for lunch and afterwards you will tell me about it." They lunched together at the Somerset Club, then after lunch crossed Beacon Street and sat on a bench in Boston Common overlooking the Frog Pond. And Frankfurter asked Arthur Hill if he would undertake this final appeal of the Sacco–Vanzetti case to the Supreme Court.

Arthur Hill said, "If the president of the biggest bank in Boston came to me and said that his wife had been convicted of murder, but he wanted me to see if there was any possible relief in the Supreme Court of the United States and offered me a fee of $50,000 to make such an effort, of course I would take the retainer as would, I suppose, everybody else at the bar. It would be a perfectly honorable thing to see whether there was anything in the record which laid a basis for an appeal to the Federal Court."

"I do not see how I can decline a similar effort on behalf of Sacco and Vanzetti simply because they are poor devils against whom the feeling of the community is strong and they have no money with which to hire me. I

_____
* See testimony from the Sacco-Vanzetti case at page 598 infra—ed.

don't particularly enjoy the proceedings that will follow, but I don't see how I can possibly refuse to make the effort."

Arthur Hill took it as a law case. To him it was a case, not a cause. He was not the partisan, he was the advocate. I want to add just one other thing, which Arthur Hill said to me, years later. It sets a sort of seal upon his conduct in the case, as a case, and not a cause. I used to meet him fairly often walking downtown, because we both often stopped at the Boston Athenaeum and we would go on downtown together. One morning I was stupid enough to ask him an indiscreet question. I had expressed my own opinion on the guilt or innocence of Sacco and Vanzetti. I said I thought that on the whole it seemed to me probable that they had been guilty, and asked Arthur what he thought. Arthur looked at me—it was years later, twenty years later—smiled, and said, "I have never said, and I cannot say, what I think on that subject because, you see, Charlie, I was their counsel."

I met Judge Thayer once. This, too, was some years after the trial. We were in his chambers in Boston settling an automobile accident case then on trial before him. We were all standing, and he was standing between me and the window, so that when I looked out the window behind him I saw the top of the Charlestown Jail where the death house was in the background of a sort of living portrait of Judge Thayer framed by the window. I wasn't thinking anything much about it until I realized that Judge Thayer was no longer talking about our case, but strutting up and down and boasting that he had been fortunate enough to be on the bench when those sons of bitches were convicted. I had a chill, and I comforted and warmed myself over thoughts of Arthur Hill.

I have talked lovingly about the practice of the law. I have spoken unsparingly, as I would to another lawyer. In a way the practice of the law is like free speech. It defends what we hate as well as what we most love. For every lawyer whose conscience may be pricked, there is another whose virtue is tickled. Every case has two sides, and for every lawyer on the wrong side, there's another on the right side. I don't know any other career that offers an ampler opportunity for both the enjoyment of virtue and the exercise of vice, or, if you please, the exercise of virtue and the enjoyment of vice....

QUESTIONS

1. Compare Curtis's description of the adversary process with the description of the advocacy paradigm by Fuller and Randall in the ABA-AALS Joint Conference Report, supra Chapter 6. How are they different? Do you agree with Curtis's definition of justice?

2. How does Curtis's focus on the "satisfaction of the parties" shape his view of a lawyer's role in an adversary proceeding?

3. Consider Curtis's handling of the situation where he was a trustee under a will and was selling real estate for the trust. How would you resolve the problem?

4. In what way is civil litigation today similar to trial by battle in medieval times? Look back at *Lucido v. Cravath,* supra Chapter 5. Did that case become a trial by battle? Who won?

5. Curtis observes that a lawyer's loyalty to a client requires him "to treat outsiders as if they were barbarians and enemies." Is this statement hyperbole? What are the dangers inherent in such an approach to representation?

6. Was Lord Brougham overstepping the bounds of proper advocacy when he implicitly threatened to disclose King George's earlier marriage contract if the Lords granted the King a divorce from Queen Caroline? See Model Rule 3.4(e).

7. It is remarkable that in the *Sacco and Vanzetti* case (about which you will read more later in this Chapter) Arthur Hill, counsel for Sacco and Vanzetti in the appeal, was less willing than Webster Thayer, the presiding judge, to talk about the merits of the case. Was Hill's objectivity a good characteristic for an advocate?

8. In a recent antitrust case in New Jersey, the plaintiffs' lawyer "repeatedly expressed his opinion as to the merits of [the] case, the credibility of witnesses, and the culpability of [the defendant] even as to claims not legitimately set forth by plaintiffs. On more than one occasion, [the] Court admonished [plaintiffs' lawyer] to refrain from including his personal opinion in his argument; despite such orders, he continued to assert his views with vigor." Fineman v. Armstrong World Indus., 774 F.Supp. 266, 271 (D.N.J.1991), aff'd in part and rev'd in part, vacated in part, remanded for a new trial, 980 F.2d 171 (3d Cir. 1992). The Third Circuit concurred in the district court's order granting a new trial because of this and other lawyer misconduct. As Curtis correctly observes, it is "improper for a lawyer to assert in argument his personal belief in his client's innocence or in the justice of his cause." Why?

9. Curtis poses another hypothetical in a later part of his discussion: "An attorney is in court with his client, who has been convicted, when he comes up for sentence. The clerk, or whoever it is that has the criminal records, tells the judge that this man has no record, and the judge then puts him on probation. As a matter of fact, he has a record, and his attorney knows it. Is it the attorney's duty to speak up?"

B. Gathering Evidence

Douglass Harcleroad, B.A. University of Iowa 1970; J.D. University of Oregon 1973; Assistant District Attorney for Lane County, Oregon, 1974–85; Lane County District Attorney since 1985 (ran unopposed three times) (lists among his "accomplishments as District Attorney" that "[i]n excess of 95% of the defendants charged with crimes by the Lane County District Attorney's Office are convicted either by negotiated guilty pleas or trials."); former President of the Oregon District Attorneys Association; Adjunct

Professor at the University of Oregon School of Law (teaches the Prosecution Clinic in the evening).

State of Oregon v. Conan Wayne Hale

(Case No. 10–96–04830) (1996)

THE DISTRICT COURT OF THE STATE OF
OREGON FOR LANE COUNTY

STATE OF OREGON)
) AFFIDAVIT FOR SEARCH WARRANT
COUNTY OF LANE)

I, Dennis A. Williams, being first duly sworn on oath, do hereby depose and say:

That I am a Detective with the Eugene Police Department and have been employed in law enforcement for over 24 years . . . . .

. . . I was assigned to assist in an investigation involving the murder of three youths, Brandon M. Williams, Kristal R. Bendele, and Patrick M. Finley, which occurred during the late evening hours of December 20, 1995 or the early morning hours of December 21, 1995.

In connection with this investigation I have spoken to Lane County Sheriff's Deputies, other Eugene Police Detectives, Oregon State Police officers and District Attorney Investigator Tom Yates. I have learned from investigative team briefings and specifically from Sgt Earl McMullen, Lane County Sheriff's office, that one of the victims of the murder was Patrick M. Finley. That when Patrick Finley's body was discovered in a remote area near McGowan Creek that he was wearing a coat from the burglary which occurred on December 19, 1995 at 1268 Brookside Drive, Eugene, Lane County, Oregon. Additionally, that the bullets which caused the death of Brandon M. Williams and Kristal R. Bendele appear to be .38 cal semi wadcutter bullets. A .38 cal pistol was stolen in the burglary at 1268 Brookside, Eugene, Oregon. Additionally, a quantity of ammunition was stolen which has been subsequently described by the [burglary] victim to be hand loaded semi wadcutter ammunition contained in a green plastic container.

In connection with the investigation of the murders of these individuals, a person identified as Michael Black, has informed Lane County Sheriff's detectives that he observed Brandon Williams, Kristal Bendele and Patrick Finley, enter a Suburban truck about 11:30 p.m. on the night of December 20, 1995. That Conan Wayne Hale was a person who was riding in the truck and invited the three victims to get into the truck at that time.

I have been told by Tom Yates and Jeff Carley, LCSO detective, that Jonathan Wayne Susbauer has admitted to being the driver of the Suburban truck during this incident, and that after the three persons were picked up by Conan Wayne Hale and himself, that the five of them drove to a remote area near McGowen Creek and that while at that location, both he and Conan Wayne Hale participated in killing the three individuals. That during the incident, Conan Wayne Hale was wearing a black trench coat and brown leather gloves. That the weapon used to kill the three victims was a .38 cal pistol that was taken in the burglary at 1268 Brookside along with football collectors cards and a football helmet. That he and Conan Wayne Hale sold items in this burglary at Action City Sportcards in the incident described above.

Jonathan Wayne Susbauer stated that during the shooting of the three victims a number of rounds of ammunition were fired by himself and Conan Wayne Hale from the .38 cal pistol. Mr. Susbauer believed the number to be 11. That during the incident the three victims were required to disrobe before they were shot. That at one point a rabbit fur jacket taken from 1268 Brookside was removed from the vehicle and ultimately was left at the scene of the murder. I learned from Sgt. McMullen that when Patrick Finley was discovered, he was wearing the rabbit fur jacket identified as coming from the 1268 Brookside burglary. A receipt with the [burglary] victim's name was located in the pocket of the coat.

Jonathan Wayne Susbauer told Detectives Yates and Carley that Conan Wayne Hale had engaged in numerous sexual acts with Kristal Bendele prior to her death. . . .

Jonathan Wayne Susbauer told Detectives Yates and Carley that he and Conan Wayne Hale had placed the clothing, floormats and garbage from the suburban into plastic garbage sacks and that the two individuals planned for Hale to dispose of the sacks and Susbauer to dispose of the .38 cal pistol.

. . . .

On December 24, 1995, the Suburban vehicle was located with the assistance of Jonathan Susbauer. That vehicle was impounded at the Oregon State Police Crime Lab. A search warrant was obtained and executed on the Suburban vehicle on December 25, 1995. Two of the seat belts had been cut, the ashtrays, lighter and floor mats had been removed.

On December 26, 1995, a search warrant was executed at the residence of Conan Wayne Hale. Located at the residence were two seat belts, two ashtrays and a lighter that are consistent with those missing from the Suburban. The search is continuing and items not recovered include .38 cal casings, clothing in garbage bags and some items from the Wilshire and Brookside burglaries.

On December 26, 1995, I received information from Springfield Police Detective John Umenhofer that Conan Wayne Hale had been seen with a .38 cal revolver after the time of the murders. The description of this gun is consistent with the one seized by police from Jon Susbauer.

Criminalist Gordon Rutter of the Oregon State Police has tested .38 caliber slugs found at the crime scene and determined that they were fired from the .38 cal revolver seized by police and which has been identified as the gun taken in the 1268 Brookside burglary.

Criminalist Bradford Putnam of the Oregon State Police has processed the [samples] taken from Kristal Bendele at her autopsy. The samples tested positive for seminal fluid.

. . . .

Based on the aforesaid information, your affiant has probable cause to believe, and does believe, that evidence of the crimes of rape, sodomy, sexual abuse, murder and aggravated murder to wit, blood, saliva exemplars and oral swabs can be found in the person of Conan Wayne Hale, dob 12/28/75, described as a white male, 5'10" tall, 190 lbs, brown hair, with hazel eyes and can be seized at the above described facility.

Efforts have been made in the last 24 hours to locate Conan Wayne Hale without success. His mother, Katie Long Brown, has indicated that he is in hiding. Efforts to locate Hale include going to his residence and contacting all known relatives and associates. It is unknown when Conan Wayne Hale will be located. Therefore, I am requesting authorization to execute this search warrant at any time of the day or night.

THEREFORE, your affiant respectfully requests the court review this affidavit in it entirety, and issue a search warrant to seize the above described person for such time as is required to obtain the exemplars and search him for the above described evidence.

/s/ Dennis A. Williams
DENNIS A. WILLIAMS

Subscribed and sworn to before me this 26th day of Dec., 1995, at 8:47 P.M.

/s/ Bryan T. Hodges
DISTRICT COURT JUDGE

SEARCH WARRANT

IN THE NAME OF THE STATE OF OREGON

TO ANY POLICE OFFICER, GREETINGS:

Information on oath having this day been laid before me that evidence of the crime of rape, sodomy, sexual abuse, murder and aggravated murder: to wit, blood, saliva, exemplars and oral swabs are currently located in the person of Conan Wayne Hale, dob 12/28/75, further described as a white male, 5'10", 190 lbs, brown hair with hazel eyes.

You are hereby commanded to seize the person of Conan Wayne Hale and to transport him to the Lane County Adult Corrections Facility and to obtain the exemplars and swabs as described above.

And if you find the same, or any part thereof, to seize the items and to return this warrant and an inventory of items seized to me at my office in the Lane County Courthouse, Eugene, Lane County, Oregon no later than five (5) days following the execution of the warrant.

( ) This warrant to be executed between 7:00 a.m. and 10:00 p.m.

(X) This warrant to be executed at any time of the day or night.

Dated at Eugene, Lane County, Oregon this 26th day of Dec., 1995 at 8:47 PM o'clock.

/s/ Bryan T. Hodges
DISTRICT COURT JUDGE

THE DISTRICT COURT OF THE STATE OF
OREGON FOR LANE COUNTY

STATE OF OREGON)
) AFFIDAVIT FOR SEARCH WARRANT
COUNTY OF LANE   )

I, Jeffrey James Carley, being first duly sworn on oath, hereby depose and say, that:

I am a detective with the Lane County Sheriff's Office and have been employed in law enforcement for 18 years.

I have been assigned to investigate the murder of three individuals who were killed on or about December 21, 1995 in Lane County, Oregon, on a logging landing near McGowan Creek. Jonathan Wayne Susbauer has been indicted for those murders and other related crimes in Lane County Circuit Court Case No. 10–96–00479. Conan Wayne Hale has been identified as a suspect in the murders and is being held at the Lane County Adult Corrections Facility on burglary and theft charges in Lane County Circuit Court Case No. 10–96–00478.

Attached as exhibit A is a copy of an affidavit and search warrant related to this case authorized by Judge Hodges of the Lane County District Court on December 26, 1995 and executed on December 27, 1995. That affidavit outlines the factual background of this investigation.

I interviewed Conan Wayne Hale on December 27, 1995, after the time of the affidavit in exhibit A. Conan Hale has told me that he was at the logging landing when the three victims were killed. He admitted hitting the two males with a baseball bat but denied firing the .38 revolver which killed them. I have reviewed the medical examiner's report and there is no physical evidence to corroborate Conan Hale's statement that he hit the males with the baseball bat. Conan Hale's DNA sample did not match the DNA recovered from Kristal Bendele's body and clothing. Conan Hale has admitted his involvement in the two burglaries and the thefts described in exhibit A.

Conan Wayne Hale has been lodged at the Lane County Adult Corrections Facility since December 27, 1995 except for times he was transported to Marion County on other charges. During Conan Hale's stay at the Lane County Adult Corrections Facility his phone calls and visits have been recorded pursuant to ORS 165–540(2)(a). I have reviewed many of the audio cassette tapes of these visits and phone calls. Conan Hale is aware that his visits are being recorded. He has demonstrated his awareness that visits are recorded by holding up signs that communicate information to the visiting party and advising that person not to repeat the information over the phone. [HANDWRITTEN, INITIALED ADDITION: My review of these tapes was prior to April 22, 1996, in which Hale demonstrated his awareness that conversations were being recorded.]

I learned from Sgt. Bud Spencer, supervisor at the Lane County Adult Corrections Facility, that on or before April 18, 1996 Conan Wayne Hale made arrangements to have a Catholic priest visit him on April 22, 1996 for the purpose of making a confession. On April 22, 1996 at 9:35 a.m. Conan Hale met with Father Mockaitis of St. Paul's Catholic Church in the visiting booths at the jail. That conversation was conducted via phone between the two rooms separated by glass. The conversation was recorded on an audio cassette tape per usual practice and was delivered to me by jail personnel who retrieved it from the recording machine. The tape is currently in the custody of the District Attorney's office where it is sealed and secured.

I know from my experience and training that the Catholic confession is an integral part of Catholicism. It is a sacrament. The basic tenet of confession is that a person is absolved of his or her wrongdoing upon making a full and complete acknowledgment of what that wrongdoing is. After the person gives that acknowledgment of what he or she has done wrong, the priest prescribes a penance. Upon performance of the penance, a person is absolved of his or her sins.

Based on the aforesaid information, your affiant has probable cause to believe, and does believe, that evidence of the crime of murder, to wit: a statement by Conan Wayne Hale can be seized from an audio tape located in the office of the Lane County District Attorney, 125 East 8th Avenue, Eugene, Oregon.

Wherefore, your affiant respectfully requests the court to review this affidavit in its entirety, and issue a search warrant to search the above described audio tape for the above described evidence.

/s/ Jeffrey James Carley
Jeffrey James Carley

Subscribed and sworn to before me this 23rd day of April, 1996 at 11:35 a.m.

/s/ Bryan T. Hodges
DISTRICT COURT JUDGE

SEARCH WARRANT

IN THE NAME OF THE STATE OF OREGON

To any police officer, greeting:

Information on oath having this day been laid before me that evidence of the crime of murder, to wit: the contents of an audio cassette recording of the confession made by Conan Wayne Hale to Father Mockaitis located at the Lane County District Attorney's Office at 125 East 8th Avenue, Eugene, Lane County, Oregon.

you are therefore hereby commanded to search the above described audio cassette tape for the above described evidence.

and if you find the same, or any part thereof, to return this warrant and an inventory of items seized to me at my office in the Lane County Courthouse, Eugene, Oregon, no later than five (5) days following execution of this warrant.

(X) This warrant to be executed between 7:00 a.m. and 10:00 p.m.

( )This warrant to be executed at any time of day or night.

Dated this 23rd day of April, 1996, at 11:35 a.m.

/s/ Bryan T. Hodges
DISTRICT COURT JUDGE

Statement of Doug Harcleroad

May 22, 1996.

In late December, 1995, three young people were murdered in the McGowan Creek area of Lane County. An extensive law enforcement investigation was launched to apprehend the perpetrator or perpetrators of these crimes. That investigation is continuing. I take very seriously my obligation to vigorously apprehend and prosecute the killer or killers.

On January 17, 1996, Jonathan Wayne Susbauer was indicted by the Lane County Grand Jury for these crimes. Conan Wayne Hale was indicted on the same date for other crimes but not for the murder of the three young people; he remains a suspect in the murder case.

On April 22, 1996, I authorized the taping at the Lane County Jail of a private conversation between Conan Hale and Father Tim Mockaitis, a Catholic Priest.

I was wrong to authorize taping that conversation. There are some things which are legal and ethical but are simply not right. I have concluded that tape recording confidential clergy-penitent communications falls within the zone of societally unacceptable conduct.

It is important that our citizens have confidence in our justice system and the methods we employ. I believe that taping a clergy-penitent conversation in a jail shakes that confidence and must be corrected. I will be supportive of legislation revising Oregon law to protect such conversations.

Regarding the tape: Our office will not attempt to use this information in any way nor derive any evidence from it whatsoever. The one and only existing tape and the one and only transcript have been delivered to the Circuit Court and the presiding Circuit Court Judge has entered an Order sealing them. Hopefully, there will come a time when they may be legally destroyed.

At no time did I nor any of the lawyers in my office intend any disrespect to the Catholic Church or Father Mockaitis or to any people of faith. Our intention was to find the truth about the murder of the three young people. This is still our intention, but this method was wrong. I apologize to Father Mockaitis and to the others who are offended, and to the extent I am able, I will not allow this method to be used again.

The public discussion that has occurred over the last few weeks has been instructive, enlightening and humbling. I am deeply impressed by how dearly Oregonians and Americans care about any infringement they perceive on their rights, including their religious freedoms.

[Letterhead of the Attorney General for the State of Oregon]

June 3, 1996

Honorable F. Douglass Harcleroad
District Attorney
400 Lane County Courthouse
125 E. 8th Avenue
Eugene, OR 97401
Re: Legal Issues Involving Tape–Recording of Inmate Conversation
Dear District Attorney Harcleroad:

You have asked the Department of Justice for its advice regarding the state's statutory authority to audio tape record a conversation between an inmate in the Lane County jail and a Catholic priest.

. . . . .

You have asked us under Oregon law: (1) whether monitoring and recording the conversation was authorized; (2) what your duties and responsibilities are with respect to preserving the tape recording; and (3) what other considerations might bear on the propriety of preserving the tape. Our answers are set out briefly below.

Authority to Intercept the Conversation Under Oregon Law

Under ORS 165.540, Lane County corrections personnel were authorized to intercept and record the telephone conversation in question. That statute generally prohibits intercepting telephone conversations. Subsection (2)(a), however, exempts jails and correctional institutions from the prohibition, except for communications or conversations between an attorney and the client. There is no exception for an inmate's conversations with a priest or other religious advisor. The statute's terms are clear and unambiguous. Lane County personnel acted within their statutory authority to monitor and record the conversation in question.

Duty to Preserve the Recording and Transcript: Criminal Case Procedures

We believe that you have a legal obligation to preserve the tape recording and transcript, one that flows at a minimum from your statutory and constitutional discovery obligations. Prosecutors have a statutory duty under ORS 135.815 (2) to "disclose" any recording of an oral statement made by the defendant. The duty to disclose encompasses not only providing the defendant an opportunity to inspect or copy the material (ORS 135.805 (2)), but also preserving the evidence to the extent possible. Your obligation under the statute was triggered by the defendant's recent indictment for murder. *See* ORS 135.845. It also may arguably have arisen in connection with charges that were pending against the defendant prior to that time. Our understanding is that defendant's attorney on those other charges has demanded that the tape be preserved. Under all these circumstances, to destroy the tape recording and transcription would violate your statutory discovery obligations. Moreover, if you have any reason to know or to believe that the tape contains exculpatory information, your obligation to preserve and provide access to the tape recording arises under the federal constitution as well.

Duty to Preserve the Tape Recording and Transcript: Oregon Public Records Law

While the tape recording was in your custody, you also had responsibilities to preserve it under the public records law. The tape recording qualifies as a public record. ORS 192.410(4) and (5). For several reasons, it may not be subject to public inspection. For example, it may relate to a criminal investigation, you may reasonably anticipate litigation pertaining to it, or it may be of a personal nature such that public inspection would create an unreasonable invasion of privacy. *See generally* ORS 192.502. But even when public records are not subject to inspection, they must be preserved for whatever period is prescribed by the State Archivist. *See* ORS 192.001 through 192.190. We are unsure of the particular schedule or schedules that might apply in this instance, because the tape recording may fall into more than one category (*i.e.*, criminal investigatory materials, records pertaining to anticipated litigation, court records, county corrections records). The State Archivist would be responsible for making that determination. Now that the tape recording and the transcript are in the custody of the court, it is the court's responsibility to preserve it for whatever period applies. Most public records must be preserved for a period of several years.

The Need to Preserve the Tape to Protect the Public Interest Generally

Apart from actual duties to preserve the tape recording, there is a practical need to do so to preserve the integrity of the murder prosecution against the defendant. As we have indicated, we believe that making the tape was authorized under state law. Even so, defendant may raise questions about its legality at trial. In addition, defendant may raise questions about the legality of other evidence you may produce against him, by theorizing that the other evidence was somehow derived as a result of information that you obtained from the tape recording. Such claims may be entirely without merit. The only way for you to establish that they have no merit, however, might be to produce the tape or the transcript of the conversation. Destruction of the tape therefore would potentially jeopardize the prosecution on what is, without question, extraordinarily serious charges. If defendant is convicted of the charges, that concern will remain until he has exhausted all of his appeals and collateral remedies (*e.g.*, state post-conviction review and federal habeas corpus review), which likely could span several years.

In Summary

To summarize our answers, they are as follows. First, the interception and recording of the conversation in the jail was lawful under ORS 154.540(2)(a). Second, now that the tape recording and transcript exist, you have duties to preserve them arising under state (and perhaps constitutional) law relating to your disclosure obligations in criminal prosecutions. You also have a duty to preserve the tape recording and transcript, so long as they are in your custody, pursuant to the public records law, although they may be protected from public disclosure. Third, your prosecution of defendant on highly serious criminal charges could be jeopardized if the tape recording and transcript were to be destroyed. Until defendant's criminal case is final and no longer subject to collateral attack, it would be advisable to preserve the tape.

Very truly yours,

/s/ Virginia L. Linder
Virginia L. Linder
Solicitor General

Maybe the Lane D.A. Was Right to Tape

by David Schuman
The Oregonian.
Wednesday, May 22, 1996.

. . . . I honor religious freedom. I respect the sanctity of the confessional. I condemn government overreaching. I would support legislation absolutely prohibiting the practice that District Attorney Doug Harcleroad engaged in.

But as of now there is no such legislation, and in his position I very well might have done the same thing. And I might have been right.

Imagine what must have been running through the district attorney's mind. He learns that the suspect in custody has requested a conference with a priest, and he has probable cause to believe that during this conference the suspect will say things that help the state's case: self-incriminating statements, the whereabouts of evidence such as guns or bloody clothes, the identity of co-perpetrators.

The D.A. also knows the jailer can capture the contents of this conversation on tape, and that he must decide quickly whether or not to do so. How does the D.A. balance his respect for religious freedom with his desire to get a conviction?

First—presuming what we have no reason to doubt: that Doug Harcleroad is a decent and conscientious public servant—he realizes the sensitivity of the situation and that listening to the conversation is an insult to society's conventional respect for religion, not to mention its respect for privacy. But then some countervailing considerations begin to trickle into his moral calculus.

He recalls the enormous pressures to successfully prosecute the gruesome, random and highly publicized murder of three children. He remembers the crime scene in all of its gore. He remembers the victims' parents.

And more. He remembers that he lives in a town that has recently rallied around two vigilante assassins: one who killed a young man suspected of selling marijuana and making verbal threats, the other a man suspected of tampering with a parked car.

He remembers that he lives in a state that is so obsessed with crime that it has over the last decade shifted its spending priorities from schools to prisons.

He remembers that the public has never objected to the many casual deceptions that are a routine part of police practice: wiretaps, paid informers, decoys; good-cop bad-cop interrogations. He remembers that the public, his constituents, persistently urge him to start respecting victims and stop coddling criminals.

And then he stops thinking like a politician and starts thinking like a lawyer. He remembers that the United States Supreme Court, in a case originating in Oregon*, announced that when the demands of law enforcement conflict with an individual's sincere desire to engage in a bona fide religious sacrament, the individual and religion lose. He remembers that the Supreme Court has announced that convicts sacrifice, along with their freedom, many of their constitutional rights.

He remembers that state law, while not authorizing the surreptitious interception of jailhouse conversations between priest and penitent, at least makes such taping noncriminal. He remembers that even though there's only a slight chance that he can use the suspect's confession itself against the suspect, there's a pretty good likelihood he'll be able to use it against

---

* [The author refers to Employment Div., Dep't of Human Resources v. Smith, 494 U.S. 872 (1990) (holding that State of Oregon employees fired for using peyote, a hallucinogenic drug, for sacramental purposes in a ceremony of the Native American Church, could be denied unemployment compensation). The Supreme Court's decision in *Smith* ultimately led to the passage of the Religious Freedom Restoration Act (RFRA).]—ed.

co-defendants and that he'll be able to use evidence that the confession leads to.

And he remembers that most people believe—maybe he even believes it himself—that in fighting crime, law enforcement officers can legally do anything they want as long as they don't violate some explicit constitutional command.

All of these considerations, in sum, might leave him as ambivalent as he was to begin with. Eavesdropping on this conversation may be morally repugnant, but sometimes the people enact laws that permit the state to act in a morally repugnant fashion in order to serve what they see as a higher morality.

So what does he do? He decides to activate the tape recorder and seal the tape until he taken his dilemma where it belongs—to a judge.

Under our system of government, the district attorney is a member of the executive branch. His duty is to faithfully execute the law—not to decide what the law is; that is the people's duty, through our legislators or directly by initiative. Nor is it his duty to decide what the law means; that is the duty of the judiciary.

In this situation, the people have already spoken, and their message has been unequivocal: Cuff 'em and stuff 'em; lock 'em up and throw away the keys; three strikes and they're out; if they do the crime they should do the time; impeach liberal judges. It should therefore come as no surprise that when the judge authorized Harcleroad to listen to the tape, he did so.

I do not mean to absolve the district attorney of all responsibility. He is a free moral agent, and could have chosen not to tape, or not to listen, and maybe should have. But before we demonize him for his decision, we should recognize that the decision was not entirely his.

The last word came, not from him but from a judge who, as far as I can tell, has completely escaped reproach. And the first work—the most insistent and the most culpable—came from those citizens and politicians among us who demand that law-enforcement officials wage a war on crime when one of that war's strategies is to denigrate a sacred right if the person who happens to be exercising it is an accused criminal.

David Schuman teaches constitutional law at the University of Oregon School of Law. Professor Schuman was appointed Deputy Attorney General for the State of Oregon in November of 1996.

The next problem the courts faced was deciding whether the tape should be destroyed. Lane County Circuit Judge Jack Billings, over the Church's protests, allowed Hale's lawyers, Terri Wood and Steve Miller, to listen to the tape. As the New York Times reported, destruction of the tape might have cost the state the entire case:

> Whether Ms. Wood uses the tape or not, it seems likely that it will be preserved until the trial and any subsequent appeals have ended. David Schuman ... said Ms. Wood might need to play the tape in court, if

she wanted to try to prove that prosecutors used information on it to build a case against Mr. Hale.

But Father Maslowsky rejects Mr. Schuman's reasoning. "If the defense attorneys want to know what was on that tape, they could just ask Mr. Hale," he said. Representing the Archdiocese, he will continue his argument in Federal District Court in a hearing that will continue on Monday that the tape should be destroyed.

"That argument is going nowhere," Mr. Schuman said. "Even if making the tape was wrong, the tape is evidence in an ongoing prosecution. And if the state destroyed it, they'd have to dismiss all charges against Mr. Hale."

Despite Protests, Lawyers Hear Recording of Confession to a Priest, The New York Times, August 4, 1996, at 23.

The Reverend Timothy Mockaitis, and The Most Reverend Francis E. George, O.M.I., Plaintiffs-Appellants, v. F. Douglass Harcleroad, The Honorable Jack A. Billings, The Honorable Kip W. Leonard, Conan Wayne Hale, Jonathan Wayne Susbauer, and John Does Nos. 1–5, Defendants-Appellees.

9th Cir. January 27, 1997.
104 F.3d 1522.

Counsel:

Thomas V. Dulcich and Bradley I. Nye of Schwabe, Williamson & Wyatt, Portland, Oregon, for the plaintiffs-appellants.

Theodore R. Kulongoski, Virginia L. Linder, Eleanor E. Wallace and Timothy A. Sylwester of the Oregon Attorney General's office, Salem, Oregon, for defendants-appellees Harcleroad, Judge Billings, Judge Leonard.

■ Before: JOHN T. NOONAN, JR., DAVID R. THOMPSON and ANDREW J. KLEINFELD, CIRCUIT JUDGES.

■ NOONAN, CIRCUIT JUDGE:

The Reverend Timothy Mockaitis (Mockaitis) and the Most Reverend Francis E. George, O.M.I. (George) appeal the dismissal by the district court of their suit against F. Douglass Harcleroad (Harcleroad); the Honorable Jack A. Billings (Billings); the Honorable Kip W. Leonard (Leonard); Conan Wayne Hale (Hale); Jonathan Wayne Susbauer (Susbauer); and John Does Nos. 1–5. We reverse the district court and remand for entry of an injunction.

FACTS

We summarize the pertinent facts as presented by stipulation, affidavits, exhibits and uncontested testimony in the district court:

Mockaitis is a Catholic priest of the archdiocese of Portland, Oregon. On occasion he has administered the Sacrament of Penance to inmates of the Lane County Jail. George is the Catholic archbishop of Portland and is responsible for the proper celebration of Catholic sacraments within his archdiocese, which includes Lane County.

Harcleroad is the District Attorney for Lane County and is responsible for the prosecution of crimes within the county. Leonard and Billings are circuit judges of the county. In the spring of 1996 Hale and Susbauer were both inmates of the county jail. Hale was twenty years old at the time of the events in the case.

On April 23, 1996 Jeffrey James Carley, a detective in the county sheriff's office, filed an affidavit in support of a search warrant. The affidavit was prepared with the assistance of Trish Furlow and Joseph Kosydar of Harcleroad's office. According to the affidavit, Hale was a suspect in the murder on the night of December 20 or the early morning of December 21, 1995 of Kristal R. Bendele, Patrick M. Finley and Brandon M. Williams. In support of that belief, Carley stated that he had interviewed Hale a week after the crimes and that Hale had admitted to having been at the logging landing in a remote area near McGowan Creek with the three victims when they were killed and had admitted to striking Finley and Williams with a baseball bat, although he denied shooting them. Carley's affidavit incorporated an affidavit made out by Dennis A. Williams of the Eugene Police Department on December 26, 1995. According to Williams, Susbauer had admitted to two detectives from the county sheriff's office that both he and Hale had participated in the three killings, each of them taking turns firing a single .38 calibre pistol. A witness confirmed seeing the three victims entering a truck where Hale was a passenger near the time of the murders.

The affidavits of Carley and Williams made evident a connection between the murders and two burglaries committed in the city of Eugene, Lane County, one on December 14, 1995 and the other on December 19, 1995. A description of the .38 calibre pistol stolen in the December 19 burglary matched the gun used in the murders. The body of Patrick Finley was clothed in a rabbit fur jacket stolen in this burglary. Sales of the property stolen had been traced to both Susbauer and Hale. Susbauer had admitted to the police that he and Hale had committed both burglaries. Hale had admitted to Detective Carley his involvement in both burglaries. Susbauer had already been indicted for the three murders.

The information in Carley's and William's affidavits, if true, provided a strong basis for believing that Hale was guilty of killing the three youthful victims, Bendele, Finley and Williams. Hale had been in the county jail since December 27, 1995. According to Carley, he had reviewed many of the tapes made of Hale's phone calls and conversations with visitors. Hale had "demonstrated his awareness that his visits are being recorded." On the basis of the information in the affidavits, Carley sought the search warrant for a new tape made on April 22, 1996 for the reason best described in his own words:

"I learned from Sgt. Bud Spencer, supervisor at the Lane County Adult Corrections Facility, that on or before April 18, 1996 Conan Wayne Hale made arrangements to have a Catholic priest visit him on April 22, 1996 for the purpose of making a confession. On April 22, 1996 at 9:35 a.m. Conan Hale met with Father Mockaitis of St. Paul's Catholic Church in the visiting booths at the jail. That conversation was conducted via phone between the two rooms separated by glass. The conversation was recorded on an audio cassette tape per usual practice and was delivered to me by jail personnel who retrieved it from the recording machine. The tape is currently in the custody of the District Attorney's office where it is sealed and secured.

I know from my experience and training that the Catholic confession is an integral part of Catholicism. It is a sacrament. The basic tenet of confession is that a person is absolved of his or her wrongdoing upon making a full and complete acknowledgment of what that wrongdoing is. After the person gives that acknowledgment of what he or she has done wrong, the priest prescribes a penance. Upon performance of the penance, a person is absolved of his or her sins.

Based on the aforesaid information, your affiant has probable cause to believe, and does believe, that evidence of the crime of murder, to wit: a statement by Conan Wayne Hale can be seized from an audio tape located in the office of the Lane County District Attorney, 125 East 8th Avenue, Eugene, Oregon."

Unmentioned in the affidavit were the following facts disclosed in this case: The jail monitored about 90% of Hale's conversations, except conversations with his counsel. Hale "communicated with visitors in writing when he did not want jailers to monitor his conversations." In the sign-in area for visitors was an order of the sheriff that "no recording equipment" was allowed in the visiting area. Father Mockaitis did not know that his encounter with Hale was being recorded nor did he have reason to believe that it would be recorded. Hale was not a Catholic. He was a baptized Christian. In Catholic belief all baptized persons are eligible to participate in the Sacrament of Penance.

Bryan Hodges, district court judge for Lane County, issued the warrant requested by Carley, who executed it. The tape was transcribed into a typed document. Two deputy district attorneys, Kosydar and Patricia Perlow, listened to it.

PROCEEDINGS

The taping soon became known to the press and public. On May 7, 1996 representatives of the archdiocese met with Harcleroad to request the tape's destruction and a guarantee of no further taping of sacramental confession in the jail. On May 22, 1996 Harcleroad moved the county court to retain and seal the tape and to prohibit anyone who knew its contents from divulging them without further order of the court. Without a hearing or notice to anyone else, Judge Leonard granted the order.

On June 12, 1996 Father Mockaitis and Archbishop George filed a petition and motion in the county circuit court seeking the destruction of the tape and a continuation of the order as to the secrecy of the tape's contents. They asserted that the taping and its preservation violated both the federal and the state constitutions and federal and state statutes. They supported their claim with an affidavit as to the Sacrament of Penance in Catholic belief, filed by the Reverend Michael Maslowsky, a representative of Archbishop George, and by Father Mockaitis's own affidavit, in which he stated that as long as the tape remained in existence, "I feel uncomfortable in administering the Sacrament of Penance (Reconciliation) in the Lane County Jail."

This petition was routed to another judge of the circuit, Judge Billings, to whom Hale's case had been assigned, Hale having been indicted on May 30 for aggravated murder. Judge Billings immediately wrote counsel for the petitioners as follows:

RE: State v. Conan Wayne Hale

Case No. 10–96–04830

Dear Mr. Dulcich:

The packet of papers which you submitted to the Court yesterday were routed to my chambers by the clerk's office, since it was not clear what should be done with them. To the extent that the Petition which you have submitted on behalf of the clergy attempts to intervene in the pending criminal case involving the above-named defendant that is not permitted by law. ORS 131.025.

To the extent that the documents you have presented to the Court represent an effort to commence some separate proceeding they do not state a justiciable controversy. They are, therefore, not suitable for filing. Accordingly, I'm returning your papers to you, together with your filing fee.

Finally, I enclose for your information a copy of an Order I have entered this date, upon the Motion of the above-named defendant, with the concurrence of the District Attorney, the parties to the criminal case. Please be advised that except upon further motion of one or both of the parties, or upon directive of some higher court, this Court will not consider, under any circumstances, the action which your clients desire.

> Sincerely yours,
> Jack A. Billings
> Circuit Judge

The accompanying order, entered at the request of Hale, without notice to the priest and archbishop, read as follows:

"THIS CAUSE coming before the Court on Defendant's motion to preserve evidence, in which the State concurs, and the Court being fully advised in the premises:

IT IS HEREBY ORDERED that all judicial officers and agents of the State who are now in possession or who may come into possession of a tape recording and transcript thereof of a conversation between Defendant and the Rev. Timothy Mockaitis which occurred on or about April 22, 1996 at the Lane County Jail are to preserve those items as evidence in the above-styled cause during the pendency of these proceedings."

On June 27, 1996 Father Mockaitis and Archbishop George filed this suit in the district court, setting out five claims based on the taping and retention of its contents: First, a claim under 42 U.S.C. § 1983, alleging violation of the right under the First Amendment to the free exercise of religion; second, also under § 1983, alleging violation of the Fourth Amendment; third, violation of the Religious Freedom Restoration Act (RFRA), 42 U.S.C. § 2000bb et seq.; fourth, violation of the Wiretapping Act, 18 U.S.C. § 2510 et seq.; and fifth, violation of the Constitution of Oregon, Article I, Sections 2 and 3. They sought an order destroying the tape and transcript and prohibiting publication of its contents; an injunction prohibiting Harcleroad and all agents of the Lane County District Attorney's office from future interception and taping of the Sacrament of Penance "and similar religious communications at the Lane County Jail"; and a judgment declaring ORS § 165.540(2)(a) to violate the First Amendment and the Oregon Constitution if used to monitor confidential religious communications. They asked for their attorney fees and expenses under 42 U.S.C. § 1988(b). The state defendants answered, denying the plaintiffs' claims and asserting that "law enforcement officers in the ordinary course of their duties intercepted the conversation between plaintiff Mockaitis and defendant Hale." Hale answered, objecting to the requested destruction of the tape as impairing his defense to the capital charge of murder. Susbauer answered similarly.

In the course of the proceeding, the affidavit of the Reverend Bertram F. Griffin, J.C.D. was received as to the canon law and theology of the Catholic Church on the Sacrament of Penance. It was noted that "prior to the commencement of the action Lane County agreed not to intercept or tape conversations between Catholic clergy and inmates at the Lane County Jail." Harcleroad, Hale, and Susbauer all argued for the preservation of the tape. It was noted that counsel for Hale and Susbauer had already listened to the tape. On August 8, 1996 Hale filed an affidavit stating as follows:

"During my conversation with Father Mockaitis at the Lane County Jail on or about April 22, 1996, I made confession and asked for God to forgive me for the following transgressions: (1) for crimes of burglary which I committed with Jonathan Susbauer; (2) for being angry with and unable to forgive Susbauer for Susbauer having killed the three teenagers and for lying to the authorities about my involvement; and (3) for being angry with the District Attorney for believing Susbauer instead of me. I told Father Mockaitis that I did not commit any of the crimes people were accusing me of except the burglaries."

"The tape recording at issue would be much more accurate than my recollection of what was said during this conversation, because the conversation took place a long time ago and I do not remember everything that I said or that Father Mockaitis said. By the time of my trial, my memory of this conversation will be even worse."

"I want the tape to be preserved and for my attorneys to be able to use it as evidence in my defense, because people may not believe what I say about it. Lots of people think that I confessed to killing the victims, because of the news reports about the tape, but I didn't confess to that because I didn't do it."

It was agreed that as Hale was charged with aggravated murder he would be subject, on conviction, to the death penalty, and that Harcleroad had given notice that he would seek the death penalty. Harcleroad stated that at the conclusion of the state proceedings against Hale and Susbauer the tape would be destroyed.

After receiving evidence and hearing argument the district court on August 15, 1996 dismissed the plaintiffs' claims. The court began by observing that the plaintiffs were "justifiably outraged" by Harcleroad's actions. The court added:

"Harcleroad himself admits that the taping was wrong: 'There are some things which are legal and ethical but are simply not right. I have concluded that tape recording confidential clergy-penitent communications falls within the zone of societally unacceptable conduct.'"

The court agreed with Harcleroad that the taping had been wrong.

Nonetheless the court, invoking Younger v. Harris, 401 U.S. 37, 27 L.Ed.2d 669, 91 S.Ct. 746 (1971), concluded that the duty of the federal court was to abstain from exercising jurisdiction where such exercise would interfere with the ongoing prosecution by the state of a criminal case. After coming to this conclusion against exercising any judicial power, the district court then undertook to "balance the equities" and held that Hale's and Susbauer's rights to a fair trial outweighed the First Amendment rights of Mockaitis and George. A judgment dismissing the action was entered against the plaintiffs.

Father Mockaitis and Archbishop George appeal.

ANALYSIS

Abstention. In abstaining from determining the merits of the case, the district court did not literally apply Younger, for a key requirement of Younger is that the party seeking relief in federal court "has an adequate remedy at law and will not suffer irreparable injury if denied equitable relief." Younger, 401 U.S. at 43–44. Mockaitis and George have no remedy at law and at least a portion of the injuries they have alleged will be irreparable without the equitable intervention of the federal courts. The county circuit court has held that they are not parties to the state's murder case against Hale. The county court has held that their petition and motion to destroy the tape did not state a cause of action under Oregon law. Alleging injuries under federal law, as they do, they are not compelled to speculate as to whether a higher Oregon court would grant them relief. They are free to seek federal remedies in the federal courts.

In addition, much of the relief they seek would not interfere with the ongoing state prosecution. We do not decide whether, had the complaint sought only destruction of evidence in a pending criminal trial, Younger abstention would have been necessary. That is not all the complaint sought. The complaint also sought an injunction against future interception and recording of sacramental confessions in the jail and a declaratory judgment that any such interception and taping was unconstitutional. An injunction and declaratory judgment limited to such relief would not interfere at all with the pending criminal prosecution of Hale and Susbauer, so Younger did not require abstention from the entire case. We need not decide whether the district court erred in abstaining under Younger from deciding whether to order destruction of the tape and nondisclosure of the contents, because we deny that relief as well, though on different grounds.

Focusing on the requested destruction of the tape, the district court in effect overlooked what the plaintiffs asked. The virtually unflagging obligation of a federal court to exercise jurisdiction when it has it makes it error to abstain from deciding this case where serious violations of the laws and Constitution of the United States are alleged and substantial relief can be afforded without disruption of a state criminal trial.

*The Violation Of The Religious Freedom Restoration Act.** Mindful of our obligation to decide a case on statutory grounds if possible, we begin with the plaintiffs' claims under RFRA.

In RFRA Congress finds: "Laws, 'neutral' toward religion may burden religious exercise as surely as laws intended to interfere with religious exercise." RFRA, 42 U.S.C. § 2000bb(a). Congress prescribes:

(a) In general

Government shall not substantially burden a person's exercise of religion even if the burden results from a rule of general applicability, except as provided in subsection (b) of this section.

(b) Exception

Government may substantially burden a person's exercise of religion only if it demonstrates that application of the burden to the person

(1) is in furtherance of a compelling governmental interest; and

(2) is the least restrictive means of furthering that compelling governmental interest.

Id. § 2000bb–1(a) and (b).

A person whose religious exercise is burdened in violation of this section "may assert that violation as a claim or defense ... and obtain

---

* The Supreme Court will rule on the constitutionality of RFRA during the summer of 1997. See Flores v. City of Boerne, 73 F.3d 1352 (5th Cir.), cert. granted, 117 S.Ct. 293 (1996).

appropriate relief against a government." Id. (c). "Government" includes
an agency or official of the United States or any state or subdivision of a
state. "Demonstrates" means to meet "the burdens of going forward with
the evidence and of persuasion." "Exercise of religion" means "the
exercise of religion under the First Amendment to the Constitution." Id.
§ 2000bb–2(1), (3) and (4). Nothing in this chapter "shall be construed to
affect, interpret, or in any way address that portion of the First Amendment prohibiting laws respecting the establishment of religion." Id.
§ 2000bb–4.

Before we can consider the impact of the statute we are confronted by
Harcleroad's contention that the statute is unconstitutional. The problem
is, as he explains, that the statute goes beyond what is required of a state
by the First Amendment, as incorporated in the Fourteenth Amendment
and as interpreted by Employment Div., Oregon Dep't of Human Resources
v. Smith, 494 U.S. 872, 108 L.Ed.2d 876, 110 S.Ct. 1595 (1990). Under
Smith the guarantee of the free exercise of religion does not relieve an
individual "of the obligation to comply with a valid and neutral law of
general applicability" on the ground that the law prescribes or proscribes
conduct interfering with the individual's exercise of religion. Id. at 879.
The valid and neutral law of general applicability on which the prosecutor
relies is ORS 165.540(2)(a), which the prosecutor argues implicitly authorizes those in charge of a jail to intercept and record conversations between
inmates and all visitors save their counsel. The prosecutor adds that he
has an affirmative obligation under Oregon law to disclose to a criminal
defendant all of his recorded statements, ORS 135.815, and to prevent the
destruction of physical evidence, ORS 162.295. These statutes, too, are
asserted to be valid, neutral, and generally applicable. If RFRA invalidates
the application of these laws here, Harcleroad argues, then the state is
being subjected to the First Amendment beyond what Smith permits and
RFRA must be held unconstitutional. The prosecutor completes his argument with the invocation of New York v. United States, 505 U.S. 144, 120
L.Ed.2d 120, 112 S.Ct. 2408 (1992) where the Low-Level Radioactive Waste
Policy Amendments Act of 1985, 42 U.S.C. § 2021b et seq. was held to
violate the Tenth Amendment by commanding the states to implement
legislation enacted by Congress.

Harcleroad has an additional challenge to the constitutionality of
RFRA, a challenge deadly in its implications for religious liberty. It is that
RFRA, because it advances the exercise of religion, is an establishment of
religion and therefore offensive to that portion of the First Amendment
which reads, "Congress shall make no law respecting an establishment of
religion, or prohibiting the free exercise thereof." Harcleroad cites the
three-pronged test of Lemon v. Kurtzman, 403 U.S. 602, 29 L.Ed.2d 745, 91
S.Ct. 2105 (1971), which he claims the advancement of religion accomplished by RFRA fails. He adds for good measure that enforcement of the
federal statute necessitates an "excessive entanglement" of the government
with religion and so runs up against "the Establishment Clause jurisprudence" of Lemon.

The United States has exercised its right to intervene as a party where the constitutionality of a federal statute is attacked, and it has vigorously defended the validity of the law, enacted by Congress without a dissenting vote in the House, 139 Cong. Rec. H8713 (November 3, 1993), only three dissents in the Senate, 139 Cong. Rec. S14471 (October 27, 1993) and signed by President Clinton on November 16, 1993.

We reject Harcleroad's challenge to RFRA for three reasons. The first two reasons explain why Harcleroad's facial attack on the constitutionality of the statute fails. The third reason responds to his challenge to the statute as applied.

First. There is no doubt that Congress under Section 5 of the Fourteenth Amendment has the power to enforce the provisions of the Bill of Rights that the Fourteenth Amendment incorporates and makes binding on the states. Section 5 is "a positive grant of legislative power authorizing Congress to exercise its discretion in determining whether and what legislation is needed to secure the guarantees of the Fourteenth Amendment." Katzenbach v. Morgan, 384 U.S. 641, 651, 16 L.Ed.2d 828, 86 S.Ct. 1717 (1966). The legislative power is not confined to ratifying restrictions placed on the states by the judiciary construing the Bill of Rights; such a narrow reading of the power granted "would depreciate both congressional resourcefulness and congressional responsibility for implementing the Amendment." Id. at 648. The legislative power granted is as broad as the power of Congress under the Necessary and Proper Clause of Article I, § 8, cl. 18. Id. at 650.

Second. Harcleroad's Establishment theory is that whenever Congress exempts religion from generally applicable law it unconstitutionally advances and therefore unconstitutionally establishes a religion; at the same time in order to effect the exemption Congress must get excessively involved in determining what is a religion. The exemptions and deductions of the Internal Revenue Code, §§ 501(c) and 170(c)(2)(B) must be bad. The deferments of the Selective Service Act, 50 Ap.U.S.C. § 456(g) must be invalid. The creation of chaplaincies in Congress and in the armed forces—particularly striking promotions of religion—must be suspect. The narrow logic of this attack is refuted by the experience of the nation. Of course the statutory protection of the free exercise of religion is good for religion. Neither the benefit nor the means are contrary to the first liberty assured by the First Amendment and made concrete by RFRA. Of course, application of RFRA, like the application of the First Amendment itself and any objection made under this amendment, requires a court to determine what is a religion and to define an exercise of it. There is no excessive entanglement. We join the other courts of appeal that have considered this challenge and rejected it. Sasnett v. Sullivan, 91 F.3d 1018 (7th Cir.1996); EEOC v. Catholic University, 317 U.S.App.D.C. 343, 83 F.3d 455 (D.C.Cir. 1996); Flores v. City of Boerne, 73 F.3d 1352 (5th Cir.1996), cert. granted 117 S.Ct. 293.

Third. The acts of the prosecutor here that are at the core of the plaintiffs' complaint did not amount to the neutral application of any

Oregon statute but were an attempt to use the statutory authorization to monitor inmate conversations in order to gain access to a confession expected to be given in accordance with a religious rite. As Carley put it, he expected the confession to contain "a full and complete acknowledgment" by Hale as a condition of his receiving absolution; Carley believed that the confession would contain "evidence of the crime of murder." The search warrant sought to use the sacramental confession as a tool to establish Hale's guilt. Deliberately, the religious rite was focussed upon and preserved for exploitation as state's evidence.

No question exists that Harcleroad is an official of a subdivision of the State of Oregon. No question exists that he has substantially burdened Father Mockaitis's exercise of religion as understood in the First Amendment. Father Mockaitis was exercising his religion in a priestly function. He was seeking to participate in the Sacrament of Penance understood by the Catholic Church to be a means by which God forgives the sins of a repentant sinner and restores the sinner to life in God's grace. It is a sacrament that from experience the Catholic Church has surrounded with extraordinary safeguards so that the content of the penitent's confession will not be revealed unless the penitent himself chooses to reveal it; and these safeguards have the evident reason that the knowledge, belief, or suspicion that freely-confessed sins would become public would operate as a serious deterrent to participation in the sacrament and an odious detriment accompanying participation. When the prosecutor asserts the right to tape the sacrament he not only intrudes upon the confession taped but threatens the security of any participation in the sacrament by penitents in the jail; he invades their free exercise of religion and doing so makes it impossible for Father Mockaitis to minister the sacrament to those who seek it in the jail.

Harcleroad is provided with a statutory defense if he can prove that his actions were "in furtherance of a compelling governmental interest" and that he used "the least restrictive means" of furthering that interest. RFRA, 42 U.S.C. § 2000bb–1(b). Taping a sacramental confession was an easy way to secure additional evidence if the detective's hunch about what would be confessed was right. But the ordinary means of proving a case by good police work were "the least restrictive means" of furthering the prosecutor's desirable goal. Understandably, Harcleroad does not even attempt to dispute this point and offers no defense when RFRA is applied to the taping itself.

A question does exist as to the preservation of the tape until the termination of the proceedings against Hale and Susbauer; or rather, there may be two questions: Does preservation substantially burden Mockaitis's exercise of religion? Does Harcleroad have a defense under RFRA? As to the first, Mockaitis has stated that the continued existence of the tape gives him discomfort and that every new public reference to it is hurtful to him. His reaction is understandable. Out of nowhere, as it must have seemed to him, the performance of a rite that he believed was enshrined in secrecy became a matter for the media, for the courts, for the public at large. His sense of betrayal is reinforced by each reference to the confession's existence on the tape. But it is hard to see that these unpleasant reminders substantially burden his free exercise of religion any more than memory of the first intrusion must rankle. Hale has chosen, as was his undisputed right as a penitent, to disclose in the district court the contents of his confession. Mockaitis does not and cannot seek to destroy this disclosure. Mockaitis knew that such voluntary disclosure by Hale was possible. Hale asks that the recorded counterpart of his disclosure be kept in existence for his criminal trial. The psychological burden thereby put on Mockaitis is not a burden on his religion or its exercise. It is, therefore, unnecessary to consider the defense under the statute that Harcleroad offers.

The reasoning as to the burden imposed on Father Mockaitis applies analogously to the burden imposed on Archbishop George. No substantial burden is imposed on him by the preservation of a confession whose contents the penitent himself has chosen to make public. A substantial burden is imposed on his free exercise of religion as the responsible head of the archdiocese of Portland by the intrusion into the Sacrament of Penance by officials of the state, an intrusion defended in this case by an assistant attorney-general of the state as not contrary to any law. Archbishop George has justifiable grounds for fearing that without a declaratory judgment and an injunction in this case the administration of the Sacrament of Penance for which he is responsible in his archdiocese will be made odious in jails by the intrusion of law enforcement officers.

We take note of the stipulation that Lane County Jail has "agreed not to intercept or tape conversations between Catholic clergy and inmates at the Lane County Jail." The stipulation is far from satisfactory. It does not state to whom Lane County Jail made this promise, or who at the jail made it, or how long the promise is good; and it appears to accord a blanket immunity to conversations with Catholic clergy not extended to clergy of other faiths. The stipulation does not remedy the violations of RFRA, or moot out the case.

The Alleged Violation Of The Wiretap Act. 18 U.S.C. § 2511 makes it a federal felony wilfully to intercept any wire communication or to disclose or use such wilful interception, but the statute does not apply to interceptions "by an investigative or law enforcement officer in the ordinary course of his duties." 18 U.S.C. § 2510(5)(a). According to the stipulated facts, Lane County jailers taped about 90% of Hale's conversations. The plaintiffs have made no showing that the taping of Father Mockaitis was not done in the ordinary course of the jailors' duties, nor have the plaintiffs challenged the status of the jailors as law enforcement officers within the meaning of § 2510(5)(a). The taping of the confession was a violation of RFRA and so should not have been part of the ordinary course of duty of any law enforcement officer; but that the taping was done in ordinary course negates the wilfulness required by the statute. See Cheek v. United States, 498 U.S. 192, 201–02, 112 L.Ed.2d 617, 111 S.Ct. 604 (1991). The interception was therefore not a violation of the Wiretap Act and Harcleroad's subsequent retention of it was therefore not a felony.

The Violation of the Fourth Amendment. Mockaitis had two bases for a reasonable expectation of privacy in his encounter with Hale: First, ORS Evidence Code § 40.260, Rule 506, "Member of clergy-penitent privilege," provides that "[a] member of the clergy shall not, without the consent of the person making the communication, be examined as to any confidential communication made to the member of the clergy in the member's professional character." As Mockaitis could not be examined directly in court on a confession it was reasonable for him to suppose that the prohibition of Rule 506 could not be easily circumvented by the prosecutor taping a confession made to him.

Secondly, the history of the nation has shown a uniform respect for the character of sacramental confession as inviolable by government agents interested in securing evidence of crime from the lips of a criminal. The first known case in the United States to consider such an attempt is famous for the court's rejection of the invasion and for the court's reason for its rejection. DeWitt Clinton, later Governor of New York and at the time Mayor of New York City, a noted statesman and astute analyst of the spirit of the new republic, speaking for the Court of General Sessions, declared:

"A provision conceived in a spirit of the most profound wisdom, and the most exalted charity, ought to receive the most liberal construction. Although by the constitution of the United States, the powers of congress do not extend beyond certain enumerated objects; yet to prevent the danger of constructive assumptions, the following amendment was adopted: "Congress shall make no law respecting an establishment of religion, or prohibiting the free exercise thereof." In this country there is no alliance between church and state; no established religion; no tolerated religion— for toleration results from establishment—but religious freedom guaranteed by the constitution, and consecrated by the social compact."

"It is essential to the free exercise of a religion, that its ordinances should be administered—that its ceremonies as well as its essentials should be protected. The sacraments of a religion are its most important elements. We have but two in the Protestant Church—Baptism and the Lord's Supper—and they are considered the seals of the covenant of grace. Suppose that a decision of this court, or a law of the state should prevent the administration of one or both of these sacraments, would not the constitution be violated, and the freedom of religion be infringed? Every man who hears me will answer in the affirmative. Will not the same result follow, if we deprive the Roman catholic of one of his ordinances? Secrecy is of the essence of penance. The sinner will not confess, nor will the priest receive his confession, if the veil of secrecy is removed: To decide that the minister shall promulgate what he receives in confession, is to declare that there shall be no penance; and this important branch of the Roman catholic religion would be thus annihilated."

People v. Phillips, N.Y.Ct.Gen.Sess. (1813), as reported by a lawyer who participated in the case as amicus curiae and as reprinted in Privileged Communications to Clergymen, 1 Cath. Lawyer 199, 207 (1955).

The evidentiary privilege as it has existed in the United States has been broadly recognized and affirmed in dicta by the Supreme Court. So Justice Field remarked for a unanimous court that "suits cannot be maintained which would require a disclosure of the confidences of the confessional, or those between husband and wife." Totten v. United States, 92 U.S. 105, 107, 23 L.Ed. 605 (1875). So Chief Justice Burger, a century later, observed approvingly, again for a unanimous court, that the priest-penitent privilege, like the privileges between attorney and client and between physician and patient, was "rooted in the imperative need for confidence and trust." Trammel v. United States, 445 U.S. 40, 51, 63 L.Ed.2d 186, 100 S.Ct. 906 (1980). The privilege has been stated broadly as embracing any "confession by a penitent to a minister in his capacity as such to obtain such spiritual aid as was sought and held out in this instance" and so applied to reverse a criminal conviction where a Lutheran communicant had confessed her crime to a minister as a condition for receiving communion and his testimony had been used to convict her. Mullen v. United States, 105 U.S.App.D.C. 25, 263 F.2d 275, 277 (D.C.Cir. 1958).

All fifty states have enacted statutes "granting some form of testimonial privilege to clergy-communicant communications. Neither scholars nor courts question the legitimacy of the privilege, and attorneys rarely litigate the issue." Developments In The Law—Privileged Communications, 98 Harv.L.Rev. 1450, 1556 (1985); W.Va. Code § 57–3–9. It would be strange if a privilege so generally recognized could be readily subverted by the governmental recording of the privileged communication and the introduction of the recording into evidence.

Against these reasons for objectively concluding that Father Mockaitis's subjective belief in the secrecy of the confession was well-founded, there was the fact that Oregon had legislated against the interception of conversation between a prisoner and his attorney but had not done so against the interception of a confidential communication from an inmate to a member of the clergy; there was also the fact that the Wiretap Act did not criminalize recordings made by law enforcement officers in the ordinary course of their duties. We do not believe that the expectation of Father Mockaitis can be made to depend on what a statute fails to forbid. If the inviolability of religious confession to the clergy were not the law of the land, the expectation of every repentant sinner, and the assured confidence of every minister of God's grace, a prosecutor would have a cheap and sometimes helpful way of uncovering evidence of crime by obtaining a court order under § 2516 of the Wiretap Act to wire a church known to be frequented, say, by families or other persons believed to be associated with a criminal organization. On Harcleroad's reasoning such bugging would be lawful because authorized by a judge in accordance with statute and not unlawful because contrary to the reasonable expectations of the participants. Such a fear does not exist because no one expects any prosecutor to engage in such a strategy.

Harcleroad has cited no case in the United States in which a court has given approval to the invasion of the Catholic rite of confession by an agency of government. Our own research has discovered none. A comprehensive study of the issue done as the thesis at Boalt Hall reports none in this country. Jacob M. Yellin, The History and Current Status of the Clergy-Penitent Privilege, 23 Santa Clara L. Rev. 95 (1983). Hard as a negative is to prove, it must be concluded that no evidence has been offered that would have led a priest in Father Mockaitis's shoes to expect that his participation in the Sacrament of Penance would be bugged. He was reasonable in relying on the Oregon law of evidence and the nation's history of respect for religion in general and respect for the sanctity of the secrets of confession in particular, and so had a reasonable expectation of privacy.

Harcleroad argues that Hale did not have such an expectation. Stipulated facts include the fact that Hale did know that his meetings with visitors were recorded and made signals to his visitors to warn them not to speak of matters that Hale did not want disclosed. The contents of Hale's confession, as revealed in his affidavit, are highly suggestive that he knew he was being recorded. He admitted to burglaries that he had already confessed to the police. The centerpiece of his confession was an accusation against Susbauer as the murderer and a protestation of his own innocence. The accusation and the protestation were given the form of a confession by being dressed up in Hale's asserted sorrow for his anger; but it may be doubted that he had any reason to repent anger if in fact his anger had been a response to a false accusation of murder. From the contents of the confession itself it is reasonable to infer that Hale hoped that his words would be recorded and preserved; and his subsequent actions confirm the inference.

It is neither logically nor factually impossible for one party to a communication to have an expectation of privacy and the other not to have one. Hale's expectation does not destroy Mockaitis's. But it does affect the remedy. There is no reason to protect Hale's confession from publication when he desires it. There is reason to protect Father Mockaitis's expectation of privacy in hearing confessions. Archbishop George's expectation is, analogously, equally reasonable.

The Violation Of The Civil Rights Act. The plaintiffs also seek relief under the more general Civil Rights Act, 42 U.S.C. § 1983, which provides redress for the deprivation of any right "secured by the Constitution and laws." As our analysis under RFRA and the Fourth Amendment indicates, Harcleroad has violated the civil rights of the plaintiffs secured by RFRA and by the Fourth Amendment. Proving their case under these heads, the plaintiffs have also proved their case under the Civil Rights Act, with the exception already noted as to their case for destruction of the tape.

The Oregon Constitutional Claims. The plaintiffs' rights are so secured by federal statutes and the Fourth Amendment that it is unnecessary for us to pass on these claims which were not addressed by the district court.

The Remedies. We remand for a grant of the plaintiffs' request for declaratory relief, holding that the taping of Father Mockaitis's encounter with Hale and its subsequent seizure by Harcleroad violated RFRA and the Fourth Amendment. We remand to the district court for the issuance of an injunction in favor of Father Mockaitis and Archbishop George. The injunction may be tailored to fit the expectation of clergy under ORS Evidence Code, Rule 506 and so should restrain Harcleroad and his agents and employees from further violation of RFRA and the Fourth Amendment by assisting, participating in or using any recording of a confidential communications from inmates of the Lane County Jail to any member of the clergy in the member's professional character. We also remand to the district court to take evidence as to the attorney fees to which the plaintiffs are entitled under the Civil Rights Act for both the litigation in the district court and on this appeal. They have prevailed, not as to all the relief sought but nevertheless substantially, on the one claim on which attorney fees may be awarded.

The judgment of the district court is REVERSED and the case is REMANDED for proceedings in accordance with this opinion.

QUESTIONS

1. Was it ethical for Harcleroad to tape Hale's confession to Father Mockaitis? Was it legal?

2. Did Harcleroad's tape recording of Hale's confession violate the Religious Freedom Restoration Act?

3. Should Judge Hodges have signed the search warrant commanding "any police officer" to examine for evidence "the contents of an audio cassette recording of the confession made by Conan Wayne Hale to Father Mockaitis"?

4. The Oregon Solicitor General, in her memorandum to Harcleroad, set forth the legal justification for both taping the confession and preserving the tapes. Should she have said anything about whether taping the confession was ethical? Should she have addressed whether the taping violated the Religious Freedom Restoration Act?

5. David Schuman was the Associate Dean at the University of Oregon, where Harcleroad taught the prosecution clinic as an adjunct professor. Is Schuman's argument on behalf of Harcleroad convincing?

6. Judge Billings wrote to the lawyers representing Father Mockaitis and the Catholic Church that the papers filed on their behalf were "not suitable for filing" and returned the papers along with the filing fee. Should he have instead formally ruled on the motion?

7. In his statement of May 22, 1996, Harcleroad said "I was wrong to authorize taping that conversation. There are some things which are legal and ethical but are simply not right." Was Harcleroad equating professional ethics with legality?

8. Who was responsible for this incident? Does Harcleroad's statement acknowledge or obfuscate and avoid issues of personal responsibility? How about the responses of the Oregon courts, the Oregon Solicitor General and Professor, now Deputy Attorney General, David Schuman?

9. Harcleroad stated among his "accomplishments as District Attorney" that "[I]n excess of 95% of the defendants charged with crimes by the Lane County District Attorney's Office are convicted either by negotiated guilty pleas or trials." What are the dangers of evaluating a prosecutor's performance by his conviction rate? How does this standard influence prosecutors' views of their professional responsibilities?

PROBLEMS

As Professor Schuman observes, prosecutors sometimes face situations in which they must decide how much to allow outside opinion to influence their decisions. What decisions would you make in each of the following situations:

1. A newly elected United States Senator has made enemies by disagreeing with influential members of his own party on appointments for federal judgeships. Several of his political opponents approach the U.S. Attorney (a member of the same political party) and suggest that he investigate an alleged bribe paid to the Senator two years ago, while he was a Congressman. The Senator's political opponents give the prosecutor a list of persons who claim to be witnesses to the alleged bribery and suggest that the prosecutor subpoena these witnesses to testify before a grand jury. The U.S. Attorney begins an investigation, but quickly discovers that one of the witnesses has lost or destroyed the only documentary evidence of the alleged bribe (a handwritten note from the then Congressman to a campaign contributor). The U.S. Attorney also knows that further investigation is very unlikely to prove wrongdoing. Should he convene the grand jury proceeding anyway? Should the views of persons wanting to go forward with the investigation play a role in his decision?

2. A prosecutor does not believe that the death penalty is justified in a particular case and does not want to accept personal responsibility for the prisoner's execution. However, the prosecutor is under pressure to seek the death penalty anyway because public opinion favors it. Should he do so? See John T. Noonan, Jr., Horses of the Night, Harris V. Vasquez, 45 Stan. L. Rev. 1011, 1022 (1993) (California prosecutors who sought the execution of Robert Alton Harris "cooperated with the infliction of death, they were as much responsible for it as the warden who dropped the lever releasing the gas pellets. There is nothing sinful or shameful in such responsibility if the death penalty is morally justified.").

Relevant Background
Prosecutorial Discretion

A prosecutor has wide discretion in deciding how to gather evidence, who to investigate and who to prosecute. As illustrated by *State v. Hale*, some of these decisions are made quickly without much time to reflect. Sometimes, these decision are also made under real or perceived public pressure.

A prosecutor should "refrain from prosecuting a charge that the prosecutor knows is not supported by probable cause." Model Rule 3.8(a); see also DR 7–103(A). However, apart from the probable cause requirement, rules of professional conduct usually give little guidance on when and who to prosecute.

Evenhandedness in exercising prosecutorial discretion is inherent in prosecutors' roles as "ministers of justice." See Model Rule 3.8, comment 1; EC 7–13. This duty to "do justice," however, is inherently vague and allows each prosecutor to individually determine what is "just," leading to inconsistencies in the prosecutorial system. Fred C. Zacharias, Structuring Ethics of Prosecutorial Trial Practice: Can Prosecutors Do Justice? 44 Vand. L. Rev. 45, 48 (1991). In the best exercise of this power, a prosecutor will try to resolve tension between the need for consistency in charging people with crimes and the need to be flexible and tailor charges to the circumstances of a particular offense. See Norman Abrams, Internal Policy: Guiding the Exercise of Prosecutorial Discretion, 19 UCLA Rev. 1, 2–4 (1971). In the worst cases, discretion becomes prosecutorial vindictiveness, selective charging, overcharging, and discrimination based on factors such as race or nationality. See Bennett L. Gershman, The New Prosecutors, 53 U. Pitt. L. Rev. 393, 408 (1992).

A prosecutor's office may have formal guidelines that define charging criteria, particularly in complex areas of criminal law. See Theodora Galacatos, The United States Department of Justice Environmental Crimes Section: A Case Study of Inter- and Intrabreach Conflict Over Congressional Oversight and the Exercise of Prosecutorial Discretion, 64 Fordham L. Rev. 587, 645 (1995); National Prosecution Standards § 9.4(A). A prosecutor's conscience, however, will often tell her something formal guidelines cannot: when she is prosecuting a case for the wrong reason, without a reasonable likelihood of success, or in a discriminatory manner. Even where formal policies permit a decision to prosecute, the prosecutor sometimes will know that she should not do so.

The No–Contact Rule

The priest-penitent privilege at issue in the *Hale* case is litigated far less often than the lawyer-client privilege. Perhaps this is because, despite Judge Ardery's advice to Edward Prichard that he "go to his pastor" about his pending indictment for election fraud (see *United States v. Prichard*, Chapter 2 supra), litigants consult lawyers more often than they consult the clergy. Apart from the "no-contact rule" discussed below, the issues surrounding the lawyer-client privilege are discussed in Chapter 2 supra.

The "no-contact rule" is set out in DR 7–104(A)(1):

During the course of his representation of a client a lawyer shall not:

(1) Communicate or cause another to communicate on the subject of the representation with a party the lawyer knows to be repre-

sented by a lawyer in that matter unless he has the prior consent of the lawyer representing such other party or is authorized to do so.

See also Mode Rule 4.2. This no-contact rule was first promulgated by the ABA in 1908, and its primary objectives are to protect the attorney-client relationship and to prevent attorneys from taking unfair advantage of laypersons. See Alafair S. R. Burke, Note: Reconciling Professional Ethics and Prosecutorial Power: The No–Contact Rule Debate, 46 Stan. L. Rev. 1635, 1638 (1994) (explaining history and rationale for the no-contact rule).

United States v. Hammad, 858 F.2d 834 (2d Cir.1988), applied the no-contact rule to pre-indictment, non-custodial conduct. In *Hammad*, a prosecutor caused an informant to elicit incriminating information from an arson suspect known to be represented by counsel by using a counterfeit grand jury subpoena. The government argued that DR 7–104(A)(1) was coextensive with the Sixth Amendment and therefore did not apply until "the onset of adversarial proceedings." The Second Circuit, however, disagreed and held that the no-contact rule also extends to pre-indictment, investigatory contact, although in most circumstances such contact would fall within the "authorized by law" exception. Although the court declined to further define what was "authorized by law," id. at 839, the court ruled that "the employment of a specious and contrived subpoena is the sort of egregious misconduct that, even before Sixth Amendment protections attach, violates DR 7–104(A)(1)." Id. at 840. However, because the law in this area was not yet settled, the court ruled that barring the admission of the prosecutor's videotapes and recordings was an inappropriate remedy. Id. at 842.

Notwithstanding *Hammad*, many courts agree with the government's position that DR 7–104(A)(1) parallels the Sixth Amendment right to counsel and thus does not apply until the commencement of adversarial proceedings. See United States v. Ryans, 903 F.2d 731, 739 (10th Cir.1990) ("We are not convinced that the language of the rule calls for its application to the investigative phase of law enforcement."); United States v. Powe, 9 F.3d 68 (9th Cir.1993). See also Neals–Erik William Delker, Ethics and the Federal Prosecutor: The Continuing Conflict over the Application of Model Rule 4.2 to Federal Attorneys, 44 Am. U. L. Rev. 855, 863 (1995); Pamela S. Karlan, Discrete and Relational Criminal Representation: The Changing Vision of the Right to Counsel, 105 Harv. L. Rev. 670, 701 (1992) ("A broad interpretation of the no-contact rule would provide a powerful incentive for criminal actors to seek relational representation because having an ongoing relationship with an attorney could insulate them from several of the most effective law enforcement techniques for investigating complex crime."). In fact, the commentary to ABA Model Rule 4.2 states:

> Communications with represented criminal suspects prior to initiation of formal judicial proceedings as part of a noncustodial investigation by government agents or with informants generally are not considered subject to the anti-contact rule. The rationale is usually that the rule is

coextensive with the accused's Sixth Amendment right to counsel, and that the contact is within the "authorized by law" exception.

Id. (quoted in United States v. Ward, 895 F.Supp. 1000, 1004 (N.D.Ill. 1995))

In the "Thornburgh Memorandum" Attorney General Richard Thornburgh responded to the *Hammad* decision. See Memorandum from Attorney General Richard Thornburgh to All Justice Department Litigators (June 8, 1989). The Attorney General asserted that defense lawyers were seeking through a disciplinary rule what they could not get through the Constitution: "a right to counsel at the investigative stage of a proceeding" Id. at 2. Therefore, "[I]t ... [was] the Department's position ... that where the Constitution and federal law permit legitimate investigative contact, DR 7–104 does not present an obstacle." Id. at 5.

Regulations issued by Attorney General Janet Reno in 1994 continued the controversy over whether federal prosecutors must comply with state versions of the no-contact rule that bar preindictment communications. See Burke, supra, at 1655–56 (stating that the new regulations "broadly authorize government attorneys to communicate directly with represented persons prior to arrest or indictment."). These regulations have been met with sharp criticism. See Delker, supra, at 872 (stating that "the new regulation suffers from the fatal flaw of holding federal prosecutors to a different ethical standard than state prosecutors ..."). The 1994 regulations also challenge the disciplinary role of state bar associations, by stating that "[o]nly if the Attorney General finds that a Department attorney has willfully violated these new rules would that attorney continue to be subject to the full measure of state disciplinary jurisdiction." Communications with Represented Persons, 59 Fed. Reg. 39,910, 39,912 (28 C.F.R. Pt. 77) (1994). As an area where the federal government has sought to encroach on the traditional power of the states to regulate lawyers, the Attorney General's efforts to exempt federal prosecutors from at least the *Hammad* Court's interpretation of the no-contact rule will provide fertile ground for future litigation. See United States v. Cutler, 91 F.3d 427 (3d Cir. 1996) (avoiding the issue by holding that New Jersey's no-contact rule "is inapplicable to contacts made by prosecutors or their agents with criminal suspects in the course of a pre-indictment investigation.").

The No–Contact Rule in Civil Litigation and Nonlitigated Matters

The no-contact rule also applies to civil litigation. The Rule thus precludes attorneys from gathering information from a party in a case except with the permission of the party's attorney or through the formal discovery process authorized by law. Although formal discovery is often cumbersome and opposing counsel often refuses to allow informal interviews, violation of the no-contact rule can lead not only to discipline, but also to exclusion of evidence and other sanctions in the case itself.

Generally, the rule also prohibits contacting certain high level employees of a represented party. See Wright v. Group Health Hosp., 103 Wash. 2d 192, 691 P.2d 564 (1984) (no-contact rule limited to employees in positions of "managing-speaking" for the organization). However, an issue that remains unresolved is whether a former employee is also a party that cannot be contacted without permission of the former employer's lawyer. Although many courts do not extend the no contact rule to former employees, some courts hold that the no contact rule does apply to former employees who have had extensive exposure to privileged information. See Rentclub, Inc. v. Transamerica Rental Finance Corp., 811 F.Supp. 651, 658 (M.D.Fla.1992); Camden v. Maryland, 910 F.Supp. 1115, 1124 (D.Md.1996). ("But it is not enough that Plaintiff be prevented from using [the former employee's] testimony in court. [Plaintiff's law firm] has listened in at the legal confessional. It has gained access to confidential information that is damaging to Defendants ... the Court will grant Defendants' Motion to Disqualify [plaintiff's law firm] from these proceedings.")

Finally, the no-contact rule extends to nonlitigated matters as well. "This Rule applies to communications with any person, whether or not a party to a formal adjudicative proceeding, contract or negotiation, who is represented by counsel concerning the matter to which the communication relates." Model Rule 4.2, comment 3. Whether closing a sale of real estate, planning a corporate transaction, or settling a will, if a lawyer knows that a person is represented by another lawyer in the matter, the lawyer should discuss the matter with the other lawyer, not with the represented person directly. The two lawyers may, and often do, work out an arrangement whereby one or more lawyers may contact another lawyer's client directly (for example, a "due diligence" site visit preceding a corporate acquisition or a sale of securities). The no-contact rule of course does not extend to communications concerning matters outside the scope of the matter for which a represented person is known to have retained counsel.

Communication With Eligible Class Members in a Class Action

Application of the no-contact rule is particularly problematic in class action lawsuits. Many courts prohibit communications by defense counsel with class members both before and after certification. "[T]he imbalance in knowledge and skill which exists between class members and defense counsel presents an extreme potential for prejudice to class members' rights. This problem has long been recognized and remedied by the proscription against such communications found in DR 7–104." Bower v. Bunker Hill Co., 689 F.Supp. 1032, 1034 (E.D.Wash.1985). See also Resnick v. American Dental Association, 95 F.R.D. 372 (N.D.Ill.1982) (communications by defense counsel with class members prohibited); and Tedesco v. Mishkin, 629 F.Supp. 1474 (S.D.N.Y.1986) (attorney sanctioned for mailing letters to class members suggesting that they "opt out" of the class action). On the other hand, communications by attorneys seeking to protect the interests of class members or various subclass members should fall outside of the reach of the no-contact rule. For example, communications of the type Derrick Bell made with parents of children in school desegregation class actions, see Chapter 6 supra, are not only proper, but raise important issues about the quality of the representation provided by class counsel.

QUESTIONS

1. At trial, defense lawyers help finders of fact distinguish between innocent and guilty defendants. However, defense lawyers' involvement in the investigatory stage of criminal cases may help guilty defendants more than it helps innocent ones. See William J. Stuntz, Lawyers, Deception and Evidence Gathering, 79 Va. L. Rev. 1903, 1955 (1993). Would innocent defendants be better off, or at least little worse off, in a system that restricted lawyers' roles in the criminal justice process (for example by suspending the no-contact rule) during the time that the government gathers most of its evidence? Why or why not?

2. Does the no-contact rule give more protection to a criminal defendant who has a lawyer than to a defendant who does not have a lawyer?

3. What are the legal and ethical obligations of a prosecutor in questioning a suspect who, after being advised of his right to counsel, asks to see a lawyer? See Miranda v. Arizona, 384 U.S. 436 (1966).

4. Does the no-contact rule interfere with cost effective discovery in civil cases?

PROBLEM

1. Dave Jones is a driver for Emerald City Distributers, a distributer of beverages. Dave, accompanied by a trainee, was making a delivery when he collided with another vehicle. You are the attorney for the driver of the vehicle with which Dave collided. Tina, the trainee, witnessed the accident but was not driving. Which of the following may you privately interview without the consent of Emerald's attorney: (i) Dave, (ii) Tina, and (iii) the Operations Officer of Emerald who supervised driver training and deliveries?

Garrard R. Beeney, b. New Rochelle, N.Y. 1954; B.A. Swarthmore 1976; J.D. University of Pennsylvania 1979; admitted to the New York bar 1980; associate at Sullivan & Cromwell 1979–87; partner since 1987.

Matter of Beiny.

129 A.D.2d 126, 517 N.Y.S.2d 474 (1987).

■ Before MURPHY, P.J., and KUPFERMAN, MILONAS, KASSAL and WALLACH, JJ.

PER CURIAM:

The present motion for suppression of allegedly improperly obtained material and disqualification of counsel comes in the context of a trust accounting proceeding commenced by petitioner Martin Wynyard. Wynyard and his family are the beneficiaries of the trust in question which has as its corpus 45% of the voting shares of the Antique Company of New York (ACNY). The trustee of this trust and respondent to the Wynyard petition is Wynyard's sister, Rotraut L.U. Beiny (hereinafter the Trustee). In addition to being Trustee of the Wynyard trust, Ms. Beiny is herself the beneficiary of trusts containing 55% of the voting and non-voting shares in ACNY and is ACNY's president and chief executive officer.

Wynyard alleges, inter alia, that valuable assets of ACNY, including antique porcelains, Renaissance jewelry and other art objects have, since 1972, been diverted from ACNY without consideration and placed in two trusts situated in Leichtenstein created by the parties' parents, Hans and Elisabeth Weinberg, but now controlled exclusively by the Trustee and her immediate family. Obviously, the ownership of the allegedly diverted assets in the Leichtenstein trusts is critical to the outcome of the accounting proceeding.

It is petitioner's contention that ACNY's ownership of the assets as to which the claim of wrongful diversion is made is traceable to the parties' father, Hans Weinberg, who amassed a large collection of antique porcelains and other art objects in pre-Nazi Germany. In 1939, Weinberg emigrated to London where he established a business dealing in porcelains, and substantially increased his collection. Petitioner maintains that before leaving London in 1957 to take up residence and center his business in the United States, Weinberg transferred ownership of his entire personal holdings of porcelains to a Panamanian company known as Michelle, the stock of which was owned by his wife Elisabeth. Michelle was liquidated in the early 1960's and its inventory transferred first to a revocable trust created by Elisabeth Weinberg for the benefit of the parties herein, and then to the newly established ACNY. In consideration for the Michelle inventory, ACNY stock was issued to four irrevocable trusts created by Elisabeth Weinberg: the Wynyards were the beneficiaries of two of these trusts which together contained 45% of the voting and non-voting ACNY stock, while the Beinys were the beneficiaries of the remaining two trusts together containing 55% of the ACNY voting and non-voting shares. It is as co-trustee of the Wynyard trust having as its corpus 45% of the ACNY voting shares that Beiny appears in the within accounting proceeding.

Beginning with the liquidation of Michelle in 1964 and in subsequent transactions pursuant to which the Michelle inventory came to be owned by ACNY, Hans Weinberg, his family, and his business were represented by the law firm of Greenbaum, Wolff & Ernst. The Greenbaum firm's representation of the Weinberg interests continued until 1973. Hans Weinberg died in 1976.

In March, 1985, after the commencement of the within proceeding, Garrard Beeney, of the firm of Sullivan & Cromwell, petitioner's counsel, twice telephoned John Wiener, the liquidator of the by then defunct Greenbaum firm. Beeney explains that he contacted Wiener "because counsel believed that the Greenbaum firm possessed factual information concerning ownership of the antiques presently held by Beiny in Europe." Wiener refused to give out any information over the phone and indicated that he had no authorization from the executor of the Weinberg estate or anyone else to permit Beeney the access he requested to Greenbaum's files. Thereafter, Beeney issued a combined notice of deposition and subpoena duces tecum commanding Wiener as Greenbaum's liquidator to appear for deposition in two weeks and to bring with him all documents within his control "which reflect, refer or relate to Hans Weinberg, Martin Wynyard, Ruth Wynyard, Rotraut Weinberg Beiny, the Antique Company of New York, Inc., the Antique Porcelain Company, Michelle, Inc., and/or the Antique Porcelain Company, Ltd., London." Accompanying the subpoena was a cover letter representing that the subpoena was served on behalf of Sullivan & Cromwell's client, Martin Wynyard, who the letter states "is the executor and an heir to Mr. Weinberg's will."

Upon receiving the subpoena, which it is conceded was not served on notice to the Trustee, Wiener states that he contacted Beeney and inquired whether the Trustee's authorization was not necessary for the release of the files. Wiener further states that he was assured that the files would be made available to the Trustee's attorneys. According to Wiener, once he had received this assurance, he retrieved the extensive Weinberg files from the Greenbaum warehouse and delivered them to Sullivan & Cromwell. This was done about one week prior to the date of the planned deposition. Shortly after the materials had been turned over, Wiener received notification that his deposition had been cancelled.

From April 1 through April 9, 1985, the Trustee was deposed by Sullivan & Cromwell in London. Documents obtained from the Greenbaum liquidator without the knowledge of the Trustee or her attorneys were used extensively to surprise her during her deposition testimony. In view of the Trustee's claim that the documents as to which she was being deposed contained confidential attorney-client communications or evidence thereof, it was stipulated that the Trustee's response to inquiries based on those documents would not constitute a waiver of her claim of privilege. When questioned by the Trustee's counsel, Beeney refused to divulge where or how he had obtained the documents. Only upon returning to New York and conducting his own investigation did the Trustee's counsel learn that Wiener had turned over the Greenbaum firm's Weinberg files pursuant to the covertly issued subpoena.

Following the Trustee's substitution of counsel in June, 1985, her new attorneys contacted Beeney and requested the production of the documents obtained from Wiener. Beeney refused to make the documents available, except in exchange for discovery concessions. The present motion for suppression of the subject documents and disqualification of Sullivan & Cromwell followed in August, 1985. As of the time of the motion the Trustee still had not been permitted access to the documents obtained from Wiener, which it must be noted were the originals, and consequently had no way of knowing the extent of the disclosure made.

.   .   .   .

There can be no question that Sullivan & Cromwell did not properly obtain the Greenbaum firm's files on the Weinbergs. Where, as here, discovery is conducted as against a non-party, adverse parties must be afforded notice. If the discovery is to be by means of deposition, notice must be given pursuant to CPLR 3107: A party desiring to take the deposition of any person upon oral examination shall give to each party twenty days' notice, unless the court orders otherwise. (emphasis added) Clearly, petitioner's counsel failed to abide by this very basic rule when it served the March 8, 1985 combined notice of deposition and subpoena duces tecum upon the Greenbaum liquidator without notice to the Trustee.

Sullivan & Cromwell makes the rather obscure argument that its obligation to notify the Trustee pursuant to CPLR 3107 was somehow excused by the deposition's cancellation. Obviously, this is not the case. The statute is quite clear: the Trustee was entitled to 20 days' notice of Wiener's deposition. The notice obligation was already overdue at the time of the subpoena's issuance as the deposition demanded in the subpoena was scheduled to be held in 14, not 20, days' time. The subsequent decision to cancel the deposition did not retrospectively excuse Sullivan & Cromwell's utter failure initially to comply with the statute's notice requirements. For Sullivan & Cromwell to describe its performance in this regard as "an earnest, even if mistaken, attempt to comply with the specific requirements of CPLR 3107", is preposterous.

It is, in addition, particularly disingenuous to suggest, as Sullivan & Cromwell does, that cancellation of Wiener's deposition in the circumstances here obtaining rendered the failure to give notice pursuant to CPLR 3107 harmless. It would be one thing if no discovery had been obtained, but that is not the case. At the time the deposition was cancelled, Sullivan & Cromwell had already received the materials requested in the combined notice of deposition and subpoena duces tecum.

Manifestly, Sullivan & Cromwell had little interest in deposing Wiener who had already informed Beeney that he had no information to give concerning the matters in which the Greenbaum firm represented the Weinbergs. As the cancellation of Wiener's deposition demonstrates with consummate clarity, Sullivan & Cromwell's real interest was in obtaining the Greenbaum files. Although Sullivan & Cromwell professes to know of no rule preventing it from using an attorney's subpoena, as it did, to compel the clandestine production of documents from a non-party who is not to be deposed, the law is otherwise. CPLR 3120(b) sets forth the proper procedure for obtaining discovery and production without deposition from a non-party:

R 3120 Discovery and production of documents and things for inspection, testing, copying or photographing.

. . . .

(b) As against non-party. A person not a party may be directed by order to do whatever a party may be directed to do under subdivision (a). *The motion for such order shall be on notice to all adverse parties*; the non-party shall be served with the notice of motion in the same manner as a summons. (emphasis added)

We do not think that this provision, designed to assure that non-parties will not be unduly burdened with discovery demands and that discovery from non-parties is conducted in a fair and open manner, can be avoided by resorting to the use of covertly issued attorneys' subpoenas. (See, Siegal, Practice Commentaries, McKinney's Cons.Laws of N.Y., Book 7B, CPLR 3102 [C3102:2], 3111 [C3111:1], 3120 [C3120:12], at 262, 409, 522; see also 3A Weinstein–Korn–Miller, N.Y.Civ.Prac. P 3120.08.) Sullivan & Cromwell's contention to the contrary is not worthy of further comment.

The above-cited rules governing the conduct of discovery and dictating that parties be notified of deposition and disclosure demands made upon non-parties, are well known. Indeed, as the Surrogate observed in her decision disposing of the Trustee's original motion, "[i]t is hornbook law that a party is entitled to a notice of deposition when a subpoena is served on a non-party witness." We do not believe that Sullivan & Cromwell was ignorant of these rules, nor would its ignorance be excusable. These are not trivial or seldom invoked provisions; they are fundamental to the orderly and fair conduct of pretrial litigation and are daily put to use by litigants and the courts.

The inference which sadly follows is that, far from making an "earnest" attempt to comply with the rules, Sullivan & Cromwell chose to chart a course which it knew to be at variance with acceptable discovery practice so as to obtain by stealth that which could not be readily obtained through proper channels. This inference unfortunately derives substantial support from our consideration of the entire sequence of events pursuant to which the Greenbaum files came into Sullivan & Cromwell's possession and were thereafter retained and used.

. . . .

[The Court then expounded at length on what it perceived to be Sullivan & Cromwell's motives for obtaining the Greenbaum files the way it did]

The question now arises whether the suppression ordered by the Surrogate adequately protects the Trustee against further use of the information improperly culled by Sullivan & Cromwell from the Greenbaum files, and whether, given the blatant abuse with which we are here confronted, involving willful disregard of procedural rules, deceit, and the covert acquisition of otherwise unobtainable privileged material, suppression is sufficient to deter such conduct and insure the integrity of the process. We conclude that suppression, while necessary, does not adequately address these concerns and accordingly, that Sullivan & Cromwell must be disqualified from further participation in this trust accounting proceeding.

. . . .

■ All concur except Kupferman, J. who dissents [from the order disqualifying Sullivan & Cromwell].

In *Rotraut L.U. Beiny v. Martin Wynyard*, 132 A.D.2d 190, 522 N.Y.S.2d 511 (1987), the Appellate Division reacted angrily to Sullivan & Cromwell's motion for leave to appeal, reiterated that the firm had engaged in blatantly unethical conduct and referred the proceeding to the Department

Disciplinary Committee for investigation. Justice Kupferman in dissenting stated, "I would grant leave to appeal. Moreover, I cannot subscribe to the hyperbole in the court's memorandum. The Surrogate, who was fully familiar with the situation, imposed a sanction germane to the problem."

QUESTIONS

1. A subpoena is signed by a lawyer as an officer of the court and has the legal effect of compelling the person named therein to testify or produce documents under penalty of contempt of court. How is a subpoena different than a search warrant signed by a judge, such as that in *State of Oregon v. Hale*? How is a subpoena similar? Why is it particularly important that a lawyer exercising the subpoena power do so in a manner that is fair to all parties concerned?

2. In portions of its opinion (omitted here) and particularly in its ruling on Sullivan & Cromwell's motion for leave to appeal, the Appellate Division chastised Sullivan & Cromwell for what appears to be primarily the conduct of one of its lawyers. Justice Kupferman dissented. To what extent should firms be held responsible for the conduct of individual lawyers? See discussion of New York's new rule allowing discipline of law firms as well as individual lawyers (chapter 12 infra). Is there anything Sullivan & Cromwell could have done to prevent what happened here?

Relevant Background

Abuse of the Subpoena Power

A litigant's right to call witnesses and collect evidence is recognized by giving attorneys the power to subpoena as officers of the court. However, the subpoena power is easily abused, whether to obtain evidence covertly as in *Matter of Beiny*, to delay a trial or to harass witnesses. See e.g. Board of Educ. v. Farmingdale Classroom Teachers Ass'n, 38 N.Y.2d 397, 380 N.Y.S.2d 635, 343 N.E.2d 278 (N.Y.1975) (school board could sue for abuse of process where lawyer for teachers' union subpoenaed 87 teachers to appear to testify on the same day to force school board to hire substitute teachers). A subpoena, like a complaint, is a form of process, and, as pointed out in Chapter 2 supra, abuse of process gives rise to a claim in tort. See Draft Rest.3d Law Governing Lawyers § 78 cmt. d.; Rest.2d torts § 682 (abuse of process is the use of "legal process, whether criminal or civil, against another primarily to accomplish a purpose for which it is not designed."). Model Rule 4.4 also prohibits a lawyer from using "means that have no substantial purpose other than to embarrass, delay, or burden a third person." Finally, many states view abuse of process as contempt of court. See Fabricant v. Superior Court of Los Angeles County, 104 Cal. App.3d 905, 916, 163 Cal.Rptr. 894, 901, citing Cal. Civ. Code § 1209 ("misuse of the court's subpoena power" can be "the basis for contempt proceedings").

Subpoena of an Attorney

The *Beiny* case discusses the subpoena of an attorney in a civil context. In criminal cases, prosecutors can also obtain evidence from attorneys, using one of the most powerful instruments at their disposal: the grand jury subpoena. Indeed, prosecutors have wide discretion in exercising this subpoena power, and the number of attorney subpoenas has risen sharply in recent years. Defense attorneys are becoming increasingly agitated by the effect this new trend may have on the quality of their work and on lawyer-client communication. Charles J. Ogletree, Symposium: Limitations on the Effectiveness of Criminal Defense Counsel: Legitimate Means or "Chilling Wedges?" 136 U. Pa. L. Rev. 1903, 1908 (1988).

The evidence sought from an attorney in a subpoena of course must concern matters outside the scope of the attorney client privilege. Such unprivileged documents and testimony, for example, may concern fee arrangements and client conduct such as perjury, obstruction of justice, or conspiracy during the legal representation (see Chapter 2, supra, for discussion of what types of client communications fall outside the scope of the privilege). See Roger C. Cramton & Lisa K. Udell, Symposium: State Ethics Rules and Federal Prosecutors: The Controversies over the Anti-Contact and Subpoena Rules, 53 U. Pitt. L. Rev. 291, 360 (1992); Matter of Grand Jury Subpoenas, 959 F.2d 1158 (2nd Cir.1992) (prosecutor could subpoena a corporate client's telephone bills that had been turned over to the client's lawyer).

Model Rule 3.8(f) provides that a prosecutor shall not "subpoena a lawyer to present evidence about a past or present client" unless the prosecutor reasonably believes that the information sought is not privileged, the information is "essential to the successful completion of an ongoing investigation or prosecution," and "there is no other feasible alternative to obtain the information." A prior version of Rule 3.8(f) had required the prosecutor to obtain "prior judicial approval after an opportunity for an adversarial hearing," but this provision won little support from state courts and was deleted from the Rule at the ABA House of Delegates August 1995 annual meeting.

Defense attorneys fear that prosecutors may abuse this power to fish for information or to diminish a defense attorney's effectiveness. Fred C. Zacharias, A Critical Look at Rules Governing Grand Jury Subpoenas of Attorneys, 76 Minn. L. Rev. 917, 924, (April, 1992). The possibility of being subpoenaed furthermore may lead attorneys to refuse cases they might otherwise accept, and responding to subpoenas may expose actual or potential conflicts, forcing defense attorneys to withdraw. Fred C. Zacharias, Specificity in Professional Responsibility Codes: Theory, Practice, and the Paradigm of Prosecutorial Ethics, 69 Notre Dame L. Rev. 223, 287 and 309 (1993). Another fear is that attorney subpoenas may interfere with attorney-client communications and foster mistrust between attorney and client. Gregory I. Massing, The Fifth Amendment, the Attorney–Client Privilege, and the Prosecution of White Collar Crime, 75 Va. L. Rev. 1179, 1215 (1989).

Tactics for Gathering Evidence

In a trial, disputed questions of fact are resolved after presentation of evidence supporting each litigant's position. To enhance the probability of success or induce a favorable settlement, an attorney gathers the most persuasive evidence available and presents it to the opposing party, judge or jury. Attorneys thus often go to great lengths to obtain information that supports a client's position. See Stephen McG. Bundy & Ebner Richard Elhauge, Do Lawyers Improve the Adversary System? A General Theory of Litigation Advice and its Regulation, 79 Cal. L. Rev. 313, 320–35 (1991). Unfortunately, attorneys sometimes go too far.

Restrictions on attorney contact with represented persons (see discussion of the no-contact rule supra) parallel other rules that protect unrepresented persons from manipulation by attorneys gathering evidence for their clients. "In dealing on behalf of a client with a person who is not represented by counsel, a lawyer shall not state or imply that the lawyer is disinterested. When the lawyer knows or reasonably should know that the unrepresented person misunderstands the lawyer's role in the matter, the lawyer shall make reasonable efforts to correct the misunderstanding." Model Rule 4.3. See also DR 7–104(A)(2). "In the case of a potential civil defendant, for example, a lawyer communicating with such a person would be required to disclose the fact that he contemplated filing a lawsuit. In most cases this would be sufficient warning to assure that lay persons would at least know enough to keep silent until they could consult counsel and thus come within the protection of Rule 4.2 [the no-contact rule]" 2 Geoffrey C. Hazard, Jr. & W. William Hodes, The Law of Lawyering § 4.3:102 at 747 (2 ed. Supp. 1991).

Unfortunately, unanswered questions abound. For example, once an attorney makes the required disclosure, is she free to "press on and cajole an unfavorable settlement or exact damaging admissions[?]" Id. at 748. The Comment to Rule 4.3 bars giving "advice to an unrepresented person other than the advice to obtain counsel," but many communications to unrepresented persons have persuasive power without falling within the ambit of "advice." A court deciding what evidentiary consequences should ensue from statements of an unrepresented party to another party's attorney, may take into account whether the attorney took unfair advantage of the unrepresented party.

A lawyer should also respect the rights of witnesses and other participants in a matter. Model Rule 4.4 thus provides that "in representing a client, a lawyer shall not use means that have no substantial purpose other than to embarrass, delay, or burden a third person, or use methods of obtaining evidence that violate the legal rights of such a person." Types of conduct that the rule was designed to discourage include harassment, threats, infiltration and gathering evidence through subterfuge. 2 Hazard & Hodes § 4.4:101 at 754–764. For example, Vermont attorney William Knight, at the urging of his boss John Harrington, sought to gain damaging evidence for a divorce proceeding. Knight participated in both "electronic eaves-dropping and the taking of photographs of [a] meeting between the [party] in the proposed divorce action and the young woman hired by Harrington to effect a compromising situation with the [party]." In re William J. Knight, 129 Vt. 428, 281 A.2d 46, 47 (Vt.1971). Knight was suspended from the practice of law with leave to reapply in three months.

However, not all conduct falls so neatly within the scope of Model Rule 4.4. For example, courts generally do not have authority to sanction private investigators for using unethical, but not illegal, tactics to gather information. William J. Stuntz, Lawyers, Deception, and Evidence Gathering, 79 Va. L. Rev. 1903, 1916 (1993). Private investigators thus may use deceptive tactics while the attorneys who hire them look the other way. Although discipline may or may not be imposed on the attorney, an attorney's reputation will certainly suffer from her willingness to condone deceptive tactics. Furthermore, some deceptive tactics, such as recording a conversation without consent, carry criminal sanctions regardless of who the perpetrator is. 2 Hazard & Hodes § 4.4:105 at 764.2 (Supp. 1996).

Destruction of Evidence

If evidence is very damaging to a lawyer's client, its destruction could reward the client, even at the expense of the truth finding function of a tribunal. As officers of the court, attorneys presumably should not take part in such destruction of evidence. Until litigation is contemplated, however, a client may have a legal right to destroy some documents in the regular course of business, and in some circumstances an attorney may believe that she should advise a client to do so. See Lawrence B. Solum, Stephen J. Marzen, Truth and Uncertainty: Legal Control of the Destruction of Evidence, 36 Emory L. J. 1085, 1138, (Fall 1987); Philip A. Lionberger, Comment, Interference With Prospective Civil Litigation By Spoliation of Evidence: Should Texas Adopt a New Tort?, 21 St. Mary's L.J. 209, 229 (1989); and Ricardo G. Cedillo, David Lopez, Symposium—Consumer Protection and the Texas Deceptive Trade Practices Act: Document Destruction in Business Litigation from a Practitioner's Point of View: The Ethical Rules vs. Practical Realities, 20 St. Mary's L.J. 637, 642 (1989).

In both the civil and criminal context, Model Code, DR 7–102 (A)(3) prohibits concealment of information that a lawyer is required by law to reveal, and DR 7–109(A) prohibits suppression of evidence that a lawyer or her client has a legal obligation to reveal or produce. Neither Disciplinary Rule, however, specifically prohibits advising a client to destroy evidence in situations in which doing so is not illegal (for example, a routine document destruction program at a corporate client). See also Model Rule 3.4(a) (providing that "[a] lawyer shall not (a) unlawfully obstruct another party's access to evidence or unlawfully alter, destroy or conceal a document or other material having potential evidentiary value. A lawyer shall not counsel or assist another person to do any such act.") Although the Model Rule, like the Code, only refers to unlawful acts, the comment to the Rule underscores an important point: "Applicable law in many jurisdictions makes it an offense to destroy material for purpose of impairing its availability in a pending proceeding or one whose commencement can be foreseen." Furthermore, destruction of evidence in such circumstances would almost certainly be "conduct prejudicial to the administration of justice." Model Rule 8.4(d). Procuring the absence of a witnesses is also forbidden. See Snyder v. State Bar, 18 Cal.3d 286, 133 Cal.Rptr. 864, 555 P.2d 1104 (1976)(lawyer disbarred for misconduct including advising his client not to appear for a deposition notwithstanding a court order).

Some jurisdictions also recognize "intentional spoliation of evidence" as a tort when evidence relevant to pending or probable civil or criminal litigation is destroyed. See Smith v. Superior Court, 151 Cal.App.3d 491, 494, 198 Cal.Rptr. 829, 831 (1984) (action for damages available against automobile dealer which, while having custody of parts removed from a van involved in an accident, "destroyed, lost or transferred said physical evidence, making it impossible for the Smith's experts to inspect and test those parts in order to pinpoint the cause of the failure of the wheel assembly on the van"). Negligent destruction of evidence is also actionable by the party deprived of the benefit of the evidence in some states including California. See Velasco v. Commercial Bldg. Maintenance Co., 169 Cal. App.3d 874, 215 Cal.Rptr. 504 (1985) (plaintiffs injured by an exploding bottle alleged they took the bottle fragments to an attorney who put them in an unmarked bag left on his desk; plaintiffs could assert a cause of action for negligent destruction of evidence against defendant maintenance company whose employees negligently disposed of the bag while cleaning the attorney's office.) See also James F. Thompson, Spoliation of Evidence: A Troubling New Tort, 37 U. Kan. L. Rev. 563, 592, (1989); John Fedders & Lauryn Guttenplan, Document Retention and Destruction: Practical, Legal and Ethical Considerations, 56 Notre Dame L. Rev. 5 (1980).

PROBLEM

1. A lawyer defending a medical malpractice case suspects that the plaintiff is faking his injuries. The lawyer hires a private investigator to go to the plaintiff's home posing as a door-to-door salesman of exercise machines. The plaintiff falls for the ruse and tells the "salesman" that he is in "excellent" shape. Is it ethical for the lawyer thus to "defensively" use fraud to detect another person's fraud? Does the lawyer's conduct violate the no-contact rule? See William J. Stuntz, Lawyers, Deception and Evidence Gathering, 79 Va. L. Rev. 1902, 1910 (1993); DR 1–102(A)(4) (A lawyer shall not "[e]ngage in conduct involving dishonesty, fraud, deceit, or misrepresentation"); Model Rule 4.1(a) ("In the course of representing a client a lawyer shall not knowingly: (a) make a false statement of material fact or law to a third person").

2. Assume that you are the plaintiff's attorney in the above action. One afternoon, you receive an envelope of documents from the defendant's insurance company. Upon examining the documents, you realize that they were not intended for your review. Moreover, the materials identify a witness who would be beneficial to your case. May you keep the documents and interview the witness?

C.   Fair and Unfair Argument at the Criminal Bar

Rex v. Raleigh (a special court, 1603)

"In 1581 a new star appeared in the court firmament, dim at first but rising meteor-like to a dazzling brilliance. **Walter Raleigh**, son of a small Devon Squire, adventurer in France and Ireland, rose, like Hatton [a prominent courtier to Elizabeth I] solely by a personal magnetism which entranced the Queen. Within a few years he received substantial grants of land, the Warden-ship of the Stannaries in Cornwall, and in 1587 the Captaincy of the Guard. Yet in the end he did not penetrate the inner sanctum of the Council. Royal indignation at his marriage—in sharp contrast to her tolerance of Leicester's or Essex's matches—excluded him from court for several crucial years. Raleigh too, like Sidney and Essex, hankered after another sort of career than the courtier's; the wilds of Virginia or of Guiana held more attraction for him than the gardens of Hampton Court or Nonsuch." Wallace MacCaffrey, Elizabeth I 173 (1993).

Raleigh studied at Oxford, but left to fight in France. He also studied law for a brief period of time, and during the reign of Elizabeth, Raleigh participated in several forays against Spanish holdings, including Cadiz in 1596, and the Azores in 1597. After his trial, Raleigh spent thirteen years in the Tower, his execution indefinitely postponed by King James I. In 1616, James freed Raleigh to sail to South America in search of treasure, but, seeking peace with Spain, prohibited Raleigh from raiding Spanish settlements. In March of 1617, Raleigh's fleet ignored these orders and invaded and sacked a Spanish settlement. King James, at the urging of the Spanish, ordered the 1603 death sentence to be carried out, and Raleigh was beheaded on October 29, 1618.

Henry Brooke, eighth Lord Cobham, b. unknown, d. 1619; son of William, seventh Lord Cobham and a favorite of Queen Elizabeth; M.P. for Kent (1588–89) and for Hedon (1592–93); warden of the Cinque Ports 1597; knight of the Garter 1599; accused in 1600 of political dishonesty by Lord Essex, who later acknowledged that the accusations were untrue; arrested in July 1603 for participation in a plot on behalf of Catholics on evidence provided by Sir Walter Releigh; tried and convicted of treason in November 1603 and sentenced to death; remained in the Tower under a suspended sentence until 1617, when he was allowed to go to Bath to cure a sickness that ended in his death.

Sir Edward Coke, b. Norfolk 1552, d. 1634; attended the Norwich free school; Master of Arts, Trinity College, Cambridge 1570; entered as a student of municipal law in the Inner Temple in 1572; called to the bar in 1578; engaged in *Shelley's Case* 1 Rep. 94 (a leading case in real property law); appointed attorney general in 1593; began in 1600 publishing the first volume of *The Reports*; prosecuted the treason trials of the Earls of Essex and Southampton in 1600, Sir Walter Raleigh in 1603 and of the gunpowder plotters in 1605; made chief justice of the common pleas in 1606;

removed from the bench by King James I in 1616 amid charges that he uttered contemptuous speeches from the bench, threatened juries and behaved disrespectfully to the King.

Robert Cecil, first Earl of Salisbury, b. Westminster 1563, d. 1612; entered St. John's College, Cambridge in 1581; M.P. for Westminster in 1584 and 1586; knighted and sworn into the Privy Council in 1591; appointed chancellor of Cambridge University in 1600.

Sir John Popham, b. Huntworth, Somerset 1531, d. 1607; educated at Balliol College, Oxford; entered the Middle Temple in 1568; made a privy councillor in 1571; appointed solicitor general in 1578; succeeded Sir Christopher Wray as Lord Chief Justice and knighted in 1592.

Catherine Drinker Bowen, The Lion and the Throne

CHAPTER FIFTEEN

Trial of Sir Walter Ralegh (Part I)*

On the seventeenth of November, 1603, Ralegh was taken down the hill for trial. When he came with his guard to the Bishop's palace, the old stone hall was crowded. People sat in the minstrels' gallery, leaned against the stone pillars until their legs must have ached. Some of them had been there since dawn; many had waited all night in the street before the doors. Lady Arabella Stuart—*Arbella*, everyone called her—sat with the old Earl of Nottingham. Before the day was out she would have her say; the indictment was full of her name. Poor Arbella—forever the center of plots she had not conceived! One look at her seemed enough to turn men's ambitions elsewhere. Lord Cobham had said that once he saw Arbella he "resolved never to hazard his estate for her." Yet she was herself to die a prisoner in the Tower. Here in the Bishop's palace, Cobham lay imprisoned beneath the courtroom or in some turret chamber. And Cobham was Ralegh's only accuser, the single witness on whom the prosecution must build its case.

A Special Commission of Oyer and Terminer had been appointed for the trial; it included seven laymen and four judges: Popham (Chief Justice of King's Bench), Justice Anderson of Common Pleas and the puisne judges, Gawdy and Warburton. The laymen were Mountjoy (Lord Deputy of Ireland), who had said he would flee England rather than come under the file of Coke's tongue; Sir William Waad (Clerk of the Privy Council), a zealous and unscrupulous trapper of recusants who had escorted Ralegh in the coach from London; the Earl of Suffolk, who had fought with Ralegh at Cadiz; Sir John Stanhope of the King's household. And lastly, to the eternal shame of the King, who had approved his appointment, sat Sir Walter's greatest enemy, the man that had poisoned James's mind against him: Lord Henry Howard, who four times changed his religion and in whom the truth did not dwell.

---

* The author uses an alternative spelling of Sir Walter Raleigh's name.—ed.

The jury of twelve knights had been brought down from Middlesex County. Such a panel was considered harsh and somewhat biased; King James himself remarked that he would not wish to be tried by a Middlesex jury. There was rumor that Sir Edward Darcy, Ralegh's friend and neighbor, had been named and removed overnight from the panel.* But there is no proof that the jury was packed, though the mere fact of Lord Henry Howard's presence as commissioner is suspicious. Ralegh declined to challenge a single juror. He "thought them all honest and Christian men and knew his own innocence." He had however one request. His memory was never good, sickness in prison had weakened him. Might he answer questions severally, as they came up, rather than all at once? Coke objected, as he had with Essex. The King's evidence, "ought not to be broken or dismembered, whereby it might lose much of its grace and vigor."

The judges conceded the point to Ralegh. Yet Coke's remark concerning the King's evidence came as no surprise in Winchester Hall. A threat to the sovereign was a threat to every English subject, dangerous moreover to a Protestant Reformation which even yet was not secure. The King's evidence (not the prisoner's) must serve as focal point. To bring out this evidence was the business of the Attorney General. Unfortunately for Ralegh, his four judges considered it their business too, as did the seven lay commissioners who sat upon the dais with the judges. The majority of these men already knew the evidence by heart. Since the moment of Ralegh's arrest (and likely a month before) they had been searching it out, fitting part to part until confession matched confession. In Essex's case such "preparation" had been easy; hundreds saw his armed passage through London. With Ralegh the evidence was slim. Moreover, the court considered that it had here a knight far cleverer than Essex, one who by common parlance was an easy liar; in Coke's own words, "the father of wiles."

Ralegh's judges plainly were part of the prosecution, determined from the start to prove the prisoner guilty. Yet there could have been no question of collusion; Popham, old Judge Anderson, Gawdy, Warburton were neither venal nor corrupt. On the contrary, they were men of high character who sat to do their duty. And judicial duty, in the year 1603 (and for two centuries after) meant bringing forward every damaging fact of character and circumstance which could be gathered in the King's favor— hearsay evidence, gossip at third hand, the confession of confederates. In treason cases smoke was hot as fire and bare suspicion tantamount to the act overt. Those keeping company with traitors were *ipso facto* guilty; any evidence could pass. Yet Coke, Chief Justice Popham, and Robert Cecil, who sat with the commissioners, took pride in the English legal tradition, pride even in their system of trial at common law. Was not such trial by accusation rather than inquisition, as in France and Spain? Was it not, by general agreement, speedy, open, viewed by any citizen who cared to come?

---

* The manuscript of the original panel shows three erasures, elaborately scratched out and written over by new names.

Above all, was not the accused permitted to speak in his own defense, holding, if he wished, a day-long altercation with judges, commissioners, Attorney General? "Sir Walter Ralegh," wrote Cecil to a Privy Councilor before the trial, "yet persists in denial of the main treason. Few men can conceive it comes from a clear heart. Always, he shall be left to the law, which is the right all men are born unto."

Cecil believed what he said. Moreover he was to be the only man in Winchester courtroom who stood out for Sir Walter in the matter of his legal rights and privileges.

Ralegh's indictment, read aloud by the Clerk, was short: Sir Walter had conspired to "kill the King, raise a rebellion with intent to change religion and subvert the government." The overt acts charged were listening to Spanish bribes, conferring with Lord Cobham concerning Arabella Stuart's claim, together with promises, plans, statements and conspiracies to that end.

Serjeant Heale opened for the Crown. He was brief, his speech is remembered only for a startlingly facetious peroration where he remarked that as for the Lady Arabella, upon his conscience she had no more title to the Crown than he had himself, "which, before God," he finished, "I utterly renounce." Even Ralegh smiled. It was the last time he would smile that day.

Coke followed and spoke at length. Foul treasons had been unearthed, though no torture was employed to find them, and no "rigorous usage." (The prosecution invariably took care to make this claim in treason trials and the audience took care to disbelieve it.) "This great and honorable assembly," Coke said, "doth look to hear this day what before hath been carried on the rack of scattering reports . . ."

There was no telling who might be listening, hidden in some dark gallery. Arthur's Hall, up the hill, had a pipe in the wall behind the judges' dais, leading to a little chamber where kings had anciently sat concealed, their ear to all that passed. People knew about it, knew also that James was visiting at a nearby country house. Those who had witnessed Essex's trial recalled the sudden appearance of Cecil from the parted arras. . . .

Two conspiracies had been discovered, Coke reminded the jury; the *Bye Plot* and the *Main*,* they were called. The Bye was the Priests' Plot, hatched by Watson and Clarke; the Main was Ralegh's conspiracy. As Coke continued, it became plain he was describing, not Ralegh's plot at all, but the Bye, a business far more flagrant and more foolish. Ralegh broke in, addressing the jury: "I pray you, Gentlemen, remember that I am not charged with the *Bye*, which was the treason of the priests."

No, Coke said; Sir Walter was not so charged. Yet all these treasons, "like Sampson's foxes, were joined together at the tails, though their heads

---

* These names meant nothing more than Main Plot and By-plot or Secondary Plot. The fact that the Bye had been perpetrated, chronologically, before the Main, was only one of a dozen ambiguities drawn by the prosecution over a murky legal trail.

were severed." Coke went on to describe and define the law of treason, and was proceeding reasonably enough until, after a sugary panegyric on the character of James, he suddenly turned on Ralegh and demanded, "To whom, Sir Walter, did you bear malice? To the royal children?"

It was the first of Coke's attacks, unexpected, startling, brought on perhaps by Ralegh's quick positive denial of Coke's charge, perhaps by the realization that here was a prisoner equipped to defend himself with skill and passion. "Mr. Attorney," Ralegh answered, "I pray you, to whom or to what end speak you all this? I protest I do not understand what a word of this means, except it be to tell me news. What is the treason of Markham and the priests to me?"

COKE: I will then come close to you; I will prove you to be the most notorious traitor that ever came to the bar! You are indeed upon the Main, but you have followed them of the Bye in imitation; I will charge you with the words.

RALEGH: Your words cannot condemn me; my innocency is my defense. I pray you go to your proofs. Prove against me any one thing of the many that you have broken, and I will confess all the indictment, and that I am the most horrible traitor that ever lived, and worthy to be crucified with a thousand torments.

COKE: Nay, I will prove all. Thou art a monster! Thou hast an English face but a Spanish heart.... I look to have good words from you, and purpose not to give you worse than the matter press me unto. But if you provoke me, I will not spare you and I have warrant for it.... You would have stirred England and Scotland both. You incited the Lord Cobham....

Cobham, rich, discontented and apparently somewhat of a fool, had been one of the "diabolical triplicity" which, according to Lord Henry Howard, met at Durham House to conspire the King's death and set Arbella in his place. Cobham planned to cross the Channel and obtain money for the support of Arbella's title—a bargain which included promise of a "toleration of the Popish religion in England." All this, said Coke, Lord Cobham had confessed: dealing with Aremberg, the Spanish agent; Aremberg's offer of 600,000 crowns. Ralegh, Coke urged, pretended the money was merely a Spanish offer "to forward the peace." Yet if the Spanish King had in mind such an offer, would he have chosen a recipient like Cobham, who was "neither politician nor swordsman?" No! It required a Ralegh to carry through these plans. "Such," said Coke, "was Sir Walter's secrecy and Machiavellian policy that he would confer with none but Cobham, 'because,' saith he, 'one witness can never condemn me.' It will be stood upon Sir Walter Ralegh today," Coke continued, "that we have but one witness. But I will show your Lordships that it is not necessary to have two witnesses."

On this point, so crucial to Ralegh, Coke was securely within the law. It was true that during the reign of Edward VI (1547–1552), statutes had been enacted, declaring for two witnesses. But on the accession of Mary Tudor, these statutes were repealed (1553), and since then, one witness was held sufficient in cases of felony tried under the common law. This was the legal view as known to every barrister who had argued in Westminster Hall. Nevertheless, the country at large clung stubbornly to the old two-witness rule. The Bible declared for it, and was not Holy Scripture corroborative of the common law?

Coke, in this first long offensive, did not stop upon the point. It would come up again and could more properly be dealt with by the judges. "In our case in hand," Coke proceeded, "we have more than two witnesses. For when a man, in his accusation of another, shall by the same accusation also condemn himself and make himself liable to the same punishment, this is by our law more forcible than many witnesses, equal to the inquest of twelve men. For *the law presumes that a man will not accuse himself in order to accuse another*."

Coke turned now to the jury and repeated the charge of setting up Arbella as "titular queen." On Ralegh's interrupting, Coke retorted angrily that he did not wonder to see Sir Walter "moved." "Nay," Ralegh replied, "you fall out with yourself. I have said nothing to you. I am in no case to be angry."

As the reporter's bare account moves forward, it is hard to see why Ralegh's calm interpolations were to Coke so palpably infuriating. Was it something in Sir Walter's manner, the old easy arrogance, impossible of description, which for thirty years had earned a host of enemies? Whatever it was, it caused Coke to lose control again and again, spitting out words shameful, unworthy, never to be forgotten. After Ralegh's quiet rebuke, Coke reverted once again to the Bye plot, of which the prosecution well knew that Sir Walter was innocent, yet which, as the tale unfolded, seemed to implicate the prisoner by the very telling. As Coke talked, his anger mounted. "And now," he informed the jury, "you shall see the most horrible practices that ever came out of the bottomless pit of the lowest hell...."

There followed the recitation of an involved, fantastic maneuver of Cobham's, turning on a forged letter "placed in a Spanish Bible," an answer forged and falsely dated.

RALEGH: What is that to me? Here is no treason of mine done. If my Lord Cobham be a traitor, what is that to me?

COKE: All that he did was by thy instigation, thou viper: For I *thou* thee, thou traitor! I will prove thee the rankest traitor in all England.

RALEGH: No no, Mr. Attorney, I am no traitor! Whether I live or die, I shall stand as true a subject as any the King hath. You may call me a traitor at your pleasure, yet it becomes not a man of quality and virtue to do so. But I take comfort in it, it is all you can do, for I do not yet hear that you charge me with any treason.

CHIEF JUSTICE POPHAM: Sir Walter Ralegh, Mr. Attorney speaks out of zeal of his duty for the service of the King, and you for your life. Be patient on both sides.

Coke now ordered the Clerk to read Cobham's confession from the Tower, dated July twentieth. It was almost a repetition of the formal indictment, but more impressive, coming direct from Cobham: "Confesseth: that he had conference with the Count Aremberg about procuring 500 or 600,000 crowns, and a passport to go into Spain to deal with the King, and to return by Jersey. And that nothing should be done until he had spoken with Sir Walter Ralegh for distribution of the money to them which were discontented in England. Being shown a note under Ralegh's hand [Cobham], when he had perused the same, brake forth, saying, 'O traitor! O villian! I will now tell you all the truth!' And then said that he had never entered into these courses but by Ralegh's instigation, and that he [Ralegh] would never let him alone."

Coke directed the Clerk to repeat the last words—"Sir Walter would never let Cobham alone." As for the "note under Ralegh's hand," so disturbing to Cobham, it was to prove one of the deadliest facts toward Ralegh's conviction. Written in July, before Sir Walter's imprisonment, it was addressed to Cecil. Coke explained the occasion. At Windsor, when Ralegh first was questioned by the Privy Council, he had said he knew of no plots between Cobham and the Spanish agent. But later the same afternoon, Sir Walter, riding home to London, remembered an incident of early spring, after Cobham had spent an evening at Durham House. Cobham had left by the water gate, and Ralegh, looking out a turret window, saw the barge turn upstream, glide past Cobham's own stairs and stop at the house of La Rensi, a Spanish agent. As soon as Sir Walter returned from Windsor, he wrote out the story and sent it to Cecil.

To the jury, this action of Ralegh's was positively damning. Why should Sir Walter, this early in the game, have taken it on himself gratuitously to inform against his friends, unless as a guilty man he hoped by such betrayal to save his own skin? Cobham, when first arrested, had sworn to Ralegh's innocence of all plots and "conversations." Only when shown this letter, had Cobham broken down and accused Ralegh of treason.

Sir Walter, in rebuttal, asked to see Cobham's confession. While it was being carried to him, he addressed the court: "Gentlemen of the Jury, this is absolutely all the evidence that can be brought against me. This is that which must either condemn me or give me life, which must free me or send my wife and children to beg their bread about the streets. This is that which must prove whether I am a notorious traitor or a true subject to the King...." Having read Cobham's confession, Sir Walter answered at once concerning his own July letter to Cecil. Yes, he had written it. But it revealed to Cecil nothing new. Long since, in the late Queen's time, said Ralegh, it was known that Cobham had dealings with agents from the Low Countries. Even Cecil's father, Lord Burghley, had been aware of it. Cobham, glimpsing this letter in the Tower, had jumped, added Ralegh, to wild unwarranted conclusions. Were not Lord Cobham's bitter railings well known? The man's passions, indeed, had "such violence," said Ralegh, "that his best friends could never temper them."

The note was never produced in court. Apparently, it had vanished, or at least it made no part of the bundle of depositions at Coke's disposal. Chief Justice Popham now intervened. He himself had been in Cobham's Tower cell when Cobham saw this letter. The Lords of Council had brought it at the exact moment when Cobham was signing his first statement of innocence. (Actually, Cobham had balked at signing. Subscription was like taking an oath. And noblemen, Cobham protested, were not required to swear to documents, their bare word being considered sufficient.) At Popham's insistence however, Cobham took up a pen—and as he wrote his name the Lords walked in the door, bearing Ralegh's note "of betrayal." Cobham looked at it and burst into fury, calling out upon Sir Walter as a wretch and a traitor. "Hath he used me thus? Nay then, I will tell you all!" Cobham's face as he said it (testified Popham) was the face of a man speaking truth; his face and all his actions.

The testimony of a Chief Justice is not easy to disregard. Clearly, Popham believed in Cobham's word, which meant he disbelieved in Ralegh's. And upon this point—which man spoke truth, Ralegh or Cobham—the trial hung, and Ralegh's life. To the jury in Winchester courtroom, Ralegh's word was if anything less reliable than Cobham's. Both were liars, opportunists. Sir Walter by all reports was much the cleverer and stronger. Did it not follow he was also the more guilty?

It was now Ralegh's turn to speak in full. He had two lines to pursue: (1) show that Cobham's word was not to be trusted; (2) convince the jury that his own circumstances made the alleged plots ridiculous, his past history being incompatible with such ill-timed and evil machinations. He began with the second argument, and what he said covers three printed pages; it is instinct with poetry and dignity, and, throughout, magnificently reasonable. By nature his voice was low; in Parliament men had complained they could not hear him when he spoke. Why, he asked now, if he desired to plot with Spain, would he have chosen this time of all times, when England was strengthened by a union with Scotland, the Irish rebels quieted, the Low Countries at peace with England, Denmark's friendship assured by the royal marriage—and on the English throne, "instead of a Lady whom time had surprised, we had now an active King, a lawful successor to the Crown who was able to attend to his own business?"

Elizabeth, the old Queen! *A Lady whom time had surprised.* No man had said it half so well. The phrase would be repeated, would become famous. "I was not such a madman," Ralegh was saying, "as to make myself in this time a Robin Hood, a Wat Tyler, a Kett, or a Jack Cade. I knew also the state of Spain well, his weakness and poorness and humbleness at this time. I knew that he was discouraged and dishonoured. I knew that six times we had repulsed his forces, thrice in Ireland, thrice at sea, and once at Cadiz on his own coast. Thrice had I served against him myself at sea, wherein for my country's sake I expended of my own properties, four thousand pound. I knew that where beforetime he was wont to have forty great sails at the least in his ports, now he hath not past six or seven; and for sending to his Indies he was driven to hire strange vessels—a thing contrary to the institutions of his proud ancestors, who straitly forbad, in case of any necessity, that the Kings of Spain should make their case known to strangers. I knew ..."

It was a saga, as Ralegh told it; it was the story of England's glory unrolling. Men who had forgotten Drake, forgotten Hawkins, remembered them now and for one quick moment remembered also the days before '88, when England, a small and feeble island, had lived in terror of the Spaniard. Ralegh had never lost his broad Devon accent. It was impressive, here in the courtroom; it breathed of the sailor, not the courtier.

"What pawn had we to give the King of Spain?" Ralegh went on, passionately. "What did we offer him?" He turned to Coke. "And to show I was not *Spanish*, as you term me, I had written at this time a Treatise to the King's Majesty of the present state of Spain, and reasons against the peace...."

The jury listened. ("Never," wrote a spectator, "any man spoke so well in times past nor would do in the world to come.") Yet as Ralegh left his own history and came to Cobham's dubious character—his second argument—what he said seemed less convincing. Sir Walter acknowledged an intimacy with Cobham, an "inwardness," he called it. But their frequent meetings had been concerned only with private business; Cobham had wished advice about his estate. Moreover, Ralegh argued, if he himself desired a treasonable confederate, why would he have chosen Cobham, one of the richest noblemen of England? Discontented earls, such as Bothwell and Westmoreland, were easily available—"men of better understanding than Cobham, ready to beg their bread."

Poverty or riches, the condition of a man's estate, played a large part in treason trials. Rich men seldom make revolutions. As had been said of the Essex affair, "Poverty soonest plungeth the English into rebellion." Essex's final act of violence had come when the Queen took away his monopoly of sweet wines and he felt himself nearing destitution. Ralegh finished speaking, and Cobham's second Examination was read by the Clerk: When he had been about to return from Spain with the 600,000 crowns, Cobham had feared to stop at Jersey and confer according to plan. At Jersey he would have been wholly in Ralegh's power, and Ralegh "might well have delivered him and all the money to the King."

Was Ralegh, then, doubly nefarious, mistrusted even by his accomplices, ready to play his cards both ways and betray his own confederate for credit with the King? Even if Cobham lied, these plots and counterplots were shocking, disturbing. They could not be all invention.... Had Cobham, Sir Walter asked quickly, put his signature to this second statement in the Tower? No, Coke replied. A declaration given in the presence of Privy Councilors needed no subscription to be valid.

RALEGH: Surely, Mr. Attorney, you would not allow a bare scroll to have credit with a jury?

COKE: Sir Walter, you say the Lord Cobham's accusing you was upon heat and passion. This is manifestly otherwise; for after that the Lord

Cobham had twice called for the letter and twice paused a good while upon it and saw that his dealing with Count Aremberg was made known, then he thought himself discovered and after said, 'O wretch and traitor, Ralegh!' As to improbability, is it probable that my Lord Cobham would turn the weapon against his own bosom and overthrow himself in estate, in honour and in all his fortunes, out of malice to accuse you? ... If he feared that you would betray him, there must of necessity be a trust between you. No man can betray another but he that is trusted, to my understanding.... You seek to wash away all that is said, by affirming the evidence against you to be but a bare accusation, without circumstances or reason to confirm it. That I will fully satisfy. For as my Lord Cobham's confession stands upon many circumstances, and concerns many others, I will, by other means, prove every circumstance thereof to be true.

RALEGH: But, my Lords, I claim to have my accuser brought here face to face to speak. And though I know not how to make my best defence by law, yet since I was a prisoner, I have learned that by the law and statutes of this realm in case of treason, a man ought to be convicted by the testimony of two witnesses if they be living. I will not take it upon me to defend the matter upon the statute *25th Edward III*, though that requires an overt act....

Ralegh referred, of course, to the great statute of 1351, upon which, for six hundred years, subsequent statutes were based and which defined treason as "compassing or imagining the king's death, levying war against the king, and adhering to the king's enemies." Not the killing of a king but the compassing or imagining his death—*intent to kill him*: this was treason. For centuries therefore the question was to arise: Whether mere words, when plainly evident of intent to kill the king (or to subvert the state), could be construed as an overt act? In times of national emergency, courts invariably have so construed them. In times of peace and national security, the overt act takes narrower construction, and courts require deeds as well as words before they will convict of treason. On this vital question, Coke as Chief Justice was himself to alter, on occasion, his own interpretation, giving, under Stuart kings, far greater latitude to the accused than he gave to Ralegh or even to Essex—and not only in the matter of the act overt but the rule concerning two witnesses.

Sir Walter went on to cite the statutes of Edward VI (1547, 1548) concerning two witnesses. "Mr. Attorney," he said, "if you proceed to condemn me by bare inference, without an oath, without a subscription, without witnesses, upon a paper accusation, you try me by the Spanish inquisition. If my accuser were dead or abroad, it were something. But he liveth and is in this very house!"

Ralegh turned to the Commissioners. "Consider, my Lords, it is no rare case for a man to be falsely accused, aye, and falsely condemned, too! And my Lords the Judges—remember, I beseech you, what one of yourselves said in times past. I mean Fortescue, a reverend Chief Justice of this kingdom, touching the remorse of his conscience for proceeding upon such slender proof. '*So long as he lived* [he said] *he should never purge his conscience of that deed.'* And my Lords, remember too the story of Susannah; she was falsely accused. . . . I may be told that the statutes I before named be repealed, for I know the diversity of religion in the Princes of those days caused many changes. Yet the equity and reason of those laws remains. They are still kept to illustrate how the common law was then taken and ought to be expounded. By the Law of God therefore, the life of man is of such price and value that no person, whatever his offence is, ought to die unless he be condemned on the testimony of two or three witnesses."

It was a long speech and there was more, referring not only to Deuteronomy but to St. Paul. How the judges were to receive it would presently be seen, but to the audience it was supremely effectual. Ralegh, in calling on the Law of God, appealed not alone to religious faith but to the national conception of LAW as apart from *the laws*—a distinction sharp in English minds: *the laws* were made by men and could be found in statute book or in judicial maxim and decision. LAW was deeper, higher, derived from God. LAW antedated *the laws* and would exist if every man-made statute were expunged. It was a native conception, part of the common inheritance. Sir Walter had presented the law as plain citizens knew it in their minds and held it in their hearts, no matter what construction had been put upon it by legalists now or in Queen Mary Tudor's time.

"If then," Ralegh finished, "by the statute law, by the civil law and by God's word it be required that there be two witnesses at the least, bear with me if I desire one. Prove me guilty of these things by one witness only, and I will confess the indictment. If I have done these things I deserve not to live, whether they be treasons by the law or no. Why then, I beseech you, my Lords, let Cobham be sent for! Let him be charged upon his soul, upon his allegiance to the King. And if he then maintain his accusation to my face, I will confess myself guilty."

CHAPTER SIXTEEN

Trial of Sir Walter Ralegh (Part II).

It was now midday, the trial was half over. Through high windows, light drifted down; on stone floors the rushes were pulled around chilly feet. Ralegh had argued brilliantly from the statutes but his judges were quick with refutation. The laws quoted did not apply, later statutes had repealed them. "I marvel, Sir Walter," Judge Warburton said, "that you being of such experience and wit, should stand on this point; for many horse-stealers should escape if they may not be condemned without witnesses. By law, a man may be condemned upon presumption and circumstances, without any witness to the main fact. As, if the King (whom God defend!) should be slain in his chamber, and one is shown to come forth of the chamber with his sword drawn and bloody, were not this evidence both in law and opinion without further inquisition?"

RALEGH: Yet by your favour, my Lord, the trial of fact at the common law is by jury and witnesses.

POPHAM: No! The trial at the common law is by *examination*. If three conspire a treason and they all confess it, here is never a witness, and yet they may all be condemned of treason.

RALEGH: I know not, my Lord, how you conceive the law; but if you affirm it, it must be a law to all posterity.

POPHAM: Nay, we do not conceive the law. We know the law.

RALEGH: Notwithstanding, my Lords, let me have thus much for my life. For though the law may be as your Lordships have stated it, yet is it a strict and rigorous interpretation of the law. Now the King of England at his coronation swears to observe the equity and not the rigour of the law. And if ever we had a just and good King, it is his Majesty; and such doth he wish his ministers and judges to be. Though, therefore, by the rigour and severity of the law, this may be sufficient evidence, without producing the witness, yet your Lordships, as Ministers of the King, are bound to administer the law in equity.

POPHAM: Equity must proceed from the King. You can only have justice from us.

Popham was confident in what he said. To him as to every lawyer in the hall, Sir Walter's trial had proceeded according to law. Should the King, after Ralegh's condemnation, pardon him, it would be done by virtue of his Majesty's prerogative. That was what Ralegh implied by "equity," and to the judges it was confusion deliberately created. The spectators reacted otherwise; to them these fancy distinctions meant nothing. Sir Walter had shown himself not only eloquent but reasonable; he seemed to know more law than the judges. Many in the hall had sat at Essex's trial, an occasion when the Attorney General made much of overt acts, stating that conviction in England was by the act overt, never on bare words alone. Yet where here was an overt act? The jury waited.

To Coke, Ralegh's arguments were mere casuistry. Laymen who talked law were irritating and Sir Walter, in this respect, was worse than Essex. Ralegh had lived in rooms at the Temple when Coke was a student; yet it did not follow Sir Walter had studied the law. These swordsmen and sailors who skimmed the cream of knowledge—these swashbuckling poetical lords and Queen's favorites with their persuasive tongues—spouted law as the devil quotes Scripture.

"The Crown," Coke said, "shall never stand one year on the head of the King if a traitor may not be condemned by circumstances.... *Scientia sceleris est mera ignorantia* [the wisdom of a scoundrel is pure ignorance]. You, Sir Walter, have read the letter of the law but understood it not."

It was the old contention, the old debate between lawyers and laymen: Which shall prevail, law or justice? To Ralegh's audience the words were not synonymous. Yet in the centuries-old calendar of criminal courts, no crime had been more difficult to construe than treason. Sir Walter's judges could cite a whole array of recent statutes, passed to strengthen Queen Elizabeth's position and to give to the Crown all advantage in the struggle against Spain, France, Rome, and against such domestic extremists as cherished ambition to alter the government and religion of England. When statutes, being new, were doubtful of application, the Crown was always favored, not the suspect. Sir Walter's judges saw no reason to take a new position.

Ralegh's own words were now produced, as taken down in the Tower on August thirteenth: "He confesseth the Lord Cobham offered him 10,000 crowns of the [Spanish] money for furthering the peace between England and Spain, and that he should have it within three days; but said, 'When I see the money I will make you an answer,' for [Ralegh] thought it one of [Cobham's] idle conceits and therefore made no account thereof."

To the jury, this was a serious acknowledgment: Ralegh had actually listened to an offer from Spain. That he had not accepted the money—had never even seen it—they promptly forgot. Men who listened to bribes were tainted men, dangerous, vulnerable. . . . Ralegh's "confession" (which in truth confessed nothing) upset this jury of Middlesex knights who knew little of the tangled politics of faction, the bargains by which courtiers lived and moved and the shifting of loyalties with each wind that blew from Europe. (Cecil himself was later to accept a pension from Spain.) Ralegh saw that he had lost ground and urged again that Cobham be produced in court. "Were the case but for a small copyhold, you would have witnesses or good proof to lead the jury to the verdict. And I am here for my life!" Once more the Chief Justice refused: "Sir Walter, you plead hard for yourself, but the laws plead as hard for the King." Cecil interposed. Might he hear the opinion of all the Judges on this point?

The judges all answered that in respect it might be a means to cover many treasons and might be prejudicial to the King, therefore by law it was not sufferable.

As the afternoon wore on, spectators showed themselves restless; the temper of the hall was seen to alter. ("Sir Walter behaved himself so worthily, so wisely, so temperately, that in half a day the mind of all the company was changed from the extremist hate to the greatest pity.") Ralegh had employed no histrionics but bore himself with simplicity, abusing no one beyond his own accuser, Cobham, and keeping his argument to the law and the state of the realm. Coke, on the other hand, digressed into any field that seemed fruitful. One of the indicted priests, Watson, had quoted in the Tower words spoken by some nobleman (unnamed), suggesting annihilation of James and his family. Coke let the words roll from his tongue, managing, during the recital, to repeat them three times: "Now let us destroy the King and all his cubs, not leaving one!"

RALEGH: O barbarous! Do you bring the words of these hellish spiders against me? If they, like unnatural villains, used those words, shall I be charged with them?

COKE: Thou art thyself a spider of hell, for thou dost confess the King to be a most sweet and gracious Prince, yet thou hast conspired against him.

The matter of a treasonable book was next. In Ralegh's library a manuscript had been found, written by a lawyer in the 1580's to justify Queen Elizabeth's proceedings against Mary Queen of Scots. By inference it argued against James's title to the English crown. Ralegh acknowledged possession but said he had borrowed the book years ago from Lord Treasurer Burghley. "I marvel," Ralegh said, "that it should now be urged as a matter so treasonable in me to have such books, when it is well known there comes out nothing in these times but I have it and might as freely have it as another. And as my Lord Cecil hath said of his library, I think a man might find in my house all the libels that have been made against the late Queen."

COKE: You were no Councillor of State, Sir Walter, and I hope never shall be.

CECIL: Sir Walter Ralegh was truly no *sworn* Councillor of State. Yet he hath been often called to consultations.

Coke now produced, with something of a flourish, his only oral witness of the trial, an English sailor, a pilot named Dyer, who put his hand on the Bible and testified that last July, in Lisbon, he had heard "a Portugal gentleman say that King James would never be crowned, for Don Cobham and Don Ralegh would cut his throat first."

Nobody was impressed; such a fellow could palpably be bought for a few pounds. The sailor retreated. Ralegh spoke contemptuously: "This is the saying of some wild Jesuit or beggarly priest. But what proof is it against me?"

COKE: It must perforce arise out of some preceding intelligence and shows that your treason had wings.

Again it was the old tactic of the treason trial, wherein the prosecution quotes damaging statements made by anybody at all, and then, by hinting association, or merely by constant repetition of the words, hypnotizes a jury into laying on the prisoner the initial responsibility for what was said. Robert Cecil, at this point, rose to remark that two innocent names had been implicated. Count Aremberg, the Ambassador, should not be blamed for "what others said to him or presumed of him, but of how far he consented or approved." (Ralegh, hearing this, must truly have despaired; he was himself being tried on nothing beyond "what others said to him or presumed.") Among the auditory, Cecil went on, was a noble lady whose name should be cleared, seeing the indictment charged a plot to set her on the throne. All eyes turned to the box where sat Arbella with the Earl of Nottingham. The old Earl rose. "The Lady," he said, "doth here protest upon her salvation that she never dealt in any of these things."

That, apparently, disposed of Arbella, a lady habitually dragged into public notice and then summarily dismissed. Coke, however, had reserved his two best points of evidence. He now produced the first one: a confession by Cobham, under date of October 13, saying that Ralegh had sent a letter to the Tower, bidding Cobham not be dismayed because "one witness could not condemn him." If they both kept silence, both were safe. The man who carried it was Kemys, a soldier and sea captain who had accompanied Ralegh to Guiana in 1595.

RALEGH: I deny the writing of any such letter! For Kemys, I never sent him on any such message. This poor man hath been a close prisoner these eighteen weeks and hath been threatened with the rack to make him confess, but I dare stand upon it he will not say it now.

Instant clamor broke among the commissioners; the lords all spoke at once. There had been no torturing of any prisoner. The King had given order that "no rigor should be used."

RALEGH: Was not the keeper of the rack sent for and he threatened with it?

SIR WILLIAM WAAD, from the commissioner's bench: When Mr. Solicitor [Fleming] and myself examined Kemys, we told him he deserved the rack but did not threaten him with it.

COMMISSIONERS: That was more than we knew.

The matter was dropped, but not until Kemys's own confession had been read, wherein he swore he had delivered the letter to Cobham. This time it was Ralegh's word against his own servant, a man known to be both faithful and brave. To the jury it looked as if Mr. Attorney had trapped Sir Walter into a lie. For the last time, Ralegh begged to have Cobham brought into court. "It is you, then, Mr. Attorney, that should press his testimony, and I ought to fear his producing, if all that be true which you have alleged." Cecil supported Sir Walter. Could not the proceedings be delayed while the judges sent to ascertain the King's pleasure in this matter?

But the judges resolved that the proceedings must go on and receive an end.... Whereupon Sir Walter Ralegh addressed himself to the Jury and used a speech to this effect....

What Sir Walter said now included little of law or logic. It was a simple, eloquent appeal: "You, Gentlemen of the jury ... you see my only accuser is the Lord Cobham, who with tears hath lamented his false accusing me, and repented of it as if it had been an horrible murder. I will not expect anything of you but what reason, religion and conscience ask for every man.... Remember what St. Augustine saith, 'So judge as if you were about to be judged yourselves, for in the end there is but one Judge and one Tribunal for all men.' .... Now if you yourselves would like to be hazarded in your lives, disabled in your posterities—your lands, goods and all you have confiscated—your wives, children and servants left crying to the world; if you should be content all this should befall you upon a trial by suspicions and presumptions—upon an accusation not subscribed by your accuser, without the open testimony of a single witness—then so judge me as you would yourselves be judged!"

Serjeant Phillips, ordered by Popham to sum up for the Crown, repeated the charges briefly, adding that Cobham had confessed to all of them. "Now the question is," Phillips said, "whether Sir Walter Ralegh be guilty as inciting or procuring the Lord Cobham to this treason. If the Lord

Cobham say truth, Sir Walter Ralegh is guilty. If Sir Walter Ralegh say true, then he is free; so which of them says true is the whole question. Sir Walter Ralegh hath no proof for his acquittal, though he hath as much wit as man can have. But he uses only his bare denial. But the denial of a criminal is not sufficient to clear him, neither is the evidence on oath of a defendant in his own cause allowed to clear him in any Court of law or equity, much less therefore in matters of treason.''

Now the business, [wrote the reporter] seemed to be at an end. Then said Sir Walter Ralegh, "Mr. Attorney, have you done?''

COKE: Yes, if you have no more to say.

RALEGH: If you have done, then I have somewhat more to say.

COKE: Nay, I will have the last word for the King.

RALEGH: Nay, I will have the last word for my life.

COKE: Go to, I will lay thee upon thy back for the confidentest traitor that ever came to the bar!

CECIL: Be not so impatient, good Mr. Attorney. Give him leave to speak.

COKE: I am the King's sworn servant and must speak. If I may not be patiently heard, you discourage the King's Counsel and encourage traitors.

Was it now the spectators hissed? (A spectator, writing afterward, said the auditory hissed at Coke, not specifying the moment.)

Mr. Attorney, [says the reporter] sat down in a chafe and would speak no more until the Commissioners urged and entreated him. After much ado, he went on and made a long repetition of the evidence for the direction of the jury. And at the repeating of some things, Sir Walter Ralegh interrupted him and said he did him wrong.

It was here that Coke lost all control, speaking words which are held forever to his shame. Nor were they phrases a man can whisper. Coke stood directly in front of Ralegh. Sir Edward was a big man and, at fifty-two, still in the prime of strength and vigor; his full dark robes made him seem even larger. Long afterward, it was said he shook his fist at Ralegh, though no eyewitness mentioned it. Nevertheless, Coke's voice must have filled the hall: "Thou are the most vile and execrable traitor," he shouted, "that ever lived!''

RALEGH: You speak indiscreetly, uncivilly and barbarously.

COKE: Thou art an odious fellow! Thy name is hateful to all the realm of England for thy pride.

RALEGH: It will go near to prove a measuring cast between you and me, Mr. Attorney.

COKE: Well, I will now lay you open for the greatest traitor that ever was. This, my Lords, is he that hath set forth so gloriously his services against the Spaniard, and hath ever so detested him! This is he that hath written a book against the peace [with Spain]. I will make it appear to the world that there never lived a viler viper on the face of the earth than thou!

I will show you wholly Spanish, and that you offered yourself a pensioner to Spain for intelligence. Then let all that have heard you this day judge what you are, and what a traitor's heart you bear, whatever you pretended.

During the terrible exchange, Coke carried in his hand a scroll. It was his final evidence, a surprise card he had withheld, a last damning word against Ralegh, given by Cobham only yesterday from his prison cell. Coke's first words would indicate he held the paper up so all could view it. "See, my Lords, what it hath pleased God to work in the heart of my Lord Cobham, even since his coming hither to Winchester! He could not sleep quietly till he had revealed the truth to the Lords, and therefore voluntarily wrote the whole matter to them, but yesterday. And to discover you, Ralegh, and all your Machiavelian tricks, hear what the Lord Cobham hath written under his own hand, which I will read with a loud voice, though I be not able to speak this the night after."

Turning to the audience, Coke began to read Cobham's words, "commenting," says the reporter, "as he went along":

"Sir Walter Ralegh, four nights before my coming from the Tower, caused a letter, inclosed in an apple, to be thrown in at my chamber window, desiring me to set down under my hand and send to him an acknowledgment that I had wronged him, and renouncing what I had formerly accused him of. His first letter I made no answer to; the next day he wrote me another, praying me, for God's sake, if I pitied him, his wife and children, that I would answer him in the points he set down, informing me that the Judges had met at Mr. Attorney's house, and putting me in hope that the proceedings against me would be stayed. Upon this I wrote him a letter as he desired. I since have thought how he went about only to clear himself by betraying me. Whereupon I have resolved to set down the truth, and under my hand to retract what he cunningly got from me, craving humble pardon of his Majesty and your Lordships for my double dealing. . . ."

"The truth"—as Cobham saw it in this last retraction—was Ralegh's bargain with Aremberg for a flat yearly pension of 1500 pounds in return for spying service, "to tell and advertise what was intended by England against Spain, the Low Countries or the Indies." To the jury this was new and shocking. Bribes had been mentioned, but nothing so damning as a continuous, yearly payment. As instance—Cobham wrote further—Sir Walter, returning one night from the palace at Greenwich, revealed "what was agreed upon betwixt the King and the Low Countrymen, that I should impart it to Count Aremberg. . . . And Sir Walter in his last letter advised me not to be overtaken by confessing to any preacher as the Earl of Essex had. . . ."

Here Coke broke off his reading, and turning to Ralegh, spoke in passion: "O damnable athetist! He counsels not to confess to preachers, as the Earl of Essex did! That noble Earl died indeed for his offence, but he died the child of God, and God honored him at his death. Thou, Ralegh, wast by when he died. *Et lupus et turpes instant morientibus ursae!*"

Wolves and bears press close upon the dying. The Latin, rolling out, was like a curse; it was anathema, incantation, and, considering Coke's own part in Essex's trial, was least excusable. This was not law but rabble-rousing. It was the stones and mire hurled once more at Ralegh. Whatever the jury thought of it, they could not disregard the new evidence—a letter written at Winchester not twenty-four hours past. Tomorrow or next day, Cobham himself would stand trial in this very hall. Impossible that a man with death so close upon him would lie thus to the Lords. What had he to gain thereby? Was any favor, Popham inquired of the commissioners, "promised or offered" to Cobham for the writing of this letter? No, Cecil replied; to his knowledge there was none. "I dare say not," Ralegh interposed drily. "But my Lord Cobham received a letter from his wife that there was no way to save his life but to accuse me."

This, to the jury, was beside the point. "The Lord Cobham's confession," wrote the reporter, "seemed to give great satisfaction and cleared all the former evidence, which stood very doubtful." Coke's triumph was plain. For him, the trial was over. The withholding of this evidence until the end had been wise, he could tell himself—especially in dealing with a man of Ralegh's skill. Now it was too late for denial. No trick of Sir Walter's, no appeal of eloquence could counteract this final accusation of his enemy. Ralegh, said the reporter, stood "much amazed."

"Now, Ralegh," Coke said, "if thou has the grace, humble thyself to the King and confess thy treasons."

But Coke (though for the last time) underestimated his adversary. Sir Walter too had reserved a surprise. By-and-by, [wrote the reporter] Sir Walter Ralegh seemed to gather his spirits again, and said: "I pray you hear me a word. You have heard tale of a strange man. . . . Before my Lord Cobham's coming from the Tower, I was advised by some of my friends to get a confession from him. Therefore I wrote to him thus, 'You or I must go to trial. If I first, then your accusation is the only evidence against me!' Therefore it was not ill of me to beg him to say the truth. But his first letter was not to my contenting. I wrote a second, and then he wrote me a very good letter."

Ralegh thrust a hand in his breast and produced a folded small sheet. "It is true," he said, "I got a poor fellow in the Tower to cast up an apple with the letter in it, at Lord Cobham's window; which I am loath to mention lest Mr. Lieutenant of the Tower might be blamed, though I protest Sir George Harvey is not to blame for what passed. No keeper in the world could so provide but it might happen. But I sent him his letter again, because I heard it was likely now he should be first tried. But the Lord Cobham sent me the letter a second time, saying it was not unfit I should have such a letter."

Ralegh held up the paper. "And here you may see it, and I pray you read it."

The Clerk came forward to take the note. The jury watched. In the history of trials, had evidence ever been so given and retracted, so sworn and forsworn? No matter what this new note of Cobham's might say, Ralegh, in producing it, confessed what he had earlier denied—communication with Cobham in the Tower. "But what say you," Popham interposed, "to the pension of 1500 pounds a year?"

He could not deny it, Ralegh replied, though it was never his purpose to accept it. "It was my fault I did conceal it, and this fault of concealing, I acknowledge. But for attempting or conspiring any treason against the King or the State, I still deny it to the death and it can never be proved against me."

"I perceive," Popham said gravely, "you are not so clear a man as you have protested all this while, for you should have discovered this matter to the King."

The Clerk, during this exchange, stood waiting, Cobham's letter in his hand. "Hear now, I pray you," Ralegh said, "what Cobham hath written to me."

Mr. Attorney would not have this letter read, saying that it was unfairly obtained from Lord Cobham. And upon Lord Cecil's advising to hear it, he said, "My Lord Cecil, mar not a good cause!"

CECIL: Mr. Attorney, you are more peremptory than honest. You must not come here to show me what to do.

RALEGH: I pray my Lord Cecil particularly to read the letter, as he knoweth my Lord Cobham's hand.

Then was read the letter of the Lord Cobham to Sir Walter Ralegh, to this effect: "Now that the arraignment draws near, not knowing which should be first, I or you, to clear my conscience, satisfy the world with truth and free myself from the cry of blood, I protest upon my soul and before God and his angels, I never had conference with you in any treason, nor was ever moved by you to the things I heretofore accused you of. And for any thing I know, you are as innocent and as clear from any treasons against the King as is any subject living. Therefore I wash my hands and pronounce with Daniel, *Purus sum a sanguine bujus.* ['I am innocent of this blood.'] And so God deal with me and have mercy on my soul, as this is true!"

It was impressive; this was a day when men did not lightly call upon God's name. Ralegh followed it quickly. "My Masters of the Jury," he said, "this is a confession made under oath, and the deepest protestations a Christian man can make." Yet the jury was weary with these retractions and denials of retractions; they came too late. Cobham's confession of yesterday, as read aloud by Coke, invalidated this earlier statement, eloquent though it had been. Too much lay counter to it—notes tied to apples, servants bearing secret letters, connivance and what looked like deliberate falsehood in court. "The acknowledging," wrote the reporter, "of this 1500 pounds a year pension made the rest of the Lord Cobham's accusation the better credited...." Chief Justice Popham addressed Ralegh direct. "In my conscience I am persuaded that Cobham accused you truly. I observed his manner of speaking. I protest before the living God I am persuaded he spoke nothing but the truth.''

The prosecution rested its case. Coke's three points had been stated, embellished, gone over until twelve knights of Middlesex knew them by heart: (1) Ralegh's July letter to Cecil, informing of Cobham's midnight visit to La Rensi; (2) Ralegh's letter to Cobham in the Tower, reminding Cobham that two witnesses were necessary for conviction and urging that as long as Cobham kept silence, they both were safe; (3) Cobham's confession of November 16, given from his cell in Winchester. The first two points were hearsay, the letters never seen by the jury, never produced in court. Yet testimony which the judges accepted, the jury accepted also. As for Point 2, the fact that Ralegh denied the writing of such a letter seemed only to enhance his guilt; Kemys had confessed to delivery of it. That Cobham had three times retracted his testimony proved only that he was, like all traitors, untrustworthy and should be destroyed. The Attorney General had trapped Sir Walter into a lie concerning communication with Cobham in the Tower. And though Magna Carta said that no man should be forced to testify against himself, in the jury's mind Coke's harsh questioning was no derogation of this law. On the contrary, the prisoner had been given every opportunity to reply and clear himself of guilt.

The day was done, the light was gone. Winchester gates were shut and barred. On its hillside the ancient Hall of Arthur loomed in shadow; lanterns swung behind the tall grilled gates that led to the cells and dungeon far below....

The Jury were willed to go together; who departed and stayed not a quarter of an hour, when they returned, bringing in their verdict, GUILTY OF TREASON.

Ralegh was led to the bar. Chief Justice Popham stood up, bare-headed. In his hand he held the black cap that signified a death sentence. "Sir Walter Ralegh," he said, "I am sorry to see this fallen upon you this day. You have always been taken for a wise man. And I cannot but marvel to see that a man of your wit, as this day you have approved it, could be entangled with so many treasons. I grieve to find that a man of your quality would have sold yourself for a spy to the enemy of your country for 1500 pounds a year. This covetousness is like a canker, that eats the iron place where it lives...."

There was more; to Ralegh it must have been well nigh unendurable. "O God!" he had written his wife from the Tower, "I cannot live to think how I am derided, the scorns I shall receive, the cruel words of lawyers, the infamous taunts and despites, to be made a wonder and a spectacle! O death, destroy the memory of these and lay me up in dark forgetfulness!"

Of all these cruel taunts, Popham's solemn pronouncement was the worst. Coke had raved but Ralegh could answer him. Now, for Ralegh, denial and affirmation were forever blocked. What the Chief Justice said, the world (or so thought Ralegh) would take as truth. "It now comes to my mind," Popham continued, "why you may not have your accuser brought face to face: for such an one is easily brought to retract when he seeth there is no hope of his own life.... It now only remaineth to pronounce the judgment, which I would to God you had not to receive this day of me. I never saw the like trial, and I hope I shall never see the like again."

Raising both hands with the deliberation of an aged man, Popham set the black cap on his head. "Sir Walter Ralegh," he said, "since you have been found guilty of these horrible treasons, the judgment of this court is, That you shall be had from hence to the place whence you came, there to remain until the day of execution. And from thence you shall be drawn upon a hurdle through the open streets to the place for execution, there to be hanged and cut down alive, and your body shall be opened, your heart and bowels plucked out, and your privy members cut off and thrown into the fire before your eyes. Then your head to be stricken off from your body, and your body shall be divided into four quarters, to be disposed of at the King's pleasure."

"And God have mercy upon your soul."

Copyright © by Catherine Drinker Bowen. By permission of Little Brown and Company.

QUESTIONS

1. Suspicious circumstances surround this trial:

(a) crucial evidence, Raleigh's letter to Cecil, was lost or destroyed while in the hands of the prosecution;

(b) Cobham's initial accusation against Raleigh was not in writing, and Cobham does not appear to testify and be cross examined by Raleigh; and

(c) Cobham committed the same offense of which he now accuses Raleigh—treason.

What do these circumstances suggest about the character of the prosecution? How credible is Raleigh's accuser, Lord Cobham?

2. What are the differences between the "trial by accusation" described here and "trial by inquisition," a method presumably favored in much of Continental Europe at the time?

3. How does this trial differ from the paradigm of the adversary process described by Curtis in Its Your Law?

4. How does this trial differ from the advocacy paradigm described by Lon Fuller and John Randall in the ABA/AALS Joint Report (Chapter 6 supra)?

Relevant Background

Investigative Tactics in Criminal Trials

Bowen writes that prosecutors would routinely claim that in questioning suspects "no rigour was used," and that jurors would routinely disbelieve this claim. Although physical abuse may not be so common in the modern police station, aggressive questioning and deceptive tactics are prevalent. Common, but ethically questionable, techniques include mischaracterizing to a defendant statements made by a witness, telling a defendant that another accused person is about to "confess" when there is no basis for such a statement, and misrepresenting to a defendant the nature or existence of documentary evidence. See William J. Stuntz, Lawyers, Deception and Evidence Gathering, 79 Va. L. Rev. 1903, 1919–21 (1993).

The state has always played a part in investigation of crimes, but the role of prosecutors in these investigations has expanded to include the planning of major undercover investigations. In the 1980's Abscam investigation, prosecutors helped create a fictitious Middle Eastern corporation, and undercover agents acted as representatives of the corporation seeking to bribe public officials. The result: a United States Senator, six members of Congress, a mayor and other public officials were all convicted of bribery. Bennett L. Gershman, The New Prosecutors, 53 U. Pitt. L. Rev. 393, 396–97 (1992). "Abscam was a deceit perpetrated by the government, in colloquial terms a 'sting' or operation in which would-be swindlers would be made dupes themselves. . . . Never before in history had movies been made of government officials being paid off." John T. Noonan, Jr., Bribes 605 (1984).

Occasionally, prosecutors go so far that courts have little choice but to dismiss their charges altogether. In Jacobson v. United States, 503 U.S. 540 (1992) the government for over two years solicited Jacobson to purchase a child pornography magazine before he did so. Jacobson's defense of entrapment was upheld when the government failed to show that he had been predisposed to illegally receive child pornography before undercover agents make their initial contact with him. Even where such a defense of entrapment would fail, there is also legitimate concern over how far ethical standards permit prosecutors to go in deceiving suspected perpetrators of crime.

Concealment of Witnesses

Lord Coke could have produced Lord Cobham at trial but did not. The judges assented in this decision. Raleigh was thus convicted on Cobham's alleged written and oral statements standing alone and was denied a chance to cross examine. Clearly, the prosecution was concerned about how Cobham might testify, and its concealment of this critical witness was highly prejudicial to the outcome of the trial.

Prosecutors still occasionally conceal witnesses, although courts today are not as receptive to this tactic. For example, in United States v. Kojayan, 8 F.3d 1315 (9th Cir.1993), an Assistant United States Attorney (AUSA) in Los Angeles tried Chake Kojayan, a middle-aged Lebanese woman, for smuggling into the United States cocaine sewn into a bag. An alleged co-conspirator, Krikor Nourian, arranged for sale of the cocaine to buyers who turned out to be DEA agents. At the "sale" immediately before Kojayan's arrest, Nourian and Kojayan spoke to a third alleged co-conspirator, Hratch Kalfayan. The conversation was partly in English and partly in Armenian, a language the DEA agent on the scene did not understand. At trial,

Kojayan and Kalfayan each claimed that the other had orchestrated the deal while they themselves did not know that the cocaine was sewn into the bag. Their alleged co-conspirator, Nourian, "was whisked away by the government, never to be seen again by Kalfayan and Kojayan." Id. at 1316.

Although, "[q]uite obviously, Nourian was at the heart of this affair" and "Nourian might have been able to clarify who, if either, of the two defendants was telling the truth," Nourian was not produced at trial. "Instead the government introduced his statements (both taped and untaped) under Fed. R. Evid. 801(d)(2)(E), as the statements of a co-conspirator." Id. at 1317. Although the defendants' lawyers sought to know Nourian's whereabouts, they were rebuffed by the government. Nourian had negotiated a deal with the government to testify completely and truthfully in the case, but for some reason, presumably because Nourian's testimony would have undercut the government's case, the AUSA chose not to produce him as a witness at trial.

The defense attorneys suspected that this might be the case and argued to the jury that Nourian was a critical witness and that the prosecution could have called Nourian but did not because his testimony would not have been helpful. The AUSA in turn argued to the jury that the defense lawyers were "asking the jury to speculate" and that Nourian "has the right to remain silent. . . . Don't be misled that the government could have called Nourian." Id. at 1317–18. Of course, it was the AUSA that was misleading the jury, as the government had already cut a deal with Nourian under which the AUSA could call him to testify at any time.

Not only did the AUSA make this misleading statement in his rebuttal argument at trial, but he did not correct his misstatement when the defense attorneys in a colloquy with the judge once again raised their suspicion that Nourian had entered into a cooperation agreement. The AUSA also did not respond when the issue was brought up yet again in a defendants' motion for retrial. Even in his brief on appeal, the AUSA upbraided the defense lawyers for arguing outside the record and reiterated that "[t]he prosecutor's comments . . . were all supported by the record before the jury." Id. at 1319. Only at oral argument to the Ninth Circuit, in response to a direct question from the bench, did the AUSA disclose that Nourian had entered into a cooperation agreement.

"How," Judge Kozinski asked in his opinion in *Kojayan*, "can it be that a serious claim of prosecutorial misconduct remains unresolved—even unaddressed—until oral argument in the Court of Appeals?" Id. at 1320. Not only did the AUSA mislead the jury at trial, but "the United States Attorney allowed the filing of a brief in our court that did not own up to the problem, a brief that itself skated perilously close to misrepresentation." Id. After expounding at some length on the responsibility of the United States Attorney and senior deputies to supervise subordinate attorneys, the Ninth Circuit remanded the case to the district court to determine whether to retry the case or dismiss the indictment on account of the government's concealment of this critical witness's availability for testimony.

Concealment of Evidence

Raleigh's letter to Cecil relating Cobham's meeting with the Spanish agent instigated the prosecution of Raleigh for treason. Coke, however, did not have Raleigh's letter at the trial; presumably it had been lost or destroyed. Alternatively, the prosecution chose to withhold the letter because it contained exculpatory evidence. In either case, there are serious deficiencies in the way this letter was handled.

A prosecutor has an ethical obligation to preserve evidence in its unaltered form. See Price v. State Bar, 30 Cal.3d 537, 179 Cal.Rptr. 914, 638 P.2d 1311 (1982) (prosecutor suspended for five years for altering information on a taxi-trip ticket to conform to testimony given by a prosecution witness). In addition to the possibility that destruction of evidence is a tort or a violation of professional conduct norms, see discussion at page 564 supra, intentional destruction of evidence relevant to a criminal prosecution, whether by the prosecutor, defense attorney or anybody else, is itself a crime: See 18 U.S.C., § 1503 (obstruction of justice).

Constitutional due process rights of the accused are not violated unless a prosecutor destroys evidence that has apparent exculpatory value before its destruction, and the defendant cannot obtain similar evidence by other means. California v. Trombetta, 467 U.S. 479 (1984). However, courts have broad discretion to correct any injustice which destruction or loss of evidence may bring about. See State v. Langlet, 283 N.W.2d 330 (Iowa 1979) (presumption that the evidence destroyed was unfavorable to the party which destroyed it); and State of Oregon v. Smith, 42 Or.App. 543, 600 P.2d 949 (1979) (because television tape showing defendant performing sobriety tests was destroyed by prosecutor and would have been admissible to rebut breathalyzer evidence, drunk driving charges were dismissed).

Under Model Code, DR 7–103(B) a prosecutor also must "make timely disclosure to counsel for the defendant, or to the defendant if he has no counsel, of the existence of evidence, known to the prosecutor or other government lawyer, that tends to negate the guilt of the accused, mitigate the degree of the offense, or reduce the punishment." See also Model Rule 3.8(d). These rules are grounded in the due process rights of the accused. In Brady v. Maryland, 373 U.S. 83 (1963), the state disclosed every statement made by a co-defendant except the co-defendant's admission to the murder with which the defendant was charged. The Court held that the prosecutor must on request disclose to the defense such exculpatory evidence that is "material either to guilt or to punishment." Id. at 87. In *Brady*, the court extended due process protection to such disclosures regardless "of the good faith or bad faith of the prosecution." Id. See also United States v. Agurs, 427 U.S. 97, 112–14 (1976) (prosecutor must disclose evidence that creates a reasonable doubt as to defendant's guilt even if the defendant does not specifically request such evidence); United States v. Bagley, 473 U.S. 667, 682 (1985) (to justify retrial, a reasonable probability must exist that, had the evidence been disclosed, the result of the trial would be different); Pennsylvania v. Ritchie, 480 U.S. 39, 59 (1987) (specifying limits on defense requests for exculpatory evidence, and noting that a defendant "has no constitutional right to conduct his own search of the State's files to argue relevance [of the exculpatory evidence]"). Although a prosecutor must disclose all material exculpatory evidence, the initial determination of whether such evidence is material and exculpatory thus lies with the state.

Defense attorneys are not under this same mandate to inform the prosecution of the existence of evidence incriminating their clients. However, a defense attorney who has received from a client or a third party *physical* evidence connected with an alleged crime generally has an obligation to turn the evidence over to the prosecution. If attorneys were allowed to keep such physical evidence from the prosecution, criminals could conceal evidence simply by turning it over to their attorneys. As the Washington Supreme Court has observed:

> "The attorney should not be a depository for criminal evidence (such as a knife, other weapons, stolen property, etc.), which in itself has little, if any, material value for the purposes of aiding counsel in the preparation of the defense of his client's case. Such evidence given the attorney during legal consultation for information purposes and used by the attorney in preparing the defense of his client's case whether or not the case ever goes to trial, could clearly be withheld for a reasonable period of time. It follows that the attorney, after a reasonable period, should, as an officer of the court, on his own motion turn the same over to the prosecution.
>
> ... the state, when attempting to introduce such evidence at the trial, should take extreme precautions to make certain that the source of the evidence is not disclosed in the presence of the jury and prejudicial error is not committed."

State v. Olwell, 64 Wash.2d 828, 833–34, 394 P.2d 681, 684–85 (1964). See also Morrell v. State, 575 P.2d 1200, 1210 (Alaska 1978) (" ...a criminal defense attorney must turn over to the prosecution real evidence that the attorney obtains from his client.").

Some states have criminally prosecuted defense attorneys who conceal evidence from prosecutors, although some laws in this area are impermissibly vague. See Commonwealth v. Stenhach, 356 Pa.Super. 5, 514 A.2d 114 (1986), appeal denied, 517 Pa. 589, 534 A.2d 769 (1987), citing 18 Pa.C.S. § 5105(a)(3) (hindering prosecution), and § 4910(1) (tampering with physical evidence), but finding these statutes to be overbroad when used to criminally prosecute defense attorneys for concealing a murder weapon from prosecutors. See also Norman Lefstein, Incriminating Physical Evidence, The Defense Attorney's Dilemma, and the Need for Rules, 64 N.C.L. Rev. 897 (1986).

Attorneys often can avoid disclosing physical evidence by refusing to accept possession of it, and some courts even allow attorneys to avoid disclosure by returning evidence to the client or to wherever else they may have obtained it. Some jurisdictions also limit or prohibit prosecutors from serving search warrants on law offices. See, e.g., O'Connor v. Johnson, 287 N.W.2d 400 (Minn.1979) (search warrants issued on law offices are unreasonable and unenforceable when the attorney is not accused of wrongdoing and there is no risk that the evidence will be destroyed); Eugene R. Gaetke, Lawyers as Officers of the Court, 42 Vand. L. Rev. 39, 72 (1989).

A similar dilemma arises when attorneys defending white collar crime cases come to possess documents which incriminate their clients. In Fisher v. United States, 425 U.S. 391 (1976), the Supreme Court held that documents in the hands of an attorney are protected from subpoena by the government in circumstances where requiring the client himself to produce the documents would violate the Fifth Amendment privilege against self incrimination. Even though most client papers, even if they contain incriminating information, are not privileged under the Fifth Amendment, nowhere in *Fisher* did the Court imply that the attorney had an obligation to come forward with unprivileged documents in the absence of a subpoena. Some commentators have suggested that *Fisher's* treatment of documents in white collar crime cases is inconsistent with the general requirement that physical evidence be produced on the attorney's own motion. See Kevin Reitz, Clients, Lawyers and the Fifth Amendment: the Need for a Projected Privilege, 41 Duke L.J. 572, 575 (1991) (urging "adoption of a new 'projected' Fifth Amendment privilege that would permit lawyers to assert their clients' self-incrimination privilege with respect to incriminating evidence and information lawfully acquired during the representation.")

The Prisoners' Dilemma

The predicament of Raleigh and Cobham is strikingly familiar to a popular paradigm in game theory known as the "Prisoners' Dilemma." Such paradigms present a highly stylized analysis of a situation and do not consider the complexities involved, but still may answer some questions about the interaction of participants in the legal system. See Douglas G. Baird, et al., Game Theory and the Law (1994). The Prisoners' Dilemma game, for example, may explain why Raleigh and Cobham were so concerned about what the other would say, why Cobham vacillated so much in his own strategies, and why Raleigh tried so earnestly to communicate with Cobham.

It is apparent from Catherine Drinker Bowen's account that Cobham would profess innocence if assured that Raleigh would do the same, but would confess and implicate Raleigh if he believed that Raleigh was going to betray him. In his letter to Cecil, Raleigh initially sought to implicate Cobham in a plot, presumably to save himself from prosecution, but quickly switched to a consistent strategy of denying further knowledge of any such plot. Although there is no way of knowing for certain why the two prisoners chose these strategies, or what was said to Raleigh and Cobham in prison, they could have confronted something resembling the following scenario:

> Raleigh and Cobham are accused of treason. Both prisoners are held in separate rooms in the Tower of London. Lord Coke approaches Cobham and says, "we know that you plotted with the Spanish to over-

throw the King. If you sign a confession implicating Raleigh, we will release you, and Raleigh is certain to be executed immediately. If you do not sign a confession, and Raleigh does, we will execute you and release Raleigh. If you both sign a confession, you will both be sentenced to death and held in the Tower until the King decides to release you or carry out the death sentence, at his pleasure. If neither of you sign a confession, we will try each of you on the circumstantial evidence, and there is at least an even chance you will be found guilty. If you are found guilty, you will be sentenced to death and held in the Tower until the King decides to release you or carry out the death sentence, at his pleasure. You should also know that we are offering the same deal to Raleigh.''

This is in essence the "Prisoners' Dilemma." Each player has to decide how to play based on how they think the other player will play. The game can be illustrated as follows:

Raleigh

		Silence	Talk
Cobham	Silence	trial, trial	death, Release
	Talk	Release, death	death sentence death sentence

Release > (is better than) trial > death sentence > death

The first word or phrase in each box refers to Cobham's "payoff" (here, the deal he will get). The second word or phrase refers to Raleigh's "payoff." The game starts in the upper left hand quadrant. However, only if both prisoners stay silent, will they both get a trial on circumstantial evidence only, an outcome preferable to the death sentence. Although we have no way of knowing what Raleigh and Cobham were each told while imprisoned in the Tower, this model would roughly fit the story so long as each believed that he was best off if he talked while the other remained silent and worst off if he remained silent while the other talked. Furthermore, the way this model relates the story, both Cobham and Raleigh are better off if they both stay silent than if they both talk.

If the prisoners do not collude beforehand, the game will probably gravitate to the lower right hand quadrant, as they each choose to talk (looking at the diagram, it is clear that each prisoner is better off talking, no matter what the other does). If the prisoners do collude beforehand, it is possible that they might agree to remain silent and trust that each other will honor the agreement. Communication between the prisoners is thus critical to fostering the cooperation between them that will move them from the lower right hand quadrant to the upper left. This cooperation, however, is delicate and can dissolve the moment one prisoner loses trust and fears that the other will defect by exchanging his compatriot's certain death for his own release.

Cooperation is more likely if the game is played on repeated occasions (multiple "rounds" of play) and the players have an opportunity to see each other cooperate (here, by remaining silent). Early defection on the other hand, may foster distrust and reinforce later rounds of defection. Indeed, the several rounds "played" while Raleigh and Cobham were both imprisoned were preceded by an initial round in which Raleigh was questioned by the Privy Council and released. Although Raleigh at this time was not threatened with the dire alternatives shown in the diagram above, he presumably believed for one reason or another that he would be better off if he wrote Cecil about Cobham's excursion to see the Spanish agent. Raleigh, in this initial round, chose to defect, and for both players this defection would prove fatal. Raleigh's defection led Cobham to defect in the next round of "play" by confessing a plot involving Raleigh. Raleigh was then arrested and turned his energies belatedly to convincing Cobham once again to play cooperatively and deny the existence of a plot.

Bowen's account refers to numerous instances where communication between the prisoners was attempted, for the most part by Raleigh trying to reach Cobham. However, it of course was in the Crown's interest that Raleigh and Cobham not cooperate with each other. Cooperation could be frustrated by shutting off avenues of communication, as by separating the two prisoners in the Tower. Lord Coke also could impose an evidentiary penalty for attempts to communicate and for concealment of attempts to communicate. The jury thus could make negative inferences from "notes tied to apples, servants bearing secret letters, connivance and what looked like deliberate falsehood in court." Finally, the prosecution could endeavor to foster distrust between the two prisoners, as by bringing Cobham the accusatory letter presumably written by Raleigh but never introduced in open court.

The end result was sporadic and ineffectual cooperation between Raleigh and Cobham. Cobham in the final round of this "game" probably would have professed innocence; why else would Lord Coke not bring him forward as a live witness? However, Raleigh's betrayal of Cobham in the first round of the game, carefully exploited by the prosecution in later rounds, led Cobham to make damaging statements about Raleigh that were then introduced into evidence as hearsay. By the time Cobham realized that Raleigh would stick to his denial of the accusation and recanted his own accusation of Raleigh, it was too late. Raleigh got his trial on the circumstantial evidence, but with Cobham's hearsay thrown in. This was enough to convict Raleigh, although the King (perhaps because there were no witnesses against Raleigh) held Raleigh's sentence in abeyance for fifteen years.

QUESTIONS

1. Using the Prisoners' Dilemma model as a paradigm, what benefit does the prosecution derive from the following strategies:

(a) lying to each prisoner about the testimony that will be given by the other;

(b) offering to reduce a prisoner's punishment if he will testify against the other;

(c) lying to each prisoner about the plea bargain arrangement being offered to the other; and

(d) listening in on conversations between the two prisoners.

Which of these strategies are ethically acceptable conduct for a prosecutor?

2. Raleigh was not represented by a lawyer and instead represented himself at his trial. Presumably, Cobham did the same. Would communication between them have been facilitated if they had each been represented by counsel? How?

3. Look back at *Wheat v. United States*, Chapter 6 supra. If counsel had been available to them, would Raleigh and Cobham have benefitted from being represented by the same lawyer? Is there a reason why the prosecution, like the prosecution in *Wheat*, would not have wanted them to be represented by the same lawyer? Does the Prisoners' Dilemma paradigm change your view on whether defendants should have the right to be represented by the same lawyer if they so choose?

PROBLEMS

1. You are the attorney for one of two drivers involved in an automobile accident. You believe that your client is probably at fault. The doctor hired by your client, during her examination of the driver of the other vehicle, discovers injuries not detected by the other driver's physicians. Must you disclose your doctor's findings?

2. You are the attorney for a man charged with a double murder. A friend of the accused delivers to you the knife apparently used in the crime which she discovered at the home of the accused. Must you turn the knife over to the police? If so, must you testify as to the source of the evidence? Is the answer different if the accused gives you the knife?

Commonwealth v. Nicola Sacco and Bartolomeo Vanzetti (1921)

Felix Frankfurter (1882–1965) was a professor at Harvard Law School at the time of the Sacco and Vanzetti trials. A more complete biography of Frankfurter is in Chapter 10 infra.

Nicola Sacco, b. Adriatic region of Italy 1891; came to the United States in 1908; employed at 3K shoe factory in Stoughton, Massachusetts; found guilty of murder in 1921 and executed at the Massachusetts Death House in 1927.

Bartolomeo Vanzetti, b. Piedmont, Italy 1888; came to the United States in 1908; employed in various jobs at manual labor in and around Stoughton, Massachusetts; found guilty of murder in 1921 and executed at the Massachusetts Death House in 1927.

Felix Frankfurter, The Case of Sacco and Vanzetti
A Critical Analysis

(1927).

Chapter I

For more than six years the Sacco–Vanzetti case has been before the courts of Massachusetts. Such extraordinary delay, in a state where ordinarily murder trials are promptly dispatched, in itself challenges attention. A long succession of disclosures has aroused interest far beyond the boundaries of Massachusetts and even of the United States, until the case has become one of those rare *causes célèbres* which are of international concern. . . .

At about three o'clock in the afternoon of April 15, 1920, Parmenter, a paymaster, and Berardelli, his guard, were fired upon and killed by two men armed with pistols, as they were carrying two boxes containing the pay roll of the shoe factory of Slater and Morrill, amounting to $15,776.51, from the company's office building to the factory through the main street of South Braintree, Massachusetts. As the murder was being committed a car containing several other men drew up to the spot. The murderers threw the two boxes into the car, jumped in themselves, and were driven away at high speed across some near-by railroad tracks. Two days later this car was found abandoned in woods at a distance from the scene of the crime. Leading away from this spot were the tracks of a smaller car. At the time of the Braintree holdup the police were investigating a similar crime in the neighboring town of Bridgewater. In both cases a gang was involved. In both they made off in a car. In both eyewitnesses believed the criminals to be Italians. In the Bridgewater holdup the car had left the scene in the direction of Cochesett. Chief Stewart of Bridgewater was therefore, at the time of the Braintree murders, on the trail of an Italian owning or driving a car in Cochesett. He found his man in one Boda, whose car was then in a garage awaiting repairs. Stewart instructed the garage proprietor, Johnson, to telephone to the police when anyone came to fetch it. Pursuing his theory, Stewart found that Boda had been living in Cochesett with a radical named Coacci. Now on April 16, 1920, which was the day after the

Braintree murders, Stewart, at the instance of the Department of Justice, then engaged in the rounding-up of Reds, had been to the house of Coacci to see why he had failed to appear at a hearing regarding his deportation. He found Coacci packing a trunk and apparently very anxious to get back to Italy as soon as possible. At the time (April 16), Coacci's trunk and his haste to depart for Italy were not connected in Chief Stewart's mind with the Braintree affair. But when later the tracks of a smaller car were found near the murder car, he surmised that this car was Boda's. And when he discovered that Boda had once been living with Coacci, he connected Coacci's packing, his eagerness to depart, his actual departure, with the Braintree murders, and assumed that the trunk contained the booty. In the light of later discoveries Stewart jumped to the conclusion that Coacci, Boda's pal, had "skipped with the swag." As a matter of fact, the contents of the trunk, when it was intercepted by the Italian police on arrival, revealed nothing. In the meantime, however, Stewart continued to work on his theory, which centered around Boda: that whosoever called for Boda's car at Johnson's garage would be suspect of the Braintree crime. On the night of May 5, Boda and three other Italians did in fact call.

To explain how they came to do so let us recall here the proceedings for the wholesale deportation of Reds under Attorney-General Palmer in the spring of 1920. In particular the case of one Salsedo must be borne in mind—a radical who was held incommunicado in a room in the New York offices of the Department of Justice on the fourteenth floor of a Park Row building. Boda and his companions were friends of Salsedo. On May 4 they learned that Salsedo had been found dead on the sidewalk outside the Park Row building, and, already frightened by the Red raids, bestirred themselves to "hide the literature and notify their friends against the federal police." For this purpose an automobile was needed and they turned to Boda. Such were the circumstances under which the four Italians appeared on the evening of May 5 at the Johnson garage. Two of them were Sacco and Vanzetti. Mrs. Johnson telephoned the police. The car was not available and the Italians left, Sacco and Vanzetti to board a street car for Brockton, Boda and the fourth member, Orciani, on a motor cycle. Sacco and Vanzetti were arrested on the street car, Orciani was arrested the next day, and Boda was never heard of again.

Stewart at once sought to apply his theory of the commission of the two "jobs" by one gang. The theory, however, broke down. Orciani had been at work on the days of both crimes, so he was let go. Sacco, in continuous employment at a shoe factory in Stoughton, had taken a day off (about which more later) on April 15. Hence, while he could not be charged with the Bridgewater crime, he was charged with the Braintree murders; Vanzetti, as a fish peddler at Plymouth and his own employer, could not give the same kind of alibi for either day, and so he was held for both crimes. Stewart's theory that the crime was committed by these Italian radicals was not shared by the head of the state police, who always maintained that it was the work of professionals.

Charged with the crime of murder on May 5, Sacco and Vanzetti were indicted on September 14, 1920, and put on trial May 31, 1921, at Dedham, Norfolk County. The setting of the trial, in the courthouse opposite the old home of Fisher Ames, furnished a striking contrast to the background and antecedents of the prisoners. Dedham is a quiet residential suburb, inhabited by well-to-do Bostonians with a surviving element of New England small farmers. Part of the jury was specially selected by the sheriff's deputies from persons whom they deemed "representative citizens," "substantial" and "intelligent." The presiding judge was **Webster Thayer** of Worcester.* The chief counsel for these Italians, **Fred H. Moore**, was a Westerner, himself a radical and a professional defender of radicals. In opinion, as well as in fact, he was an "outsider." Unfamiliar with the traditions of the Massachusetts bench, not even a member of the Massachusetts bar, the characteristics of Judge Thayer unknown to him, Moore found neither professional nor personal sympathies between himself and the Judge. So far as the relations between court and counsel seriously, even if unconsciously, affect the temper of a trial, Moore was a factor of irritation and not of appeasement. Sacco and Vanzetti spoke very broken English, and their testimony shows how often they misunderstood the questions put to them. A court interpreter was used, but his conduct raised such doubts** that the defendants brought their own interpreter to check his questions and answers. The trial lasted nearly seven weeks, and on July 14, 1921, Sacco and Vanzetti were found guilty of murder in the first degree.

Chapter II

So far as crime is concerned we are dealing with a conventional case of payroll robbery resulting in murder. At the trial the killing of Parmenter and Berardelli was undisputed. The only issue was the identity of the murderers. Were Sacco and Vanzetti two of the assailants of Parmenter and Berardelli, or were they not? This was the beginning and the end of the inquiry at the trial; this is the beginning and the end of any judgment now on the guilt or innocence of these men. Every other issue, no matter how worded, is relevant only as it helps to answer that central question....

Jeremiah McAnarney assisted Fred Moore in representing Sacco and Vanzetti.

Frederick Gunn Katzmann, b. Roxbury, Massachusetts 1875; prepared at Boston Latin School; A.B. Harvard University 1896; LL.B. Boston University 1902 (studied law at night school while a meter-reader for Boston Edison); elected Representative in the Massachusetts Legislature in 1907 and 1908; appointed Assistant District Attorney for the Counties of Norfolk and Plymouth in 1909; elected District Attorney for the same district in 1916 and again in 1919; began a private law practice in 1923; Master of Hyde Park Masonic Lodge; member of Norfolk County Republican Club; later President of the Hyde Park Savings Bank.

---

* [*See* Charles Curtis's account in *The Advocate, supra*, of his discussion of this case years later with Judge Thayer]—ed.

** Some time after the trial this interpreter was convicted of larceny.

Cross–Examination of Nicola Sacco in Commonwealth v. Sacco (1921)

See 255 Mass. 369, 151 N.E. 839 (1927).

Nicola Sacco, Sworn.

THE COURT. Let me suggest, Mr. Sacco, to you, the same as I did to Mr. Vanzetti, if you do not understand any questions put to you either by Mr. Moore or by,—either in direct examination or by Mr. Katzmann in cross-examination, it is your right to say so and have the questions put so that you may understand each one and all. You may proceed, Mr. Moore.

Q. [By Moore.] Mr. Sacco, state your name in full, please.

A. Nicola Sacco.

Q. Where were you born?

A. Toremaggione, Italy.

Q. What year were you born?

A. 1891.

Q. Your father, what business was he in there?

A. He is a business man of olive oil.

Q. Raising olives?

A. No, buy olive oil.

Q. How long did you go to school?

A. Seven to fourteen.

Q. And why did you leave school?

A. Well, my father was need very bad on our property,—vineyards.

Q. Needed working on the vineyards?

A. Yes.

Q. How many children were there in your family?

A. Seventeen.

Q. And after you quit school at fourteen, what did you do then?

A. I went to work in,—after fourteen I went to work with my father.

Q. After fourteen you went to work with your father?

A. Yes.

Q. How long did you continue to work at the family place?

A. I continued to work until fourteen to sixteen.

Q. Then what happened, Mr. Sacco?

A. Well, I did not like very much agriculture.

Q. You did not like farm work?

A. No.

Q. No ...

A. No, so I went and learned mechanic.

Q. Where did you go to take up mechanical work?

A. In the same town.

Q. When did you leave Italy to come for the United States, what year?

A. 1917.

Q. No. What year did you leave Italy?

A. 1908.

Q. And how did you happen to come here? What was the occasion of your coming here? Who did you come with?

A. Well, my father got some friend here when he was young. This friend, he baptize most of the people in the family, so my brother—who is Sabeno—he was in army three years and he served in the army for about thirty-six months.

Q. In the Italian army?

A. Yes, so he came back. My father's friend live in Milford and he liked very much to see my brother, so my brother when he came back from the army, he desired to come to this country, so I was crazy to come to this country because I was liked a free country, call a free country, I desire to come with him.

Q. So you two came together, did you?

A. Yes.

Q. How old were you at that time?

A. Seventeen years old.

Q. Do you know at what port you landed? Where did you come into the United States, at what city?

A. Milford.

Q. No, I mean what—...

A. Massachusetts.

Q. Where did you land in the United States, what harbor, what city did you come into when you came in on the boat?

A. In Boston,—White Star Line.

Q. Where did this friend of your father's live?

A. He is dead now, but the folks live in Milford yet.

Q. You and your brother went where upon your arrival here?

A. To Boston.

Q. You and your brother Sabeno, where did you go?

A.   We got a steamboat to Naples to Boston the last of April. We reached Boston about twelve,—no, the last of March. We reach Boston at twelve of April, 12th of April, 1908.

Q.   And then where did you go immediately on arrival here?

A.   Start to Milford the same night.

Q.   And you were what age at the time of your arrival in this country?

A.   What year?

Q.   What age were you, how old were you?

A.   Seventeen years old.

Q.   When you went to Milford, what kind of work did you first take up?

A.   Well, my brother Sabeno, after next day—

MR. KATZMANN. One moment, if your Honor please.

THE WITNESS. All right.

Q.   What kind of work did you take up?

A.   I loaf a couple of weeks. I had an idea to go in a shoe factory to learn a job, but that time in the shoe factory was very slack and I go to see if I could go get another job. I was kind of sick.

Q.   What kind of work did you take up first?

A.   Water boy.

Q.   In what character of work was that, construction work, do you mean?

A.   Contractor work, sanitary for Milford. Who done the work, the contractor was the Draper Company.

Q.   How long did you follow that line of work?

A.   About six months, six or seven months, anyway. I am not certain.

Q.   Then what did you do?

A.   In the winter time, it was kind of cold, you know, so I decided to work in the factory.

MR. KATZMANN. I object, if your Honor please. The answer is not responsive.

Q.   What did you do after you go through with this work as a water boy?

A.   I got a job in Draper, in the foundry.

Q.   At Milford?

A.   Yes, sir. No, well, five cent ride to Milford, to Draper to Hopedale.

Q.   Hopedale?

A.   Yes.

Q.   Now, how long did you work in the foundry at Hopedale?

A. I should say about a year, pretty near, not certain, but pretty near.

Q. Then what did you do?

A. So I decided, my brother want to come back to the old country.

MR. KATZMANN. I object, if your Honor please.

Q. Not what your brother did, Mr. Sacco. What you did . . .

A. I decided to learn a job, a trade, so I did.

Q. Where did you learn edge trimming?

A. Michael Kelly, 3–K. He used to run the little factory over there at that time. He used to do about eighty dozen a day.

MR. KATZMANN. I ask that be stricken out, if your Honor please.

THE COURT. It may be.

Q. Were you paid to learn that trade?

A. Yes, sir.

Q. After you had learned the trade, Mr. Sacco, what did you do then?

A. After three months, I got a job in Webster.

Q. Massachusetts?

A. Massachusetts, yes, sir.

Q. How long did you work there?

A. All winter; about six or seven months.

Q. And that was at edge trimming?

A. Yes, sir.

Q. And then what did you do?

A. A friend of mine wrote to me a special delivery.

MR. KATZMANN. I object, if you honor please.

Q. Wait. What did you do, not what some one else do, but what did you do?

A. I left the job at Webster. I took a job at Milford Shoe Company, Milford.

Q. Milford Shoe Company at Milford?

A. Yes.

Q. As an edge trimmer?

A. As an edge trimmer.

Q. When did you start in there as an edge trimmer?

A. You mean the year?

Q. Yes . . .

A. 1910.

Q. 1910?

A.   Yes, sir.

Q.   How long did you work at the Milford Shoe Company as an edge trimmer?

A.   Until 1917. . . .

MR. JEREMIAH MCANARNEY. I am only going to put this question and follow it up and close the incident.

THE COURT. If there is only one question, I might allow that even though I might violate some rule of the law of evidence.

MR. JEREMIAH MCANARNEY. I want to get this man's frame of mind as a result of the questions that we asked of him.

THE COURT. I will allow you to get that, but I am a little inclined to feel that you were trying to get at the frame of mind of the Chief.

MR. JEREMIAH MCANARNEY. I wouldn't intimate the Chief's frame of mind.

Q.   As a result of questions that were asked of you by the Chief, did you form any opinion as to why you were apprehended that night of May 5th?

A.   No, sir.

Q.   You did not form any opinion?

A.   No.

Q.   You were not informed as to what the charge was?

A.   I thought it was a Radical charge.

Q.   You thought it was a Radical charge?

A.   Yes.

Q.   Then I don't understand your previous answer. Without calling the interpreter, did you form the opinion that you were arrested because of Radical work?

A.   Yes.

Q.   Now, when you were interrogated by Stewart, did you tell Stewart the truth?

A.   No, sir.

Q.   When you were interrogated by the district attorney, did you tell him the truth, or did you lie to him?

A.   I did not tell him the truth.

Q.   You did not tell him the truth?

A.   No.

Q.   Why not?

A.   Well, because I was,—I wouldn't give him all that work we had done.

Q.   What is that?

A. All the work we had done to get the literature, not to name my friends to get them in trouble.

MR. JEREMIAH MCANARNEY. I think that is all.

If your Honor please, the District Attorney is having trouble getting a hat here.

MR. KATZMANN. Not in getting it, but in getting the man, who has been on duty, and we have telephoned for him. He was to be here at 9:30 this morning.

MR. JEREMIAH MCANARNEY. I believe he has not the cap and coat yet.

MR. KATZMANN. Neither have I.

MR. JEREMIAH MCANARNEY. We better get it through you. When it does come, we would like the privilege of recalling this witness to testify.

THE COURT. I think there ought not to be any difficulty on that, inasmuch as both counsel,—that is, counsel on both sides seem to be desirous of having the cap, so I think between you you might succeed in getting it.

[Conference at bench between Court and counsel.]

Q. [By Mr. Katzmann.] Did you say yesterday you love a free country?

A. Yes, sir.

Q. Did you love this country in the month of May, 1917?

A. I did not say,—I don't want to say I did not love this country.

Q. Did you love this country in the month of May, 1917?

A. If you can, Mr. Katzmann, if you give me that,—I could explain—

Q. Do you understand that question?

A. Yes.

Q. Then will you please answer it?

A. I can't answer in one word.

Q. You can't say whether you loved the United States of America one week before the day you enlisted for the first draft?

A. I can't say in one word, Mr. Katzmann.

Q. You can't tell this jury whether you loved the country or not?

MR. MOORE. I object to that.

A. I could explain that, yes, if I loved—

Q. What?

A. I could explain that, yes, if I loved, if you give me a chance.

Q. I ask you first to answer that question. Did you love this United States of America in May, 1917?

A. I can't answer in one word.

Q. Don't you know whether you did or not?

MR. MOORE. I object, your Honor.

THE COURT. What say?

MR. MOORE. I object to the repetition of this question without giving the young man an opportunity to explain his attitude.

THE COURT. That is not the usual method that prevails. Where the question can be categorically answered by yes or no, it should be answered. The explanation comes later. Then you can make any inquiry to the effect of giving the witness an opportunity of making whatever explanation at that time he sees fit to make, but under cross-examination counsel is entitled to get an answer either yes or no, when the question can be so answered. You may proceed, please.

Q. Did you love this country in the last week of May, 1917?

A. That is pretty hard for me to say in one word, Mr. Katzmann.

Q. There are two words you can use, Mr. Sacco, yes or no. Which one is it?

A. Yes.

Q. And in order to show your love for this United States of America when she was about to call upon you to become a soldier you ran away to Mexico?

MR. JEREMIAH MCANARNEY. Wait.

THE COURT. Did you?

Q. Did you run away to Mexico?

THE COURT. He has not said he ran away to Mexico. Did you go?

Q. Did you go to Mexico to avoid being a soldier for this country that you loved?

A. Yes.

Q. You went under an assumed name?

A. No.

Q. Didn't you take the name of Mosmacotelli?

A. Yes.

Q. That is not your name, is it?

A. No.

Q. How long did you remain under the name of Mosmacotelli?

A. Until I got a job over to Mr. Kelley's.

Q. When was that?

A. The armistice.

Q. After the war was practically over?

A. Yes, sir.

Q. Then, for the first time, after May, 1917, did you become known as Sacco again?

A. Yes, sir.

Q. Was it for the reason that you desired to avoid service that when you came back in four months you went to Cambridge instead of to Milford?

A. For the reason for not to get in the army.

Q. So as to avoid getting in the army.

A. Another reason why, I did not want no chance to get arrested and one year in prison.

Q. Did not want to get arrested and spend one year in prison for dodging the draft. Is that it?

A. Yes.

Q. Did you love your country when you came back from Mexico?

A. The first time?

THE COURT. Which country did you say? You said—

Q. United States of America, your adopted country?

A. I did not say already.

Q. When you came back, I asked you. That was before you went . . .

A. I don't think I could change my opinion in three months.

Q. You still loved America, did you?

A. I should say yes.

Q. And is that your idea of showing your love for this Country?

A. [Witness hesitates.]

Q. Is that your idea of showing your love for America?

A. Yes.

Q. And would it be your idea of showing your love for your wife that when she needed you you ran away from her?

A. I did not run away from her.

MR. MOORE. I object.

THE WITNESS. I was going to come after if I need her.

THE COURT. He may answer. Simply on the question of credibility, that is all.

Q. Would it be your idea of love for your wife that you were to run away from her when she needed you?

MR. JEREMIAH McANARNEY. Pardon me. I ask for an exception on that.

THE COURT. Excluded. One may not run away. He has not admitted he ran away.

Q.   Then I will ask you, didn't you run away from Milford so as to avoid being a soldier for the United States?

A.   I did not run away.

Q.   You mean you walked away?

A.   Yes.

Q.   You don't understand me when I say "run away," do you?

A.   That is vulgar.

Q.   That is vulgar?

A.   You can say a little intelligent, Mr. Katzmann.

Q.   Don't you think going away from your country is a vulgar thing to do when she needs you?

A.   I don't believe in war.

Q.   You don't believe in war?

A.   No, sir.

Q.   Do you think it is a cowardly thing to do what you did?

A.   No, sir.

Q.   Do you think it is a brave thing to do what you did?

A.   Yes, sir.

Q.   Do you think it would be a brave thing to go away from your own wife?

A.   No.

Q.   When she needed you?

A.   No.

Q.   What wages did you first earn in this country?

A.   Wage?

Q.   Wages, money, pay?

A.   I used to get before I leave?

Q.   When you first came to this country?

A. $1.15.

Q.   Per day?

A.   Yes.

Q.   What were you getting at the 3–K factory when you got through?

A.   Sometimes sixty, fifty, seventy, eighty, forty, thirty, twenty-five, thirty-five. Depends on how much work was.

Q.   That was within eight years after you first came to this country, isn't it?

A.   After seven years,—no, after twelve years.

Q.   1908. I beg your pardon. That is my mistake, Mr. Sacco. I did not mean that. That is within thirteen years?

A.   Yes, sir.

Q.   From the time you came to this country?

A.   Yes.

Q.   From $1.15 a day to $5 a day or better?

A.   Yes.

Q.   And your child was born in this country, wasn't it?

A.   Yes.

Q.   And your marriage took place in this country?

A.   Yes.

Q.   Is Italy a free country? Is it a republic?

A.   Republic, yes.

Q.   Why didn't you stay down in Mexico?

A.   Well, first thing, I could not get my trade over there. I had to do any other job.

Q.   Don't they work with a pick and shovel in Mexico?

A.   Yes.

Q.   Haven't you worked with a pick and shovel in this country?

A.   I did.

Q.   Why didn't you stay there, down there in that free country, and work with a pick and shovel?

A.   I don't think I did sacrifice to learn a job to go and pick and shovel in Mexico.

Q.   Is it because,—is your love for the United States of America commensurate with the amount of money you can get in this country per week?

A.   Better conditions, yes.

Q.   Better country to make money, isn't it?

A.   Yes.

Q.   Mr. Sacco, that is the extent of your love for this country, isn't it, measured in dollars and cents?

MR. JEREMIAH MCANARNEY. If your Honor please, I object to this particular question.

THE COURT. You opened up this whole subject.

MR. JEREMIAH MCANARNEY. If your Honor please, I object to this question. That is my objection.

THE COURT. The form of it?

MR. JEREMIAH MCANARNEY. To the substance and form.

MR. KATZMANN. I will change the form, if your Honor please.

THE COURT. Better change that.

Q.   Is your love for this country measured by the amount of money you can earn here?

MR. JEREMIAH MCANARNEY. To that question I object.

THE COURT. Now, you may answer.

A.   I never loved money.

MR. JEREMIAH MCANARNEY. Save my exception.

THE COURT. Certainly.

Q.   What is the reason then?—

THE COURT. I allow this on the ground that the defendants opened it up.

Q.   What is the reason you came back?

MR. JEREMIAH MCANARNEY. My exception lies just the same.

THE COURT. Certainly.

MR. JEREMIAH MCANARNEY. Both defendants.

THE COURT. Certainly.

Q.   What is the reason you came back from Mexico if you did not love money, then?

A.   The first reason is all against my nature, is all different food over there, different nature, anyway.

Q.   That is the first reason. It is against your nature. The food isn't right.

A.   Food, and many other things.

Q.   You stood it for four months, didn't you?

A.   Three months.

Q.   Three months?

A.   Yes.

Q.   You came back all right physically, didn't you?

A.   I should say yes.

Q.   And you had Italian food there, didn't you?

A.   Yes, made by ourselves.

Q.   You could have had it all the time if you sent for it, couldn't you?

A.   Not all the time. I don't know.

Q.   Did you fail to have it at any time in the three months you were there?

A.   Yes, sir. Different.

Q.   What is the difference about it?

A.   Oh, different food that we did not like.

Q.   It was Italian food, wasn't it?

A.   No, sir.

Q.   Didn't you say it was?

A.   Sometimes after.

Q.   You could have had it all the time if you sent for it, couldn't you?

A.   Could have had beans sometimes and any other vegetable.

MR. KATZMANN. I ask that be stricken out and the witness required to answer the question.

Q.   Could you have had it by sending for it?

A.   Could not get it all the time.

Q.   Why couldn't you get it in Mexico the same as you get it here?

A.   I suppose Mexico is not very much industries as in this country.

Q.   Couldn't you send to Boston to get Italian food sent to Monterey, Mexico?

A.   If I was a D. Rockefeller I will.

Q.   Then, I take it, you came back to the United States first to get something to eat. Is that right? Something that you liked?

A.   No, not just for eat.

Q.   Didn't you say that was the first reason?

A.   The first reason—

Q.   Didn't you say that was the first reason?

A.   Yes.

Q.   All right. That wasn't a reason of the heart, was it?

A.   The heart?

Q.   Yes.

A.   No.

Q.   That was a reason of the stomach, wasn't it?

A.   Not just for the stomach, but any other reason.

Q.   I am talking first about the first reason. So, the first reason your love of America is founded upon is pleasing your stomach. Is that right?

A.   I will not say yes.

Q.   Haven't you said so?

A.   Not for the stomach. I don't think it is a satisfaction just for the stomach.

Q.   What is your second reason?

A.   The second reason is strange for me, the language.

Q.   Strange language?

A.   Yes.

Q. Were you in an Italian colony there?

A. If I got them. I can't get that, Mr. Katzmann.

Q. Pardon me. Were you in a group of Italians there?

A. Yes.

Q. When you came to America in 1908, did you understand English?

A. No.

Q. A strange language here, wasn't it?

A. Yes.

Q. What is the third reason, if there is one?

A. A third reason, I was far away from my wife and boy.

Q. Couldn't you have sent for your wife and your boy?

A. I wouldn't send for my wife and boy over there, because it was the idea to come back here.

Q. I know that. You are back here. My question is, couldn't you have sent for Mrs. Sacco and your boy?

A. Extreme condition, it would be bad. I could not go back in this United States, why I would get my wife and my boy.

Q. Your answer means, does it not, you could have had Mrs. Sacco and the boy come down there to live with you?

A. Yes.

Q. You preferred to come back to this country?

A. Yes.

Q. But you preferred to remain under the name of Mosmacotelli until the armistice was signed, didn't you?

A. Yes.

Q. Now, is there any other besides those three reasons why you loved the United States of America?

A. Well, I couldn't say. Over here there is more accommodation for the working class, I suppose, than any other people, a chance to be more industrious, and more industry. Can have a chance to get anything he wants.

Q. You mean to earn more money, don't you?

A. No, no, money, never loved money.

Q. Never loved money?

A. No, money never satisfaction to me.

Q. Money was never a satisfaction to you?

A. No.

Q. What was the industrial condition that pleased you so much here if it wasn't a chance to earn bigger money?

A. A man, Mr. Katzmann, has no satisfaction all through the money, for the belly.

Q. For the what?

A. For the stomach, I mean.

Q. We got away from the stomach. Now, I am talking about money.

A. There is lots of things.

Q. Well, let us have them all. I want to know why you loved America so that after you got to the haven of Mexico when the United States was at war you came back here?

A. Yes.

Q. I want all the reasons why you came back?

A. I think I did tell you already.

Q. Are those all?

A. Yes. Industry makes lots of things different.

Q. Then there is food, that is one?

A. Yes.

Q. Foreign language is two?

A. Yes.

Q. Your wife and child is three?

A. Yes.

Q. And better industrial conditions?

A. Yes.

Q. Is that all?

A. That is all.

Q. Among those four reasons, Mr. Katzmann, then, do you find any one that is called love of country? Have you named that reason?

MR. MOORE. I object to that question. The others are reasons, I take it.

THE COURT. Read it, please.

[The question is read.]

THE COURT. That last remark does not belong in your question.

MR. KATZMANN. "Have you named them?" No, I suppose not.

THE COURT. Leave that off, and you may ask it.

MR. KATZMANN. All right.

Q. Did you find love of country among those four reasons?

A. Yes, sir.

Q. Which one is love of country?

A. All together.

Q. All together?

A. Yes, sir.

Q. Food, wife, language, industry?

A. Yes.

Q. That is love of country, is it?

A. Yes.

Q. Is standing by a country when she needs a soldier evidence of love of country?

MR. JEREMIAH MCANARNEY. That I object to, if your Honor please. And I might state now I want my objection to go to this whole line of interrogation?

THE COURT. I think you opened it up.

MR. JEREMIAH MCANARNEY. No, if your Honor please, I have not.

THE COURT. It seems to me you have. Are you going to claim much of all the collection of the literature and the books was really in the interest of the United States as well as these people and therefore it has opened up the credibility of the defendant when he claims that all that work was done really for the interest of the United States in getting this literature out of the way?

MR. JEREMIAH MCANARNEY. That claim is not presented in anything tantamount to the language just used by the Court, and in view of the record as it stands at this time I object to this line of inquiry.

THE COURT. Is that not your claim, that the defendant, as a reason that he has given for going to the Johnson house, that they wanted the automobile to prevent people from being deported and to get this literature all out of the way? Does he not claim that that was done in the interest of the United States, to prevent violation of the law by the distribution of this literature? I understood that was the—

MR. JEREMIAH MCANARNEY. Are you asking that as a question of me?

THE COURT. Yes.

MR. JEREMIAH MCANARNEY. Absolutely we have taken no such position as that, and the evidence at this time does not warrant the assumption of that question.

THE COURT. Then you are not going to make that claim?

MR. JEREMIAH MCANARNEY. I am going to make whatever claim is legitimate.

THE COURT. I want to know what that is. You are going to claim in argument—

MR. JEREMIAH MCANARNEY. I am going to claim this man and Vanzetti were of that class called Socialists. I am going to claim that riot was running a year ago last April, that men were being deported, that twelve to fifteen hundred were seized in Massachusetts.

THE COURT. Do you mean to say you are going to offer evidence on that?

MR. JEREMIAH MCANARNEY. I am going to claim—

THE COURT. I am asking the claim. You must know when I ask the claim I mean a claim that is founded on fact, evidence introduced in the case, and not upon anything else.

MR. JEREMIAH MCANARNEY. We have not concluded the evidence, if your Honor please.

THE COURT. Do you say you are going to introduce evidence to that effect?

MR. JEREMIAH MCANARNEY. We have witnesses which we may introduce here. I do not know whether we will introduce them or not.

THE COURT. When you address me, I wish you would direct yourself to either evidence introduced or evidence you propose to introduce.

MR. JEREMIAH MCANARNEY. Your honor now sees—

THE COURT. So I can pass judgment then upon that, and I cannot pass judgment as to the competency of something that may not be introduced and never come before me for consideration.

MR. JEREMIAH MCANARNEY. Your Honor now sees the competency of my remarks, when I said to your Honor that I objected to the question in the present state of the evidence?

THE COURT. Are you going to claim that what the defendant did was in the interest of the United States?

MR. JEREMIAH MCANARNEY. Your Honor please, I now object to your Honor's statement as prejudicial to the rights of the defendants and ask that this statement be withdrawn from the jury.

THE COURT. There is no prejudicial remark made that I know of, and none were intended. I simply asked you, sir, whether you propose to offer evidence as to what you said to me.

MR. JEREMIAH MCANARNEY. If your Honor please, the remarks made with reference to the country and whether the acts that he was doing were for the benefit of the country. I can see no other inference to be drawn from those except prejudicial to the defendants.

THE COURT. Do you intend to make that claim?

MR. JEREMIAH MCANARNEY. What claim, please?

THE COURT. The one that I am suggesting.

MR. JEREMIAH MCANARNEY. When this evidence is closed, if your Honor please, I shall argue what is legitimate in the case.

THE COURT. All I ask is this one question, and it will simplify matters very much. Is it your claim that in the collection of the literature and the books and papers that that was done in the interest of the United States?

MR. JEREMIAH MCANARNEY. No, I make no such broad claim as that.

THE COURT. Then I will hear you, Mr. Katzmann, on the competency of this testimony.

MR. KATZMANN: I am sorry I did not hear what Mr. McAnarney said.

THE COURT. Mr . McAnarney says it is not his claim, as I got it, he does not propose to make the claim that the collection and distribution of this literature was any matter to be done by either or both of the defendants in the interest of the United States.

MR. KATZMANN. Then, if your Honor please, I offer the line of cross-examination I have started upon as tending to attack the credibility of this man as a witness.

THE COURT. As to what part of his testimony?

MR. KATZMANN. As to any part of his testimony to affect his credibility as a witness *in toto*.

THE COURT. You can't attack a witness's credibility *in toto* excepting concerning some subject matter about which he has testified.

MR. KATZMANN. Well, he stated in his direct examination yesterday that he loved a free country, and I offer it to attack that statement made in his examination by his own counsel.

THE COURT. That is what I supposed, and that is what I supposed that remark meant when it was introduced in this cross-examination, but counsel now say they don't make that claim.

MR. KATZMANN. They say they don't make the claim that gathering up the literature on May 5th at West Bridgewater was for the purpose of helping the country, but that is a different matter, not related to May 5th.

THE COURT. I will let you inquire further first as to what he meant by the expression.

MR. MOORE. If your Honor please, with all due respect to the Court, I desire to reserve an exception to the question that was asked,—interrogation that was asked as to the purpose of the testimony that was introduced on behalf of the defendant with reference to the issue of love of country; reserve an exception with all due respect to the Court.

THE COURT. Of course, gentlemen, you understand, and you should understand by this time, that the Court is simply to pass upon the competency of testimony that is offered. The Court has no opinion of any facts. You heard me say so. The Court has no opinion in reference to this matter. I made simply the inquiry with a view of ascertaining what the claim of counsel might be, what might be argued, and inasmuch as counsel said they made no such claim, then I have reserved the right to pass upon the competency after inquiry has been made with reference to said testimony of the witness. I think you should know, and I repeat it, anyhow, there is no disposition, nothing has been said to do the slightest thing in any manner whatsoever to prejudice the rights of either of these defendants, and anything that has been said you will not consider it if anybody can draw such an inference. You will give it not the slightest consideration in the world. It deserves none, and you will give it none. The only question I was passing upon was the competency of testimony and nothing else. Questions are not evidence. Statements of counsel are not evidence. Statements by the Court are not evidence. You will be governed by absolutely nothing but testimony that is admitted and heard by you from the witnesses upon the stand. You may proceed.

Q. What did you mean when you said yesterday you loved a free country?

A. First thing I came in this country—

Q. No, pardon me. What did you mean when you said yesterday you loved a free country?

A. Give me a chance to explain.

Q. I am asking you to explain now.

A. When I was in Italy, a boy, I was a Republican, so I always thinking Republican has more chance to manage education, develop, to build some day his family, to raise the child and education, if you could. But that was my opinion; so when I came to this country I saw there was not what I was thinking before, but there was all the difference, because I been working in Italy not so hard as I been work in this country. I could live free there just as well. Work in the same condition, but not so hard, about seven or eight hours a day, better food. I mean genuine. Of course, over here is good food, because it is a bigger country, to any those who got money to spend, not for the working and laboring class, and in Italy is more opportunity to laborer to eat vegetable, more fresh, and I came in this country. When I been started work here very hard and been work thirteen years, hard worker, I could not been afford much a family the way I did have the idea before. I could not put any money in the bank . . . I could no push my boy some to go to school and other things. I teach over here men who is with me. The free idea gives any man a chance to profess his own idea, not the supreme idea, not to give any person, not to be like Spain in position, yes, about twenty centuries ago, but to give a chance to print and education, literature, free speech, that I see it was all wrong. I could see the best men, intelligent, education, they been arrested and sent to prison and died in prison for years and years without getting them out, and Debs, one of the great men in his country, he is in prison, still away in prison, because he is a Socialist. He wanted the laboring class to have better conditions and better living, more education, give a push his son if he could have a chance some day, but they put him in prison. Why? Because the capitalist class, they know, they are against that, because the capitalist class, they don't want our child to go to high school or to college or Harvard College. There would not be no chance, there would not be no,—they don't want the working class educationed; they want the working class to be a low all the times, be underfoot, and not to be up with the head. So, sometimes, you see, the Rockefellers, Morgans, they give fifty,—mean they give five hundred thousand dollars to Harvard College, they give a million dollars for another school. Everybody say, "Well, D. Rockefeller is a great man, the best in the country?'' I want to ask him who is going to Harvard College? What benefit the working class they will get by those millions dollars they give by Rockefeller, D. Rockefellers. They won't get, the poor class, they won't have no chance to go to Harvard College because men who is getting $21 a week or $30 a week, I don't care if he gets $80 a week, if he gets a family of five children he can't live and send his child and go to Harvard College if he wants to eat anything nature will give him. If he wants to eat like a cow, and that is the best thing, but I want men to live like men. I like men to get everything that nature will give best, because they belong,—we are not the friend of any other place, but we are belong to nations. So that is why my idea has been changed. So that is why I love people who labor and work and see better conditions every day develop, makes no more war. We no want fight by the gun, and we don't want to destroy young men. The mother been suffering for building the young man. Some day need a little more bread, so when the time the mother get some bread or profit out of that boy, the Rockefellers, Morgans, and some of the peoples, high class, they send to war. Why? What is war? The war is not shoots like Abraham Lincoln's and Abe Jefferson, to fight for the free country, for the better education, to give chance to any other peoples, not the white people but the black and the others, because they believe and know they are mens like the rest, but they are war for the great millionaire. No war for the civilization of men. They are war for business, million dollars come on the side. What right we have to kill each other? I been work for the Irish, I have been working with the German fellow, with the French, many other peoples. I love them people just as I could love my wife, and my people for that did receive me. Why should I go kill them men? What he done to me? He never done anything, so I don't believe in no war. I want to destroy those guns. All I can say, the Government put the literature, give us educations. I remember in Italy, a long time ago, about sixty years ago, I should say, yes, about sixty years ago, the Government they could not control very much these two,—devilment went on, and robbery, so one of the government in the cabinet he says, "If you want to destroy those devilments, if you want to take off all those criminals, you ought to give a chance to Socialist literature, education of people, emancipation. That is why I destroy governments, boys." That is why my idea I love Socialists. That is why I like people who want education and living, building, who is good, just as much as they could. That is all.

Q.   And that is why you love the United States of America?

A. Yes.

Q.   She is back more than twenty centuries like Spain, is she?

A. At the time of the war they do it.

Q.   Are we in time of war now?

A. No.

Q.   Were we in time of war when you came back from Mexico?

A. Yes.

Q. What did you come back for, then?

A. I told the reason why I came back.

Q. All right. You don't get a good education in this country?

A. I don't see why they have a chance.

Q. Do you get a better chance for education in Italy, I take it, from what you said?

A. I don't say Italy better education in this country.

Q. You said you could work less hours over in Italy?

A. Yes.

Q. You could get fresher vegetables?

A. Yes.

Q. Better food, and it was a republic?

A. For the working class.

Q. Why didn't you go back there?

A. Pretty hard for men to change when he establish in one place.

Q. Why, you were to go back, weren't you?

A. Yes.

Q. Why didn't you intend to stay back there when you went back?

A. Italy?

Q. Yes, your native country?

A. I could not stay or not, because—

Q. Have you said whether you were going to stay or not?

A. Yes, I was going to go.

Q. Were you coming back?

A. I do not know, Mr. Katzmann.

Q. Did you tell me you were coming back?

A. I couldn't say so.

Q. Can't you remember what you said to me over in the Brockton police station?

A. I could not remember all the words, but I do remember some conversation between me and Mr. Kelley.

Q. Never mind Kelley. I am talking about myself now. Didn't you tell me that you were coming back to this country in two or three months?

A. Well, if I did—

Q. Did you?

A. I could not remember, Mr. Katzmann, if I did.

Q. Wasn't that your intention to come back?

A. I couldn't say yes, because probably I could remain in Italy because my father is old. I could get his business over there.

Q.   Were you going to have your father support you?

A. What? Support me, my father?

Q.   Yes.

A. No.

Q.   Were you going to take your wife and child over?

A. Yes.

Q.   You could not go back to Italy, you say, because it would be a hardship, but you could take your wife and child back for a vacation; is that right?

A. No, not vacation.

Q.   Wasn't it a vacation?

A. No, sir.

Q.   Were you going to work while you were over there?

A. Certainly. I could not work without work. I love work.

Q.   You love work?

A. Yes.

Q.   Do you love it as much as you love this country?

A. Well, I think men is a great work,—greater profit for the country, too.

Q.   When you came over to this country, you had certain ideas, didn't you of what was here?

A. No.

Q.   Didn't you say when you came over you were thinking about education, building for your family, and raising a family?

A. Yes, but I was a Republican in my country.

Q.   Didn't you say that you had those ideas of this country when you came here?

A.   Yes.

Q.   And didn't you say when you came you saw a difference?

A. Yes.

Q.   And the things were better in Italy than they were here?

A. No, not that.

Q.   In substance, haven't you said that in this long answer you gave.

A. No. Buy fruit more fresh for the working class, but no education and other things. It is just the same.

Q.   Didn't you say you did not have to work so hard in Italy?

A. Yes.

Q.   That you could live just as well in Italy?

A. Yes.

Q.   And that there was better food?

A. Yes.

Q.   And fresher vegetables in Italy?

A. Yes.

Q.   Why didn't you go back?

A. Well, I say already—

Q.   Say it again. Why didn't you go back when you were disappointed in those things?

A. I say men established in this country, it is pretty hard to go back, change mind to go back.

Q.   Pretty hard to change your mind?

A. Yes.

Q.   You say on April 15, 1920, you were in Boston getting a passport to go back with your wife and children?

A. Yes. That is not the reason I go back to the old country, for the fruit, but to see my father. For twelve years I never saw him, my brother, my sister, or my folks.

Q.   It is just as easy, isn't it, to go back to see your father as to go back for fruit. You go back in either case?

A. I do the greatest sacrifice in the life to go there.

Q.   To go back to a country where you get those things and could not get them here,—is that a sacrifice?

A. No. The great sacrifice is to see my folks.

Q.   The great sacrifice. All right. Do you believe in obedience to constituted governmental authority?

Mr. Jeremiah McAnarney. I object, if your Honor please.

Mr. Katzmann. Pause a moment. There is an objection.

The Court. I would like to see counsel at the bench.

[Conference between Court and counsel at bench.]

[Short recess.]

Q.   Do you remember speaking of educational advantages before the recess?

A. Yes, sir.

Q.   Do you remember speaking of Harvard University?

A. Yes, sir.

Q. Do you remember saying that you could not get an education there unless you had money? I do not mean you used those exact words. I do not contend you did, but, in substance, didn't you say that?

A. They have to use money is the rule of the Government.

Q. No. You don't understand. Did you hear it, perhaps?

A. I can't understand.

Q. I will raise my voice a little bit. Did you say in substance you could not send your boy to Harvard?

A. Yes.

Q. Unless you had money. Did you say that?

A. Of course.

Q. Do you think that is true?

A. I think it is.

Q. Don't you know Harvard University educates more boys of poor people free than any other university in the United States of America?

MR. JEREMIAH McANARNEY. I object.

THE COURT. You may answer.

MR. JEREMIAH McANARNEY. Save an exception.

THE COURT. You may answer—if he knows.

Q. Do you know that to be the fact?

A. How many there are?

Q. What?

A. How many.

Q. How many? Don't you know that each year there are scores of them that Harvard educates free?

MR. JEREMIAH McANARNEY. I object.

THE COURT. Wait until he finishes the question.

MR. JEREMIAH McANARNEY. I thought he had.

MR. KATZMANN: That was the end of it.

THE COURT. He may answer yes or no, whether he knows or not.

MR. JEREMIAH McANARNEY. Save an exception.

Q. The question is, do you know?

A. I can't answer that question, no.

Q. So without the light of knowledge on that subject, you are condemning even Harvard University, are you, as being a place for rich men?

MR. JEREMIAH McANARNEY. Wait one minute.

THE COURT. It does not follow.

Q. Do you intend to condemn Harvard College?

THE COURT. He may answer.

MR. JEREMIAH MCANARNEY. Save an exception.

THE COURT. Certainly.

A.   No, sir.

Q.   Were you ready to say none but the rich could go there without knowing about offering scholarhsips?

MR. JEREMIAH MCANARNEY. To that I object.

THE COURT. He may answer.

MR. JEREMIAH MCANARNEY. Save an exception.

THE COURT. He made a statement in cross-examination with reference to statements that the witness himself made. He may answer.

A.   Yes.

Q.   Does your boy go to the public schools?

A. Yes.

Q.   Are there any schools in the town you came from in Italy that compare with the school your boy goes to?

MR. JEREMIAH MCANARNEY. I object.

THE COURT. Isn't this quite a good way now from that? Of course, I see, or think I see, what you have in mind eventually, but it seems to me the boy going to school is quite a considerable distance.

Q.   Does your boy go to the public school?

A. Yes.

Q.   Without payment of money.

A. Yes.

Q.   Have you free nursing where you come from in Stoughton?

A. What do you mean?

Q.   A district nurse?

A. For the boys?

Q.   For anybody in your family who is ill?

A. I could not say. Yes, I never have them in my house.

Q.   Do you know how many children the city of Boston is educating in the public schools?—

MR. JEREMIAH MCANARNEY. I object.

Q.   [Continued.]—free?

THE COURT. Ask him if he knows.

MR. KATZMANN. I did.

THE COURT. Answer yes or no.

Q.   Do you know?

A. I can't answer yes or no.

Q. Do you know it is close to one hundred thousand children?

MR. JEREMIAH MCANARNEY. I object.

A. I know millions of people don't go there.

MR. JEREMIAH MCANARNEY. Wait. When there is objection, don't answer. I object to that question.

THE COURT. He says he doesn't know.

MR. JEREMIAH MCANARNEY. I object to that answer. I object to the question and the answer

THE COURT. The question may stand, and the answer also.

MR. JEREMIAH MCANARNEY. Will your Honor save an exception.

Q. Did you have some circulars and books in your house on May 5th?

A. Yes.

Q. How long had you had them there?

A. Well, I buy little by little when I have a chance to buy books.

Q. How long?

A. When I have money to buy.

Q. How long in all had you had them there?

A. In the house?

Q. Yes.

A. I should say beginning when I came to this country, some books. Always were there right along after.

Q. Are they written in English?

A. Some.

Q. And in what other language?

A. Italian. The most of them.

Q. Printed in this country or in Italy?

A. I couldn't say, but the most they are printed in Europe.

Q. The continent you left behind you?

A. And some is printed in America.

Q. Yes. And do you subscribe to any papers?

A. Literature?

Q. Yes, literature in the sense of not books. I was trying to distinguish.

A. Yes?

Q. What papers?

MR. JEREMIAH MCANARNEY. I object.

THE COURT. You may answer.

MR. JEREMIAH McANARNEY. Will your Honor save an exception?

THE COURT. Certainly.

A.   You mean a paper or books?

Q.   Papers?

A. You mean I could say the paper I get every day?

    .   .   .

Subsequent Developments

Abbot Lawrence Lowell (1856–1943), the President of Harvard University, was appointed to a state commission to review the case after Sacco and Vanzetti were convicted of murder and sentenced to death. Lowell had previously been active in public affairs, including as a signer of the letter from fifty-five Boston lawyers opposed to the nomination of Louis Brandeis (supra Chapter 6). The Lowell Committee, in a report written by Lowell, found that the Sacco and Vanzetti trial had been fair.

Felix Frankfurter later observed:

"[w]hat is essential to what you call the 'drama of Sacco–Vanzetti' was expressed in a remark made to me by John F. Moors about 'two wops.' Moors was a Yankee of Yankees, a Bostonian of Bostonians, an intimate, close personal friend; indeed a Harvard classmate of President Lowell and a member of the Harvard Corporation. His friendship with Lowell survived without strain despite Moors's nonconformist attitude, and indeed he fought hard for the cause of Sacco–Vanzetti.... [Moors] said about his friend, Lawrence Lowell, this: 'Lawrence Lowell was incapable of seeing that two wops could be right and the Yankee judiciary could be wrong.' "

"That posed a dilemma for Lowell which his mind couldn't overreach, clear and hurdle with ease. His crowd, the Yankees, were right, and the alien immigrants were what they were—pacifists and draft dodgers. He was incapable of doing what men have done, namely, say their crowd was wrong."

Harlan B. Phillips, Felix Frankfurter Reminisces 202–03 (1960).

QUESTIONS

1.   The direct examination elicited an admission from Sacco that he did not tell the truth to Stewart or to the District Attorney. Why did Fred Moore want to address his own client's untruthfulness on direct examination? Was the direct examination effective at explaining why Sacco did not tell the truth upon his arrest?

2.   Katzmann elicited statements from Sacco showing that he dodged the draft, had materialist instincts, had negative feelings toward Harvard University, and had socialist political principles. Were these facts relevant to the central issue of fact in this trial?

3. Was the cross examination designed to reveal the truth or to undermine Sacco's self confidence and induce him to make statements that would prejudice the jury against him?

4. At what points in the cross examination did Sacco fail to understand the questions he was being asked? When Sacco did not understand a question, and answered it anyway, what should Judge Thayer have done? Was it enough merely to tell Sacco that he had an opportunity, if he did not understand a question, "to say so and have the questions put so that you may understand each one and all"?

5. What was Katzmann's purpose in pursuing the line of questioning about why Sacco came to the United States? What was his purpose in asking Sacco why he went to Mexico and why he returned?

6. Judge Thayer stated that he allowed much of this questioning because the defense "opened up the whole subject." What subject did the defense supposedly open up? Assume Judge Thayer was right that "a reason that [Sacco] has given for going to the Johnson house, [was] that they wanted the automobile to prevent people from being deported and to get this literature all out of the way ... That that was done in the interest of the United States, to prevent violation of the law by the distribution of this literature." What line of relevant cross examination would have been proper for the prosecution to refute this claim? Was the cross examination here relevant?

7. Even if a line of questioning is relevant, are there limits on the extent and duration of cross examination? How many times should a lawyer ask a witness the same question? In the Warren Trust matter, Chapter 6 supra, Samuel Warren shot himself after 27 days of cross-examination by Sherman Whipple. What were the effects on Sacco of Katzmann's questioning here?

8. Was Sacco's long monologue on politics exactly what the prosecution was hoping for? What was the probable effect of Sacco's monologue on the jury? Should Judge Thayer have interjected?

9. Was it proper for Judge Thayer to ask defense counsel in the presence of the jury about the evidence that the defense intended to introduce?

10. Did Judge Thayer make remarks in the jury's presence that were prejudicial to the defendants? What were those remarks? Is it likely that the jury believed Judge Thayer's statement that "the Court has no opinion in reference to this matter"?

11. Catherine Drinker Bowen, in her account of Sir Walter Ralegh's trial, observes that in times of national emergency, courts interpreting treason statutes construed words alone to be an overt act, whereas "in times of peace and national security, the overt act takes narrower construction, and courts require deeds as well as words before they will convict of treason." Once England's fear of Catholic invasion died down, "Coke as Chief Justice was himself to alter, on occasion, his own interpretation, giving under Stuart kings far greater latitude to the accused than he gave to Ralegh or even to Essex—and not only in the matter of the act overt but the rule concerning two witnesses." See page 575 supra.

Felix Frankfurter also refers to a fearful political climate, the Red Scare in the United States following the First World War and the 1917 Russian Revolution. What specific evidentiary rulings by Judge Thayer on the cross examination of Sacco accommodated the prevailing fear of foreigners and socialists? How is the integrity of the judicial system affected when judges expand and contract their interpretations of legal norms on account of the political climate?

12. Charles Curtis observes in Its Your Law that "[A] criminal trial, it has been well said, should have the atmosphere of the operating room. The presiding judge determines the atmosphere." How well did this trial conform to Curtis's analogy? What atmosphere did Judge Thayer determine for the trial?

13. The Commonwealth of Massachusetts now requires that:

"In appearing in his professional capacity before a tribunal, a lawyer shall not ... [e]ngage in conduct manifesting bias or prejudice based on race, sex, religion, national origin, disability, age, or sexual orientation against any party, witness, counsel or other person. This Disciplinary Rule does not preclude legitimate advocacy when race, sex, national origin, disability, age, or sexual orientation, or another similar factor, is an issue in the proceeding."

Massachusetts Canons of Ethics and Disciplinary Rules DR 7–106(C)(8)(1972). See Eva S. Nilsen, The Criminal Defense Lawyer's Reliance on Bias and Prejudice, 8 Geo. J. Legal Ethics 1, 24 n. 98 (1994). Was Sacco's national origin an issue in his trial? Did Katzmann, in his cross examination of Sacco, engage in conduct that would violate this rule?

Relevant Background

It is clearly improper for a prosecutor to appeal to factors such as class, wealth, and race in order to obtain a conviction. See United States ex rel. Haynes v. McKendrick, 481 F.2d 152, 156 (2d Cir. 1973) (prosecutor's description to the jury of how African Americans have certain mannerisms and habits "introduced race prejudice into the trial and thereby denied petitioner his constitutional right under the due process clause to a fair trial"); Fred Zacharias, Structuring the Ethics of Prosecutorial Trial Practice: Can Prosecutors Do Justice?, 44 Vand. L. Rev. 45, 88–89 (1991) ("When a prosecutor relies on inadmissible evidence or plays to prejudice, she seeks what might be called 'reverse jury nullification'—conviction when the evidence and law technically may not support that result."), citing United States v. Socony–Vacuum Oil Co., 310 U.S. 150, 239–40 (1940) (improper appeal to class prejudice) and United States v. Stahl, 616 F.2d 30, 31–33 (2d Cir.1980) (improper reference to defendant's wealth). Another source of prejudice is a criminal defendant's exercise of his Fifth Amendment right against self-incrimination. See Lime v. State, 479 P.2d 608 (Okl.Crim.App.1971) (remand for a new trial required where prosecutors, in arguing to the jury, made specific reference to the nontestifying defendants charged with murder and stated that "there is no excuse and they offer you no excuse whatsoever for the manner in which this was done.").

Katzmann's cross-examination of Nicola Sacco displayed multiple breaches of these standards. Indeed, almost all of the subject matter discussed, from the defendant's taste in food, his reasons for coming to the United States, his leaving for Mexico during World War I, to what he thought of Harvard, had nothing to do with the offense with which he was charged and had everything to do with inflaming the prejudices of the jury against immigrants and draft resisters.

It being unethical for a prosecutor to manipulate juror bias, it is difficult to see how it would be more ethical for a defense lawyer to do the same thing. "Jury nullification," an acquittal by jurors who are convinced that the defendant has committed the crime, occasionally has its place where prosecutors' conduct has been egregious, the defendant's conduct has been exemplary in other respects, or the punishment for the crime is unconscionable. However, factors such as race, religion or ethnic background are hardly legitimate reasons for a jury to acquit. But See Paul Butler, Racially Based Jury Nullification: Black Power in the Criminal Justice System, 105 Yale L.J. 677 (1995) (African Americans should acquit African American defendants who are guilty of nonviolent victimless offenses such as drug possession, and should consider nullification where African–American defendants are charged with non-violent crimes such as theft from the very rich); Andrew D. Leipold, The Dangers of Race–Based Jury Nullification: A Response to Professor Butler, 44 UCLA L. Rev. 109, 111–12 (1996) (Professor Butler's proposal "misconstrues the lessons history teaches about jury nullification" and in the end would make the criminal jury system less fair to African Americans). Whatever the merits or demerits of race based nullification, a lawyer arguing such a theory to a jury treads dangerously close to violating acceptable standards of professional conduct. See Model Code, DR 7–106(C)(1) (a lawyer should not "allude to any matter that he has no reasonable basis to believe is relevant to the case or that will not be supported by admissible evidence."); see also Model Rule 3.4(e).

D. Fair and Unfair Argument at the Civil Bar

Harold Laski, b. Manchester, England 1893, d. 1950; raised in an Orthodox Jewish household; first class degree in 1914 from New College, Oxford (where he joined the socialist Fabian Society and was active in the women's suffrage movement); editorial writer for the Daily Herald 1914–15; Lecturer in History at McGill College in Montreal, Canada 1915–16; wrote extensively for the New Republic in 1915–16; recruited by Professor Felix Frankfurter to be a Lecturer in History at Harvard and to enroll as a student at Harvard Law School from 1916–20 (where he met Justice Oliver Wendell Holmes and published three notes for the Harvard Law Review);

appointed to a post at the London School of Economics in 1920 and eventually became known as one of the School's most famous and influential teachers (also corresponded frequently with Justice Holmes and later with Justice Frankfurter); published thirty books and hundreds of scholarly and popular articles during his lifetime; member of the Labour Party's Executive Committee 1934–49; became Labour Party Chairman in 1945.

Laski became a central figure in the political campaign before the 1945 General Election in which Clement Attlee's Labour Party defeated Winston Churchill's Conservatives. Laski gave over sixty speeches over five weeks of the campaign. Tory loyalists attended Laski's speeches in the hope that they could lure him into revealing his seemingly dangerous theories. Soon, an opportunity presented itself, and the Newark Advertiser, a Tory newspaper owned by the Beaverbrook interests, quoted Laski as saying that if Labor were obstructed, "we shall have to use violence even if it means revolution." Laski issued a writ for libel against the newspaper.

The case was heard by a "special" jury of seven persons (until special juries were abolished by the 1949 Juries Bill, either party could request that a case with complicated subject matter be heard by jurors with more property holdings than "common" jurors). At trial, Laski's 1933 book Democracy in Crisis became the subject of lengthy questioning in his cross examination by Sir Patrick Hastings.

See Isaac Kramnick and Barry Sheerman, Harold Laski, A Life on the Left (1993).

Sir Patrick Hastings was Attorney General in McDonald's Labor Government in the early 1920's and had occasionally attended Fabian meetings at which Laski would speak. He abandoned socialism in the 1920's and became one of England's most skilled trial lawyers. He was the author of two autobiographies and counsel for the Beaverbrook newspapers, including the Newark Advertiser.

G.O. Slade, England's foremost expert on libel law, represented Laski in the 1945 libel trial. **Sir Valentine Holmes** was Slade's assistant for the trial.

Lord Chief Justice Rayner Goddard, a former unsuccessful Tory candidate for Parliament and a strong advocate of capital punishment, was appointed by Prime Minister Attlee's Labour Government to ease fears of conservatives. Goddard was the presiding Judge in the libel trial and played an active role in the cross-examination of Laski. Goddard came across to many observers as favoring the defense.

Transcript of Closing Speeches in Laski v. Newark Advertising Company., Ltd. and Parlby

(King's Bench 1945).

Closing Speech Of Sir Patrick Hastings

* * *

Slade has told us he is not going to say anything of the sort. All that was gone. Malice has gone. All you have to consider is: were the words spoken? Or, if you do not think they were, as I am going to suggest they were, is it on the whole a fair and accurate report of this rather uncivil exchange—I think "exchange of incivilities" was the expression used by one witness—on some night at this particular place during the course of a "General Election".

Of course, Members of the Jury, I gathered that Mr. Slade, certainly when treason felony was looming in front of us—and possibly still—was asking for very very heavy damages. All I want to say about that is this: this paper in this little town in Nottingham is being asked to pay these terrific damages for treason felony at one time, and all that by this gentleman, because it is said that his character has been ruined apparently by what has been said about him.

Now, Members of the Jury, if words about revolution were said about some people, it is very difficult to think of anyone who could be above all such suspicion that they would not be very damaging to him; but let me take the highest person I can think of. Let me think that they were said about Mr. Slade—that he had been guilty of treason felony. Well, I can quite understand people saying that that is a very serious allegation against him which he would naturally resent. But revolution does not mean quite the same to Mr. Laski: he has written about nothing else for 30 years. I have it in front of me: *Reflections on Revolution in our Time*,[2] and things of that sort.

Were these words said? You have had evidence *ad nauseam*. I am going to do no more than just to remind you of what I venture to think are admitted facts. Do not let us bother about controversy for one moment. Look at what is admitted. We know that in the meeting *everything* that appears in this letter—every single thing as far as I know except that one sentence—is admitted to have been said. All these things you may think are very different or you may think they are very very much the same. You know—"great changes"—"so urgent"—"if they are not made by consent they would be made by violence". That is admitted; that is all admitted. "When 25 percent of the people have inadequate nutrition, it does become intolerable. It did not become possible to prevent what was not given by generosity being taken by the people". All that is admitted. That was said, anyhow; and there is only just one line which is said to be inaccurate.

Now, Members of the Jury, am I not right in saying that it is admitted—admitted by Mr. Laski himself—that that is what he thinks, that the words here complained of are what he thinks and what he has said himself over and over again. Now, I promise you I am not going to refer to those books again. I gave you I think the four passages in the volume you have got where, if you want to look up the sentences, you can see them. But

---

2. [Sir Patrick Hastings refers to Laski's book Reflections on the Revolution of our Time]—ed.

let me remind you of what he said himself in the witness box. You have not got a copy of the shorthand note. You are very fortunate in that regard. But his Lordship has, and there is just one passage to which I want to refer to you. I am going to ask you whether you do not think yourselves that it is exactly what he thinks. It is page 18 of the Second Day—just a few sentences of what he says about his writing. He was writing a book called *The State in Theory and Practice* in 1934. There is a sentence which begins: "This view"—that is the view he is expressing—"is one that naturally disturbs many generous minds. It postulates the inevitability of revolution as the midwife of a social change." Now, if anybody had said that you or I had said that, we should probably be angry. We would not have dreamt of saying it. But this is what he said: "(Q.) At that time your view was: 'The only thing is force, violence'?" This is his answer: "At that time my view was that the relationship between classes, the decline in the well being of the worker, was such as to make it inevitable that if the condition continued, the relationship between classes would be resolved by force." I really do not understand the difference between that and what we say he says at the meeting. "(Q.) Inevitable revolution by violence? (A.) Yes. (Q.) That was because of the condition when you wrote? (A.) Yes. (Q.) When did that condition change, so that your view changes? (A.) I think the condition began to change with the advent of full employment during the war, with the emphasis on the victory of democracy at the close of the war." So that that is what his view was right up to this particular war.

Then I asked him another question, because his answers were very long. "(Q.) We will just keep to my question, which was dates. Never mind about speeches about it. You, at the time you wrote, believed honestly this: 'At this stage of economic development, the difference between classes can only be settled by force.' You believed that honestly? (A.) Yes, if those conditions deteriorated. (Q.) You believed that honestly? (A.) Certainly. (Q.) What was the date on which you changed your mind? (A.) The date when I changed my mind was at the beginning of the war."—He wrote that in 1934 and he has never changed it in a book, not a word ever saying he disagreed with it.

Then there was a gentleman who was a Communist and I asked him. There was a little hesitation, and I thought we would not press it any further because we are not dealing with political matters. But which Party do you think he was referring to? He did not mention the Labour Party, but who else was going to start it? Was it even the Liberal Party? There it is: it is admitted by Mr. Poole that in substance that is what he said. I think Mr. Poole was one of the first witnesses called; he was released quite quickly and went back to this town where no doubt he was suitably reproved for having given away something which was not entirely desired. However I dare say he is not here now and it is not always very wise to say exactly what you remember.

Now, Members of the Jury, look at the last admission. I do not know whether you think this is right or whether you do not, but I thought it right to call Lord Hinchingbrooke before you, because, you know, when you read things out of a paper it never carries as much weight as if you see the person himself. What did Lord Hinchingbrooke say? He said: "In a serious discussion between three of us on socialistic matters, Professor Laski said: 'I do not for one moment say that it is certain you can arrive at socialism through the processes solely of discussion.'" Well, that means to say you cannot get it peaceably. And both Lord Hinchingbrooke and Sir Malcolm Darling said: "But, Laski, are you seriously suggesting that you must use either the whip or the rifle?" Now, here is this gentleman who says it is such an awful thing if anyone suggests that he ever said that. I mean it is a shocking thing. He says: "I want enormous damages." And, remember, he was speaking then in the hearing of millions of his supporters, and he had either got to say: "I do mean that." Or, "I do not mean that," and indignantly deny it, or say nothing. Of course, if he indignantly denied it, all his millions of supporters might have said: "What has happened?"

LORD CHIEF JUSTICE: It is not quite accurate to say "millions of supporters," because the evidence was that the broadcast was not a broadcast to this country.

PATRICK HASTINGS: My Lord, I am much obliged—whatever country people live in who are interested in such things as revolution in England. Anyhow, it goes out. Now, Professor Laski may have been faced, if he had said "I never said anything of the sort" with this, that an enormous number of his supporters would say: "What has happened to Laski? Well, it is what he has been telling us for years." He could not say, "Yes, I do mean that," because that might have been stopped. He said nothing. His only answer was "Let us be realists. I have never known a case in which a governing class has surrendered the ultimate possession of power without fighting for it;" and he took Charles I and the French aristocracy and the Russian nobility as example. What does that mean?—"You will never get socialism without violence and I mean it."....

* * *

You know, Members of the Jury, this is not very far away from a storm in a teacup—this case. If there had not been an imminent Election, it would have passed, Mr. Laski would have gone home and his supporters no doubt would have said: "Good old Laski, he's at it again;" but because there is an Election do not you think somebody said: "Laski, you have got to stop this at once?" And once you start issuing writs, you know, you have to go on. Probably there is no one in this Court, with all the time that has been taken—even you—who so deeply regrets that he issued this writ than the gentleman sitting in front of me now who is the Plaintiff in this action. If he could get out of it, do not you think he would be only too pleased? He never wanted to bring it. It is what he said over and over and over again. It is what he said then, and perhaps in the heat of the moment.

. . . .

Now, Members of the Jury, I told you I was only going to be a few minutes. I have been 15, and I am afraid that is too long. I wish you good luck in the hope that Mr. Slade will not be four times as long. Whether you will get that good luck or not, I do not know. I doubt it. All I say to you is this: If you really think that this gentleman has been harmed in the slightest degree by what we said he said, then of course you will say so, but I ask you to say that in common sense he said no more on that cart than he has said for years, and he is now sorry that he said it. Not that he does not think it bad because he is put to all this trouble. Whether or not he objects to a little more publicity to his writings and to his views I do not know. It may well be that when he goes back to the next Labour Meeting he will find his reception is even more warm-hearted from some members than it was before. Of course, you know, it must not be thought that anyone in this court on this side suggests that the Socialist Party believes in this rubbish. They are the last people to do so. But there are a few—perhaps people who have not got houses and want very little incitement to go and take them; a few who have not got comforts and who want very little incitement indeed to roar in the streets. Those are the people and the only people to whom he is dangerous.

I venture to suggest to you that a man of his attainments might well be ashamed of some of the doctrines that he scatters so recklessly to people who are in a state of misfortune—perhaps some of the 25 per cent who he himself says are suffering from malnutrition. There are great minds, advanced minds, perhaps you may think socialistic minds, at this moment working their best and achieving enormous results for those people who are in poverty and suffering; but they are not helped by a man who comes and decries the things they believe in and levels them into the mud. I see Mr. Slade making a note, and he is welcome to do so. But I say he brings these things into the mud by advocating this sort of horror, shouting about Russian Revolution with all the horrors of that, the misery and—Well, I had better not put it too strongly or I might be carried away myself. He is doing no great good to the cause which he says he supports.

Members of the Jury, I want to correct one little inaccuracy in what I said to you. That is with regard to the book which he wrote in 1934. You know. It is the one, as I told you, in which he said he had altered his mind. It was republished in an edition in 1945 with those words in it which he says he then believed in and he has not the courage to stick to, and says now: "I did then, but I have changed my mind." There is the edition; I have it here in my hand. I am told it is 1946, but that no doubt was in anticipation of this litigation; so I will not say any more about that.

Members of the Jury, that is the whole of this case. I am going to ask you to say that those words were spoken and in addition, that the whole of this Report is a fair and accurate Report of what was said on that murky evening when incivilities were so happily exchanged between these two gentlemen one of whom read his questions from the publicly issued *Conservative Handbook*.

Members of the Jury, I have taken up even more of your time than I intended. I ask you to say that this action ought never to have been brought and probably no one regrets it more than the Plaintiff himself.

Closing Speech Of Mr. Slade

Mr. Slade: May it please your Lordship, Members of the Jury, I am not going to try and emulate my friend Sir Patrick Hastings, because I am quite certain I could not do it successfully if I were to try. Amongst others of my shortcomings, I am not gifted with the same amount of imagination. Even just now he told you that I was making a note or deducted that I was making a note about something he was saying. In point of fact, I was putting square brackets round that portion of the innuendo in regard to which in your absence the Lord Chief Justice has ruled that the words are not capable of having that meaning, so that my friend flatters himself if he thinks I was paying any particular attention to that remark of his; and when I come to deal with the issue of damages I shall have something to say to you about the way in which this case has been conducted.

I content myself for the moment by telling you this: that when I opened this case asking for exemplary damages, I did not do it because Professor Laski requires money. I did it—and I will return to it when I come to the issue of damages—because when you accuse a person of having committed criminal offenses and you persist in that plea and you conduct the case suggesting that he has acted in a criminal manner, then, if you find it true, well, there is an end of the action, but if you find that the whole of these charges are untrue, then the proper and indeed the only way in which you can mark your sense of the fact that that sort of conduct does not pay is by giving what in these Courts we call exemplary damages for the purpose of showing that that is the case. I shall return to that when I recapitulate for you, quite briefly, some of the matters, the highly irrelevant but highly prejudicial matters that Counsel for the Newspaper in this case has deliberately introduced; because I shall submit that those also are matters which you are invited to take into your consideration in assessing the damages. But I hope I shall do it more dispassionately.

Now, first of all, let me try and remind you what the questions are that you have to try. I hope I am not doing Sir Patrick an injustice if I tell you that no one would ever be able to deduce from anything that he has told you the entire difference between the two questions that the Defendants have themselves seen fit to raise in this action. I believe I can explain to you in quite simple words so that there can be no possible shadow of doubt about it. You will take anything I say about the law—and I shall say very little about the law, as I told you before—subject to the direction of my Lord; but I do think there can be no possible two views about this, and I will give you an illustration.

Suppose a person gets up in the local Council Chamber. We will call him "A." He is talking about "B;" and he says that "B" is a thief. Now, if there are Newspaper reporters there reporting that meeting, they will say this in the local Newspaper: "At the Council Meeting last Saturday night 'A' said that 'B' was a thief." If "B" sues the newspaper for libel, the Newspaper can do either or both of two things. The Newspaper: we are merely there to report what goes on, and what we reported was fair and accurate. " 'A' did say that 'B' was a thief. We are not suggesting that 'B' was a thief. We are merely reporting that 'A' said it." If they succeed in that Defense, there is not the slightest point in their going further.

That is a wholly different thing—and I am sure you will appreciate it— from saying what these Defendants have come here to say in this Court and to support by an extremely gross attack upon Mr. Laski. "Oh," they say, "we are not content with coming here to say that Mr. Wentworth Day did ask these questions and did receive those answers. We are not coming here content to say that Mr. Laski did use those words. We are coming here (if I may take my analogy of the council Meeting) to say not only did someone say that he was thief, but we are going to prove that in fact he was a thief."

Now, the second of those two defenses is known in law in libel or in slander as the defense of justification, and the words which are used to set up the second defense are these: "The words are true"—the words which are used to set up the other defense have nothing whatever to do with the truth of the words and it does not in the slightest matter whether they are true or false, the other defense is merely that "We are a Newspaper reporting a public meeting, and if you want to vindicate your character you must not come against us, because we merely report what was said. You must sue the person who said it."

I hope I have made that clear, because I am going to tell you now what are the matters, subject to my Lord's direction, to which you have to devote your minds in this case, and I hope I shall make it abundantly clear what is the distinction between those two wholly separate issues, which I repeat: "A" said that "B" was a thief. That is No. 1. "B" is a thief. That is No. 2. Those are two wholly different things.

The Defendants say firstly that what they published in the *Newark Advertiser* was merely a fair and accurate report of what people said there. If they are right, then they win this action; and you may therefore ask yourselves this: why, if they are sufficiently certain that they are right in that, have they taken upon themselves the burden of saying: Well, even if we are wrong about that, that is to say, even if that was not said at the meeting, we are going to try and escape from the consequences of what we published by saying: although it was not said it is true. Just think that out, will you, in your minds, because that is what they are doing here.

Furthermore, they say: if the words mean, as it is quite clear they can mean, a charge of crime, that is to say, crime in the form of sedition or breach of peace, then you have committed those crimes, if that is what the words mean. They say: We deny that the words bear that more serious meaning, but, if they do, we say that you are a criminal.

Sir Patrick Hastings has said over and over again in his airy way: "Oh, we are not charging the Professor with crime." On Day 2, page 15, this is one of Sir Patrick's questions. I will refer to this again when I come to the issue of damages. Referring to one of Professor Laski's writings, Sir Patrick Hastings says: "When you wrote that, was it a criminal statement, in your view, a threat to the Conservatives?" The suggestion he was conveying was, of course, that when he wrote that particular part of his work which he was referring to he was encouraging sedition or committing some other criminal offense. That is what the word "criminal" means. . . .

[Slade proceeded to argue that the *Newark Advertiser* had not published a "fair and accurate report" of what transpired at the meeting at which Laski spoke. Slade then went on to address the defendant's "justification" argument: that even if its report of what was said at the meeting was inaccurate, its description of Laski's political ideology was true. There then followed a colloquy with Justice Goddard over a separate "defamatory" statement appearing in the same newspaper article—that Laski was a coward and guilty of dereliction of duty for having avoided military service during World War I. At trial, the defense had sought to justify this libel also in order to buttress its argument that its statements concerning Laski's advocacy of revolution were justified. Laski, however, had chosen not to sue on the allegedly defamatory statements about his war record, and Slade was frustrated to see that this subject matter had still come into the trial. Slade began arguing that the defendant's statements about Laski's military record were also defamatory, but was firmly told by Justice Goddard that embarking on further discussion of this subject matter in his closing argument would be improper unless Sir Patrick Hastings were given a chance to respond.]

* * *

Now, Members of the Jury, I pass to the issue of damages. When I opened this case I ventured to suggest what you were entitled to take into consideration in assessing the damages; and I am now going to read to you about six lines of what a very well known Judge, Lord Esher, said in the Court of Appeal. I am quoting from page 183 of Fraser: "In actions for libel . . . the Jury, in assessing damages, are entitled to look at the whole conduct of the Defendant from the time the libel was published down to the time they give their verdict. They may consider what his conduct has been before action, after action, and in Court during the trial."

The words "and in Court during the trial" include the manner in which the case is conducted on the Defendants' behalf.

Now, if you find these words are true, the question of damages will not arise, and if you find that they are a fair and accurate report, the question of damages will not arise. Therefore I am only addressing you upon the assumption that your verdict will be in favour of Professor Laski. Upon that assumption means this, that Professor Laski, having been seriously libelled, comes into Court to vindicate his character. There are two ways, as I have pointed out to you, of defending that action. One was for the Defendants to content themselves with saying: "Well, we merely reported what Mr. Wentworth Day said." If they had sufficient confidence in that, there was no need to go on and say that what Mr. Wentworth Day said was true. That is what they have done, and this is the reception or some instances of the reception that Mr. Laski got in the witness-box when he came here to vindicate a character which, upon my assumption, had been seriously assailed.

I will just give you a few illustrations. Day 1, page 10, and as I read this out I want you to ask yourselves why you think these questions were put in cross-examination to Mr. Laski. "(Q.) Well, let us take some of the more important ones. One of the great things that some people in England have revered for centuries has been English law and justice? (A.) Yes. (Q.) Do you? (A.) Yes. (Q.) It would be a most dangerous thing, would it not, to instill into the minds of the proletariat contempt for the Bench or for juries or for people who have to administer justice, even lawyers—well, leave lawyers out; there are so many sorts. Just tell me whether you agree with this: One of the methods of administering justice is this, is it not, to call a jury at great inconvenience to themselves who are sworn to do justice as between man and man and to administer justice fairly and impartially—you know that, do you not? (A.) Oh indeed." Rather a long question.

"(Q.) Do you think they do it? (A.) On the whole, yes. (Q.) Let me just read a sentence to you and ask you to tell me whether you think you agree with this: 'A London jury is fairly certain to award damages for libel to a Tory Member of Parliament, but it is also fairly certain to assume that a Labour sympathizer cannot be libelled.' Do you hear that? (A.) Yes. (Q.) Would you agree with me that that is unfair, stupid and offensive? (A.) No. I think this is an accurate summary of the history of political libel actions in London from some such period as the treason trials of 1794 down to some such period as 1924. (Q.) Will you try and keep within a century or two, Prof. Laski. What I am suggesting to you is that you write offensive, unfair and violent things about anyone that you do not like in order to please what you think are your political supporters. What do you say to that? (A.) I say that is wholly and quite definitely untrue."

Members of the Jury, why do you think those questions were asked? What had they got to do with this case?

Now I will go on: "(Q.) Let me take the Bench in generality and let me see what is your view of an English Judge—who, hitherto, of course, the people of England have been rather inclined to respect. Listen to this: 'What occurs in any State where there are great material differences between classes is simply a perversion of the end of the State to the interests of the rich. Their power compels the agents of the State to make their wishes the first object of consideration' etc. etc. (reading to the words) 'by the lessons of history they mean the deposit of their experience'—I do not know what that means. 'Anyone who considers, for example, the history of the interpretation of Trade Union law by the Judges in England' etc. etc. (reading to the words) 'needs of the working classes'. Is that offensive, unfair and thoroughly unjust? (A.) I think not. I think that is an historical summary of the types of case to which it refers."

Again I ask you: what possible object had that question, and what had it to do with this case, except, of course, to create prejudice in your minds?

Then at page 19, the same day, this question: "I think you do not approve of taking machine guns to Income Tax Inspectors, but you can take machine guns to more important people if the situation becomes intolerable; you have told us that, have you not? (A.) No. (Q.) Well, we shall come to that a little later on."

Did we come to that a little later on? What atom of foundation was there for the suggestion: "I think you do not approve of taking machine guns to Income Tax Inspectors, but you can take machine guns to more important people if the situation becomes intolerable"?

Now, religious beliefs, Day 2, pages 8 and 9. And just before I come to religious beliefs, I cannot forbear to repeat to you the passage which immediately precedes it. You will remember this: Sir Patrick asked Mr. Laski this "Are there any privileged in the Socialist Party?" And Mr. Laski said: "Why, indeed, Sir Patrick, when you were a member."—I think at least I should have said "Touché" if that answer had been given to me; but listen to the question, will you: "Are there any privileged in the Socialist Party?" Was that a sneer, or was it a question to which an answer was desired? He gave the answer I have just read out to you, and Sir Patrick said: "Do not be rude;" to which Mr. Laski said: "It is the last thing I want in the world." You will judge for yourselves whether he was rude in the witness-box.

"(Q.) It may be difficult for you to be courteous, but do not be rude. (A.) Not in the least. (Q.) You are rude to everybody, are you not? (A.) I do not think so. (Q.) I will just ask you a question which I was not proposing to ask you. You know that some people in this country possess religious beliefs, do you not? (A.) Yes. (Q.) I want to read one short sentence which is the most offensive thing I suggest that you have ever said; it is in a book I think called *Threat is Constitution*,[3] or something of that sort. Just listen to this, it is only four lines: 'Nor was it an accident that no influence was more persuasive than that of Wesley'—Wesley was the Nonconformist Minister and reformer, was he not?—'in inducing the masses in England to accept the grim discipline of the new factories'—that is the hardships of the old factory life; just listen to this—'in return for the dubious consolation of an unproved and unprovable eternal bliss'. By that passage, addressed to people who had some religious beliefs, you mean that it was rubbish, and that Wesley blackmailed the workers to accept conditions in the old factories by promising them eternal life? (A.) That is fantastic rhetorical exaggeration, Sir Patrick. What I meant by that was that, as is well known by all historians and is set out with particular emphasis in the classic books of Mr. and Mrs. J. L. Plant, at the time of the industrial revolution Wesleyanism deflected the sense of men's indignation with their conditions in the new factories to religion as a consolation for the sorrows of this life, and that I thought that in the light of the historical problem presented by Wesleyanism that was an unjustifiable thing to do. (Q.) Of course, when you are rude to other people, Mr. Laski, you think that is argument: when people say something about you, you bring actions for libel."

3. [The book to which Sir Patrick Hastings refers is Laski's The Crisis and the Constitution (1931)]—ed.

Now, the question is, what has that got to do with this case, and why are those questions asked?

Day 2, page 16: "(Q.) There is just one other thing that I would like to ask you, and tell me whether you agree. It is only a sentence. I do not think anyone need bother to follow it. It is one sentence on page 5 of this book. It is a passage which you wrote in an attack on Mr. Churchill, apparently, in the *Chicago Sun*. I do not know why you attacked Mr. Churchill at that time. It was in 1943. It was the middle of the war period, was it not? (A.) Yes."

Mr. Laski was asked in re-examination to deal with the attitude he had adopted towards Mr. Churchill, you will remember and at page 50 this was said when Sir Valentine was re-examining him about that passage: "(Q.) Throughout all these books during the war, have you given the highest possible praise to Mr. Winston Churchill? (A.) I have indeed. I still feel the deepest respect and admiration for Mr. Churchill's immense achievement during the war. (Q.) And you have expressed that time and time again in your writings during the war? (A.) I have." But what has that got to do with this case?

I have already referred you to the question in which the word "criminal" was used, Day 2, page 15. The last one is at the foot of page 20: "(Q.) Do not for a moment think that that is the Labour view, but in your view, if the Socialist Party think the State are not doing what is right for them, they are entitled to resist by violence? (A.) Where they come to the conclusion that there is no other way, certainly. (Q.) You do not think that is a terrifying theory, do you? (A.) It is a theory that Mr. Abraham Lincoln—." He got as far as that and then Sir Patrick said: "Never mind about him. He is not in Court. Let us keep to ourselves;" and the Lord Chief Justice said: "I think the witness is entitled to answer in that way."

Now, only two more things. Sir Patrick Hastings told you or suggested in so many words and quite unequivocally that this action had been brought on first because the *Newark Advertiser* was a small newspaper and was therefore the less in a position to bear the expense and brunt of a libel action than the three other newspapers which are being sued. There is not an atom of foundation for that suggestion. My Lord will correct me if I am wrong, because the application was made to him. Sir Patrick Hastings made the application in the last month and I was present. The application was that this case should be taken first and that the other three actions should go over to next sittings. That was Sir Patrick's own application, and the suggestion that I actually threw out in open court when that suggestion was made, which I said was a perfectly reasonable one, was that my clients would like to have the four actions consolidated, in which case they would have been tried together. You will consider what justification there was for making that statement.

And my last word: Sir Patrick Hastings said two or three times in his closing speech, almost in so many words, that no one must be regretting that he had brought this action more than Mr. Laski, and he suggested that the only purpose of bringing it was to stop discussion at the time of the

General Election. There is not only no substance in that, but there is no evidence before you at all upon which any such suggestion can be based.

Now, Members of the Jury, I ask you to take all those matters into consideration together with the plea of justification which has been persisted in right up to this moment, and if you come to the conclusion that the Plaintiff is entitled to succeed—and it is only in that event that you have to consider the question of damages at all—I say, subject to my Lord's direction, that you are entitled to take into consideration the whole of the matters I have mentioned in aggravation of damages, so that when a man comes to vindicate his character he shall not be subjected to treatment of this kind, and I ask you to do so. That is why I ask you, if you are in Mr. Laski's favour, to award him exemplary damages, as I say, not for the purpose of the money itself, but so as to make your reprobation of that treatment of a Plaintiff who comes to these Courts for the purpose, as I say, of vindicating his character. That is all I desire to say.

* * *

Subsequent Developments:

Harold Laski lost this case after the jury deliberated for forty minutes. Under the "English rule" of awarding costs, 12,000 pounds was awarded to the Newark Advertiser against Laski for the fee of Sir Patrick Hastings and court costs. Much of the money was raised for Laski by various Labour party leaders through a fund to which several American notables, including Albert Einstein and New York's Mayor Fiorella La Guardia, contributed. The trial itself was a defining moment for Laski. As Ian McIntyre observed fifty years later in The Times, "In five hours of brutal cross-examination, Sir Patrick Hastings destroyed him. 'He wept,' [Laski's wife] Frida said, 'as I have never seen a man weep.' Afterwards he wrote of himself as a pariah, and within three years he was dead." Ian McIntyre, Chairman Laski's Big Red Books, The Times, June 17, 1993.

QUESTIONS

1. In Its Your Law, supra, Charles Curtis quotes Charles Wyzanski as saying, "[a] political libel suit is the modern substitute for ordeal by battle. It is the means which society has chosen to induce bitter partisans to wager money instead of exchanging bloody noses." What elements of an ordeal by battle are reflected in Laski's libel trial?

2. Does Sir Patrick Hastings clearly state the newspaper's ground for defending this libel action? How closely does his argument stick to his purported line of defense?

3. Does Justice Goddard effectively reign in Sir Patrick when his argument strays into irrelevant and prejudicial matter? Does Justice Goddard appear to favor one side in this case?

4. Presumably, the defendant in a libel action should be allowed to argue in the alternative: "We merely wrote about what someone else said without reporting whether or not it was true, and, now that you raise the issue, we can also show that it was true." To what extent does this defense compound the libel?

5. If such a defense fails, should the plaintiff be entitled to additional damages for the injury done to his reputation by the attempt to prove the truth of the libel at trial? If so, who is responsible for this additional injury, the defendant or its lawyer?

6. Slade refers to "the highly irrelevant but highly prejudicial matters that counsel for the newspaper has introduced." How might each of the following statements by Sir Patrick Hastings in examining Laski fit that description?

(a) After citing examples of Laski's writings on political libel trials, Hastings asks, "Would you agree with me that that is unfair, stupid and offensive?"

(b) He asks, "[y]ou write offensive, unfair, and violent things about anyone you do not like?"

(c) As to Laski's characterization of judicial rulings under trade union laws, he asks "[i]s that offensive, unfair and thoroughly unjust?"

(d) He says, "[i]t may be difficult for you to be courteous, but do not be rude. You are rude to everybody are you not?"

(e) Hastings asks, "You meant it [religion] was rubbish and that [Methodist Church founder John] Wesley blackmailed the workers." Laski replies, "That is fantastic rhetorical exaggeration, Sir Patrick."

(f) Sir Patrick says, "I do not know why you attacked Mr. Churchill at that time" [1943, in the midst of the War].

7. At one point in his questioning of Laski, Sir Patrick states "[y]ou can take machine guns to more important people if the situation becomes intolerable; you have told us that have you not ... We shall come to that a little later on." Here, Hastings refers to nonexistent evidence that he never comes to later on. Where else does he do this same thing? How should Justice Goddard have responded?

8. This trial is a political battle in which the lawyers, particularly Sir Patrick Hastings, assume vicarious responsibility as if their clients' beliefs are their own (compare the other extreme of objectivity shown by Sacco and Vanzetti's appellate counsel, Arthur Hill, who would not even express to Charles Curtis an opinion about his clients' guilt or innocence). What consequences follow from justifying a client's position vicariously? Should the lawyers in the *Laski* trial have exerted more effort to restrain themselves?

9. Reread the material in Chapter 1 on the "English rule" and the "American rule" for allocating costs. Did the English rule produce a fair result in this case?

10. Although the libel alleged in this lawsuit concerns Laski's advocation of violence to achieve socialism, there is a second libel lurking in the background concerning Laski's cowardice and dereliction of duty in World War I. Similar allegations of "cowardice" and "draft dodging" surfaced in Massachusetts's 1921 trial of Sacco and Vanzetti for murder. Both trials took place shortly after a war in which the Allies experienced heavy casualties. Should Justice Goddard have taken more care to make sure that this subject matter either stayed out of the trial or that Laski's counsel was given more of an opportunity to respond?

Relevant Background

Civility in the Courtroom

Sir Patrick Hastings's treatment of Harold Laski and Frederick Katzmann's treatment of Nicola Sacco clearly demonstrate that ad hominem attacks are nothing new to civil or criminal litigation. Indeed, Lord Coke's examination of Sir Walter Raleigh almost four hundred years ago was an even more blatant example of substituting ad hominem attack for proof of the matter asserted. In all three of these cases, the judges displayed tolerance, if not outright endorsement, of the tactics used.

Today, concern over decline in professional courtesy has led some bar associations to adopt guidelines for courtroom behavior. The Los Angeles County Bar Association Litigation Guidelines, for example, state two guidelines: come to court appearances punctually and prepared, and treat everyone in the courtroom with courtesy and civility. Virginia's Principles of Professional Courtesy are more detailed, and include specific pronouncements such as that lawyers should be courteous toward courthouse staff and the press, should be tolerant of inept opposing counsel and should even give opposing counsel advance warning of situations that might prove embarrassing. Catherine Therese Clarke, Missed Manners in Courtroom Decorum, 50 Md. L. Rev. 945, 1018, 1019 (1991).

Some lawyers, however, still view litigation as Lord Coke and Sir Patrick Hastings apparently did: as a form of warfare. For example, Charles Curtis perpetuates this view by beginning his discussion of the adversary process with an analogy to trial by battle. See Charles P. Curtis, The Advocate, supra. "Playing hardball" in this context may be seen as "consistent with fair play—and scorched earth." Stephanie B. Goldberg, Playing Hardball, A.B.A. J., July 1987 at 48, 50. "Battle," "hardball" and "scorched earth," however, are not terms that sound congruent with the objective of the advocacy paradigm—justice. Furthermore, as evident from the *Laski, Sacco and Vanzetti* and *Raleigh* trials, lawyers who are too intent on winning sometimes focus on subject matter that has little to do with the issue before the trier of fact. Such tactics sometimes do work—the lawyers substituting ad hominem attack for proof won in each of these three trials. However, they did not "win" in the sense of establishing their own reputation for good lawyering and playing fair. Also, the judges who allowed such behavior while presiding over these trials created the appearance that they were biased and unwilling to insist that lawyers rely on factual proof rather than name calling.

Other lawyers and judges, however, view litigation as "a means of dispute resolution that has been carefully crafted to be non-warlike." Robert N. Sayler, Rambo Litigation: Why Hardball Tactics Don't Work, A.B.A. J., March 1988 at 78, 80 ("no one has ever constructed a rationale for believing that the adversarial process is somehow purified by a shouting match"). Rather than a battle, a trial may be an effort—however imperfect that effort may be—to discern the truth and do what is right. This view is perhaps most eloquently articulated by Lon Fuller and John Randall in the ABA—AALS Joint Conference Report, supra chapter 6.

CHAPTER 9

THE INFORMED TRIBUNAL

A. DISINGENUOUS ARGUMENT—MISREPRESENTATION OF FACTS

Louis J. Greenberg, b. 1902; J.D. New York Law School 1925; practiced in Jersey City, New Jersey; represented the estate of Walter Shellhammer, the foreman of car inspectors for the Lehigh Valley Railroad who was decapitated by a train moving out of the Jersey City railyard.

Chief Justice Arthur T. Vanderbilt was Dean of New York University School of Law before he was appointed to the New Jersey Supreme Court in 1948. Serving as Chief Justice until 1957, Vanderbilt was a leader in court reform and a mentor to a younger justice on the Court, William J. Brennan Jr., who in 1956 was appointed by President Eisenhower to the United States Supreme Court.

In re Greenberg

15 N.J. 132, 104 A.2d 46 (1954).

George Warren, Trenton, by direction of the court, argued the order to show cause.

Louis J. Greenberg, Jersey City, appearing pro se in opposition to the order to show cause.

The opinion of the court was delivered by

■ VANDERBILT, C.J.

The respondent in his brief and in his oral argument in Shellhammer v. Lehigh Valley Railroad Company, 14 N.J. 341, 102 A.2d 602, 605 (1954) contended that:

> "it is shown by 'uncontradicted evidence' that 'an interval of 15 to 20 minutes had elapsed between the all-clear signal, followed by the air-brake test, which took thirty seconds, and the actual starting of the train by Hann, the defendant's engineer;' that 'no one was assigned to check up and take any steps to ascertain if a change of status had occurred during that 15 to 20 minute interval during which no check-up or investigation had been made to prove it was safe to start the train,' 'as to whether or not the decedent or any one else was working at or about the train or between the cars,' and the 'engineer started the train relying solely on an all-clear signal which had been given to him 15 to 20 minutes earlier.' "

In dealing with this question which is the crucial, indeed, the only issue in the case, Mr. Justice Heher speaking for the court held:

> "The Court's preargument examination of the record revealed no ground whatever for the statement that between 15 to 20 minutes intervened between the giving of the all-clear signal and the movement of the train; and on the oral argument, when counsel was asked to point out the evidential justification for this factual assertion, he was unable to do so and then agreed that it had no basis in the record. In ostensible support of this affirmation of fact, the brief cites evidence tending to show that there was an interval of 15 minutes between 'the time of the last coupling' of cars 'until the time the train moved out of the yard, started to move,' a radically different thing. Thus, the basic factor in the charge of negligence made on the brief is not sustained by the proofs. The train went into timely motion in accordance with the only signal given; there was no interval calling for a renewal of the signal before the train was actually put into operation. A finding of culpable negligence in these circumstances would be purely conjectural and utterly devoid of the factual substance requisite for liability under the statute."

The court thereupon issued an order calling on the respondent to show cause

> "why he should not be disciplined for a misrepresentation of fact in the presentation of the cause of his client, censurable as in disregard of his professional duty to his client and to the Court."

On the return of the order to show cause it appeared that the respondent had nothing to do with the earlier stages of the case beyond introducing New York counsel to the court. Specifically it appeared that he did not prepare the briefs or argue the cause in the Appellate Division of the Superior Court, both of these matters being attended to by New York counsel.

The respondent was delegated by the law office with which he was then associated to prepare a petition for certification and, after certification was granted, to draft the brief and argue the appeal here. The respondent frankly concedes that he did not examine the transcript of the trial or the appendix used in the Appellate Division, but merely condensed the statement of facts in the brief used there. Nor did he check the cases in the brief in the Appellate Division which he adopted for use here. He says that it was not until two of the justices queried him at the oral argument as to the foundation in fact in the record for the basic position asserted by him that he realized that his position was untenable. On returning to his office he examined the transcript and became convinced of his error.

In extenuation the respondent pleads that the error was not discovered by his adversary either in the Appellate Division of the Superior Court, in the proceedings in this court for certification, or in the briefs or on the oral argument here. We are convinced of the good faith of the respondent and of the entire lack of any intention on his part to deceive the court. Yet it is so obvious as not to require the citation of authorities that the work of our appellate courts cannot go on satisfactorily if we cannot rely on the representations of counsel to us both as to the facts and as to the law. It is because of the necessity of such reliance that in this State only counselors-at-law are allowed to submit briefs and argue appeals in our appellate courts.

This fundamental responsibility of our appellate bar is not to be construed as in any way curtailing the legitimate argument of counsel. He may assert any inferences from the facts of the case that seem to him arguable, but he cannot present his inferences from the facts as if they were the very facts themselves. When he is indulging, as he has every right to do, in inferences or reasoning from the facts, he must say so—there are many words in the English language fitted to express this process of inference—and to be effective he should state the facts in the record from which he is making his inferences. A fortiori, if, as here, there are no facts on which to predicate a statement or from which he may reason or argue, he makes such false statement of facts or false inferences from such non-existing facts at his peril. The failure of his adversary to discover his mistake here or below is no excuse for what may turn out to be an imposition on the court, even if it can be attributed merely to carelessness and lack of thoroughness in the preparation of the appeal. The facts of a case are or should be peculiarly within the knowledge of the counsel who are arguing the appeal and there is great likelihood of error by the court and of consequent injustice to the parties, if counsel do not adequately present the true facts of the case.

Similarly, if counsel is responsible, as he is under the Canons of Professional Ethics, for making known to the court any decisions in the State adverse to his cause in the event his opponent fails to cite them, it necessarily follows that he is even more responsible for citing authorities which cannot conceivably be taken to stand for the proposition for which he cites them, although as in the matter of presenting facts he is permitted to argue freely every inference that can be legitimately drawn from the cases he cites provided he does not misrepresent to the court the contents of such cases.

The opinions of the American Bar Association Committee on Professional Ethics and Grievances on the question of a lawyer's duty to disclose adverse decisions are not without significance to our present discussion. In answering the question

> "Is it the duty of a lawyer appearing in a pending case to advise the court of decisions adverse to his client's contentions that are known to him and unknown to his adversary?"

The Committee on July 17, 1935 gave its Opinion 146:

> "A lawyer is an officer of the court. His obligation to the public is no less significant than his obligation to his client. His oath binds him to the highest fidelity to the court as well as to his client. It is his duty to aid the court in the due administration of justice."

"The conduct of the lawyer before the Court and with other lawyers should be characterized by candor and fairness. Canon 22.''

"We are of the opinion that this Canon requires the lawyer to disclose such decisions to the court. He may, of course, after doing so, challenge the soundness of the decisions or present reasons which he believes would warrant the court in not following them in the pending case."

This opinion has been criticized as too broad in an article by Robert B. Tunstall of the Virginia bar, who advocates that the rule be limited to "controlling authorities," 35 A.B.A.J. 5 (January, 1949), which in effect would mean that it would not be mandatory to cite decisions that the court was not required to follow.

Thereafter, on June 18, 1949, Opinion 280 was handed down by the Committee, which states in part:

"We would not confine the Opinion to 'controlling authorities',—i.e., those decisive of the pending case,—but, in accordance with the tests hereafter suggested, would apply it to a decision directly adverse to any proposition of law on which the lawyer expressly relies, which would reasonably be considered important by the judge sitting on the case. * * *

"In a case involving a right angle collision or a vested or contingent remainder, there would seem to be no necessity whatever of citing even all the relevant decisions in the jurisdiction, much less those from other states or by inferior courts. Where the question is a new or novel one, such as the constitutionality or construction of a statute, on which there is a dearth of authority, the lawyer's duty may be broader. The test in every case should be: Is the decision which opposing counsel has overlooked one which the court should clearly consider in deciding the case? Would a reasonable judge properly feel that a lawyer who advanced, as the law, a proposition adverse to the undisclosed decision, was lacking in candor and fairness to him? Might the judge consider himself misled by an implied representation that the lawyer knew of no adverse authority."

We adopt the view expressed in Opinion 280, limiting it, however, to decisions of the courts of this State and, with respect to federal questions, to decisions of the courts of the United States.

There is, of course, no charge here of misquoting or of suppressing decisions. That question is presented simply because it is an integral part of any discussion of the fundamental relations of appellate counsel and the court. The process of deciding cases on appeal involves the joint efforts of counsel and the court. It is only when each branch of the profession performs its function properly that justice can be administered to the satisfaction of both the litigants and society and a body of decisions developed that will be a credit to the bar, the courts and the state.

The underlying philosophy of this phase of the relations between court and counsel has been aptly summarized by a leading authority on legal ethics:

"The extent to which it is regarded as counsel's duty to advise the court as to matters relevant to the proper decision of the case of which opposing counsel is ignorant or which he has overlooked turns on the degree to which the old idea that litigation is a game between the lawyers has been supplanted by the more modern view that the lawyer is a minister of justice. Always, however, must be borne in mind the principle that the theory of our system is still that justice is best accomplished by having all the facts and arguments on each side investigated and presented with maximum vigor by opposing counsel, for decision by the court and jury." Drinker, Legal Ethics (1953), p. 76.

These problems have never, to our knowledge, come before our courts in a disciplinary matter, but they are of transcendent importance in the administration of justice. In view of our findings with reference to the good faith of the respondent, it would be manifestly unfair to impose discipline on him. Nevertheless, the case should serve as a warning to all that the bar is expected to live up in full measure to its professional obligations in the delicate and difficult process of molding the law of the state insofar as it is embodied in the decisions of the appellate courts to the needs of the time. It necessarily follows that any future transgressions in this field must meet with severe disciplinary action, if the courts and the bar alike are to perform their duties to litigants and the public.

And it may not be amiss in view of what happened in the courts below in the Shellhammer case to remind the bar that vouching for out-of-state attorneys in order to enable them to appear Pro hac vice in our courts is not a mere formality, but entails responsibility for the good conduct of such attorneys according to Our standards of professional conduct.

The order to show cause is discharged but without costs.

For discharge of order: Chief Justice Vanderbilt, and Justices Heher, Oliphant, Wachenfeld, Burling, Jacobs and Brennan—7.

Opposed: None.

QUESTIONS

1. Greenberg "merely condensed the statement of facts in the brief" prepared by New York counsel for argument in the Appellate Division. He did not check the factual allegations in the brief against the trial transcript and did not check the cases cited in the brief. Why was it wrong for Greenberg to rely on the work of another lawyer without checking the work himself?

2. Would Greenberg have been justified in relying on a brief prepared by a lawyer acting as co-counsel and also licensed in New Jersey? Would it make any difference if the brief had been prepared by another lawyer in Greenberg's firm?

3. The opinion observes that a lawyer "cannot present his inferences from the facts as if they were the very facts themselves," and should clearly "state the facts in the record from which he is making his inferences." How specifically did Greenberg fail in these respects?

4. Go back and review the closing arguments from Harold Laski's libel trial. Were inferences and facts confused there as well? Should any of the lawyers have been sanctioned?

B. DISINGENUOUS ARGUMENT—MISREPRESENTATION OF LEGAL AUTHORITY

Relevant Background

The following version of Federal Rules of Civil Procedure, Rule 11 was effective until December 1, 1993:

Signing of Pleadings, Motions, and Other Papers; Representations to Court; Sanctions

Every pleading, motion, and other paper of a party represented by an attorney shall be signed by at least one attorney of record in the attorney's individual name, whose address shall be stated. A party who is not represented by an attorney shall sign the party's pleading, motion, or other paper and state the party's address. Except when otherwise specifically provided by rule or statute, pleadings need not be verified or accompanied by affidavit. The rule in equity that the averments of an answer under oath must be overcome by the testimony of two witnesses or of one witness sustained by corroborating circumstances is abolished. The signature of an attorney or party constitutes a certificate by the signer that the signer has read the pleading, motion, or other paper; that to the best of the signer's knowledge, information, and belief formed after reasonable inquiry it is well grounded in fact and is warranted by existing law or a good faith argument for the extension, modification, or reversal of existing law, and that it is not interposed for any improper purpose, such as to harass or to cause unnecessary delay or needless increase in the cost of litigation. If a pleading, motion, or other paper is not signed, it shall be stricken unless it is signed promptly after the omission is called to the attention of the pleader or movant. If a pleading, motion or other paper is signed in violation of this rule, the court, upon motion or upon its own initiative, shall impose upon the person who signed it, a represented party, or both, an appropriate sanction, which may include an order to pay to the other party or parties the amount of the reasonable expenses incurred because of the filing of the pleading, motion, or other paper, including a reasonable attorney's fee.

Kirkland & Ellis (est. 1908) is a Chicago based firm of over 450 attorneys and has offices in Los Angeles, Denver, Washington, D.C., New York and London. Kirkland & Ellis was lead counsel for the defendant in the action below.

Crosby, Heafey, Roach & May, P.C. (est. 1900) is an Oakland, California based firm of over 200 lawyers and has offices in Los Angeles, San

Francisco and Santa Rosa. Crosby, Heafey, Roach & May was local counsel for the defendant in the action below.

Golden Eagle Distributing Corporation v. Burroughs Corporation

103 F.R.D. 124 (N.D.Cal.1984).

MEMORANDUM OF OPINION AND ORDER

Plaintiff brought this action in Minnesota state court for fraud, negligence, and breach of contract against Burroughs Corporation, the manufacturer of an allegedly defective computer system sold to plaintiff. Defendant removed to federal court in Minnesota on the basis of diversity of citizenship, and that court, on defendant's motion, transferred the action to this Court pursuant to 28 U.S.C. § 1404 (a). Defendant then moved for summary judgment on the ground that all four claims are time-barred under California law. While conceding that the breach of contract claim is time-barred by the terms of the sales agreement, plaintiff argued that the limitations period for the remaining claims was governed by Minnesota law under which they would not be time-barred. Defendant also moved to dismiss plaintiff's claim for economic loss arising from negligent manufacture as being barred by California law.

At the hearing on defendant's motion, the Court denied it for lack of merit and directed counsel for defendant responsible for the filing of the motion[1] to submit a memorandum explaining why sanctions should not be imposed under Rule 11.

The Statute of Limitations Issue

Counsel for defendant have submitted an excellent brief in defense of their position. It articulates the argument they sought to present in support of their motion with exemplary clarity and fairness. The difficulty is that this is not the argument presented when the motion was made. Had it been made then, there would be no question that it would have qualified under Rule 11 as "a good faith argument for the extension . . . of existing law" and the issue of sanctions would never had arisen. Instead of doing what they have now done, counsel presented an argument calculated to lead the Court to believe that it was "warranted by existing law." Nothing demonstrates the point more clearly than a comparison of the key portions

---

1. At the hearing, an associate of the Chicago firm of Kirkland & Ellis acknowledged responsibility for the preparation of the motion although it was signed by local counsel. One reason for requiring the association of an attorney who is a member of the bar of this court (see Local Rule 110–2 (a)) is to assure that standards of professional conduct will be met. (See Local Rule 110–3) Accordingly local counsel has an obligation to satisfy himself before signing a paper that it complies with applicable requirements. However, in the absence of an indication of active participation in the preparation or decision to file a paper by local counsel—of which there is none here—it does not seem appropriate to subject them to sanctions other than criticism for their apparent neglect.

of the argument made in the memorandum in support of the motion with those in the memorandum in opposition to Rule 11 sanctions.[2] Counsel's argument was two-pronged. The first prong was that a Minnesota court would have dismissed the action under the doctrine of forum non conveniens. The second was that a federal court, following a change of venue, would not have applied the longer Minnesota statute to plaintiff's claims because Minnesota would not have done so.

Minnesota Law Argument

Opening Memorandum

The doctrine of *forum non conveniens* is well settled in Minnesota and was recently reaffirmed by the Minnesota Supreme Court in *Bongards' Creameries v. Alfa–Laval, Inc.*, 339 N.W.2d 561 (Minn.1983).

* * *

The Minnesota courts have repeatedly applied the doctrine of *forum non conveniens* to dismiss claims of nonresident plaintiffs in circumstances strikingly similar to those in this case. All of these [relevant] factors are equally present here, and it would have been an abuse of discretion for a Minnesota

Rule 11 Memorandum

The premise of Burroughs' choice-of-law argument was that a Minnesota court would have dismissed the complaint under the Minnesota doctrine of *forum non conveniens*. There is precedent to support Burroughs' assertion that Minnesota courts apply this doctrine to claims like Golden Eagle's having no nexus with that state. *See, e.g., Bongards' Creameries v. Alfa–Laval, Inc.*, 339 N.W.2d 561 (Minn.1983); *Willoughby v. Hawkeye–Security Insurance Co.*, 189 N.W.2d 165 (Minn.1971). Even Golden Eagle did not dispute that a Minnesota court would ordinarily dismiss a complaint where, as here, (1) both parties are non-citizens of Minnesota, (2) none of the witnesses reside in Minnesota, (3) all documents and other sources of proof are outside Minnesota, (4) no part of the transaction was consummated in Minnesota, (5) no damages were suffered in Minnesota, and (6) the substantive law of another state governs the parties' dispute.

The unsettled question raised by this case is whether a Minnesota court would have refused to apply this doctrine to Golden Eagle's complaint solely because it would be time-barred if filed in other jurisdictions. As evidenced by the Minnesota cases cited in both parties' briefs, the Minnesota courts have not given

---

2. Counsel's reply memorandum, being essentially of the same tenor as the opening memorandum, will not be separately addressed here.

Opening Memorandum

trial court not to dismiss Golden Eagle's Complaint. * * * Because this action would have been dismissed by a Minnesota state court, application of the Minnesota statute of limitations by a federal court would violate the *Erie* doctrine of uniformity between state and federal rules of decision in diversity cases. *See, Van Dusen v. Barrack, supra*, 376 U.S. 612, 638–639.

* * *

Here, Golden Eagle would not have had the benefit of the six-year Minnesota statute of limitations in Minnesota state court since its Complaint would have been dismissed. Thus, for this Court to apply the Minnesota limitation period would make the outcome differ from that in state court, contrary to *Erie*. For this reason, the exception noted in *Van Dusen* applies here, and Golden Eagle's Complaint must be dismissed for failure to comply with the three-year California statute of limitations.

Rule 11 Memorandum

a clear answer to this question. Thus, while no decision has expressly applied the doctrine under these precise circumstances there are no cases in which a Minnesota court has refused to dismiss for this reason.

* * *

Counsel recognizes that courts in other jurisdictions have hesitated or refused to dismiss on *forum non conveniens* grounds where a plaintiff's claim would be barred as a result. The relevant inquiry in this case, however, is what a *Minnesota* court would do applying the law and policy of the state of Minnesota. Given the vigor with which Minnesota has applied the *forum non conveniens* doctrine and the state's particular interest in avoiding inundation by unrelated transitory claims, it is plausible that a Minnesota court would have dismissed this complaint. [footnote omitted]

Federal Law Argument

Opening Memorandum

Neither the Supreme Court nor the Ninth Circuit has ever held that a transferee court must apply the choice-of-law rules of a forum whose own courts would have refused to entertain the suit. The leading case on the law to be applied by the transferee court after a change of venue under Section 1404(a) is *Van Dusen v. Barrack*, 376 U.S. 612, 84 S.Ct. 805, 11 L.Ed.2d 945 (1964). In *Van Dusen*, the Supreme Court declined to state a *per se* rule requiring a transferee court to apply the original forum's choice-of-law rules under all circumstances. Although the Court held that in that

Rule 11 Memorandum

The second step in counsel's argument was that a federal court, following a change of venue, should not apply the choice-of-law rules of a state whose own courts would not have applied them to plaintiff's claim. This is an issue of first impression in this circuit. The Supreme Court in *Van Dusen* expressly left open the question of which state's law would apply following a § 1404 (a) transfer "if it was contended that the transferor State would simply have dismissed the action on the ground of *forum non conveniens*." 376 U.S. at 640. No subsequent Supreme Court decision

Opening Memorandum

case the transferee court should apply the state law that would have applied had there been no change of venue, the Court stated specifically that the original state's law would not necessarily apply "if it was contended that the transferor State would simply have dismissed the action on the ground of *forum non conveniens*." *Id.* at 640. This case falls squarely within the *forum non conveniens* exception noted by the Court in *Van Dusen*.

Rule 11 Memorandum

has resolved this question. Neither the Ninth Circuit nor any district court in California has ever ruled on the law to be applied under these circumstances. In sum, there is no "controlling" precedent on this issue.

Although several cases in other circuits have addressed this issue in dicta, only one of the decisions cited by Golden Eagle actually held that the transferor forum's choice-of-law rules apply even though that state's own courts would have dismissed under *forum non conveniens*.

* * *

This is not an issue on which only one result is possible as a matter of law. The Supreme Court went out of its way in *Van Dusen* to identify the choice of law in a case such as this as an open question. Few federal courts have subsequently addressed the question, and even fewer have given it any analysis. At least one federal district judge has stated, albeit in dictum, that the original forum's law does *not* control where that state's courts would have dismissed under *forum non conveniens*. *Mayers v. Northbrook Insurance Co.*, No. 77 C 4358 (N.D.Ill. January 19, 1979) ... Burroughs' motion was based on a plausible view of the proper choice-of-law rule in this case.

The contrast between the two memoranda speaks for itself. It is a dramatic illustration of the sort of practice at which Rule 11 is aimed and of the result it seeks to achieve. There would be little point to Rule 11 if it tolerated counsel making an argument for the extension of existing law disguised as one based on existing law. The certification made by counsel signing the motion is not intended to leave the court guessing as to which argument is being made, let alone to permit counsel to lead the court to believe that an argument is supported by existing law when it is not.

The duty of candor is a necessary corollary of the certification required by Rule 11. A court has a right to expect that counsel will state the controlling law fairly and fully; indeed, unless that is done the court cannot perform its task properly. A lawyer must not misstate the law, fail to disclose adverse authority (not disclosed by his opponent), or omit facts critical to the application of the rule of law relied on.

These are settled principles.[3] Rule 3.3 of the ABA's Model Rules states that:

> A lawyer shall not knowingly: (1) make a false statement of material fact or law to a tribunal.... Model Rules of Professional Conduct Rule 3.3 (1983).

The accompanying comment states in part:

> The advocate's task is to present the client's case with persuasive force. Performance of that duty while maintaining confidences of the client is qualified by the advocate's duty of candor to the tribunal.
>
> * * *
>
> Legal argument based on a knowingly false representation of law constitutes dishonesty toward the tribunal. A lawyer is not required to make a disinterested exposition of the law, but must recognize the existence of pertinent legal authorities. Furthermore, as stated in paragraph (a) (3), an advocate has a duty to disclose directly adverse authority in the controlling jurisdiction which has not been disclosed by the opposing party. The underlying concept is that legal argument is a discussion seeking to determine the legal premises properly applicable to the case. Model Rules of Professional Conduct Rule 3.3 comment (1983).

Ethical Consideration 7–23 under the former ABA Model Code further explains:

> The complexity of law often makes it difficult for a tribunal to be fully informed unless the pertinent law is presented by the lawyers in the cause. A tribunal that is fully informed on the applicable law is better able to make a fair and accurate determination of the matter before it. The adversary system contemplates that each lawyer will present and argue the existing law in the light most favorable to his client. Where a lawyer knows of legal authority in the controlling jurisdiction directly adverse to the position of his client, he should inform the tribunal of its existence unless his adversary has done so, but, having made such disclosure, he may challenge its soundness in whole or in part. Model Code of Professional Responsibility EC 7–23 (1979).

3. The Advisory Committee Notes to Rule 11 state that "[t]he new language is intended to reduce the reluctance of courts to impose sanctions ... by emphasizing the responsibilities of the attorney and reenforcing those obligations by the imposition of sanctions." 97 F.R.D. 165, 198 (1983).

The most elemental rationale of this branch of Rule 11 is that fair decisions cannot be expected if the deciding tribunal is not fully informed, let alone if it is misled. It is as badly misled by an argument purporting to reflect existing law when such law does not exist as by a failure to disclose adverse authority. The misleading character of defendant's counsel's memorandum is convincingly demonstrated by their subsequent memorandum. That is a sufficient basis for finding a violation of Rule 11, regardless of their purpose and whether they may have acted in good faith. The absence of a purpose to cause unnecessary delay or needless expense—or, for that matter, the absence of bad faith—is irrelevant to the imposition of sanctions under the first prong of Rule 11.

The Economic Loss Issue

In support of the motion to dismiss plaintiff's claim for economic loss, counsel quoted from Seely v. White Motor Co., 45 Cal. Rptr. 17, 23 (Sup.Ct.1965), that "in actions for negligence, a manufacturer's liability is limited to damages for physical injuries and there is no recovery for economic losses alone." Counsel failed to cite the California Supreme Court's recent opinion in J'Aire Corp. v. Gregory, 157 Cal. Rptr. 407 (1979), in which the court held economic loss to be recoverable in a negligence action against a contractor, saying:

> This court has held that a plaintiff's interest in prospective economic advantage may be protected against injury occasioned by negligent as well as intentional conduct. For example, economic losses such as lost earnings or profits are recoverable as part of general damages in a suit for personal injury based on negligence. * * * Where negligent conduct causes injury to real or personal property, the plaintiff may recover damages for profits lost during the time necessary to repair or replace the property.
>
> * * *
>
> Even when only injury to prospective economic advantage is claimed, recovery is not foreclosed. Where a special relationship exists between the parties, a plaintiff may recover for loss of expected economic advantage through the negligent performance of a contract although the parties were not in contractual privity.

157 Cal. at 410 (citations omitted)

It is true that J'Aire, inexplicably, did not cite Seely. But inasmuch as the later decision is on its face at least inconsistent with the former, it cannot be ignored in a discussion of the claim for economic loss, even if it can be distinguished.

Further, the effect of J'Aire on Seely was specifically considered in two recent decisions of the California intermediate appellate court, the Court of Appeal. In Pisano v. American Leasing, 194 Cal. Rptr. 77 (Cal.App. Aug.18, 1983), the court reversed a summary judgment for defendant manufacturer holding that plaintiff, to whom defendant had supplied a defective sander, could recover economic loss suffered in his business as a result of the supplier's negligence. The court appears to have reasoned that J'Aire rather than Seely, both of which are cited, controlled. Pisano was followed in Huang v. Garner, 203 Cal. Rptr. 800 (Cal.App.1984), again citing both Seely and J'Aire.

Counsel distinguished J'Aire in their reply only after it was cited in plaintiff's opposition. They did not cite either Pisano or Huang while asserting in their reply that Seely [sic] "has never been overruled." That statement, while technically correct, becomes misleading in the light of two intermediate appellate decisions which relied on J'Aire in explaining away Seely.

In their Rule 11 memorandum counsel offer a "principled basis" for distinguishing J'Aire. Again, the argument made there in support of the continuing vitality of Seely is entirely acceptable but it is not the argument made in the earlier memorandum.

Moreover, the failure to cite, if not Huang, at least Pisano, decided almost a year earlier, is a violation of counsel's "duty to disclose directly adverse authority." See pp. 127–128 above. Counsel claim to have been "unaware of [those cases] until the oral argument on the motion." For counsel to have been unaware of those cases means that they did not Shepardize their principal authority, Seely; as early as February 1984, Shepard lists Pisano under Seely as "distinguished." In some circumstances a failure to discover adverse authority after a reasonable search has been made may be excusable. Counsel's declaration does not specify what search was made here, but their Rule 11 memorandum bespeaks their capacity to find supporting authority, such as the Lexis copy of an unreported district court decision and a decision of the California Court of Appeal issued on July 13, 1984. Thus their failure to cite adverse authority is not excusable.

Conclusion

Accordingly the Court finds and concludes, first, that defendant's memorandum in support of its motion based on the statute of limitations was not warranted by existing law, contrary to the representation made therein by counsel, and, second, that counsel failed to make a reasonable inquiry to determine whether the motion to dismiss the economic loss claim was warranted by existing law. The memorandum therefore was signed in violation of Rule 11.

Counsel for plaintiff are directed to submit a declaration setting forth the record of plaintiff's reasonable expenses, including reasonable attorney's fees, incurred in opposing the motion. The Court will thereafter issue its order specifying the amount assessed as sanctions.

Sanctions shall be paid by the firm of Kirkland & Ellis and shall not be reimbursed by the defendant. In addition, both Kirkland & Ellis and Crosby, Heafey, Roach & May, local counsel, shall submit a statement certifying that a copy of this opinion was given to each partner and associate of each firm.

IT IS SO ORDERED.

DATED: September 18, 1984

William W. Schwarzer
United States District Judge

Judge Schwarzer was reversed on appeal. Part V of the Ninth Circuit's opinion follows:

Golden Eagle Distributing Corporation v. Burroughs Corporation

801 F.2d 1531 (9th Cir.1986).

V. The Application of Rule 11 in this Case

The district court's application of Rule 11 in this case strikes a chord not otherwise heard in discussion of this Rule. The district court did not focus on whether a sound basis in law and in fact existed for the defendant's motion for summary judgment. Indeed it indicated that the motion itself was nonfrivolous. 103 F.R.D. at 126. Rather, the district court looked to the manner in which the motion was presented. The district court in this case held that Rule 11 imposes upon counsel an ethical "duty of candor." Golden Eagle, 103 F.R.D. at 127. The court drew its principles from Rule 3.3 of the ABA's Model Rules and the accompanying comment. It said:

> The duty of candor is a necessary corollary of the certification required by Rule 11. A court has a right to expect that counsel will state the controlling law fairly and fully; indeed, unless that is done the court cannot perform its task properly. A lawyer must not misstate the law, fail to disclose adverse authority (not disclosed by his opponent), or omit facts critical to the application of the rule of law relied on.

Golden Eagle, 103 F.R.D. at 127.

With the district court's salutary admonitions against misstatements of the law, failure to disclose directly adverse authority, or omission of critical facts, we have no quarrel. It is, however, with Rule 11 that we must deal. The district court's interpretation of Rule 11 requires district courts to judge the ethical propriety of lawyers' conduct with respect to every piece of paper filed in federal court. This gives us considerable pause.

We need not here definitively resolve the problems of the proper role of the courts in enforcing the ethical obligations of lawyers. We must consider only whether Rule 11 requires the courts to enforce ethical standards of advocacy beyond the terms of the Rule itself.

The district court's invocation of Rule 11 has two aspects. The first, which we term "argument identification" is the holding that counsel should differentiate between an argument "warranted by existing law" and an argument for the "extension, modification, or reversal of existing law."

The second is the conclusion that Rule 11 is violated when counsel fails to cite what the district court views to be directly contrary authority. We deal with each in turn, noting at the outset that many of our observations are applicable to both aspects of the court's interpretation of Rule 11.

A. "Argument Identification"

We look first to the text of Rule 11. It requires that the lawyer certify that a pleading, motion or other paper is "warranted by existing law or a good faith argument for the extension, modification, or reversal of existing law." The district court held that the lawyer in this case had a good faith argument for the extension of the law, but violated Rule 11 when he characterized his position as warranted by existing law.

The text of the Rule, however, does not require that counsel differentiate between a position which is supported by existing law and one that would extend it. The Rule on its face requires that the motion be either one or the other. Moreover, there is nothing in any of the statements of the proponents of the amended Rule or in the authorities we have surveyed since its adoption which suggests such a requirement.

The district court's ruling appears to go even beyond the principle of Rule 3.3 of the ABA Model Rules which proscribes "knowing" false statements of material fact or law. The district court made no finding of a knowing misstatement, and, given the well-established objective nature of the Rule 11 standard, such a requirement would be inappropriate. Both the earnest advocate exaggerating the state of the current law without knowingly misrepresenting it, and the unscrupulous lawyer knowingly deceiving the court, are within the scope of the district court's interpretation.

This gives rise to serious concerns about the effect of such a rule on advocacy. It is not always easy to decide whether an argument is based on established law or is an argument for the extension of existing law. Whether the case being litigated is or is not materially the same as earlier precedent is frequently the very issue which prompted the litigation in the first place. Such questions can be close.

Sanctions under Rule 11 are mandatory. *See, e.g., Eastway*, 762 F.2d at 254 n.7.* In even a close case, we think it extremely unlikely that a judge, who has already decided that the law is not as a lawyer argued it, will also decide that the loser's position was warranted by existing law. Attorneys who adopt an aggressive posture risk more than the loss of the motion if the district court decides that their argument is for an extension of the law which it declines to make. What is at stake is often not merely the monetary sanction but the lawyer's reputation.

The "argument identification" requirement adopted by the district court therefore tends to create a conflict between the lawyer's duty zealously to represent his client, Model Code of Professional Responsibility Canon

---

* [Rule 11 was subsequently amended in 1993 to make sanctions discretionary, *see* Relevant Background section below]—ed.

7, and the lawyer's own interest in avoiding rebuke. The concern on the part of the bar that this type of requirement will chill advocacy is understandable. As the appellant points out in its appellate brief, courts "should not be empowered to sanction for the level of assurance used by the briefwriter."

Such an effect on advocacy was one of the principal risks associated with the 1983 amendments. It is an effect which the proponents of the amended Rule sought to avoid. In re Yagman, 796 F.2d 1165, 1182 (9th Cir.1986). The language of the Rule thus refers to whether the document being filed is "well grounded in fact and is warranted by ... law." The Advisory Committee Note charged courts to look to "what was reasonable to believe at the time the ... paper was submitted." It said that the Rule is "not intended to chill an attorney's enthusiasm or creativity...." Advisory Committee Note, 97 F.R.D. at 199.

The imposition of the district court's requirement appears to be at cross purposes with the Rule 11 amendments in still another fundamental respect. The key objective of the amendments to the Rule was to reduce cost and delay in the courts. See materials cited in Part III supra. Asking judges to grade accuracy of advocacy in connection with every piece of paper filed in federal court multiplies the decisions which the court must make as well as the cost for litigants.

Moreover, Rule 11 does not apply to the mere making of a frivolous argument. The Rule permits the imposition of sanctions only when the "pleading, motion, or other paper" itself is frivolous, not when one of the arguments in support of a pleading or motion is frivolous. Nothing in the language of the Rule or the Advisory Committee Notes supports the view that the Rule empowers the district court to impose sanctions on lawyers simply because a particular argument or ground for relief contained in a non-frivolous motion is found by the district court to be unjustified. In short, the fact that the court concludes that one argument or sub-argument in support of an otherwise valid motion, pleading, or other paper is unmeritorious does not warrant a finding that the motion or pleading is frivolous or that the Rule has been violated.

Litigation on the issue of sanctions, like any litigation, is expensive. In this case, for example, the underlying legal issues which prompted the sanctions have now been briefed three times: first in the motion; second, at the court's request, in the Rule 11 responses; third, on this appeal. It is not unusual for lawyers involved in sanction proceedings to hire other lawyers to represent them. Here the appellant is a prominent Chicago law firm represented in this appeal by a prominent San Francisco firm. Litigation expenses already must have exceeded, many times over, the few thousand dollars of sanctions imposed. In another case, the law firm appealing an order of sanctions imposed by the same district judge, obtained the services of the reporter for the Rule 11 amendments. See Huettig & Schromm, Inc. v. Landscape Contractors Council, 790 F.2d 1421 (9th Cir.1986).

The district court's interpretation makes the Rule more complex than it needs to be and creates costly obstacles for lawyers. We agree with the recent comment of one knowledgeable observer who has followed the development of the Rules of Civil Procedure as closely as anyone in America: "More and 'better' rules may not be the answer. Rules require sanctions. Sanctions require enforcement proceedings. These absorb resources of time, energy, and money that it is the very purpose of the rules to spare." Rosenberg, The Federal Civil Rules After Half A Century, 36 Me. L. Rev. 243, 244 (1984).

There is another risk when mandatory sanctions ride upon close judicial decisions. The danger of arbitrariness increases and the probability of uniform enforcement declines. The Federal Judicial Center recently studied the application of Rule 11 in fairly routine cases involving issues far less sophisticated than those involved in this case. The conclusion was as follows:

> Overall, we found that although the 1983 amendments appear to have increased judges' readiness to enforce the new certification requirements, their success thus far has been limited. Of specific concern are the findings that there is a good deal of interjudge disagreement over what actions constitute a violation of the rule, only partial compliance with the desired objective standard, inaccurate and systematically biased normative assumptions about other judges' reactions to frivolous actions, and a continued neglect of alternative, nonmonetary means of response.

S.M. Kassin, [An Empirical Study of Rule 11 Sanctions (Federal Judicial Center 1985)] at xi.

Although this is the first reported case to require a differentiation between arguments based on existing law and arguments calling for an extension of existing law, most existing authority implicitly rejects such an interpretation by looking to whether or not a basis in law or fact exists. We said in Zaldivar that sanctions should not have been imposed where a "plausible good faith argument can be made." Zaldivar, 780 F.2d at 832. The district court's ruling here is not reconcilable with that view. Nor is the district court's ruling supported by or consistent with presently controlling law, since Zaldivar applied the rule to the pleading or motion itself and not to the particular supporting grounds advanced.

B. The Failure to Cite Adverse Authority

We turn now to the aspect of the district court's ruling which sanctioned the attorneys for failing to cite contrary authority. Many of the same considerations discussed above apply with at least equal force to it. The district court imposed sanctions not for the filing of a motion or pleading it believed violated terms of the rule, but because it believed additional cases should have been discussed.

Were the scope of the rule to be expanded as the district court suggests, mandatory sanctions would ride on close decisions concerning whether or not one case is or is not the same as another. We think Rule 11 should not impose the risk of sanctions in the event that the court later decides that the lawyer was wrong. The burdens of research and briefing by a diligent lawyer anxious to avoid any possible rebuke would be great. And the burdens would not be merely on the lawyer. If the mandatory provisions of the Rule are to be interpreted literally, the court would have a duty to research authority beyond that provided by the parties to make sure that they have not omitted something.

The burden is illustrated in this case where the district court based its imposition of sanctions in part upon Kirkland & Ellis's failure to cite authorities which the court concluded were directly adverse to a case it did cite. The district court charged the appellant with constructive notice of these authorities because they were identified in Shepard's as "distinguishing" the case Kirkland & Ellis relied on.

This use of Rule 11, far from avoiding excess litigation, increases it. We must not interpret Rule 11 to create two ladders for after-the-fact review of asserted unethical conduct: one consisting of sanction procedures, the other consisting of the well-established bar and court ethical procedures. Utilizing Rule 11 to sanction motions or pleadings not well-grounded in fact or law, or papers filed for improper purposes, gives full and ample play to the 1983 amendments.

In rejecting the district court's broad interpretation of Rule 11, we do not suggest that the court is powerless to sanction lawyers who take positions which cannot be supported. A lawyer should not be able to proceed with impunity in real or feigned ignorance of authorities which render his argument meritless. See, e.g., Rodgers v. Lincoln Towing Service, Inc., 771 F.2d 194, 205 (7th Cir.1985). In addition, Rule 11 is not the only tool available to judges in imposing sanctions on lawyers. However, neither Rule 11 nor any other rule imposes a requirement that the lawyer, in addition to advocating the cause of his client, step first into the shoes of opposing counsel to find all potentially contrary authority, and finally into the robes of the judge to decide whether the authority is indeed contrary or whether it is distinguishable. It is not in the nature of our adversary system to require lawyers to demonstrate to the court that they have exhausted every theory, both for and against their client. Nor does that requirement further the interests of the court. It blurs the role of judge and advocate. The role of judges is not merely to

> match the colors of the case at hand against the colors of many sample cases spread out upon their desk.... It is when the colors do not match, when the references in the index fail, when there is no decisive precedent, that the serious business of the judge begins.

B. Cardozo, The Nature of the Judicial Process 21 (1922). In conducting this "serious business," the judge relies on each party to present his side of the dispute as forcefully as possible. The lawyers cannot adequately perform their role if they are required to make predeterminations of the kind the district court's approach to Rule 11 would necessitate.

* * *

There was strong disagreement on the Ninth Circuit about its reversal of Judge Schwarzer. Judge Noonan, joined by Judges Sneed, Anderson, and Kozinski, dissented from the denial of a sua sponte request for en banc hearing. As their dissent pointed out:

> The opinion is mistaken in its analysis of the action of the district court. The opinion says that the district judge sanctioned the Kirkland, Ellis brief after the judge had "looked not to the merits of the position originally taken by the plaintiff, but to the manner in which the position was advocated." Id. at 1535. But this account does not do justice to the district judge. The district judge had in front of him a brief which did three things. The brief flatly misrepresented Minnesota law as having definitively decided the issue of forum non conveniens in a way favorable to the defendant. The brief insinuated that federal law on the same issue was definitively established the way the defendant would have liked. The brief set out California law without qualifications and without mention of later authority which for purposes of the present opinion is assumed to have been "directly contrary." The court sanctioned Kirkland, Ellis for these three statements of law, each of which was not "warranted." The truth or falsity of a statement is not merely a matter of "the manner" in which a position is presented. A false statement presented as a true statement is simply a misstatement. It is not warranted. It should be sanctionable.

809 F.2d 584, 585 (9th Cir.1987). The dissent went on to observe that:

> The [majority] opinion contradicts Rule 11. Rule 11 requires that a lawyer certify that what he files with the court is "warranted by existing law or a good faith argument for the extension, modification or reversal of existing law." In this case what Kirkland, Ellis had filed was a brief arguing for summary judgment because of the law of California, applicable under Erie Railroad Co. v. Tompkins, 304 U.S. 64, 82 L. Ed. 1188, 58 S. Ct. 817 (1938). The opinion assumes that the California cases which Kirkland, Ellis failed to cite were "directly contrary" to the argument it was making. Id. at 1536. But the opinion concludes that Kirkland, Ellis' failure was not a violation of Rule 11. Id. at 1542.

> How can a brief be warranted by existing law if its argument goes in the face of "directly contrary" authority from the highest court of the jurisdiction whose law is being argued? How can a brief be warranted to be "a good faith argument for the extension, modification, or reversal of existing law" where there is not the slightest indication that the brief is arguing for extension, modification or reversal?

> To ask these questions is to answer them. An argument in the teeth of uncited and undistinguishable contrary authority is not warranted by existing law. An argument that does not mention directly-contrary authority is not a good faith argument for its modification or reversal. The [majority] opinion contradicts the Rule. The opinion

repeals the Rule's requirement that a brief be warranted by existing law or a good faith argument for the law's amendment or reversal.

Id. The Third Circuit later agreed with the Ninth Circuit's interpretation of Rule 11. Mary Ann Pensiero, Inc. v. Lingle, 847 F.2d 90 (3d Cir. 1988). However, the Eleventh Circuit agreed with the dissent in *Golden Eagle*. DeSisto College, Inc. v. Line, 888 F.2d 755, 766 (11th Cir.1989) (Rule 11 requires "differentiation between arguments warranted by existing law and arguments for extending, modifying or reversing existing law").

QUESTIONS

1. Is the purpose of Rule 11 merely to discourage frivolous claims and defenses (see discussion of Rule 11 at page 37, supra)? Alternatively is the purpose of Rule 11 to require that pleadings filed with a federal court are not misleading as to law or fact?

2. Does the Ninth Circuit majority opinion support the proposition that, so long as a good faith argument exists for a motion, any brief filed in support of that motion meets Rule 11 standards?

3. Is a false argument by a lawyer just as bad as false testimony by a witness (see Chapter 1 supra)?

4. Judge Schwarzer's sanctions were directed at Kirkland & Ellis and Crosby, Heafey, Roach & May, the two law firms who represented the defendant, rather than at any particular lawyers within these firms. Although a Kirkland & Ellis associate acknowledged responsibility for preparing the motion signed by local counsel, it is not entirely clear which other lawyers within these firms were responsible for the motion papers. Should state disciplinary rules, like Rule 11, allow imposition of sanctions on law firms as well as on individual attorneys? See discussion of New York's new rule allowing discipline of law firms, Chapter 12 infra.

Relevant Background

Rule 11 was amended in 1993. The Rule now provides:

(a) *Signature.* Every pleading, written motion, and other paper shall be signed by at least one attorney of record in the attorney's individual name, or, if the party is not represented by an attorney, shall be signed by the party. Each paper shall state the signer's address and telephone number, if any. Except when otherwise specifically provided by rule or statute, pleadings need not be verified or accompanied by affidavit. An unsigned paper shall be stricken unless omission of the signature is corrected promptly after being called to the attention of the attorney or party.

(b) *Representations to Court.* By presenting to the court (whether by signing, filing, submitting, or later advocating) a pleading, written motion, or other paper, an attorney or unrepresented party is certifying that to the best of the person's knowledge, information, and belief, formed after an inquiry reasonable under the circumstances,—

(1) it is not being presented for any improper purpose, such as to harass or to cause unnecessary delay or needless increase in the cost of litigation;

(2) the claims, defenses, and other legal contentions therein are warranted by existing law or by a nonfrivolous argument for the extension, modification, or reversal of existing law or the establishment of new law;

(3) the allegations and other factual contentions have evidentiary support or, if specifically so identified, are likely to have evidentiary support after a reasonable opportunity for further investigation or discovery; and

(4) the denials of factual contentions are warranted on the evidence or, if specifically so identified, are reasonably based on a lack of information or belief.

(c) *Sanctions*. If, after notice and a reasonable opportunity to respond, the court determines that subdivision (b) has been violated, the court may, subject to the conditions stated below, impose an appropriate sanction upon the attorneys, law firms, or parties that have violated subdivision (b) or are responsible for the violation.

(1) *How Initiated.*

(A) *By Motion*. A motion for sanctions under this rule shall be made separately from other motions or requests and shall describe the specific conduct alleged to violate subdivision (b). It shall be served as provided in Rule 5, but shall not be filed with or presented to the court unless, within 21 days after service of the motion (or such other period as the court may prescribe), the challenged paper, claim, defense, contention, allegation, or denial is not withdrawn or appropriately corrected. If warranted, the court may award to the party prevailing on the motion the reasonable expenses and attorney's fees incurred in presenting or opposing the motion. Absent exceptional circumstances, a law firm shall be held jointly responsible for violations committed by its partners, associates, and employees.

(B) *On Court's Initiative*. On its own initiative, the court may enter an order describing the specific conduct that appears to violate subdivision (b) and directing an attorney, law firm, or party to show cause why it has not violated subdivision (b) with respect thereto.

(2) *Nature of Sanction; Limitations*. A sanction imposed for violation of this rule shall be limited to what is sufficient to deter repetition of such conduct or comparable conduct by others similarly situated. Subject to the limitations in subparagraphs (A) and (B), the sanction may consist of, or include, directives of a non-monetary nature, an

order to pay a penalty into court, or, if imposed on motion and warranted for effective deterrence, an order directing payment to the movant of some or all of the reasonable attorneys' fees and other expenses incurred as a direct result of the violation.

(A) Monetary sanctions may not be awarded against a represented party for a violation of subdivision (b)(2).

(B) Monetary sanctions may not be awarded on the court's initiative unless the court issues its order to show cause before a voluntary dismissal or settlement of the claims made by or against the party which is, or whose attorneys are, to be sanctioned.

(3) *Order.* When imposing sanctions, the court shall describe the conduct determined to constitute a violation of this rule and explain the basis for the sanction imposed.

(d) *Inapplicability to Discovery.* Subdivisions (a) through (c) of this rule do not apply to disclosures and discovery requests, responses, objections, and motions that are subject to the provisions of Rules 26 through 37.

QUESTIONS

1. What are the differences between the pre–1993 and post–1993 versions of Rule 11?

2. The amended Rule 11, section (b), specifically refers to the "claims, defenses, and other legal contentions" within a "pleading, written motion or other paper." How would *Golden Eagle* be decided under this new version of Rule 11?

3. Why might judges be reluctant to impose sanctions under Rule 11? Does the amended Rule 11 reduce the likelihood that sanctions will be imposed?

4. The Private Securities Litigation Reform Act of 1995, Public Law Number 104–67, 109 Stat. 737, amends the 1934 Securities Exchange Act to provide that "[i]n any private action arising under this title, upon final adjudication of the action, the court shall include in the record specific findings regarding compliance by each party and each attorney representing any party with each requirement of Rule 11(b) of the Federal Rules of Civil Procedure as to any complaint, responsive pleading, or dispositive motion." Id., Section 101. If the court finds that a violation did occur, "the court *shall* impose sanctions on such party or attorney in accordance with Rule 11" and

> the court shall adopt a presumption that the appropriate sanction (i) for failure of any responsive pleading or dispositive motion to comply with any requirement of Rule 11(b) ... is the award to the opposing party of the reasonable attorney's fees and other expenses incurred as a direct result of the violation; and (ii) for substantial failure of any complaint to comply with any requirement of Rule 11(b) ... is an

award to the opposing party of the reasonable attorney's fees and other expenses incurred in the action.

Id. at Section 101(c)(3). Congress has considered making Rule 11 sanctions mandatory for other types of litigation as well.

(a) The Private Securities Litigation Reform Act addresses what Congress and many businesspeople, particularly executives in high technology related industries, perceive to be a serious problem—frivolous lawsuits by investors against issuers, underwriters and accountants alleging fraud in the sale of securities. (See discussion of frivolous litigation in Chapter 1 supra.) What costs are imposed on investors by frivolous lawsuits? What costs are imposed on investors by frivolous defenses to lawsuits?

(b) Will mandatory Rule 11 findings and sanctions discourage defrauded investors from filing meritorious lawsuits?

David L. Curl, b. 1951 in Illinois; A.B. Illinois 1973; J.D. Southern Illinois 1977; admitted to the bar in Illinois in 1977, Arizona in 1980 and Texas in 1988; Assistant State Attorney in Vermilion County, Illinois; Member of Illinois Trial Lawyers' Association; member of the Grievance Committee of Pima County Arizona; currently a partner of Studdard & Melby in El Paso, Texas.

In re Disciplinary Action, David L. Curl, Respondent, International Harvester Credit Corporation v. Johnny E. Henry

803 F.2d 1004 (9th Cir.1986).

David L. Curl, Barassi & Curl, P.C., Tucson, Ariz., for defendant/appellant.

Before NELSON, CANBY and JOHN T. NOONAN, JR., Circuit Judges.

■ NOONAN, Circuit Judge.

David L. Curl is a 34 year old lawyer, a partner in a small firm in Tucson, Arizona. He has an A.B. from Illinois University and a J.D., class of 1977, from Southern Illinois University. He has served as Assistant State Attorney in Vermilion County, Illinois. He is a member of the state bars of Illinois and Arizona, the Illinois Trial Lawyers' Association, and the American Bar Association. He is on the Grievance Committee of Pima County, Arizona.

On July 22, 1986, this court issued an order to David L. Curl that he show cause why sanctions should not be imposed on him for a misrepresentation made by him as counsel for Johnny E. Henry in the case of International Harvester Credit Corporation (Harvester) v. Henry, decided by this court July 22, 1986. David L. Curl responded with an affidavit seeking to excuse his misrepresentation. We now impose a sanction.

Background. On September 8, 1980, Henry executed a contract with Wes–Tex Equipment Company for the purchase of a drilling rig and water tank truck. Wes–Tex assigned the contract to Harvester. Henry paid $49,962.54 as a down payment and financed the remaining balance of $283,121.09. When Henry purchased the equipment he told Wes–Tex that he needed Bills of Sale and Manufacturer's Statements of Origin to register the equipment in California. Wes–Tex supplied these documents. He made payments totaling $45,355.51 on the equipment, but in August 1981, defaulted. The next month he secreted the equipment through a sham sales transaction, and took it to Mexico. Before the Third Civil Court of Sonora, Harvester sought to foreclose upon Henry. That court, basing its decision solely on Henry's answer, which alleged he had made payment in full, decided in his favor on March 24, 1983. On appeal before the Supreme Court of Sonora, the judgment was, in the words of that court, "modified" ("se modifica"). The foreclosure action ("la via ejecutiva") was found to have failed because of Harvester's failure to tender a return of the down payments. Harvester was condemned to pay the costs of the trial. All rights of Harvester were preserved to be asserted as appropriate ("por lo que se dejan a salvo sus derechos para que los haga valer en la via y forma correspondiente").

After the decision by the lower Mexican court and before the appeal was heard, Harvester served Henry in the United States. Henry sought summary judgment asking that the lower court decision in Mexico be accorded comity. Judge Alfredo C. Marquez denied this motion on May 31, 1984. Trial was scheduled for October 10, 1984. The day before the trial David L. Curl, Henry's counsel, presented a certified copy of the decision of the Supreme Court of Sonora in Spanish. In open court, Curl told Judge Marquez that the decision "affirms the lower court's order." The trial proceeded before a jury, which gave a verdict in favor of Harvester.

On appeal, Curl contended that there should have been no trial because the lower Sonora court decision should have barred Harvester's suit. "The Appellee here brought his original action in the Mexican court system and lost," his brief asserted.

This court found that no genuine issue was presented by Henry's appeal; that Harvester's rights had been expressly preserved by the decree of the Supreme Court of Sonora; and that Henry's appeal, based on the assertion of a Mexican judgment in his favor, had rested on a mischaracterization of the judgment. Attorney's fees and double costs were awarded Harvester against Henry. We then issued the show cause order directed to the more serious question of Curl's responsibility for the appeal.

Curl's Response. On August 18, 1986 Curl filed an affidavit in which he swore that, when he first received the judgment of the Supreme Court of Sonora, he "contacted his client," who told him that Raul Encinas, a Mexican lawyer from Hermosillo, had told Henry that the judgment "upheld the trial court in its entirety"; that Curl then had the judgment translated; that he then saw that it appeared that "the appeal had been dismissed without prejudice"; that Curl again contacted Henry who in turn contacted Encinas, who continued to maintain that Henry "had won the appeal in its entirety"; that after judgment against Henry in the federal district court and before taking this appeal, Curl spoke to another Mexican lawyer for Henry, Arturo Serrano of Aqua Prieta and that Curl speaking in "broken Spanish" and Serrano in "broken English," Serrano assured him that the Sonora judgment was entirely in Henry's favor, that "the bar to foreclosing on the property was bar to gaining possession of the property," and that Serrano would so testify if called as a witness. In summary, Curl swore that he and Henry were "misled by at least two Mexican attorneys."

Curl further pointed out that he had submitted the Sonoran judgment in Spanish and an accurate English translation of it to this court, leaving this court "free to decide what the interpretation of the Mexican Judgment" was. He added that it was his "duty to his client to represent him, within the bounds of ethics, and to take a position which may be sustained by evidence."

Discussion. A lawyer's duty to an appellate court consists in more than not putting false evidence before the court. Curl complied with the elementary obligation of not falsifying the record by providing the Sonoran judgment in Spanish with an accurate English translation. But Curl's obligations were greater. He had a duty not to misrepresent the evidence in argument before the court.

Curl in his brief for Henry stated that "the Mexican judgment had been rendered in favor of Defendant–Appellant Johnny Bo Henry in the appropriate amount of $370,000." Appellant's Brief, p. 5. Curl noted that the judgment had then been taken to a higher Mexican court. His appeal to our court was from the district court's failure "to recognize the Mexican judgments." Appellant's Brief, p. 2.

In his "Statement of Facts and Issues," Curl cited the words of the lower Mexican court that Henry had "payed the price of the transaction." He then stated that the Supreme Court of Sonora had "affirmed the lower court." Appellant's Brief, p. 4. In his "Summary of Argument," Curl began: "Since International Harvester voluntarily brought its action before the Mexican court system and lost, the doctrines of comity, collateral estoppel and res judicata should bar an attempt to relitigate the matter in the U.S. court system." Appellant's Brief, p. 5. The rest of the brief was a development of this position which rested squarely on the bar created by the judgment of the Supreme Court of Sonora.

Curl reiterated his basic position that "the Mexican Court" had "entered its finding that the Defendant had paid for the property and absolved Defendant of the claims of Plaintiff." Appellant's Brief, p. 8. This judgment, Curl reported, "had been made final by a decision of the Third Section of the Supreme Tribunal of Justice of Hermosillo (akin to state supreme court)." Appellant's Brief, p. 10. "As a result," he continued, "the Mexican proceedings are conclusive—Plaintiff was barred by the doctrine of res judicata from relitigating his claim here." Id. His 26 page brief presented variations on this theme. At no point did Curl in any fashion indicate that there was ambiguity or uncertainty in his reading of the judgment of the Supreme Court of Sonora. His assertions were completely affirmative and unqualified. Harvester, he maintained, was absolutely barred by the Mexican judgment against it. At oral argument, Curl took the same line.

If by some piece of legal ingenuity or quirk of Mexican law, the Sonoran judgment could have been construed as a judgment on the merits, it was Curl's duty to explain the inference by which one could reach this conclusion:

> [A lawyer] may assert any inferences from the facts of the case that seem to him arguable, but he cannot present his inferences from the facts as if they were the very facts themselves. When he is indulging, as he has every right to do, in inferences or reasoning from the facts, he must say so—there are many words in the English language fitted to express this process of inference—and to be effective he should state the facts in the record from which he is making his inferences. A fortiori, if, as here, there are no facts on which to predicate a statement or from which he may reason or argue, he makes such false statement of facts or false inferences from such non-existing facts at his peril. The failure of his adversary to discover his mistake here or below is no excuse for what may turn out to be an imposition on the court, even if it can be attributed merely to carelessness and lack of thoroughness in the preparation of the appeal. In re Greenberg, 15 N.J. 132, 104 A.2d 46 (1954) (per Vanderbilt, C.J.).

When Curl chose to state as a fact what was at the best a guess and a hope, he engaged in misrepresentation.

Curl misrepresented the judgment on which his appeal depended. If we accept his affidavit, he did so in part because of statements made to him by his client, Henry. Curl had no reason to believe Henry, an oil driller, on a matter of law. Henry's basic story, that he had paid Harvester, was disbelieved by the jury in this case, and was wholly implausible. At oral argument Curl acknowledged that Henry's story was "wild." We do not address here the duty of a lawyer never to put on the witness stand a client he has reason to know is committing perjury. See Nix v. Whiteside, 475 U.S. 157, 164, 106 S.Ct. 988, 995, 89 L.Ed.2d 123 (1986). But the implausibility of Henry's story bears on the reasonableness of Curl relying on him. No reasonable lawyer would have taken Henry's word for what another lawyer said was the meaning of a foreign judgment.

Curl's other reliance was on a lawyer with whom he conversed with difficulty because neither could speak the other's language fluently. On a matter of central importance to his case it was reckless for Curl to depend on his understanding of the broken English of Serrano responding to questions framed by him in broken Spanish. Ordinary prudence required Curl to get a written opinion of the meaning of the judgment, especially so when his own reading of it, like ours, showed him that the judgment was procedural only. Recklessly, Curl chose to hear what he wanted to hear and charged ahead.

Curl's excuses do not relieve him of responsibility for having brought an appeal that should never have been brought, for subjecting Harvester to the burden of appellate litigation, and for having put this court to the task of reading, analyzing, and judging his baseless arguments. Curl's conduct has been professionally irresponsible in violation of the standards of legal ethics and his duty to this court. Sanctions are appropriate and indeed required.

By Rule 5 of the Rules of this court, the Federal Rules of Civil Procedure, "whenever relevant" are part of the rules of this court. Rule 11, Fed.R.Civ.P. prescribes that "the signature of an attorney" constitutes "a certificate by him" that to the "best of his knowledge, information, and belief formed after reasonable inquiry," the paper he is filing with the court is "well grounded in fact." The brief filed by Curl was not well-grounded in fact and he had not made reasonable inquiry. Rule 11 prescribes that in such a situation the court "shall impose" "an appropriate sanction" upon the attorney. The imposition of sanctions is mandatory. Golden Eagle Distributing Corp. v. Burroughs Corp., 801 F.2d 1531 (9th Cir.1986); Eastway Construction Corp. v. City of New York, 762 F.2d 243 at 254 n. 7.

A majority of this court believes the public admonishment of this opinion is sufficient sanction. The majority is willing to believe that Curl did not intentionally attempt to perpetrate a fraud on this court. There is no evidence that Curl has been subject to prior disciplinary proceedings. The court will not hesitate to sanction future negligence with substantial monetary fines, suspension, or disbarment from practice before our court.

QUESTIONS

1. Was David Curl's conduct more or less culpable than that of Louis Greenberg?

2. What specifically was misleading about Curl's representations to the Court of Appeals?

3. What was Curl's own initial reading of the Mexican judgment? Why didn't Curl trust his own reading of the judgment more than that of his client, Johnny Henry?

4. The Court mentions that Curl should have obtained a written opinion from Mexican counsel explaining the meaning of the judgment. What other steps could he have taken to ascertain whether he had grounds for filing an appeal?

Relevant Background

Arguing a False Inference to a Jury

A lawyer, and particularly a prosecutor, should not argue false inferences to a jury. See George L. Scott v. Dale Foltz, 612 F.Supp. 50 (E.D.Mich.1985) (defendant granted writ of habeas corpus requiring that he be given a new trial on armed robbery charges because of the prosecutor's failure to disclose a plea bargain with a prosecution witness and his failure to correct a false inference from the witness's testimony that no promise had been made to her in return for her guilty plea); Frederick Dukes v. State of Florida, 356 So.2d 873, 875 (Fla.App.1978) ("[W]hen the prosecutor frames his questions to suggest as a fact that the accused was previously convicted of a certain offense, and the inference is false, the trial court must at least emphatically charge the jury to dispel the inference. Other remedies may be necessary if a corrective instruction is ineffective or if a prosecutor knowingly or recklessly plants a false inference.")

In some respects, criminal defense lawyers are not held to as high a standard. A defense lawyer "may permissibly cross-examine a witness known to be telling the truth in an effort to persuade the jury not to believe the witness." Charles W. Wolfram, Modern Legal Ethics 651–52 (1986), citing Justice White's opinion in United States v. Wade, 388 U.S. 218, 257–58 (1967) (after describing the adversarial role of a criminal defense lawyer at trial, Justice White observes that counsel playing such a role would do nothing to increase the reliability of pre trial lineups and for this reason he dissents from the Court's holding that a defendant's Sixth Amendment right to counsel extends to lineups). It has even been argued that a defense attorney at trial "may create false inferences so long as this is not accomplished through false evidence because the prosecution bears the burden of proof." Richard H. Underwood & William H. Fortune, Trial Ethics 365 (1988). However, a criminal defense attorney should also be cognizant of the Supreme Court's condemnation of false evidence in *Nix v. Whiteside*, supra Chapter 1. A lawyer arguing a false inference in some ways does the same thing as a lawyer arguing perjured testimony or other false evidence: she is trying to persuade the trier of fact to believe an assertion that the lawyer knows is untrue.

PROBLEMS

1. In a bank robbery trial, there is testimony that a security camera was activated during the robbery, but no photographs are introduced into evidence and no reference is made to photographs in any of the testimony. The prosecution does not introduce any evidence explaining why there were no photographs, although both the prosecution and defense attorneys know that there are no photographs because the camera was broken. Once the evidence is closed, the prosecution is forbidden to go outside the record and tell the jury that the camera was broken. Is it proper for the defense attorney to take advantage of the prosecution's failure to introduce evidence about the camera's malfunction and suggest in closing arguments that the prosecution did not introduce photographs because they would have shown that the defendant was not the robber? See United States v. Latimer, 511 F.2d 498 (10th Cir.1975).

2. Your client, aged 19, is arrested for shoplifting from a drugstore a can of hairspray priced at two dollars. She had ten dollars in her pocket at the time of arrest. In your office, she tells you that she took the hairspray because she needed it and wanted to spend the ten dollars on going to a dance club with her friends. You fear that she might perjure herself at trial and decide not to put her on the stand (if you wonder why, you should review chapter 1). The prosecution introduces unrefuted testimony that your client walked out of the store with the hairspray without paying and that she had ten dollars in her pocket at the time. An associate in your office has drafted two closing arguments for you to choose from:

First Version: The prosecution claims that my client stole the hairspray because she walked out of the store with it without paying. They also claim that my client *intended* to walk out of the store without paying, in essence to permanently deprive the store owner of his property. Well, maybe she did, but maybe she didn't. Were you there? No. The prosecution's witnesses were there, but all they can testify to is the fact that my client walked out of the store with the hairspray without paying. They can't testify as to whether she intended to because they could not get inside her mind. Indeed, she had ten dollars in her purse, which was more than enough to pay for the hairspray. She just walked right out of the store without stopping at the cashier; perhaps you have come close to doing the same thing by mistake. My point is that, after you have heard all this evidence, you are left with the conclusion "maybe she intended to steal the hairspray, maybe she didn't." "Maybe" is not "probably" or "most likely" and certainly is not "beyond a reasonable doubt." The prosecution simply cannot carry its burden of proving my client guilty.

Second Version: The prosecution claims that my client walked out of the store with the intention of not paying for the hairspray. Why, however, would my client, with ten dollars in her purse, steal a two dollar can of hairspray? Isn't it just as likely, or perhaps even more likely, that she was in a rush to leave the store and forgot to stop by the cashier? At least, don't you have a reasonable doubt about whether she really intended to steal the hairspray?

Is either or both of these two closing arguments intended to create a false impression in the minds of the jury? Is there a difference between the two? Is there a difference between using these arguments and putting perjured testimony on the stand? If you think neither of these arguments is ethical, what closing argument can you make on behalf of your client? See Harry Subin , The Criminal Lawyer's "Different Mission": Reflections on the "Right" to Present a False Case, 1 Geo. J. Legal Ethics 125 (1987); John Mitchell, Reasonable Doubts Are Where You Find Them: A Response to Professor Subin's Position on the Criminal Lawyer's "Different Mission," 1 Geo. J. Legal Ethics 339, (1987); Harry Subin, Is This Lie Necessary? Further Reflections on the Right to Present a False Defense, 1 Geo. J. Legal Ethics 689 (1988).

3. How would you answer the following question: "Does defense counsel have an ethical duty to advise the trial judge that she is relying on a misunderstanding of the law or overlooking settled law in handling her client's case?"

Marilyn Bednarski, Disclosing Adverse Authority and Correcting Judicial Misunderstanding, in Ethical Problems Facing the Criminal Defense Lawyer 184 (Rodney J. Uphoff Ed.) (ABA 1995).

4. How would you answer the following question: "Must defense counsel correct a trial judge who in sentencing the defendant indicates he is relying on the prosecutor's statement that the client has no prior record when counsel knows the defendant has a prior record?"

William Talley, Jr., Setting the Record Straight: The Client with Undisclosed Prior Convictions, in Ethical Problems Facing the Criminal Defense Lawyer, supra, at 194.

CHAPTER 10

THE INFLUENCED TRIBUNAL

A.   EX-PARTE CONTACTS WITH THE JUDICIARY

Justice Frankfurter once observed that the responsibilities given to lawyers come with important obligations:

> "From a profession charged with such responsibilities there must be exacted those qualities of truth-speaking, of a high sense of honor, of granite discretion, of the strictest observance of fiduciary responsibility, that have, throughout the centuries, been compendiously described as 'moral character.'"

Schware v. Board of Bar Examiners, 353 U.S. 232, 247 (1957) (concurring opinion). Frankfurter, however, like all persons, was fallible. As you read the following selections, ask yourself whether Frankfurter's discretion and observance of fiduciary responsibilities were as strong as they should have been.

Felix Frankfurter, b. Vienna, Austria 1882, d. 1965; immigrated to the United States in 1894; attended the College of the City of New York; LL.B. Harvard University 1906; assistant to Henry Stimson, Office of the United States Attorney 1906–09; legal officer, Bureau of Insular Affairs 1911–13; Professor of Law, Harvard University 1914–39; Associate Justice of the United States Supreme Court 1939–62; author of numerous articles and books including The Case of Sacco and Vanzetti (1927) (see Chapter 8 supra)

Harlan B. Phillips, Felix Frankfurter Reminisces

(1960)

Stettler v. O'Hara and *Simpson v. O'Hara*[1] were both argued twice. They were first argued on December 16 and 17, 1914. The Court evidently was divided so they were restored to the docket for reargument on June 12, 1916, and the cases were re-argued on January 18 and 19, 1917 and were decided on April 9, 1917.

---

1. Stettler v. O'Hara, 139 P. 743 (Or. 1914), aff'd 243 U.S. 629 (1917) (the Supreme Court split 4–4 to uphold an Oregon law regulating hours and wages for women); Simpson v. O'Hara, 141 P. 158 (Or.1914), aff'd 243 U.S. 629 (1917) (same divided court upheld an Oregon minimum wage statute). Both of these cases involved challenges under the fourteenth amendment to acts passed by the Oregon Legislature.—ed.

It required a good deal of contrivance on the part of Mrs. Kelley[2] to get the state of Oregon to invite us to be of counsel because the litigation was in the hands of the attorney general of the state. The controlling counsel who was called the attorney of record was the attorney general. He's the fellow who would represent the state on the records of the Court, the responsible person on whom papers were to be served in the first place, and it required getting friends in the state to persuade the attorney general either to share the argument or to turn the argument over to Brandeis in the Muller case and later on to Professor Frankfurter in the Bunting and O'Hara cases. That was done. One day, looking as was my custom at one of the back pages of the *New York Times* for what had happened the day before in the Supreme Court—the Journal is printed in small type, as you may have noted—I noticed that the O'Hara cases were submitted on briefs by both sides. The attorney general without telling me about it, or consulting me, or informing me, or asking me, had agreed with counsel on the other side just to submit on briefs. When I read that I nearly passed out because the brief that he would submit would be just flimsy stuff. This was precisely the kind of a case in which you need, if anything can help, the impact of argument, of personality upon the Court to goad them into an awareness of what is involved.

When I saw that the attorney general of Oregon had submitted these cases I was in the doldrums and began to think what could I do about it. What could I do about it? I thought and thought. I thought of the two men I knew on the Court. Mr. Justice Holmes. Well, I didn't want to bother the old gentleman. I couldn't talk to Brandeis. He had been of counsel. I worried much about it. I assumed that the attorney general of the state wasn't unaffected by the fact that the counsel on the other side was a fellow named Fulton, a former United States Senator of considerable influence. I don't mean to suggest corruption or anything, but just good fellowship—you know, with Fulton saying, "Jim"—or whatever the name of the attorney general was—"Washington's a hell of a way off. Why don't we just leave it on the briefs?"

He had nothing to lose by that. The attorney general would say, "We'll save the fare to go to Washington."

I thought and thought and finally I concocted a night letter, a telegram, to the then Chief Justice whom I had known pleasantly, Chief Justice White who was a very gracious, charming Southern gentleman. He was a massive man, a charming gentleman and a devout Catholic. I forget whether I sent this telegram to the Supreme Court or to his house. He had a house on New Hampshire Avenue, a few blocks away from where the present Catholic Cathedral is, and I sent him the following telegram: MY DEAR MR. CHIEF JUSTICE I SHALL CALL AT YOUR HOUSE AT ABOUT NINE O'CLOCK SATURDAY MORNING NEXT IN THE HOPE THAT YOU'LL BE FREE TO SEE ME ON A MATTER OF CONSIDER-

2. Florence Kelley of the National Consumers League coordinated efforts to obtain outside counsel to argue the case defending the Oregon legislation.—ed.

ABLE PUBLIC IMPORTANCE. RESPECTFULLY YOURS FELIX
FRANKFURTER.

Knowing the kind of gentleman he was, I thought that would at least
arouse his curiosity—you know, why should I want to see him on "a matter
of considerable public importance?" Well, I took the Federal from Boston
and turned up at the house. His man at the door said, "Yes, the Chief
Justice is waiting for you." He greeted me cordially. He hadn't seen me
since I went up to Harvard. He asked me how I liked it and then said,
"How many Southern students have you got, students from the South?"

Luckily I knew at that time with great particularity the composition of
our student body and so I told him. He was perfectly delighted to hear that
so large a percentage of our students came from the South. Then he spent a
considerable time descanting on the ruin that the Civil War had wrought in
the South. They were just about then emerging from all its devastation and
the consequences of such a war. He tried to tell me what it would mean in
terms of the North if all the railroad tracks were ripped up and so on, and
so on. I'd give anything if that had been taken down. It was so eloquent.
White came from Louisiana, and he was essentially an orator, eloquent and
illuminating. As Holmes says somewhere, "His big frame was meant for
politics rather than the law."

He had been a United States Senator and was an impressive fellow.
Then he sort of moved his chair a little forward and said, "Well, son, tell
me what brings you here. Tell me what's on your mind."

Then one of these special interventions, divine interventions if one
must conceive it, put just the right thought into my head. It is more or less
a habit of mine to let things stew around inside of me and trust to the
moment to express it, having the right words come. It's my good fortune to
believe in the moment instead of preparing rigidly. I prepare thoughts but
not words. As he said, "My son, what brings you here?" the happy thought
struck me to say, "Mr. Chief Justice, I am not at all sure that I have a right
to be here. I am not at all clear that I should put to you the matter that I'm
about to put to you, but I come to you as though in the confessional."

Well, that was a master stroke. I felt at once as though the whole
church was enfolding me. He came near, more intimately, he said, "Tell
me. Just speak freely."

Well, then I told him. There were these two cases on the calendar of
the Court. I was to argue them. I was the counsel, but not the attorney of
record. The attorney general of Oregon had exercised his prerogative of
submitting them, by agreement with counsel on the other side, on briefs.
As a student of the Court I was convinced these were precisely the kind of
cases in which the Court should have the benefit of oral argument. I
thought it very bad for the Court to be confronted with merely the briefs
which were perhaps inadequate without the benefit of the give-and-take of
argument and questions from the Court to bring out the difficulties of the
cases.

"Well," he said, and there were briefs and records strewn all around his big living room, "now suppose—mind you, just supposin'—the Court were to hand down an order next Monday saying that in numbers so-and-so, whatever they are, the motion for leave to submit without oral argument is denied, and the case is set down for oral argument. Now, supposin'—now you see I'm just one of nine, just one of nine—but supposin' the Court were to do that, would that meet the situation?"

After the necessary moment of deliberation, deep thought led me to say very promptly, "I think that would absolutely deal with the situation just as it should be dealt with. I think that would take care of the situation entirely."

"Now, I'm supposin'. I'm just supposin'. I'm just one of nine, but supposin' the Court were to take that position would that meet the situation?"

"I think, Mr. Chief Justice, that would take care of the situation quite adequately."

I made my getaway as soon as I could in warm cordiality. He took me to the door and let me out. I climbed a telephone pole. On Monday that order came down. He was going to conference within an hour or so after I left him. I always regard that as my single most successful professional achievement. That's what is called *ex parte* practice.

Philip Elman, b. 1918 in Paterson, New Jersey; A.B. City College of New York 1936; LL.B. Harvard University 1939 (Editor, Harvard Law Review); law clerk to Judge Calvert Magruder, United States Court of Appeals for the First Circuit 1939–40; attorney with the Federal Communications Commission 1940–41; law clerk to Justice Felix Frankfurter 1941–43; assistant Chairman, Office of Economic Coordination, Department of State 1943–44; assistant to the Solicitor General 1944–61 (handled civil rights cases in the Supreme Court in which the United States was a party or amicus curiae); commissioner of the Federal Trade Commission 1961–70; Professor of Law, Georgetown University 1970–76.

The Solicitor General's Office, Justice Frankfurter, and Civil Rights Litigation, 1946–1960: An Oral History

(Philip Elman interviewed by Norman Silber).
100 Harv. L. Rev. 817 (1987).

Philip Elman was law clerk to Justice Felix Frankfurter in the 1941 and 1942 Terms, and he remained, in the Justice's words, his "law clerk for life." What follows is an edited excerpt from a much larger interview with Mr. Elman, conducted for the Columbia Oral History Project by Norman Silber, about Mr. Elman's career of public service, his relationship with Justice Frankfurter, and his view of American legal culture and institutions since the 1930s.

In June 1945, when Charles Fahy became Legal Adviser to General Dwight D. Eisenhower, the United States Military Governor in Germany, Mr. Elman went along as his assistant. This part of the memoir takes up upon his return to the Solicitor General's office in the fall of 1946.

* * *

Elman: Now, at just about this time the NAACP began to bring its cases attacking segregation in public elementary schools. There were cases all over the country. . . . The Court was nowhere near ready to take on the issue. The Justices (except for Black and Douglas) were deliberately pursuing a strategy of procrastination. The Court's strategy, and this was the Frankfurter–Jackson strategy, was to delay, delay, delay—putting off the issue as long as possible.

Q: That strategy has bothered quite a few observers since.

Elman: Any other strategy would have been disastrous for everybody— the Court, the country, and most sadly of all, the blacks themselves. Frankfurter wanted the Court to deal with the issue openly, directly, wisely, courageously, and more than anything else, unanimously. He did not want the segregation issue to be decided by a fractured Court, as it then was; he did not want a decision to go out with nine or six or four opinions. He wanted the Court to stand before the country on this issue united and speaking in a single voice. He felt that whatever it did had to go out to the country with an appearance of unity, so that the Court as an institution would best be able to withstand the attacks that inevitably were going to be made on it. And, what was crucial at that time—1952— Frankfurter could not count five sure, or even probable, votes for overruling Plessy. So Frankfurter, along with Jackson, wanted to postpone as long as he possibly could.

. . . .

Jackson's view was that whatever the Court did, it should do as a united Court; and what he wanted to do was erase Plessy v. Ferguson, simply erase it. Neither say it's wrong nor say it's right. Jackson's view was that integration of public school systems in almost half of the states was too enormous a job for the federal judiciary, that the Court should tell Congress to take it on. Looking at the fourteenth amendment's section five, which specifically gives Congress the power to enforce its provisions, Jackson said, in substance, "Congress has abdicated, leaving enforcement of the fourteenth amendment entirely to us, and I don't think that's right. Let them enforce the fourteenth amendment in this area, because it involves radically transforming the educational institutions of twenty-one states, with enormous social, administrative, and political complexities and dangers. Let Congress deal with the problem; it's too difficult for judges. We can't preside over so massive a reconstruction of state educational systems. The issue is basically 'political,' inappropriate for article III courts." And he wanted, until the very end, for the Court to be honest and admit that it was rendering a political (as he called it) decision. That was

Jackson's view, not the one expressed (and falsely attributed to Jackson) in that famous memo Rehnquist wrote as his law clerk.

Q: How could Frankfurter be so sure that unanimity was worth waiting for?

Elman: Frankfurter has written letters, after Brown v. Board of Education came down in May 1954, that I've seen quoted. He wrote a letter to Learned Hand, for example, in which he said that if the two "great libertarians," Black and Douglas, had had their way in 1952, "we would have been in the soup." What he meant was that Black and Douglas wanted to decide the issue the first time it was presented, when Vinson was still the Chief Justice, when Truman was still President, when the Court was still hopelessly divided, when the Department of Justice would not have participated in the case, as Frankfurter knew from me. It would have been disastrous. Frankfurter thought that even though they might have eked out a bare five-to-four majority to overrule Plessy, it would have gone out to the country in the worst possible way.

The opposition would have been massive, it would have been more than interposition. Even Frankfurter didn't foresee that federal troops, the United States Army, would have to be called out to enforce the Court's decision, as it turned out they had to be in the Little Rock case. [Cooper v. Aaron, 358 U.S. 1 (1958)] To him that was inconceivable and, if it should happen, might bring on a national crisis. That the Court, after making the decision, should be unable to enforce it was the last thing he wanted.

So Frankfurter felt we would have been in the soup if Black and Douglas, who simply said, "Let's overrule Plessy," had had their way. He told me that what those two really wanted was for the Court to uphold Plessy so they could dissent and become the heroes of the liberals. I don't know about that, but I'm sure Hugo Black at least would have been happier in the role of dissenter. He was scared to death—and he scared everybody else on the Court—of the political turmoil in the South that would follow from a decision ending racial segregation in public schools.

Well, when this came up the first time early in 1952, Perlman was the Solicitor General. Perlman had had no problem signing his name to all our briefs in Henderson, Sweatt, and McLaurin arguing that Plessy v. Ferguson was wrong and should be overruled. So when Briggs came up, I went into his office and said, "Let's do in this case what we've done in all the others and argue to overrule Plessy." Much to my surprise—and dismay—Perlman's response was, "No, it's much too early to end segregation in public schools. You can't have little black boys sitting next to little white girls. The country isn't ready for that. This would lead to miscegenation and mongrelization of the races." All that stuff. When I pointed out that several times already we had taken a position on this issue, he replied that never before had we had any case involving an elementary school or a high school. As to law schools, he said, that was okay, but as to public schools, absolutely not. And we were stuck. Perlman was absolutely adamant. All the letters to the Attorney General, all the telephone calls, all the visits that were paid to him didn't make him budge. Perlman said no, the line has to be drawn. Trains, dining cars, law schools, graduate schools, yes—but not public schools; no sir! So there we were.

Q: Stuck. . . .

Elman: And along came the first of the kind of miracles that Frankfurter—who knew from me that the Court no longer could count on the United States to support overruling Plessy—was waiting for. J. Howard McGrath, the Attorney General, got into trouble. A man by the name of Newbold Morris had been appointed by Truman to investigate corruption in the administration. There was corruption in the Internal Revenue Service, and there were some indications that things were not completely kosher in the Department of Justice. Morris sent a detailed questionnaire to McGrath. McGrath didn't like it and didn't fill it out. So he was fired and replaced as Attorney General by James P. McGranery, an old friend of Truman's who had served with him in Congress and was then a federal district judge in Philadelphia. McGranery, to put it as simply as I can, was a kind of nut. He was very unstable and given to emotional outbursts. There were people in the Department of Justice who thought he was off his rocker and told stories about his erratic behavior in meetings. Well, Perlman and McGranery did not get along, and Perlman quit as soon as he could.

So there we were in the fall of 1952 with the Brown group of cases coming up for argument before the Supreme Court. Frankfurter then did something unprecedented in the District of Columbia case, Bolling v. Sharpe, which was not yet before the Court. It was still in the lower courts. Frankfurter had the Court put out an order inviting counsel in the case to file a petition for certiorari which, the order said, would be granted so that the Court would have the case before it along with the cases coming from Kansas, Delaware, South Carolina, and Virginia. The cases were scheduled for argument early in December 1952.

Q: Did the Justice Department want to get involved?

Elman: Perlman's departure was sort of an act of God. If Morris hadn't sent that questionnaire, if McGrath hadn't left as Attorney General, if Perlman had remained as Solicitor General, we wouldn't have filed anything. The United States would have stayed out of the segregation cases. But as it happened, Perlman left and Robert L. Stern, First Assistant to the Solicitor General, became Acting Solicitor General.

The two of us went in to see McGranery. We told McGranery, who hated Perlman, who had been very happy to see him go, that Perlman, even though the Department had consistently taken the position that Plessy was wrong and should be overruled, had refused to participate as amicus in the pending school segregation cases. We told him the Department of Justice should stick to its position and file an amicus brief in the Court. McGranery's immediate response was, "You're right, boys. Go ahead and write a brief."

So that's how we happened to file the first brief in Brown v. Board of Education in December 1952, signed by McGranery as Attorney General and by me. You notice the brief wasn't signed by the Solicitor General. The reason is that when the brief had to be filed, Bob Stern was no longer Acting Solicitor General. Walter Cummings, Jr.'s appointment as Solicitor General had just been announced, but he had had nothing to do with this brief. There we were, the brief was in page proof, and the question was whether we should hold it up. McGranery's executive assistant at that time was James Browning, who is now the Chief Judge of the Court of Appeals for the Ninth Circuit. I called Browning, who was very much with us in this whole enterprise, and asked, "What do we do? Walter Cummings is now the Solicitor General. Does he have to approve this brief before we file it?" Browning said, "No, you send it to the printer just as it is with McGranery's name on it and yours, and if any question is raised, tell them McGranery okayed it." So that's how it was done, and it became the position of the Truman administration.

I told Richard Kluger—when he interviewed me for Simple Justice—that this first brief we filed in December 1952 is the one thing I'm proudest of in my whole career. Not because it's a beautifully written brief; I don't think it is. Rather, it's because we were the first to suggest, and all the parties and amici on both sides rejected it after the government proposed it, that if the Court should hold that racial segregation in public schools is unconstitutional, it should give district courts a reasonable period of time to work out the details and timing of implementation of the decision. In other words, "with all deliberate speed."

The reason I'm so proud of that proposal is that it offered the Court a way out of its dilemma, a way to end racial segregation without inviting massive disobedience, a way to decide the constitutional issue unanimously without tearing the Court apart. For the first time the Court was told that it was not necessarily confronted with an all-or-nothing choice between reaffirming separate but equal, as urged by the states, and overruling Plessy and requiring immediate integration of public schools in all states, as urged by the NAACP. We proposed a middle ground, separating the constitutional principle from the remedy—a proposal that nobody had previously suggested and that, when we made it, both sides opposed.

It was entirely unprincipled, it was just plain wrong as a matter of constitutional law, to suggest that someone whose personal constitutional rights were being violated should be denied relief. It was saying to Linda Brown and all the other children in these cases, "Yes, you're right, your constitutional rights are being violated and ignored, you are not being allowed to go to a public school of your choice because of your race, and we agree that's unconstitutional. But we're not going to do a damn thing for you. You go back to that same segregated school you're going to. We'll take care of your children, perhaps. Or your grandchildren. But we're not going to do a damn thing for you. By the time we get around to doing something for kids like you, you will have graduated from school." That's what we were arguing, even though the Supreme Court had held again and again that constitutional rights are personal, that if an individual's constitutional rights are being violated, he is entitled to immediate relief. As a matter of constitutional principle, what we were arguing in this brief was simply indefensible.

Now, where did this idea come from? Not from Frankfurter; he never expressed anything along those lines. But it did grow out of my many conversations with him over a period of many months. He told me what he thought, what the other Justices were telling him they thought. I knew from him what their positions were. If the issue was inescapably presented in yes-or-no terms, he could not count five votes on the Court to overrule Plessy. Black, who was a sure vote to overrule Plessy, was frightening the other Justices the most. He was saying to them, "Now, look, I have to vote to overrule Plessy, but this would mean the end of political liberalism in the South. Politicians like Lister Hill will be dead. It will bring the Bilbos and the Talmadges out of the woodwork; the Klan is going to be riding again. It will be the end of liberalism in the South."

Burton and Minton didn't say very much. As it turned out, when the votes were finally cast, they were on the right side, but of course when they voted, they were not voting for immediate relief. Nobody on the Court ever voted for immediate implementation, for opening up all the public schools in the whole country, tomorrow morning at nine o'clock, all nonsegregated.

Q: Aren't you exaggerating? Was that really the alternative that the petitioners placed in front of the Court?

Elman: Yes. That was the stark issue posed to the Court by the parties—which the Justices never had to reach, because the United States as amicus curiae offered a way out, and they grabbed it. If they had not had that alternative offered to them, one that came to them with the seal of approval of both the Democratic Truman and Republican Eisenhower administrations, who knows what would have happened. It would, in Frankfurter's judgment, have been an incredible godawful mess: possibly nine different opinions, nine different views on the Court. It would have set back the cause of desegregation; it would have hurt the public school systems everywhere; and it would have damaged the Court.

Vinson was clearly for leaving the Constitution as it was. Plessy and separate but equal had been the law of the land for over a half-century, and he was not ready to change it. Let them amend the Constitution or let Congress do something, but Vinson was not going to overrule Plessy. He had Tom Clark with him, at least initially in 1952. True, Clark voted the other way in the end—after "with all deliberate speed" had been added to the choices before the Court—but Clark was then with Vinson. At least Frankfurter said so. Reed kept quiet publicly, but he was certainly with Vinson.

So as Frankfurter saw it when the cases came up, he would be the fifth man. He saw Vinson, Clark, and Reed for simply affirming Plessy; Jackson for leaving it to Congress. On the other side, although Frankfurter wasn't sure of Minton, he had Black, Douglas, and Burton for overruling Plessy, with Black screaming it would be a political disaster to do so. So I began looking around for something that would get Jackson, that would hold

Frankfurter, that would even get a strong majority to hold racial segregation unconstitutional but would provide some kind of cushion, something to avoid the immediate impact, some insurance against the inevitable fallout of a Court decision requiring immediate integration everywhere. So that is why I made this "indefensible" argument in point four of the 1952 brief. None of this was based on what I thought was right—I had no idea whether it would have been better educationally or politically to do it immediately—I was simply counting votes on the Supreme Court. I was trying to come up with a realistic formula that would win the case, that would overrule Plessy, that would knock out separate but equal, that would not damage the Court or public educational systems. It was as simple as that. I repeat: I had had no discussion about it with Frankfurter beforehand.

Q: You said you were talking with him all the way along?

Elman: Sure, but I had no discussion with Frankfurter beforehand with respect to the position I was going to take in point four of this brief. I just didn't want to take a chance on telling him—because of what might happen if I did. I was on very shaky legal ground. As I said, it was insupportable in dealing with individual constitutional rights, and I didn't want Frankfurter to tell me so. I was relying on antitrust cases, where the Court had ordered the dissolution of large monopolies and said that, because it would take time, the Court would allow time. There are other situations where courts allow time, such as boundary disputes between states. The expression "with all deliberate speed" was used first by Holmes in a case called Virginia v. West Virginia. [222 U.S. 17, 20 (1911)].

Q: Was that phrase in your brief?

Elman: No. The phrase made its first appearance in Brown in [Assistant Attorney General J. Lee] Rankin's oral argument in 1953. But the idea was the same as in our brief. Frankfurter wrote it into the draft opinion circulated by Earl Warren, and he got it from this old Holmes opinion.

Well, going back to that brief in December of 1952, I had been a great hero of the NAACP and all these other people who were fighting to end racial segregation, but after that brief was filed, I wasn't a hero anymore. They thought point four was gradualism, and to them gradualism meant never. Unlike Frankfurter and me, they couldn't or didn't count the votes on the Court. When that brief was filed, Frankfurter called me up and said, "Phil, I think you've rendered a real service to your country." That's the way I felt about it then, and that's the way I feel about it now, even though many people think that "with all deliberate speed" was a disaster. It broke the logjam. It was the formula that the Court needed in order to bring all the Justices together to decide the constitutional issue on the merits correctly. Without "all deliberate speed" in the remedy, the Court could never have decided the constitutional issue in the strong, forthright, unanimous way that it did; and it was essential for the Court to do so if its decision was to be accepted and followed throughout the country.

The Justices couldn't decide at the 1952 Term. Eisenhower became President in January 1953, and Herbert Brownell became Attorney General; we had no Solicitor General for a while. Lee Rankin was running the S.G.'s office for Brownell, and Rankin was very pleasantly surprised by the caliber of the lawyers he found there. . . .

Q: What was happening that spring in the Brown case?

Elman: Well, what the Court did in the segregation cases in June of 1953 was to set them down for reargument. The Justices discussed the cases in conference, but they never took a vote; they just expressed their views. Some of their conference notes are now available, and it's not altogether clear who said what or when. Tom Clark, for example, said long afterward that, oh yes, he was for overruling Plessy. But that's not the way I heard it from Frankfurter.

There's no question that the grand strategist in all this inside the Court was F.F. He was writing memos to his colleagues and having his clerk, Alex Bickel, do research into the legislative history of the fourteenth amendment, the results of which he then circulated to the Court. To use the Yiddish word that Frankfurter used all the time, he was the Kochleffel. It means cooking spoon, stirring things up; the man stirring everything up inside the Court was Frankfurter. They couldn't decide the cases, they didn't know what to do with them, they had no majority, and they hadn't even taken a formal vote, because they didn't want to harden anybody's position.

So in the summer of 1953 before they adjourned, they set the cases down for reargument: they asked five questions of the parties, and they invited the Attorney General of the United States and the attorneys general of all the states requiring or authorizing segregation to file briefs and present oral argument. Well, that order setting the cases down for reargument brought misery to the Department of Justice. The new people in the Eisenhower administration had been waiting on the sidelines for the Court to decide. They had had nothing to do with the cases, they had never taken a position on the issue, they didn't want to get involved, and here the Supreme Court was asking the Attorney General of the United States to file a brief and present oral argument. Well. . . .

Q: Excuse me, do you know how that invitation came about? Whose idea it was?

Elman: It was Frankfurter's.

Q: You had nothing to do with it?

Elman: Oh, he might have told me about it. It came as no surprise to me, but reargument was his idea. What he kept telling me was, "These cases are just sitting, Phil, nothing's happening." I knew that. Incidentally, I must emphasize to you that I never mentioned my conversations with Frankfurter to anyone. He didn't regard me as a lawyer for any party; I was still his law clerk. He needed help, lots of help, and there were things I could do in the Department of Justice that he couldn't do, like getting the support of both administrations, Democratic and Republican, for the position that he wanted the Court to come out with, so that it would not become a hot political issue. When the Court announced its decision, he wanted both the present and former Presidents of the United States to be publicly on record as having urged the Court to take the position it had. And that's exactly the way it worked out.

Q: What happened in the Eisenhower Department of Justice after the order for reargument was issued in June 1953?

Elman: Brownell called a meeting of his high command to discuss what to do in view of this order inviting him to file an amicus brief. Stern, who was Acting Solicitor General, and I attended the meeting, along with William P. Rogers, who was then Deputy Attorney General and later became Attorney General and Secretary of State. Others at the meeting included Warren Burger, who was then Assistant Attorney General in charge of the Civil Division, Warren Olney IV, Assistant Attorney General in charge of the Criminal Division, and other assistant A.G.'s, particularly Rankin.

Stern and I said, "When the Supreme Court invites you, that's the equivalent of a royal command. An invitation from the Supreme Court just can't be rejected. Besides, if you turn it down, how are you going to explain it to the press? Does this mean you're not supporting the position taken by the prior administration?" My recollection is that Rankin, Stern, and I were the only ones at the meeting who recommended that the government accept the Court's invitation. Rogers said an invitation is only an invitation, which we could either accept or refuse, and he saw no reason why we should accept. I do not recall Burger's saying very much. When the meeting ended, Brownell said he would have to think about it.

Some time later, I think much later—I remember writing a letter to Frankfurter during the summer telling him that nothing, absolutely nothing, was going on in the Department of Justice—Rankin called me into his office and said that he had gotten the green light from Brownell. I'm sure Brownell had talked to Eisenhower about it. The feeling we all had at the time was that Eisenhower would not be sympathetic to the idea, because he was known to believe that public education was something for the states, the federal government should stay out of it, and this problem was the Court's and not his as President. So I give Brownell and Rankin the most credit for the Eisenhower administration's decision to participate.

I think the administration would have looked terribly bad had it stayed out. At any rate, Rankin told me to organize a team to prepare the government's brief. The Court had asked what the legislative history of the fourteenth amendment showed about the intent of Congress and of the ratifying state legislatures concerning racial segregation of public school students. It was relatively easy to go through the congressional debates and determine what had been in the minds of the members of Congress. We didn't know, at least we didn't know officially, that Alex Bickel had already done that job as Frankfurter's clerk. It all appeared much later in an article that Bickel published on the legislative history of the fourteenth amendment in Congress. The big research job was to go to the state legislatures. We were very fortunate, because at that time the Office of Alien Property in the Department of Justice was being dismantled. Some able lawyers in it were being fired, or riffed as the bureaucratic jargon puts it, and I recommended to Rankin that they be hired to work on the historical research. We had five or six lawyers assigned to this chore.

I was relieved of most of my other duties in the S.G.'s office and put in charge of writing the brief, mainly editing what others wrote and putting it all together. We came up with a draft that was read by Rankin, who made almost no changes and then turned it over to Brownell. Brownell reviewed that draft, read every word of it with me beside him, over a period of weeks. Whenever Brownell had some free time, he sent for me. We would sit there, and he would read it, and if there was something he didn't understand or agree with, he would stop and ask me to explain or justify it. We did a little rewriting in his office.

Now there's some controversy over the position taken in the early drafts of the brief. Tony Lewis—Anthony Lewis of The New York Times—says that I told him or that he knew, because he had his own independent sources in the department, that my draft stated that "the United States submits that Plessy v. Ferguson is erroneous and should be overruled"—that it took a position on the merits. As it was finally filed, the brief said nothing like that; it simply answered the five questions asked by the Court and said nothing about the government's position on the merits. Lewis has written somewhere that Brownell took it out. Brownell has said that the brief that came to him did not have it in it. I don't remember. I don't have the early drafts. I've asked the people who worked on the brief, and their recollection is that the brief as it left me and went to Rankin and Brownell did express the position and that it was taken out somewhere afterward.

Q: You had included that view, you said, in the December 1952 brief. You said there that Plessy was wrong.

Elman: Oh, yes.

Q: So it was not at all unlikely that it would appear again?

Elman: I would have put it in again unless I had been instructed not to put it in. And I don't remember whether I was so instructed, in which case I would have left it out, or whether I had put it in and it was taken out later. But it was not in the final draft as it went to the White House.

Now, this second brief was long, and as I talk about it, I can't help thinking that I must sound like a devious fellow. For example, as to the intent of Congress regarding racial segregation in public schools, the fact of the matter is that there was not a word on schools in the legislative history of the fourteenth amendment. So if you wanted to divine the intent of Congress, you had to do so without the benefit of any specific reference to schools. Well, the conclusion of the brief, which was the only part that was shown to Eisenhower, simply said, "The legislative history of the fourteenth amendment is inconclusive with respect to segregation of schools." That was innocuous, and there was no reason why Eisenhower should object to it. But in the earlier section of the brief, which dealt with the legislative history of the amendment in Congress, we said that although the legislative history was inconclusive, it was clear that the framers of the amendment had intended to eliminate all distinctions based upon race and color with respect to all government institutions and that there was no indication that they had meant to exclude public schools. The same Congress that had adopted the fourteenth amendment, however, also had appropriated funds for the District of Columbia public schools, which were then segregated. John W. Davis argued that this showed that Congress had not intended to wipe out racial segregation even in the District of Columbia, where no constitutional amendment would have been necessary to do so. If you looked at the meat of the brief, then, it presented strong arguments against segregation. But if you looked only at the conclusion, it was innocuous.

Another thing I did with respect to this brief that slipped by my superiors, Rankin and Brownell, was that I called it Supplemental Brief for the United States on Reargument. The word "supplemental" meant that it was a supplement to the first brief, the Truman brief, so the December 1952 brief still stood. It did not replace the first brief but added to it. That's what the word "supplemental" meant to the Court, but you can be sure the folks in the White House didn't realize its significance.

Q: No, I don't think I would have either. Anyway, you must have worked as hard in preparing for the oral argument as you had in writing the brief.

Elman: Well, Rankin was going to argue the case, and I was coaching him. This was to be Rankin's first argument in the Supreme Court, and he was scared to death. He spent lots and lots of time preparing for it. He was enormously awed by the historic significance of this event in which we were participating. He never lost sight of what this was really all about. Remember, the government was in the case but had not taken a square position in the brief. And I asked him, "What are you going to do in oral argument before the Court when you're asked, 'What's the position of the United States on overruling Plessy?' " As it happened, Douglas was the one who asked Rankin the question; he beat Frankfurter to it. Rankin knew he was going to be asked and got his instructions from Brownell, who presumably had cleared them with Eisenhower. The instructions were: "Don't volunteer. We answered the Court's questions in our brief, and that's it. However, if you're asked, and only if you're asked, then you say, 'We adhere to the position previously taken by the United States.' "

. . . .

The lawyers who won Brown, the NAACP, Thurgood Marshall, Jack Greenberg, Spottswood Robinson, William Coleman, and all the other lawyers who were part of the NAACP team, emerged in the end with a unanimous decision, a victory that changed the whole course of race relations in the United States, the most important Supreme Court decision in this century. [See Brown v. Board of Educ., 347 U.S. 483 (1954) (Brown I)] Well, I don't want to tarnish or demean the majestic grandeur of their historic victory, but the way I see it, they brought these cases at the wrong time—much too soon. The votes on the Supreme Court simply weren't there, and they brought these cases in the wrong places. Instead of going to South Carolina or Virginia, about which the Court was terribly worried, they should have concentrated on the District of Columbia, where the Court would have had no problem at all with ending school segregation immediately. And they made the wrong arguments. The NAACP strategy was: we'll put it to the Court so they can't squirm out of it. We're going to concede that there is physical equality, and we're going to insist on immediate integration, on opening up all the schools in every state to everybody tomorrow morning at nine o'clock. That was the one thing that couldn't possibly command a majority on the Supreme Court. In Frankfurter's opinion and mine, even Black and Douglas didn't want to join a decision ordering immediate integration. They wanted to dissent from a decision adhering to Plessy. So the NAACP made the wrong arguments at the wrong time in the wrong cases, yet they won.

Q: Wouldn't you say then that at least they didn't do much damage to their case?

Elman: No, they didn't, as it turned out. But I haven't told you yet how and why the cases were won. Let me tell you first about one of the NAACP's expert witnesses, a man who received a lot of applause for his role in the school segregation cases, a psychologist named Kenneth Clark, who had a doll test. Do you know about the doll test? You show little black kids brown dolls and white dolls and ask them, "Which doll do you like better, which do you think is smarter?" They almost always pick the white doll, and Clark said this proved that the black kids, as a result of school segregation laws, had feelings of inferiority, that their self-esteem had been damaged. That was what these laws did. I have no doubt that his basic point was valid. But Clark felt that it had to be proved "scientifically," and he relied on his doll test for proof. By doing so, he trivialized the basic truth and opened himself and the NAACP to ridicule.

John W. Davis, the great advocate and dean of the American bar, was the lawyer for South Carolina. And he demolished the doll test. He cited an article by Clark stating that they had given this test not only to black kids in southern states where schools were segregated but also to black kids in the northern states where the schools were integrated, and the strange result was that the southern kids were significantly less likely to reject the brown doll than were the northern kids. So if any conclusion were to be drawn from the doll tests, it would have been the absurd one that education in a segregated school is less, not more, likely to damage a black child's self esteem! Davis poured ridicule on the black lawyers, and they did not have the courage and the good sense to stand up there and say, "We do not need scientific proof. Regardless of whether we can prove that racially segregated schools are better or worse for black children, regardless of whether we can prove that racial segregation generates feelings of inferiority, in the United States you simply cannot have governmental institutions in which people are segregated by law on the basis of race and color. It's as simple as that. That's what we stand on. This is not a country in which you can have racial apartheid."

This is the argument that I made in the racial gerrymander case, Gomillion v. Lightfoot [364 U.S. 339 (1960)]. There is no reason that they couldn't have made precisely the same argument in Brown: that we don't care that segregated schools may be better, that the black kids may even get a better education or come out of it with greater opportunities; it doesn't make any difference. Because we can't have black schools and white schools and green schools and yellow schools in the United States. It's incompatible with the Constitution to have distinctions, imposed by government, that are drawn on the basis of race or color. That was our argument in the United States brief. The blacks were the ones who were most affected by it, yet their lawyers felt they had to prove that segregated schools were inferior. In my book the NAACP arguments, indeed, their whole strategy, was unwise; yet in the end, thanks to God and luck, they won.

After Brown was decided in 1954 and the Court set down the case for further argument on the issue of relief, Frankfurter wrote me from his summer place in Charlemont, Massachusetts on July 21, 1954:

Every reasonable effort to keep the litigation that remains out of politics is indispensable. The forethoughtful endeavor to prevent such entanglements has brought us where we are. And I don't mind telling you that this was mainly due to the clear thinking, skillful maneuvering, and disinterested persistence of Jackson J. and FF. I shudder to think the disaster we would have suffered—the country, that is—if the "libertarians", the heir of Jefferson [Black] and the heir of Brandeis [Douglas] had had their way! Nor are some of us resting on our oars in regard to the task ahead.

Q: Did you try and coordinate the government brief in Brown with other briefs? Or was that not appropriate?

Elman: No, not at all, no coordination of any sort with anyone.

I've been telling you about the Department of Justice and about the oral arguments, but I've left out the one thing that made all the difference, the thing that made everything possible. . . .

Elman: A few weeks after the Rosenberg case, the word came that Vinson had died, very suddenly. Frankfurter was then in New England where he spent the summer. The Justices all came back to Washington to attend the funeral services. I met Frankfurter, I think at Union Station, and he was in high spirits. I shouldn't really report all this, but this is history and as he used to say, history has its claims. Frankfurter said to me, "I'm in mourning," sarcastically. What he meant was that Vinson's departure from the Court was going to remove the roadblock in Brown. As long as Vinson was Chief Justice, they could never get unanimity or anything close to it. If Vinson dissented, Reed would surely join him, Tom Clark probably would too, and Jackson would write that the issue should be left to Congress. Anyway, Frankfurter happily said to me, "I'm in mourning." And, with that viselike grip of his, he grabbed me by the arm and looking me straight in the eye said, "Phil, this is the first solid piece of evidence I've ever had that there really is a God."

Q: That's a piece of bittersweet agnosticism.

Elman: He was right. Without God, we never would have had Brown, a unanimous decision that racial segregation is unconstitutional. Without God, the Court would have remained bitterly divided, fragmented, unable to decide the issue forthrightly. The winning formula was God plus "all deliberate speed." God won Brown v. Board of Education, not Thurgood Marshall or any other lawyer or any other mortal. God intervened. God takes care of drunks, little children, and the American people. He took care of the American people and little children and Brown by taking Fred Vinson when He did.

Vinson was replaced by Warren. Warren had no problems with Brown. There was now a clear majority because, thanks to "all deliberate speed," the Court could separate the constitutional decision on the merits from what to do about it, the remedy. Jackson could go along with the simple proposition that racial segregation violates the fourteenth amendment and Plessy should be overruled. He could go along with that on May 17, 1954, because he thought he would have an opportunity the following year to say, "Well, we've rendered our decision. We've told the Congress what the fourteenth amendment means. Now Congress ought to enforce it."

Q: Jackson's attitude was very cautious. Did you and Frankfurter agree with him?

Elman: I remember arguing with Frankfurter. He was very sympathetic to Jackson. Frankfurter felt, for reasons going beyond the segregation cases, that Congress ought to exercise its section five power to enforce the fourteenth amendment, as it later did in the Civil Rights Act of 1964, long after he had moved out of the picture. So he was very sympathetic to the Jackson position.

I used to say to him, "Now look, the fourteenth amendment has been on the books since 1868, and its legislative history shows that it was adopted to remove doubts about the constitutionality of the Civil Rights Act of 1866, which had given black freedmen all the rights of white men in dealing with property and everything else. The blacks were the group for whom the amendment was written; it was intended for their protection. And since 1868, everybody else has come to the Court invoking the protection of the fourteenth amendment. Corporations and Chinese and aliens and everybody else come in and claim they've been denied equal protection of the laws. They come to the Supreme Court of the United States, and you listen to them. And if you find that their rights have been violated, you take care of them. But when the one group for whose protection the fourteenth amendment was adopted, the blacks, comes in and asks you for relief, Jackson wants you to say, 'Yes, your constitutional rights have been violated. But don't come to us. You go across the street and ask Congress to give you relief; we're not going to give you a damn thing. All we're going to do is tell you that your rights have been violated.' How can you do that?''

So that was the trouble with Jackson's position, I think. And Frankfurter was torn. Anyway, Jackson never had a chance to express it, because he died. He came out of the hospital to sit on the bench on May 17th, because he wanted the whole world to see that the Court was unanimous. Of course, you know, Reed dissented until almost the very last day. Warren went to see him. Reed didn't write anything or note his dissent, but he never agreed with the decision.

Well, on May 17, 1954, after holding racial segregation in public schools to be unconstitutional, the Court set the cases down for further reargument on the question of the relief to be ordered. By this time, Simon Sobeloff was Solicitor General, and the third brief we filed was almost an anticlimax; it was essentially the same brief we had written twice before. The only thing interesting about the third brief, which was filed in November 1954 and signed by Brownell, Sobeloff, Rankin, me, and another lawyer named Alan Rosenthal, was the contribution made to it by the President of the United States. The page proofs were taken over to the White House by Judge Sobeloff. Eisenhower read them and wrote in some changes in longhand on pages seven and eight. I punctuated and put his language in more readable form. These are Eisenhower's sentences, edited by me. Where I wrote that the Court had outlawed a social institution that had existed for a long time in many areas throughout the country, he added this language (as cleaned up by me):

[Segregation is] an institution, it may be noted, which during its existence not only has had the sanction of decisions of this Court but has been fervently supported by great numbers of people as justifiable on legal and moral grounds. The Court's holding in the present cases that segregation is a denial of constitutional rights involved an express recognition of the importance of psychological and emotional factors; the impact of segregation upon children, the Court found, can so affect their entire lives as to preclude their full enjoyment of constitutional rights. In similar fashion, psychological and emotional factors are involved—and must be met with understanding and good will—in the alterations that must now take place in order to bring about compliance with the Court's decision.

As I look at it now, thirty years later, I'm astonished at the liberties that I, a young lawyer in the Solicitor General's office, felt free to take with the language of the President of the United States, which he wasn't going to have an opportunity to change, because it went from me to the printer. It shows the degree of what seems to me now astonishing self-confidence, or even arrogance, I had at that time. Anyway, it was the first and only instance I know of in which the President of the United States was coauthor of a brief in the Supreme Court. I think the point he made was a valid one. I wish I had thought of it first.

Well, what the Court did was write a second opinion saying that in view of all the difficulties they would leave it to the district courts to decide how quickly compliance with the Court's decision should be carried out.

Warren's opinion used the phrase "with all deliberate speed." Scholars were paid by the NAACP to try to find out where "with all deliberate speed" had come from. Everybody knew it was Holmes, but the question was, where had Holmes gotten it? In the case in which he had used the phrase he had modified it by saying, "in the language of the English Chancery." Holmes apparently had thought that he was using an equity expression familiar to English lawyers. But when inquiry was made, it turned out that English lawyers and judges had never heard of it. So the NAACP retained legal historians in England to find out where Holmes had gotten it. They went through old case books and treatises. They couldn't find it anywhere in the British legal literature. The accepted view now is that Holmes, who read poetry, had forgotten where he had read it. It appears in Francis Thompson's The Hound of Heaven, in which he speaks of "[d]eliberate speed, majestic instancy." So Holmes got it from Francis Thompson, Frankfurter got it from Holmes, Warren got it from Frankfurter, and that's how it got into Brown II.

Q: You talked about ongoing private conversations with Frankfurter about pending civil rights cases in which you were involved as a lawyer for the government. How do you respond to what I guess might be considered post-Watergate morality—or something of that nature—that could suggest that in a sense, Frankfurter was receiving a government brief all along, from you, to which Davis never had a chance to reply?

Elman: Yes, I suppose there's a point there. I have no easy, snappy response to that. In Brown I didn't consider myself a lawyer for a litigant. I considered it a cause that transcended ordinary notions about propriety in a litigation. This was not a litigation in the usual sense. The constitutional issue went to the heart of what kind of country we are, what kind of Constitution and Supreme Court we have: whether, almost a century after the fourteenth amendment was adopted, the Court could find the wisdom and courage to hold that the amendment meant what it said, that black people could no longer be singled out and treated differently because of their color, that in everything it did, government had to be color-blind. I don't defend my discussions with Frankfurter; I just did what I thought was right, and I'm sure he didn't give it much thought. I regarded myself, in the literal sense, as an amicus curiae.

The personal relationship that existed between Justice Frankfurter and me was very close. I was his law clerk emeritus, and he regarded me as his law clerk no matter where I was and what I did. That continued to be the case until the day he died. Here is a little note he wrote me on February 1, 1959, after I congratulated him on his twentieth anniversary on the Court:

Dear Phil: You have sent me gayly and encouragingly off for the next course—whatever its distance. For the period I have completed you have been, almost for the whole of it, my sympathetic companion and that rarest of collaborators—a stimulating and constructive critic. Continue that role. Gratefully, FF.

I don't know whether I mentioned this to you, but over the years—I'm talking now not just about the two years that I was at the Court but about the entire length of our relationship from 1941 to 1965 when he died—the Justice and I would talk on the phone a good deal. He would call me almost every Sunday night at home. He would have gone through the Sunday papers, and after dinner he liked to talk, or shmoos, as he would say. We'd have a long, relaxed, gossipy conversation for an hour and a half sometimes. And he had code names for other Justices.

Q: Give us the code.

Elman: Well, for example, Douglas was Yak or Yakima, because he came from Yakima, Washington. Hugo Black was Lafayette, his middle name. Stone was Vermont. Hughes was Whiskers. Minton was Shay. Stanley Reed was the Chamer, which means fool, or dolt, or mule in Hebrew; now that might be very difficult for somebody to decipher. The others wouldn't have been. Murphy was the Saint. Roberts was the Squire. He was the country Squire. Jackson was Jamestown, the town in upstate New York that Jackson came from. Francis Biddle, the Attorney General, was Frawn-cis. They were all pretty transparent.

Q: Did you ever say, "I don't want to know this, I'm not supposed to know it?"

Elman: Well, there were certain unspoken restrictions. We never discussed a case that I had argued. Never, other than his calling up my wife afterward and telling her how good or how funny I was or what a great answer I had given to so and so. Brown v. Board of Education, which we fully discussed, was an extraordinary case, and the ordinary rules didn't apply. In that case I knew everything, or at least he gave me the impression that I knew everything, that was going on at the Court. He told me about what was said in conference and who said it.

As I look back now, I can see myself in Brown v. Board of Education as having been his junior partner, or law clerk emeritus, in helping him work out the best solution for the toughest problem to come before the Court in this century. He succeeded in the end—but it was nip and tuck—and I would like to think that I contributed an important assist.

I'll be immodest. In a letter to McGeorge Bundy dated May 15, 1964, Justice Frankfurter wrote:

Everyone who is cognizant of the course of litigation which ended in the Supreme Court decision on discrimination in public schools knows that Phil Elman was the real strategist of the litigation.... [H]e was largely responsible for blocking the leaders of the colored people who proposed a remedy which not only would not have succeeded with the Court but, what is even worse, would have had disastrous consequences to the National interest.... It was Phil who proposed what the Supreme Court finally decreed, namely, that the Court should not become a school board for the whole country, that the question of how non-discrimination should be brought about should be left primarily to the local school boards, and that any dissatisfaction with their plans should go to the local federal courts.

Q: Let me ask you about the civil rights cases other than the housing and school cases. Were you just as much of an outside advocate in those?

Elman: Why don't I tell you now about Naim v. Naim. . . .

QUESTIONS

1.   What was the constitutional issue in *Brown*? Did the political feasibility of a remedy influence the Court's approach to the constitutional issue? Should it have?

2.   Justice Jackson complained that "Congress has abdicated, leaving enforcement of the fourteenth amendment entirely to us, and I don't think that's right ... Let Congress deal with the problem; it's too difficult for judges." In what ways could the Justices' approach to their own professional responsibilities have been affected by the fact that Congress was abdicating its responsibility to enforce the fourteenth amendment?

3.   Frankfurter revealed to Elman that he delayed overturning *Plessy* because "he did not want a decision to go out with nine or six or four opinions. He wanted the Court to stand before the country on [desegregating public schools] united and speaking in a single voice." Frankfurter was "buying time ... waiting for public opinion to form." Should a court, particularly the Supreme Court of the United States, take political considerations and public opinion into account in rendering its decisions? Would it have been unrealistic to expect the Court to ignore political considerations in this case?

4.   Philip Perlman, the Solicitor General, also sought to delay overruling *Plessy* by refusing to sign briefs in school desegregation cases: "You can't have little black boys sitting next to little white girls. The country isn't ready for that." Paradoxically, Perlman previously supported desegregation in "[t]rains, dining cars, law schools, [and] graduate schools." Was Perlman abdicating his professional responsibility as Solicitor General to uphold the laws of the United States? Does the Administration's selective enforcement of civil rights law raise the same issues as the Nixon Administration's selective enforcement of antitrust law in the ITT case (see Chapter 3)? When should the Justice Department take political considerations into account in deciding when and how to litigate?

5.   A government brief in the first *Brown v. Board* case in 1952 was signed by the new Attorney General, James P. McGranery. The brief was not signed by the Solicitor General, the Justice Department's chief litigator before the Supreme Court. Do you agree with James Browning's decision to go ahead and file the brief without consulting the Solicitor General? What are the risks of going over the head of an important government official in this manner?

6.   Elman suggested in the government's amicus brief that the Court "should give district courts a reasonable period of time to work out the details and timing of implementation of the decision." Elman was "proud" of the proposal despite it being, in his own words, "entirely unprincipled

[and] just plain wrong as a matter of constitutional law." Elman freely acknowledges that "the Supreme Court had held again and again ... that if an individual's constitutional rights are being violated, he is entitled to immediate relief" and that the position in the brief was "simply indefensible." Was Elman acting unprofessionally if, at the time he filed the brief, he believed the position advocated therein was "indefensible" and he did not acknowledge in the brief that his argument was contrary to existing law? (See discussion of F.R.C.P. Rule 11 in Chapter 9.) Does the fact that the Court actually adopted this "indefensible" position in *Brown* suggest that lawyers should not be discouraged from making arguments contrary to existing law?

7. Did the circumstances here give *Brown* some of the qualities of a legislative proceeding once it was clear that the separate but equal doctrine in *Plessy* had to go? In what ways was the case still a judicial proceeding?

8. Why do we allow lawyers and lobbyists to make ex parte contacts with legislators but not with judges?

9. Was Elman essentially giving the Court "a government brief all along ... to which Davis never had a chance to reply?" Did Linda Brown have a chance to reply? How were her rights affected by Elman's "with all deliberate speed" formula?

10. Elman, who was Justice Frankfurter's law clerk in the 1941 and 1942 terms, continued to have access to the Supreme Court through Frankfurter well into the 1950s. Was Elman misusing their friendship?

11. When challenged by the interviewer, Norman Silber, Elman justified his ex-parte contacts with Frankfurter:

> I considered [*Brown*] a cause that transcended ordinary notions about propriety in a litigation ... The personal relationship that existed between Justice Frankfurter and me was very close. I was his law clerk emeritus, and he regarded me as his law clerk no matter where I was and what I did. That continued to be the case until the day he died ...

The ease with which Elman excused himself and Justice Frankfurter from "the ordinary rules" was somewhat incongruent with their reference to the other Justices by code names, often employed by actors who have something to hide. Would they have wanted the other Justices to know what they were discussing at the time? Why?

12. In *Brown*, Elman and Frankfurter "count[ed] the votes on the Court ... in order to bring all the Justices together." Elman justified this collaboration between them by indicating that Justice Frankfurter "didn't regard [Elman] as a lawyer for any party; [he] was still his law clerk." In a later part of the interview, Elman said that he "was not a lawyer for a litigant but a lawyer for the public interest in its broadest sense, that [he] was not just a lawyer in the Department of Justice but that [he] continued to be Justice Frankfurter's law clerk for life." Elman's view of his own role in this case appears similar to Louis Brandeis's view of himself as "lawyer for the situation" rather than for a specific client (*see* question 3 following the *Brief in Opposition* in Chapter 6 *supra*). What are the pitfalls to this approach? Do Elman's actions, and his disclosure years after Justice Frankfurter's death of having circumvented "the ordinary rules," suggest that both at the time *Brown* was decided and later Elman believed himself to be responsible for orchestrating a successful resolution to this difficult problem? Was he a lawyer for his own ego as much as for the public interest?

13. When *Brown* returned to the Court in 1953, Elman submitted a second brief from the Solicitor General's Office in which a statement in the first brief that *Plessy* was "erroneous and should be overruled" was "not in the final draft [of the second brief] as it went to the [Eisenhower] White House." However, Elman entitled the brief *Supplemental Brief for the United States on Reargument*, clearly telling the Court that the Truman Administration's "1952 brief [characterizing *Plessy* as 'erroneous'] still stood." Elman almost enjoyed making the observation that "the folks in the White House didn't realize its significance." While reading the brief, President Eisenhower wrote in some changes, which Elman then edited without further presidential review. Upon reflection, Elman was "astonished at the liberties that [he], a young lawyer in the Solicitor General's office, felt free to take with the language of the President of the United States." How was Elman's handling of the White House in this politically sensitive case similar to Attorney General Kleindienst's handling of the President's orders in the ITT case? Did Elman and his colleagues in the Solicitor General's office overstep their bounds in their dealings with the President?

14. Professor Jeffrey Stempel maintains that "Justice Frankfurter was, in essence, informing Elman ... of the positions of the Justices regarding segregation, and advising Elman as to how best involve the Government in the litigation...." Jeffrey W. Stempel, Rehnquist, Recusal and Reform, 53 Bklyn.L.Rev. 589, 624 (1987). Stempel characterizes Elman's defense of the collusion as "unpersuasive" and recognizes the ends as "laudable," but not the "ex parte contacts." Id. at 625. Elman and Frankfurter "violated the ideal of impartiality, ... attempted to shape Court decisions through means other than debate among Justices upon the case record [and] revealed deliberative confidences of other Justices." Id. Stempel warns that "[w]ere Justice Frankfurter's conduct widely imitated, the Court would lose much of its moral authority to render binding decisions." Id.

Joseph Rauh, who had been a law clerk to Frankfurter in the 1930's, states that "[a]lthough one must assume [the contact] was indiscreet and wrong, it was without venality and possibly inescapable in light of the nature of the relationship between the two men." Joseph L. Rauh, Jr., Historical Perspectives: An Unabashed Liberal Looks at a Half–Century of the Supreme Court, 69 N.C.L.Rev. 213, 230 (1990). Rauh, like Elman, justifies the means with the ends: the unanimous decision in *Brown* "was one of the greatest moments in the nation's constitutional history and lots of people contributed to it [including] the Frankfurter–Elman connection." Id. With which of these two commentators do you agree?

15. Elman says that John W. Davis, whom he describes as "the great advocate and dean of the American bar," "poured ridicule on the black lawyers, [who] did not have the courage and the good sense to stand up there and say ... [that, whether or not segregated schools are better or worse, they are unconstitutional]." Elman prides himself on his role in achieving racial equality, yet goes out of his way to emphasize Davis's superiority over the black lawyers, one of whom later became an Associate Justice of the Supreme Court. Does Elman's extremely critical view of the NAACP's strategy underscore the value of his own contribution to *Brown,* or reveal the type of arrogance that Derrick Bell attributes to civil rights lawyers from outside the affected communities (see Chapter 6 supra)?

Relevant Background

Ex Parte Contact With Judges

Ex parte contact is contact "done for, in behalf of, or on the application of, one party only." Black's Law Dictionary 576 (6th ed. 1990). The principal problem with ex parte contact is that it may lead a judge to consider communications from one party without giving the other party a chance to respond, and thus, "give the appearance of granting undue advantage to one party [over another]." Model Code of Professional Responsibility EC 7–35 (1980).

A lawyer is generally prohibited from communicating ex parte with a judge about the merits of a case. Model Code DR 7–110 provides:

"(B) In an adversary proceeding, a lawyer shall not communicate, or cause another to communicate, as to the merits of the cause with a judge or an official before whom the proceeding is pending, except:

(1) In the course of official proceedings in the cause.

(2) In writing if he promptly delivers a copy of the writing to opposing counsel or to the adverse party if he is not represented by a lawyer.

(3) Orally upon adequate notice to opposing counsel or to the adverse party if he is not represented by a lawyer."

Model Rule 3.5 provides:

"A lawyer shall not:

(a) seek to influence a judge, juror, prospective juror or other official by means prohibited by law;

(b) communicate ex parte with such a person except as permitted by law...."

Where an *ex parte* proceeding is permitted by law, Model Rule 3.3(d) requires a lawyer to affirmatively disclose material facts that will enable the tribunal to make an informed decision, whether or not those facts help the lawyer's case.

Concerning a judge's handling of an ex parte communication, the Model Code of Judicial Conduct Canon 3 provides:

"B(7) ... A judge shall not initiate, permit, or consider ex parte communications, or consider other communications made to the judge outside the presence of the parties concerning a pending or impending proceeding except that:

(a) Where circumstances require, ex parte communications for scheduling, administrative purposes or emergencies that do not deal with substantive matters or issues on the merits are authorized; provided:

(i) the judge reasonably believes that no party will gain a procedural or tactical advantage as a result of the ex parte communication, and

(ii) the judge makes provision promptly to notify all other parties of the substance of the ex parte communication and allows an opportunity to respond.

. . . .

(d) A judge may, with the consent of the parties, confer separately with the parties and their lawyers in an effort to mediate or settle matters pending before the judge.

(e) A judge may initiate or consider any ex parte communications when expressly authorized by law to do so."

See In re Bell, 294 Or. 202, 655 P.2d 569 (1982) (lawyer suspended for thirty days for procuring a judge's signature on a decree still in dispute by the parties in the absence of opposing counsel). As Philip Elman and Justice Frankfurter both should have known, a lawyer need not represent a party in a dispute to be prohibited from making *ex parte* communications with the court. See Florida Bar v. Mason, 334 So.2d 1 (Fla.1976) (lawyer who submitted an amicus brief to the Florida Supreme Court suspended for one year for making ex-parte contacts with the justices of the Court, including discussing the case with one justice during a golf game and sending a note to another justice detailing the issues in the case).

B. EX-PARTE CONTACT WITH ADMINISTRATIVE TRIBUNALS

Robert B. Choate, b. 1898, d. 1963; attended Harvard College 1917–19; managing editor of the Boston Herald from 1928–40; named publisher and general manager of the Boston Herald in 1941; Chairman of Boston Herald–Traveler Corporation and president of television and radio station WHDH; elected president of the Boston Herald–Traveler Corporation in 1960; member of the Pulitzer Prize Committee and the board of directors of the Associated Press.

Leverett Saltonstall, b. Chestnut Hill, Massachusetts 1892, d. 1979; B.A. Harvard University 1914, J.D. Harvard University 1918; admitted to the Massachusetts state bar in 1919; assistant district attorney of Middlesex County 1921–22; member of the Massachusetts House of Representatives

1923–36 (speaker 1929–36); Governor of Massachusetts 1939–45; United States Senator from Massachusetts 1945–67; Republican whip 1949–57.

John F. Kennedy, b. Brookline, Massachusetts 1917, d. 1963; B.S. Harvard University 1940; author of Why England Slept (1940) and Profiles in Courage (1956–awarded Pulitzer prize 1957); served three terms in the House of Representatives from 1947–53; United States Senator from Massachusetts 1953–60 (although a Democrat, Kennedy gave only token support to Saltonstall's opponent in the 1954 and 1960 elections); President of the United States 1961–63 (first Roman Catholic elected to the presidency); assassinated in November 1963.

George C. McConnaughey, b. Hillsboro, Ohio 1896, d. 1966; B.A. Denison University 1918; LL.B. Case Western Reserve University 1923; admitted to the bar in Ohio 1924; private practice 1924–26; assistant director of law, City of Cleveland 1926–28; practice of corporate law in Cleveland 1928–39; Chairman, Ohio Public Utilities Commission 1939–45; Chairman, Renegotiation Board 1953–54; Chairman, FCC 1954–57; member of Laylin, McConnaughey & Stradley in Columbus, Ohio 1958–66.

Hearing Examiner's Report and Decision of the Commission in the Matter of WHDH

20 FR 397 (FCC) (1960).

Extract from the Initial Decision of Hearing Examiner Horace Stern

Issue 2—Did any person or persons influence or attempt to influence any member of the Commission with respect to the proceedings resulting in the award of the construction permit for Channel 5, Boston, in any manner whatsoever except by the recognized and public processes of adjudication?

A. First as to the Boston Herald–Traveler Corporation, sole owner of WHDH, Inc., the successful applicant for the permit.

Robert B. Choate,—director and vice-president of the Boston Herald–Traveler Corporation, publisher and editor of the Boston Herald and Traveler newspapers, and president of WHDH,—had two lunch meetings with Chairman McConnaughey, although the latter remembers only one of them. In view of the lapse of time since they took place and the informal nature of the conversation that would ordinarily characterize such occasions it is no wonder that although all the participants impressed the Examiner as being entirely honest and sincere in their desire to recall exactly what was said, they vary to some extent in their recollections, especially as to minor details.

Accordingly to Choate the first luncheon was with McConnaughey and Charles F. Mills, a mutual friend, at either the Raleigh or Willard Hotel in late 1954 or early 1955. Choate identified himself as an applicant for a permit but it was purely a social affair and there was no discussion whatever of the Channel 5 case. The second luncheon meeting was in the public room of the Statler Hotel at either the end of March or the early part of April, 1956, at which there were also present Mills and Thomas M. Joyce, who was a lawyer for the Herald–Traveler Corporation but was not there in that capacity. Choate had sought this meeting in order to show McConnaughey the draft of a proposed "Dempsey Amendment" to the Communications Act (hereinafter explained), together with a supporting memorandum, and in that same connection to talk to him about the testimony which he, McConnaughey, had given on the subject involved before a Subcommittee of the House Committee on Interstate and Foreign Commerce. However, at the very first suggestion of this purpose he was stopped by McConnaughey, the draft and memorandum were not shown, there followed only a general social conversation, and at no time was the Channel 5 case discussed in any manner.

According to Chairman McConnaughey he had only one luncheon meeting with Choate, probably in mid-March, 1956, at either the Statler or the Mayflower Hotel, and he did not remember anyone else being present. He confirmed Choate's statement that he would not allow him to talk about the then pending legislation. Nothing was said about the Channel 5 case "even indirectly;" he *presumed* that Choate wanted merely to "put his best foot forward" as "everybody" tries to do, to "make a good impression" as being "a capable, responsible person," *though he never said it "in so many words."*

Charles Mills' version was that Choate asked him to arrange a luncheon meeting with McConnaughey, who had just been appointed, because he would like to "size up"—form an impression of—this new head of the Commission. The conversation at the Raleigh Hotel was only of a general, social nature but, while he said he had only a poor recollection of what transpired at the luncheon, he believed that Choate asked how long such proceedings usually took and as to what the general procedure would be after the Examiner made a ruling. He did not recall Joyce being present at the second luncheon, which he also arranged and which he placed at sometime in 1956, nor did he recall any discussion in reference to legislation. He thought that Choate said there had been a ruling by the Examiner and he would be interested in knowing when it might be reviewed and what the subsequent procedure would be, and there was then some conversation about procedure. Neither Choate nor McConnaughey had any recollection of this, and Mills frankly stated that he was not interested in the conversation and did not pay close attention to it. Even if, however, such inquiries as to procedure were in fact made by Choate he could well say—as Othello to the signiors of Venice—

> "The very head and front of my offending
> Hath this extent, no more,"

for certainly by no stretch of the imagination could they be stigmatized as amounting to an attempt to influence McConnaughey with reference to his application.[3] What is of real importance is the statement of Mills—agreed to by all—that there was no discussion of the merits of the Channel 5 case.

---

3. There has never been thought to be any impropriety in ex parte conversations with a judge in reference merely to noncon- troversial questions of procedure. Judges are frequently so consulted as a matter of course.

From all of this testimony the Examiner finds the facts to have been that there were two luncheon meetings, Mills acting as the host on both occasions. That the first was in the winter of 1954–55. That the conversation was purely social and the Channel 5 case was not discussed in any manner whatsoever. That Choate may have inquired as to the usual length of time of such proceedings and the procedure following a ruling by the hearing examiner. That the second luncheon was in March or April, 1956. That it was held at Choate's request for the purpose of presenting to McConnaughey a draft of the "Dempsey Amendment" and explaining its proposed effect on the legislation then being considered by the House Subcommittee on Interstate and Foreign Commerce. That Joyce was present in a purely personal capacity. That again the Channel 5 case was not even remotely referred to. That Choate made no representations at either luncheon as to the caliber of his people, nor attempted in any way to "impress" McConnaughey. That any question concerning procedure was mentioned casually if at all. That there was no discussion of the legislation or of the Dempsey Amendment because Chairman McConnaughey refused to allow it, and that only general, social conservation was indulged in.[4] Since, however, Choate had had in mind to bring up the subject an explanation in regard to it is in order.

There then was, and for some time had been, considerable discussion in Congress, in the radio and television industry, in the press, in the Federal Communications Commission, and in the courts, as to whether, and to what extent, the question of diversification of ownership of media of mass communications should properly play a part in the consideration of comparative proceedings of the award of a radio or television license. [Choate, who was justified in wanting to know whether newspapers were barred from receiving permits for television stations and whether his case was therefore hopeless from the start, wrote to Senator Saltonstall asking if he could give the matter his attention and, if the Commission would consider applications of newspapers for the remaining open channels at least with impartiality, —in other words a statement as to its general policy. Saltonstall thereupon wrote to Chairman Hyde, calling attention to the Herald's interest and anxiety in the matter, but asking only that "all applicants be given a fair and equal opportunity," which he "was certain the Commission would do." Chairman Hyde promptly gave such an assurance, and furnished information to show that there was no predisposition of the Commission against newspaper applicants].... In the winter and early spring of 1956 hearings were had before a House Subcommittee of

---

4. The argument that McConnaughey should have made his lunches with Choate and Mills a matter of record and have notified the other parties in regard to them is, to say the least, wholly without merit in view of the fact that the luncheons did not involve any discussion of the Channel 5 case or even of the proposed general legislation on the subject of diversification. Judges are not required to record and to notify other parties in regard to any lunches or meetings they might have with a litigant or a lawyer in the case where no discussions took place there in reference to the case and only a social relation prevailed.

the Committee on Interstate and Foreign Commerce on the "Harris–Beamer" bills which provided that the Commission could not adopt any rule which would discriminate against applicants because of their interest in any medium primarily engaged in the gathering and dissemination of information, nor deny any application solely because of such interest. Naturally the entire newspaper industry was greatly in favor of the bills, and a representative of the American Newspaper Publishers Association testified in support of the proposed legislation. On the other hand Chairman McConnaughey voiced opposition to the bills on the ground that they were unnecessary because it was the Commission's policy to treat the question of diversification, not as controlling, but as only one of the many factors which it had to evaluate, and it never disqualified an applicant solely for the reason that it was engaged in the dissemination of news. McConnaughey also thought that some of the terms in the bills were vague and ambiguous.

Such, then, being the situation, the Herald–Traveler Corporation had its counsel, William J. Dempsey, prepare an amendment or substitute bill designed to cure the ambiguities to which Chairman McConnaughey referred in his testimony, but which also safeguarded the applicability of the antitrust laws. Senator Kennedy presented the amendment to the Subcommittee, and it was a draft of this amendment and a supporting memorandum that Choate had intended to show McConnaughey at their lunch meeting in order that, if he found it satisfactory and would therefore withdraw his opposition to the legislation, there would be a better chance of its enactment. However, as previously stated, McConnaughey refused even to look at the draft much less discuss it, and the bills themselves ultimately failed of passage.

In accordance with the views expressed by the present Hearing Examiner with respect to similar activities of North Dade Video, Inc. in the case of the Miami Channel 10 award, it is not thought that there was any impropriety in the efforts of the Herald–Traveler Corporation to obtain legislation by Congress that would definitely prevent the refusal of a permit for a radio or television station solely because of the applicant being engaged in the dissemination of news. There was no reason why it could not seek, in conjunction with the newspaper world generally, the legislative establishment of a public policy governing the subject of the control of media of mass communications. It was therefore well within its rights in having Senator Kennedy present the amendment to the Congressional Subcommittee in order to secure the desired legislation, and it was equally in order for Choate to interview Chairman McConnaughey for the same general purpose, which would not, of course, have been within the jurisdictional scope of the Commission in the Channel 5 proceedings but only for action by Congress. It must be borne in mind that Choate's intended appeal to McConnaughey was not to be directed to him as a Commissioner in the Channel 5 case, but only because he had appeared and testified before the Subcommittee in opposition to the enactment of the legislation, and it was solely in his role as a hostile witness there that Choate sought to remove his objections and have him approve the Dempsey Amendment, just as he could or might have done in the case of any other person who had similarly tried to block the legislation in question. . . .

From all of the testimony, therefore, the Examiner finds that neither at his luncheon meetings with Chairman McConnaughey nor on any other occasion did Choate make any culpable attempt to influence his vote in the Channel 5 proceedings nor did in fact exert any such influence. And while he may have had some casual social contacts, as at lunches, receptions, and the like, with other Commissioners and with men in public life generally, some of whom he knew intimately for many years, there is no evidence that he or any other representative of the Herald–Traveler Corporation ever asked or received from any of them any improper help in connection with the application of WHDH for the Channel 5 permit. Incidentally, it may not be amiss to remark that mere normal social relations with public officials are not taboo, for they, like other human beings, are not required to live in ivory towers,—subject always, of course, to the fundamental condition that there be no attempt on the part of a litigant or applicant for some judicial or quasi-judicial favor to take advantage of such acquaintanceships or intimacies by using them for the advancement of his cause. It is only marked attention and unusual hospitality on the part of a lawyer or litigant to a judge that is reprehensible: Canon 3 of Professional Ethics of the American Bar Association. In the present case there was no such excessive hospitality on the part of Choate; indeed, there was none at all, for both Choate and McConnaughey were the guests of Mills at both of the luncheons, which, incidentally, took place more than a year apart, and even the "return" courtesy of Choate's invitation to the others to a Gridiron Club dinner was ultimately declined by McConnaughey because of a previous engagement. Nor was there anything secretive or sinister merely in the holding of these brief luncheon meetings, the real question being, of course, the nature and content of the conversation which occurred there, and as to that it must once again be repeated, for it goes to the very heart of the present issues, that there is not a shred of credible evidence that there was any attempt there on the part of Choate to present the merits of the Herald application, the qualifications of the Herald organization, or anything in derogation of the other applicants,—in short, nothing that either in law or codes of professional or judicial ethics could justifiably be regarded as impairing the validity or propriety of the award which was subsequently made by the Commission.

B.   As to Massachusetts Bay Telecasters, Inc.

Forrester A. Clark—director and vice-president of Massachusetts Bay Telecasters,—either alone or together with another stockholder of the company, during the years 1954–1956 visited several persons in high public positions,—Henry Cabot Lodge, Sinclair Weeks, Robert Cutler, Senator Saltonstall, Leonard Hall, Representatives Bates and Curtis,—to tell them that there were rumors of political activity on the part of other applicants, to urge "neutrality" on their part, and to seek their advice. Another stockholder wrote in the same vein to Representatives Martin and Wigglesworth, and still another saw Max Rabb. None of the persons thus interviewed was asked to contact, or did contact, any of the Commissioners, nor did any of them interfere in the proceedings in any way. It is true that Clark gave Cutler a memorandum urging that a concentration of ownership of newspaper and television control should be avoided, and Cutler showed this memorandum to Sherman Adams, who, however, promptly called the Chairman of the Commission and notified him that he could rest on the assurance that there would be no interference whatever from the White House; the memorandum, therefore, never reached any of the Commissioners.

Claiming that the rumors continued, Clark, in February, 1956, had a lunch meeting with Chairman McConnaughey at the Mayflower Hotel. He revealed the position of the Massachusetts Bay Telecasters as an applicant for the permit but told McConnaughey that all they wanted was fair play according to the rules and that they themselves had no political affiliation of any kind. He denies that he tried to "show that they were responsible people" or that he "wanted to put his best foot forward," as McConnaughey, without further explanation, stated that he did, but he did call attention to some of the prominent members of his group in order to show, as he claimed, that it was not a politically partisan organization. McConnaughey testified that he would not let Clark enter upon any of the merits of the case, but did not think, in that connection, that what he said about the personnel of the Massachusetts Bay Telecasters was objectionable. Clark later wrote to McConnaughey urging him to read the Massachusetts Bay brief which had been filed in the proceedings; however he had previously suggested to him to read *all* the briefs.

Accepting Clark's testimony as true,—which the Hearing Examiner does,—it would thus seem that, while his activities were essentially directed toward making sure that no political or other improper influence could be successfully exerted by any of the other parties, he may have stepped somewhat out of bounds in the presentation he made to McConnaughey of the merits of his associates.

WHDH, Inc., et al.

Decision

(Adopted July 14, 1960).

By the Commission: Commissioner Craven absent.

PRELIMINARY STATEMENT

1. On April 25, 1957, the Commission released a decision (22 FCC 761) resolving a comparative hearing for a new television station on channel 5, Boston, Mass., in favor of WHDH, Inc., and denying the competing applications of Greater Boston Television Corp.; Massachusetts Bay Telecasters, Inc.; and Allen B. DuMont Laboratories, Inc. Appeals to the U.S. Court of Appeals for the District of Columbia Circuit were filed by Greater Boston and Massachusetts Bay, and on July 31, 1958, that court

released its decision affirming the Commission on the basis of the record on which the Commission had decided the case, but remanding for inquiry into factors not in the original record.

2. The court noted that, subsequent to the Commission's disposition of the proceeding, testimony by a member of the Commission before the House Subcommittee on Legislative Oversight indicated that various individuals connected with some of the parties to the proceeding had conferred with him with reference to the case while the matter was still under consideration by the Commission. In light of this testimony the court remanded the case to the Commission with direction to make findings of fact on the following issues:

> Whether or not any member of the Commission should have disqualified himself in the present case;

> Whether any person or persons influenced or attempted to influence any member of the Commission in any manner whatsoever except by the recognized and public process of adjudication * * *, and, if so the full facts and circumstances;

> Whether any party to the proceeding before the Commission directly or indirectly secured, aided, confirmed or ratified, or knew of any misconduct which may be found by the Commission to have occurred;

> Whether or not in the light of such findings, the grant of a permit for channel 5, Boston was void ab initio, and if not, is voidable and action should be taken to set it aside, and whether any one applicant or more than one may have been disqualified to receive a grant of its application; and

> Whether the conduct of any applicant, if not of a disqualifying character, has been such as to reflect adversely upon such applicant from a comparative standpoint.

3. The court indicated that the Commission's findings and conclusions on the specified issues should form the basis of a "report" which would "supplement the record upon which [the] appeal had so far been based." However, the court observed that "it is to be understood that it is for the Commission initially to determine, subject to review in usual course, the competence of its individual members to have participated in the award, but with appropriate findings with respect to the ultimate conclusions. We deem it the Commission's proper duty and function to determine the basic qualifications of each of the four named parties...."

. . . .

FINDINGS OF FACT

WHDH

5. Originally this proceeding involved a comparison of the applications of WHDH, Inc.; Greater Boston Television Corp.; Massachusetts Bay Telecasters, Inc.; Allen B. DuMont Laboratories, Inc.; Columbia Broadcast-

ing System; and Post Publishing Co. In the spring of 1954, shortly before the consolidation of the applications for hearing, Senator Saltonstall, at the behest of Robert B. Choate, director and vice president of the Boston Herald–Traveler Corp., publisher and editor of the Boston Herald and Traveler newspapers and president of WHDH, Inc., wrote to the Chairman of the Commission stating that the Herald Traveler was concerned with the Commission's diversification policy as it applied to newspapers, and asked that "all applicants be given a fair and equal opportunity." In the letter no preference for any of the applicants was urged.

6. On October 4, 1954, George C. McConnaughey commenced his service as Chairman of the Commission. The evidence in this proceeding is concerned in large part with certain conversations held with Mr. McConnaughey by officers of two of the applicant corporations. The examiner noted, as do we, certain minor discrepancies in the testimony of the witnesses as to details of the events which transpired. He, having an opportunity to observe the demeanor of the witnesses and to evaluate their testimony in the light of his wide judicial experience, expressed the view that all of them were "entirely honest and sincere," and reconciled their testimony into his findings of fact. Our examination of the cold record furnishes no case to disturb the examiner's basic findings as to the honesty of the witnesses, and we attribute such discrepancies as appear to confusion as to the meaning of questions; to legitimate failure of exact recollection; or to improper phraseology in spontaneous answers. However, as hereinafter noted, while we accept the honesty of the testimony so far as it went, we do not believe that all the witnesses disclosed fully their actions and motives.

7. In late 1954 or early 1955, Mr. Charles F. Mills, a friend of Choate who had previously served with McConnaughey on the Renegotiation Board, arranged a luncheon meeting for himself, Choate, and McConnaughey, who had not theretofore met.... [describes the first lunch]

8. In March or April of 1956, a second luncheon took place attended by McConnaughey, Choate, Mills, and Thomas M. Joyce, a lawyer for the Herald–Traveler Corp. who did not, however, attend the luncheon in that capacity.... [describes the second lunch]

9. The only other encounters between Choate and McConnaughey have been at large social gatherings which both attended but not as members of the same party....

. . . .

Massachusetts Bay

10. During the years 1954–56, certain officers and stockholders of Massachusetts Bay, including Forrester A. Clark, director and vice-president, communicated with prominent political figures in Washington, to advise them that there were rumors of "political activity" on the part of other applicants and to urge their neutrality. However, none of the persons contacted were asked to or did approach any Commissioner with the exception of Sherman Adams, whose only act was to call the Chairman of

the Commission and advise him that there would be no interference whatever from the White House.

11.   In February of 1956, Clark arranged a luncheon meeting with McConnaughey whereat he told the Chairman that Massachusetts Bay had no political affiliation of any kind and was only seeking fair play under the rules governing comparative hearings....

Globe Newspaper Co.

14.   Globe Newspaper Co. was not an applicant in the channel 5 proceedings and its only interest therein was to prevent an award to WHDH, a subsidiary of its competitor in the newspaper publishing business in Boston. In pursuit of this objective, William Davis Taylor and John S. Taylor, president and vice president, respectively, went to Washington in December of 1956 and called on a number of prominent political figures....

15.   The Taylors then made calls on each of the Commissioners who, on being told by the Taylors that they were not applicants, listened briefly to their complaint. Chairman McConnaughey told them that they had no right to be heard and there was nothing they could do in the matter, and none of the Commissioners indicated how he had voted or intended to vote or expressed any opinion concerning the channel 5 case.

16.   On January 30, 1957, Globe filed a petition to intervene, and subsequently Greater Boston and Massachusetts Bay filed petitions to have the record reopened to permit the introduction of evidence in support of the allegations contained in Globe's petition to intervene. These allegations were to the effect that the Herald–Traveler Corp. had used its radio station to give it an unfair competitive advantage; that it proposed to operate the television station it sought in the same manner; that it had threatened to drive Globe out of business....

CONCLUSIONS

1.   The object of this proceeding is to determine whether the grant to WHDH is void or voidable and, if so, the status of the parties for the purpose of such further proceedings as may be appropriate.

2.   Patently, in determining whether the grant is void ab initio or voidable we are concerned only with the actions by or attributable to the grantee, for it would manifestly be improper to penalize an innocent grantee for the conduct of its competitors. If the evidence indicates that the grant was actually obtained by improper means, its very foundation would be destroyed and it would, in our view, be void ab initio. If, on the other hand, the evidence indicates that the grantee attempted to exert improper influence but that such attempt did not contribute to the award, the basic foundation of the grant would be unimpaired, but a question would be raised as to whether the integrity of the Commission's processes had not been jeopardized requiring the voiding of the grant. In the event that the foregoing tests reveal the grant to be void ab initio or voidable, a comparative reevaluation of the applicants would be required. If the record has

disclosed that any party attempted improperly to influence the Commission's decision, such a finding, at the very least, must reflect adversely on such party and on its qualifications as a licensee. The circumstances surrounding such attempt would determine whether the party was disqualified as an applicant or merely suffered a demerit in the overall comparative balance.

3. We turn first to the activities of Robert Choate of WHDH. The record indicates that Choate and McConnaughey were unacquainted in the fall of 1954, when Mr. McConnaughey was appointed to the Commission. Shortly thereafter Choate remedied that situation by arranging through a mutual friend to meet the new Chairman for lunch. While there was no attempt to discuss the merits of the Boston case then pending before the Commission's hearing examiner, Choate was identified as an applicant in Boston and there was some discussion of comparative proceedings in general. Subsequently, Choate attempted to profit by the acquaintance thus established by again meeting McConnaughey for lunch with a view toward presenting the Chairman with a brief on proposed legislation dealing with the subject matter of a key issue in the Boston case.

4. No other contacts were made on behalf of WHDH,[5] and on such evidence we do not hold the grant to be void ab initio. Mr. McConnaughey did not even recall the first meeting and he refused to accept or read the brief tendered by Choate at the second luncheon. Under such circumstances it would be unrealistic to conclude that he was influenced by Choate's contacts or that the grant was actually secured as a result of improper activities.

5. However, we do conclude that Choate demonstrated an attempted pattern of influence. He indicates that his reason for the initial meeting with McConnaughey was to "size up" the new Chairman but, accepting that as true as far as it goes, it does not appear to be a full disclosure of his motives. While the Herald–Traveler had a legitimate interest in the views of the new Chairman of the agency regulating its radio station and the television station it soon hoped to have, in the normal course of events its contacts with the Commission would be conducted through its professional representatives and its appraisal of the individual Commissioners would be formulated from the opinions of these gentlemen. The record contains no persuasive explanation of why Choate felt it necessary to seek a personal relationship with McConnaughey, and we conclude that his reason was to afford the Chairman an opportunity to "size him up;" that is, to demonstrate by his demeanor and presence that he was a responsible man representing responsible interests who merited favorable consideration of their application to conduct an operation in the public interest.

6. This view of Choate's motive in arranging the first luncheon is buttressed by the fact of the second luncheon and its admitted purpose of

---

5. We do not deem the sending of a routine letter by a Member of Congress without urging any favoritism on the Commission as being of sufficient materiality to warrant discussion in these conclusions.

providing an opportunity to present McConnaughey with a brief on the Dempsey amendment. While WHDH undoubtedly had a right to express its views to the Commission on communications legislation concerning it, its attempted method of presentation must be judged in the light of the circumstances then prevailing. It could not have escaped Choate's attention that the subject of the legislation was an important issue in the pending adjudicatory proceeding, nor could he have believed that McConnaughey might read such a brief without perceiving the pertinence of its arguments to the disposition of the Boston case. If he felt it necessary to present such a brief to the Commission at that time, he must be presumed to have been aware of the relevance of the brief to the pending case, and, if he wished to escape the stigma of ex parte representation, the presentation should have been in such form as would afford his opponents an opportunity to make such reply as they might deem appropriate. Further, there is no persuasive explanation of why Choate, who is not shown to be a specialist in communications law, should consider himself, rather than the draftsman of the proposed legislation or some other experienced counsel, to be the proper person to present a brief on so technical and complex a subject. That McConnaughey did not accept and, therefore, could not have been influenced by the brief is irrelevant to the fact that Choate attempted, in effect to influence the outcome of the case by presenting argument on a portion thereof to a member of the Commission ex parte.

7. The very attempt to establish such a pattern of influence does violence to the integrity of the Commission's processes. Such an attack on the integrity of the processes of any adjudicatory body brings into play its inherent right to protect such processes, and one of the remedial measures available is its discretion in the voiding of any previous action that may have been tainted by such attempt. The facts revealed on this record persuade us that the Commission's processes can best be protected in this instance by exercising our discretion to void the grant to WHDH.

8. It follows that we must now determine our ultimate disposition of the construction permit for channel 5 in Boston, and the role, if any, WHDH should play in such disposition. There is no question that the attempted pattern of influence disclosed on this record reflects adversely on WHDH, but we do not believe in light of all the circumstances that the public interest would be best served by the disqualification of that applicant. Mr. Choate is not guilty of offering any material inducement to influence the outcome of the proceeding or of actually arguing the merits of the case ex parte, but rather of attempting to establish a personal relationship with a member of the Commission with the hope of creating a favorable bias in that gentleman's mind which might be calculated to operate in favor of WHDH in the event of a close decision and of attempting to present to a member of the Commission ex parte a legal brief on a matter so intimately concerned with the then-pending hearing that he must have been aware of the applicability of the general problem discussed therein to the specific issue at stake in the Boston hearing. Such conduct, while reflecting adversely on WHDH and weakening its comparative posi-

tion vis-a-vis its competitors in the proceeding, does not demonstrate such a complete lack of character as to require absolute disqualification.

9. Our conclusions as to Massachusetts Bay are not unlike those with respect to WHDH, for we deem Clark's activities to be essentially similar to Choate's. We cannot lend full credence to his statement that he only sought to offset rumored "political activity" by other applicants, for, if he believed such rumors and believed that the Commission could actually be influenced by such activity, he could not seriously have believed that his mild protest at a social luncheon would have altered the course of events. We deem his mission to have been similar to Choate's; that is, to demonstrate the responsible nature of the individuals owning the applicant he represented. In his own case such demonstration was tacit by exposing McConnaughey to his personality, but he went even further by intruding into the conversation the names of stockholders who had achieved distinction and national prominence in their own fields. Such conduct does not dictate absolute disqualification, but it does reflect adversely on the applicant and, in a comparative evaluation, weakens that applicant relative to its opponents.

10. We have not discussed the activities of Globe because we do not deem them relevant to our decision. Globe was not an applicant nor did its representatives act in connivance with any applicant. That the Taylors succeeded in interviewing individual Commissioners and expressing their views cannot be held to require the vacating of the entire proceeding, for such a ruling would imply that any entity not party to a proceeding could influence such proceeding to its own ends by the simple device of communicating its views to individual Commissioners, who could never know in advance the purpose of a visit, and thereby force them to disqualify themselves....

11. The grant to WHDH being voided, we must make a new comparative evaluation of the applicants in order to determine the ultimate comparative effect of the adverse conclusions made on this record with respect to WHDH and Massachusetts Bay. Neither is disqualified, although each stands in a less advantageous position vis-a-vis its opponents, and it remains to be determined on the basis of a comparison of both the conventional criteria contained in the original record of this proceeding and the facts disclosed on the remanded record which applicant would best serve the public interest. We believe that our final decision should be postponed until we have the benefit of the parties' views through the media of briefs and oral argument....

Accordingly, *It is ordered*, that the Commission's decision of April 24, 1957, granting a construction permit on channel 5, Boston, Mass., to WHDH, Inc., *Is vacated*, and its grant *Is set aside* ...

QUESTIONS

1. Is the FCC proceeding here intended to resemble a judicial or a legislative proceeding? When should agency officials act like judges? When should they act like legislators?

2. Does the intervention by Senators Saltonstall and Kennedy encroach on the FCC's adjudicative function? Is there anything wrong with the Senators' actions?

3. What is the difference between Choate "presenting himself" and presenting his case? What type of person did he present himself to be?

4. What should a competitor do to offset improper political activity by a rival? Did Globe Newspapers handle the situation properly?

5. Should McConnaughey have gone to the lunches? Even if there was no ex-parte contact about the WHDH proceeding at the lunches, was there an appearance of impropriety?

6. Why did McConnaughey refuse to take the Dempsey amendment from Choate?

7. What measures did McConnaughey and the FCC take to prevent improper influence? Were those measures effective?

8. Should McConnaughey have disqualified himself once he attended the lunches?

9. Looking at the biographies of the various players in this episode, who were the real Washington "insiders?" Was it possible that McConnaughey, by openly meeting with powerful figures from the Boston media establishment, was trying to impress people with more influence in politics than he had?

10. What procedural rules govern an ex parte communication with a judge? What ethical rules? Are there any specific procedural or ethical rules governing the contacts made with the FCC in this case? Should there be?

Relevant Background

Lawyers come before administrative agencies to argue, lobby and even share their expertise with regulators. Administrative law is thus created through informal consultations by regulators with attorneys in the rulemaking context as much as through formal hearings in which diametrically opposing positions are argued before a tribunal. See George C. Hoffman, The Lawyer as Lobbyist, 1963 U. Ill. L.F. 16 (1963) (noting that lawyers are ordinarily more qualified than others to make suggestions concerning new legislation or regulation). Standards for lawyer conduct before administrative agencies are in some contexts similar to ethical standards for lobbyists and others seeking to influence the rulemaking process, but in other contexts similar to ethical standards for adversarial proceedings in a courtroom. See Harold L. Marquis, An Appraisal of Attorneys' Responsibilities Before Administrative Agencies, 26 Case W. Res. L. Rev. 285, 305–306 (1976). Furthermore, administrative agencies like courts can be subjected to improper influence. For example, Chairman McConnaughey had legitimate reasons for consulting with members of the communications bar in formulating the FCC's policy on media diversification and the FCC's response to the Dempsey Amendment in Congress, but he should have avoided discussing these issues, and probably should have avoided any ex parte contact, with media companies whose applications were pending before the FCC.

The more difficult aspects of attorney conduct before an agency generally are not addressed by statute, and in many cases, not even by administrative rules. See Marquis, supra at 306. However, Model Rule 3.9 does give some guidance: "A lawyer representing a client before a legislative or administrative tribunal in a nonadjudicative proceeding shall disclose that the appearance is in a representative capacity and shall conform to the provisions of rules 3.3(a) through (c) [candor toward the tribunal], 3.4(a) through (c) [prohibiting obstruction of access to and destruction of evidence, falsification of evidence and disobedience of the rules of a tribunal], and 3.5 [prohibiting attempts to unduly influence a tribunal, ex-parte contacts and disruptive conduct]." As the Comment to Model Rule 3.9 points out:

> "In representation before bodies such as legislatures, municipal councils, and executive and administrative agencies acting in a rule-making or policy-making capacity, lawyers present facts, formulate issues and advance argument in the matters under consideration. The decision-making body, like a court, should be able to rely on the integrity of the submissions made to it. A lawyer appearing before such a body should deal with the tribunal honestly and in conformity with applicable rules of procedure."

Model Rule 3.9 cmt.

In 1976, the Supreme Court of New Jersey suspended Harry L. Sears, a prominent attorney, from practice for three years for his participation in an effort by International Control Corporation (ICC), a corporation controlled by financier Robert Vesco, to influence an SEC investigation into various securities law violations. Sears approached Attorney General John Mitchell, told Mitchell "that Vesco intended to make a substantial contribution of an undetermined amount of money up to $500,000" to President Nixon's reelection campaign and asked Mitchell to arrange a meeting with SEC Chairman William Casey. "At the subsequent meeting Sears received personal assurances from [Casey] that ICC would be afforded an opportunity to respond to the findings of the SEC investigation and that Casey would personally review ICC allegations of SEC harassment." In the Matter of Harry L. Sears, 71 N.J. 175, 364 A.2d 777, 780–81 (N.J.1976). Sears was indicted by a grand jury investigating Mitchell and others and accepted an offer of transactional immunity in return for his testimony at a trial in which Mitchell was ultimately acquitted. Chairman Casey somehow managed to escape scrutiny. After New Jersey imposed its suspension, the United States District Court for the District of New Jersey also suspended Sears from practice before it for three years. District Judge Stern dissented, urging the Court to convene its own investigation and, if the results of that investigation were consonant with the findings of the New Jersey Ethics Committee, impose a penalty of disbarment. In the Matter of Harry L. Sears, 425 F.Supp. 1190, 1190–91 (D.N.J.1977).

In addition to state professional conduct rules, lawyers must also look to relevant federal and state statutes as well as the rules of the particular agency before which they are practicing. See 5 U.S.C.A. section 557(d)(1) (1996) (barring ex parte communications with hearing officers of federal administrative agencies); Note, Ex Parte Contacts Under the Constitution and Administrative Procedure Act, 80 Colum. L. Rev. 379 (1980) (analyzing due process and APA limitations on the freedom of agencies to entertain ex parte communications in the informal rulemaking context). Some agencies promulgate their own rules of professional conduct for lawyers practicing before them, while others require lawyers to comply with ABA rules. The Patent and Trademark Office (PTO), for example, may prescribe rules governing the "conduct of agents, attorneys, or other persons representing applicants," see 35 U.S.C.A. § 31 (1984), and has chosen to amend its rules governing practice before the PTO (which formerly only required attorneys appearing before the PTO to adhere to the ABA's Code of Professional Responsibility) to establish a PTO Code of Professional Responsibility. See 37 C.F.R. §§ 10.20–10.112 (1996).

The Lobbying Disclosure Act of 1995, 2 U.S.C.A. §§ 1601–1612 (Supp. 1996), requires registration of lobbyists and disclosure of lobbying activities to influence the federal government, including agencies under the executive branch. A "lobbyist" is any person employed by a client for lobbying activities that constitute 20 percent or more of the time engaged in services for that client. Id. § 1602. Some of the work a lawyer does, such as Armand D'Amato's lobbying for Unisys Corporation, see Chapter 1 supra, may exceed this 20 percent threshold and put the lawyer within this definition of "lobbyist." The Act requires semiannual disclosure by a lobbyist of the names of her clients, the lobbyist's contacts with Congress or federal agencies, the specific issues with respect to which the lobbyist is employed by each client, and a good faith estimate of all income received from each client. Id. § 1604.

Bribery of agency officials is clearly a criminal offense. See 18 U.S.C.A. § 201 (Supp.1996), Bribery of Public Officials and Witnesses.

QUESTIONS AND PROBLEMS

1. What do the Model Code's Disciplinary Rules and Ethical Considerations say about lawyer conduct before administrative agencies? Do the Model Code and the Model Rules provide clear guidance as to what type of behavior is unacceptable?

2. A public official is generally prohibited from receiving personal gifts over a certain amount from persons other than family members. If an official has legal problems arising out of his official duties, the government usually pays for representation, but an official confronted with high legal expenses on a personal matter must pay his own lawyer and cannot accept a gift of money or a donation of legal services in excess of the allowable amount. One solution to this problem is to set up a legal defense fund into which individuals may make donations not in excess of the specified maximum individual gift. See Editorial, The President's Legal Bills, Washington Post, December 26, 1994, at A28 (describing a legal defense fund established in June of 1994 to accept contributions of $1000 or less from individuals—but not from corporations, government employees, political action committees or lobbyists—to defray mounting legal expenses of President and Mrs. Clinton in a federal investigation of Arkansas land and banking transactions and a sexual harassment suit brought against the President by a former Arkansas state employee). Should lawyers contribute to such a fund if they represent clients before agencies that report to the President? In what other ways could such a fund create the appearance of impropriety? Are there any better solutions to the problem?

3.   You have a successful white collar criminal defense practice in Chicago and represent clients under investigation by the SEC for securities fraud. Your law school classmate Steve used to work for the SEC and is now an attorney practicing securities law in Washington, D.C. He tells you that he has friends at the SEC and that if you ever need to get an SEC investigation to come out the right way, all you need to do is retain him as co-counsel. What should you do? What do the Model Code and the Model Rules say about Steve's proposal?

C.   THE BIASED TRIBUNAL

Henry Chapin, a judge of the probate court in Worcester, Massachusetts, appointed his wife's brother **Edward C. Thayer** administrator of the estate of **Warren Hunt**, a deceased person. Judge Chapin's wife's father **Joseph Thayer** was a principal creditor of the estate.

Alvin Hall v. Edward C. Thayer
105 Mass. 219 (1870).

Appeal from a decree of the probate court dismissing a petition of Alvin Hall for the appointment of an administrator with the will annexed of the estate of Warren Hunt; submitted to the determination of the full court on these facts agreed:

"Warren Hunt, late of Douglas, died June 7, 1867, leaving a last will and testament, which was admitted to probate July 2, 1867, in the probate court for the county of Worcester, and a decree approving and allowing said will was entered, and letters testamentary were issued thereon to Francis W. Hunt, the executor named therein, who gave a probate bond in the ordinary form and took upon himself the execution of the trust. Said executor represented the estate insolvent, December 30, 1868; and on January 5, 1869, commissioners were appointed to receive and examine claims. On February 16, 1869, Francis W. Hunt resigned the trust, and was discharged therefrom by the judge of said court.

"On March 2, 1869, Edward C. Thayer and Fenner Batcheller were upon their own application appointed by said judge administrators with the will annexed of the estate of the deceased not already administered, and gave bonds for the discharge of the trust, and letters of administration were issued to them. At a meeting of the commissioners, Joseph Thayer, of Uxbridge, presented a claim against the estate for $3939.34, consisting of two promissory notes made by the deceased in his lifetime; and the same was allowed by the commissioners, who afterwards made their report into the court allowing it, and the report was accepted by said judge. The claim was held by Joseph Thayer at the decease of Warren Hunt; and he has ever since been, and is now, the holder thereof. The estate of the deceased is insufficient to pay his debts in full.

"Henry Chapin, Esquire, was during all said time, and is now, the judge of said court, and sat and acted as such judge in all said proceedings, signed said decree, issued and signed the letters testamentary and letters of administration, and approved the probate bonds, which run to him by name in the usual form of such bonds. During said time the judge was related to Joseph Thayer and to Edward C. Thayer, as follows: the wife of the judge was the daughter of Joseph Thayer and the sister of Edward C. Thayer, the latter being the son of Joseph Thayer.

"On October 8, 1869, the appellant, being a creditor of the deceased, signed and filed in said court the following paper: 'In the matter of the will of Warren Hunt, deceased. And now Alvin Hall, of Douglas, in the county of Worcester, comes and objects that Henry Chapin, Esquire, judge of probate and insolvency for said county, is disqualified from acting in said matter, for the following reasons, namely: 1. That Joseph Thayer, of Uxbridge, in said county, is a creditor of the estate of said Hunt, to the amount of four thousand dollars, and said Thayer is the father in law of the said judge. 2. That Edward C. Thayer, of said Uxbridge, claims to be the administrator with the will annexed of said estate, and is unlawfully acting as such, and is the brother in law of the said judge.'

"The appellant at the same time presented in said court a petition, dated October 5, 1869, 'that the will of Warren Hunt, late of Douglas, in said county, deceased, was duly proved and allowed on July 2, 1867, in said court, and Francis W. Hunt appointed executor thereof, and that said executor was removed from said office upon his own petition to said court, without having fully executed said will; that the petitioner is a creditor of the deceased; and that his claim is not disputed; wherefore your petitioner prays that Horace Leland, of Sutton, in said county, or some other suitable person, may be appointed administrator with the will annexed of the estate of the deceased not already administered.'

" 'On November 25, 1869, a decree dismissing this petition was entered in said court' by Charles Mattoon, Esquire, the judge of probate for the county of Franklin, acting in the place and at the request of the judge for the county of Worcester, at a probate court on that day held at Worcester, 'it appearing,' in the language of the decree, 'that the will of said deceased was duly proved and allowed on the second day of July, A.D. 1867, by said court, and that on the second day of March, A.D. 1869, Edward C. Thayer and Fenner Batcheller were duly appointed administrators with the will annexed of said estate, and gave bonds accordingly, and that said Thayer and Batcheller have not resigned nor been removed from said trust, but are still in the performance thereof; and all parties interested having been notified according to the order of the court, and objecting said Thayer and Batcheller thereto.'

"On December 17, 1869, Hall claimed an appeal in due form to this court from said decree, and gave due notice thereof in said probate office and filed therein his reasons of appeal, and gave due notice thereof to the said Edward C. Thayer and Fenner Batcheller, who appeared to oppose said petition." The reasons were as follows: "1. Because the facts set forth in said petition are true, and the prayer thereof ought to have been granted. 2. Because Edwin C. Thayer and Fenner Batcheller were never duly and legally appointed administrators with the will annexed of said estate, and never gave bond for the discharge of said trust; nor was any bond given by them duly approved, nor any letters of administration with the will annexed upon said estate legally issued and granted to them by any judge of probate having jurisdiction of said estate, and any such bond and letters of administration are illegal, void, of no force or validity."

G.   F. Hoar & T. L. Nelson, for the appellant.

P.   E. Aldrich, for the appellees.

CHAPMAN, C. J. The provision of art. 29 of our Declaration of Rights, that "it is the right of every citizen to be tried by judges as free, impartial and independent of the lot of humanity will admit," rests upon a principle so obviously just, and so necessary for the protection of the citizen against injustice, that no argument is necessary to sustain it, but it must be accepted as an elementary truth. The impartiality which it requires incapacitates one to act as a judge in a matter in which he has any pecuniary interest, or in which a near relative or connection is one of the parties. It applies to civil as well as criminal causes; and not only to judges of courts of common law and equity and probate, but to special tribunals, and to persons authorized on a special occasion to decide between parties in respect to their rights. It existed under the common law from the earliest times. Thus sheriffs by whom jurors were selected in England, and jurors, were subject to it, and it was held that consanguinity between the sheriff or juror and either of the parties, or affinity by marriage of either party himself with the cousin of the sheriff or a juror, or *converso*, were principal causes of challenge to the array or to the polls. Bac. Ab. Juries, E.

This court has had occasion to consider this constitutional provision in a variety of its aspects, and to state some of its limitations.

In *Williams* v. *Robinson*, 6 Cush. 333, the principle is stated in application to a police court; and where the judge had heard the plaintiff state the facts in a case and thereupon had a bias or prejudice in his favor, it was held that he properly declined to act in the case, and called in the special justice, on the ground that he could not properly take jurisdiction.

In *Sigourney* v. *Sibley*, 21 Pick. 101, it was held that, where a judge of probate had a claim against the estate of a deceased person, he had no jurisdiction as to the settlement of the estate, though he did not intend to enforce his demand. It was held that the amount of his claim was immaterial, till a statute was passed limiting the disqualification to cases where his claim exceeded one hundred dollars, exclusive of interest. Gen. Sts. *c.* 119, § 4. This is perhaps a reasonable limitation. If the judge is interested as a debtor to the estate, he is disqualified. *Gay* v. *Minot*, 3 Cush. 352. So if he is a creditor merely in his capacity of executor of another estate. *Bacon, appellant*, 7 Gray 391. But the interest must be legal or beneficiary, and not a mere general interest in the prosperity of the town he lives in. *Northampton v. Smith*, 11 Met. 390.

The principle applies to county commissioners, though they are not judicial officers. It was decided that the interest which an inhabitant of a town has in the laying out of a highway, which was partly through the town, did not disqualify him from acting as a commissioner in laying out the way; nor the fact that his brother was one of the signers of a petition for laying out the way. *Wilbraham* v. *County Commissioners*, 11 Pick 322. But yet long after this decision was made, the legislature passed an act, which is still in force, disqualifying a commissioner from acting in respect to a road, if any part of it lies within the town where he resides. Gen. Sts. *c.* 17, § 12. *Tolland* v. *County Commissioners*, 13 Gray 12.

The principle applies to a juror. *Davis* v. *Allen*, 11 Pick. 466. Also to an appraiser of land set off on execution. The sheriff appointed a brother in law of the creditor as an appraiser; and the levy was held void, for that reason. *Wolcott* v. *Ely*, 2 Allen, 338. *McGough* v. *Wellington*, 6 Allen, 505. It applies to a referee, though referees are selected by the parties, unless the objection is known and waived. *Fox* v. *Hazelton*, 10 Pick. 275. *Strong* v. *Strong*, 9 Cush. 560, 574.

These decisions show that the provision is to have no technical or strict construction, but is to be broadly applied to all classes of cases where one is appointed to decide the rights of his fellow-citizens. It is not necessary to cite other cases from this or other states, or from England, to explain or illustrate the principle.

There can be no doubt that it applies to this case, if the judge of probate passed upon matters in which his father in law or his brother in law had a pecuniary interest adverse to other persons who were to be affected by his decision.

The facts stated are, that Warren Hunt had died testate; the will had been proved; the executor named in the will had taken upon himself the trust, and had represented the estate insolvent; commissioners had been appointed to receive and examine claims; and then the executor had resigned his trust, and was discharged. Soon afterwards, namely, March 2, 1869, Edward C. Thayer and Fenner Batcheller were upon their own application appointed administrators with the will annexed. Thayer was a brother of the judge's wife, and her father was, and had been from the first, a large creditor of the estate, and proved his claim before the commissioners.

A creditor, though he is interested as such in the administration of the estate, is not thereby disqualified to be administrator. On the contrary, by Gen. Sts. *c.* 94, § 1, a principal creditor has a right to be appointed, if the widow and next of kin do not act: and it is generally the case that administration is committed to persons having not only a pecuniary interest in the estate, but being related to the parties in interest. But the duties of the office are executive, and not judicial; and in all his acts an executor or administrator is strictly accountable to the judge of probate, at the instance of any party interested. If no one appears to take administration, the judge of probate appoints such person as he deems fit.

It is an office to which a pecuniary value is attached, and adverse interests may be involved, not only in the appointment but in all the proceedings of the administrator. As to many of the questions that arise the judge must act judicially: for example, whether the applicant is a suitable person; what shall be the amount of the bond to be given; who are sufficient sureties; what notices shall be given; and what proceedings shall be had in cases of alleged fraud or embezzlement; also, all matters of account, and many other matters requiring the decision of questions in which the interest of adverse parties is involved. The whole proceeding requires impartiality on the part of the judge; an impartiality that disqualifies him to act where a father in law or a brother in law is a party, and takes away his jurisdiction.

The defect is uncurable. It does not depend upon the motives with which the judge acted. No wrong motives are imputed to the judge in this case. But it is said by Chief Justice Shaw, in *Gay* v. *Minot*, 3 Cush. 352, 354, that the case being *coram non judice*, the first probate was not voidable merely, but void; incapable of being made good by confirmation, waiver or ratification on the part of those interested. The same is true as to county commissioners. *Tolland* v. *County Commissioners*, 13 Gray 12. This was said in application to a case where the judge was merely indebted to the estate in a small note, secured by mortgage, and the executors had been named by the testator, and after probate of the will they had sold the note for its full value. We cannot doubt that this case is within that principle; and that some other judge should have been called to act, in conformity with the provisions of the statute.

The appointment of Thayer and Batcheller being void, the petition of Hall, the appellant, was properly presented; and, it having been dismissed by the judge of probate who acted, he had a right of appeal to this court. It cannot be acted upon in this court without a hearing before a single justice. It must therefore

Stand for a hearing.

Velorous Taft, a county commissioner of Worcester county, took part in adjudications of the county commissioners on construction of a highway over land of his sister's husband, **Moses H. Bullard**, entitling Bullard to receive payment for the taking.

Franklin Taylor v. County Commissioners of Worcester
105 Mass. 225 (1870).

Petition for a writ of *certiorari* to quash proceedings of the county commissioners of Worcester laying out a highway in the towns of Holden and Princeton; heard by *Morton, J.*, and reported for the consideration of the full court. The following are the material parts of the report:

"It appeared that in May 1866 certain citizens of Holden and Princeton presented a petition to the county commissioners to lay out and build a new county road in said towns. Upon this petition the county commissioners issued notices, held meetings, adjudicated that the common necessity and convenience required said road, laid and located the same, and did other acts in regard to the matter. During the pendency of these proceedings before the board of county commissioners, Velorous Taft, Esquire, was a member thereof, and participated in all the proceedings had under the petition.

"Moses H. Bullard, of Princeton, was one of the original signers of the petition. The road as prayed for, and as located, passed through a farm owned and occupied by him, and damages were awarded to him by the county commissioners in their final decree locating the road and assessing damages therefor. Bullard wrote the petition, and circulated it to some extent; and appeared before the board in behalf of the petitioners, and managed the case for them at the several hearings. The wife of Bullard, during all the time of the pendency of these proceedings, and who had an inchoate right to dower and homestead, was the sister of said Velorous Taft.

"The laying out of the road was opposed by the town of Princeton; and Taylor, the present petitioner, was a legal voter of Princeton, was present as a witness at the hearing as to the common convenience and necessity of the road, and was also present at the subsequent meetings and at the time of the location. The commissioners, at a regular meeting held July 1, 1869, made the decree laying out and locating the road, and ordering the towns of Princeton and Holden to construct the same before July 1, 1870. The next regular meeting of the board was on the second Tuesday of September 1869, and at an adjournment thereof, held September 30, 1869, Taylor filed his petition for a jury to revise the proceedings of the commissioners laying out and locating said road, and the award of damages to him therefor, and recognized for costs, as required by law, and at another adjournment thereof, held October 22, 1869, by consent of counsel for respondents said petition was amended. All this was done by Taylor for the purpose of saving his rights. At the time said petition was filed, or just before, Taylor's counsel informed Taft that Taylor objected to the proceedings in regard to the road, on account of Taft's relationship to Bullard. After the petition and bond were filed, Taylor did nothing more in regard to it, did not then or afterwards otherwise ask or move for an order for a jury or the issue of the warrant therefor, and no such order was made or warrant issued, and the said meeting adjourned without day in December 1869, no action being had on said petition. No notice in relation to said petition was given to the petitioner or to the towns. No order for such notice was passed, and no order was passed for arresting the work; nor was such notice or order applied for except as herein appears. The usage of the county commissioners as to ordering a jury in this class of cases is, that the petition for the jury is filed, and when the petitioner asks for the warrant to issue the court directs the clerk to issue it.

"During all the proceedings, there were two special commissioners for the county. But no objection was made to the competency of Taft to act as commissioner, at any stage of the proceedings.

"The road is 461 rods in Princeton, 252 rods in Holden, 77 rods on Bullard's land. Bullard and others told the commissioners that they should charge nothing for their land, but they might give them what they pleased for fencing; but no release of damages on the part of Bullard was ever executed. It appeared on the trial that Bullard was ready to release all damages by reason of the location of the road on his land.

"Taylor lived about quarter of a mile from Bullard, and knew of the relationship between Taft and Bullard's wife, before these proceedings. Taylor testified that it was not present in his mind, at the hearings, that the relationship existed, nor did he suppose that it made any difference with his rights. The relationship was generally known in the town of Princeton, and both towns were represented by committees at the hearing. Taylor was informed by his counsel, when he filed his petition for a jury, that the relationship aforesaid made the proceedings void."

W.   W. Rice & T. L. Nelson, for the petitioner.

P.   E. Aldrich & H. B. Staples, for the respondents.

CHAPMAN, C. J. As one of the county commissioners was a brother in law of Bullard, over whose land the highway was located, and who was entitled to damages, the proceeding was *coram non judice* and utterly void, and no subsequent waiver, consent or release could render it valid. *Hall* v. *Thayer, ante*, 219.

Writ for certiorari to issue.

QUESTIONS

1. Why should the actions of the Worcester County probate judge in *Hall* and of the County Commissioners in *Taylor* be void instead of merely voidable at the option of one of the parties? Should ethical standards be "waivable" by litigants and other participants in the justice system?

2. Why was the judge in *Hall* held to a higher standard than the executor?

3. In these cases the Supreme Judicial Court of Massachusetts reviewed proceedings of Worcester County's probate court (*Hall*) and County Commissioners (*Taylor*). These proceedings took place in the same year and both involved impermissible conflicts of interest. If lax ethical standards are tolerated in one branch of local government, they are likely to appear in other branches as well. For example, *Prichard v. United States* (Chapter 2 supra) describes a much worse situation in Bourbon County, Kentucky in the 1940s: election fraud followed by the culprit's use of his friendship with a judge's son to foster ex-parte communications. In what other cases appearing in this casebook does improper conduct appear on multiple levels in the same geographic location, family or political administration?

Robert F. Collins, b. 1931; B.A. Dillard University 1951 (graduated first in his class); J.D. Louisiana State University (LSU) 1954 (one of the first African Americans to graduate from LSU); admitted to the Louisiana bar in 1954; leading civil rights lawyer in the 1960's; senior partner in Collins, Douglas & Elie, New Orleans 1960–72; judge of the magistrate section, Criminal District, Orleans Parish, Louisiana 1971–78; U.S. District Judge 1978–93 (one of the South's first African American federal judges) (convicted in 1991 of taking $15,000 in return for leniency in a drug sentencing) (resigned in 1993 rather than face impeachment proceedings in Congress).[6]

Collins spent much of the 1960's representing CORE and other civil rights groups in school desegregation and freedom march cases in Louisiana. Upon his appointment to the federal bench by President Carter in 1977, Collins recalled the dramatic moments of his earlier law practice and one incident in particular in which he and CORE director James Farmer fled Louisiana state troopers charging on horseback into a crowd of about a thousand civil rights demonstrators in Plaquemines Parish, Louisiana:

> It was the most terrifying experience of my life. ... We were talking in back of this little church when the state police all of a sudden started throwing teargas. It was like wartime.... We crawled on our hands and knees across the town square and [in] turn through a cornfield to escape. The state police were [chasing] us on horseback with cattle prods.

Bill Peterson, From CORE to U.S. Bench, The Washington Post, November 3, 1977, at A3. Collins practiced law for 18 years before being nominated to the federal bench. He had argued and appeared on the briefs in several civil rights cases before the United States Supreme Court. See Carter v. West

---

6. Although The Times–Picayune, New Orleans's leading newspaper, repeatedly stated that Collins was the first federal judge ever to be convicted of taking a bribe, he was not. In 1939, Martin T. Manton, a judge of the United States Court of Appeals for the Second Circuit, was convicted of conspiracy "to defraud the United States" and sentenced to two years in jail. Arrangement and acceptance of bribes were the overt acts by which Manton was shown to have carried out

the conspiracy. From 1932 to 1938, Manton "received large sums of money from litigants in at least a dozen cases—six patent suits, three receiverships, two criminal prosecutions, and one stockholders' suit. His payors included two poultry dealers; an insurance salesman; an engineer; a brewer; two lawyers; a fence for stolen bonds; a movie executive (Harry Warner of Warner Brothers); and several presidents of closely held companies." John T. Noonan, Jr., Bribes 568 (1984).

Feliciana Parish Sch. Bd., 396 U.S. 290 (1970) and Brown v. Louisiana, 383 U.S. 131 (1966).

John A. Liljeberg, Jr., Petitioner v. Health Services Acquisition Corp.

486 U.S. 847 (1988).

■ Justice STEVENS delivered the opinion of the Court.

In 1974 Congress amended the Judicial Code "to broaden and clarify the grounds for judicial disqualification." 88 Stat. 1609. The first sentence of the amendment provides: "Any justice, judge, or magistrate of the United States shall disqualify himself in any proceeding in which his impartiality might reasonably be questioned." 28 U.S.C.A. § 455(a) as amended. In the present case, the Court of Appeals for the Fifth Circuit concluded that a violation of § 455(a) is established when a reasonable person, knowing the relevant facts, would expect that a justice, judge, or magistrate knew of circumstances creating an appearance of partiality, notwithstanding a finding that the judge was not actually conscious of those circumstances. Moreover, although the judgment in question had become final, the Court of Appeals determined that under the facts of this case, the appropriate remedy was to vacate the court's judgment. We granted certiorari to consider its construction of § 455(a) as well as its remedial decision. 480 U.S. 915, 107 S.Ct. 1368, 94 L.Ed.2d 684 (1987). We now affirm.

I

In November 1981, respondent Health Services Acquisition Corp. brought an action against petitioner John Liljeberg, Jr., seeking a declaration of ownership of a corporation known as St. Jude Hospital of Kenner, Louisiana (St. Jude). The case was tried by Judge Robert Collins, sitting without a jury. Judge Collins found for Liljeberg and, over a strong dissent, the Court of Appeals affirmed. Approximately 10 months later, respondent learned that Judge Collins had been a member of the Board of Trustees of Loyola University while Liljeberg was negotiating with Loyola to purchase a parcel of land on which to construct a hospital. The success and benefit to Loyola of these negotiations turned, in large part, on Liljeberg prevailing in the litigation before Judge Collins.

Based on this information, respondent moved pursuant to Federal Rule of Civil Procedure 60(b)(6) to vacate the judgment on the ground that Judge Collins was disqualified under § 455(a) at the time he heard the action and entered judgment in favor of Liljeberg....

II

Petitioner, John Liljeberg, Jr., is a pharmacist, a promoter, and a half-owner of Axel Realty, Inc., a real estate brokerage firm. In 1976, he became interested in a project to construct and operate a hospital in Kenner,

Louisiana, a suburb of New Orleans. In addition to providing the community with needed health care facilities, he hoped to obtain a real estate commission for Axel Realty and the exclusive right to provide pharmaceutical services at the new hospital. The successful operation of such a hospital depended upon the acquisition of a "certificate of need" from the State of Louisiana; without such a certificate the hospital would not qualify for health care reimbursement payments under the federal medicare and medicaid programs. Accordingly, in October 1979, Liljeberg formed St. Jude, intending to have the corporation apply for the certificate of need at an appropriate time.

During the next two years Liljeberg engaged in serious negotiations with at least two major parties. One set of negotiations involved a proposal to purchase a large tract of land from Loyola University for use as a hospital site, coupled with a plan to rezone adjoining University property. The proposed benefits to the University included not only the proceeds of the real estate sale itself, amounting to several million dollars, but also a substantial increase in the value to the University of the rezoned adjoining property. The progress of these negotiations was regularly reported to the University's Board of Trustees by its Real Estate Committee and discussed at Board meetings. The minutes of those meetings indicate that the University's interest in the project was dependent on the issuance of the certificate of need.

Liljeberg was also conducting serious negotiations with respondent's corporate predecessor, Hospital Affiliates International (HAI), a national health management company. In the summer of 1980, Liljeberg and HAI reached an agreement in principle, outlining their respective roles in developing the hospital. The agreement contemplated that HAI would purchase a tract of land in Kenner (not owned by the University) and construct the hospital on that land; prepare and file the certificate of need; and retain Liljeberg as a consultant to the hospital in various capacities. In turn, it was understood that Liljeberg would transfer St. Jude to HAI. Pursuant to this preliminary agreement, various documents were executed, including an agreement by HAI to purchase the tract of land from its owner for $5 million and a further agreement by HAI to place $500,000 in escrow. In addition, it was agreed that Axel Realty, Inc., would receive a $250,000 commission for locating the property. Eventually, Liljeberg signed a "warranty and indemnity agreement," which HAI understood to transfer ownership of St. Jude to HAI. After the warranty and indemnity agreement was signed, HAI filed an application for the certificate of need.

On August 26, 1981, the certificate of need was issued and delivered to Liljeberg. He promptly advised HAI, and HAI paid the real estate commission to Axel Realty. A dispute arose, however, over whether the warranty and indemnity agreement did in fact transfer ownership of St. Jude to HAI. Liljeberg contended that the transfer of ownership of St. Jude—and hence, the certificate of need—was conditioned upon reaching a final agreement concerning his continued participation in the hospital project. This contention was not supported by any written instrument. HAI denied that there was any such unwritten understanding and insisted that, by virtue of the warranty and indemnity agreement, it had been sole owner of St. Jude for over a year. The dispute gave rise to this litigation.

Respondent filed its complaint for declaratory judgment on November 30, 1981. The case was tried by Judge Collins, sitting without a jury, on January 21 and 22, 1982. At the close of the evidence, he announced his intended ruling, and on March 16, 1982, he filed a judgment (dated March 12, 1982) and his findings of fact and conclusions of law. He credited Liljeberg's version of oral conversations that were disputed and of critical importance in his ruling.

During the period between November 30, 1981, and March 16, 1982, Judge Collins was a trustee of Loyola University, but was not conscious of the fact that the University and Liljeberg were then engaged in serious negotiations concerning the Kenner hospital project, or of the further fact that the success of those negotiations depended upon his conclusion that Liljeberg controlled the certificate of need. To determine whether Judge Collins' impartiality in the Liljeberg litigation "might reasonably be questioned," it is appropriate to consider the state of his knowledge immediately before the lawsuit was filed, what happened while the case was pending before him, and what he did when he learned of the University's interest in the litigation.

After the certificate of need was issued, and Liljeberg and HAI became embroiled in their dispute, Liljeberg reopened his negotiations with the University. On October 29, 1981, the Real Estate Committee sent a written report to each of the trustees, including Judge Collins, advising them of "a significant change" concerning the proposed hospital in Kenner and stating specifically that Loyola's property had "again become a prime location." App. 72. The Committee submitted a draft of a resolution authorizing a University vice president "to continue negotiations with the developers of the St. Jude Hospital." Id., at 73. At the Board meeting on November 12, 1981, which Judge Collins attended, the trustees discussed the connection between the rezoning of Loyola's land in Kenner and the St. Jude project and adopted the Real Estate Committee's proposed resolution. Thus, Judge Collins had actual knowledge of the University's potential interest in the St. Jude hospital project in Kenner just a few days before the complaint was filed.

While the case was pending before Judge Collins, the University agreed to sell 80 acres of its land in Kenner to Liljeberg for $6,694,000. The progress of negotiations was discussed at a Board meeting on January 28, 1982. Judge Collins did not attend that meeting, but the Real Estate Committee advised the trustees that "the federal courts have determined that the certificate of need will be awarded to the St. Jude Corporation." Id., at 37. Presumably this advice was based on Judge Collins' comment at the close of the hearing a week earlier, when he announced his intended ruling because he thought "it would be unfair to keep the parties in doubt as to how I feel about the case." App. to Pet. for Cert. 41a.

The formal agreement between Liljeberg and the University was apparently executed on March 19. App. 50–58. The agreement stated that it was not in any way conditioned on Liljeberg's prevailing in the litigation "pending in the U.S. District Court for the Eastern District of Louisiana . . . involving the obtaining by [Liljeberg] of a Certificate of Need," id., at 55, but it also gave the University the right to repurchase the property for the contract price if Liljeberg had not executed a satisfactory construction contract within one year and further provided for nullification of the contract in the event the rezoning of the University's adjoining land was not accomplished. Thus, the University continued to have an active interest in the outcome of the litigation because it was unlikely that Liljeberg could build the hospital if he lost control of the certificate of need; moreover, the rezoning was in turn dependent on the hospital project.

The details of the transaction were discussed in three letters to the trustees dated March 12, 15, and 19, 1982, but Judge Collins did not examine any of those letters until shortly before the Board meeting on March 25, 1982. Thus, he acquired actual knowledge of Loyola's interest in the litigation on March 24, 1982. As the Court of Appeals correctly held, "Judge Collins should have recused himself when he obtained actual knowledge of that interest on March 24." 796 F.2d, at 801.

In considering whether the Court of Appeals properly vacated the declaratory relief judgment, we are required to address two questions. We must first determine whether § 455(a) can be violated based on an appearance of partiality, even though the judge was not conscious of the circumstances creating the appearance of impropriety, and second, whether relief is available under Rule 60(b) when such a violation is not discovered until after the judgment has become final.

III

Title 28 U.S.C.A. § 455 provides in relevant part:

"(a) Any justice, judge, or magistrate of the United States shall disqualify himself in any proceeding in which his impartiality might reasonably be questioned." (b) He shall also disqualify himself in the following circumstances:

* * *

"(4) He knows that he, individually or as a fiduciary, or his spouse or minor child residing in his household, has a financial interest in the subject matter in controversy or in a party to the proceeding, or any other interest that could be substantially affected by the outcome of the proceeding.

* * *

"(c) A judge should inform himself about his personal and fiduciary financial interests, and make a reasonable effort to inform himself about the personal financial interests of his spouse and minor children residing in his household."

Scienter is not an element of a violation of § 455(a). The judge's lack of knowledge of a disqualifying circumstance may bear on the question of remedy, but it does not eliminate the risk that "his impartiality might reasonably be questioned" by other persons. To read § 455(a) to provide that the judge must know of the disqualifying facts, requires not simply ignoring the language of the provision—which makes no mention of knowledge—but further requires concluding that the language in subsection (b)(4)—which expressly provides that the judge must know of his or her interest—is extraneous. A careful reading of the respective subsections makes clear that Congress intended to require knowledge under subsection (b)(4) and not to require knowledge under subsection (a). Moreover, advancement of the purpose of the provision—to promote public confidence in the integrity of the judicial process, see S.Rep. No. 93–419, p. 5 (1973); H.R.Rep. No. 93–1453, p. 5 (1974)—does not depend upon whether or not the judge actually knew of facts creating an appearance of impropriety, so long as the public might reasonably believe that he or she knew. As Chief Judge Clark of the Court of Appeals explained:

> "The goal of section 455(a) is to avoid even the appearance of partiality. If it would appear to a reasonable person that a judge has knowledge of facts that would give him an interest in the litigation then an appearance of partiality is created even though no actual partiality exists because the judge does not recall the facts, because the judge actually has no interest in the case or because the judge is pure in heart and incorruptible. The judge's forgetfulness, however, is not the sort of objectively ascertainable fact that can avoid the appearance of partiality. Hall v. Small Business Administration, 695 F.2d 175, 179 (5th Cir.1983). Under section 455(a), therefore, recusal is required even when a judge lacks actual knowledge of the facts indicating his interest or bias in the case if a reasonable person, knowing all the circumstances, would expect that the judge would have actual knowledge."

796 F.2d at 802.

Contrary to petitioner's contentions, this reading of the statute does not call upon judges to perform the impossible—to disqualify themselves based on facts they do not know. If, as petitioner argues, § 455(a) should only be applied prospectively, then requiring disqualification based on facts the judge does not know would of course be absurd; a judge could never be expected to disqualify himself based on some fact he does not know, even though the fact is one that perhaps he should know or one that people might reasonably suspect that he does know. But to the extent the provision can also, in proper cases, be applied retroactively, the judge is not called upon to perform an impossible feat. Rather, he is called upon to rectify an oversight and to take the steps necessary to maintain public confidence in the impartiality of the judiciary. If he concludes that "his impartiality might reasonably be questioned," then he should also find that the statute has been violated. This is certainly not an impossible task. No one questions that Judge Collins could have disqualified himself and vacated his judgment when he finally realized that Loyola had an interest in the litigation. The initial appeal was taken from his failure to disqualify himself and vacate the judgment after he became aware of the appearance of impropriety, not from his failure to disqualify himself when he first became involved in the litigation and lacked the requisite knowledge.

In this case both the District Court and the Court of Appeals found an ample basis in the record for concluding that an objective observer would have questioned Judge Collins' impartiality. Accordingly, even though his failure to disqualify himself was the product of a temporary lapse of memory, it was nevertheless a plain violation of the terms of the statute.

A conclusion that a statutory violation occurred does not, however, end our inquiry. As in other areas of the law, there is surely room for harmless error committed by busy judges who inadvertently overlook a disqualifying circumstance. There need not be a draconian remedy for every violation of § 455(a). It would be equally wrong, however, to adopt an absolute prohibition against any relief in cases involving forgetful judges.

IV

Although § 455 defines the circumstances that mandate disqualification of federal judges, it neither prescribes nor prohibits any particular remedy for a violation of that duty. Congress has wisely delegated to the judiciary the task of fashioning the remedies that will best serve the purpose of the legislation. In considering whether a remedy is appropriate, we do well to bear in mind that in many cases—and this is such an example—the Court of Appeals is in a better position to evaluate the significance of a violation than is this Court. Its judgment as to the proper remedy should thus be afforded our due consideration. A review of the facts demonstrates that the Court of Appeals' determination that a new trial is in order is well supported. . . .

. . . .

Like the Court of Appeals, we accept the District Court's finding that while the case was actually being tried Judge Collins did not have actual knowledge of Loyola's interest in the dispute over the ownership of St. Jude and its precious certificate of need. When a busy federal judge concentrates his or her full attention on a pending case, personal concerns are easily forgotten. The problem, however, is that people who have not served on the bench are often all too willing to indulge suspicions and doubts concerning the integrity of judges. The very purpose of § 455(a) is to promote confidence in the judiciary by avoiding even the appearance of impropriety whenever possible. See S.Rep. No. 93–419, at 5; H.R.Rep. No. 93–1453, at 5. Thus, it is critically important in a case of this kind to identify the facts that might reasonably cause an objective observer to question Judge Collins' impartiality. There are at least four such facts.

First, it is remarkable that the judge, who had regularly attended the meetings of the Board of Trustees since 1977, completely forgot about the University's interest in having a hospital constructed on its property in

Kenner. The importance of the project to the University is indicated by the fact that the 80–acre parcel, which represented only about 40% of the entire tract owned by the University, was sold for $6,694,000 and that the rezoning would substantially increase the value of the remaining 60%. The "negotiations with the developers of the St. Jude Hospital" were the subject of discussion and formal action by the trustees at a meeting attended by Judge Collins only a few days before the lawsuit was filed. App. 35.

Second, it is an unfortunate coincidence that although the judge regularly attended the meetings of the Board of Trustees, he was not present at the January 28, 1982, meeting, a week after the 2–day trial and while the case was still under advisement. The minutes of that meeting record that representatives of the University monitored the progress of the trial, but did not see fit to call to the judge's attention the obvious conflict of interest that resulted from having a University trustee preside over that trial. These minutes were mailed to Judge Collins on March 12, 1982. If the judge had opened that envelope when he received it on March 14 or 15, he would have been under a duty to recuse himself before he entered judgment on March 16.

Third, it is remarkable—and quite inexcusable—that Judge Collins failed to recuse himself on March 24, 1982. A full disclosure at that time would have completely removed any basis for questioning the judge's impartiality and would have made it possible for a different judge to decide whether the interests—and appearance—of justice would have been served by a retrial. Another 2–day evidentiary hearing would surely have been less burdensome and less embarrassing than the protracted proceedings that resulted from Judge Collins' nonrecusal and nondisclosure. Moreover, as the Court of Appeals correctly noted, Judge Collins' failure to disqualify himself on March 24, 1982, also constituted a violation of § 455(b)(4), which disqualifies a judge if he "knows that he, individually or as a fiduciary, . . . has a financial interest in the subject matter in controversy or in a party to the proceeding, or any other interest that could be substantially affected by the outcome of the proceeding." This separate violation of § 455 further compels the conclusion that vacatur was an appropriate remedy; by his silence, Judge Collins deprived respondent of a basis for making a timely motion for a new trial and also deprived it of an issue on direct appeal.

Fourth, when respondent filed its motion to vacate, Judge Collins gave three reasons for denying the motion,[7] but still did not acknowledge that he had known about the University's interest both shortly before and shortly

---

7. These were his three reasons: "First, Loyola University was not and is not a party to this litigation, nor was any of its real estate the subject matter of this controversy. Second, Loyola University is a non-profit, educational institution, and any benefits [inuring] to that institution would not benefit any individual personally. Finally, and most significantly, this Judge never served on either the Real Estate or Executive Committees of the Loyola University Board of Trustees. Thus, this Judge had no participation of any kind in negotiating Loyola University's real estate transactions and, in fact, had no knowledge of such transactions." App. to Pet. for Cert. 50a.

after the trial. Nor did he indicate any awareness of a duty to recuse himself in March 1982.

These facts create precisely the kind of appearance of impropriety that § 455(a) was intended to prevent. The violation is neither insubstantial nor excusable. Although Judge Collins did not know of his fiduciary interest in the litigation, he certainly should have known. In fact, his failure to stay informed of this fiduciary interest may well constitute a separate violation of § 455. See § 455(c). Moreover, providing relief in cases such as this will not produce injustice in other cases; to the contrary, the Court of Appeals' willingness to enforce § 455 may prevent a substantive injustice in some future case by encouraging a judge or litigant to more carefully examine possible grounds for disqualification and to promptly disclose them when discovered. It is therefore appropriate to vacate the judgment unless it can be said that respondent did not make a timely request for relief, or that it would otherwise be unfair to deprive the prevailing party of its judgment.

If we focus on fairness to the particular litigants, a careful study of Judge Rubin's analysis of the merits of the underlying litigation suggests that there is a greater risk of unfairness in upholding the judgment in favor of Liljeberg than there is in allowing a new judge to take a fresh look at the issues. Moreover, neither Liljeberg nor Loyola University has made a showing of special hardship by reason of their reliance on the original judgment. Finally, although a delay of 10 months after the affirmance by the Court of Appeals would normally foreclose relief based on a violation of § 455(a), in this case the entire delay is attributable to Judge Collins' inexcusable failure to disqualify himself on March 24, 1982; had he recused himself on March 24, or even disclosed Loyola's interest in the case at that time, the motion could have been made less than 10 days after the entry of judgment. "The guiding consideration is that the administration of justice should reasonably appear to be disinterested as well as be so in fact." Public Utilities Comm'n of D.C. v. Pollak, 343 U.S. 451, 466–467, 72 S.Ct. 813, 822–823, 96 L.Ed. 1068 (1952) (Frankfurter, J., in chambers). In sum, we conclude that Chief Judge Clark's opinion of the Court of Appeals reflects an eminently sound and wise disposition of this case.

The judgment of the Court of Appeals is accordingly

Affirmed.

■ Chief Justice REHNQUIST, with whom Justice WHITE and Justice SCALIA join, dissenting.

The Court's decision in this case is long on ethics in the abstract, but short on workable rules of law. The Court first finds that 28 U.S.C.A. § 455(a) can be used to disqualify a judge on the basis of facts not known to the judge himself. It then broadens the standard for overturning final judgments under Federal Rule of Civil Procedure 60(b). Because these results are at odds with the intended scope of § 455 and Rule 60(b), and are likely to cause considerable mischief when courts attempt to apply them, I dissent. . . .

Subsection (b) of § 455 sets forth more particularized situations in which a judge must disqualify himself. Congress intended the provisions of § 455(b) to remove any doubt about recusal in cases where a judge's interest is too closely connected with the litigation to allow his participation. Subsection (b)(4), for example, disqualifies a jurist if he knows that he, his spouse, or his minor children have a financial interest in the subject matter in controversy. Unlike the more open-ended provision adopted in subsection (a), the language of subsection (b) requires recusal only in specific circumstances, and is phrased in such a way as to suggest a requirement of actual knowledge of the disqualifying circumstances.

The purpose of § 455 is obviously to inform judges of what matters they must consider in deciding whether to recuse themselves in a given case. The Court here holds, as did the Court of Appeals below, that a judge must recuse himself under § 455(a) if he should have known of the circumstances requiring disqualification, even though in fact he did not know of them. I do not believe this is a tenable construction of subsection (a). A judge considering whether or not to recuse himself is necessarily limited to those facts bearing on the question of which he has knowledge. To hold that disqualification is required by reason of facts which the judge does not know, even though he should have known of them, is to posit a conundrum which is not decipherable by ordinary mortals. While the concept of "constructive knowledge" is useful in other areas of the law, I do not think it should be imported into § 455(a).

At the direction of the Court of Appeals, Judge Schwartz of the District Court for the Eastern District of Louisiana made factual findings concerning the extent and timing of Judge Collins' knowledge of Loyola's interest in the underlying lawsuit. See ante, at 2197–2198. Judge Schwartz determined that Judge Collins had no actual knowledge of Loyola's involvement when he tried the case. Not until March 24, 1982, when he reviewed materials in preparation for a Board meeting, did Judge Collins obtain actual knowledge of the negotiations between petitioners and Loyola.

Despite this factual determination, reached after a public hearing on the subject, the Court nevertheless concludes that "public confidence in the impartiality of the judiciary" compels retroactive disqualification of Judge Collins under § 455(a). This conclusion interprets § 455(a) in a manner which Congress never intended. As the Court of Appeals noted, in drafting § 455(a) Congress was concerned with the "appearance" of impropriety, and to that end changed the previous subjective standard for disqualification to an objective one; no longer was disqualification to be decided on the basis of the opinion of the judge in question, but by the standard of what a reasonable person would think. But the facts and circumstances which this reasonable person would consider must be the facts and circumstances known to the judge at the time. In short, as is unquestionably the case with subsection (b), I would adhere to a standard of actual knowledge in § 455(a), and not slide off into the very speculative ground of "constructive" knowledge. . . .

■ Justice O'CONNOR, dissenting.

For the reasons given by Chief Justice REHNQUIST, ante, at 871–873, I agree that "constructive knowledge" cannot be the basis for a violation of 28 U.S.C.A. § 455(a). The question then remains whether respondent is entitled to a new trial because there are other "extraordinary circumstances," apart from the § 455(a) violation found by the Fifth Circuit, that justify "relief from the operation of the judgment." See Fed.Rule Civ.Proc. 60(b)(6).... I believe the issue should be addressed in the first instance by the courts below. I would therefore remand this case with appropriate instructions.

QUESTIONS

1. The dissent argues that the Court's opinion is "long on ethics in the abstract, but short on workable rules of law." Does the dissent's proposed rule of law hold federal judges to a high enough standard?

2. Courts and bar disciplinary committees require lawyers to avoid successive and concurrent conflicts of interest (see Chapters 4 and 6 supra). A lawyer's knowledge of a conflict usually need not be proven to sanction or disqualify the lawyer for an impermissible conflict, particularly if the lawyer was careless in checking for conflicts. Should judges be held to as high a standard?

3. Why did Judge Collins fail to stay informed of his fiduciary interest in the litigation?

4. The "representatives of the University monitored the progress of the trial, but did not see fit to call to the judge's attention the obvious conflict of interest that resulted from having a University trustee preside over that trial." Why not?

5. Why did Judge Collins not recuse himself once he knew of the conflict?

6. Collins's early law practice took place in a setting where the law was applied differently to blacks than to whites, and the incident he described to the Washington Post illustrates the seeming powerlessness of black lawyers at a time when force sometimes overshadowed the rule of law. In many cases, civil rights gains emerged from the federal judiciary looking to what the law said was right while many state judges and law enforcement officials were absorbed by local prejudices. When Collins ultimately became a federal judge, did he remain faithful to the task of upholding the law without distinction between persons? Could his failings in the *Liljeberg* case have signaled other more serious failings yet to come?

7. Did Collins fulfill his calling as a lawyer more faithfully than as a judge? Why?

PROBLEMS

1. Judge presides over a bench trial in which X Corp. sues Y Corp. Judge rules for X Corp., and judgment is affirmed on appeal. Ten years later, Y Corp. learns that unbeknownst to it, Judge owned fifty shares of stock in X

Corp., although it is quite clear that Judge had forgotten that he owned the stock at the time of trial. Should the final judgment in X Corp.'s favor be set aside? (Justice Rehnquist's dissent in *Liljeberg*, supra, uses this hypothetical).

2. How is the above hypothetical different from what happened in the *Liljeberg* case? Are hypotheticals like this one helpful for developing workable, and fair, rules of law?

Relevant Background

Judicial Conflicts of Interest

An unbiased tribunal is an inherent part of the right to due process under the Fourteenth Amendment. In re Murchison, 349 U.S. 133, 136 (1955). Codes of judicial conduct preserve this right by setting forth standards for judges to observe in avoiding real *or perceived* bias, and both federal and state statutes provide litigants with procedures for disqualifying judges who fail to observe those standards.

Disqualification of a federal judge is provided for in 28 U.S.C.A. § 144 (1993): "Whenever a party to any proceeding in a district court makes and files a timely and sufficient affidavit that the judge before whom the matter is pending has a personal bias or prejudice either against him or in favor of any adverse party, such judge shall proceed no further therein, but another judge shall be assigned to hear such proceeding." In order for a judge's bias to disqualify him, it "must stem from an extrajudicial source and result in an opinion on the merits on some basis other than what the judge learned from his participation in the case." United States v. Grinnell Corp., 384 U.S. 563, 583 (1966). See Berger v. United States, 255 U.S. 22 (1921) (creating this "extrajudicial source doctrine"). In addition, 28 U.S.C.A. § 455(b) enumerates circumstances in which bias is presumed to exist regardless of an extrajudicial source (for example, if the judge, her spouse or children have a financial interest in the subject matter of a case). See Christopher R. Carton, Comment, Disqualifying Federal Judges for Bias: A Consideration of the Extrajudicial Bias Limitation for Disqualification under 28 U.S.C. § 455(a), 24 Seton Hall L.Rev. 2057 (1994).

28 U.S.C.A. § 455(e) allows litigants to waive a judge's disqualification in instances when a judge disqualifies himself because his impartiality might be reasonably questioned. Full disclosure on the record of the basis for disqualification, however, must be made to the litigants before waiver can be granted. Also, if all available judges have an interest in a matter in controversy, it may become necessary for one or more of them to hear the case, even though there could be an appearance of bias. See United States v. Will, 449 U.S. 200 (1980) (all federal judges, including the Justices of the Supreme Court, cannot be barred from hearing challenge under the Compensation Clause to Congress's revocation of pay increases previously bestowed on federal judges).

Whereas financial interests of a judge and positions he has on boards of trustees and similar bodies can be grounds for disqualifying the judge from a case, a judge's political affiliations usually are insufficient grounds for disqualification, absent a close personal affiliation with one of the parties. Furthermore, personal religious beliefs cannot be used as grounds for disqualification absent an objective showing that "incapacitating prejudice flows from religious belief." Feminist Women's Health Center v. Codispoti, 69 F.3d 399, 400 (9th Cir. 1995) (Noonan, J.) (plaintiffs' motion for recusal denied) ("The plaintiffs seek to qualify the office of federal judge with a proviso: no judge with religious beliefs condemning abortion may function in abortion cases. The sphere of action of these judges is limited and reduced. The proviso effectively imposes a religious test on the federal judiciary [in contravention of the Constitution, Article VI].") Id.

State statutes and rules of court set the standards for disqualification of state judges. Many states have adopted the ABA Model Code of Judicial Conduct (1990), of which Canon 3E resembles 28 U.S.C.A. §§ 144 and 455:

"(1) A judge shall disqualify himself or herself in a proceeding in which the judge's impartiality might reasonably be questioned, including but not limited to instances where:

(a) the judge has a personal bias or prejudice concerning a party or a party's lawyer, or personal knowledge of disputed evidentiary facts concerning the proceeding;

(b) the judge served as a lawyer in the matter in controversy, or a lawyer with whom the judge previously practiced law served during such association as a lawyer concerning the matter, or the judge has been a material witness concerning it;

(c) the judge knows that he or she, individually or as a fiduciary, or the judge's spouse, parent or child wherever residing, or any other member of the judge's family residing in the judge's household, has an economic interest in the subject matter in controversy or in a party to the proceeding or has any other more than de minimis interest that could be substantially affected by the proceeding;

(d) the judge or the judge's spouse, or a person within the third degree of relationship to either of them, or the spouse of such a person:

(i) is a party to the proceeding, or an officer, director or trustee of a party;

(ii) is acting as a lawyer in the proceeding;

(iii) is known by the judge to have a more than de minimis interest that could be substantially affected by the proceeding;

(iv) is to the judge's knowledge likely to be a material witness in the proceeding.

(2) A judge shall keep informed about the judge's personal and fiduciary economic interests, and make a reasonable effort to keep informed about the personal economic interests of the judge's spouse and minor children residing in the judge's household."

Model Code of Judicial Conduct Canon 2B states that a judge "shall not allow family, social, political or other relationships to influence the judge's judicial conduct or judgment." Also, a judge "shall disqualify himself or herself in a proceeding in which the judge's impartiality might reasonably be questioned...." Model Code of Judicial Conduct Canon 3E(1). For example, "if a judge were in the process of negotiating for employment with a law firm, the judge would be disqualified from any matters in which that law firm appeared...." Id., cmt.

Loans and Gifts

The general rule is that a judge is prohibited from accepting gifts or loans from persons other than family members and close personal friends. Model Code of Judicial Conduct Canon 4 provides:

"D(5) A judge shall not accept, and shall urge members of the judge's family residing in the judge's household, not to accept, a gift, bequest, favor or loan from anyone except for:

(a) a gift incident to a public testimonial, books, tapes and other resource materials supplied by publishers on a complimentary basis for official use, or an invitation to the judge and the judge's spouse or guest to attend a bar-related function or an activity devoted to the improvement of the law, the legal system or the administration of justice;

(b) a gift, award or benefit incident to the business, profession or other separate activity of a spouse or other family member of a judge residing in the judge's household, including gifts, awards and benefits for the use of both the spouse or other family member and the judge (as spouse or family member), provided the gift, award or benefit could not reasonably be perceived as intended to influence the judge in the performance of judicial duties;

(c) ordinary social hospitality;

(d) a gift from a relative or friend, for a special occasion, such as a wedding, anniversary or birthday, if the gift is fairly commensurate with the occasion and the relationship;

(e) a gift, bequest, favor or loan from a relative or close personal friend whose appearance or interest in a case would in any event require disqualification under Section 3E;

(f) a loan from a lending institution in its regular course of business on the same terms generally available to persons who are not judges;

(g) a scholarship or fellowship awarded on the same terms and based on the same criteria applied to other applicants; or

(h) any other gift, bequest, favor or loan, only if: the donor is not a party or other person who has come or is likely to come or whose interest have come or are likely to come before the judge; and, if its value exceeds $150.00, the judge reports it in the same manner as the judge reports compensation in Section 4H."

See In re Vaccaro, 409 N.Y.S.2d 1009 (1977) (judge suspended for six months without pay for improper conduct including accepting a weekend stay at a hotel paid for by a law firm); Matter of Anderson, 312 Minn. 442, 252 N.W.2d 592 (1977) (judge suspended for three months without pay for improper conduct including receiving a loan of money from attorneys involved in cases before him). See Steven Lubet, Regulation of Judges' Business and Financial Activities, 37 Emory L.J. 1, 40–43 (1988). Examples of illegal payments include cash given to a judge by a criminal defense lawyer after dismissal of charges against two of his clients, Florida Bar v. Saxon, 379 So.2d 1281 (Fla.1980)(judge's rejection of the cash does not prevent suspension of the offering attorney for violation of DR 7–110(A)), and kickbacks given to a probate judge by court appointed appraisers, In re Bartholet, 293 Minn. 495, 198 N.W.2d 152 (Minn.1972)(judge disbarred for accepting the same). Another startling example is of course Judge Albert Johnson's receipt through his sons of kickbacks from court appointed receivers in bankruptcy cases throughout the 1930s (see Chapter 2 supra). Although Judge Johnson was forced to resign to escape impeachment, his prolonged pattern of bribe taking did not result in a criminal conviction for bribery.

Judge Johnson's crime, of course, required the complicity of the lawyers practicing before him, including Hoyt Moore. Although Moore appears to have gotten away with it, bribery is a serious crime, see 18 U.S.C.A. § 201 (Supp.1996) (criminalizing bribery of and by federal officials). The Model Code of Professional Responsibility DR 7–110 also specifically addresses gifts and loans to judicial officials:

> "(A) A lawyer shall not give or lend any thing of value to a judge, official, or employee of a tribunal, [except as permitted by Model Code of Judicial Conduct Canon 4D(5)], but a lawyer may make a contribution to the campaign fund of a candidate for judicial office in conformity with [Model Code of Judicial Conduct Canon 5C(2), see below]."

See also Model Rules 3.5 ("A lawyer shall not (a) seek to influence a judge, juror, prospective juror or other official by means prohibited by law"), and 8.4 ("It is professional misconduct for a lawyer to ... (f) knowingly assist a judge or judicial officer in conduct that is a violation of applicable rules of judicial conduct or other law.").

Campaign Contributions

A majority of states elect at least some of their judges. Many potential campaign contributors are lawyers, and the Model Code of Judicial Conduct Canon 5C(2) permits a non-appointed judicial candidate to set up, and lawyers to contribute to, campaign committees organized for the election of judges. However, a candidate for judicial office may not personally accept campaign contributions, and a lawyer should not offer such contributions to a candidate personally. Furthermore, the commentary to Canon 5C(2) indicates that campaign contributions by lawyers who appear before a judge may be relevant to disqualification under Canon 3E if the judge has knowledge of such contributions. See Hans A. Linde, The Judge as Political Candidate, 40 Clev. St. L. Rev. 1, 6–10 (1992); Stuart Banner, Disqualifying Elected Judges from Cases Involving Campaign Contributors, 40 Stan. L. Rev. 449, 474 (1988).

IV. Cooperation With the Political System

CHAPTER 11

The Profession and the Political System

Alexis de Tocqueville, b. 1805, d. 1859 (Tocqueville's family was of aristocratic Norman ancestry and narrowly escaped execution in the Terror following the French Revolution); educated at the lycee in Metz; trained in law and became a magistrate at Versailles under the restored Bourbon monarchy; served as a lawyer and judge under Louis Philippe and in 1831 traveled to the United States to study the American criminal justice system; author of Democracy in America (1835); deputy in the Chamber of Deputies beginning in 1839; member of the Constituent Assembly of the Second Republic 1848; minister of foreign affairs 1849.

Causes Which Mitigate the Tyranny of the Majority in the United States, from Democracy in America (1835)

Alexis de Tocqueville.
Translated by Henry Reeve (1838)

THE PROFESSION OF THE LAW IN THE UNITED STATES SERVES TO COUNTERPOISE THE DEMOCRACY

In visiting the Americans and in studying their laws, we perceive that the authority they have entrusted to members of the legal profession, and the influence which these individuals exercise in the Government, is the most powerful existing security against the excesses of democracy.

This effect seems to me to result from a general cause which it is useful to investigate, since it may produce analogous consequences elsewhere.

The members of the legal profession have taken an important part in all the vicissitudes of political society in Europe, during the last five hundred years. At one time they have been the instruments of those who were invested with political authority, and at another they have succeeded in converting political authorities into their instrument. In the Middle Ages they afforded a powerful support to the Crown; and since that period they have exerted themselves to the utmost to limit the royal prerogative. In England they have contracted a close alliance with the aristocracy; in France they have proved to be the most dangerous enemies of that class. It is my object to inquire whether, under all these circumstances, the members of the legal profession have been swayed by sudden and momentary impulses; or whether they have been impelled by principles which are inherent in their pursuits, and which will always recur in history. I am incited to this investigation by reflecting that this particular class of men will most likely play a prominent part in that order of things to which the events of our time are giving birth.

Men who have more especially devoted themselves to legal pursuits derive from those occupations certain habits of order, a taste for formalities, and a kind of instinctive regard for the regular connection of ideas, which naturally render them very hostile to the revolutionary spirit and the unreflecting passions of the multitude.

The special information which lawyers derive from their studies ensures them a separate station in society; and they constitute a sort of privileged body in the scale of intelligence. This notion of their superiority perpetually recurs to them in the practice of their profession: they are the masters of a science which is necessary, but which is not very generally known; they serve as arbiters between the citizens; and the habit of directing the blind passions of parties in litigation to their purpose, inspires them with a certain contempt for the judgment of the multitude. To this it may be added that they naturally constitute a body; not by any previous understanding, or by an agreement which directs them to a common end; but the analogy of their studies and the uniformity of their proceedings connect their minds together, as much as a common interest could combine their endeavors.

A portion of the tastes and of the habits of the aristocracy may consequently be discovered in the characters of men in the profession of the law. They participate in the same instinctive love of order and of formalities; and they entertain the same repugnance to the actions of the multitude, and the same secret contempt of the government of the people. I do not mean to say that the natural propensities of lawyers are sufficiently strong to sway them irresistibly; for they, like most other men, are governed by their private interests and the advantages of the moment.

In a state of society in which the members of the legal profession are prevented from holding that rank in the political world which they enjoy in private life, we may rest assured that they will be the foremost agents of revolution. But it must then be inquired whether the cause which induces them to innovate and to destroy is accidental, or whether it belongs to some lasting purpose which they entertain. It is true that lawyers mainly contributed to the overthrow of the French Monarchy in 1789; but it remains to be seen whether they acted thus because they had studied the laws, or because they were prohibited from co-operating in the work of legislation.

Five hundred years ago the English nobles headed the people, and spoke in its name; at the present time, the aristocracy supports the throne, and defends the royal prerogative. But aristocracy has, notwithstanding this, its peculiar instincts and propensities. We must be careful not to confound isolated members of a body with the body itself. In all free governments, of whatsoever form they may be, members of the legal profession will be found at the head of all parties. The same remark is also applicable to the aristocracy; for almost all the democratic convulsions which have agitated the world have been directed by nobles.

* * *

I am therefore convinced that the prince who, in presence of an encroaching democracy, should endeavor to impair the judicial authority in his dominions, and to diminish the political influence of lawyers, would commit a great mistake. He would let slip the substance of authority to grasp at the shadow. He would act more wisely in introducing men connected with the law into the government; and if he entrusted them with the conduct of a despotic power, bearing some marks of violence, that power would most likely assume the external features of justice and of legality in their hands.

The government of democracy is favorable to the political power of lawyers; for when the wealthy, the noble, and the prince are excluded from the government, they are sure to occupy the highest stations in their own right, as it were, since they are the only men of information and sagacity, beyond the sphere of the people, who can be the object of the popular choice. If, then, they are led by their tastes to combine with the aristocracy and to support the Crown, they are naturally brought into contact with the people by their interests. They like the government of democracy, without participating in its propensities and without imitating its weaknesses; whence they derive a twofold authority, from it and over it. The people in democratic states does not mistrust the members of the legal profession, because it is well known that they are interested in serving the popular cause; and it listens to them without irritation, because it does not attribute to them any sinister designs. The object of lawyers is not, indeed, to overthrow the institutions of democracy, but they constantly endeavor to give it an impulse which diverts it from its real tendency, by means which are foreign to its nature. Lawyers belong to the people by birth and interest, to the aristocracy by habit and by taste, and they may be looked upon as the natural bond and connecting link of the two great classes of society.

The profession of the law is the only aristocratic element which can be amalgamated without violence with the natural elements of democracy, and which can be advantageously and permanently combined with them. I am not unacquainted with the defects which are inherent in the character of that body of men; but without this admixture of lawyer-like sobriety with the democratic principle, I question whether democratic institutions could long be maintained; and I cannot believe that a republic could subsist at the present time, if the influence of lawyers in public business did not increase in proportion to the power of the people.

This aristocratic character, which I hold to be common to the legal profession, is much more distinctly marked in the United States and in England than in any other country. This proceeds not only from the legal studies of the English and American lawyers, but from the nature of the legislation, and the position which those persons occupy in the two countries. The English and the Americans have retained the law of precedents; that is to say, they continue to found their legal opinions and the decisions of their courts upon the opinions and the decisions of their forefathers. In the mind of an English or American lawyer, a taste and a reverence for what is old is almost always united to a love of regular and lawful proceedings.

This predisposition has another effect upon the character of the legal profession and upon the general course of society. The English and American lawyers investigate what has been done; the French advocate inquires what should have been done; the former produce precedents, the latter reasons. A French observer is surprised to hear how often an English or an American lawyer quotes the opinions of others, and how little he alludes to his own; whilst the reverse occurs in France. There, the most trifling litigation is never conducted without the introduction of an entire system of ideas peculiar to the counsel employed; and the fundamental principles of law are discussed in order to obtain a perch of land by the decision of the court. This abnegation of his own opinion, and this implicit deference to the opinion of his forefathers which are common to the English and American lawyer, this subjection of thought which he is obliged to profess, necessarily give him more timid habits and more sluggish inclinations in England and America than in France.

The French codes are often difficult of comprehension, but they can be read by every one; nothing, on the other hand, can be more impenetrable to the uninitiated than a legislation founded upon precedents. The indispensable want of legal assistance which is felt in England and in the United States, and the high opinion which is generally entertained of the ability of the legal profession, tend to separate it more and more from the people, and to place it in a distinct class. The French lawyer is simply a man extensively acquainted with the statutes of his country; but the English or American lawyer resembles the hierophants of Egypt, for, like them, he is the sole interpreter of an occult science.

The station which lawyers occupy in England and America exercises no less an influence upon their habits and their opinions. The English aristocracy, which has taken care to attract to its sphere whatever is at all analogous to itself, has conferred a high degree of importance and of authority upon the members of the legal profession. In English society lawyers do not occupy the first rank, but they are contented with the station assigned to them; they constitute, as it were, the younger branch of the English aristocracy, and they are attached to their elder brothers, although they do not enjoy all their privileges. The English lawyers consequently mingle the tastes and the ideas of the aristocratic circles in which they move, with the aristocratic interests of their profession.

And indeed the lawyer-like character which I am endeavoring to depict is most distinctly to be met with in England: there, laws are esteemed not so much because they are good, as because they are old; and if it be necessary to modify them in any respect, or to adapt them to the changes which time operates in society, recourse is had to the most inconceivable contrivances in order to uphold the traditionary fabric, and to maintain that nothing has been done which does not square with the intentions, and complete the labors, of former generations. The very individuals who conduct these changes disclaim all intention of innovation, and they had rather resort to absurd expedients than plead guilty to so great a crime. This spirit appertains more especially to the English lawyers; they seem indifferent to the real meaning of what they treat, and they direct all their attention to the letter, seeming inclined to infringe the rules of common sense and of humanity, rather than to swerve one tittle from the law. The English legislation may be compared to the stock of an old tree, upon which lawyers have engrafted the most various shoots, with the hope that, although their fruits may differ, their foliage at least will be confounded with the venerable trunk which supports them all.

In America there are no nobles or literary men, and the people is apt to mistrust the wealthy; lawyers consequently form the highest political class, and the most cultivated circle of society. They have therefore nothing to gain by innovation, which adds a conservative interest to their natural taste for public order. If I were asked where I place the American aristocracy, I should reply without hesitation, that it is not composed of the rich, who are united together by no common tie, but that it occupies the judicial bench and the bar.

The more we reflect upon all that occurs in the United States, the more shall we be persuaded that the lawyers as a body form the most powerful, if not the only, counterpoise to the democratic element. In that country we perceive how eminently the legal profession is qualified by its powers, and even by its defects, to neutralize the vices which are inherent in popular government. When the American people is intoxicated by passion, or carried away by the impetuosity of its ideas, it is checked and stopped by the almost invisible influence of its legal counselors, who secretly oppose their aristocratic propensities to its democratic instincts, their superstitious attachment to what is antique to its love of novelty, their narrow views to its immense designs, and their habitual procrastination to its ardent impatience.

The courts of justice are the most visible organs by which the legal profession is enabled to control the democracy. The judge is a lawyer, who, independently of the taste for regularity and order which he has contracted in the study of legislation, derives an additional love of stability from his own inalienable functions. His legal attainments have already raised him to a distinguished rank amongst his fellow-citizens; his political power completes the distinction of his station, and gives him the inclinations natural to privileged classes.

Armed with the power of declaring the laws to be unconstitutional, the American magistrate perpetually interferes in political affairs. He cannot force the people to make laws, but at least he can oblige it not to disobey its own enactments, or to act inconsistently with its own principles. I am aware that a secret tendency to diminish the judicial power exists in the United States; and by most of the constitutions of the several States the Government can, upon the demand of the two houses of the legislature, remove the judges from their station. By some other constitutions the members of the tribunals are elected, and they are even subjected to frequent re-elections. I venture to predict that these innovations will sooner or later be attended with fatal consequences; and that it will be found out at some future period, that the attack which is made upon the judicial power has affected the democratic republic itself.

It must not, however, be supposed that the legal spirit of which I have been speaking has been confined, in the United States, to the courts of justice; it extends far beyond them. As the lawyers constitute the only enlightened class which the people does not mistrust, they are naturally called upon to occupy most of the public stations. They fill the legislative assemblies, and they conduct the administration; they consequently exercise a powerful influence upon the formation of the law, and upon its execution. The lawyers are, however, obliged to yield to the current of public opinion, which is too strong for them to resist it, but it is easy to find indications of what their conduct would be, if they were free to act as they chose. The Americans, who have made such copious innovations in their political legislation, have introduced very sparing alterations in their civil laws, and that with great difficulty, although those laws are frequently repugnant to their social condition. The reason of this is, that in matters of civil law the majority is obliged to defer to the authority of the legal profession, and that the American lawyers are disinclined to innovate when they are left to their own choice.

It is curious for a Frenchman, accustomed to a very different state of things, to hear the perpetual complaints which are made in the United States against the stationary propensities of legal men, and their prejudices in favor of existing institutions.

The influence of the legal habits which are common in America extends beyond the limits I have just pointed out. Scarcely any question arises in the United States which does not become, sooner or later, a subject of judicial debate; hence all parties are obliged to borrow the ideas, and even the language, usual in judicial proceedings in their daily controversies. As most public men are, or have been legal practitioners, they introduce the customs and technicalities of their profession into the affairs of the country. The jury extends this habitude to all classes. The language of the law thus becomes, in some measure, a vulgar tongue; the spirit of the law, which is produced in the schools and courts of justice, gradually penetrates beyond their walls into the bosom of society, where it descends to the lowest classes, so that the whole people contracts the habits and the tastes of the magistrate. The lawyers of the United States form a party which is but little feared and scarcely perceived, which has no badge peculiar to itself, which adapts itself with great flexibility to the exigencies of the time, and accommodates itself to all the movements of the social body: but this party extends over the whole community, and it penetrates into all classes of society; it acts upon the country imperceptibly, but it finally fashions it to suit its purposes.

Trial by Jury in the United States Considered as a Political Institution

. . . . To look upon the jury as a mere judicial institution, is to confine our attention to a very narrow view of it; for however great its influence may be upon the decisions of the law courts, that influence is very subordinate to the powerful effects which it produces on the destinies of the community at large. The jury is above all a political institution, and it must be regarded in this light in order to be duly appreciated.

By the jury, I mean a certain number of citizens chosen indiscriminately, and invested with a temporary right of judging. Trial by jury, as applied to the repression of crime, appears to me to introduce an eminently republican element into the government, upon the following grounds:

The institution of the jury may be aristocratic or democratic, according to the class of society from which the jurors are selected; but it always preserves its republican character, in as much as it places the real direction of society in the hands of the governed, or of a portion of the governed, instead of leaving it under the authority of the Government. Force is never more than a transient element of success; and after force comes the notion of right. A government which should only be able to crush its enemies upon a field of battle would very soon be destroyed. The true sanction of political laws is to be found in penal legislation, and if that sanction be wanting, the law will sooner or later lose its cogency. He who punishes infractions of the law, is therefore the real master of society. Now, the institution of the jury raises the people itself, or at least a class of citizens, to the bench of judicial authority. The institution of the jury consequently invests the people, or that class of citizens, with the direction of society.

In England the jury is returned from the aristocratic portion of the nation; the aristocracy makes the laws, applies the laws, and punishes all infractions of the laws; everything is established upon a consistent footing, and England may with truth be said to constitute an aristocratic republic. In the United States the same system is applied to the whole people. Every American citizen is qualified to be an elector, a juror, and is eligible to office. The system of the jury, as it is understood in America, appears to me to be as direct and as extreme a consequence of the sovereignty of the people as universal suffrage. These institutions are two instruments of equal power, which contribute to the supremacy of the majority. All the sovereigns who have chosen to govern by their own authority, and to direct society instead of obeying its direction, have destroyed or enfeebled the institution of the jury. The monarchs of the House of Tudor sent to prison jurors who refused to convict, and Napoleon caused them to be returned by his agents.

However clear most of these truths may seem to be, they do not command universal assent, and in France, at least, the institution of trial by jury is still very imperfectly understood. If the question arises as to the proper qualification of jurors, it is confined to a discussion of the intelligence and knowledge of the citizens who may be returned, as if the jury was merely a judicial institution. This appears to me to be the least part of the subject. The jury is pre-eminently a political institution; it must be regarded as one form of the sovereignty of the people; when that sovereignty is repudiated, it must be rejected; or it must be adapted to the laws by which that sovereignty is established. The jury is that portion of the nation to which the execution of the laws is entrusted, as the Houses of Parliament constitute that part of the nation which makes the laws; and in order that society may be governed with consistency and uniformity, the list of citizens qualified to serve on juries must increase and diminish with the list of electors. This I hold to be the point of view most worthy of the attention of the legislator; and all that remains is merely accessory.

I am so entirely convinced that the jury is pre-eminently a political institution that I still consider it in this light when it is applied in civil causes. Laws are always unstable unless they are founded upon the manners of a nation; manners are the only durable and resisting power in a people. When the jury is reserved for criminal offences, the people only witnesses its occasional action in certain particular cases; the ordinary course of life goes on without its interference, and it is considered as an instrument, but not as the only instrument, of obtaining justice. This is true *à fortiori* when the jury is only applied to certain criminal causes.

When, on the contrary, the influence of the jury is extended to civil causes, its application is constantly palpable; it affects all the interests of the community; everyone co-operates in its work: it thus penetrates into all the usages of life, it fashions the human mind to its peculiar forms, and is gradually associated with the idea of justice itself.

The institution of the jury, if confined to criminal causes, is always in danger, but when once it is introduced into civil proceedings it defies the aggressions of time and of man. If it had been as easy to remove the jury from the manners as from the laws of England, it would have perished under Henry VIII, and Elizabeth, and the civil jury did in reality, at that period, save the liberties of the country. In whatever manner the jury be applied, it cannot fail to exercise a powerful influence upon the national character; but this influence is prodigiously increased when it is introduced into civil causes. The jury, and more especially the civil jury, serves to communicate the spirit of the judges to the minds of all the citizens; and this spirit, with the habits which attend it, is the soundest preparation for free institutions. It imbues all classes with a respect for the thing judged, and with the notion of right. If these two elements be removed, the love of independence is reduced to a mere destructive passion. It teaches men to practice equity, every man learns to judge his neighbor as he would himself be judged; and this is especially true of the jury in civil causes; for, whilst the number of persons who have reason to apprehend a criminal prosecution is small, every one is liable to have a civil action brought against him. The jury teaches every man not to recoil before the responsibility of his own actions, and impresses him with that manly confidence without which political virtue cannot exist. It invests each citizen with a kind of magistracy; it makes them all feel the duties which they are bound to discharge towards society, and the part which they take in the Government. By obliging men to turn their attention to affairs which are not exclusively their own, it rubs off that individual egotism which is the rust of society.

The jury contributes most powerfully to form the judgment, and to increase the natural intelligence of a people, and this is, in my opinion, its greatest advantage. It may be regarded as a gratuitous public school ever open, in which every juror learns to exercise his rights, enters into daily communication with the most learned and enlightened members of the upper classes, and becomes practically acquainted with the laws of his country, which are brought within the reach of his capacity by the efforts of the bar, the advice of the judge, and even by the passions of the parties. I think that the practical intelligence and political good sense of the Americans are mainly attributable to the long use which they have made of the jury in civil causes.

I do not know whether the jury is useful to those who are in litigation; but I am certain it is highly beneficial to those who decide the litigation; and I look upon it as one of the most efficacious means for the education of the people which society can employ.

What I have hitherto said applies to all nations; but the remark I am now about to make is peculiar to the Americans and to democratic peoples. I have already observed that in democracies the members of the legal profession, and the magistrates, constitute the only aristocratic body which can check the irregularities of the people. This aristocracy is invested with no physical power, but it exercises its conservative influence upon the minds of men, and the most abundant source of its authority is the institution of the civil jury. In criminal causes, when society is armed against a single individual, the jury is apt to look upon the judge as the passive instrument of social power, and to mistrust his advice. Moreover, criminal causes are entirely founded upon the evidence of facts which common sense can readily appreciate; upon this ground the judge and the jury are equal. Such, however, is not the case in civil causes; then the judge appears as a disinterested arbiter between the conflicting passions of the parties. The jurors look up to him with confidence, and listen to him with respect, for in this instance their intelligence is completely under the control of his learning. It is the judge who sums up the various arguments with which their memory has been wearied out, and who guides them through the devious course of the proceedings; he points their attention to the exact question of fact which they are called upon to solve, and he puts the answer to the question of law into their mouths. His influence upon their verdict is almost unlimited.

If I am called upon to explain why I am but little moved by the arguments derived from the ignorance of jurors in civil causes, I reply, that in these proceedings, whenever the question to be solved is not a mere question of fact, the jury has only the semblance of a judicial body. The jury sanctions the decision of the judge; they by the authority of society which they represent, and he by that of reason and of law.

In England and in America the judges exercise an influence upon criminal trials which the French judges have never possessed. The reason of this difference may easily be discovered; the English and American magistrates establish their authority in civil causes, and only transfer it afterwards to tribunals of another kind, where that authority was not acquired. In some cases (and they are frequently the most important ones) the American judges have the right of deciding causes alone.* Upon these occasions they are accidentally placed in the position which the French judges habitually occupy, but they are still surrounded by the reminiscence of the jury, and their judgment has almost as much authority as the voice of the community at large, represented by that institution. Their influence extends beyond the limits of the courts; in the recreations of private life as well as in the turmoil of public business, abroad and in the legislative assemblies, the American judge is constantly surrounded by men who are accustomed to regard his intelligence as superior to their own; and after having exercised his power in the decision of causes, he continues to influence the habits of thought and the characters of the individuals who took a part in his judgment.

The jury, then, which seems to restrict the rights of magistracy, does in reality consolidate its power; and in no country are the judges so powerful as there, where the people partakes their privileges. It is more especially by means of the jury in civil causes that the American magistrates imbue all classes of society with the spirit of their profession. Thus the jury, which is the most energetic means of making the people rule, is also the most efficacious means of teaching it to rule well.

QUESTIONS

1. Tocqueville describes how the legal system vests extraordinary power with lawyers in the United States and England. To what ends does Tocqueville envision lawyers using this power?

---

* The Federal judges decide upon their own authority almost all the questions most important to the country.

2. How did each of the following lawyers use the power entrusted to him or her: John Adams, Daniel Webster, Abraham Lincoln, Elihu Root, Louis Brandeis, Hoyt Moore, Philip Elman and Elizabeth Hishon?

3. What are the differences Tocqueville perceives between the way Anglo–American lawyers and judges think about the law and the approach of their French counterparts? What aspects of your own legal education reflect the way in which law is analyzed in our country?

4. What are the advantages of the Anglo–American approach of relying on precedent in looking at the law? What are the problems inherent in this approach?

5. Would the French legal system be more likely than the American legal system to depart from a precedent that judges knew to be morally and legally wrong? (See Philip Elman's discussion of how some of the Supreme Court's justices simply wanted to "erase" the sixty-year precedent established by *Plessy v. Ferguson*, Chapter 10 supra).

6. What are the dangers of the legal profession allying itself with a particular social class, as Tocqueville describes? To what extent is the legal profession today allied with a particular social class?

7. Tocqueville describes jury service as an inherent part of the democratic process: "By the jury I mean a certain number of citizens chosen indiscriminately, and invested with a temporary right of judging." Lawyers, however, often seek to manipulate the makeup of jury panels to further their cause (see, for example, the impaneling of the jury in the trial of Sir Walter Raleigh, Chapter 8 supra, and the impaneling of juries in the Boston Massacre trials, Chapter 7 supra). Sometimes preemptory challenges make the jury system less fair (for example when race, sex and religion are the basis for excusing jurors), but sometimes preemptory challenges make the jury system fairer (for example, by excluding jurors who might be biased against a criminal defendant). In cases where preemptory challenges may facilitate impaneling an unbiased jury, which priority is more important— impaneling the unbiased jury or allowing everyone to participate in what Tocqueville identifies as a fundamental part of the democratic process?

Mary Ann Glendon, b. 1938; B.A. University of Chicago 1959, J.D. University of Chicago 1961, M.C.L. University of Chicago 1963; associated with Mayer, Brown & Platt in Chicago 1963–68; professor at Boston College School of Law 1968–86; Learned Hand Professor at Harvard Law School since 1986.

A Nation Under Lawyers

Mary Ann Glendon (1994)

* * *

The disoriented state of the country's legal profession cannot help but have consequences for our law-dependent democratic experiment, as well as for individual attorneys and clients. Lawyers of all sorts, for better or worse, will continue to have much influence on how America deals with the great issues of our time—the deterioration of natural and social environments, crime, poverty, education, race relations, the plight of child-raising families, decaying infrastructure, intense international competition, and so on. Traditionally, the country has depended on the legal profession to supply most of our needs for consensus builders, problem solvers, troubleshooters, dispute avoiders, and dispute settlers. The country's need for talented persons in such roles is greater than it has ever been. The opportunities for satisfaction and a sense of personal accomplishment are unparalleled. The potential of the alternative dispute resolution movement, for example, has barely been tapped. For some thirty years, however, those creative and useful activities have been devalued while litigation has been exalted.

It will not do to say the profession has always been a mixed bag, for the proportions in the mix are of far-reaching significance, as is the relative prestige of various legal activities. Imagine the American legal profession spread out in the manner of a weather map. If we color its order-affirming activities yellow and its adversarial activities blue, the map will be a study in chartreuse. But the shades of green will vary. The yellowish "trader" hue (to reprise Jane Jacobs's heuristic)* will be predominant, because (contrary to television images) most lawyers, most of the time, are engaged in planning, prevention, and problem solving. Relatively close-knit legal

---

* As Professor Glendon earlier explains:

"[Jane] Jacobs maintains that human beings have had basically only two ways of making a living from prehistoric times to the present. One way of life is concerned with acquiring and protecting territories, the other with trading and producing for trade. By a process resembling natural selection, humankind has developed its approaches to the ethics of making a living around two (and only two) matrices. . . .

"To Jacobs, lawyers were a puzzle. They are associated with both guardian and commercial ethics, often switching from one role to another depending on the task. In some contexts, an honesty-based ethic seems to prevail; in others, loyalty seems to be the highest value. Their official canons of ethics are an ambiguous blend of court officer and client service ideals. In the best scientific tradition, Jacobs treated this strange profession that did not fit her theory as an invitation to further investigation and possible discovery.

"She noted with interest that the culture of English barristers, historically at least, had a strong raider cast. . . . Endowed with a virtual monopoly on lawyers' most raiderlike activity—the planning and conduct of courtroom battles—barristers went to great lengths to shun trading. They did not discuss payment for their services (their clerks did it) and would not sue to collect their fee. On the back of the barrister's gown there is still a little pocket that in former times enabled him to be paid without actually seeing or handling money. Unlike solicitors, barristers chiefly belonged to social circles that looked down on persons 'in trade.'

"American conditions, however, were different from the beginning. Lawyers often had to be barristers and solicitors rolled into one. Many of them even sat as justices of the peace, or filled in, on occasion, for an absent judge. Abraham Lincoln's legal career, to take one famous example, involved him in all of those roles. Nor is there any reason to think Lincoln was unique in his ability to perform as a peacemaker among neighbors one day, a zealous advocate for the Illinois Central Railroad on another, and an impartial magistrate on the next. . . ." Mary Ann Glendon, A Nation Under Lawyers 63–65 (1994), citing Jane Jacobs, Systems of Survival: A Dialogue on the Moral Foundations of Commerce and Politics (1992), pp. xi, 130.

communities like Becky Klemt's will be brightest. Several parts of the profession, however, will have a more bluish "guardian/raider" tinge: litigators and those who work in specialties such as plaintiff's personal injury, domestic relations, and criminal law.

Now place our map next to one reflecting the proportions of order-affirming and adversarial activities, say, thirty years ago. Over time, the yellow-green areas have shrunk somewhat and dimmed in brightness. The spread of blue pigments is striking, but equally striking is the fact that the sunny trader hue still predominates. What the maps do not reveal is that the prestige of adversarial activities has risen at an even greater rate than the numbers of lawyers engaged in them. True, those activities have come under intense criticism in recent years. But the profession's connoisseurs of conflict have also been lionized more than ever. Their more numerous brothers and sisters, the artisans of order, receive little recognition from their colleagues or the public. That interesting situation has important personal and political consequences.

Consider first the political implications. The legal profession has always needed its innovators nipping at the heels of its traditionalists, and its heroic advocates alongside its peacemakers and preventive planners. But if Tocqueville was right that lawyers' special attachment to formality, order, and continuity made the legal profession a linchpin of democracy's social checks and balances, a major shift in the proportion and prestige of lawyers who share that attachment is admonitory. It is difficult to say more. History affords no example of what happens to a highly law-dependent polity when the traditional predominance of counselors, planners, and problem solvers is challenged by swelling ranks of innovators, iconoclasts, and adversarial advocates. We are the example.

The declining prestige accorded to order-affirming and peacemaking activities of lawyers has personal effects as well. Few lawyers are virtuoso courtroom performers or full-time vindicators of political and civil rights. Sadly, in recent years, the artisans of order in small and large firms, in government agencies, in corporate legal departments, have received little encouragement and respect. They lack even the cold comforts held out to their ancestors by Holmes, who understood a practitioner's fears and doubts, and respected the dignity of the legal craftsman's everyday labor. No wonder many are dejected.

Yet competent accomplishment of the everyday tasks of lawyers deserves to be celebrated in our complex, pluralistic nation oriented to the rule of law, representative government, and fundamental freedoms. Lawyers cannot claim to have a monopoly on any of the following qualities, but no other occupational group in American society displays the ensemble to the same degree. For that reason, no other group has more to offer American society simply by building on what it has always done best.

The Eye for the Issue. Lawyers like to think—and often it is true—that their training and experience make them handy to have around when people are deliberating about how to reach a common objective, or when they are at odds but need to go on living together—in the neighborhood, workplace, club, church, city, or nation. What makes a lawyer a skillful collaborator or consensus builder is more than just the clean mental slate of any intelligent onlooker. It is his practice in discerning the precise issues in controversy, whether the disagreement is about means to an end or about ends themselves. A trained eye for the issue enables lawyers to constructively disagree with their own clients as well as to narrow the scope of conflict between antagonists. It suits lawyers for the increasingly important roles of mediators. "Can any discipline be more valuable today," constitutional scholar Paul Freund once asked, "than one that teaches us to look through the great antinomies that present themselves like gladiators for our favors—individualism and collectivism, liberty and authority, secularism and clericalism—to look through these in order to discover the precise issue in controversy, the precise consequences of one decision or another, and the possibility of an accommodation by deflating the isms and narrowing the schisms?"

The Feel for Common Ground. The lawyer's experience in delineating the issues that divide people, and in grasping just what is essential or expendable to each party in a discussion, also gives her a feel for the common ground that even determined opponents may share—and the ability to frame a settlement in terms that antagonists can accept. Often it is a lawyer who, in public or private negotiations, comes up with the face-saving compromise that everyone can live with. Effective mediation in situations where deep grievances prevent the partisans from thinking clearly requires mastering the facts, listening exhaustively to all sides, understanding the positions, and patient searching for the scraps of territory on which accord can be constructed. Interestingly, regular users of mediation services are finding that lawyers with extensive practice backgrounds often make better mediators than long-time judges.

The Eye to the Future. When issues are clarified and agreements reached in principle, someone still has to give inchoate understandings a concrete form that will stand the test of time. By training and experience lawyers are accustomed to making shrewd guesses about where trouble is most likely to arise in the future, and adept at creating arrangements to avoid those situations or minimize harm if they occur. As Yale's Anthony Kronman puts it: "The ability to fashion hypothetical cases and empathically to explore both real and invented ones is the lawyer's professional forte." A specialized, cultivated foresight often helps a lawyer to supply the right words, the time-tested formula, the reliable procedural safeguards, the safe passage through stormy straits.

Mastery of the Apparatus. "So what is it that lawyers and judges know that philosophers and economists do not?" former Solicitor General Charles Fried once asked rhetorically. "The answer is simple," he said. "The law." Fried was not being a smart aleck. There's no getting around the fact that a regulatory state with a complex economy requires an array of specialists in interpreting, explaining, applying, and coordinating the rules, principles, and standards emanating from sources as diverse as the local zoning board and the United States Congress. Obvious? Yes, but sometimes we lose sight of the obvious—especially as some law schools begin to neglect the teaching of law in favor of philosophy, economics, and other subjects that are useful adjuncts to, but no substitutes for, legal training. Mastery of the apparatus includes care for the apparatus, its history, its maintenance and proper functioning; awareness of its range of uses; and understanding of its limitations.

Legal Architecture. Without institutional structures and frameworks, the torrent of laws, regulations, and decisions spilling out from legislatures, courts, administrative agencies, and private associations would not constitute a legal system, but only a regulatory deluge. A country's constitution, of course, provides the basic framework. But the never-ending legal construction that goes on within that framework requires architects as well as carpenters. The authors of well-crafted corporate charters and bylaws, collective bargaining agreements, leases, trusts and estate plans, parliamentary procedures, constitution-like regulatory schemes, and so on, have extraordinary opportunities to affect for better or worse the quality of everyday life in our large commercial republic. Theirs is the delicate job of providing structure and order while leaving as much room as possible for spontaneity and creativity. That's why an older generation of legal educators had such great respect for those who negotiate and draft such instruments. Only someone who has never negotiated a long-term agreement and tried to reduce it to writing can regard the exercise as an easy one. It is this aspect of legal work, Paul Freund once wrote, that "most nearly resembles the enterprise of the artist."

Procedure. The history of law, to a great extent, is the record of a search for means to enable people to order their lives together according to principles that can be understood and accepted by affected parties and onlookers—even when the outcomes go against their interests or desires. Disputes must not only be settled, but settled in such a way as to minimize festering resentment and the renewed eruption of conflict. Good lawyers will try hard to accomplish this result without ever going to court. But when all other methods of dispute resolution fail, the legal system is our alternative to private force. Adjudication in advanced societies means, at a minimum, a commitment to hearing both sides, impartial judges, reason-giving in arguments and judgments, and procedures that help to minimize arbitrariness. Though lawyers did not invent procedure, they have become its high priests and protectors. It was lawyers who developed reliable procedures in place of ordeal and torture for the investigation and trial of facts; courtroom protocols for the presentation of arguments; and the law of evidence with its ever more sophisticated understanding of relevance, probability, and human cognition. Procedure pervades the lawyer's world. Love of procedure makes the most diverse members of the legal profession cousins, if not siblings, under the skin. Proceduralism radiates from the law to every corner of American business, political, and associational life.

Problem Solving. Many of the most rewarding moments of law practice occur when a lawyer devises a viable solution to a problem that has brought a client to wit's end, or when lawyers for antagonists resolve the conflict in a way that expands the pie for all concerned. Even in nonlegal settings—the PTA, the corporate boardroom, the town finance committee, the church council—when everyone else has given up, it is often the lawyer who fashions the strategy that works. If the key to success in problem solving were individual ingenuity or common sense, lawyers would be of no special use. The added value that lawyers bring to the table, besides specialized training, is a vast fund of inherited experience. The humble form book (or the firm's computer bank) is every lawyer's endowment, a record of the trials and errors, successes and failures of others in a huge range of variants on recurring human problems. Faced with a new variant, a lawyer typically invents little, but adds, adapts, and rearranges much. Some of the most ingenious legal devices from the medieval trust to the Uniform Probate Code, from the United States Constitution to the federal securities legislation, have been produced in just that way.

Strong Tolerance. Representing other people, in both friendly and adversarial situations, promotes in lawyers an ability to enter empathically into another person's way of seeing things while retaining a certain detachment. That cast of mind in turn fosters a sturdier form of tolerance than that produced by mere relativism or pacts of nonaggression. Strong tolerance can be attentive, protective, and respectful to the other person without being "nonjudgmental." Some such qualities, Learned Hand thought, would greatly aid the country's adjustment to a larger and more varied population. No one can say for certain whether the American design for government will weather the twin challenges of bigness and heterogeneity, but it would help if the sails of the ship of state were billowed by the spirit of which Hand wrote: a "temper which does not press a partisan advantage to the bitter end, which can understand and will respect the other side, which feels a unity between all citizens—real and not the factitious product of propaganda—which recognizes their common fate and their common aspirations."

Incremental Change. As a great lawyer once pointed out: "A state without the means of some change is without the means of its conservation." Nevertheless, Edmund Burke went on, "it is with infinite caution that any man ought to venture upon pulling down an edifice which has answered in any tolerable degree for ages the common purposes of society, and on building again without a pattern." The American Founders, most of them steeped in the same legal traditions as Burke, designed durable political institutions that contained within themselves the means of change. For two hundred years, the American legal profession has provided the polity with a reliable supply of citizens especially attuned to the twin necessities of conserving hard-won achievements and imaginatively adapting old arrangements to new circumstances. Like architects, lawyers are usually at their best when working with existing materials—reshaping, recycling, reshuffling, and adding to the usable past, rather than destroying and starting afresh. In Anthony Kronman's words, they "know how to extend and revise the traditions of their craft in ways that are faithful to the meaning and spirit of those traditions themselves."

Now, returning to the problem of feeling bad when one ought to be feeling good, an attentive reader may have noticed that all of the foregoing traits have one feature in common. The more fully a lawyer excels in them, the less likely it is that his or her work will receive acclaim beyond the circle of those immediately benefited. Peacemaking, problem-solving lawyers are the legal profession's equivalent of doctors who practice preventive medicine. Their efforts are generally overshadowed by the heroics of surgeons and litigators. The plain fact is that much of what lawyers do best is exacting, unglamourous, and unadvertised—the reasonable settlement that averts costly litigation, the creditors' arrangement that permits a failing business to regain its health, the patient drafting of model legislation within the National Conference of Commissioners on Uniform State Laws and the American Law Institute.

The exaltation of litigation, moneymaking, and efforts to achieve social transformation through law in recent years has been at the expense of the useful services that have always given lawyers in the aggregate their best chance to achieve personal satisfaction while contributing to the well-being of their fellow citizens. The law schools and the organized bar have responded only slowly to the need to develop lawyers' capacities for creative problem solving.

Meanwhile, the current devaluation of the ordinary activities to which most lawyers still devote most of their attention, day in and day out, must be an important reason why so many lawyers feel bad when they should be feeling good. They are torn between their complex obligations to client and court, on the one hand, and their fear, on the other, of being blindsided by competitors, adversaries, and even colleagues, who no longer acknowledge those obligations. Attorneys in all sorts of roles are under pressure to transform themselves on the model of hardball litigators. Many transactional lawyers now want to be participants in deals, rather than advisers to deal-makers.

Yet why should a lawyer not take pride and pleasure in achievements akin to those of a skilled practitioner of preventive medicine, a builder whose house will last for generations, or a parent whose children grow into happy adults and productive citizens? The question that is so often debated—whether the United States has too many lawyers—is the wrong question altogether. Whether a society has too many lawyers depends entirely on what its lawyers are doing and how they imagine the good life. If all lawyers followed Lincoln's advice to be peacemakers among neighbors, there could never be too many lawyers. And there would still, as Lincoln said, be business enough.

The Once and Future of the Legal Profession

(Book Review).
Michael M. Uhlmann.
1995 Public Interest Law Review 173

Glendon's critique of the legal profession is in some respects a continuation of themes she broached in her widely praised 1991 book, *Rights Talk:*

The Impoverishment of Political Discourse. There, she lamented our diminished sense of political community and the degeneration of constitutional debate into a feckless logomachy about whose rights trump whose. Although the narrow focus of her new book is what lawyers think about themselves and their chosen occupation, its broad theme is the self-denigration of the legal profession and what that means to a nation whose roots are uniquely intertwined with the rule of law. Appropriately enough, Professor Glendon begins with Tocqueville's praise of lawyers and lawyering in the early Republic. Lawyers were, he said, the closest thing to an aristocratic class that he had observed in America. They brought continuity and stability to a society whose tendencies were otherwise turbulent and centrifugal. Tocqueville was acutely aware—in ways that we are not—of the ancient skepticism concerning democracy. According to this view, democratic regimes were preoccupied with short-term, venal interests and inclined to volatility and envy. For these reasons, they tended to be weak and often short-lived: if they did not crumble from within, they were apt to be overrun from without. When the Framers undertook to create, in James Madison's words, "a republican remedy for the diseases most incident to republican government,"* they believed that the rule of law as solemnly embodied in the Constitution could overcome the ancient prejudice against the deficiencies of popular government. As Martin Diamond once put it, they believed that a properly constituted government could make democracy safe for the world.

This emphatic reliance on the rule of law in the American regime necessarily enhanced the social and political dignity of the lawyer, which is one reason why Tocqueville hoped that lawyers would act as ballast for the democratic ship of state. For the better part of our history, Glendon argues, the best lawyers were esteemed not merely because they were clever rhetoricians or wealthy pillars of the community, but because they exercised a conspicuously important public trust as stewards of the rule of law. To be sure, not all lawyers thought or acted in such high-minded terms, but the ideal was proclaimed by school and bench and bar alike. There were scalawags aplenty, but they wouldn't have dreamed of defending their behavior in public, nor would their cunning have been acclaimed in the popular media. This older dispensation, however, appears to have gone the way of parchment and quill. The new order, says Glendon, is represented by a series of propositions utterly inconsistent with the earlier tradition (p.6):

> that we live under a rule of men, not law; that the Constitution is just an old text that means whatever the current crop of judges says it does; that all rules (including the rules of professional ethics) are infinitely manipulable; that law is a business like any other; and that business is just the unrestrained pursuit of self-interest.

The remarkable thing, says Glendon, is not that these opinions are new (they are not), but that they now have a sizable following and are openly advanced and defended by many leading lights of the law.

---

* THE FEDERALIST, No. 10, at 84 (James Madison) (Clinton Rossiter ed., 1961).

The world of private practice has absorbed the new doctrine all too well. Professor Glendon, who practiced in Chicago for some years before turning to teaching, has a good feel for life in the modern firm and how it has changed over the past generation. She eschews the overworked distinction between "trade" and "profession" which has dominated public discussion of late and relies instead on Jane Jacobs' distinction between "raider" ethics (which prize combative strength and cunning) and "trader" ethics (which prize conciliation and reasoned discourse). Acknowledging that the law has always had its share of both types, Glendon worries that the raider mentality now exercises a talismanic hold on today's practitioners. The result has been in many cases "a mutually destructive war of all against all" (p. 286). She notes the moral ambivalence that so often attends discussions of professional ethics today, throwing the lawyer back upon his own instinct, which in turn seldom moves beyond an unreflective calculation of his own self-interest. But where self-interest reigns supreme, in what is a lawyer to vest personal pride? Alas, it seems to be litigation, the pursuit of billable hours, and the celebration of politically fashionable causes. These goals have been achieved, she says, "at the expense of the useful services that have always given lawyers in the aggregate their best chance to achieve personal satisfaction while contributing to the well-being of their fellow citizens" (p. 108).

Business as a Calling: Work and the Examined Life

By Michael Novak (1996).

Four Characteristics of a Calling

First, each calling is unique to each individual. Not everyone wants to be a psychiatrist ... Nor, for that matter, does everyone want to work in business. Each of us is unique in our calling ...

Second, a calling requires certain preconditions. It requires more than desires; it requires talent. Not everyone can be, simply by desiring it, an opera singer, or professional athlete, or leader of a large enterprise. For a calling to be right, it must fit our abilities. Another precondition is love—not just love of the final product but, as the essayist Logan Pearsall Smith once put it, "The test of a vocation is love of drudgery it involves." Long hours, frustrations, small steps forward, struggles: unless these too are welcomed with a certain joy, the claim to being called has a hollow ring.

Third, a true calling reveals its presence by the enjoyment and sense of renewed energies its practice yields us. This does not mean that sometimes we do not groan inwardly at the weight of the burdens imposed on us or that we never feel reluctance about reentering bloody combat. Facing hard tasks necessarily exacts dread. Indeed, there are times when we wish we did not have to face every burden our calling imposes on us. Still, finding ourselves where we are and with the responsibilities we bear, we know it is our duty—part of what we were meant to do—to soldier on.

Enjoying what we do is not always a feeling of enjoyment; it is sometimes the gritty resolution a man or woman shows in doing what must be done—perhaps with inner dread and yet without whimpering self-pity. These are things a grown man or woman must do. There is an odd satisfaction in bearing certain pains. . . .

A fourth truth about callings is also apparent: they are not usually easy to discover. Frequently, many false paths are taken before the satisfying path is at last uncovered. Experiments, painful setbacks, false hopes, discernment, prayer, and much patience are often required before the "light goes on."

QUESTIONS

1. Lon Fuller and John Randall describe the legal profession as a "calling." See Report of the Joint Conference on Professional Responsibility, Chapter 6 supra. What does Alexis de Tocqueville perceive to be the profession's calling? What does Mary Ann Glendon view lawyers' calling to be?

2. Glendon notes that "[m]any transactional lawyers now want to be participants in deals, rather than advisers to deal-makers." What are the dangers of a lawyer becoming too involved with her client's affairs? Does such involvement sacrifice a lawyer's objectivity?

3. Do you agree with Glendon's assessment of instruction in law schools? How do you think law school instruction could better prepare lawyers for their professional lives?

Richard L. Abel, b. 1941; B.A. Harvard University 1962; LL.B. Columbia University 1965; Ph.D. University of London 1974; Assistant and Associate Professor at Yale Law School 1968–74; attorney with New Haven Legal Assistance Association 1971–72; Connell Professor of Law at U.C.L.A. School of Law since 1974.

United States: The Contradictions of Professionalism

By Richard L. Abel
From Lawyers in Society: I
(Richard L. Abel & Philip S.C. Lewis Eds., 1988).

The trajectory of professionalism among American lawyers is unusual in several respects. They began to professionalize later than lawyers in almost any other nation—not until the end of the nineteenth century. They embarked on this project with fewer resources, because the political rupture with England a century earlier and the late Jacksonian attack on privilege disrupted traditional procedures for qualifying as a solicitor or barrister. The United States differed in this from those common law countries that preserved their ties to England much longer—Canada, Australia, New Zealand, and India, whose barristers often were called to the English Bar and whose solicitors followed an apprenticeship quite similar to that of their English counterparts. Indeed, the United States displays a surprising parallel to continental European legal systems (which some late nineteenth century educational reformers consciously sought to emulate) in that the rise of professionalism coincided with the expansion of the university.

If the legal profession rose from humble beginnings, however, it achieved everything promised by the paradigmatic American fables of Abraham Lincoln and Horatio Alger—greater wealth and political influence than are enjoyed by any other national legal profession, although, like other parvenus, an uncertain social status. This qualified success also was typically American in that it was coveted by many but achieved by few; most American lawyers proudly claim the hollow title of "professional" but share few of its perquisites. As a result, the internal differentiation of the profession has reproduced—indeed, magnified—the heterogeneous backgrounds of American lawyers, which are an inevitable reflection of the national experience.

These unique features in the history of American lawyers serve to reveal—indeed, highlight—the many contradictions within the professional project. An occupation becomes a profession by controlling the supply of those who produce its services while justifying such control in terms of the public interest. Whereas the object of American physicians was to eliminate competing schools of healers, the problem for American lawyers was to establish *any* controls over production, which were virtually nonexistent until the last quarter of the nineteenth century. Yet, although bar associations eventually succeeded in controlling both the numbers who qualified as lawyers and the background characteristics of those who did so, this very success had long-term consequences that threatened to undermine the professional project. Limits on entry never achieved anything like total homogeneity, and the ascriptive differences that emerged, when superimposed on professional stratification, belied professional claims of community and meritocracy. The virtual exclusion of women and minorities until the late 1960s temporarily may have enhanced the status and income of white male lawyers but at a considerable cost in legitimacy. Moreover, the experience of the last two decades dramatically demonstrates that efforts to control supply cannot prevail indefinitely against the economic forces of a market economy and the political attack on ascriptive barriers under the banner of the dominant liberal ideology.

Having controlled entry into the profession, lawyers sought to suppress competition among qualified producers by promulgating restrictive practices in the guise of ethical codes. But whereas the struggle to erect entry barriers tended to unify the profession (if lawyers from different strata disagreed about the urgency of the campaign and the tactics to be used), the attempt to dampen competition aggravated internal tensions—economic differences between those who wished to compete and those who did not—and ideological disagreements between those seeking to elevate the status of the profession by giving it a noncommercial tone and others relatively unconcerned about status. Furthermore, restrictive practices become increasingly difficult to justify in a society that at least pays lip service to laissez-faire ideology and extols consumer sovereignty.

With the erosion of professional control over the production *of* producers of legal services and *by* those producers, lawyers have turned increasingly to market strategies that seek to augment demand; but these are even more problematic. First, whereas control over supply seeks to reduce intraprofessional competition (if with only limited success), efforts to stimulate demand inevitably intensify such competition. Second, to the extent that the profession successfully persuades the state to subsidize demand or constructs private schemes for third-party payment, it inescapably sacrifices some control to those new paymasters. Third, demand creation undermines the profession's legitimacy insofar as it belies professional pretensions to altruism, noncommercialism, and independence. Fourth, by proclaiming and documenting the "unmet need" for legal services, lawyers open themselves to the reasonable request that they satisfy such need, with pay or without. Finally, it is very doubtful that the demand for legal services, particularly among individual consumers, can be expanded significantly.

American lawyers pursued the project of market control through their professional organizations, and they justified those institutions by the axiomatic identification of professionalism with self-regulation. But the actual experience of self-regulation has tended to undermine the profession's claim to privileged immunity from external oversight. Controls over misconduct were established quite late. They were ineffective in detecting, investigating, and punishing misconduct, and the public was fully aware of these failings. Both the substantive rules and the disciplinary process have been unresponsive to consumer grievances, especially since neither does anything to ensure continuing technical competence among lawyers. Discipline also has aggravated tensions within the profession, because ethical rules stigmatize the behavior of low-status lawyers while tolerating the functional equivalent among the elite. As external dissatisfaction with professional self-regulation has accumulated, courts, legislatures, administrative agencies, and consumers have asserted increasing control over lawyers.

Professions emerge out of the functional division of labor among occupations and persist only as long as they reflect some coherent, unitary category within that functional differentiation. I argued above that the unity of the American legal profession always has been qualified by the diverse backgrounds of its members, a heterogeneity that has increased in the last two decades with the entry of women and racial minorities. These ascriptive differences are unequally distributed across a set of roles that have undergone progressive differentiation, both functional and structural. Until after World War II, a single role dominated the profession—the private practitioner, working independently or with a partner or associate. Since then, however, several changes have threatened this clear professional identity. First, the number of employed lawyers has increased to the point where it approaches the number of independent practitioners. Second, as law firms have expanded, many independent practitioners have become employers of numerous subordinates and members of large bureaucratic organizations. Third, several distinct subgroups have grown in both size and coherence: judges, government employees, lawyers employed in business enterprises, and law professors. These changes have profound implications for the profession. Increasing differentiation and stratification undermine the sense of professional community and threaten the capacity of lawyers to engage in self-governance. They also enhance the importance of those institutions (primarily formal education) that allocate lawyers to professional roles.

With the erosion of control over supply, heightened competition, loss of independence to public and private third-party paymasters, growth of external regulation, the flight into employment, and the dissolution of community, the professional project of the first half of the twentieth century is in serious disarray.

CONTROLLING THE PRODUCTION OF LAWYERS

Although the newly independent United States had more than its share of lawyers, many of whom played a major role in establishing and staffing the nascent state and federal governments, they were not a profession. The entry barriers, which distinguish a profession from an occupation, remained poorly defined for the first hundred years of independence. Although colonial American lawyers had qualified in much the same way as their English counterparts, those paths were closed. After the Revolution there was no point in being called to the Bar at one of the Inns of Court in London, and America possessed no comparable institutions. Like English solicitors, some American lawyers did continue to serve an apprenticeship of up to five years, but even in England this was enforced only loosely at the end of the eighteenth century.

When the Jacksonians attacked privilege and monopoly in the 1840s, therefore, they encountered little resistance. Professional associations of lawyers had been weakened by the flight of the Tory elite following the Revolution. In any case, they were organized by city or county, whereas only state governments could control entry to the profession. The frontier functioned as a safety valve for the overproduction of lawyers, offering the alternative of migration to those who could not find sufficient work on the eastern seaboard. Consequently, whereas fourteen out of nineteen American jurisdictions required lawyers to complete an apprenticeship in 1800, only nine out of thirty-nine did so in 1860. Formal education, liberal or professional, was neither demanded of lawyers nor acquired by most of them until the end of the nineteenth century. For there were few postsecondary institutions, and the new nation lacked a highly rationalized body of legal doctrine that either called for, or rewarded, extensive study. As late as the eve of the Civil War, there were fewer than 1,000 law students throughout the country, most of them enrolled in small schools, of indifferent quality, offering short courses of a year or two. No jurisdiction insisted on law school training, and only a few even allowed academic study to substitute for whatever period of apprenticeship they required. In 1891 it was estimated that 80 percent of all practicing lawyers never had attended law school.

Yet, formal legal education began to expand about 1890 and rapidly displaced apprenticeship as the mode of qualification. This was not the result of state coercion. Although the number of jurisdictions requiring apprenticeship rose from nine out of thirty-nine in 1860 to sixteen out of thirty-nine in 1881, only six of these even granted law students any reduction of the mandatory apprenticeship, and as late as 1923, not a single jurisdiction insisted on any academic legal education. Nevertheless, the number of law schools doubled between 1890 and 1910, and the number of law students increased fourfold. By the end of the next decade virtually no one was entering the profession by means of apprenticeship. The significance of this transformation cannot be overestimated, although the reasons for it remain obscure . . . .

There is an irony in this evolution from apprenticeship to the academy. Apprenticeship is a highly particularistic institution, in which entrants are selected on the basis of personal contacts and ascribed characteristics; however, it is less effective as a sorting device that justifies the ultimate location of the lawyer within the professional hierarchy. Formal education is far more universalistic, either admitting all applicants or selecting among them on the basis of more or less objective measures of performance, but its imprint is more permanent. The hierarchy of educational institutions has a profound impact on the allocation of graduates to positions within the stratified profession. The displacement of apprenticeship by the academy thus admitted a more heterogeneous group of entrants but also did more to legitimate inequality among them.

. . . .

Control over the production of lawyers not only limits their numbers but also defines their characteristics. Cost is a central mechanism. The decline of part-time education made the legal profession much less accessible to those who needed to work in order to support themselves and pay for their education. Full-time institutions also entailed greater living expenses (because students could not live at home) and demanded much higher tuition. Furthermore, the tuition charged by full-time institutions has increased tenfold in the last fifty years—thirtyfold at some schools—and most rapidly since the 1960s. The total annual cost of attending a private law school now approaches $20,000, and even the minority of public institutions cost almost half as much. True, this rise has been accompanied by the growth of financial assistance, from both the schools themselves and the federal government; however, most of that assistance has taken the form of loans. As a result, lawyers begin practice with tens of thousands of dollars of debt accumulated during seven years of postsecondary education, which strongly influences the range of career alternatives they were willing to consider.

* * *

We strongly associate professions with a licensing examination required by the state, which serves as both the fundamental guarantee of quality and the principal mechanism for controlling numbers. Yet the bar examination has performed those functions for American lawyers only at certain times and with respect to particular categories of entrants. For a long time attending law school and passing the bar examination were alternatives rather than sequential hurdles. During the last quarter of the nineteenth century many jurisdictions automatically admitted graduates of law schools situated within their own borders and even those from out-of-state schools. Naturally, this so-called diploma privilege was favored by the schools themselves, which enjoyed higher enrollments as a result, and was opposed by the organized profession, which wanted to control entry. The profession gradually prevailed, and the number of jurisdictions granting the diploma privilege dwindled to fifteen in 1949 and five in 1973, with the result that the proportion of entrants admitted in this fashion dropped from 10 percent in the 1930s to 2 percent today.

Even after the bar examination was required, it was not always a significant obstacle. Written examinations first were introduced only in 1870 and did not become widespread until the end of the century. They were administered locally, allowing applicants to shop around for the most lenient within their own states. Only four out of forty-nine jurisdictions had central examination boards in 1890, but the number rose to thirty-seven by 1917. Even then, examiners were poorly paid and few in number. Although there was a slight decline in the pass rates during the first two decades of the twentieth century, the rates fluctuated widely. Only toward the end of this period did a distinction emerge between the industrialized states on one hand, characterized by major cities, substantial immigration, large and growing populations, sizable legal professions, a high proportion of part-time law students, and considerable pressure to enter the profession—which had lower and declining pass rates—and the more rural states on the other hand, either agricultural or frontier, with relatively homogeneous native populations, little immigration or population growth, a small legal profession, and little pressure for entry—which had constant and high pass rates.

The Great Depression affected both categories. Between 1929 and 1930, pass rates fell in fourteen states and rose in only six (out of the thirty-six for which figures are available). Three-quarters of all jurisdictions had lower pass rates in 1933 than in 1927, although the number taking the examination actually had decreased. In many jurisdictions the decline was precipitous—a fall of up to 40 percentage points. It was widely recognized, and just as widely accepted, that bar examiners were imposing a quota in light of the reduced demand for lawyers' services. Pass rates reached a low point in 1935, which also was the bottom of the Great Depression, and then began to climb as the number of examinees dropped. Even when rates were lowest, the examination may not have been a barrier to the persistent; several studies estimated that 90 percent of repeaters ultimately passed.

* * *

The aspirant who has completed prelegal education, gained admission to law school, graduated, and passed the bar examination still has three other hurdles to overcome. In 1909 the ABA applauded the decision by some state bars to exclude noncitizens from practice and urged the other jurisdictions to follow suit. By 1946, all forty-eight states had done so. Yet, patently ascriptive criteria was very difficult to defend within a liberal polity, and this one was struck down by the U.S. Supreme Court in 1973. Each state bar also erected protectionist barriers against out-of-state lawyers, limiting their appearances in particular matters and insisting that they become residents before taking the bar examination or being admitted to practice. These rules were strengthened between 1930 and 1960, as part of the project of supply control. States began to relax them in the 1970s, however, and the U.S. Supreme Court struck them down in 1985,* although some jurisdictions responded by eliminating the reciprocity they previously had extended to others. Finally, most state bars introduced or elaborated character examinations in the 1920s and 1930s in order to discourage or exclude immigrants from entering the profession. However, these also were difficult to justify, had little impact, were attacked in court in the 1960s and 1970s, and have minimal significance today.

Each mechanism of supply control discussed above displays the same general pattern: increasing stringency until the 1960s and relaxation thereafter. More prelegal education was required, but the growth of public universities made it more widely available. Law school became obligatory, and most part-time programs were eliminated, but the number of ABA-approved law schools expanded, and their enrollments increased. Attrition among law students, once quite high, fell sharply. The bar examination was introduced to limit numbers, but increasing proportions of law students passed it. In addition, the requirements of citizenship, residence, and "character" have been eliminated or relaxed. Perhaps the central irony of this narrative is the fact that, in constructing its project of supply control on the foundation of the university, the profession ultimately lost control over supply to the university, whose interests diverge significantly from those of lawyers.

QUESTIONS

1. Richard Abel clearly differs from both Alexis de Tocqueville and Mary Ann Glendon in his view of the legal profession, and indeed professionalism in general. Professionalism, for Abel, is essentially economic protectionism. Do lawyers behave as an economic interest group in their approach to issues such as bar admission requirements and regulation of legal fees? To what extent are the ideological norms of the profession shaped by economics?

2. Abel postulates that "[a]n occupation becomes a profession by controlling the supply of those who produce its services while justifying such

---

* See *Virginia v. Friedman,* infra.—ed.

control in terms of the public interest." Is he right? What do you think makes an occupation a profession?

3. Abel states that "[d]iscipline also has aggravated tensions within the profession, because ethical rules stigmatize the behavior of low-status lawyers while tolerating the functional equivalent among the elite." This casebook begins with two lower "status" lawyers who behaved admirably, appointed defense counsel Gary Robinson, who in *Nix v. Whiteside* refused to condone client perjury, and Idaho Legal Aid attorney Charles Johnson, who in *Evans v. Jeff D.* personally bore costs of litigation after waiving his fee to obtain a settlement in the best interests of the children he was representing. By contrast, many of the cases later in this casebook show high status lawyers, such as Cravath's Hoyt Moore, engaging in blatantly unethical conduct such as participation in bribing a federal judge. Does Abel's view of the profession's rules adequately explain why unethical behavior by high status lawyers is often tolerated?

4. Is Abel's analysis one dimensional? Is he arguing the very proposition that Professor Glendon denounces: "that law is a business like any other; and that business is just the unrestrained pursuit of self-interest[?]" Mary Ann Glendon, A Nation Under Lawyers 6 (1994).

5. Assuming law is another form of business, consider the following:

> "People in business are not merely 'rational economic agents.' Each is also a human being in search of his calling. All are trying to live fulfilled lives, eager to mix their own identity with their work and their work with their identity. They want more satisfactions from work than money." Michael Novak, Business as a Calling 40 (1996).

Does Abel's analysis sufficiently consider the noneconomic motivations of lawyers and other professionals?

6. Does Abel's discussion explain the role of the legal profession in the advocacy paradigm? How does the advocacy paradigm fit into his analysis?

7. Abel discusses two approaches to legal training: the apprenticeship and the academy? What are the advantages of each? Should the third year of law school be modeled after the apprenticeship?

8. Abel mentions the shift of financial assistance for law students from grants to loans. How does high debt load influence the career choices that law students make? Does the high debt load of young lawyers exacerbate the unequal distribution of legal services?

Geographic Restrictions on Law Practice

Myrna E. Friedman, b. 1949, B.A. University of Illinois 1969; J.D. Indiana University School of Law 1977; admitted to the Illinois bar in 1977 and the District of Columbia Bar in 1980; Department of the Navy in Arlington, Virginia 1977–81; private practice in Washington, D.C. 1982–86; associate general counsel of ERC International, Inc. in Vienna, Virginia 1986–89; general counsel of Huntmar Associates Ltd., a real estate development firm based in the District of Columbia beginning in 1989; currently a member of Sargeant & Friedman, P.C. in Arlington, Virginia (specializing in government contracts, corporate law and personnel policies).

Supreme Court of Virginia and David B. Beach, Its Clerk, Appellants, v. Myrna E. Friedman

487 U.S. 59 (1988).

■ Justice KENNEDY delivered the opinion of the Court.

Qualified lawyers admitted to practice in other States may be admitted to the Virginia Bar "on motion," that is, without taking the bar examination which Virginia otherwise requires. The State conditions such admission on a showing, among other matters, that the applicant is a permanent resident of Virginia. The question for decision is whether this residency requirement violates the Privileges and Immunities Clause of the United States Constitution, Art. IV, § 2, cl. 1. We hold that it does.

I

Myrna E. Friedman was admitted to the Illinois Bar by examination in 1977 and to the District of Columbia Bar by reciprocity in 1980. From 1977 to 1981, she was employed by the Department of the Navy in Arlington, Virginia, as a civilian attorney, and from 1982 until 1986, she was an attorney in private practice in Washington, D.C. In January 1986, she became associate general counsel for ERC International, Inc., a Delaware corporation. Friedman practices and maintains her offices at the company's principal place of business in Vienna, Virginia. Her duties at ERC International include drafting contracts and advising her employer and its subsidiaries on matters of Virginia law.

From 1977 to early 1986, Friedman lived in Virginia. In February 1986, however, she married and moved to her husband's home in Cheverly, Maryland. In June 1986, Friedman applied for admission to the Virginia Bar on motion.

The applicable rule, promulgated by the Supreme Court of Virginia pursuant to statute, is Rule 1A:1. The Rule permits admission on motion of attorneys who are licensed to practice in another jurisdiction, provided the other jurisdiction admits Virginia attorneys without examination. The applicant must have been licensed for at least five years and the Virginia Supreme Court must determine that the applicant: "(a) Is a proper person to practice law." "(b) Has made such progress in the practice of law that it would be unreasonable to require him to take an examination." "(c) Has become a permanent resident of the Commonwealth." "(d) Intends to practice full time as a member of the Virginia bar."

In a letter accompanying her application, Friedman alerted the Clerk of the Virginia Supreme Court to her change of residence, but argued that her application should nevertheless be granted. Friedman gave assurance that she would be engaged full-time in the practice of law in Virginia, that she would be available for service of process and court appearances, and that she would keep informed of local rules. She also asserted that "there appears to be no reason to discriminate against my petition as a nonresident for admission to the Bar on motion," that her circumstances fit within the purview of this Court's decision in Supreme Court of New Hampshire v. Piper, 470 U.S. 274, 105 S.Ct. 1272, 84 L.Ed.2d 205 (1985), and that accordingly she was entitled to admission under the Privileges and Immunities Clause of the Constitution, Art. IV, § 2, cl. 1. See App. 34–35.

The Clerk wrote Friedman that her request had been denied. He explained that because Friedman was no longer a permanent resident of the Commonwealth of Virginia, she was not eligible for admission to the Virginia Bar pursuant to Rule 1A:1. He added that the court had concluded that our decision in Piper, which invalidated a residency requirement imposed on lawyers who had passed a State's bar examination, was "not applicable" to the "discretionary requirement in Rule 1A:1 of residence as a condition of admission by reciprocity." App. 51–52.

Friedman then commenced this action, against the Supreme Court of Virginia and its Clerk, in the United States District Court for the Eastern District of Virginia. She alleged that the residency requirement of Rule 1A:1 violated the Privileges and Immunities Clause. The District Court entered summary judgment in Friedman's favor, holding that the requirement of residency for admission without examination violates the Clause.

The Court of Appeals for the Fourth Circuit unanimously affirmed. 822 F.2d 423 (1987)....

The Supreme Court of Virginia and its Clerk filed a timely notice of appeal. We noted probable jurisdiction, 484 U.S. 923, 108 S.Ct. 283, 98 L.Ed.2d 244 (1987), and we now affirm.

II

Article IV, § 2, cl. 1, of the Constitution provides that the "Citizens of each State shall be entitled to all Privileges and Immunities of Citizens in the several States." The provision was designed "to place the citizens of each State upon the same footing with citizens of other States, so far as the advantages resulting from citizenship in those States are concerned." Paul v. Virginia, 8 Wall. 168, 180, 19 L.Ed. 357 (1869). See also Toomer v. Witsell, 334 U.S. 385, 395, 68 S.Ct. 1156, 1162, 92 L.Ed. 1460 (1948) (the Privileges and Immunities Clause "was designed to insure to a citizen of State A who ventures into State B the same privileges which the citizens of State B enjoy"). The Clause "thus establishes a norm of comity without specifying the particular subjects as to which citizens of one State coming within the jurisdiction of another are guaranteed equality of treatment." Austin v. New Hampshire, 420 U.S. 656, 660, 95 S.Ct. 1191, 1194, 43 L.Ed.2d 530 (1975).

While the Privileges and Immunities Clause cites the term "Citizens," for analytic purposes citizenship and residency are essentially interchangeable. See United Building & Construction Trades Council v. Mayor and Council of Camden, 465 U.S. 208, 216, 104 S.Ct. 1020, 1026, 79 L.Ed.2d 249

(1984). When examining claims that a citizenship or residency classification offends privileges and immunities protections, we undertake a two-step inquiry. First, the activity in question must be " 'sufficiently basic to the livelihood of the Nation' . . . as to fall within the purview of the Privileges and Immunities Clause. . . ." Id., at 221–222, 104 S.Ct., at 1029, quoting Baldwin v. Montana Fish & Game Comm'n, 436 U.S. 371, 388, 98 S.Ct. 1852, 1863, 56 L.Ed.2d 354 (1978). For it is " '[o]nly with respect to those "privileges" and "immunities" bearing on the vitality of the Nation as a single entity' that a State must accord residents and nonresidents equal treatment." Supreme Court of New Hampshire v. Piper, 470 U.S., at 279, 105 S.Ct., at 1276, quoting Baldwin, supra, 436 U.S., at 383, 98 S.Ct., at 1860. Second, if the challenged restriction deprives nonresidents of a protected privilege, we will invalidate it only if we conclude that the restriction is not closely related to the advancement of a substantial state interest. Piper, supra, 470 U.S., at 284, 105 S.Ct., at 1278. Appellants assert that the residency requirement offends neither part of this test. We disagree.

A

Appellants concede, as they must, that our decision in Piper establishes that a nonresident who takes and passes an examination prescribed by the State, and who otherwise is qualified for the practice of law, has an interest in practicing law that is protected by the Privileges and Immunities Clause. Appellants contend, however, that the discretionary admission provided for by Rule 1A:1 is not a privilege protected by the Clause for two reasons. First, appellants argue that the bar examination "serves as an adequate, alternative means of gaining admission to the bar." Brief for Appellants 20. In appellants' view, "[s]o long as any applicant may gain admission to a State's bar, without regard to residence, by passing the bar examination," id., at 21, the State cannot be said to have discriminated against nonresidents "as a matter of fundamental concern." Id., at 19. Second, appellants argue that the right to admission on motion is not within the purview of the Clause because, without offense to the Constitution, the State could require all bar applicants to pass an examination. Neither argument is persuasive.

We cannot accept appellants' first theory because it is quite inconsistent with our precedents. We reaffirmed in Piper the well-settled principle that " 'one of the privileges which the Clause guarantees to citizens of State A is that of doing business in State B on terms of substantial equality with the citizens of that State.' " Piper, supra, at 280, 105 S.Ct., at 1276, quoting Toomer v. Witsell, supra, 334 U.S., at 396, 68 S.Ct., at 1162. See also United Building & Construction Trades Council, supra, 465 U.S., at 219, 104 S.Ct., at 1028 ("Certainly, the pursuit of a common calling is one of the most fundamental of those privileges protected by the Clause"). After reviewing our precedents, we explicitly held that the practice of law, like other occupations considered in those cases, is sufficiently basic to the national economy to be deemed a privilege protected by the Clause. See Piper, supra, 470 U.S., at 280–281, 105 S.Ct., at 1276–1277. The clear import of Piper is that the Clause is implicated whenever, as is the case here, a State does not permit qualified nonresidents to practice law within its borders on terms of substantial equality with its own residents.

Nothing in our precedents, moreover, supports the contention that the Privileges and Immunities Clause does not reach a State's discrimination against nonresidents when such discrimination does not result in their total exclusion from the State. . . . Indeed, as the Court of Appeals correctly noted, the New Hampshire rule struck down in Piper did not result in the total exclusion of nonresidents from the practice of law in that State. 822 F.2d, at 427 (citing Piper, supra, 470 U.S., at 277, n. 2, 105 S.Ct., at 1274, n. 2).

Further, we find appellants' second theory—that Virginia could constitutionally require that all applicants to its bar take and pass an examination—quite irrelevant to the question whether the Clause is applicable in the circumstances of this case. A State's abstract authority to require from resident and nonresident alike that which it has chosen to demand from the nonresident alone has never been held to shield the discriminatory distinction from the reach of the Privileges and Immunities Clause. Thus, the applicability of the Clause to the present case no more turns on the legality vel non of an examination requirement than it turned on the inherent reasonableness of the fees charged to nonresidents in Toomer and Ward. The issue instead is whether the State has burdened the right to practice law, a privilege protected by the Privileges and Immunities Clause, by discriminating among otherwise equally qualified applicants solely on the basis of citizenship or residency. We conclude it has.

B

Our conclusion that the residence requirement burdens a privilege protected by the Privileges and Immunities Clause does not conclude the matter, of course; for we repeatedly have recognized that the Clause, like other constitutional provisions, is not an absolute. See, e.g., Piper, supra, at 284, 105 S.Ct., at 1278; United Building & Construction Trades Council, 465 U.S., at 222, 104 S.Ct., at 1029; Toomer, 334 U.S., at 396, 68 S.Ct., at 1162. The Clause does not preclude disparity in treatment where substantial reasons exist for the discrimination and the degree of discrimination bears a close relation to such reasons. See United Building & Construction Trades Council, supra, 465 U.S., at 222, 104 S.Ct., at 1029. In deciding whether the degree of discrimination bears a sufficiently close relation to the reasons proffered by the State, the Court has considered whether, within the full panoply of legislative choices otherwise available to the State, there exist alternative means of furthering the State's purpose without implicating constitutional concerns. See Piper, supra, 470 U.S., at 284, 105 S.Ct., at 1278.

Appellants offer two principal justifications for the Rule's requirement that applicants seeking admission on motion reside within the Commonwealth of Virginia. First, they contend that the residence requirement assures, in tandem with the full-time practice requirement, that attorneys admitted on motion will have the same commitment to service and familiarity with Virginia law that is possessed by applicants securing admission upon examination. Attorneys admitted on motion, appellants argue, have "no personal investment" in the jurisdiction; consequently, they "are entitled to no presumption that they will willingly and actively participate in bar activities and obligations, or fulfill their public service responsibilities to the State's client community." Brief for Appellants 26–27. Second, appellants argue that the residency requirement facilitates enforcement of the full-time practice requirement of Rule 1A:1. We find each of these justifications insufficient to meet the State's burden of showing that the discrimination is warranted by a substantial state objective and closely drawn to its achievement.

We acknowledge that a bar examination is one method of assuring that the admitted attorney has a stake in his or her professional licensure and a concomitant interest in the integrity and standards of the bar. A bar examination, as we know judicially and from our own experience, is not a casual or lighthearted exercise. The question, however, is whether lawyers who are admitted in other States and seek admission in Virginia are less likely to respect the bar and further its interests solely because they are nonresidents. We cannot say this is the case. While Piper relied on an examination requirement as an indicium of the nonresident's commitment to the bar and to the State's legal profession, see Piper, supra, at 285, 105 S.Ct., at 1279, it does not follow that when the State waives the examination it may make a distinction between residents and nonresidents.

Friedman's case proves the point. She earns her living working as an attorney in Virginia, and it is of scant relevance that her residence is located in the neighboring State of Maryland. It is indisputable that she has a substantial stake in the practice of law in Virginia. Indeed, despite appellants' suggestion at oral argument that Friedman's case is "atypical," Tr. of Oral Arg. 51, the same will likely be true of all nonresident attorneys who are admitted on motion to the Virginia Bar, in light of the State's requirement that attorneys so admitted show their intention to maintain an office and a regular practice in the State. See Application of Brown, 213 Va. 282, 286, n. 3, 191 S.E.2d 812, 815, n. 3 (1972) (interpreting full-time practice requirement of Rule 1A:1). This requirement goes a long way toward ensuring that such attorneys will have an interest in the practice of law in Virginia that is at least comparable to the interest we ascribed in Piper to applicants admitted upon examination. Accordingly, we see no reason to assume that nonresident attorneys who, like Friedman, seek admission to the Virginia bar on motion will lack adequate incentives to remain abreast of changes in the law or to fulfill their civic duties.

Further, to the extent that the State is justifiably concerned with ensuring that its attorneys keep abreast of legal developments, it can protect these interests through other equally or more effective means that do not themselves infringe constitutional protections. While this Court is not well positioned to dictate specific legislative choices to the State, it is sufficient to note that such alternatives exist and that the State, in the exercise of its legislative prerogatives, is free to implement them. The Supreme Court of Virginia could, for example, require mandatory attendance at periodic continuing legal education courses. See Piper, supra, 470 U.S., at 285, n. 19, 105 S.Ct., at 1279, n. 19. The same is true with respect to the State's interest that the nonresident bar member does his or her share of volunteer and pro bono work. A "nonresident bar member, like the resident member, could be required to represent indigents and perhaps to participate in formal legal-aid work." Piper, supra, at 287, 105 S.Ct., at 1280 (footnote omitted).

We also reject appellants' attempt to justify the residency restriction as a necessary aid to the enforcement of the full-time practice requirement of Rule 1A:1. Virginia already requires, pursuant to the full-time practice restriction of Rule 1A:1, that attorneys admitted on motion maintain an office for the practice of law in Virginia. As the Court of Appeals noted, the requirement that applicants maintain an office in Virginia facilitates compliance with the full-time practice requirement in nearly the identical manner that the residency restriction does, rendering the latter restriction largely redundant. 822 F.2d, at 429. The office requirement furnishes an alternative to the residency requirement that is not only less restrictive, but also is fully adequate to protect whatever interest the State might have in the full-time practice restriction.

III

We hold that Virginia's residency requirement for admission to the State's bar without examination violates the Privileges and Immunities Clause. The nonresident's interest in practicing law on terms of substantial equality with those enjoyed by residents is a privilege protected by the Clause. A State may not discriminate against nonresidents unless it shows that such discrimination bears a close relation to the achievement of substantial state objectives. Virginia has failed to make this showing. Accordingly, the judgment of the Court of Appeals is affirmed.

It is so ordered.

■ Chief Justice REHNQUIST, with whom Justice SCALIA joins, dissenting.

Three Terms ago the Court invalidated a New Hampshire Bar rule which denied admission to an applicant who had passed the state bar examination because she was not, and would not become, a resident of the State. Supreme Court of New Hampshire v. Piper, 470 U.S. 274, 105 S.Ct. 1272, 84 L.Ed.2d 205 (1985). In the present case the Court extends the reasoning of Piper to invalidate a Virginia Bar rule allowing admission on motion without examination to qualified applicants, but restricting the privilege to those applicants who have become residents of the State.

For the reasons stated in my dissent in Piper, I also disagree with the Court's decision in this case. I continue to believe that the Privileges and Immunities Clause of Article IV, § 2, does not require States to ignore residency when admitting lawyers to practice in the way that they must ignore residency when licensing traders in foreign goods, Ward v. Maryland, 12 Wall. 418, 20 L.Ed. 449 (1871), or when licensing commercial shrimp fishermen, Toomer v. Witsell, 334 U.S. 385, 68 S.Ct. 1156, 92 L.Ed. 1460 (1948).

I think the effect of today's decision is unfortunate even apart from what I believe is its mistaken view of the Privileges and Immunities Clause. Virginia's rule allowing admission on motion is an ameliorative provision, recognizing the fact that previous practice in another State may qualify a new resident of Virginia to practice there without the necessity of taking another bar examination. The Court's ruling penalizes Virginia, which has at least gone part way towards accommodating the present mobility of our population, but of course leaves untouched the rules of those States which allow no reciprocal admission on motion. Virginia may of course retain the privilege of admission on motion without enforcing a residency requirement even after today's decision, but it might also decide to eliminate admission on motion altogether.

QUESTIONS

1.   Was Virginia's residency requirement for admission on motion an example of the economic protectionism described by Professor Abel?

2.   Alternatively, could the requirement have been motivated by parochialism (in particular, hostility to attorneys living in the District of Columbia) and/or hostility to litigation on behalf of unpopular causes by out-of-state lawyers?

3.   The dissenting opinion distinguishes between the legal profession and other types of businesses, but does not explain why lawyers should be treated differently for purposes of the Privileges and Immunities Clause. Are there any reasons for allowing a state to discriminate in favor of its own residents when regulating the legal profession?

4.   Do restrictions on lawyer mobility from state to state facilitate or hinder the profession's fulfillment of the calling described by Tocqueville?

Relevant Background

Through the late 1970s, many states required residency for admission to the bar. See generally Note, A Constitutional Analysis of State Bar Residency Requirements Under the Interstate Privileges and Immunities Clause of Article IV, 92 Harv. L. Rev. 1461, 1461–64 (1979). In 1978, however, the Court redirected its attention to the Privileges and Immunities Clause of Article IV in Hicklin v. Orbeck, 437 U.S. 518 (1978) and Baldwin v. Fish & Game Commission, 436 U.S. 371 (1978). Then, in 1985 the Court used Article IV to invalidate New Hampshire's bar admission residency requirement. Supreme Court of New Hampshire v. Piper, 470 U.S. 274 (1985). The Court found that both commercial and noncommercial roles for the legal profession gave law practice the status of a protected privilege. In particular, the Court noted the role out-of-state lawyers have in representing clients with unpopular causes. Id. at 281–82.

The New Hampshire Supreme Court in *Piper* had relied on four justifications for refusing bar admission to nonresidents: (i) nonresident lawyers would be less likely to be familiar with local rules of procedure; (ii) they would be less likely to behave ethically; (iii) they would be less likely to be available for court proceedings; and (iv) they would be less likely to do pro bono work. The United States Supreme Court found none of these arguments convincing enough to justify the residency requirement. *Piper,* 470 U.S. at 285.

After the *Friedman* holding, in Frazier v. Heebe, 482 U.S. 641 (1987), the Court used its supervisory role over lower federal courts to invalidate a residency requirement in the local rules of a Louisiana federal district court. The Court observed that "there is no reason to believe that nonresident attorneys who have passed the Louisiana bar examination are less competent than resident attorneys." Id. at 647. See also Barnard v. Thorstenn, 489 U.S. 546, 551–52 (1989) (Virgin Islands residency requirement for admission to the district court bar invalid under the Privileges and Immunities Clause as extended to the Virgin Islands by statute).

U.S. v. Altstoetter

Military Tribunal III (1947)
From: Trials of War Criminals Before the Nuernberg Military Tribunals (Volume III, "The Justice Case")

CONTROL COUNCIL LAW NO. 10

PUNISHMENT OF PERSONS GUILTY OF WAR CRIMES, CRIMES AGAINST PEACE AND AGAINST HUMANITY

In order to give effect to the terms of the Moscow Declaration of 30 October 1943 and the London Agreement of 8 August 1945, and the Charter issued pursuant thereto and in order to establish a uniform legal basis in Germany for the prosecution of war criminals and other similar offenders, other than those dealt with by the International Military Tribunal, the Control Council enacts as follows: . . . .

Article II

1. Each of the following acts is recognized as a crime:

(a) Crimes against Peace. Initiation of invasions of other countries and wars of aggression in violation of international laws and treaties, including but not limited to planning, preparation, initiation or waging a war of aggression, or a war of violation of international treaties, agreements or assurances, or participation in a common plan or conspiracy for the accomplishment of any of the foregoing.

(b) War Crimes. Atrocities or offences against persons or property constituting violations of the laws or customs of war, including but not limited to, murder, ill treatment or deportation to slave labour or for any other purpose, of civilian population from occupied territory, murder or ill

treatment of prisoners of war or persons on the seas, killing of hostages, plunder of public or private property, wanton destruction of cities, towns or villages, or devastation not justified by military necessity.

(c) Crimes against Humanity. Atrocities and offences, including but not limited to murder, extermination, enslavement, deportation, imprisonment, torture, rape, or other inhumane acts committed against any civilian population, or persecutions on political, racial or religious grounds whether or not in violation of the domestic laws of the country where perpetrated.

(d) Membership in categories of a criminal group or organization declared criminal by the International Military Tribunal.

2. Any person without regard to nationality or the capacity in which he acted, is deemed to have committed a crime as defined in paragraph 1 of this Article, if he was *(a)* a principal or *(b)* was an accessory to the commission of any such crime or ordered or abetted the same or *(c)* took a consenting part therein or *(d)* was connected with plans or enterprises involving its commission or *(e)* was a member of any organization or group connected with the commission of any such crime or *(f)* with reference to paragraph 1 *(a)*, if he held a high political, civil or military (including General Staff) position in Germany or in one of its Allies, co-belligerents or satellites or held high position in the financial, industrial or economic life of any such country.

3. Any person found guilty of any of the Crimes above mentioned may upon conviction be punished as shall be determined by the tribunal to be just. Such punishment may consist of one or more of the following:

(a) Death.

(b) Imprisonment for life or a term of years, with or without hard labour.

(c) Fine, and imprisonment with or without hard labour, in lieu thereof.

(d) Forfeiture of property.

(e) Restitution of property wrongfully acquired.

(f) Deprivation of some or all civil rights.

Any property declared to be forfeited or the restitution of which is ordered by the tribunal shall be delivered to the Control Council for Germany, which shall decide on its disposal.

4. *(a)* The official position of any person, whether as Head of State or as a responsible official in a Government Department, does not free him from responsibility for a crime or entitle him to mitigation of punishment.

(b) The fact that any person acted pursuant to the order of his Government or of a superior does not free him from responsibility for a crime, but may be considered in mitigation.

5. In any trial or prosecution for a crime herein referred to, the accused shall not be entitled to the benefits of any statute of limitation in respect of the period from 30 January 1933 to 1 July 1945, nor shall any

immunity, pardon or amnesty granted under the Nazi regime be admitted as a bar to trial or punishment.

Article III

Each occupying authority, within its Zone of occupation,

(a) shall have the right to cause persons within such Zone suspected of having committed a crime, including those charged with crime by one of the United Nations, to be arrested and shall take under control the property, real and personal, owned or controlled by said persons, pending decisions as to its eventual disposition.

(b) shall report to the Legal Directorate the names of all suspected criminals, the reasons for and the places of their detention, if they are detained, and the names and locations of witnesses.

(c) shall take appropriate measures to see that witnesses and evidence will be available when required.

(d) shall have the right to cause all persons so arrested and charged, and not delivered to another authority as herein provided, or released, to be brought to trial before an appropriate tribunal. Such tribunal may, in the case of crimes committed by persons of German citizenship or nationality against other persons of German citizenship or nationality, or stateless persons, be a German Court, if authorized by the occupying authorities.

2. The tribunal by which persons charged with offenses hereunder shall be tried and the rules and procedure thereof shall be determined or designated by each Zone Commander for his respective Zone. Nothing herein is intended to, or shall impair or limit the jurisdiction or power of any court or tribunal now or hereafter established in any Zone by the Commander thereof, or of the International Military Tribunal established by the London Agreement of 8 August 1945.

* * *

U.S. v. Altstoetter et al.

I. Indictment.

. . . .

Count Two—War Crimes

8. Between September 1939 and April 1945 all of the defendants herein unlawfully, willfully, and knowingly committed war crimes, as defined by Control Council Law No. 10, in that they were principals in, accessories to, ordered, abetted, took a consenting part in, and were connected with plans and enterprises involving the commission of atrocities and offenses against persons and property, including, but not limited to, plunder of private property, murder, torture, and illegal imprisonment of, and brutalities, atrocities, and other inhumane acts against thousands of persons. These crimes included, but were not limited to, the facts set out in

paragraphs 9 to 19, inclusive, of this indictment, and were committed against civilians of occupied territories and members of the armed forces of nations then at war with the German Reich and who were in the custody of the German Reich in the exercise of belligerent control.

9.   Extraordinary irregular courts, superimposed upon the regular court system, were used by all of the defendants for the purpose of and in fact creating a reign of terror to suppress political opposition to the Nazi regime. This was accomplished principally through the People's Court (Volksgerichtshof) and various Special Courts (Sondergerichte), which subjected civilians of the occupied countries to criminal abuse of judicial and penal process including repeated trials on the same charges, criminal abuse of discretion, unwarranted imposition of the death penalty, prearrangement of sentences between judges and prosecutors, discriminatory trial processes, and other criminal practices, all of which resulted in murders, cruelties, tortures, atrocities, plunder of private property, and other inhumane acts.

10.   Special Courts subjected Jews of all nationalities, Poles, Ukrainians, Russians, and other nationals of the Occupied Eastern Territories, indiscriminately classed as "gypsies", to discriminatory and special penal laws and trials, and denied them all semblance of judicial process. These persons who had been arbitrarily designated "asocial" by conspiracy and agreement between the Ministry of Justice and the SS were turned over by the Ministry of Justice, both during and after service of prison sentences, to the SS to be worked to death. Many such persons were given a summary travesty of trial before extraordinary courts, and after serving the sentences imposed upon them, were turned over to the Gestapo for "protective custody" in concentration camps. Jews discharged from prison were turned over to the Gestapo for final detention in Auschwitz, Lublin, and other concentration camps. The above-described proceedings resulted in the murder, torture, and ill-treatment of thousands of such persons. The defendants von Ammon, Engert, Klemm, Schlegelberger, Mettgenberg, Rothenberger, and Westphal are charged with special responsibility for and participation in these crimes.

11.   The German criminal laws, through a series of expansions and perversions by the Ministry of Justice, finally embraced passive defeatism, petty misdemeanors and trivial private utterances as treasonable for the purpose of exterminating Jews or other nationals of the occupied countries. Indictments, trials and convictions were transparent devices for a system of murderous extermination, and death became the routine penalty.... Rauthaug [and] Rothenberger ... are charged with special responsibility for and participation in these crimes.

12.   The Justice Ministry aided and implemented the unlawful annexation and occupation of Czechoslovakia, Poland, and France. Special Courts were created to facilitate the extermination of Poles and Jews and the suppression of political opposition generally by the employment of summary procedures and the enforcement of Draconic penal laws. Sentences were limited to death or transfer to the SS for extermination. The People's Court and Special Courts were projected into these countries, irregular

prejudicial regulations and procedures were invoked without notice (even in violation of the Reich Criminal Code as unlawfully extended to other occupied territories), sentences were prearranged, and trial and execution followed service of the indictment within a few hours. . . .

13.   The Ministry of Justice participated with the OKW and the Gestapo in the execution of Hitler's decree of "Night and Fog" (Nacht und Nebel) whereby civilians of occupied territories who had been accused of crimes of resistance against occupying forces were spirited away for secret trial by certain Special Courts of the Justice Ministry within the Reich, in the course of which the victims' whereabouts, trial, and subsequent disposition were kept completely secret, thus serving the dual purpose of terrorizing the victims' relatives and associates and barring recourse to any evidence, witnesses, or counsel for defense. The accused was not informed of the disposition of his case, and in almost every instance those who were acquitted or who had served their sentences were handed over by the Justice Ministry to the Gestapo for "protective custody" for the duration of the war. . . .

14.   Hundreds of non-German nationals imprisoned in penal institutions operated by the Reich Ministry of Justice were unlawfully executed and murdered. Death sentences were executed in the absence of the necessary official orders, and while clemency pleas were pending. Many who were not sentenced to death were executed. In the face of Allied military advances so-called "inferior" or "asocial" prison inmates were, by Ministry order, executed regardless of sentences under which they served. In many instances these penal institutions were operated in a manner indistinguishable from concentration camps. . . . Rothenberger [is] charged with special responsibility for and participation in these crimes.

15.   The Ministry of Justice participated in the Nazi program of racial purity pursuant to which sterilization and castration laws were perverted for the extermination of Jews, "asocials", and certain nationals of the occupied territories. In the course of the program thousands of Jews were sterilized. Insane, aged, and sick nationals of occupied territories, the so-called "useless eaters," were systematically murdered. . . .

16.   The Ministry of Justice granted immunity to and amnesty following prosecutions and convictions of Nazi Party members for major crimes committed against civilians of occupied territories. Pardons were granted to members of the Party who had been sentenced for proved offenses. . . .

17.   By decrees signed by the Reich Minister of Justice and others, the citizenship of all Jews in Bohemia and Moravia was forfeited upon their change of residence by deportation or otherwise; and upon their loss of citizenship their properties were automatically confiscated by the Reich. There were discriminatory changes in the family and inheritance laws by which Jewish property was forfeited at death to the Reich with no compensation to the Jewish heirs . . .

18.   The Ministry of Justice through suspension and quashing of criminal process, participated in Hitler's program of inciting the German

civilian population to murder Allied airmen forced down within the Reich. . . .

19.   The said war crimes constitute violations of international conventions, particularly of Articles 4–7, 23, 43, 45, 46, and 50 of the Hague Regulations, 1907, and of articles 2, 3, and 4 of the Prisoner of War Convention (Geneva, 1929), the laws and customs of war, the general principles of criminal law as derived from the criminal laws of all civilized nations, the internal penal laws of the countries in which such crimes were committed, and of Article II of Control Council Law No. 10.

Count Three—Crimes Against Humanity

20.   Between September 1939 and April 1945 all of the defendants herein unlawfully, willfully, and knowingly committed crimes against humanity as defined by Control Council Law No. 10, in that they were principals in, accessories to, ordered, abetted, took a consenting part in, and were connected with plans and enterprises involving the commission of atrocities and offenses, including but not limited to murder, extermination, enslavement, deportation, illegal imprisonment, torture, persecution on political, racial and religious grounds, and ill-treatment of and other inhumane acts against German civilians and nationals of occupied countries.

[Paragraphs 21–30 restate the factual allegations in paragraphs 9–18, supra]

31.   The said crimes against humanity constitute violations of international conventions, including article 46 of the Hague Regulations, 1907, the laws and customs of war, the general principles of criminal law as derived from the criminal laws of all civilized nations, the internal penal laws of the countries in which such crimes were committed, and of article II of Control Council Law No. 10.

Count Four

Membership in Criminal Organizations

[charging several of the defendants with membership in the SS, and defendant Rothaug with membership in the Leadership Corps of the Nazi Party]

Wherefore, this indictment is filed with the Secretary General of the Military Tribunals and the charges herein made against the above-named defendants are hereby presented to the Military Tribunals.

Acting on Behalf of the United States of America

Telford Taylor
Brigadier General, U. S. Army
Chief of Counsel for War Crimes

Nuremberg, 4 January 1947

* * *

II.   Arraignment

[Each defendant indicated that he was represented by counsel, and each pleaded "Not guilty" to the charges of the indictment against him.]

* * *

III.   Opening Statements

A.   Opening Statement for the Prosecution

BRIGADIER GENERAL TAYLOR: This case is unusual in that the defendants are charged with crimes committed in the name of the law. These men, together with their deceased or fugitive colleagues, were the embodiment of what passed for justice in the Third Reich.

Most of the defendants have served, at various times, as judges, as state prosecutors, and as officials of the Reich Ministry of Justice. All but one are professional jurists; they are well accustomed to courts and courtrooms, though their present role may be new to them.

But a court is far more than a courtroom; it is a process and a spirit. It is the house of law. This the defendants know, or must have known in times past. I doubt that they ever forgot it. Indeed, the root of the accusation here is that those men, leaders of the German judicial system, consciously and deliberately suppressed the law, engaged in an unholy masquerade of brutish tyranny disguised as justice, and converted the German judicial system to an engine of despotism, conquest, pillage, and slaughter.

The methods by which these crimes were committed may be novel in some respects, but the crimes themselves are not. They are as old as mankind, and their names are murder, torture, plunder, and others equally familiar. The victims of these crimes are countless, and include nationals of practically every country in Europe.

But because these crimes were committed in the guise of legal process, it is important at the outset to set forth certain things that are not, here and now, charged as crimes.

The defendants and their colleagues distorted, perverted, and finally accomplished the complete overthrow of justice and law in Germany. They made the system of courts an integral part of dictatorship. They established and operated special tribunals obedient only to the political dictates of the Hitler regime. They abolished all semblance of judicial independence. They brow-beat, bullied, and denied fundamental rights to those who came before the courts. The "trials" they conducted became horrible farces, with vestigial remnants of legal procedure which only served to mock the hapless victims....

In summary, the defendants are charged with judicial murder and other atrocities which they committed by destroying law and justice in Germany, and by then utilizing the emptied forms of legal process for persecution, enslavement, and extermination on a vast scale. It is the purpose of this proceeding to hear these charges and to render judgment according to the evidence under law.

The true purposes of this proceeding, therefore, are broader than the mere visiting of retribution on a few men for the death and suffering of many thousands. I have said that the defendants know, or should know, that a court is the house of law. But it is, I fear, many years since any of the defendants have dwelt therein. Great as was their crime against those who died or suffered at their hands, their crime against Germany was even more shameful. They defiled the German temple of justice, and delivered Germany into the dictatorship of the Third Reich, "with all its methods of terror, and its cynical and open denial of the rule of law."

The temple must be reconsecrated. This cannot be done in the twinkling of an eye or by any mere ritual. It cannot be done in any single proceeding or at any one place. It certainly cannot be done at Nuernberg alone. But we have here, I think, a special opportunity and grave responsibility to help achieve this goal. We have here the men who played a leading part in the destruction of law in Germany. They are about to be judged in accordance with the law. It is more than fitting that these men be judged under that which they, as jurists, denied to others. Judgment under law is the only just fate for the defendants; the prosecution asks no other.

The German Judicial System

There are fifteen defendants in the box, all of whom held high judicial office, and all but one of whom are trained lawyers. To understand this case, it is necessary to understand the general structure of the German judicial system and the places occupied by the several defendants within that system. . . .

Judicial Organization Prior to 1933

Because Germany was divided into a multitude of states and provinces until modern times, German law is not the product of a continuous or uniform development. However, while some elements of old Germanic law have survived, German law has for many centuries been based primarily on the principles of Roman law. As is the case in most continental nations, German law today is enacted to a substantial degree in the form of codes.

Even at the present time, the principal source of German criminal law is the Criminal Code of 1871. Amendments have been frequent, but it has never been completely overhauled. For our present purpose, it is sufficient to note the code's threefold division of criminal offenses. Serious crimes, punishable with death or imprisonment for more than 5 years, are called "crimes" (Verbrechen); lesser offenses, punishable with imprisonment or substantial fines, are called "delicts" (Vergehen); and minor offenses are called "contraventions" (Uebertretungen). Questions of criminal procedure are regulated by the Code of Criminal Procedure of February, 1877; matters of jurisdiction and of court organization are prescribed in the General Judicature Act of January, 1877.

Under both the German Empire and the Weimar Republic, the authority to appoint judges and prosecutors and the power to execute sentences were jealously guarded prerogatives of the individual German states. The Reich Ministry of Justice, therefore, remained predominantly a ministry of federal legislation. The anomaly of a highly unified federal law, as contrasted with a court system administered by the individual states, endured until after the advent of Hitler.

In spite of the fact that the authority for supervision and appointment of judges rested with the numerous states, the German court system was well organized and highly unified before Hitler came to power. The basis of the court system was the local courts (Amtsgerichte), of which there were over 2,000, which had original jurisdiction over minor civil suits and over the less serious criminal offenses ("delicts" and "contraventions"). Original jurisdiction in the more important civil and criminal cases was exercised by the district courts (Landgerichte), of which there were some 180.

The principal appellate courts in Germany were called the district courts of appeal (Oberlandesgerichte). Of those there were 26, or generally one to each state and province. The district courts of appeal entertained civil appeals from all decisions of the local and district courts, and second criminal appeals from cases originally heard in the local courts. The president of the district court of appeals (Oberlandesgerichtspraesident) was also the administrative head of all the courts in his district.

The Supreme Court of the Reich (Reichsgericht) in Leipzig formed the apex of the judicial pyramid. It determined important legal questions involving the interpretation of Reich laws, and entertained appeals from the decisions of the district courts of appeal and from criminal cases originally heard in the district courts. It was also the court of first and last instance for important treason cases.

The judges of the Reich Supreme Court were appointed by the President of the Reich. The judges of the lower courts were appointed by the respective state governments. Before the advent of national socialism, a judge could not be removed by the government, but only by formal action before a disciplinary court composed of his peers. This security of tenure was guaranteed by articles 102 and 104 of the Weimar constitution.

Judicial Organization of the Third Reich

The impact of Hitler's seizure of power on the German judicial system was swift and drastic. The Enabling Law of 24 March 1933 authorized the executive to issue decrees with the force of law and provided that these "decree laws" could deviate from the Weimar constitution, the civil rights provision of which had already been suspended by a decree of 28 February 1933. For practical purposes, therefore, legislative and executive powers were merged in Hitler's cabinet, and the constitution was robbed of all practical effect.

In 1934, the administration of justice was taken entirely out of the hands of the German states and was concentrated exclusively in the government of the Reich. The first law for the transfer of the administration of justice to the Reich was proclaimed 16 February 1934; it provided that thereafter all courts should pronounce judgment in the name of the German people, vested in the President of the Reich all clemency powers formerly held by the states, and authorized the Reich Minister of Justice to issue regulations for the transfer of the administration of justice to the Reich. This general directive was put into execution by the second and third laws for the transfer of the administration of justice to the Reich, promulgated in December 1934 and January 1935, respectively. The Justice Ministries of the several states were thereby abolished, and all their functions and powers were concentrated in the Reich Ministry of Justice, which became the supreme judicial authority, under Hitler, in the Reich. Hitler had already proclaimed himself the "Supreme Law Lord of the German people" in his speech to the Reichstag defending the killings which occurred during the suppression of the Roehm putsch.

1. *The Reich Ministry of Justice (Reichsjustizministerium)*—The centralization of the German administration of justice brought about, of course, a great increase in the scope and functions of the Reich Ministry of Justice. Its more important divisions are shown in the composite chart on the wall of the courtroom; a more detailed chart of the Ministry alone is included in the expository brief.

.   .   .   .

The Ministry of Justice controlled a variety of other judicial institutions, including various Special Courts and the examining office for candidates for admission and qualification of judges and lawyers. It controlled the Academy for German Law and various other associations of attorneys, as well as a special training camp for the Nazi indoctrination of young attorneys. Most important of all, it supervised and administered the entire court system from the Reich Supreme Court clear down to the local courts. This function included the assignment, transfer, and promotion of all judges.

2. *The Hierarchy of regular courts*—The centralization of judicial administration in the Reich Ministry of Justice did not at first have any pronounced effect upon the structure of the regular court system. The established hierarchy of courts—local courts, district courts, district courts of appeal, and the Reich Supreme Court—continued in effect. The most important development in the early years of the Third Reich was the creation of extraordinary and special courts, which increasingly cut into the jurisdiction of the regular courts.

Under the impact of war, however, the system of regular courts was substantially altered, although its general outlines remained the same. These alterations were intended for economy and expedition, and to reduce the number of judicial personnel. This was accomplished chiefly in two ways: by reduction in the number of judges required to hear particular kinds of cases, and by drastic curtailment of the right of appeal.

Many of these changes were made at the outbreak of war in 1939. Thereafter, all cases in the local courts and all civil cases in the district courts were heard by one judge only; criminal cases in the district courts were heard by three judges, but the president of the court could hear such cases alone if the issues were simple. Criminal cases heard by the local courts could be appealed only as far as the district courts; civil cases heard in the local courts could be appealed directly to the district court of appeals, bypassing the district court.

Further drastic curtailments of the right of appeal occurred in 1944 and 1945. In general, appeals could only be taken by permission of the court which heard the case, and permission was granted only to settle legal questions of fundamental importance. The judicial functions of the district courts of appeal were almost, if not entirely, eliminated, although their supervisory administrative functions continued.

3. *Extraordinary courts*—The most crucial and radical change in the judicial system under the Third Reich, however, was the establishment of various extraordinary courts. These irregular tribunals permeated the entire judicial structure, and eventually took over all judicial business which touched political issues or related to the war.

Within a matter of weeks after the seizure of power, by a decree of 21 March 1933, "Special Courts" (Sondergerichte) were established. One Special Court was set up within the district of each district court of appeal. Each court was composed of three judges drawn from the judges of the particular district. They were given jurisdiction over offenses described in the emergency decree of 28 February 1933, which included inciting to disobedience of government orders, crimes in the nature of sabotage, and acts "contrary to the public welfare." There were drastic provisions for the expedition of proceedings before the special courts, and no appeal whatsoever lay from their decisions.

A few weeks later, special military courts, which had been abolished by the Weimar constitution, were reestablished and given jurisdiction over all offenses committed by members of the armed forces. In July 1933, special "Hereditary Health Courts" more generally known as "Sterilization Courts" were established at the seats of the local courts, with special appellate "Hereditary Health Courts" above them.

But the most notorious Nazi judicial innovation was the so-called "People's Court" (Volksgerichtshof), established by the decree of 24 April 1934, after the Reich Supreme Court's acquittal of the defendants in the Reichstag fire trial. The People's Court replaced the Supreme Court as the court of first and last instance for most treason cases.

The People's Court sat in divisions, or "senates," of five members each. Two of the five had to be qualified judges; the other three were trusted Nazi laymen selected from high ranking officers of the Wehrmacht (armed forces) and SS, or from the party hierarchy. They were appointed for 5–year terms by Hitler, on the recommendation of the Minister of Justice. Six "senates" were established, each of which heard cases from a particular geographical section of Germany. In 1940 a "special senate" was established to retry cases where, in the judgment of the chief public prosecutor of the Reich, an inadequate punishment had been imposed.

As time went on, the concept of "treason" was much enlarged by a variety of Nazi decrees, and both the Special Courts and the People's Court were given jurisdiction to try a great variety of offenses. In 1936, for example, the smuggling of property out of Germany was proclaimed an offense against the national economy, and the People's Court was given jurisdiction over such cases. In 1940, a new decree defined the jurisdiction of the Special Courts and the People's Court, and all sorts of offenses, such as evasion of conscription and listening to foreign broadcasting stations, were brought within their purview.

Toward the end of the war, by a decree of February 1945, emergency civil courts martial (Standgerichte) were set up in areas "menaced by the approaching enemy." Each consisted of three members appointed by the Reich Defense Commissar, usually the Gauleiter (regional leader) of the district; the president was a professional judge, who sat with one associate judge from the Nazi Party, and one from the Wehrmacht or SS. These courts martial could only condemn the accused to death, acquit him, or transfer the case to a regular tribunal. . . .

Three of the defendants were judges of the Special Courts ... the defendant Rothaug was president of the Special Court in Nuernberg. . . .

4. *Public prosecutors*—The prosecution of criminal offenses, under the Third Reich, was handled by a special group of state attorneys (Staatsanwaltschaft) directed by the Ministry of Justice. Increasingly under the Third Reich there was interchange of personnel among judges and prosecutors.

The defendant Rothaug, for example, left the bench of the Special Court at Nuernberg to become a senior public prosecutor of the Reich (Reichsanwalt). . . .

* * *

The Defendant Rothenberger

From his own sworn statements we derive the following information concerning the defendant Rothenberger. He joined the NSDAP on 1 May 1933 "for reasons of full conviction." From 1937 until 1942 he held the position of Gau Rechtsamtleiter. He states: "As such I also belonged to the Leadership Corps." Parenthetically, it should be stated that the organization within the Leadership Corps to which he belonged has been declared criminal by the judgment of the first International Military Tribunal, and that membership therein with knowledge of its illegal activities is a punishable crime under C. C. Law 10. We consider the interesting fact of his membership in the Leadership Corps no further, solely because defendant Rothenberger was not charged in the indictment with membership in a criminal organization. He was a Dienstleiter in the NSDAP during 1942 and 1943. From 1934 to 1942 he was Gaufuehrer in the National Socialist Jurists' League. In 1931 he became Landgerichtsdirektor, and in 1933 Justiz–Senator in Hamburg. From 1935 to 1942 he was president of the district court of appeals in Hamburg. In 1942 he was appointed Under Secretary in the Ministry of Justice under Thierack. He remained in that office until he left the Ministry in December 1943, after which he served as a notary in Hamburg. Thus, it is established by his own evidence that while serving as president of the district court of appeals he was also actively engaged as a Party official. Other evidence discloses the wide extent to which the interests and demands of the Ministry of Justice, the Party, the Gau Leadership, the SS, the SD, and the Gestapo affected his conduct in matters pertaining to the administration of justice. Rothenberger took over the Gau Leadership of the National Socialist Lawyers' League at the request of Gauleiter Kauffmann, who was the representative of German sovereignty in the Gau and who was, for all intents and purposes, a local dictator. As Gaufuehrer during the period following the seizure of power, Rothenberger had ample opportunity to learn of the corruption which permeated the administration of justice.

. . . .

In August 1939, on the eve of war, Rothenberger was in conference with officials of the SS and expressed to them the wish to be able to fall back on the information apparatus of the SD, and offered to furnish to the SD copies of "such sentences as are significant on account of their importance for the carrying-out of the National Socialist ideas in the field of the administration of justice." Rothenberger testified that during the first few years after the seizure of power, there was the usual system of SD informers in Hamburg. The unsatisfactory personnel in the SD was removed by Reichstatthalter Kauffmann, and the defendant Rothenberger nominated in their place individuals who, he said, "were judges and who I knew would never submit reports which were against the administration of justice." He states also:

> "In the meantime, the directive had been sent down from the Reich Ministry of Justice to the effect that the SD should be considered and used as a source of information of the State by agencies of the administration of justice."

While he was president of the district court of appeals at Hamburg, and during the war, this ardent advocate of judicial independence was not adverse to acting as the agent of Gauleiter Kauffmann. On 19 September 1939 Kauffmann, as Reichstatthalter and defense commissioner, issued an order as follows:

> "The president of the Hanseatic Court of Appeals, Senator Dr. Rothenberger, is acting on my order and is entitled to demand information in matters concerning the special courts and to in-

spect documents of every kind. All administrative offices as well as the offices of the NSDAP are requested to assist him in his work."

On 26 September 1939 Rothenberger, as president of the Hanseatic Court of Appeals, notified the Prosecutor General of Kauffmann's order and requested that a copy of the indictment "in all politically important cases or cases which are of special interest to the public should be sent to him." In a report to Schlegelberger of 11 May 1942 he spoke of the "crushing effect" of the Fuehrer's speech of 26 April 1942 and of the feeling of consequent insecurity on the part of the judges....

By reference to his own words we have already set forth Rothenberger's expressed convictions as to the duty of a judge as the "vassal" of the Fuehrer to decide cases as the Fuehrer would decide. The conclusion which we are compelled to draw from a great mass of evidence is not that Rothenberger objected to the exertion of influence upon the courts by Hitler, the party leaders, or the Gestapo, but that he wished that influence to be channeled through him personally rather than directed in a more public way at each individual judge. On the one hand he established liaison with the Party officials and the police, and on the other he organized the system of guidance of the judges who were his subordinates in the Hamburg area. He testifies that he considered the system of conferences between judges and prosecutors before trial, during trial and sometimes after trial, but before the consultation of the judges, to be wrong, and states that he considered it more correct, in view of the situation, that such a discussion should take place a long time before the trial and not between individual judges and the prosecutor, "but on a higher level, namely, between the chiefs of the offices, so that there would be no possibility to exert an influence on the individual judge in any way." Concerning his dictatorial attitude toward the other judges, Rothenberger testified: "Of course, guidance is guidance, and absolute and complete independence of the judge is possible only in normal conditions of peace, and we did not have these conditions after the Hitler speech."

The guidance system instituted by the defendant Rothenberger was not limited to conferences concerning pending cases of political importance before trial. We are convinced from the evidence that he used his influence with the subordinate judges in his district to protect Party members who had been charged or convicted of crime....

He especially required of the judges that they report to him concerning penal cases against Poles, Jews, and other foreigners, and "penal and civil cases in which persons are involved who are State or Party officials, or NSDAP functionaries, or who hold some other eminent position in public life."

One will seek in vain for any simple, frank, or direct statement by Rothenberger relative to any of the abuses of the Nazi system. His real attitude can only be extracted from the ambiguities of his evasive language. We quote from the record of the report made by Rothenberger to the judges on 27 January 1942 (*NG–1106, Pros. Ex. 462*):

"With regard to the matter it had to be considered whether or not any material claims made by the Jews could still be answered in the affirmative. Concerning this question, it might, however, be practical to maintain a certain reserve."

In an early report to the Hamburg judges, Rothenberger discussed the opinion of the Ministry concerning the legal treatment of Jews. He stated that the fact that a debtor in a civil case is a Jew should as a rule be a reason for arresting him; that Jews may be heard as witnesses but extreme caution is to be exercised in weighing their testimony. He requested that no verdict should be passed in Hamburg when a condemnation was exclusively based on the testimony of a Jew, and that the judges be advised accordingly.

On 21 April 1943, as a result of a long period of interdepartmental discussions, a conference of the state secretaries was held. Rothenberger was at the time State Secretary in the Ministry of Justice and participated in the conference concerning the limitation of legal rights of Jews. Kaltenbrunner also participated. At this meeting consideration was given to drafts of a decree which had long been under discussion. Modifications were agreed upon and the result was the promulgation of the infamous 13th regulation under the Reich Citizenship Law which provided that criminal actions committed by Jews shall be punished by the police and that after the death of a Jew his property shall be confiscated.

We next consider Rothenberger's activity concerning the deprivation of the rights of Jews in civil litigation. In the report of 5 January 1942 the defendant wrote:

"The lower courts do not grant to Jews the right to participate in court proceedings in *forma pauperis*. The district court suspended such a decision in one case. The refusal to grant this right of participation in court proceedings in *forma pauperis* is in accordance with today's legal thinking. But since a direct legal basis is missing, the refusal is unsuitable. We therefore think it urgently necessary that a legal regulation or order is given on the basis of which the rights of a pauper can be denied to a Jew." (*Pros. Ex. 373, NG–392, document books 5–D, p. 331.*)

. . . .

The foregoing narrative takes on additional significance when summarized. First, Rothenberger recommends to the Minister of Justice that it is desirable to deny to Jews the right to proceed in *forma pauperis*, but that such denial is admissible because there is no law to justify it. He recommends the passage of such a law. About 3 weeks later, no law having been passed, he recommends that the judges take a uniform line depriving the Jew of the right to proceed in *forma pauperis*. A specific case now arises in which the right was granted to a Jew, and the defendant Rothenberger receives veiled suggestions from the Gau economic advisor to the effect that defendants should not be allowed to compromise a case brought against them by a Jewish plaintiff because the court should decide against the Jew in any event on political grounds. Concerning this suggestion Rothenberger ventures no comment. The defendant in the Prenzlau case takes his cue from the advice of the economic advisor and denies liability; the court grants to the Jew the right to proceed in *forma pauperis*. Rothenberger criticizes this action, although the lower court had acted in strict conformity with the law. In March the awaited law excluding the Jew from the benefit of the poor-law is passed. In May, Rothenberger overrules the protest of a judge and directs the canceling of the order which was made by the lower court. This dictation by the defendant Rothenberger to other courts and judges of his district was not done in the course of a legal appeal from the lower court to the court over which he presided. It was done after the manner of a dictator directing an administrative inferior how to proceed.

Rothenberger not only participated in securing the enactment of a discriminatory law against Jews; he enforced it when enacted and, in the meantime, before its enactment, upon his own initiative he acted without authority of any law in denying to Jewish paupers the aid of the courts.

It is true that the denial of Jews of the right to proceed in civil litigation without advancement of costs appears to be a small matter compared to the extermination of Jews by the millions under other procedures. It is nevertheless a part of the government-organized plan for the persecution of the Jews, not only by murder and imprisonment but by depriving them of the means of livelihood and of equal rights in the courts of law.

The defendant Rothenberger testified that various judges reported to him "that they had heard rumors to the effect that everything was not quite all right in the concentration camps" and that they wished to inspect one. Accordingly, Rothenberger and the other judges visited the concentration camp at Neuengamme. He testified that they inquired about food conditions, accommodations, and the methods of work, and spoke to some inmates, and he asserts that they did not discover any abuses. This was in 1941. Again in 1942, according to his own testimony, the defendant visited Mauthausen concentration camp in company with Kaltenbrunner, who was later in charge of all concentration camps in Germany and has since suffered death by hanging. At Mauthausen concentration camp the defendant Rothenberger again inspected installations, conferred with inmates, and inquired as to the cause of detention of the inmates with whom he had talked. He states that from his spot checks he "could not find out that there was any case of a sentence being 'corrected.'" Upon inquiry as to what the defendant meant by the "correction of sentences," he answered:

> "By correcting of a sentence we mean that when the court had pronounced a sentence, for example, had condemned somebody to be imprisoned for a term of 5 years—if the police now, after these 5 years had been served, if the police arrested this man and put him into a concentration camp—this is only an example of a correction. Or even if, and this is clearer, it happened that a person was acquitted by a court, and in spite of that the police put

this man into a concentration camp. These are examples of correction of sentences."

The defendant stated that he did not observe and could not discover any abuse at Mauthausen.

.   .   .   .

It follows that the defendant Rothenberger, contrary to his sworn testimony, must have known that the inmates of the Mauthausen concentration camp were there by reason of the "correction of sentences" by the police, for the inmates were in the camp either without trial, or after acquittal, or after the expiration of their term of imprisonment.

It must be borne in mind that this inspection by the defendant Rothenberger was made at Mauthausen concentration camp, an institution which will go down in history as a human slaughter house and was made in company with the man who became the chief butcher.

We are compelled to conclude that Rothenberger was not candid in his testimony and that in denying knowledge of the institution of protective custody in its relationship with the concentration camps he classified himself as either a dupe or a knave. Nor can we believe that his trips to the camps were merely for pleasure or for general education. He also advised other judges to make like investigations. We concede that the concentration camps were not under the direct jurisdiction of the Reich Minister of Justice, but are unable to believe that an Under Secretary in the Ministry, who makes an official tour of inspection, is so feeble a person that he could not even raise his voice against the evil of which he certainly knew.

If the defendant Rothenberger disapproved of protective custody and the consequent employment of concentration camps, it must be because of a change in heart concerning which we have had no evidence.

.   .   .   .

In conclusion, the evidence discloses a personality full of complexities, contradictions, and inner conflict. He was kind to many half-Jews, and occasionally publicly aided them, yet he was instrumental in denying them the rights to which every litigant is entitled. He fulminated publicly against the "Schwarze Korps" for attacking the courts, yet he reproached judges for administering justice against Party officials and unquestionably used his influence toward achieving discriminatory action favorable to high Party officials and unfavorable to Poles and Jews. He wrote learnedly in favor of an independent judiciary, yet he ruled the judges of Hamburg with an iron hand. He protested vehemently against the practice of Party officials and Gestapo officers who interfered with the judges in pending cases, but he made arrangements with the Gestapo, the SS, and the SD whereby they were to come to him with their political affairs and then he instituted "preview and review" of sentences with the judges who were his inferiors. He thought concentration camps wrong but concluded that they were not objectionable if third degree methods did not become a habit.

Rothenberger was not happy with his work in Berlin. In his farewell speech on leaving Hamburg, he exuberantly exclaimed that he had been "an uncrowned king" in Hamburg, but he would have us believe that he received a crown of thorns in Berlin. Soon he learned of the utter brutality of the Nazi system and the cynical wickedness of Thierack and Himmler, whom he considered his personal enemies. He could not stomach what he saw, and they could not stomach him. The evidence satisfies us that Rothenberger was deceived and abused by his superiors; that evidence was "framed" against him; and that he was ultimately removed, in part at least, because he was not sufficiently brutal to satisfy the demands of the hour. He was retired to the apparently quiet life of a notary in Hamburg, but even then we find that he was receiving some pay as an Under Secretary and was assisting Gauleiter Kauffmann in political matters in that city.

The defendant Rothenberger is guilty of taking a minor but consenting part in the Night and Fog program. He aided and abetted in the program of racial persecution, and notwithstanding his many protestations to the contrary he materially contributed toward the prostitution of the Ministry of Justice and the courts and their subordination to the arbitrary will of Hitler, the Party minions, and the police. He participated in the corruption and perversion of the judicial system. The defendant Rothenberger is guilty under counts two and three of the indictment.

The Defendant Rothaug

Oswald Rothaug was born 17 May 1897. His education was interrupted from 1916 to 1918 while he was in the army. He passed the final law examination in 1922 and the State examination for the higher administration of justice in 1925.

He joined the NSDAP in the spring of 1938 and the membership was made effective from May 1937.

Rothaug was a member of the National Socialist Jurists' League and the National Socialist Public Welfare Association. In his affidavit he denies belonging to the SD. However, the testimony of Elkar and his own admission on the witness stand establishes that he was an "honorary collaborator" for the SD on legal matters.

In December 1925 he began his career as a jurist, first as an assistant to an attorney in Ansbach and later as assistant judge at various courts. In 1927 he became public prosecutor in Hof in charge of criminal cases. From 1929 to 1933 he officiated as counsellor at the local court in Nuernberg. In June 1933 he became senior public prosecutor in the public prosecution in Nuernberg. Here he was the official in charge of general criminal cases, assistant of the Chief Public Prosecutor handling examination of suspensions of proceedings and of petitions for pardon. From November to April 1937 he officiated as counsellor of the district court in Schweinfurt. He was legal advisor in the civil and penal chamber and at the Court of Assizes, as well as chairman of the lay assessors' court. From April 1937 to May 1943 he was director of the district court in Nuernberg, except for a period in

August and September of 1939 when he was in the Wehrmacht. During this time he was chairman of the Court of Assizes, of a penal chamber, and of the Special Court.

From May 1943 to April 1945 he was public prosecutor of the public prosecution at the People's Court in Berlin. Here, as head of Department I he handled for a time cases of high treason in the southern Reich territory, and from January 1944 cases concerning the undermining of public morale in the Reich territory.

Crimes charged in the indictment, as heretofore stated in this opinion, have been established by the evidence in this case. The questions, therefore, to be determined as to the defendant Rothaug are: first, whether he had knowledge of any crime so established; and second, whether he was a participant in or took a consenting part in its commission.

Rothaug's sources of knowledge have, with those of all the defendants, already been pointed out. But Rothaug's knowledge was not limited to those general sources. Rothaug was an official of considerable importance in Nuernberg. He had many political and official contacts; among these—he was the friend of Haberkern, Gau inspector of the Gau Franconia; he was the friend and associate of Oeschey, Gau legal advisor for the Gau Franconia; and was himself Gauwalter of the Lawyers' League. He was the "honorary collaborator" for the SD. According to the witness Elkar, [Rothaug was] the agent of the SD for Nuernberg and vicinity, this position was more important than that of a confidential agent, and an honorary collaborator was active in SD affairs. He testifies that Rothaug took the SS oath of secrecy.

. . . .

The evidence as to the character and activities of the defendant is voluminous. We shall confine ourselves to the question as to whether or not he took a consenting part in the plan for the persecution, oppression, and extermination of Poles and Jews.

His attitude of virulent hostility toward these races is proved from many sources and is in no wise shaken by the affidavits he has submitted on his own behalf.

The evidence in this regard comes from his own associates—the judges, prosecutors, defense counsel, medical experts, and others with whom he dealt. Among, but not limited to these, we cite the evidence of Doebig, Ferber, Bauer, Dorfmueller, Elkar, Engert, Groben, and Markl. In particular the testimony of Father Schosser is important. He testified as to many statements made by the defendant Rothaug during the trial of his own case, showing the defendant's hostility to Poles and his general attitude toward them. He stated that concerning the Poles in general, Rothaug expressed himself in the following manner:

> "If he (Rothaug) had his way, then no Pole would be buried in a German cemetery, and then he went on to make the remark which everybody heard in that courtroom—that he would get up from his

coffin if there was a Pole being buried near to him. Rothaug himself had to laugh because of this mean joke, and he went on to say, 'You have to be able to hate, because according to the Bible, God is a hating God.' "

The testimony of Elkar is even more significant. He testifies that Rothaug believed in severe measures against foreigners and particularly against Poles and Jews, whom he felt should be treated differently from German transgressors. Rothaug felt there was a gap in the law in this respect. He states that Rothaug asserted that in his own court he achieved this discrimination by interpretation of existing laws but that other courts failed to do so. Such a gap, according to Rothaug, should be closed by singling out Poles and Jews for special treatment. Elkar testifies that recommendations were made by the defendant Rothaug, through the witness, to higher levels and that the subsequent decree of 1941 against Poles and Jews conformed to Rothaug's ideas as expressed and forwarded by the witness Elkar through SD channels to the RSHA.

. . . .

Concerning his participation in the Nazi policy of persecution and extermination of persons of these races, we shall confine our discussions to three cases which were tried by Rothaug as presiding judge.

The first case to be considered is that of Durka and Struss. Our knowledge of this case is based primarily upon the evidence of Hans Kern, the defense counsel of one of these defendants; Hermann Markl, the prosecutor in the case; and the testimony of the defendant Rothaug.

The essential facts are in substance as follows: Two Polish girls—one, according to the testimony of Kern, 17 years of age, the other somewhat older—were accused of starting a fire in an armament plant in Bayreuth. This alleged fire did not do any material damage to the plant, but they were in the vicinity when it started and were arrested and interrogated by the Gestapo. Both gave alleged confessions to the Gestapo. Almost immediately following this occurrence, they were brought to Nuernberg by the Gestapo for trial before the Special Court.

Upon their arrival the prosecutor in the case, Markl, was directed to draw up an indictment based upon the Gestapo interrogation. This was at 11 o'clock of the day they were tried.

The witness Kern was summoned by the defendant Rothaug to act as defense counsel in the case approximately 2 hours before the case came to trial. He informed Rothaug that he would not have time to prepare a defense. According to Kern, Rothaug stated that if he did not take over the defense, the trial would have to be conducted without a defense counsel. According to Rothaug, he told Kern that he would get another defense counsel. In either event the trial was to go on at once.

The trial itself, according to Kern, lasted about half an hour; according to the defendant, approximately an hour; according to Markl, it was conducted with the speed of a court martial.

The evidence consisted of the alleged confessions which one of the defendants repudiated before the court. Rothaug states that he thereupon called the Gestapo official who had obtained these alleged confessions and questioned him under oath. According to Rothaug the Gestapo official stated that the interrogations were perfectly regular. There was also a letter in evidence which it was said the defendants had tried to destroy before their capture. The witness Kern stated on cross-examination that this letter had little materiality.

The defendant attempts to justify the speed of this trial upon the legal requirements in existence at this time. He states, in contradiction to the other witnesses, that a clear case of sabotage was established. This Tribunal is not inclined to accept the defendant Rothaug's version of the facts which were established. Under the circumstances and in the brief period of the trial, the Tribunal does not believe the defendant could have established those facts from evidence.

According to the witness Kern, one of the defendants was 17 years of age. This assertion as to age was not disputed. A German 18 years of age or thereunder would have come under the German Juvenile Act and would not have been subject to trial before a Special Court or to capital punishment. Whatever the age of the defendants in this case, they were tried under the procedure described in the ordinance against Poles and Jews which was in effect at this time, by a judge who did not believe the statements of Polish defendants, according to the testimony in this case. These two young Polish women were sentenced to death and executed 4 days after trial. In the view of this Tribunal, based upon the evidence, these two young women did not have what amounted to a trial at all but were executed because they were Polish nationals in conformity with the Nazi plan of persecution and extermination.

The second case to be considered is the Lopata case. This was a case in which a young Polish farmhand, approximately 25 years of age, is alleged to have made indecent advances to his employer's wife.

He first was tried in the district court at Neumarkt. That court sentenced him to a term of 2 years in the penitentiary. A nullity plea was filed in this case before the Reich Supreme Court, and the Reich Supreme Court returned the case to the Special Court at Nuernberg for a new trial and sentence. The Reich Supreme Court stated that the judgment of the lower court was defective, since it did not discuss in detail whether the ordinance against public enemies was applicable and stated that if such ordinance were applicable—a thing which seemed probable, a much more severe sentence was deemed necessary.

The case was therefore again tried in violation of the fundamental principles of justice that no man should be tried twice for the same offense.

In the second trial of the case, the defendant Rothaug obligingly found that the ordinance against public enemies had been violated.

In its reasons, the court states the facts on which the verdict was based as follows:

"The wife of farmer Schwenzl, together with the accused and a Polish girl, chopped straw in the barn. The accused was standing on the right-hand side of the machine to carry out the work. Suddenly, in the middle of the work, the accused, without saying anything, touched with his hand the genitals of the wife of farmer Schwenzl, through her skirt. When she said, after this unexpected action of the defendant, 'You hog, do you think I am not disgusted about anything; you think you can do that because my husband is sick,' the accused laughed and in spite of this dissuasion touched again the genitals of the farmer's wife above her skirt. The wife of farmer Schwenzl slapped him after that. In spite of this, the accused continued with his impertinent behavior; for a third time he touched the genitals of the farmer's wife above the skirt.

.   .   .   .

"The accused did not make a complete confession. He states that he only once, for fun, touched the farmer's wife's genitals above the skirt.

"The court is convinced, on account of the testimony given by the witness Therese Schwenzl, who makes a trustworthy impression, that the affair occurred exactly as described by the witness. Therefore, its findings were arrived at according to the testimony given by her."

The Polish woman who was present at the time of this alleged assault is not listed as a witness. Rothaug has stated in his testimony before this Court that he never had a Polish witness.

As for the reasons for bringing the defendant under the public enemy ordinance, the following facts are stated in the reasons for the verdict: Lopata having had some minor difficulties with the farmer Schwenzl refused to eat his noon meal and induced the Polish servant maid to do likewise. Thereupon, farmer Schwenzl, his employer, called him to account in the stable. The defendant put up resistance to the farmer's "admonitions" by arming himself with a dung fork. It is further stated that the Pole, at the threshold of the farm hallway, again turned against his employer and let him go only when attacked by the sheep dog which the farmer kept.

As to the actual reasons for the sentence of this Polish farmhand to death, the following paragraphs are more significant:

"Thus, the defendant gives the impression of a thoroughly degenerate personality, which is marked by excitability and a definite trend to mendacity, or to lying. The whole inferiority of the defendant, I would say, lies in the sphere of character and is obviously based on his being a part of Polish subhumanity, or in his belonging to Polish subhumanity.

"The drafting of men into the armed forces effected a heavy labor shortage in all spheres of life at home, last but not least in agriculture. To compensate this, Polish laborers, among others, had to be used to a large extent, mainly as farmhands.

"These men cannot be supervised by the authorities to such an extent as would be necessary due to their insubordinate and criminal disposition.

. . . .

"The action of the defendant constitutes a considerable disturbance of the peace of the persons immediately concerned by his mean actions. The rural population has the right to expect that the strongest measures will be taken against such terrorization by foreign elements. But beyond disregarding the honor of the wife of farmer Schwenzl, the attack of the defendant is directed against the purity of the German blood. Looking at it from this point of view, the defendant showed such insubordination within the German living space that his action has to be considered as especially significant.

"Accordingly, as outlined in article III, paragraph 2, second sentence of the ordinance against Poles and Jews, the crime of the defendant, which in connection with his other behavior shows a climax of unheard-of impudence, has to be considered as especially serious so that the death sentence had to be passed as the only just expiation, which is also necessary in the interest of the Reich security to deter Poles of similar mentality."

The defendant was sentenced under the ordinance against Poles and Jews in the Incorporated Eastern Territories. The verdict was signed by the defendant Rothaug, and an application for clemency was disapproved by him.

When on the witness stand, the defendant Rothaug was asked the following question by the court:

". . . if Lopata had been a racial German, all other facts being the same as they were in the Lopata case, is it your judgment that the nullity plea would have been invoked and that the Supreme Court would have ordered the case sent back to you for another trial? I should like your opinion on that."

Rothaug replied as follows to this question:

"Mr. President, this question is very interesting, but I cannot even imagine that possibility even theoretically, because the very elements which are of the greatest importance could not be the same in the case of a German."

Lopata was sentenced to death and subsequently executed.

The third case to be considered is that of Leo Katzenberger. The record in this case shows that Lehmann Israel Katzenberger, commonly called Leo Katzenberger, was a merchant and head of the Jewish community in Nuernberg; that he was "sentenced to death for an offense under paragraph 2, legally identical with an offense under paragraph 4 of the decree against public enemies in connection with the offense of racial pollution."

The trial was held in the public session on 13 March 1942. Katzenberger's age at that time was over 68 years.

The offense of racial pollution with which he was charged comes under article 2 of the Law for the Protection of German Blood and Honor. This sections reads as follows:

"Sexual intercourse (except in marriage) between Jews and German nationals of German or German-related blood is forbidden."

The applicable sections of the Decree Against Public Enemies reads as follows:

"Section 2

"Crimes During Air Raids

"Whoever commits a crime or offense against the body, life, or property, taking advantage of air raid protection measures, is punishable by hard labor of up to 15 years, or for life, and in particularly severe cases, punishable by death.

. . . .

"Section 4

"Exploitation of the State of War a Reason for More Severe Punishment

"Whoever commits a criminal act exploiting the extraordinary conditions caused by war is punishable beyond the regular punishment limits with hard labor of up to 15 years, or for life, or is punishable by death if the sound common sense of the people requires it on account of the crime being particularly despicable."

The evidence in this case, aside from the record, is based primarily upon the testimony of Hans Groben, the investigating judge who first investigated the case; Hermann Markl, the official who prosecuted the case; Karl Ferber, who was one of the associate judges in the trial; Heinz Hoffman, who was the other associate judge in the trial; Armin Baur, who was medical expert in the trial; Georg Engert, who dealt with clemency proceedings; and Otto Ankenbrand, another investigating judge.

The salient facts established in connection with this case are in substance as follows: Sometime in the first half of the year 1941 the witness Groben issued a warrant of arrest against Katzenberger, who was accused of having had intimate relations with the photographer Seiler. According to the results of the police inquiry, actual intercourse had not been proved, and Katzenberger denied the charge. Upon Groben's advice, Katzenberger agreed that he would not move against the warrant of arrest at that time but would await the results of further investigation. These further investigations were very lengthy, although Groben pressed the public prosecutor for speed. The police, in spite of their efforts, were unable to get further material evidence, and it became apparent that the way to clarify the situation was to take the sworn statement of Seiler, and this was done.

In her sworn statement she said that Katzenberger had known both her and her family for many years before she had come to Nuernberg and that his relationship to her was a friendly and fatherly one and denied the charge of sexual intercourse. The evidence also showed that Katzenberger had given Seiler financial assistance on various occasions and that he was administrator of the property where Seiler lived, which was owned by a firm of which he was a partner. Upon Seiler's statement, Groben informed Dr. Herz, counsel for Katzenberger, of the result and suggested that it was the right time to move against the warrant of arrest.

When this was done, Rothaug learned of it and ordered that the Katzenberger case be transferred from the criminal divisional court to the Special Court. The first indictment was withdrawn, and another indictment was prepared for the Special Court.

The witness Markl states that Rothaug dominated the prosecution, especially through his close friendship with the senior public prosecutor, Dr. Schroeder, who was the superior of Markl.

The indictment before the Special Court was prepared according to the orders of Rothaug, and Katzenberger was not charged only with race defilement in this new indictment, but there was also an additional charge under the decree against public enemies, which made the death sentence permissible. The new indictment also joined the Seiler woman on a charge of perjury. The effect of joining Seiler in the charge against Katzenberger was to preclude her from being a witness for the defendant, and such a combination was contrary to established practice. Rothaug at this time told Markl that there was sufficient proof of sexual intercourse between Seiler and Katzenberger to convince him, and that he was prepared to condemn Katzenberger to death. Markl informed the Ministry of Justice of Rothaug's intended procedure against Katzenberger and was told that if Rothaug so desired it, the procedure would be approved.

Prior to the trial, the defendant Rothaug called on Dr. Armin Baur, medical counsellor for the Nuernberg Court, as the medical expert for the Katzenberger case. He stated to Baur that he wanted to pronounce a death sentence and that it was, therefore, necessary for the defendant to be examined. This examination, Rothaug stated, was a mere formality since Katzenberger "would be beheaded anyhow." To the doctor's reproach that Katzenberger was old, and it seemed questionable whether he could be charged with race defilement, Rothaug stated:

"It is sufficient for me that the swine said that a German girl had sat upon his lap."

The trial itself, as testified to by many witnesses, was in the nature of a political demonstration. High party officials attended, including Reich Inspector Oexle. Part of the group of Party officials appeared in uniform.

During the proceedings, Rothaug tried with all his power to encourage the witnesses to make incriminating statements against the defendants.

Both defendants were hardly heard by the court. Their statements were passed over or disregarded. During the course of the trial, Rothaug took the opportunity to give the audience a National Socialist lecture on the subject of the Jewish question. The witnesses found great difficulty in giving testimony because of the way in which the trial was conducted, since Rothaug constantly anticipated the evaluation of the facts and gave expression to his own opinions.

Because of the way the trial was conducted, it was apparent that the sentence which would be imposed was the death sentence.

After the introduction of evidence was concluded, a recess was taken, during which time the prosecutor Markl appeared in the consultation room and Rothaug made it clear to him that he expected the prosecution to ask for a death sentence against Katzenberger and a term in the penitentiary for Seiler. Rothaug at this time also gave him suggestions as to what he should include in his arguments.

The reasons for the verdict were drawn up by Ferber. They were based upon the notes of Rothaug as to what should be included. Considerable space is given to Katzenberger's ancestry and the fact that he was of the Mosaic faith, although that fact was admitted by Katzenberger. Such space is also given to the relationship between Katzenberger and Seiler. That there was no proof of actual sexual intercourse is clear from the opinion. The proof seems to have gone little farther than the fact that the defendant Seiler had at times sat upon Katzenberger's lap and that he had kissed her, which facts were also admitted. Many assumptions were made in the reasons stated which obviously are not borne out by the evidence. The court even goes back to the time prior to the passage of the law for the protection of German Blood and Honor, during which Katzenberger had known Seiler. It draws the conclusion apparently without evidence, that their relationship for a period of approximately 10 years, had always been of a sexual nature. The opinion undertakes to bring the case under the decision of the Reich Supreme Court that actual sexual intercourse need not be proved, provided the acts are sexual in nature.

Having wandered far afield from the proof to arrive at this conclusion as to the matter of racial pollution, the court then proceeds to go far afield in order to bring the case under the decree against public enemies. Here the essential facts proved were that the defendant Seiler's husband was at the front and that Katzenberger, on one or possibly two occasions, had visited her after dark. On both points the following paragraphs of the opinion are enlightening (*NG–154, Pros. Ex. 152*):

> "Looked at from this point of view, Katzenberger's conduct is particularly contemptible. Together with his offense of racial pollution he is also guilty of an offense under paragraph 4 of the ordinance against people's parasites.* It should be noted here that the national community is in need of increased legal protection

---

* Popular name for the decree against public enemies.

from all crimes attempting to destroy or undermine its inner cohesion.

"On several occasions since the outbreak of war the defendant Katzenberger crept into Seiler's flat after dark. In those cases the defendant exploited the measures taken for the protection in air raids. His chances were further improved by the absence of the bright street lighting which exists in the street along Spittlertorgraben in peacetime. He exploited this fact fully aware of its significance because thus he instinctively escaped during his excursions being observed by people in the street.

"The visits paid by Katzenberger to Seiler under the protection of the black-out served at least the purpose of keeping relations going. It does not matter whether during these visits extra-marital sexual relations took place or whether they only conversed as when the husband was present, as Katzenberger claims. The request to interrogate the husband was therefore overruled. The court holds the defendant's actions, done with a purpose within a definite plan, amount to a crime against the body according to paragraph 2 of the ordinance against people's parasites. The law of 15 September 1935 has been passed to protect German blood and German honor. The Jew's racial pollution amounts to a grave attack on the purity of German blood, the object of the attack being the body of a German woman. The general need for protection therefore makes appear as unimportant the behavior of the other partner in racial pollution who anyway is not liable to prosecution. The fact that racial pollution occurred up to at least 1939–1940 becomes clear from statements made by the witness Zeuschel to whom the defendant repeatedly and consistently admitted that up to the end of 1939 and the beginning of 1940 she was used to sitting on the Jew's lap and exchanging caresses as described above.

"Thus, the defendant committed an offense also under paragraph 2 of the ordinance against people's parasites.

"The personal character of the male defendant also stamps him as a people's parasite. The racial pollution practiced by him through many years grew, by exploiting wartime conditions, into an attitude inimical to the nation, into an attack on the security of the national community, during an emergency.

"This was why the defendant Katzenberger had to be sentenced both on a charge of racial pollution and of an offense under paragraphs 2 and 4 of the ordinance against people's parasites, the two charges being taken in conjunction according to paragraph 73 of the criminal code."

. . . .

QUESTIONS

1. How did the German judicial system during the Weimar period (prior to 1933) resemble the judicial system in the United States? How was it different?

2. How specifically did the Nazis change the German judicial system?

3. What is the significance of each of the following features of the Nazi judicial system:

(a) close supervision of the judicial system by party officials;

(b) correction of sentences and use of protective custody;

(c) removal of judges not favored by party officials;

(d) creation of special courts to try political offenses and offenses by persons of certain races and nationalities; and

(e) ex parte communications between prosecutors and judges.

4. Rothenberger enthusiastically endorsed the refusal to Jews of *forma pauperis* rights at trial, and in all three of the criminal cases tried by Rothaug, Polish and Jewish witnesses were afforded no credibility. What was the justification that Rothenberger and Rothaug used for applying different evidentiary and procedural rules to different ethnic groups?

5. Did Rothenberger know what was happening in the concentration camps? Did he want to know?

6. Rothaug distorts religion to justify hate and distorts law to carry out a political program. Why does he feel a need to hate? How does political ideology dominate his sense of right and wrong?

7. "Proof" played a relatively unimportant role in the three criminal cases tried by Rothaug, all three of which ended with imposition of the death penalty. Is there a relationship between burdens of proof and preservation of a democratic society?

8. Where does the Military Tribunal get the authority to try and sentence the defendants at Nuernberg? Were these trials justified?

9. In *State v. Marshall*, Chapter 2 supra, the Alabama Supreme Court applied a law that allowed the death penalty to hinge on the defendant's status as a slave and admitted Breeden's testimony about his communications with his client. How was the reasoning used by the Alabama court to deprive Marshall of his right to the attorney-client privilege in a capital case different from the reasoning used by Rothenberger and Rothaug to deprive Jews and Poles of procedural rights in capital cases?

10. The Alabama Supreme Court in *Marshall* found that a new trial was warranted because the jury had probably been misled. Even in an evil legal system, an appellate court placed some value on the life of a defendant and there was at least some semblance of procedure. What was the function of appellate courts in the Nazi judicial system? What was the purpose of having any judicial procedure at all?

The Believer and the Powers That Are

John T. Noonan, Jr. (1987)

Thomas Wolsey (1475–1530) was "the great cardinal," who in person unified ecclesiastical interests and the power of the state, enjoying the special privileges of a papal legate as well as the almost unlimited confidence of young Henry VIII, and ruling as chief minister from 1515 until his abrupt fall in October 1529. Wolsey's pursuit of personal profit, his failure to reform recognized abuses in the Church, his cynical and unrealistic attempt to have Henry's marriage to Catherine of Aragon annulled set the stage on which the constitutional change occurred....

Thomas More (1477–1535) succeeded Wolsey as chancellor, the first layman ever to hold the office. Ironically, as it was to seem, the very appointment of a layman was a signal by Henry VIII of the king's new turn of mind. More was fifty-two, a London lawyer's son, who had gone from a successful legal practice to service as a royal counselor in 1518. In his *Utopia*, published before he held high office, he had imagined a Nowhere where no one was molested for his religious opinion, although disbelievers in God or a future life were barred from office. In the 1520s he had become a polemicist against the new heretics, and as chancellor he encouraged enforcement of the statute against heresy. The king knew from the start that More did not believe in his case for an annulment and for a time tolerated his noncooperation here while other agents continued to press the case in Rome.

The matter of the marriage, an accident on which so much was to turn, was constitutionally within the jurisdiction of the Church; and at the apex of that jurisdiction was the pope, who had awarded Henry for his anti-Lutheran writing the title of "Defender of the Faith." Exasperated by delay, seeing clearly that whatever the legal merits of his case (they were little) the pope would never decide in his favor because the pope was politically under the thumb of the Emperor Charles, Henry soured on his propapal attitude and listened to the counsels of those who proposed a new and daring course. The chief counselors were Thomas Cromwell (1485–1540) and Thomas Cranmer (1489–1556)....

In May 1532, the Convocation asked the king to protect the liberties of the Church: Magna Carta was invoked. Henry, steeled by his more radical counselors, replied by demanding subservience, and the cowed clerics surrendered, the Convocation passing a declaration entitled "The Submission of the Clergy," granting the king power to approve or disapprove their canons.... Thomas More resigned the day after it was passed; it may reasonably be inferred that he read the concession as fatal and foresaw the course the king would now follow. Parliament passed a statute whose preamble referred to England as an empire "governed by one supreme head and king," beneath whom there was a "spirituality [sic] and temporalty [sic]" (24 Hen. VIII c. 12 [4 Pick. Stat. 257], 1532). The germ of revolution was planted....

Parliament then passed the Act of Succession declaring Henry and Catherine's marriage void and Henry and Anne's marriage "perfect," and requiring from every adult male an oath of allegiance to Anne and her issue; to refuse was to be guilty of "misprision of high treason" (25 Hen. VIII c. 22 [4 Pick. Stat. 305], 1533). Commissioners to enact the oath were appointed, and on April 17, 1534, Thomas More, two years in retirement, was summoned to take the oath. The remarkable letter that follows was written soon afterward, addressed to Margaret, his oldest daughter, aged 29. It is, of course, not an unqualified defense of the supremacy of conscience; but it is a defense of even a doubtful conscience against coercion by the secular power.

More's silence sealed his fate. In November 1534, under Cromwell's management, a special bill of attainder was passed condemning him to death for his failure. . . .

More himself was not disposed of by the bill of attainder, but was proceeded against under the Treason Act. Convicted in June 1535 of denying the king's supremacy over the church, he was executed on July 6, 1535; he was canonized as a martyr in 1933.

The following letter is from the Correspondence of Thomas More, edited by Elizabeth Frances Rogers (Princeton, 1947).

Thomas More to His Daughter Margaret

(Tower of London).
(C. 17 April 1534).

When I was before the Lords at Lambeth, I was the first that was called in, although Master Doctor the Vicar of Croydon had come before me, and several others. After the cause of my being sent for was declared to me (whereof I somewhat marveled in my mind, considering that they sent for no more temporal men but me) I desired the sight of the oath, which they showed me under the great seal. Then I desired the sight of the Act of Succession, which was delivered to me in a printed roll. After which I read separately by myself and considered the oath with the act, and I showed them that my purpose was not to put any fault either on the act or any man that made it, upon the oath or any man that swore it, nor to condemn the conscience of any other man. But as for myself in good faith my conscience so moved me in the matter that though I would not refuse to swear to the succession, yet unto the oath that there was offered me I could not swear without the risking of my soul to perpetual damnation. And that if they doubted whether I would refuse the oath only for·the grudge of my conscience, or for any other fantasy, I was ready therein to satisfy them by my oath. Which if they trusted not, what should they be the better to give me any oath? And if they trusted that I would therein swear true, then trusted I that of their goodness they would not move me to swear the oath that they offered me, perceiving that the swearing was against my conscience.

Unto this my Lord Chancellor said that they all were sorry to see me say this and see me thus refuse the oath. And they all said that on their faith I was the very first that ever refused it; which would cause the King's Highness to conceive great suspicion of me and great indignation toward me. And therewith they showed me the roll and let me see the names of the lords and the commons who had sworn and subscribed their names already. Which notwithstanding, when they saw that I refused to swear the same myself, not blaming any other man that had sworn, I was in conclusion commanded to go down into the garden and thereupon I tarried in the old burned chamber that looks into the garden and would not go down because of the heat. . . .

When they had played their pageant and were gone out of the place, then was I called in again. And then was it declared to me what a number had sworn, even since I went aside, and gladly without any sticking. Wherein I laid no blame on any man but for my own self answered as before. . . .

My Lord of Canterbury taking hold upon that which I had said, that I condemned not the conscience of them that swore, said to me that it appeared well that I did not take it for a very sure and certain thing that I might not lawfully swear, but rather as a thing uncertain and doubtful. But then, said my Lord, you know for a certainty and a thing without doubt that you are bound to obey your sovereign lord, your King, and therefore you are bound to leave the doubt of your unsure conscience in refusing the oath and take the sure way in obeying your prince, and swear it. Now it was all so in my own mind I thought myself not defeated, yet this argument seemed suddenly so subtle and with such authority coming out from so noble a prelate's mouth that I could answer nothing thereto but only that I thought myself I might not well do so, because in my conscience this was one of the cases in which I was bound that I should not obey my prince, since whatever other folk thought in the matter (whose conscience and learning I would not condemn nor take upon myself to judge), yet in my conscience the truth seemed on the other side. Wherein I had not informed my conscience suddenly nor slightly but at long leisure and with diligent search in the matter. And of truth if that reason is conclusive, then have we a ready way to avoid all perplexities. For in whatsoever matters the doctors stand in great doubt the King's commandment given upon whatever side he chooses, resolves all the doubts.

Then said my Lord of Westminster to me that howsoever the matter seemed to my mind, I had cause to fear that my own mind was erroneous when I saw the Great Council of the Realm determine the contrary of my mind, and that, therefore, I ought to change my conscience. To that I answered that if there were no men but myself upon my side, and the whole Parliament upon the other, I would be sore afraid to lean to my own mind alone against so many. But on the other side, if it so be that in some things for which I refuse the oath, I have (as I think I have) upon my part as great a Council and a greater too, I am not then bound to change my conscience and would conform it to the Council of one realm against the

General Council of Christendom. Upon this, Master Secretary (as one that tenderly favors me) said and swore a great oath that he would rather that his only son (who is in truth a goodly young gentleman and shall I trust come to much worship) had lost his head than that I should thus have refused the oath. For surely the King's Highness would now conceive a great suspicion against me and think of the matter of the nun of Canterbury was all contrived by my drift. To which I said that the contrary was true and well known and whatsoever should mishap me, it lay not in my power to help it without peril of my soul. Then did my Lord Chancellor repeat before me my refusal to Mister Secretary, as to him that was going unto the King's Grace. And in the rehearsing, this Lordship repeated again that I denied not but was content to swear to the succession. Whereunto I said that as for that point I would be content so that I might see my oath in that point so framed in such a manner as might stand with my conscience.

Then said my Lord: "Mary! Master Secretary mark that too that he will not swear that either only in some certain manner." "Verily no, my Lord," quote I, "but that I will see it made in such wise first as I shall myself see that I shall neither be foresworn nor swear against my conscience." Surely as to swear to the succession I see no peril, but I thought and think it reason, that to my own oath I myself look well and be of counsel in the fashion, and never intend to swear for a piece and set my hand to the whole oath. How be it (as help me God) as touching the whole oath, I never withdrew any man from it nor never advised any to refuse it nor never put, nor will, any scruple in any man's head, but leave every man to his own conscience. And me thinks in good faith that so were it good reason that every man should leave me to mine.

QUESTIONS

1.   Why was Thomas More willing to swear to the Act of Succession, but not to take the oath of allegiance to Anne and her issue?

2.   Thomas More, on the one hand, and Rothaug and Rothenberger, on the other, were polar opposites in the way they defined their own relationship to the law. More was willing to lose his life rather than affirm an act by Henry VIII that he believed was immoral and unlawful. Rothaug and Rothenberger were willing to take the lives of other people in transforming Germany's laws and judicial system into instruments of state-sanctioned murder. All three of these men were lawyers. Where did each of them derive their understanding of the meaning of law?

3.   Although the King and Parliament had the power to promulgate laws in England, did Thomas More in his death define the meaning of law? How?

4.   How did the rationalizations that the Lords of Canterbury and Westminster offered to More resemble rationalizations commonly used to justify doing something one believes to be wrong? Do ethical actions hinge upon the power of conscience over rationalization?

5.   Does legal training make a person more prone or less prone to rationalization?

CHAPTER 12

DISCIPLINE AND REGULATION OF LAWYERS AND LAW FIRMS

A. THE GRIEVANCE PROCESS

Report of the Commission on Evaluation of Disciplinary Enforcement (The "McKay Commission").[1]

(1991).
Reprinted by Permission of the American Bar Association.

Executive Summary

In 1970, the ABA Special Committee on Evaluation of Disciplinary Enforcement (Clark Committee) published its report—the first nationwide evaluation of lawyer disciplinary procedures. The legal profession has undergone considerable change since then. The profession has grown. Not only are there more lawyers practicing in this country but many of them practice in more than one state. There has also been a growth in the size of law firms. This has produced an expansion of the type and scope of service offered to clients with many firms offering ancillary business services.

At the same time, in an attempt to advance consumer interests, our courts have authorized advertising and solicitation of clients and a general promotion of competition among lawyers. Greater emphasis has been placed on the marketing of legal services. These changes have produced tensions between traditional notions of professionalism and the expectations and demands of clients. These changes have also produced a growing mistrust of secret, self-regulated systems of lawyer discipline.

Much progress has been made in the enforcement of lawyer discipline since the Clark Committee's report. Almost without exception, disciplinary systems are staffed by full-time professional disciplinary counsel having statewide jurisdiction. In most jurisdictions, many of the recommendations made by the Clark Committee have been implemented. In addition, a majority of jurisdictions have adopted the Model Rules of Professional Conduct promulgated by the American Bar Association in 1983. In spite of all of these efforts, the public continues to be critical of lawyer regulation. Efforts are made on a recurring basis to remove authority for the regula-

---

1. [Professor Robert McKay (1919–90), former dean of the New York University Law School, was Chair of the ABA's Commission on Evaluation of Disciplinary Enforcement from 1989–90.]—ed.

tion of lawyers from the judicial branch and to transfer it to the legislative or executive branches of government.

This Commission has studied these challenges to regulation of the legal profession by the judiciary. We have found no convincing evidence that lawyers would be better regulated by the legislative or executive branches. The Commission concludes, on the contrary, that the regulation of lawyers must be lodged with the judicial branch of government. Judicial regulation of lawyers is essential to the independence of the judiciary and to the proper discharge of the role of the lawyer in a democratic society. Lawyers are called on to champion unpopular causes and to challenge the will of the majority. Lawyers must remain free from political oppression and the fear of reprisal. Lawyers are officers of the court and it is essential that the court retain the authority to regulate their conduct.

If judicial regulation of the legal profession is to be preserved, that system of regulation must withstand the charge of inherent conflict of interest and appearance of impropriety. Regulation of lawyer conduct must be exercised by the judiciary and not by the organized bar. The courts must take more direct and active control of the disciplinary system. Reform is required to insulate disciplinary counsel from control or influence by the organized bar. Lawyers have a legitimate role to play in an appropriately structured disciplinary system, but the management and control of the system must rest with the courts. Central intake and statewide jurisdiction are essential to avoid charges of cronyism and the familiar criticism that the fox is guarding the henhouse. Non-lawyers must be given a significant role in the administration of the system. Adequate resources must be provided to insure a thorough and comprehensive system of regulation.

The Commission's research convinces us that disciplinary systems are fair to both respondents and complainants, but there is a high level of public distrust. Secret proceedings are the greatest cause of distrust. If public trust is to be promoted, disciplinary systems can no longer operate secretly. Florida and West Virginia's disciplinary records are open to the public when a charge is filed or a complaint is dismissed. Oregon's records are public when a complaint is made. These open disciplinary systems have proven that lawyers are not harmed by them. Gag rules have already been declared unconstitutional by a number of courts. Without gag rules confidentiality is no longer tenable. An open system of discipline will foster greater respect for the integrity of the system.

At the same time, resort to a disciplinary system must not be discouraged by fear of reprisal. Absolute immunity must be provided to complainants. The prospect of being sued by the lawyer who is the subject of the complaint discourages the filing of legitimate complaints.

Despite the considerable progress made since the Clark Report, there is still room for improvements in the functioning of disciplinary systems. Lawyers charged with misconduct are entitled to basic due process. At the same time, summary procedures and consent procedures are appropriate to insure prompt disposition of complaints. Expedited processing of minor complaints will unburden the system and permit greater attention to more serious charges. In all cases, the disciplinary system must react in a timely fashion to protect the public against continued misconduct. Interim suspension procedures must be available. There must be expedited processes for reciprocal discipline and for discipline upon conviction of crime. Preventive measures must be adopted. Measures such as the mandatory reporting of trust account overdrafts and random audit of trust accounts have proven to be effective in the prevention of misconduct. All jurisdictions need to adopt them.

Finally, and perhaps most importantly, the scope of judicial regulation must be expanded to cover the thousands of complaints that are routinely dismissed each year. These complaints are dismissed because they do not allege ethical violations. Yet in many of these cases, while the lawyer's conduct may not have been unethical, the complaint deserves attention and response. In some jurisdictions, a response has been provided by the organized bar such as fee dispute arbitration. In a few of these jurisdictions, arbitration is mandatory for the lawyer. Some bar associations have offered mediation and voluntary arbitration services to resolve minor disputes. In some jurisdictions, continuing legal education is mandatory.

However, these efforts are not coordinated or offered in any structured, integrated way. The Commission recommends a multi-door system of lawyer regulation which affords a variety of responses to the needs of the public and the profession in addressing these problems. The Commission recognizes that implementation of its recommendations will not still the voices of criticism. Criticism of the legal profession will continue because of the kind of work lawyers do. The challenge is to address the changing needs of the public and the profession. The Commission hopes that its recommendations will be viewed as an extension of the principles of professionalism evidenced by the considerable efforts over the last twenty years to implement the Clark Committee recommendations.

. . . .

Summary of Recommendations

. . . .

Be it resolved, that the American Bar Association adopts the following recommendations:

Recommendation 1: Regulation of the profession by the judiciary

Regulation of the legal profession should remain under the authority of the judicial branch of government.

Recommendation 2: Supporting judicial regulation and professional responsibility

2.1 The American Bar Association should continue to place the highest priority on promoting, developing, and supporting judicial regulation of the legal profession and professional responsibility.

2.2 The Association should continue to provide adequate funding and staffing for activities to support judicial regulation and professional responsibility.

2.3 To promote the most efficient allocation of resources, the Association should establish written policies to insure that all of its judicial regulation and professional responsibility activities are coordinated, regardless of the Association entity conducting the activity.

Recommendation 3: Expanding the scope of public protection

[Each state's highest court (the Court)] should establish a system of regulation of the legal profession that consists of:

3.1 component agencies, including but not limited to:

(a) lawyer discipline; (b) a client protection fund; (c) mandatory arbitration of fee disputes; (d) voluntary arbitration of lawyer malpractice claims and other disputes; (e) mediation; (f) lawyer practice assistance; (g) lawyer substance abuse counseling; and

3.2 a central intake office for the receipt of all complaints about lawyers, whose functions should include:

(a) providing assistance to complainants in stating their complaints; (b) making a preliminary determination as to the validity of the complaint; (c) dismissing the complaint or determining the appropriate component agency or agencies to which the complaint should be directed and forwarding the complaint; (d) providing information to complainants about available remedies, operations and procedures, and the status of their complaints; and (e) coordinating among agencies and tracking the handling and disposition of each complaint.

Recommendation 4: Lawyer Practice Assistance Committee

4.1 The Court should establish a Lawyer Practice Assistance Committee. At least one third of the members should be non-lawyers. The Lawyer Assistance Committee should consider cases referred to it by the disciplinary counsel and the Court and should assist lawyers voluntarily seeking assistance. The Committee should provide guidance to the lawyer including, when appropriate: (a) review of the lawyer's office and case management practices and recommendations for improvement; and (b) review of the lawyer's substantive knowledge of the law and recommendations for further study.

4.2 In cases in which the lawyer has agreed with disciplinary counsel to submit to practice assistance, the Committee may require the lawyer to attend continuing legal education classes, to attend and successfully complete law school courses or office management courses, to participate in substance abuse recovery programs or in psychological counseling, or to take other actions necessary to improve the lawyer's fitness to practice law.

Recommendation 5: Independence of disciplinary officials

All jurisdictions should structure their lawyer disciplinary systems so that disciplinary officials are appointed by the highest court of the jurisdiction or by other disciplinary officials who are appointed by the Court. Disciplinary officials should possess sufficient independent authority to conduct the lawyer discipline function impartially.

5.1 Elected bar officials, their appointees and employees should provide only administrative and other services for the disciplinary system that support the operation of the system without impairing the independence of disciplinary officials.

5.2 Elected bar officials, their appointees and employees should have no investigative, prosecutorial, or adjudicative functions in the disciplinary process.

5.3 The budget for the office of disciplinary counsel should be formulated by disciplinary counsel. The budget for the statewide disciplinary board should be formulated by the board. Disciplinary budgets should be approved or modified directly by the Court or by an administrative agency of the Court disciplinary counsel and the disciplinary board should be accountable for the expenditure of funds only to the Court, except that bar associations may provide accounting and other financial services that do not impair the independence of disciplinary officials.

5.4 Disciplinary counsel and staff, disciplinary adjudicators and staff, and other disciplinary agency personnel should be absolutely immune from civil liability for all actions performed within the scope of their duties, consistent with ABA MRLDE [Model Rules for Lawyer Disciplinary Enforcement (1993)] 12A.

Recommendation 6: Independence of disciplinary counsel

6.1 The Court alone should appoint and for cause remove disciplinary counsel and should provide sufficient authority for prosecutorial independence and discretion. The Court should also promulgate rules providing that disciplinary counsel shall: (a) have authority to employ and terminate staff, formulate a budget and approve expenditures subject only to the authority of the Court; (b) have authority to determine after investigation whether probable cause exists to believe misconduct has been committed and to dismiss a case or file formal charges against respondent lawyers; (c) have authority, in cases involving allegations of minor incompetence, neglect, or misconduct, to resolve a matter with the consent of the respondent by administrative procedures established by the Court; (d) have authority to appeal a decision of a hearing committee or the disciplinary board; (e) be compensated sufficiently to attract competent counsel and retain experienced counsel; and (f) be prohibited from providing advisory ethics opinions, either orally or in writing.

6.2 The Court should adopt a rule providing that no disciplinary adjudicative official (including hearing committee members, disciplinary board members, or members of the Court) shall communicate ex parte with disciplinary counsel regarding an ongoing investigation or disciplinary matter, except about administrative matters or to report information alleging the misconduct of a lawyer.

Recommendation 7: Fully public discipline process

All records of the lawyer disciplinary agency except the work product of disciplinary counsel should be available to the public from the time of the complainant's initial communication with the agency, unless the complainant or respondent, upon a showing of grounds that would be sufficient in a civil proceeding, obtains a protective order for specific documents or records. All proceedings except adjudicative deliberations should be public.

Recommendation 8: Complainant immunity

8.1 Complainants should be absolutely immune from civil suit for all communications with the disciplinary agency and for all statements made within the disciplinary proceeding. Consideration should be given to making it a misdemeanor to knowingly file a false complaint with the disciplinary agency.

8.2 When informing the public about the existence and operations of the disciplinary agency the agency should emphasize and explain the nature of a complainant's absolute immunity.

Recommendation 9: Complainant's rights

9.1 Complainants should receive notice of the status of disciplinary proceedings at all stages of the proceedings. In general, a complainant should receive, contemporaneously, the same notices and orders the respondent receives as well as copies of respondent's communications to the agency, except information that is subject to another client's privilege.

9.2 Complainants should be permitted a reasonable opportunity to rebut statements of the respondent before a complaint is summarily dismissed.

9.3 Complainants should be notified in writing when the complaint has been dismissed. The notice should include a concise recitation of the specific facts and reasoning upon which the decision to dismiss was made.

9.4 Disciplinary counsel should issue written guidelines for determining which cases will be dismissed for failure to allege facts that, if true, would constitute grounds for disciplinary action. These guidelines should be sent to complainants whose cases are dismissed.

9.5 Complainants should be notified of the date, time, and location of the hearing. Complainants should have the right to personally appear and testify at the hearing.

9.6 All jurisdictions should afford a right of review to complainants whose complaints are dismissed prior to a full hearing on the merits, consistent with ABA MRLDE 11B(3) and 31.

Recommendation 10: Procedures in lieu of discipline for minor misconduct

All jurisdictions should adopt procedures in lieu of discipline for matters in which a lawyer's actions constitute minor misconduct, minor incompetence, or minor neglect. The procedures should provide:

10.1   The Court shall define criteria for matters involving minor misconduct, minor incompetence, or minor neglect that may be resolved by non-disciplinary proceedings or dismissal.

10.2   If disciplinary counsel determines that a matter meets the criteria established by the Court, disciplinary counsel may reach agreement with the respondent to submit the matter to non-disciplinary proceedings. Such proceedings may consist of fee arbitration, arbitration, mediation, lawyer practice assistance, substance abuse recovery programs, psychological counseling, or any other non-disciplinary proceedings authorized by the Court. Disciplinary counsel shall then refer the matter to the agency or agencies authorized by the Court to conduct the proceedings.

10.3   If the lawyer does not comply with the terms of the agreement, disciplinary counsel may resume disciplinary proceedings.

10.4   If the lawyer fulfills the terms of the agreement, the disciplinary counsel shall dismiss the disciplinary proceeding.

Recommendation 11: Expedited procedures for minor misconduct

All jurisdictions should adopt simplified, expedited procedures to adjudicate cases in which the alleged misconduct warrants less than suspension or disbarment or other restriction on the right to practice. Expedited procedures should provide:

11.1   The Court shall define minor violations of the rules of professional conduct that shall subject the respondent to sanctions not constituting restrictions on the right to practice law, consistent with the ABA Standards for Imposing Lawyer Sanctions.

11.2   Disciplinary counsel shall determine upon investigation whether probable cause exists to file charges alleging a minor violation of the rules of professional conduct and, if so, shall file charges with the Court.

11.3   A hearing shall be held by a single adjudicator [member of a hearing committee].

11.4   The adjudicator shall make concise, written findings of fact and conclusions of law and shall either dismiss the case or impose a sanction that does not constitute a restriction on the respondent's right to practice.

11.5   Respondent and Disciplinary counsel shall have the right to appeal the decision to a second adjudicator [member of the statewide disciplinary board], who shall either adopt the decision below or make written findings. The appellate adjudicator shall either dismiss the case or impose a sanction that does not constitute a restriction on the respondent's right to practice.

11.6   The decision of the appellate adjudicator may be reviewed at the discretion of the Court upon application by respondent or Disciplinary counsel. The Court shall grant review only in cases involving significant issues of law or upon a showing that the decision below constituted an abuse of discretion. The Court shall either adopt the decision below or make written findings. The Court shall either dismiss the case or impose a sanction that does not constitute a restriction on the respondent's right to practice.

11.7   Upon final disposition of the case, the written findings of the final adjudicator shall be published in an appropriate journal or reporter and a copy shall be mailed to the respondent and the complainant and to the ABA National Discipline Data Bank.

Recommendation 12: Disposition of cases by a hearing committee, the Board, or Court

The statewide disciplinary board should not review a determination of the hearing committee except upon a request for review by the disciplinary counsel or respondent or upon the vote of a majority of the Board. The Court should not review a matter except: (a) within its discretion upon a request for review of the determination of the Board by the disciplinary counsel or respondent; or (b) upon the vote of a majority of the Court to review a determination of the hearing committee or Board. The Court should exercise its jurisdiction only in the capacity of appellate review. In any matter finally determined by a hearing committee or the Board, the Court should by per curiam order adopt the findings and conclusions contained in the written report of the committee or Board.

Recommendation 13: Interim suspension for threat of harm

The immediate interim suspension of a lawyer should be ordered upon a finding that a lawyer poses a substantial threat of serious harm to the public, contrary to the provision of MRLDE 20A requiring a showing of "irreparable harm."

Recommendation 14: Funding and staffing

The Court should insure that adequate funding and staffing is provided for the disciplinary agency so that: (a) disciplinary cases are screened, investigated, prosecuted and adjudicated promptly; (b) the work load per staff person permits careful and thorough performance of duties; (c) professional and support staff are compensated at a level sufficient to attract and retain competent personnel; (d) sufficient office and data processing equipment exist to efficiently and quickly process the work load and manage the agency; (e) adequate office space exists to provide a productive working environment; and (f) staff and volunteers are adequately trained in disciplinary law and procedure.

Recommendation 15: Standards for resources

15.1   Each jurisdiction should keep case load and time statistics to assist in determining the need for additional staff and resources. Case load and time statistics should include, at the minimum: (a) time records for all counsel and investigators, tracked by case or other task including time spent on non-disciplinary functions; (b) the number of pending cases at each stage in the disciplinary process for each counsel and for the whole agency; (c) the number of new cases assigned to each counsel during the year and the total for the agency; (d) the number of cases carried over from the prior year for each counsel and the total for the agency; (e) the number of cases closed by each counsel during the year and the total for the agency; (f) the number of cases of special difficulty or complexity at each stage in the proceedings; and (g) the ratio of staff turnover.

15.2 The American Bar Association, National Organization of Bar Counsel, and disciplinary agencies in each jurisdiction should cooperate to develop standards for: (a) staffing levels and case load per professional and support staff member; (b) case processing time at all stages of disciplinary proceedings; and (c) compensation of professional and support staff.

Recommendation 16: Field investigations

Disciplinary counsel should have sufficient staff and resources to: (1) fully investigate complaints, by such means as sending investigators into the field to interview witnesses and examine records and evidence; and (2) regularly monitor sources of public information such as news reports and court decisions likely to contain information about lawyer misconduct.

Recommendation 17: Random audit of trust accounts

The Court should adopt a rule providing that disciplinary counsel may audit lawyer trust accounts selected at random without having grounds to believe misconduct has occurred.

Recommendation 18: Burden of proof in fee disputes

The court should adopt a rule to provide that where there is no written agreement between the lawyer and the client, the lawyer shall bear the burden of proof of all facts, including the competency of the work and the absence of neglect or delay, and the lawyer shall be entitled to no more than the reasonable value of services for the work completed or, if the failure to complete the work was caused by the client, for the work performed.

Recommendation 19: Mandatory malpractice insurance study

The American Bar Association should continue studies to determine whether a model program and model rule should be created to: (a) make appropriate levels of malpractice insurance coverage available at a reasonable price; and (b) make coverage mandatory for all lawyers who have clients.

Recommendation 20: Effective date of disbarment and suspension orders

The Court should adopt a rule providing that orders of disbarment and suspension shall be effective on a date [15] days after the date of the order except where the Court finds that immediate disbarment or suspension is necessary to protect the public, contrary to the provisions of MRLDE 27E.

Recommendation 21: National Discipline Data Bank

The American Bar Association should provide or seek adequate funding to automate the dissemination of reciprocal discipline information by means of electronic data processing and telecommunications, so that:

21.1 appropriate discipline, bar admissions, and other officials in each jurisdiction can directly access and query the National Discipline Data Bank via a computer telecommunications network;

21.2 a uniform data format and software are developed permitting automated cross-checking of jurisdictions' rosters of licensed lawyers against the National Discipline Data Bank's contents;

21.3 a listing of the contents of the National Discipline Data Bank is disseminated to discipline officials quarterly or semi-annually on an electronic data processing medium suitable for automated comparison with a jurisdiction's roster of lawyers.

Recommendation 22: Coordinating interstate identification

22.1 The American Bar Association and the appropriate officials in each jurisdiction should establish a system of assigning a universal identification number to each lawyer licensed to practice law.

22.2 The highest court in each jurisdiction should require all lawyers licensed in the jurisdiction to (a) register annually with the agency designated by the Court stating all other jurisdictions in which they are licensed to practice law, and (b) immediately report to the agency designated by the Court changes of law license status in other jurisdictions such as admission to practice, discipline imposed, or resignation.

Introduction

. . . .

Progress Since the Clark Report

Twenty years ago, the ABA Special Committee on Evaluation of Disciplinary Enforcement (the Clark Committee) published *Problems and Recommendations in Disciplinary Enforcement* (1970)(the Clark Report). The Clark Committee conducted the first nationwide examination of lawyer disciplinary procedures in the United States.

The Clark Committee warned of a "scandalous situation" in professional discipline and called for "the immediate attention of the profession." Today this Commission can report that most states have resolved many of the problems identified by the Clark Committee. Our detailed findings are set out in Appendix A: Implementation of Clark Report Recommendations.

It is no exaggeration to say that revolutionary changes have occurred. Twenty years ago, most states conducted lawyer discipline at the local level with no professional staff. Lawyer discipline was a secretive procedural labyrinth of multiple hearings and reviews. At the national level, there was the ABA's Model Code of Professional Responsibility, but little coordination, guidance, or research.

Today almost all states have professional disciplinary staff with statewide jurisdiction. Most have eliminated duplicative procedures. In over half the states, disciplinary hearings are public. Several national organizations exist, including the ABA Center For Professional Responsibility, the ABA

Standing Committee on Professional Discipline, and the National Organization of Bar Counsel. These groups formulate standards, conduct research, present educational programs, compile statistics, and consult with disciplinary officials. The ABA Center and the Bureau of National Affairs publish a comprehensive reference manual on professional responsibility. The Center also operates a national data bank on disciplined lawyers. In the two decades since the Clark Report, most states and the ABA have adopted most of its recommendations.

The Need to Expand Regulation to Protect the Public and Assist Lawyers

Times, however, have changed. The expectations of the public and the client have changed. The existing system of regulating the profession is narrowly focused on violations of professional ethics. It provides no mechanisms to handle other types of clients' complaints. The system does not address complaints that the lawyer's service was overpriced, incompetent, unreasonably slow, or negligent. It does not address complaints that the lawyer promised services that were not performed or billed for services that were not authorized. Some jurisdictions dismiss up to ninety per cent of all complaints. Most are dismissed because the conduct alleged does not violate the rules of professional conduct. The Commission has gathered much information about these dismissed complaints. It convinces us that many of them do state legitimate grounds for client dissatisfaction. The disciplinary system does not address these tens of thousands of complaints annually. The public is left with no practical remedy. While some states have created fee arbitration and other programs, additional avenues must be created in all states to resolve these complaints.

The disciplinary process also does nothing to improve the inadequate legal or office management skills that cause many of these complaints. Many state bar associations have mandatory continuing legal education, substance abuse counseling, and other programs. However, these programs usually are not coordinated with the disciplinary process. Lawyers with substandard skills often need more help than these programs can provide. The judiciary and profession must create new programs and coordinate all such programs with the disciplinary system.

The Need to Strengthen Regulation of the Profession by the Judiciary

Neither the profession nor the judiciary can permit this situation to continue. Clients, the public, the justice system, and the profession are suffering harm from this state of affairs. If it does continue the public may remove the authority of the judiciary to regulate lawyers. There have been several attempts to do so in the last twenty years. The failure of the profession and the judiciary to act imperils the inherent power of the court to regulate its officers. It threatens the independence of counsel. The judiciary must expand the regulatory structure and improve the disciplinary system. This is necessary to protect the public and to insure the judiciary's power to regulate the profession.

The Need for Direct and Exclusive Judicial Control of Lawyer Discipline

To strengthen judicial regulation of the profession, it must be distinguished from *self*-regulation. Control of the lawyer discipline system by elected officials of bar associations is self-regulation. It creates an appearance of conflicts of interest and of impropriety. In many states, bar officials still investigate, prosecute, and adjudicate disciplinary cases. The state high court must control the disciplinary process *exclusively*. It must appoint disciplinary officials who are independent of the organized bar. The Court must oversee the disciplinary system with as much care and attention as it devotes to deciding cases.

The Need to Increase Public Confidence in the Disciplinary System

Secret disciplinary records and proceedings generate the most criticism of the system. It is ironic that this attempt to shield honest lawyers' reputations has made the profession look so bad. What does the public think of hearings held behind closed doors? What does the public think when the disciplinary agency threatens the complaining party with imprisonment for speaking publicly about the complaint? These do not sound like the judicial proceedings of a free society. Indeed, several federal and state courts have held that such provisions violate federal or state constitutional provisions. The public will never accept the claim that lawyers must protect their reputations by gag rules and secret proceedings.

In many states, not only does the disciplinary agency threaten the complainant, the respondent lawyer can file a libel suit. Disciplinary counsel summarily dismiss complaints with no explanation of the decision. Complainants have no right to have the decision reviewed. The way many disciplinary systems treat complainants does not inspire confidence in the process.

The Need to Expedite the Disciplinary Process

Most complaints allege minor incompetence, minor neglect, or other minor misconduct. Most disciplinary agencies do not consider single instances of incompetence or neglect to be grounds for disciplinary action, although technically these do violate the rules of professional conduct. *See* Model Rules of Professional Conduct 1.1, 1.3. Disciplinary counsel routinely dismiss these complaints.

When a lawyer shows a pattern of incompetence, neglect or minor misconduct, most disciplinary agencies have only two options. They can (1) negotiate a private admonition or public reprimand with the respondent's consent, or (2) hold a formal hearing.

Dismissing valid complaints does nothing to correct the lawyer's behavior or compensate the client. Dismissing so many complaints casts suspicion on the disciplinary process. An admonition or reprimand may motivate the lawyer to change, but provides no guidance on how to change. Formal disciplinary proceedings cost time and money out of proportion to the minor nature of the offense. They divert resources from serious cases.

In these cases, the complainant needs a remedy and the lawyer needs additional skills and guidance. Programs must be created to provide them. When discipline is appropriate, the system needs expedited procedures commensurate with the sanctions (admonition or reprimand) involved.

The Need to Provide Adequate Resources

In the last twenty years, lawyers have volunteered hundreds of thousands of hours to carry out Clark Committee reforms. Lawyers also have paid millions of dollars to fund disciplinary agencies. Still, funding and staffing have not kept pace with the growth of the profession. Most agencies handle cases of serious misconduct effectively, but some agencies are so underfunded and understaffed that they offer little protection against unethical lawyers. The highest courts in these states must provide the funds needed to operate their disciplinary systems effectively.

The Need for Preventive Measures

Every year, millions of dollars of clients' money are stolen by a relatively few lawyers. Yet, most disciplinary systems lack authority to take basic preventive measures such as auditing trust account records or monitoring trust account overdrafts.

Fee disputes generate many disciplinary complaints. These complaints clog the disciplinary process. Most are summarily dismissed, because the lawyers' conduct did not violate the rules of professional conduct. This is a continuing source of the public's dissatisfaction with the profession. Written fee agreements could prevent many fee disputes or at least simplify resolution of them.

The Need to Improve Interstate Enforcement

With admirable prescience, the Clark Committee called for the creation of a National Discipline Data Bank. The American Bar Association created the Data Bank in 1968 to help states share disciplinary information. However, since the Clark Report was published, the number of lawyers in the United States has more than doubled. Today, more lawyers are licensed in more than one state. The increasing number of lawyers has created new problems.

It is no longer practical for disciplinary counsel to manually compare the Data Bank's annual report to the state's roster of lawyers. There is no efficient way to know that a name on the report and the roster identifies the same lawyer. A recent survey of disciplinary counsel shows that they seldom use the Data Bank report because of these limitations. Most reciprocal disciplinary actions result from ad hoc communications between disciplinary counsel, not from the Data Bank lists. Under present conditions, a lawyer could be disbarred in one state and continue practicing elsewhere without detection.

The Need to Fully Implement Essential Provisions of the Model Rules of Lawyer Disciplinary Enforcement

The Clark Report reshaped lawyer discipline in the United States. Yet some states have not adopted basic reforms. Some recommendations of the

Clark Committee were modified or eliminated in the ABA Model Rules of Lawyer Disciplinary Enforcement (MRLDE). See Appendix A. We refer here to those basic reforms that have withstood the test of twenty years. No court can afford to keep rules that impede enforcement, especially when effective procedures exist that have been tested in other jurisdictions. The profession and the judiciary must finish the work started by the Clark Committee.

. . . .

Regulation of the Profession by the Judiciary

. . . .

Judicial regulation of the profession and professional responsibility must remain the highest priorities of the ABA. The ABA must implement this recommendation in its most concrete form—in difficult decisions allocating people, money, and time. We recognize that many interests compete for ABA resources. However, judicial regulation of the profession is essential to both the courts and the profession. Professional responsibility is equally essential. Lawyers must never forget that they are members of a profession, not a business. Lawyers' primary responsibility is to serve the client, the justice system, and the public.

. . . .

Expanding Regulation to Protect the Public and Assist Lawyers

Existing regulation, while generally effective in disciplining serious misconduct, does not adequately protect the public from lawyer incompetence and neglect. This failure is having severe repercussions for the legal profession.

In 1988, over forty-four thousand disciplinary complaints were summarily dismissed. In some jurisdictions up to ninety per cent of all complaints filed were summarily dismissed. Most of these were dismissed for failing to allege unethical conduct. Some of these complaints may have been without merit, but the huge number shows a gap exists between client expectations and existing regulation. It is clear that tens of thousands of dissatisfied clients are being turned away. The disciplinary system was not designed to address complaints about the quality of lawyers' services or fee disputes. Yet in all but a few states it is the only regulatory body available to complainants.

The incompetence and neglect of relatively few lawyers must not continue to sully the image of the rest. We cannot afford to let legitimate disagreements between lawyers and clients go unresolved. Without a mechanism to resolve these complaints and disputes, clients are harmed and the profession's reputation unnecessarily suffers.

The consequences of continuing to ignore these problems are clear. The Federal Trade Commission has made several attempts to gain jurisdiction over some complaints against lawyers. State legislatures have made forays into lawyer regulation with increasing frequency. Legal consumer organizations have grown in membership and in political activism.

Disciplinary proceedings, reimbursement from client protection funds, and civil suits for legal malpractice are all that exists in most jurisdictions to redress client injury. These are insufficient in several respects.

Discipline primarily offers prospective protection to the public. It either removes the lawyer from practice or seeks to change the lawyer's future behavior. Protection of clients already harmed is minimal. Respondents are sometimes ordered to pay restitution in disciplinary cases. However, in many states, the failure of a lawyer to make restitution ordered in a disciplinary proceeding will not bar subsequent readmission to practice.

Clients can seek restitution from client protection funds in those states that have them. Client protection funds are an innovation of the legal profession unmatched by any other profession. Every year lawyers, through payments into the funds, reimburse millions of dollars to clients harmed by unethical lawyers. The profession can truly be proud of this achievement.

However, the ability of client protection funds to compensate clients is limited. Restitution is generally available only when a lawyer has stolen client funds. Many client protection funds have limitations on the amounts that will be paid on any one claim. Many client protection funds require a finding of misconduct by the disciplinary agency before a claim will be considered, delaying reimbursement sometimes for years.

Not only are disciplinary agencies and client protection funds limited in the types of remedies they provide but, except for the most egregious cases, they do not address lawyer incompetence and neglect. Most jurisdictions treat individual instances of incompetence and neglect as not violative of the rules of professional conduct or as a minimal violation not worthy of disciplinary action. Yet these types of cases constitute a large proportion of all complaints filed with disciplinary agencies against lawyers.

Other lawyer conduct not regulated by discipline mechanisms is that which generates fee disputes. Fee disputes may arise because a lawyer fails to provide services in the manner promised, delays performance, fails to clarify the computation of the fee, gives an unrealistic initial estimate of the fee, or behaves in other ways that are unfair to the client and unprofessional. This behavior, while perhaps not a violation of the rules of professional conduct, is clearly a legitimate ground for complaint from a client's perspective. Only a handful of jurisdictions mandate that the lawyer submit to arbitration when there is a prima facie legitimate fee dispute. In all other jurisdictions, most clients who have a legitimate dispute are without an economically feasible remedy. Their only options are to sue or to not pay the fee and be sued by the lawyer. The sum involved may be substantial to the client, but often the cost to litigate will be more than the amount in dispute. The client often files a complaint with the disciplinary agency, but the claim is dismissed. The National Organization of Bar Counsel[2] reports that fee dispute issues constitute the second largest category of complaints dismissed for lack of jurisdiction. The profession can no longer afford to ignore these complaints. For every such complaint filed and dismissed, undoubtedly many more clients simply give up without filing a complaint and then blame the profession.

In most jurisdictions, the only option for aggrieved clients other than the disciplinary agency or the client protection fund is a malpractice suit. While the Commission has heard claims that lawyers are unwilling to sue other lawyers, there is ample evidence to suggest that a client with a reasonable claim for large enough damages will be able to find representation. The problem is not the willingness of lawyers to handle malpractice cases but that the time and expense of a civil suit make only large claims economically feasible. Even when the claim is for a large sum, full civil proceedings are a slow and expensive method of resolving the dispute. Also, many types of lawyer conduct that are legitimate grounds for client dissatisfaction and dispute may not constitute malpractice.

The profession's attempts to deal with substandard practice have not worked. The "code of professionalism" is valuable only to those predisposed to improve their practice. Peer review programs have not been accepted. Mandatory continuing legal education programs may keep lawyers' legal skills current, but they were not designed to remedy substandard skills. While legal malpractice is a growing specialization, it must surely be the least desirable means of self-regulation. What is required is a variety of methods to address the different types of problems and circumstances that create disputes between lawyers and clients. *See chart [on next page].*

Relevant Background

In July of 1995, Minnesota adopted a complaint diversion system modeled on some of the suggestions in the McKay Report. Client complaints diverted to mediation include complaints alleging "noncommunication, short-term neglect, rude and insensitive behavior, and failure to return client files or other property." 7 Prof. Law 20 (1995). Minnesota also adopted a system of mandatory arbitration for fee disputes under $7500. Id.

Probably the most controversial recommendation of the McKay Report is that disciplinary proceedings be opened to the public as soon as a complaint is filed. Mary M. Devlin, The Development of Lawyer Disciplinary Procedures in the United States, 7 Geo. J. Legal Ethics 911, 931 (1994). By contrast, the confidentiality of attorney disciplinary proceedings is well established in many jurisdictions. See McLaughlin v. Philadelphia Newspapers, Inc., 465 Pa. 104, 348 A.2d 376 (1975) (court may prevent newspaper from obtaining access to the impounded court records of disciplinary proceedings against a private attorney later appointed to public office). "This rule . . . reflects the considered judgment that there is nothing to be

---

2. The National Organization of Bar Counsel's membership includes over 400 lawyer disciplinary counsel representing more than 60 state and federal disciplinary jurisdictions in the United States and Canada.

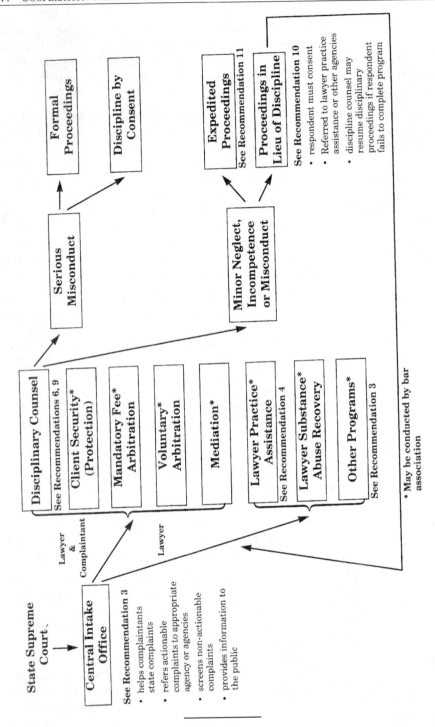

* May be conducted by bar association

gained and much to be lost, where an attorney's reputation and livelihood are concerned, by opening to the public the record of proceedings concerning allegations of professional misconduct which are ultimately found to be groundless." Id. at 114, 348 A.2d at 381 (footnote omitted). See also Conn. P.B., 27F(e) (well-settled procedure of keeping the complaint and investigation confidential unless and until there has been a finding of probable cause). In the parallel arena of judicial disciplinary proceedings, the United States Supreme Court has identified three public interests served by rules that require confidentiality: (1) protecting complainants and witnesses against recrimination or retaliation, (2) protecting judges from publication of frivolous or unwarranted complaints, and (3) maintaining confidence in the courts by avoiding premature announcement of groundless claims of judicial misconduct. Landmark Communications, Inc. v. Virginia, 435 U.S. 829, 835 (1978).

Some jurisdictions have gradually moved away from strict confidentiality in the discipline process, and the McKay Report cites thirty-one jurisdictions where disciplinary hearings are public. Devlin, supra at 932, n.184. Oregon follows the practice recommended in the McKay Report of making disciplinary proceedings public as soon as a complaint is filed. See Or. BR 2.5 (1985). Nonetheless in 1992 the ABA House of Delegates amended this recommendation to state that records of disciplinary proceedings should be confidential until a finding of probable cause that misconduct occurred. Devlin, supra at 932, n.183, citing Commission on Evaluation of Disciplinary Enforcement, Am. Bar Ass'n, Lawyer Regulation for a New Century 35 (1992).

QUESTIONS

1.   The McKay Commission recommended adoption of the Oregon rule. What are the advantages and disadvantages of making disciplinary proceedings public at the accusatory stage?

2.   How convincing are the arguments in the McKay Report in favor of continued regulation of the legal profession by the judiciary?

3.   Why is it important that even minor complaints of lawyer misconduct receive prompt attention?

B.   DISCIPLINE OF LAW FIRMS

The following Report of the Association of the Bar of the City of New York discusses Model Code provisions concerning supervision of lawyers in law firms, as well as a proposal to make disciplinary sanctions directly available against law firms.

Discipline of Law Firms, Report of the Committee on Professional Responsibility

48 The Record of the Association of the Bar of the City of New York 628 (1993).
Copyright 1993 by the Bar of the City of New York.

New York's system of professional discipline for lawyers is, like that of other states, oriented almost exclusively toward individual lawyers, not the firms in which they practice. Most of the Disciplinary Rules refer to lawyers only, not to firms. With respect to the handful of Disciplinary Rules which do refer to the conduct of law firms, procedures for enforcing those rules are virtually nonexistent.

Outside of the realm of attorney discipline, however, the situation is very different—in an increasing number of instances, law firms, as well as individual lawyers, have been found liable for professional misconduct in tort, under the securities laws and under other statutes. Law firms have also been subjected to sanctions by administrative agencies for alleged professional misconduct by partners and associates.* The Disciplinary Rules, as currently implemented, thus lag behind developments in other areas of the law governing law firms. The rules provide inadequate guidance, and even less by way of sanctions, to correct those law firm practices and procedures which expose firms to liability.

This Committee believes that the Disciplinary Rules should set forth and enforce standards for law firm conduct which will minimize the chances that lawyers practicing in firms will violate the Disciplinary Rules. More emphasis on law *firm* (as distinct from individual lawyer) responsibility in the Disciplinary Rules should also help firms avoid exposure to legal liability for conduct which could have been avoided. Both specific standards of conduct for law firms and procedures for disciplining law firms, therefore, should be integrated into the Disciplinary Rules and the statutes providing for enforcement of those rules.

A. *Reasons for Extending the Disciplinary Rules to Law Firm Conduct*

There are a number of reasons why law firms should be included in the Disciplinary Rules and the procedures used to enforce those rules.

(1) *Improving the Practice Environment.* A possible disciplinary sanction directed against the firm will create a practice environment for lawyers which discourages ethical violations. As stated in Model Rule 5.1 comment 2 (1989): "The ethical atmosphere of a firm can influence the conduct of its members." Of course, even in the absence of direct discipline, a law firm which fails to create a positive ethical atmosphere will most likely experience a higher number of ethical violations by attorneys, which may result in sanctions against the attorneys and adverse publicity for the firm. Standards for firm conduct, however, add a positive reinforcement to a firm's desire to avoid adverse publicity, not to mention the disciplinary sanction itself. If an attorney in a firm is disciplined, the firm can always attempt to distance itself from the lawyer's individual act; not so if the firm itself is disciplined. The threat of direct discipline on the firm thus provides an important incentive to improve firm-wide compliance with ethical norms. This should help cut down on *all* ethical violations, including those for which the firm would not itself be sanctioned.

* [The Report cites examples, including the attachment of Kaye, Scholer's assets by the Office of Thrift Supervision and the subsequent settlement of the underlying action for $42 million. See Chapter 2 supra.]—ed.

(2) *Self-Policing.* By making compliance with the Disciplinary Rules a collective effort within a firm, the possibility of direct discipline against law firms will further the model of self-governance, which is a cornerstone of the legal profession.

Self-policing by the profession is a goal already sought in DR 1–103, which requires a lawyer to report to a tribunal or other investigative authority any knowledge that raises a substantial question as to another lawyer's honesty, trustworthiness or fitness in other respects as a lawyer. If a law firm were subject to discipline, the firm itself would have an incentive to be attendant to ethical lapses by attorneys within the firm, as well as to firm-wide practices which may encourage, or insufficiently regulate, the possibility of individual ethical violations. Although the reporting of ethical lapses of attorneys to the appropriate supervisory persons or committees within firms is not a substitute for the reporting requirement of DR 1–103, such internal reporting and corrective action is needed to supplement the external reporting required by DR 1–103.

(3) *Joint Responsibility and Supervision.* The orientation of the Disciplinary Rules toward individual lawyers is at odds with the realities of the modern practice environment in which many lawyers are no longer responsible only for themselves.

The Disciplinary Rules are the product of a time in which law was practiced differently than it is today. In 1951, 60 percent of lawyers practiced alone. By contrast, as of 1985, two-thirds of lawyers worked in law firms or other organizations such as corporations. In some firms, the ratio of associates to partners has risen as high as four-to-one, creating an obvious need for supervision.[4]

DR 1–104 makes a lawyer responsible for a violation of the Disciplinary Rules by an associate or employee if that lawyer orders the conduct in question, or if the lawyer has "supervisory authority" over the violator and knew or should have known of the conduct at a time when its consequences could be avoided and fails to take remedial action. In some cases, however, there may be nobody with supervisory authority, such as where the more junior lawyer undertakes a representation on his or her own initiative. Some areas of supervision may also be the responsibility of the entire firm, not just a supervising lawyer. Examples include: supervision of a lawyer's overall caseload; determination of the number of practice areas in which a lawyer is expected to work; policies on signing pleadings; policies on minimum billable hours; safeguards to prevent overbilling; conflict-check procedures; and the use of performance reviews to identify those areas in which a lawyer's work fails to meet minimum standards. In areas such as these, supervision is a collective effort and should be reinforced by collective responsibility.

---

4. T. Schneyer, Professional Discipline for Law Firms? 77 Cornell L. Rev. 1, 4–5 (1991).

(4) *Supervision of Non–Lawyers.* Centralized law firm management increasingly includes non-lawyer administrators, such as accountants and clerical personnel, who cannot be directly controlled through the disciplinary process. Once again, the mandate in DR 1–104 requiring adequate supervision of non-lawyers extends only to individual attorneys, not to the firm itself, and the rule is presumably unenforceable where a particular attorney with supervisory authority over the non-lawyer cannot be identified. This identification of a responsible attorney is most impractical in the very cases where ethical lapses by non-lawyers are most likely to occur: where the firm clearly has a duty to supervise the non-lawyer's work but there is no agreement or firm policy as to who should do the supervising, the result being that the non-lawyer's work goes unsupervised.

(5) *The Difficulty of Assessing Blame to Individual Lawyers.* When a firm commits wrongdoing, courts and disciplinary authorities often have difficulty assigning blame to individual lawyers. This is particularly true in larger firms where many tasks, such as document production, are assigned to teams. Teaming tends to obscure responsibility and may encourage lawyers to take ethical risks.[5] A firm which uses teaming should have an incentive to implement policies, such as identification of work done by each team member and random checks on work product, which discourage team members from taking ethical risks. The availability of sanctions against firms for ethical violations will create the incentive to implement such safeguards.

(6) *Discouraging Lawyers who Encourage Violations.* Courts and disciplinary authorities may be reluctant to sanction a lawyer who only did what others would have done to further the firm's interests. This may be particularly true where an associate commits an ethical breach under the implicit encouragement of one or more partners. Where the partners in question do not have supervisory authority over the work in question sufficient to trigger DR 1–104, and where their encouragement is not sufficiently explicit to justify finding a violation on their part, the wrong may go unpunished. The possibility of discipline of the firm itself in appropriate cases will rectify this gap in enforcement.

(7) *Addressing Organization Problems.* A law firm's organization and operating procedure may be what is at fault—not the individual lawyers. This is particularly likely to be the case with conflict of interest problems, billing procedures and handling of client funds. A firm's policies with respect to leverage through partner/associate ratios and caseload management may also encourage mishandling of cases. If the problem is the firm, and not any individual attorney, then it is the firm which should be disciplined.

. . . .

C. Disciplinary Rules Which Should Be Applicable to Law Firms

This Committee believes that a number of Disciplinary Rules which do not currently purport to govern the conduct of law firms should do so.

---

5. See Schneyer, supra note 4.

Among these is DR 1–104 governing the responsibilities of a supervising lawyer. As pointed out above, supervision of attorney work product is a task which requires sound firm policies with respect to performance reviews, billing, case load and specialization. The extent of supervision of a junior lawyer by other lawyers is also a decision which may be made on a firm-wide basis.

This Committee believes that a law firm itself, not just individual lawyers who work within the firm, should be accountable for adequate supervision of the work of lawyers and non-lawyers who work at the firm. The mandated level of supervision should be what is reasonable under the circumstances, and supervision should not be required only where there is a superior-subordinate relationship; under some circumstances, partners should supervise each other's work. DR 1–104 should therefore be amended to add a Section (B) to read:

> B. A law firm shall adequately supervise the work of all partners, associates and non-lawyers who work at the firm. The degree of supervision required is that which is reasonable under the circumstances, taking into account factors such as the experience of the person whose work is being supervised, the amount of work involved in a particular matter, and the likelihood that ethical problems might arise in the course of working on the matter.*....

Other areas where law firm involvement should be required include the use of client funds and the avoidance of conflicting representations. These are problems which sometimes arise out of intentional breaches of the Code, but which sometimes also arise out of negligence. Mistakes could often be avoided if the firm as well as the responsible attorney takes steps to assure that all representation is undertaken free of conflicts (or with appropriate waivers) and that client funds are appropriately maintained and segregated....

An amended DR 5–105, however, should not tell firms precisely how to assist their lawyers in avoiding conflicts; rather, it should only tell firms that it must be done. The proposed amendment would add a new Section (E) stating:

> (E) A law firm shall keep detailed and accurate records of prior engagements and have a written policy implementing a system by which proposed engagements are checked against previous engagements, so as to render effective assistance to lawyers within the firm in complying with Section (D) of this Rule. Failure to keep records or to have a written policy which complies with this Section (E), whether or not a violation of Section (D) of this Rule occurs, shall be a violation by the firm. In cases where a violation of this Section (E) by the firm is a substantial factor in causing a violation of Section (D) of this Rule, the

---

* [As discussed infra, New York's Appellate Division in 1996 adopted 22 NYCRR Part 1200, § 1200.5(c), using language essentially identical to that suggested here in this Report]—ed.

firm as well as the individual lawyer, shall also be responsible for the violation of Section (D).*

. . . .

Likewise, law firms should be required to implement procedures for keeping track of client funds. DR 9–102[13] sets forth detailed standards for the management of client funds. While the provisions of this rule set forth the procedures which should be implemented by lawyers practicing in firms, DR 9–102(I), the provision for disciplinary action, says nothing of law firms. It is the individual lawyer (although exactly which individual lawyer is unclear), not the firm, which is ultimately responsible for compliance.

This Committee proposes that DR 9–102(I) be amended as follows:

(I) Disciplinary Action

> A lawyer who *or law firm which* does not maintain and keep the accounts and records as specified and required by this Disciplinary Rule, or [who] does not produce any such records pursuant to this Rule, shall be deemed in violation of these Rules and shall be subject to disciplinary proceedings. *In appropriate circumstances, disciplinary proceedings may be commenced under this Rule against both a law firm and the lawyer or group of lawyers within such firm who were responsible for the violation.*

The revised DR 9–102(I) thus provides for disciplinary proceedings against firms in the one area of professional responsibility which many lawyers delegate almost exclusively to a particular lawyer or accountant, or, in many large firms, to an accounting department. The firm, as well as the individual lawyers, should be held accountable for assuring that the procedures which the firm uses to handle client funds are reliable and well documented. It should also be possible to enforce compliance with these requirements without identifying a particular lawyer within the firm who must be held responsible.

The Committee notes that the term "law firm" is defined in the Code of Professional Responsibility as including, but "not limited to, a professional legal corporation, the legal department of a corporation or other organization and a legal services organization." With respect to discipline of law firms, we note that some difficult questions may arise such as whether lawyers who share offices or services constitute a firm on which discipline can be imposed. We believe that the definition of "law firm" provided in the Code will give courts and disciplinary committees sufficient flexibility to confront these problems when they arise. We suggest that the definition of a law firm, for disciplinary purposes, should depend on whether a group of lawyers hold themselves out to the public as practicing

---

* [New York's Appellate Division in 1996 adopted 22 NYCRR Part 1200, § 1200.24(e), using language similar to that suggested here in this Report]—ed.

13. Preserving Identity of Funds and Property of Others; Fiduciary Responsibility: Maintenance of Bank Accounts; Record-keeping; Examination of Records.

together. If several lawyers hold themselves out as an independent entity, then they can fairly be treated as such for disciplinary purposes.

Finally, this Committee believes that an additional Disciplinary Rule should be enacted stating that, under appropriate circumstances, a law firm as well as an individual lawyer may be disciplined for a violation by one of its lawyers of any of the Disciplinary Rules.* Such a rule is necessary to encourage more aggressive, firm-wide compliance with *all* of the provisions of the Code of Professional Responsibility.

Conclusion

The revisions to the Disciplinary Rules and to the Judiciary Law proposed in this Report are not intended to impose obligations on law firms which the lawyers who practice in those firms do not already have. The proposed revisions are also not intended to increase the potential liability of law firms for professional misconduct. This Committee furthermore does not wish to suggest that the individual lawyer should be absolved of responsibility for violations of the Disciplinary Rules in situations in which a responsible lawyer can be identified.

Rather, the proposed revisions make clear where there is a collective as well as an individual responsibility. The proposed statutory revisions also provide for direct sanctions against law firms where the firms do not comply with the Disciplinary Rules. This Committee believes that the inclusion of law firms in the disciplinary process will improve firm practices and procedures in a way which reduces the number of violations of the Disciplinary Rules by both firms and their attorneys. The end result is that law firms will be less, rather than more, likely to be faced with the far more draconian sanctions available to plaintiffs and administrative agencies outside the disciplinary arena.

* * *

We therefore conclude that the Disciplinary Rules be amended in the manner set forth in this Report, to provide for direct discipline of law firms.

May 1993

Committee on Professional Responsibility

Daniel J. Capra, *Chair*

Karen B. Burrows *   Richard W. Painter *

* Co–Authors of this Report.

* [New York's Appellate Division in 1996 adopted 22 NYCRR Part 1200, section 1200.3, amending DR 1–102 (Misconduct) to provide that a "lawyer *or law firm* shall not," engage in misconduct, including violation of a Disciplinary Rule or circumvention of a Disciplinary Rule through the actions of another]—ed.

Subsequent Developments:

In May of 1996, New York became the first state in the United States to adopt rules allowing disciplinary charges to be brought against law firms as well as individual lawyers. See Edward A. Adams, New Rule Authorizes Discipline of Law Firms, New York Law Journal, June 4, 1996 at 1. New York's four Appellate Division presiding justices approved changes to DR 1–102, DR 1–104 and DR 5–105 to require, among other things that law firms adequately supervise the work of their lawyers and keep adequate records of potential conflicts of interest. The text of the order reads:

Joint Order of the Appellate Divisions of the Supreme Court

The Appellate Divisions of the Supreme Court, pursuant to the authority vested in them, do hereby, effective immediately, amend the Disciplinary Rules of the Code of Professional Responsibility, (22 NYCRR Part 1200) as follows;

§ 1200.3 Misconduct

(a) A lawyer or law firm shall not: [there follows the text of DR 1–102 prohibiting violation of a Disciplinary Rule and other forms of misconduct]

§ 1200.5 [amending DR 1–104] Responsibilities of a Partner or Supervisory Lawyer

(a) A law firm shall make reasonable efforts to ensure that all lawyers in the firm conform to the disciplinary rules.

(b) A lawyer with management responsibility in the law firm or direct supervisory authority over another lawyer shall make reasonable efforts to ensure that the other lawyer conforms to the disciplinary rules.

(c) A law firm shall adequately supervise, as appropriate, the work of partners, associates and nonlawyers who work at the firm. The degree of supervision required is that which is reasonable under the circumstances, taking into account factors such as the experience of the person whose work is being supervised, the amount of work involved in a particular matter, and the likelihood that ethical problems might arise in the course of working on the matter.

(d) A lawyer shall be responsible for a violation of the disciplinary rules by another lawyer or for the conduct of a nonlawyer employed or retained by or associated with the lawyer that would be a violation of the disciplinary rules if engaged in by a lawyer if:

(1) The lawyer orders, or directs the specific conduct, or with knowledge of the specific conduct, ratifies it; or

(2) The lawyer is a partner in the law firm in which the other lawyer practices or the nonlawyer is employed, or has supervisory authority over the other lawyer or the nonlawyer, and knows of such conduct, or in the exercise of reasonable management or supervisory authority should have known of the conduct so that reasonable remedial action could be or could have been taken at a time when its consequences could be or could have been avoided or mitigated.

§ 1200.24 Refusing to Accept or Continue Employment if the Interests of Another Client May Impair the Independent Professional Judgment of the Lawyer. [see DR 5–105]

(e) A law firm shall keep records of prior engagements, which records shall be made at or near the time of such engagements and shall have a policy implementing a system by which proposed engagements are checked against current and previous engagements, so as to render effective assistance to lawyers within the firm in complying with subdivision (d) of this disciplinary rule. Failure to keep record or to have a policy which complies with this subdivision, whether or not a violation of subdivision (d) of this disciplinary rule occurs, shall be a violation by the firm. In cases where a violation of this subdivision by the firm is a substantial factor in causing a violation of subdivision (d) by a lawyer, the firm as well as the individual lawyer, shall also be responsible for the violation of subdivision (d).

Edward A. Adams, New Rule Authorizes Discipline of Law Firms, New York Law Journal, June 4, 1996 at 1.

QUESTIONS

1.   The Appellate Division was undecided on whether to allow disciplinary authorities to impose fines on law firms for violations of disciplinary rules. Absent fines, what forms of discipline can realistically be imposed on law firms? Should disciplinary authorities be empowered to levy fines against law firms?

2.   Should a law firm be exempt from discipline if it has implemented a system for monitoring and disciplining its own lawyers and, in appropriate circumstances (see Model Rule 8.3), for reporting lawyer misconduct to the bar?

C.   ADMINISTRATIVE AGENCY DISCIPLINE AND ENFORCEMENT PROCEEDINGS

Lawyers who represent clients that are themselves regulated by an administrative agency can be subject to proceedings to suspend or disbar lawyers from practicing before the agency. Occasionally, lawyers may also be subject to enforcement proceedings for violating, or aiding and abetting a violation of, the substantive regulations of the agency.

A lawyer representing a regulated client should be familiar with the substantive regulations, rules of professional conduct and disciplinary procedures of the relevant agency. The Patent and Trademark Office, the Department of the Treasury and the Federal Trade Commission are only a few of the federal agencies that have their own procedures for disciplining lawyers who practice before them. The following brief excerpt from a law review article gives an overview of enforcement options available to the Securities and Exchange Commission (SEC) against lawyers and accountants. The SEC's standards for lawyer conduct are briefly discussed in Chapter 2 supra.

Lawyer Disclosure of Corporate Fraud: Establishing a Firm Foundation

Richard W. Painter and Jennifer E. Duggan.*
50 SMU Law Review 225 (1996).

II B. The SEC Enforcement Arsenal Against Professionals

With the Supreme Court's limitation of Section 10–b civil liability to knowing or reckless conduct that amounts to a primary violation,[25] the SEC's enforcement arsenal against professionals becomes all the more important as a deterrent to professional malfeasance or omission. Indeed, the narrower scope of civil liability may encourage the SEC to fill the perceived void with stepped up enforcement actions.

In addition to prosecuting primary violations of the securities laws, the SEC may sanction professionals in a variety of ways, including Rule 2(e) disciplinary proceedings, cease and desist orders, or using its authority to prosecute aiders and abetters under the 1995 [Private Securities Litigation Reform] Act....

1. Rule 2(e) Disciplinary Proceedings:

SEC Rule 2(e) proceedings are more common than proceedings against professionals by other administrative agencies, although infrequent relative to the number of lawyers and accountants working on securities offerings.[29] Rule 2(e)(1) provides:

> [T]he [SEC] may deny, temporarily or permanently, the privilege of appearing or practicing before it in any way to any person who is found by the [SEC] after notice of an opportunity for hearing in the matter (i) not to possess the requisite qualifications to represent others, or (ii) to be lacking in character or integrity or to have engaged in unethical or improper professional conduct, or (iii) to have willfully violated, or willfully aided and abetted the violation of any provision of the Federal securities laws, or the rules and regulations thereunder.[30]

* Associate, Porter, Scott, Weiberg and Delehant, Sacramento, California.

25. [See Ernst & Ernst v. Hochfelder, 425 U.S. 185 (1976) (knowing or reckless conduct required to assert a claim under 1934 Act, Section 10(b)); Central Bank of Denver v. First Interstate Bank, 511 U.S. 164 (1994) (no private cause of action for aiding and abetting under Section 10(b)).]

29. There had been a total of roughly 139 reported Rule 2(e) cases as of 1991. These cases involved 147 individual lawyers and four law firms. Robert W. Emerson, Rule 2(e) Revisited: SEC Disciplining of Attorneys Since *In Re Carter*, 29 Am. Bus. L.J. 155, 175 (1991). During the "peak years" 1975–1977, 53 individual attorneys (36% of the total) and three law firms (75% of the total) were subject to such proceedings. Id. at 176. By contrast, only 26 lawyers went through rule 2(e) proceedings during the 1980's. Id. at 176–77, 211–12.

30. SEC Procedural Rules § 2(e)(1); 17 C.F.R. § 201.2(e)(1)(1996).

Although the SEC used Rule 2(e) to define professional standards for attorneys through the early 1980s, it has since retreated from this position and has only started Rule 2(e) disciplinary proceedings against attorneys who have *already* been found by a court or the SEC to have violated the securities laws.

2. Cease and Desist Orders Under the Remedies Act

The SEC also may sanction attorneys and accountants pursuant to the Remedies Act under which the Commission may:

> [E]nter an order requiring [a person who has or is about to violate the securities laws], and any other person that is, was or would be a cause of the violation, due to an act or omission the person knew or should have known would contribute to such violation, to cease and desist from committing or causing such violation and any future violation of the same provision, rule, or regulation.[32]

Although the Commission has occasionally used the Remedies Act against professionals,[33] the statutory language states that there must be, or about to be, a violation of the securities laws before the Commission may enter an order to cease and desist. Accordingly, this limits the Commission's options since professional misconduct can only be sanctioned *after* a finding that a violation has occurred or is about to occur *and* the lawyer or accountant is found to be the violator or the "cause" of the violation. Nonetheless, the statutory language potentially authorizes the sanctioning of professionals for a wide range of conduct, depending on what the SEC and the courts view as conduct that "causes" a violation to occur.

3. Prosecution of Aiders and Abetters

The [Private Securities Litigation] Reform Act of 1995, Section 104, amends Section 20 of the 1934 [Exchange] Act to expressly grant the Commission authority to prosecute persons who aid and abet violations of the securities laws:

> [F]or purposes of any action brought by the Commission under paragraph (1) or (3) of Section 21(d), any person that knowingly provides substantial assistance to another person in violation of a provision of this title, or of any rule or regulation issued under this title, shall be deemed to be in violation of such provision to the same extent as the person to whom such assistance is provided.[36]

Although the Supreme Court ruled in *Central Bank of Denver* that private

32. 1933 Securities Act, § 8A; 1934 Securities Exchange Act, § 21C.

33. See In Re Feldman, Securities Act Release No. 33–7014, 55 SEC Docket (CCH) 9, 12 (Sept. 20, 1993) (lawyer for three Pakistani banks "aided and abetted and caused" violations of Sections 5(a) and (c) of the 1933 Act by incorrectly advising his client that offering of rupee-denominated foreign exchange bearer certificates did not involve securities required to be registered prior to sale in U.S.).

36. Private Securities Litigation Reform Act of 1995, § 104.

litigants may not assert aiding and abetting claims under the 1934 Act,[37] the SEC has long believed itself to have the authority to prosecute aiders and abetters as well as primary violators. This provision of the 1995 Reform Act reaffirms that view. . . .

* * *

The above Article proceeds to describe the findings of fact and conclusions of law by the SEC in *In re Carter and Johnson* and several other Rule 2(e) disciplinary proceedings (some of which are discussed briefly in Chapter 2 supra), the SEC's enforcement action in *In re George Kern* (also discussed in Chapter 2 supra), and the SEC's proceeding against lawyers as aiders and abetters in S.E.C. v. National Student Marketing, 457 F.Supp. 682 (D.D.C.1978). An excerpt from Arthur Solmssen's novel The Comfort Letter, which is based on the *National Student Marketing* case, also appears in Chapter 2 supra. The primary concern raised in the above Article, and in a comment letter sent by its authors to the SEC in October of 1996, is that existing rules in this area are uncertain, SEC disciplinary proceedings are unpredictable, and courts have not articulated a clear standard setting forth what a lawyer must, may and may not do when confronted with client fraud.

D.   Lawyer Advertising and Solicitation

Although many state bar associations prohibited lawyer advertising until the late 1970's, the Supreme Court, in Bates v. State Bar of Arizona, 433 U.S. 350 (1977), held that the First Amendment does not permit a state to ban advertising of routine legal services. Regulation of attorney advertising has changed significantly since *Bates*, and rules differ significantly from state to state.

Under the Model Rules, a lawyer "shall not make a false or misleading communication about the lawyer or the lawyer's services." Model Rule 7.1. A misleading statement includes a comparison of "the lawyer's services with other lawyers' services, unless the comparison can be factually substantiated." Id. Model Rule 7.2 states that "[a] lawyer may advertise services through public media, such as a telephone directory, legal directory, newspaper or other periodical, outdoor advertising, radio or television, or through written or recorded communication." However, the attorney must keep a copy or recording of the advertising for at least two years. Id.

Listing a Specialization

Although a lawyer may advertise that the lawyer practices in a particular field of law, Model Rule 7.4 provides that a lawyer may not "state or imply that the lawyer has been recognized or certified as a specialist in a particular field of law." Exceptions to this rule include licensed patent

---

37. [See *Central Bank of Denver v. First Interstate Bank, supra* note 25.]

attorneys, admiralty lawyers and lawyers who have actually been certified for a particular practice area by a regulatory authority in their jurisdiction.

However, the Supreme Court's holding in Peel v. Attorney Registration & Disciplinary Commission of Illinois, 496 U.S. 91 (1990) casts doubt on the constitutionality of such restrictions. Peel stated on his letterhead that he was a "Certified Trial Specialist By the National Board of Trial Advocacy." Id. at 96. A plurality opinion by Justice Stevens noted that Peel's advertising was neither actually nor potentially misleading and therefore was protected by the first amendment. "Misleading advertising may be prohibited entirely. But the [s]tates may not place an absolute prohibition on . . . potentially misleading information . . . if the information may also be presented in a way that is not deceptive." Peel, 496 U.S. at 100, quoting In re R.M.J., 455 U.S. 191, 203 (1982). As Justice Stevens pointed out, the public was well aware that certificates, unlike licenses, were issued by private organizations and that the certification was not supported by the State of Illinois. Id. at 103.

In Person and Direct-mail Solicitation

Unlike advertising, in person solicitation of clients is subject to stringent restraints. Model Rule 7.3(a) provides that "[A] lawyer shall not by in-person or live telephone contact solicit professional employment from a prospective client with whom the lawyer has no family or prior professional relationship when a significant motive for the lawyer's doing so is the lawyer's pecuniary gain." The comment to Model Rule 7.3 notes that "[t]here is a potential for abuse inherent in direct in-person or live telephone contact by a lawyer with a prospective client known to need legal services . . . [which] justifies its prohibition, particularly since lawyer advertising and written and recorded communication permitted under [Model] Rule 7.2 offer alternative means of conveying necessary information to those who may be in need of legal services." Model Rule 7.3(b) furthermore provides that a lawyer shall not solicit professional employment "even when not otherwise prohibited by paragraph (a), if: 1) the prospective client has made known to the lawyer a desire not to be solicited by the lawyer; or 2) the solicitation involves coercion, duress or harassment." See also Model Code, DR 2–103(A).

In Ohralik v. Ohio State Bar Ass'n, 436 U.S. 447 (1978), attorney Ohralik sought to represent two young automobile accident victims. Ohralik approached one of the victims in person at her home, and the other in person while she was hospitalized. The Court held that the Ohio State Bar did not violate Ohralik's First Amendment rights by enforcing its ban on in-person solicitation. Ohio had an interest in protecting recipients of solicitation from "potential for overreaching," and the likelihood of "speedy and perhaps uninformed decisionmaking," with "no opportunity for intervention or counter-education by agencies of the Bar, supervisory authorities, or persons close to the solicited individual." Id. at 457.

Ten years later, in Shapero v. Kentucky Bar Association, 486 U.S. 466 (1988), attorney Shapero sought to send a letter to potential clients that had foreclosure suits filed against them, stating:

> "It has come to my attention that your home is being foreclosed on. If this is true, you may be about to lose your home. Federal law may allow you to keep your home by ORDERING your creditor [sic] to STOP and give you more time to pay them. You may call my office . . . for FREE information. . . . Call NOW, don't wait. . . . Remember it is FREE, there is NO charge for calling." Id. at 469.

The Kentucky State Bar Association did not find that the letter was false or misleading. Nonetheless, the bar ruled that the letter violated a Kentucky Supreme Court rule prohibiting direct solicitation of clients. Id.

The Supreme Court, however, struck down Kentucky's rule, distinguishing between this restriction on direct-mail solicitation and the restriction on direct in-person solicitation upheld in *Ohralik*. The Court found that direct-mail solicitation did not involve two dangers of face-to-face solicitation: first, the risk of "overreaching, invasion of privacy, the exercise of undue influence, and outright fraud," and second, lack of visibility or openness to public scrutiny. The Court pointed out that states could regulate direct-mail solicitation by requiring lawyers to file copies of solicitation letters with the bar, but that an outright ban violated the First Amendment. Id. at 475–76.

Some state courts have carved out an exception to this holding by finding that the First Amendment does not protect mailings targeted at recent accident victims. A New Jersey attorney was publicly reprimanded after sending a letter to the family of a victim of Pan Am Flight 103 two weeks after the crash and one day after the body had been identified. In re Anis, 126 N.J. 448, 599 A.2d 1265 (N.J. 1992), cert. denied, 504 U.S. 956 (1992). The attorney had violated New Jersey's rule prohibiting communication with prospective clients if a lawyer "knows or reasonably should know that the physical, emotional or mental state of the person is such that the person could not exercise reasonable judgment in employing a lawyer." Id. at 1272. The New Jersey Supreme Court distinguished *Anis* from *Shapero* by the impact of the direct contact on the recipient, stating, "[t]he form of solicitation at issue here is so universally condemned that its intrusiveness can hardly be disputed." Id. at 1269. See Jeffrey S. Kinsler, Targeted, Direct–Mail Solicitation: Shapero v. Kentucky Bar Association Under Attack, 25 Loy. U. Chi. L.J. 1 (1993).

In the following case, the Supreme Court rules on a Florida version of Model Rule 7.4 that does not allow attorneys to solicit victims or relatives of victims for 30 days following an accident or disaster.

Went For It, Inc. was a lawyer referral service wholly owned by **G. Stewart McHenry**, a plaintiffs' accident lawyer who was admitted to the Florida bar in 1975. In 1985, McHenry was publicly reprimanded for repeatedly referring to a Pasco County judge's courtroom as a "star chamber" while defending a drunk driving case. See Florida Bar v. McHenry, 478 So.2d 50 (Fla.1985). In 1988, McHenry was again publicly reprimanded for abusive conduct toward a paralegal. See Florida Bar v. McHenry, 536 So.2d 245 (Fla.1988). In September of 1992, McHenry was disbarred for fondling one female client under the guise of a "physical exam" and for masturbating in front of that client and one other female client. Florida Bar v. McHenry, 605 So.2d 459 (Fla.1992).

John T. Blakely, a partner of Johnson, Blakely, Pope, Bokor, Ruppel and Burns P.A. was substituted for McHenry in this case after McHenry's disbarment.

Florida Bar v. Went for It, Inc., and John T. Blakely

115 S.Ct. 2371 (1995).

■ Justice O'CONNOR delivered the opinion of the Court.

Rules of the Florida Bar prohibit personal injury lawyers from sending targeted direct-mail solicitations to victims and their relatives for 30 days following an accident or disaster. This case asks us to consider whether such rules violate the First and Fourteenth Amendments of the Constitution. We hold that in the circumstances presented here, they do not.

I

In 1989, the Florida Bar completed a 2–year study of the effects of lawyer advertising on public opinion. After conducting hearings, commissioning surveys, and reviewing extensive public commentary, the Bar determined that several changes to its advertising rules were in order. In late 1990, the Florida Supreme Court adopted the Bar's proposed amendments with some modifications. The Florida Bar: Petition to Amend the Rules Regulating the Florida Bar—Advertising Issues, 571 So.2d 451 (Fla. 1990). Two of these amendments are at issue in this case. Rule 4–7.4(b)(1) provides that "[a] lawyer shall not send, or knowingly permit to be sent, ... a written communication to a prospective client for the purpose of obtaining professional employment if: (A) the written communication concerns an action for personal injury or wrongful death or otherwise relates to an accident or disaster involving the person to whom the communication is addressed or a relative of that person, unless the accident or disaster occurred more than 30 days prior to the mailing of the communication." Rule 4–7.8(a) states that "[a] lawyer shall not accept referrals from a lawyer referral service unless the service: (1) engages in no communication with the public and in no direct contact with prospective clients in a manner that would violate the Rules of Professional Conduct if the communication or contact were made by the lawyer." Together, these rules create a brief 30–day blackout period after an accident during which lawyers may not, directly or indirectly, single out accident victims or their relatives in order to solicit their business.

In March 1992, G. Stewart McHenry and his wholly owned lawyer referral service, Went For It, Inc., filed this action for declaratory and injunctive relief in the United States District Court for the Middle District of Florida challenging Rules 4.7–4(b)(1) and 4.7–8 as violative of the First and Fourteenth Amendments to the Constitution. McHenry alleged that he routinely sent targeted solicitations to accident victims or their survivors within 30 days after accidents and that he wished to continue doing so in the future. Went For It, Inc. represented that it wished to contact accident victims or their survivors within 30 days of accidents and to refer potential clients to participating Florida lawyers. In October 1992, McHenry was disbarred for reasons unrelated to this suit, The Florida Bar v. McHenry, 605 So.2d 459 (Fla.1992). Another Florida lawyer, John T. Blakely, was substituted in his stead.

The District Court referred the parties' competing summary judgment motions to a Magistrate Judge, who concluded that the Florida Bar had substantial government interests, predicated on a concern for professionalism, both in protecting the personal privacy and tranquility of recent accident victims and their relatives and in ensuring that these individuals do not fall prey to undue influence or overreaching. . . .

The District Court rejected the Magistrate Judge's report and recommendations and entered summary judgment for the plaintiffs, 808 F.Supp. 1543 (M.D.Fla.1992), relying on Bates v. State Bar of Arizona, 433 U.S. 350, 97 S.Ct. 2691, 53 L.Ed.2d 810 (1977), and subsequent cases. The Eleventh Circuit affirmed on similar grounds, 21 F.3d 1038 (1994). . . . We granted certiorari . . . and now reverse.

II

A

Constitutional protection for attorney advertising, and for commercial speech generally, is of recent vintage. Until the mid–1970s, we adhered to the broad rule laid out in Valentine v. Chrestensen, 316 U.S. 52, 54, 62 S.Ct. 920, 921, 86 L.Ed. 1262 (1942), that, while the First Amendment guards against government restriction of speech in most contexts, "the Constitution imposes no such restraint on government as respects purely commercial advertising." In 1976, the Court changed course. In Virginia State Bd. of Pharmacy v. Virginia Citizens Consumer Council, Inc., 425 U.S. 748, 96 S.Ct. 1817, 48 L.Ed.2d 346, we invalidated a state statute barring pharmacists from advertising prescription drug prices. . . .

. . . . In Bates v. State Bar of Arizona, supra, the Court struck a ban on price advertising for what it deemed "routine" legal services: "the uncontested divorce, the simple adoption, the uncontested personal bankruptcy, the change of name, and the like." Id., 433 U.S., at 372, 97 S.Ct., at 2703. Expressing confidence that legal advertising would only be practicable for such simple, standardized services, the Court rejected the State's proffered justifications for regulation.

Nearly two decades of cases have built upon the foundation laid by Bates. It is now well established that lawyer advertising is commercial speech and, as such, is accorded a measure of First Amendment protection. See, e.g., Shapero v. Kentucky Bar Assn., 486 U.S. 466, 472, 108 S.Ct. 1916,

1921, 100 L.Ed.2d 475 (1988); Zauderer v. Office of Disciplinary Counsel of Supreme Court of Ohio, 471 U.S. 626, 637, 105 S.Ct. 2265, 2274, 85 L.Ed.2d 652 (1985); In re R.M.J., 455 U.S. 191, 199, 102 S.Ct. 929, 935, 71 L.Ed.2d 64 (1982). Such First Amendment protection, of course, is not absolute. We have always been careful to distinguish commercial speech from speech at the First Amendment's core. " '[C]ommercial speech [enjoys] a limited measure of protection, commensurate with its subordinate position in the scale of First Amendment values,' and is subject to 'modes of regulation that might be impermissible in the realm of noncommercial expression.' " . . . .

Mindful of these concerns, we engage in "intermediate" scrutiny of restrictions on commercial speech, analyzing them under the framework set forth in Central Hudson Gas & Electric Corp. v. Public Service Comm'n of N.Y., 447 U.S. 557, 100 S.Ct. 2343, 65 L.Ed.2d 341 (1980). Under Central Hudson, the government may freely regulate commercial speech that concerns unlawful activity or is misleading. Id., at 563–564, 100 S.Ct., at 2350. Commercial speech that falls into neither of those categories, like the advertising at issue here, may be regulated if the government satisfies a test consisting of three related prongs: first, the government must assert a substantial interest in support of its regulation; second, the government must demonstrate that the restriction on commercial speech directly and materially advances that interest; and third, the regulation must be " 'narrowly drawn.' " Id., at 564–565, 100 S.Ct., at 2350–51.

B

"Unlike rational basis review, the Central Hudson standard does not permit us to supplant the precise interests put forward by the State with other suppositions," Edenfield v. Fane, 507 U.S. 761, ___, 113 S.Ct. 1792, 1798, 123 L.Ed.2d 543 (1993). The Florida Bar asserts that it has a substantial interest in protecting the privacy and tranquility of personal injury victims and their loved ones against intrusive, unsolicited contact by lawyers. See Brief for Petitioner 8, 25–27; 21 F.3d, at 1043–1044. This interest obviously factors into the Bar's paramount (and repeatedly professed) objective of curbing activities that "negatively affec[t] the administration of justice." The Florida Bar: Petition to Amend the Rules Regulating the Florida Bar—Advertising Issues, 571 So.2d, at 455; see also Brief for Petitioner 7, 14, 24; 21 F.3d, at 1043 (describing Bar's effort "to preserve the integrity of the legal profession"). Because direct mail solicitations in the wake of accidents are perceived by the public as intrusive, the Bar argues, the reputation of the legal profession in the eyes of Floridians has suffered commensurately. See Pet. for Cert. 14–15; Brief for Petitioner 28–29. The regulation, then, is an effort to protect the flagging reputations of Florida lawyers by preventing them from engaging in conduct that, the Bar maintains, " 'is universally regarded as deplorable and beneath common decency because of its intrusion upon the special vulnerability and private grief of victims or their families.' " Brief for Petitioner 28, quoting In re Anis, 126 N.J. 448, 458, 599 A.2d 1265, 1270 (1992).

We have little trouble crediting the Bar's interest as substantial. On various occasions we have accepted the proposition that "States have a compelling interest in the practice of professions within their boundaries, and ... as part of their power to protect the public health, safety, and other valid interests they have broad power to establish standards for licensing practitioners and regulating the practice of professions." Goldfarb v. Virginia State Bar, 421 U.S. 773, 792, 95 S.Ct. 2004, 2016, 44 L.Ed.2d 572 (1975)....

Under Central Hudson's second prong, the State must demonstrate that the challenged regulation "advances the Government's interest 'in a direct and material way.'"... In Edenfield [113 S. Ct., at 1592], the Court invalidated a Florida ban on in-person solicitation by certified public accountants (CPAs). We observed that the State Board of Accountancy had "present[ed] no studies that suggest personal solicitation of prospective business clients by CPAs creates the dangers of fraud, overreaching, or compromised independence that the Board claims to fear."....

The direct-mail solicitation regulation before us does not suffer from such infirmities. The Florida Bar submitted a 106–page summary of its 2–year study of lawyer advertising and solicitation to the District Court. That summary contains data—both statistical and anecdotal—supporting the Bar's contentions that the Florida public views direct-mail solicitations in the immediate wake of accidents as an intrusion on privacy that reflects poorly upon the profession. As of June 1989, lawyers mailed 700,000 direct solicitations in Florida annually, 40% of which were aimed at accident victims or their survivors. Summary of the Record in No. 74,987 (Fla.) on Petition to Amend the Rules Regulating Lawyer Advertising (hereinafter Summary of Record), App. H, p. 2. A survey of Florida adults commissioned by the Bar indicated that Floridians "have negative feelings about those attorneys who use direct mail advertising." Magid Associates, Attitudes & Opinions Toward Direct Mail Advertising by Attorneys (Dec. 1987), Summary of Record, App. C(4), p. 6. Fifty-four percent of the general population surveyed said that contacting persons concerning accidents or similar events is a violation of privacy. Id., at 7. A random sampling of persons who received direct-mail advertising from lawyers in 1987 revealed that 45% believed that direct-mail solicitation is "designed to take advantage of gullible or unstable people"; 34% found such tactics "annoying or irritating"; 26% found it "an invasion of your privacy"; and 24% reported that it "made you angry." Ibid. Significantly, 27% of direct-mail recipients reported that their regard for the legal profession and for the judicial process as a whole was "lower" as a result of receiving the direct mail. Ibid.

The anecdotal record mustered by the Bar is noteworthy for its breadth and detail. With titles like "Scavenger Lawyers" (The Miami Herald, Sept. 29, 1987) and "Solicitors Out of Bounds" (St. Petersburg Times, Oct. 26, 1987), newspaper editorial pages in Florida have burgeoned with criticism of Florida lawyers who send targeted direct mail to victims shortly after accidents. See Summary of Record, App. B, pp. 1–8 (excerpts from articles); see also Peltz, Legal Advertising—Opening Pandora's Box,

19 Stetson L.Rev. 43, 116 (1989) (listing Florida editorials critical of direct-mail solicitation of accident victims in 1987, several of which are referenced in the record). The study summary also includes page upon page of excerpts from complaints of direct-mail recipients. For example, a Florida citizen described how he was " 'appalled and angered by the brazen attempt' " of a law firm to solicit him by letter shortly after he was injured and his fiancee was killed in an auto accident. Summary of Record, App. I(1), p. 2. Another found it " 'despicable and inexcusable' " that a Pensacola lawyer wrote to his mother three days after his father's funeral. Ibid. Another described how she was " 'astounded' " and then " 'very angry' " when she received a solicitation following a minor accident. Id., at 3. Still another described as " 'beyond comprehension' " a letter his nephew's family received the day of the nephew's funeral. Ibid. One citizen wrote, " 'I consider the unsolicited contact from you after my child's accident to be of the rankest form of ambulance chasing and in incredibly poor taste.... I cannot begin to express with my limited vocabulary the utter contempt in which I hold you and your kind.' " Ibid.

In light of this showing—which respondents at no time refuted, save by the conclusory assertion that the rule lacked "any factual basis," Plaintiffs' Motion for Summary Judgment and Supplementary Memorandum of Law in No. 92–370–Civ. (MD Fla.), p. 5—we conclude that the Bar has satisfied the second prong of the Central Hudson test....

In reaching a contrary conclusion, the Court of Appeals determined that this case was governed squarely by Shapero v. Kentucky Bar Assn., 486 U.S. 466, 108 S.Ct. 1916, 100 L.Ed.2d 475 (1988)....

While some of Shapero's language might be read to support the Court of Appeals' interpretation, Shapero differs in several fundamental respects from the case before us. First and foremost, Shapero's treatment of privacy was casual. Contrary to the dissent's suggestions, post, at 2382, the State in Shapero did not seek to justify its regulation as a measure undertaken to prevent lawyers' invasions of privacy interests. See generally Brief for Respondent in Shapero v. Kentucky Bar Assn., O.T.1987, No. 87–16. Rather, the State focused exclusively on the special dangers of overreaching inhering in targeted solicitations. Ibid. Second, in contrast to this case, Shapero dealt with a broad ban on all direct-mail solicitations, whatever the time frame and whoever the recipient. Finally, the State in Shapero assembled no evidence attempting to demonstrate any actual harm caused by targeted direct mail. The Court rejected the State's effort to justify a prophylactic ban on the basis of blanket, untested assertions of undue influence and overreaching. 486 U.S., at 475, 108 S.Ct., at 1922–1923. Because the State did not make a privacy-based argument at all, its empirical showing on that issue was similarly infirm.

We find the Court's perfunctory treatment of privacy in Shapero to be of little utility in assessing this ban on targeted solicitation of victims in the immediate aftermath of accidents. While it is undoubtedly true that many people find the image of lawyers sifting through accident and police reports in pursuit of prospective clients unpalatable and invasive, this case targets a different kind of intrusion. The Florida Bar has argued, and the record reflects, that a principal purpose of the ban is "protecting the personal privacy and tranquility of [Florida's] citizens from crass commercial intrusion by attorneys upon their personal grief in times of trauma." Brief for Petitioner 8; cf. Summary of Record, App. I(1) (citizen commentary describing outrage at lawyers' timing in sending solicitation letters). The intrusion targeted by the Bar's regulation stems not from the fact that a lawyer has learned about an accident or disaster (as the Court of Appeals notes, in many instances a lawyer need only read the newspaper to glean this information), but from the lawyer's confrontation of victims or relatives with such information, while wounds are still open, in order to solicit their business. In this respect, an untargeted letter mailed to society at large is different in kind from a targeted solicitation; the untargeted letter involves no willful or knowing affront to or invasion of the tranquility of bereaved or injured individuals and simply does not cause the same kind of reputational harm to the profession unearthed by the Florida Bar's study.

Nor do we find Bolger v. Youngs Drug Products Corp., 463 U.S. 60, 103 S.Ct. 2875, 77 L.Ed.2d 469 (1983), dispositive of the issue, despite any superficial resemblance. In Bolger, we rejected the Federal Government's paternalistic effort to ban potentially "offensive" and "intrusive" direct-mail advertisements for contraceptives. Minimizing the Government's allegations of harm, we reasoned that "[r]ecipients of objectionable mailings . . . may 'effectively avoid further bombardment of their sensibilities simply by averting their eyes.' " Id., at 72, 103 S.Ct., at 2883, quoting Cohen v. California, 403 U.S. 15, 21, 91 S.Ct. 1780, 1786, 29 L.Ed.2d 284 (1971). We found that the " 'short, though regular, journey from mail box to trash can . . . is an acceptable burden, at least so far as the Constitution is concerned.' " 463 U.S., at 72, 103 S.Ct., at 2883 (ellipses in original), quoting Lamont v. Commissioner of Motor Vehicles, 269 F.Supp. 880, 883 (S.D.N.Y.), summarily aff'd, 386 F.2d 449 (C.A.2 1967). Concluding that citizens have at their disposal ample means of averting any substantial injury inhering in the delivery of objectionable contraceptive material, we deemed the State's intercession unnecessary and unduly restrictive.

Here, in contrast, the harm targeted by the Florida Bar cannot be eliminated by a brief journey to the trash can. The purpose of the 30–day targeted direct-mail ban is to forestall the outrage and irritation with the state-licensed legal profession that the practice of direct solicitation only days after accidents has engendered. The Bar is concerned not with citizens' "offense" in the abstract, see post, at 2382–2383, but with the demonstrable detrimental effects that such "offense" has on the profession it regulates. See Brief for Petitioner 7, 14, 24, 28. Moreover, the harm posited by the Bar is as much a function of simple receipt of targeted solicitations within days of accidents as it is a function of the letters' contents. Throwing the letter away shortly after opening it may minimize the latter intrusion, but it does little to combat the former. We see no basis in Bolger, nor in the other, similar cases cited by the dissent, post, at 2382–2383, for dismissing the Florida Bar's assertions of harm, particularly given the unrefuted empirical and anecdotal basis for the Bar's conclusions.

Passing to Central Hudson's third prong, we examine the relationship between the Florida Bar's interests and the means chosen to serve them. See Board of Trustees of State University of N.Y. v. Fox, 492 U.S., at 480, 109 S.Ct., at 3034–3035. With respect to this prong, the differences between commercial speech and noncommercial speech are manifest. In Fox, we made clear that the "least restrictive means" test has no role in the commercial speech context. Ibid. "What our decisions require," instead, "is a 'fit' between the legislature's ends and the means chosen to accomplish those ends," a fit that is not necessarily perfect, but reasonable; that represents not necessarily the single best disposition but one whose scope is " 'in proportion to the interest served,' that employs not necessarily the least restrictive means but ... a means narrowly tailored to achieve the desired objective." Ibid. (citations omitted)....

Respondents levy a great deal of criticism, echoed in the dissent, post, at 2384–2386, at the scope of the Bar's restriction on targeted mail.... First, the rule does not distinguish between victims in terms of the severity of their injuries. According to respondents, the rule is unconstitutionally overinclusive insofar as it bans targeted mailings even to citizens whose injuries or grief are relatively minor. Id., at 15. Second, the rule may prevent citizens from learning about their legal options, particularly at a time when other actors—opposing counsel and insurance adjusters—may be clamoring for victims' attentions. Any benefit arising from the Bar's regulation, respondents implicitly contend, is outweighed by these costs.

We are not persuaded by respondents' allegations of constitutional infirmity. We find little deficiency in the ban's failure to distinguish among injured Floridians by the severity of their pain or the intensity of their grief. Indeed, it is hard to imagine the contours of a regulation that might satisfy respondents on this score. Rather than drawing difficult lines on the basis that some injuries are "severe" and some situations appropriate (and others, presumably, inappropriate) for grief, anger, or emotion, the Florida Bar has crafted a ban applicable to all postaccident or disaster solicitations for a brief 30–day period. Unlike respondents, we do not see "numerous and obvious less-burdensome alternatives" to Florida's short temporal ban. Cincinnati, supra, at ___, n. 13, 113 S.Ct., at 1510, n. 13. The Bar's rule is reasonably well-tailored to its stated objective of eliminating targeted mailings whose type and timing are a source of distress to Floridians, distress that has caused many of them to lose respect for the legal profession.

Respondents' second point would have force if the Bar's rule were not limited to a brief period and if there were not many other ways for injured Floridians to learn about the availability of legal representation during that time. Our lawyer advertising cases have afforded lawyers a great deal of leeway to devise innovative ways to attract new business. Florida permits lawyers to advertise on prime-time television and radio as well as in newspapers and other media. They may rent space on billboards. They may send untargeted letters to the general population, or to discrete segments thereof. There are, of course, pages upon pages devoted to lawyers in the

Yellow Pages of Florida telephone directories. These listings are organized alphabetically and by area of specialty. See generally Rule 4–7.2(a), Rules Regulating The Florida Bar ("[A] lawyer may advertise services through public media, such as a telephone directory, legal directory, newspaper or other periodical, billboards and other signs, radio, television, and recorded messages the public may access by dialing a telephone number, or through written communication not involving solicitation as defined in rule 4–7.4"); The Florida Bar: Petition to Amend the Rules Regulating The Florida Bar—Advertising Issues, 571 So.2d, at 461. These ample alternative channels for receipt of information about the availability of legal representation during the 30–day period following accidents may explain why, despite the ample evidence, testimony, and commentary submitted by those favoring (as well as opposing) unrestricted direct-mail solicitation, respondents have not pointed to—and we have not independently found—a single example of an individual case in which immediate solicitation helped to avoid, or failure to solicit within 30 days brought about, the harms that concern the dissent, see post, at 2385. In fact, the record contains considerable empirical survey information suggesting that Floridians have little difficulty finding lawyers when they need one. See, e.g., Summary of Record, App. C(4), p. 7; id., App. C(5), p. 8. Finding no basis to question the common-sense conclusion that the many alternative channels for communicating necessary information about attorneys are sufficient, we see no defect in Florida's regulation.

III

Speech by professionals obviously has many dimensions. There are circumstances in which we will accord speech by attorneys on public issues and matters of legal representation the strongest protection our Constitution has to offer. [citations omitted] This case, however, concerns pure commercial advertising, for which we have always reserved a lesser degree of protection under the First Amendment. Particularly because the standards and conduct of state-licensed lawyers have traditionally been subject to extensive regulation by the States, it is all the more appropriate that we limit our scrutiny of state regulations to a level commensurate with the " 'subordinate position' " of commercial speech in the scale of First Amendment values. Fox, 492 U.S., at 477, 109 S.Ct., at 3033, quoting Ohralik, 436 U.S., at 456, 98 S.Ct., at 1918–1919.

We believe that the Florida Bar's 30–day restriction on targeted direct-mail solicitation of accident victims and their relatives withstands scrutiny under the three-part Central Hudson test that we have devised for this context. The Bar has substantial interest both in protecting injured Floridians from invasive conduct by lawyers and in preventing the erosion of confidence in the profession that such repeated invasions have engendered. The Bar's proffered study, unrebutted by respondents below, provides evidence indicating that the harms it targets are far from illusory. The palliative devised by the Bar to address these harms is narrow both in scope and in duration. The Constitution, in our view, requires nothing more.

The judgment of the Court of Appeals, accordingly, is reversed.

■ Justice KENNEDY, with whom Justice STEVENS, Justice SOUTER, and Justice GINSBURG join, dissenting.

Attorneys who communicate their willingness to assist potential clients are engaged in speech protected by the First and Fourteenth Amendments. That principle has been understood since Bates v. State Bar of Arizona, 433 U.S. 350, 97 S.Ct. 2691, 53 L.Ed.2d 810 (1977). The Court today undercuts this guarantee in an important class of cases and unsettles leading First Amendment precedents, at the expense of those victims most in need of legal assistance. With all respect for the Court, in my view its solicitude for the privacy of victims and its concern for our profession are misplaced and self-defeating, even upon the Court's own premises.

. . . .

I

As the Court notes, the first of the Central Hudson factors to be considered is whether the interest the State pursues in enacting the speech restriction is a substantial one. . . .

To avoid the controlling effect of Shapero in the case before us, the Court seeks to declare that a different privacy interest is implicated. As it sees the matter, the substantial concern is that victims or their families will be offended by receiving a solicitation during their grief and trauma. But we do not allow restrictions on speech to be justified on the ground that the expression might offend the listener. . . .

. . . .

In the face of these difficulties of logic and precedent, the State and the opinion of the Court turn to a second interest: protecting the reputation and dignity of the legal profession. The argument is, it seems fair to say, that all are demeaned by the crass behavior of a few. The argument takes a further step in the amicus brief filed by the Association of Trial Lawyers of America. There it is said that disrespect for the profession from this sort of solicitation (but presumably from no other sort of solicitation) results in lower jury verdicts. In a sense, of course, these arguments are circular. While disrespect will arise from an unethical or improper practice, the majority begs a most critical question by assuming that direct mail solicitations constitute such a practice. The fact is, however, that direct solicitation may serve vital purposes and promote the administration of justice, and to the extent the bar seeks to protect lawyers' reputations by preventing them from engaging in speech some deem offensive, the State is doing nothing more (as amicus the Association of Trial Lawyers of America is at least candid enough to admit) than manipulating the public's opinion by suppressing speech that informs us how the legal system works. The disrespect argument thus proceeds from the very assumption it tries to prove, which is to say that solicitations within 30 days serve no legitimate purpose. This, of course, is censorship pure and simple; and censorship is antithetical to the first principles of free expression.

II

Even were the interests asserted substantial, the regulation here fails the second part of the Central Hudson test, which requires that the dangers the State seeks to eliminate be real and that a speech restriction or ban advance that asserted State interest in a direct and material way. Edenfield, 507 U.S., at ___[113 S.Ct., at 1800]. The burden of demonstrating the reality of the asserted harm rests on the State. Ibid. Slight evidence in this regard does not mean there is sufficient evidence to support the claims. Here, what the State has offered falls well short of demonstrating that the harms it is trying to redress are real, let alone that the regulation directly and materially advances the State's interests. The parties and the Court have used the term "Summary of Record" to describe a document prepared by the Florida Bar, one of the adverse parties, and submitted to the District Court in this case. See ante, at 2377. This document includes no actual surveys, few indications of sample size or selection procedures, no explanations of methodology, and no discussion of excluded results. There is no description of the statistical universe or scientific framework that permits any productive use of the information the so-called Summary of Record contains. The majority describes this anecdotal matter as "noteworthy for its breadth and detail," ante, at 2377, but when examined, it is noteworthy for its incompetence. . . .

III

The insufficiency of the regulation to advance the State's interest is reinforced by the third inquiry necessary in this analysis. Were it appropriate to reach the third part of the Central Hudson test, it would be clear that the relationship between the Bar's interests and the means chosen to serve them is not a reasonable fit. The Bar's rule creates a flat ban that prohibits far more speech than necessary to serve the purported state interest. Even assuming that interest were legitimate, there is a wild disproportion between the harm supposed and the speech ban enforced. It is a disproportion the Court does not bother to discuss, but our speech jurisprudence requires that it do so. Central Hudson, 447 U.S., at 569–571, 100 S.Ct., at 2353–2354; Board of Trustees of State University of N.Y. v. Fox, 492 U.S. 469, 480, 109 S.Ct. 3028, 3034–3035, 106 L.Ed.2d 388 (1989).

To begin with, the ban applies with respect to all accidental injuries, whatever their gravity. The Court's purported justification for the excess of regulation in this respect is the difficulty of drawing lines between severe and less serious injuries, see ante, at 2380, but making such distinctions is not important in this analysis. Even were it significant, the Court's assertion is unconvincing. . . .

There is, moreover, simply no justification for assuming that in all or most cases an attorney's advice would be unwelcome or unnecessary when the survivors or the victim must at once begin assessing their legal and financial position in a rational manner. With regard to lesser injuries, there is little chance that for any period, much less 30 days, the victims will become distraught upon hearing from an attorney. It is, in fact, more likely a real risk that some victims might think no attorney will be interested enough to help them. It is at this precise time that sound legal advice may be necessary and most urgent.

Even as to more serious injuries, the State's argument fails, since it must be conceded that prompt legal representation is essential where death or injury results from accidents.... The telephone book and general advertisements may serve this purpose in part; but the direct solicitation ban will fall on those who most need legal representation: for those with minor injuries, the victims too ill-informed to know an attorney may be interested in their cases; for those with serious injuries, the victims too ill-informed to know that time is of the essence if counsel is to assemble evidence and warn them not to enter into settlement negotiations or evidentiary discussions with investigators for opposing parties....

IV

It is most ironic that, for the first time since Bates v. State Bar of Arizona, the Court now orders a major retreat from the constitutional guarantees for commercial speech in order to shield its own profession from public criticism. Obscuring the financial aspect of the legal profession from public discussion through direct mail solicitation, at the expense of the least sophisticated members of society, is not a laudable constitutional goal. There is no authority for the proposition that the Constitution permits the State to promote the public image of the legal profession by suppressing information about the profession's business aspects. If public respect for the profession erodes because solicitation distorts the idea of the law as most lawyers see it, it must be remembered that real progress begins with more rational speech, not less....

QUESTIONS

1. In the majority opinion, Justice O'Connor applied an intermediate level of scrutiny to restrictions on commercial speech and used the three part *Hudson* test for regulating commercial speech: "first the government must assert a substantial interest in support of its regulation; second, the government must demonstrate that the restriction on commercial speech directly and materially advances that interest; and third, the regulation must be 'narrowly drawn.'" Id., citing Central Hudson Gas & Electric Corp. v. Public Service Comm'n of N.Y., 447 U.S. 557, 564–565 (1980). The Court found that the Florida Bar had met all of these requirements. Do you agree?

2. Justice O'Connor distinguished this case from *Shapero* by saying that *Shapero* dealt with a broad ban on all direct mail solicitations, and that the state in *Shapero* had no evidence to demonstrate actual harm caused by targeted direct mail. Do these distinctions justify the different result here?

3. This case induced several "lawyer jokes" from the justices during oral argument. Justice O'Connor was not impressed with the respondent's name "Went For It, Inc.," and she and the other justices must have known at least some of the details surrounding McHenry's disbarment. The Florida Bar certainly had an ideal case to test how far it could go in restricting lawyer advertising. Nonetheless, Justice Kennedy's dissent, joined by Justices Stevens, Souter and Ginsburg, argues that the bar is seeking to protect its own public image at the expense of both the First Amendment and accident victims. Do you agree?

4. The opinion states that "newspaper editorial pages in Florida have burgeoned with criticism of Florida lawyers who send targeted direct mail to victims shortly after accidents." Is this criticism a legitimate reason to prohibit such mailings?

5. Does the dissenting opinion adequately consider the emotional impact of direct mail solicitations on accident victims and their families?

Relevant Background

Solicitation of Class Members

Solicitation of potential class members may be necessary for successful maintenance of a class action. Rules requiring a minimum number of plaintiffs and opt-in rules often require plaintiffs' lawyers to solicit eligible class members. However, lawyers are subject to solicitation rules that vary from state to state, and in federal court to the Federal Rules of Civil Procedure, Rule 23, under which the court monitors communications with class members.

Solicitation of class members is generally excepted from prohibitions against client solicitation. In Gulf Oil Company v. Bernard, 452 U.S. 89 (1981), the Supreme Court upheld the right of counsel in Rule 23 class actions to communicate with eligible class members and to notify them of the commencement of the action, even before class certification. See also Zauderer v. Office of Disciplinary Counsel, 471 U.S. 626, 638 (1985) (advertisement soliciting Dalkan Shield class members must be allowed where no false or misleading statements were made).

Bernard and similar cases are limited to Rule 23 class actions, and some federal causes of action are tied to specific statutory procedures. For example, the Private Securities Litigation Reform Act of 1995, section 101, prevents attorneys from recruiting "professional plaintiffs" (persons who have been lead plaintiff in five or more securities class actions during a three–year period). Class actions brought under the Age Discrimination in Employment Act ("ADEA"), use the procedures of the Fair Labor Standards Act ("FLSA"). *See* ADEA at 29 U.S.C.A. § 626(b) and (c); and FLSA at 29 U.S.C.A. § 216(b). Some courts have prohibited class counsel in ADEA suits from contacting prospective class members. See McKenna v. Champion International Corporation, 747 F.2d 1211 (8th Cir.1984) (class counsel in ADEA suit may not solicit class members in a manner that would violate DR 2–103).

For discussion of communication by labor unions, public interest groups and other nonlawyer "lay intermediaries" with class members, see Chapter 6 supra. See also In re Primus, 436 U.S. 412 (1978) (solicitation of prospective litigants by nonprofit organizations is political expression entitled to First Amendment protection); NAACP v. Button, 371 U.S. 415

(1963) (same); and Vance G. Camisa, The Constitutional Right to Solicit Potential Class Members in a Class Action, 25 Gonz. L.Rev. 95 (1989).

Internet Advertising

There are at least three separate ways attorneys may advertise on the Internet: law firm servers (or "homepages"), electronic mail (or "e-mail") to newsgroups, and e-mail directly to potential clients. One of the most significant issues a lawyer using any of these methods has to confront is when an advertisement turns into an attorney-client relationship. For example, such a relationship may be formed by a potential client's request to a homepage for more information or response to an attorney's e-mail. If so, confidentiality requirements, conflicts rules and other obligations may apply from that point forward.

Many law firms advertise through a homepage from which an interested party can retrieve information. A law firm can put on its homepage resumes of its attorneys, lists of clients and copies of firm memoranda to clients. Restrictions, under state ethics rules are generally limited to requiring that the information be truthful and not misleading.

Attorneys can also advertise on the Internet by sending e-mail messages to newsgroups. In April, 1994, a Phoenix law firm, Canter & Siegel, sent advertisements offering assistance with acquiring federal green cards to over 6000 Internet newsgroups. In return, Canter and Siegel received numerous scathing messages, called "flames," and their home addresses were listed with threats to post their credit reports. Eventually they were shut off the Internet when their incoming mail caused 15 crashes of their Internet supplier. However, this intense negative response from Internet users did not prevent Canter and Siegel from earning $100,000 in new legal business or from publishing a book entitled How to Make a Fortune on the Information Superhighway. See Peter H. Lewis, Arizona Lawyers Form Company for Internet Advertising, N.Y. Times, May 7, 1994, at B1.

Finally, an attorney may want to send e-mail directly to a potential client. In some ways, e-mail is analogous to sending a United States Postal Service letter, only faster. An alternative analogy is to a direct personal contact with the potential client. Which analogy do you think is the most appropriate? Why does it matter?

E. PUBLIC STATEMENTS OF ATTORNEYS

Public Comment on a Case

Restrictions on pre-trial publicity define the border between the First and Sixth Amendments. As the comment to Model Rule 3.6 points out, "[I]t is difficult to strike a balance between protecting the right to a fair trial and safeguarding the right of free expression. Preserving the right to a fair trial necessarily entails some curtailment of the information that may be disseminated about a party prior to trial, particularly where trial by jury is involved."

Model Rule 3.6 states that "[a] lawyer who is participating or has participated in the investigation or litigation of a matter shall not make an extrajudicial statement that a reasonable person would expect to be disseminated by means of public communication if the lawyer knows or reasonably should know that it will have a substantial likelihood of materially prejudicing an adjudicative proceeding in the matter." The comment to Model Rule 3.6 recognizes that "the likelihood of prejudice may be different depending on the type of proceeding," and specifically points out that "criminal jury trials will be most sensitive to extrajudicial speech."

Model Rule 3.6(b) carves out some exceptions to this broad prohibition, including that a lawyer may state the "claim, offense or defense involved," "information contained in a public record," "a request for assistance in obtaining evidence," as well as, in criminal cases, "the identity, residence, occupation and family status of the accused" and certain information about the arrest and arresting officers. Model Rule 3.6(c) provides another exception: "a lawyer may make a statement that a reasonable lawyer would believe is required to protect a client from the substantial undue prejudicial effect of recent publicity" initiated by someone other than the lawyer or the lawyer's client. Model Rule 3.6(d) extends prohibitions on pre-trial publicity to law firms, prosecutors' offices and other organizations. "No lawyer associated in a firm or government agency with a lawyer subject to [these prohibitions on pre-trial comments] shall make a statement prohibited [thereby]." Id. See also Model Code, DR 7–107.

Although Model Rule 3.6 is phrased in general terms, many jurisdictions specifically prohibit pretrial comments on such things as the character or criminal record of a party or witness, expected testimony, admissibility of evidence and plea bargain negotiations. Prospective jurors, for example, could view the possibility of a plea bargain as an admission of guilt, even if plea bargain negotiations fall through. Some jurisdictions prohibit pre-trial release by prosecutors of information about a suspect's confession or refusal to talk. See H. Morley Swingle, Warning: Pretrial Publicity May be Hazardous to Your Bar License, 50 Jour. of the Missouri Bar 335 (1994). Some jurisdictions also have special confidentiality rules governing juvenile, domestic relations, mental disability and other proceedings. Rule 3.6, cmt.

In Gentile v. State Bar, 501 U.S. 1030 (1991), the Supreme Court ruled on the constitutionality of such restrictions, particularly when applied to criminal defense attorneys. Nevada's Disciplinary Board reprimanded Gentile for holding a press conference hours after his client was indicted on charges of stealing $300,000 in travelers checks and large amounts of cocaine from a vault used in connection with an undercover operation. At the press conference, Gentile made statements "to the effect that (1) the evidence demonstrated his client's innocence, (2) the likely thief was a police detective, Steve Scholl, and (3) the other victims were not credible, as most were drug dealers or convicted money launderers...." Id. at 1045. Gentile made these comments out of concern that "unless some of the weaknesses in the State's case were made public, a potential jury venire would be poisoned by repetition in the press of information being released by the police and prosecutors ..." Id. at 1042. The United States Supreme

Court reversed the judgment of the Nevada Supreme Court, which had upheld the reprimand. Justice Kennedy's opinion for the Court found that Nevada's restriction on pretrial publicity as applied to Gentile violated the First Amendment because Gentile had spoken at a time and in a manner that did not create any real prejudice to the trial. The Court also found Nevada's rule to be unconstitutionally vague because it allowed a lawyer to "state without elaboration ... the general nature of the ... defense" without defining precisely the difference between a "general" statement and "elaboration." Id. at 1048. Model Rule 3.6(b), which allows a lawyer to state "the claim, offense or defense involved" without specifying how far a lawyer may go in doing so, could have a similar problem of vagueness.

Prejudicial pretrial comments by prosecutors, however, raise different constitutional problems which may require reversal of a criminal conviction. See Sheppard v. Maxwell, 384 U.S. 333, 363 (1966) (habeas petition granted to prisoner convicted of murder because the "trial judge did not fulfill his duty to protect Sheppard from the inherently prejudicial publicity which saturated the community and to control disruptive influences in the courtroom"); Rideau v. Louisiana, 373 U.S. 723 (1963)(due process required trial court to grant Rideau's motion for change of venue after a film of a jailhouse "interview" in which he made admissions to bank robbery, kidnaping, and murder was broadcast over a local television station). Other consequences of prejudicial pretrial publicity include declaration of a mistrial and discipline of the prosecutor. See Zimmerman v. Board of Professional Responsibility, 764 S.W.2d 757 (Tenn.1989) (prosecutor reprimanded for violating DR 7–107(B) by making statements to the press about a medical examiner's report and other evidence that had not yet been introduced in a murder trial, and for violating DR 7–107(E) by making post-trial statements to the press that were likely to affect sentencing). Also, if a court has imposed a specific gag order, violation of that order by any lawyer is punishable as contempt of court.

Public Accusations Against a Judge

Elizabeth Holtzman, b. New York 1941; A.B. Radcliffe College 1962; J.D. Harvard University 1965; admitted to the bar in New York 1966; Democratic State Committeewoman 1970–72; U.S. Congresswoman 1973–81; District Attorney, Kings County, 1982–89; New York City Comptroller 1990–93; of counsel to Herrick, Feinstein LLP since 1993.

In the Matter of Elizabeth Holtzman, an Attorney, Appellant. Grievance Committee for the Tenth Judicial District, Respondent.

78 N.Y.2d 184, 573 N.Y.S.2d 39, 577 N.E.2d 30 (1991).

■ PER CURIAM.

Petitioner brought this proceeding pursuant to 22 NYCRR 691.6(a) to vacate a Letter of Reprimand issued by the Grievance Committee for the Tenth Judicial District.

The charge of misconduct that is relevant to this appeal was based on the public release by petitioner, then District Attorney of Kings County, of a letter charging Judge Irving Levine with judicial misconduct in relation to an incident that allegedly occurred in the course of a trial on criminal charges of sexual misconduct (Penal Law § 130.20), and was reported to her some six weeks later. Specifically, petitioner's letter stated that:

"Judge Levine asked the Assistant District Attorney, defense counsel, defendant, court officer and court reporter to join him in the robing room, where the judge then asked the victim to get down on the floor and show the position she was in when she was being sexually assaulted. * * * [T]he victim reluctantly got down on her hands and knees as everyone stood and watched. In making the victim assume the position she was forced to take when she was sexually assaulted, Judge Levine profoundly degraded, humiliated and demeaned her."

The letter, addressed to Judge Kathryn McDonald as Chair of the Committee to Implement Recommendations of the New York State Task Force on Women in the Courts, was publicly disseminated after petitioner's office issued a "news alert" to the media.

Following a dispute over the truth of the accusations, Robert Keating, as Administrative Judge of the New York City Criminal Court, conducted an investigation into the allegations of judicial misconduct. His report, dated December 22, 1987, concluded that petitioner's accusations were not supported by the evidence. Upon receipt of the report, Albert M. Rosenblatt, then Chief Administrative Judge, referred the matter to the Grievance Committee for inquiry as to whether petitioner had violated the Code of Professional Responsibility.

Some six months later, the Grievance Committee sent petitioner a private Letter of Admonition in which it stated that "the totality of the circumstances presented by this matter require that you be admonished for your conduct." Petitioner's misconduct, the Committee concluded, violated DR 8–102(B), DR 1–102(A)(5), (6) and EC 8–6 of the Code of Professional Responsibility.

In July 1988, after petitioner requested a subcommittee hearing pursuant to 22 NYCRR 691.6(a), she was served with three formal charges of misconduct under DR 8–102(B) and 1–102(A)(5) and (6). Charge 1 alleged that petitioner had engaged in conduct that adversely reflected on her fitness to practice law in releasing a false accusation of misconduct against Judge Levine. Charge 2 related to petitioner's subsequent videotaping of the complaining witness's statement under oath, and release of the audio portion of the tape to the media, despite her knowledge that the complainant would be a necessary witness in other investigations. Charge 3 related to a later press release in which petitioner stated that she had knowledge of other allegations of misconduct involving the Judge, thereby further demeaning him. Only Charge 1 is in issue on this appeal.

The conduct set forth in Charge 1, allegedly demonstrating petitioner's unfitness to practice law, included release of the letter to the media (1) prior to obtaining the minutes of the criminal trial, (2) without making any effort to speak with court officers, the court reporter, defense counsel or any other person present during the alleged misconduct, (3) without meeting with or discussing the incident with the trial assistant who reported it, and (4) with the knowledge that Judge Levine was being transferred out of the Criminal Court, and the matter would be investigated by the Court's Administrative Judge as well as the Commission on Judicial Conduct (to which the petitioner had complained).

After hearings, the subcommittee submitted its findings to the full Grievance Committee. The Committee sustained the first and third charges and issued petitioner a Letter of Reprimand, which was also private (22 NYCRR 691.6 [a]). The letter, dated October 19, 1989, stated that the Committee sustained Charges 1 and 3, and concluded that petitioner's conduct was "prejudicial to the administration of justice and adversely reflects on [her] fitness to practice law in violation of DR 1–102(A)(5) and (6) of the Code of Professional Responsibility." No mention was made of DR 8–102(B).

Petitioner then brought this proceeding seeking to vacate the Letter of Reprimand. The Appellate Division concluded that the record supported the Committee's findings as to Charge 1, more specifically that petitioner's conduct violated DR 8–102 and 1–102(A)(6). We now affirm, agreeing with both the Grievance Committee and the Appellate Division that petitioner's conduct violated DR 1–102(A)(6), and we reach no other question.

Petitioner relies primarily on two arguments. First, she asserts that the allegations concerning Judge Levine's conduct were true or at least not demonstrably false. Second, petitioner asserts that her conduct violates no specific disciplinary rule and further that DR 1–102(A)(6), if applicable, is unconstitutionally vague. These contentions are without merit.

The factual basis of Charge 1 is that petitioner made false accusations against the Judge. This charge was sustained by the Committee and upheld by the Appellate Division, and the factual finding of falsity (which is supported by the record) is therefore binding on us.

As for the contention that petitioner's conduct did not violate any provision of the Code, DR 1–102(A)(6) (now DR 1–102[A][7]) provides that a lawyer shall not "[e]ngage in any other conduct that adversely reflects on [the lawyer's] fitness to practice law." As far back as 1856, the Supreme Court acknowledged that "it is difficult, if not impossible, to enumerate and define, with legal precision, every offense for which an attorney or counselor ought to be removed" (Ex parte Secombe, 19 How. [60 U.S.] 9, 14, 15 L.Ed. 565). Broad standards governing professional conduct are permissible and indeed often necessary (see, In re Charges of Unprofessional Conduct Against N.P., 361 N.W.2d 386, 395 [Minn.], appeal dismissed 474 U.S. 976, 106 S.Ct. 375, 88 L.Ed.2d 330).

Such standards are set forth in Canon 1 and particularly in DR 1–102. An earlier draft of the Code listed "conduct degrading to the legal profession" as a basis for a finding of misconduct under DR 1–102, but this provision was replaced by the "fitness" language of DR 1–102(A)(6) and the "prejudicial to the administration of justice" standard of DR 1–102(A)(5) (see, Annotated Code of Professional Responsibility, Textual and Historical Notes, at 12). The drafters of the Code refined the provisions to provide attorneys with proper ethical guidelines. Were we to find such language impermissibly vague, attempts to promulgate general guidelines such as DR 1–102(A)(6) would be futile.

Rather than an absolute prohibition on broad standards, the guiding principle must be whether a reasonable attorney, familiar with the Code and its ethical strictures, would have notice of what conduct is proscribed (see, Committee on Professional Ethics & Conduct v. Durham, 279 N.W.2d 280, 283–284 [Iowa]; see also, In re Ruffalo, 390 U.S. 544, 554–555, 88 S.Ct. 1222, 1227–28, 20 L.Ed.2d 117 [White, J., concurring]; Matter of Cohen, 139 A.D.2d 221, 530 N.Y.S.2d 830).

Applying this standard, petitioner was plainly on notice that her conduct in this case, involving public dissemination of a specific accusation of improper judicial conduct under the circumstances described, could be held to reflect adversely on her fitness to practice law. Indeed, her staff, including the person assigned the task of looking into the ethical implications of release to the press, counseled her to delay publication until the trial minutes were received.

Petitioner's act was not generalized criticism but rather release to the media of a false allegation of specific wrongdoing, made without any support other than the interoffice memoranda of a newly admitted trial assistant, aimed at a named Judge who had presided over a number of cases prosecuted by her office (see, Matter of Terry, 271 Ind. 499, 502–503, 394 N.E.2d 94, 95–96, cert. denied 444 U.S. 1077, 100 S.Ct. 1025, 62 L.Ed.2d 759). Petitioner knew or should have known that such attacks are unwarranted and unprofessional, serve to bring the Bench and Bar into disrepute, and tend to undermine public confidence in the judicial system (see, Matter of Bevans, 225 App.Div. 427, 431, 233 N.Y.S. 439).

Therefore, petitioner's conduct was properly the subject of disciplinary action under DR 1–102(A)(6), and it is of no consequence that she might be charged with violating DR 8–102(B) based on this same course of conduct (see, In re Huffman, 289 Or. 515, 522, 614 P.2d 586, 589; Committee on Professional Ethics & Conduct v. Durham, 279 N.W.2d, at 285, supra; Matter of Terry, 271 Ind., at 501, 394 N.E.2d, at 94, supra). Indeed, in the present case there are factors that distinguish petitioner's conduct from that prohibited under DR 8–102(B)—most notably, release of the false charges to the media—and make it particularly relevant to her fitness to practice law.

Petitioner contends that her conduct would not be actionable under the "constitutional malice" standard enunciated by the Supreme Court in New York Times Co. v. Sullivan, 376 U.S. 254, 84 S.Ct. 710, 11 L.Ed.2d 686. Neither this Court nor the Supreme Court has ever extended the Sullivan standard to lawyer discipline and we decline to do so here.

Accepting petitioner's argument would immunize all accusations, however reckless or irresponsible, from censure as long as the attorney uttering them did not actually entertain serious doubts as to their truth (see, St. Amant v. Thompson, 390 U.S. 727, 731, 88 S.Ct. 1323, 20 L.Ed.2d 262; Trails West v. Wolff, 32 N.Y.2d 207, 219, 344 N.Y.S.2d 863, 298 N.E.2d 52). Such a standard would be wholly at odds with the policy underlying the rules governing professional responsibility, which seeks to establish a "minimum level of conduct below which no lawyer can fall without being subject to disciplinary action." (Code of Professional Responsibility, Preliminary Statement.)

Unlike defamation cases, "[p]rofessional misconduct, although it may directly affect an individual, is not punished for the benefit of the affected person; the wrong is against society as a whole, the preservation of a fair, impartial judicial system, and the system of justice as it has evolved for generations." (Matter of Terry, 271 Ind., at 502, 394 N.E.2d, at 95, supra.) It follows that the issue raised when an attorney makes public a false accusation of wrongdoing by a Judge is not whether the target of the false attack has been harmed in reputation; the issue is whether that criticism adversely affects the administration of justice and adversely reflects on the attorney's judgment and, consequentially, her ability to practice law (see, In re Disciplinary Action Against Graham, 453 N.W.2d 313, 322 [Minn.], cert. denied 498 U.S. 820, 111 S.Ct. 67, 112 L.Ed.2d 41).

In order to adequately protect the public interest and maintain the integrity of the judicial system, there must be an objective standard of what a reasonable attorney would do in similar circumstances (see, Louisiana State Bar Assn. v. Karst, 428 So.2d 406, 409 [La.]). It is the reasonableness of the belief, not the state of mind of the attorney, that is determinative.

Petitioner's course of conduct satisfies any standard other than "constitutional malice," and therefore Charge 1 must be sustained.

We have examined petitioner's remaining contentions and conclude that they are without merit.

Accordingly, the order of the Appellate Division should be affirmed, without costs.

■ Simons, Kaye, Alexander, Titone, Hancock and Bellacosa, JJ., concur in Per Curiam opinion.

■ Wachtler, C.J.*, taking no part.

---

* Although Holtzman's accusations in this case were apparently groundless, there are some shocking examples of male judges harassing women both inside and outside the courtroom. Eighteen months after this holding, in November, 1992, New York Court of Appeals Chief Judge Sol Wachtler was arrested by the FBI for stalking his ex-lover, Joy

Order affirmed, without costs.

QUESTIONS

1. Does this holding discourage lawyers from speaking out when they believe litigants or witnesses are being treated unfairly in court?

2. Holtzman was legitimately concerned about a problem: rude treatment of women litigants and lawyers in some judges' courtrooms. However, in this case, Holtzman was too zealous in addressing the problem. Are there other cases in this book where overzealousness has led lawyers to make accusations that were probably untrue?

3. Holtzman's staff had advised her to delay dissemination of the press release until she received the trial minutes. Why did she decide to make the accusation without this critical evidence of what actually occurred?

4. Charge 3 against Holtzman, not at issue in this appeal, "related to a later press release in which petitioner stated that she had knowledge of other allegations of misconduct involving the Judge, thereby further demeaning him." Is it ever appropriate for a lawyer to allege that a judge or another lawyer has engaged in misconduct without specifying exactly what her allegations are?

Relevant Background

Model Code, DR 8–102(B) states that "[a] lawyer shall not knowingly make false accusations against a judge or other adjudicatory officer." Under Model Rule 8.2(a), "[a] lawyer shall not make a statement that the lawyer knows to be false or with reckless disregard as to its truth or falsity concerning the qualifications or integrity of a judge. . . ."

The Model Rule uses language similar to that of the Supreme Court in a libel case, *New York Times v. Sullivan*, 376 U.S. 254 (1964). In *Sullivan*, a newspaper advertisement stated that an Alabama police official used violent tactics to put down protests. The Court held that such a statement about a public official could be grounds for a libel action only if made "with knowledge that it was false or with reckless disregard of whether it was false or not." Id. at 280. Despite the similarity in language between the Model Rule and the *Sullivan* opinion, however, the *Sullivan* standard applies only to civil and criminal defamation actions. Lawyer discipline potentially has a broader reach. As the New York Court of Appeals said in *Holtzman*, "neither this Court nor the Supreme Court has ever extended the *Sullivan* standard to lawyer discipline and we decline to do so here." 573 N.Y.S. 2d at 43.

In *Garrison v. Louisiana*, 379 U.S. 64 (1964), Jim Garrison, a New Orleans district attorney, held a press conference at which he alleged that eight local judges refused to authorize disbursements for undercover inves-

---

Silverman, disguising his voice on the telephone, mailing threats to Silverman, and following her dressed in disguises. He pled guilty to threatening to kidnap Silverman's daughter and served eleven months in federal prison.—ed.

tigation of vice. He went on to say that "[t]his raises interesting questions about the racketeer influences on our eight vacation-minded judges." Id. at 66. Garrison was tried and convicted of criminal defamation, and the United States Supreme Court reversed. The Court reaffirmed the *Sullivan* standard and held that Garrison's accusations were protected speech unless made with knowledge or reckless disregard of their falsity. Id. at 74. Under this standard, the Louisiana criminal defamation statute was unconstitutional because it directed "punishment of true statements made with actual malice" and allowed punishment of any untrue statements, whether made with or without malice. Id. at 78.

In re Evans, 801 F.2d 703 (4th Cir.1986), by contrast, was a disciplinary proceeding instead of a libel suit or criminal action. Attorney Paul Evans responded to a federal magistrate's adverse report in a tort case with a letter to the magistrate stating in part, "I feel that your Report was either the result of your incompetence in the matter or perhaps worse and reflected a Jewish bias in favor of the Kaplan firm [opposing counsel] whose actions were in my judgment inexcusable in this cause." Id. at 704. The District Court found that this letter violated DR 1–102(A)(5) ("A lawyer shall not engage in conduct that is prejudicial to the administration of justice."), DR 7–106(C)(6) ("In appearing in his professional capacity before a tribunal, a lawyer shall not engage in undignified or discourteous conduct which is degrading to a tribunal") and DR 8–102(B) ("A lawyer shall not knowingly make false accusations against a judge or other adjudicatory officer"). The District Court disbarred Evans from practice before it. The Fourth Circuit affirmed, holding that Evans "knew or reasonably should have known" that these accusations were false, and that his failure to investigate the charges "demonstrates his lack of integrity and fitness to practice law." Id. at 706. The Court also suggested that a different standard was appropriate here where the issue was "the qualification of appellant to practice law in the district court of Maryland," than if this had been an action for contempt. Id. See also In re Graham, 453 N.W.2d 313 (Minn.1990) (belief in the truth of accusations does not excuse reckless disregard for their truth in making a statement about a judge); Louisiana State Bar Ass'n v. Karst, 428 So.2d 406 (La.1983) (same).

Untrue accusations directed at a judge in a brief are also improper. Such accusations, for example, sometimes occur when an attorney overzealously argues a motion for recusal. In United States v. Cooper, 872 F.2d 1 (1st Cir.1989), the First Circuit warned that an attorney filing a motion to recuse a judge must do so in good faith and may not "seek refuge within his own First Amendment right of free speech to fill a courtroom with a litany of speculative accusations and insults which raise doubts as to a judge's impartiality." Id. at 3. Appellate briefs are another area where criticism of a court's decision can cross the line into personal attacks on its judges. In Ramirez v. State Bar, 28 Cal.3d 402, 169 Cal.Rptr. 206, 207, 619 P.2d 399, 400 (Cal.1980), the California Supreme Court upheld discipline of a lawyer for filing a brief with the Ninth Circuit Court of Appeals alleging, without support by credible facts, that the justices of the California Court of Appeal, when ruling against his clients, had "acted 'unlawfully' and 'illegally' and had become 'parties to the theft' of property belonging to [his] clients." Id. at 404.

There is more latitude for criticism of the legal system in general, or even of the proceedings in a particular case, than of an individual judge. In In re Sawyer, 360 U.S. 622 (1959), attorney Harriet Sawyer gave a speech attacking the credibility of a conspiracy trial under the Smith Act (aimed at alleged Communist activity). Sawyer said, among other things that the defendants, her clients, were on trial for the books they had read, that the FBI "spent too much time investigating people's minds," that the prosecution would "do anything and everything necessary to convict," that the government used perjured testimony, and that "there's no such thing as a fair trial in a Smith Act case." Id. at 628–29. Sawyer also said that "all rules of evidence have to be scrapped or the government can't make a case," and referred to some "shocking and rather horrible things that go on at the trial." Id. at 628. Judge Wiig, who presided over the trial, was not mentioned by name in Sawyer's speech. The Supreme Court of Hawaii nonetheless ordered Sawyer suspended for one year because these statements constituted "a willful oral attack upon the administration of justice in and by the [federal district court] and by direct statement and implication impugned the integrity of the judge presiding therein ... and thus tended to also create disrespect for the courts of justice and judicial officers generally...." Id. at 626. The United States Supreme Court reversed, holding that the record did not support the finding that Sawyer's statements impugned Judge Wiig's integrity. As Justice Brennan observed, "Judge Wiig remained equally protected from statements impugning him, and petitioner remained equally free to make critical statements that did not cross that line." Id. at 636.

Finally, in jurisdictions where judges are elected, lawyers may be tempted to engage in political rhetoric directed against a specific judge. The more responsible approach is to avoid comments that could be interpreted as trying to influence a pending trial (see Model Rule 3.6) and to preface remarks about a judge with a clear explanation that the statement is opinion rather than a factual allegation. See In re Baker, 218 Kan. 209, 542 P.2d 701 (1975) (challenger in an election for judicial office could criticize the incumbent's record so long as criticism was accurate, but could be censured for statements concerning incumbent judge's eligibility for a disability pension that challenger knew or should have known were false).

QUESTION

1. The Florida Supreme Court pointed out in In re Shimek, 284 So.2d 686, 689 (Fla.1973), that an attorney's untrue statement that a judge was not performing his sworn duty "cast a cloud of suspicion upon the entire judiciary ... and is totally unbecoming a member of the bar." In In re Woodward, 300 S.W.2d 385 (Mo.1957), the Court observed that a lawyer, as an officer of the court and a member of a regulated profession, cannot exercise free speech rights to a point where he violates standards of professional ethics. However, Professor Wolfram suggests that "[a]ny argument that lawyer criticism of judges is entitled to a lesser protection than nonlawyer criticism ... proceeds on the readily rejectable premise that [either] lawyers are not entitled to the normal rights of citizens or ... [that] there is a substantial and compelling state interest in requiring lawyers to protect judges...." C.W. Wolfram, Modern Legal Ethics 602 (1986). Which of these positions is more persuasive?

Courtroom Demeanor

Anonymous, Dyer 188B, Note

(1631).

"Richardson ch. Just. de C. Banc. al Assises at Salisbury in Summer 1631, fuit assault per prisoner la condemne pur felony que puis son condemnation ject un Brickbat a le dit Justice que narrowly mist, & per ceo immediately fuit Indictment drawn per Noy envers le prisoner, & son Dexter manus ampute & fix al Gibbet sur que luy mesme immediatement hange in presence de Court."

Quoted in Z. Chafee & E. Re, Cases and Materials on Equity 37 (4th ed. 1957).

Disrespectful courtroom demeanor is not punished as severely today, and even the most disruptive defendants are given more due process than was given at Salisbury in 1631. Consider the following exchange that took place in a Pennsylvania state court during the 1966 trial of charges stemming from a prison riot:

"Mr. Mayberry [defendant]: I would like to have a fair trial of this case and like to be granted a fair trial under the Sixth Amendment.

"The Court: You will get a fair trial.

"Mr. Mayberry: It doesn't appear that I am going to get one the way you are overruling all our motions and that, and being like a hatchet man for the State.

"The Court: This side bar is over.

"Mr. Mayberry: Wait a minute, Your Honor.

"The Court: It is over.

"Mr. Mayberry: You dirty sonofabitch."

Mayberry v. Pennsylvania, 400 U.S. 455, 456 (1971). The trial court found that the petitioner and two codefendants, all representing themselves pro se, had committed similar contempts on 11 out of the 21 days of the trial. They were each given stiff prison sentences for contempt. Id. at 455. One of the defendants actually "told the judge if he did not get access to his papers at night he'd 'blow your head off.' " Id. at 458. Nonetheless, the Supreme Court observed that "such insults were apt to strike 'at the most vulnerable and human qualities of a judge's temperament.' " Id. at 466, quoting Bloom v. Illinois, 391 U.S. 194, 202 (1968). The Due Process Clause of the Fourteenth Amendment therefore required that "a defendant in criminal contempt proceedings should be given a public trial before a judge other than the one reviled by the contemnor." Id. at 466.

Abusive conduct toward a judge on a lawyer's part can result in disciplinary sanction as well as a proceeding for contempt. As Judge Weinfeld observed over twenty years ago in finding a criminal defense lawyer guilty of criminal contempt:

> It is one thing for counsel to strongly and persistently pursue a contention; it is quite another to continue in actions that debase the trial when warned to refrain from obstructive tactics.... That the Court made adverse rulings to the defense, even if counsel disagreed, did not justify contumacious behavior or disrespectful outbursts, or the repeated specious challenges to the Court's integrity, and the motions for mistrial on the ground that it was biased, prejudiced and unfair to the defense, a number of which were made in the presence of the jury.

In the Matter of Stanley S. Cohen, 370 F. Supp. 1166, 1175–76 (S.D.N.Y. 1973).

The Federal Circuit more recently heard a dispute over a patent claim culminate in an outburst by the appellant's counsel at oral argument:

> While [appellant] was entitled to appeal the denial of its claim, its counsel was not entitled to disrupt the oral argument with a display of temper. During his rebuttal argument, counsel turned around, pointed a finger at opposing counsel, and heatedly said: "These two lawyers are bad lawyers. They deceived the examiners, they deceived the trial judge, and then they pull this here." This court is accustomed to hearing forceful argument. However, counsel's outburst was unacceptable. Strong conviction concerning the merits of one's case is not justification for losing one's composure at oral argument and making pointed accusations at opposing counsel.

Nordberg, Inc. v. Telsmith, Inc., 82 F.3d 394, 398 (Fed.Cir.1996) (appellant's counsel admonished and put on notice that future infractions would be sanctioned under Fed R. App. P. 46(c)).

In addition to conducting themselves respectfully in the courtroom, lawyers should follow the directions of a presiding judge on procedural matters and should attend hearings when requested to do so. See In re Yengo, 84 N.J. 111, 417 A.2d 533 (1980), *cert. denied*, 449 U.S. 1124 (1981) (defense attorney held in contempt and fined $500 for missing two days of trial).

F.   UNAUTHORIZED PRACTICE OF LAW

Beginning in the 1930's, bar associations made a concerted effort to restrict nonlawyers from practicing law. By 1938, for example, over 400 bar associations had established committees charged with enforcing prohibitions on unauthorized practice. Deborah L. Rhode, Policing the Professional Monopoly: A Constitutional and Empirical Analysis of Unauthorized

Practice Prohibitions, 34 Stan. L. Rev. 1, 8 (1981)(citing Otterbourg, Collection Agency Activities: The Problem from the Standpoint of the Bar, 5 Law and Contemp. Prob. 35 (1938)). Proponents of this effort argue that it protects the public from incompetent legal assistance. Opponents, however, argue that such prohibitions are an attempt by licensed lawyers to monopolize the market for legal services, limit competition and extract high fees. Thomas D. Morgan, The Evolving Concept of Professional Responsibility, 90 Harv. L. Rev. 702, 707–712 (1977).

"Practice of law" is defined differently in each state. New Mexico's Supreme Court has held that practice of law includes:

"(1) representation of parties before judicial or administrative bodies, (2) preparation of pleadings and other papers incident to actions and special proceedings, (3) management of such action and proceeding, and non-court related activities such as (4) giving legal advice and counsel, (5) rendering a service that requires the use of legal knowledge or skill, (6) preparing instruments and contracts by which legal rights are secured."

State ex rel. Norvell v. Credit Bureau of Albuquerque, Inc., 85 N.M. 521, 514 P.2d 40, 45 (1973). Some courts have defined "practice of law" even more broadly. In R.J. Edwards, Inc. v. Hert, for example, the Oklahoma Supreme Court held that the practice of law is "the rendition of services requiring the knowledge and application of legal principles and technique to serve the interests of another with his consent." 504 P.2d 407, 416 (Okl.1972).

Where the amount in controversy is minimal, some jurisdictions allow non-lawyers to engage in activities that clearly are practicing law, such as representing a party at a hearing. In Hunt v. Maricopa County Employees Merit System Commission, a county employee was allowed to be represented by a nonlawyer union official at an appeal from disciplinary action taken by her employer. The Court noted that the amount in controversy (lost pay from a four-day work suspension) was small enough to make hiring an attorney impractical. 127 Ariz. 259, 619 P.2d 1036, 1040 (Ariz.1980). In Henize v. Giles, the Ohio Supreme Court held that representing a party at hearings of the Ohio Unemployment Compensation Board of Review was not unauthorized practice of law. 22 Ohio St.3d 213, 490 N.E.2d 585, 587 (1986). In Florida Bar v. Brumbaugh, the Florida Supreme Court held that the proprietor of a secretarial service could sell and fill out preprinted legal forms for "do-it-yourself" divorces so long as she "only cop[ied] the information given to her in writing by her clients." 355 So.2d 1186, 1194 (1978). Many states also have specific rules allowing supervised court appearances by law students and recent law school graduates not yet admitted to the bar. Such persons, however, should be careful both in and outside the courtroom not to cross the line into unauthorized practice, a transgression that could later adversely affect their application for admission to the bar.

Sanctions for unauthorized practice of law include penalties for contempt of court and, in some jurisdictions, penalties under the criminal code.

For example, in Florida Bar v. Furman a non-lawyer was held in contempt for helping clients obtain uncontested divorces. 376 So.2d 378 (Fla.1979). Other states have enacted legislation specifying that unauthorized practice of law is a misdemeanor. In California, "[a]ny person advertising or holding himself or herself out as practicing or entitled to practice law or otherwise practicing law who is not an active member of the State Bar, is guilty of a misdemeanor." Cal. Bus. & Prof. Code Sec. 6126 (West 1996). See *Rhode,* supra, at 11.

Finally, a lawyer who practices law in a jurisdiction where he is not licensed or who assists a nonlawyer with unauthorized practice may be subject to discipline. Model Rule 5.5 provides that a lawyer shall not:

"(a) practice law in a jurisdiction where doing so violates the regulation of the legal profession in that jurisdiction; or

(b) assist a person who is not a member of the bar in the performance of activity that constitutes the unauthorized practice of law."

This rule "does not prohibit lawyers from providing professional advice and instruction to nonlawyers whose employment requires knowledge of law, for example claims adjusters, employees of financial or commercial institutions, social workers, accountants and persons employed in government agencies." In addition, "a lawyer may counsel nonlawyers who wish to proceed pro se." Rule 5.5, cmt. See also Model Code, DR 3–101(A) (same); Model Code, EC 3–5 (where professional judgment is not involved, "nonlawyers, such as court clerks, police officers, abstracters, and many governmental employees, may engage in occupations that require a special knowledge of law in certain areas."). Rules prohibiting unauthorized practice of law also do not apply to persons who seek to represent themselves. See Model Code, EC 3–7. Indeed, in criminal cases defendants have a constitutional right to represent themselves if they choose to. See Faretta v. California, 422 U.S. 806 (1975).

Critics of restrictions on unauthorized practice sometimes point out that, despite the large number of lawyers in our society, legal services for the general public are both expensive and in short supply. Deborah L. Rhode, The Delivery of Legal Services by Non–Lawyers, 4 Geo. J. Legal Ethics 209, 228–233 (1990). For example, one survey found that 50% of the time lawyers spend representing individual clients goes to persons with incomes in the top 15% of the population, and that "only 10% of American attorneys' time is devoted to persons in the bottom third of the economy." Id. Another survey found that 43% of low-income households experienced some sort of legal difficulty in 1988, and that a lawyer was not available for roughly 50% of those problems. Id. Professor Rhode and others have suggested that one solution to this problem would be to allow lay-persons to handle simple legal problems, presumably at lower cost than a lawyer would charge for the same services. Id. at 231.

In 1983 Washington State began to license nonlawyers. See Wash. Ct. Rules, Admission to Practice R. 12(a) (1983) (allowing "certain lay persons to select, prepare and complete legal documents" for real estate closings).

In 1990 California created a Commission on Legal Technicians which recommended that the California Supreme Court allow nonlawyers to assist clients in bankruptcy, family, and landlord and tenant law. See Kathleen E. Justice, Note, There Goes the Monopoly: The California Proposal to Allow Nonlawyers to Practice Law, 44 Vand. L. Rev. 179 (1991). The Commission proposed a separate regulatory and licensing system for nonlawyers providing these services. Id. at 201–06.

G. INTERSTATE AND INTERNATIONAL LAWYERING

Interstate Lawyering

Many lawyers and law firms have offices in several states. Besides obvious logistical difficulties of practicing law in more than one jurisdiction, conflicting professional responsibility standards can be confusing. Not only do rules differ on many important issues, but it may not be entirely clear which jurisdiction's rules apply to a specific situation.

Rules on maintaining client confidences, for example, can be particularly problematic. "If you are in Wilmington, Delaware, confronted by a client's intended fraudulent conduct that will likely cause substantial financial harm, and you practice law also in Pennsylvania and New Jersey, you are subject to three different rules. New Jersey requires disclosure to the proper authorities. Delaware forbids disclosure. Pennsylvania permits but does not require disclosure." Harris Weinstein, Attorney Liability in the Savings and Loan Crisis, 1993 U. Ill. L. Rev. 53, 64 (1993). Compare, for example, Model Rule 1.6 with Model Code, DR 4–101.

Contingent fees and lawyer advertising are two other areas prone to differing standards. For example, under the Model Code, DR 5–103(B) an attorney or firm that advances expenses of litigation, such as court costs, must be repaid by the client who "remains ultimately liable for such expenses." Model Rule 1.8(e)(1), by contrast, provides that repayment of such expenses can be made "contingent on the outcome of the matter." With respect to lawyer advertising, the Model Rules allow a lawyer to compare herself to other lawyers, so long as "the comparison can be factually substantiated." New Jersey, however, forbids any advertisement that "compares the lawyer's services with other lawyers' services." N.J. Court Rules, 1969 R. RPC 7.1(a)(3) (1996). See Duncan T. O'Brien, Multistate Practice and Conflicting Ethical Obligations, 16 Seton Hall L. Rev. 678, 690–91 (1986).

Choice of law problems are often difficult. Model Rule 8.5(b) provides that, for conduct in connection with a court proceeding, the professional conduct rules of the jurisdiction in which the court sits shall be applied unless rules of court provide otherwise. For any other conduct, if a lawyer is licensed to practice only in one jurisdiction, that jurisdiction's rules apply. If the lawyer is licensed to practice in more than one jurisdiction, the applicable rules are the rules of the jurisdiction in which the lawyer "principally practices," unless "particular conduct clearly has its predominant effect in another jurisdiction in which the lawyer is licensed to practice," in which case that jurisdiction's rules shall apply.

This choice of law rule is significantly different from general choice of law rules and some commentators have questioned whether lawyers need a different rule. Professor Kathleen Clark points out that lawyers ought to understand traditional choice of law analysis, and that there is little inherent in lawyer discipline that makes standard choice of law analysis inappropriate. Kathleen Clark, Is Discipline Different? An Essay on Choice of Law and Lawyer Conduct, 36 S. Tex. L. Rev. 1069, 1071–72 (1995). See also Jeffrey L. Rensberger, Jurisdiction, Choice of Law, and the Multistate Attorney, 36 S. Tex. L. Rev. 799, 827–28 (1995).

Appearance Pro Hac Vice

The term *pro hac vice* means "for this turn" and refers to admission of an out-of-state lawyer to represent a client in a particular trial. However, in most jurisdictions, admission *pro hac vice* is not automatically granted. In Leis v. Flynt, 439 U.S. 438 (1979), the Supreme Court held that a state has discretion in deciding whether to allow a litigant to be represented by lawyers licensed in other jurisdictions. "[T]he asserted right of an out-of-state lawyer to appear *pro hac vice* in an Ohio court does not fall among those interests protected by the Due Process Clause of the Fourteenth Amendment." Id. at 438.

New Jersey permits out-of-state lawyers to appear *pro hac vice*, but requires that all papers filed with the court be signed by "an attorney of record authorized to practice in this State, who shall be held responsible for them and for the conduct of the cause and of the admitted attorney therein." N.J. Court Rules, 1969 R. 1:21–2(b)(4) (1996). By contrast, New York allows an attorney admitted in "another state, territory, district or foreign country" to be admitted "in the discretion of any court of record, to participate in the trial or argument of any particular cause in which the attorney may be for the time being employed." 22 N.Y.C.R.R. § 520.10(a)(4)(e)(1)(1996). Oregon has six requirements for an out-of-state attorney to appear *pro hac vice*: (1) certification of good standing in the foreign jurisdiction; (2) disclosure of any disciplinary proceedings pending against the attorney; (3) "association" with an active member of the Oregon bar in good standing; (4) certification that the attorney will comply with applicable Oregon rules; (5) certification of insurance covering the attorney's work in Oregon; and (6) agreement to advise the court of any changes in insurance or other status. Marilyn Lindgren Cohen, Preparing Parachutes, A New Rule for Out-of-State Attorneys, 56 Nov. Or. St. B. Bull. 31 (1995), citing Uniform Trial Court Rule 3.170 (1995).

Admission *pro hac vice* may be revoked, usually at the discretion of the court granting it in the first place. See Johnson v. Trueblood, 629 F.2d 302 (3d Cir.1980), cert. denied, 450 U.S. 999 (1981). In *Johnson*, a Chicago attorney was admitted to represent a plaintiff in a Pennsylvania civil trial in which the jury found for the defendants. The district judge revoked the attorney's *pro hac vice* status while an appeal was pending. The revocation, ordered sua sponte without opportunity for notice and hearing, was made retroactive to the date of the verdict because of "the attorney's conduct during the trial." Id. at 302. The Third Circuit vacated the order, observing that "some type of notice and an opportunity to respond are necessary when a district court seeks to revoke an attorney's *pro hac vice* status." Id. at 303.

Paramount Communications Inc. v. QVC Network Inc., 637 A.2d 34 (Del.1994), is noted for its holding that Paramount directors violated their fiduciary duties in implementing defensive measures against a takeover bid by QVC. However, in an addendum to its opinion, the Delaware Supreme Court pointed out that out-of-state counsel should get themselves admitted *pro hac vice* before representing their clients at depositions in Delaware proceedings. The immediate focus of the Court's concern was serious misconduct by Joseph D. Jamail of the Texas bar in representing Paramount director J. Hugh Liedtke in a deposition, and acquiescence in Jamail's misconduct by Peter C. Thomas of the New York bar, who attended the deposition on behalf of Paramount. Although the deposition was taken by William Johnston, a Delaware lawyer representing QVC, "[t]here was no [other] Delaware lawyer and no lawyer admitted *pro hac vice* present at the deposition representing any party." Id. at 53, n. 27. During the course of the deposition, the following exchange occurred:

A. [Mr. Liedtke] I vaguely recall [Mr. Oresman's letter].... I think I did read it, probably.

     . . . .

Q. (By Mr. Johnston [Delaware counsel for QVC]) Okay. Do you have any idea why Mr. Oresman was calling that material to your attention?

MR. JAMAIL: Don't answer that.

How would he know what was going on in Mr. Oresman's mind?

Don't answer it. Go on to your next question.

MR. JOHNSTON: No, Joe—

MR. JAMAIL: He's not going to answer that. Certify it. I'm going to shut it down if you don't go to your next question.

MR. JOHNSTON: No. Joe, Joe—

MR. JAMAIL: Don't "Joe" me, asshole. You can ask some questions, but get off of that. I'm tired of you. You could gag a maggot off a meat wagon. Now, we've helped you every way we can.

MR. JOHNSTON: Let's just take it easy.

MR. JAMAIL: No, we're not going to take it easy. Get done with this.

MR. JOHNSTON: We will go on to the next question.

MR. JAMAIL: Do it now.

MR. JOHNSTON: We will go on to the next question. We're not trying to excite anyone.

MR. JAMAIL: Come on. Quit talking. Ask the question. Nobody wants to socialize with you.

MR. JOHNSTON: I'm not trying to socialize. We'll go on to another question. We're continuing the deposition.

MR. JAMAIL: Well, go on and shut up.

MR. JOHNSTON: Are you finished?

MR. JAMAIL: Yeah, you—

MR. JOHNSTON: Are you finished?

MR. JAMAIL: I may be and you may be. Now, you want to sit here and talk to me, fine. This deposition is going to be over with. You don't know what you're doing. Obviously someone wrote out a long outline of stuff for you to ask. You have no concept of what you're doing.

Now, I've tolerated you for three hours. If you've got another question, get on with it. This is going to stop one hour from now, period. Go.

MR. JOHNSTON: Are you finished?

MR. THOMAS [representing Paramount]: Come on, Mr. Johnston, move it.

MR. JOHNSTON: I don't need this kind of abuse.

MR. THOMAS: Then just ask the next question.

Q.   (By Mr. Johnston) All right. To try to move forward, Mr. Liedtke, . . . I'll show you what's been marked as Liedtke 14 and it is a covering letter dated October 29 from Steven Cohen of Wachtell, Lipton, Rosen & Katz including QVC's Amendment Number 1 to its Schedule 14D–1, and my question—

A.   No.

Q.—to you, sir, is whether you've seen that?

A.   No. Look, I don't know what your intent in asking all these questions is, but, my God, I am not going to play boy lawyer.

Q.   Mr. Liedtke—

A.   Okay. Go ahead and ask your question.

Q.—I'm trying to move forward in this deposition that we are entitled to take. I'm trying to streamline it.

MR. JAMAIL: Come on with your next question. Don't even talk with this witness.

MR. JOHNSTON: I'm trying to move forward with it.

MR. JAMAIL: You understand me? Don't talk to this witness except by question. Did you hear me?

MR. JOHNSTON: I heard you fine.

MR. JAMAIL: You fee makers think you can come here and sit in somebody's office, get your meter running, get your full day's fee by asking stupid questions. Let's go with it.

(JA 6002–06). *Id.* at 54.

In the addendum to its opinion in *Paramount*, the Delaware Supreme Court observed that "the Court finds this unprofessional behavior to be outrageous and unacceptable. If a Delaware lawyer had engaged in the kind of misconduct committed by Mr. Jamail on this record, that lawyer would have been subject to censure or more serious sanctions." Id. at 55. The problem, of course, was that none of the lawyers at the deposition besides Mr. Johnston were subject to the authority of the Delaware courts. The Court observed that "the Paramount defendants should have been represented at the deposition by a Delaware lawyer or a lawyer admitted *pro hac vice*," and that "[a] Delaware lawyer or a lawyer admitted *pro hac vice* would have been expected to put an end to the misconduct in the Liedtke deposition." Id. at 55, 56. Instead, Mr. Thomas, also beyond the reach of the Delaware courts, "passively let matters proceed as they did, and at times even added his own voice to support the behavior of Mr. Jamail." Id. at 56.

The Court went on to observe that "one of the principal purposes of the *pro hac vice* rules is to assure that, if a Delaware lawyer is not to be present at a deposition, the lawyer admitted *pro hac vice* will be there. As such, he is an officer of the Delaware Court, subject to control of the Court to ensure the integrity of the proceeding." Id. "[I]n the future the Court expects that counsel in Mr. Thomas's position will have been admitted *pro hac vice* before participating in a deposition. As an officer of the Delaware Court, counsel admitted *pro hac vice* are now clearly on notice that they are expected to put an end to conduct such as that perpetrated by Mr. Jamail on this record." Id., n. 38.

QUESTION

1. In Ford v. Israel, 701 F.2d 689 (7th Cir.), cert. denied, 464 U.S. 832 (1983), Jesse James Ford was charged with murder in Wisconsin. Ford's parent hired a Chicago lawyer to represent him but refused to pay also for local counsel to affiliate on the case. Wisconsin's *pro hac vice* rule required all non resident counsel to appear with local counsel. Ford ended up being represented by the public defender and was convicted. Judge Posner upheld the Wisconsin rule, reasoning that the rule prevents a party from dragging out proceedings by arguing that their out-of-state counsel denied them adequate representation because of unfamiliarity with the state's law. Id. at 692–93. Do you think Wisconsin's *pro hac vice* rule imposes undue restrictions on the right to counsel of one's choice? Would your answer be different for a civil as opposed to a criminal trial?

International Lawyering

Transnational Law Practice

Richard L. Abel.
44 Case W. Res. 737 (1994).

Although transnational law practice is not new—Coudert opened its Paris office more than a century ago—most of the growth has occurred in the last two decades, and most of that since the 1980s. Lawyers practicing across national boundaries elicit considerable media attention, especially from the new legal journalism. Transnational lawyering possesses some of the glamor that air travel enjoyed half a century ago. Firms proudly announce the opening of each new office abroad, even the acquisition of each new lawyer, though they are often more discreet about the contraction and closure of offices. Law firms and bar associations become equally exercised about regulatory barriers and regulatory lacunae. It is essential, therefore, to place the phenomenon in proper perspective: transnational law practice is numerically a trivial component of all national legal professions and will remain so for the foreseeable future. Even in the American legal profession, generally characterized as the most aggressively competitive and internationalist, foreign branches contain fewer than 2000 lawyers—or less than a quarter of a percent of the profession (and many of them are foreign qualified lawyers practicing local law). The only other country that even approaches that proportion is the United Kingdom. Elsewhere no more than a handful of firms have even the barest toehold outside their borders.

. . . .

The response of local governments, legal associations and lawyers to the foreign "invasion" evokes the experience of American states, as well as the components of other federal polities such as Canada, Australia, Germany, and Switzerland. Indeed, we can chronicle a continuous succession of protectionist strategies: lawyers against non-lawyers; lawyers admitted to one court against those admitted to others; lawyers performing one function against those performing others (e.g., barristers and solicitors; avocats, avoues, and conseils juridiques); and lawyers from one geographic jurisdiction against those from others. Given national differences of law, language, history, and culture, there is every reason to expect foreign lawyers to provoke more intense protectionism.

. . . .

The growth of transnational practice raises a number of troubling ethical questions, although not the ones usually invoked as rationalizations for protectionism. Competition may increase the quality and reduce the price of legal services, but it has other less attractive consequences. In the international market, where quality is difficult or impossible to gauge, firms are forced to compete on the surrogate indices touted by the new legal journalism, which are easy to calculate. These typically include billings or profits (aggregate or per partner), size, and growth rates. In order to elevate these, firms must augment leverage by increasing either the ratio of associates to partners or billable hours or both. The heightened competition for partnership makes associates even more compliant and uncritical. The race to bill hours makes the lip service firms pay to pro bono or deo activities even more hypocritical. As service to individual clients is driven out by more lucrative commercial work, firms lose the basic competence to represent ordinary people. Updating Veblen, firms may compete for prestige in the domestic market by rendering conspicuous public service: Skadden's public interest fellowships, Arnold and Porter's declaration that all lawyers could spend 15% of their time on pro bono activities, and Piper & Marbury's branch office. There is no comparable incentive for altruism in the international market. As far as I know, foreign branch offices perform *no* public interest work.

Lawyers pride themselves on their "independence." Private practitioners often invoke this shibboleth to claim superiority to house counsel. Firms note that they rarely depend on a single client for more than five percent of their gross income. Robert Nelson, however, has demonstrated that individual lawyers in large American firms typically earn thirty to forty percent of their fees from a single client.[28] Foreign branch offices are closer to the latter situation than the former. Many opened at the behest of a single client—sometimes the national or local government—to which they may be obligated for special privileges (e.g., White & Case). All have a much smaller client base than the home office. This situation is likely to breed a worrying clientelism.

Finally, foreign lawyers have a different relation to professional associations from their domestic counterparts. Foreigners depend on local professional associations for their right to practice, but most do not belong, unless fully admitted locally, and even fewer participate in governance, although an American and a Spanish lawyer have just been elected to the barreau of Paris. International associations remain weak. Some, like the Conseil des Barreaux de la Communaute Europeenne (CCBE), are merely federations of national bodies. Even the International Bar Association (IBA), which has individual members, remains relatively small. There are few effective organizations within the face-to-face communities of foreign lawyers practicing in a single city. Even their interests may diverge if some have been grandfathered into the local bar, or enjoy the privileges of a former metropole, or are EC members. Unlike domestic professional bodies, international associations do not encourage pro bono activities, support legal aid (which is administered nationally), ensure standards of competence or ethical behavior, certify educational institutions, or help to reform legal institutions or rules.[29] I know of no efforts to ensure proportional representation of women or racial minorities, grant maternity leave or provide re-entry schemes. Transnational lawyers are significantly deprofessionalized. In this they increasingly resemble their competitors in offices of

---

28. *See* Robert L. Nelson, Partners with Power: The Social Transformation of the Large Law Firm 250–51 (1988) (exploring the development and structure of large law firms).

29. *Cf.* Michael J. Powell, From Patrician to Professionally Elite: The Transformation of the New York City Bar Association 150–75 (1988) (discussing how the Association of the Bar of the City of New York [is] involved in many of these areas). *See* generally Terence C. Halliday, Beyond Monopoly: Lawyers, State Crises, and Professional Empowerment (1987) (exploring the role of the Chicago Bar Association in the reform of legal rules and institutions between 1950 and 1970).

house counsel and accounting firms, as well as their predecessors—lawyers before the emergence of strong professional associations.

QUESTIONS

1.   In this article, economic motivations and protectionism once again play a central role in Abel's analysis of the legal profession. See Abel, The Contradictions of Professionalism, Chapter 11 supra. In contrasting American professional associations to their foreign counterparts, however, does Abel acknowledge important noneconomic facets of the profession?

2.   Abel suggests that billings, profits, size and growth are more likely to motivate lawyers in the international market than in the domestic market. Are many of his observations, however, also true of lawyers working in large American cities?

3.   Abel points out problems that arise when a lawyer's practice depends upon a single client. What specific cases discussed in this casebook are good examples of the dangers of dependence on a single client?

4.   In 1988, a Code of Conduct for Lawyers in the European Community (the "CCBE Code of Conduct") was adopted by delegates from the European Community's twelve member countries. See Laurel S. Terry, An Introduction to the European Community's Legal Ethics Code, Part I: An Analysis of the CCBE Code of Conduct, 7 Geo. J. Legal Ethics 1 (1993), and Part II: Applying the CCBE Code of Conduct, 7 Geo. J. Legal Ethics 345 (1993). "Although the CCBE Code of Conduct does not currently apply to most American lawyers practicing in Europe" some European countries are considering requiring American lawyers to agree to abide by the CCBE Code of Conduct to the extent it does not conflict with provisions in the lawyers' home jurisdictions. Id. at 347. To what extent are rules of professional conduct derived from the cultural values of the jurisdictions in which lawyers practice? How likely is it that most jurisdictions will be able to agree on the same rules of professional conduct?

H.   Lawyers and Laypersons

Laypersons as Employees

Lawyers typically employ assistants such as paralegals, secretaries, lobbyists, investigators and accountants. "Such assistants, whether employees or independent contractors, act for the lawyer in rendition of the lawyer's professional services." ABA Model Rules of Professional Conduct Rule 5.3, cmt. (1995). See also In re Opinion No. 24 of the Committee on the Unauthorized Practice of Law, 128 N.J. 114, 607 A.2d 962 (N.J. 1992) (independent paralegals working on a contract basis must be supervised by an attorney, but the evidence does not support a categorical ban on all independent paralegals in New Jersey); Cameo Convalescent Center, Inc. v. Senn, 738 F.2d 836, 846 (7th Cir.1984) (allowing compensation for law clerks as part of an award of attorneys' fees "encourages cost effective delivery of legal services by reducing the spiraling cost of litigation").

Model Rule 5.3(a) requires a partner in a law firm to implement "measures giving reasonable assurance that [the conduct of laypersons employed by the firm] is compatible with the professional obligations of the lawyer." Model Rule 5.3(b) requires an attorney, when delegating tasks to a nonlawyer, to "make reasonable efforts to ensure that the layperson's conduct is compatible with the professional obligations of the lawyer." Model Rule 5.3(c) makes the supervising attorney responsible for the layperson's work product, when: "(1) the lawyer orders or, with the knowledge of the specific conduct, ratifies the conduct involved; or (2) the lawyer is a partner in the law firm in which the person is employed, or has direct supervisory authority over the person, and knows of the conduct at a time when its consequences can be avoided or mitigated but fails to take reasonable remedial action." See In re Galbasini, 163 Ariz. 120, 786 P.2d 971, 974 (Ariz. 1990) (quoting a substantially similar Arizona rule); The Florida Bar v. Carter, 502 So.2d 904, 905 (Fla.1987) ("Failure of supervising attorney to examine and be responsible for all work delegated to nonlawyer personnel warrants disciplinary proceedings").

Laypersons as Partners

An attorney is prohibited from forming a partnership with a nonlawyer if the "activities of the partnership consist of the practice of law." Model Rule 5.4. See also Model Code, DR 3–103(A)(same); The Florida Bar v. James, 478 So.2d 27 (Fla.1985) (lawyer suspended from practice for forming with a nonlawyer a partnership that engaged in part in the practice of law). This restriction is presumably designed to preserve the professional independence of the attorney, Model Rule 5.4, cmt, and has withstood challenges under the Sherman Antitrust Act and the First Amendment. Lawline v. American Bar Ass'n, 956 F.2d 1378 (7th Cir.1992), cert. denied, 510 U.S. 992 (1993). A few jurisdictions, however, have liberalized their restrictions on laypersons' participation as partners of law firms. See District of Columbia Rule 5.4(b) (1996) (allowing nonlawyers to participate as partners of law firms if, among other conditions, the partnership's sole purpose is providing legal services to clients, and all persons having managerial authority or a financial interest in the firm abide by the District's Rules of Professional Conduct).

Model Rule 5.4(a) prohibits a lawyer from sharing legal fees with a nonlawyer. This rule, like the prohibition on forming with a layperson a partnership to practice law, is designed to safeguard the lawyer's independence of judgment. Model Rule 5.4 cmt. Many jurisdictions allow three exceptions: (1) payments by a firm to a lawyer's estate, or specified persons, upon the lawyer's death; (2) payments by the purchaser of the practice of a deceased, disabled, or disappeared lawyer of the specified purchase price for the lawyer's ownership interest in his firm; and (3) payments to a layperson employee as part of a compensation or retirement plan. Model Rule 5.4(a)(1)-(3). Fee splitting with other lawyers is discussed in Section E of

Chapter 1 supra and fee splitting with legal service organizations, labor unions and other lay intermediaries in Section D of Chapter 6 supra (see Brotherhood of R.R. Trainmen v. Virginia ex rel. Va. State Bar, 377 U.S. 1 (1964)).

Law Firms and Ancillary Businesses

In an increasingly competitive marketplace, many law firms are expanding into areas such as consulting, real estate, lobbying and accounting. The mail fraud charge stemming from Armand D'Amato's concealment of his lobbying activity for Unisys, see Chapter 1 supra, is only one example of the problems that arise when lawyers do something for their clients other than practice law.

First, as a lawyer's business interests become more diversified, her independent professional judgment may be compromised, and her clients "may not be able to rely on the lawyer's objectivity to the extent they could if the lawyer were fully independent." L. Harold Levinson, Making Society's Legal System Accessible to Society: The Lawyer's Role and Its Implications, 41 Vand. L. Rev. 789, 803, (1988). A second problem is that, as the power of an ancillary business increases, nonlawyers focusing primarily on profit may make decisions about how the law firm is run and which clients to accept.

A third concern is jeopardizing client confidentiality. For example, the client of an ancillary business might tell an affiliated lawyer a confidence under the mistaken impression that it is privileged, or a legal client might tell a nonlawyer in the ancillary business a confidence under the same misapprehension. Dennis J. Block, Irwin H. Warren & George F. Meierhofer, Jr., Model Rule of Professional Conduct 5.7: Its Origin and Interpretation, 5 Geo. J. Legal Ethics 739, 760 (1992). A confidence could also be told to a lawyer in front of a nonlawyer, thereby destroying the attorney-client privilege. See discussion of the privilege in Chapter 2 supra. A fourth problem that may arise is the unauthorized practice of law. Under Model Rule 5.5(b), "[a] lawyer shall not assist a person who is not a member of the bar in the performance of activity that constitutes the unauthorized practice of law." As the line dividing law and other professions is blurred, persons affiliated with lawyers may be more likely to give legal advice. Block, supra, at 763. Improper solicitation of clients is a fifth point of concern. Model Rule 7.3 restricts direct solicitation of prospective clients, yet ancillary businesses could create a "feeder operation" for attracting business to the law firm. Id. at 761.

There are, however, some arguments in favor of ancillary businesses. First, ancillary businesses can make good business sense, and it may be a "myth to say that lawyers do not work for money, or that money making is not an inherent component of professionalism." Gary A. Munneke, Dances With Nonlawyers: A New Perspective on Law Firm Diversification, 61 Fordham L. Rev. 559, 575 (1992). Second, there is precedent for combining nonlegal services with law practice. For example, lawyers have for a long time prepared tax returns for their clients. Problems usually do not arise so long as an ancillary business is conducted in a manner consistent with lawyers' professional responsibilities and is not used to secure legal work. William B. Dunn, Legal Ethics and Ancillary Business, 74 Mich. B.J. 154, 160 (1995); Block, supra at 747. Third, there is not always a clear distinction between what is and is not legal work, and many lawyers believe that this distinction is becoming more artificial. See Marjorie Meeks, Alter[ing] People's Perceptions: The Challenge Facing Advocates of Ancillary Business Practices, 66 Ind. L.J. 1031, 1041, 1049 (1991).

Model Rule 5.7 states that lawyers "shall be subject to the Rules of Professional Conduct" when performing "law-related services," which are defined as services "that might reasonably be performed in conjunction with and in substance are related to the provision of legal services," but that "are not prohibited as unauthorized practice of law when provided by a nonlawyer." Rules concerning client confidences, successive and concurrent conflicts, fees and other matters thus would all apply to law related services. Model Rule 5.7 excepts from such coverage law related services provided in circumstances that are distinct from a lawyer's provision of legal services to clients. A lawyer seeking to remove law related services from the reach of professional conduct rules thus must make sure that, even if the services are provided by a separate entity controlled by the lawyer, her client knows that the services are not legal services and "that the protections of the client-lawyer relationship do not exist."

Washington D.C.'s Arnold & Porter has implemented a system of self-regulation for its ancillary businesses that begins with a screening of all potential clients of an ancillary business to discern conflicts of interest with the law firm's clients. If any conflicts do exist, they are resolved by the law firm, not the business. All promotional literature for the ancillary businesses is cleared by the law firm first, and all ties of the businesses to the law firm are disclosed to clients in writing. Finally, clients of the ancillary businesses are told that they may use any law firm they want to if the need for legal representation should arise. See Stephen R. Ripps, Law Firm Ownership of Ancillary Businesses in Ohio—A New Era?, 27 Akron L. Rev. 1, 16 (1993).

Lawyers as Directors

Harold B. Finn III, formerly a law clerk to Justice Stanley F. Reed and Chief Justice Earl Warren, is the managing partner of Finn, Dixon & Herling in Stamford, Connecticut. From 1994 to 1997, Mr. Finn was Co-Chair and then Chair of the Banking Law Committee of the American Bar Association.

Mission Intractable?

By Harold B. Finn III
The Connecticut Law Tribune
May 15, 1995.

A well-known lawyer recently reported to me with enthusiasm that he had been elected as a director of a local bank. When asked whether he was concerned about the attendant risks, he assured me that risk was not a problem: His bank is well-capitalized . . . .

My friend might also have taken comfort from the frequently stated assurances of representatives of the Federal Deposit Insurance Corp. that the FDIC will not commence an action against directors of a failed bank or thrift unless such directors have participated in illegal acts or were grossly negligent in the performance of their duties.

Unfortunately, those assurances are meaningless as a matter of law and are typically ignored by those who have the power and responsibility to prosecute cases against directors of failed financial institutions. Perhaps it is true, as often claimed, that the board of directors of the FDIC will not authorize the initiation of a suit against directors of a failed bank unless the case against such directors is based on allegedly illegal or grossly negligent conduct. Nonetheless, the FDIC's complaints against directors of failed financial institutions almost universally allege simple negligence as well as gross negligence.

Moreover, in settlement negotiations, the representatives of the FDIC repeatedly and unabashedly threaten to prosecute cases on the ground that the directors, if nothing else, were negligent (albeit only simply so) and, therefore, are liable to the FDIC as the receiver for the failed bank. Faced with the prospect of bearing enormous legal-defense costs, to say nothing of the risk of being held jointly and severally liable for the losses that were suffered by the failed bank, it is no wonder that directors of failed banks regularly choose the alternative of settling with the FDIC, even if they are convinced—with good reason—that they performed their duties as directors diligently and in good faith.

Perhaps my friend also derived comfort from his familiarity with § 212(k) of the Financial Institutions Reform, Recovery and Enforcement Act of 1989 (FIRREA), 12 U.S.C.A. § 1821(k), which specifies that:

> A director . . . of an insured depository institution may be held person-ally liable for monetary damages in any civil action by [the FDIC] acting as conservator or receiver of such institution . . . for gross negligence, including any similar conduct or conduct that demonstrates a greater disregard of a duty of care (than gross negligence) including intentional tortious conduct, as such terms are defined and determined under applicable State law. Nothing in this paragraph shall impair or affect any right of the [FDIC] under other applicable law.

Negligence

At first blush, one might think that the plain language of § 1821(k) precludes the FDIC from asserting a claim seeking monetary damages against a director of an insured financial institution unless it can show that the director's conduct amounted to gross negligence or worse. A number of circuit courts have held, however, that § 1821(k) does not prevent the FDIC (or its counterpart, the Resolution Trust Corp.) from asserting state law claims for monetary damages against directors of state banks and thrifts for allegedly negligent conduct.

Moreover, the courts are divided on the question of whether the FDIC or the RTC can assert a state-law, simple-negligence claim for monetary damages against directors of failed federally chartered banks or thrifts....*

A Higher Standard

My friend might also have had the arrogance to assume that he could perform his duties as a director in a manner that could pass muster even under a simple-negligence standard. But the reality is that many representatives of the FDIC believe that directors of banks and thrifts must personally approve all significant loans that are made by the depository institution (including loans that have already been approved by the loan committee) and must, in doing so, apprise themselves of all facts relevant to the making of the loan. Those facts include the reputation and financial circumstances of the borrower, the sufficiency of the security for the loan, and the legality of the loan under applicable state and federal law. In theory, such a standard may be laudable, but directors who meet but once a month for limited periods of time cannot expect to live up to such a standard.

In addition, the task of fulfilling the FDIC's expectations is even more difficult for directors who have professional expertise, such as lawyers: Lawyers are held to a higher standard because the representatives of the FDIC presume that such professionals are in a better position to know and understand the applicable law and the risks of lending. Moreover, if a lawyer-director used her expertise to serve the bank in a capacity other than that of a director, such as in representing the bank in lending transactions, her risk increases exponentially, since she may be deemed to have a duty to investigate whether the information provided to the directors was accurate and whether a transaction that has been approved by the directors complies with all applicable law.

Finally, my friend might have taken comfort from the fact that his bank was fortunate enough to have directors-and-officers liability insurance. Unfortunately, most D & O policies now contain a regulatory exclusion provision under which the insurance company is not liable for losses arising out of claims by regulatory agencies. Also, even if such exclusion is not applicable, nearly all D & O policies are written on a "claims-made" basis, and directors of failed banks and thrifts often find that the regulatory agency does not assert a claim against them until long after the insurance policy has lapsed.

. . . .

---

* In Atherton v. FDIC, 117 S.Ct. 666 (1997), the Supreme Court held that, apart from § 1821(k), there is no federal common law creating a general standard of care for officers and directors of federally insured savings institutions. "[S]tate law sets the standard of conduct as long as the state standard (such as simple negligence) is stricter than that of the federal statute. The federal statute nonetheless sets a 'gross negligence' floor, which applies as a substitute for state standards that are more relaxed." Id. The FDIC thus may not bring suit against an institution's officers or directors for simple negligence unless the institution's main office or principal place of business is located in a state that imposed such a standard.—ed.

In short, if my friend had been willing to listen, I would have told him that he was living in a fool's paradise to think that he could serve as a director of either a federal or state bank or thrift without substantial risk of loss of his mental and financial well-being.

QUESTIONS

1. Should lawyers be held to a higher standard of care than other corporate directors concerning such matters as whether the corporation is complying with regulatory requirements?

2. What are the advantages to a corporation of having an outside lawyer on its board of directors? What are the disadvantages?

3. The Cravath firm traditionally discouraged its lawyers from serving as directors. See Swaine's discussion of the Cravath system, Chapter 5 supra. How is serving on a client's board of directors likely to complicate a lawyer's practice? Why do some lawyers do it anyway?

A biographical sketch of **George D. Reycraft** is included in Chapter 4 supra preceding *General Motors v. City of New York*.

Conflicts of Interest and Effective Representation: The Dilemma of Corporate Counsel

George D. Reycraft.
39 Hastings L.J. 605 (1988).
Copyright 1988 by the University of California, Hastings College of Law.

In April of 1986, the New York law firm of Rogers & Wells agreed to the largest malpractice settlement ever reported, paying $40 million to settle 330 lawsuits that charged the firm with aiding and abetting fraud committed by a client investment company. The lawsuits maintained that Rogers & Wells had failed to notify regulatory authorities and had continued to represent the investment company after learning of its securities law violations.

In March of 1987, the New York law firm of Fried, Frank, Harris, Shriver & Jacobson (Fried Frank) and one of its members were named as defendants in an action brought by limited partners in Ivan F. Boesky's arbitrage partnership.[2] The limited partners alleged, among other things, that Fried Frank and its member had (1) participated in the offer and sale of unregistered securities in violation of sections 5 and 12(1) of the Securities Act of 1933, (2) assisted in the offer and sale of partnership securities by means of false and misleading offering materials in violation of section 12(2) of the Securities Act of 1933 and section 10(b) of the Securities Exchange Act of 1934, and (3) breached their fiduciary duty to the limited partners. In July of 1987, the court denied Fried Frank's motions to dismiss.[7]

In June of 1987, the Securities and Exchange Commission (SEC) charged that a partner of Sullivan & Cromwell had failed to advise his

---

2. Arden Way Assocs. v. Boesky, No. 87 Civ. 1865 (S.D.N.Y. filed Mar. 20, 1987).

7. Arden Way Assocs. v. Boesky, 664 F. Supp. 855, 858 (S.D.N.Y. 1987).

client to promptly disclose confidential takeover negotiations in accordance with securities laws.[8] The lawyer was a director of a company that was the target of a hostile takeover. The lawyer also served as corporate counsel to the target and was allegedly responsible for the decision not to disclose the target's merger negotiations with a white knight. As of this writing, these charges are pending.

These cases are but a few examples of a growing number of lawsuits being brought against lawyers and law firms engaged in the practice of corporate and securities law. Such lawsuits often involve lawyers who are alleged to have assisted their clients in the commission of securities law violations. An ever increasing number of suits, however, arise out of routine services provided by corporate and securities lawyers, such as preparing offering materials, issuing opinions, and determining the substance and timing of disclosures. Moreover, suits against lawyers are more frequently being brought by persons who were not themselves clients of the lawyers, but who nonetheless claim that the lawyers have breached a duty owed to them.

. . . .

A large number of these cases involve investors who claim that they relied on false or misleading offering materials. Such investors claim that the lawyer for the issuer assisted in the offer and sale of securities by means of offering materials that the lawyer knew contained material misstatements or omissions. Investors have argued that lawyers were instrumental in the sale of securities by (1) soliciting investors, (2) making misrepresentations regarding the investment, or (3) structuring the offering to avoid disclosure requirements. . . . Those allegations, coupled with the pleading of scienter, have been held sufficient to state a claim against lawyers.

. . . .

The mergers and takeovers context is conducive to claims against lawyers for involvement in the organizational client's securities violations. To preserve their own positions, the incumbent management or board of directors may be reluctant to make certain disclosures. A lawyer's failure to advise in favor of required disclosures to the SEC may lead to securities violation claims against him. A material misrepresentation or omission to shareholders by management in defending against a hostile tender offer may also result in a securities violation claim against a lawyer. Finally, a lawyer's failure to disclose to shareholders his potential self-interest in a merger could also result in a securities violation.

Conclusion

The recent onslaught of lawsuits against corporate and securities lawyers signals a warning to lawyers to be increasingly vigilant in their

---

8. In re Allied Stores Corp., Fed. Sec. L. Rep. (CCH) P84,142 (June 29, 1987). [The charges in this case, later designated In Re Kern, were later dropped on jurisdictional grounds. *See* discussion of the *Kern* case in Chapter 2 supra]—ed.

representation of organizational clients. The ethical problems faced by corporate and securities lawyers now present the additional risk that such problems may result in steep liability. Recent decisions make clear that lawyers are more vulnerable to lawsuits when they step out of their professional role and take a more active part in their client's business by promoting deals, soliciting investors, conducting meetings at the firm's premises, and becoming tied to client companies as directors or general partners. Such conduct makes lawyers appear less like advisors and more like principals, who may be charged with participating in and furthering the client's wrongful conduct. Yet there are no clear-cut guidelines for resolving many of the complex ethical dilemmas that arise for corporate counsel. The corporate and securities bar should initiate revisions to the Model Code and Model Rules to guide counsel through the minefield of conflicts in corporate representation.

QUESTIONS

1. Review the excerpt from The Comfort Letter in Chapter 2 supra and the discussion in Chapter 2 of the *National Student Marketing, Carter and Johnson* and *Kern* cases. How are problems similar to those faced by the lawyers in these cases exacerbated if a lawyer also sits on a client's board of directors?

2. Why is it easier to sue a lawyer who sits on a client's board of directors than it is to sue a lawyer who does not serve as a director? Should a lawyer-director be held to a higher standard than a nonlawyer-director when the corporation commits fraudulent or tortious acts?

3. The corporate interest represented by the lawyer as a director is usually congruent with the corporate interest represented by the lawyer as the corporation's counsel. George Reycraft's own experience, however, illustrates that in some situations a lawyer should not undertake two different roles concerning the same subject matter, even if the lawyer is working on behalf of congruent interests. See *General Motors v. City of New York*, Chapter 4 supra. In what specific situations should a lawyer serving as a director recuse himself from the board's deliberations and decisions? When should he resign from the board?

4. The board of directors is the highest authority that speaks for a corporate lawyer's client. See Del. Gen. Corp. Law, section 141(a) ("The business and affairs of every corporation organized under this chapter shall be managed by or under the direction of a board of directors. . . ."). Should a lawyer manage the affairs of a client in addition to advising the client? Do many lawyers already participate in managing the affairs of their clients, even if they do not sit on clients' boards? See Richard W. Painter, The Moral Interdependence of Corporate Lawyers and Their Clients, 67 S. Cal. L. Rev. 507, 520–53 (1994).

INDEX

References are to pages

†